D0086713

IMPROVE YOUR GRADE!

STUDENTS START HERE ▶

PERSONALIZED STUDY PLANS STRENGTHEN STUDENT COMPREHENSION

Diagnostic pre- and post-assessment quizzes identify gaps in knowledge and help you develop a Personalized Study Plan. The plan provides practice with links to videos, eBook content, and other multimedia tools.

SUCCESSFULLY COMPLETE HOMEWORK ONLINE

All end-of-chapter problems and exercises are available online with hints and links to tools. These additional review opportunities help you effectively complete assignments. You can easily view assignments completed, due dates, and current grades from one convenient screen.

GAMES REINFORCE CONCEPTS

Interactive accounting games reinforce key concepts and provide you with immediate feedback.

eBOOK BRINGS CONTENT TO LIFE

ThomsonNOW features a full-color eBook, allowing you to reference pages from homework assignments and end-of-chapter activities. This immediate and convenient access to the text is ideal for study and review.

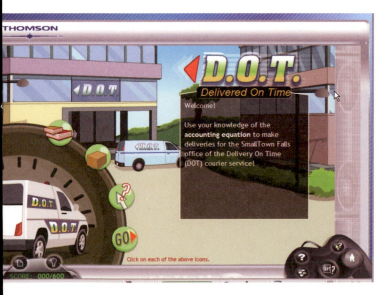

TENTH EDITION

FINANCIAL
ACCOUNTING

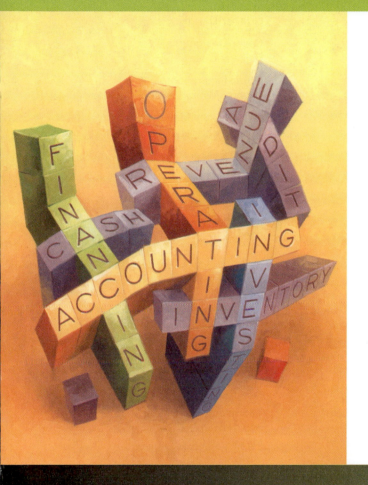

W. STEVE ALBRECHT
PhD, CPA, CIA, CFE
Brigham Young University

•

EARL K. STICE
PhD
Brigham Young University

•

JAMES D. STICE
PhD
Brigham Young University

THOMSON
™
SOUTH-WESTERN

Australia · Brazil · Canada · Mexico · Singapore · Spain · United Kingdom · United States

THOMSON

SOUTH-WESTERN

Financial Accounting, 10e
W. Steve Albrecht, Earl K. Stice, and James D. Stice

VP/Editorial Director:
Jack W. Calhoun

Publisher:
Rob Dewey

Executive Editor:
Sharon Oblinger

Developmental Editor:
Aaron Arnsparger

Marketing Manager:
Kristen Hurd

Content Project Manager:
Starratt E. Alexander

Manager of Technology, Editorial:
John Barans

Technology Project Editor:
Sally Nieman

Manufacturing Coordinator:
Doug Wilke

Production House/Composition:
Litten Editing and Production, Inc. and GGS Information Services

Printer:
R R Donnelley
Willard Manufacturing Division

Art Director:
Bethany Casey

Internal Designer:
C Miller Design

Cover Designer:
Bethany Casey

Cover Illustrations:
© Larry Moore, Scott Hull Associates

Photography Manager:
Deanna Ettinger

Photo Researcher:
Robin Samper

Library of Congress Control Number:
2006937998

For more information about our products, contact us at:

Thomson Learning Academic Resource Center

1-800-423-0563

Thomson Higher Education
5191 Natorp Boulevard
Mason, OH 45040
USA

TAKE A LOOK AT THE BEST GAME IN TOWN

FINANCIAL ACCOUNTING, 10E
WHERE FUTURE BUSINESS CHAMPIONS BEGIN

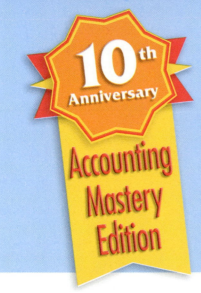

Staying on top of the game in today's competitive world means consistently looking for ways to improve, building upon existing strengths, and maximizing every opportunity. **Financial Accounting, 10e** *does just that to give you and your students a competitive edge in accounting today. See for yourself how proven accounting leaders Albrecht, Stice, and Stice have improved this edition to help you and your students achieve your personal best — in today's classroom and the business world beyond.*

A STRATEGY FOR SUCCESS

Financial Accounting, 10e continues to build upon a winning strategy designed to help you meet the diverse needs of both accounting majors and non-majors in your course. The text's solid presentation of procedures blends with a balanced emphasis on business activities. Students learn how to effectively use and prepare accounting information.

With an emphasis on the activities of a business, **Financial Accounting, 10e** demonstrates accounting in action using a wealth of actual examples from numerous leading companies throughout the world. Student-focused learning features place concepts within a business context. No matter what your students' career choices, this edition has the coverage to make them winners in the game of life.

THE WINNING SOLUTION – STRONGER WITH EVERY ROUND

Building on the strengths that make this a market-leading text, this edition takes the accounting experience to a new level. The flexibility of expanded coverage, new applications in every chapter, reorganized and streamlined content, and the innovative online ThomsonNOW™ course management system are everything you need to put your students ahead of the game!

Now It's Your Turn.
Take a look for yourself!

SEE page iv

GO

YOU WIN WITH FLEXIBILITY TAILORED TO YOUR COURSE NEEDS

Always a hallmark of this text, **expanded coverage within each chapter,** in addition to solid **basic coverage** of essential accounting concepts, allows you to choose how much depth you wish for exploring advanced topics. The result is maximum flexibility for your class.

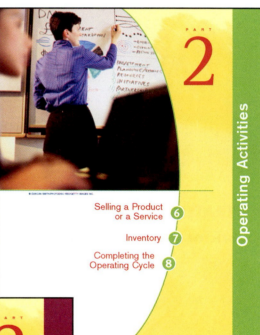

ORGANIZATION PLAYS TO TODAY'S BUSINESS STRENGTHS

The text's unique approach, emphasizing business activities, provides a solid framework for understanding how an organization performs its primary business activities. This realistic approach makes it easier for students to understand accounting's role.

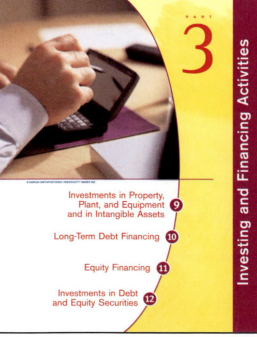

STREAMLINED SOLUTIONS
ADD UP TO SUCCESS

FINANCIAL CHAPTERS LEAVE NOTHING TO CHANCE

■ Based on your feedback, **the financial statement analysis chapter appears as the last chapter** (Ch. 14). This now serves as a capstone chapter, getting students into analysis.

■ The **unique chapter on financial statement integrity** (now Ch. 5) provides a strong ethical foundation for students to better understand the impact of the Sarbanes-Oxley Act and today's increased focus on earnings management.

Ensuring the Integrity of Financial Information

After studying this chapter, you should be able to:

LEARNING OBJECTIVES

① **Identify the types of problems that can appear in financial statements.** *Mechanical errors in the recording or posting process and mistakes in accounting estimates can result in incorrect financial statement numbers. Financial statements can also be intentionally misstated by managers seeking to fraudulently deceive investors and creditors.*

② **Describe the safeguards employed to ensure that financial statements are free from problems.** *Ethical and careful managers are much more likely to establish conditions and procedures that result in fair financial statements. Such managers insist on a carefully designed accounting system that captures all company transactions. These managers also ensure that internal checks and balances prevent accidental loss and intentional theft and fraud.*

③ **Understand the concept of earnings management and why it occurs.** *Managers of companies sometimes are motivated to manage reported earnings in order to meet internal targets and to look good to outsiders. When a manager decides to manage earnings, he or she can fall into a downward spiral of deception which can result in a massive loss of reputation for the manager and the company.*

④ **Understand the major parts of the Sarbanes-Oxley Act and how it impacts financial reporting.** *The Sarbanes-Oxley Act was passed by Congress in 2002 in response to the public uproar over a rash of large corporate accounting scandals. The Act places a personal responsibility on corporate managers to produce reliable financial reports. The Act also raises the standards for external auditors.*

⑤ **Describe the role of auditors and how their presence affects the integrity of financial statements.** *Auditors increase the reliance that users can place on financial reports. Internal auditors monitor accounting processes in a company on an ongoing basis. External auditors certify that the financial statements released to the public are a fair representation of the company's financial position and performance.*

⑥ **Explain the role of the Securities and Exchange Commission in adding credibility to financial statements.** *The SEC has legal authority to set financial accounting standards in the United States; in practice, the SEC allows the FASB to set these standards. The SEC also oversees the certification of external auditors. The SEC requires publicly-traded companies to provide quarterly financial statements to the public.*

© SPENCER PLATT/GETTY IMAGES INC.

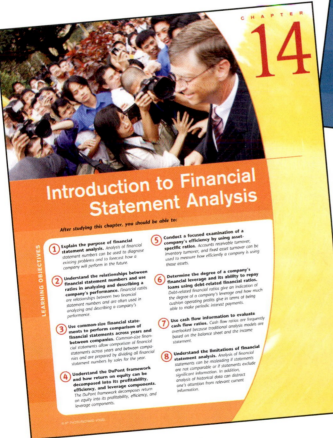

Introduction to Financial Statement Analysis

After studying this chapter, you should be able to:

LEARNING OBJECTIVES

① **Explain the purpose of financial statement analysis.** *Analysis of financial statement numbers can be used to diagnose existing problems and to forecast how a company will perform in the future.*

② **Understand the relationships between financial statement numbers and use ratios in analyzing and describing a company's performance.** *Financial ratios are relationships between two financial statement numbers and are often used in analyzing and describing a company's performance.*

③ **Use common-size financial statements to perform comparison of financial statements across years and between companies.** *Common-size financial statements allow comparison of financial statements across years and between companies and are prepared by dividing all financial statement numbers by sales for the year.*

④ **Understand the DuPont framework and how return on equity can be decomposed into its profitability, efficiency, and leverage components.** *The DuPont framework decomposes return on equity into its profitability, efficiency, and leverage components.*

⑤ **Conduct a focused examination of a company's efficiency by using asset-specific ratios.** *Accounts receivable turnover, inventory turnover, and fixed asset turnover can be used to measure how efficiently a company is using those assets.*

⑥ **Determine the degree of a company's financial leverage and its ability to repay loans using debt-related financial ratios.** *Debt-related financial ratios give an indication of the degree of a company's leverage and how much cushion operating profits give in terms of being able to make periodic interest payments.*

⑦ **Use cash flow information to evaluate cash flow ratios.** *Cash flow ratios are frequently overlooked because traditional analysis models are based on the balance sheet and the income statement.*

⑧ **Understand the limitations of financial statement analysis.** *Analysis of financial statements can be misleading if statements are not comparable or if statements exclude significant information. In addition, analysis of historical data can distract one's attention from relevant current information.*

MODIFIED TABLE OF CONTENTS

Based on your feedback, the table of contents has been modified to introduce topics similar to the order they are presented on the balance sheet.

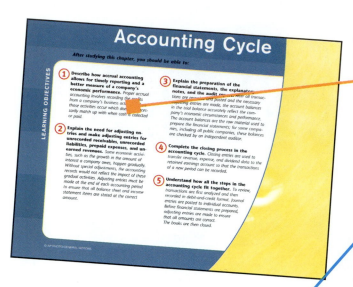

LEARNING FEATURES STUDENTS REALLY USE

NEW! **Brief Explanations that accompany Learning Objectives** at the beginning of every chapter direct students' attention while reading. They are an ideal resource to refresh student understanding before lectures and tests.

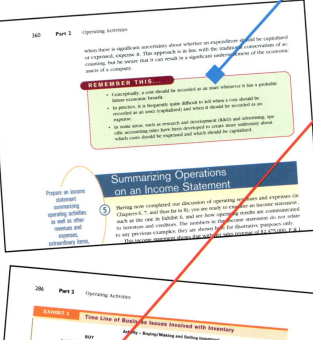

NEW! **Revised *Remember This... Summaries*** at the end of each topical section of the chapter highlight the most important material within that section. Bulleted lists assist with retention, while tables visually demonstrate important relationships or connections.

NEW! **Improved Chapter-Opening Exhibits** place events in context, while showing both the timeline of events for a particular business activity and the impact of these events on the financial statements. These enhanced exhibits provide a clear visual aid as students begin to conceptualize the relationships between various activities of a business and the proper accounting procedures that accompany them.

FYI boxes draw examples from real business events or situations to show students the immediate relevance of the information they are learning.

Stop and Think features highlight thought-provoking issues or concepts that reinforce the importance of developing critical-thinking skills for success in today's competitive business world.

Caution boxes remind students of the important points to consider when resolving more difficult situations or learning more complex concepts.

FROM NOVICE TO PROFESSIONAL

A **variety of homework and assignment opportunities** at the end of each chapter provides a wealth of hands-on, focused practice.

Practice exercises offer quick-hit concept checks ideal for in-class practice.

Exercises and Problems delve deeper into concepts, testing students' retention of critical topics and procedures.

NEW!

Margin References to Learning Objectives have been added to all exercise and problem materials for quick reference and focused practice.

NEW!

Analytical Assignments, following the problems in each chapter, provide dynamic new discussion and critical-thinking activities. From discussion cases and judgment calls, to assignments that require the analysis of real company financial statements, this new section is a source for assignments that take learning a step beyond the typical.

Bonus Round

End-of-chapter practice exercises and problems are now available online through the innovative **ThomsonNOW™ for Financial Accounting, 10e** with instant grading and homework management capabilities!

JUST WHAT YOU NEED TO
KNOW AND DO **NOW**

IT'S YOUR TURN TO SAVE TIME AND ENSURE INTERACTIVE LEARNING

■ **Assign Online Homework** – All end-of-chapter problems and exercises are available online with hints and links to the eBook. This helps students to effectively complete assignments.

■ **Check Course Credibility and Compliance** – ThomsonNOW identifies assignment and test bank questions as they relate to AACSB and AICPA standards with customizable reports that allow you to track progress as well as course content.

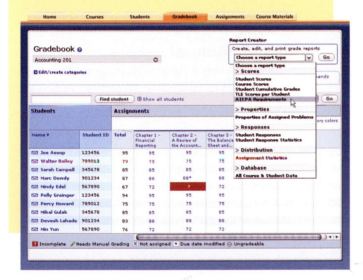

■ **Manage Your Gradebook with Ease** – ThomsonNOW automatically grades homework and tests and provides students with immediate results. Students take responsibility for their own assignments as they can easily view assignments completed, due dates, and current grades from one convenient screen. You can even weight grades to best fit your overall course plan.

■ **Integrated eBook Brings Content to Life** – Students can read the latest edition sequentially or follow links from specific assignments and end-of-chapter activities for remedial review.

■ **Interactive Learning Games and Assignments Reinforce Key Concepts** – Multimedia games provide a fun way to learn accounting concepts. Both creative and challenging, these games reinforce core content and provide immediate feedback to help students improve knowledge and skills.

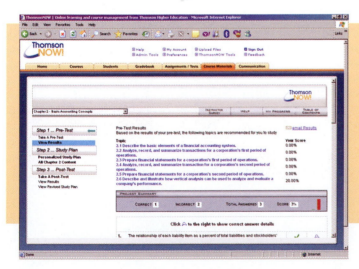

■ **Personalized Study Plans Reinforce Student Comprehension** – Diagnostic pre- and post-assessment quizzes identify gaps in knowledge and help students develop Personalized Study Plans that provide practice with links to tutorials, demonstration exercises, videos, eBook content, accounting games and other multimedia tools.

QUALITY RESOURCES HELP SOLVE
THE ACCOUNTING PUZZLE!

FULL SUITE OF INSTRUCTOR SUPPORT GIVES YOU THE WINNING HAND

A complete selection of reliable supplements, including PowerPoint® slides and a revised Test Bank edited personally by the authors, ensures consistency throughout your course and full continuity with the text! In addition to the innovative new technology offered with ThomsonNOW™, **Financial Accounting, 10e** delivers a wealth of choices for your teaching convenience. Here are just a few highlights from the complete package:

- **Improved Test Bank** now tags questions to **AACSB** and **AICPA** standards so you can efficiently monitor student progress. This is particularly valuable during the accreditation process or when your school wants to standardize assessment. Test bank questions are also identified as **easy, moderate,** and **difficult** to help you create exams best suited for your individual students.

- **ExamView® Electronic Testing Software** allows you to easily generate and customize tests from the reliable test bank questions for traditional or online quizzes or exams.

Study Guide

- **Instructor's Manual** includes an overview of chapter Learning Objectives, detailed lecture outlines, descriptions of key illustrations and boxed items with page references, and a topical overview grid of end-of-chapter assignments with assignments classified by level of difficulty and estimated time of completion.

- **Companion Web Site**

www.thomsonedu.com/accounting/albrecht

Find all of the resources you and your students need on the text's companion Web site. Online, password-protected access allows you to easily download numerous valuable resources and teaching tools, including Solutions Manual, Instructor's Manual, PowerPoint® slides, and Spreadsheet Solutions.

Students can easily access Student Spreadsheet Templates. They can test their understanding with interactive online quizzes and other interactive learning tools.

ACKNOWLEDGMENTS

The tenth edition of *Financial Accounting* reflects many comments from colleagues and students, all of which are deeply appreciated. In particular we would like to thank the following:

Laurie Hays
Western Michigan University

Samuel Tiras
University of Buffalo

Bob Hartman
University of Iowa

Cathy Lumbattis
Southern Illinois University-Carbondale

Hubert Glover
Howard University

Diane Tanner
University of North Florida

Kem Edwards
Bryant College

James Bannister
University of Hartford

Linda Chase
Baldwin Wallace College

K.D. Hatheway-Dial
University of Idaho

Doug Asbury
University of Findlay

Louann Cummings
University of Findlay

Josie Mathias
Mercer County Community College

Ibrahim Badawi
St. John's University

Christie Comunale
Long Island University-C.W. Post

Keren Deal
Auburn University

Rafik Elias
California State University-Los Angeles

Marian Boscia
Kings College

Mary MacAusland
Reading Area Community College

Bonnie Slager
Santiago Canyon College

Joey Styron
Augusta State University

Robert Holtfreter
Central Washington University

Donald Raux
Siena College

William Braberry
Bluefield State College

William Goodman
Bluefield State College

Anne Rich
Quinnipac University

Paul Holt
Texas A&M University-Kingsville

Ralph Lindeman
Kent State University

Susan Minke
Indiana University-Purdue University at Fort Wayne

Lynne Shoaf
Belmont Abbey College

In addition, we would like to thank the following content providers and verifiers for their professional services and consideration in providing a more concise, higher-quality product.

Content Providers:

Cameron Pratt
Brigham Young University

Jason Bond
Brigham Young University

Michael and Becky Blue
Bloomsburg University

David O'Dell
McPherson College

Dave Cottrell
Brigham Young University

Verifiers:

James Emig
Villanova University

Beth Woods
Howell, MI

W. Steve Albrecht
James D. Stice
Earl K. Stice

W. Steve Albrecht

W. Steve Albrecht is the Associate Dean of the Marriott School of Management and Andersen Professor at Brigham Young University. Dr. Albrecht, a certified public accountant, certified internal auditor, and certified fraud examiner, came to BYU in 1977 after teaching at Stanford and at the University of Illinois. Earlier, he worked as a staff accountant for Deloitte & Touche. Prior to becoming associate dean of the Marriott School, Dr. Albrecht served for nine years as the director of the School of Accountancy and Information Systems at BYU.

Dr. Albrecht received a bachelor's degree in accounting from Brigham Young University and his MBA and PhD degrees from the University of Wisconsin at Madison. He is past President of the American Accounting Association and the Association of Certified Fraud Examiners. He was a former member of the Board of Regents of the Institute of Internal Auditors and the Board of Directors of the Utah Association of CPAs. He was also president of the Accounting Program Leadership Group (chairs of accounting departments and programs) and served on the task force of the American Institute of CPAs that wrote a fraud auditing standard. He was a member of the Committee of Sponsoring Organizations (COSO) from 1997–2000 and is past president of Beta Alpha Psi, the national accounting honors fraternity. He was a member of the AICPA Council and chaired their Pre-Certification Executive Education Committee.

Dr. Albrecht has done extensive research on business fraud. His research has resulted in the publication of over one hundred articles in academic and professional journals. He is the author or co-author of over 20 books or monographs, several of which are on fraud. His financial and principles of accounting textbooks are in their 10th editions. In 2000, he completed a major study (Accounting Education: Charting the Course through a Perilous Future) on the future of accounting education in the United States. His fraud textbook is currently in its second edition. He is a frequent speaker on the topics of fraud examination, accounting education, and personal financial planning.

Dr. Albrecht has received numerous awards and honors, including BYU's highest faculty honor, the Karl G. Maeser Distinguished Faculty Lecturer Award for superior scholarship and teaching. He has also received the BYU School of Management's Outstanding Faculty Award and the BYU Outstanding Researcher Award. He has been recognized by Beta Alpha Psi, the Federation of Schools of Accountancy, the Auditing Section of the American Association and the AICPA as Educator of the Year. He has also received awards for outstanding teaching at Stanford University, the University of Illinois, and the University of Wisconsin. In 1997, 2001, 2002, and 2003 he was chosen as one of the 100 most influential accounting professionals in the United States by *Accounting Today* magazine. In 1998, he received the Cressey Award from the Association of Certified Fraud Examiners, the highest award given for a lifetime of achievement in fraud detection and deterrence. (Past winners were Jane Bryant Quinn of *Newsweek* magazine and Rudolph Giuliani, past United States Attorney for the Southern District of New York and past mayor of New York City.) In 2002, in honor of his contribution in fighting fraud, the Association of Certified Fraud Examiners named one of the buildings at their headquarters after Dr. Albrecht. And in 2001, in recognition of his contributions to BYU and to academia, an anonymous donor endowed the W. Steve Albrecht Professorship in Accounting.

Dr. Albrecht has consulted with numerous organizations, including a variety of Fortune 500 companies, major financial institutions, the United Nations, FBI, and other organizations, and he has been an expert witness in some of the largest fraud cases in America. He currently serves on the audit committees and boards of directors of four public and three private companies. Dr. Albrecht is married to the former LeAnn Christiansen, and they have six children and ten grandchildren.

Earl K. Stice

Earl K. Stice is the PricewaterhouseCoopers Professor of Accounting in the School of Accountancy and Information Systems at Brigham Young University where he has been on the faculty since 1998. He holds bachelor's and master's degrees from Brigham Young University and a PhD from Cornell University.

Dr. Stice has taught at Rice University, the University of Arizona, Cornell University, and the Hong Kong University of Science and Technology (HKUST). He won the Phi Beta Kappa teaching award at Rice University and was twice selected at HKUST as one of the ten best lecturers on campus. Dr. Stice has also taught in a variety of executive education and corporate training programs in the United States, Hong Kong, China, and South Africa, and he is currently on the executive MBA faculty of the China Europe International Business School in Shanghai. He has published papers in the *Journal of Financial and Quantitative Analysis, The Accounting Review, Review of Accounting Studies, Issues in Accounting Education*, and the *Journal of Accounting Education*, and his research on stock splits has been cited in *Business Week, Money*, and *Forbes*. Dr. Stice has presented his research results at seminars in the United States, Finland, Taiwan, Australia, and Hong Kong. He is co-author of *Intermediate Accounting, 16th edition* and *Financial Accounting: Reporting and Analysis, 7th Edition*. Dr. Stice and his wife, Ramona, are the parents of seven children: Derrald, Han, Ryan Marie, Lorien, Lily, Taraz, and Kamila.

James D. Stice

James D. Stice is the Distinguished Teaching Professor in the Marriott School of Management at Brigham Young University. He is currently the Director of the Marriott School's MBA Program. He holds bachelor's and master's degrees from BYU and a PhD from the University of Washington, all in accounting. Professor Stice has been on the faculty at BYU since 1988. During that time, he has been selected by graduating accounting students as "Teacher of the Year" on numerous occasions, he was selected by his peers in the Marriott School at BYU to receive the "Outstanding Teaching Award" in 1995, and in 1999 he was selected by the University to receive its highest teaching award, the Maeser Excellence in Teaching Award. Professor Stice has taught at INSEAD in France and at the China Europe International Business School in Shanghai. Professor Stice has published articles in *The Journal of Accounting Research, The Accounting Review, Decision Sciences, Issues in Accounting Education, The CPA Journal*, and other academic and professional journals. In addition to this textbook, he has published two other textbooks: *Financial Accounting: Reporting and Analysis*, and *Intermediate Accounting*. In addition to his teaching and research, Dr. Stice has been involved in executive education for such companies as IBM, Bank of America, Ernst & Young, RSM McGladrey and currently serves on the board of directors of Nutraceutical Corporation. Dr. Stice and his wife, Kaye, have seven children: Crystal, J.D., Ashley, Whitney, Kara, Skyler, and Cierra and two grandchildren.

SUPPLEMENTS

For the Instructor.......

ThomsonNOW™ for *Financial Accounting, 10e*

Description:

Save time and ensure all of your students—regardless of their major—have the understanding they need of accounting procedures and concepts with the integrated, online innovation of ThomsonNOW™. This integrated online course management and learning system combines the best of current technology to save you time in planning your course and managing student assignments. You can teach with the latest built-in technology support, reinforce comprehension with customized student learning paths, and efficiently test and automatically grade assignments with reports that correspond to AACSB, AICPA and IMA standards. ThomsonNOW™ is effective for the standard lecture-based course or can serve as a strong foundation for full distance-learning programs. For your convenience, ThomsonNOW™ is even compatible with WebCT® and Blackboard®.

For more information, visit **www.thomsonedu.com/thomsonnow**.

Instructor's Manual

Description:

Simplify class preparation with these detailed lecture outlines, overview of Learning Objectives, descriptions of key illustrations and boxed items with page references, and topical overview grid of end-of-chapter assignments with assignments classified by level of difficulty and estimated time of completion. Available online or on the Instructor's Resource CD-ROM.

Instructor's Resource CD-ROM
ISBN: 0324645783

Description:

Place all of the key teaching resources you need for a winning course at your fingertips with this all-in-one source. Find everything you need to plan, teach, grade and assess student understanding and progress. This CD includes the Solutions Manual, Instructor's Manual, Test Bank in Word and ExamView®, PowerPoint® slides, spreadsheet solutions, and solutions to the Cumulative Spreadsheet Analysis assignments from the textbook.

PowerPoint® Presentation Slides

Description:

Bring your lectures to life and clarify difficult concepts with these slides for this edition to capture and keep your students' attention. Ideal as guides for student note-taking and study, you can print the slides or simply use with an overhead projector. Available online or on the Instructor's Resource CD-Rom.

Solutions Manual
ISBN: 0324648308

Description:

Carefully verified to ensure accuracy, these solutions and answers to all end-of-chapter materials from the textbook help you easily plan, assign, and efficiently grade assignments.

Solutions Transparencies
ISBN: 0324645848

Description:

Clarify learning for students with these acetate masters that detail solutions for the exercises and problems from the text. These are specifically created for instructors who wish to use overheads in class.

Test Bank
ISBN: 0324645775

Description:

This revised test bank helps you efficiently assess your students' understanding with problems and questions that are now tagged to AACSB and AICPA standards. This is particularly valuable during the accreditation process or when your school wants to standardize assessment. Test bank questions are also identified by easy, medium, or challenging level of difficulty for easy selection.

ExamView® 5.0 Computerized Test Bank

Description:

This easy-to-use test-creation program for Microsoft® Windows or Macintosh contains all questions from the printed Test Bank with AACSB, AICPA, and standards and level of difficulty indicated for each question. It's simple to customize tests to your specific class needs as you edit or create questions and store customized exams. This is an ideal tool for online testing. Available on the IRCD.

WebTutor™ Toolbox for Blackboard® and WebCT
ISBN: 0534272401 (Blackboard) or 053427241x (WebCT)

Description:

Leverage the power of the Internet and bring your course to life with this course management program. You or your students can use this wealth of interactive resources with those on the text's companion Web site to supplement the classroom experience and ensure positive outcomes. Use this effective resource as an integrated solution for your distance learning or web-enhanced course. Visit **http://webtutor.swlearning.com.**

Working Papers t/a Financial Accounting (Chapters 1–14)
ISBN: 0324648227

Description:
Verified by the text authors to ensure accuracy and quality consistent with the text, the working papers for problems from the financial accounting chapters in the textbook are provided together in one convenient resource.

Albrecht/Stice/Stice's *Financial Accounting, 10e* Companion Web Site
URL: **http://www.thomsonedu.com/accounting/albrecht**

Description:
Now you and your students can reach the top of your game in accounting with immediate access to a rich array of teaching and learning resources at *Financial Accounting, 10e*'s interactive companion Web site. This resource features chapter-by-chapter online tutorial quizzes, a final exam, chapter outlines

and review, online learning games, flashcards, expanded coverage of certain topics not found in the textbook, and more! Easily download the instructor resources you need from the password-protected, instructor-only section of the site.

For Students….

Companion Web Site

Description:
Now you can stay on top of your game, master the procedures and concepts of accounting and earn the grade you want in your accounting course with the rich array of learning resources at the *Financial Accounting, 10e* interactive companion Web site. Designed specifically for your accounting needs, this Web site features chapter-by-chapter online quizzes and solutions, learning games, flashcards, expanded coverage of topics not covered in the text, and more!

Working Papers t/a Financial Accounting (Chapters 1–14)
ISBN: 0324648227

Description:
The working papers for problems from the textbook are provided together in one resource for your convenience. Verified by the text authors to ensure accuracy and consistent quality, you'll find the tools you need to enhance your learning experience.

BRIEF CONTENTS

CONTENTS

▶ PART TWO

OPERATING ACTIVITIES 223

▶ PART THREE

INVESTING AND FINANCING ACTIVITIES 387

EXPANDED *material*

EXPANDED
material

▶ PART FOUR

OTHER DIMENSIONS OF FINANCIAL REPORTING 611

APPENDICES

INDEXES

TENTH EDITION

FINANCIAL
ACCOUNTING

PART
1

Financial Reporting and the Accounting Cycle

Accounting Information: Users and Uses

After studying this chapter, you should be able to:

© AP PHOTO/RON EDMONDS

LEARNING OBJECTIVES

(1) Describe the purpose of accounting and explain its role in business and society. *Accounting is the recording of the day-to-day financial activities of a company and the organization of that information into summary reports used by people inside and outside the company to make decisions.*

(2) Identify the primary users of accounting information. *Among the users of accounting information are lenders, investors, company management, suppliers, customers, employees, competitors, government agencies, politicians, and the press.*

(3) Describe the environment of accounting, including the effects of generally accepted accounting principles, international business, ethical considerations, and technology. *The practice of accounting involves adherence to the established national and (increasingly) international accounting rules as well as the use of judgment. Because accounting data are typically captured and summarized by computer systems, the practice of accounting requires familiarity with information technology.*

(4) Analyze the reasons for studying accounting. *Every job requires you to prepare, use, respond to, or be evaluated using accounting data. Those people who better understand accounting are better able to function in any organization.*

In 1913, a young CPA named Arthur Andersen partnered with a gentleman named Clarence DeLany to form the public accounting firm of **Andersen, DeLany & Co**. At the time, there were only about 2,200 CPAs in the United States, and at the age of 23, Mr. Andersen was one of the youngest. Mr. DeLany later left the firm, and in 1918 it was renamed **Arthur Andersen**. From that beginning, the company grew to the point where in 2001, Andersen had operations in 84 countries and over 85,000 employees. Revenues for 2002 were $9.3 billion. Some of the companies whose financial statements were audited by Andersen included **Colgate-Palmolive**, **Delta Air Lines**, **FedEx Corp.**, **Hershey Foods**, **Hilton Hotels**, and **Merck**.

On August 31, 2002, Arthur Andersen closed its doors and ceased to be an auditor of the financial statements of companies whose stock was traded on public stock exchanges. How did this dramatic "about face" occur? In a word—Enron. Arthur Andersen was the external auditor for a Texas-based energy company named **Enron**.[1] To make its financial statements appear as though the company was performing better than it actually was, Enron officials created several companies, established partnerships with those companies, and then used those partnerships to hide hundreds of millions of dollars in debt. Andersen officials knew about these companies and approved the accounting for the transactions. While the details of the accounting for these transactions are far beyond the scope of this accounting class, suffice it to say that it was complicated.

When the SEC began investigating the Enron scandal, Arthur Andersen undertook a series of events that led to its eventual demise. Company officials ordered that documents relating to the Enron audit be shredded, and Andersen attorneys asked that certain internal correspondence with Enron officers that had not yet been made public be changed to hide the firm's knowledge of certain transactions. Investigation by the SEC into charges of obstruction of justice by Andersen officials led to the firm closing its doors in August of 2002.

I**n this textbook, you will begin your study of accounting. You will learn to speak and understand accounting, "the language of business." Without an understanding of accounting, business investments, taxes, and money management will be like a foreign language to you. In brief, an understanding of accounting facilitates the interpretation of financial information, which allows for better economic decisions.**

interpret and use financial information prepared using accounting techniques and procedures. With the knowledge you obtain from this exposure to accounting, you will be able to "read" the financial statements of companies, understand the information that is being conveyed, and use accounting information to make good business decisions. Also, through discussion of the business environment in which accounting is used, you will increase your understanding of general business concepts such as corporations, leases, annuities, leverage, investments, and so forth.

You will become convinced that accounting is not "bean counting." Time after time you will see that accountants must exercise judgment about how to best summarize and report the results of business transactions. This judgment was at the heart of the Enron, WorldCom, and other scandals. As a result, you will gain a respect for the complexity of accounting and develop a healthy skepticism about the precision of any financial reports you see.

> ### ⃠ CAUTION
>
> Don't be too concerned with all the new and unfamiliar terms you see in the first chapter of the book. Learning a "new language" takes time. Be patient. Before too long, you will be speaking the "language of business" (accounting) quite fluently.

The major objectives of this text are to provide you with a basic understanding of the language of accounting and with the ability to

---

[1] In addition to Enron, several other Andersen clients including WorldCom, Qwest, Sunbeam, and Waste Management also had major financial statement frauds. These near-term failures also contributed to Andersen's demise.

Finally, you will see the power of accounting. Financial statements are not just paper reports that get filed away and forgotten. As an example, the misleading financial statement numbers associated with Enron, WorldCom, and Tyco (another financial statement fraud) resulted in tens of thousands of employees being laid off and investors losing billions of dollars. You will see that financial statement numbers, and, indirectly, the accountants who prepare them, determine who receives loans and who doesn't, which companies attract investors and which don't, which managers receive salary bonuses and which don't, and which companies are praised in the financial press and which aren't.

So, let's get started.

What's the Purpose of Accounting?

Describe the purpose of accounting and explain its role in business and society.

1 Imagine a long distance telephone company with no system in place to document who calls whom and how long they talk. Or a manager of a 300-unit apartment complex who has forgotten to write down which tenants have and have not paid this month's rent. Or an accounting professor who, the day before final grades are due, loses the only copy of the disk containing the spreadsheet of all the homework, quiz, and exam scores. Each of these scenarios illustrates a problem with bookkeeping, the least glamorous aspect of accounting. **Bookkeeping** is the preservation of a systematic, quantitative record of an activity. Bookkeeping systems can be very primitive—cutting notches in a stick to tally how many sheep you have or moving beads on a string to track the score in a billiards game. But the importance of routine bookkeeping cannot be overstated; without bookkeeping, business is impossible.

bookkeeping

The preservation of a systematic, quantitative record of an activity.

Rudimentary bookkeeping is ancient, probably predating both language and money. The modern system of double-entry bookkeeping still in use today (described in Chapter 3) was developed in the 1300s–1400s in Italy by the merchants in the trading and banking centers of Florence, Venice, and Genoa. The key development in accounting in the last 500 years has been the use of the bookkeeping data, not just to keep track of things, but to evaluate the performance and health of a business.

This use of bookkeeping data as an evaluation tool may seem obvious to you, but it is a step that is often not taken. Let's consider a bookkeeping system with which most of us are familiar—a checking account. Your checking account involves (or should involve) careful recording of the dates and amounts of all checks written and all deposits made, the maintenance of a running account total, and reconciliations with the monthly bank statement. Now, assume that you have a perfect checking account bookkeeping system. Will the system answer the following questions?

- Are you spending more for groceries this year than you did last year?
- What proportion of your monthly expenditures are fixed, meaning that you can't change them except through a drastic change in lifestyle?
- You plan to study abroad next year; will you be able to save enough between now and then to pay for it?

accounting system

The procedures and processes used by a business to analyze transactions, handle routine bookkeeping tasks, and structure information so it can be used to evaluate the performance and health of the business.

In order to answer these kinds of evaluation questions, each check must be analyzed to determine the type of expenditure, your checks must then be coded by type of expenditure, the data must be boiled down into summary reports, and past data must be used to forecast future patterns. How many of us use our checking account data like this? Not many. We do the bookkeeping (usually), but we don't structure the information to be used for evaluation.

In summary, an **accounting system** is used by a business to (1) analyze transactions, (2) handle routine bookkeeping tasks, and (3) structure information so it can be used to evaluate the performance and health of the business. Exhibit 1 illustrates the three functions of the accounting system.

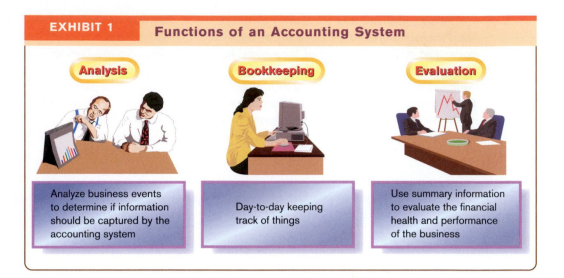

EXHIBIT 1   Functions of an Accounting System

Analysis

Analyze business events to determine if information should be captured by the accounting system

Bookkeeping

Day-to-day keeping track of things

Evaluation

Use summary information to evaluate the financial health and performance of the business

---

accounting

A system for providing quantitative, financial information about economic entities that is useful for making sound economic decisions. Accounting is often called the "language of business" because it provides the means of recording and communicating business activities and the results of those activities.

Accounting is formally defined as a system for providing "quantitative information, primarily financial in nature, about economic entities that is intended to be useful in making economic decisions."[2] The key components of this definition are:

- *Quantitative.* Accounting relates to numbers. This is a strength because numbers can be easily tabulated and summarized. It is a weakness because some important business events, such as a toxic waste spill and the associated lawsuits and countersuits, cannot be easily described by one or two numbers.
- *Financial.* The health and performance of a business are affected by and reflected in many dimensions—financial, personal relationships, community and environmental impact, and public image. Accounting focuses on just the financial dimension.
- *Useful.* The practice of accounting is supported by a long tradition of theory. U.S. accounting rules have a theoretical conceptual framework. Some people actually make a living as accounting theorists. However, in spite of its theoretical beauty, accounting exists only because it is useful.
- *Decisions.* Although accounting is the structured reporting of what has already occurred, this past information can only be useful if it impacts decisions about the future.

Making good decisions is critical for success in any business enterprise. When an important decision must be made, it is essential to use a rational decision-making process. The process is basically the same no matter how complex the issue. First, the issue or question must be clearly identified. Next, the facts surrounding the situation must be gathered and analyzed. Then, several alternative courses of action should be identified and considered before a decision is finally reached. This decision-making process is summarized in Exhibit 2.

---

[2] Statement of the Accounting Principles Board No. 4, "Basic Concepts and Accounting Principles Underlying Financial Statements of Business Enterprises," New York: American Institute of Certified Public Accountants, 1970, par. 40.

One must be careful to make a distinction between a good decision and a good outcome. Often, many factors outside the control of the decision maker affect the outcome of a decision. The decision-making process does not guarantee a certain result; it only ensures that a good decision is made. The outcome always has an element of chance. Part of business is learning how to protect yourself against bad outcomes. The first step in achieving a favorable outcome begins with making a good decision.

business

An organization operated with the objective of making a profit from the sale of goods or services.

nonprofit organization

An entity without a profit objective, oriented toward providing services efficiently and effectively.

Accounting plays a vital role in the decision-making process. An accounting system provides information in a form that can be used to make knowledgeable financial decisions. The information supplied by accounting is in the form of quantitative data, primarily financial in nature, and relates to specific economic entities. An economic entity may be an individual, a business enterprise, or a non-profit organization. A **business**, such as a grocery store or a car dealership, is operated with the objective of making a profit for its owners. The goal of a **nonprofit organization**, such as a city government or a university, is to provide services in an effective and efficient manner. Every entity, regardless of its size or purpose, must have a way to keep track of its economic activities and measure how well it is accomplishing its goals. Accounting provides the means for tracking activities and measuring results.

The Relationship of Accounting to Business

Business is the general term applied to the activities involved in the production and distribution of goods and services. Accounting is used to record and report the financial effects of business activities. Thus, as mentioned earlier, accounting is often called the "language of business." It provides the means of recording and communicating the successes and failures of business organizations. Without accounting information, many important financial decisions would be made blindly. Investors, for example, would have no way to distinguish between a profitable company and one that is on the verge of failure; bankers could not evaluate the riskiness of potential loans; corporate managers would have no basis for controlling costs, setting prices, or investing the company's resources; and governments would have no basis for taxing income.

All business enterprises have some activities in common. As shown in Exhibit 3, one common activity is the acquisition of monetary resources. These resources, often referred to as "capital," come from three sources: (1) investors (owners), (2) creditors (lenders), and (3) the business itself in the form of earnings that have been retained. Once resources are obtained, they are used to buy land, buildings, and equipment; to purchase materials and supplies; to pay employees; and to meet any other operating expenses involved in the production and marketing of goods or services. When the product or service is sold, additional monetary resources (revenues) are generated. These resources can be used to pay loans, to pay taxes, and to buy new materials, equipment,

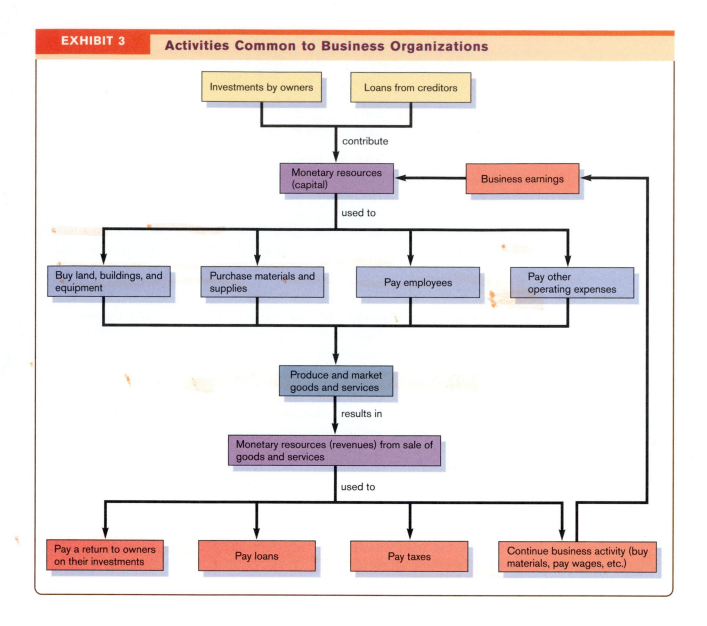

EXHIBIT 3 | **Activities Common to Business Organizations**

and other items needed to continue the operations of the business. In addition, some of the resources may be distributed to owners as a return on their investment. **Wal-Mart**, for example, uses the earnings from its operations to open new stores and purchase inventory for those new stores. Once the new stores are opened, they produce more funds that can then be used to open more stores. Wal-Mart also distributes many of its resources back to its owners. Owners also receive a return on their investment through increases in the value of the stock.

Accountants play two roles with regard to these activities. First, they measure and communicate (report) the results of these activities—in other words, accountants keep score. In order to measure these results as accurately as possible, accountants follow a fairly standard set of procedures, usually referred to as the **accounting cycle**. The cycle includes several steps, which involve analyzing, recording, classifying, summarizing, and reporting the transactions of a business. These steps are explained in detail in Chapters 3 and 4. Second, accountants advise managers on how to structure these activities so as to achieve the goals of the business—be those goals to generate a profit, to minimize costs, to provide efficient services, etc.

accounting cycle

The procedure for analyzing, recording, classifying, summarizing, and reporting the transactions of a business.

REMEMBER THIS...

- Accounting is a service activity designed to accumulate, measure, and communicate financial information about businesses and other organizations and to provide information for making informed decisions about how to best use available resources.
- Accounting is often called the "language of business."

Who Uses Accounting Information?

Identify the primary users of accounting information.

2 The accounting system generates output in the form of financial reports. As shown in Exhibit 4, there are two major categories of reports: internal and external. Internal reports are used by those who direct the day-to-day operations of a business enterprise. These individuals are collectively referred to as "management," and the related area of accounting is called **management accounting** (see page 10 for definition). Management accounting focuses on the information needed for planning, implementing plans, and controlling costs. Managers and executives who work inside a company have access to specialized management accounting information that is not available to outsiders. For example, the management of **McDonald's Corporation** has detailed management accounting data on exactly how much it costs to produce each food and drink item on the menu. Further, if **Burger King** or **Wendy's** starts a local burger price war in, say, Missouri, McDonald's managers can request daily sales summaries for each store in the area to measure the impact.

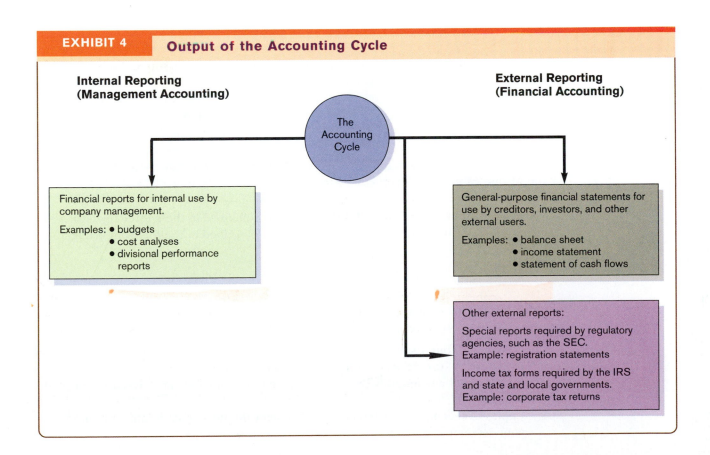

EXHIBIT 4   Output of the Accounting Cycle

Internal Reporting (Management Accounting)

External Reporting (Financial Accounting)

The Accounting Cycle

Financial reports for internal use by company management.

Examples: • budgets
• cost analyses
• divisional performance reports

General-purpose financial statements for use by creditors, investors, and other external users.

Examples: • balance sheet
• income statement
• statement of cash flows

Other external reports:

Special reports required by regulatory agencies, such as the SEC.
Example: registration statements

Income tax forms required by the IRS and state and local governments.
Example: corporate tax returns

management accounting

The area of accounting concerned with providing internal financial reports to assist management in making decisions.

annual report

A document that summarizes the results of operations and financial status of a company for the past year and outlines plans for the future.

financial statements

Reports such as the balance sheet, income statement, and statement of cash flows, which summarize the financial status and results of operations of a business entity.

financial accounting

The area of accounting concerned with reporting financial information to interested external parties.

Other examples of decisions made using management accounting information are whether to produce a product internally or purchase it from an outside supplier, what prices to charge, and which costs seem excessive. Consider those companies that produce computers. Most computers are shipped with an operating system already installed. More than 90% of computers have **Microsoft's** Windows pre-installed. The computer makers must decide whether to develop their own operating system or pay Microsoft a licensing fee to use Windows. Most computer manufacturers have determined it is cost effective to license from Microsoft. Companies such as **Sears** and **Radio Shack** often use products produced by outside suppliers rather than manufacture the products themselves. The products are then labeled with the "Kenmore" or "Realistic" brand names and sold to customers. These are just two examples of decisions that must be made by management given available financial information.

External financial reports, included in the firm's **annual report**, are used by individuals and organizations that have an economic interest in the business but are not part of its management. Information is provided to these "external users" in the form of general-purpose **financial statements** and special reports required by government agencies. The general-purpose information provided by **financial accounting** is summarized in the three primary financial statements: balance sheet, income statement, and statement of cash flows (more formally introduced in Chapter 2), and explanatory notes and discussion that supports these statements.

- The *balance sheet*—reports the resources of a company (the assets), the company's obligations (the liabilities), and the owners' equity, which represents the difference between what is owned (assets) and what is owed (liabilities).
- The *income statement*—reports the amount of net income earned by a company during a period, with annual and quarterly income statements being the most common. Net income is the excess of a company's revenues over its expenses; if the expenses are more than the revenues, then the company has suffered a loss for the period. The income statement represents the accountant's best effort at measuring the economic performance of a company.
- The *statement of cash flows*—reports the amount of cash collected and paid out by a company in the following three types of activities: operating, investing, and financing. The statement of cash flows is the most objective of the financial statements because, as you will see in subsequent chapters, it involves fewer accounting estimates and judgments.

Examples of external users of the information contained in these three financial statements, along with other available information, are described in the following paragraphs.

Lenders

Lenders (creditors) are interested in one thing—being repaid, with interest. If you were to approach a bank for a large loan, the bank would ask you for the following types of information in order to evaluate whether you would be able to repay the loan:

- A listing of your assets and liabilities
- Payroll stubs, tax returns, and other evidence of your income
- Details about any monthly payments (car, rent, credit cards, etc.) you are obligated to make
- Copies of recent bank statements to document the flow of cash into and out of your account

In essence, the bank would be asking you for a balance sheet, an income statement, and a statement of cash flows. Similarly, banks use companies' financial statements in making decisions about commercial loans. The financial statements are useful because they help the lender predict the future ability of the borrower to repay the loan.

In the case of Wal-Mart, a review of its balance sheet indicates that the company has several formal lenders. In addition, Wal-Mart reports a balance in its "accounts payable" account. This amount represents amounts owed to vendors from whom Wal-Mart has purchased on credit. Considering Wal-Mart's reputation, this "lending" is very low risk.

Investors

Investors want information to help them estimate how much cash they can expect to receive in the future if they invest in a business now. Financial statements, coupled with a knowledge of business plans, market forecasts, and the character of management, can aid investors in assessing these future cash flows. Many companies have broad ownership with a few individuals owning a large portion of the company's stock. At Wal-Mart, the Walton Family (the founders of Wal-Mart) own 1,701,604,926 shares (40.8% of total shares outstanding).

Obviously, millions of Americans invest in McDonald's, Wal-Mart, **Cisco Systems**, **General Electric**, and other public companies without ever seeing the financial statements of these companies. Investors can feel justifiably safe in doing this because large companies are followed by armies of financial analysts who would quickly blow the whistle if they found information suggesting that investors in these companies were at serious risk. But what about investing in a smaller company, one that the financial press doesn't follow, or in a local family business that is seeking outside investors for the first time? In cases such as these, investing without looking at the financial statements is like jumping off the high dive without looking first to see if there is any water in the pool.

FYI

One of the concerns with online "day trading" in stocks is that investors make significant investment decisions without ever seeing, or even thinking about, a company's reported financial position.

Management

In addition to using management accounting information available only to those within the firm, managers of a company can use the general financial accounting information that is also made available to outsiders. Company goals are often stated in terms of financial accounting numbers, such as a target of sales growth in excess of 5%. Also, reported "net income" is frequently used in calculating management bonuses. Finally, managers of a company can analyze the general-purpose financial statements (using the techniques introduced in Chapter 6 and discussed in detail in Chapter 14) in order to pinpoint areas of weakness about which more detailed management accounting information can be sought.

Other Users of Financial Information

There are many other external users of financial information, including suppliers, customers, employees, competitors, government agencies, and the press. These are described below.

Suppliers and Customers In some settings, suppliers and customers are interested in the long-run staying power of a company. On the supplier side, if **Boeing** receives an order from an airline for 30 new 747s over the next 10 years, Boeing wants to know whether the airline will be around in the future to take delivery of and pay for the planes. On the customer side, a homeowner who has foundation repair work done wants to know whether the company making the repairs will be around long enough to honor its 50-year guarantee. Financial statements provide information that suppliers and customers can use to assess the long-run prospects of a company.

Employees   Employees are interested in financial accounting information for a variety of reasons. As mentioned earlier, financial statement data are used in determining employee bonuses. In addition, financial accounting information can help an employee evaluate the likelihood that the employer will be able to fulfill its long-run promises, such as pensions and retiree health-care benefits. Financial statements are also important in contract negotiations between labor unions and management.

Competitors   If you were a manager at **PepsiCo**, would you be interested in knowing the relative profitability of **Coca-Cola**'s operations in the United States, Brazil, Japan, and France? Of course you would, because that information could help you identify strategic opportunities for marketing efforts where potential profits are high or where your competitor is weak. Wal-Mart can use the information in financial statements to track its competitors and identify new opportunities to grow and use its market share in retail to increase its revenues in other ventures.

Government Agencies   Federal and state government agencies make frequent use of financial accounting information. For example, to make sure that investors have sufficient information to make informed investment decisions, the Securities and Exchange Commission monitors the financial accounting disclosures of companies (both U.S. and foreign) whose stocks trade on U.S. stock exchanges. The International Trade Commission uses financial accounting information to determine whether the importation of Ecuadorian roses or Chinese textiles is harming U.S. companies through unfair trade practices. The Justice Department uses financial statement data to evaluate whether companies (such as Microsoft) are earning excessive monopolistic profits. In Microsoft's case, from 2003 to 2005, it reported profits of $0.26 on every dollar of sales. During that same period, General Electric, one of America's most admired companies, generated profits of $0.12 on every dollar of sales.

The Press   Financial statements are a great place for a reporter to find background information to flesh out a story about a company. For example, a story about Wal-Mart can be enhanced by using the sales data shown in its annual report. In addition, a surprising accounting announcement, such as a large drop in reported profits, is a trigger for an investigative reporter to write about what is going on in a company.

In summary, who uses financial accounting information? Everyone does, or at least everyone should. External financial reports come within the area of accounting referred to as financial accounting. Most of the data needed to prepare both internal and external reports are provided by the same accounting system. A major difference between management and financial accounting is the types of financial reports prepared. Internal reports are tailored to meet the needs of management and may vary considerably among businesses. General-purpose financial statements and other external reports, however, follow certain standards or guidelines and are thus more uniform among companies. The first fourteen chapters of *Accounting: Concepts and Applications* focus on financial accounting, specifically on the primary financial statements (discussed and illustrated in Chapter 2). The remaining chapters, 15 through 23, focus on management accounting.

REMEMBER THIS...

- Management accounting focuses on providing reports for INTERNAL use by management to assist in making operating decisions and in planning and controlling a company's activities.
- Financial accounting provides information to meet the needs of EXTERNAL users.
- The three general-purpose financial statements are the balance sheet, the income statement, and the statement of cash flows.
- The financial statements are used by interested external parties such as investors, creditors, suppliers, customers, employees, competitors, the government, and the press.

Describe the environment of accounting, including the effects of generally accepted accounting principles, international business, ethical considerations, and technology.

Within What Kind of Environment Does Accounting Operate?

③ Accounting functions in a dynamic environment. Changes in technology as well as economic and political factors can significantly influence accounting practice. For example, the downfall of Enron and WorldCom and the resulting demise of Arthur Andersen have significantly changed the way accounting is done. As a result of these scandals, the U.S. government has taken a more active role in the development of accounting rules and oversight of the accounting industry. Four particularly important factors that influence the environment in which accounting operates are the development of "generally accepted accounting principles" (GAAP), international business, ethical considerations, and technology.

The Significance and Development of Accounting Standards

Imagine a company that compensates a key employee in the following ways:

- Paying a cash salary of $80,000.
- Offering the option to become, a year from now, a 10% owner of the company in exchange for an investment of $200,000.

If the company does well in the coming year, the company will increase in value, the $200,000 price tag for 10% ownership will look like a great deal, and the employee will exercise the option. If the company does poorly, it will decline in value, the $200,000 price will be too high, and the employee will throw the option away and forget the whole thing. Assume the company then sells the ownership option to interested outside investors for $25,000.

The accounting question is how to summarize in one number the company's compensation cost associated with this employee. We would probably all agree to include the $80,000 cash salary as compensation. What about the option? Both of the following arguments could be put forward:

1. If the employee were to buy the option from the company, just like any other outside investor, the employee would have to pay $25,000. Therefore, giving the option to the employee is just like paying him or her $25,000 cash. The $25,000 value of the option should be added to compensation cost.
2. The option doesn't cost the company a thing. In fact, the option merely increases the probability that the employee will invest $200,000 in the company in the future. The option doesn't add a penny to compensation cost.

So, which argument is right? Should each company decide for itself whether to include the $25,000 option value as part of compensation cost, or should there be an overall accounting standard followed by all companies? And if there is a standard, who sets it?[3]

There are many situations in business, such as the option compensation case just described, in which reasonable people can disagree about how certain items should be handled for accounting purposes. And, since financial accounting information is designed to be used by people outside a company, it is important that outsiders understand the rules and assumptions used by the company in constructing its financial statements. This would be extremely difficult and costly for outsiders to find out if every company formulated its own set of accounting rules. Accordingly, in most countries in the world, there exists a committee or board that establishes the accounting rules for that country.

---

[3] The answer to this surprisingly controversial question of the accounting for option compensation is given in Chapter 8. Just to show how influential accounting can be, this exact issue was debated on the floor of the U.S. Senate.

The Financial Accounting Standards Board

In the United States, accounting standards for publicly listed companies are set by the **Financial Accounting Standards Board (FASB)**. The FASB is based in Norwalk, Connecticut, and its seven full-time members are selected from a variety of backgrounds—professional accounting, business, government, and academia. An important thing to note about the FASB is that it is not a government agency; the FASB is a private body established and supported by fees received from companies that are audited by public accounting firms. Because the FASB is not a government agency, it has no legal power to enforce the accounting standards it sets. The FASB gets its authority to establish rules from the Securities and Exchange Commission (discussed later).

Financial Accounting Standards Board (FASB)

The private organization responsible for establishing the standards for financial accounting and reporting in the United States.

The FASB maintains its influence as the accounting standard setter for the United States (and the most influential accounting body in the world) by carefully protecting its prestige and reputation for setting good standards. In doing so, the FASB must walk a fine line between constant improvement of accounting practices to provide more full and fair information for external users and practical constraints on financial disclosure to appease businesses that are reluctant to disclose too much information to outsiders. To balance these opposing forces, the FASB seeks consensus by requesting written comments and sponsoring public hearings on all its proposed standards. The end result of this public process is a set of accounting rules that are described as being **generally accepted accounting principles (GAAP)**.

generally accepted accounting principles (GAAP)

Authoritative guidelines that define accounting practice at a particular time.

As you study this text, you will be intrigued by the interesting conceptual issues the FASB must wrestle with in setting accounting standards. The FASB has deliberated over the correct way to compute motion picture profits, the appropriate treatment of the cost of dismantling a nuclear power plant, the best approach for reflecting the impact of changes in foreign currency exchange rates, and the proper accounting for complex financial instruments such as commodity futures and interest rate swaps. And since U.S. companies are always suspicious that any change in the accounting rules will make them look worse on paper, almost all FASB decisions are made in the midst of controversy.

STOP & THINK

Why is it important for the FASB to remain completely independent?

Other Organizations

In addition to the FASB, several other organizations affect accounting standards and are important in other ways to the practice of accounting. Some of these organizations are discussed below.

Securities and Exchange Commission   In response to the Stock Market Crash of 1929, Congress created the **Securities and Exchange Commission (SEC)** to regulate U.S. stock exchanges. Part of the job of the SEC is to make sure that investors are provided with full and fair information about publicly-traded companies. The SEC is not charged with protecting investors from losing money; instead, the SEC seeks to create a fair information environment in which investors can buy and sell stocks without fear that companies are hiding or manipulating financial data.

Securities and Exchange Commission (SEC)

The government body responsible for regulating the financial reporting practices of most publicly-owned corporations in connection with the buying and selling of stocks and bonds.

As part of its regulatory role, the SEC has received from Congress specific legal authority to establish accounting standards for companies soliciting investment funds from the American public. Generally, the SEC refrains from exercising this authority and allows the FASB to set U.S. accounting standards. However, as a result of the accounting scandals of the early 2000s, the SEC was given more responsibility and authority to monitor financial reporting. Congress provided this

certified public accountant (CPA)

A special designation given to an accountant who has passed a national uniform examination and has met other certifying requirements.

American Institute of Certified Public Accountants (AICPA)

The national organization of CPAs in the United States.

additional authority with the Sarbanes-Oxley Act. This Act created, among other things, a Public Company Accounting Oversight Board. The Act also required the SEC to implement many changes in the way corporations are governed.

While the FASB is charged with creating the rules that dictate financial reporting practices, the SEC is always looming in the background, legally authorized to take over the setting of U.S. accounting standards should the FASB lose its credibility with the public.

American Institute of Certified Public Accountants   The label "CPA" has two different uses—there are individuals who are CPAs and there are CPA firms. A **certified public accountant (CPA)** is someone who has taken a minimum number of college-level accounting classes, has passed the CPA exam administered by the **American Institute of Certified Public Accountants (AICPA)**, and has met other requirements set by his or her state. In essence, the CPA label guarantees that the person has received substantial accounting training.

The second use of the label "CPA" is in association with a CPA firm. A CPA firm is a company that performs accounting services, just as a law firm performs legal services. Obviously, a CPA firm employs a large number of accountants, not all of whom have received the training necessary to be certified public accountants. CPA firms help companies establish accounting systems, formulate business plans, redesign their operating procedures, and just about anything else you can think of. A good way to think of a CPA firm is as a freelance business-advising firm with a particular strength in accounting issues.

CPA firms are also hired to perform independent audits of the financial statements of a company. The important role of the independent audit in ensuring the reliability of the financial statements is discussed in Chapter 5.

 F Y I

Other tasks accountants perform are planning for acquisitions and mergers, measuring efficiency improvements from new technology, managing quality, and developing accounting software.

 F Y I

Besides CPAs, other accounting-related certifications also exist. Examples include the Certified Management Accountant (CMA), Certified Internal Auditor (CIA), and the Certified Fraud Examiner (CFE).

Internal Revenue Service   Financial accounting reports are designed to provide information about the economic performance and health of a company. Income tax rules are designed to tax income when the tax can be paid and to provide concrete rules to minimize inefficient arguing between taxpayers and the **Internal Revenue Service (IRS)**. Financial accounting and tax accounting involve different sets of rules because they are designed for different purposes. The implication of these two different sets of rules is that companies must maintain two sets of books—one set from which the financial statements can be prepared and the other set to comply with income tax regulations. There is nothing shady or underhanded about this. Individuals studying accounting often confuse financial accounting standards and income tax regulations. Keep in mind that what is done for accounting purposes is not necessarily accounted for in the same way for tax purposes.

Internal Revenue Service (IRS)

A government agency that prescribes the rules and regulations that govern the collection of tax revenues in the United States.

International Business

One of the significant environmental changes in recent years has been the expansion of business activity on a worldwide basis. As consumers, we are familiar with the wide array of products from other countries, such as electronics from Japan

© GETTY IMAGES INC.

and clothing made in China. On the other hand, many U.S. companies have operating divisions in foreign countries. Other American companies are located totally within the United States but have extensive transactions with foreign companies. The economic environment of today's business is truly based on a global economy. As an example, in 2005 almost 62% of **IBM**'s sales were to individuals and companies located outside the United States.

Accounting practices among countries vary widely. Attempts are being made to make those practices more consistent among countries. In an attempt to harmonize conflicting national standards, the **International Accounting Standards Board (IASB)** was formed in 1973 to develop worldwide accounting standards. The IASB includes representatives from the eight major accounting standard-setting boards around the world including the United States. Like the FASB, the IASB develops proposals, circulates them among interested organizations, receives feedback, and then issues a final pronouncement.

The accounting standards produced by the IASB are referred to as International Financial Reporting Standards (IFRS's). IFRS's are envisioned to be a set of standards that can be used by all companies regardless of where they are based. In the extreme, IFRS's could supplement or even replace standards set by national standard setters such as the FASB. IASB standards are gaining increasing acceptance throughout the world. Thus far, however, the SEC has not recognized IASB standards and has barred foreign companies from listing their shares on U.S. stock exchanges unless those companies agree to provide financial statements in accordance with U.S. accounting rules (or at least provide a reconciliation between IASB GAAP and U.S. GAAP). Disclosure requirements in the United States are the strictest in the world, and foreign companies are reluctant to submit to the SEC requirement. This conflict between IASB GAAP and U.S. GAAP will be interesting to watch in the coming years: Will the SEC maintain a hard line and ultimately force U.S. accounting rules on the rest of the world? Or will the IASB standards gain increasing acceptance and become the worldwide standard? We'll see.

At numerous points throughout this text, we will point out certain international applications of accounting as well as some differences that might exist in accounting rules between the United States and other countries. In addition, each chapter includes a case in the end-of-chapter material dealing with an international accounting issue.

International Accounting Standards Board (IASB)

The committee formed in 1973 to develop worldwide accounting standards.

 F Y I

Since international accounting standards often differ from GAAP, foreign companies may be required to adjust their books to be listed on the New York Stock Exchange. For example, when Germany's **Daimler-Benz** (makers of Mercedes Benz) became a NYSE-listed company in 1994, its GAAP-adjusted books showed a loss of $748 million, whereas its German standard books reported earnings of $636 million. Note: Daimler-Benz subsequently merged with **Chrysler** to become **DaimlerChrysler**.

F Y I

In 2001, the IASB restructured itself as an independent body with closer links to national standard-setting bodies. At that time, the IASB adopted its current name and dropped its original name of the International Accounting Standards Committee (IASC).

Ethics in Accounting

Another environmental factor affecting accounting, and business in general, is the growing concern over ethics. This concern has been a focus of the accounting scandals of the early 2000s. Enron, WorldCom, and Tyco (to name a few) each resulted from upper management's falsifying financial reports (with the help of the company's internal accountants) and external auditors not detecting those falsifications. Accounting rules and the resulting information are designed to capture and reflect the underlying performance of a company. When management is tempted to use accounting numbers to misrepresent a company's performance, accountants (both inside and outside the company) are perceived by the public as being responsible for ensuring that the misrepresentation does not occur. The public's confidence in the accounting profession was weakened when these scandals came to light with the common denominator being that accounting information was used to mislead the public.

As mentioned previously, the SEC has taken action to see that public confidence in the accounting profession is restored. In addition, other organizations (like the Auditing Standards Board and the major stock exchanges) have taken measures to increase the public's confidence in the role of accountants and auditors and to restore the image of the accounting professional as being ethical and competent.

This concern over ethics and the accounting profession was highlighted in an almost prophetic speech given by then chairman of the SEC, Arthur Levitt, in September 1998 and was reinforced in 2001 with the business failures of Enron and WorldCom. In his speech, entitled "The Number's Game," Chairman Levitt identified several major accounting techniques that he believed were being used to undermine the integrity of financial reporting. As you will find, accounting involves significant judgment. Chairman Levitt expressed concern that this accounting judgment was giving way to pressure to "meet the numbers." In other words, Wall Street's expectations about a company, rather than the company's actual business performance, were driving the reported accounting numbers.

The ethical dilemmas facing businesses and their accountants often revolve around pressures placed on companies by investors, creditors, and potential investors and creditors. As Chairman Levitt mentioned, these pressures can sometimes cause company officials to become involved in "accounting hocus-pocus." Because accounting involves judgment, the reported accounting numbers can differ significantly depending on the assumptions made by those preparing the financial statements. As a simple example of how this can occur, consider again the case of Microsoft. When a customer buys a Microsoft product, part of the purchase price relates to promised customer service and future product upgrades. So the question is this: How much of the sales price should Microsoft report as a "sale" on the date of the sale, and how much relates to future services to be provided? As you can imagine, that is a difficult question to answer, and any answer will involve an estimate.

To quote again from Chairman Levitt's speech, accounting principles "allow for flexibility to adapt to changing circumstances." It is this flexibility that creates many of the ethical dilemmas faced by accountants. As businesses come under pressure to report favorable performance, accountants may also come under pressure to "flex" the rules just a little too far.

Don't let yourself naively think that ethical dilemmas in business are rare. Such issues occur quite frequently. To help prepare you to enter the business world and to recognize and deal with ethical issues, we have included at least one accounting-related ethics case at the end of each chapter. Ethics is an important topic that should be considered carefully, with the ultimate goal of improving individual and collective behavior in society.

Technology

Few developments have changed the way business is conducted as much as computers have. Computer technology allows businesses to do things that 20 years ago were unimaginable. Consider being able to use your desktop computer to track the status of a package shipped from Los Angeles to New York. Companies such as **UPS** and **FedEx** incorporate this type of technology as an integral part of their business. Financial institutions use computer technology to wire billions of dollars each day to locations around the world.

So how have computers changed the way accounting is done? That question can be addressed on several levels. First, computer technology allows companies to easily gather vast amounts of information about individual transactions. For example, information relating to the customer, the salesperson, the product being sold, and the method of payment can be easily gathered for each transaction using computer technology.

Second, computer technology allows large amounts of data to be compiled quickly and accurately, thereby significantly reducing the likelihood of errors. As you will soon discover, a large part of the mechanics of accounting involves moving numbers to and from various accounting records as well as adding and subtracting a lot of figures. Computers have made this process virtually invisible. What once occupied a large part of an accountant's time can now be done in an instant.

Third, in the precomputer world of limited analytical capacity, it was essential for lenders and investors to receive condensed summaries of a company's financial activities. Now, lenders and investors have the ability to receive and process gigabytes of information, so why should the report of Wal-Mart's financial performance be restricted to three short financial statements? Why can't Wal-Mart provide access to much more detailed information online? In fact, why can't Wal-Mart allow investors to directly tap into its own internal accounting database? Information technology has made this type of information acquisition and analysis possible; the question accountants face now is how much information companies should be required to make available to outsiders. Ten years ago, the only way you could get a copy of Wal-Mart's financial statements was to call or write to receive paper copies in the mail. Now you can download those summary financial statements from Wal-Mart's Web site. How will you get financial information 10 years from now? No one knows, but the rapid advances in information technology guarantee that it will be different from anything we are familiar with now.

Finally, and most importantly, although technology has changed the way certain aspects of accounting are carried out, on a fundamental level the mechanics of accounting

THE SECRETS TO DOING WELL
in an Accounting Class

Step one in succeeding in an accounting class is to stay current with your studies and with your assignments. Many of the concepts in accounting are new, and some time is required between the introduction of a new concept and the mastery of that concept. Some students try to "cram" all their accounting study into a short period of time right before an exam, and they almost always find, through sad experience, that the cramming strategy doesn't work in accounting. Some of you may be skeptical of this advice because you have successfully used the cramming strategy in other courses. For you, we suggest the following experiment: pair up with a classmate, with one of you

studying your accounting on a regular basis and the other waiting until two days before the first exam to start studying. We guarantee that the "crammer" will have a humbling experience on that first exam whereas the regular studier will have reasonable success. We also strongly suggest that if you try this experiment, you take the role of the regular studier and let your friend be the crammer.

Second, realize that many of the concepts in accounting build on one another. As a result, missing class or skipping a couple of homework assignments can be catastrophic. An initial concept must be understood before a subsequent concept can be attempted.

are still the same as they were 500 years ago. People are still required to analyze complex business transactions and input the results of that analysis into the computer. Technology has not replaced judgment.

So if you are asking "Why do I need to understand accounting—can't computers just do it?"—the answer is a resounding "No!" You need to know what the computer is doing if you are to understand and interpret the information resulting from the accounting process. You need to understand that since judgment was required when the various pieces of information were put into the accounting systems, judgment will be required to appropriately use that information. We have included numerous end-of-chapter opportunities for you to experience how technology helps in the accounting process. These opportunities will illustrate the important role that technology can play in the accounting process as well as emphasize the critical role that the accountant plays as well.

REMEMBER THIS...

- The rules governing financial accounting are called generally accepted accounting principles (GAAP).
- In the United States, GAAP is set by a private, nongovernmental group called the Financial Accounting Standards Board (FASB).
- Worldwide GAAP is set by the International Accounting Standards Board (IASB) based in London.
- Other U.S. organizations that are important to the practice of accounting are the SEC, the AICPA, and the IRS.
- Because the practice of accounting requires professional judgment, accountants are frequently faced with ethical dilemmas.
- Technology has changed the way accounting information is collected, analyzed, and used. However, computers have not replaced the accountant nor eliminated the need for qualified decision makers.

For example, imagine trying to learn to do algebra after having skipped the lessons on addition and subtraction. Similarly, jumping into Chapter 6 in this book is a difficult feat if you don't understand the material covered in Chapter 3.

The third step in having a good experience in your accounting class is to make sure you understand the big picture. We have included learning objectives to cover each major point in the chapter. The introductions associated with each learning objective should help you understand WHY you are studying the issue in addition to HOW to do accounting. In most cases, when you understand the "why" of something, you find it much easier to grasp the "how."

Finally, if you need help, don't delay in finding it. Your instructor is a valuable resource and you should take advantage of his or her office hours. (Note: Instructors love students who come in with written lists of specific questions. On the other hand, instructors get frustrated with students who view office hours as a time for the instructor to repeat, for an audience of one, a lecture that the student missed.) In addition, many students find that accounting study groups are beneficial. A well-organized study group is an example of the classic economic concept of specialization and trade; group members can rotate in taking the lead in studying difficult concepts and then explaining them to the rest of the group.

Good luck, and enjoy the ride!

So, Why Should I Study Accounting?

4 You may still be asking, "But why do I need to study accounting?" Even if you have no desire to be an accountant, at some point in your life you will need financial information to make certain decisions, such as whether to buy or lease an automobile, how to budget your monthly income, where to invest your savings, or how to finance your (or your child's) college education. You can make each of these decisions without using financial information and then hope everything turns out okay, but that would be bad decision making. As noted in the discussion of Exhibit 3, a good decision does not guarantee a good outcome, but a bad decision guarantees one of two things—a bad outcome or a lucky outcome. And you cannot count on lucky outcomes time after time. On a personal level, each of us needs to understand how to collect and use accounting information.

Odds are that each of you will have the responsibility of providing some form of income for yourself and your family. Would you prefer to work for a company that is doing well and has a promising future or one that is on the brink of bankruptcy? Of course we all want to work for companies that are doing well. But how would you know? Accounting information will allow you to evaluate your employer's short- and long-term potential.

When you graduate and secure employment, it is almost certain that accounting information will play some role in your job. Whether your responsibilities include sales (where you will need information about product availability and costs), production (where you will need information regarding the costs of materials, labor, and overhead), quality control (where you will need information relating to variances between expected and actual production), or human resources (where you will need information relating to the costs of employees), you will use accounting information. The more you know about where accounting information comes from, how it is accumulated, and how it is best used, the better you will be able to perform your job.

Everyone is affected by accounting information. Saying you don't need to know accounting doesn't change the fact that you are affected by accounting information. Ignoring the value of that information simply puts you at a disadvantage. Those who recognize the value of accounting information and learn how to use it to make better decisions will have a competitive advantage over those who don't. It's as simple as that.

F Y I

The AICPA provides a Web site that introduces students to career opportunities in accounting. The Web site is **http://www.startheregoplaces.com**.

REMEMBER THIS...

- Everyone is affected by accounting.
- Each individual needs some accounting skills in order to organize his or her personal finances.
- Each person in a business, charity, or other organization can use accounting information to make better decisions.

REVIEW OF LEARNING OBJECTIVES

(1) Describe the purpose of accounting and explain its role in business and society.

- Accounting is a service activity designed to accumulate, measure, and communicate financial information about businesses and other organizations to provide information for making informed decisions about how to best use available resources.
- Accounting is often called the "language of business."

(2) Identify the primary users of accounting information.

	Managerial Accounting	Financial Accounting
Focus	Internal reporting	External reporting
Reports	Budgets	Balance sheet
	Cost analyses	Income statement
	Performance reports	Statement of cash flows
Users	Company management	Investors
		Creditors
		Suppliers
		Customers
		Employees
		Competitors
		The government
		The press

(3) Describe the environment of accounting, including the effects of generally accepted accounting principles, international business, ethical considerations, and technology.

- Generally accepted accounting principles (GAAP)
  - Set by the FASB in the United States.
  - Set by the IASB worldwide.
- Other U.S. organizations that are important to the practice of accounting:
  - SEC—regulates U.S. stock exchanges and requires financial disclosures by companies listed on those exchanges.
  - AICPA—national association of professional accountants in the United States.
  - IRS—government agency responsible for tax accounting rules.
- Do accountants need ethics? Yes, because they are called on to make accounting judgments and estimates which impact the reported performance of a company.
- Do accountants use computers? Yes, computers have changed the way accounting information is collected, analyzed, and used. However, computers have not replaced the accountant nor eliminated the need for qualified decision makers.

(4) Analyze the reasons for studying accounting.

- Everyone is affected by accounting.
- Each individual needs some accounting skills in order to organize his or her personal finances.
- Each person in a business, charity, or other organization can use accounting information to make better decisions.

KEY TERMS & CONCEPTS

DISCUSSION QUESTIONS

1. What are the three functions of an accounting system?

2. What are the essential elements in decision making, and how does accounting fit into the process?

3. What types of personal decisions have required you to use accounting information?

4. What does the term *business* mean to you?

5. Why is accounting often referred to as the "language of business"?

6. In what ways are the needs of internal and external users of accounting information the same? In what ways are they different?

7. What are generally accepted accounting principles (GAAP)? Who currently develops and issues GAAP? What is the purpose of GAAP?

8. Why is it important for financial statements and other external reports to be based on generally accepted accounting principles?

9. What are the respective roles of the Securities and Exchange Commission (SEC) and the Internal Revenue Service (IRS) in the setting of accounting standards?

10. For you as a potential investor, what is the problem with different countries having different accounting standards? For you as the president of a multinational company, what is the problem with different countries having different accounting standards?

11. Ethical considerations affect all society. Why are ethical considerations especially important for accountants?

12. Given significant technological advances, can we expect to see less demand for accountants and accounting-type services?

13. Other than that it is a requirement for your major or that your mom or dad is making you, why should you study accounting?

EXERCISES

E 1-1   **The Role and Importance of Accounting**

LO1   Assume that you are applying for a part-time job as an accounting clerk in a retail clothing establishment. During the interview, the store manager asks how you expect to contribute to the business. How would you respond?

E 1-2   **Bookkeeping Is Everywhere**

LO1   Describe how bookkeeping is applied in each of the following settings:
   a. Your college English class.
   b. The National Basketball Association.
   c. A hospital emergency room.
   d. Jury selection for a major murder trial.
   e. Four college roommates on a weekend skiing trip.

E 1-3   **Accounting Information and Decision Making**

LO1   You are the owner of Automated Systems, Inc., which sells **Apple** computers and related data processing equipment. You are currently trying to decide whether to continue selling the Apple computer line or to distribute the Windows-based computers instead. What information do you need to consider in order to determine how successful your business is or will be? What information would help you decide whether to sell the Apple or the

(continued)

Windows-based personal computer line? Use your imagination and general knowledge of business activity.

E 1-4
LO1

Allocation of Limited Resources

Assume you are a small business owner trying to increase your company's profits. How can accounting information help you efficiently allocate your limited resources to maximize your business profit?

E 1-5
LO2

Users of Financial Information

Why might each of the following individuals or groups be interested in a firm's financial statements? (a) The current stockholders of the firm; (b) the creditors of the firm; (c) the management of the firm; (d) the prospective stockholders of the firm; (e) the Internal Revenue Service (IRS); (f) the SEC; (g) the firm's major labor union.

E 1-6
LO2

Structuring Information for Use in Evaluation

You work in a small convenience store. The store is very low-tech; you ring up the sales on an old-style cash register that merely records the amount of the sale. The store owner uses this cash register tape at the end of each day to verify that the correct amount of cash is in the cash register drawer.

In addition to verifying the cash amount, how else could the information on the cash register tape be used to evaluate the store's operation? What additional bookkeeping procedures would be necessary to make these additional uses possible?

E 1-7
LO2

Investing in the Stock Market

Assume your grandparents have just given you $20,000 on the condition that you invest the money in the stock market. As you contemplate making your investment choices, what accounting information do you want to help identify companies that will have high future rates of return?

E 1-8
LO2

Management versus Financial Accounting

This chapter discusses two areas of accounting: management and financial accounting. Contrast management and financial accounting with respect to the following:

- Overall purpose
- Type of financial reports used (i.e., external, internal, or both)
- Users of the information

Also, in what ways are these two fields of accounting similar?

E 1-9
LO2

The Role of the SEC

It is not often that the federal government has allowed the private sector to govern itself, but that is exactly what has happened with the field of accounting. The SEC has delegated the responsibility of rule making to the FASB, a group of seven individuals who are hired full-time to discuss issues, research areas of interest, and determine what GAAP is and will be. What are the advantages of allowing the private sector to determine accounting standards? Identify any advantages that the SEC might gain if it established the rules that govern the practice of accounting.

E 1-10
LO2

Why Two Sets of Books?

This past year you were married. This coming April you will be faced with preparing your first tax return since mom and dad said "you are now on your own." As you review the IRS regulations, you notice several differences from what you learned in your accounting class. It appears that businesses must keep two sets of books: one for the IRS and one in accordance with GAAP. Why aren't GAAP and IRS rules the same?

E 1-11
LO2

Career Opportunities in Accounting

You are scheduled to graduate from college with a degree in accounting, and your mother would like to know what you plan to do with the rest of your life. She assumes

(continued)

that your only option is to be a bookkeeper like Bob Cratchit in the story *A Christmas Carol*. What can you tell Mom regarding the options available to you with your degree in accounting?

E 1-12
LO3

Differences in Accounting across Borders

In the United States, accounting for inventory is a difficult issue. Inventory is comprised of those items either purchased or manufactured to be resold at a profit. Numerous methods are available to account for inventory for financial reporting purposes. A very commonly used method—called LIFO (last-in, first-out)—minimizes a company's tax obligation. In the United Kingdom, however, LIFO is not permitted for tax purposes and thus is not used very often for financial reporting. In Turkey, the use of LIFO is severely restricted, and in Russia, LIFO is a foreign term. Only in Germany, where the tax laws have been modified to allow the use of LIFO, is LIFO being adopted. Different accounting methods are available for numerous other issues in accounting. Identify some major problems associated with comparing the financial statements of companies from different countries.

E 1-13
LO3

Ethics in Accounting

The text has pointed out that ethics is an important topic, especially for CPAs. Derek Bok, former law professor and president of Harvard University, has suggested that colleges and universities have a special opportunity and obligation to train students to be more thoughtful and perceptive about moral and ethical issues. Other individuals have concluded that it is not possible to "teach" ethics. What do you think? Can ethics be taught? If you agree that colleges and universities can teach ethics, how might the ethical dimensions of accounting be presented to students?

E 1-14
LO3

Challenges to the Accounting Profession

As the business world continues to change the way in which business is conducted, accountants are faced with the challenge of accounting for these changes. Who, for example, could have anticipated the risks associated with asbestos? Or the decline of communism? Or the increasingly litigious environment in the United States? Each of these events, and many more, has influenced business—which has, in turn, influenced accounting. From your general understanding of accounting and the current business environment, what are some of the challenges you see facing the accounting profession?

E 1-15
LO4

Why Do I Need to Know Accounting?

One of your college friends recently graduated from school with a major in music (specifically piano). He has told you that he is going to start his own piano instructional business. He plans to operate the business from home. You ask him how he is going to account for his business, and his reply is, "I graduated in music, not accounting. I am going to teach music, not number crunching. I didn't need accounting in college and I don't need it now!" Is your friend right? What financial information might he find useful in operating his business?

ANALYTICAL ASSIGNMENTS

AA 1-16
DISCUSSION

To Lend or Not To Lend—That Is the Question

Sam Love is vice president and chief lending officer of the Meeker First National Bank. Recently, Bill McCarthy, a new farmer, moved to town. Sam has not dealt with Bill previously and knows little about the Mountain Meadow Ranch that Bill operates. Bill would like to borrow $100,000 to purchase some equipment and yearling steers for his ranch. What information does Sam need to help make the lending decision? What type of information should Bill collect and analyze before even requesting the loan?

AA 1-17
DISCUSSION

Information Needs to Remain Competitive

In 2005, **Intel** owned the microprocessor industry with a market share of over 80%. Its nearest competition was **Advanced Micro Devices (AMD)** with a market share of 17.6%.

(continued)

What type of information, accounting or otherwise, do you think the management of AMD may want and need as they try to compete with Intel and other companies?

AA 1-18
DISCUSSION

International Happenings

July 1, 1997, marked a historic date as Hong Kong reverted to political and economic control by mainland China. The Stock Exchange of Hong Kong offers the opportunity to invest in both local Hong Kong companies and in "red-chip offerings," which are stocks of companies that are listed in Hong Kong but controlled by mainland China interests. As an international investor, what accounting information might be helpful as you consider investing in the Hong Kong stock market? For which variables in this situation is accounting information unlikely to be very helpful?

AA 1-19
DISCUSSION

Is Better Accounting the Solution to All of Life's Problems?

Your friend has just completed an introductory accounting course. She has heard that you are now taking accounting, and she has come to give you the benefit of her experience. You discover that your friend is enamored with the field of accounting, and she now believes that most business problems can be easily solved through better accounting. In fact, your friend believes that most government, social, and spiritual problems can also be solved by a better application of good accounting principles. Given what you have read in Chapter 1, do you agree with your friend? Explain.

AA 1-20
DISCUSSION

We Don't Have Time for Good Accounting!

Your sister and her business partner have just launched their own software company. They have developed software that compresses and packages email text and voice messages, allowing email and phone messages to be safely transmitted over a wireless network even while flying in a commercial airliner. Orders for the software have been pouring in, and your sister and her business partner estimate that they will make at least $10 million within the next three months. You suggest to your sister that she hire an accountant and begin to set up an accounting system within her new company. Your sister replies that accounting systems are for old-fashioned companies such as **General Motors** and **Procter & Gamble**; she wants to focus her time on hiring new software developers and on working on ideas for her company's next generation of software products. Is your sister correct? Explain.

AA 1-21
DISCUSSION

Is the Proposed Electricity Rate Increase Fair?

The governor of your state has just appointed you to the state's public utility rate commission. Your job is to set fair prices for the electricity and natural gas sold to residents of the state by a select number of public utilities. The state's primary electric utility has just proposed a 5.3% rate increase. How should you use accounting information to evaluate this proposed rate hike?

AA 1-22
JUDGMENT CALL

You Decide: How much education is necessary for an accountant?

You are at your family reunion when some relatives start asking you about your studies and plans after school. Upon learning your intentions to be an accountant, everyone was alarmed that it took five to six years to get a master's degree in accounting. Your uncle says, "All you have to do is go to a computer store and pick up a copy of QuickBooks. Computers do everything these days. The computer will do all the work and you can collect a paycheck!" Is five to six years too much time and effort to prepare to be an accountant, or is it necessary?

AA 1-23
JUDGMENT CALL

You Decide: Should the Emerging Issues Task Force (a group organized to assist the FASB in developing accounting positions) be allowed to have members of large corporations sit on their committee and vote on accounting issues that are facing today's companies, or should it be left to the accounting firms?

That is what happened with **J.P. Morgan** at a June 2002 meeting of the EITF (Emerging Issues Task Force), an extension of the FASB. J.P. Morgan blocked a vote that would have barred companies from recognizing immediate profits or losses upon entering an energy-trading contract, a move that is critical to the financial statements of J.P. Morgan and others in its industry.

AA 1-24
REAL COMPANY
ANALYSIS

Wal-Mart

In Appendix A at the back of this text is **Wal-Mart's** Form 10-K for the year ended January 31, 2006. Review the Form 10-K and identify its major areas. How many pages of the Form 10-K are devoted to a narrative of the prior three years' performance? How many pages focus on explaining technical accounting and business-related issues and procedures? In your opinion, given your limited knowledge of accounting, what is the most interesting part of the Form 10-K? What is the least interesting?

AA 1-25
REAL COMPANY
ANALYSIS

General Motors

Below is a condensed listing of the assets and liabilities of **General Motors** as of December 31, 2005. All amounts are in millions of U.S. dollars.

Assets		Liabilities	
Cash	$ 50,452	Payables	$315,663
Loans receivable	218,236	Pensions	11,304
Inventories	14,354	Other retiree benefits	33,997
Property & equipment	82,740	Other liabilities	99,478
Other assets	110,296		
Total assets	$476,078	Total liabilities	$460,442

1. Among its assets, General Motors lists more than $218 billion in loans receivable. This represents loans that General Motors has made and expects to collect in the future. This is exactly the kind of asset reported among the assets of banks. Given what you know about General Motors' business, how do you think the company acquired these loans receivable?

2. The difference between the reported amount of General Motors' assets and liabilities is $15.636 billion ($476.078 – $460.442). What does this difference represent?

AA 1-26
INTERNATIONAL

Should the SEC Choose the FASB or the IASB?

The SEC has received from Congress the legal authority to set accounting standards in the United States. Historically, the SEC has allowed the FASB to set those standards. In addition, the SEC has refused to allow foreign companies to seek investment funds in the United States unless they agree to provide U.S. investors with financial statements prepared using FASB rules.

The number of foreign companies seeking to list their shares on U.S. stock exchanges is increasing. Even more would likely sell stock to the American public if the SEC were to agree to accept financial statements prepared according to usually less stringent IASB standards.

Why do you think the SEC has so far insisted on financial statements prepared using FASB rules? Do you agree with its policy? Explain.

AA 1-27
ETHICS

Disagreement with the Boss

You recently graduated with your degree in accounting and have accepted an entry-level accounting position with BigTec, Inc. One of your first responsibilities is to review expense reports submitted by various executives. The expense reports include such items as receipts for taking clients to dinner and hotel receipts for business travel. In conducting this review, you note that your boss has submitted for reimbursement several items that are clearly outside the established guidelines of the corporation. In questioning your boss about the items, he told you to process the items and not worry about them. What would you do?

AA 1-28
WRITING

The Language of Business

Accounting is known as the "language of business." Prepare a one- to two-page paper explaining why all business students should have some accounting education. Also include a discussion of how accounting applies to at least five different types of businesses, such as a grocery store, a university, or a movie theater.

AA 1-29
WRITING

Visiting an Accounting Professional

Select a field of accounting you are interested in. Visit a professional who works in that area and discuss the career opportunities available in that specific accounting field. After the visit, prepare a one- to two-page paper summarizing what you learned from your discussion with the accounting professional.

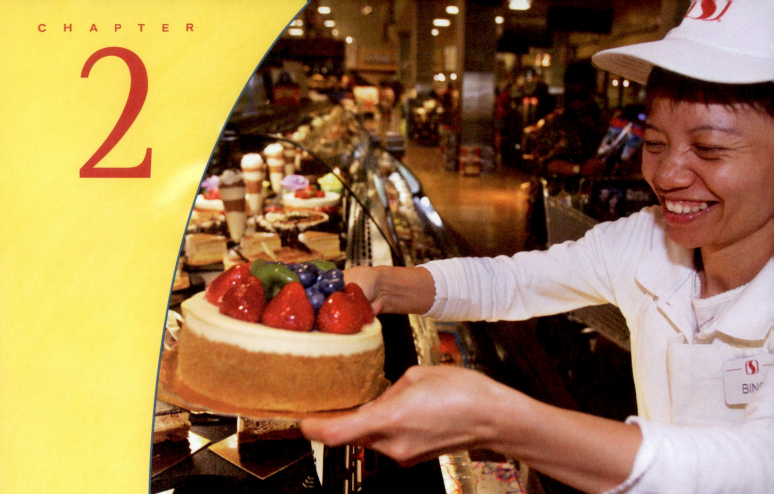

© AP PHOTO/BEN MARGOT

Financial Statements: An Overview

(1) Understand the basic elements, uses, and limitations of the balance sheet. *The balance sheet reports a company's financial position at a point in time and lists the company's resources (assets), obligations (liabilities), and net ownership interest (owners' equity).*

(2) Understand the basic elements and uses of the income statement. *The income statement describes a company's financial performance for a period of time. A company's expenses are subtracted from its revenues in computing net income.*

(3) Understand the categories and uses of the statement of cash flows and see how the primary financial statements tie together. *The statement of cash flows details how a company obtained and spent cash during a period of time. All of a company's cash transactions are categorized as either operating, investing, or financing activities.*

(4) Recognize the need for financial statement notes and identify the types of information included in the notes. *The notes to the financial statements provide information on the accounting assumptions used in preparing the statements and also provide supplemental information not included in the statements themselves.*

(5) Describe the purpose of an audit report and the incentives the auditor has to perform a good audit. *An audit performed by accountants from outside the company increases the reliance that users can place on the information in the company's financial statements. The audit firm does a thorough and fair audit in order to protect its reputation and to reduce the risk of a costly lawsuit.*

(6) Explain the fundamental concepts and assumptions that underlie financial accounting. *The financial statements are prepared for the business itself, excluding items related strictly to the personal affairs of the owner or owners. The dollar amounts recorded in the financial statements come from market transactions and are assumed to be a fair reflection of the underlying value of the items exchanged.*

In addition to founding the brokerage firm of **Merrill Lynch**, in 1926 Charles Merrill was instrumental in the consolidation of several grocery store chains in the western United States to form one big holding company called **Safeway**. In 1955, control of Safeway passed to Robert Magowan, Merrill's son-in-law. Under Magowan's leadership, Safeway expanded to become, in 1971, the largest supermarket chain in the United States.

During the 1970s, Safeway became too cautious and conservative (in the view of many). In 1980, Robert Magowan's 37-year-old son, Peter (who had started out in Safeway as a teenager bagging groceries), became chairman of the board of directors. As he assumed leadership of Safeway, Magowan faced a host of problems: an overall decrease in the size of the grocery market due to an increased tendency by Americans to eat at fast-food restaurants; union contracts that resulted in higher labor costs for Safeway than many of its competitors; high corporate overhead; and stores that were too small and too close together.

Under Peter Magowan's leadership, Safeway eliminated 2,000 office and warehouse jobs and embarked upon an impressive program of new construction and remodeling. During much of the early 1980s, Safeway spent more on capital expenditures than any other U.S. company, averaging nearly $600 million per year. In November 1986, Safeway was acquired by **Kohlberg, Kravis, Roberts & Co. (KKR)** for $5.3 billion in what was then the second-largest debt-financed buyout of all time.

So, how is Safeway doing today? In the 2005 Fortune 500 survey, Safeway, with 2004 sales of $35.8 billion, ranks as the fourth-largest food and drug chain in the United States, behind **Kroger** ($56.4 billion in sales), **Albertson's** ($40.1 billion in sales)[1], and **Walgreen** ($37.5 billion in sales). Sales volume isn't the only financial measure that can be used to evaluate a company. For example, Safeway reported net income in 2004 of ($560) million, compared to the net loss reported by Kroger ($128 million) and net income reported by Albertson's ($444 million) and Walgreen ($1,360 million). Also, Safeway's cash income ("cash from operations") was $2,226 million.

To adequately answer the question of how Safeway is doing today, one must have a working knowledge of financial statements. In this chapter, you will learn that the financial statements are summary reports that show how a business is doing and what its successes and failures are. The financial statements covered in this chapter are the same as those used every day by millions of business owners, investors, and creditors to evaluate how well or poorly organizations are doing.

Hopefully, you will come away from this chapter convinced that the purpose of accounting is not to fill out dull reports that are then filed away in dusty cabinets, but rather to prepare summary financial performance measures to be used as the basis for thousands of economic decisions every day.

The Financial Statements

The job of a mortgage loan officer is to evaluate each mortgage applicant to determine the likelihood that he or she will repay the mortgage loan. A key piece of evidence in each applicant's file is the financial information included as part of the loan application. A loan officer can use this information to evaluate whether an applicant will generate enough income to make the monthly mortgage payments and continue to make the required payments on other obligations. In fact, it is difficult to imagine how a mortgage loan officer could make an informed decision without this financial information.

Gaining access to an applicant's financial information clearly helps the mortgage lender make a better loan decision, but the applicant also benefits from making these

---

[1] In 1999, Albertson's merged with **American Stores** to form what was, at the time, the largest supermarket chain in the United States. Coincidentally, American Stores traces its roots back to the Skaggs family, whose stores also formed the backbone of the original Safeway chain organized by Charles Merrill in 1926.

primary financial statements

The balance sheet, income statement, and statement of cash flows, used by external groups to assess a company's economic standing.

balance sheet (statement of financial position)

The financial statement that reports a company's assets, liabilities, and owners' equity at a particular date.

income statement (statement of earnings)

The financial statement that reports the amount of net income earned by a company during a period.

statement of cash flows

The financial statement that reports the amount of cash collected and paid out by a company during a period of time.

financial disclosures. If no financial disclosures were provided, lenders would be forced to make loan decisions in the absence of reliable financial information about applicants. With greater uncertainty about applicants' ability to repay loans, a lender's risk would increase, causing the lender to raise the interest rate charged on loans. Thus, disclosure of financial information allows a lender to make better lending decisions and also allows an applicant to reduce the lender's uncertainty, leading to a lower interest rate on the loan.

The financial statements prepared by companies yield the same benefits as do the financial disclosures provided by mortgage applicants. Financial statement information provides potential lenders and investors with a reliable basis for evaluating the past performance and future prospects of a company. Because financial statements are used by so many different groups (investors, creditors, managers, etc.), they are sometimes called *general-purpose financial statements*. The three **primary financial statements** are the balance sheet, the income statement, and the statement of cash flows. These statements provide answers to the following questions:

1. What is the company's current financial status?
2. What were the company's operating results for the period?
3. How did the company obtain and use cash during the period?

The **balance sheet** (or **statement of financial position**) reports the resources of a company (assets), the company's obligations (liabilities), and the difference between what is owned (assets) and what is owed (liabilities), called owners' equity.

The **income statement** (or **statement of earnings**) reports the amount of net income earned by a company during a period, with annual and quarterly income statements being the most common. (Net income is discussed later in the chapter.) The income statement represents the accountant's best effort at measuring the economic performance of a company.

The **statement of cash flows** reports the amount of cash collected and paid out by a company in the following three types of activities: operating, investing, and financing.

For illustrative purposes, we will reference **Wal-Mart**'s financial statements in this chapter and throughout the rest of the book. Those financial statements can be found in the back of the text in Appendix A.

The Balance Sheet

1 Understand the basic elements, uses, and limitations of the balance sheet.

In the movie *The Princess Bride*, the hero, Wesley, was "mostly dead all day" until being revived by a miracle pill. Wesley was immediately challenged to come up with a plan to stop the imminent marriage of his true love, Buttercup, to the evil Prince Humperdinck. In formulating his plan, Wesley's first question to his conspirators was "What are our liabilities?" followed by "What are our assets?" In essence, the recently revived hero was saying, "Let me see a balance sheet." Similarly, the first questions asked about any business by potential investors and creditors are "What are the resources of the business?" and "What are its existing obligations?" The balance sheet answers these questions.

The three categories of the balance sheet—assets, liabilities, and owners' equity—are each explained on the following page.

assets

Economic resources that are owned or controlled by a company.

Assets

Assets are economic resources that are owned or controlled[2] by a company. Exhibit 1 contains a list of common assets along with a brief explanation of each asset. To be summarized and aggregated on a balance sheet, each asset must be assigned a dollar amount. A balance sheet wouldn't be very useful with the following asset listing: one bank account, two warehouses full of goods, three trucks, and four customers who owe us money. As emphasized throughout this text, the monetary measurement and valuation of assets is an area in which accountants must exercise considerable professional judgment.

F Y I

The insurmountable difficulties in valuing some assets can cause important economic assets to be excluded from a company's balance sheet. For example, how does one put a monetary value on the worldwide reputation of Coca-Cola or on the genius and leadership of Bill Gates? These assets, though incredibly valuable, are not listed in the balance sheets of **The Coca-Cola Company** or of **Microsoft**.

Liabilities

Liabilities are obligations to pay cash, transfer other assets, or provide services to someone else. Your personal liabilities might include unpaid phone bills, the remaining balance on an automobile loan, or an obligation to complete work for which you have already been paid. Exhibit 2 includes a listing of some of the more common liabilities. Like assets, liabilities must be measured in dollars or whatever the currency being used is (monetary amounts.) And, as with assets, quantifying the amount of a liability can require extensive judgment. As one example, consider the difficulties faced by a company to quantify its obligation to clean up a particular toxic waste site when the cleanup will take years to complete; the exact extent of the environmental damage at the site is still in dispute; and legal responsibility for the toxic mess is still being debated in the courts. Properly valuing a company's liabilities is one of the biggest (if not *the* biggest) challenges that an accountant faces.

liabilities

Obligations to pay cash, transfer other assets, or provide services to someone else.

Owners' Equity

The remaining claim against the assets of a business, after the liabilities have been deducted, is **owners' equity**. Thus, owners' equity is a

owners' equity

The ownership interest in the net assets of an entity; equals total assets minus total liabilities.

EXHIBIT 1	Common Assets

Common Assets

Asset	Definition	Example
Cash	Coins, currency, checks.	The amount in a company's checking account.
Accounts Receivable	Amounts owed to a company that sold goods or services to a customer on credit.	If you have a balance on your credit card, the credit card company classifies the amount you owe them as an account receivable.
Inventory	Items that are purchased or manufactured by a company and are resold.	The items you see on the shelves in **Wal-Mart** are considered by Wal-Mart as inventory.
Buildings	Structures used in the operations of a business.	To continue the previous example, the store itself is classified by Wal-Mart as a building.

---

[2] An example of an asset that a company technically does not own, but does economically control, is a building that the company uses under a long-term, noncancelable lease agreement.

EXHIBIT 2	Common Liabilities	

Common Liabilities

Liability	Definition	Example
Accounts Payable	Amount owed as a result of the purchase of goods and services on credit.	The amount owed by a company for inventory that was purchased on credit and has not been paid for yet.
Taxes Payable	Amount owed to federal and state governments resulting from the application of tax laws.	Corporate income tax owed but not yet paid; employment taxes owed but not yet paid.
Mortgage Payable	Amount owed relating to the purchase of property.	The loan associated with the purchase of a home or building would be called a Mortgage Payable.
Unearned Revenue	When customers pay for service or product in advance, the company owes service or product (not money) to the customer.	If you pay for a 12-month magazine subscription, the publishing company owes you magazines.

net assets

The owners' equity of a business; equal to total assets minus total liabilities.

residual amount; it represents the **net assets** (total assets minus total liabilities) available after all obligations have been satisfied. Exhibit 3 contains a listing of common sources of owners' equity. Obviously, if there are no liabilities (an unlikely situation, except at the start of a business), then the total assets are exactly equal to the owners' claims against those assets—the owners' equity.

In order to get a business started, investors transfer resources, usually cash, to the business in return for part ownership. Ownership of a company can be restricted to one person (a sole proprietorship), to a small group (a partnership), or to a diverse group of owners who often don't even know one another (a corporation). When owners initially invest money in a corporation, they receive evidence of their ownership in the form of shares of stock, represented by stock certificates. These shares of stock may then be privately traded among existing owners of the corporation, privately sold to new owners, or traded publicly on an organized stock exchange such as the New York Stock Exchange (NYSE) (where **Safeway's** shares are traded) or the NASDAQ exchange (where Microsoft's shares are traded). The owners of a corporation are called **stockholders** or **shareholders**, and the

stockholders (shareholders)

The owners of a corporation.

EXHIBIT 3	Sources of Owners' Equity *aka net assets*	

Sources of Owners' Equity

Owners' Equity	Definition	Example
Capital Stock	The amount given by shareholders to obtain shares of stock from a company.	A company sells shares of stock to the public. The amount the company receives is Capital Stock. Capital Stock is usually divided into two accounts: Common Stock and Additional Capital Stock that will be explained later.
Retained Earnings	Earnings that are retained in the business.	If a company reports net income for the year of $100,000 and reinvests the entire amount in the business (doesn't distribute dividends to its owners), retained earnings is $100,000.

stockholders' equity

The owners' equity section of a corporate balance sheet.

owners' equity section of a corporate balance sheet is sometimes referred to as **stockholders' equity**.

Owners' equity is increased when owners make additional investments in a business or when the business generates profits that are retained in the business. Owners' equity is decreased when the owners take back part of their investment. If the business is a corporation, distributions to the owners (stockholders) are called **dividends**. Owners' equity can also be decreased if operations generate a loss instead of a profit. In the extreme, very poor performance can result in the loss of all the assets originally invested by the owners. For a corporation, the amount of accumulated earnings of the business that have not been distributed to owners is called **retained earnings**. The portion of owners' equity contributed by owners in exchange for shares of stock is called **capital stock**. The amount of retained earnings plus the amount of capital stock equals the corporation's total owners' equity.

F Y I

Although the emphasis in this book is on corporations, most of the same principles also apply to proprietorships and partnerships. Differences in accounting for proprietorships and partnerships are explained in detail in this text's website at **http://www.thomsonedu.com/accounting/albrecht**.

dividends

Distributions to the owners (stockholders) of a corporation.

retained earnings

The amount of accumulated earnings of the business that have not been distributed to owners.

Accounting Equation   The balance sheet presents information based on the basic **accounting equation**:

$$\text{Assets} = \text{Liablities} + \text{Owners' Equity}$$

In fact, the name *balance sheet* comes from the fact that a proper balance sheet must always balance—total assets must equal the total of liabilities and owners' equity. The accounting equation is not some miraculous coincidence; it is true by definition. Liabilities and owners' equity are just the methods used to finance the purchase of assets; that is, they are the claims (creditors' claims and owners' claims) against the assets. They can also be thought of as the sources of the funds that were used to purchase the assets. So, another way to view the accounting equation is that the total amount of the assets is equal to the total amount of financing needed to buy the assets. The total resources, therefore, equal the claims against those resources. This is illustrated in Exhibit 4.

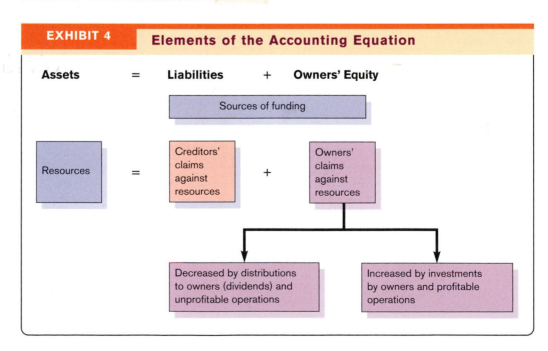

EXHIBIT 4   **Elements of the Accounting Equation**

capital stock

The portion of stockholders' equity that represents investment by owners in exchange for shares of stock. Also referred to as paid-in capital.

accounting equation

An algebraic equation that expresses the relationship between assets (resources), liabilities (obligations), and owners' equity (net assets, or the residual interest in a business after all liabilities have been met): Assets = Liabilities + Owners' Equity.

double-entry accounting

A system of recording transactions in a way that maintains the equality of the accounting equation.

classified balance sheet

A balance sheet in which assets and liabilities are subdivided into current and long-term categories.

current assets

Cash and other assets that can be easily converted to cash within a year.

The accounting equation is presented here merely to give you a glimpse of **double-entry accounting**. Chapter 3 gives an in-depth discussion of the equation elements and the mechanics of double-entry accounting.

The Format of a Balance Sheet   A balance sheet, adapted from Safeway's 2005 balance sheet is shown in Exhibit 5. Note that a balance sheet is presented for a particular date because it reports a company's financial position at a point in time.

As illustrated, the balance sheet is divided into the major sections we have described: assets, liabilities, and owners' equity. The asset section identifies the types of assets owned by Safeway (cash, for example) and the monetary amounts associated with those assets. The liability section defines the extent and nature of Safeway's debts (income taxes not yet paid, for example).

Owners' equity completes the balance sheet. This section identifies the portion of Safeway's resources that were contributed by owners, either in exchange for shares of stock or as undistributed earnings since Safeway's inception. Together with liabilities, owners' equity indicates how a company is financed (whether by borrowing or by owner contributions and operating profits). You can see that Safeway has been financed primarily through liabilities. Because total liabilities are over 70% of Safeway's total assets, we can say that most of Safeway's assets are financed using some form of liabilities.

Classified and Comparative Balance Sheets   Imagine that two people each owe you $10,000. You ask to see the balance sheets of each. Borrower A has assets of $10,000 in the form of cash. Borrower B has assets of $10,000 in the form of undeveloped land. If you need to collect the loan in the next two weeks, which of the two borrowers is more likely to be able to pay you back? Borrower A is more likely to be able to repay you quickly because the assets of A are more *liquid*, meaning that they are in the form of cash or can be easily converted into cash. Assets such as undeveloped land are said to be *illiquid* in that it takes time and effort to convert them into cash. This illustration shows that not all assets are the same. For some purposes, it is very important to distinguish between current assets, which are generally more liquid, and long-term assets. A balance sheet that distinguishes between current and long-term assets is called a **classified balance sheet**.

Note that in the balance sheet in Exhibit 5, Safeway's assets are classified as current, or short-term, and long-term. **Current assets** include cash and other assets that are expected to be converted to cash within a year. Current assets generally are listed in decreasing order of **liquidity** (see page 36 for definition); cash is listed first, followed by the other current assets, such as accounts receivable. **Long-term assets**, such as land, buildings, and equipment, are those that a company needs in order to operate its business over an extended period of time (see page 37 for definition).

Like assets, liabilities usually are classified as either **current liabilities** (obligations expected to be paid within a year) or **long-term liabilities** (see page 37 for definitions). Accounts payable, for example, usually would be paid within 30 to 60 days, whereas a mortgage may remain on the books for 20 to 30 years before it is fully paid.

Safeway's balance sheet in Exhibit 5 includes financial information for both the current year and the preceding year. Most companies prepare such **comparative financial statements** so that readers can identify any significant changes in particular items (see page 37 for definition). For example, notice that Safeway's

CAUTION

Don't worry about fully understanding all the items in Safeway's classified balance sheet, such as the "Obligations under capital leases" and the "Accumulated other comprehensive income." If there was nothing else to learn, this book would be much shorter and this accounting class would last only two weeks.

EXHIBIT 5	Classified Balance Sheets for Safeway

Safeway, Inc.
Comparative Balance Sheet
Year-End 2005 and 2004
(amounts in millions)

	2005	2004
ASSETS		
Current assets:		
Cash and equivalents	$ 373.3	$ 266.8
Receivables	350.6	339.0
Merchandise inventories, net of LIFO reserve of $48.4 and $48.6	2,766.0	2,740.7
Prepaid expenses and other current assets	212.5	251.2
Total current assets	$ 3,702.4	$ 3,597.7
Property, plant & equipment:		
Land	$ 1,413.9	$ 1,396.0
Plant and equipment	14,714.9	13,646.7
	$16,128.8	$15,042.7
Less accumulated depreciation and amortization	(7,031.7)	(6,353.3)
Total property, net	$ 9,097.1	$ 8,689.4
Goodwill	2,402.4	2,406.6
Other assets	555.0	683.7
Total assets	$15,756.9	$15,377.4
LIABILITIES AND STOCKHOLDERS' EQUITY		
Current liabilities:		
Current portion of long-term debt	$ 753.3	$ 639.7
Accounts payable	2,151.5	1,759.4
Accrued salaries and wages	526.1	426.4
Income taxes	124.2	270.3
Other accrued liabilities	708.8	696.3
Total current liabilities	$ 4,263.9	$ 3,792.1
Long-term debt:		
Notes and debentures	$ 4,961.2	$ 5,469.7
Obligations under capital leases	644.1	654.0
Total long-term debt	$ 5,605.3	$ 6,123.7
Deferred income taxes	223.1	463.6
Accrued claims and other liabilities	744.9	691.1
Total liabilities	$10,837.2	$11,070.5
Stockholders' equity:		
Common stock: par value $0.01 per share; 1,500 shares authorized; 580.1 and 578.5 shares outstanding	$ 5.8	$ 5.8
Additional capital stock and other	3,445.1	3,357.9
Treasury stock at cost; 130.7 and 130.8 shares	(3,875.7)	(3,879.7)
Accumulated other comprehensive income	172.8	144.9
Retained earnings	5,171.7	4,678.0
Total stockholders' equity	$ 4,919.7	$ 4,306.9
Total liabilities and stockholders' equity	$15,756.9	$15,377.4

liquidity

The ability of a company to pay its debts in the short run.

total assets increased by $379.5 million ($15,756.9 − $15,377.4) from 2004 to 2005. In addition, notice that Safeway's total liabilities decreased by $233.3 million. An increase in total assets coupled with a decrease in total liabilities often indicates a company is doing well. The fact that the company reported net income of $561.1 million confirms that the company is having success.

Limitations of a Balance Sheet   Although the balance sheet is useful in showing the financial status of a company, it does have some limitations. The primary limitation of

long-term assets

Assets that a company needs in order to operate its business over an extended period of time.

current liabilities

Liabilities expected to be satisfied within a year or the current operating cycle, whichever is longer.

long-term liabilities

Liabilities that are not expected to be satisfied within a year.

comparative financial statements

Financial statements in which data for two or more years are shown together.

market value

The value of a company as measured by the number of shares of stock outstanding multiplied by the current market price of the stock; the current value of a business.

book value

The value of a company as measured by the amount of owners' equity; that is, assets less liabilities.

the balance sheet is that it does not reflect the current value or worth of a company. Refer to the balance sheet numbers for Wal-Mart in the appendix. If the balance sheet were perfect, meaning that it included all economic assets reported at their current market values, then the amount of owners' equity would be equal to the market value of the company. In the case of Wal-Mart, the value of the company would be $70.8 billion, which is the amount of assets that would remain after all the liabilities were repaid. The actual market value of Wal-Mart on May 9, 2006, however, was $200 billion. How could the balance sheet be so wrong?

The discrepancy between recorded balance sheet value and actual market value is the result of the following two factors:

1. Accountants record many assets at their purchase cost, not at their current market value. **Market value** is the price that would have to be paid to buy the same asset today. For example, if land was obtained ten years ago, it would still be reported on the balance sheet at its original cost, even though its market value may have increased dramatically.
2. Not all economic assets are included in the balance sheet. For example, some of the most important economic assets of Wal-Mart are its distribution channels, its name recognition, and its reputation for low prices. These intangible factors are all very valuable economic assets. In fact, they are by far the most valuable assets Wal-Mart has. Nevertheless, these important economic assets are outside the normal accounting process.

Because the balance sheet can underreport the value of some long-term assets, and not report other important economic assets, the accounting **book value** of a company (measured by the amount of owners' equity) is usually less than the company's market value, measured by the market price per share times the number of shares of stock. This is illustrated in Exhibit 6 using data for the ten largest companies (in terms of market value) in the United States.

Despite its deficiencies, the balance sheet is a useful source of information regarding the financial position of a business. A lender would never loan a company money without knowing what assets the company has and what other loans the company is already obligated to repay. An investor shouldn't pay money in exchange for ownership in a company without knowing something about the company's existing resources and obligations. When a balance sheet is classified, and when comparative data are provided, the balance sheet provides an informative picture of a company's financial position.

> **REMEMBER THIS...**
>
> - Balance sheet—a summary of the financial position of a company at a particular date
> - Asset—economic resource owned or controlled by a company
> - Liability—economic obligation to deliver assets or provide a service
> - Equity—equal to total assets minus total liabilities and representing the book value of the assets that belongs to the owners after the liability obligations have been satisfied; stems from direct owner investment and past profits retained in the business
> - Accounting equation—Assets = Liabilities + Owners' Equity
> - Format—in the balance sheet, assets and liabilities are typically separated into current and long-term items with data for both the current and the preceding year reported for comparison
> - Limitations—the balance sheet reflects assets acquired at their historical cost, thus frequently ignoring changes in value and gradual development of intangible assets

| EXHIBIT 6 | Book Value and Market Value for the Ten Largest U.S. Firms |||

Rank	Company	Book Value*	Market Value*†
1	ExxonMobil	$101.76	$405.25
2	General Electric	110.82	372.14
3	Microsoft	74.83	273.75
4	Citigroup	109.29	247.66
5	Wal-Mart	19.40	218.56
6	Pfizer	68.28	197.99
7	Johnson & Johnson	31.81	194.68
8	Bank of America	99.65	188.77
9	American Intl. Group	80.61	173.99
10	International Business Machines	29.75	152.76

* Accounting book value and market value are in billions of dollars.

†On page 37 we noted that Wal-Mart's market value was $200 billion on May 9, 2006. In this exhibit, Wal-Mart's value is listed as $218.56 billion as of February 28, 2005.

Source: Forbes 2000 listing, 2005. Market values are as of February 28, 2005. Accounting book values are for the end of the immediately preceding fiscal year.

The Income Statement

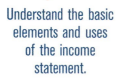

Understand the basic elements and uses of the income statement. ②

Almost every day, *The Wall Street Journal* includes articles detailing the income forecasts of many publicly-traded companies. The stock prices of companies go up or down depending on whether information disclosed about a company has a positive or negative impact on the firm's expected earnings. For example, on March 31, 2006, the following events occurred:

- **Google**'s stock price fell $6.54 per share on news that the Internet search giant would sell 5.3 million new shares. Additional stock raises concerns about dilution for current shareholders, so the market reacted negatively.
- **Ruby Tuesday**'s stock price rose by $1.58 per share. The casual-dining chain's fiscal third-quarter earnings were better than expected. In addition, the restaurant-level profit margins exceeded predictions. This announcement means investors earned more return on their investment than expected and will continue to do so since profit margins are higher than expected. Because of this announcement, the market reacted positively.

As companies provide additional information about revenue and income numbers, it is apparent that investors find these accounting numbers useful in evaluating the health and performance of a business.

Net income is reported in the income statement. The income statement shows the results of a company's operations for a period of time (a month, a quarter, or a year). The income statement summarizes the revenues generated and the costs incurred (expenses) to generate those revenues. The "bottom line" of an income statement is net income (or net loss), the difference between revenues and expenses. To help you understand an income statement, we must first define its elements—revenues, expenses, and net income (or net loss).

revenue

Increase in a company's resources from the sale of goods or services.

Revenues   Revenue is the amount of assets created through business operations. Think of revenue as another way for a company to acquire assets. In the same way that assets can be acquired by borrowing or by owners' investment, assets can also be acquired by providing a product or service for which customers are willing to pay. Manufacturing and merchandising companies receive revenues from the sale of merchandise. For example, Safeway's revenue is the cash that customers pay in exchange for groceries. A service enterprise generates revenues from the fees it charges for the services it performs. Companies might also earn revenues from other activities, such as charging interest or collecting rent. When goods are sold or services performed, the resulting revenue is in the form of cash or accounts receivable (a promise from the buyer to pay for the goods or services by a specified date in the future). Revenues thus generally represent an increase in total assets. These new assets are not tied to any liability obligation; therefore, the assets belong to the owners and thus represent an increase in owners' equity.

expenses

Costs incurred in the normal course of business to generate revenues.

Expenses   Expenses are the amount of assets consumed through business operations. Expenses are the costs incurred in normal business operations to generate revenues. Employee salaries and utilities used during a period are two common examples of expenses. For Safeway, the primary expense is the wholesale cost of the groceries that it sells to its customers at retail. Just as revenues represent an increase in assets and equity, expenses generally represent a decrease in assets and in equity.

> In considering revenues and expenses, remember that not all inflows of assets are revenues; nor are all outflows of assets considered to be expenses. For example, cash may be received by borrowing from a bank, which is an increase in a liability, not a revenue. Similarly, cash may be paid for supplies, which is an exchange of one asset for another asset, not an expense. The details of properly identifying revenues and expenses will be discussed further in Chapter 3.

net income (net loss)

An overall measure of the performance of a company; equal to revenues minus expenses for the period.

Net Income (or Net Loss)   Net income, sometimes called earnings or profit, is an overall measure of the performance of a company. Net income reflects the company's accomplishments (revenues) in relation to its efforts (expenses) during a particular period of time. If revenues exceed expenses, the result is called net income (revenues − expenses = net income). If expenses exceed revenues, the difference is called **net loss**. Because net income results in an increase in resources from operations, owners' equity is also increased; a net loss decreases owners' equity. Exhibit 7 lists the ten U.S. companies with the highest net incomes in 2004.

It is important to note the difference between revenues and net income. Both concepts represent an increase in the net assets (assets - liabilities) of a firm. However, revenues represent total resource increases; expenses are subtracted from revenues to derive net income or net loss. Thus, whereas revenue is a "gross" concept, income (or loss) is a "net" concept.

It is also important to note the difference between revenues and assets. Revenues are one activity of a company that generates assets. For example, selling a product (which is revenue) results in an asset (either cash or an accounts receivable). Assets can also be generated by other activities. For example, borrowing money from a bank would not be considered a revenue-generating activity, but it would result in an asset—cash. To summarize, activities involving revenue result in assets, but assets can result from many different activities.

The Format of an Income Statement   Comparative income statements for Safeway are presented in Exhibit 8. In contrast to the balance sheet, which is "as of" a particular date, the income statement refers to the "year ended." Remember, the income statement covers a period of time; the balance sheet is a report at a point in time. The multi-step format illustrated here highlights several profit measurements including gross profit, operating income, and net income.

EXHIBIT 7	Top Ten U.S. Companies, Ranked by Net Income

Company Name	Net Income*
ExxonMobil	$25,330
Citigroup	17,046
General Electric	16,593
Bank of America Corp.	14,143
ChevronTexaco	13,328
Pfizer	11,361
American Intl. Group	11,050
Wal-Mart Stores	10,267
Altria Group	9,416
Johnson & Johnson	8,509

*Net income is in millions of dollars.

Source: Fortune 500 listing, 2005.

EXHIBIT 8	Adapted Comparative Income Statements for Safeway

Safeway, Inc.

Comparative Income Statement

For Years Ended 2005 and 2004

(amounts in millions)

	2005	2004
Sales	$ 38,416.0	$ 35,822.9
Cost of goods sold	(27,303.1)	(25,227.6)
Gross profit	$ 11,112.9	$ 10,595.3
Operating and administrative expense	(9,898.2)	(9,422.5)
Operating profit	$ 1,214.7	$ 1,172.8
Interest expense	(402.6)	(411.2)
Other income, net	36.9	32.3
Income from continuing operations before income taxes	$ 849.0	$ 793.9
Income taxes	(287.9)	(233.7)
Net income (loss)	$ 561.1	$ 560.2
BASIC (LOSS) EARNINGS PER SHARE:	$1.25	$1.26

The income statement usually shows two main categories, revenues and expenses, although several subcategories may also be presented (as illustrated). Revenues are listed first. Typical operating expenses for most businesses are employee salaries, utilities, and advertising. For Safeway, as with any retail firm, the largest expense is for cost of goods sold. The difference between sales and cost of goods sold represents the difference between the retail price Safeway receives from a grocery sale and the wholesale cost of the groceries that are sold. This difference (sales − cost of goods sold) is called **gross profit** or **gross margin**.

gross profit (gross margin)

The excess of net sales revenue over the cost of goods sold.

Expenses are sometimes divided into operating and nonoperating categories. The primary nonoperating expenses are interest and income taxes. These expenses are called nonoperating because they have no connection with the specific nature of the operation of the business. For example, Safeway and Wal-Mart deal with interest and income taxes in a similar way, even though the two companies operate using different strategies.

gains (losses)

Money made or lost on activities outside the normal operation of a company.

Two other items that frequently appear in the income statement are **gains** and **losses**. Gains and losses refer to money made or lost on activities outside the normal business of a company. For example, when Safeway receives cash for selling groceries, it is called revenue. But when Safeway makes money by selling an old delivery truck, the amount is called a gain, not revenue, because Safeway is not in the business of selling trucks.

earnings (loss) per share (EPS)

The amount of net income (earnings) related to each share of stock; computed by dividing net income by the number of shares of stock outstanding during the period.

One final bit of information required on the income statements of corporations is **earnings (loss) per share (EPS)**. This EPS amount is computed by dividing the net income (earnings or loss) for the current period by the number of shares of stock outstanding during the period. Earnings per share information tells the owner of a single share of stock how much of the net income for the year belongs to him or her. Often two EPS figures are disclosed—basic and diluted. Basic EPS is based on historical transactions and involves dividing net income by actual average shares outstanding during the period. Diluted EPS is a bit more complicated and involves estimating what EPS would be if certain stock transactions (that will be discussed later) had occurred.

 F Y I

Recently, companies have been providing an additional measure of income—comprehensive income. The wealth of a company is affected in a variety of ways that have nothing to do with the business operations of the company. **Comprehensive income** is the number used to reflect an overall measure of the change in a company's wealth during the period. The most common examples of items included in comprehensive income include changes in foreign currency exchange rates, changes in the value of certain investment securities, and changes in the value of certain derivative financial instruments. Each of these items is affected by market conditions, affects a company's reported assets and liabilities yet cannot be influenced in any large degree by the company. Therefore, they are reported as part of a firm's comprehensive income.

Like the balance sheet, the income statement usually shows the comparative results for two or more periods, allowing investors and creditors to evaluate how profitable an enterprise has been during the current period as compared with earlier periods. For example, examination of Safeway's comparative income statements in Exhibit 8 shows that net income in 2005 was over $0.9 million higher ($561.1 − $560.2) than in 2004. Further analysis of the income statement is reinforced throughout the text.

The Statement of Retained Earnings

In addition to an income statement, corporations sometimes prepare a **statement of retained earnings** (see page 42 for definition). This statement identifies changes in retained earnings from one accounting period to the next. Exhibit 9 illustrates the statement of retained earnings for Safeway. The statement shows a beginning retained earnings balance, the net income for the period, a deduction for any dividends paid (which were $67.4 million for Safeway), and an ending retained earnings balance.

comprehensive income

A measure of the overall change in a company's wealth during a period; consists of net income plus changes in wealth resulting from changes in investment values and exchange rates.

Note how the accounting equation is affected by the elements reported in the statement of retained earnings. Net income results in an increase in net assets and a corresponding increase in Retained Earnings, which increases Owners' Equity.

$$(\uparrow)\text{Assets} = \text{Liabilities} + \text{Owners' Equity } (\uparrow)$$

Capital Stock   Retained Earnings $(\uparrow)$

Dividends reduce net assets (e.g., cash) and similarly reduce Retained Earnings, which reduces Owners' Equity.

$$(\downarrow)\text{Assets} = \text{Liabilities} + \text{Owners' Equity } (\downarrow)$$

Capital Stock   Retained Earnings $(\downarrow)$

EXHIBIT 9	Illustrated Statement of Retained Earnings for Safeway

Safeway, Inc.
Illustrated Statement of Retained Earnings
For the Year Ended December 31, 2005
(in millions)

Retained earnings, January 1, 2005	$4,678.0
Plus net income for the year	561.1
	$5,239.1
Less dividends	(67.4)
Retained earnings, December 31, 2005	$5,171.7

statement of retained earnings

A report that shows the changes in retained earnings during a period of time.

It is worth taking a moment to review just what exactly Retained Earnings is and what Retained Earnings isn't. Retained Earnings is the amount of earnings of a business that have been retained in the business (hence, the name Retained Earnings). The earnings that have not been retained in the business have been distributed to owners in the form of a dividend. The earnings that have been retained have been reinvested back into the business to become inventory and equipment and to pay down debt. To see where a company has reinvested the earnings it has retained would require you to examine the assets on the firm's balance sheet. Odds are that many of those assets will have been provided by the earnings that have been reinvested in the business.

Now, what isn't Retained Earnings? Retained Earnings is not cash. Some of the earnings that have been retained in a business may be retained in the form of cash, but it is more likely that the cash has been used to purchase other assets or to pay off liabilities. Students often make the mistake of assuming that if a company has Retained Earnings, the company has cash. That is not true. To determine how much cash a company has, you would examine the balance in the company's cash account—not the balance in the company's retained earnings account.

Corporations sometimes present a *statement of stockholders' equity* instead of a statement of retained earnings. The statement of stockholders' equity is more detailed and includes changes in capital stock as well as changes in retained earnings.

REMEMBER THIS...

- Income statement—a report of a company's performance for a particular period of time
- Revenue—an INCREASE in a company's resources through a normal business transaction
- Expense—a DECREASE in a company's resources through a normal business transaction
- Net income—equal to revenues minus expenses and represents the net amount of assets created through business operations during a particular period of time
- Format—usually several years of income statement data are reported side by side for comparison
- Computation of retained earnings—retained earnings is equal to the total earnings that have been retained in the company; this amount accumulates each year and is computed as beginning retained earnings plus net income minus dividends

The Statement of Cash Flows

③ Understand the categories and uses of the statement of cash flows and see how the primary financial statements tie together.

Net income is the single best measure of a company's economic performance. However, anyone who has paid rent or college tuition knows that bills must be paid with cash, not with "economic performance." Accordingly, in addition to net income, investors and creditors also desire to know how much actual cash a company's operations generate during a period and how that cash is used. The statement of cash flows shows the cash inflows (receipts) and cash outflows (payments) of an entity during a period of time. As shown in Exhibit 10, companies receive cash primarily by selling goods or providing services, by selling other assets, by borrowing, and by receiving cash from investments by owners. Companies use cash to pay current operating expenses such as wages, utilities, and taxes; to purchase additional buildings, land, and otherwise expand operations; to repay loans; and to pay their owners a return on the investments that have been made.

In the statement of cash flows, individual cash flow items are classified according to three main activities: operating, investing, and financing.

operating activities

Activities that are part of the day-to-day business of a company.

Operating Activities Operating activities are those activities that are part of the day-to-day business of a company. Cash receipts from selling goods or from providing services are the major operating cash inflow. Major operating cash outflows include payments to purchase inventory and to pay wages, taxes, interest, utilities, rent, and similar expenses.

investing activities

Activities associated with buying and selling long-term assets.

Investing Activities The primary investing activities are the purchase and sale of land, buildings, and equipment. You can think of investing activities as those activities associated with buying and selling long-term assets.

financing activities

Activities whereby cash is obtained from or repaid to owners and creditors.

Financing Activities Financing activities are those activities whereby cash is obtained from or repaid to owners and creditors. For example, cash received from owners' investments, cash proceeds from a loan, or cash payments to repay loans would all be classified under financing activities.

Conceptually, the statement of cash flows is the easiest to prepare of the three primary financial statements. Imagine examining every check and deposit slip you have written in the past year and sorting them into three piles—operating, investing, and financing. You would have to exercise some judgment in deciding which pile some items go into (for example, is the payment of interest an operating or a financing activity?). But overall, the three-way categorization of cash flows is not that difficult. In essence, this is all that is involved in the preparation of a statement of cash flows. As you will see in Chapter 13, however, actual preparation of a statement of cash flows can sometimes be challenging.

Exhibit 11 contains the statement of cash flows for Safeway for 2005 and 2004. As with balance sheets and income statements, companies usually provide comparative statements of cash flows.

How can Safeway report such a small amount of income on the income statement and yet be generating almost $2 billion in cash flow from operating activities? The simple answer is that Safeway reported a large number of noncash expenses on its 2005 income statement. This issue gets at the heart of accrual accounting which is introduced in Chapter 4. The details relating to the statement of cash flows will be explored in Chapter 13.

EXHIBIT 10   **Cash Flows**

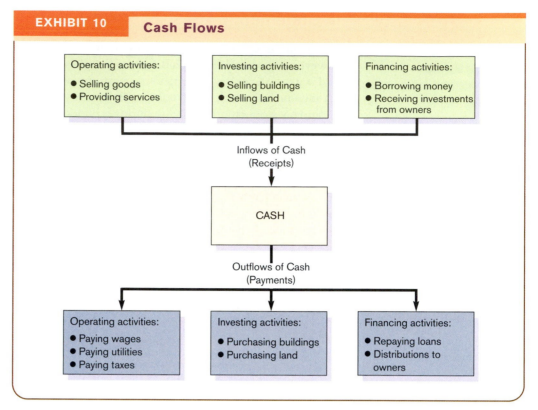

EXHIBIT 11   **Statement of Cash Flows for Safeway, Inc.**

Safeway Inc. and Subsidiaries
Consolidated Statements of Cash Flows
For Year Ended December 2005 and 2004*

CASH FLOWS FROM OPERATING ACTIVITIES	2005	2004
Cash collected from customers	$ 38,404.4	$ 35,867.1
Cash paid for		
Inventory	(26,936.3)	(25,076.3)
Operating and administrative expenses	(8,550.6)	(8,085.8)
Interest	(412.1)	(434.8)
Taxes	(624.4)	(43.8)
NET CASH FLOWS FROM OPERATING ACTIVITIES	1,881.0	2,226.4
CASH FLOWS FROM INVESTING ACTIVITIES		
Cash paid for property additions	(1,383.5)	(1,212.5)
Proceeds from sale of property	105.1	194.7
Other	(35.1)	(52.5)
NET CASH FLOWS USED BY INVESTING ACTIVITIES	(1,313.5)	(1,070.3)
CASH FLOWS FROM FINANCING ACTIVITIES		
Additions to short-term borrowings	13.0	11.2
Payments on short-term borrowings	(23.8)	(1.5)
Additions to long-term borrowings	754.5	1,173.5
Payments on long-term borrowing	(1,188.6)	(2,278.6)
Purchase of treasury stock	(1.5)	(0.4)
Dividends paid	(44.9)	–
Other	30.3	31.7
NET CASH FLOWS USED BY FINANCING ACTIVITIES	(461.0)	(1,064.1)
INCREASE IN CASH FOR THE PERIOD	$ 106.5	$ 92.0

*Adapted.

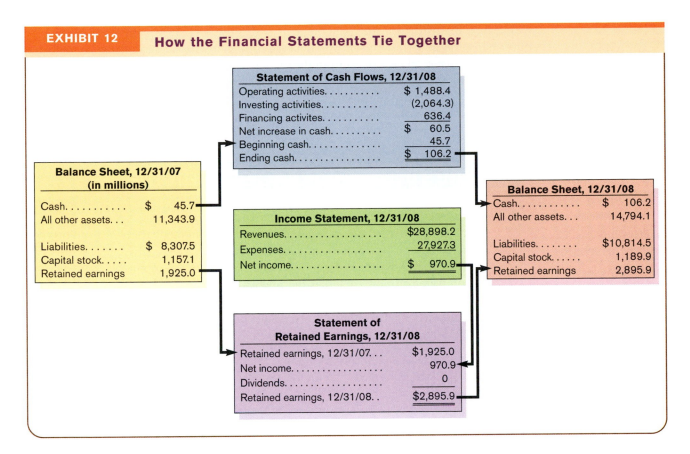

EXHIBIT 12 **How the Financial Statements Tie Together**

Statement of Cash Flows, 12/31/08

Operating activities.	$ 1,488.4
Investing activities.	(2,064.3)
Financing activites.	636.4
Net increase in cash.	$ 60.5
Beginning cash.	45.7
Ending cash.	$ 106.2

Balance Sheet, 12/31/07 (in millions)

Cash.	$ 45.7
All other assets. . .	11,343.9
Liabilities.	$ 8,307.5
Capital stock.	1,157.1
Retained earnings	1,925.0

Income Statement, 12/31/08

Revenues.	$28,898.2
Expenses.	27,927.3
Net income.	$ 970.9

Balance Sheet, 12/31/08

Cash.	$ 106.2
All other assets. . .	14,794.1
Liabilities.	$10,814.5
Capital stock.	1,189.9
Retained earnings	2,895.9

Statement of Retained Earnings, 12/31/08

Retained earnings, 12/31/07. . .	$1,925.0
Net income.	970.9
Dividends.	0
Retained earnings, 12/31/08. .	$2,895.9

How the Financial Statements Tie Together

Although we have introduced the primary financial statements as if they were independent of one another, they are interrelated and tie together. In accounting language, they "articulate." **Articulation** refers to the relationship between an operating statement (the income statement or the statement of cash flows) and comparative balance sheets, whereby an item on the operating statement helps explain the change in an item on the balance sheet from one period to the next.

Exhibit 12 shows how the financial statements tie together. Note that the beginning amount of cash from the 2004 balance sheet is added to the net increase

articulation

The interrelationships among the financial statements.

REMEMBER THIS...

- Statement of cash flows—a report of a company's cash inflows and outflows categorized into operating, investing, and financing activities
- Operating activities—activities that are part of a company's day-to-day business; examples include collecting cash from customers, paying employees, and purchasing inventory
- Investing activities—activities involving the purchase and sale of long-term assets such as buildings, trucks, and equipment
- Financing activities—activities surrounding acquiring the capital needed to purchase the company's assets; examples include getting cash from loans, repaying loans, receiving invested cash from owners, and paying dividends
- Format—usually several years of cash flow data are reported side by side for comparison
- Articulation—the three primary financial statements tie together as follows:
  - the income statement explains the change in the retained earnings balance in the balance sheet
  - the statement of cash flows explains the change in the cash balance in the balance sheet

or decrease in cash (from the statement of cash flows) to derive the cash balance as reported on the 2005 balance sheet. Similarly, the retained earnings balance as reported on the 2005 balance sheet comes from the beginning retained earnings balance (2004 balance sheet) plus net income for the period (from the income statement) less dividends paid. As you study financial statements, these relationships will become clearer and you will understand the concept of articulation better.

Notes to the Financial Statements

Recognize the need for financial statement notes and identify the types of information included in the notes.

④ The three primary financial statements contain a lot of information. Still, three summary reports cannot possibly tell financial statement users everything they want to know about a company. Additional information is given in the **notes to the financial statements**. In fact, in a typical annual report, the notes go on for 15 pages or more, whereas the primary financial statements fill only 3 pages. The notes tell about the assumptions and methods used in preparing the financial statements and also give more detail about specific items.

The financial statement notes are of the following four general types:

1. Summary of significant accounting policies.
2. Additional information about the summary totals found in the financial statements.
3. Disclosure of important information that is not recognized in the financial statements.
4. Supplementary information required by the Financial Accounting Standards Board (FASB) or the Securities and Exchange Commission (SEC).

notes to the financial statements

Explanatory information considered an integral part of the financial statements.

Summary of Significant Accounting Policies

As mentioned earlier, accounting involves making assumptions, estimates, and judgments. In addition, in some settings, there is more than one acceptable method of accounting for certain items. For example, there are a variety of acceptable ways of estimating how much a building depreciates (wears out) in a year. In order for financial statement users to be able to properly interpret the three primary financial statements, they must know what procedures were used in preparing those statements. This information about accounting policies and practices is given in the financial statement notes.

FYI

In its 1920 annual report, **IBM** included zero pages of notes (and the dollar amounts were carried out to the penny). In 1966, there were four pages of notes (and dollar amounts were rounded to the nearest dollar). In 2005, IBM's annual report included 46 pages of notes (and dollar amounts were rounded to the nearest million).

Additional Information about Summary Totals

For a large company, such as **Wal-Mart** or **Safeway**, one summary number in the financial statements represents literally thousands of individual items. For example, the $4.961 billion in long-term notes and debentures included in Safeway's 2005 balance sheet (see Exhibit 5) represents loans comprised of mortgages, senior secured debentures, senior subordinated debentures, commercial paper, short-term unsecured bank borrowings, an unsecured bank credit agreement, and more. The balance sheet includes only one number, with the details in the notes.

Disclosure of Information Not Recognized

One way to report financial information is to include the estimates and judgments in the financial statements. This is called *recognition*. The key assumptions and estimates are then described in a note to the financial statements. Another approach is to not include

---

EXHIBIT 13   **Safeway's Note Disclosure**

NOTE L: COMMITMENTS AND CONTINGENCIES

LEGAL MATTERS In July 1988, there was a major fire at the Company's dry grocery warehouse in Richmond, California. Through March 1, 2006, in excess of 126,000 claims for personal injury and property damage arising from the fire have been settled for an aggregate amount of approximately $125 million. The Company's loss as a result of the fire damage to its property and settlement of the above claims was substantially covered by insurance.

As of March 1, 2006, there were still pending approximately 175 claims against the Company for personal injury (including punitive damages), arising from the smoke, ash and embers generated by the fire. A substantial percentage of these claims have been asserted in lawsuits against the Company filed in the Superior Court for Alameda County, California. There can be no assurance that the pending claims will be settled or otherwise disposed of for amounts and on terms comparable to those settled to date. Safeway continues to believe that coverage under its insurance policy will be sufficient and available for resolution of all remaining personal injury and property damage claims arising out of the fire.

---

estimates and judgments in the financial statements but instead to explain them in the notes to the financial statements. This is called *disclosure*. Disclosure is the accepted way to convey information to users when the information is too uncertain to be recognized. For example, in July 1988, Safeway suffered a fire in one of its warehouses in Richmond, California. As of March 1, 2006, there were still 175 unsettled personal injury lawsuits against Safeway stemming from the fire. It is impossible to summarize the complexity of the potential outcome of these lawsuits in a number that can be reported on the financial statements; so, Safeway describes the situation, in some detail, in the notes to the financial statements. The related note from Safeway's annual report is included in Exhibit 13.

Supplementary Information

The FASB and SEC both require supplementary information that must be reported in the financial statement notes. For example, the FASB requires the disclosure of quarterly financial information and of business segment information. A sample of this type of disclosure can be seen in Wal-Mart's Form 10-K in Appendix A. In the notes to its financial statements, Wal-Mart reports that almost 20% of its 2006 revenue was generated outside of the United States.

REMEMBER THIS...

The notes to the financial statements contain additional information not included in the financial statements themselves. The notes:

- explain the company's accounting assumptions and practices,
- provide details of financial statement summary numbers and additional disclosure about complex events, and
- report supplementary information required by the SEC or the FASB.

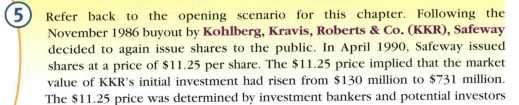

Describe the purpose of an audit report and the incentives the auditor has to perform a good audit.

The External Audit

(5) Refer back to the opening scenario for this chapter. Following the November 1986 buyout by **Kohlberg, Kravis, Roberts & Co. (KKR), Safeway** decided to again issue shares to the public. In April 1990, Safeway issued shares at a price of $11.25 per share. The $11.25 price implied that the market value of KKR's initial investment had risen from $130 million to $731 million. The $11.25 price was determined by investment bankers and potential investors

after examining the financial statements of Safeway. Now, consider the following questions:

- Who controlled the preparation of the Safeway financial statements used by investors in arriving at the $11.25 price? The owners and managers of Safeway, led by KKR.
- Did KKR have any incentive to bias the reported financial statement numbers? Absolutely. The better the numbers, the higher the stock offering price and the more money raised by KKR.
- Since KKR had control of the preparation of the financial statements and stood to benefit substantially if those statements looked overly favorable, how could the financial statements be trusted? Good question.

This situation illustrates a general truth: the owners and managers of a company have an incentive to report the most favorable results possible. Poor reported financial performance can make it harder to get loans, can lower the amount that managers receive as salary bonuses, and can lower the stock price when shares are issued to the public. With these incentives to stretch the truth, the financial statements would not be reliable unless they were reviewed by an external party.

audit report

A report issued by an independent CPA that expresses an opinion about whether the financial statements fairly present a company's financial position, operating results, and cash flows in accordance with generally accepted accounting principles.

To provide this external review, a company's financial statements are often audited by an independent certified public accountant (CPA). A CPA firm issues an **audit report** that expresses an opinion about whether the statements fairly present a company's financial position, operating results, and cash flows in accordance with generally accepted accounting principles. Note that the financial statements are the responsibility of a company's management and not of the CPA. Although not all company records have to be audited, audits are needed for many purposes. For example, a banker may not make a loan without first receiving audited financial statements from a prospective borrower. As another example, most securities cannot be sold to the general public until they are registered with the SEC. Audited financial statements are required for this registration process.

Though an audit report does not guarantee accuracy, it does provide added assurance that the financial statements are not misleading since they have been examined by an independent professional. However, the CPA cannot examine every transaction upon which the summary figures in the financial statements are based. The accuracy of the statements must remain the responsibility of the company's management. An example of a typical audit report is found in Wal-Mart's 2006 financial statements in-

? F Y I

Notice that **Wal-Mart**'s audit report is dated March 25, 2006. This means that it took less than two months (from the end of the fiscal year on January 31) for the completion of the audit. Obviously, much audit work was conducted during the year to make this happen.

cluded in the appendix. Wal-Mart's financial statements were audited by **Ernst & Young LLP**, one of the large international audit firms.

One final question: Who hires and pays Ernst & Young to do the audit of Wal-Mart's financial statements? Wal-Mart does. At first glance, this situation appears to be similar to allowing students in an accounting class to choose and pay the graders of the examinations. However, two economic factors combine to allow us to trust the quality of the audit, even though the auditor was hired by the company being audited:

- *Reputation.* Ernst & Young, as one of the large accounting firms, has a reputation for doing high-quality audits (as do almost all independent auditors in the United States). It would be very reluctant to risk this reputation by signing off on a questionable set of financial statements.
- *Lawsuits.* Auditors are sued all the time, even when they conduct a good audit. Investors who lose money claim that they lost the money by relying on bogus financial statements that were certified by an external auditor. If even honest auditors

get sued, then an auditor who intentionally approves a false set of financial statements is at great risk of losing a big lawsuit.

The business scandals of the early 2000s have reinforced the important role that auditors play in ensuring the integrity of financial statements. We will discuss the role of auditing and auditors in much greater detail in Chapter 5.

REMEMBER THIS...

- An audit report is issued by an independent CPA firm and verifies that a set of financial statements has been prepared in accordance with generally accepted accounting principles.
- CPA firms have an economic incentive to perform good audits in order to preserve their reputations and avoid lawsuits.

Fundamental Concepts and Assumptions

Explain the fundamental concepts and assumptions that underlie financial accounting.

6 Certain fundamental concepts and assumptions underlie financial accounting practice and the resulting financial statements. These ideas are so fundamental to any economic activity that they usually are taken for granted in conducting business. Nevertheless, it is important to be aware of them because these assumptions, together with certain basic concepts and procedures, determine the rules and set the boundaries of accounting practice. They indicate which events will be accounted for and in what manner. In total, they provide the essential characteristics of the traditional **accounting model**.

This section will describe the **separate entity concept**, the assumption of arm's-length transactions, the cost principle, the monetary measurement concept, and the going concern assumption. The concept of double-entry accounting was already introduced on page 35 as the basis for the accounting equation. Remember that accounting is the language of business, and it takes time to learn a new language. The terms and concepts we introduce here will become much more familiar as your study continues.

The Separate Entity Concept

accounting model

The basic accounting assumptions, concepts, principles, and procedures that determine the manner of recording, measuring, and reporting a company's transactions.

Because business involves the exchange of goods or services between entities, it follows that accounting records should be kept for those entities. For accounting purposes, an **entity** is defined as the organizational unit for which accounting records are maintained—for example, **IBM Corporation**. It is a focal point for identifying, measuring, and communicating accounting data. Furthermore, the entity is considered to be separate from its individual owners.

separate entity concept

The idea that the activities of an entity are to be separated from those of the individual owners.

The Assumption of Arm's-Length Transactions

Accounting is based on the recording of economic transactions. Viewed broadly, **transactions** include not only exchanges of economic resources between separate entities, but also events that have an economic impact on a business independently (see page 50 for definition). The borrowing and lending of money and the sale and purchase of goods or services are examples of the former. The loss in value of equipment due to obsolescence or fire is an example of the latter. Collectively, transactions provide the data that are included in accounting records and reports.

entity

An organizational unit (a person, partnership, or corporation) for which accounting records are kept and about which accounting reports are prepared.

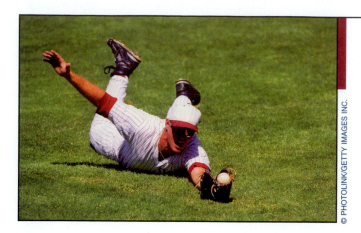

© PHOTOLINK/GETTY IMAGES INC.

The balance sheets of major league sports teams are based on historical costs. The market value of the teams is often much higher than is reflected on the books.

Accounting for economic transactions enables us to measure the success of an entity. However, the data for a transaction will not accurately represent that transaction if any bias is involved. Therefore, unless there is evidence to the contrary, accountants assume **arm's-length transactions**. That is, they make the assumption that both parties—for example, a buyer and a seller—are rational and free to act independently; each trying to make the best deal possible in establishing the terms of the transaction.

The Cost Principle

To further ensure objective measurements, accountants record transactions at **historical cost**, the amount originally paid or received for goods and services in arm's-length transactions. The historical cost is assumed to represent the fair market value of the item at the date of the transaction because it reflects the actual use of resources by independent parties. In accounting, this convention of recording transactions at cost is often referred to as the **cost principle**.

The historical cost figure may be modified in the future to reflect new information. While historical cost is a reliable number in that it results from an arm's-length transaction, it may not always provide information that is as relevant as financial statement users would like.

> ## ! CAUTION
>
> When reading accounting reports, remember that many reported values are historical costs, reflecting exchange prices at various transaction dates.

transactions

Exchange of goods or services between entities (whether individuals, businesses, or other organizations), as well as other events having an economic impact on a business.

arm's-length transactions

Business dealings between independent and rational parties who are looking out for their own interests.

historical cost

The dollar amount originally exchanged in an arm's-length transaction; an amount assumed to reflect the fair market value of an item at the transaction date.

The Monetary Measurement Concept

Accountants do not record all the activities of economic entities. They record only those that can be measured in monetary terms. Thus, the concept of **monetary measurement** becomes another important characteristic of the accounting model. For example, employee morale cannot be measured directly in monetary terms and is not reported in the accounting records. Wages paid or owed, however, are quantifiable in terms of money and are reported. In accounting, all transactions are recorded in monetary amounts, whether or not cash is involved. In the United States, the dollar is the unit of exchange and is thus the measuring unit for accounting purposes.

The Going Concern Assumption

The **Safeway** balance sheet in Exhibit 5 was prepared under the assumption that Safeway would continue in business for the foreseeable future. This is called the **going concern assumption**. Without this assumption, preparation of the balance sheet would be much more difficult. For example, the $2.8 billion inventory for Safeway in 2005 is reported at the cost originally paid to purchase the inventory. This is a reasonable figure because, in the normal course of business, Safeway can expect to sell the inventory for this amount, plus some profit. But if it were assumed that Safeway

cost principle

The idea that transactions are recorded at their historical costs or exchange prices at the transaction date.

monetary measurement

The idea that money, as the common medium of exchange, is the accounting unit of measurement, and that only economic activities measurable in monetary terms are included in the accounting model.

going concern assumption

The idea that an accounting entity will have a continuing existence for the foreseeable future.

would go out of business tomorrow, the inventory would suddenly be worth a lot less. The going concern assumption allows the accountant to record assets at what they are worth to a company in normal use, rather than what they would sell for in a liquidation sale.

> **REMEMBER THIS...**
>
> - Entity concept—Financial statements are prepared for a specific economic entity; the private affairs of the owners are not to be mixed in with the business transactions.
> - Arm's-length transaction—A market price accurately reflects underlying value when the transaction occurs between two unrelated parties, each bargaining for his or her own interests.
> - Cost principle—In general, financial statement items are measured at their cost on the original transaction date.
> - Monetary measurement concept—In order to be included in the financial statements, the value of an item must be measurable in terms of dollars.
> - Going concern assumption—When preparing the financial statements, the accountant assumes that the business will survive for the foreseeable future. Without this assumption, balance sheet items would be recorded at emergency liquidation amounts.

REVIEW OF LEARNING OBJECTIVES

(1) Understand the basic elements, uses, and limitations of the balance sheet.

Assets	=	Liabilities	+	Owners' Equity

Sources of funding

Resources	=	Creditors' claims against resources	+	Owners' claims against resources

- In the balance sheet, assets and liabilities are typically separated into current and long-term items with data for both the current and the preceding year reported for comparison.
- The balance sheet reflects assets acquired at their historical cost, thus frequently ignoring changes in value and gradual development of intangible assets.

(2) Understand the basic elements and uses of the income statement.

INCOME STATEMENT	
REVENUE	an INCREASE in a company's resources through a normal business transaction
− EXPENSE	a DECREASE in a company's resources through a normal business transaction
= NET INCOME	equal to revenues minus expenses and representing the net amount of assets created through business operations during a particular period of time

- Format—usually several years of income statement data are reported side by side for comparison

STATEMENT OF RETAINED EARNINGS	
RETAINED EARNINGS, BEGINNING	cumulative retained earnings from all prior years
+ NET INCOME	the net amount of assets created through business operations during the year; these assets belong to the owners
− DIVIDENDS	amount of business profits (usually in the form of cash) paid out to the owners during the year
= RETAINED EARNINGS, ENDING	as of the end of the year, the amount of the company's assets that have come through owners' reinvestment of their profits into the business

(3) Understand the categories and uses of the statement of cash flows and see how the primary financial statements tie together.

STATEMENT OF CASH FLOWS	
+ Operating Activities	activities that are part of a company's day-to-day business; examples include collecting cash from customers, paying employees, and purchasing inventory
+ Investing Activities	activities involving the purchase and sale of long-term assets such as buildings, trucks, and equipment
+ Financing Activities	activities surrounding acquiring the capital needed to purchase the company's assets; examples include getting cash from loans, repaying loans, receiving invested cash from owners, and paying dividends
= Net Change in Cash	change in the cash balance from the beginning of the period to the end of the period

- Format—usually several years of cash flow data are reported side by side for comparison
- Articulation—the three primary financial statements tie together as follows:
  - the income statement explains the change in the retained earnings balance in the balance sheet
  - the statement of cash flows explains the change in the cash balance in the balance sheet

(4) Recognize the need for financial statement notes and identify the types of information included in the notes.

- The notes to the financial statements contain additional information not included in the financial statements themselves.
- The notes explain the company's accounting assumptions and practices, provide details of financial statement summary numbers and additional disclosure about complex events, and report supplementary information required by the SEC or the FASB.

(5) Describe the purpose of an audit report and the incentives the auditor has to perform a good audit.

- An audit report is issued by an independent CPA firm and verifies that a set of financial statements has been prepared in accordance with generally accepted accounting principles.
- CPA firms have an economic incentive to perform good audits in order to preserve their reputations and avoid lawsuits.

Explain the fundamental concepts and assumptions that underlie financial accounting.

FUNDAMENTAL CONCEPT OR ASSUMPTION	DESCRIPTION
Entity concept	Financial statements are prepared for a specific economic entity; the private affairs of the owners are not to be mixed in with the business transactions.
Arm's-length transaction	A market price accurately reflects underlying value when the transaction occurs between two unrelated parties, each bargaining for his or her own interests.
Cost principle	In general, financial statement items are measured at their cost on the original transaction date.
Monetary measurement concept	In order to be included in the financial statements, the value of an item must be measurable in terms of dollars.
Going concern assumption	When preparing the financial statements, the accountant assumes that the business will survive for the foreseeable future. Without this assumption, balance sheet items would be recorded at emergency liquidation amounts.

KEY TERMS & CONCEPTS

accounting
   equation, 35
accounting model, 49
arm's-length
   transactions, 50
articulation, 45
assets, 32
audit report, 48
balance sheet
   (statement
   of financial
   position), 31
book value, 37
capital stock, 35
classified balance
   sheet, 35
comparative financial
   statements, 37

comprehensive
   income, 41
cost principle, 51
current assets, 35
current
   liabilities, 37
dividends, 34
double-entry
   accounting, 35
earnings (loss) per
   share (EPS), 41
entity, 49
expenses, 39
financing
   activities, 43
gains (losses), 41
going concern
   assumption, 51

gross profit (gross
   margin), 40
historical cost, 50
income statement
   (statement of
   earnings), 31
investing activities, 43
liabilities, 32
liquidity, 36
long-term assets, 37
long-term liabilities, 37
market value, 37
monetary
   measurement, 51
net assets, 33
net income (net loss), 39
notes to the financial
   statements, 46

operating activities, 43
owners' equity, 32
primary financial
   statements, 31
retained earnings, 34
revenue, 38
separate entity
   concept, 49
statement of cash
   flows, 31
statement of retained
   earnings, 42
stockholders
   (shareholders), 33
stockholders'
   equity, 34
transactions, 50

REVIEW PROBLEM

The Income Statement and the Balance Sheet

Shirley Baum manages The Copy Shop. She has come to you for help in preparing an income statement and a balance sheet for the year ended December 31, 2009. Several amounts, determined as of December 31, 2009, are presented below. No dividends were paid this year.

(continued)

Capital stock (10,000		Mortgage payable		$72,000
shares outstanding)	$ 40,000	Accounts payable		6,000
Retained earnings (12/31/08)	12,400	Land		24,000
Advertising expense	2,000	Supplies		2,000
Cash	17,000	Salary expense		20,000
Rent expense	2,400	Revenues		42,000
Building (net)	100,000	Other expenses		1,300
Interest expense	700	Accounts receivable		3,000

Required:

1. Prepare an income statement for the year ended December 31, 2009, including EPS.
2. Determine the amount of retained earnings at December 31, 2009.
3. Prepare a classified balance sheet as of December 31, 2009.

Solution

1. Income Statement

The first step in solving this problem is to separate the balance sheet items from the income statement items. Asset, liability, and owners' equity items reflect the company's financial position and appear on the balance sheet; revenues and expenses are reported on the income statement.

Balance Sheet Items

Capital stock
Retained earnings
Cash
Building (net)
Mortgage payable
Accounts payable
Land
Supplies
Accounts receivable

Income Statement Items

Advertising expense
Rent expense
Interest expense
Salary expense
Revenues
Other expenses

After the items have been separated, the income statement and the balance sheet may be prepared using a proper format.

The Copy Shop
Income Statement
For the Year Ended December 31, 2009

Revenues		$42,000
Expenses:		
Advertising expense	$ 2,000	
Rent expense	2,400	
Interest expense	700	
Salary expense	20,000	
Other expenses	1,300	26,400
Net income		$15,600
EPS = $15,600 ÷ 10,000 shares = $1.56		

(continued)

2. Retained Earnings

The amount of Retained Earnings at December 31, 2009, may be calculated as follows:

Retained earnings (12/31/08)	$12,400
Add: Net income for year	15,600
Subtract: Dividends for year	0
Retained earnings (12/31/09)	$28,000

Since no dividends were paid during 2009, the ending balance in Retained Earnings is simply the beginning balance plus net income for the year.

3. Balance Sheet

The Copy Shop
Balance Sheet
December 31, 2009

Assets			**Liabilities and Owners' Equity**		
Current assets:			**Current liabilities:**		
Cash	$ 17,000		Accounts payable	$ 6,000	
Accounts receivable	3,000				
Supplies	2,000	$ 22,000	**Long-term liabilities:**		
			Mortgage payable	72,000	
Long-term assets:			Total liabilities		$ 78,000
Land	$ 24,000				
Building (net)	100,000	124,000	**Owners' equity:**		
			Capital stock	$ 40,000	
			Retained earnings	28,000*	68,000
Total assets		$146,000	Total liabilities and owners' equity		$146,000

*See item 2 for calculation.

DISCUSSION QUESTIONS

1. As an external user of financial statements, perhaps an investor or creditor, what type of accounting information do you need?
2. What is the major purpose of:
    a. A balance sheet?
    b. An income statement?
    c. A statement of cash flows?
3. Assume you want to invest in the stock market, and your friends tell you about a company's stock that is "guaranteed" to have an annual growth rate of 150%. Should you trust your friends and invest immediately, or should you research the company's financial statements before investing? Explain.
4. Why are classified and comparative financial statements generally presented in annual reports to shareholders?
5. Why are owners' equity and liabilities considered the "sources" of assets?
6. Owners' equity is not cash; it is not a liability; and it generally is not equal to the current worth

of a business. What is the nature of owners' equity?
7. What are the limitations of the balance sheet? Why is it important to be aware of them when evaluating a company's growth potential?
8. Some people feel that the income statement is more important than the balance sheet. Do you agree? Why or why not?
9. How might an investor be misled by looking only at the "bottom line" (the net income or EPS number) on an income statement?
10. Why is it important to classify cash flows according to operating, investing, and financing activities?
11. You are thinking of investing in one of two companies. In one annual report, the auditor's opinion states that the financial statements were prepared in accordance with generally accepted accounting principles. The other makes no such claim. How important is that to you? Explain.

12. Some people think that auditors are responsible for ensuring the accuracy of financial statements. Are they correct? Why or why not?

13. What are the four general types of financial statement notes typically included in annual reports to stockholders?

14. Explain why each of the following is important in accounting:
    a. The separate entity concept
    b. The assumption of arm's-length transactions
    c. The cost principle
    d. The monetary measurement concept
    e. The going concern assumption

PRACTICE EXERCISES

PE 2-1   **Total Assets**
LO1   Using the following information, compute total assets.

Equipment	$10,000
Accounts payable	900
Capital stock	1,500
Cash	800
Loan payable	9,000
Wages payable	500
Accounts receivable	1,000
Retained earnings	3,400
Inventory	3,500

PE 2-2   **Total Liabilities**
LO1   Refer to the data in PE 2-1. Compute total liabilities.

PE 2-3   **Total Owners' Equity**
LO1   Refer to the data in PE 2-1. Compute total owners' equity.

PE 2-4   **The Accounting Equation**
LO1   For the following four cases, use the accounting equation to compute the missing quantity.

	Assets	Liabilities	Owners' Equity
Case A	$10,000	$ 4,000	A
Case B	8,000	B	$3,500
Case C	C	5,500	7,000
Case D	13,000	15,000	D

PE 2-5   **Balance Sheet**
LO1   Using the data in PE 2-1, prepare a balance sheet.

PE 2-6   **Current Assets**
LO1   Using the following information, compute total current assets.

Land	$7,000
Machinery	1,300
Accounts payable	1,600
Cash	625
Buildings	7,500
Accounts receivable	800
Retained earnings	2,200
Inventory	2,100

PE 2-7 **Current Liabilities**
LO1 Using the following information, compute total current liabilities.

Inventory	$ 9,000
Loan payable (due in 14 months)	1,100
Capital stock	1,750
Cash	400
Mortgage payable (due in 30 years)	10,000
Loan payable (due in 6 months)	250
Accounts payable	700
Retained earnings	5,000

PE 2-8 **Book Value and Market Value of Equity**
LO1 For the following four cases, compute (1) the book value of equity and (2) the market value of equity.

	Assets	Liabilities	Number of Shares of Stock Outstanding	Market Price per Share
Case A	$ 10,000	$ 4,000	1,000	$15
Case B	8,000	7,000	500	10
Case C	13,500	5,500	300	20
Case D	100,000	150,000	1,000	7

PE 2-9 **Total Revenues**
LO2 Using the following information, compute total revenues. Caution: Not all of the items listed should be included in the computation of total revenues.

Cost of goods sold	$10,200	Wages payable	$ 475
Interest revenue	900	Accounts receivable	950
Advertising expense	2,150	Retained earnings	6,400
Cash	700	Consulting revenue	2,700
Sales	13,600		

PE 2-10 **Total Expenses**
LO2 Using the data in PE 2-9, compute total expenses. Caution: Not all of the items listed should be included in the computation of total expenses.

PE 2-11 **Computation of Net Income**
LO2 For the following four cases, compute net income (or net loss). Caution: Not all of the items listed should be included in the computation of net income.

	Case A	Case B	Case C	Case D
Cost of goods sold	$ 60,000	$ 30,000	$60,000	$110,000
Interest expense	18,000	47,000	25,000	31,000
Cash	3,000	4,500	2,100	6,000
Retained earnings	50,000	15,000	31,000	70,000
Sales	100,000	150,000	70,000	200,000
Accounts payable	12,000	20,000	5,000	38,000
Rent revenue	5,000	1,000	12,000	10,000
Machinery	175,000	60,000	50,000	185,000

PE 2-12 **Income Statement**
LO2 Using the following information, prepare an income statement.

(continued)

Cost of goods sold	$ 7,300
Interest expense	1,200
Wage expense	900
Cash	600
Sales	12,000
Accounts payable	400
Accounts receivable	750
Retained earnings	3,300
Income tax expense	800

PE 2-13
LO2

Computation of Ending Retained Earnings

For the following four cases, compute the ending amount of retained earnings. Caution: Not all of the items listed should be included in the computation of ending retained earnings.

	Case A	Case B	Case C	Case D
Capital stock	$ 60,000	$ 30,000	$60,000	$110,000
Long-term loan payable	18,000	47,000	25,000	31,000
Dividends	3,000	4,500	2,100	6,000
Retained earnings (beginning)	50,000	15,000	31,000	70,000
Inventory	100,000	150,000	70,000	200,000
Cash	12,000	20,000	5,000	38,000
Net income (loss)	5,000	1,000	12,000	(10,000)
Machinery	175,000	60,000	50,000	185,000

PE 2-14
LO2

Expanded Accounting Equation

For the following four cases, use the expanded accounting equation to compute the missing quantity.

	Assets	Liabilities	Capital Stock	Retained Earnings
Case A	$23,000	$11,000	A	$ 4,500
Case B	17,500	B	$ 4,500	3,600
Case C	C	14,000	11,000	27,000
Case D	45,000	29,000	18,000	D

PE 2-15
LO3

Computing Cash from Operating Activities

Using the following data, compute cash flow from operating activities.

	Cash Inflow (Outflow)	
a.	Cash received from sale of a building	$ 5,600
b.	Cash paid for interest	(450)
c.	Cash paid to repay a loan	(1,000)
d.	Cash collected from customers	10,000
e.	Cash paid for dividends	(780)
f.	Cash paid for income taxes	(1,320)
g.	Cash received upon the issuance of new shares of stock	3,000
h.	Cash received from tenants renting part of a building	600
i.	Cash paid to purchase land	(12,000)

PE 2-16
LO3

Computing Cash from Investing Activities

Refer to the information in PE 2-15. Use that information to compute cash flow from investing activities.

PE 2-17
LO3

Computing Cash from Financing Activities

Refer to the information in PE 2-15. Use that information to compute cash flow from financing activities.

PE 2-18 **Preparing a Statement of Cash Flows**

LO3 Refer to the information in PE 2-15. Use that information to prepare a complete statement of cash flows. The beginning cash balance for the year was $2,000.

PE 2-19 **Financial Statement Articulation**

LO3 For the following four cases, use the principle of financial statement articulation to compute the missing amounts.

	Case A	Case B	Case C	Case D
Dividends	$ 6,500	$ 7,300	$ 800	G
Cash, beginning	13,000	C	4,200	$ 22,000
Retained earnings, ending	A	16,000	15,500	35,000
Net increase (decrease) in cash	8,200	5,300	E	(6,300)
Net income (loss)	18,000	25,000	F	(11,000)
Retained earnings, beginning	41,000	D	22,000	51,000
Cash, ending	B	21,000	1,600	H

EXERCISES

E 2-20 **Classification of Financial Statement Elements**

LO1 Indicate for each of the following items whether it would appear on a balance sheet (BS) or an income statement (IS). If a balance sheet item, is it an asset (A), a liability (L), or an owners' equity item (OE)?

1. Accounts Payable
2. Sales Revenue
3. Accounts Receivable
4. Advertising Expense
5. Cash
6. Supplies
7. Consulting Revenue
8. Land
9. Capital Stock
10. Rent Expense
11. Equipment
12. Interest Receivable
13. Mortgage Payable
14. Notes Payable
15. Buildings
16. Salaries & Wages Expense
17. Retained Earnings
18. Utilities Expense

E 2-21 **Accounting Equation**

LO1 Compute the missing amounts for companies A, B, and C.

	A	B	C
Cash	$31,000	$ 8,400	$13,000
Accounts receivable	14,000	13,000	16,500
Land and buildings	95,000	?	67,000
Accounts payable	?	16,000	23,000
Mortgage payable	80,000	31,000	41,500
Owners' equity	45,000	17,000	?

E 2-22 **Comprehensive Accounting Equation**

LO1, LO2 Assuming no additional investments by or distributions to owners, compute the missing amounts for companies X, Y, and Z.

	X	Y	Z
Assets: January 1, 2009	$360	$?	$230
Liabilities: January 1, 2009	280	460	?
Owners' equity: January 1, 2009	?	620	150
Assets: December 31, 2009	380	?	310
Liabilities: December 31, 2009	?	520	90
Owners' equity: December 31, 2009	?	720	?
Revenues in 2009	80	?	400
Expenses in 2009	100	116	?

E 2-23
LO1, LO2

Computing Elements of Owners' Equity

From the information provided, determine:

1. The amount of retained earnings at December 31.
2. The amount of revenues for the period.

Totals	January 1	December 31
Current assets	$ 10,000	$ 15,000
All other assets	190,000	180,000
Liabilities	65,000	45,000
Capital stock	60,000	?
Retained earnings	75,000	?

Additional data:

Expenses for the period were $75,000.

Dividends paid were $11,500.

Capital stock increased by $10,000 during the period.

E 2-24
LO1, LO2

Balance Sheet Relationships

Correct the following balance sheet.

Canfield Corporation
Balance Sheet
December 31, 2009

Assets		Liabilities and Owners' Equity	
Cash	$ 55,000	Buildings	$325,000
Accounts payable	65,000	Accounts receivable	75,000
Interest receivable	20,000	Mortgage payable	150,000
Capital stock	200,000	Sales revenue	350,000
Rent expense	60,000	Equipment	85,000
Retained earnings	145,000	Utilities expense	5,000
		Total liabilities	
Total assets	$545,000	and owners' equity	$990,000

E 2-25
LO1, LO2

Balance Sheet Preparation

From the following data, prepare a classified balance sheet for Taylorsville Construction Company at December 31, 2009.

Accounts payable	$ 74,300
Accounts receivable	113,500
Buildings	512,000
Owners' equity, 1/1/09	314,300
Cash	153,600
Distributions to owners during 2009	48,100
Supplies	4,250
Land	90,000
Mortgage payable	423,400
Net income for 2009	109,450
Owners' equity, 12/31/09	?

E 2-26
LO2

Income Statement Computations

Following are the operating data for an advertising firm for the year ended December 31, 2009.

(continued)

Revenues	$175,000
Supplies expense	45,000
Salaries expense	70,000
Rent expense	1,500
Administrative expense	6,000
Income taxes (30% of income before taxes)	?

For 2009, determine:

1. Income before taxes.
2. Income taxes.
3. Net income.
4. Earnings per share (EPS), assuming there are 15,000 shares of stock outstanding.

E 2-27
LO2

Income Statement Preparation

The following selected information is taken from the records of Pickard and Associates.

Accounts payable	$ 143,000
Accounts receivable	95,000
Advertising expense	14,500
Cash	63,000
Supplies expense	31,500
Rent expense	12,000
Utilities expense	2,500
Income taxes (30% of income before taxes)	?
Miscellaneous expense	5,100
Owners' equity	215,000
Salaries expense	78,000
Fees (revenues)	476,000

1. Prepare an income statement for the year ended December 31, 2009. (Assume that 11,000 shares of stock are outstanding.)
2. Explain what the EPS ratio tells the reader about Pickard and Associates.

E 2-28
LO2

Income and Retained Earnings Relationships

Assume that retained earnings increased by $375,000 from December 31, 2008, to December 31, 2009, for Jarvie Distribution Corporation. During the year, a cash dividend of $135,000 was paid.

1. Compute the net income for the year.
2. Assume that the revenues for the year were $830,000. Compute the expenses incurred for the year.

E 2-29
LO2

Retained Earnings Computations

During 2009, Edgemont Corporation had revenues of $230,000 and expenses, including income taxes, of $190,000. On December 31, 2008, Edgemont had assets of $350,000, liabilities of $80,000, and capital stock of $210,000. Edgemont paid a cash dividend of $25,000 in 2009. No additional stock was issued. Compute the retained earnings on December 31, 2008, and 2009.

E 2-30
LO2

Preparation of Income Statement and Retained Earnings Statement

Prepare an income statement and a statement of retained earnings for Big Sky Corporation for the year ended June 30, 2009, based on the following information:

(continued)

Capital stock (1,500 shares @ $100)		$150,000
Retained earnings, July 1, 2008		76,800
Dividends		6,500
Ski rental revenue		77,900
Expenses:		
Rent expense	$ 6,000	
Salaries expense	38,600	
Utilities expense	2,400	
Advertising expense	7,500	
Miscellaneous expense	7,700	
Income taxes	2,100	64,300

E 2-31   **Articulation: Relationships between a Balance Sheet and an Income Statement**

LO2   The total assets and liabilities of Omni Company at January 1 and December 31, 2009, are presented below.

	January 1	December 31
Assets	$103,000	$167,000
Liabilities	72,000	88,000

Determine the amount of net income or loss for 2009, applying each of the following assumptions concerning the additional issuance of stock and dividends paid by the firm. Each case is independent of the others.

1. Dividends of $12,100 were paid and no additional stock was issued during the year.
2. Additional stock of $18,000 was issued and no dividends were paid during the year.
3. Additional stock of $72,000 was issued and dividends of $12,400 were paid during the year.

E 2-32   **Cash Flow Computations**

LO3   From the following selected data, compute:

1. Net cash flow provided (used) by operating activities.
2. Net cash flow provided (used) by investing activities.
3. Net cash flow provided (used) by financing activities.
4. Net increase (decrease) in cash during the year.
5. The cash balance at the end of the year.

Cash receipts from:	
Customers	$270,000
Investments by owners	54,000
Sale of building	90,000
Proceeds from bank loan	60,000
Cash payments for:	
Wages	$ 82,000
Utilities	3,000
Advertising	4,000
Rent	36,000
Taxes	67,000
Dividends	20,000
Repayment of principal on loan	40,000
Purchase of land	106,000
Cash balance at beginning of year	$386,000

E 2-33   **Cash Flow Classifications**

LO3   For each of the following items, indicate whether it would be classified and reported under the operating activities (OA), investing activities (IA), or financing activities (FA) section of a statement of cash flows:

a. Cash receipts from selling merchandise
b. Cash payments for wages and salaries

(continued)

    c. Cash proceeds from sale of stock

    d. Cash purchase of equipment

    e. Cash dividends paid

    f. Cash received from bank loan

    g. Cash payments for inventory

    h. Cash receipts from services rendered

    i. Cash payments for taxes

    j. Cash proceeds from sale of property no longer needed as expansion site

E 2-34
LO4

Notes to Financial Statements

Refer to **Wal-Mart's** Form 10-K in Appendix A at the end of the book. How important are the notes to financial statements? What are the major types of notes that Wal-Mart includes in its Form 10-K?

E 2-35
LO6

The Cost Principle

On January 1, 2009, Save-More Construction Company paid $150,000 in cash for a parcel of land to be used as the site of a new office building. During March, the company petitioned the city council to rezone the area for professional office buildings. The city council refused, preferring to maintain the area as a residential zone. After nine months of negotiation, Save-More Construction convinced the council to rezone the property for commercial use, thus raising its value to $200,000.

    For accounting purposes, what value should be used to record the transaction on January 1, 2009? At what value would the property be reported at year-end, after the city council rezoning? Explain why accountants use historical costs to record transactions.

E 2-36
LO6

The Monetary Measurement Concept

Many successful companies, such as **Ford Motor Company**, **ExxonMobil**, and **Marriott Corporation**, readily acknowledge the importance and value of their employees. In fact, the employees of a company are often viewed as the most valued asset of the company. Yet in the asset section of the balance sheets of these companies there is no mention of the asset Employees. What is the reason for this oversight and apparent inconsistency?

E 2-37
LO6

The Going Concern Assumption

Assume that you open an auto repair business. You purchase a building and buy new equipment. What difference does the going concern assumption make with regard to how you would account for these assets?

PROBLEMS

P 2-38
LO1

Balance Sheet Classifications and Relationships

Stoker and Co. has the following balance sheet elements as of December 31, 2009.

Land	$136,000		Mortgage payable	$253,000
Cash	?		Capital stock	200,000
Building	225,000		Retained earnings	186,000
Accounts payable	101,000		Inventory	72,000
Notes payable (short-term)	98,000		Accounts receivable	119,000
Equipment	215,000			

Required:

Compute the total amount of:

1. Current assets.

2. Long-term assets.

3. Current liabilities.

4. Long-term liabilities.

5. Stockholders' equity.

P 2-39
LO1, LO2

Preparation of a Classified Balance Sheet

Following are the December 31, 2009, account balances for Siraco Company.

Cash	$ 1,950
Accounts receivable	2,500
Supplies	1,800
Equipment	11,275
Accounts payable	3,450
Wages payable	250
Dividends paid	1,500
Capital stock	775
Retained earnings, January 1, 2009	12,000
Revenues	10,000
Miscellaneous expense	1,550
Supplies expense	3,700
Wages expense	2,200

Required:

1. Prepare a classified balance sheet as of December 31, 2009.
2. **Interpretive Question:** On the basis of its 2009 earnings, was this company's decision to pay dividends of $1,500 a sound one?

P 2-40
LO1

Balance Sheet Preparation with a Missing Element

The following data are available for Schubert Products Inc., as of December 31, 2009.

Cash	$ 7,500
Accounts payable	24,000
Capital stock	42,000
Accounts receivable	20,000
Building	49,500
Supplies	2,000
Retained earnings	?
Land	20,000

Required:

1. Prepare a balance sheet for Schubert Products Inc.
2. Determine the amount of retained earnings at December 31, 2009.
3. **Interpretive Question:** In what way is a balance sheet a depiction of the basic accounting equation?

P 2-41
LO2

Income Statement Preparation

Listed below are the results of Rulon Candies' operations for 2008 and 2009. (Assume 4,000 shares of outstanding stock for both years.)

	2009	2008
Sales	$300,000	$350,000
Utilities expenses	15,000	8,500
Employee salaries	115,000	110,000
Advertising expenses	10,000	20,000
Income tax expense	9,000	36,500
Interest expense	25,000	15,000
Cost of goods sold	115,000	85,000
Interest revenue	10,000	10,000

Required:

1. Prepare a comparative income statement for Rulon Candies, Inc., for the years ended December 31, 2009, and 2008. Be sure to include figures for gross margin, operating income, income before taxes, net income, and earnings per share.

(continued)

2. **Interpretive Question:** What advice would you give Rulon Candies, Inc., to improve its profitability for the year 2010?

P 2-42

LO2

Income Statement Preparation

The following information is taken from the records of Wadley's Car Wash for the year ended December 31, 2009.

Income taxes	$ 45,000
Service revenues	210,000
Rent expense	6,000
Salaries expense	41,000
Miscellaneous expense	970
Utilities expense	4,300
Supplies expense	10,300

Required:

Prepare an income statement for Wadley's Car Wash for the year ended December 31, 2009. (Assume that 3,000 shares of stock are outstanding.)

P 2-43

LO1, LO2

Expanded Accounting Equation

At the end of 2009, Spencer Systems, Inc., had a fire that destroyed the majority of its accounting records. Spencer Systems, Inc., was able to gather the following financial information for 2009.

a. Retained earnings was changed only as a result of net income and a $25,000 dividend payment to Spencer's investors.

b. All other account changes for the year are listed below. The amount of change for each account is shown as a net increase or decrease.

	Increase or (Decrease)
Cash	$ 12,500
Interest receivable	(7,500)
Inventory	50,000
Accounts receivable	(11,750)
Building	157,500
Accounts payable	22,500
Mortgage payable	137,500
Wages payable	(35,250)
Capital stock	26,250

Required:

Using the accounting equation, compute Spencer's net income for 2009.

P 2-44

LO2

Income Statement Preparation

Precision Corporation has been a leading supplier of magnetic storage disks for three years. Following are the results of Precision's operations for 2009.

Sales revenue	$68,000
Advertising expense	1,530
Income taxes	4,360
Delivery expense	480
Packaging expense	355
Salaries expense	18,350
Supplies expense	8,410
EPS	3.45

Required:

1. Prepare an income statement for the year ended December 31, 2009.
2. How many shares of stock were outstanding?

P 2-45
LO2

Net Income

A summary of the operations of Streuling Company for the year ended May 31, 2009, is shown below.

Advertising expense	$ 2,760
Supplies expense	37,820
Rent expense	1,500
Salaries expense	18,150
Miscellaneous expense	4,170
Dividends	12,400
Retained earnings (6/1/08)	156,540
Income taxes	21,180
Consulting fees (revenues)	115,100
Administrative expense	7,250

Required:

1. Determine the net income for the year by preparing an income statement. (Assume that 3,000 shares of stock are outstanding.)
2. **Interpretive Question:** Assuming an operating loss for the year, is it a good idea for Streuling to still pay its shareholders dividends?

P 2-46
LO2

Net Income and Statement of Retained Earnings

A summary of the operations of Quincy Company for the year ended May 31, 2009, is shown below.

Advertising expense	$ 4,650
Supplies expense	38,410
Rent expense	2,400
Salaries expense	25,340
Miscellaneous expense	10,200
Dividends	19,500
Retained earnings (6/1/08)	175,670
Income taxes	20,760
Consulting fees (revenues)	176,400
Administrative expense	13,900

Required:

1. Determine the net income for the year by preparing an income statement. (There are 8,000 shares of stock outstanding.)
2. Prepare a statement of retained earnings for the year ended May 31, 2009.
3. Prepare a statement of retained earnings assuming that Quincy had a net loss for the year of $38,000.
4. **Interpretive Question:** Assuming a loss as in (3), is it a good idea for Quincy to still pay its shareholders dividends?

P 2-47
LO1, LO2

Comprehensive Financial Statement Preparation

The following information was obtained from the records of Wilcox, Inc., as of December 31, 2009.

Land	$ 42,500
Buildings	197,550
Salaries expense	125,350
Utilities expense	5,250
Accounts payable	38,050
Revenues	389,950
Supplies	72,500
Retained earnings (1/1/09)	311,000

(continued)

Capital stock (2,000 shares outstanding)	$ 65,000
Accounts receivable	90,000
Supplies expense	110,600
Cash	?
Notes payable (long-term)	63,800
Rent expense	21,200
Dividends in 2009	95,500
Other expenses	11,250
Income taxes	35,000

Required:

1. Prepare an income statement for the year ended December 31, 2009.
2. Prepare a classified balance sheet as of December 31, 2009.
3. **Interpretive Question:** Why is the balance in Retained Earnings so large as compared with the balance in Capital Stock?

P 2-48

LO1, LO2

Elements of Comparative Financial Statements

The following report is supplied by Maxwell Sons Company.

Maxwell Sons Company

Comparative Balance Sheets

As of December 31, 2009 and 2008

Assets	2009	2008	Liabilities and Owners' Equity	2009	2008
Cash	$ 28,000	$19,000	Accounts payable	$ 9,000	$ 8,000
Accounts receivable	21,000	14,000	Salaries and commissions		
Notes receivable	10,000	12,000	payable	11,000	12,000
Land	43,000	43,000	Notes payable	32,000	35,000
			Capital stock	15,000	15,000
			Retained earnings	35,000	18,000
			Total liabilities and		
Total assets	$102,000	$88,000	owners' equity	$102,000	$88,000

Operating expenses for the year included utilities of $5,700, salaries and commissions of $38,700, and miscellaneous expenses of $2,200. Income taxes for the year were $4,500, and the company paid dividends of $8,000.

Required:

1. Compute the total expenses, including taxes, incurred in 2009.
2. Compute the net income or net loss for 2009.
3. Compute the total revenue for 2009.
4. **Interpretive Question:** Why are comparative financial statements generally of more value to users than statements for a single period?

P 2-49

LO3

Statement of Cash Flows

Pratt & Jordan Development, Inc., constructs homes and offices and sells them to customers. The financial information shown below was gathered from its accounting records for 2009. Assume any increase or decrease in the balances from 1/1/09 to 12/31/09 resulted from either receiving or paying cash in the transaction. For example, during 2009 the balance on loans for land holdings increased $75,000 because the company received $75,000 in cash by taking out an additional loan on the land.

(continued)

Items	Balance as of 1/1/09	Balance as of 12/31/09
Cash	$130,000	$175,000
Cash receipts from customers	–	750,000
Loans on land holdings	225,000	300,000
Cash distributions to owners	–	60,000
Loan on building	130,000	80,000
Investments in securities	600,000	845,000
Cash payments for other expenses	–	32,000
Cash payments for taxes	–	43,000
Cash payments for operating expenses	–	215,000
Cash payments for wages and salaries	–	135,000

Required:

1. Prepare a statement of cash flows for Pratt & Jordan Development, Inc., for the year ended December 31, 2009.

2. **Interpretive Question:** Does Pratt & Jordan Development, Inc., appear to be in good shape from a cash flow standpoint? What other information would help you analyze the situation?

P 2-50

LO3

Statement of Cash Flows

The cash account for Esplin Enterprises shows the following for the year ended December 31, 2009.

Beginning cash balance	$?
Cash receipts during year from:	
Services	2,214,000
Investments by owners	93,000
Sale of land	194,000
Cash payments during year for:	
Operating expenses	1,735,000
Taxes	207,000
Purchase of building	352,000
Distributions to owners	68,000
Ending cash balance	815,000

Required:

Prepare a statement of cash flows for Esplin Enterprises for the year ended December 31, 2009.

ANALYTICAL ASSIGNMENTS

AA 2-51

DISCUSSION

Creditor and Investor Information Needs

Ink Spot is a small company that has been in business for two years. Wilford Smith, the president of the company, has decided that it is time to expand. He needs $10,000 to purchase additional equipment and to pay for increased operating expenses. Wilford can either apply for a loan at First City Bank, or he can issue more stock (1,000 shares are outstanding) to new investors. Assuming that you are the loan officer at First City Bank, what information would you request from Ink Spot before deciding whether to make the loan? As a potential investor in Ink Spot, what information would you need to make a good investment decision?

AA 2-52

DISCUSSION

Analyzing Trends and Key Financial Relationships

An investor may choose from several investment opportunities: the stocks of different companies; rental property or other real estate; or savings accounts, money market certificates, and similar financial instruments. When considering an investment in the stock of a particular

(continued)

company, comparative financial data presented in the annual report to stockholders help an investor identify key relationships and trends. As an illustration, comparative operating results for Prime Properties, Inc., from its 2009 annual report are provided. (Dollars are presented in thousands except for earnings per share.)

	Year Ended December 31		
	2009	**2008**	**2007**
Revenues:			
Property management fees	$ 58,742	$ 63,902	$ 66,204
Appraisal fees	55,641	60,945	62,320
Total revenues	$114,383	$124,847	$128,524
Expenses:			
Selling and advertising	$ 64,371	$ 75,403	$ 80,478
Administrative expenses	30,671	31,115	31,618
Other expenses	9,265	9,540	9,446
Interest expense	2,047	1,468	26
Total expenses	$106,354	$117,526	$121,568
Income before taxes	$ 8,029	$ 7,321	$ 6,956
Income taxes	2,409	2,196	2,087
Net income	$ 5,620	$ 5,125	$ 4,869
Earnings per share*	$2.25	$2.05	$1.95

*2.5 million shares outstanding

What trends are indicated by the comparative income statement data for Prime Properties, Inc.? Which of these trends would be of concern to a potential investor? What additional information would an investor need in order to make a decision about whether to invest in this company?

AA 2-53

DISCUSSION

How Many Accounting Equations Are There?

You have recently completed Chapter 2 in your introductory accounting course and have been enthusiastically explaining the accounting equation to all of your friends. One of your friends reports that he took accounting last year and that actually there isn't just one accounting equation. For example, he says that in addition to the equation Assets = Liabilities + Owners' Equity, there are also the equations Revenues = Assets, Net Income = Cash from Operating Activities, and Retained Earnings = Cash. Comment on these three additional accounting "equations" listed by your friend.

AA 2-54

DISCUSSION

Can Financial Statement Information Be Used to Successfully Pick Stocks?

For most companies, the only reliable source of information about the company's performance is found in the company's financial statements. However, for the 15,000 publicly-traded companies in the United States (those whose ownership shares can be bought and sold on a stock exchange), there is much information generated by business reporters and financial analysts to supplement the financial statements. In addition, ownership shares of these publicly-traded companies are bought and sold by investors, large and small, every day. For these publicly-traded companies, can the financial statements be used to pick winning and losing stocks, that is, those stocks that will go up in value and those that will decline in value in the future? Explain.

AA 2-55

DISCUSSION

Who Audits American Companies?

Your sister is a biochemist, but she prides herself on keeping a close eye on the business news. It is her opinion that the U.S. federal government should increase the amount that it pays to the auditors of the financial statements of U.S. companies. She is convinced that taxpayers would support this increase, even if it means increased income taxes. She thinks that

(continued)

increased government audit fees will attract more qualified auditors and will result in a dramatic rise in the reliability of the financial statements released by U.S. companies. This increased reliability will help U.S. companies compete in the global marketplace. Comment on your sister's opinion.

AA 2-56
DISCUSSION

Accounting for the Proper Entity

You have been hired to prepare the financial reports for White River Building Supply, a proprietorship owned by Bill Masters. Upon encountering several payments made from the company bank account to a nearby university, you contact Bill Masters to find out how to classify these payments. Masters explains that those checks were written to pay his daughter's tuition and to purchase her textbooks and miscellaneous supplies. He then tells you to include the payments with other expenses of the business. "This way," he explains, "I can deduct the payments on my tax return. Why not, since it all comes out of the same pocket?" How would you respond to Masters?

AA 2-57
JUDGMENT CALL

You Decide: **What is the most important number in the financial statements–net income or EPS?**

You were talking with some of your friends, who are finance majors, and they said that the most important number in the financial statements is the earnings per share figure on the income statement. One friend said, "EPS is the only number Wall Street cares about!" Some of your fellow students in accounting believe, however, that net income and the income statement are much more important than a single EPS figure.

AA 2-58
JUDGMENT CALL

You Decide: **Is the cash flow statement necessary?**

You were at dinner with some family and friends when one of them started talking about the long hours he has been putting in at work—a local waste management company. He said that cash flows have been bad and he has been staying up late trying to figure out the problem. When asked about the condition of his statement of cash flows, he said, "We don't have one of those statements to assess cash flows, we just use EBITDA (earnings before interest, taxes, depreciation, and amortization). Besides, everything I need to know is in either the balance sheet or income statement." Is a statement of cash flows necessary, or is the information it contains redundant of the balance sheet and income statement?

AA 2-59
JUDGMENT CALL

You Decide: **Should Wall Street place so much importance on the EPS figure or not?**

Recently, your mom came to you with questions about some of her investments. A year ago, she made an investment in 10 companies that are traded on the S&P 500. She tried to pick enough different companies to "diversify" her portfolio. Last week, one of her companies came out with "lower than expected EPS." In the two days following the news, the stock price dropped almost 30%! She wanted to know why so many people cared about one number. How do you respond?

AA 2-60
JUDGMENT CALL

You Decide: **Are the notes to the financial statements necessary?**

Do the notes to the financial statements add value to investors, or have they evolved from tradition? You were listening to talk radio on your way home from work a couple weeks ago when you heard someone say, "Everything you need to know about a company should be either in the balance sheet, income statement, or statement of cash flows. If you can't find it in there, it is not worth knowing! Besides that, the notes are too complex to understand!" Do you agree with this assumption?

AA 2-61
REAL COMPANY ANALYSIS

Wal-Mart

The 2006 Form 10-K for **Wal-Mart** can be found in Appendix A. Answer the following questions:

1. Locate Wal-Mart's 2006 balance sheet. What percentage of its total assets consists of cash and cash equivalents? How much long-term debt does Wal-Mart have?

(continued)

2. Find Wal-Mart's 2006 income statement. Have revenues increased or decreased over the last three years? Is the rate of increase rising?

3. Find Wal-Mart's statement of stockholders' equity. Did Wal-Mart pay a dividend in 2006? Did Wal-Mart buy or sell any stock in 2006?

4. Review Wal-Mart's statement of cash flows. What activity generates most of Wal-Mart's cash? What is Wal-Mart doing with all its money—buying back its own stock, investing in other companies, or something else?

AA 2-62

REAL COMPANY ANALYSIS

Safeway

At the start of this chapter you learned a little about **Safeway** and its history. Now let's take a look at the company's financial performance in recent years. Refer back to Safeway's income statement (on page 40), the balance sheet (on page 36), and the statement of cash flows (on page 44).

Based on information contained in these financial statements, answer the following questions:

1. As a percentage of total assets, did current assets increase or decrease from 2004 to 2005? What was the primary reason for the change?

2. Divide gross profit by sales for 2004 and 2005. For which year is the gross profit percentage higher? What does that change represent?

3. In 2005, did Safeway generate enough cash from operations to fund all of its investing activities? Looking at the financing activities section of the statement of cash flows, would you predict that long-term debt on the balance sheet went up or down in 2005?

AA 2-63

INTERNATIONAL

Diageo

Diageo is a United Kingdom (UK) consumer products firm, best known in the United States for the following brand names: Smirnoff, Johnnie Walker, J&B, Gordon's, Guinness, Pillsbury, and Häagen-Dazs. Diageo's 2005 balance sheet is shown on the next page.

(continued)

Diageo

Consolidated Balance Sheet

30 June 2005

(in millions of pounds)

Fixed assets		
Intangible assets	4,252	
Tangible assets	2,097	
Investment in associates	1,334	
Other investments	719	
		8,402
Current assets		
Stocks	2,335	
Debtors–due within one year	1,664	
Debtors–due after one year	68	
Cash at bank and liquid resources	817	
	4,884	
Creditors–due within one year		
Borrowings	(869)	
Other creditors	(3,183)	
	(4,052)	
Net current (liabilities)/assets		832
Total assets less current liabilities		9,234
Creditors–due after one year		
Borrowings	(3,677)	
Other creditors	(98)	
		(3,775)
Provisions for liabilities and charges		(723)
Post employment charges		(902)
Net Assets		3,834
Capital and reserves		
Called-up share capital		883
Share premium account	1,337	
Revaluation reserve	111	
Capital redemption reserve	3,060	
Profit and loss account	(1,750)	
Reserves attributable to equity shareholders		2,758
Shareholders' funds		3,641
Minority interests		193
		3,834

1. Can you identify any major differences between Wal-Mart's and Diageo's balance sheets in terms of the order in which major categories are displayed?
2. What is Diageo's total assets? Is it as easy to determine as Wal-Mart's total assets?
3. Take a look at the following list of accounts and identify, given your knowledge of assets, liabilities, and owners' equity, what the American equivalent of those accounts might be (you might want to reference Wal-Mart's balance sheet for comparison):
   - Stocks
   - Debtors
   - Called-up share capital
   - Profit and loss account

AA 2-64

ETHICS

Violating a Covenant

Often banks will require a company that borrows money to agree to certain restrictions on its activities in order to protect the lending institution. These restrictions are called "debt covenants." An example of a common debt covenant is requiring a company to maintain its current ratio (which is current assets ÷ current liabilities) at a certain level, say, 2.0.

(continued)

Your boss has just come to you and asked, "How can you make our current ratio higher?" You know that the company has a line of credit with a local bank that requires the company to maintain its current ratio at 1.5. You also know that the company was dangerously close to violating this covenant during the previous quarter. The end of the fiscal period is next week, and some action must be taken to increase the current ratio. If the covenant is violated, the lending agreement allows the bank to significantly modify the terms of the debt (in the bank's favor) and also gives the bank a seat on the company's board of directors. Management would prefer not to have the bank involved in the day-to-day affairs of the business, nor do they want to alter the terms of the lending agreement.

Identify ways in which the current ratio can be increased. Would any of the alternatives you identify be good for the business, e.g., selling equipment might raise the current ratio but would that be good for the business? Should a company engage in these types of transactions?

AA 2-65
WRITING

The Most Important Financial Statement

As you have discovered, there are three primary financial statements—balance sheet, income statement, and statement of cash flows. In no more than two pages, answer the following question: If you could have access to only one of the primary financial statements, which would it be and why? As you provide support for the financial statement of your choice, also provide reasons as to why you would not pick the other two statements.

AA 2-66
CUMULATIVE SPREADSHEET PROJECT

Creating a Balance Sheet and Income Statement

Starting with this chapter, each chapter in this text will include a spreadsheet assignment based on the financial information of a fictitious company named Handyman. The first assignments are simple—in this chapter you are asked to do little more than set up financial statement formats and input some numbers. In succeeding chapters, the spreadsheets will get more complex so that by the end of the course you will have constructed a spreadsheet that allows you to forecast operating cash flow for five years in the future and adjust your forecast depending on the operating parameters that you think are most reasonable.

So, let's get started with the first spreadsheet assignment.

1. The following numbers are for Handyman Company for 2009:

Short-Term Loans Payable	$ 10	Long-Term Debt	$207
Interest Expense	9	Income Tax Expense	4
Capital Stock	50	Retained Earnings (as of 1/1/06)	31
Cash	10	Receivables	27
Dividends	0	Sales	700
Accumulated Depreciation	9	Accounts Payable	74
Inventory	153	Property, Plant, & Equipment	199
Cost of Goods Sold	519	Other Operating Expenses	160

Your assignment is to create a spreadsheet containing a balance sheet and an income statement for Handyman Company.

2. Handyman is wondering what its balance sheet and income statement would have looked like if the following numbers were changed as indicated:

	Change	
	From	To
Sales	700	730
Cost of Goods Sold	519	550
Other Operating Expenses	160	165

Create a second spreadsheet with the numbers changed as indicated. *Note:* After making these changes, your balance sheet may no longer balance. Assume that any discrepancy is eliminated by increasing or decreasing Short-Term Loans Payable as much as necessary.

The Mechanics of Accounting

After studying this chapter, you should be able to:

LEARNING OBJECTIVES

(1) Understand the process of transforming transaction data into useful accounting information. *Transforming raw transaction data into useful accounting information involves analyzing, recording, and summarizing a large amount of transaction data so that financial reports can be prepared.*

(2) Analyze transactions and determine how those transactions affect the accounting equation (step one of the accounting cycle). *Accountants analyze transactions using debits and credits. Whether a debit or credit represents an increase or decrease depends on the type of account being considered. The accounting equation (Assets = Liabilities + Owners' Equity) represents the fact that the amount of a company's assets is always equal to the amount of financing (from investors and creditors) used to acquire those assets.*

(3) Record the effects of transactions using journal entries (step two of the accounting cycle). *Journal entries are the accountant's way of recording the debit and credit effects of both simple and complex business transactions. Journal*

entries are recorded in the journal which is a chronological listing of transactions coded in debit and credit language.

(4) Summarize the resulting journal entries through posting and prepare a trial balance (step three of the accounting cycle). *Once journal entries are made, their effects must be sorted and copied, or posted, to the individual accounts. All of the individual accounts are collected in the ledger. A trial balance lists all of the accounts in the ledger, along with their balances.*

(5) Describe how technology has affected the first three steps of the accounting cycle. *Computers now take care of the routine aspects of bookkeeping, such as posting, trial balance preparation, and analysis of common transactions. Knowledge of the process helps one understand the flow of information within a company.*

Ray Kroc, a 51-year-old milkshake machine distributor, first visited the McDonald brothers' drive-in (in San Bernardino, California) in July of 1954 because he wanted to know why a single "hamburger stand" needed 10 milkshake machines. That first day, Kroc spent the lunch rush hour watching the incredible volume of business the small drive-in was able to handle. By the time he left town, Kroc had received a personal briefing on the "McDonald's Speedee System" from Dick and Mac McDonald and had secured the rights to duplicate the system throughout the United States.

Ray Kroc opened his first outlet in Chicago in 1955, and 50 years later the number of McDonald's locations had expanded to over 31,500. The essence of **McDonald's** business seems fairly simple: revenues come from selling Big Macs, Happy Meals, Chicken McNuggets, etc.; operating costs include the costs of the raw materials to produce the food items, labor costs, building rentals, income taxes, and so forth. But the magnitude of McDonald's operations in terms of volume (sales average over $100 million per day) as

accounting cycle

The procedure for analyzing, recording, summarizing, and reporting the transactions of a business.

well as geography (McDonald's has locations in 121 countries throughout the world) makes compiling this information a challenge. In order to prepare its year-end financial reports, McDonald's must accumulate financial information from its various locations throughout the world, summarize that information according to U.S. accounting standards, and make the report available to the public within a short time (45 days beginning in 2007) after the end of the year. In fact, McDonald's annual report for the period ended December 31, 2005, was finished on February 20, 2006.

With the number of transactions that occur on a daily basis, the accounting for McDonald's would be impossible were it not for a systematic method for analyzing these transactions and collecting and recording transaction related information. What is the process by which McDonald's and other entities transform raw transaction data into useful information? Certainly, shareholders and others would not understand how McDonald's has performed if the company merely published volumes of raw transaction data. How are millions of transactions summarized and eventually reported in the primary financial statements? This transformation process is referred to as the **accounting cycle**, or the bookkeeping part of accounting.

I n the first two chapters, we provided an overview of accounting. We discussed the environment of accounting and its objectives, some basic concepts and assumptions of accounting, and the primary financial statements. Now we begin our study of the "accounting cycle."

This simply means that we will examine the procedures for analyzing, recording, summarizing, and reporting the transactions of a business. In this chapter, we describe the first three steps in the cycle. The remaining step (preparing reports for external users) is explained in Chapter 4.

How Can We Collect All This Information?

Understand the process of transforming transaction data into useful accounting information.

1 Suppose you were asked, "What was the total cost, to the nearest dollar, of your college education last year?" To answer this question would require that you (1) gather information (in the form of receipts, credit card statements, and canceled checks) for all your expenditures, (2) analyze that information to determine which outflows relate to your college education, and (3) summarize those outflows into one number—the cost of your college education. Once you have answered that question, answer this one, "How much did you spend on food last year?" Again you would have to go through the same process of

© GHISLAIN & MARIE DAVID DELOSSY/GETTY IMAGES INC.

Businesses, such as a college bookstore, have many exchange transactions in which they trade one thing for another—like textbooks for cash.

collecting data, analyzing the information to identify those expenditures relating to food, and then summarizing those expenditures into one number. From these two examples you can see that, without a method for gathering and organizing day-to-day financial data, answers to seemingly routine questions can get quite complex.

Now you may be thinking, "Doesn't my checkbook allow me to easily answer these questions?" Your checkbook (also known as your check register) would certainly help, but it is limited in that it tracks only the transactions that go through your checking account. It does not track the cash in your pocket, in your savings accounts, or in other investment accounts. It also is not yet summarized.

Now consider the dilemma for businesses. They typically have far more transactions than you, and the kinds of transactions are more varied. Businesses buy and sell goods or services; borrow and invest money; pay wages to employees; purchase land, buildings, and equipment; distribute earnings to owners; and pay taxes to the government. These activities are referred to as "exchange transactions" because the entity is actually trading (exchanging) one thing for another. A college bookstore, for example, exchanges textbooks for cash. **Business documents**, such as a sales invoice, a purchase order, or a check stub, are often used (1) to confirm that a transaction has occurred, (2) to establish the amounts to be recorded, and (3) to facilitate the analysis of business events.

business documents

Records of transactions used as the basis for recording accounting entries; include invoices, check stubs, receipts, and similar business papers.

To determine how well an entity is managing its resources, the results of transactions must be analyzed. The accounting cycle makes the analysis possible by recording and summarizing an entity's transactions and preparing reports that present the summary results. Exhibit 1 shows the sequence of the accounting cycle. Later, we will discuss these general categories and the specific steps of the cycle.

Keeping track of a company's transactions requires a system of accounting that is tailor-made to the needs of that particular enterprise. Obviously, the accounting system of a large multinational corporation with millions of business transactions each day will be much more complex than the system needed by a small Internet start-up company. The more complex and detailed the accounting system, the more likely it is to be automated. Even small companies generally use some type of inexpensive accounting software. Such software helps reduce the number of routine clerical functions and improves the accuracy and timeliness of the accounting records.

Although a computer-based system is faster and requires less labor than a manual system, the steps in the process are basically the same for both: transactions are first recorded on source documents; they are then analyzed, journalized, and posted to the accounts; and the resulting information is summarized, reported, and used for evaluation purposes. The difference lies in who (or what) does the work. With a computer-based system, the software transforms the recorded data, summarizes the data into categories, and prepares the financial statements and other reports. Nevertheless,

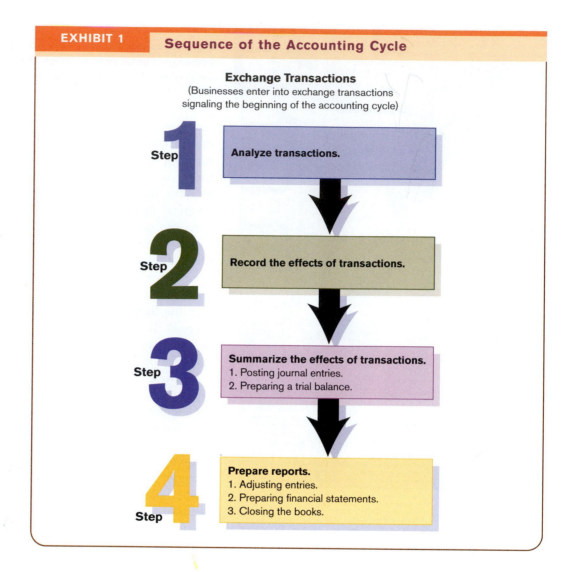

EXHIBIT 1   Sequence of the Accounting Cycle

Exchange Transactions
(Businesses enter into exchange transactions signaling the beginning of the accounting cycle)

Step **1**   **Analyze transactions.**

Step **2**   **Record the effects of transactions.**

Step **3**   **Summarize the effects of transactions.**
1. Posting journal entries.
2. Preparing a trial balance.

Step **4**   **Prepare reports.**
1. Adjusting entries.
2. Preparing financial statements.
3. Closing the books.

human judgment is still essential in analyzing and recording transactions, especially those of a non-routine nature.

Because a manual accounting system is easier to understand, we will use a manual system for the examples in this text. As you begin studying the steps in the accounting cycle, it is important that you understand the accounting equation and double-entry accounting more fully. This concept was briefly introduced in Chapter 2. You will recall that the accounting model is built on this basic equation. You now need to learn how to use the equation in accounting for the transactions of a business.

REMEMBER THIS...

Accounting is designed to accumulate and report in summary form the results of a company's transactions, thereby transforming the financial data into useful information for decision making. The four steps in the accounting cycle are as follows.

1. Analyze transactions.
2. Record the effects of transactions.
3. Summarize the effects of transactions.
4. Prepare reports.

How Do Transactions Affect the Accounting Equation?

Analyze transactions and determine how those transactions affect the accounting equation (step one of the accounting cycle).

② Often, the most difficult aspect of accounting is determining which events are to be reflected in the accounting records and which are not. Suppose, for example, that **Burger King** introduced a Big Mac clone at half the Big Mac price. The proliferation of Big Mac clones could have a serious impact on the future of **McDonald's**. However, as discussed in Chapter 2, events that cannot be measured in monetary terms will not be reflected in the financial statements. It would be virtually impossible to reliably quantify the impact that Big Mac clones could have on the future profitability of McDonald's, and thus, that information would not be reflected in the financial statements.

Now you may be saying to yourself, "We have an obligation to inform financial statement users about this attack on the Big Mac." We would all agree that this information should be shared, but the financial statements are not the place to do it. As you review a company's annual report to shareholders, you will notice that the financial statements are only one part of the information provided to users. Information relating to the competitive environment, product development, and marketing and sales efforts is included in the annual report, but not as part of the accounting information.

After determining the amount of a transaction, the event must be analyzed to determine if an arm's-length transaction has occurred. Accounting is concerned primarily with reflecting the effects of transactions between two independent entities. So **Delta Air Lines** signing a contract with **Boeing** to purchase airplanes in the future would not be reflected in the financial statements until the airplanes are manufactured and Delta has contracted to pay for the planes. Transactions between independent parties must be analyzed to determine their effect on the accounting equation. This analysis is often what separates an accountant from a bookkeeper. While many transactions are routine, some business events are quite complex and require a comprehensive analysis to determine how the event should be reflected in the financial statements. Consider the following example:

- A company buys a building. In addition to paying $20,000 cash, the company agrees to pay $10,000 per year for the next 10 years. The company will also pay a $2,000 property tax bill associated with the building from last year. As part of the purchase, the company gave the former owners of the building 500 shares of stock. Finally, the building will require $23,000 worth of repairs and renovations before it can be used. How much should be recorded as the cost of the building?

As this example illustrates, transactions can become quite complex. The good news is that the transaction analysis framework introduced in this chapter allows you to break complex transactions into manageable pieces and also provides a self-checking mechanism to ensure that you haven't forgotten anything. Once a transaction is properly analyzed and the affected accounts identified (along with the direction of those effects), the remainder of the accounting cycle can proceed without much difficulty.

The Accounting Equation

So let's begin our analysis of transactions by first reviewing some of the basics. Recall that the fundamental accounting equation is:

Assets	=	**Liabilities**	+	**Owners' Equity**
[Resources]		[A method of financing resources that requires repayment]*		[A method of financing resources that does not require repayment and represents ownership interests in the business]

---

*Not all liabilities represent a method of financing assets. In some cases, liabilities arise during the course of business that are not associated with the financing of assets. For example, an obligation to clean up a toxic waste spill is not associated with an asset but still represents a liability. Still, the majority of liabilities are incurred to finance assets.

The accounting equation must always remain in balance. To see how this balance is maintained when accounting for business transactions, consider the following activities:

Business Activity (Transaction)	Effect in Terms of the Accounting Equation
1. Investment of $50,000 by owners	Increase asset (Cash), increase owners' equity (Capital Stock): A ↑ $50,000 = OE ↑ $50,000
2. Borrowed $25,000 from bank	Increase asset (Cash), increase liability (Notes Payable): A ↑ $25,000 = L ↑ $25,000
3. Purchased $14,000 worth of inventory on credit (will pay later). The inventory is to be resold at a later date.	Increase asset (Inventory), increase liability (Accounts Payable): A ↑ $14,000 = L ↑ $14,000
4. Purchased equipment costing $15,000 for cash	Decrease asset (Cash), increase asset (Equipment): A ↓ $15,000 = A ↑ $15,000

For each of the transactions, the terms in parentheses are the specific accounts affected by the transactions, as will be explained in the next section.

In each case, the equation remains in balance because an identical amount is added to both sides, subtracted from both sides, or added to and subtracted from the same side of the equation. Following each transaction, we can ensure that the accounting equation balances. Note how the following spreadsheet keeps track of the equality of the accounting equation for these four transactions:

TRANSACTION #	ASSETS		LIABILITIES		OWNERS' EQUITY
Beginning Balance	$ 0	=	$ 0	+	$ 0
1	+50,000				+50,000
Subtotal	$50,000	=	$ 0	+	$50,000
2	+25,000		+25,000		
Subtotal	$75,000	=	$25,000	+	$50,000
3	+14,000		+14,000		
Subtotal	$89,000	=	$39,000	+	$50,000
4	+15,000				
	−15,000				
Total	$89,000	=	$39,000	+	$50,000

Using Accounts to Categorize Transactions

In Chapter 2, the balance sheet and the income statement were introduced as two of the three primary financial statements, the third being the statement of cash flows. We learned that the elements of the balance sheet are assets, liabilities, and owners' equity; the elements of the income statement are revenues and expenses. Now we must learn how each of these elements is comprised of many different accounts.

An **account** is a specific accounting record that provides an efficient way to categorize similar transactions. Thus, we may designate asset accounts, liability accounts, and owners' equity accounts. Examples of asset accounts are Cash, Inventory, and Equipment. Liability accounts include Accounts Payable and Notes Payable. The equity accounts for a corporation are Capital Stock and Retained

account

An accounting record in which the results of transactions are accumulated; shows increases, decreases, and a balance.

Earnings. You can think of an individual account as a summary of every transaction affecting a certain item (such as cash); the summary may be recorded on one page of a book or in one column of a spreadsheet (seen as follows).

| Transaction # | ASSETS | | | | LIABILITIES | | | OWNER'S EQUITY |
	Cash	Inventory	Equipment		Accounts Payable	Notes Payable		Capital Stock
Beginning Balance	$ 0	$ 0	$ 0	=	$ 0	$ 0	+	$ 0
1	+50,000							+50,000
Subtotal	$50,000	$ 0	$ 0	=	$ 0	$ 0	+	$50,000
2	+25,000					+25,000		
Subtotal	$75,000	$ 0	$ 0	=	$ 0	$25,000	+	$50,000
3		+14,000			+14,000			
Subtotal	$75,000	$14,000	$ 0	=	$14,000	$25,000	+	$50,000
4	−15,000		+15,000					
Total	$60,000	$14,000	$15,000	=	$14,000	$25,000	+	$50,000

Using the previous transactions, we can easily see how the accounting equation can be expanded to include specific accounts under the headings of assets, liabilities, and owners' equity. We can also see that after each transaction, the equality of the accounting equation can be determined simply by adding up the balances of all the asset accounts and comparing the total to the sum of all the liability and owners' equity accounts.

Now suppose that a company has 200 accounts and 10,000 transactions each month. Obviously, this spreadsheet would quickly get very big. Today, computers help in compiling this massive amount of data. Five hundred years ago, when double-entry accounting was formalized, all the adding and subtracting was done by hand. You can imagine the difficulties of tracking multiple accounts, involving hundreds of transactions, using the spreadsheet method described above while doing all the computations by hand. Mixing "+" and "−" in one column would provide ample opportunity to make mistakes.

T-account

A simplified depiction of an account in the form of a letter T.

This problem was solved by separating the "+" and the "−" for each account into separate columns, totaling each column, and then computing the difference between the columns to arrive at an ending balance. The simplest, most fundamental format is the configuration of the letter T. This is called a **T-account**. Note that a T-account is an abbreviated representation of an actual account (illustrated later) and is used as a teaching and learning tool. The following are examples of T-accounts, representing the transactions described previously.

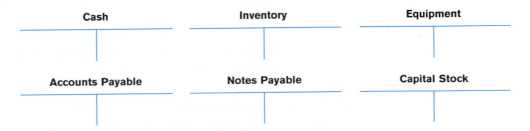

debit

An entry on the left side of a T-account.

The account title (Cash, for example) appears at the top of the T-account. Transaction amounts may be recorded on both the left side and the right side of the T-account. Instead of using the terms left and right to indicate which side of a T-account is affected, terms unique to accounting were developed. **Debit (abbreviated Dr)** is used to indicate the left side of a T-account, and

credit

An entry on the right side of a T-account.

credit (abbreviated Cr) is used to indicate the right side of a T-account. Debit means left, credit means right—nothing more, nothing less.

Besides representing the left and right sides of an account, the terms *debit* and *credit* take on additional meaning when coupled with a specific account. By convention, for asset accounts, debits refer to increases and credits to decreases. For example, to increase the cash account, we debit it; to decrease the cash account, we credit it. Since we expect the total increases in the cash account to be greater than the decreases, the cash account will usually have a debit balance after accounting for all transactions. Thus, we can make this generalization—asset accounts will usually have debit balances. The opposite relationship is true of liability and owners' equity accounts; they are decreased by *debits* and increased by *credits*. As a result, liability and owners' equity accounts will typically have credit balances. The effect of this system is shown here, with an increase indicated by (+) and a decrease by (−).

Assets		=	Liabilities		+	Owners' Equity	
DR	CR		DR	CR		DR	CR
(+)	(−)		(−)	(+)		(−)	(+)

 FYI

Where does the "DR" come from when the term debit doesn't have an "r" in it? Recall that accounting, as we know it today, was formalized in the 1500s in Italy. The Italian and Latin (a common language back then) verb forms of debit are *addebitare* and *debere,* respectively. Thus, the "DR" represents an Italian or Latin abbreviation of debit.

 CAUTION

Just a reminder that asset accounts will typically have debit balances, whereas liabilities and owners' equity accounts will typically have credit balances.

In addition to assets equaling liabilities and owners' equity, debits should always also equal credits. If you fully grasp the meaning of these two equalities, you are well on your way to mastering the mechanics of accounting or learning the language of accounting. Debits and credits allow us to take a shortcut to ensure that the accounting equation balances. **If, for every transaction, debits equal credits, then the accounting equation will balance.**

To understand why this happens, keep in mind three basic facts regarding double-entry accounting:

1. Debits are always entered on the left side of an account and credits on the right side.
2. For every transaction, there must be at least one debit and one credit.
3. Debits must always equal credits for each transaction.

Now notice what this means for one of the business transactions shown earlier (page 80): investment by owners. An asset account (Cash) is debited; it is increased. An owners' equity account (Capital Stock) is credited; it is also increased. There is both a debit and a credit for the transaction, and we have increased accounts on both sides of the equation by an equal amount, thus keeping the accounting equation in balance.

Be careful not to let the general, non-accounting meanings of the words *credit* and *debit* confuse you. In general conversation, credit has an association with plus and debit with minus. But on the asset side of the accounting equation, where debit means increase and credit means decrease, this association can lead you astray. In accounting, debit simply means left and credit simply means right. To make sure you understand the relationship between debits and credits, the various accounts, and the accounting equation, let us examine further the transactions listed on page 80.

Business Activity (Transaction)	Effect in Terms of the Accounting Equation						
	Assets		=	Liabilities	+	Owners' Equity	
1. Investment by owners	Cash DR (+)					Capital Stock CR (+)	
2. Borrowed money from bank	Cash DR (+)			Notes Payable CR (+)			
3. Purchased inventory on credit	Inventory DR (+)			Accounts Payable CR (+)			
4. Purchased equipment for cash	Equipment DR (+)	Cash CR (−)					

Note that every time an account is debited, other accounts have to be credited for the same amount. This is the major characteristic of the double-entry accounting system: *the debits must always equal the credits*. This important characteristic creates a practical advantage: the opportunity for "self-checking." If debits do not equal credits, an error has been made in analyzing and recording the entity's activities.

Before proceeding any further, let's stop for a moment and review the relationship between the various types of accounts and debits and credits. It is in your best interest not to go on until you understand these very important relationships.

Account Type			Debit or Credit?	Ending Balance
Asset	Increase	results in	Debit	Debit
	Decrease	results in	Credit	
Liability	Increase	results in	Credit	Credit
	Decrease	results in	Debit	
Owners' Equity	Increase	results in	Credit	Credit
	Decrease	results in	Debit	

Expanding the Accounting Equation to Include Revenues, Expenses, and Dividends

At this point, we must bring revenues and expenses into the picture. Obviously, they are part of every ongoing business. Revenues provide resource inflows; they are increases in resources from the sale of goods or services. Expenses represent resource outflows; they are costs incurred in generating revenues. Note that revenues are not synonymous with cash or other assets, but are a way of describing where the assets came from. For example, cash received from the sale of a product would be considered revenue. Cash received by borrowing from the bank would not be revenue, but an increase in a liability. By the same token, expenses are a way of describing how an asset has been used. Thus, cash paid for interest on a loan is an expense, but cash paid to buy a building represents the exchange of one asset for another.

CAUTION

We stated previously that owners' equity accounts will have credit balances. However, expenses, a component of Retained Earnings, will almost always have debit balances. Since revenues will usually exceed expenses, the net effect on Retained Earnings will result in a credit balance.

How do revenues and expenses fit into the accounting equation? Remember that revenues minus expenses equals net income; and net income is a major source of change in owners' equity from one accounting period to the next. Revenues and expenses, then, may be thought of as *temporary* subdivisions of owners' equity. Revenues increase owners' equity and so, like all owners' equity accounts, are increased by credits. Expenses reduce owners' equity and are therefore increased by debits. As will be explained in Chapter 4, all revenue and expense accounts are "closed" into the retained earnings account at the end of the accounting cycle.

dividends

Distributions to the owners (stockholders) of a corporation.

One other temporary account affects owners' equity. It is the account that shows distributions of earnings to owners. For a corporation, this account is called **Dividends**. Since dividends reflect payments to the owners, thereby reducing owners' equity, the dividends account is increased by a debit and decreased by a credit. The dividends account, like revenues and expenses, is also "closed" into the retained earnings account.

Just a warning here: students who have trouble grasping debits and credits usually get hung up on the revenue and expense accounts. Remember that revenues and expenses are subcategories of Retained Earnings. When you credit a revenue account, you are essentially increasing Retained Earnings. When you debit an expense account, you are increasing the amount of expense, which in turn reduces Retained Earnings.

Using the corporate form of business as an example, the accounting equation may be expanded to include revenues, expenses, and dividends, as shown in Exhibit 2.

Why Should I Understand the Mechanics of Accounting?

If computers now take care of all the routine accounting functions, why does a businessperson need to know anything about debits, credits, journals, posting, T-accounts, and trial balances? Good question. First of all, even though computers now do most of

EXHIBIT 2   **Expanded Accounting Equation**

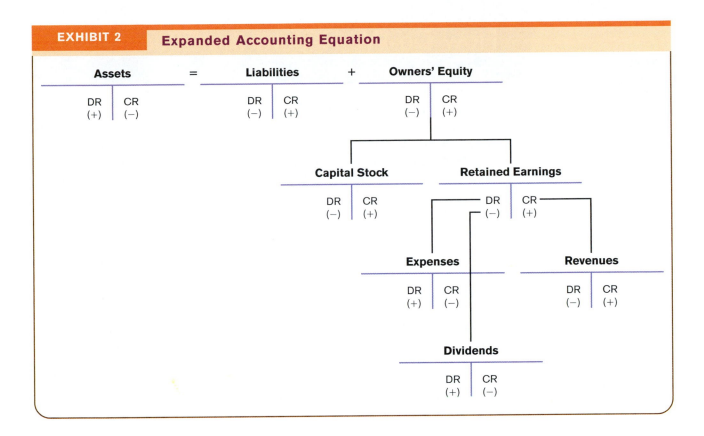

the dirty work, the essence of double-entry accounting is unchanged from the days of quill pens and handwritten ledgers. Thus, understanding the process explained in this chapter is still relevant to a computer-based accounting system. In addition, with or without computers, the use of debits, credits, and T-accounts still provides an efficient and widely used shorthand method of analyzing transactions. At a minimum, all businesspeople should be familiar enough with the language of accounting to understand, for example, why a credit balance in Cash or a debit balance in Retained Earnings is something unusual enough to merit investigation. Finally, an understanding of the accounting cycle—analyzing, recording, summarizing, and preparing—gives one insight into how information flows within an organization. And great advantages accrue to those who understand information flow.

REMEMBER THIS...

	Debit	Credit
Asset	↑	↓
Liability	↓	↑
Owners' Equity	↓	↑
Revenue	↓	↑
Expense	↑	↓
Dividend	↑	↓

- Revenues increase owners' equity.
- Expenses decrease owners' equity.
- Dividends decrease owners' equity.
- If debits = credits, then Assets = Liabilities + Owners' Equity

Record the effects of transactions using journal entries (step two of the accounting cycle).

How Do We Record the Effects of Transactions?

③ With our knowledge of the different types of accounts (assets, liabilities, and owners' equity) and the use of the terms *debit* and *credit* (debit means left and credit means right), we are now ready to actually record the effects of transactions.

The second step in the accounting cycle is to record the results of transactions in a **journal**. Journals provide a chronological record of all transactions of a business. They show the dates of the transactions, the amounts involved, and the particular accounts affected by the transactions. Sometimes a detailed description of the transaction is also included.

This chronological recording of transactions in a journal (sometimes called a book of original entry) provides a company with a complete record of its activities. If amounts were recorded directly in the accounts, it would be difficult, if not impossible, for a company to trace a transaction that occurred, say, six months previously.

Smaller companies, such as a locally owned pizza restaurant, may use only one journal, called a "general journal," to record all transactions. Larger companies having thousands of transactions each year may use special journals (for example, a cash receipts journal) as well as a general journal.

A specific format is used in **journalizing** (recording) transactions in a general journal. The debit entry is listed first; the credit entry is listed second and is indented to the right. Normally, the date and a brief explanation of the transaction are considered essential parts of the **journal entry**. (In the text, we often ignore dates and explanations to simplify the examples.) Dollar signs usually are omitted. Unless otherwise noted, this format will be used whenever a journal entry is presented.

journal

An accounting record in which transactions are first entered; provides a chronological record of all business activities.

journalizing

Recording transactions in a journal.

journal entry

A recording of a transaction where debits equal credits; usually includes a date and an explanation of the transaction.

General Journal Entry Format

Date   Debit Entry   xx
          Credit Entry   xx
             Explanation.

Exhibit 3 is a partial page from a general journal, showing typical journal entries. Study this exhibit carefully because the entire accounting cycle is based on journal entries. If journal entries are incorrect, the resulting financial information will be inaccurate.

To give you additional exposure to analyzing transactions and recording journal entries, we are going to start our own business. Rather than spend the summer flipping burgers at the local hamburger house, you decide that you want to have an outdoor job—one that allows you to enjoy the summer sun, engage in rigorous physical activity, and sharpen your skills as an entrepreneur. You are going to start your own landscaping business. This business will involve mowing lawns, pulling weeds, trimming and planting shrubs, and so forth. We will use your new business to illustrate the journal entries used to record some common transactions of a business enterprise.[1] These transactions fit into the following four general categories: acquiring cash, acquiring other assets, selling goods or providing services, and collecting cash and paying obligations. Obviously, we cannot present all possible transactions in this chapter. In studying the illustrations, strive to understand the conceptual basis of transaction analysis rather than memorizing specific journal entries. Pay particular attention to the dual effect of each transaction on the company in terms of the basic accounting equation (that is, its impact on assets and on liabilities and owners' equity). Remember that business activity involves revenues, expenses, and distributions to owners as well, and that these accounts eventually increase or decrease the retained earnings account in owners' equity.

---

[1] Normally, a small business like this one would be started as a sole proprietorship or as a partnership. We assume a corporation here to show a complete set of transactions.

| EXHIBIT 3 | **General Journal** |

JOURNAL   Page 1

Date	Description	Post. Ref.	Debits	Credits
2009 July 1	Cash		2,000	
	Capital Stock			2,000
	Issued 200 shares of capital stock at $10 per share.			
5	Truck		800	
	Cash			800
	Purchased a used truck.			
5	Equipment		250	
	Accounts Payable			250
	Purchased a lawnmower on account.			
5	Supplies		180	
	Cash			180
	Purchased supplies for cash.			

Acquiring Cash, Either from Owners or by Borrowing

Your first task in starting this business is to acquire cash, either through owners' investments or by borrowing. Your parents indicate that they will match any funds that you are going to put into your business. You have $1,000 in savings, and coupled with your parents' matching funds, you decide to issue 200 shares of stock.

Example 1   The following transaction illustrates investments by owners:

assets (+)
owners' equity (+)

Cash 2,000
    Capital Stock   2,000
    Issued 200 shares of capital stock at $10 per share.

This transaction increases cash as a result of capital stock being issued to investors, or stockholders. The cash account is debited, and the capital stock account is credited. The economic impact of this situation may be summarized as follows:

	ASSETS					=	LIABILITIES		+	OWNERS' EQUITY
Transaction	**Cash**	**Inventory**	**Equipment**	**Supplies**	**Truck**	=	**Accounts Payable**	**Notes Payable**	+	**Capital Stock**
Beginning Balance	$ 0	$0	$0	$0	$0	=	$0	$0	+	$ 0
Invested money in the business	2,000	—	—	—	—		—	—		2,000
Subtotal	$2,000	$0	$0	$0	$0	=	$0	$0	+	$2,000

Example 2   Suppose that in addition to coming up with the money yourself or from your parents, you went to a bank and convinced the loan officer to lend you the money. The journal entry for such a transaction would be:

assets (+)
liabilities (+)

Cash 2,000	
Notes Payable	2,000
Borrowed $2,000 from First National Bank, signing a	
12-month note at 12% interest.	

Here, the cash account is debited, and the notes payable account is credited. The accounting equation captures the economic impact of borrowing the money as follows:

	ASSETS					=	LIABILITIES		+	OWNERS' EQUITY
Transaction	Cash	Inventory	Equipment	Supplies	Truck		Accounts Payable	Notes Payable		Capital Stock
Beginning Balance	$ 0	$0	$0	$0	$0	=	$0	$ 0	+	$ 0
Invested money in the business	2,000	—	—	—	—		—	—		2,000
Borrowed money from a bank	2,000	—	—	—	—		—	2,000		—
Subtotal	$4,000	$0	$0	$0	$0	=	$0	$2,000	+	$2,000

Acquiring Other Assets

Now that you have obtained the funds necessary to start your business, either from owner investment or by borrowing, you can use that money to acquire other assets needed to operate the business. Such assets include supplies (such as fertilizer), inventory (perhaps shrubs that you will plant), and equipment (for example, a lawnmower and a truck for hauling). These assets may be purchased with cash or on credit. Credit purchases require payment after a period of time, for example, 30 days. Normally, interest expense is incurred when assets are bought on a time-payment plan that extends beyond two or three months. (To keep our examples simple here, we will not include interest expense. We will show how to account for interest on page 94, where we discuss the payment of obligations.) Examples of transactions involving the acquisition of noncash assets follow.

Example 1   The first thing you need is a lawnmower and some form of transportation. You find an old 1988 pickup truck for sale for $800, and you buy it paying cash.

assets (+)
assets (−)

Truck 800	
Cash	800
Purchased a used truck.	

The accounting equation shows:

Transaction	Cash	Inventory	Equipment	Supplies	Truck	=	Accounts Payable	Notes Payable	+	Capital Stock
			ASSETS			=	LIABILITIES		+	OWNERS' EQUITY
Beginning Balance	$ 0	$0	$0	$0	$ 0	=	$0	$ 0	+	$ 0
Invested money in the business	2,000	–	–	–	–		–	–		2,000
Borrowed money from a bank	2,000	–	–	–	–		–	2,000		–
Purchased a truck paying cash	–800	–	–	–	800		–	–		–
Subtotal	$3,200	$0	$0	$0	$800	=	$0	$2,000	+	$2,000

Next, you drive to the local Sears store and purchase a Craftsman lawnmower and gas can for $250. Instead of paying for the mower with cash, you open a charge account, which will allow you to pay for the mower in 30 days with no interest charge. (If you wait and pay beyond this 30-day grace period, an interest charge will apply.) The journal entry to record this purchase is:

assets (+)   Equipment 250

liabilities (+)   Accounts Payable 250

            Purchased a lawnmower and gas can on account.

The accounting equation is shown below. When you pay for the mower, cash will be reduced, and the liability, Accounts Payable, will also be reduced, thus keeping the equation in balance.

Transaction	Cash	Inventory	Equipment	Supplies	Truck	=	Accounts Payable	Notes Payable	+	Capital Stock
			ASSETS			=	LIABILITIES		+	OWNERS' EQUITY
Beginning Balance	$ 0	$0	$ 0	$0	$ 0	=	$ 0	$ 0	+	$ 0
Invested money in the business	2,000	–	–	–	–		–	–		2,000
Borrowed money from a bank	2,000	–	–	–	–		–	2,000		–
Purchased a truck paying cash	–800	–	–	–	800		–	–		–
Purchased a mower on account	–	–	250	–	–		250	–		–
Subtotal	$3,200	$0	$250	$0	$800	=	$250	$2,000	+	$2,000

Example 2 Off you go to the neighborhood Home Depot store to purchase fertilizer, gloves, a rake, a shovel, and other assorted supplies. The total cost is $180, which you pay in cash; an increase in one asset (supplies) results in a decrease in another asset (cash).

assets (+)	Supplies	180	
assets (−)	Cash		180
	Purchased supplies for cash.		

The accounting equation shows:

Transaction		ASSETS				=	LIABILITIES		+	OWNERS' EQUITY
	Cash	Inventory	Equipment	Supplies	Truck		Accounts Payable	Notes Payable		Capital Stock
Beginning Balance	$ 0	$0	$ 0	$ 0	$ 0	=	$ 0	$ 0	+	$ 0
Invested money in the business	2,000	—	—	—	—		—	—		2,000
Borrowed money from a bank	2,000	—	—	—	—		—	2,000		—
Purchased a truck paying cash	−800	—	—	—	800		—	—		—
Purchased a mower on account	—	—	250	—	—		250	—		—
Purchased supplies for cash	−180	—	—	180	—		—	—		—
Subtotal	$3,020	$0	$250	$180	$800	=	$250	$2,000	+	$2,000

Example 3 On your way home from the hardware store, you drive past a greenhouse and notice a big sign advertising a "50% off" sale on shrubs. Since you anticipate that planting shrubs will be part of your business, you stop and purchase for cash $150 worth of shrubs as inventory. You plan to make money in two ways with the shrubs: (1) revenue from the labor associated with planting them and (2) a profit on selling the shrubs for more than you paid. (This is fair; after all, you are saving your client the time and trouble of having to go to the greenhouse.)

assets (+)	Inventory	150	
assets (−)	Cash		150
	Purchased inventory for cash.		

The accounting equation is shown at the top of the following page.

| Transaction | ASSETS | | | | | = | LIABILITIES | | + | OWNERS' EQUITY |
	Cash	Inventory	Equipment	Supplies	Truck	=	Accounts Payable	Notes Payable	+	Capital Stock
Beginning Balance	$ 0	$ 0	$ 0	$ 0	$ 0	=	$ 0	$ 0	+	$ 0
Invested money in the business	2,000	–	–	–	–		–	–		2,000
Borrowed money from a bank	2,000	–	–	–	–		–	2,000		–
Purchased a truck paying cash	–800	–	–	–	800		–	–		–
Purchased a mower on account	–	–	250	–	–		250	–		–
Purchased supplies for cash	–180	–	–	180	–		–	–		–
Purchased inventory for cash	–150	150	–	–	–		–	–		–
Subtotal	$2,870	$150	$250	$180	$800	=	$250	$2,000	+	$2,000

Selling Goods or Providing Services

Now that you have your lawnmower, your transportation, your supplies, and your inventory, it is time to go to work. The next category of common transactions involves the sale of services or merchandise. Revenues are generated and expenses incurred during this process. Sometimes services and merchandise are sold for cash; at other times, they are sold on credit (on account to be collected later), and a receivable is established for collection at a later date. Therefore, revenues indicate the source not only of cash but of other assets as well, all of which are received in exchange for the merchandise or services provided. Similarly, expenses may be incurred and paid for immediately by cash, or they may be incurred on credit—that is, they may be "charged," with a cash payment to be made at a later date. Illustrative transactions follow. Note the effect of revenues and expenses on owners' equity is indicated in brackets for each transaction.

Example 1 As soon as people find out that you are in the lawn care and landscaping business, your phone begins ringing off the hook. Although most of your clients pay you immediately when you perform the service, some prefer to pay you once a month. As a result, a portion of your revenues is received immediately in cash, while the balance becomes receivables. The journal entry to record your first week's revenue for lawn care services is:

assets (+)	Cash	270	
assets (+)	Accounts Receivable	80	
revenues (+) [equity (+)]	Lawn Care Revenue		350
	To record revenue for lawn care services.		

compound journal entry

A journal entry that involves more than one debit or more than one credit or both.

As the journal entry illustrates, more than two accounts can be involved in recording a transaction. This type of entry is called a **compound journal entry**. Because revenues increase owners' equity, the accounting equation shows:

Assets	=	Liabilities	+	Owners' Equity (Revenues)
(increase $350)		(no change)		(increase $350)

The detailed effect of this transaction and of each of the following transactions is summarized in Exhibit 4 on page 96.

Example 2   One of your customers asks if you will plant some shrubs in her backyard. You mention that you have some shrubs and describe them to her; she is thrilled that you have just the shrubs she wants, thereby saving her a trip to the greenhouse. You use one-half of your inventory of shrubs in this customer's yard, and it takes you three hours to complete the job. She pays you in cash. In this instance, we are dealing with two different types of revenue—profit from the sale of the shrubs and revenue from your labor. Let's deal with each type of revenue separately.

Sale of Shrubs.   Sales, whether made on account or for cash, require entries that reflect not only the sale, but also the cost of the inventory sold. The "cost of goods sold" is an expense and, as such, is offset with the sales revenue to determine the profitability of sales transactions. The special procedures for handling inventory are described in Chapter 7. It is sufficient here to show an example of the impact of the transaction on the accounting equation.

In this example, you charged your customer $90 for one-half of the shrubs you purchased earlier.

assets (+)	Cash	90
revenues (+) [equity (+)]	Sales Revenue	90
expenses (+) [equity (−)]	Cost of Goods Sold	75
assets (−)	Inventory	75
	To record the cost of inventory sold and to reduce inventory for its cost.	

STOP & THINK

Could the two journal entries relating to the sale of inventory be combined into one journal entry?

In this example, inventory costing you $75 is being sold for $90. The effect on the accounting equation for each transaction is:

Sales on Account

Assets	=	Liabilities	+	Owners' Equity (Revenues)
(increase $90)		(no change)		(increase $90)

Cost of Goods Sold

Assets	=	Liabilities	+	Owners' Equity (Expenses)
(decrease $75)		(no change)		(decrease $75)

Labor for Planting.   In addition to making a profit on the sale of the shrubs, you also generated revenue planting them. The journal entry to record this revenue is:

assets (+)

revenues (+) [equity (+)]

Cash	45	
Landscaping Revenue		45
To record revenue for landscaping services.		

The effect of the transaction on the accounting equation is:

Assets	=	Liabilities	+	Owners' Equity (Revenues)
(increase $45)		(no change)		(increase $45)

Example 3   In addition to expenses relating to the sale of inventory, other expenses are also incurred in operating a business. Examples include gas for your lawnmower and your truck and the wages you agreed to pay your little brother for working for you (Mom said you had to let him help). The following journal entries illustrate how these expenses would be accounted for:

expenses (+) [equity (−)]

   assets (−)

Gasoline Expense	50	
Cash		50
Paid cash for gas for the truck and the mower.		

expenses (+) [equity (−)]

   assets (−)

Wages Expense	60	
Cash		60
Paid wages expense.		

The effect on the accounting equation of the gasoline expense is:

Assets	=	Liabilities	+	Owners' Equity
(decrease $50)		(no change)		(decrease $50)

The entry for Wages Expense affects the equation in the same manner, the only difference being the amount, $60.

Collecting Cash and Paying Obligations

Obviously, once merchandise or services are sold on account, the receivables must be collected. The cash received is generally used to meet daily operating expenses and to pay other obligations. Excess cash can be reinvested in the business or distributed to the owners as a return on their investment.

Example 1   The collection of accounts receivable is an important aspect of most businesses. Receivables are created when you allow certain customers to pay for your services at a later date. When receivables are collected, that asset is reduced and cash is increased, as shown here.

assets (+)

assets (−)

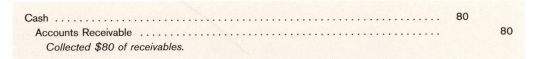

Cash	80	
Accounts Receivable		80
Collected $80 of receivables.		

The effect of collecting the receivables on the accounting equation is:

Assets	=	Liabilities	+	Owners' Equity
(increase $80; decrease $80)		(no change)		(no change)

Note that no revenue is involved here. Revenue is recorded when the original sales transaction creates the accounts receivable. The cash collection on account merely involves exchanging one asset for another.

Example 2   Remember that lawnmower and gas can you purchased on account? Well, now you have to pay for them. The entry to record the payment of obligations with cash is:

liabilities (−)	Accounts Payable	250	
assets (−)	Cash		250
	Paid $250 for the lawnmower and gas can previously purchased.		

After payment of accounts payable, the accounting equation shows:

Assets	=	Liabilities	+	Owners' Equity
(decrease $250)		(decrease $250)		(no change)

Remember that two parties are always involved in exchange transactions. What one buys, the other sells. When sales are on credit, the seller will record a receivable and the buyer will record a payable. The two accounts are inversely related. The seller of merchandise records a receivable and a sale, and simultaneously records an expense for the cost of goods sold and a reduction of inventory (as in Example 2 on page 92). The buyer records the receipt of the merchandise and, at the same time, records an obligation to pay the seller at some future time. When payment is made, the buyer reduces Accounts Payable and Cash (as in this example), whereas the seller increases Cash and reduces Accounts Receivable (as in Example 1 on page 93).

Example 3   On page 88, we showed the entry required when cash was borrowed from the bank. In that entry, you borrowed $2,000 to be paid over 12 months. Suppose you are required to make monthly loan payments of $178 with a portion of each payment being attributed to interest and a portion to reducing the liability—just like a mortgage on a house. As the following compound journal entry shows, a note payable or similar obligation requires an entry for payment, as well as for the interest due. Note that "interest" is the amount charged for using money, as will be more fully explained in later chapters.

liabilities (−)	Notes Payable..	158	
expenses (+) [equity (−)]	Interest Expense	20	
assets (−)	Cash..		178
	Paid first monthly payment on note with interest ($2,000 × 0.12 × 1/12).		

Analysis of this transaction reveals that assets have decreased for two reasons. First, a portion of a liability has been paid with cash. Second, interest expense at 12% for one month on the note payable has been paid. This relationship will generally be present in most long-term and some short-term liability transactions. Since the interest charge is an expense and decreases owners' equity, the impact of the entry on the accounting equation is:

STOP & THINK

Why are dividends NOT considered to be an expense?

Assets	=	Liabilities	+	Owners' Equity (Expenses)
(decrease $178)		(decrease $158)		(decrease $20)

Example 4 Recall that you obtained financing in two ways to start your business—investors (you, Mom, and Dad) and the bank. In the previous journal entry, we illustrated how the bank receives a return on its investment. Well, Mom and Dad would like a return as well. Corporations that are profitable generally pay dividends to their stockholders. "Dividends" represent a distribution to the stockholders of part of the earnings of a company. The following entry illustrates the payment of a cash dividend:

dividends (+) [equity (−)]	Dividends	50	
assets (−)	Cash		50
	Paid a $50 cash dividend.		

As noted earlier, dividends, like revenues and expenses, affect owners' equity. Unlike revenues and expenses, dividends are a distribution of profits and, therefore, are not considered in determining net income. Because dividends reduce the retained earnings accumulated by a corporation, they decrease owners' equity. The payment of a $50 dividend affects the accounting equation as follows:

Assets	=	Liabilities	+	Owners' Equity (Dividends)
(decrease $50)		(no change)		(decrease $50)

See Exhibit 4 on the next page for a summary of the transactions shown in this chapter and their effect on the accounting equation.

FYI

Many students have a little trouble getting used to debits, credits, and journal entries. So you are not alone if you are feeling a little overwhelmed. But remember, riding a bike wasn't easy the first time either. Like riding a bike, you will soon find that debits, credits, and journal entries aren't that difficult.

A Note on Journal Entries

When preparing a journal entry, a systematic method may be used in analyzing every transaction. A journal entry involves a three-step process:

1. Identify which accounts are involved.
2. For each account, determine if it is increased or decreased.
3. For each account, determine by how much it has changed.

The answer to step 1 tells you if the accounts involved are asset, liability, or owners' equity accounts. The answer to step 2, when considered in light of your answer to step 1, tells you if the accounts involved are to be debited or credited. Consider the instance where $25,000 is borrowed from a bank. The two accounts involved are Cash and Notes Payable. Cash increased, and since Cash is an asset and assets increase with debits, then Cash must be debited. Notes Payable increased (we owe more money), and since Notes Payable is a liability and liabilities increase with credits, then Notes Payable must be credited. The answer to step 3 completes the journal entry. Cash is debited for $25,000, and Notes Payable is credited for $25,000.

EXHIBIT 4	Summary of Transactions

		ASSETS					=	LIABILITIES	
	Cash	Accounts Receivable	Inventory	Equipment	Supplies	Truck		Accounts Payable	Notes Payable
Balance (from page 91)	$2,870	–	$150	$250	$180	$800	=	$ 250	$2,000
Revenue from lawn care	270	80	–	–	–	–		–	–
Sold inventory for cash	90	–	–75	–	–	–		–	–
Revenue from landscaping	45	–	–	–	–	–		–	–
Paid for gasoline	–50	–	–	–	–	–		–	–
Paid wages	–60	–	–	–	–	–		–	–
Collected receivables	80	–80	–	–	–	–		–	–
Paid accounts payable	–250	–	–	–	–	–		–250	–
Paid loan payment	–178	–	–	–	–	–		–	–158
Paid dividend	–50	–	–	–	–	–		–	–
Total	$2,767	$ 0	$ 75	$250	$180	$800	=	$ 0	$1,842

This three-step process will always work, even for complex transactions. Consider the case where inventory costing $60,000 is sold on account for $75,000. Using the three-step process results in the following:

1. *Step 1:* What accounts are involved?
   - Accounts Receivable (an asset), Inventory (an asset), Cost of Goods Sold (an expense—part of owners' equity), and Sales Revenue (a revenue account—part of owners' equity).
2. *Step 2:* Did the accounts increase or decrease?
   - Accounts Receivable increased (customers owe us more money). Since Accounts Receivable is an asset, it is increased with a debit.
   - Inventory decreased (we don't have it anymore). Since Inventory is an asset, it is decreased with a credit.
   - Cost of Goods Sold increased (an expense causing owners' equity to decrease). Since owners' equity decreases with a debit, Cost of Goods Sold must be debited.
   - Sales Revenue increased (a revenue causing owners' equity to increase). Since owners' equity increases with a credit, Sales Revenue must be credited.
3. *Step 3:* By how much did each account change?
   - The answer to step 3 results in the following journal entries:

Accounts Receivable	75,000	
Sales Revenue		75,000
Cost of Goods Sold	60,000	
Inventory		60,000

+		OWNERS' EQUITY							
		Retained Earnings							
	Capital Stock	Lawn Care Revenue	Sales Revenue	Landscaping Revenue	Cost of Goods Sold*	Gasoline Expense*	Wages Expense*	Interest Expense*	Dividends*
+	$2,000	–	–	–	–	–	–	–	–
	–	350	–	–	–	–	–	–	–
	–	–	90	–	–75	–	–	–	–
	–	–	–	45	–	–	–	–	–
	–	–	–	–	–	–50	–	–	–
	–	–	–	–	–	–	–60	–	–
	–	–	–	–	–	–	–	–	–
	–	–	–	–	–	–	–	–	–
	–	–	–	–	–	–	–	–20	–
	–	–	–	–	–	–	–	–	–50
+	$2,000	$350	$90	$45	–$75	–$50	–$60	–$20	–$50

*Recall that an increase in these accounts actually decreases owners' equity, hence the – (minus sign).

REMEMBER THIS...

Making a journal entry involves the following three steps:

1. Identify which accounts are involved.
2. For each account, determine if it is increased or decreased.
3. For each account, determine by how much it has changed.

Posting Journal Entries and Preparing a Trial Balance

Summarize the resulting journal entries through posting and prepare a trial balance (step three of the accounting cycle).

④ Once transactions have been analyzed and recorded in a journal, it is necessary to classify and group all similar items. This is accomplished by the bookkeeping procedure of **posting** all the journal entries to appropriate accounts (see page 98 for definition). As indicated earlier, accounts are records of like items. They show transaction dates, increases and decreases, and balances. For example, all increases and decreases in cash arising from transactions recorded in the journal are accumulated in one account called Cash. Similarly, all sales transactions are grouped together in the sales revenue account.

Posting is no more than sorting all journal entry amounts by account and copying those amounts to the appropriate account. No analysis is needed; all the necessary analysis is performed when the transaction is first recorded in the journal.

posting

The process of transferring amounts from the journal to the ledger.

ledger

A book of accounts in which data from transactions recorded in journals are posted and thereby summarized.

chart of accounts

A systematic listing of all accounts used by a company.

All accounts are maintained in an accounting record called a "ledger." A **ledger** (the main ledger is called a general ledger) is a "book of accounts." Exhibit 5 shows how the three cash transactions in the general journal would be posted to the cash account in the general ledger, with arrows depicting the posting procedures. Observe that a number has been inserted in the "posting reference" column in both books. This number serves as a cross-reference between the general journal and the accounts in the general ledger. In the journal, it identifies the account to which the journal entry has been posted. In the ledger, it identifies the page on which the entry appears in the general journal. For example, the GJ1 notation in the cash account for the July 1 entry means that the $2,000 has been posted from page 1 of the general journal. As you will discover, these posting references are useful in tracking down mistakes. With a computer system, the software automatically generates these posting references.

A particular company will have as many (or as few) accounts as it needs to provide a reasonable classification of its transactions. The list of accounts used by a company is known as its **chart of accounts**. The normal order of a chart of accounts is assets (current and long-term), then liabilities (current and long-term), followed by owners' equity, sales, and expenses. Exhibit 6 on page 100 shows some accounts that might appear in a typical company's chart of accounts.

 CAUTION

Common mistakes when manually posting include posting a debit to the credit side of an account, transposing numbers (e.g., a 45 magically becomes a 54), and posting to the wrong account (e.g., Supplies instead of Inventory). The lesson—be very careful or mistakes will creep into your work. Thankfully, posting is a task done almost exclusively by computers these days.

Determining Account Balances

At the end of an accounting period, the accounts in the general ledger are reviewed to determine each account's balance. Asset, expense, and dividend accounts normally have debit balances; liability, owners' equity, and revenue accounts normally have credit balances. In other words, the balance is normally on the side that increases the account.

To illustrate how to determine an account balance, consider the following T-account depicting all the cash transactions from our landscaping business (with dates being added). The beginning cash account balance plus all Cash debit entries, less total credits to Cash, equals the ending balance in the cash account.

Cash

Beg. Bal.	0		
7/1	2,000		
7/1	2,000	7/5	800
7/9	270	7/5	180
7/14	90	7/7	150
7/14	45	7/18	50
7/30	80	7/23	60
		7/31	250
		7/31	178
		7/31	50
	4,485		(1,718)
	(1,718)		
End. Bal.	2,767		

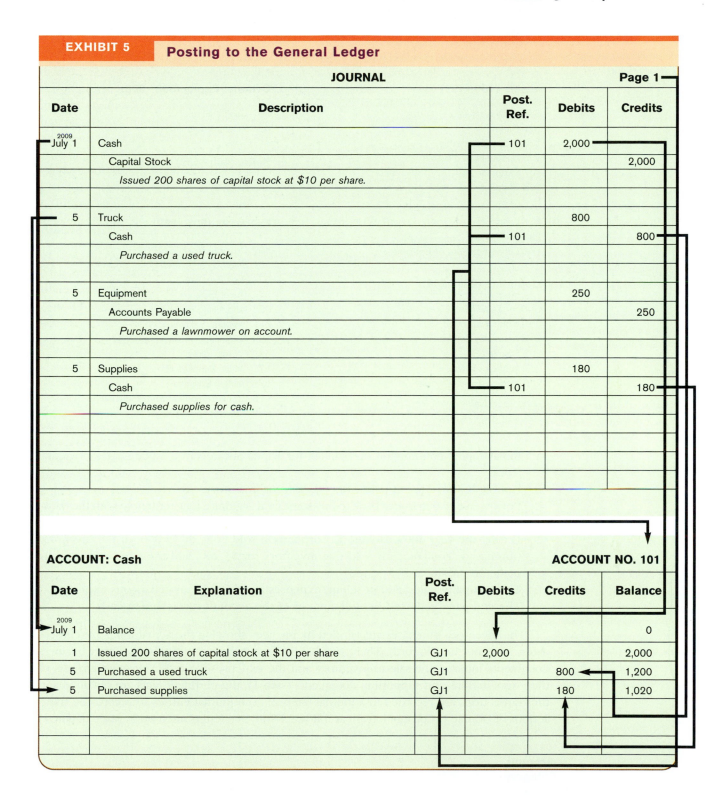

EXHIBIT 5	**Posting to the General Ledger**				

JOURNAL   Page 1

Date	Description	Post. Ref.	Debits	Credits
2009 July 1	Cash	101	2,000	
	Capital Stock			2,000
	Issued 200 shares of capital stock at $10 per share.			
5	Truck		800	
	Cash	101		800
	Purchased a used truck.			
5	Equipment		250	
	Accounts Payable			250
	Purchased a lawnmower on account.			
5	Supplies		180	
	Cash	101		180
	Purchased supplies for cash.			

ACCOUNT: Cash   **ACCOUNT NO. 101**

Date	Explanation	Post. Ref.	Debits	Credits	Balance
2009 July 1	Balance				0
1	Issued 200 shares of capital stock at $10 per share	GJ1	2,000		2,000
5	Purchased a used truck	GJ1		800	1,200
5	Purchased supplies	GJ1		180	1,020

Illustration of the First Three Steps in the Accounting Cycle

We have introduced the first three steps in the accounting cycle. A simple illustration will help reinforce what you have learned about the relationship of assets, liabilities, and owners' equity, as well as revenues, expenses, and dividends, and the mechanics of double-entry accounting. Katherine Kohler established the Double K Corporation in 2009. The following transactions occurred.

EXHIBIT 6   **Chart of Accounts for a Typical Company**

Assets (100–199)

Current Assets (100–150):
101 Cash
103 Notes Receivable
105 Accounts Receivable
107 Inventory
108 Supplies

Long-Term Assets (151–199):
151 Land
152 Buildings
154 Office Furniture or Equipment

Liabilities (200–299)

Current Liabilities (200–219):
201 Notes Payable
202 Accounts Payable
203 Salaries Payable
204 Interest Payable
206 Income Taxes Payable

Long-Term Liabilities (220–239):
222 Mortgage Payable

Owners' Equity (300–399)

301 Capital Stock
330 Retained Earnings

Sales (400–499)

400 Sales Revenue

Expenses (500–599)

500 Cost of Goods Sold
501 Sales Salaries and Commissions
523 Rent Expense
525 Travel Expense
528 Advertising Expense
551 Officers' Salaries
553 Administrative Salaries
570 Payroll Taxes
571 Office Supplies Expense
573 Utilities Expense
578 Office Equipment Rent Expense
579 Accounting and Legal Fees

---

a. Initial capital contribution of $20,000, for which she received 1,000 shares of capital stock.
b. Double K Corporation paid $10,000 cash for inventory.
c. Borrowed $20,000 from a bank to buy some land, signing a long-term note with the bank.
d. Land was purchased for $25,000 cash.
e. During the year 2009, Double K Corporation sold 20%, or $2,000, of the inventory purchased. The company sold that inventory for $3,200, and the sale was originally made on credit.
f. The company paid $200 in selling expenses and $100 in miscellaneous expenses.
g. The company collected the full amount of the account receivable in cash.

The inventory purchases are verified by invoices showing the actual items purchased, dates, amounts, and so forth. There is a $20,000 note payable to the bank. Other business documents indicate the sale of inventory and the expenses incurred. Through analysis of these transactions and supporting documents (step 1), the pertinent facts are obtained and the transactions are recorded in a journal (step 2). The journal entries to record the transactions of Double K Corporation are as follows. (Note that letters are used in place of dates.)

Business Transaction	Account Category and Direction	Journal Entries	Debits	Credits
Issued stock	assets (+)	(a) Cash	20,000	
	owners' equity (+)	(a) Capital Stock		20,000
		Issued 1,000 shares of capital stock for $20,000.		
Purchased	assets (+)	(b) Inventory	10,000	
inventory	assets (−)	(b) Cash		10,000
		Purchased $10,000 of inventory for cash.		

(continued)

Business Transaction	Account Category and Direction	Journal Entries	Debits	Credits
Borrowed	assets (+)	(c) Cash	20,000	
money	liabilities (+)	(c) Notes Payable		20,000
		Borrowed $20,000 from a bank.		
Purchased	assets (+)	(d) Land	25,000	
land	assets (−)	(d) Cash		25,000
		Purchased land for cash.		
Sold inventory	assets (+)	(e) Accounts Receivable	3,200	
	revenues (+)	(e) Sales Revenue		3,200
		Sold inventory for $3,200 on account.		
	expenses (+)	(e) Cost of Goods Sold	2,000	
	assets (−)	(e) Inventory		2,000
		To record the cost of goods or inventory sold.		
Paid expenses	expenses (+)	(f) Selling Expenses	200	
	expenses (+)	(f) Miscellaneous Expenses	100	
	assets (−)	(f) Cash		300
		Paid selling and miscellaneous expenses.		
Collected cash	assets (+)	(g) Cash	3,200	
	assets (−)	(g) Accounts Receivable		3,200
		Collected accounts receivable.		

Next, the transactions are posted to the ledger accounts (step 3, part 1). T-accounts are used to illustrate this process, with the letters (a) through (g) showing the cross-references to the journal entries. A balance is shown for the end of the period. (Where only one transaction is involved, the amount of the transaction is also the account balance.)

	Cash				Accounts Receivable			Inventory				Land	
(a)	20,000	(b)	10,000	(e)	3,200	(g)	3,200	(b)	10,000	(e)	2,000	(d)	25,000
(c)	20,000	(d)	25,000										
(g)	3,200	(f)	300	Bal.	0			Bal.	8,000				
Bal.	7,900												

	Notes Payable			Capital Stock			Sales Revenue	
		(c)	20,000		(a)	20,000		(e)	3,200

	Cost of Goods Sold			Selling Expenses			Miscellaneous Expenses	
(e)	2,000		(f)	200		(f)	100	

The effect of these transactions can also be visualized using a spreadsheet format as shown in Exhibit 7.

EXHIBIT 7	Effects of Business Transactions on the Accounting Equation

	ASSETS				=	LIABILITIES	+	OWNERS' EQUITY				
Transaction	Cash	Inventory	Land	Accounts Receivable		Notes Payable		Capital Stock	Retained Earnings			
										Sales Revenue	Cost of Goods Sold*	Selling Expenses*	Misc. Expenses*
Beginning Balance	$ 0	$ 0	$ 0	$ 0	=	$ 0	+	$ 0	—	—	—	—
A	20,000	—	—	—		—		20,000	—	—	—	—
B	−10,000	10,000	—	—		—		0	—	—	—	—
C	20,000	—	—	—		20,000		—	—	—	—	—
D	−25,000	—	25,000	—		—		—	—	—	—	—
E	—	−2,000	—	3,200		—		—	3,200	−2,000	—	—
F	−300	—	—	—		—		—	—	—	−200	−100
G	3,200	—	—	−3,200		—		—	—	—	—	—
Total	$ 7,900	$ 8,000	$25,000	$ 0	=	$20,000	+	$20,000	$3,200	−$2,000	−$200	−$100

*Recall that an increase in these accounts actually decreases owners' equity, hence the − (minus sign).

trial balance

A listing of all account balances; provides a means of testing whether total debits equal total credits for all accounts.

After the account balances have been determined, a trial balance is usually prepared (step 3, part 2). A **trial balance** lists each account with its debit or credit balance, as shown in Exhibit 8. By adding all the debit balances and all the credit balances, the accountant can see whether total debits equal total credits. Even if the trial balance does show total debits equal to total credits, there may be errors. A transaction may have been omitted completely, or it may have been recorded incorrectly or posted to the wrong account. These types of errors will not be discovered by preparing a trial balance; additional analysis would be required. In this case, total debits equal total credits.

EXHIBIT 8	Trial Balance

Double K Corporation
Trial Balance
December 31, 2009

	Debits	Credits
Cash	$ 7,900	
Accounts Receivable	0	
Inventory	8,000	
Land	25,000	
Notes Payable		$20,000
Capital Stock		20,000
Sales Revenue		3,200
Cost of Goods Sold	2,000	
Selling Expenses	200	
Miscellaneous Expenses	100	
Totals	$43,200	$43,200

Thus, the accounting equation is in balance. The balances are taken from each ledger account.

Students frequently mistake a trial balance and the balance sheet for one another. In fact, they are very different reports. A trial balance is strictly an internal document used to summarize all of the account balances (assets, liabilities, owners' equity, revenues, expenses, and dividends) in a company's accounting system. Few people outside a company's accounting department ever see the trial balance; most businesspeople never see a real trial balance during their entire business career. The balance sheet, on the other hand, is a more formal summary document that is frequently provided to interested parties both inside and outside a company.

From the data in the trial balance, an income statement and a balance sheet can be prepared. Exhibit 9 shows these two financial statements for Double K Corporation. Notice that there is no retained earnings account in the trial balance but there is one on the balance sheet. The reason for this is that all the income statement accounts such as Revenue, Cost of Goods Sold, and expenses are eventually accumulated into Retained Earnings. That is, earnings are reflected on the income statement. The business then decides the amount of those earnings to be retained. Those earnings that are to be retained are then disclosed on the balance sheet.

Also, the statement of cash flows can be prepared by categorizing the items in the cash account as operating, investing, or financing, as shown in Exhibit 10.

Three final notes: First, the preparation of financial statements is rarely so simple. In reality, the procedure also involves the adjustment of some ledger accounts, which need to be brought current before they can be included in the balance sheet or the income statement. In Chapter 4, we will explain how accounts are adjusted (step 4, part 1) so that the financial statements will accurately reflect the current financial position and operating results of an enterprise.

EXHIBIT 9	**Income Statement and Balance Sheet**

Double K Corporation

Income Statement

For the Year Ended December 31, 2009

Sales revenue		$3,200
Expenses:		
Cost of goods sold	$2,000	
Selling expenses	200	
Miscellaneous expenses	100	2,300
Net income		$ 900
EPS ($900 ÷ 1,000 shares)		$ 0.90

Double K Corporation

Balance Sheet

December 31, 2009

Assets		**Liabilities and Owners' Equity**	
Cash	$ 7,900	Notes payable	$20,000
Inventory	8,000	Capital stock (1,000 shares)	20,000
Land	25,000	Retained earnings	900*
Total assets	$40,900	Total liabilities and	
		owners' equity	$40,900

*Beginning retained earnings plus net income minus dividends.

EXHIBIT 10	Statement of Cash Flows

Double K Corporation
Statement of Cash Flows
For the Year Ended December 31, 2009

Operating activities:		
Collections from customers.	$ 3,200	
Purchase of inventory	(10,000)	
Paid expenses.	(300)	$ (7,100)
Investing activities:		
Purchased land.		(25,000)
Financing activities:		
Issued stock	$20,000	
Borrowed from bank	20,000	40,000
Net increase in cash.		$ 7,900
Beginning cash balance		0
Ending cash balance		$ 7,900

Second, net income does not usually equal the ending retained earnings balance. Only in the first year of a company's operations would this be the case. Double K Corporation began operations in 2009 and paid no dividends during the year; so, its $900 net income on the income statement equals the retained earnings figure on the balance sheet. In future years, the figures would be different, since retained earnings is an accumulation of earnings from past years adjusted for dividends and other special items.

REMEMBER THIS...

- Posting involves sorting and copying the journal entry items to individual accounts.
- Account balances are computed by summing the debit and credit entries in each account.
- A trial balance is prepared by listing each account along with its balance.
- An income statement and a balance sheet can be prepared from this trial balance.
- A statement of cash flows is prepared by analyzing the inflows and outflows of cash as detailed in the cash account.

Where Do Computers Fit In All This?

Describe how technology has affected the first three steps of the accounting cycle.

(5) Students often ask, "Do I really need to know the difference between a debit and a credit? Haven't computers taken care of that?" Computers have greatly facilitated a business's ability to quickly process huge amounts of information without making mathematical errors. Most computers can make millions of calculations per second and produce more documents in 10 minutes than a person could in an entire week. The time spent posting journal entries and summarizing accounts into a trial balance has been greatly reduced as a result of computers.

But computers still can't think. That's your job. Walk up to a computer terminal and show it a sales invoice and the computer will just sit there and wait.

Wait for what? For the answers to three questions: (1) What accounts are involved? (2) Did those accounts increase or decrease? (3) By how much did each account change?

Let's consider how the best-selling money management software package, Quicken®, has changed the accounting process. Quicken works a lot like a check register. For each check, you indicate the date, the check number, the payee, and the amount. Quicken then prompts you to indicate the nature of the expenditure by selecting from a list of accounts. For example, if the expenditure relates to your purchase of groceries, you would select the account "Food." Thus, all your transactions relating to "Food" will be grouped together, allowing you to quickly determine all food expenditures.

Now let's review what Quicken has done. First of all, since you indicated the transaction involved a check, Quicken knows that cash decreased. Quicken is programmed to know that when cash decreases, it involves a credit to the cash account. Quicken also has been programmed to know that debits have to equal credits, and since Cash was credited, the program knows that something was debited. Since you indicated "Food" (an expense) was the other account, Quicken debits that account, causing your expense account to increase (we now know that expenses increase with debits). Instead of telling Quicken which accounts to debit and credit, you are required to identify the accounts (question 1) and indicate if they increased or decreased (question 2). Quicken is able to determine, based on the answer to these two questions, which accounts were debited and which accounts were credited.

So has Quicken fundamentally changed the accounting process? No. It has increased the accuracy and speed with which the posting process is done, as well as the speed with which a variety of reports can be prepared. Quicken has also eliminated the need for the user to specify debit or credit. Because computers are so fast, the two-step process of identifying accounts and the direction of their change can be done as quickly as you can say "credit Cash." So why don't accountants get rid of these 500-year-old terms, debit and credit? The reason is that all accountants are familiar with and comfortable using these terms. When someone says "credit Cash," accountants everywhere know exactly what that means. Thus, debit and credit provide a useful shorthand method of communication.

The computer has also enhanced step 3 of the accounting cycle—summarizing. In fact, only in the smallest of businesses will you find the posting of journal entries and the preparation of a trial balance being done by hand. But in every business, from the largest to the smallest, you will find accountants still actively involved in analyzing transactions and turning those transactions into journal entries and eventually into useful accounting reports.

REMEMBER THIS...

- Computers have made posting and the preparation of reports and statements much easier.
- Computers have *not* replaced the need for accountants to analyze transactions and determine their effect on the accounting equation.

REVIEW OF LEARNING OBJECTIVES

① **Understand the process of transforming transaction data into useful accounting information.** The objective of the accounting process is to gather and transform transaction data into useful information that measures and communicates the results of business activity. The four steps in the accounting cycle are as follows:

Step 1.   Analyze transactions.
Step 2.   Record the effects of transactions.
Step 3.   Summarize the effects of transactions.
Step 4.   Prepare reports.

② **Analyze transactions and determine how those transactions affect the accounting equation (step one of the accounting cycle).**

Assets	=	Liabilities	+	Owners' Equity
DR CR		DR CR		DR CR
(+) (−)		(−) (+)		(−) (+)

The following types of accounts are sub-categories of Retained Earnings which is an Owners' Equity account.

Expenses	Dividends	Revenues
DR CR	DR CR	DR CR
(+) (−)	(+) (−)	(−) (+)

- More expense, a debit, means less owners' equity.
- More dividends, a debit, means less owners' equity.
- More revenue, a credit, means more owners' equity.

③ **Record the effects of transactions using journal entries (step two of the accounting cycle).** Making a journal entry involves the following three steps:

1. Identify which accounts are involved.
2. For each account, determine if it is increased or decreased.
3. For each account, determine by how much it has changed.

④ **Summarize the resulting journal entries through posting and prepare a trial balance (step three of the accounting cycle).**
- Posting involves sorting and copying the journal entry items to individual accounts.
- Account balances are computed by summing the debit and credit entries in each account.
- A trial balance is prepared by listing each account along with its balance.
- An income statement and a balance sheet can be prepared from this trial balance.
- A statement of cash flows is prepared by analyzing the inflows and outflows of cash as detailed in the cash account.

⑤ **Describe how technology has affected the first three steps of the accounting cycle.**
- Computers have made posting and the preparation of reports and statements much easier.
- Computers have ***not*** replaced the need for accountants to analyze transactions and determine their effect on the accounting equation.

KEY TERMS & CONCEPTS

account, 80
accounting cycle, 76
business documents, 77
chart of accounts, 98

compound journal
 entry, 92
credit, 82
debit, 81

dividends, 84
journal, 86
journal entry, 86
journalizing, 86

ledger, 98
posting, 98
T-account, 81
trial balance, 102

REVIEW PROBLEM

The First Three Steps in the Accounting Cycle

Journal entries are given below for January 2009, the first month of operation for the Svendsen Service Company.

Jan. 2	Cash		40,000	
	Capital Stock			40,000
	Issued capital stock for cash.			
2	Insurance Expense		500	
	Cash			500
	Purchased a one-month insurance policy.			
2	Rent Expense		750	
	Cash			750
	Paid rent for the month of January.			
3	Shop Equipment		8,000	
	Cash			8,000
	Purchased shop equipment for cash.			
4	Supplies		3,000	
	Accounts Payable			3,000
	Purchased shop supplies on account.			
5	Automotive Equipment		11,500	
	Cash			3,500
	Notes Payable			8,000
	Purchased a truck. Paid $3,500 cash and issued			
	a 30-day note for the balance.			
8	Cash		1,750	
	Service and Repair Revenue			1,750
	Received cash for repairs.			
9	Advertising Expense		300	
	Cash			300
	Paid cash for radio spot announcements.			
12	Automotive Expense		200	
	Cash			200
	Paid gas, oil, and service costs on the truck.			
14	Accounts Payable		3,000	
	Cash			3,000
	Paid $3,000 on account.			
16	Accounts Receivable		1,200	
	Service and Repair Revenue			1,200
	Repaired truck for Acme Drilling Company on account.			
18	Telephone Expense		75	
	Cash			75
	Paid for installation and telephone service for one month.			
19	Automotive Expense		180	
	Cash			180
	Paid for minor repairs on the truck.			
20	Cash		1,000	
	Notes Receivable		1,450	
	Service and Repair Revenue			2,450
	Collected $1,000 cash from Jones for truck repairs;			
	accepted a 60-day note for the balance.			

(continued)

Jan. 24	Repairs and Maintenance Expense	150	
	Cash		150
	Paid cleaning and painting expenses on the building.		
25	Cash	1,500	
	Service and Repair Revenue		1,500
	Received cash for repairs and services from Hamilton, Inc.		
27	Supplies	2,500	
	Cash		2,500
	Purchased shop supplies.		
29	Office Equipment	1,250	
	Cash		1,250
	Purchased a computer.		
30	Cash	1,200	
	Accounts Receivable		1,200
	Collected receivables from Acme Drilling Company.		
31	Utilities Expense	900	
	Cash		900
	Paid the monthly utility bill.		
31	Automotive Expense	350	
	Cash		350
	Paid for gas, oil, and servicing of the truck.		

Required:

Set up T-accounts, post all journal entries to the accounts, balance the accounts, and prepare a trial balance.

Solution

The first step in solving this problem is to set up T-accounts for each item; then post all journal entries to the appropriate ledger accounts, as shown. Once the amounts are properly posted, account balances can be determined.

Cash			
1/2	40,000	1/2	500
1/8	1,750	1/2	750
1/20	1,000	1/3	8,000
1/25	1,500	1/5	3,500
1/30	1,200	1/9	300
		1/12	200
		1/14	3,000
		1/18	75
		1/19	180
		1/24	150
		1/27	2,500
		1/29	1,250
		1/31	900
		1/31	350
Bal.	23,795		

Notes Receivable		
1/20	1,450	

Accounts Receivable			
1/16	1,200	1/30	1,200
Bal.	0		

Supplies		
1/4	3,000	
1/27	2,500	
Bal.	5,500	

Shop Equipment		
1/3	8,000	

Automotive Equipment		
1/5	11,500	

Office Equipment		
1/29	1,250	

Notes Payable		
	1/5	8,000

Accounts Payable			
1/14	3,000	1/4	3,000
		Bal.	0

Capital Stock		
	1/2	40,000

Service and Repair Revenue		
	1/8	1,750
	1/16	1,200
	1/20	2,450
	1/25	1,500
	Bal.	6,900

Insurance Expense		
1/2	500	

Rent Expense		
1/2	750	

Advertising Expense		
1/9	300	

Automotive Expense		
1/12	200	
1/19	180	
1/31	350	
Bal.	730	

(continued)

Telephone Expense		Repairs and Maintenance Expense		Utilities Expense	
1/18	75	1/24	150	1/31	900

The final step is to prepare a trial balance to see whether total debits equal total credits for all accounts. List all the accounts with balances; then enter the balance in each account.

Svendsen Service Company
Trial Balance
January 31, 2009

	Debits	Credits
Cash	$23,795	
Accounts Receivable	0	
Notes Receivable	1,450	
Supplies	5,500	
Shop Equipment	8,000	
Automotive Equipment	11,500	
Office Equipment	1,250	
Accounts Payable		$ 0
Notes Payable		8,000
Capital Stock		40,000
Service and Repair Revenue		6,900
Insurance Expense	500	
Rent Expense	750	
Advertising Expense	300	
Automotive Expense	730	
Telephone Expense	75	
Repairs and Maintenance Expense	150	
Utilities Expense	900	
Totals	$54,900	$54,900

DISCUSSION QUESTIONS

1. What is the basic objective of the accounting cycle?
2. Explain the first three steps in the accounting cycle.
3. What are the advantages of a computer-based accounting system? Does such a system eliminate the need for human judgment? Explain.
4. In a double-entry system of accounting, why must total debits always equal total credits?
5. Explain the increase/decrease, debit/credit relationship of asset, liability, and owners' equity accounts.
6. How are revenues, expenses, and dividends related to the basic accounting equation?
7. In what ways are dividend and expense accounts similar, and in what ways are they different?
8. How does understanding the mechanics of accounting help a businessperson who has no intention of practicing accounting?
9. Distinguish between a journal and a ledger.
10. Assume that Company A buys $1,500 of merchandise from Company B for cash. The merchandise originally cost Company B $1,000. What entries should the buyer and seller make, and what is the relationship of the accounts for this transaction?
11. Indicate how each of the following transactions affects the accounting equation.
    a. Purchase of supplies on account.
    b. Payment of wages.
    c. Cash sales of goods for more than their cost.
    d. Payment of monthly utility bills.
    e. Purchase of a building with a down payment of cash plus a mortgage.
    f. Cash investment by a stockholder.
    g. Payment of a cash dividend.
    h. Sale of goods on account for more than their cost.
    i. Sale of land at less than its cost.
12. What is a chart of accounts? What is its purpose?
13. If a trial balance appears to be correct (debits equal credits), does that guarantee complete accuracy in the accounting records? Explain.

14. What is the difference between a trial balance and a balance sheet?

15. Have computers eliminated the need to analyze transactions? Explain.

PRACTICE EXERCISES

For PE 3-1 through 3-5, do the following for each transaction:
a. List the accounts impacted by the transaction.
b. For each account, indicate whether the transaction increased or decreased the account.
c. For each account, indicate how much the transaction increased or decreased the account.
d. Compute the impact of the transaction on total assets, total liabilities, and total owners' equity.

PE 3-1   **Impact of a Transaction**
LO2   The company borrowed $85,000 in cash from Eastern Bank.

PE 3-2   **Impact of a Transaction**
LO2   The company used $45,000 in cash to purchase land on the west side of Hatu Lake.

PE 3-3   **Impact of a Transaction**
LO2   The company used $30,000 in cash to repay a portion of its bank loan (see PE 3-1). For simplicity, assume that there is no interest on the loan.

PE 3-4   **Impact of a Transaction**
LO2   The company received $75,000 in cash as an additional investment by the stockholders (owners) of the company.

PE 3-5   **Impact of a Transaction**
LO2   The company purchased a building for $130,000. The company paid $50,000 of the purchase price in cash and signed a mortgage contract obligating it to pay the remaining $80,000 over the next 10 years.

PE 3-6   **Computing Ending Account Balances**
LO2   Refer to PE 3-1 through 3-5. Construct a spreadsheet similar to the one shown on page 91. Enter each transaction into the spreadsheet and compute the ending balance in each account.

PE 3-7   **Understanding Debits**
LO2   Below is a list of accounts. For each account, indicate whether a *debit* increases or decreases the account balance.

	Account	Debit
0.	Cash	Increases
1.	Accounts Payable	
2.	Capital Stock	
3.	Land	
4.	Inventory	
5.	Loan Payable	
6.	Mortgage Payable	
7.	Building	

PE 3-8
LO2

Understanding Credits

Below is a list of accounts. For each account, indicate whether a credit increases or decreases the account balance.

Account	Credit
0. Cash	Decreases
1. Accounts Receivable	
2. Capital Stock	
3. Equipment	
4. Inventory	
5. Accounts Payable	
6. Building	
7. Notes Payable	

PE 3-9
LO2

Understanding Debits, Credits, and Retained Earnings

Below is a list of accounts and whether the account is being debited or credited. For each item, indicate whether the account balance will be increased or decreased.

Account	Debit or Credit	Account Balance
0. Salary Expense	Debit	Increased
1. Sales Revenue	Credit	
2. Retained Earnings	Debit	
3. Insurance Expense	Credit	
4. Dividends	Credit	
5. Interest Revenue	Debit	
6. Advertising Expense	Debit	
7. Rent Revenue	Credit	

PE 3-10
LO2

Understanding Retained Earnings

Below is a list of accounts with corresponding balances. Using these accounts, along with the fact that the beginning balance in Retained Earnings is $9,000, compute the ending balance in Retained Earnings. *Note:* Not all of the listed account balances enter into the calculation of Retained Earnings.

Account	Account Balance
a. Insurance Expense	$1,600
b. Cash	1,200
c. Sales Revenue	7,500
d. Advertising Expense	1,800
e. Accounts Payable	2,100
f. Dividends	600
g. Interest Revenue	350

PE 3-11
LO3

Journal Entries

Refer to PE 3-1. Make the journal entry necessary to record the transaction.

PE 3-12
LO3

Journal Entries

Refer to PE 3-2. Make the journal entry necessary to record the transaction.

PE 3-13
LO3

Journal Entries

Refer to PE 3-3. Make the journal entry necessary to record the transaction.

PE 3-14
LO3

Journal Entries

Refer to PE 3-4. Make the journal entry necessary to record the transaction.

PE 3-15   **Journal Entries**

LO3   Refer to PE 3-5. Make the journal entry necessary to record the transaction.

PE 3-16   **Journal Entries with Revenues, Expenses, and Dividends**

LO3   Make the journal entries necessary to record the following eight transactions.

a.   Purchased inventory on account for $130,000.

b.   Sold goods for $100,000 cash. The goods originally cost $65,000.

c.   Paid $27,000 cash for employee wages.

d.   Paid $12,500 cash for advertising.

e.   Sold goods for $25,000 cash and $60,000 on account (a total of $85,000). The goods originally cost $57,000.

f.   Collected cash of $47,000 from the $60,000 receivable on account; the remaining $13,000 is expected to be collected later.

g.   Paid cash of $55,000 on the $130,000 payable on account; the remaining $75,000 is expected to be paid later.

h.   Paid cash dividends of $8,500.

PE 3-17   **Posting**

LO4   Refer to the journal entries made in PE 3-11 through PE 3-15. Construct a T-account representing each account impacted by those five transactions. Post all of the journal entries to these T-accounts. Compute the ending balance in each account. Assume that the beginning balance in each T-account is zero.

PE 3-18   **Posting with Revenues, Expenses, and Dividends**

LO4   Refer to the journal entries made in PE 3-16. Construct a T-account representing each account impacted by those eight transactions. Post all of the journal entries to these T-accounts. Compute the ending balance in each account. Assume that the beginning balance in each T-account is zero.

PE 3-19   **Preparing a Trial Balance**

LO4   Refer to the T-accounts constructed in PE 3-17 and PE 3-18. Using the ending balances in those T-accounts, construct a trial balance. *Note:* The only account that is common to these two sets of T-accounts is the cash account; add the two cash account balances together to get the total balance.

PE 3-20   **Using a Trial Balance to Prepare an Income Statement**

LO4   Using the trial balance given below, prepare an income statement.

	Debit	Credit
Cash	$ 68,000	
Accounts Receivable	126,000	
Inventory	216,000	
Land	90,000	
Building	200,000	
Accounts Payable		$ 150,000
Loan Payable		270,000
Capital Stock		250,000
Dividends	17,000	
Sales Revenue		370,000
Cost of Goods Sold	244,000	
Utilities Expense	54,000	
Rental Expense	25,000	
Totals	$1,040,000	$1,040,000

PE 3-21
LO4
Using a Trial Balance to Prepare a Balance Sheet
Using the trial balance given in PE 3-20, prepare a balance sheet. *Note:* The ending retained earnings balance is equal to the beginning balance (which is assumed to be $0) plus the amount of net income less the amount of dividends.

PE 3-22
LO4
Preparing a Statement of Cash Flows
Refer to the transactions described in PE 3-1 through PE 3-5 as well as to the eight transactions in PE 3-16. Using all of these transactions, prepare a statement of cash flows. *Note:* For the building purchase described in PE 3-5, the portion of the purchase financed with the mortgage ($80,000) is considered to be a noncash transaction; accordingly, the only portion of the transaction that impacts the statement of cash flows is the $50,000 cash down payment.

EXERCISES

E 3-23
LO2
Basic Accounting Equation
The fundamental accounting equation can be applied to your personal finances. For each of the following transactions, show how the accounting equation would be kept in balance. Example: Paid for semester's tuition (decrease assets: cash account; decrease owners' equity: expense account increases).
  1. Took out a school loan for college.
  2. Paid this month's rent.
  3. Sold your old computer for cash at what it cost to buy it.
  4. Received week's paycheck from part-time job.
  5. Received interest on savings account.
  6. Paid monthly payment on car loan (part of the payment is principal; the remainder is interest).

E 3-24
LO2
Accounting Elements: Increase/Decrease, Debit/Credit Relationships
The text describes the following accounting elements: assets, liabilities, owners' equity, capital stock, retained earnings, revenues, expenses, and dividends. Which of these elements are increased by a debit entry, and which are increased by a credit entry? Give a transaction for each item that would result in a net increase in its balance.

E 3-25
LO2
Expanded Accounting Equation
Payless Department Store had the following transactions during the year:
  1. Purchased inventory on account.
  2. Sold merchandise for cash, assuming a profit on the sale.
  3. Borrowed money from a bank.
  4. Purchased land, making cash down payment and issuing a note for the balance.
  5. Issued stock for cash.
  6. Paid salaries for the year.
  7. Paid a vendor for inventory purchased on account.
  8. Sold a building for cash and notes receivable at no gain or loss.
  9. Paid cash dividends to stockholders.
  10. Paid utilities.

Using the following column headings, identify the accounts involved and indicate the net effect of each transaction on the accounting equation (+ increase; − decrease; 0 no effect). Transaction 1 has been completed as an example.

Transaction	Assets	=	Liabilities	+	Owners' Equity
1	+		+		0
	(Inventory)		(Accounts Payable)		

E 3-26
LO2

draw. T-account

Classification of Accounts

For each of the accounts listed, indicate whether it is an asset (A), a liability (L), or an owners' equity (OE) account. If it is an account that affects owners' equity, indicate whether it is a revenue (R) or expense (E) account.

1. Cash	8. Salaries and Wages	14. Interest Receivable
2. Sales	Expense	15. Notes Payable
3. Accounts Receivable	9. Retained Earnings	16. Equipment
4. Cost of Goods Sold	10. Salaries Payable	17. Office Supplies
5. Insurance Expense	11. Accounts Payable	18. Utilities Expense
6. Capital Stock	12. Interest Revenue	19. Interest Payable
7. Mortgage Payable	13. Inventory	20. Rent Expense

E 3-27
LO2

Normal Account Balances

For each account listed in E 3-26, indicate whether it would normally have a debit (DR) balance or a credit (CR) balance.

E 3-28
LO2

Relationships of the Expanded Accounting Equation

Skibbe, Inc., had the following information reported. From these data, determine the amount of:

1. Capital stock at December 31, 2008.
2. Retained earnings at December 31, 2009.
3. Revenues for the year 2009.

	December 31, 2008	December 31, 2009
Total assets	$125,000	$150,000
Total liabilities	30,000	35,000
Capital stock	?	25,000
Retained earnings	75,000	?
Revenues for 2009		?
Expenses for 2009		102,500
Dividends paid during 2009		2,500

E 3-29
LO3

Journalizing Transactions

Record each of the following transactions in Raintree's general journal. (Omit explanations.)

1. Issued capital stock for $90,000 cash.
2. Borrowed $45,000 from a bank. Signed a note to secure the debt.
3. Paid salaries and rent of $53,000 and $4,100, respectively.
4. Purchased inventory from a supplier on credit for $6,300.
5. Paid the supplier for the inventory purchased in (4) above.
6. Sold inventory that cost $1,350 for $2,400 on credit.
7. Collected $2,400 from customers on transaction (6) above.

E 3-30
LO3

Journalizing Transactions

Silva Company had the following transactions:

1. Purchased a new building, paying $20,000 cash and issuing a note for $50,000.
2. Purchased $15,000 of inventory on account.
3. Sold inventory costing $5,000 for $6,000 on account.
4. Paid for inventory purchased on account (item 2).
5. Issued capital stock for $25,000.

(continued)

6. Collected $4,500 of accounts receivable.
7. Paid utility bills totaling $360.
8. Sold old building for $27,000, receiving $10,000 cash and a $17,000 note (no gain or loss on the sale).
9. Paid $2,000 cash dividends to stockholders.

Record the above transactions in general journal format. (Omit explanations.)

E 3-31
LO3

Journal Entries

During July 2009, Krogue, Inc., completed the following transactions. Prepare the journal entry for each transaction.

July	2	Received $320,000 for 80,000 shares of capital stock.
	4	Purchased $90,000 of equipment, with 75% down and 25% on a note payable.
	5	Paid utilities of $2,300 in cash.
	9	Sold equipment for $15,000 cash (no gain or loss).
	13	Purchased $250,000 of inventory, paying 40% down and 60% on credit.
	14	Paid $6,000 cash insurance premium for July.
	18	Sold inventory costing $62,000 for $81,000 to customers on account to be paid at a later date.
	20	Collected $7,500 from accounts receivable.
	24	Sold inventory costing $32,000 for $43,000 to customers for cash.
	27	Paid property taxes of $1,200.
	30	Paid $150,000 of accounts payable for inventory purchased on July 13.

E 3-32
LO3

Challenging Journal Entries

The accountant for Han Company is considering how to journalize the following transactions:

a. The employees of Han Company earned $105,000. The employees received $90,000 in cash and were promised that they will receive the remaining $15,000 as a pension payment on the date that they retire.

b. On August 1, 2009, Han Company paid $1,800 cash for one year of rent on a building it is using. This one year of rent is scheduled to be in effect for the 12 months starting on August 1, 2009.

1. What journal entry should be made on the books of Han Company to record the employee compensation information in (a)?
2. Describe any assumptions necessary in making the employee compensation journal entry in (1).
3. Make the necessary journal entry on Han Company's books on August 1 to record the payment for the building rent described in (b).
4. Consider the journal entry made in (3). Is any adjustment to Han's books necessary as of December 31, 2009, as a consequence of the rent journal entry made on August 1?

E 3-33
LO3

Journal Entries

The following transactions are for the Pickard Construction Company:

a. The firm bought equipment for $64,000 on credit.
b. The firm purchased land for $450,000, $160,000 of which was paid in cash and a note payable signed for the balance.

(continued)

   c. The firm paid $41,000 it owed to its suppliers.

   d. The firm arranged for a $225,000 line of credit (the right to borrow funds as needed) from the bank. No funds have yet been borrowed.

   e. The firm sold some of its products for $34,000—$18,000 for cash, the remainder on account.

   f. Cost of sales in (e) are $22,000.

   g. The firm borrowed $84,000 on its line of credit.

   h. The firm paid a $10,000 cash dividend to its stockholders.

   i. An investor invested an additional $60,000 in the company in exchange for additional capital stock.

   j. One of the primary investors borrowed $90,000 from a bank. The loan is a personal loan.

   k. The firm repaid $16,000 of its line of credit.

   l. The firm received a $1,000 deposit from a customer for a product to be sold and delivered to that customer next month.

Analyze and record the transactions as journal entries. (Omit explanations.)

E 3-34

LO3

Analysis of Journal Entries

The following journal entries are from the books of Kara Elizabeth Company:

		Debit	Credit
a.	Buildings	90,000	
	Cash		35,000
	Mortgage Payable		55,000
b.	Cash	25,000	
	Capital Stock		25,000
c.	Cash	40,000	
	Loan Payable		40,000
d.	Salary Expense	12,000	
	Cash		12,000
e.	Inventory	12,500	
	Accounts Payable		12,500
f.	Accounts Receivable	84,000	
	Sales		84,000
	Cost of Goods Sold	51,000	
	Inventory		51,000
g.	Cash	62,000	
	Accounts Receivable		62,000
h.	Accounts Payable	38,000	
	Cash		38,000

For each of the journal entries, prepare an explanation of the business event that is being represented.

E 3-35

LO3

Journal Entry to Correct an Error

Legolas Company paid $5,000 cash for executive salaries. When the journal entry to record this $5,000 payment was made, the payment was mistakenly added to the cost of land purchased by Legolas. The $5,000 should have been recorded as salary expense. Make the journal entry necessary to correct this error.

E 3-36
LO3, LO4

Journalizing and Posting Transactions

Given the following T-accounts, describe the transaction that took place on each specified date during July:

	Cash		
7/5	9,500	7/1	3,420
7/28	8,000	7/23	2,000
		7/25	5,000
		7/30	5,500
Bal.	1,580		

	Accounts Receivable		
7/14	18,000	7/5	9,500
		7/28	8,000
Bal.	500		

	Inventory		
7/10	20,000	7/14	15,000
Bal.	5,000		

	Equipment	
7/30	1,500	

	Land	
7/30	4,000	

	Accounts Payable		
7/25	5,000	7/10	20,000
		Bal.	15,000

	Sales Revenue	
	7/14	18,000

	Cost of Goods Sold	
7/14	15,000	

	Rent Expense	
7/23	2,000	

	Advertising Expense	
7/1	3,420	

E 3-37
LO4

Posting Journal Entries

Post the journal entries prepared in E 3-31 to T-accounts, and determine the final balance for each account. (Assume all beginning account balances are zero.)

E 3-38
LO4

Trial Balance

The account balances from the ledger of Arigato, Inc., as of July 31, 2009, are listed here in alphabetical order. The balance for Retained Earnings has been omitted. Prepare a trial balance, and insert the missing amount for Retained Earnings.

Accounts Payable	$ 10,300		Land	$31,000
Accounts Receivable	8,100		Miscellaneous Expenses	1,300
Buildings	44,000		Mortgage Payable (due 2012)	32,000
Capital Stock	21,000		Rent Expense	4,300
Cash	19,600		Retained Earnings	?
Equipment	22,000		Salary Expense	11,000
Fees Earned	44,500		Supplies	550
Insurance Expense	5,100		Utilities Expense	1,150

E 3-39
LO4

Trial Balance

Assume you work in the accounting department at Marshall, Inc. Your boss has asked you to prepare a trial balance as of November 30, 2009, using the following account balances from the company's ledger. Prepare the trial balance and insert the missing amount for Cost of Goods Sold.

(continued)

Accounts Payable	$ 55,000	Notes Payable	$250,000
Accounts Receivable	25,000	Notes Receivable	20,000
Advertising Expense	5,000	Other Expenses	1,000
Buildings	150,000	Property Tax Expense	1,500
Capital Stock	173,000	Rent Expense	7,500
Cash	35,000	Retained Earnings	40,000
Cost of Goods Sold	?	Salaries Expense	155,000
Equipment	55,000	Salaries Payable	2,000
Inventory	200,000	Sales Revenue	375,000
Land	125,000	Short-Term Investments	15,000
Mortgage Payable	95,000	Utilities Expense	7,000

PROBLEMS

P 3-40

LO2, LO3

Transaction Analysis and Journal Entries

Browne Motors, Inc., entered into the following transactions during the month of June:

a. Purchased a total of eight new cars and trucks from Jerry's Motors, Inc., for a total of $105,600, one-half of which was paid in cash. The balance is due within 45 days. The total cost of the vehicles to Jerry's Motors was $91,000.

b. Purchased $3,300 of supplies on account from White Supply Company. The cost of the supplies to White Supply Company was $2,400.

c. Paid $720 to Mountain Electric for the monthly utility bill.

d. Sold a truck to Dave's Delivery, Inc. A $2,800 down payment was received with the balance of $14,500 due within 30 days. The cost of the delivery truck to Browne Motors was $13,200.

e. Paid $4,950 to Steve's Automotive for repair work on cars for the current month.

f. Sold one of the new cars purchased from Jerry's Motors to the town mayor, Rachel Mecham. The sales price was $16,250, and was paid by Mecham upon delivery of the car. The cost of the particular car sold to Mecham was $11,800.

g. Borrowed $25,000 from a local bank to be repaid in one year with 12% interest.

Required:

1. For each of the transactions, make the proper journal entry on the books of Browne Motors. (Omit explanations.)

2. For each of the transactions, make the proper journal entry on the books of the other party to the transaction, for example, (a) Jerry's Motors, Inc., (b) White Supply Company. (Omit explanations.)

3. **Interpretive Question:** Why do some of the journal entries for Browne Motors and other companies involved appear to be "mirror images" of each other?

P 3-41

LO3, LO4

Journal Entries and Trial Balance

As of January 1, 2009, Gammon Corporation had the following balances in its general ledger:

	Debits	Credits
Cash	$ 63,000	
Accounts Receivable	47,000	
Inventory	184,000	
Office Building	416,000	
Accounts Payable		$ 33,000
Mortgage Payable		360,000
Notes Payable		137,000
Capital Stock		115,000
Retained Earnings		65,000
Totals	$710,000	$710,000

(continued)

Gammon had the following transactions during 2009. All expenses were paid in cash, unless otherwise stated.

a. Collected $42,000 of receivables.

b. Accounts Payable as of January 1, 2009, were paid off.

c. Purchased inventory for $70,000 cash.

d. Paid utilities of $12,600.

e. Sold $370,000 of merchandise, 90% for cash and 10% for credit. The Cost of Goods Sold was $197,000.

f. Paid $50,000 mortgage payment, of which $30,000 represents interest expense.

g. Paid salaries expense of $120,000.

h. Paid installment of $10,000 on note.

Required:

1. Prepare journal entries to record each listed transaction. (Omit explanations.)

2. Set up T-accounts with the proper account balances at January 1, 2009, post the journal entries to the T-accounts, and prepare a trial balance for Gammon Corporation at December 31, 2009.

3. **Interpretive Question:** If the debit and credit columns of the trial balance are in balance, does this mean that no errors have been made in journalizing the transactions? Explain.

P 3-42

LO3, LO4

Journalizing and Posting

Assume you are interviewing for a part-time accounting job at Spilker & Associates, Inc., and the interviewer gives you the following list of company transactions in September 2009.

Sept. 1	Received $150,000 for capital stock issued.
2	Paid $20,000 cash to employees for wages earned in September 2009.
4	Purchased $75,000 of running shoes and clothing on account for resale.
5	Paid utilities of $1,800 for September 2009.
9	Paid $1,500 cash for September's insurance premium.
11	Sold inventory of running shoes and clothing costing $35,000 for $70,000, with $20,000 received in cash and the remaining balance on credit.
15	Purchased $2,500 of supplies on account.
21	Received $25,000 from customers as payments on their accounts.
25	Paid $75,000 of accounts payable.

Using this list, you have been asked to do the following in the interview:

Required:

1. Journalize each of the transactions for September. (Omit explanations.)

2. Set up T-accounts, and post each of the journal entries made in (1).

3. **Interpretive Question:** If the business owners wanted to know at any given time how much cash the company had, where would you tell the owners to look? Why?

P 3-43

LO3, LO4

Journal Entries from Ledger Analysis

T-accounts for JCB Industries, Inc., are shown below.

	Cash				Accounts Receivable				Inventory		
(a)	140,000	(b)	70,000	(e)	35,000	(i)	22,000	(d)	43,000	(e)	25,000
(c)	60,000	(d)	8,000								
(e)	35,000	(f)	18,000								
(i)	22,000	(g)	63,000								
		(h)	35,000								

(continued)

Building		Accounts Payable			Mortgage Payable	
(b) 210,000		(h) 35,000	(d) 35,000			(b) 140,000

Notes Payable		Capital Stock		Sales Revenue	
(g) 60,000	(c) 60,000		(a) 140,000		(e) 70,000

Cost of Goods Sold		Interest Expense		Wages Expense	
(e) 25,000		(g) 3,000		(f) 18,000	

Required:

1. Analyze these accounts and detail the appropriate journal entries that must have been made by JCB Industries, Inc. (Omit explanations.)
2. Determine the amount of net income/loss from the account information.

P 3-44

LO3, LO4

Journalizing and Posting Transactions

Anna Regina, owner of Anna's Beauty Supply, completed the following business transactions during March 2009.

Mar. 1   Purchased $26,500 of inventory on credit.
   4   Collected $2,500 from customers as payments on their accounts.
   5   Purchased equipment for $1,500 cash.
   6   Sold inventory that cost $15,000 to customers on account
        for $20,000.
   10   Paid rent for March, $525.
   15   Paid utilities for March, $50.
   17   Paid a $150 monthly salary to the part-time helper.
   20   Collected $16,500 from customers as payments on their accounts.
   25   Paid property taxes for March of $600.
   26   Sold inventory that cost $10,000 to customers for $15,000 cash.
   28   Paid $26,500 cash on account payable. (See March 1 entry.)

Required:

1. For each transaction, give the entry to record it in the company's general journal. (Omit explanations.)
2. Set up T-accounts, and post the journal entries to their appropriate accounts.

P 3-45

LO3, LO4

Unifying Concepts: Compound Journal Entries, Posting, Trial Balance

Shaw Mercantile Company had the following transactions during 2009.

a. Jon Shaw began business by investing the following assets, receiving capital stock in exchange:

Cash	$ 30,000
Inventory	34,000
Land	20,000
Building	165,000
Equipment	13,500*
Totals	$262,500

*A note of $6,000 on the equipment was assumed by the company.

(continued)

b. Sold merchandise that cost $32,000 for $52,000; $20,000 cash was received immediately, and the other $32,000 will be collected in 30 days.

c. Paid off the note of $6,000 plus $500 interest.

d. Purchased merchandise costing $14,000, paying $6,000 cash and issuing a note for $8,000.

e. Exchanged $6,000 cash and $6,000 in capital stock for office equipment costing $12,000.

f. Purchased a truck for $25,000 with $5,000 down and a one-year note for the balance.

Required:

1. Journalize the transactions. (Omit explanations.)
2. Post the journal entries using T-accounts for each account.
3. Prepare a trial balance at December 31, 2009.

P 3-46   **Unifying Concepts: Journal Entries, T-Accounts, Trial Balance**

LO3, LO4

Jethro Company, a retailer, had the following account balances as of April 30, 2009:

Cash	$ 5,050	
Accounts Receivable	2,450	
Inventory	8,000	
Land	13,000	
Building	12,000	
Furniture	2,000	
Notes Payable		$12,500
Accounts Payable		6,000
Capital Stock		15,000
Retained Earnings		9,000
Totals	$42,500	$42,500

During May, the company completed the following transactions.

May 3	Paid one-half of 4/30/09 accounts payable.
4	Purchased inventory on account, $5,000.
6	Collected all of 4/30/09 accounts receivable.
7	Sold inventory costing $3,850 for $3,000 cash and $2,000 on account.
8	Sold one-half of the land for $6,500, receiving $4,000 cash plus a note for $2,500.
15	Paid installment of $2,500 on notes payable (entire amount reduces the liability account).
21	Issued additional capital stock for $1,000 cash.
23	Sold inventory costing $2,000 for $3,750 cash.
25	Paid salaries of $1,000.
26	Paid rent of $250.
29	Purchased desk for $250 cash.

Required:

1. Prepare the journal entry for each transaction.
2. Set up T-accounts with the proper account balances at April 30, 2009, and post the entries to the T-accounts.
3. Prepare a trial balance as of May 31, 2009.

P 3-47   **Unifying Concepts: First Steps in the Accounting Cycle**

LO3, LO4

The following balances were taken from the general ledger of Holland Company on January 1, 2009:

(continued)

	Debits	Credits
Cash	$14,500	
Short-Term Investments	9,000	
Accounts Receivable	17,500	
Inventory	22,000	
Land	30,000	
Buildings	70,000	
Equipment	15,000	
Notes Payable		$15,500
Accounts Payable		19,500
Salaries and Wages Payable		7,500
Mortgage Payable		32,500
Capital Stock (7,000 shares outstanding)		70,000
Retained Earnings		33,000

During 2009, the company completed the following transactions:

a. Purchased inventory for $95,000 on credit.
b. Issued an additional $40,000 of capital stock (4,000 shares) for cash.
c. Paid property taxes of $5,200 for the year 2009.
d. Paid advertising and other selling expenses of $6,500.
e. Paid utilities expense of $4,800 for 2009.
f. Paid the salaries and wages owed for 2008. Paid additional salaries and wages of $23,000 during 2009.
g. Sold merchandise costing $111,000 for $167,000. Of total sales, $38,000 were cash sales and $129,000 were credit sales.
h. Paid off notes of $15,500 plus interest of $1,200.
i. On November 1, 2009, received a loan of $15,000 from the bank.
j. On December 30, 2009, made annual mortgage payment of $3,300 and paid interest of $700.
k. Collected receivables for the year of $132,000.
l. Paid off accounts payable of $110,500.
m. Received dividends and interest of $1,100 on short-term investments during 2009. (Record as Miscellaneous Revenue.)
n. Purchased additional short-term investments of $12,000 during 2009. (*Note:* Short-term investments are current assets.)
o. Paid 2009 corporate income taxes of $6,300.
p. Paid cash dividends of $6,100.

Required:

1. Journalize the 2009 transactions. (Omit explanations.)
2. Set up T-accounts with the proper account balances at January 1, 2009, and post the journal entries to the T-accounts.
3. Determine the account balances, and prepare a trial balance at December 31, 2009.
4. Prepare an income statement and a balance sheet. (Remember that the dividends account and all revenue and expense accounts are temporary retained earnings accounts.)
5. **Interpretive Question**: Why are revenue and expense accounts used at all?

P 3-48

LO2, LO4

Unifying Concepts: T-Accounts, Trial Balance, and Income Statement

The following list is a selection of transactions from Trafalga, Inc.'s business activities during 2009, the first year of operations.

a. Received $50,000 cash for capital stock.
b. Paid $5,000 cash for equipment.

(continued)

c. Purchased inventory costing $18,000 on account.

d. Sold $25,000 of merchandise to customers on account. Cost of goods sold was $15,000.

e. Signed a note with a bank for a $10,000 loan.

f. Collected $9,500 cash from customers who had purchased merchandise on account.

g. Purchased land, $10,000, and a building, $60,000, for $15,000 cash and a 30-year mortgage of $55,000.

h. Made a first payment of $2,750 on the mortgage principal plus $2,750 in interest.

i. Paid $12,000 of accounts payable.

j. Purchased $1,500 of supplies on account.

k. Paid $2,500 of accounts payable.

l. Paid $7,500 in wages earned during the year.

m. Received $10,000 cash and $3,000 of notes in settlement of customers' accounts.

n. Received $3,250 in payment of a note receivable of $3,000 plus interest of $250.

o. Paid $600 cash for a utility bill.

p. Sold excess land for its cost of $3,000.

q. Received $1,500 in rent for an unused part of a building.

r. Paid off $10,000 note, plus interest of $1,200.

Required:

1. Set up T-accounts, and appropriately record the debits and credits for each transaction directly in the T-accounts. Leave room for a number of entries in the cash account.

2. Prepare a trial balance.

3. Prepare an income statement for the period. (Ignore income taxes and the EPS computation.)

P 3-49
LO4

Correcting a Trial Balance

The following trial balance was prepared by a new employee.

Trial Balance Jeppson Company, Inc. For the Year Ended November 30, 2009	Credits	Debits
Cash	$ 19,000	
Mortgage Payable		$ 75,200
Advertising Expense	9,600	
Capital Stock	110,000	
Equipment		36,900
Notes Payable		197,350
Inventory		142,000
Wages Expense	87,900	
Notes Receivable		12,000
Accounts Payable		23,450
Accounts Receivable	5,300	
Rent Expense		8,750
Wages Payable	12,000	
Furniture		18,000
Other Expenses	1,950	
Sales Revenue	225,600	
Buildings	110,700	
Cost of Goods Sold		113,650
Property Tax Expense	1,300	
Land		95,850
Retained Earnings		21,400
Utilities Expense	2,100	
Totals	$584,150	$745,850

(continued)

Required:
Prepare the corrected company trial balance. (Assume all accounts have "normal" balances and the recorded amounts are correct.)

ANALYTICAL ASSIGNMENTS

AA 3-50
DISCUSSION

How Does Wal-Mart (and Other Companies) Do It?
Wal-Mart's revenues exceeded $312 billion in 2005. These revenues were generated by millions of transactions all over the world: in the United States, Canada, Europe, South America, and Asia. What is the process used by Wal-Mart to transform this tremendous amount of transaction data into summarized information reported to the general public in the form of financial statements?

AA 3-51
DISCUSSION

Advantages and Disadvantages of a Computerized Accounting System
Your soon-to-be father-in-law owns a small retail store. He has manually kept his business accounting records for over 20 years, but he is currently thinking about switching to a computerized accounting system. What advice would you give him about the advantages and the disadvantages of using a computerized accounting system?

AA 3-52
DISCUSSION

When Is a Debit a Debit?
Your new roommate, Susan, is confused. She has just received a notice from her bank indicating that her account has been debited for the cost of new checks. This has reduced her cash account. Susan just learned in her introductory accounting class that debiting Cash increases the account. She wonders why the bank has reduced her account by debiting it. How can you help Susan understand this situation?

AA 3-53
DISCUSSION

Understanding the Mechanics of Accounting
As the CFO (chief financial officer) of Rollins Engineering Company, you are looking for someone to fill the position of office manager. Part of the job description is to maintain the company's accounting records. This means that the office manager must be able to journalize transactions, post them to the ledger accounts, and prepare monthly trial balances. You have just interviewed the first applicant, Jay McMahon, who claims that he has studied accounting. As an initial check on his understanding of the basic mechanics of accounting, you give Jay a list of accounts randomly ordered and with assumed balances and ask him to prepare a trial balance. Jay prepares the following.

Trial Balance		
	Debits	**Credits**
Accounts Payable		$ 4,500
Salaries Expense		175,000
Consulting Revenues	$269,000	
Cash	82,100	
Utilities Expense	12,000	
Accounts Receivable		44,000
Supplies	11,000	
Rent Expense	30,000	
Capital Stock		77,000
Supplies Expense	33,000	
Office Equipment	15,000	
Retained Earnings		24,000
Other Expenses	6,400	
Salaries Payable	34,000	
Totals	$492,500	$324,500

(continued)

Based solely on your assessment of Jay McMahon's understanding of accounting, would you hire him as office manager? Explain. Prepare a corrected trial balance that you can use as a basis for your discussion with Jay and future applicants. Explain how the basic accounting equation and the system of double-entry accounting provide a check on the accounting records.

AA 3-54
DISCUSSION

Exercising Accounting Judgment

You have recently started business as an accounting consultant. Companies come to you when they face difficult decisions about how to make certain journal entries. You are currently working on the following two problems, which are independent of one another.

a. Baggins Company sells hamburgers for $1.00 each. The cost of the materials used to make each hamburger is 30 cents. Baggins has a compensation plan in which its employees are paid in the form of cash and hamburgers. During 2009, Baggins paid cash salaries of $500,000 and also issued certificates to employees entitling them to 200,000 free hamburgers. The certificates are not redeemable until 2010. What journal entry or entries should Baggins make in 2009 to record this employee compensation information?

b. Radagast Company purchased a building for $100,000 cash on January 1, 2009. Because of poor business decisions, as of December 31, 2009, the building is worthless. Make all journal entries necessary in 2009 in connection with this building.

AA 3-55
JUDGMENT CALL

You Decide: Is understanding the accounting cycle essential to being a good accountant, or is it a waste of time?

John, a family friend who didn't go to college, was talking to you about his job, as bookkeeper, at a local bookstore. "It is no longer necessary to learn the accounting cycle to be a good accountant," he said. "Computers do most of the work anyway. Unless you work in a small family-owned business, it doesn't make any sense to learn the correct method for posting debits and credits. If you just understand the financial statements, you will be ok!" Do you agree or disagree? Explain.

AA 3-56
JUDGMENT CALL

You Decide: If you major in accounting, will you enjoy a rewarding career, or will the field be extinct in 20 years?

I thought an accounting degree would give me the solid, fundamental understanding of business I was looking for but some of my friends seem to think that accountants won't have jobs a few years from now. They argue that as computers become smarter and more powerful, they will develop enough capacities to make good business decisions. They say I am making a mistake by majoring in a field that will not be around in 20 years. What do you think?

AA 3-57
REAL COMPANY
ANALYSIS

Wal-Mart

The 2006 Form 10-K for **Wal-Mart** is included in Appendix A. Locate that Form 10-K and consider the following questions:

1. Find Wal-Mart's 2006 income statement. Assume that operating, selling, general, and administrative expenses were paid in cash. What journal entry did Wal-Mart make in 2006 to record these expenses?

2. Find Wal-Mart's 2006 cash flow statement. What journal entry did Wal-Mart make in 2006 to record the issuance of long-term debt?

3. Again, looking at the cash flow statement, what journal entry did Wal-Mart make in 2006 to record the purchase of property and equipment?

AA 3-58
REAL COMPANY
ANALYSIS

McDonald's

A brief history of the origin of the **McDonald's Corporation** is given at the start of this chapter. The following questions are adapted from information appearing in McDonald's 2005 annual report.

1. In 2005, total sales at all McDonald's stores worldwide were $54.3 billion. There were 31,886 McDonald's stores operating in 2005. Estimate how many customers per day visit an average McDonald's store.

2. For the stores owned by the McDonald's Corporation (as opposed to those owned by franchisees), total sales in 2005 were $15.4 billion, and total cost of food and packaging

(continued)

was $5.207 billion. What journal entries would McDonald's make to record a $10 sale and to record the cost of food and packaging associated with the $10 sale?

3. McDonald's reported payment of cash dividends of $842.0 million in 2005. What journal entry was required?

4. McDonald's reported that the total income tax it owed for 2005 was $1,137.7 million. However, only $795.1 million in cash was paid for taxes during the year. What compound journal entry did McDonald's make to record its income tax expense for the year?

AA 3-59
INTERNATIONAL

Shanghai Petrochemical Company Limited

In July 1993, **Shanghai Petrochemical Company Limited** became the first company organized under the laws of the People's Republic of China to publicly issue its shares on the worldwide market. Shanghai Petrochemical's shares now trade on the stock exchanges in Shanghai, Hong Kong, and New York. The following questions are adapted from information appearing in Shanghai Petrochemical's 1995 annual report.

1. In 1995, Shanghai Petrochemical reported sales of 11.835 billion renminbi (US$ 1 = 8.33 RMB) and cost of sales of RMB 9.016 billion. Make the necessary journal entries, using renminbi as the currency.

2. In 1995, Shanghai Petrochemical declared cash dividends of RMB 851.5 million. However, cash paid for dividends during the year was only RMB 818.8 million. Make the necessary compound journal entry to record the declaration and payment of cash dividends for the year.

3. In China, a 17% value added tax (VAT) is added to the invoiced value of all sales. This VAT is collected by the seller from the buyer and then held to be forwarded to the government. What journal entry would Shanghai Petrochemical make to record the sale, on account, of crude oil with an invoice sales value of $100 and a cost of $70?

AA 3-60
ETHICS

Should You Go the Extra Mile?

You work in a small convenience store. The store is very low-tech; you ring up the sales on an old-style cash register that merely records the amount of the sale. The store owner uses this cash register tape at the end of each day to verify that the correct amount of cash is in the cash register drawer. On a day-to-day basis, no other financial information is collected about store operations.

Since you started studying accounting, you have become a bit uneasy about your job because you see many ways that store operations could be improved through the gathering and use of financial information. Even though you are not an expert, you are quite certain that you could help the store owner set up an improved information system. However, you also know that this will take extra effort on your part, with no real possibility of receiving an increase in pay.

Should you say anything to the store owner, or should you just keep quiet and save yourself the trouble?

AA 3-61
WRITING

Accounting Is Everywhere!

Financial accounting information is frequently used in newspaper and magazine articles to provide background data on companies. Prepare a one-page report on the use of financial accounting data by the press. Proceed as follows:

1. Scan the articles in a recent copy of one of the popular business periodicals (such as *The Wall Street Journal*, *Forbes*, *Fortune*, or *Business Week*) for examples of the use of financial accounting data.

2. Identify and describe three interesting examples:
   • Detail the nature of the accounting data used.
   • Outline the point that the writer is trying to make by using the particular accounting data.

AA 3-62
CUMULATIVE
SPREADSHEET
PROJECT

Analyzing Transactions

This spreadsheet assignment is a continuation of the spreadsheet assignment given in Chapter 2. If you completed that spreadsheet, you have a head start on this one.

Determine the impact of each of the following transactions on total assets, total liabilities, and total owners' equity. Treat each transaction independently, meaning that before determining the impact of each new transaction, you should reset the financial statement values to their original amounts. Each of the hypothetical transactions is assumed to occur on the last day of the year.

a. Collected $20 cash from customer receivables.
b. Purchased $30 in inventory on account.
c. Purchased $100 in property, plant, and equipment. The entire amount of the purchase was financed with a mortgage. Principal repayment for the mortgage is due in 10 years.
d. Purchased $100 in property, plant, and equipment. The entire amount of the purchase was financed with new stockholder investment.
e. Borrowed $20 with a short-term loan payable. The $20 was paid out as a dividend to stockholders.
f. Received $20 as an investment from stockholders. The $20 was paid out as a dividend to stockholders.

Completing the Accounting Cycle

After studying this chapter, you should be able to:

LEARNING OBJECTIVES

(1) Describe how accrual accounting allows for timely reporting and a better measure of a company's economic performance. *Proper accrual accounting involves recording the profits from a company's business activities when those activities occur which does not necessarily match up with when cash is collected or paid.*

(2) Explain the need for adjusting entries and make adjusting entries for unrecorded receivables, unrecorded liabilities, prepaid expenses, and unearned revenues. *Some economic activities, such as the growth in the amount of interest a company owes, happen gradually. Without special adjustments, the accounting records would not reflect the impact of these gradual activities. Adjusting entries must be made at the end of each accounting period to ensure that all balance sheet and income statement items are stated at the correct amount.*

(3) Explain the preparation of the financial statements, the explanatory notes, and the audit report. *After all transactions are recorded and posted and the necessary adjusting entries are made, the account balances in the trial balance accurately reflect the company's economic circumstances and performance. The account balances are the raw material used to prepare the financial statements; for some companies, including all public companies, these balances are checked by an independent auditor.*

(4) Complete the closing process in the accounting cycle. *Closing entries are used to transfer revenue, expense, and dividend data to the retained earnings account so that the transactions of a new period can be recorded.*

(5) Understand how all the steps in the accounting cycle fit together. *To review, transactions are first analyzed and then recorded in debit-and-credit format. Journal entries are posted to individual accounts. Before financial statements are prepared, adjusting entries are made to ensure that all amounts are correct. The books are then closed.*

General Motors, the brainchild of William Durant, was formed through the acquisition of a number of preexisting car makers. **Buick** and **Oldsmobile** were acquired in 1908; **Cadillac** and **Pontiac** (originally called **Oakland**) were added in 1909. With so many acquisitions in those early years, General Motors' financing was quickly depleted, and Durant lost control of his company. With Durant fighting to regain the reins of General Motors, the company was in such turmoil that, at one point, **Chevrolet Motor Company** (another Durant creation) owned a majority of GM stock. After many deals, Durant found himself back in charge in 1916, and Chevrolet became a subsidiary of GM in 1918.

Following the end of World War I, an economic slowdown stretched Durant's financial resources past the breaking point, and in 1920 he lost control of General Motors for good. Under the direction of Alfred P. Sloan, General Motors eventually became the dominant car maker in the world, a position it still holds.

Although General Motors' global market share has declined with stiff competition from Japanese (**Toyota, Honda,** etc.), European (including **DaimlerChrysler**), and domestic (**Ford**) competitors, General Motors still sells more cars and trucks than any other company in the world. In 2005, GM sold 65 million vehicles, nearly 14% of the worldwide total. GM also remains one of the largest private employers in the United States with 325,000 employees at the end of 2005.

But recent stiff competition has resulted in General Motors falling on hard times. In 2005, the company reported a net loss of over $10.5 billion. During the same period it was reporting this huge loss on its income statement, GM reported an even larger negative cash flow from operations on its cash flow statement. In fact, in 2005, GM's negative cash flow from operations was $16.9 billion. In 2004, GM reported net income of $2.8 billion and cash flow from operations of $9.4 billion.

How can a company incur such a large loss on the income statement and an even larger negative cash flow and still stay in business? Why the large discrepancy in 2004 and 2005 between net income (loss) and cash flow from operations? The differences came from business expenses that General Motors incurred but which required no cash or had either paid for in earlier years or would pay for in subsequent years. As an example, consider postretirement benefits. These benefits are recorded as expenses (a cost of doing business) to the company now as employees work, but General Motors won't actually have to make the cash payments related to these benefits until the employees retire in the future. Proper accounting requires recording now all business expenses—both those that are paid in cash and those that involve promises of payment in the future.

As the General Motors scenario illustrates, adjustments or true-ups (to the original transaction data recorded in the accounts) usually are needed so that the financial statements will accurately reflect a company's economic performance during the period and its economic condition as of the end of the period. This is a part of completing the accounting cycle. In addition to the true-up adjustments, certain accounts must be "closed" (brought to a zero balance) at the end of an accounting period to prepare the records for a new accounting cycle. The nature of year-end adjustments and the remaining steps in the accounting cycle are discussed in this chapter.

Accrual Accounting

Describe how accrual accounting allows for timely reporting and a better measure of a company's economic performance.

(1) In 2008, two brothers sign a contract for a consulting project. The total contract price is $20,000. The brothers do most of the consulting work in 2008 and finish the job in 2009. They receive a $2,000 cash payment from the contract in 2008 and receive the remaining $18,000 cash in 2009. On December 31, 2008, the brothers prepare a 2008 income statement to use in applying for a bank loan. What amount of revenue should the brothers report for 2008?

This simple example illustrates why accounting is much more than merely tabulating cash receipts and cash payments. A proper measure of the brothers' economic performance in 2008 requires estimating the amount of the work completed in 2008; to report 2008 revenue as only the $2,000 cash received grossly understates the actual economic output produced during the year. In addition, the need for the year-end income statement means that the brothers can't wait until after the final contract payment is received before preparing a summary of their activities; the bank wants the income statement now.

Accrual accounting is the process of recording expenses and revenues when incurred and earned, regardless of when cash is received and of adjusting original transaction data into refined measures of a firm's past economic performance and current economic condition. As the following sections explain, this accrual process is necessary because a business requires periodic, timely financial reports and accrual information better measures a firm's performance than do cash flow data.

The difficulty in using accrual accounting to generate a performance measure is represented in Exhibit 1. Each horizontal bar in the exhibit represents a business deal such as the production and sale of a car, the delivery of legal services for a specific lawsuit, or the development, delivery, and support of a piece of software. Some deals last less than a day from start to finish, such as when a barber provides a haircut in exchange for cash. The obligations and responsibilities associated with other deals can stretch on for years. For example, when you buy a **General Motors** car, the deal is not done from your standpoint until four or five years later after you have received all of the GM warranty services promised to you. And, from GM's standpoint, the deal is not done until 40 or 50 years later after GM has paid the assembly-line workers all of the pension benefits they earned through the labor hours spent assembling your car. Even though the economic loose ends of some business deals extend for years, financial statement users still require periodic reports about a company's operating performance. As you can see in Exhibit 1, the beginning and the end of a year are arbitrary breaks in the life of an ongoing business. The job of accountants is to consider all business deals that were at least partially completed during a year and to measure the revenues, expenses, and profit associated with those deals. This profit is then reported as net income for the year. As you can see, accrual accounting is much more than mere "bean counting."

Periodic Reporting

All businesses, large or small, periodically issue their financial statements so that users can make sound economic decisions. Current owners, prospective investors, bankers, and others need up-to-date reports in order to compare and judge a company's financial position and operating results on a continuing, timely basis. They need to know the financial position of a company (from the balance sheet), the relative success or failure of

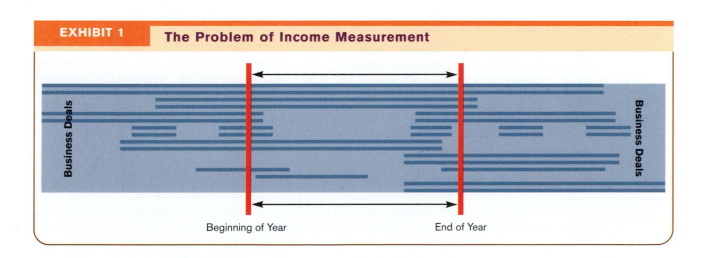

EXHIBIT 1 **The Problem of Income Measurement**

Business Deals

Business Deals

Beginning of Year   End of Year

time-period concept

The idea that the life of a business is divided into distinct and relatively short time periods so that accounting information can be timely.

fiscal year

An entity's reporting year, covering a 12-month accounting period.

calendar year

An entity's reporting year, covering 12 months and ending on December 31.

current operations (from the income statement), and the nature and extent of cash flows (from the statement of cash flows).

The financial picture of a company—its success or failure in meeting its economic objectives—cannot really be complete until the "life" of a business is over. However, managers, owners, and creditors cannot wait 10, 20, or 100 years to receive an exact accounting of a business. In order to provide timely accounting information, the **time-period concept** divides the life of an enterprise into distinct and relatively short (generally 12 months or less) accounting periods. The 12-month accounting period is referred to as the **fiscal year**. When an entity closes its books on December 31, its reports are based on a **calendar year**.

Most large corporations, and even many small companies, issue a report to stockholders as of a fiscal year-end. Also, most corporations prepare reports on a quarterly basis as well. As noted in Chapters 1 and 2, this annual report includes the primary financial statements (balance sheet, income statement, and statement of cash flows) and other financial data, such as a management discussion and analysis of operations.

Although periodic reporting is vital to a firm's success, the frequency of reporting forces accountants to use some data that are based on judgments and estimates. Ideally, accounting judgments are made carefully and estimates are based on reliable evidence, but the limitations of accounting reports should be understood and kept in mind.

? F Y I

About two-thirds of large U.S. companies choose December 31 as the end of their fiscal year.

Accrual- versus Cash-Basis Accounting

Closely related to the time-period concept is the concept of **accrual-basis accounting**. This important characteristic of the traditional accounting model simply means that—

accrual-basis accounting

A system of accounting in which revenues and expenses are recorded as they are earned and incurred, not necessarily when cash is received or paid.

revenues are recognized (recorded) when earned without regard for when cash is received; expenses are recorded as incurred without regard for when they are paid. Accrual accounting requires that revenues and expenses be assigned to their proper accounting periods, which do not necessarily coincide with the periods in which cash is received or paid.

○ STOP & THINK

Since almost all companies have their financial records on computer, what stops them from preparing financial statements every day?

Revenue Recognition   How do we assign revenues to particular periods? First, we must determine when revenues have actually been earned. The **revenue recognition principle** states that revenues are recorded when two main criteria have been met.

1. The earnings process is substantially complete; generally, a sale has been made or services have been performed.
2. Cash has been collected or collectibility is reasonably assured.

These two criteria ensure that both parties to the transaction have fulfilled their commitment or are formally obligated to do so. In simple terms, satisfying the first criterion demonstrates that the seller has done something; satisfying the second criterion demonstrates that the buyer has done something. The seller generally records sales revenue when goods are shipped or when services are performed. When this occurs, the seller has

revenue recognition principle

The idea that revenues should be recorded when (1) the earnings process has been substantially completed and (2) cash has either been collected or collectibility is reasonably assured.

completed his or her part of the transaction. The seller assumes, when shipment is made or services performed, that the buyer has given a valid promise to pay (if this promise is not implied, then the seller probably will not ship). The promise to pay, or the actual payment, would complete the buyer's part of the transaction. If, for example, General Motors sold and shipped $800 million of cars in 2009, but will not receive the cash proceeds until 2010, the $800 million would still be recognized as revenue in 2009, when it is earned and a promise of payment is received. Both of the revenue recognition principle criteria have been met. On the other hand, if General Motors is paid in 2009 for cars to be shipped in 2010, it would not record those payments as revenues until the cars are actually shipped. Referring back to the example that began this section, the two brothers would recognize as consulting revenue the amount associated with the proportion of the job that was completed in 2008. For example, if an objective estimate indicated that 80% of the consulting project was completed in 2008, then it would be appropriate for the brothers to recognize $16,000 ($20,000 × 0.8) as revenue in 2008—assuming that they felt they had received a valid promise that they would be paid for the consulting work.

F Y I

Determining when to recognize revenues is usually the most difficult accounting decision most companies have to make. And, there have been more financial statement frauds involving improper revenue recognition than any other type of financial statement misstatement.

The Matching Principle   Once a company determines which revenues should be recognized during a period, how does it identify the expenses that have been incurred? The **matching principle** requires that all costs and expenses incurred to generate revenues must be recognized in the same accounting period as the related revenues. The cost of the merchandise sold, for example, should be matched to the revenue derived from the sale of that merchandise during the period. Expenses that cannot be matched with revenues are assigned to the accounting period in which they are incurred. For example, the exact amount of electricity used to make an automobile generally cannot be determined, but since the amount used for a month or a year is known, that amount can be matched to the revenues earned during the same period.

matching principle

The concept that all costs and expenses incurred in generating revenues must be recognized in the same reporting period as the related revenues.

As shown in Exhibit 2, this process of matching expenses with recognized revenues determines the amount of net income reported on the income statement. Net income is the most widely used indicator of how well a company has performed during a period. The subject of income determination, including revenue recognition and expense matching, is discussed more completely in Chapters 6, 7, and 8.

To illustrate the difference between cash- and accrual-basis accounting, and to demonstrate why accrual-basis accounting provides a more meaningful measure of income, assume that during 2009, Karas Brothers billed clients $50,500 for consulting

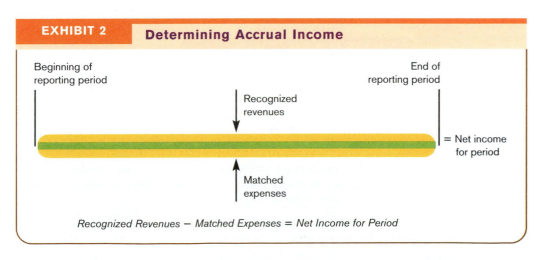

EXHIBIT 2   Determining Accrual Income

Beginning of reporting period

End of reporting period

Recognized revenues

= Net income for period

Matched expenses

Recognized Revenues − Matched Expenses = Net Income for Period

services performed in 2009. By December 31, Karas had received $22,000 in cash from customers, with the $28,500 balance expected in 2010. During 2009, Karas paid $21,900 for various expenses that had been incurred. At December 31, 2009, Karas still owed $11,200 for additional expenses incurred. These expenses will be paid during January 2010. How much income should Karas Brothers report for 2009? The answer depends on whether cash-basis or accrual-basis accounting is used. As shown below, with cash-basis accounting, reported income would be $100. With accrual-basis accounting, reported income would be $17,400.

Karas Brothers
Reported Income for 2009

Cash-Basis Accounting		Accrual-Basis Accounting	
Cash receipts	$22,000	Revenues earned	$50,500
Cash disbursements	21,900	Expenses incurred	33,100
Income	$ 100	Income	$17,400

cash-basis accounting

A system of accounting in which transactions are recorded and revenues and expenses are recognized only when cash is received or paid.

How do we explain this $17,300 difference? Under **cash-basis accounting**, Karas Brothers would report only $22,000 in revenue, the total amount of cash received during 2009. Similarly, the company would report only $21,900 of expenses (the amount actually paid) during 2009. The additional $11,200 of expenses incurred but not yet paid would not be reported. Using accrual-basis accounting, however, Karas earned $50,500 in revenues, which is the total increase in resources for the period (an increase of $22,000 in cash plus $28,500 in receivables). Similarly, Karas incurred a total of $33,100 in expenses, which should be matched with revenues earned to produce a realistic income measurement. The combined result of increasing revenues by $28,500 while increasing expenses by only $11,200 creates the $17,300 difference in net income ($28,500 − $11,200 = $17,300).

 CAUTION

Although accrual-basis net income is the measure of Karas Brothers' economic performance for the year, the cash flow information is useful in evaluating the need to obtain short-term loans, the ability to repay existing loans, and the like. The statement of cash flows is an essential companion to the accrual-basis income statement.

As this example shows, accrual-basis accounting provides a more accurate picture of a company's profitability. It matches earned revenues with the expenses incurred to generate those revenues. This helps investors, creditors, and others to better assess the operating results of a company and make more informed judgments concerning its profitability and earnings potential. Accrual-basis accounting is required by generally accepted accounting principles (GAAP).

REMEMBER THIS...

- Accrual accounting is the process of recording expenses and revenues when incurred and earned, regardless of when cash is received. Accrual accounting is required by GAAP because it provides a better measure of performance than does cash-basis accounting.

- The revenue recognition principle states that revenue is reported when the work is done which is often not the same time period as when the cash is collected.

- The matching principle states that expenses are reported when the corresponding asset or service is used which is often not the same time period as when cash is paid.

Adjusting Entries

Explain the need for adjusting entries and make adjusting entries for unrecorded receivables, unrecorded liabilities, prepaid expenses, and unearned revenues.

② As discussed in Chapter 3, transactions generally are recorded in a journal in chronological order and then posted to the ledger accounts. The entries are based on the best information available at the time. Although the majority of accounts are up-to-date at the end of an accounting period and their balances can be included in the financial statements, some accounts require adjustment to reflect current circumstances. In general, these accounts are not updated throughout the period because it is impractical or inconvenient to make such entries on a daily or weekly basis. At the end of each accounting period, in order to report all asset, liability, and owners' equity amounts properly and to recognize all revenues and expenses for the period on an accrual basis, accountants are required to make any necessary adjustments prior to preparing the financial statements. The entries that reflect these adjustments are called **adjusting entries**. It is important to note that adjusting entries are not made based on transactions; rather, they are the entries needed after careful analysis of revenues earned and expenses incurred.

adjusting entries

Entries required at the end of each accounting period to recognize, on an accrual basis, revenues and expenses for the period and to report proper amounts for asset, liability, and owners' equity accounts.

One difficulty with adjusting entries is that the need for an adjustment is not signaled by a specific event such as the receipt of a bill or the receipt of cash from a customer. Rather, adjusting entries are recorded on the basis of an analysis of the circumstances at the close of each accounting period.

This analysis involves just two steps:

1. Determine whether the amounts recorded for all assets and liabilities are correct. If not, debit or credit the appropriate asset or liability account. In short, fix the balance sheet.
2. Determine what revenue or expense adjustments are required as a result of the changes in recorded amounts of assets and liabilities indicated in step 1. Debit or credit the appropriate revenue or expense account. In short, fix the income statement.

It should be noted that these two steps are interrelated and may be reversed. That is, revenue and expense adjustments may be considered first to fix the income statement, indicating which asset and liability accounts need adjustment to fix the balance sheet. As you will see, *each adjusting entry involves at least one income statement account and one balance sheet account*. T-accounts are helpful in analyzing adjusting entries and will be used in the illustrations that follow.

The areas most commonly requiring analysis to see whether adjusting entries are needed are:

1. Unrecorded receivables
2. Unrecorded liabilities
3. Prepaid expenses
4. Unearned revenues

As we illustrate and discuss adjusting entries, remember that the basic purpose of adjustments is to make account balances current in order to report all asset, liability, and owners' equity amounts properly and to recognize all revenues and expenses for the period on an accrual basis. This is done so that the income statement and the balance sheet will reflect the proper operating results and financial position, respectively, at the end of the accounting period.

Unrecorded Receivables

In accordance with the revenue recognition principle of accrual accounting, revenues should be recorded when earned, regardless of when the cash is received. If revenue is earned but not yet collected in cash, a receivable exists. To ensure that all receivables are properly reported on the balance sheet in the correct amounts, an analysis should be made at the end of each accounting period to see whether there are any revenues that have been earned but have not yet been collected or recorded. These **unrecorded receivables** are earned and represent amounts that are receivable in the future; therefore, they should be recognized as assets.

unrecorded receivables

Revenues earned during a period that have not been recorded by the end of that period.

To illustrate, we will pick up with the landscaping business we started in Chapter 3. Recall that we mow lawns, pull weeds, plant shrubs, and perform other related services. We are able to provide these services year round because we live in a region with a very mild climate. Our company reports on a calendar-year basis and has determined the following on December 31, 2009:

On November 1, we entered into a year-long contract with an apartment complex to provide general landscaping services each week and bill the customer every three months. The terms of the contract state that we will earn $400 per month. As of December 31, Lawn Care Revenue of $800 ($400 for November and $400 for December) has not been recorded and will not be billed or received until the end of January 2010. No entry has been made since the end of October with respect to this contract.

As of year-end, no asset has been recorded, but an $800 receivable exists ($400 × 2), because two months' worth of revenue has been earned. To record this receivable, we must debit (increase) the asset Accounts Receivable for $800. With the debit, we have accomplished step 1 by fixing the balance sheet with regard to this transaction. Step 2 requires that we use the other half of the adjusting entry, the credit of $800, to fix the income statement. We know that the credit must be to either a revenue or an expense account, and the nature of the transaction suggests that we should credit Lawn Care Revenue for $800. The adjusting entry is:

Dec. 31	Accounts Receivable.	800	
	Lawn Care Revenue.		800
	To record two months of earned revenue not yet received.		

Adjusting entries are recorded in the general journal and are posted to the accounts in the general ledger in the same manner as other journal entries. Again note that each adjusting entry must involve at least one balance sheet account and at least one income statement account.

After this adjusting entry has been journalized and posted, the receivable will appear as an asset on the balance sheet, and the lawn care revenue is reported on the income statement. Through the adjusting entry, the asset (receivable) accounts are properly stated and revenues are appropriately reported.

Unrecorded Liabilities

Just as assets are created from revenues being earned before they are collected or recorded, liabilities can be created by expenses being incurred prior to being paid or recorded. These expenses, along with their corresponding liabilities, should be recorded when incurred, no matter when they are paid. Thus, adjusting entries are required at the end of an accounting period to recognize any **unrecorded liabilities** in the proper period and to record the corresponding expenses. As the expense is recorded (increased by a debit), the offsetting liability is also recorded (increased by a credit), showing the entity's obligation to pay for the expense.

unrecorded liabilities

Expenses incurred during a period that have not been recorded by the end of that period.

If such adjustments are not made, the net income measurement for the period will not reflect all appropriate expenses and the corresponding liabilities will be understated on the balance sheet.

To illustrate, we will assume that on December 31, 2009, our landscaping company has determined the following:

1. Your brother has worked for the company since its inception. He is paid every two weeks. The next payday is on Friday, January 5, 2010. On that day, your brother will be paid $700, the amount he earns every two weeks. Since December 31 falls halfway through the pay period, one-half of his wages should be allocated to 2009.
2. Recall from Chapter 3 that one of our options for financing our company was to borrow money from a bank. We borrowed $2,000 with the promise that on the first of every month we would make a $178 payment—a portion of that payment being attributed to interest[1] and a portion to principal. Our next payment is due on January 1, 2010, but the interest expense associated with that payment should be attributed to the period in which the money was actually used—December 2009. Assume that interest of $20 must be recognized on December 31, 2009.

To represent its current financial position and earnings, our landscaping company must record the impact of these events in the accounts, even though cash transactions have not yet occurred. The wages will not be paid until 2010. Under accrual-basis accounting, however, these costs are expenses of 2009 and should be recognized on this year's income statement, with the corresponding liability shown on the balance sheet as of the end of the year. To fix the balance sheet, Wages Payable must be credited (increased) for $350; recognition of this liability ensures that the balance sheet properly reports this liability, which was created during 2009 and exists as of the end of the year. The debit of this adjusting entry is to Wages Expense, resulting in the proper inclusion of this expense in the 2009 income statement. The adjusting journal entry is as follows:

Dec. 31	Wages Expense	350	
	Wages Payable.		350
	To record obligation for wages.		

The liability for the interest for the month of December is recorded by a credit (increase) to Interest Payable; this fixes the balance sheet. The debit of the adjusting entry is to Interest Expense, which properly includes this expense on the 2009 income statement. The adjusting entry is:

Dec. 31	Interest Expense	20	
	Interest Payable.		20
	To record interest incurred.		

The wages expense and interest expense would be reported on the income statement for the year ended December 31, and the liabilities (wages payable and interest payable) would be reported on the balance sheet as of December 31. Because of the adjusting entries, both the income statement

CAUTION

A liability is not recorded for the total amount of interest that will have to be paid over the entire life of the loan. If we repay the loan on December 31, the future interest will not have to be paid, but the interest for the month of December that has passed will still be due.

---

[1] As noted in Chapter 3, interest is the cost of using money. The amount borrowed or lent is the principal. The interest rate is an annual rate stated as a percentage. The period of time involved may be stated in terms of a year. For example, if interest is to be paid for 3 months, time is 3/12, or 1/4 of a year. If interest is to be paid for 90 days, time is 90/365 of a year. Thus, the formula for computing interest is Interest = Principal × Interest Rate × Time (fraction of a year).

and the balance sheet will more accurately reflect the financial situation of our landscaping company.

Prepaid Expenses

prepaid expenses

Payments made in advance for items normally charged to expense.

Payments that a company makes in advance for items normally charged to expense are known as **prepaid expenses**. An example would be the payment of an insurance premium for the next 18 months. Theoretically, every resource acquisition is an asset, at least temporarily. Thus, the entry to record an advance payment should be a debit to an asset account (Prepaid Expenses) and a credit to Cash, showing the exchange of cash for another asset.[2]

An expense is the using up of an asset. For example, when supplies are purchased, they are recorded as assets; when they are used, their cost is transferred to an expense account. The purpose of making adjusting entries for prepaid expenses is to show the complete or partial consumption of an asset. If the original entry is to an asset account, the adjusting entry reduces the asset to an amount that reflects its remaining future benefit and at the same time recognizes the actual expense incurred for the period.

> **! CAUTION**
>
> Prepaid Expenses is a tricky name for an asset. Assets are reported in the balance sheet. Don't make the mistake of including Prepaid Expenses with the expenses on the income statement.

For the unrecorded assets and liabilities discussed earlier, there was no original entry; the adjusting entry was the first time these items were recorded in the accounting records. For prepaid expenses, this is not the case. Because cash has already been paid (in the case of prepaid expenses), an original entry has been made to record the cash transaction. Therefore, the amount of the adjusting entry is the difference between what the updated balance should be and the amount of the original entry already recorded.

To illustrate adjustments for Prepaid Expenses, we will assume the following about our landscaping company:

1. On November 1, 2009, we purchased a six-month insurance policy on our old truck, paying a $600 premium.
2. On December 15, 2009, we purchased several months' of supplies (fertilizer, weed killer, etc.) at a total cost of $350. At year-end, $225 worth of supplies were still on hand.

For the prepaid insurance, we record the payment of $600 on November 1 as follows:

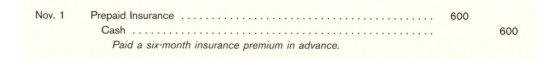

Nov. 1	Prepaid Insurance	600	
	Cash		600
	Paid a six-month insurance premium in advance.		

This entry shows that one asset (Cash) has been exchanged for another asset (Prepaid Insurance). Over the next six months we will use the auto insurance and the asset, Prepaid Insurance, will slowly be used up. As the asset is used, its cost is recorded as an expense.

At year-end, only those assets that still offer future benefits to the company should be reported on the balance sheet. Thus, an adjustment is required to reduce the prepaid

---

[2] It is also possible that the initial expenditure could be recorded with a debit to an expense account. This would require a different adjusting entry. This possibility is discussed in the web material associated with the text at **http://www.thomsonedu.com/accounting/albrecht**.

insurance account to reflect the fact that only four months of prepaid insurance remain. See the following time line.

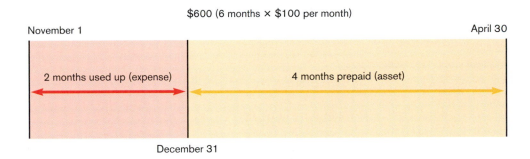

The adjusting journal entry to bring the original amounts to their updated balances at year-end is:

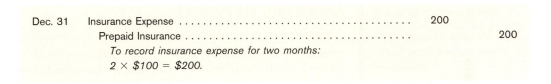

Dec. 31	Insurance Expense	200	
	Prepaid Insurance		200
	To record insurance expense for two months:		
	2 × $100 = $200.		

When the adjusting entry is journalized and posted, the proper amount of insurance expense ($200) will be shown as an expense on the income statement and the proper amount of prepaid insurance ($400) will be carried forward to the next period as an asset on the balance sheet. This is illustrated in the following T-accounts:

	Prepaid Insurance		**Cash**		**Insurance Expense**	
Original entry (11/1/09)	600		600			
Adjusting entry (12/31/09)		200			200	
Updated balances (12/31/09)	400				200	
	To balance sheet				To income statement	

 CAUTION

The terms *supplies* and *inventory* are often confused. Supplies include such items as paper, pencils, and soap that might be used in an office or a warehouse. Inventory includes only those items held for resale to customers or for direct use in the manufacture of products.

When supplies are consumed in the normal course of business, the asset account (Supplies on Hand) must be adjusted and the used up portion charged as an operating expense (Supplies Expense) on the income statement. Thus, the adjustment for supplies is handled the same way as for any other prepaid asset.

We initially recorded $350 of supplies as an asset:

Dec. 15	Supplies on Hand	350	
	Cash		350
	Purchased supplies.		

At year-end, an adjustment must be made to recognize that only $225 of supplies remains. This also implies that $125 ($350 − $225) of the supplies have been used and should be charged to expense. The entries are summarized in the following T-accounts:

	Supplies on Hand		Cash		Supplies Expense	
Original entry (12/15/09)	350		350			
Adjusting entry (12/31/09)		125			125	
Updated balances (12/31/09)	225				125	
	To balance sheet				To income statement	

The adjusting entry is:

Dec. 31	Supplies Expense	125	
	Supplies on Hand		125
	To record the use of supplies.		

Unearned Revenues

unearned revenues

Cash amounts received before they have been earned.

Amounts received before the actual earning of revenues are known as **unearned revenues**. They arise when customers pay in advance of the receipt of goods or services. Because the company has received cash but has not yet given the customer the purchased goods or services, the unearned revenues are in fact liabilities. That is, the company must provide something in return for the amounts received. For example, a building contractor may require a deposit before proceeding on construction of a house. Upon receipt of the deposit, the contractor has unearned revenue, a liability. The contractor must construct the house to earn the revenue. If the house is not built, the contractor will be obligated to repay the deposit.

 CAUTION

Unearned Revenue is a tricky name for a liability. Liabilities are reported in the balance sheet. Don't make the mistake of including Unearned Revenue with the revenues on the income statement.

To illustrate the adjustments for unearned revenues, we will assume the following about our landscaping company:

> On December 1, a client pays you $225 for three months of landscaping services to be provided for the period beginning December 1, 2009, and ending February 28, 2010. This client is going to Hawaii for an extended vacation and would like you to take care of the grounds in her absence.

Typically, the original entry to record unearned revenue involves a debit to Cash and a credit to a liability account.[3] In our example of landscaping revenue received three months in advance, the liability account would be Unearned Revenue, as shown below.

Dec. 1	Cash..	225	
	Unearned Revenue		225
	Received three months' revenue in advance:		
	$75 × 3 = $225.		

The credit to the liability account, Unearned Revenue, is logically correct; until we provide the landscaping service, the revenue received in advance is unearned and is thus an obligation (liability).

---

[3] It is also possible that the initial expenditure could be recorded with a credit to a revenue account. This would require a different adjusting entry. This possibility is discussed in the web material associated with the text at **http://www.thomsonedu.com/accounting/albrecht**.

The deposit received by a building contractor prior to the construction of a house is classified as unearned revenue.

© RUSSELL ILLIG/PHOTODISC GREEN/GETTY IMAGES INC.

The next step is to compute the updated balances at year-end. As illustrated with the following time line, on December 31, two months' services (2 × $75 = $150) are still unearned and should be shown as a liability, Unearned Revenue, on the balance sheet. At the same time, $75, or one month's services, has been earned (1 × $75 = $75) and should be reported as Landscaping Revenue on the income statement.

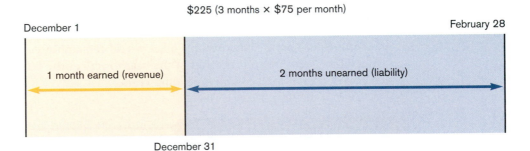

Step 1 of the adjusting entry is to fix the balance sheet. The reported liability of $225 is too much since some of the unearned revenue has been earned. The remaining obligation is $150 (2 × $75), so the liability must be reduced (debited) by $75 ($225 − $150). The second half of the adjusting entry is used to correct the income statement. The $75 credit is made to Landscaping Revenue, reflecting the fact that one month's revenue has now been earned. The appropriate adjusting entry is:

Dec. 31	Unearned Revenue	75	
	Landscaping Revenue		75
	To record landscaping revenue for one month:		
	$75 × 1 month = $75.		

These results are illustrated in the following T-accounts:

	Unearned Revenue		Cash		Landscaping Revenue	
Original entry (12/1/09)		225	225			
Adjusting entry (12/31/09)	75					75
Updated balances (12/31/09)		150				75
		To balance sheet				To income statement

After the adjusting entry has been made on December 31, our accounts show $225 of cash received. Of this amount, $75 has been earned (1 month's service at $75) and would be reported as Landscaping Revenue on the income statement; $150 will not be earned until the next reporting period and would be shown as a liability on the balance sheet.

We should emphasize two characteristics of adjusting entries. First, **_adjusting entries made at the end of an accounting period do not involve cash_**. Cash has either changed hands prior to the end of the period (as is the case with prepaid expenses or unearned revenues), or cash will change hands in a future period (as is the case with many unrecorded receivables and unrecorded liabilities). It is precisely because cash is _not_ changing hands on the last day of the accounting period that most adjusting entries must be made.

Second, **_each adjusting entry involves a balance sheet account and an income statement account_**. In each case requiring adjustment, we are either generating an asset, using up an asset, recording an incurred but unrecorded expense, or recording revenue that has yet to be earned. Knowing that each adjusting entry has at least one balance sheet and one income statement account makes the adjustment process a little easier. Once you have determined that an adjusting entry involves a certain balance sheet account, you can then focus on identifying the corresponding income statement account that requires adjustment.

The 2005 financial statements for **General Motors** offer several illustrations of the potential impact of failing to make adjusting entries. GM reports that, as of December 31, 2005, it had unearned revenue totaling $13.611 billion. If GM had failed to make the adjustment necessary to record this unearned revenue, total revenue for 2005 would have been overstated by $13.611 billion, or 7%. In addition, GM reported that its total warranty liability as of December 31, 2005, was $9.128 billion. This warranty liability falls in the category of unrecorded liabilities that are not reported in the financial statements unless an appropriate adjusting entry is made. Finally, GM also reported a $29.889 billion asset related to future tax deductions; this asset would remain unrecorded unless a special adjusting entry were made at the end of the year to reflect the future tax benefits of events that had occurred in 2005 and preceding years.

REMEMBER THIS...

Two-step analysis in making journal entries:

- determine what adjustments are necessary to ensure that all asset and liability amounts have been properly recorded, and
- determine which revenues or expenses must be adjusted to correspond with the changes in assets and liabilities recorded in step 1.

Unrecorded receivables

- Debit asset
- Credit revenue

Unrecorded liabilities

- Debit expense
- Credit liability

Prepaid expenses

- Debit expense
- Credit asset

Unearned revenues

- Debit liability
- Credit revenue

Preparing Financial Statements

Explain the preparation of the financial statements, the explanatory notes, and the audit report.

3 Once all transactions have been analyzed, journalized, and posted and all adjusting entries have been made, the accounts can be summarized and presented in the form of financial statements. Financial statements can be prepared directly from the data in the adjusted ledger accounts. The data must be organized into appropriate sections and categories so as to present them as simply and clearly as possible. The following process describes how the financial statements are prepared from the information taken from the trial balance:

1. Identify all revenues and expenses—these account balances are used to prepare the income statement.
2. Compute net income—subtract expenses from revenues.
3. Compute the ending retained earnings balance—this process was described in Chapter 2 and is illustrated here. Retained Earnings from the previous period is the starting point. Net income (computed in step 2) is added to the beginning retained earnings balance, and dividends for the period are subtracted.
4. Prepare a balance sheet using the balance sheet accounts from the trial balance and the modified retained earnings balance computed from step 3.

Note: No account on the trial balance shows up on both the income statement and the balance sheet.

CAUTION

Students often make the mistake of using the beginning retained earnings balance on the end-of-year balance sheet. As we shall see in the next section, the ending retained earnings balance is arrived at when the books are closed for the year.

Once the financial statements are prepared, explanatory notes are written. These notes clarify the methods and assumptions used in preparing the statements. In addition, the auditor must review the financial statements to make sure they are accurate, reasonable, and in accordance with generally accepted accounting principles. Finally, the financial statements are distributed to external users who analyze them in order to learn more about the financial condition of the company.

Financial Statement Preparation

To illustrate the preparation of financial statements from adjusted ledger accounts, a simplified adjusted trial balance for **General Motors** as of December 31, 2005, is provided in Exhibit 3.

From these data, an income statement and a balance sheet may be prepared for General Motors, as shown in Exhibits 4 and 5.

The ending retained earnings balance for General Motors for 2005 ($2,361), as reported on the balance sheet, is computed as follows:

Beginning retained earnings balance	$14,062
(from the adjusted trial balance)	
Add: Net income (loss) for the period	(10,567)
(from the income statement)	
Subtract: Dividends for the period	(1,134)
(from the adjusted trial balance)	
Ending retained earnings balance	$ 2,361

This follows the computation of retained earnings discussed in Chapter 2.

EXHIBIT 3   **Simplified Adjusted Trial Balance**

General Motors Corporation
Simplified Adjusted Trial Balance
December 31, 2005
(in millions)

	Debits	Credits
Cash	$ 30,726	
Investments	23,017	
Receivables	218,236	
Inventories	14,354	
Property and Equipment	78,401	
Intangible Assets	4,339	
Deferred Taxes	29,889	
Other Assets	77,116	
Accounts Payable		$ 29,913
Notes and Loans Payable		285,750
Pensions and Other Retirement Benefits		45,301
Accrued Expenses and Other Liabilities		99,478
Capital Stock and Other		17,267
Accumulated Other Comprehensive Loss	3,992	
Retained Earnings		14,062
Dividends	1,134	
Net Sales and Revenues		192,604
Cost of Sales and Other Expenses	170,547	
Selling, General and Administrative Expenses	22,734	
Interest Expense	15,768	
Income Tax (Benefit) Expense		5,878
Totals	$690,253	$690,253

EXHIBIT 4   **Income Statement**

General Motors Corporation
Statement of Income
For the Year Ended December 31, 2005
(in millions)

Net sales and revenues		$192,604
Cost of sales and other expenses	$170,547	
Selling, general and administrative expenses	22,734	
Total operating expenses		193,281
Operating income		$ (677)
Interest expense	$ 15,768	
Income tax (benefit) expense	(5,878)	
Total other expenses		9,890
Net loss		$ (10,567)

A statement of cash flows is not shown here. To prepare a statement of cash flows, we need more detailed information about the nature of the cash receipts and cash disbursements during the year. The preparation of a statement of cash flows will be illustrated in Chapter 13.

EXHIBIT 5	Balance Sheet

General Motors Corporation
Balance Sheet
December 31, 2005
(in millions)

Assets

Cash	$ 30,726	
Investments	23,017	
Receivables	218,236	
Inventories	14,354	
Total current assets		$286,333
Property and equipment	$ 78,401	
Intangible assets	4,339	
Deferred taxes	29,889	
Other assets	77,116	
Total long-term assets		189,745
Total assets		$476,078

Liabilities and Owners' Equity

Accounts payable	$ 29,913	
Accrued expenses and other liabilities	99,478	
Total current liabilities		$129,391
Notes and loans payable		285,750
Pensions and other retirement benefits		45,301
Total liabilities		$460,442
Owners' equity		
Capital stock and other	$ 17,267	
Accumulated other comprehensive loss	(3,992)	
Retained earnings	2,361	
Total owners' equity		15,636
Total liabilities and owners' equity		$476,078

Note: This balance sheet is not an exact replica of General Motors' actual balance sheet due to simplifying modifications for this exhibit.

The Notes

As discussed in Chapter 2, the notes to the financial statements tell about the assumptions and methods used in preparing the financial statements and also give more detail about specific items. A sample of the kind of information that appears in the notes for General Motors' financial statements is illustrated in Exhibit 6. The first note on revenue recognition illustrates how financial statement notes can summarize the accounting policies and assumptions that underlie the financial statements. The second note, on the debt associated with GM's financing subsidiary (GMAC), provides detailed information about a summary number that was reported in the financial statements. The third note, on GM's labor force, provides information that is deemed to be important to financial statement users, such as future labor costs, but that does not directly affect any of the reported historical financial statement numbers.

The financial statement notes serve to augment the summarized, numerical information contained in the financial statements. To highlight the importance of the notes, many financial statements have the following message printed at the bottom: "The notes are an integral part of these financial statements."

EXHIBIT 6 | **General Motors: Notes to the Financial Statements**

General Motors Corporation
Notes to the Financial Statements (partial list)
For the Year Ended December 31, 2005

Revenue Recognition: Sales generally are recorded when products are shipped . . . to independent dealers or other third parties.

Debt: For Automotive and Other Operations, long-term debt and loans payable were as follows (dollars in millions):

	Weighted-Average Interest Rate		December 31,	
	2005	2004	2005	2004
Long-term debt and loans payable				
Payable within one year:				
Current portion of long-term debt	5.8%	5.7%	$ 564	$ 584
All other	7.4%	3.0%	955	1,478
Total loans payable			$ 1,519	$ 2,062
Payable beyond one year	6.9%	6.8%	31,084	30,425
Unamortized discount			(97)	(103)
Mark to market adjustment			27	138
Total long-term debt			31,014	30,460
Total long-term debt and loans payable			$32,533	$32,522

Labor Force: GM, on a worldwide basis, has a concentration of its labor supply in employees working under union collective bargaining agreements, of which certain contracts expired in 2003.

The Audit

As mentioned in Chapter 2, an independent audit, by CPAs from outside the company, is often conducted to ensure that the financial statements have been prepared in conformity with generally accepted accounting principles. With respect to the financial statements of General Motors, the audit procedures conducted by the external auditor, **Deloitte & Touche**, would probably include the following checks.

Review of Adjustments   As you learned in the first part of this chapter, adjusting entries usually require more analysis, and more judgment, than do the regular journal entries recorded throughout the year. As part of the audit, the auditor will review these adjusting entries.

When conducting the audit of the financial statements, auditors are concerned that accounts are properly adjusted. Auditors are able to focus their efforts as illustrated in Exhibit 7. Companies usually are more concerned about and make sure that assets

---

EXHIBIT 7 | **How Auditors Spend Their Time**

	Too much recorded	Too little recorded
Assets	Auditors must critically scrutinize each recorded amount to ensure it does not overstate the asset's value.	Little worry for the auditor—companies themselves will work hard to make sure that assets are not understated.
Liabilities	Little worry for the auditor—companies themselves will work hard to make sure that liabilities are not overstated.	Auditors must search for unrecorded liabilities as a company might not work as hard in an effort to increase its own liabilities.

are not UNDERstated and that liabilities are not OVERstated. Auditors will make special effort to ensure that assets are not OVERstated and that liabilities are not UNDERstated.

Sample of Selected Accounts

For a number of accounts, the auditor undertakes a sampling process to see whether the items reported in the balance sheet actually exist. For example, General Motors reports an ending cash and equivalents balance of $30,726,000,000. The auditor will ask to see bank statements and will probably call the bank(s) to verify the existence of the cash. For inventory, the auditor will ask to physically see the inventory and will conduct a spot check to see whether the company inventory records match what is actually in the warehouse.

Review of Accounting Systems

The auditor will also evaluate General Motors' accounting systems. If a company has a good accounting system, with all transactions being recorded in an efficient, orderly way, then the auditor has greater reason to be confident that the financial statements are reliable. On the other hand, if the company's accounting system is haphazard, with many missing documents and unexplained discrepancies, then the auditor must do more detailed work to verify the financial statements.

If the auditor finds that the financial statements have been prepared in conformance with generally accepted accounting principles, then the auditor provides a report to that effect. This report is attached and distributed as part of the financial statements. The audit report is discussed in more detail in Chapter 5.

work sheet

A tool used by accountants to facilitate the preparation of financial statements.

Using a Work Sheet

A **work sheet** is a tool used by accountants to facilitate the preparation of financial statements. Unlike the financial statements, work sheets are for internal use only; they are not distributed to "outsiders." Although the use of work sheets is optional, most accountants find them helpful for organizing large quantities of data. Many work sheets are now prepared on electronic spreadsheets, using a software package such as Lotus 1-2-3, Excel, or Quattro Pro. Using a work sheet to assist in the preparation of financial statements is explained in detail on the text Web site at **http://www.thomsonedu.com/accounting/albrecht**.

Financial Statement Analysis

Financial statements are prepared so that they can be used. Once the balance sheet, income statement, and statement of cash flows of a company are completed, the whole package is distributed to bankers, suppliers, and investors to be used in evaluating the company's financial health.

Financial statement analysis involves the examination of both relationships among financial statements numbers and the trends in those numbers over time. One purpose of financial statement analysis is to use the past performance of a company to predict how well it will do in the future. Another purpose of financial statement analysis is to evaluate the performance of a company with an eye toward identifying problem areas. Financial statement analysis is both diagnosis, identifying where a firm has problems, and prognosis, predicting how a firm will perform in the future.

Relationships between financial statement amounts are called financial ratios. For example, net income divided by sales is a financial ratio called "return on sales." Return on sales tells you how many pennies of profit a company makes on each dollar of sales. There are hundreds of different financial ratios, each shedding light on a different aspect of the health of a company.

In subsequent chapters, we will introduce a variety of ratios that help financial statement users evaluate a company's financial health. In Chapter 14, we will provide a comprehensive overview of financial statement analysis.

REMEMBER THIS...

- The adjusted trial balance provides the raw material for the preparation of the balance sheet and the income statement. Accounts in the adjusted trial balance are reported in either the balance sheet or the income statement, but not both.
- The notes to the financial statements provide further information about the methods and assumptions used in preparing the financial statements as well as further detail about certain financial statement items.
- The audit is conducted by a CPA from outside the company who reviews the adjusting entries, performs tests to check the balances of selected accounts, and reviews the condition of the accounting systems.
- Financial statement analysis involves examining the relationship of financial statement numbers across time for the same company and across companies at the same point in time.

Closing the Books

Complete the closing process in the accounting cycle.

④ We have almost reached the end of the accounting cycle for a period. Thus far, the accounting cycle has included analyzing documents, journalizing transactions, posting to the ledger accounts, determining account balances, preparing a trial balance, making adjusting entries, and preparing the financial statements. Just two additional steps are needed: (1) journalizing and posting closing entries and (2) preparing a post-closing trial balance.

Real and Nominal Accounts

real accounts

Accounts that are not closed to a zero balance at the end of each accounting period; permanent accounts appearing on the balance sheet.

nominal accounts

Accounts that are closed to a zero balance at the end of each accounting period; temporary accounts generally appearing on the income statement.

To explain the closing process, we must first define two new terms. Certain accounts are referred to as **real accounts**. These accounts report the cumulative increases and decreases in certain account balances from the date the company was organized. Real accounts (assets, liabilities, and owners' equity) appear on the balance sheet and are permanent; they are not closed to a zero balance at the end of each accounting period. Balances existing in real accounts at the end of a period are carried forward to the next period.

Other accounts are known as **nominal accounts**. These accounts (revenues, expenses, and dividends) are temporary; they are really just subcategories of Retained Earnings and are reduced to a zero balance through the closing process at the end of each accounting period. Thus, nominal accounts begin with a zero balance at the start of each accounting cycle. Transactions throughout the period (generally a year) are journalized and posted to the nominal accounts. These are used to accumulate and classify all revenue and expense items, and also dividends, for that period. At the end of the accounting period, adjustments are made, the income statement is prepared, and the balances in the temporary accounts are then closed to Retained Earnings, a permanent account.

Closing entries bring the income statement accounts back to a zero balance, which makes the accounts ready for a new accounting period. In addition, the closing entries transfer the net income or loss for the accounting period to Retained Earnings and reduce Retained Earnings for any dividends. Without closing entries, revenue and expense balances would extend from period to period, making it difficult to isolate the operating results of each accounting period.

Closing Entries

Unlike adjusting entries, the actual mechanics of the closing process are not complicated. Revenue accounts normally have credit balances and are closed by being debited; expense accounts generally have debit balances and are closed by being credited. The difference between total revenues and total expenses represents the net income (or net loss) of the entity. For a corporation, net income is credited to Retained Earnings because income increases owners' equity. A net loss would be debited to Retained Earnings because a loss decreases owners' equity.

To illustrate the closing process, we will again refer to **General Motors**' financial information as discussed earlier on pages 143–146. The closing journal entry is:

Dec. 31	Net Sales and Revenues	192,604	
	Cost of Sales and Other Expenses		170,547
	Selling, General and Administrative Expenses		22,734
	Interest Expense		15,768
	Income Tax Expense	5,878	
	Retained Earnings	10,567	
	To close revenues and expenses to Retained Earnings.		

closing entries

Entries that reduce all nominal, or temporary, accounts to a zero balance at the end of each accounting period, transferring their preclosing balances to a permanent balance sheet account.

Closing entries must be posted to the appropriate ledger accounts. Once posted, all nominal accounts will have a zero balance; that is, they will be "closed."

The dividends account is also a nominal (temporary) account that must be closed at the end of the accounting period. However, dividends are not expenses and will not be reported on an income statement; they are distributions to stockholders of part of a corporation's earnings. Thus, dividends reduce retained earnings. When dividends are declared by the board of directors of a corporation, the amount that will be paid is debited to Dividends and credited to a liability account, Dividends Payable, or to Cash if paid immediately. Because Dividends is a temporary account, it must be closed to Retained Earnings at the end of the accounting period. The dividends account is closed by crediting it and by debiting Retained Earnings, thereby reducing owners' equity, as illustrated below for General Motors.

Dec. 31	Retained Earnings	1,134	
	Dividends		1,134
	To close Dividends to Retained Earnings.		

The books are now ready for a new accounting cycle. The closing process for the revenues, expenses, and dividends of a corporation is shown schematically in Exhibit 8.

Preparing a Post-Closing Trial Balance

An optional last step in the accounting cycle is to balance the accounts and to prepare a **post-closing trial balance** (see page 150 for definition). The accounts are to be

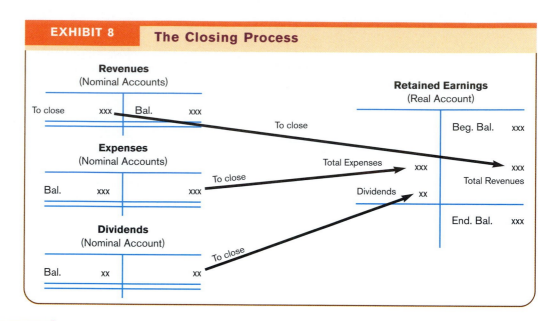

EXHIBIT 8   The Closing Process

---

balanced—debits and credits added and a balance determined—only after the closing entries have been recorded and posted in the general ledger. The information for the post-closing trial balance is then taken from the ledger. The nominal accounts will not be shown since they have been closed and thus have zero balances. Only the real accounts will have current balances. This step is for internal purposes only and is designed to provide some assurance that the previous steps in the cycle have been performed properly, prior to the start of a new accounting period. Exhibit 9 illustrates a post-closing trial balance for General Motors Corporation.

EXHIBIT 9   Post-Closing Trial Balance

General Motors Corporation
Post-Closing Trial Balance
December 31, 2005
(in millions)

	Debits	Credits
Cash	$ 30,726	
Investments	23,017	
Receivables	218,236	
Inventories	14,354	
Property and Equipment	78,401	
Intangible Assets	4,339	
Deferred Taxes	29,889	
Other Assets	77,116	
Accounts Payable		$ 29,913
Notes and Loans Payable		285,750
Pensions and Other Retirement Benefits		45,301
Accrued Expenses and Other Liabilities		99,478
Capital Stock and Other		17,267
Accumulated Other Comprehensive Loss	3,992	
Retained Earnings		2,361
Totals	$480,070	$480,070

REMEMBER THIS...

- Nominal (temporary) accounts = revenues, expenses, and dividends
- Real (permanent) accounts = assets, liabilities, and owners' equity
- Two objectives of closing entries:
  - Close all revenue, expense, and dividend accounts to zero in preparation for the start of a new period.
  - Transfer all revenue, expense, and dividend balances to Retained Earnings.

A Summary of the Accounting Cycle

Understand how all the steps in the accounting cycle fit together.

(5) We have now completed our discussion of the steps that are performed each period in the accounting cycle. By way of review, Exhibit 10 lists the sequence of the accounting cycle (presented earlier in Chapter 3). Many of the steps, such as analyzing transactions, occur continuously. Other steps, such as preparing the financial statements, generally occur only once during the cycle.

The financial statements that result from the accounting cycle provide useful information to investors, creditors, and other external users. These statements are included in the annual reports provided to stockholders. As illustrated earlier

EXHIBIT 10   Sequence of the Accounting Cycle

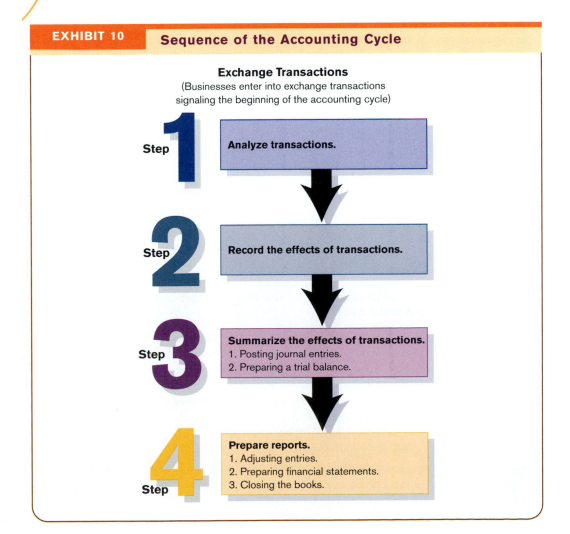

Exchange Transactions
(Businesses enter into exchange transactions
signaling the beginning of the accounting cycle)

Step **1** Analyze transactions.

Step **2** Record the effects of transactions.

Step **3** Summarize the effects of transactions.
1. Posting journal entries.
2. Preparing a trial balance.

Step **4** Prepare reports.
1. Adjusting entries.
2. Preparing financial statements.
3. Closing the books.

in the chapter, once the financial statements are made available to users, they can then be analyzed and compared to the financial statements of similar firms to detect strengths and weaknesses.

REMEMBER THIS...

The four steps in the accounting cycle are as follows:

1. Analyze transactions.
2. Record the effects of transactions.
3. Summarize the effects of transactions.
4. Prepare reports, with the following detailed steps as covered in this chapter.
   - Adjusting entries
   - Financial statements
   - Closing entries

REVIEW OF LEARNING OBJECTIVES

(1) Describe how accrual accounting allows for timely reporting and a better measure of a company's economic performance. Accrual-basis accounting means that:

- revenues are recognized as they are earned, not necessarily when cash is received;
- expenses are recognized as they are incurred, not necessarily when cash is paid.

Accrual-basis accounting provides a more accurate picture of a company's financial position and operating results than does cash-basis accounting.

(2) Explain the need for adjusting entries and make adjusting entries for unrecorded receivables, unrecorded liabilities, prepaid expenses, and unearned revenues.

Adjusting entry for	Debit	Credit
Unrecorded receivable	Asset	Revenue
Unrecorded liability	Expense	Liability
Prepaid expense	Expense	Asset
Unearned revenue	Liability	Revenue

(3) Explain the preparation of the financial statements, the explanatory notes, and the audit report.

- The adjusted trial balance provides the raw material for the preparation of the balance sheet and the income statement. Accounts in the adjusted trial balance are reported in either the balance sheet or the income statement, but not both.
- The notes to the financial statements provide further information about the methods and assumptions used in preparing the financial statements as well as further detail about certain financial statement items.
- The audit is conducted by a CPA from outside the company who:
  - reviews the adjusting entries,
  - performs tests to check the balances of selected accounts, and
  - reviews the condition of the accounting systems.

Financial statements are prepared to be used. Financial statement analysis exams relationships between financial numbers across companies at the same point in time and across time for the same company.

 Complete the closing process in the accounting cycle.

Closing entry for	Debit	Credit
Revenue	Revenue	Retained Earnings
Expense	Retained Earnings	Expense
Dividends	Retained Earnings	Dividends

Understand how all the steps in the accounting cycle fit together. The accounting cycle consists of specific steps to analyze, record, classify, summarize, and report the transactions of a business. The three detailed steps of "reporting" covered in this chapter are:

- making adjusting entries,
- preparing financial statements, and
- making closing entries.

KEY TERMS & CONCEPTS

accrual-basis
  accounting, 132
adjusting entries, 135
calendar year, 132
cash-basis
  accounting, 134

closing entries, 149
fiscal year, 132
matching principle, 133
nominal accounts, 148
post-closing trial
  balance, 150

prepaid expenses, 138
real accounts, 148
revenue recognition
  principle, 133
time-period
  concept, 132

unearned revenues, 140
unrecorded
  liabilities, 136
unrecorded
  receivables, 136
work sheet, 147

REVIEW PROBLEM

The Accounting Cycle

This review problem provides a useful summary of the entire accounting cycle. The following post-closing trial balance is for Sports Haven Company as of December 31, 2008.

Sports Haven Company Post-Closing Trial Balance December 31, 2008		
	Debits	**Credits**
Cash	$17,500	
Accounts Receivable	17,000	
Inventory	28,800	
Supplies on Hand	1,200	
Prepaid Building Rental	24,000	
Accounts Payable		$18,000
Capital Stock (3,600 shares outstanding)		54,000
Retained Earnings		16,500
Totals	$88,500	$88,500

(continued)

Following is a summary of the company's transactions for 2009.

a. At the beginning of 2009, the company issued 1,500 new shares of stock at $20 per share.
b. Total inventory purchases were $49,500; all purchases were made on credit and are recorded in the inventory account.
c. Total sales were $125,000; $102,900 were on credit, the rest were for cash. The cost of goods sold was $47,500; the inventory account is reduced at the time of each sale.
d. In December, a customer paid $3,500 cash in advance for merchandise that was temporarily out of stock. The advance payments received from customers are initially recorded as liabilities. The $3,500 is not included in the sales figures in (c) above.
e. The company paid $66,500 on accounts payable during the year.
f. The company collected $102,000 of accounts receivable during the year.
g. The company purchased $600 of supplies for cash during 2009, debiting Supplies on Hand.
h. The company paid $850 for advertising during the year, debiting Prepaid Advertising.
i. Total salaries paid during the year were $45,000.
j. The company paid $650 during the year for utilities.
k. Dividends of $7,500 were paid to stockholders in December.

On December 31, 2009, the company's accountant gathers the following information to adjust the accounts:

l. As of December 31, salaries of $750 had been earned by employees but will not be paid until January 3, 2010.
m. A count at December 31 shows $800 of supplies still on hand.
n. The prepaid advertising paid during 2009 includes $400 paid on December 1, 2009, for a series of radio advertisements to be broadcast throughout December 2009 and January 2010. The balance in the account, $450, represents advertisements that were broadcast during 2009.
o. On December 31, 2008, the company rented an office building for two years and paid $24,000 in cash (the full rental fee for 2009 and 2010). The payment was recorded with a debit to Prepaid Building Rental. No entries have been made for building rent in 2009.
p. On December 20, 2009, a bill for $150 was received for utilities. No entry was made to record the receipt of the bill, which is to be paid on January 4, 2010.
q. As of December 31, 2009, the merchandise paid for in advance [transaction (d)] was still out of stock. The company expects to receive the merchandise and fill the order by January 15, 2010.
r. The company's income is taxed at a rate of 15%.

Required:
1. Make entries in the general journal to record each of the transactions [items (a) through (k)].
2. Using T-accounts to represent the general ledger accounts, post the transactions recorded in the general journal. Enter the beginning balances in the accounts that appear in the December 31, 2008, post-closing trial balance before posting 2009 transactions. When all transactions have been posted to the T-accounts, determine the balance for each account.
3. Prepare a trial balance as of December 31, 2009.
4. Record adjusting entries [items (l) through (r)] in the general journal; post these entries to the general ledger (T-accounts).
5. Prepare an income statement and balance sheet for 2009.
6. Record closing entries [label (s) and (t)] in the general journal; post these entries to the general ledger (T-accounts).
7. Prepare a post-closing trial balance.

(continued)

Solution

1. Following are the journal entries to record the transactions for the year. Several of these are summary entries representing numerous individual transactions.

(a) Cash 30,000
      Capital Stock 30,000

The company issued additional shares of stock, so Capital Stock must be credited to reflect the increase in owners' equity. Since the company received cash of $30,000 (1,500 shares at $20 per share), Cash is also increased.

(b) Inventory 49,500
      Accounts Payable 49,500

The company purchased $49,500 of goods on credit. Inventory is increased (debited) for this amount. Accounts Payable is credited to show the increase in liabilities.

(c) Accounts Receivable 102,900
     Cash 22,100
      Sales Revenue 125,000

Total sales were $125,000, so Sales Revenue must be increased (credited) by that amount. Of this amount, $102,900 were on credit, and $22,100 were cash sales. We increase the asset accounts, Accounts Receivable and Cash, by debiting them.

(c) Cost of Goods Sold 47,500
      Inventory 47,500

The cost of the merchandise sold during the year was $47,500. Cost of Goods Sold (expense) must be increased (debited) by this amount. Since the goods were sold, Inventory (asset) must be reduced by a credit of $47,500.

(d) Cash 3,500
      Unearned Sales Revenue 3,500

Cash is debited (increased) by the amount received from the customer. The company recorded the advance payments for merchandise by crediting a liability account, Unearned Sales Revenue.

(e) Accounts Payable 66,500
      Cash 66,500

The company's payments on its accounts reduce the amount of its obligation to creditors, so Accounts Payable (liability) is debited to decrease it by the amount paid. Cash must also be decreased (credited).

(f) Cash 102,000
      Accounts Receivable 102,000

Since the company has collected some of its receivables from customers, Accounts Receivable is credited to show a decrease. Cash is increased (debited).

(g) Supplies on Hand 600
      Cash 600

The company purchased $600 of supplies. By debiting Supplies on Hand, an increase is shown in that asset account. Cash must be credited to show a decrease.

(h) Prepaid Advertising 850
      Cash 850

The company purchased $850 of advertising and chose to initially debit an asset account, Prepaid Advertising. Since cash was paid, it must be reduced by a credit.

(i) Salaries Expense 45,000
      Cash 45,000

(continued)

| (j) | Utilities Expense | 650 | |
| | Cash | | 650 |

For transactions (i) and (j), an expense account must be debited to show that expenses have been incurred. Cash must be credited (reduced).

| (k) | Dividends | 7,500 | |
| | Cash | | 7,500 |

Dividends must be debited to show a decrease in owners' equity resulting from a distribution of earnings. Cash must be reduced by a credit.

2. T-accounts with the beginning balances and journal entries posted are shown here. (Note that accounts with more than one entry must be "balanced" by drawing a rule and entering the debit or credit balance below it.)

Cash

Beg.		(e)	66,500
bal.	17,500	(g)	600
(a)	30,000	(h)	850
(c)	22,100	(i)	45,000
(d)	3,500	(j)	650
(f)	102,000	(k)	7,500
Updated			
bal.	54,000		

Accounts Receivable

Beg.		(f)	102,000
bal.	17,000		
(c)	102,900		
Updated			
bal.	17,900		

Inventory

Beg.		(c)	47,500
bal.	28,800		
(b)	49,500		
Updated			
bal.	30,800		

Supplies on Hand

Beg.			
bal.	1,200		
(g)	600		
Updated			
bal.	1,800		

Prepaid Building Rental

| Beg. | | | |
| bal. | 24,000 | | |

Prepaid Advertising

| (h) | 850 | | |

Accounts Payable

(e)	66,500	Beg.	
		bal.	18,000
		(b)	49,500
		Updated	
		bal.	1,000

Unearned Sales Revenue

| (d) | 3,500 | | |

Capital Stock

		Beg.	
		bal.	54,000
		(a)	30,000
		Updated	
		bal.	84,000

Retained Earnings

| | | Beg. | |
| | | bal. | 16,500 |

Dividends

| (k) | 7,500 | | |

Sales Revenue

| | | (c) | 125,000 |

Cost of Goods Sold

| (c) | 47,500 | | |

Salaries Expense

| (i) | 45,000 | | |

Utilities Expense

| (j) | 650 | | |

3. The balance of each account is entered in a trial balance. Each column in the trial balance is totaled to determine that total debits equal total credits.

(continued)

Sports Haven Company
Trial Balance
December 31, 2009

	Debits	Credits
Cash	$ 54,000	
Accounts Receivable	17,900	
Inventory	30,800	
Supplies on Hand	1,800	
Prepaid Building Rental	24,000	
Prepaid Advertising	850	
Accounts Payable		$ 1,000
Unearned Sales Revenue		3,500
Capital Stock		84,000
Retained Earnings		16,500
Dividends	7,500	
Sales Revenue		125,000
Cost of Goods Sold	47,500	
Salaries Expense	45,000	
Utilities Expense	650	
Totals	$230,000	$230,000

4. The adjusting entries for Sports Haven Company are presented in journal form and explained. Updated T-accounts are provided showing the posting of the adjusting entries.

(l)	Salaries Expense	750	
	Salaries Payable		750

As of December 31, there is an unrecorded liability and expense of $750 for salaries owed to employees. Because the salaries were earned in 2009, the liability and related expense must be recorded in 2009.

(m)	Supplies Expense	1,000	
	Supplies on Hand		1,000

Supplies on Hand (asset) has a debit balance before adjustment of $1,800 [beginning balance of $1,200 plus $600 of supplies purchased during the year, transaction (g)]. Since $800 of supplies are on hand at the end of the year, Supplies on Hand should be reduced (credited) by $1,000. Supplies Expense must be debited to show that $1,000 of supplies were used during the period.

(n)	Advertising Expense	650	
	Prepaid Advertising		650

Prepaid Advertising has a debit balance before adjustment of $850, the total amount paid for advertising during the year [transaction (h)]. This amount includes $400 that was paid for radio advertising throughout December 2009 and January 2010. Only that portion that applies to 2010 should be shown as Prepaid Advertising, $200 ($400 ÷ 2 months), since it is not an expense of the current year. The remainder, $650, is advertising expense for the period. Thus, the asset account, Prepaid Advertising, must be credited for $650, and Advertising Expense must be increased by a debit of $650.

(o)	Building Rent Expense	12,000	
	Prepaid Building Rental		12,000

The original entry at the end of 2008 was a debit to the asset account, Prepaid Building Rental, and a credit to Cash. An adjusting entry is needed to record rent expense of $12,000 for 2009 ($24,000 ÷ 2 years). The expense account must be debited and the asset account must be reduced by a credit. The remaining $12,000 in Prepaid Building Rental reflects the portion of the total payment for building rent expense in 2010.

(p)	Utilities Expense	150	
	Utilities Payable		150

(continued)

As of December 31, 2009, there is an unrecorded liability and expense of $150 for utilities. Because the expense was incurred in 2009, an adjusting entry is needed to record the liability and related expense.

(q)   No entry required.

The original entry to record the advance payment from a customer was made by crediting a liability [transaction (d)]. As of December 31, no revenue has been earned. The company still has an obligation to deliver goods or refund the advanced payment. Therefore, no adjustment is required, since the liability is already properly recorded.

(r)	Income Tax Expense	2,595	
	Income Taxes Payable		2,595

The remaining adjustment is for income taxes. The difference between total revenues and total expenses is the amount of income before taxes, $17,300. This amount is multiplied by the applicable tax rate of 15% to determine income taxes for the period. The expense account is debited to show the income taxes incurred for the year and the liability account is credited to show the obligation to the government.

Cash

Beg.		(e)	66,500
bal.	17,500	(g)	600
(a)	30,000	(h)	850
(c)	22,100	(i)	45,000
(d)	3,500	(j)	650
(f)	102,000	(k)	7,500
Updated			
bal.	54,000		

Accounts Receivable

Beg.		(f)	102,000
bal.	17,000		
(c)	102,900		
Updated			
bal.	17,900		

Inventory

Beg.		(c)	47,500
bal.	28,800		
(b)	49,500		
Updated			
bal.	30,800		

Supplies on Hand

Beg.		(m)	1,000
bal.	1,200		
(g)	600		
Updated			
bal.	800		

Prepaid Building Rental

Beg.		(o)	12,000
bal.	24,000		
Updated			
bal.	12,000		

Prepaid Advertising

(h)	850	(n)	650
Updated			
bal.	200		

Accounts Payable

(e)	66,500	Beg.	
		bal.	18,000
		(b)	49,500
		Updated	
		bal.	1,000

Salaries Payable

		(l)	750

Utilities Payable

		(p)	150

Income Taxes Payable

		(r)	2,595

Unearned Sales Revenue

		(d)	3,500

Capital Stock

		Beg.	
		bal.	54,000
		(a)	30,000
		Updated	
		bal.	84,000

(continued)

Retained Earnings		**Dividends**		**Sales Revenue**	
	Beg. bal. 16,500	(k) 7,500			(c) 125,000

Cost of Goods Sold		**Salaries Expense**		**Utilities Expense**	
(c) 47,500		(i) 45,000		(j) 650	
		(l) 750		(p) 150	
		Updated bal. 45,750		Updated bal. 800	

Advertising Expense		**Supplies Expense**		**Building Rent Expense**	
(n) 650		(m) 1,000		(o) 12,000	

Income Tax Expense	
(r) 2,595	

5. Data for the financial statements may be taken from the adjusted ledger accounts and reported as follows:

Sports Haven Company
Income Statement
For the Year Ended December 31, 2009

Sales revenue	$125,000	
Less cost of goods sold	47,500	
Gross profit		$77,500
Less operating expenses:		
Salaries expense	$ 45,750	
Utilities expense	800	
Advertising expense	650	
Supplies expense	1,000	
Building rent expense	12,000	60,200
Income before income taxes		$17,300
Income tax expense		2,595
Net income		$14,705

Earnings per share:
$14,705 ÷ 5,100 shares = $2.88 (rounded)

(continued)

Sports Haven Company
Balance Sheet
December 31, 2009

Assets

Cash	$54,000	
Accounts receivable	17,900	
Inventory	30,800	
Supplies on hand	800	
Prepaid building rental	12,000	
Prepaid advertising	200	
Total assets		$115,700

Liabilities and Owners' Equity

Liabilities:

Accounts payable	$ 1,000	
Salaries payable	750	
Utilities payable	150	
Income taxes payable	2,595	
Unearned sales revenue	3,500	
Total liabilities		$ 7,995
Owners' equity:		
Capital stock (5,100 shares outstanding)	$84,000	
Retained earnings	23,705*	
Total owners' equity		107,705
Total liabilities and owners' equity		$115,700

*Note that in preparing the balance sheet, net income must be added to the beginning balance in Retained Earnings and dividends must be subtracted ($16,500 + $14,705 − $7,500 = $23,705).

6. The next step is to record the closing entries in the general journal and then post those entries to the general ledger (T-accounts). T-accounts are shown with all previous entries and the closing entries [items (s) and (t)] posted.

     The first entry is to close the revenue account and each of the expense accounts. Sales Revenue has a credit balance; it is debited to reduce the balance to zero. The expense accounts are closed by crediting them. The difference in total revenues and total expenses is $14,705 (net income for the period). Net income represents an increase in retained earnings. All of this is captured in the single, compound closing entry(s), as follows:

(s)	Sales Revenue	125,000	
	Cost of Goods Sold		47,500
	Salaries Expense		45,750
	Utilities Expense		800
	Advertising Expense		650
	Supplies Expense		1,000
	Building Rent Expense		12,000
	Income Tax Expense		2,595
	Retained Earnings		14,705

Second, Dividends, a nominal account, must also be closed to Retained Earnings.

(t)	Retained Earnings	7,500	
	Dividends		7,500

(continued)

Cash			
Beg.		(e)	66,500
bal.	17,500	(g)	600
(a)	30,000	(h)	850
(c)	22,100	(i)	45,000
(d)	3,500	(j)	650
(f)	102,000	(k)	7,500
Updated			
Bal.	54,000		

Accounts Receivable			
Beg.		(f)	102,000
bal.	17,000		
(c)	102,900		
Updated			
bal.	17,900		

Inventory			
Beg.		(c)	47,500
bal.	28,800		
(b)	49,500		
Updated			
bal.	30,800		

Supplies on Hand			
Beg.		(m)	1,000
bal.	1,200		
(g)	600		
Updated			
bal.	800		

Prepaid Building Rental			
Beg.		(o)	12,000
bal.	24,000		
Updated			
bal.	12,000		

Prepaid Advertising			
(h)	850	(n)	650
Updated			
bal.	200		

Accounts Payable			
(e)	66,500	Beg.	
		bal.	18,000
		(b)	49,500
		Updated	
		bal.	1,000

Salaries Payable		
	(l)	750

Utilities Payable		
	(p)	150

Income Taxes Payable		
	(r)	2,595

Unearned Sales Revenue		
	(d)	3,500

Capital Stock			
		Beg.	
		bal.	54,000
		(a)	30,000
		Updated	
		bal.	84,000

Retained Earnings			
(t)	7,500	Beg.	
		bal.	16,500
		(s)	14,705
		Updated	
		bal.	23,705

Dividends			
(k)	7,500	(t)	7,500

Sales Revenue			
(s)	125,000	(c)	125,000

Cost of Goods Sold			
(c)	47,500	(s)	47,500

Salaries Expense			
(i)	45,000	(s)	45,750
(l)	750		

Utilities Expense			
(j)	650	(s)	800
(p)	150		

Advertising Expense			
(n)	650	(s)	650

Supplies Expense			
(m)	1,000	(s)	1,000

Building Rent Expense			
(o)	12,000	(s)	12,000

Income Tax Expense			
(r)	2,595	(s)	2,595

(continued)

7. The final (optional) step in the accounting cycle is to prepare a post-closing trial balance. This procedure is a check on the accuracy of the closing process. It is a listing of all ledger account balances at year-end. Note that only real accounts appear because all nominal accounts have been closed to a zero balance in preparation for the next accounting cycle.

Sports Haven Company
Post-Closing Trial Balance
December 31, 2009

	Debits	Credits
Cash	$ 54,000	
Accounts Receivable	17,900	
Inventory	30,800	
Supplies on Hand	800	
Prepaid Building Rental	12,000	
Prepaid Advertising	200	
Accounts Payable		$ 1,000
Salaries Payable		750
Utilities Payable		150
Income Taxes Payable		2,595
Unearned Sales Revenue		3,500
Capital Stock		84,000
Retained Earnings		23,705
Totals	$115,700	$115,700

DISCUSSION QUESTIONS

1. Why are financial reports prepared on a periodic basis?
2. Distinguish between reporting on a calendar-year and on a fiscal-year basis.
3. When are revenues generally recognized (recorded)?
4. What is the matching principle?
5. Explain why accrual-basis accounting is more appropriate than cash-basis accounting for most businesses.
6. Why are accrual-based financial statements considered somewhat tentative?
7. Why are adjusting entries necessary?
8. Since there are usually no source documents for adjusting entries, how does the accountant know when to make adjusting entries and for what amounts?
9. The analysis process for preparing adjusting entries involves two basic steps. Identify the two steps and explain why both are necessary.

10. Why are supplies not considered inventory? What type of account is Supplies on Hand?
11. Cash is not one of the accounts increased or decreased in an adjusting entry. Why?
12. Which are prepared first: the year-end financial statements or the general journal adjusting entries? Explain.
13. Of what value are the notes to the financial statements and the audit report, both of which are usually included in the annual report to shareholders?
14. Distinguish between real and nominal accounts.
15. What is the purpose of closing entries?
16. What is the purpose of the post-closing trial balance? Explain where the information for the post-closing trial balance comes from.

PRACTICE EXERCISES

PE 4-1
LO1

Periodic Reporting

Which one of the following statements is true with respect to periodic reporting?
a. All companies in the United States are required to have a fiscal year that ends on December 31.
b. The issuance of frequent periodic financial reports reduces the need for accountants to make estimates and judgments.
c. In the United States, only large businesses (those with total assets in excess of $650 million) prepare periodic financial statements.
d. Some financial reports may be prepared on a daily basis.
e. The Securities and Exchange Commission (SEC) requires all publicly-traded companies in the United States to file monthly financial statements.

PE 4-2
LO1

Revenue Recognition

In which one of the following situations should revenue be recognized?
a. The earnings process has begun and cash collectibility is reasonably assured.
b. The earnings process has begun and cash has been collected.
c. The earnings process is substantially complete and cash collectibility is not yet reasonably assured.
d. The earnings process will soon begin and cash has been collected.
e. The earnings process is substantially complete and cash collectibility is reasonably assured.

PE 4-3
LO1

Matching

Select the one phrase below that best completes the following statement: According to the matching principle, . . .
a. The amount of cash collected should be matched and recognized in the same period as the related revenue.
b. Expenses should be matched and recognized in the same period as the related revenue.
c. The amount of cash collected should be matched and recognized in the same period as the related expense.
d. Revenue should be matched and recognized in the same period as the related cash collection.
e. Expenses should be matched and recognized in the same period as the related shareholder investment.

PE 4-4
LO1

Cash-Basis Accounting

A lawn care company started business on January 1, 2009. The company billed clients $85,000 for lawn care services completed in 2009. By December 31, the company had received $61,000 cash from the customers, with the $24,000 balance expected to be collected in 2010. During 2009, the company paid $58,000 cash for various expenses. At December 31, the company still owed $29,000 for additional expenses incurred which have not yet been paid in cash. These expenses will be paid during January 2010. How much income should the company report for 2009? Note: The company computes income using cash-basis accounting.

PE 4-5
LO1

Accrual-Basis Accounting

Refer to PE 4-4. Compute income for 2009 assuming that the company uses accrual-basis accounting.

PE 4-6
LO2

Unrecorded Receivable: Original Entry

Greg operates a sizeable newspaper delivery service. On the last day of each month, Greg receives a statement from the newspaper publisher detailing how much money Greg earned

(continued)

that month from delivering papers. On the 10th day of the following month, Greg receives the cash for the preceding month's deliveries. On December 10, Greg received $12,300 cash for deliveries made in November. Make the journal entry necessary on Greg's books on December 10 to record the receipt of this cash, assuming that Greg did not make any adjusting entry as of the end of November.

PE 4-7
LO2
Unrecorded Receivable: Adjusting Entry
Refer to PE 4-6. On December 31, Greg received a statement from the newspaper publisher notifying him that he had earned $13,700 for his December deliveries. Because December 31 is the end of Greg's fiscal year, he makes adjusting entries at that time. (1) Make the adjusting journal entry necessary on Greg's books on December 31 to record the $13,700 in delivery revenue earned during December and (2) make the journal entry necessary on Greg's books on January 10 to record the receipt of the $13,700 in cash. Note: When making the January 10 entry, don't forget the adjusting entry that was made on December 31.

PE 4-8
LO2
Unrecorded Liability: Original Entry
On May 1, the company borrowed $75,000 from Bank of Salt Lake. The loan is for five years and bears an annual interest rate of 9%. Interest on the loan is to be paid in cash each year on April 30; the $75,000 loan amount is to be repaid in full after five years. Make the journal entry necessary on the company's books to record the receipt of this loan on May 1.

PE 4-9
LO2
Unrecorded Liability: Adjusting Entry
Refer to PE 4-8. (1) Make the adjusting entry necessary on the company's books with respect to this loan on December 31. (2) Make the journal entry necessary on the company's books on the following April 30 to record payment of interest for the first year of the loan. Note: When making this April 30 entry, don't forget the adjusting entry that was made on December 31.

PE 4-10
LO2
Prepaid Expense: Original Entry
On August 1, the company paid $72,000 cash for a four-year insurance policy. The policy went into effect on August 1. Make the journal entry necessary on the company's books to record the payment for the insurance on August 1.

PE 4-11
LO2
Prepaid Expense: Adjusting Entry
Refer to PE 4-10. (1) Make the adjusting entry necessary on the company's books on December 31 with respect to this insurance policy and (2) compute the ending balance in the prepaid insurance account; assume that the balance as of the beginning of the year was $0.

PE 4-12
LO2
Unearned Revenue: Original Entry
The company provides security services to its clients. On April 1, the company received $270,000 cash for a three-year security contract. The contract went into effect on April 1. Make the journal entry necessary on the company's books to record the receipt of the payment for the contract on April 1.

PE 4-13
LO2
Unearned Revenue: Adjusting Entry
Refer to PE 4-12. (1) Make the adjusting entry necessary on the company's books on December 31 with respect to this security contract and (2) compute the ending balance in the unearned security revenue account; assume that the balance as of the beginning of the year was $0.

PE 4-14
LO2
Wages Payable: Adjusting Entry and Subsequent Payment
The company pays its employees at the end of the day Friday for work done during that five-day work week. Total wages for a week are $24,000. In the current year, December 31 occurred on a Tuesday. (1) Make the adjusting entry necessary on the company's books on December 31 with respect to unpaid employee wages and (2) make the journal entry necessary on Friday, January 3, of the following year to record the cash payment of wages for the

(continued)

week. Ignore the new year's holiday season and assume that employees worked each of the five days. Note: When making the January 3 entry, don't forget the adjusting entry that was made on December 31.

PE 4-15
LO2

Supplies: Original Purchase and Adjusting Entry

On January 1, the company had office supplies costing $4,600. On March 23, the company bought additional office supplies costing $8,200; the company paid cash. On December 31, a physical count of office supplies revealed that supplies costing $2,900 remained. (1) Make the journal entry necessary on the company's books on March 23 to record the purchase of office supplies and (2) make the adjusting entry necessary on December 31 with respect to office supplies.

PE 4-16
LO3

Preparing an Adjusted Trial Balance

Before any adjusting entries were made, the company prepared the following trial balance as of December 31:

	Debit	Credit
Cash	$ 68,000	
Notes Receivable	126,000	
Prepaid Rent	216,000	
Building	290,000	
Accounts Payable		$ 150,000
Unearned Fee Revenue		270,000
Capital Stock		150,000
Retained Earnings		100,000
Dividends	17,000	
Fee Revenue		370,000
Wages Expense	244,000	
Utilities Expense	79,000	
Totals	$1,040,000	$1,040,000

In order to make the adjusting entries, the following information has been assembled:

a. The notes receivable were issued on June 1. The annual interest rate on the notes is 12%. Interest is to be received each year on May 31; accordingly, no interest has been received.

b. The unearned fee revenue represents cash received in advance on February 1. This $270,000 relates to a three-year contract which began on February 1. It is expected that the fees will be earned evenly over the three-year contract period. As of December 31, no revenue had yet been recognized on this contract.

c. The prepaid rent represents cash paid in advance on October 1. This $216,000 relates to a five-year rental agreement that began on October 1. As of December 31, no expense had yet been recognized in association with this rental agreement.

d. As of December 31, unpaid (and unrecorded) wages totaled $22,000.

(1) Prepare the necessary adjusting journal entries and (2) prepare an adjusted trial balance.

PE 4-17
LO3

Using an Adjusted Trial Balance to Prepare an Income Statement

Refer to PE 4-16. Using the adjusted trial balance prepared in part (2), prepare an income statement for the year.

PE 4-18
LO3

Using an Adjusted Trial Balance to Prepare a Balance Sheet

Refer to PE 4-16. Using the adjusted trial balance prepared in part (2), prepare a balance sheet as of the end of the year. Note: The ending retained earnings balance is equal to the beginning balance plus the amount of net income less the amount of dividends.

PE 4-19

LO3

Adjusting Entries and the Audit

Consider the auditor's review of a company's adjusting entries. For which one of the following would a concerned auditor be required to make a search of items not included in the accounting records?

a. Overstated assets
b. Overstated liabilities
c. Understated assets
d. Understated liabilities

PE 4-20

LO4

Closing Entries: Revenues

Below is a list of accounts with corresponding ending balances.

	Account	Account Balance
a.	Prepaid Insurance	$3,200
b.	Cash	1,650
c.	Sales Revenue	5,500
d.	Retained Earnings	4,100
e.	Accounts Payable	2,300
f.	Capital Stock	1,000
g.	Interest Revenue	100

Prepare one summary entry to close those accounts that should be closed at the end of the year.

PE 4-21

LO4

Closing Entries: Expenses

Below is a list of accounts with corresponding ending balances.

	Account	Account Balance
a.	Insurance Expense	$1,300
b.	Cash	750
c.	Accounts Receivable	4,000
d.	Cost of Goods Sold	2,300
e.	Interest Payable	1,500
f.	Building	450
g.	Interest Receivable	200

Prepare one summary entry to close those accounts that should be closed at the end of the year.

PE 4-22

LO4

Closing Entries: Everything

Below is a list of accounts with corresponding ending balances.

	Account	Account Balance
a.	Inventory	$1,800
b.	Dividends	900
c.	Sales Revenue	7,900
d.	Wages Expense	5,100
e.	Cash	1,900
f.	Cost of Goods Sold	3,200
g.	Rent Revenue	800
h.	Retained Earnings (beginning)	1,300

(1) Prepare all entries necessary to close those accounts that should be closed at the end of the year and (2) compute the ending balance in the retained earnings account.

PE 4-23

LO4

Post-Closing Trial Balance

Refer to PE 4-16. Prepare a post-closing trial balance. For this exercise, ignore the adjustments described in PE 4-16; just use the reported trial balance.

EXERCISES

E 4-24
LO1

Reporting Income: Cash versus Accrual Accounting

On December 31, 2009, Matt Morgan completed the first year of operations for his new computer retail store. The following data were obtained from the company's accounting records:

Sales to customers	$197,000
Collections from customers	145,000
Interest earned and received on savings accounts	2,500
Cost of goods sold	98,500
Amounts paid to suppliers for inventory	103,000
Wages owed to employees at year-end	3,500
Wages paid to employees	40,000
Utility bill owed: to be paid next month	1,100
Interest due at 12/31 on loan to be paid in March of next year	1,200
Amount paid for one and one-half years' rent, beginning Jan. 1, 2009	17,500
Income taxes owed at year-end	4,000

1. How much net income (loss) should Matt report for the year ended December 31, 2009, according to (a) cash-basis accounting and (b) accrual-basis accounting?
2. Which basis of accounting provides the better measure of operating results for Matt?

E 4-25
LO1

Reporting Income: Cash versus Accrual Accounting

On December 31, Daniel McGrath completed the first year of operations for his new business. The following data are available from the company's accounting records:

Sales to customers	$265,000
Collections from customers	185,000
Interest earned and received on savings accounts	1,100
Amount paid on January 1 for one and one-half years' rent	18,000
Utility bill owed: to be paid next month	1,350
Cost of goods sold	123,000
Amount paid to suppliers for materials	104,500
Wages paid to employees	71,000
Wages owed to employees at year-end	3,500
Interest due at 12/31 on a loan to be paid the middle of next year	950

1. How much net income (loss) should Daniel report for the year ended December 31 according to (a) cash-basis accounting and (b) accrual-basis accounting?
2. Which basis of accounting provides the better measure of operating results for Daniel?

E 4-26
LO2

Classifications of Accounts Requiring Adjusting Entries

For each type of adjustment listed, indicate whether it is an unrecorded receivable, an unrecorded liability, an unearned revenue, or a prepaid expense at December 31, 2009.
1. Property taxes that are for the year 2009, but are not to be paid until 2010.
2. Rent revenue earned during 2009, but not collected until 2010.
3. Salaries earned by employees in December 2009, but not to be paid until January 5, 2010.
4. A payment received from a customer in December 2009 for services that will not be performed until February 2010.
5. An insurance premium paid on December 29, 2009, for the period January 1, 2010, to December 31, 2010.
6. Gasoline charged on a credit card during December 2009. The bill will not be received until January 15, 2010.
7. Interest on a certificate of deposit held during 2009. The interest will not be received until January 7, 2010.
8. A deposit received on December 15, 2009, for rental of storage space. The rental period is from January 1, 2010, to December 31, 2010.

E 4-27   **Adjusting Entries: Prepaid Expenses and Unearned Revenues**

LO2   Kearl Associates is a professional corporation providing management consulting services. The company initially debits assets in recording prepaid expenses and credits liabilities in recording unearned revenues. Give the entry that Kearl would use to record each of the following transactions on the date it occurred. Prepare the adjusting entries needed on December 31, 2009.

1. On July 1, 2009, the company paid a three-year premium of $5,400 on an insurance policy that is effective July 1, 2009, and expires June 30, 2012.
2. On February 1, 2009, Kearl paid its property taxes for the year February 1, 2009, to January 31, 2010. The tax bill was $2,400.
3. On May 1, 2009, the company paid $360 for a three-year subscription to an advertising journal. The subscription starts May 1, 2009, and expires April 30, 2012.
4. Kearl received $3,600 on September 15, 2009, in return for which the company agreed to provide consulting services for 18 months beginning immediately.
5. Kearl rented part of its office space to Davis Realty. Davis paid $900 on November 1, 2009, for the next six months' rent.
6. Kearl loaned $80,000 to a client. On November 1, the client paid $14,400, which represents two years' interest in advance (November 1, 2009, through October 31, 2011).

E 4-28   **Adjusting Entries: Prepaid Expenses and Unearned Revenues**

LO2   Erickson Group provides computer network consulting services. The company initially debits assets in recording prepaid expenses and credits liabilities in recording unearned revenues. Give the appropriate entry that Erickson would use to record each of the following transactions on the date it occurred. Prepare the adjusting entries needed on December 31, 2009. (Round all numbers to the nearest dollar.)

1. On March 15, 2009, Erickson received $35,000 for a contract to provide consulting services for 18 months beginning immediately.
2. On April 1, 2009, the company paid $350 for a two-year subscription to a computer networking journal. The subscription starts April 1, 2009, and expires March 31, 2011.
3. On May 1, 2009, Erickson paid $4,500 in property taxes for the year May 1, 2009, to April 30, 2010.
4. Erickson rented part of its office building to Boss Graphics, LLC. Boss paid $1,900 on August 1, 2009, for the next six months' rent.
5. On September 1, 2009, the company paid a two-year premium of $20,000 on an insurance policy that is effective September 1, 2009, and expires August 31, 2011.
6. Erickson loaned $250,000 to a client. On October 1, 2009, the client paid $21,000 for interest in advance (October 1, 2009, to September 30, 2010).

E 4-29   **Adjusting Entries**

LO2

Shop Rite Services is ready to prepare its financial statements for the year ended December 31, 2009. The following information can be determined by analyzing the accounts:

1. On August 1, 2009, Shop Rite received a $4,800 payment in advance for rental of office space. The rental period is for one year beginning on the date payment was received. Shop Rite recorded the receipt as unearned rent.
2. On March 1, 2009, Shop Rite paid its insurance agent $3,000 for the premium due on a 24-month corporate policy. Shop Rite recorded the payment as prepaid insurance.
3. Shop Rite pays its employee wages the middle of each month. The monthly payroll (ignoring payroll taxes) is $22,000.
4. Shop Rite received a note from a customer on June 1, 2009, as payment for services. The amount of the note is $1,000 with interest at 12%. The note and interest will be paid on June 1, 2011.
5. On December 20, 2009, Shop Rite received a $2,500 check for services. The transaction was recorded as unearned revenue. By year-end, Shop Rite had completed three-fourths

(continued)

of the contracted services. The rest of the services won't be completed until at least the middle of January 2010.

6. On September 1, Shop Rite purchased $500 worth of supplies. At December 31, 2009, one-fourth of the supplies had been used. Shop Rite initially recorded the purchase of supplies as an asset.

Where appropriate, prepare adjusting journal entries at December 31, 2009, for each of these items.

E 4-30
LO2

Adjusting Entries

Consider the following two independent situations:

1. On June 1, Hatch Company received $3,600 cash for a two-year subscription to its monthly magazine. The term of the subscription begins on June 1. Make the entry to record the receipt of the subscription on June 1. Also make the necessary adjusting entry at December 31. The company uses an account called Unearned Subscription Revenue.

2. Clark Company pays its employees every Friday for a five-day workweek. Salaries of $150,000 are earned equally throughout the week. December 31 of the current year is a Tuesday.
   a. Make the adjusting entry at December 31.
   b. Make the entry to pay the week's salaries on Friday, January 3, of the next year. Assume that all employees are paid for New Year's Day.

E 4-31
LO2

Adjusting Entries

Consider the following items for Williams Company:

1. On July 1 of the current year, Williams Company borrowed $300,000 at 9% interest. As of December 31, no interest expense has been recognized.

2. On September 1 of the current year, Williams Company rented to another company some excess space in one of its buildings. Williams Company received $24,000 cash on September 1. The rental period extends for six months, starting on September 1. Williams Company credited the account Unearned Rent Revenue upon receipt of the rent paid in advance.

3. At the beginning of the year, Williams Company had $750 of supplies on hand. During the year, another $3,900 of supplies were purchased for cash and recorded in the asset account Office Supplies. At the end of the year, Williams Company determined that $980 of supplies remained on hand.

4. On February 1 of the current year, Williams Company loaned Botts Company $125,000 at 8% interest. The loan amount, plus accrued interest, will be repaid in one year.

For each of the items, make the appropriate adjusting journal entry, if any, necessary in Williams Company's books as of December 31.

E 4-32
LO2

Adjusting Entries

Davis Company opened a Web page design business on January 1 of the current year. The following information relates to Davis Company's operations during the current year:

1. On February 1, Davis Company rented a new office. Before moving in, it prepaid a year's rent of $24,000 cash.

2. On March 31, Davis Company borrowed $50,000 from a local bank at 15%. The loan is to be repaid, with interest, after one year. As of December 31, no interest payments had yet been made.

3. Davis Company bills some of its customers in advance for its design services. During the year, Davis received $60,000 cash in advance from its customers. As of December 31, Davis's accountant determined that 40% of that amount had not yet been earned.

(continued)

4. On June 15, Davis Company purchased $1,400 of supplies for cash. On September 14, Davis made another cash purchase of $1,100. As of December 31, Davis's accountant determined that $1,700 of supplies had been used during the year.

5. Before closing its books, Davis Company found a bill for $800 from a free-lance programmer who had done work for the company in November. Davis had not yet recorded anything in its books with respect to this bill. Davis plans to pay the bill in January of next year.

For each of the items, make the initial entry, where appropriate, to record the transaction and, if necessary, the adjusting entry at December 31.

E 4-33
LO2

Adjusting Entries

Wallin Enterprises disclosed the following information on December 31, 2009 (before any adjusting entries were made):

1. In June, Wallin purchased an insurance premium for $54,000 for the 18 months beginning July 1, 2009.

2. On November 1, Wallin received $12,000 from Judy Phan for six months of rent beginning on November 1.

3. On February 1, Wallin borrowed $50,000 at 10% interest. Wallin has not recognized any interest expense this year.

4. On October 1, Wallin loaned Chris Spiker $15,000 at 12% interest. No interest revenue has been collected or recorded.

For each item listed, prepare the necessary adjusting entries to be made on December 31, 2009.

E 4-34
LO2

Adjusting Entries

Consider the following information related to the Timmy Thompson Company:

1. At the beginning of the year, the company had $460 in supplies on hand. During the year, the company purchased $5,300 in supplies. At the end of the year, the company had $1,320 in supplies on hand.

2. The company pays its employees on the 15th of each month. The monthly payroll (ignoring payroll taxes) is $19,000.

3. On November 1, the company received a $10,000 check for services. The transaction was recorded as unearned revenue. By year-end, the Timmy Thompson Company had completed one-fourth of the required work related to this service. Timmy expects to complete the rest of the work within the first two months of the next year.

4. On December 15, Timmy paid $4,800 for factory rental related to January of the next year.

For each item listed, prepare the necessary adjusting entries to be made on December 31.

E 4-35
LO2

Adjusting Entries

Consider the following information related to Pendleton Consulting:

1. On October 1, 2009, Pendleton Consulting entered into an agreement to provide consulting services for six months to Soelberg Company. Soelberg agreed to pay Pendleton $750 for each month of service. Payment will be made at the end of the contract (March 31, 2010).

2. On April 30, Pendleton borrowed $40,000 from a local bank at 12%. The loan is to be repaid, with interest, after one year. As of December 31, no interest expense had been recognized.

3. On February 25, Pendleton paid $36,000 for 12 months of rent beginning on March 1. On February 25, Pendleton made a journal entry debiting Prepaid Rent Expense.

(continued)

4. At the beginning of 2009, Pendleton had $825 in supplies on hand. During 2009, Pendleton purchased $7,290 in supplies. On December 31, 2009, Pendleton had $1,035 in supplies on hand.

For each item listed, prepare the necessary adjusting entries to be made on December 31, 2009.

E 4-36
LO2

Analysis of Accounts

Answer the following questions:

1. If office supplies on hand amounted to $3,500 at the beginning of the period and total purchases of office supplies during the period amounted to $18,000, determine the ending balance of office supplies on hand if office supplies expense for the period amounted to $19,500.

2. If beginning and ending accounts receivable were $22,000 and $26,000, respectively, and total sales made on account for the period amounted to $73,000, determine the amount of cash collections from customers on account for the period.

3. Assume all rent revenues are received in advance and accounted for as unearned rent, and beginning and ending balances of unearned rent are $4,000 and $4,500, respectively. If total rent revenue for the period amounts to $18,000, determine the amount of rent collections in advance for the period.

E 4-37
LO3

Classifying Account Balances

For each of the following accounts, indicate whether it would be found in the income statement or in the balance sheet.

1. Cash	10. Interest Receivable	19. Sales Revenue
2. Inventory	11. Capital Stock	20. Insurance Expense
3. Salaries Expense	12. Accounts Payable	21. Machinery
4. Prepaid Salaries	13. Buildings	22. Land
5. Retained Earnings	14. Mortgage Payable	23. Salaries Payable
6. Office Supplies Expense	15. Interest Expense	24. Prepaid Insurance
7. Accounts Receivable	16. Accounts Payable	25. Notes Payable
8. Cost of Goods Sold	17. Notes Receivable	26. Dividends
9. Maintenance Expense	18. Office Supplies	

E 4-38
LO4

Real and Nominal Accounts

Classify each of the following accounts as either a real account (R) or a nominal account (N):

1. Cash	14. Prepaid Salaries
2. Sales Revenue	15. Utilities Expense
3. Accounts Receivable	16. Notes Payable
4. Cost of Goods Sold	17. Inventory
5. Prepaid Insurance	18. Property Tax Expense
6. Capital Stock	19. Rent Expense
7. Retained Earnings	20. Interest Payable
8. Insurance Expense	21. Income Taxes Payable
9. Salaries Payable	22. Dividends
10. Interest Expense	23. Buildings
11. Insurance Premiums Payable	24. Office Supplies
12. Salaries Expense	25. Income Tax Expense
13. Accounts Payable	

E 4-39

LO4

Closing Entry

The income statement for Roberts Enterprises for the year ended June 30, 2009, is provided.

Roberts Enterprises	
Income Statement	
For the Year Ended June 30, 2009	
Sales revenue	$ 263,000
Cost of goods sold	(148,000)
Selling and general expenses	(21,300)
Income before income taxes	$ 93,700
Income tax expense	(33,000)
Net income	$ 60,700

1. Prepare a journal entry to close the accounts to Retained Earnings.
2. What problem may arise in closing the accounts if the information from the income statement is used?

E 4-40

LO4

Closing Entry

Revenue and expense accounts of Reschke Training Services for November 30, 2009, are given as follows. Prepare a compound journal entry that will close the revenue and expense accounts to the retained earnings account.

	Debit	Credit
Sales Revenue		$372,000
Cost of Goods Sold	$189,500	
Salaries Expense	42,000	
Interest Expense	2,500	
Rent Expense	12,600	
Insurance Expense	2,800	
Property Tax Expense	900	
Supplies Expense	1,600	
Advertising Expense	13,000	

E 4-41

LO4

Closing Entries

Johstoneaux, Inc. reports the following numbers for 2009:

Johstoneaux, Inc.	
Income Statement	
For the Year Ended December 31, 2009	
Sales	$ 420,300
Cost of goods sold	(230,000)
Insurance expense	(3,000)
Selling and administrative expenses	(90,000)
Income before taxes	$ 97,300
Income tax expense	(30,100)
Net income	$ 67,200

Prepare journal entries to close the revenue and expense accounts to the retained earnings account.

E 4-42 **Closing Entries**

LO4 The following information relates to the Wycherly Company:

Wycherly Company	
Income Statement	
For the Year Ended December 31, 2009	
Sales revenue	$ 906,000
Interest revenue	23,000
Net revenue	$ 929,000
Cost of goods sold	(450,000)
Selling and administrative expenses	(140,000)
Income before taxes	$ 339,000
Income tax expense	(135,600)
Net income	$ 203,400

Prepare journal entries to close the revenue and expense accounts to the retained earnings account.

E 4-43 **Closing Dividends and Preparing a Post-Closing Trial Balance**

LO4 A listing of account balances taken from the adjusted ledger account balances of The Miners' Guild shows the following:

Cash	$ 45,160	Salaries Payable	$ 18,000
Accounts Receivable	112,960	Taxes Payable	48,800
Inventory	156,720	Unearned Rent	30,400
Prepaid Insurance	13,040	Mortgage Payable	180,000
Land	272,000	Capital Stock	88,000
Accounts Payable	57,280	Dividends	40,000
Notes Payable	80,000	Retained Earnings	137,400

All revenue and expense accounts have been closed to Retained Earnings. Dividends has not yet been closed.

Prepare (1) the closing entry for Dividends and (2) a post-closing trial balance for December 31, 2009.

E 4-44 **Closing Dividends and Preparing a Post-Closing Trial Balance**

LO4 Below is a listing of account balances taken from the adjusted ledger account balances of Jolley Manufacturing Corporation.

Cash	$ 16,400	Income Taxes Payable	$ 7,000
Accounts Receivable	23,500	Mortgage Payable	82,500
Inventory	71,000	Notes Payable	23,000
Prepaid Advertising	4,000	Unearned Rent	4,200
Building	110,000	Capital Stock	80,000
Land	45,000	Dividends	14,800
Accounts Payable	24,000	Retained Earnings	56,000
Wages Payable	8,000		

All revenues and expense accounts have been closed to Retained Earnings. Dividends has not yet been closed.

Prepare (1) the closing entry for Dividends and (2) a post-closing trial balance for December 31, 2009.

PROBLEMS

P 4-45
LO1

Cash- and Accrual-Basis Accounting

In the course of your examination of the books and records of Karen Company, you find the following data:

Salaries earned by employees in 2009	$ 61,000
Salaries paid in 2009	53,000
Total sales revenue in 2009	927,000
Cash collected from sales in 2009	952,000
Utilities expense incurred in 2009	7,500
Utility bills paid in 2009	6,300
Cost of goods sold in 2009	602,000
Cash paid on purchases in 2009	613,000
Inventory at December 31, 2009	416,000
Tax assessment for 2009	6,210
Taxes paid in 2009	5,930
Rent expense for 2009	36,000
Rent paid in 2009	41,000

Required:

1. Compute Karen's net income for 2009 using cash-basis accounting.
2. Compute Karen's net income for 2009 using accrual-basis accounting.
3. **Interpretive Question:** Why is accrual-basis accounting normally used? Can you see any opportunities for improperly reporting income under cash-basis accounting? Explain.

P 4-46
LO2

Adjusting Entries

The information presented below is for MedQuest Pharmacy, Inc.

a. Salaries for the period December 26, 2009, through December 31, 2009, amounted to $17,840 and have not been recorded or paid. (Ignore payroll taxes.)
b. Interest of $5,225 is payable for three months on an 11%, $190,000 loan and has not been recorded.
c. Rent of $36,000 was paid for six months in advance on December 1 and debited to Prepaid Rent.
d. Rent of $76,000 was credited to an unearned revenue account when received. Of this amount, $42,100 is still unearned at year-end.
e. The expired portion of an insurance policy is $2,400. Prepaid Insurance was originally debited.
f. Interest revenue of $400 from a $4,000 note has been earned but not collected or recorded.

Required:

Prepare the adjusting entries that should be made on December 31, 2009. (Omit explanations.)

P 4-47
LO2

Adjusting Entries

The information presented below is for Susan's Sweet Shop.

a. Interest of $9,600 is payable for September 2009 through December 2009 on a 9%, $320,000 loan and has not been recorded.
b. Rent of $93,500 was credited to an unearned revenue account when received. Of this amount, $42,250 is still unearned at year-end.
c. Interest revenue of $9,450 from a $105,000 note has been earned but not collected or recorded.
d. The expired portion of an insurance policy is $4,960. Prepaid Insurance was originally debited.
e. Rent of $30,000 was paid for six months in advance on November 15, 2009, and debited to Prepaid Rent.

(continued)

f.   Salaries for the period December 26, 2009, to December 31, 2009, amounted to $15,300 and have not been recorded or paid. (Ignore payroll taxes.)

Required:
Prepare the adjusting entries that should be made on December 31, 2009. (Omit explanations.)

P 4-48
LO2

Year-End Analysis of Accounts

An analysis of cash records and account balances of Wells, Inc., for 2009 is as follows:

	Account Balances Jan. 1, 2009	Account Balances Dec. 31, 2009	Cash Received or Paid in 2009
Wages Payable	$2,600	$3,000	
Unearned Rent	4,500	5,000	
Prepaid Insurance	100	120	
Paid for wages			$29,600
Received for rent			12,000
Paid for insurance			720

Required:
Determine the amounts that should be included on the 2009 income statement for (1) wages expense, (2) rent revenue, and (3) insurance expense.

P 4-49
LO2

Year-End Analysis of Accounts

An analysis of cash records and account balances of Apartment Renters, Inc., for 2009 is as follows:

	Account Balances Jan. 1, 2009	Account Balances Dec. 31, 2009	Cash Received or Paid in 2009
Salaries Payable	$15,600	$18,400	
Unearned Rent	10,350	14,100	
Prepaid Insurance	3,300	2,000	
Paid for salaries			$134,000
Received for rent			48,500
Paid for insurance			13,800

Required:
Determine the amounts that should be included on the 2009 income statement for (1) salaries expense, (2) rent revenue, and (3) insurance expense.

P 4-50
LO4

Account Classifications and Debit-Credit Relationships

Using the format provided, for each account identify (1) whether the account is a balance sheet (B/S) or an income statement (I/S) account; (2) whether it is an asset (A), a liability (L), an owners' equity (OE), a revenue (R), or an expense (E) account; (3) whether the account is a real or a nominal account; (4) whether the account will be "closed" or left "open" at year-end; and (5) whether the account normally has a debit or a credit balance. The following example is provided:

Account Title	(1) B/S or I/S	(2) A, L, OE, R, E	(3) Real or Nominal	(4) Closed or Open	(5) Debit/ Credit
Cash	B/S	A	Real	Open	Debit

(continued)

1. Accounts Receivable	13. Supplies on Hand
2. Accounts Payable	14. Utilities Expense
3. Prepaid Insurance	15. Income Taxes Payable
4. Mortgage Payable	16. Interest Revenue
5. Rent Expense	17. Notes Payable
6. Sales Revenue	18. Income Tax Expense
7. Cost of Goods Sold	19. Wages Payable
8. Dividends	20. Unearned Rent Revenue
9. Capital Stock	21. Land
10. Inventory	22. Unearned Consulting Fees
11. Retained Earnings	23. Interest Receivable
12. Prepaid Rent	24. Consulting Fees

P 4-51   **Closing Entries**

LO4

The income statement for Joe's Asphalt, Inc., for the year ended December 31, 2009, is as follows:

Joe's Asphalt, Inc.
Income Statement
For the Year Ended December 31, 2009

Sales revenue		$904,000
Less expenses:		
Cost of goods sold	$726,000	
Salaries expense	144,000	
Interest expense	10,500	
Office supplies expense	7,640	
Insurance expense	9,860	
Property tax expense	22,400	
Total expenses		920,400
Net loss		$(16,400)

Required:

Dividends of $36,000 were paid on December 30, 2009.

1. Give the entry required on December 31, 2009, to properly close the income statement accounts.
2. Give the entry required to close the dividends account at December 31, 2009.

P 4-52   **Closing Entries**

LO4

The income statement for Squared Carpentry, Inc., for the year ended December 31, 2009, is as follows:

Squared Carpentry, Inc.
Income Statement
For the Year Ended December 31, 2009

Sales revenue		$843,200
Less expenses:		
Cost of goods sold	$567,100	
Wages expense	102,750	
Utilities expense	4,890	
Insurance expense	6,930	
Property tax expense	10,510	
Rent expense	49,000	
Advertising expense	15,640	
Interest expense	9,800	
Total expenses		766,620
Net income		$ 76,580

(continued)

Dividends of $18,600 were paid on December 30, 2009.

Required:
1. Give the entry required on December 31, 2009, to properly close the income statement accounts.
2. Give the entry required to close the dividends account at December 31, 2009.

P 4-53

LO2, LO4

Unifying Concepts: Adjusting and Closing Entries

The unadjusted and adjusted trial balances of White Company as of December 31, 2009, are presented below.

White Company Trial Balance December 31, 2009				
	Unadjusted		Adjusted	
	Debits	Credits	Debits	Credits
Cash	$ 21,250		$ 21,250	
Accounts Receivable	11,250		11,250	
Supplies on Hand	5,195		3,895	
Prepaid Rent	17,545		7,545	
Prepaid Insurance	1,985		1,100	
Buildings (net)	95,000		95,000	
Land	45,720		45,720	
Accounts Payable		$ 9,350		$ 9,350
Wages Payable				5,700
Income Taxes Payable				580
Interest Payable		450		1,050
Notes Payable		65,000		65,000
Capital Stock		84,320		84,320
Consulting Fees Earned		142,380		142,380
Wages Expense	92,335		98,035	
Rent Expense			10,000	
Interest Expense	3,500		4,100	
Insurance Expense	585		1,470	
Supplies Expenses	4,365		5,665	
Income Tax Expense	2,770		3,350	
Totals	$301,500	$301,500	$308,380	$308,380

Required:
1. Prepare the journal entries that are required to adjust the accounts at December 31, 2009.
2. Prepare the journal entry that is required to close the accounts at December 31, 2009.

P 4-54

LO3, LO4

Unifying Concepts: Analysis of Accounts

The bookkeeper for Davey James Company accidentally pressed the wrong computer key and erased the amount of Retained Earnings. You have been asked to analyze the following data and provide some key numbers for the board of directors meeting, which is to take place in 30 minutes. With the exception of Retained Earnings, the following account balances are available at December 31, 2009.

(continued)

Cash	$ 61,000	Accounts Receivable	$ 49,000
Furniture (net)	40,000	Inventory	160,000
Accounts Payable	120,000	Notes Payable	250,000
Land	260,000	Supplies on Hand	10,000
Buildings (net)	240,000	Capital Stock	300,000
Sales Revenue	415,000	Dividends	20,000
Salaries Expense	50,000	Retained Earnings	?
Cost of Goods Sold	220,000		

Required:

1. Compute the amount of total assets at December 31, 2009.
2. Compute the amount of net income for the year ended December 31, 2009.
3. After all closing entries are made, what is the amount of Retained Earnings at December 31, 2009?
4. What was the beginning Retained Earnings balance at January 1, 2009?

P 4-55
LO5

Unifying Concepts: Analysis and Correction of Errors

At the end of November 2009, the general ledger of Peacock Clothing Company showed the following amounts:

Assets	$103,070
Liabilities	53,300
Owners' Equity	76,300

The company's bookkeeper is new on the job and does not have much accounting experience. Because the bookkeeper has made numerous errors, total assets do not equal liabilities plus owners' equity. The following is a list of errors made.

a. Inventory that cost $64,000 was sold, but the entry to record cost of goods sold was not made.
b. Credit sales of $23,400 were posted to the general ledger as $32,400. The accounts receivable were posted correctly.
c. Inventory of $14,800 was purchased on account and received before the end of November, but no entry to record the purchase was made until December.
d. November salaries payable of $4,000 were not recorded until paid in December.
e. Common stock was issued for $25,000 and credited to Accounts Payable.
f. Inventory purchased for $42,030 was incorrectly posted to the asset account as $24,500. No error was made in the liability account.

Required:
Determine the correct balances of assets, liabilities, and owners' equity at the end of November.

P 4-56
LO5

Unifying Concepts: The Accounting Cycle

The post-closing trial balance of Anderson Company at December 31, 2008, is shown here.

(continued)

Anderson Company		
Post-Closing Trial Balance		
December 31, 2008		
	Debits	**Credits**
Cash	$ 15,000	
Accounts Receivable	20,000	
Inventory	30,000	
Land	150,000	
Accounts Payable		$ 25,000
Notes Payable		35,000
Capital Stock		125,000
Retained Earnings		30,000
Totals	$215,000	$215,000

During 2009, Anderson Company had the following transactions:

a. Inventory purchases were $80,000, all on credit (debit Inventory).

b. An additional $10,000 of capital stock was issued for cash.

c. Merchandise that cost $100,000 was sold for $180,000; $100,000 were credit sales and the balance were cash sales. (Debit Cost of Goods Sold and credit Inventory for sale of merchandise.)

d. The notes were paid, including $7,000 interest.

e. $105,000 was collected from customers.

f. $95,000 was paid to reduce accounts payable.

g. Salaries expense was $30,000, all paid in cash.

h. A $10,000 cash dividend was declared and paid.

Required:

1. Prepare journal entries to record each of the 2009 transactions.

2. Set up T-accounts with the proper balances at January 1, 2009, and post the journal entries to the T-accounts.

3. Prepare an income statement for the year ended December 31, 2009, and a balance sheet as of that date. Also prepare a statement of retained earnings.

4. Prepare the entries necessary to close the nominal accounts, including Dividends.

5. Post the closing entries to the ledger accounts [label (i) and (j)] and prepare a post-closing trial balance at December 31, 2009.

ANALYTICAL ASSIGNMENTS

AA 4-57
DISCUSSION

Using Financial Statements for Investment Decisions

Several doctors are considering the purchase of a small real estate business as an investment. Because you have some training in the mechanics of the accounting cycle, they have hired you to review the real estate company's accounting records and to prepare a balance sheet and an income statement for their use. In analyzing various business documents, you verify the following data.

The account balances at the beginning of the current year were as follows:

Cash in Bank	$ 7,800
Notes Receivable (from Current Owner)	10,000
Supplies on Hand	750
Prepaid Office Rent	4,500
Accounts Payable	450
Owners' Equity	22,600

(continued)

During the current year, the following summarized transactions took place:

a. The owner paid $1,200 to the business to cover the interest on the note receivable ($10,000 × 0.12 × 1 year). Nothing was paid on the principal.

b. Real estate commissions earned during the year totaled $45,500. Of this amount, $1,000 has not been received by year-end.

c. The company purchased $500 of supplies during the year. A count at year-end shows $300 worth still on hand.

d. The $4,500 paid for office rental was for 18 months, beginning in January of this year.

e. Utilities paid during the year amounted to $1,500.

f. During the year, $400 of accounts payable were paid; the balance in Accounts Payable at year-end is $300, with the adjustment being debited to Miscellaneous Office Expense.

g. The owner paid himself $1,500 a month as a salary and paid a part-time secretary $2,400 for the year. (Ignore payroll taxes.)

On the basis of the above data, prepare a balance sheet and an income statement for the real estate business. Does the business appear profitable? Does the balance sheet raise any questions or concerns? What other information might the doctors want to consider in making this investment decision?

AA 4-58
DISCUSSION

Accounting and Ethical Issues Involving the Closing Process

Silva and Wanita Rodriques are the owners of Year-Round Landscape, Inc., a small landscape and yard service business in southern California. The business is three years old and has grown significantly, especially during the past year. To sustain this growth, Year-Round Landscape must expand operations.

In the past, the Rodriques have been able to secure funds for the business from personal resources. Now those resources are exhausted, and the Rodriques are seeking a loan from a local bank.

To satisfy bank requirements, Year-Round Landscape, Inc., must provide a set of financial statements, including comparative income statements showing the growth in earnings over the past three years. In analyzing the records, Silva notices that the nominal accounts have not yet been closed for this year. Furthermore, Silva is aware of a major contract that is to be signed on January 3, only three days after the December 31 year-end for the business. Silva suggests that the closing process be delayed one week so that this major contract can be included in this year's operating results. Silva estimates that this contract will increase current year earnings by 20%.

What accounting issues are involved in this case? What are the ethical issues?

AA 4-59
DISCUSSION

Wrestling with Your Conscience and GAAP

You are the controller for South Valley Industries. Your assistant has just completed the financial statements for the current year and has given them to you for review. A copy of the statements also has been given to the president of the company. The income statement reports net income for the year of $50,000 and earnings per share of $2.50.

In reviewing the statements, you realize the assistant neglected to record adjusting entries. After making the necessary adjustments, the company shows a net loss of $10,000. The difference is due to an unusually large amount of unrecorded expenses at year-end. You realize that these expenses are not likely to be found by the independent auditors.

You wonder if it would be better to delay the recording of the expenses until the first part of the subsequent year in order to avoid reporting a net loss on the income statement for the current year. A significant increase in revenues is expected in the coming year, and the expenses in question could be "absorbed" by the higher revenues.

What issues are involved in this case? What course of action would you take?

AA 4-60
JUDGMENT CALL

You Decide: Should deferred compensation packages be disclosed in the notes to the financial statements, or should they be recorded as liabilities?

Recently, corporate accounting scandals have brought about an increased scrutiny of executive compensation. Companies are being criticized for their role in accounting for stock

(continued)

options, inflated salaries, and personal loans to executives. However, there is one hidden treasure that should not be overlooked: deferred compensation packages for executives. These are retirement packages that will allow executives to set aside, pretax, up to 100% of their cash compensation, earning as much as a 10% return. For many companies, these deferred compensation packages represent corporate liabilities that are not in the financial statements or even disclosed in the notes. How should they be reported and/or disclosed, if at all?

AA 4-61
JUDGMENT CALL

You Decide: **Should intellectual properties be recorded as assets on the balance sheet or disclosed in the notes to the financial statements?**

Intellectual property refers to creations of the mind. Examples include inventions, symbols, names, images, logos, and designs used in commerce. For example, the annual reports for a mutual fund company will often list all fund managers with their associated professional credentials, academic history, and honors they have received. This provides useful information to the investors and helps individuals realize the value of good fund managers. Is there a way to "quantify" this type of information so that it can appear in the balance sheet as an asset to the firm?

AA 4-62
JUDGMENT CALL

You Decide: **Can wages payable be deferred to make the financial statements look better?**

It is early December and you have just been hired as an accountant for a local computer hardware store. Business is expanding due to the increased number of sales reps your boss just hired. Your boss is excited about expanding the business into other nearby communities, but will need a loan from the bank to do so. He has hired you to clean up the books and get the company's financial information ready so he can present it to the bank's loan officer after the first of the year. On December 30, your boss asks you not to record the sales force's wages for the month of December because he won't be able to pay them until mid-January. He wants the financial statements to be in good shape when he visits the loan officer. What should you do?

AA 4-63
REAL COMPANY ANALYSIS

Wal-Mart

Using **Wal-Mart's** 2006 Form 10-K contained in Appendix A, answer the following questions:

1. Find note #1 in Wal-Mart's annual report. Specifically locate the "Revenue Recognition" heading. In the case of Wal-Mart and SAM'S CLUB shopping cards, does the company recognize revenue when the card is purchased?
2. SAM'S CLUB sells 12-month membership cards. Are the revenues associated with the sale of those cards recognized when the card is sold, at the end of the 12 months, or at some other point?

AA 4-64
REAL COMPANY ANALYSIS

Home Depot

Selected financial statement information for **Home Depot** is given in the table below. Using this information, answer the following questions:

(all numbers in millions)
Retained Earnings balance—02/02/2003 $15,971 million

	Net Income	Dividends
For year ended February 1, 2004	$4,304	$595
For year ended January 30, 2005	5,001	719
For year ended January 29, 2006	5,838	857

1. Compute Home Depot's Retained Earnings balance at the end of each year.
2. Divide dividends into net income for each year. The result is termed the "dividend payout ratio." Did Home Depot's dividend payout ratio increase or decrease over time?

AA 4-65
REAL COMPANY
ANALYSIS

Campbell Soup

Information from the 2005 income statement for **Campbell Soup Company** is shown below.

(in millions, except per-share amounts)	2005	2004	2003
Net Sales	$7,548	$7,109	$6,678
Costs and expenses			
Cost of products sold	4,491	4,187	3,805
Marketing and selling expenses	1,185	1,153	1,145
Administrative expenses	571	542	507
Research and development expenses	95	93	88
Other expenses	(4)	(13)	59
Restructuring charge	–	32	–
Total costs and expenses	6,338	5,994	5,604
Earnings Before Interest and Taxes	$1,210	$1,115	$1,074
Interest expense	184	174	186
Interest income	4	6	5
Earnings before taxes	1,030	947	893
Taxes on earnings	323	300	298
Net Earnings	$ 707	$ 647	$ 595

Using the information from the income statement, perform the following:
1. Prepare the entries made by Campbell to close the 2005 revenue and expense accounts to Retained Earnings.
2. Campbell Soup paid dividends of $280 million in 2005. Provide the entry made to close the dividends account to Retained Earnings.
3. If the beginning balance in Campbell's Retained Earnings was $5,642 million, what would the ending balance be after the above closing entries have been posted?

AA 4-66
INTERNATIONAL

Exchange Rate Adjustments

Given the international economy in which many firms operate, it is not unusual for companies to have transactions with companies in foreign countries. Relatedly, it is becoming common for some of those transactions to be denominated in a foreign currency. That is, if a company in the United States makes a purchase from a company in Japan, it is possible that the U.S. company will have to pay Japanese yen when the invoice comes due.

For example, suppose American, Inc., purchased inventory from Japan, Inc., on December 15, 2008. Japan, Inc., expects to receive 1,000,000 Japanese yen in 30 days. To record a journal entry for this purchase, you would need to know what 1,000,000 yen are worth today. Suppose that on December 15, 2008, one yen is worth $0.07 (this is called an exchange rate). What journal entry would be made on American, Inc.'s books?

Since exchange rates change every day, the amount of U.S. dollars to be paid on January 15, 2009, will likely be different than the originally recorded $70,000. In addition, to correctly state the liability on December 31, 2008, an adjustment will be required. Suppose that at year-end, one Japanese yen is worth $0.08. What adjusting entry would be made to reflect this change in exchange rates as of December 31, 2008? (Hint: The accounts being adjusted with this journal entry will be the accounts payable account and an exchange gain or loss.)

When the invoice is paid on January 15, 2009, it is likely that the number of U.S. dollars required to purchase 1,000,000 Japanese yen will again have changed. Suppose exchange rates have increased to $0.09. Provide the journal entry to pay the invoice.

AA 4-67
ETHICS

Do Two Wrongs Make a Right?

Jex Varner, chief financial officer of Wyndam, Inc., is involved in a meeting with the firm's newly hired external auditors, Ernst & Price. The external auditors have noted several

(continued)

adjusting entries that they believe should be reflected in the current period's financial statements. Specifically, there are questions regarding $400,000 of cash that has been received (and recorded as revenue) but not yet earned. The auditors feel that this amount should be recognized as a liability.

Jex counters that the firm's policy has always been to recognize revenue when the cash is received. He states that $350,000 of cash was received in December of last year, earned in January, and no adjustment was made. To be consistent, he continues, he doesn't believe any adjustments should be made this year.

As a member of the external auditing team, do you agree with Jex's reasoning? If you think that an adjustment needs to be made, what journal entry would you propose? What should be done about the $350,000 that has been earned this year even though the cash was received last year?

| AA 4-68 | **Are Adjusting Entries More Trouble Than They Are Worth?** |

WRITING

You are taking an introductory accounting class. You think that making regular journal entries is not too difficult, but making adjusting entries is still a bit of a mystery. You have found that your answers to homework questions on adjusting entries are incorrect at least half the time. You mentioned your difficulties to the other members of your study group, and they all agreed—adjusting entries are brutal. As you and your study colleagues shared your frustration with adjusting entries, the following consensus formed: adjusting entries are more trouble than they are worth. You were selected by your study group to pass this sentiment along to your accounting instructor. She agreed that adjusting entries can be difficult, but she insisted that they are worth the effort. She has now given you the following writing assignment: write a one-page paper describing the value of adjusting entries.

AA 4-69

CUMULATIVE SPREADSHEET PROJECT

Preparing Forecasts

This spreadsheet assignment is a continuation of the spreadsheet assignments given in earlier chapters. If you completed those spreadsheets, you have a head start on this one.

1. Refer back to the balance sheet and income statement created using the financial statement numbers for Handyman Company for 2009 [given in part (1) of the Cumulative Spreadsheet Project assignment in Chapter 2]. With these historical numbers for 2009 as a starting point, Handyman wishes to prepare a forecasted balance sheet and a forecasted income statement for 2010. In preparing the forecasted financial statements for 2010, consider the following additional information:

    a. Sales in 2010 are expected to increase by 40% over 2009 sales of $700.

    b. In the forecasted balance sheet for 2010, cash, receivables, inventory, and accounts payable will all increase at the same rate as sales (40%) relative to 2009. These increases occur because, with the planned 40% increase in the volume of business and no plans to significantly change its methods of operation, Handyman will probably also experience a 40% increase in the levels of its current operating assets and liabilities.

    c. In 2010, Handyman expects to acquire new property, plant, and equipment costing $80.

    d. Accumulated depreciation is the cumulative amount of depreciation expense that Handyman has reported over its years in business. Thus, the forecasted amount of accumulated depreciation for 2010 can be computed as accumulated depreciation as of the end of 2009 plus the forecasted depreciation expense for 2010.

    e. New short-term loans payable will be acquired in an amount sufficient to make Handyman's current ratio (current assets divided by current liabilities) in 2010 exactly equal to 2.0.

    f. No new long-term debt will be acquired in 2010.

    g. No cash dividends will be paid in 2010. Remember that the amount of retained earnings at the end of any year is the beginning retained earnings amount plus net income minus dividends.

(continued)

h. In this exercise, the forecasted amount of paid-in capital is the "plug" figure. In other words, the forecasted balance in paid-in capital at the end of 2010 is the amount necessary to make the forecasted balance sheet balance such that forecasted total assets equal forecasted total liabilities. A key reason for preparing forecasted financial statements is to identify in advance whether any additional financing will be required.

i. The $160 in operating expenses reported in 2009 breaks down as follows: $5 depreciation expense, $155 other operating expenses.

j. In the forecasted income statement for 2010, cost of goods sold and other operating expenses will both increase at the same rate as sales (40%) relative to 2009. This is another way of saying that the amount of these expenses, relative to the amount of sales, will probably stay about the same year to year unless Handyman plans to significantly change the way it does business.

k. The amount of Handyman's depreciation expense is determined by how much property, plant, and equipment the company has. In 2009, Handyman had $5 of depreciation expense on $199 of property, plant, and equipment, meaning that depreciation was equal to 2.5% ($5/$199) of the amount of property, plant, and equipment. It is expected that the same relationship will hold in 2010.

l. Interest expense depends on how much interest-bearing debt a company has. In 2009, Handyman reported interest expense of $9 on long-term debt of $207. (Note: To simplify this exercise, we will ignore interest expense on the short-term loan payable.) Because Handyman is expected to have the same amount of long-term debt in 2010, our best guess is that interest expense will remain the same.

m. Income tax expense is determined by how much pretax income a company has. And, the most reasonable assumption to make is that a company's tax rate, equal to income tax expense divided by pretax income, will stay constant from year to year. Handyman's income tax rate in 2009 was 33% ($4/$12).

2. Repeat (1) assuming that forecasted sales growth in 2010 is 20% instead of 40%. Clearly state any assumptions that you make.

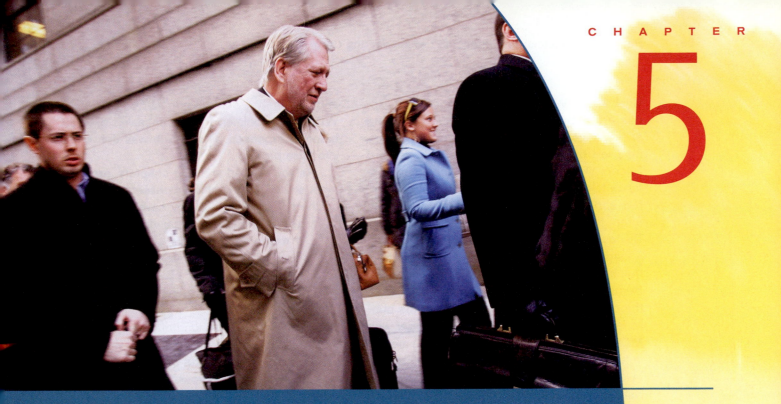

Ensuring the Integrity of Financial Information

After studying this chapter, you should be able to:

LEARNING OBJECTIVES

(1) Identify the types of problems that can appear in financial statements. *Mechanical errors in the recording or posting process and mistakes in accounting estimates can result in incorrect financial statement numbers. Financial statements can also be intentionally misstated by managers seeking to fraudulently deceive investors and creditors.*

(2) Describe the safeguards employed to ensure that financial statements are free from problems. *Ethical and careful managers are much more likely to establish conditions and procedures that result in fair financial statements. Such managers insist on a carefully designed accounting system that captures all company transactions. These managers also ensure that internal checks and balances prevent accidental loss and intentional theft and fraud.*

(3) Understand the concept of earnings management and why it occurs. *Managers of companies sometimes are motivated to manage reported earnings in order to meet internal targets and to look good to outsiders. When a manager decides to manage earnings, he or she can fall into a downward spiral of deception which can result in a massive loss of reputation for the manager and the company.*

(4) Understand the major parts of the Sarbanes-Oxley Act and how it impacts financial reporting. *The Sarbanes-Oxley Act was passed by Congress in 2002 in response to the public uproar over a rash of large corporate accounting scandals. The Act places a personal responsibility on corporate managers to produce reliable financial reports. The Act also raises the standards for external auditors.*

(5) Describe the role of auditors and how their presence affects the integrity of financial statements. *Auditors increase the reliance that users can place on financial reports. Internal auditors monitor accounting processes in a company on an ongoing basis. External auditors certify that the financial statements released to the public are a fair representation of the company's financial position and performance.*

(6) Explain the role of the Securities and Exchange Commission in adding credibility to financial statements. *The SEC has legal authority to set financial accounting standards in the United States; in practice, the SEC allows the FASB to set these standards. The SEC also oversees the certification of external auditors. The SEC requires publicly-traded companies to provide quarterly financial statements to the public.*

Until 2002, **WorldCom**, a telecom giant, appeared to be one of the greatest corporate success stories ever. In 1983, a group of partners led by former basketball coach Bernard Ebbers sketched out their idea for a long distance telephone company on a napkin in a coffee shop in Hattiesburg, Mississippi. Soon after, their company **LDDS** (Long Distance Discount Service) began providing service as a long distance reseller. For 15 years, it grew quickly through acquisitions and mergers. Bernard Ebbers was named CEO in 1985, and the company sold shares of stock to the public in August 1989. Its $40 billion merger with **MCI** in 1998 was the largest corporate merger in history at the time. The company was also a favorite with investors and Wall Street analysts. The stock reached a peak of $64.51 per share in June 1999.

Not long after, however, the success of the company's finances began to unravel with the accumulation of debt and expenses, the fall of the stock market, and drops in long distance rates and revenue. While it would take nearly two years for the extent of these problems to become public, in the end, WorldCom disclosed massive financial statement fraud and filed for Chapter 11 bankruptcy, the largest in U.S. history. In 2002, WorldCom became a horror story that involved the largest accounting fraud ever reported, SEC investigations, the resignation of CEO Bernard Ebbers, a $101.9 billion dollar bankruptcy, and a stock that was worth less than a pay phone call.[1]

While there were several different types of financial statement frauds committed by WorldCom, by far the largest was the manipulation of expenses and assets. In a court filing in New York in November 2002, the Securities and Exchange Commission (SEC) said that WorldCom admitted that it concealed over $9 billion in expenses, all of which was converted into false profits.

As you learned in earlier chapters, expenditures should be classified as assets and listed on the balance sheet if they have future value, such as expenditures for buildings or equipment. If expenditures are for current operating costs such as salaries or rent, however, you learned that they should be expensed as incurred and reported as expenses on the income statement.

In simple terms, instead of expensing costs that had been incurred, the company was listing these costs as assets and putting them on the balance sheet. These expenditures should have been subtracted from revenues on the income statement and reported as expenses when incurred. The result was that reported expenses were lower than they should have been on the income statement and reported assets and owners' equity were higher than they should have been on the balance sheet.

The simple WorldCom fraud was discovered when some obscure tips provided to the company's internal auditors were pursued by Cynthia Cooper, Gene Morse, and Glyn Smith, all internal auditors working for the company. The subsequent investigation resulted in testimony from David Myers, an accountant with WorldCom, who stated: "I was instructed on a quarterly basis by Scott Sullivan, chief financial officer, to ensure that entries were made to falsify WorldCom's books to reduce WorldCom's reported actual costs and therefore to increase WorldCom's reported earnings." He said that Scott Sullivan and he would ". . . work backward, picking the earnings numbers that they knew Wall Street analysts expected to see, and then force WorldCom's financials to match those numbers." While these shenanigans worked for a time, in the end, WorldCom's total market value (number of shares of stock times stock price) went from a high of about $120 billion to almost nothing and several individuals were indicted for fraud.

? FYI

On April 14, 2002, WorldCom announced that it was changing its name to MCI—the company it purchased in 1998. In 2005, it was sold to **Verizon** for $6.7 billion or about $20.75 per share of stock.

---

[1] CEO Bernie Ebbers was sentenced in July 2005 to 25 years in prison for his role in orchestrating the WorldCom financial statement fraud. His sentence is the longest ever for a CEO found guilty of committing corporate crimes while running a Fortune 500 company.

In Chapters 1 and 2, you were introduced to financial accounting and shown the outputs (financial statements) of the financial reporting process. You learned that the balance sheet, income statement, and statement of cash flows are reports used by organizations to summarize their financial results for various users. In Chapters 3 and 4, the accounting cycle, the method of entering and processing financial transaction information in the accounting records, was described. You learned that transaction data are captured by journal entries, journal entry data are summarized in accounts and ledgers, ledger information is summarized on trial balances, and trial balance information provides the basis for the balance sheet, income statement, and statement of cash flows.

In Chapters 1 through 4, the assumption was made that the financial reporting process always works the way it should and that the resulting financial statements are accurate. In reality, however, because of unintentional errors, as well as intentional deception or fraud (such as in the WorldCom case), the resulting financial statements sometimes contain errors or omissions that can mislead investors, creditors, and other users.

In this chapter, we show how financial statements might be manipulated, and we discuss the safeguards built into the financial reporting system to prevent these abuses. We also examine the role that auditors play in ensuring that the financial statements fairly represent the financial performance of the firm.

The Types of Problems That Can Occur

Identify the types of problems that can appear in financial statements.

1 Obviously, most businesses do not engage in massive frauds like those that occurred at **WorldCom**. Financial deception does not come about mainly for two reasons: (1) the vast majority of business managers are honest, possess integrity, and would not be associated with fraudulent activity, and (2) safeguards have been built into the accounting system to prevent and detect activities that are inconsistent with the objectives of a business. These safeguards attempt to eliminate problems from being introduced into the financial statements. However, during the past few years, there have been numerous financial statement frauds disclosed at companies such as **Enron**, **WorldCom**, **Adelphia**, **Global Crossing**, **Xerox**, **Quest**, **Waste Management**, **Cendant**, **AniCom**, **Homestore**, **Sunbeam**, **Tyco**, and others.

Before proceeding further, we need to make an important distinction regarding these problems. Problems in the financial statements can result for several different reasons.

1. *Errors*—result when unintentional mistakes are made in recording transactions, posting transactions, summarizing accounts, and so forth. Errors are *not intentional* and when detected are immediately corrected. Errors can result from sloppy accounting, bad assumptions, misinformation, miscalculations, and other factors.
2. *Disagreements*—result when different people arrive at different conclusions based on the same set of facts. Because accounting involves judgment and estimates, opportunities for honest disagreements in judgment abound. These disagreements often come about because of the different incentives that motivate those involved with producing the financial statements. An example of a disagreement might be differing views about what percentage of reported receivables will be collected or how long equipment and other assets will last.
3. *Frauds*—result from intentional errors. Fraudulent financial reporting occurs when management chooses to intentionally manipulate the financial statements to serve their own purposes, such as meeting Wall Street's earnings forecasts as was the case with WorldCom.

An accounting system should be designed to significantly reduce the possibility that problems, in whatever form, will make their way into financial statements. When it is discovered that the financial statements of public companies are wrong, for whatever reason, they must be restated (reissued with correct amounts). In recent years, the number of restatements has increased, as shown below.

Year	Number of U.S. Restatements
2000	233
2001	270
2002	330
2003	323
2004	619
2005	1295[2]

Types of Errors in the Reporting Process

Errors, and other problems, can occur in most stages of the accounting cycle. We will first describe the kinds of errors that can occur and then identify controls to minimize these errors.

Errors in Transactions and Journal Entries
Transactions, such as selling products or services, paying salaries, buying inventory, and paying taxes, are entered into the accounting records through journal entries. For example, if $5,000 is paid to an attorney for legal services, the following journal entry is made:

Legal Expense	5,000	
Cash		5,000
Paid an attorney $5,000 for legal services.		

An invoice from the law firm should support this entry. Errors could be introduced into the financial reporting process if (1) the invoice from the law firm was lost and the legal expense was not entered into the accounting records, (2) the amount entered into the accounting records was incorrect, or (3) the accounts involved were incorrectly identified.

Errors in Accounts and Ledgers
Even when journal entries properly summarize legitimate transactions, errors and misstatements can be introduced into the financial records because journal entry data are not summarized appropriately or accurately in the ledgers. Using the previous example of paying an attorney $5,000, errors could occur at the posting stage of the accounting cycle if the legal expense is entered in the wrong account in the ledger or if an incorrect amount is posted to the correct account. Posting the correct amount to the wrong expense account would result in the correct total for all expenses, but individual expense account balances would be incorrect.

A more severe error occurs at the ledger stage if amounts that should be included in asset or liability accounts are improperly included in expense or revenue accounts, or vice versa. Examples include (1) recording insurance expense as prepaid insurance (an asset), (2) recording purchases of goods for resale as inventory (an asset) when they should be reported as cost of goods sold (an expense), (3) recording money received from customers as revenue when it should be recorded as unearned revenue (a liability), or (4) not reporting supplies used as an expense.

---

[2] 1,195 of these were by U.S. companies and 100 were by foreign private issues with U.S.-listed stocks. This information comes from a 2006 Glass Lewis Report and includes restatements of both quarterly and annual financial statements.

Disagreements in Judgment

Many people think that accounting involves exactness and precision and that accountants simply record the facts, total the numbers, and present unbiased results. Nothing could be further from the truth. Accountants are constantly making judgments and estimates regarding the past and the future. Let's return to the landscaping business that we introduced in Chapters 3 and 4 to illustrate some of the judgments involved in the accounting process.

As your lawn care and landscaping business has become more and more successful, you have been able to obtain bigger and better jobs. Recently, you signed a contract to provide all the landscaping for a new condominium complex currently under construction. The terms of the contract call for payment of one-half of the contract amount up front and the remaining one-half upon completion. You begin working on the condominium landscaping in early December, but it looks as though you will not finish until well into January. To prepare financial statements at the end of December, how much of the condominium contract should you report as revenue? The answer depends on how close to completion the job is. If you are 25% complete, it makes sense to report 25% of the contract amount as revenue. If you are 75% complete, report 75% of the contract amount as revenue. The hard part is determining how much of the job has been completed.

Suppose you contact two landscapers (friendly competitors) and ask them to provide you with an estimate of how complete the landscaping job is at year-end. Would it be possible for these two people to arrive at different conclusions regarding the percentage of completion? Which one would be right? Different people can look at the same set of facts and arrive at different conclusions. They're not wrong, just different. In this case, the different estimates would result in different financial statement numbers. These different numbers could make the difference between your company showing a profit or reporting a loss.

Consider another example. Most of your customers pay promptly, but some take a little longer to pay. A few customers discontinue their lawn care service and never pay for some of the services they received. Your problem is that when you provide a service for a customer, you do not know if that customer will be a "prompt payer," a "slow payer," or a "no payer." Recognizing that a certain percentage of your customers will be "no payers," should you record a receivable (and a revenue) for the full amount of every sale? As you will learn in Chapter 6, most businesses recognize that a certain percentage of receivables will be uncollectible. How should you arrive at the amount of your receivables that won't be collected? Is it possible that your estimate will be slightly off? Could different people legitimately arrive at different estimates? Of course. These different estimates will then affect the results reported in the financial statements. There are many more estimates like these required when preparing financial statements for most companies.

Fraudulent Financial Reporting

As mentioned previously, fraudulent financial reporting is intentional. To illustrate, consider the journal entry made previously related to legal expense. Assume that a company's accountant embezzles $5,000 and prepares the following journal entry to conceal the fraud:

Legal Expense	5,000	
Cash		5,000
Paid an attorney $5,000 for legal services.		

The accountant could prepare the journal entry without supporting documentation (e.g., an invoice) or create a fictitious invoice from a phantom law firm.

Unless someone is watching closely, the theft may go undetected. Because the accountant made a fictitious entry to Legal Expense, the accounting records appear to be correct, and the accounting equation still balances. Cash, an asset, is stolen, and the recognition of an expense results in owners' equity being reduced by the same amount.

Assets	=	Liablities	+	Owners' Equity
(decreased by $5,000)				(decreased by $5,000)

While this illustration is small and the dishonest act was committed by an employee against the company, it is intentional and results in financial statements that are incorrect. More serious financial statement fraud occurs when top management intentionally manipulates the financial statements in much larger amounts.

There are many different ways for management to commit financial statement fraud. Examples are listing sales that don't exist (as was the case with **Waste Management**, the trash disposal company, which was making false entries to record revenues and receivables that overstated income by as much as 35% in 1996 and a total of $1.7 billion from 1992–1997);

not recording sales returns or uncollectible receivables (as was the case with the vacuum maker, **Regina**, which did not record the return of over 40,000 vacuums); and not recording various expenses, understating liabilities, and overstating assets such as inventory or receivables (as was the case with **Phar-Mor**, which overstated its assets by shipping products back and forth between stores when inventory was counted).

STOP & THINK

Before reading about the safeguards designed to minimize the types of problems we have just discussed, can you think of things that could be done to ensure that errors, disagreements in judgment, and fraudulent financial reporting do not occur?

REMEMBER THIS...

The financial reports for most companies are accurate.
Inaccurate financial reports can result from any one of the following:

- Unintentional errors
- Disagreements in judgment
- Fraud

Safeguards Designed to Minimize Problems

Describe the safeguards employed to ensure that financial statements are free from problems.

(2) Accounting is a language just as is English. In the same way that a falsehood can be written in English, a misleading story can be expressed by financial statements. By far, the vast majority of financial statements are as accurate as possible, and the preparers are honest. **Federal Express**, the shipping company, as do all public companies, requires that its executives annually sign off on a code of ethics that gives assurances in writing that they have no conflicts of interest or know of no improprieties. The company's policy requires that any employee involved in any kind of dishonesty be immediately terminated and prosecuted. According to FedEx's policy, ". . . magnitude is not the issue. It doesn't matter if the impropriety involves a thousand or a million dollars, our company will not tolerate anything that is done unethically or inappropriately." Almost all organizations prepare accounting records and financial reports with integrity, and in most cases, preparers are even conservative when judgments and estimates are required. To help ensure that financial

reports are accurate and to prevent problems such as those that occurred at **WorldCom**, several safeguards have been built into the financial reporting system and structure of most organizations in the United States. As a future user of accounting information, you should be aware of these safeguards and the reasons for their existence.

internal control structure

Safeguards in the form of policies and procedures established to provide management with reasonable assurance that the objectives of an entity will be achieved.

Most organizations build controls into their organization and financial reporting processes so that abuses are difficult. These safeguards, called the **internal control structure**, are internal to the organization preparing the financial statements. The American Institute of Certified Public Accountants (AICPA) has defined *internal control* as "the policies and procedures established to provide reasonable assurance that specific entity objectives will be achieved."[3] These internal controls protect investors and creditors and even help management in their efforts to run their organizations as effectively and efficiently as possible. If you encounter an organization or financial statements that do not have these controls and safeguards, you should exercise extreme care.

Most companies have the following five concerns in mind when they are designing internal controls:

1. To provide accurate accounting records and financial statements containing reliable data for business decisions.
2. To safeguard assets and records. Most companies think of their assets as including their financial assets (such as cash or property), their employees, their confidential information, and their reputation and image.
3. To effectively and efficiently run their operations, without duplication of effort or waste.
4. To follow management policies.
5. To comply with the Foreign Corrupt Practices and Sarbanes-Oxley Acts, which require companies to maintain proper record-keeping systems and controls.

Foreign Corrupt Practices Act (FCPA)

Legislation requiring any company that has publicly-traded stock to have an adequate system of internal accounting controls.

Sarbanes-Oxley Act

A law passed by Congress in 2002 that gives the SEC significant oversight responsibility and control over companies issuing financial statements and their external auditors.

The responsibility for establishing and maintaining the internal control structure belongs to a company's management. Until several years ago, this responsibility was only implied; there was no formal legal requirement. However, in the wake of illegal political campaign contributions, business frauds, and numerous illegal payments to foreign officials in exchange for business favors, in 1977, Congress passed the **Foreign Corrupt Practices Act (FCPA)**. As a result of this legislation, all companies whose stock is publicly traded are required by law to keep records that represent the firm's transactions accurately and fairly. In addition, they must maintain adequate systems of internal accounting control. Following the rash of reported financial statement frauds in 2001 and 2002, Congress passed the **Sarbanes-Oxley Act** (known as the corporate responsibility act) in 2002. This far-sweeping corporate reform act requires, among other things, that every company's annual report contain an "internal control report," which must (1) state the responsibility of management for establishing and maintaining an adequate internal control structure and procedures for financial reporting, (2) contain an assessment of the effectiveness of the internal control structure by management, (3) contain an independent auditor's assessment of the concurrence with the way management assessed the reliability of its internal controls, and (4) contain an independent assessment of the reliability of internal controls by the independent auditor.

---

[3] AU Section 319, par. 06, Codification of Statements on Auditing Standards, CCH Inc., 1994, p. 98.

(This act, by the way, requires that the CEO and CFO of every public company prepare and sign a statement to accompany their financial statements that certifies the "appropriateness of the financial statements and disclosures contained in the report.")

A company's internal control structure can be divided into five basic categories:[4] (1) the control environment, (2) risk assessment, (3) control activities, (4) information and communication, and (5) monitoring. In this chapter, we will only briefly cover the control environment and control activities (sometimes called control procedures), as well as the need for monitoring (the areas of risk assessment and information and communication are left to courses covering the details of auditing).

The Control Environment

control environment

The actions, policies, and procedures that reflect the overall attitudes of top management about control and its importance to the entity.

The **control environment** consists of the actions, policies, and procedures that reflect the overall attitudes of top management, the directors, and the owners about control and its importance to the company. In a strong control environment, management believes control is important and makes sure that everyone responds conscientiously to the control policies and procedures. In addition, a company with a good control environment generally develops an organizational structure that identifies clear lines of authority and responsibility. A complex **organizational structure** can make it easier to conceal dishonest transactions.

organizational structure

Lines of authority and responsibility.

Another element of a good control environment relates to independent oversight of significant management decisions. This oversight is generally exhibited through a board of directors which consists of individuals both internal and external to the firm.

audit committee

Members of a company's board of directors who are responsible for dealing with the external and internal auditors.

Every major company has a board of directors. A good control environment would suggest that a subset of these directors should form an **audit committee**. The audit committee should be comprised of independent, outside directors (members of the board who are not officers of the company). The internal and external auditors would then be accountable to this audit committee. Under the Sarbanes-Oxley Act, members of the audit committee must be financially literate. The audit committee must be directly responsible for the appointment, compensation, and oversight of the work of the external auditor and must have the authority to engage independent legal counsel or other advisors if it suspects any wrongdoing. External auditors who suspect wrongdoing in financial reporting should forward those concerns to the audit committee.

control activities (procedures)

Policies and procedures used by management to meet their objectives.

Control Activities (Procedures)

Control activities or **control procedures** are those policies and procedures, in addition to the control environment and accounting system, that management has adopted to provide reasonable assurance that the company's established objectives will be met and that financial reports are accurate. Generally, control activities fall into five categories: adequate segregation of duties, proper procedures for authorization, physical control over assets and records, adequate documents and records, and independent checks on performance. The first three are referred to as **preventative controls** because they "prevent" problems from occurring. The last two are referred to as **detective controls** because they help catch problems that are occurring before the problems become large.

preventative controls

Internal control activities that are designed to prevent the occurrence of errors and fraud.

detective controls

Internal control activities that are designed to detect the occurrence of errors and fraud.

---

[4] These five categories were outlined in a document created by the Committee of Sponsoring Organizations (COSO). Most companies use the COSO framework to assess the reliability of their internal controls.

Adequate Segregation of Duties

segregation of duties

A strategy to provide an internal check on performance through separation of authorization of transactions from custody of related assets, separation of operational responsibilities from record-keeping responsibilities, and separation of custody of assets from accounting personnel.

Adequate Segregation of Duties   A good internal control system should provide for the appropriate **segregation of duties**. This means that no one department or individual should be responsible for handling all or conflicting phases of a transaction. In some small businesses, this segregation is not possible because the limited number of employees prevents division of all the conflicting functions. Nevertheless, there are three functions that should be performed by separate departments or by different people whenever possible.

1. *Authorization.* Authorizing and approving the execution of transactions; for example, approving the sale of a building or land.
2. *Record keeping.* Recording the transactions in the accounting records.
3. *Custody of assets.* Having physical possession of or control over the assets involved in transactions, including operational responsibility; for example, having the key to the safe in which cash or investment securities are kept or, more generally, having control over the production function.

By separating the responsibilities for these duties, a company realizes the efficiency derived from specialization and also reduces the errors, both intentional and unintentional, that might otherwise occur.

Proper Procedures for Authorization   A strong system of internal control requires proper authorization for every transaction. In the typical corporate organization, this authorization originates with the stockholders who elect a board of directors. It is then delegated from the board of directors to upper-level management and eventually throughout the organization. While the board of directors and upper-level management possess a fairly general power of authorization, a clerk usually has limited authority. Thus, the board would authorize dividends, a general change in policies, or a merger; a clerk would be restricted to authorizing credit or a specific cash transaction. Only certain people should be authorized to enter data into accounting records and prepare accounting reports.

As an example of journal entries and misstated financial statements that were not authorized, consider the following example:

> In one of the large financial statement frauds that became public in 2002, the CFO instructed the chief accountant to increase earnings by $105 million. The chief accountant was skeptical about the purpose of these instructions, but he did not challenge them. The mechanics were left to the chief accountant to carry out. The chief accountant created a spreadsheet containing seven pages of improper journal entries that he determined were necessary to carry out the CFO's instructions. These types of fictitious and unauthorized journal entries were made over a five-year period.

physical safeguards

Physical precautions used to protect assets and records, such as locks on doors, fireproof vaults, password verification, and security guards.

Physical Control Over Assets and Records   Some of the most crucial policies and procedures involve the use of adequate **physical safeguards** to protect resources. For example, a bank would not allow significant amounts of money to be transported in an ordinary car. Similarly, a company should not leave its valuable assets or records unprotected. Examples of physical safeguards are fireproof vaults for the storage of classified information, currency, and marketable securities; and guards, fences, and remote control cameras for the protection of equipment, materials, and merchandise. Re-creating lost or destroyed records can be costly and time-consuming, so companies make backup copies of records.

Adequate Documents and Records   A key to good controls is an adequate system of documentation and records. As explained in Chapter 3, documents are the physical,

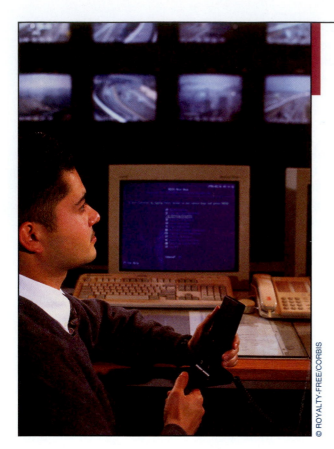

© ROYALTY-FREE/CORBIS

Many companies use physical safeguards, such as surveillance cameras, to protect their resources.

objective evidence of accounting transactions. Their existence allows management to review any transaction for appropriate authorization. Documents are also the means by which information is communicated throughout an organization. In short, adequate documentation provides evidence that the recording and summarizing functions that lead to financial reports are being performed properly. A well-designed document has several characteristics: (1) it is easily interpreted and understood, (2) it has been designed with all possible uses in mind, (3) it has been pre-numbered for easy identification and tracking, and (4) it is formatted so that it can be handled quickly and efficiently. Documents can be actual pieces of paper or information in a computer database.

Independent Checks on Performance Having **independent checks** on performance is a valuable control technique. Independent checks incorporate reviews of functions, as well as the internal checks created from a proper segregation of duties.

There are many ways to independently check performance. Using independent reviewers, such as auditors, is one of the most common. In addition, mandatory vacations, where another employee performs the vacationing person's duties, periodic rotations or transfers, or merely having someone independent of the accounting records reconcile the bank statement are all types of independent checks.

As stated previously, all public companies are required to include in their annual report a statement signed by management that describes and accepts responsibility for the internal controls of the company. The statement shown in Exhibit 1 was included in the 2005 annual report of **IBM Corporation**.

independent checks

Procedures for continual internal verification of other controls.

REMEMBER THIS...

Most organizations have an internal control system that, among other things, helps ensure integrity in financial reports. The various elements of control that relate to financial reporting are summarized as follows.

Control Environment	**Control Activities (Procedures)**
1. Management philosophy and operating style.	1. Segregation of duties (preventative control).
2. Organizational structure.	2. Proper procedures for authorization (preventative control).
3. Audit committee.	3. Physical control over assets and records (preventative control).
	4. Adequate documents and records (detective control).
	5. Independent checks on performance (detective control).

| EXHIBIT 1 | **IBM Corporation's 2005 Management Letter** |

Report of Management

Management's Report on Internal Control Over Financial Reporting

Management is responsible for establishing and maintaining adequate internal control over financial reporting of the company. Internal control over financial reporting is a process designed to provide reasonable assurance regarding the reliability of financial reporting and the preparation of financial statements for external purposes in accordance with accounting principles generally accepted in the United States of America.

The company's internal control over financial reporting includes those policies and procedures that (1) pertain to the maintenance of records that, in reasonable detail, accurately and fairly reflect the transactions and dispositions of the assets of the company; (2) provide reasonable assurance that transactions are recorded as necessary to permit preparation of financial statements in accordance with accounting principles generally accepted in the United States of America, and that receipts and expenditures of the company are being made only in accordance with authorizations of management and directors of the company; and (3) provide reasonable assurance regarding prevention or timely detection of unauthorized acquisition, use, or disposition of the company's assets that could have a material effect on the financial statements.

Because of its inherent limitations, internal control over financial reporting may not prevent or detect misstatements. Also, projections of any evaluation of effectiveness to future periods are subject to the risk that controls may become inadequate because of changes in conditions, or that the degree of compliance with the policies or procedures may deteriorate.

Management conducted an evaluation of the effectiveness of internal control over financial reporting based on the framework in Internal Control-Integrated Framework issued by the Committee of Sponsoring Organizations of the Treadway Commission (COSO). Based on this evaluation, management concluded that the company's internal control over financial reporting was effective as of December 31, 2005. Management's assessment of the effectiveness of the company's internal control over financial reporting as of December 31, 2005 has been audited by PricewaterhouseCoopers LLP, an independent registered public accounting firm, as stated in their report which is included herein.

Samuel J. Palmisano
Chairman of the Board,
President and Chief Executive Officer
February 28, 2006

Mark Loughridge
Senior Vice President,
Chief Financial Officer
February 28, 2006

Reasons for Earnings Management

Understand the concept of earnings management and why it occurs.

(3) Accountants, using the concepts of accrual accounting and the accounting standards that have been issued, add information value by using estimates and assumptions to convert the raw cash flow data into accrual data. However, the same flexibility that allows accountants to use professional judgment to produce financial statements that accurately portray a company's financial condition also allows desperate managers to "manage" the reported numbers.[5]

This section describes four reasons for managing reported earnings. These aren't necessarily good reasons. However, they do reflect the forces that are often spoken of as pushing managers to manipulate reported earnings. These four reasons are as follows:

- Meet internal targets.
- Meet external expectations.
- Income smoothing.
- Window dressing for an IPO or a loan.

---

[5] As we will learn in the subsequent discussion, extreme "earnings management" may result from fraudulent activities. But it is important to note that not all earnings management activities are fraudulent.

Meet Internal Targets

internal earnings targets

Financial goals established within a company.

Internal earnings targets are an important tool in motivating managers to increase sales efforts, control costs, and use resources more efficiently. But as with any performance measurement tool, it is a fact of life that the person being evaluated will have a tendency to forget the economic factors underlying the measurement and instead focus on the measured number itself.

Meet External Expectations

A wide variety of external stakeholders have an interest in the financial performance of a company. For example, employees and customers want a company to do well so that it can survive for the long run and make good on its long-term pension and warranty obligations. Suppliers want assurance that they will receive payment and, more importantly, that the purchasing company will be a reliable purchaser for many years into the future. For these stakeholders, signs of financial weakness, such as the reporting of negative earnings, are very bad news indeed. Accordingly, we shouldn't be surprised that in some companies when the initial computations reveal that a company will report a net loss, the company's accountants are asked to go back to the accrual judgments and estimates to see if just a few more dollars of earnings can be squeezed in order to get earnings to be positive.

Income Smoothing

Examine the time series of earnings for Company A and Company B shown in Exhibit 2. For Company A, the amount of earnings increases steadily for each year from Year 1 through Year 10. For Company B, the earnings series is like a roller coaster ride. Companies A and B have the same earnings in Year 1 and the same earnings in Year 10, and they also have the same total earnings over the 10-year period included in the graph. At the end of Year 10, if you were asked which company you would prefer to loan money to or to invest in, you would almost certainly choose Company A. The earnings stream of Company A gives you a sense of stability, reliability, and reduced risk.

Now, imagine yourself as the chief executive officer of Company B. You know that through aggressive accounting assumptions, you can strategically defer or accelerate the

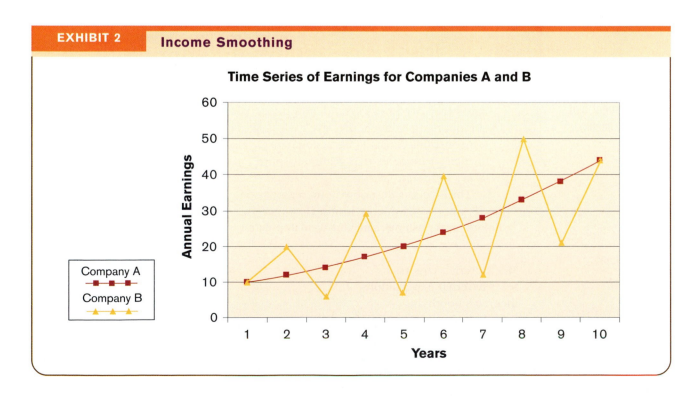

EXHIBIT 2   Income Smoothing

Time Series of Earnings for Companies A and B

income smoothing

The practice of carefully timing the recognition of revenues and expenses to even out the amount of reported earnings from one year to the next.

recognition of some revenues and expenses and smooth your reported earnings stream to be exactly like that shown for Company A. Would you be tempted to do so? The practice of carefully timing the recognition of revenues and expenses to even out the amount of reported earnings from one year to the next is called **income smoothing**. By making a company appear to be less volatile, income smoothing can make it easier for a company to obtain a loan on favorable terms and to attract investors.

Window Dressing for an IPO or a Loan

For companies entering phases where it is critical that reported earnings look good, accounting assumptions can be stretched—sometimes to the breaking point. Such phases include just before making a large loan application or just before the initial public offering (IPO) of stock. Many studies have demonstrated the tendency of managers in U.S. companies to boost their reported earnings using accounting assumptions in the period before an IPO.

With all of the incentives to manage earnings, it isn't surprising that managers occasionally do use the flexibility inherent in accrual accounting to actually manage earnings. And the more accounting training one has, the easier it is to see ways in which accounting judgments and estimates can be used to "enhance" the reported numbers. In fact, there have been nationwide seminars on exactly how to effectively manage earnings. One popular seminar sponsored by the National Center for Continuing Education in 2001 was titled, "How to Manage Earnings in Conformance with GAAP." The target audience for the two-day seminar was described as CFOs, CPAs, controllers, auditors, bankers, analysts, and securities attorneys.

F Y I

In the wake of the accounting scandals that occurred in 2001 and 2002, the National Center for Continuing Education decided to change the title of the earnings management seminar to "How to Detect Manipulative Accounting Practices." However, the course outline was exactly the same as the original "How to Manage Earnings" seminar.

The Earnings Management Continuum

Not all earnings management schemes are created equal. The continuum in Exhibit 3 illustrates that earnings management can range from savvy timing of transactions to outright fraud. The discussion in this section discusses each activity on the earnings management continuum. Keep in mind that in most companies, earnings management, if it is practiced at all, does not extend beyond the savvy transaction timing found at the left end of the continuum in Exhibit 3. However, because of the importance, and economic significance, of the catastrophic reporting failures that are sometimes associated with companies that engage in more elaborate earnings management, the entire continuum is discussed here.

EXHIBIT 3	The Earnings Management Continuum			
Savvy Transaction Timing	Aggressive Accounting	Deceptive Accounting	Fraudulent Reporting	Fraud
Strategic Matching	Change in Methods or Estimates with Full Disclosure	Change in Methods or Estimates but with Little or No Disclosure	Non-GAAP Accounting	Fictitious Transactions

Strategic Matching   As mentioned in the earlier discussion of income smoothing, through awareness of the benefits of consistently meeting earnings targets or of reporting a stable income stream, a company can make extra efforts to ensure that certain key transactions are completed quickly, or delayed, in order for them to be recognized in the most advantageous quarter.

Change in Methods or Estimates with Full Disclosure   Companies frequently change accounting estimates regarding bad debts, return on pension funds, depreciation lives, and so forth. Although such changes are a routine part of adjusting accounting estimates to reflect the most current information available, they can be used to manage the amount of reported earnings. Because the impact of such changes is fully disclosed, any earnings management motivation could be detected by financial statement users willing to do a little detective work.

Change in Methods or Estimates with Little or No Disclosure   In contrast to the accounting changes referred to in the preceding paragraph, other accounting changes are sometimes made without full disclosure. For example, in 1999 **Xerox** reported that the company changed the estimated interest rate used in recording sales-type leases without describing the change in the notes to the financial statements. While one might debate whether the new estimated interest rate was more appropriate, what is certain is that failing to disclose the impact of the change resulted in financial statement users being misled. These users evaluated the reported earnings of Xerox under the incorrect assumption that the results were compiled using a consistent set of accounting methods and estimates and could therefore be meaningfully compared to prior-year results. As indicated by the label in Exhibit 3, this constitutes deceptive accounting.

Non-GAAP Accounting   Toward the right end of the earnings management continuum lies the earnings management tool that can be politely called "non-GAAP accounting." A more descriptive label in many cases is "fraudulent reporting," although non-GAAP accounting can also be the result of inadvertent errors. For example, a brief description of some of **Enron's** accounting practices was given in Chapter 1. It is clear that some (though certainly not all) of these accounting practices were established for the express purpose of hiding information from financial statement users. In so doing, Enron violated the spirit of the accounting standards. In some cases, Enron also violated the letter of the standards by using some accounting practices that were not allowed under GAAP.

Fictitious Transactions   As mentioned previously in this chapter, **Regina** did not record the return of over 40,000 vacuums. In fact, the company rented secret warehouses in which to store returned merchandise in order to avoid recording the returns. This is an example of outright fraud, which is the deceptive concealment of transactions (like the sales returns) or the creation of fictitious transactions.

The five items displayed in Exhibit 3 also mirror the progression in earnings management strategies followed by individual companies. These activities start small and legitimate and really reflect nothing more than the strategic timing of transactions to smooth reported results. In the face of operating results that fall short of targets, a company might make some cosmetic changes in accounting estimates in order to meet earnings expectations, but would fully disclose these changes to avoid deceiving serious financial statement users. If operating results are far short of expectations, an increasingly desperate management might cross the line into deceptive accounting by making accounting changes that are not disclosed or by violating GAAP completely. Finally, when the gap between expected results and actual results is so great that it cannot be closed by any accounting assumption, a manager who is still fixated on making the target number must resort to out-and-out fraud by inventing transactions and customers. The key thing to remember is that the forces encouraging managers and accountants to manage earnings are real, and if one is not aware of those forces it is easy to gradually slip from the left side of the earnings management continuum to the right side.

Is Earnings Management Ethical?

Refer back to Exhibit 3. Everyone agrees that the creation of fictitious transactions, at the far right side of the earnings management continuum, is unethical. But there the universal agreement ends with respect to what is and is not ethical. For example, managers and their auditors frequently disagree about what constitutes fraudulent, non-GAAP reporting. In the **WorldCom** example mentioned earlier, the company's CFO vigorously defended the capitalization, rather than the expensing, of the disputed $3.8 billion in local phone access charges. The CFO reiterated this defense, based on his understanding of the appropriate accounting standards, in a multi-day series of meetings with the external auditor and the audit committee. In the view of the CFO, this "fraudulent reporting" was both ethical and in conformity with GAAP. And as one moves even further to the left on the earnings management continuum, disagreement about whether a certain act is or is not ethical increases. For example, when a company makes an accounting change, how can a bright line be drawn between sufficient and deceptive disclosure? And who is to judge whether the strategic timing of gains and losses by a company is unethical or just prudent business practice?

Exhibit 4 contains a figure called the **GAAP oval**. This oval represents the flexibility a manager has, within GAAP, to report one earnings number from among many possibilities based on different methods and assumptions. Clearly, reporting a number corresponding with points D or E, which are both outside the GAAP oval, is unethical. The difficult ethical question is whether the manager has a responsibility to try to report an earnings number exactly in the middle of the possible range, such as point B in Exhibit 4. Or does the manager have a responsibility to report the most conservative, worst-case number, like point A in the exhibit? Is it wrong for the manager to try to use accounting flexibility to report an earnings number corresponding with point C, which is the highest possible earnings number that is still in conformity with GAAP? And what cost is there, in terms of credibility, for a manager who makes a conservative

GAAP oval

A diagram that represents the flexibility a manager has, within GAAP, to report one earnings number from among many possibilities based on different methods and assumptions.

F Y I

Nonaccountants are under the impression that there is no GAAP oval. Instead, they believe that there is only a GAAP point, a single quantity that represents the one, true earnings number. Managers must be aware that because of this attitude the public can be very unforgiving of companies that are found to have "innocently" managed earnings.

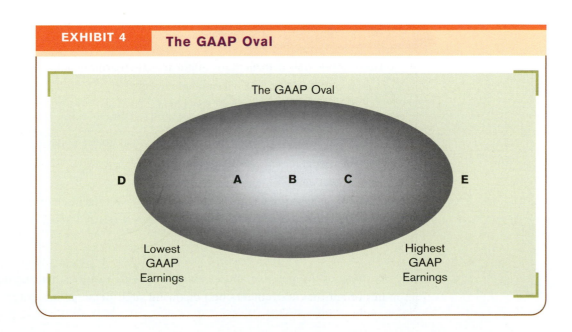

EXHIBIT 4	The GAAP Oval

The GAAP Oval

D   A   B   C   E

Lowest GAAP Earnings

Highest GAAP Earnings

set of accounting assumptions one year, perhaps when overall operating performance is good, and an aggressive set of assumptions the next year, perhaps to try to hide lackluster operating performance? Finally, note also that the boundary of the oval is fuzzy, so it sometimes is not clear whether a certain set of computations is or is not in conformity with GAAP.

Of course, whether a manager actually does manage earnings, and whether he or she crosses the line and violates GAAP to do so, is partially a function of the fear (and costs) of getting caught and of the general ethical culture of the company. But it is also a function of the personal ethics of the manager, and the manager's ability to recognize that fraudulent and deceptive financial reporting is part of a continuum that starts with innocent window dressing but can end with full-scale fraud. There is no neon sign giving a final warning saying, "Beware, don't cross this line!" Thus, each individual must be constantly aware of where he or she is with respect to the earnings management continuum in Exhibit 3 and the GAAP oval in Exhibit 4. Boards of directors and financial statement preparers should also be aware that, as a group, managers are notoriously overoptimistic about the future business prospects of their companies. Therefore, a company policy of having a consistently conservative approach to accounting is a good counterbalance to managers who might try to justify optimistic accounting assumptions on the basis of a business turnaround that is "just around the corner."

Personal Ethics

Personal ethics is not a topic one typically expects to study in a financial accounting course. However, the large number of accounting scandals in 2001 and 2002 demonstrated that personal ethics and financial reporting are inextricably connected. The GAAP oval in Exhibit 4 illustrates that there is a range of earnings numbers a company can report for a year and still be in strict conformity with GAAP. Thus, earnings management can and does occur without any violation of the accounting rules. If one takes a strictly legalistic view of the world, then it is clear that managers should manage earnings, when they have concluded that the potential costs in terms of lost credibility are outweighed by the financial reporting benefits, because earnings can be managed without violating any rules.

A contrasting view is that the practice of financial accounting is not a matter of simply applying a list of rules to a set of objective facts. Management intent often enters into the decision of how to report a particular item. For example, land is reported as a long-term

---

REMEMBER THIS...

The reasons that management might manage earnings include:

- pressure to meet internal earnings targets,
- pressure to meet external expectations,
- smoothing income, and
- preparing to apply for a loan or to offer stock to the public.

Earnings management can take the form of:

- careful timing of transactions,
- changing accounting methods or estimates with full disclosure,
- changing accounting methods or estimates WITHOUT adequate disclosure,
- non-GAAP accounting, and
- fictitious transactions.

Because of the possible abuses associated with earnings management, it is important that accountants be persons of high personal integrity.

asset in the balance sheet unless management intends to sell the land within one year of the balance sheet date. In the context of earnings management, an important consideration is whether savvy transaction timing or changes in accounting methods or estimates are done to better communicate the economic performance of the business to financial statement users or whether the earnings management techniques are used with the intent to deceive. And if earnings management is done to deceive, who is management trying to deceive? If management is trying to deceive potential investors, lenders, regulatory authorities, employees, or other company stakeholders, then managing earnings poses a real risk of lost credibility in the future. And there is one final important item to consider—most of us believe that intentionally trying to deceive others is wrong, no matter what the economic consequences.

The Sarbanes-Oxley Act

Understand the major parts of the Sarbanes-Oxley Act and how it impacts financial reporting.

(4) The Sarbanes-Oxley Act that was passed by Congress in 2002 was by far the most comprehensive legislation ever affecting the accuracy of financial reports. Because of its significance, it is important that you understand the highlights of this legislation. The major effects of this legislation can be divided into three categories: the establishment of independent oversight of auditors, constraints on auditors, and constraints on company management.

Public Company Accounting Oversight Board

Public Company Accounting Oversight Board (PCAOB)

Board of five full-time members established by the Sarbanes-Oxley Act to oversee the accounting and auditing profession.

Sarbanes-Oxley required the establishment of a **Public Company Accounting Oversight Board (PCAOB)**, with five full-time members, to oversee the accounting and auditing profession. This board is required to:

- Register all public accounting firms that provide audits for public companies.
- Establish standards relating to the preparation of audit reports for public companies.
- Conduct inspections (reviews) of accounting firms.
- Conduct investigations and disciplinary proceedings and impose appropriate sanctions on pubic accounting firms whose performance is inadequate.
- Enforce compliance with the Sarbanes-Oxley Act.

FYI

Who are Sarbanes and Oxley? Paul Sarbanes is a Democratic senator from Maryland, and Michael Oxley is a Republican member of the House of Representatives from Ohio. These two gentlemen co-sponsored this sweeping reform.

Constraints on Auditors

To ensure that external auditors remain independent, Sarbanes-Oxley requires the following:

- Accounting firms that audit public companies are prohibited from providing several non-audit services to their clients, including: (1) bookkeeping or other services related to the accounting records or financial statements, (2) financial information systems design and implementation, (3) appraisal or valuation services, (4) actuarial services, (5) internal audit outsourcing services, (6) management functions or human resources, (7) broker or dealer, investment adviser or investment banking services, (8) legal services and expert services unrelated to the audit, and (9) any other service that the Board determines is impermissible.

- Requires that audit partners on engagements be rotated off the audit every five years.
- Requires that auditors report to and be retained by the audit committee rather than the CFO or other members of the company's management.

Constraints on Management

Restoring public confidence in the financial reporting process will require that management ensure financial statement users of the steps taken to provide quality financial information. To that end, Sarbanes-Oxley requires management to do the following:

- The CEO and CFO of each public company are required to prepare a statement to accompany the audit report to certify to the appropriateness of the financial statements and disclosures. As discussed earlier, management is still required to provide an assessment of internal controls in each annual report.
- All public companies are required to develop and enforce an officer code of ethics.
- Loans to executive officers and directors are prohibited.
- Support a much stronger board and audit committee in each public company. The audit committee is a subset of the board of directors and consists only of individuals who are not part of the management team of the company.

Only time will tell how effective this law is in preventing and deterring financial statement misstatements. One thing is for sure, however, and that is that because of this legislation, public companies are taking their financial reporting responsibilities much more seriously than ever before.

REMEMBER THIS...

The Sarbanes-Oxley Act has the following major provisions.

- Public Company Accounting Oversight Board—established to oversee the certification of auditors
- Constraints on auditors—stricter rules to ensure that external auditors maintain their independence
- Constraints on management—provisions to make corporate CEOs and CFOs personally responsible for reliable financial statements

The Role of Auditors in the Accounting Process

Describe the role of auditors and how their presence affects the integrity of financial statements.

(5) Someone needs to check and make sure that the accounting system is running as designed and that the resulting financial statements fairly present the financial performance of the company. Auditors are that "someone." Auditors provide management (and stockholders) with some assurance that the internal control system is functioning properly and that the financial statements fairly represent the financial performance of the firm. Two types of auditors are typically employed by management—internal and external auditors.

Internal Auditors

Most large organizations have a staff of **internal auditors**, an independent group of experts in controls, accounting, and operations. This group's major purpose is to monitor

internal auditors

An independent group of experts (in controls, accounting, and operations) who monitor operating results and financial records, evaluate internal controls, assist with increasing the efficiency and effectiveness of operations, and detect fraud.

operating results and financial records, evaluate internal controls, assist with increasing the efficiency and effectiveness of operations, and even detect fraud. The internal audit staffs in some large organizations include over 100 individuals. The audit manager reports directly to the president (or other high-level executive officer) and to the audit committee of the board of directors. By performing independent evaluations of an organization's internal controls, the internal auditors are helping preserve integrity in the reporting process. Employees who know that internal auditors are reviewing operations and reports are less likely to manipulate records. Even if they do, their actions may be discovered by the work of the internal auditors.

Internal auditors' responsibilities vary considerably, depending upon the organization. Some internal audit staffs consist of only one or two employees who spend most of their time performing reviews of financial records or internal controls. Other organizations may have a large number of auditors who search for and investigate fraud, work to improve operational efficiency and effectiveness, and make sure their organization is complying with various laws and regulations.

Organizations that have a competent group of internal auditors generally have fewer financial reporting problems than do organizations that don't have internal auditors.

External Auditors

external auditors

Independent CPAs who are retained by organizations to perform audits of financial statements.

generally accepted auditing standards (GAAS)

Auditing standards developed by the PCAOB for public companies and AICPA for private companies.

Probably the greatest safeguard in the financial reporting system in the United States is the requirement that firms have external audits of their financial statements and internal controls. **External auditors** examine an organization's financial statements to determine if they are prepared and presented in accordance with generally accepted accounting principles and are free from material (significant) misstatement. They also issue opinions about management's assessment of the reliability of an organization's internal controls and their own assessment of the reliability of internal controls. External audits are performed by certified public accounting (CPA) firms. CPA audits are required by the Securities and Exchange Commission and the major stock exchanges for all companies whose stock is publicly traded. Even companies that are not public, however, often employ CPAs to perform audits of their financial statements. Banks and other lenders usually require audits, and audits can instill confidence in users of financial reports. In conducting audits, CPAs are required by **generally accepted auditing standards (GAAS)** to provide reasonable assurance that significant fraud or misstatement is not present in financial statements. Because CPAs cannot audit every transaction of an organization, and because detecting collusive management deception is sometimes impossible, it is not possible for auditors to guarantee that financial statements are "correct." Instead, they can only provide reasonable assurance that financial statements are "presented fairly." Even with audits, there are still a few occasions when major financial statement fraud is not detected. As we have already discussed in this chapter, the Sarbanes-Oxley Act of 2002 made major reforms in the way CPAs must conduct their audits, who they report to, and what their penalties are for not conducting proper audits.

 F Y I

As of 2006, four international public accounting firms—the "Big 4": **Ernst & Young**, **PricewaterhouseCoopers**, **Deloitte & Touche**, and **KPMG**—were responsible for auditing the majority of the Fortune 500 companies, as well as most other large, publicly-traded companies in the United States. Until 2001, there were five large firms but as you learned in Chapter 1, **Arthur Andersen's** involvement in **Waste Management**, **Enron**, and **WorldCom** dealt a one-two-three knockout punch that put Arthur Andersen out of business.

CPA audits of financial statements have become very important in the United States because of the enormous size of many

STOP & THINK

What could auditors do to ensure that the financial reporting system in a company is working properly? Be specific.

corporations. Because the stockholders, who own corporations, are usually different individuals from a company's management, audits provide comfort to these owners/investors that management is carrying out its stewardship function appropriately.

What Do Auditors Do?

While management has the primary responsibility to prepare the financial statements and ensure that the internal control system is functioning properly, internal auditors provide an independent assessment of how well the controls are working. External auditors usually study the internal control system to see if they can rely on it as they perform their audits, provide an opinion on management's assessment of the reliability of internal controls, and issue their own independent opinion about the adequacy of the internal controls. If the internal control system is functioning correctly, it increases the likelihood that the resulting financial information is reliable.

CAUTION

External auditors are responsible for evaluating the assumptions and estimates of management as well as testing the internal control system. The external auditors do not make the assumptions and estimates, nor are they responsible for designing the internal control system.

Auditors gain confidence in the quality of the reporting process using several different processes: interviews, observation, sampling, confirmation, and analytical procedures. Several of these processes are used by both internal and external auditors, while some are used primarily by external auditors. Exhibit 5 provides a summary of these procedures and indicates who uses them most often. A brief discussion of each process then follows.

Interviews Auditors *interview* employees to ensure that procedures are understood, proper documentation is being made, and proper authorization is being obtained. Through interviews, auditors identify potential weaknesses in the control system that will be examined using testing procedures.

Observation *Observation* is done to verify compliance with procedures and to ensure that accounting records agree with physical records. For example, auditors in a bank will count the cash in a vault to ensure that recorded amounts agree with the actual cash on hand. Auditors will also verify the existence of inventory by doing a physical count of product. In addition to using observation to verify the existence of assets, auditors will also use observation to ensure that employees are complying with proper procedures.

Sampling As mentioned previously, auditors cannot examine every transaction. Typically, they will select a *sample of transactions* for analysis. Based on the results of

EXHIBIT 5	Audit Processes Used by Auditors	
	Internal Auditors	**External Auditors**
Interviews	X	X
Observation	X	X
Sampling	X	X
Confirmation	–	X
Analytical procedures	–	X

their analysis of the sample, they may conclude that the internal control procedures are being complied with, resulting in reliable financial information. Auditors may also conclude from the results that the internal control system is not reliable, resulting in further testing being required.

Confirmation   Used primarily by external auditors, *confirmations* are used to verify the balances in accounts that result from transactions with outsiders. For example, customers are often contacted and asked to verify account balances. Banks are contacted to verify loan amounts, lines of credit, and other account balances. This procedure ensures that the balances listed on the financial statements do, in fact, exist.

Analytical Procedures   *Analytical procedures* are used to provide guidance to external auditors as they attempt to identify areas that may deserve attention. Analytical procedures involve the use of such techniques as comparative ratio analysis. By comparing the results of ratio analysis from one period to the next, auditors may be able to identify areas where additional investigation may be appropriate.

At the completion of an audit, the auditors issue a report that accompanies the financial statements and describes to readers, in very general terms, what was done by the audit firm and whether accounting rules were followed; the report also indicates an opinion as to whether the financial statements and the accompanying notes fairly represent the financial condition of the firm.

As an example of an auditors' report, **Wal-Mart's** 2006 independent auditors' report, taken from the company's 2006 financial statements, is included in Exhibit 6.

EXHIBIT 6	**Wal-Mart's 2006 Independent Auditors' Report**

Report of Independent Registered Accounting Firm

The Board of Directors and Shareholders of Wal-Mart Stores, Inc.

We have audited the accompanying consolidated balance sheets of Wal-Mart Stores, Inc. as of January 31, 2006 and 2005, and the related consolidated statements of income, shareholders' equity and cash flows for each of the three years in the period ended January 31, 2006. These financial statements are the responsibility of the Company's management. Our responsibility is to express an opinion on these financial statements based on our audits.

We conducted our audits in accordance with the standards of the Public Company Accounting Oversight Board (United States). Those standards require that we plan and perform the audit to obtain reasonable assurance about whether the financial statements are free of material misstatement. An audit includes examining, on a test basis, evidence supporting the amounts and disclosures in the financial statements. An audit also includes assessing the accounting principles used and significant estimates made by management, as well as evaluating the overall financial statement presentation. We believe that our audits provide a reasonable basis for our opinion.

In our opinion, the financial statements referred to above present fairly, in all material respects, the consolidated financial position of Wal-Mart Stores, Inc. at January 31, 2006 and 2005, and the consolidated results of its operations and its cash flows for each of the three years in the period ended January 31, 2006, in conformity with accounting principles generally accepted in the United States of America.

We have also audited, in accordance with the standards of the Public Company Accounting Oversight Board (United States), the effectiveness of the Wal-Mart Stores, Inc.'s internal control over financial reporting as of January 31, 2006 based on the criteria established in *Internal Control–Integrated Framework* issued by the Committee of Sponsoring Organizations of the Treadway Commission, and our report dated March 27, 2006, expressed an unqualified opinion thereon.

ERNST & YOUNG LLP
Ernst & Young LLP
Rogers, Arkansas

March 27, 2006

Are Outside (Independent) Auditors Independent?

Independent auditors are hired by the audit committee of the board of directors to make sure that the financial statements prepared by *management* fairly represent the financial performance of the company. Since the company being audited is paying the auditors, is there a danger that the auditors may not be independent? Is there a possibility that auditors will go along with whatever management says because management is paying them? That possibility exists, but there are a number of factors that work as a counterbalance.

First, recall from our discussion of the internal control structure that the Foreign Corrupt Practices and Sarbanes-Oxley acts require companies to maintain an adequate system of internal controls. If management knowingly violate this law, they can go to jail (a number of top managers have) and would be subject to personal fines. In addition, the company is subject to corporate fines. Thus, management would be taking a big risk if they interfere with the auditors.

Second, external auditors have a responsibility to financial statement users to ensure that financial statements are fairly presented. The legal system in the United States provides auditors with financial incentives to remain independent. As an example, the auditors in the **Phar-Mor** financial statement fraud case were sued by plaintiffs for over $1 billion. A jury held the audit firm liable, and that firm settled with the plaintiffs for a lesser, though undisclosed (but not insignificant), amount. Thus, external auditors are taking a big risk if they allow their independence and integrity to be compromised.

Third, auditors have a reputation to protect. The reason auditors are hired at all is because the investing public believes they provide an independent check on the reliability and integrity of the financial information. If an audit firm were no longer perceived in this manner, companies would cease to employ it. CPA firms obtain audit clients based on the quality of their reputation. Would they sell that reputation to the highest bidder? That would be very shortsighted indeed.

FYI

This give and take between the auditors and management typically results in financial statements that fairly reflect the financial performance of a business. For example, in 2004, of 6,319 audits conducted for firms listed on the New York, American, and NASDAQ stock exchanges, only 3 involved significant issues on which auditors and management could not reach agreement on disclosure.

Knowing the incentives that influence auditors to provide fair and reliable financial information, we can now begin to see how the issues relating to disagreements in judgment can work themselves out. On the one hand, we have a management team that has an incentive to provide financial statement information that portrays the company in the most favorable position possible. On the other hand, we have auditors who are responsible to ensure that the information being provided is unbiased and fair. If auditors don't live up to their charge, they can end up paying to litigants much more than they ever received in audit fees.

The Securities and Exchange Commission (SEC) and the new Public Company Accounting Oversight Board are working with public accounting firms to ensure that independence remains a keystone of the auditing profession.

If management is allowed to paint an overly optimistic picture of the firm's performance by using estimates that bias the financial reports, the audit firm will pay (via litigation) if those estimates prove to be materially wrong in the future. To protect itself, the audit firm would actually prefer that management use conservative estimates, but management will not always go along with the auditors in this regard. It is this tension, resulting from differing incentives, that provides financial statement users with information that, taken as a whole, fairly represents the financial performance of a business.

REMEMBER THIS...

- Auditors provide a check and balance to ensure that the financial statements fairly reflect the financial performance of a business.
- Internal auditors ensure integrity in the financial records and evaluate and encourage adherence to the organization's internal controls.
- External certified public accountants ensure the integrity in the financial reporting process with independent audits of financial statements.
- Independent financial statement audits are required for all public companies, and often by creditors and other users.

The Securities and Exchange Commission

Explain the role of the Securities and Exchange Commission in adding credibility to financial statements.

(6) In addition to the role of independent internal and external auditors, the U.S. government plays a role in ensuring the integrity of financial information. The **Securities and Exchange Commission (SEC)** is responsible for ensuring that investors, creditors, and other financial statement users are provided with reliable information upon which to make investment decisions.

The SEC is an agency of the federal government. The SEC was organized in the 1930s because of financial reporting and stock market abuses. One such abuse was price manipulation. It was not uncommon in the 1920s for stockbrokers or dealers to indulge in "wash sales" or "matched orders," in which successive buy and sell orders created a false impression of stock activity and forced prices up. This maneuver allowed those involved to reap huge profits before the price fell back to its true market level. Outright deceit by issuing false and misleading financial statements was another improper practice. The objective of these manipulative procedures was to make profits at the expense of unwary investors.

The Securities Act of 1933 requires most companies planning to issue new debt or stock securities to the public to submit a registration statement to the SEC for approval. The SEC examines these statements for completeness and adequacy before permitting companies to sell securities through securities exchanges. The Securities Exchange Act of 1934 requires all public companies to file detailed periodic reports with the SEC.

Securities and Exchange Commission (SEC)

The government body responsible for regulating the financial reporting practices of most publicly-owned corporations in connection with the buying and selling of stocks and bonds.

? FYI

The first chairman of the SEC was Joseph P. Kennedy, father of the late President John F. Kennedy.

The SEC requires a considerable amount of information to be included in these filings. Among other things, a company must submit financial statements that have been audited by CPAs and that contain an opinion issued by those CPAs.

Of the many reports required by the SEC, the following have the most direct impact on financial reporting:

- *Registration statements.* These include various forms that must be filed and approved before a company can sell securities through the securities exchanges.
- *Form 10-K.* This report must be filed annually for all publicly held companies. The report contains extensive financial information, including audited financial

statements by independent CPAs. The 10-K also requires additional disclosure beyond that typically provided in the audited financial statements. Examples of additional information include the executive compensation of top management and the details of property, plant, and equipment transactions.

• *Form 10-Q.* This report must be filed quarterly for all publicly held companies. It contains certain financial information and requires a CPA's involvement.

Because the SEC has statutory power to mandate any reporting requirement it feels is needed, it has considerable influence in setting generally accepted accounting principles and disclosure requirements for financial statements. Generally, the SEC accepts the accounting pronouncements of the Financial Accounting Standards Board and other bodies such as the AICPA. In addition, the SEC has the power to establish rules for any CPA associated with audited financial statements submitted to the commission.

The SEC is given broad enforcement powers under the 1934 Act. If the rules of operation for stock exchanges prove to be ineffectual in implementing the requirements of the SEC, the SEC can alter or supplement them. The SEC can suspend trading of a company's stock for not more than 10 days (a series of orders has enabled the SEC to suspend trading for extended periods, however) and can suspend all trading on any exchange for up to 90 days. If substantive hearings show that the issuer failed to comply with the requirements of the securities laws, the SEC can "de-list" any security. Brokers and dealers can be prevented, either temporarily or permanently, from working in the securities market, and investigations can be initiated, if deemed necessary, to determine violations of any of the Acts or rules administered by the SEC.

The Effect of the 1934 Act on Independent Accountants

Accountants are involved in the preparation and review of a major portion of the reports and statements required by the 1934 Act. Accountants also can be censured, and their work is subject to approval by the SEC. The financial statements in the annual report to stockholders and in the 10-K report must be audited. In addition, accountants consult and assist in the preparation of the quarterly 10-Q reports and the other periodic reports.

More recently, the Sarbanes-Oxley Act has strengthened the authority of the SEC to monitor financial reporting. Under the Act, the SEC is given more resources and authority, has oversight for the new Public Company Accounting Oversight Board, has more control over auditors and reporting companies, and, in general, has a greater responsibility to protect investors and creditors who rely on financial reports.

REMEMBER THIS...

• The Securities and Exchange Commission (SEC) is an agency of the federal government.

• The purpose of the SEC is to assist investors in public companies by regulating stock and bond markets and by requiring certain disclosures.

• The SEC has statutory authority to establish accounting principles, but it basically accepts pronouncements of the FASB and AICPA as authoritative.

• Common reports required by the SEC are registration statements and Forms 10-K and 10-Q.

• The SEC can suspend trading and even de-list securities.

REVIEW OF LEARNING OBJECTIVES

① **Identify the types of problems that can appear in financial statements.** Three types of problems can affect financial statements.

Errors	Unintentional mistakes that can enter the accounting system at the transaction and journal entry stage or when journal entries are posted to accounts
Disagreements in judgment	Differences in opinion about what numbers should be reported in the financial statements based on different estimates
Fraud	Intentional misrepresentations in the financial statements

② **Describe the safeguards employed to ensure that financial statements are free from problems.** Internal controls are safeguards built into an organization that help to protect assets and increase reliability of the accounting records. The three basic internal control structure categories are:

(1) the control environment,
(2) the accounting systems, and
(3) the control procedures.

The five types of control procedures are:

(1) segregation of duties,
(2) procedures for authorizations,
(3) documents and records,
(4) physical safeguards, and
(5) independent checks.

③ **Understand the concept of earnings management and why it occurs.**

Reasons for earnings management	• pressure to meet internal earnings targets • pressure to meet external expectations • smoothing income • preparing to apply for a loan or to offer stock to the public
Techniques of earnings management	• careful timing of transactions • changing accounting methods or estimates with full disclosure • changing accounting methods or estimates withOUT adequate disclosure • non-GAAP accounting • fictitious transactions

④ **Understand the major parts of the Sarbanes-Oxley Act and how it impacts financial reporting.**

Public Company Accounting Oversight Board (PCAOB)	• register all public accounting firms • establish auditing standards • inspect public accounting firms
Constraints on auditors	• auditors are prohibited from providing non-audit services to audit clients • audit partners must rotate every five years • auditors must report to the audit committee of the board of directors

Constraints on management	• the CEO and the CFO must personally certify the reliability of the financial statements • companies must have a code of ethics • loans to company executives are prohibited • audit committees must be strengthened

(5) Describe the role of auditors and how their presence affects the integrity of financial statements.

Internal auditors	• evaluate internal controls • monitor operating results • ensure compliance with laws and company policy • detect fraud
External auditors	Gather evidence to be able to certify the fairness of the financial statements through: • interviews • observation • sampling • confirmation • analytical procedures

• External audits are required of most public companies by the Securities and Exchange Commission.
• External audits must be performed by CPAs who are licensed by the individual states in which they practice.

(6) Explain the role of the Securities and Exchange Commission in adding credibility to financial statements.
• The SEC is the agency of the federal government charged with the responsibility of assisting investors by making sure they are provided with reliable information upon which to make investment decisions.
• The SEC was organized in the 1930s and requires certain periodic reports such as the Forms 10-Q and 10-K of companies that sell stock publicly in the United States.
• The SEC adds credibility to financial statements by:
  • requiring independent audits,
  • reviewing financial statements itself, and
  • sanctioning firms that violate its standards.

KEY TERMS & CONCEPTS

audit committee, 192

control activities (procedures), 192

control environment, 192

detective controls, 192

external auditors, 203

Foreign Corrupt Practices Act (FCPA), 191

GAAP oval, 199

generally accepted auditing standards (GAAS), 203

income smoothing, 197

independent checks, 194

internal auditors, 203

internal control structure, 191

internal earnings target, 196

organizational structure, 192

physical safeguards, 193

preventative controls, 192

Public Company Accounting Oversight Board (PCAOB), 201

Sarbanes-Oxley Act, 191

Securities and Exchange Commission (SEC), 207

segregation of duties, 193

DISCUSSION QUESTIONS

1. How can a person tell whether an entry to an expense account is payment for a legitimate expenditure or a means of concealing a theft of cash?
2. How would it be possible to overstate revenues? What effect would an overstatement of revenues have on total assets?
3. What is the Foreign Corrupt Practices Act, and how is it important to financial reporting?
4. What are the major elements of a system of internal controls?
5. Identify five different types of control procedures.
6. What are the four factors that might motivate a manager to attempt to manage earnings?
7. (a) What is the purpose of internal earnings targets? (b) What is the risk associated with internal earnings targets?
8. What is meant by the term *income smoothing*?
9. What are the five labels in the earnings management continuum (see Exhibit 3), and what general types of actions are associated with each of the labels?
10. Is there anything wrong with using a different accounting estimate this year compared to last year, as long as both estimates fall within a generally accepted range for your industry?
11. Refer to the GAAP oval in Exhibit 4. (a) In what important way is point E different from point C?

(b) In what important way is point A different from point C?
12. The Sarbanes-Oxley Act established the Public Company Accounting Oversight Board. Identify the duties of that board.
13. What constraints were placed on auditors as a result of the Sarbanes-Oxley Act?
14. As a result of the Sarbanes-Oxley Act, public companies are required to make changes in the way they do business. What practice does Sarbanes-Oxley forbid?
15. How do internal auditors add to the credibility of financial statements?
16. What is the purpose of a financial statement audit by CPAs?
17. Do you believe that outside auditors (CPAs) who examine the financial statements of a company, while being paid by that company, can be truly independent?
18. The SEC requires companies to register with it when they sell stocks or bonds and also requires periodic reporting thereafter. Which of these reports, the initial registration statements or the subsequent periodic reports, do you believe would be scrutinized more closely by the SEC?
19. What do you suspect is the relationship between the FASB and the SEC?

EXERCISES

E 5-1
LO1

Accounting Errors–Transaction Errors

How would the following errors affect the account balances and the basic accounting equation, *Assets = Liabilities + Owners' Equity*? How do the misstatements affect income?

a. The purchase of a truck is recorded as an expense instead of an asset.
b. A cash payment on accounts receivable is received but not recorded.
c. Fictitious sales on account are recorded.
d. A clerk misreads a handwritten invoice for repairs and records it as $1,500 instead of $1,800.
e. Payment is received on December 31 for the next three months' rent and is recorded as revenue.

E 5-2
LO1

Errors in Financial Statements

The following financial statements are available for Sherwood Real Estate Company:

(continued)

Balance Sheet

Assets		Liabilities	
Cash	$ 1,300	Accounts payable	$ 100,000
Receivable from sale		Mortgage payable	6,000,000
of real estate	5,000,000	Total liabilities	$ 6,100,000
Interest receivable*	180,000		
Real estate properties ...	6,000,000	**Stockholders' Equity**	
		Capital stock	$ 10,000
		Retained earnings	5,071,300
		Total stockholders' equity ...	5,081,300
		Total liabilities and	
Total assets	$11,181,300	stockholders' equity	$11,181,300

*Interest Receivable applies to Receivable from sale of real estate.

Income Statement

Gain on sale of real estate	$3,200,000
Interest income*	180,000
Total revenues	$3,380,000
Expenses	1,200,000
Net income	$2,180,000

*Interest Income applies to Receivable from sale of real estate.

Sherwood Company is using these financial statements to entice investors to buy stock in the company. However, a recent FBI investigation revealed that the sale of real estate was a fabricated transaction with a fictitious company that was recorded to make the financial statements look better. The sales price was $5,000,000 with a zero cash down payment and a $5,000,000 receivable. Prepare financial statements for Sherwood Company showing what its total assets, liabilities, stockholders' equity, and income really are with the sale of real estate removed.

E 5-3
LO1, LO3

Appropriateness of Accounting Rules

In the early 1990s, the top executive of a large oil refining company (based in New York) was convicted of financial statement fraud. One of the issues in the case involved the way the company accounted for its oil inventories. In particular, the company would purchase crude oil from exploration companies and then process the oil into finished oil products, such as jet fuel, diesel fuel, and so forth. Because there was a ready market for these finished products, as soon as the company purchased the crude oil, it would value its oil inventory at the selling prices of the finished products less the cost to refine the oil. Although the case involved fraud, the type of accounting used was also questioned because it allowed the company to recognize profit before the actual sale (and even refining) of the oil. Nevertheless, one of the large CPA firms attested to the use of this method. If you were the judge in this case, would you be critical of this accounting practice?

E 5-4
LO2

Internal Control Procedures

As an auditor, you have discovered the following problems with the accounting system control procedures of Jim's Supply Store. For each of the following occurrences, tell which of the five internal control procedures was lacking. Also, recommend how the company should change its procedures to avoid the problem in the future.

a. Jim's Supply's losses due to bad debts have increased dramatically over the past year. In an effort to increase sales, the managers of certain stores have allowed large credit sales to occur without review or approval.

(continued)

b. An accountant hid his theft of $200 from the company's bank account by changing the monthly reconciliation. He knew the manipulation would not be discovered.

c. Mark Peterson works in the storeroom. He maintains the inventory records, counts the inventory, and has unlimited access to the storeroom. He occasionally steals items of inventory and hides the theft by including the value of the stolen goods in his inventory count.

d. Receiving reports are sometimes filled out days after shipments have arrived.

E 5-5
LO5

Internal Auditing–Staffing Internal Audits

A manufacturing corporation recently reassigned one of its accounting managers to the internal audit department. He had successfully directed the western-area accounting office, and the corporation thought his skills would be valuable to the internal audit department. The director of the internal audit division knew of this individual's experience in the western-area accounting office and assigned him to audit that same office.

Should the internal auditor be assigned to audit the same office in which he recently worked? What problems could arise in this situation?

E 5-6
LO5

Internal Auditing

Which of the following is not applicable to the internal audit function?

a. Deter or catch employee fraud.

b. Issue an opinion for investors regarding the reliability of the financial statements.

c. Be guided by its own set of professional standards.

d. Help to ensure that the accounting function is performed correctly and that the financial statements are prepared accurately.

E 5-7
LO5

Internal Auditing–External Auditor's Reliance on Internal Auditors

Pierson, CPA, is planning an audit of the financial statements of Generic Company. In determining the nature, timing, and extent of the auditing procedures, Pierson is considering Generic's internal audit function, which is staffed by Shawn Goff.

1. In what ways may Goff's work be relevant to Pierson?

2. What factors should Pierson consider, and what inquiries should Pierson make in deciding whether to rely on Goff's work?

E 5-8
LO5, LO6

Ensuring the Integrity of Financial Reporting

Three college seniors with majors in accounting are discussing alternative career plans. All three want to enter careers that will help to ensure the integrity of financial reporting. The first wants to become an internal auditor. She believes that by ensuring appropriate internal controls within a company, the financial statements will be reliable. The second wants to go to work in public accounting and perform external audits of companies. He believes that external auditors are independent and can make sure that financial statements are correct. The third student believes that neither choice will be adding much value to the integrity of financial statements because, in both cases, the auditors will be receiving their pay (either directly or indirectly) from the companies they audit. He believes the only way to make a real difference is to work for the Securities and Exchange Commission, using the "arm of government regulation" to force companies to issue appropriate financial statements and then punishing them (through jail sentences and large fines) when their financial statements are misleading. In your opinion, which of these three students will make the largest contribution toward ensuring integrity in the financial statements?

E 5-9
LO5

External Auditors–Purpose of an Audit

What is the purpose of external auditors providing an opinion on a company's financial statements?

E 5-10   **Auditing Financial Statements**

LO5   The Utah Lakers professional basketball team has recently decided to sell stock and become a public company. In determining what it must do to file a registration statement with the SEC, the company realizes that it needs to have an audit opinion to accompany its financial statements. The company has recently approached two accounting students at a major university and asked them to "audit" its financial statements to be submitted to the SEC. Should the two accounting students accept the work and perform the audit?

E 5-11   **Auditing Negligence**

LO5   A few years ago, the officers of **Phar-Mor**, a discount retail chain, were convicted of issuing fraudulent financial statements. It was learned at the trial that the company overstated its inventory by moving inventory from store to store and counting the same inventory several times. For example, a case of Coca-Cola would be counted at one store and then moved to another store and counted again. In a separate civil trial, Phar-Mor's auditors were accused of performing negligent audits because they didn't catch these inventory movements. Do you believe that the external auditors were negligent in this case?

E 5-12   **Securities and Exchange Commission–Authority to Set Accounting**
LO6   **Standards**

Which organization—the Securities and Exchange Commission, the American Institute of Certified Public Accountants, or the Financial Accounting Standards Board—has federal government authority to set accounting standards and reporting requirements? Some people have argued that all accounting rule making should be done by the federal government. Do you agree? Why or why not?

E 5-13   **Securities and Exchange Commission–Role of the SEC**

LO6   Describe the role of the Securities and Exchange Commission and its influence on the practice of auditing.

E 5-14   **Securities and Exchange Commission–Information Needed for Investing**

LO6   As an investor you are considering buying stock in a relatively new company. Medical Horizons, Inc., has been in existence for 10 years and is now about to go public. The first stock offering will be listed on the New York Stock Exchange next week.

1. What kind of information would you like to know before investing in the company? Where can you find this information?
2. How does the SEC protect the securities market from companies that are fraudulent or in poor financial condition?
3. Besides stock market investors, what other parties might be interested in knowing financial data about companies?

E 5-15   **Securities and Exchange Commission**

LO6   Many people have argued that the purpose of the SEC is to protect investors. Some believe that the best way to do this is by preventing weak companies from issuing stock. Others say that the SEC should require full disclosure and then let the buyer beware. Which do you think is more appropriate: a preventive role or a disclosure role?

ANALYTICAL ASSIGNMENTS

AA 5-16
DISCUSSION

Auditing a Company

Jerry Stillwell, the owner of a small company, asked Jones, a CPA, to conduct an audit of the company's financial statements. Stillwell told Jones that the audit needed to be completed in time to submit audited financial statements to a bank as part of a loan application. Jones immediately accepted the assignment and agreed to provide an auditor's report within two weeks.

Because Jones was busy, he hired two accounting students to perform the audit. After two hours of instruction, he sent them off to conduct the audit. Jones told the students not to spend time reviewing the internal controls, but instead to concentrate on proving the mathematical accuracy of the ledgers and other financial records.

The students followed Jones's instructions, and after 10 days, they provided the financial statements, which did not include notes. Jones reviewed the statements and prepared an auditor's report. The report did not refer to generally accepted accounting principles and contained no mention of any qualifications or disclosures. Briefly describe the problems with this audit.

AA 5-17
DISCUSSION

Auditing Practice

A few years ago, the owners of an electronics wholesale company committed massive fraud by overstating revenues on the financial statements. They recorded three large fictitious sales near the end of the year to the retailers **Silo**, **Circuit City**, and **Wal-Mart**. The three transactions overstated revenues, receivables, and income by nearly $20 million. As part of the audit procedures, the external auditors sent requests for confirmation to the three stores to ensure that they did, in fact, owe the electronics company $20 million. In the meantime, the owners of the electronics company rented mailboxes in the cities where the three "customers" were headquartered, using names very similar to those of the three "customers." The requests for confirmation were sent to the mailboxes. The owners completed the confirmations and sent them back to the auditors, confirming the $20 million in receivables. With respect to the fraud, answer the following two questions:

1. What journal entries would the fraud perpetrators have entered into the financial records to overstate revenues?
2. Should the external auditors be held liable for not catching the fraud?

AA 5-18
DISCUSSION

Income Smoothing and an IPO

You are an analyst for an investment fund that invests in initial public offerings (IPOs). You are looking at the financial statements of two companies, Clark Company and Durfee Company, that plan to go public soon. Net income for the past three years for the two companies has been as follows (in thousands):

Year	Clark Net Income	Durfee Net Income
2008	$10,000	$17,000
2009	14,000	1,000
2010	20,000	26,000

If both companies issue the same number of shares and if the initial share prices are the same, which of the two companies appears to be a more attractive investment? Explain your reasoning. Also, what alternate sources of data would you look at to find out if the reported earnings amounts accurately portray the business performance of these two companies over the past three years?

AA 5-19
DISCUSSION

If It Isn't Fraud, Then It's Ethical

Cruella DeVil is the chief financial officer (CFO) of a local publicly-traded company. Cruella was recently invited to speak to accounting students at the local university. One of the students asked Cruella whether she thought earnings management was ethical. Cruella laughed and responded that her view was that anything that was not explicitly prohibited by the accounting standards or by government regulations was ethical. What do you think of Cruella's opinion?

AA 5-20
DISCUSSION

GAAP Is a Point, Not an Oval!

You are the chief financial officer (CFO) of Lorien Company, which is publicly traded. At the annual shareholders' meeting, you have been asked to discuss the company's recent reported results. As part of your presentation, you illustrated the minimum and maximum values for net income that could have been reported by Lorien using a range of accounting assumptions used by other companies in your industry. Your statement prompted a cry of outrage from one of the shareholders present at the meeting. This shareholder accused you of being an unprincipled liar. This shareholder stated that any suggestion that there is a range of possible net income values for a given company in a given year indicates an overly liberal approach to financial reporting. This shareholder has moved that your employment contract be immediately terminated because of an apparent lack of moral character. The shareholder's arguments have been persuasive to a large number of people present at the meeting. What can you say to defend yourself?

AA 5-21
JUDGMENT CALL

You Decide: **Which is more important—having a good system of internal controls or hiring honest employees?**

Is an internal control structure really necessary? Your uncle doesn't seem to think so. He works for a regional employment staffing service and recently commented, "As long as a company hires hard-working, honest people, fraud and abusive financial reporting cases will be almost nonexistent. People with integrity will always make the right choice. In the last six months, we haven't placed anyone for employment who has been fired or let go for fraudulent activity!" A friend argues, however, that anyone presented with the right pressures can commit fraud and that opportunities must be eliminated through an effective internal control structure. Who do you agree with?

AA 5-22
JUDGMENT CALL

You Decide: **Can auditors rely on client personnel to assist them with their audit?**

Should external auditors do all audit procedures themselves, or should the relationship between the auditor and the client be more friendly? You have just graduated from college and are now working as an auditor for a public accounting firm. Your first client is a major shipping company on the west coast that specializes in sending goods to China. As part of your first assignment, you are asked to count the number of metal containers in the storage warehouse and also verify their contents. As you begin, the warehouse manager (and long-time friend of the firm) comes to you and says, "Don't worry about looking inside the containers. Our guys did that last week and we are running low on time." What should you do?

AA 5-23
REAL COMPANY ANALYSIS

Wal-Mart

The 2006 Form 10-K for **Wal-Mart** is included in Appendix A. Locate that Form 10-K and consider the following questions:

1. With respect to the report of the external auditors to "the Board of Directors and Shareholders of Wal-Mart Stores, Inc.":
   a. Who is Wal-Mart's external auditor?
   b. How long after the end of Wal-Mart's fiscal year did the external auditor complete the audit?

(continued)

2. With respect to the report of management concerning the financial statements:

   a. Who is responsible for the financial statements?

   b. After reading the paragraph on internal control, indicate whether you agree or disagree with the following statement: "The purpose of an internal control system is to ensure that all transactions are always recorded and that all assets are always completely safeguarded."

   c. After looking at the description of the members of the audit committee (in the second paragraph), do you think that any members of the Walton family are members of that committee?

AA 5-24
REAL COMPANY
ANALYSIS

Circle K

At one time, **Circle K** was the second-largest convenience store chain in the United States (behind **7-Eleven**). At its peak, Circle K, based in Phoenix, Arizona, operated 4,685 stores in 32 states. Circle K's rapid expansion was financed through long-term borrowing. Interest on this large debt, combined with increased price competition from convenience stores operated by oil companies, squeezed the profits of Circle K. For the fiscal year ended April 30, 1990, Circle K reported a loss of $773 million. In May 1990, Circle K filed for Chapter 11 bankruptcy protection. Subsequently, Circle K was taken over by **Tosco**, a large independent oil company.

1. In the fiscal year ended April 30, 1989, Circle K experienced significant financial difficulty. Reported profits were down 74.5% from the year before. In the president's letter to the shareholders, Circle K explained that 1989 was a "disappointing" year and that management was seeking some outside company to come in and buy out the Circle K shareholders. How do you think all this bad news was reflected in the auditor's report accompanying the financial statements dated April 30, 1989?

2. As mentioned, Circle K reported a loss of $773 million for the year ended April 30, 1990. Just a week after the end of the fiscal year, the CEO was fired. One week after that, Circle K declared bankruptcy. The audit report was completed approximately two months later. How do you think the news of the bankruptcy was reflected in the auditor's report accompanying the financial statements dated April 30, 1990?

AA 5-25
INTERNATIONAL

Do the Financial Statements Give a True and Fair View?

Swire Pacific, Ltd., based in Hong Kong, is one of the largest companies in the world. The primary operations of the company are in the region of Hong Kong, China, and Taiwan where it has operated for over 125 years. Swire operates **Cathay Pacific Airways** and has extensive real estate holdings in Hong Kong. The 2005 auditor's report (prepared by **Pricewaterhouse-Coopers**) for Swire Pacific, dated March 9, 2006, read as follows (in part):

> An audit includes examination, on a test basis, of evidence relevant to the amounts and disclosures in the accounts. It also includes an assessment of the significant estimates and judgments made by the Directors in the preparation of the accounts, and of whether the accounting policies are appropriate to the circumstances of the Company and the group consistently applied and adequately disclosed....
>
> In our opinion the accounts give a true and fair view of the state of affairs of the company and of the group as at 31st December 2005....

Although the concept of a "true and fair view" is not part of the auditor's terminology in the United States, it is used by auditors all over the world and is also discussed as part of International Accounting Standards (IAS). The "true and fair view" concept states that an auditor must make sure that the financial statements give an honest representation of the economic status of the company, even if the company violates generally accepted accounting principles in order to do so.

(continued)

1. Review the opinion language in the auditor's report for **Wal-Mart** (see Appendix A). Does the audit report state unconditionally that Wal-Mart's financial statements are a fair representation of the economic status of the company?

2. Auditors in the United States concentrate on performing audits to ensure that financial statements are prepared in accordance with generally accepted accounting principles. What economic and legal realities in the United States would make it difficult for U.S. auditors to apply the "true and fair view" concept?

AA 5-26

ETHICS

Blowing the Whistle on Former Partners

On St. Patrick's Day in 1992, **Chambers Development Company**, one of the largest landfill and waste management firms in the United States, announced that it had been engaging in improper accounting for years. Wall Street fear (over what this announcement implied about the company's track record of steady earnings growth) sent Chambers' stock price plunging by 62% in one day.

The improper accounting by Chambers had been discovered in the course of the external audit. The auditors found that $362 million in expenses had not been reported since Chambers first became a public company in 1985. If this amount of additional expense had been reported, it would have completely wiped out all the profit reported by Chambers since it first went public. The difficult part of this situation was that a large number of the financial staff working for Chambers were former partners in the audit firm performing the audit. These accountants had first worked as independent external auditors at Chambers, then were hired by Chambers, and subsequently were audited by their old partners.

What ethical and economic issues did the auditors of Chambers Development Company face as they considered whether to blow the whistle on their former partners?

AA 5-27

WRITING

External Auditors

Visit or call a local CPA firm (or the local office of a multi-office CPA firm). Ask about career opportunities, the size of the firm's staff, who some of its major clients are, and other facts about the firm. Then, write a one-page summary of your visit.

AA 5-28

CUMULATIVE SPREADSHEET PROJECT

Analyzing the Impact of Errors

This spreadsheet assignment is a continuation of the spreadsheet assignment given in Chapter 2. If you completed that spreadsheet, you have a head start on this one.

1. Refer back to the financial statement numbers for Handyman Company for 2009 [given in part (1) of the Cumulative Spreadsheet Project assignment in Chapter 2]. Using the balance sheet and income statement created with those numbers, create spreadsheet cell formulas to compute and display values for the following ratios:
   a. Current assets divided by current liabilities (often called the current ratio)
   b. Total liabilities divided by total assets (often called the debt ratio)
   c. Sales divided by total assets (often called asset turnover)
   d. Net income divided by total stockholders' equity (often called return on equity)

   The details of these ratios will be discussed in detail in subsequent chapters.

2. To observe the impact that errors and fraudulent transactions can have on the financial statements, determine what the ratios computed in (1) would have been if (1) each of the following transactions was recorded as described and (2) the transaction was recorded correctly. Treat each transaction independently, meaning that before determining the impact of each new transaction you should reset the financial statement values to their original amounts. Each of the hypothetical transactions is assumed to occur on the last day of the year.

(continued)

a. Created receivables by creating fictitious sales of $140 all on account.
b. Purchased $80 of inventory on account but incorrectly increased the property, plant, and equipment account instead of increasing Inventory.
c. Borrowed $60 with a short-term payable. The liability was incorrectly recorded as Long-Term Debt.
d. An inventory purchase on account in the amount of $90 was not recorded until the next year.

As a recently hired accountant for a small business, Bearing, Inc., you are provided with last year's balance sheet, income statement, and post-closing trial balance to familiarize yourself with the business.

Bearing, Inc.
Balance Sheet
December 31, 2009

Assets

Cash	$22,100	
Accounts receivable	27,000	
Inventory	13,500	
Supplies	600	
Total assets		$63,200

Liabilities and Stockholders' Equity

Liabilities:

Accounts payable	$17,000	
Salaries payable	3,500	
Income taxes payable	3,200	
Total liabilities		$23,700

Stockholders' equity:

Capital stock (10,000 shares outstanding)	$20,000	
Retained earnings	19,500	
Total stockholders' equity		39,500
Total liabilities and stockholders' equity		$63,200

Bearing, Inc.
Income Statement
For the Year Ended December 31, 2009

Sales revenue	$143,000	
Rent revenue	4,000	
Total revenues		$147,000
Less cost of goods sold		85,000
Gross margin		$ 62,000
Less operating expenses:		
Supplies expense	$ 1,200	
Salaries expense	31,000	
Miscellaneous expense	6,400	38,600
Income before taxes		$ 23,400
Less income taxes		8,190
Net income		$ 15,210
Earnings per share ($15,210 ÷ 10,000 shares)		$ 1.52

Bearing, Inc.
Post-Closing Trial Balance
December 31, 2009

	Debits	Credits
Cash	$22,100	
Accounts Receivable	27,000	
Inventory	13,500	
Supplies	600	
Accounts Payable		$17,000
Salaries Payable		3,500
Income Taxes Payable		3,200
Capital Stock		20,000
Retained Earnings		19,500
Totals	$63,200	$63,200

You are also given the following information that summarizes the business activity for the current year, 2010.

a. Issued 6,000 additional shares of capital stock for $30,000 cash.
b. Borrowed $10,000 on January 2, 2010, from Metropolis Bank as a long-term loan. Interest for the year is $700, payable on January 2, 2011.
c. Paid $5,100 cash on September 1 to lease a truck for one year.
d. Received $1,800 on November 1 from a tenant for six months' rent.
e. Paid $900 on December 1 for a one-year insurance policy.
f. Purchased $250 of supplies for cash.
g. Purchased inventory for $80,000 on account.
h. Sold inventory for $105,000 on account; cost of the merchandise sold was $60,000.
i. Collected $95,000 cash from customers' accounts receivable.
j. Paid $65,000 cash for inventories purchased during the year.
k. Paid $34,000 for sales reps' salaries, including $3,500 owed at the beginning of 2010.
l. No dividends were paid during the year.
m. The income taxes payable for 2009 were paid.
n. For adjusting entries, all prepaid expenses are initially recorded as assets, and all unearned revenues are initially recorded as liabilities.
o. At year-end, $400 worth of supplies are on hand.
p. At year-end, an additional $4,000 of sales salaries are owed, but have not yet been paid.
q. Income tax expense is based on a 35% corporate tax rate.

You are asked to do the following:

1. Journalize the transactions for the current year, 2010, using the accounts listed on the financial statements and other appropriate accounts (you may omit explanations).
2. Set up T-accounts and enter the beginning balances from the December 31, 2009, post-closing trial balance for Bearing. Post all current year journal entries to the T-accounts.
3. Journalize and post any necessary adjusting entries at the end of 2010. (*Hint:* Items b, c, d, e, m, o, and p require adjustment.)
4. After the adjusting entries are posted, prepare a trial balance, a balance sheet, and an income statement for 2010. (*Hint:* Income before income taxes should equal $8,175.)
5. Journalize and post closing entries for 2010 and prepare a post-closing trial balance.

© DUNCAN SMITH/PHOTODISC RED/GETTY IMAGES INC.

PART

2

Operating Activities

Selling a Product or a Service

① Understand the three basic types of business activities: operating, investing, and financing. *Operating activities are the day-to-day activities of a business such as selling products, purchasing inventory, and paying for wages. Investing activities primarily relate to the purchase of property, plant, and equipment and the sale of those assets after they have been used. Financing activities are the borrowing of money, and its repayment, and the receipt of funds from investors and payment of dividends back to those investors.*

② Use the two revenue recognition criteria to decide when the revenue from a sale or service should be recorded in the accounting records. *Companies should recognize revenue only after they provide a good or service and after they receive a valid promise of payment. Deciding when to recognize revenue is a critical issue in accounting judgment because companies almost always want to recognize revenue sooner rather than later.*

③ Properly account for the collection of cash and describe the business controls necessary to safeguard cash. *Companies frequently sell on credit, collecting the cash after the sales revenue has already been recorded. Sales discounts are used to encourage early payment of accounts. Cash is a tempting target for theft or fraud, so adequate safeguards must be established within a business to protect the cash.*

④ Record the losses resulting from credit customers who do not pay their bills. *In order to match bad debt expense with revenue in the appropriate year, the amount of the accounts that will ultimately be uncollectible must be forecasted before individual bad debts are specifically identified. Two ways to perform this estimate are the percentage of sales and aging.*

⑤ Evaluate a company's management of its receivables by computing and analyzing appropriate financial ratios. *A company's credit policy can be evaluated by computing how quickly the company collects its receivables.*

⑥ Match revenues and expenses by estimating and recording future warranty and service costs associated with a sale. *When warranty promises are made, the total cost to be associated with those promises is estimated and recorded as an expense at the time of the sale.*

EXPANDED *material*

⑦ Reconcile a checking account. *A bank reconciliation is a detailed explanation of why the amount of cash a company or individual has in the bank differs from the amount recorded in the company or individual's own records. Most of the differences are caused by timing. For example, a company subtracts a payment amount as soon as it mails the check; the bank doesn't reduce the account balance until the check is presented for payment.*

⑧ Account for the impact of changing exchange rates on the value of accounts receivable denominated in foreign currencies. *Making sales denominated in a foreign currency exposes a company to risk because the U.S. dollar value of that currency can fluctuate between the time of the sale and the actual collection. These fluctuations create foreign currency gains and losses.*

Jerry Yang and David Filo met while graduate students at Stanford. Jerry and David's friendship was strengthened when they both went on a six-month academic exchange program to Japan in 1992. In 1993, Jerry and David were supposed to be working on their Ph.D. theses in computer-aided design at Stanford. Instead, they found themselves spending more and more research time surfing through the incredible amount of information available on the newly created "World Wide Web." Jerry and David quickly learned that the key to surfing the vast quantities of information on the Web was to be able to organize the information. They compiled a list of their favorite Web sites, which they e-mailed to friends and posted on the Web. The Web site eventually became known as "**Yahoo!**"

By 1994, thousands were using Yahoo! to access information on the Web. In fact, the demand was so great that Jerry and David were spending 20-plus hours a day on their "hobby." In addition, the resources of the Stanford computer network were being taxed by Yahoo! users, and university officials asked Jerry and David to find another computer to host their service.

F Y I

Jonathan Swift coined the word *yahoo* in his book *Gulliver's Travels*. The "yahoos" were savage humans who lived in a land where horses were the dominant species. Swift, a noted satirist, used the term yahoo to illustrate how easy it is to justify committing atrocities against people once they are categorized with an unfavorable label.

In March 1995, Jerry and David were finally convinced that their Web search hobby could actually be turned into a business. They accepted a $4 million investment from a **venture capital firm**. Realizing that they lacked business expertise, they chose Tim Koogle, another Stanford graduate who was running a $400 million high-tech equipment company, to join them in running their company. This team has turned Yahoo! into one of the most

venture capital firm

A company that provides needed cash to companies in return for an ownership interest.

recognized names among Internet companies. In January of 2000, the company was worth over $100 billion. Then the "Internet bubble" burst. The year 2000 saw many Internet companies fall by the wayside and those that remained had market value a fraction of what they once were. For example, Yahoo!'s value in May of 2006 was approximately $45.5 billion.

So what happened to Internet companies? Investors were afraid of missing out on the next "Microsoft." As a result, the value of many high-tech companies was based on rumors, beta versions, and vaporware. Once investors realized the outlandish prices being paid for these tech companies, they began focusing on the basics of a business—revenues and profits. Many Internet companies never posted a profit—Yahoo! did not report its first profitable year until 1999. Once investors began expecting companies to post profits and generate cash, many Internet companies went out of business—the "bubble" burst.

So, how does Yahoo! make money? Throughout its history, Yahoo! has generated almost all of its revenue through the sale of advertising space on its Web pages. For example, in 2005, 87% of Yahoo!'s $5.3 billion in revenue was generated through marketing services. Yahoo! has various methods of marketing and advertising and is very specific in its annual report as to how revenue is recognized for each of its revenue sources. For example, "The Company recognizes revenue related to the display of advertisements on the Yahoo! Properties as 'impressions' are delivered. An 'impression' is delivered when an advertisement appears in pages viewed by users." Another source of advertising revenue is text-link advertisements, and revenues from that source are recognized when "'click-throughs' occur. A 'click-through' occurs when a user clicks on an advertiser's listing." As you can see, companies are very careful when it comes to the recognition of revenue—and for good reason. The recent accounting scandals coupled with the bursting of the Internet bubble have placed a renewed emphasis on "when should revenue be recognized?"

SETTING THE STAGE

or Internet companies such as Yahoo!, investors are extremely interested in the amount of revenue reported in the income statement. In fact, in the gold rush of e-commerce, investors were more concerned about how much e-business a company was doing than about whether the company was able to generate immediate profits. The amount of revenue reported by an Internet company is a key indicator of how large the company is in the Internet economy. For example, until 2003, Amazon.com had never reported a profit (revenue minus expenses) in its history; the company lost $149 million in 2002 alone. Yet, because of the $3.9 billion in revenue it reported in 2002, Amazon.com was viewed as a major player in the Internet economy. As a result, Amazon.com had a market value of $12 billion in May 2003.

Exhibit 1 illustrates how the stock of both Yahoo! and Amazon.com has performed since 1998. The Internet boom peaked in January of 2000 and in one year both companies had lost significant market value. The bright side is that both of these companies are still in existence. Many Internet companies are gone.

The amount of revenue reported by traditional companies, such as General Motors, Wal-Mart, and General Electric, is also of interest to investors because increased revenues almost always lead to increased profits. Consequently, there is sometimes great pressure on companies to report as much revenue as possible. To balance this pressure, accounting rules have been established to govern exactly when it is appropriate for a company to report the revenue from a transaction in the income statement. These accounting rules are not just conceptual toys for accountants; investor concern about whether Microstrategy, a software company, was correctly applying the accounting rules associated with revenue caused the company's stock price to drop from $333 per share on March 10, 2000, to $22.25 per share just 10 weeks later.

In this chapter, you will study the accounting rules governing the proper recognition of revenue. You will also learn how to account for cash collections and how to handle customer accounts that are uncollectible. Selling goods and services, collecting the cash, and handling customer accounts are fundamental to the operation of any business. Accordingly, properly recording these activities is fundamental to the practice of accounting.

EXHIBIT 1	**Stock Performance for Yahoo! and Amazon.com**

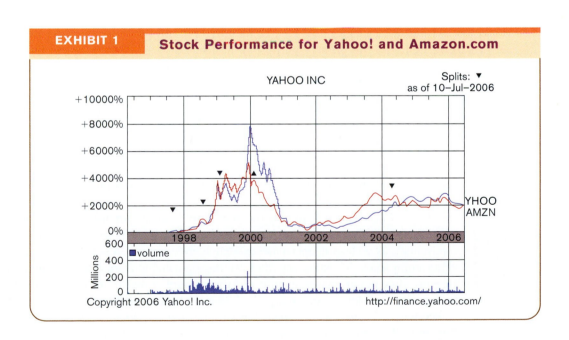

Major Activities of a Business

In the first five chapters, you were introduced to the accounting environment, the basic financial statements, and the accounting cycle (the way business transactions are entered into the accounting records). That material was necessary for you to understand some basic terminology and procedures used in accounting. Accounting has often been called the language of business. By studying the first five chapters, you should now be somewhat familiar with this new business language.

With the basics behind us, it is now time to use accounting to understand how businesses work, how the various activities of business are accounted for, and how businesses report their operating results to investors. The activities of most businesses can be divided into three groups:

- Operating activities
- Investing activities
- Financing activities

operating activities

Transactions and events that involve selling products or services and incurring the necessary expenses associated with the primary activities of the business.

Operating activities involve selling products or services, buying inventory for resale, and incurring and paying for necessary expenses associated with the primary activities of the business. The operating activities of a motel, for example, would include renting rooms (the selling activity); buying soap, shampoo, and other supplies to operate the motel; and incurring and paying for electricity, heat, water, cleaning, television and telephone service; and salaries and taxes of workers. The operating activities of a grocery store would include buying produce, meats, canned goods, and other items for resale; selling products to customers; and incurring and paying for expenses associated with the store's operations such as utilities, salaries, and taxes. The operating activities of **Yahoo!** include selling advertising space on the company's Web pages, paying employees to maintain the Yahoo! system and to develop new software, and paying to advertise the Yahoo! brand name on TV and in magazines. It is easy to identify operating activities because they are always associated with the primary purpose of a business.

In this chapter we cover the operating activities for selling products and services, the recognition of revenues from those sales, accounting for cash, and problems associated with collecting receivables arising from sales. In Chapter 7 we examine the purchase of inventory for resale to customers and the necessary accounting procedures. In Chapter 8 we conclude our discussion of operating activities by considering other operating expenses and how revenues and expenses are combined to compute the net income of a business. Incurring and paying for operating expenses such as employee compensation, insurance, advertising, research and development, and income taxes are also covered in Chapter 8.

investing activities

Transactions and events that involve the purchase and sale of property, plant, equipment, and other assets not generally held for resale.

Investing activities involve the purchase of assets for use in the business. The assets purchased as part of investing activities include property, plant, and equipment, as well as financial assets such as investments in stocks and bonds of other companies. Investing activities are distinguishable from operating activities because they occur less frequently and the amounts involved in each transaction are usually quite large. For example, while most businesses buy and sell inventory or services to customers on a daily basis (operating activities), only rarely do they buy and sell buildings, equipment, and stocks and bonds of other companies. It is important to note that buying inventory for resale is an operating activity, not an investing activity. Investing activities are covered in Chapters 9 and 12.

financing activities

Transactions and events whereby resources are obtained from, or repaid to, owners (equity financing) and creditors (debt financing).

Financing activities involve raising money to finance a business by means other than operations. In addition to earning money through profitable operations, there are two other ways to fund a business: (1) money can be borrowed from creditors (debt financing), or (2) money can be raised by selling stock or

A motel deals with operating activities on a daily basis when renting rooms, buying supplies, and paying utility expenses.

ownership interests in the business to investors (equity financing). Debt financing is the subject of Chapter 10, while equity financing will be discussed in Chapter 11.

Once you have studied Chapters 6 through 12, you will have a good understanding of how businesses operate, invest, and are financed. That knowledge should be helpful in the future if you own your own business, invest in companies as a stockholder, work for a financial institution (or other lender of funds), or work in any position where a knowledge of business is essential.

After studying the operating, investing, and financing activities of a business, you will be ready to combine your knowledge of how businesses operate with the basic accounting knowledge you gained from Chapters 1 through 5. To do this, we will study in detail the statement of cash flows, which is structured around the three activities of a business (Chapter 13). You will discover that preparation of a statement of cash flows requires a sound understanding of the balance sheet and the income statement, as well as a good grasp of how the activities of a business tie together. Throughout Chapters 6 through 12 we will be discussing how financial statement numbers are used to make decisions. In Chapter 14, we will bring together in one chapter all of the financial ratios that have been discussed as well as provide a framework for the various financial statement ratios and how they are used. Exhibit 2 provides a graphical road map of the business and reporting activities that will be discussed in the subsequent eight chapters.

Although Chapters 6 through 12 are organized around business activities, it is important to understand how these activities relate to the basic financial statements. To help you understand these relationships, at the beginning of each of the next seven chapters where possible, we present an exhibit that identifies the time line of transactions that will

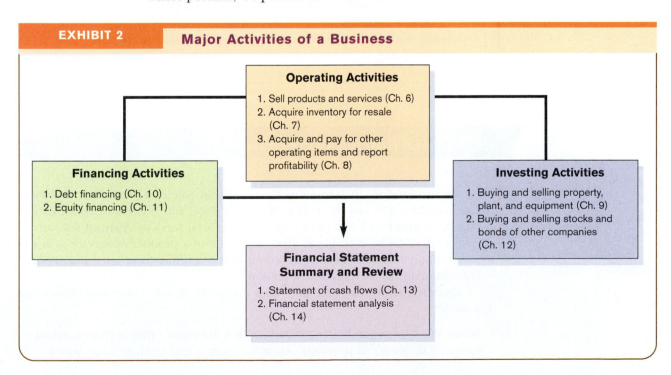

EXHIBIT 2   Major Activities of a Business

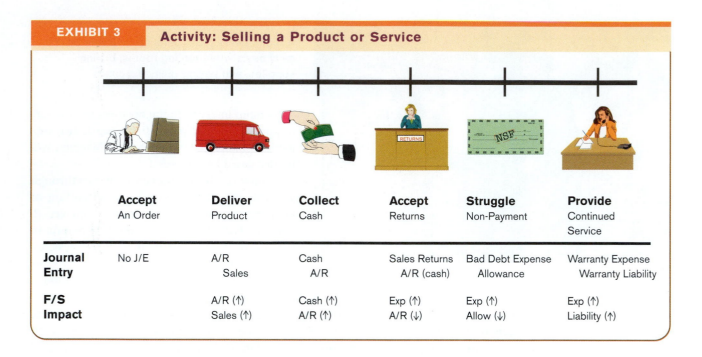

EXHIBIT 3   **Activity: Selling a Product or Service**

	Accept An Order	Deliver Product	Collect Cash	Accept Returns	Struggle Non-Payment	Provide Continued Service

Journal Entry	No J/E	A/R
		  Sales
			Cash
			  A/R
				Sales Returns
				  A/R (cash)
					Bad Debt Expense
					  Allowance
						Warranty Expense
						  Warranty Liability

F/S Impact		A/R (↑) Sales (↑)	Cash (↑) A/R (↑)	Exp (↑) A/R (↓)	Exp (↑) Allow (↓)	Exp (↑) Liability (↑)

be covered in that chapter, the specific accounts associated with those transactions, summary journal entries relating to those accounts, and how the financial statements are ultimately affected because of those transactions. As you can see in Exhibit 3, Cash, Accounts Receivable, and Warranty Liability on the balance sheet; Sales, Bad Debt Expense, and Warranty Expense on the income statement; and Receipts from Customers on the statement of cash flows are covered in Chapter 6.

REMEMBER THIS...

- Operating activities involve selling products or services, buying inventory for resale, and incurring and paying for necessary expenses associated with the primary activities of a business.
- Investing activities include purchasing assets for use in the business and making investments in such items as stocks and bonds.
- Financing activities include raising money to finance a business by means other than operations.

Recognizing Revenue

Use the two revenue recognition criteria to decide when the revenue from a sale or service should be recorded in the accounting records.

② The operations of a business revolve around the sale of a product or a service. **Mcdonald's** sells fast food; **Wal-Mart** sells food and other household goods; **Bank of America** loans money and sells financial services; **Yahoo!** sells advertising space on its Web pages. Just as the sale of a product or service is at the heart of any business, proper recording of the revenue from sales and services is fundamental to the practice of accounting.

Consideration of this time line raises a number of very interesting accounting questions:

- When should revenue be recognized—when the initial order is placed, when the good or service is provided, when the cash is collected, or later, when there is no longer any chance that the customer will return the product or demand a refund because of faulty service?

- What accounting procedures are used to manage and safeguard cash as it is collected?
- How do you account for bad debts, that is, customers who don't pay their bills?
- How do you account for the possibility that sales this year may obligate you to make warranty repairs and provide continuing customer service for many years to come?

The following sections will address these accounting issues, beginning with the important question of when to recognize revenue.

When Should Revenue Be Recognized?

revenue recognition

The process of recording revenue in the accounting records; occurs after (1) the work has been substantially completed and (2) cash collection is reasonably assured.

Revenue recognition is the phrase that accountants use to refer to the recording of a sale through a journal entry in the formal accounting records. Revenue is usually recognized when two important criteria have been met:

1. The work has been substantially completed (the company has done something), and
2. Cash, or a valid promise of future payment, has been received (the company has received something in return).

As a practical matter, most companies record sales when goods are shipped to customers. Credit sales are recognized as revenues before cash is collected, and revenue from services is usually recognized when the service is performed, not necessarily when cash is received.

To illustrate, we will assume that on a typical business day Farm Land Products sells 30 sacks of fertilizer for cash and 20 sacks on credit, all at $10 per sack. Given these data, the $500 of revenue is recorded as follows:

Cash	300	
Accounts Receivable	200	
Sales Revenue		500
Sold 30 sacks of fertilizer for cash and 20 sacks on credit.		

 F Y I

In the majority of companies, the most frequent types of journal entries are those to record sales, cash collections, purchases, and payments to suppliers. Because such transactions are so frequent, most firms maintain four separate special journals: (1) the sales journal, (2) the purchases journal, (3) the cash receipts journal, and (4) the cash disbursements journal. These journals are discussed in detail in this text's Interactive Study Center at **http://www.thomsonedu.com/accounting/albrecht**.

Although the debit entries are made to different accounts, the credit entry for the full amount is to a revenue account. Thus, accrual-basis accounting requires the recognition of $500 in revenue instead of the $300 that would be recognized if the focus were merely on cash collection.

This example is a simple illustration of how sales are recorded and revenue is recognized. In reality, sales transactions are usually more complex, involving such things as uncertainty about exactly when the transaction is actually completed and whether a valid promise of payment has actually been received from the customer. These difficulties are compounded by the fact that companies often have an understandable desire to report revenue as soon as possible in order to enhance their reported performance and make it easier to get loans or attract investors. The discussion below will further examine the two revenue recognition criteria (work done and cash collectible) to see how accountants apply these rules to ensure that reported revenue fairly reflects the economic performance of a business.

Application of the Revenue Recognition Criteria

The Farm Land example was used to illustrate a straightforward case of revenue recognition at the time a sale is made. The Farm Land customers bought $500 worth of fertilizer, paying $300 cash and promising to pay $200 later; the $500 of revenue was recognized immediately. But what if the terms of the sale had also required Farm Land to deliver the fertilizer to the customers at no extra charge? In this case, proper application of the "work done" revenue recognition criterion would require that the revenue not be recorded until actual delivery had taken place. Alternatively, assume that the fertilizer sale was accompanied by a guarantee that, within 30 days, customers could return the unused portion of fertilizer for a full refund. If very few customers ever seek a refund, revenue should still be recognized at the time of sale. But, for example, if over 70% of fertilizer customers later seek refunds, the "cash collectible" revenue recognition criterion suggests that no revenue should be recognized until the completion of the 30-day return period; Farm Land then becomes reasonably assured of the amount of cash it will collect from the $500 in sales. This situation illustrates the need for accountants to exercise professional judgment and account for the economic reality of a transaction instead of blindly relying on technical legal rules about whether a sale has taken place. Other examples of the application of the revenue recognition criteria are given below.

Yahoo!   As mentioned in the opening scenario of this chapter, **Yahoo!** derives most of its revenue from the sale of banner advertising space on its Web pages. As mentioned, Yahoo! recognizes advertising revenue as the impressions occur. This revenue recognition practice makes sense if Yahoo! is reasonably certain of collecting payment for these impressions because Yahoo! has completed its work of providing the impressions. Yahoo! often guarantees an advertiser a minimum number of impressions. To the extent that the minimum guaranteed impressions are not met as of the date the financial statements are prepared, Yahoo! delays recognizing the advertising revenue until the guaranteed number of impressions is reached.

Microsoft   The nature of the computer software industry presents several sticky revenue recognition issues. The installation of software and the promise of software upgrades require software companies to consider when the earnings process is substantially complete. Are the revenue recognition criteria satisfied at the point of sale, when the software is installed, or after promised upgrades are delivered? **Microsoft** recognizes a portion (about 80% for the Office 2003 software) of the software price as revenue immediately upon delivery of the software to you. The rest of

STOP & THINK

As you might expect, not all software companies support this revenue recognition practice; they would prefer to recognize all of the revenue from a software sale immediately at the time of the sale. Microsoft, on the other hand, has been very supportive of the rule. Why do you think Microsoft supports the accounting rule that many other software firms oppose?

the software price is recognized as revenue gradually over time as the technical support service is provided.

Boeing   **Boeing** recognizes revenue from commercial aircraft sales at the time the aircraft is delivered to the airline. For example, in 2005 Boeing recognized revenue from the delivery of 290 commercial aircraft, including 212 737s. In contrast, many of Boeing's government contracts require years of work before any product is delivered. If Boeing did not recognize any revenue during this extended production period, its economic activity for that period would be understated. Thus, the accounting rules allow Boeing to recognize revenue piecemeal as it reaches "scheduled performance milestones." This type of "proportional performance" technique is commonly used to recognize revenue from transactions that extend over a long time period, such as for highway construction projects or season tickets for a professional sports team.

Rent-A-Center   **Rent-A-Center** operates 2,753 rent-to-own stores in the United States under both its own name and the names, "Get It Now" and "ColorTyme." Customers rent furniture, VCRs, and other consumer goods under an agreement giving them ownership of the item if they continue to make their payments for the entire rental period. Rent-to-own stores attract customers who cannot afford the outright purchase of consumer goods and who anticipate difficulty in receiving credit through normal channels. Thus, a big concern for Rent-A-Center is collecting the full amount of cash due under a rental contract. In fact, Rent-A-Center states that only about 25% of its customers complete the full term of their agreement. With such a high likelihood of customers stopping payments on their rental agreements, Rent-A-Center recognizes revenue from a specific contract only gradually as the cash is actually collected.

As mentioned initially, the accounting for most sales transactions is straightforward—the revenue is recognized when the sale is made. However, as illustrated by the examples in this section, when the "work" associated with a sale extends over a significant period of time, or when cash collectibility is in doubt, the accountant must use professional judgment in applying the revenue recognition criteria to determine the proper time to record the sale.

Properly recognizing revenue is made more difficult by the fact that companies often have an understandable desire to report revenue as soon as possible. For example, for a company that is applying for a large loan or making an initial public offering of stock, it is critical that reported revenue, and thus reported net income, be as high as possible. In addition, company managers are often scrambling to make revenue or profit targets. In many cases, the managers' bonuses depend on whether these targets are met. Accordingly, managers often have great interest in making sure that revenue is recognized this year rather than waiting until next year. Receivables and revenue continue to be ripe areas for abuse or outright fraud because the associated accounting journal entry is so temptingly easy to make: debit Accounts Receivable and credit Revenue.

STOP & THINK

Many colleges and universities prepare financial statements that are released to the public. When do you think a college or university should recognize revenue from student tuition?

Cash Collection

Properly account for the collection of cash and describe the business controls necessary to safeguard cash.

③ Recall the Farm Land Products example in which fertilizer was sold, partially for cash and partially on credit. Farm Land recorded the sales as follows:

Cash	300	
Accounts Receivable	200	
Sales Revenue		500

Sold 30 sacks of fertilizer for cash and 20 sacks on credit.

Subsequent collection of the $200 accounts receivable is recorded as follows:

Cash	200	
Accounts Receivable		200

Collected cash for $200 credit sale.

Note that Sales Revenue is not credited again when the cash is collected; the revenue was already recognized when the sale was made.

The following T-accounts show that the net result of these two transactions is an increase in Cash and Sales Revenue of $500.

	Cash		Accounts Receivable		Sales Revenue	
Original sale	300		200			500
Collection of account	200			200		
Final balances	500		0			500
	To balance sheet					To income statement

These two entries illustrate simple sales and collection transactions. Many companies, however, offer sales discounts and must deal with merchandise returns. The accounting for discounts and returns is explained next.

Sales Discounts

sales discount

A reduction in the selling price that is allowed if payment is received within a specified period.

In many sales transactions, the buyer is given a discount if the bill is paid promptly. Such incentives to pay quickly are called **sales discounts**, or cash discounts, and the discount terms are typically expressed in abbreviated form. For example, 2/10, n/30 means that a buyer will receive a 2% discount from the selling price if payment is made within 10 days of the date of purchase, but that the full amount must be paid within 30 days or it will be considered past due. (Other common terms are 1/10, n/30 and 2/10, EOM. The latter means that a 2% discount is granted if payment is made within 10 days after the date of sale; otherwise the balance is due at the end of the month.) A 2% discount is a strong incentive for a customer to pay within 10 days because it is equivalent to paying an annual interest rate of about 36% to wait and pay after the discount period. In fact, if the amount owed is substantial, most firms will borrow money, if necessary, to take advantage of a sales discount. The interest rate they will have to pay a lending institution to borrow the money is considerably less than the effective interest rate of missing the sales discount.

If an account receivable is paid within a specified discount period, the entry to record the receipt of cash is different from the cash receipt entry shown earlier. Thus, if the $200 in Farm Land credit sales were made with discount terms of 2/10, n/30, and if the customers paid within the discount period, the entry to record the receipt of cash is:

Cash	196	
Sales Discounts ($200 × 0.02)	4	
Accounts Receivable		200
Collected cash within the discount period for $200 credit sale.		

contra account

An account that is offset or deducted from another account.

Sales Discounts is a **contra account** (specifically, a contra-revenue account), which means that it is deducted from sales revenue on the income statement. This account is included with other revenue accounts in the general ledger, but unlike other revenue accounts, it has a debit balance rather than a credit balance.

Sales Returns and Allowances

Customers often return merchandise, either because the item is defective or for a variety of other reasons. Most companies generally accept merchandise returns in order to maintain good customer relations. When merchandise is returned, the company must make an entry to reduce revenues and to reduce either Cash (a cash refund) or Accounts Receivable (an adjustment to the customer's account). A similar entry is required when the sales price is reduced because the merchandise was defective or damaged during shipment to the customer.

To illustrate the type of entry needed, we will assume that before any payments on account are made, Farm Land customers return goods costing $150; $100 in returns were made by cash customers, and $50 in returns were made by credit customers. The entry to record the return of merchandise is:

Sales Returns and Allowances	150	
Cash		100
Accounts Receivable		50
Received $150 of returned merchandise; $100 from cash customers		
and $50 from credit customers.		

sales returns and allowances

A contra-revenue account in which the return of, or allowance for reduction in the price of, merchandise previously sold is recorded.

The credit customers will be sent a credit memorandum for the return, stating that credit has been granted and that the balance of their accounts (in total) is now $150 ($200 original credit purchase − $50 returns). Like Sales Discounts, **Sales Returns and Allowances** is a contra account that is deducted from sales revenue on the income statement. The income statement presentation for the revenue accounts, assuming payment within the discount period on the $150 balance in Accounts Receivable, is shown on the following page.

Income Statement	
Sales revenue	$ 500
Less: Sales discounts*	(3)
Less: Sales returns and allowances	(150)
Net sales revenue	$347

*($200 − $50) × 0.02 = $3

Note that when merchandise is returned, sales discounts for the subsequent payment are granted only on the selling price of the merchandise not returned.

It might seem that the use of contra accounts (Sales Discounts and Sales Returns and Allowances) involves extra steps that would not be necessary if discounts and returns of merchandise were deducted directly from Sales Revenue. Although such direct deductions would have the same final effect on net income, the contra accounts separate initial sales from all returns, allowances, and discounts. This permits a company's management to analyze the extent to which customers are returning merchandise, receiving allowances, and taking advantage of discounts. If management find that excessive amounts of merchandise are being returned, they may decide that the company's sales returns policy is too liberal or that the quality of its merchandise needs improvement.

A company's total recorded sales, before any discounts or returns and allowances, are referred to as **gross sales**. When sales discounts or sales returns and allowances are deducted from gross sales, the resulting amount is referred to as **net sales**.

gross sales

Total recorded sales before deducting any sales discounts or sales returns and allowances.

net sales

Gross sales less sales discounts and sales returns and allowances.

cash

Coins, currency, money orders, checks, and funds on deposit with financial institutions; the most liquid of assets.

Control of Cash

Cash includes coins, currency, money orders and checks (made payable or endorsed to the company), and money on deposit with banks or savings institutions that are available for use to satisfy the company's obligations. All the various transactions involving these forms of cash are usually summarized and reported under a single balance sheet account, Cash.

Because it is the easiest asset to spend if it is stolen, cash is a tempting target and must be carefully safeguarded. Several control procedures have been developed to help management monitor and protect cash. Because cash is particularly vulnerable to loss or misuse we will discuss three important controls that are an integral part of accounting for cash.

One of the most important controls is that the handling of cash be separated from the recording of cash. The purpose of this separation of duties is that it becomes more difficult for theft or errors to occur when two or more people are involved. If the cash records are maintained by an employee who also has access to the cash itself, cash can be stolen or "borrowed," and the employee can cover up the shortage by falsifying the accounting records.

A second cash control practice is to require that all cash receipts be deposited daily in bank accounts. This disciplined, rigid process ensures that personal responsibility for the handling of cash is focused on the individual assigned to make the regular deposit. In addition, this process prevents the accumulation of a large amount of cash—even the most trusted employee can be tempted by a large cash hoard.

 F Y I

In its balance sheet (see Appendix A), **Wal-Mart** follows the common practice of combining cash and short-term investments (bonds and U.S. Treasury securities) for the total Cash amount.

A third cash control practice is to require that all cash expenditures (except those paid out of a miscellaneous petty cash fund) be made with prenumbered checks. As we all know from managing our personal finances, payments made with pocket cash are quickly forgotten and easily concealed. In contrast, payments made by check are well documented, both in our personal check registers and by our bank.

In addition to safeguarding cash, a business must ensure that cash is wisely managed. In fact, many businesses establish elaborate control and budgeting procedures for monitoring cash balances and estimating future cash needs. Companies also try to keep only minimum balances in no-interest or low-interest checking accounts; other cash is kept in more high-yielding investments such as certificates of deposit.

REMEMBER THIS...

- Net sales can be calculated as follows:

  Gross Sales
  − Sales Discounts
  − Sales Returns and Allowances
  = Net Sales

- Common cash controls include:

  - separation of duties in handling and accounting for cash,

  - daily deposits of all cash receipts, and

  - payment of all expenditures by prenumbered checks.

Accounting for Credit Customers Who Don't Pay

Record the losses resulting from credit customers who do not pay their bills.

④ The term **receivables** refers to a company's claims for money, goods, or services. Receivables are created through various types of transactions, the two most common being the sale of merchandise or services on credit and the lending of money. On a personal level, we are all familiar with credit. Because credit is so readily available, we can buy such items as cars, refrigerators, and big-screen TVs, even when we cannot afford to pay cash for them. Major retail companies such as **Sears**, oil companies such as **Shell**, and credit card companies such as **Visa, Mastercard**, and **American Express** have made credit available to almost every person in the United States. We live in a credit world—not only on the individual level, but also at the wholesale and manufacturing business levels.

In business, credit sales give rise to the most common type of receivables: accounts receivable. **Accounts receivable** are the amounts owed to a business by its credit customers and are usually collected in cash within 10 to 60 days (see page 238 for definition). Accounts receivable result from agreements between a company and its credit customers; a more formal contract, including interest on the unpaid balance, is called a note receivable. Receivables that are to be converted to cash within a year (or the normal operating cycle) are classified as current assets and listed on the balance sheet below Cash. In

receivables

Claims for money, goods, or services.

F Y I

Credit card sales can be viewed as a way for a business to reap the benefit of increased credit sales without having to set up a bookkeeping and collection service for accounts receivable. The credit card company screens customers based on their creditworthiness, sends out the bills, collects the cash, and bears the cost of any uncollectible accounts. A business that accepts credit card sales pays a fee ranging from 1 to 5% of credit card sales.

accounts receivable

A current asset representing money due for services performed or merchandise sold on credit.

bad debt

An uncollectible account receivable.

this section of the chapter, we discuss the accounting issues associated with credit customers who don't pay.

When companies sell goods and services on credit (as most do), there are usually some customers who do not pay for the merchandise they purchase; these are referred to as **bad debts**. In fact, most businesses expect a small percentage of their receivables to be uncollectible. If a firm tries too hard to eliminate the possibility of losses from nonpaying customers, it usually makes its credit policy so restrictive that valuable sales are lost. On the other hand, if a firm extends credit too easily, the total cost of maintaining the accounts receivable system may exceed the benefit gained from attracting customers by allowing them to buy on credit (due to the number of accounts to track and uncollectible receivables to try to collect). Because of this dilemma, most firms carefully monitor their credit sales and accounts receivable to ensure that their policies are neither too restrictive nor too liberal.

 F Y I

Sometimes companies need cash prior to the due dates of their receivables. Often, in these circumstances, such companies will sell or "factor" their accounts receivables to financing or factoring companies. To learn more about how companies account for the "factoring" of receivables, visit this text's Interactive Study Center at **http://www.thomsonedu.com/ accounting/albrecht**.

When an account receivable becomes uncollectible, a firm incurs a bad debt loss. This loss is recognized as a cost of doing business, so it is classified as a selling expense. There are two ways to account for losses from uncollectible accounts: the direct write-off method and the allowance method.

direct write-off method

The recording of actual losses from uncollectible accounts as expenses during the period in which accounts receivable are determined to be uncollectible.

Direct Write-Off Method

With the **direct write-off method**, an uncollectible account is recognized as an expense at the time it is determined to be uncollectible. For example, assume that during the year 2009, Farm Land Products had total credit sales of $300,000. Of this amount, $250,000 was subsequently collected in cash during the year, leaving a year-end balance in Accounts Receivable of $50,000 ($300,000 − $250,000). The summary journal entries to record this information are:

Accounts Receivable	300,000	
Sales Revenue		300,000
To record total credit sales for the year.		
Cash	250,000	
Accounts Receivable		250,000
To record total cash collections for the year.		

Assume that one credit customer, Jake Palmer, has an account balance of $1,500 that remains unpaid for several months in 2010. If, after receiving several past-due notices, Palmer still does not pay, Farm Land will probably turn the account over to an attorney or a collection agency. Then, if collection attempts fail, the company may decide that the Palmer account will not be collected and write it off as a loss. The entry to record the expense under the direct write-off method is:

Bad Debt Expense	1,500	
Accounts Receivable		1,500
To write off the uncollectible account of Jake Palmer.		

bad debt expense

An account that represents the portion of the current period's credit sales that are estimated to be uncollectible.

Bad Debt Expense is usually considered a selling expense on the income statement. Although the direct write-off method is objective (the account is written off at the time it proves to be uncollectible), it most likely would violate the matching principle, which requires that all costs and expenses incurred in generating revenues be identified with those revenues period by period. With the direct write-off method, sales made near the end of one accounting period may not be recognized as uncollectible until the next period. In this example, the revenue from the sale to Jake Palmer is recognized in 2009, but the expense from the bad debt is not recognized until 2010. As a result, expenses are understated in 2009 and overstated in 2010. This makes the direct write-off method unacceptable from a theoretical point of view. The direct write-off method is allowable only if bad debts involve small, insignificant amounts.

The Allowance Method

allowance method

The recording of estimated losses due to uncollectible accounts as expenses during the period in which the sales occurred.

The **allowance method** satisfies the matching principle because it accounts for uncollectibles during the same period in which the sales occurred. With this method, a firm uses its experience (or industry averages) to estimate the amount of receivables arising from this year's credit sales that will ultimately become uncollectible. That estimate is recorded as bad debt expense in the period of sale. Although the use of estimates may result in a somewhat imprecise expense figure, this is generally thought to be a less serious problem than the direct write-off method's failure to match bad debt expenses with the sales that caused them. In addition, with experience, these estimates tend to be quite accurate.

To illustrate the allowance method, assume that Farm Land Products estimates that the bad debts created by its $300,000 in credit sales in 2009 will ultimately total $4,500. Note that this is a statistical estimate—on average, bad debts will be $4,500, but Farm Land does not yet know exactly which customers will be the ones who will fail to pay. The entry to record this estimated bad debt expense for 2009 is:

Bad Debt Expense	4,500	
Allowance for Bad Debts		4,500
To record the estimated bad debt expense for the current year.		

allowance for bad debts

A contra account, deducted from Accounts Receivable, that shows the estimated losses from uncollectible accounts.

Bad Debt Expense is a selling expense on the income statement, and **Allowance for Bad Debts** is a contra account to Accounts Receivable on the balance sheet. An allowance account is used because the company does not yet know which receivables will not be collected. Later on, for example, in 2010, as actual losses are recognized, the balance in Allowance for Bad Debts is reduced. For example, if in 2010 Jake Palmer's receivable for $1,500 is specifically identified as being uncollectible, the entry is:

Allowance for Bad Debts	1,500	
Accounts Receivable		1,500
To write off the uncollectible account of Jake Palmer.		

Note that the write-off entry in 2010 does not affect net income in 2010. Instead, the net income in 2009, when the credit sale to Jake Palmer was originally made, already reflects the estimated bad debt expense. Think of this entry as follows: The $1,500 Jake Palmer account has been shown to be bad, so it is "thrown away" via a credit to Accounts Receivable. In addition, Allowance for Bad Debts, which is a general estimate of the amount of bad accounts, is reduced by $1,500 because the bad Palmer account has been specifically identified and eliminated. In one entry, the amounts in Accounts Receivable and Allowance for Bad Debts have been reduced. Assume that the balance in Accounts Receivable was $50,000 and the balance in Allowance for Bad Debts was $4,500 before the Palmer account was written off. The net amount in Accounts Receivable after the $1,500 write-off is exactly the same as it was before the entry, as shown here.

Before Write-Off Entry		After Write-Off Entry	
Accounts receivable	$50,000	Accounts receivable	
		($50,000 − $1,500)	$48,500
Less allowance for		Less allowance for bad	
bad debts	4,500	debts ($4,500 − $1,500)	3,000
Net balance	$45,500	Net balance	$45,500

net realizable value of accounts receivable

The net amount that would be received if all receivables considered collectible were collected; equal to total accounts receivable less the allowance for bad debts.

The net balance of $45,500 reflects the estimated **net realizable value of accounts receivable**, that is, the amount of receivables the company actually expects to collect.

The following T-account shows the kinds of entries that are made to Allowance for Bad Debts:

Allowance for Bad Debts

Actual write-offs of uncollectible accounts	Estimates of uncollectible accounts

Occasionally, a customer whose account has been written off as uncollectible later pays the outstanding balance. When this happens, the company reverses the entry that was used to write off the account and then recognizes the payment. For example, if Jake Palmer pays the $1,500 after his account has already been written off, the entries to correct the accounting records are:

Accounts Receivable	1,500	
Allowance for Bad Debts		1,500
To reinstate the balance previously written off as uncollectible.		
Cash	1,500	
Accounts Receivable		1,500
Received payment in full of previously written-off accounts receivable.		

Because customers sometimes pay their balances after their accounts are written off, it is important for a company to have good control over both the cash collection procedures and the accounting for accounts receivable. Otherwise, such payments as the previously written-off $1,500 could be pocketed by the employee who receives the cash, and it would never be missed. This is one reason that most companies separate the handling of cash from the recording of cash transactions in the accounts.

Because the amount recorded in Bad Debt Expense affects both the reported net realizable value of the receivables and net income, companies must be careful to use good estimation procedures. These estimates can focus on an examination of either the total number of credit sales during the period or the outstanding receivables at year-end to determine their collectibility.

Estimating Uncollectible Accounts Receivable as a Percentage of Credit Sales

One method of estimating bad debt expense is to estimate uncollectible receivables as a percentage of credit sales for the period. If a company uses this method, the amount of uncollectibles will be a straight percentage of the current year's credit sales. That percentage will be a projection based on experience in prior years, modified for any changes expected for the current period. For example, in the Farm Land example, credit sales for the year of $300,000 are expected to generate bad debts of $4,500, indicating that 1.5% of all credit sales are expected to be uncollectible ($4,500/$300,000 = 1.5%). Farm Land would evaluate the percentage each year, in light of its continued experience, to see whether the same percentage still seems reasonable. In addition, if economic conditions have changed for Farm Land's customers (such as the onset of a recession making it more likely that debts will remain uncollected), the percentage would be adjusted.

When this percentage of sales method is used, the existing balance (if there is one) in Allowance for Bad Debts does not affect the amount computed and is not included in the adjusting entry to record bad debt expense. The 1.5% of the current year's sales that is estimated to be uncollectible is calculated and entered separately, and then added to the existing balance. For example, if the existing credit balance is $2,000, the $4,500 will be added, making the new credit balance $6,500. The rationale for not considering the existing $2,000 balance in Allowance for Bad Debts is that it relates to previous periods' sales and reflects the company's estimate (as of the beginning of the year) of prior years' accounts receivable that are expected to be uncollectible.

In determining the percentage of credit sales that will be uncollectible, a company must estimate the total amount of loss on the basis of experience or industry averages. Obviously, a company that has been in business for several years should be able to make more accurate estimates than a new company. Many established companies use a three- or five-year average as the basis for estimating losses from uncollectible accounts.

STOP & THINK

Should a company work to reduce its bad debt expense to zero? Explain.

Estimating Uncollectible Accounts Receivable as a Percentage of Total Receivables

Another way to estimate uncollectible receivables is to use a percentage of total receivables. Using this method, the amount of uncollectibles is a percentage of the total receivables balance at the end of the period. Assume that Farm Land decides to use this method and determines that 12% of the $50,000 in the year-end Accounts Receivable will ultimately be uncollectible. Accordingly, the credit balance in Allowance for Bad Debts should be $6,000 ($50,000 × 0.12). If there is no existing balance in Allowance for Bad Debts representing the estimate of bad accounts left over from prior years, then an entry for $6,000 is made. If the account has an existing balance, however, only the net amount needed to bring the credit balance to $6,000 is added. For example, an existing credit balance of $2,000 in Allowance for Bad Debts results in the following adjusting entry:

Bad Debt Expense	4,000	
Allowance for Bad Debts		4,000
To adjust the allowance account to the desired balance		
($6,000 − $2,000 = $4,000).		

In all cases, the ending balance in Allowance for Bad Debts should be the amount of total receivables estimated to be uncollectible.

In estimating bad debt expense, the percentage of sales method focuses on an estimation based directly on the level of the current year's credit sales. With the percentage of total receivables method, the focus is on estimating total bad debts existing at the end of the period; this number is compared to the leftover bad debts from prior years, and the difference is bad debt expense, the new bad debts created in the current period. These two techniques are merely alternative estimation approaches. In practice, as a check, a company would probably use both procedures to ensure that they yield roughly consistent results.

Aging Accounts Receivable.   In the example just given, the correct amount of the ending Allowance for Bad Debts balance was computed by applying the estimated uncollectible percentage (12%) to the entire Accounts Receivable balance ($50,000). In a more refined method of estimating the appropriate ending balance in Allowance for Bad Debts, a company bases its calculations on how long its receivables have been outstanding. With this procedure, called **aging accounts receivable**, each receivable is categorized according to age, such as current, 1–30 days past due, 31–60 days past due, 61–90 days past due, 91–120 days past due, and over 120 days past due. Once the receivables in each age classification are totaled, each total is multiplied by an appropriate uncollectible percentage (as determined by experience), recognizing that the older the receivable, the less likely the company is to collect. Exhibit 4 shows how Farm Land could use an aging accounts receivable analysis to estimate the amount of its $50,000 ending balance in Accounts Receivable that will ultimately be uncollectible.

> **aging accounts receivable**
>
> The process of categorizing each account receivable by the number of days it has been outstanding.

EXHIBIT 4   Aging Accounts Receivable

Customer	Balance	Current	Days Past Due 1–30	31–60	61–90	91–120	Over 120
A. Adams	$10,000	$10,000					
R. Bartholomew	6,500			$ 5,000			$1,500
F. Christiansen	6,250	5,000	$1,250				
G. Dover	7,260			7,260			
M. Ellis	4,000	4,000					
G. Erkland	2,250				$2,250		
R. Fisher	1,500		500			$1,000	
J. Palmer	1,500		1,500				
E. Zeigler	10,740	4,000	6,740				
Totals	$50,000	$23,000	$9,990	$12,260	$2,250	$1,000	$1,500

Estimate of Losses from Uncollectible Accounts

Age	Balance	Percentage Estimated to Be Uncollectible	Amount
Current	$23,000	1.5	$ 345
1–30 days past due	9,990	4.0	400
31–60 days past due	12,260	20.0	2,452
61–90 days past due	2,250	40.0	900
91–120 days past due	1,000	60.0	600
Over 120 days past due	1,500	80.0	1,200
Totals	$50,000		$5,897*

*Receivables that are likely to be uncollectible.

The allowance for bad debts estimate obtained using the aging method is $5,897. If the existing credit balance in Allowance for Bad Debts is $2,000, the required adjusting entry is:

Bad Debt Expense	3,897	
Allowance for Bad Debts		3,897

To adjust the allowance account to the desired ending balance ($5,897 − $2,000 = $3,897).

CAUTION

The aging method is merely a more refined technique for estimating the desired balance in Allowance for Bad Debts.

The aging of accounts receivable is probably the most accurate method of estimating uncollectible accounts. It also enables a company to identify its problem customers. Companies that base their estimates of uncollectible accounts on credit sales or total outstanding receivables also often age their receivables as a way of monitoring the individual accounts receivable balances.

Real-World Illustration of Accounting for Bad Debts

The application of bad debt accounting is illustrated using the financial statements of **Yahoo!** for 2003–2005. As shown in Exhibit 5, Yahoo! reported accounts receivable at the end of 2005 of $763.6 million and a bad debt allowance for bad debts of $41.9 million. In other words, credit customers owed Yahoo! $763.6 million as of the end of 2005; however, Yahoo!'s best estimate was that $41.9 million of this amount would never be collected. This bad debt allowance amounted to 5.5% of the Accounts Receivable balance, down from 6.7% in 2004 and 10.2% in 2003. For a company operating in a stable economic environment with little change in the nature of its credit customers, this percentage would be expected to be about the same from year to year. In the case of Yahoo!, operating in the volatile Internet economy, it appears that there has been some variation in the collectibility of accounts receivable from one year to the next.

EXHIBIT 5	Bad Debt Expense for Yahoo!		
Year of	Ending Accounts Receivable	Ending Bad Debt Allowance	Bad Debt Allowance as a Percentage of Accounts Receivable
2003	$314,376*	$31,961	10.2%
2004	514,208	34,215	6.7%
2005	763,580	41,857	5.5%

*Dollar amounts are in thousands.

REMEMBER THIS...

Two ways of accounting for losses from uncollectible receivables include:

- allowance method (generally accepted)
- direct write-off method (NOT generally accepted)

Two ways of estimating losses from uncollectible receivables include:

- percentage of credit sales (existing balance is ignored)
- fraction of total outstanding receivables (often determined by aging the accounts receivable) (existing balance is considered)

Assessing How Well Companies Manage Their Receivables

(5) As introduced in Chapter 4, information from the financial statements can be used to evaluate a company's performance. An important element of overall company performance is the efficient use of assets. With regard to accounts receivable, inefficient use means that too much cash is tied up in the form of receivables. A company that collects its receivables on a timely basis has cash to pay its bills. Companies that do not do a good job of collecting receivables are often cash poor, paying interest on short-term loans to cover their cash shortage or losing interest that could be earned by investing cash.

There are several methods of evaluating how well an organization is managing its accounts receivable. The most common method involves computing two ratios, accounts receivable turnover and average collection period. The **accounts receivable turnover** ratio is an attempt to determine how many times during the year a company is "turning over" or collecting its receivables. It is a measure of how many times old receivables are collected and replaced by new receivables. Accounts receivable turnover is calculated as follows:

accounts receivable turnover

A measure used to indicate how fast a company collects its receivables; computed by dividing sales by average accounts receivable.

$$\text{Accounts Receivable Turnover} = \frac{\text{Sales Revenue}}{\text{Average Accounts Receivable}}$$

Notice that the numerator of this ratio is sales revenue, not credit sales. Conceptually, one might consider comparing the level of accounts receivable to the amount of credit sales instead of total sales. However, companies rarely, if ever, disclose how much of their sales are credit sales. For this ratio, you can think of cash sales as credit sales with a very short collection time (0 days). Also note that the denominator uses average accounts receivable instead of the ending balance. This recognizes that sales are generated throughout the year; the average Accounts Receivable balance is an approximation of the amount that prevailed during the year. If the Accounts Receivable balance is relatively unchanged during the year, then using the ending balance is acceptable and common. The following are the accounts receivable turnover ratios for two well-known companies for 2005:

Wal-Mart $\dfrac{\$312.47 \text{ billion}}{\$2.189 \text{ billion}} = 142.7$ times

Boeing $\dfrac{\$54.845 \text{ billion}}{\$4.950 \text{ billion}} = 11.1$ times

From this analysis, you can see that **Wal-Mart** turns its receivables over much more often than does **Boeing**. This is not surprising given the different nature of the two businesses. Wal-Mart sells primarily to retail customers for cash. Remember, from Wal-Mart's standpoint, a credit card sale is the same as a cash sale since Wal-Mart receives its money instantly; it is the credit card company that must worry about collecting the receivable. Boeing, on the other hand, sells to airlines and governments that have established business credit relationships with Boeing. Thus, the nature of its business dictates that Boeing has a much larger fraction of its sales tied up in the form of accounts receivable than does Wal-Mart.

Accounts receivable turnover can then be converted into the number of days it takes to collect receivables by computing a ratio called **average collection period**. This ratio is computed by dividing 365 (or the number of days in a year) by the accounts receivable turnover as follows:

average collection period

A measure of the average number of days it takes to collect a credit sale; computed by dividing 365 days by the accounts receivable turnover.

$$\text{Average Collection Period} = \frac{365}{\text{Accounts Receivable Turnover}}$$

Computing this ratio for both Wal-Mart and Boeing shows that it takes Wal-Mart only 2.6 days (365 ÷ 142.7) on average to collect its receivables, while Boeing takes an average of 32.9 days (365 ÷ 11.1).

Consider what might happen to Boeing's average collection period during an economic recession. During a recession, purchasers are often strapped for cash and try to delay paying on their accounts for as long as possible. Boeing might be faced with airlines that still want to buy airplanes but wish to stretch out the payment period. The result would be a rise in Boeing's average collection period; more of Boeing's resources would be tied up in the form of accounts receivable. In turn, Boeing would have to increase its borrowing in order to pay its own bills since it would be collecting less cash from its slow-paying customers. Proper receivables management involves balancing the desire to extend credit in order to increase sales with the need to collect the cash quickly in order to pay off your own bills.

REMEMBER THIS...

Careful management of accounts receivable is a balance between:

- extending credit to increase your sales and
- collecting cash quickly to reduce your need to borrow.

Two ratios commonly used in monitoring the level of receivables are:

- accounts receivable turnover (Sales Revenue ÷ Average Accounts Receivable) and
- average collection period (365 ÷ Accounts Receivable Turnover).

Recording Warranty and Service Costs Associated with a Sale

Match revenues and expenses by estimating and recording future warranty and service costs associated with a sale.

6 Let's return to the Farm Land example in which 50 sacks of fertilizer were sold for $500. Assume that as part of each sale, Farm Land offers to send a customer service representative to the home or place of business of any purchaser who wants more detailed instructions on how to apply the fertilizer. Historical experience suggests that the buyer of one fertilizer sack in 10 will request a visit from a Farm Land representative, and the material and labor cost of each visit averages $35. So, with 50 sacks of fertilizer sold, Farm Land has obligated itself to provide, on average, $175 in future customer service [(50 ÷ 10) × $35]. Proper matching requires that this $175 expense be estimated and recognized in the same period in which the associated sale is recognized. Otherwise, if the company waited to record customer service expense until the actual visits are requested, this period's sales revenue would be reported in the same income statement with customer service expense arising from last period's sales. The accountant is giving up some precision because the service expense must be estimated in advance. This sacrifice in precision is worth the benefit of being able to better match revenues and expenses.

The entry to recognize Farm Land's estimated service expense from the sale of 50 sacks of fertilizer is as follows:

Customer Service Expense	175	
Estimated Liability for Service		175
Estimated customer service costs on sales [(50 ÷ 10) × $35].		

The credit entry, Estimated Liability for Service, is a liability. When actual expenses are incurred in providing the customer service, the liability is eliminated with the following type of entry:

Estimated Liability for Service	145	
Wages Payable (to service employees)		100
Supplies		45
Actual customer service costs incurred.		

This entry shows that supplies and labor were required to honor the service agreements. This procedure results in the service expense being recognized at the time of sale, not necessarily when the actual service occurs.

After these two journal entries are made, the remaining balance in Estimated Liability for Service will be $30, shown as follows:

Estimated Liability for Service

Estimate at time of sale		175
Actual service costs incurred	145	
Remaining balance		30

The $30 balance represents the estimated amount of service that still must be provided in the future resulting from the sale of the 50 sacks of fertilizer. If actual experience suggests that the estimated service cost is too high, a lower estimate would be made in connection with subsequent fertilizer sales. If estimated liability for service is too low, a higher estimate is made for subsequent sales. The important point is that the accountant would not try to go back and "fix" an estimate that later proves to be inexact; the accountant merely monitors the relationship between the estimated and actual service costs in order to adjust future estimates accordingly.

The accounting just shown for estimated service costs is the same procedure used for estimated warranty costs. For example, **General Motors** promises automobile buyers that it will fix, at no charge to the buyer, certain mechanical problems for a certain period of time. GM estimates and records this warranty expense at the time the automobile sales are made. At the end of 2005, GM reported an existing liability for warranty costs of $9.1 billion. This amount is what GM estimates it will have to spend on warranty repairs in 2006 (and later years) on cars sold in 2005 (and earlier).

REMEMBER THIS...

If a company makes promises about future warranty repairs or continued customer service as part of the sale, the value of these promises should be estimated and recorded as an expense at the time of the sale. The entry has the following general format:

Expense	XXX	
Warranty Liability		XXX

Thus far the chapter has covered the main topics associated with selling goods or services, collecting the proceeds from those sales, and estimating and recording bad debt expense and service expense. The expanded material will cover two additional topics. First, an important tool of cash control, the bank reconciliation, will be explained. Second, the financial statement implications of making sales denominated in foreign currencies will be illustrated.

Reconciling the Bank Account

Reconcile a checking account.

(7) With the exception of small amounts of petty cash kept for miscellaneous purposes, most cash is kept in various bank accounts. Generally, only a few employees are authorized to sign checks, and they must have their signatures on file with the bank.

Each month the business receives a bank statement that shows the cash balance at the beginning of the period, the deposits, the amounts of the checks processed, and the cash balance at the end of the period. With the statement, the bank includes all of that month's canceled checks (or at least a listing of the checks), as well as debit and credit memos [for example, an explanation of charges for **NSF (not sufficient funds) checks** and service fees]. From a bank's perspective, customers' deposits are liabilities; hence, debit memos reduce the company's cash balance, and credit memos increase the balance.

NSF (not sufficient funds) check

A check that is not honored by a bank because of insufficient cash in the check writer's account.

The July bank statement for one of Hunt Company's accounts is presented in Exhibit 6. This statement shows all activity in the cash account as recorded by the bank and includes four bank adjustments to Hunt's balance—a bank service charge of $7 (the bank's monthly fee), $60 of interest paid by First Security Bank on Hunt's average balance, a $425 transfer into another account, and a $3,200 direct deposit made by a customer who regularly deposits payments directly to Hunt's bank account. Other adjustments that are commonly made by a bank to a company's account include:

1. *NSF (not sufficient funds).* This is the cancellation of a prior deposit that could not be collected because of insufficient funds in the check writer's (payer's) account. When a check is received and deposited in the payee's account, the check is assumed to represent funds that will be collected from the payer's bank. When a bank refuses to honor a check because of insufficient funds in the account on which it was written, the check is returned to the payee's bank and is marked "NSF." The amount of the check, which was originally recorded as a deposit (addition) to the payee's account, is deducted from the account when the check is returned unpaid.
2. *MS (miscellaneous).* Other adjustments made by a bank.
3. *ATM (automated teller machine) transactions.* These are deposits and withdrawals made by the depositor at automated teller machines.
4. *Withdrawals for credit card transactions paid directly from accounts.* These types of cards, called debit cards, are like using plastic checks. Instead of the card holder getting a bill or statement, the amount charged is deducted from the card holder's bank balance.

It is unusual for the ending balance on the bank statement to equal the amount of cash recorded in a company's cash account. The most common reasons for differences are:

1. *Time period differences.* The time period of the bank statement does not coincide with the timing of the company's postings to the cash account.
2. *Deposits in transit.* These are deposits that have not been processed by the bank as of the bank statement date, usually because they were made at or near the end of the month.
3. *Outstanding checks.* These are checks that have been written and deducted from a company's cash account but have not cleared or been deducted by the bank as of the bank statement date.
4. *Bank debits.* These are deductions made by the bank that have not yet been recorded by the company. The most common are monthly service charges, NSF checks, and bank transfers out of the account.
5. *Bank credits.* These are additions made by the bank to a company's account before they are recorded by the company. The most common source is interest paid by the bank on the account balance.

EXHIBIT 6	**July Bank Statement for Hunt Company**

First Security Bank   Statement of Account
Helena, Montana 59601

     HUNT COMPANY   Account Number 325-78126
     1900 S. PARK LANE
     HELENA, MT 59601   Date of Statement JULY 31, 2009

Check Number	Checks and Withdrawals	Deposits and Additions	Date	Balance
			6/30	13,000
620	140		7/01	12,860
621	250	1,500	7/03	14,110
622	860		7/05	13,250
623	210		7/08	13,040
		2,140	7/09	15,180
624	205		7/10	14,975
626	310		7/14	14,665
	425 T		7/15	14,240
		3,200 D	7/18	17,440
628	765		7/19	16,675
629	4,825		7/22	11,850
630	420		7/24	11,430
632	326	1,600	7/25	12,704
		2,100	7/26	14,804
633	210		7/29	14,594
635	225		7/31	14,369
	7 SC	60 I	7/31	14,422
	9,178 TOTAL CHECKS AND WITHDRAWALS	**10,600** TOTAL DEPOSITS AND ADDITIONS		**14,422** BALANCE

NSF = Not Sufficient Funds   D = Direct Deposit   I = Interest   T = Transfer Out of Account
SC = Service Charge   MS = Miscellaneous   ATM = Automated Teller Machine Transaction

6. *Accounting errors.* These are numerical errors made by either the company or the bank. The most common is transposition of numbers.

bank reconciliation

The process of systematically comparing the cash balance as reported by the bank with the cash balance on the company's books and explaining any differences.

The process of determining the reasons for the differences between the bank balance and the company's cash account balance is called a **bank reconciliation**. This usually results in adjusting both the bank statement and the book (cash account) balances. If the balances were not reconciled (if the cash balance were left as is), the figure used on the financial statements would probably be incorrect, and external users would not have accurate information for decision making. More importantly, the bank reconciliation can serve as an independent check to ensure that the cash is being accounted for correctly within the company.

We will use Hunt Company's bank account to illustrate a bank reconciliation. The statement shown in Exhibit 6 indicates an ending balance of $14,422 for the month of July. After arranging the month's canceled checks in numerical order and examining the bank statement, Hunt's accountant notes the following:

1. A deposit of $3,100 on July 31 was not shown on the bank statement. (It was in transit at the end of the month.)

EXHIBIT 7	July Bank Reconciliation for Hunt Company

Hunt Company
Bank Reconciliation
July 31, 2009

Balance per bank statement		$14,422	Balance per books		$13,937

Additions to bank balance: / *Additions to book balance:*

Deposit in transit 3,100 — Direct deposit $3,200
Total $17,522 — Interest 60 3,260
— Total $17,197

Deductions from bank balance: / *Deductions from book balance:*

Outstanding checks: 625 $326 — Service charge $ 7
631 426 — Bank transfer 425
634 185 (937) — Error in recording check No. 630
(for Jones's wages) 180 (612)

Adjusted bank balance $16,585 — **Adjusted book balance $16,585**

2. Checks No. 625 for $326, No. 631 for $426, and No. 634 for $185 are outstanding. Check No. 627 was voided at the time it was written.
3. The bank's service charge for the month is $7.
4. A direct deposit of $3,200 was made by Joy Company, a regular customer.
5. A transfer of $425 was made out of Hunt's account into the account of Martin Custodial Service for payment owed.
6. The bank paid interest of $60 on Hunt's average balance.
7. Check No. 630 for Thelma Jones's wages was recorded in the accounting records as $240 instead of the correct amount, $420.
8. The cash account in the general ledger shows a balance on July 31 of $13,937.

The bank reconciliation is shown in Exhibit 7. Since the bank and book balances now agree, the $16,585 adjusted cash balance is the amount that will be reported on the financial statements. If the adjusted book and bank balances had not agreed, the accountant would have had to search for errors in bookkeeping or in the bank's figures. When the balances finally agree, any necessary adjustments are made to the cash account to bring it to the correct balance. The entries to correct the balance include debits to Cash for all reconciling additions to the book balance and credits to Cash for all reconciling deductions from the book balance. Additions and deductions from the bank balance do not require adjustments to the company's books; the deposits in transit and the outstanding checks have already been recorded by the company, and, of course, bank errors are corrected by notifying the bank and having the bank make corrections. The adjustments required to correct Hunt's cash account are:

Cash 3,260
Accounts Receivable 3,200
Interest Revenue 60
To record the additions due to the July bank reconciliation (a $3,200 deposit made by Joy Company and $60 interest).
Custodial Expense 425
Miscellaneous Expense 7
Wages Expense 180
Cash 612
To record the deductions due to the July bank reconciliation (service charge, $7; a $180 recording error, check No. 630; bank transfer of $425 to Martin Custodial Service).

- A bank reconciliation has the following general format:

  Balance per bank
  +   Deposits in transit
  −   Outstanding checks
  +/− Bank errors or other adjustments for things that the bank doesn't yet know about
  =   Adjusted balance per bank

  Balance per books
  +   Interest received, automatic deposits, and other additions revealed in the bank statement
  −   Service fees and other subtractions revealed in the bank statement
  +/− Book errors or other adjustments for things heretofore unreflected in the books
  =   Adjusted balance per books

- The reconciliation is not done until the adjusted balance per books is equal to the adjusted balance per bank.

Foreign Currency Transactions

Account for the impact of changing exchange rates on the value of accounts receivable denominated in foreign currencies.

(8) All of the sales illustrated to this point in the text have been denominated in U.S. dollars. However, many U.S. companies do a large portion of their business in foreign countries. For example, **Wal-Mart** reports that sales in 2005 were denominated in currencies other than the U.S. dollar, including the euro, Japanese yen, British pound, and Canadian dollar. So, what would Wal-Mart have to do to record a software sale denominated in Japanese yen or British pounds? This section answers that question.

When a U.S. company sells a good or provides a service to a party in a foreign country, the transaction amount is frequently denominated in U.S. dollars. The U.S. dollar is a relatively stable currency, and buyers from Azerbaijan to Zimbabwe are often eager to avoid the uncertainty associated with payments denominated in their local currencies. For example, no matter where they are located, buyers and sellers of crude oil almost always write the contract price in terms of U.S. dollars. A U.S. company accounts for a sales contract with a foreign buyer with the sales price denominated in U.S. dollars in the way illustrated previously in this chapter; no new accounting issues are raised. However, if a U.S. company enters into a transaction in which the price is denominated in a foreign currency, the U.S. company must use special accounting procedures to recognize the change in the value of the transaction as foreign currency exchange rates fluctuate. For example, if Wal-Mart makes a credit sale with a price of 100,000 Indonesian rupiah, Wal-Mart knows that it will eventually collect 100,000 rupiah, but Wal-Mart does not know what those rupiah will be worth, in U.S. dollar terms, until the actual rupiah payment is received. Such a transaction is called a **foreign currency transaction**; the accounting for these transactions is demonstrated in the following section.

foreign currency transaction

A sale in which the price is denominated in a currency other than the currency of the seller's home country.

Foreign Currency Transaction Example

To illustrate the accounting for a sale denominated in a foreign currency, assume that American Company sold goods with a price of 20,000,000 Korean won on March 23 to one of its Korean customers. Payment in Korean won is due July 12. American Company prepares quarterly financial statements on June 30. The following exchange rates apply:

	U.S. Dollar Value of One Korean Won	Event
April 23	$0.0010	Sale
June 30	0.0007	Financial statements prepared
July 12	0.0008	Payment received on account

On April 23, each Korean won is worth one-tenth of one U.S. cent. In other words, it takes 1,000 Korean won (1/0.0010) to buy one U.S. dollar. At this exchange rate, the 20,000,000-Korean-won contract is worth $20,000 (20,000,000 × $0.0010).

On April 23, American Company records the sale and the account receivable in its books as follows:

Accounts Receivable (fc)	20,000	
Sales Revenue		20,000

Note that this journal entry is exactly the same as those illustrated earlier in the chapter. The (fc) indicates that the Accounts Receivable asset is denominated in a foreign currency and, thus, subject to exchange rate fluctuations. Because the financial statements of American Company are reported in U.S. dollars, all transaction amounts must be converted into their U.S. dollar equivalents when they are entered into the formal accounting system.

F Y I

The wide fluctuations in exchange rates in this illustration are unusual, but not unprecedented. For example, as part of the Asian financial crisis of 1997, the number of Korean won needed to purchase one U.S. dollar increased from 917.77 on October 23, 1997, to 1,952.68 on December 23, 1997.

On June 30, American Company prepares its quarterly financial statements. Because the 20,000,000-Korean-won contract price has not yet been collected in cash, American Company still has a receivable denominated in Korean won and must reflect the effect of the change in the exchange rate on the U.S. dollar value of that receivable. In this case the Korean won has decreased in value and is worth only $0.0007 on June 30. If American Company had to settle the contract on June 30, it would receive only $14,000 (20,000,000 × $0.0007). Thus, American Company must recognize an exchange loss of $6,000, or 20,000,000 × ($0.0010 − $0.0007). On July 12, American Company receives payment from its Korean customer. In the interim the value of the Korean won has increased slightly to $0.0008. When the receivable is collected, the 20,000,000 Korean won are worth $16,000 (20,000,000 × $0.0008), so now American Company has experienced a gain relative to its position on June 30. The effects of the fluctuation in the value of the Korean won can be summarized as follows:

	U.S. Dollar Value of the Receivable	Gain or Loss
April 23	$20,000	Not applicable
June 30	14,000	$6,000 loss
July 12	16,000	$2,000 gain

This information would be reported in American Company's three primary financial statements in the second quarter (ending June 30) and the third quarter (beginning July 1) as follows:

Second Quarter:

Income Statement		Balance Sheet		Statement of Cash Flows	
Sales revenue	$20,000	Accounts receivable	$14,000	Cash collected from customers	$ 0
Foreign exchange loss	(6,000)				

Third Quarter:

Income Statement		Balance Sheet		Statement of Cash Flows	
Sales revenue	$ 0	Cash	$16,000	Cash collected from customers	$16,000
Foreign exchange gain	2,000	Accounts receivable	0		

The net result of the sale in the second quarter, the collection of cash in the third quarter, and the changing exchange rates in between is to record a sale of $20,000, the collection of cash of $16,000, and a net exchange loss of $4,000 (a $6,000 loss in the second quarter and a $2,000 gain in the third quarter). The important point to note is that the sale is measured at the exchange rate on the date of sale and that any fluctuations between the sale date and the settlement date are recognized as exchange gains or losses.

What could American Company have done in the previous example to reduce its exposure to the risk associated with changing exchange rates? The easiest thing would have been to denominate the transaction in U.S. dollars. Then the risk of exchange rate changes would have fallen on the Korean company. Secondly, American Company could have locked in the price of Korean won by entering into a forward contract with a foreign currency broker. A forward contract is an example of a derivative contract. Derivatives are becoming more and more commonplace in today's business environment.

REMEMBER THIS...

- When a U.S. company makes a sale that is denominated in a foreign currency, the sale is called a foreign currency transaction.
  - Sale: measured at the exchange rate on the date of sale
  - Cash collection: measured at the exchange rate on the date of collection
- Any fluctuations between the sale date and the cash collection date are recognized as exchange gains or losses.

REVIEW OF LEARNING OBJECTIVES

(1) Understand the three basic types of business activities: operating, investing, and financing.

Operating Activities	• selling products or services
	• buying inventory for resale
	• incurring and paying for necessary expenses associated with the primary activities of a business
Investing Activities	• purchasing assets for use in the business
	• making investments in such items as stocks and bonds
Financing Activities	• borrowing money and repaying loans
	• issuing new shares of stock
	• paying cash dividends

(2) Use the two revenue recognition criteria to decide when the revenue from a sale or service should be recorded in the accounting records. Revenue is recognized after:

• the work is done **and**
• cash collectibility is reasonably assured.

Revenue for long-term contracts is recognized in proportion to the amount of the contract completed.

(3) Properly account for the collection of cash and describe the business controls necessary to safeguard cash.

• Net sales can be calculated as follows:
  Gross Sales
  − Sales Discounts
  − Sales Returns and Allowances
  = Net Sales

• Common cash controls include:
  • separation of duties in handling and accounting for cash,
  • daily deposits of all cash receipts, and
  • payment of all expenditures by prenumbered checks.

(4) Record the losses resulting from credit customers who do not pay their bills. Two ways of accounting for losses from uncollectible receivables:

• allowance method (generally accepted)
• direct write-off method (NOT generally accepted)

Two ways of estimating losses from uncollectible receivables:

• percentage of credit sales
• fraction of total outstanding receivables (often determined by aging the accounts receivable)

(5) Evaluate a company's management of its receivables by computing and analyzing appropriate financial ratios. Careful management of accounts receivable is a balance between:

• extending credit to increase your sales and
• collecting cash quickly to reduce your need to borrow.

Two ratios commonly used in monitoring the level of receivables are:

• accounts receivable turnover (Sales Revenue ÷ Average Accounts Receivable) and
• average collection period (365 ÷ Accounts Receivable Turnover).

6 **Match revenues and expenses by estimating and recording future warranty and service costs associated with a sale.** If a company makes promises about future warranty repairs or continued customer service as part of the sale, the value of these promises should be estimated and recorded as an expense (and liability) at the time of the sale.

7 **Reconcile a checking account.**

  Balance per bank
+ Deposits in transit
− Outstanding checks
+/− Bank errors or other adjustments for things that the bank doesn't yet know about
= Adjusted balance per bank

  Balance per books
+ Interest received, automatic deposits, and other additions revealed in the bank statement
− Service fees and other subtractions revealed in the bank statement
+/− Book errors or other adjustments for things heretofore unreflected in the books
= Adjusted balance per books

8 **Account for the impact of changing exchange rates on the value of accounts receivable denominated in foreign currencies.** When a U.S. company makes a sale that is denominated in a foreign currency, the sale is called a foreign currency transaction.
• Sale: measured at the exchange rate on the date of sale
• Cash collection: measured at the exchange rate on the date of collection

Any fluctuations between the sale date and the cash collection date are recognized as exchange gains or losses.

KEY TERMS & CONCEPTS

accounts receivable, 238

accounts receivable
  turnover, 244

aging accounts
  receivable, 242

allowance for bad
  debts, 239

allowance method, 239

average collection
  period, 244

bad debt, 238

bad debt expense, 239

cash, 236

contra account, 235

direct write-off
  method, 238

financing activities, 228

gross sales, 236

investing
  activities, 228

net realizable value
  of accounts
  receivable, 240

net sales, 236

operating activities, 228

receivables, 237

revenue recognition, 231

sales discounts, 234

sales returns and
  allowances, 235

venture capital firm, 226

EXPANDED *material*

bank reconciliation, 248

foreign currency
  transaction, 250

NSF (not sufficient
  funds) checks, 247

REVIEW PROBLEM

Accounting for Receivables and Warranty Obligations

Douglas Company sells furniture. Approximately 10% of its sales are cash; the remainder are on credit. During the year ended December 31, 2009, the company had net credit sales of $2,200,000. As of December 31, 2009, total accounts receivable were $800,000, and Allowance for Bad Debts had a debit balance of $1,100 prior to adjustment. In the past, approximately 1% of credit sales have proved to be uncollectible. An aging analysis of the individual accounts receivable revealed that $32,000 of the Accounts Receivable balance appeared to be uncollectible.

(continued)

The largest credit sale during the year occurred on December 4, 2009, for $72,000 to Aaron Company. Terms of the sale were 2/10, n/30. On December 13, Aaron Company paid $60,000 of the receivable balance and took advantage of the 2% discount. The remaining $12,000 was still outstanding on March 31, 2010, when Douglas Company learned that Aaron Company had declared bankruptcy. Douglas wrote the receivable off as uncollectible.

On December 31, 2009, Douglas Company estimated that it would cost $11,000 in labor and various expenditures to service the furniture it had sold (under 90-day warranty agreements) during the last three months of 2009. During January 2010, the company spent $430 in labor and $600 for supplies to perform service on defective furniture that was sold during the year 2009.

Required:

Prepare the following journal entries:

1. The sale of $72,000 of furniture on December 4, 2009, to Aaron Company on credit.
2. The collection of $58,800 from Aaron Company on December 13, 2009, assuming the company allows the discount on partial payment.
3. Record Bad Debt Expense on December 31, 2009, using the percentage of credit sales method.
4. Record Bad Debt Expense on December 31, 2009, using the aging of receivables method.
5. Record estimated warranty expense on December 31, 2009.
6. Record actual expenditures to service defective furniture under the warranty agreements on January 31, 2010.
7. Write off the balance of the Aaron Company receivable as uncollectible, March 31, 2010.

Solution

The journal entries would be recorded as follows:

1.	Dec. 4, 2009	Accounts Receivable	72,000	
		Sales Revenue		72,000
		Sold $72,000 of furniture to Aaron Company on credit.		

2.	Dec. 13, 2009	Cash	58,800	
		Sales Discounts	1,200	
		Accounts Receivable		60,000
		Collected $58,800 from Aaron Company on December 4 sale and recognized the 2% discount taken (0.02 × $60,000 = $1,200).		

3.	Dec. 31, 2009	Bad Debt Expense	22,000	
		Allowance for Bad Debts		22,000
		Recorded bad debt expense as 1% of credit sales of $2,200,000 ($2,200,000 × 0.01 = $22,000).		

Note: When using the percentage of credit sales method to estimate bad debt expense, the existing balance in the allowance for bad debts account is ignored.

4.	Dec. 31, 2009	Bad Debt Expense	33,100	
		Allowance for Bad Debts		33,100
		Recorded bad debt expense using the aging of accounts receivable method ($32,000 + $1,100 debit balance).		

Note: When using the percentage of total receivables method (e.g., by aging receivables) to estimate bad debt expense, the existing balance in Allowance for Bad Debts must be taken into consideration so that the new balance is the amount of receivables not expected to be collected.

5.	Dec. 31, 2009	Customer Service Expense	11,000	
		Estimated Liability for Service		11,000
		Estimated customer service (warranty) costs on furniture sold during the last three months of 2009. (The warranty period is 90 days.)		

(continued)

6.	Jan. 31, 2010	Estimated Liability for Service	1,030	
		Wages Payable (to service employees)		430
		Supplies		600
		Actual customer service costs incurred.		
7.	Mar. 31, 2010	Allowance for Bad Debts	12,000	
		Accounts Receivable		12,000
		Wrote off the balance in the Aaron Company account as uncollectible.		

DISCUSSION QUESTIONS

1. What are the three types of basic business activities?
2. Why is the purchase of inventory for resale to customers classified as an operating activity rather than an investing activity?
3. When should revenues be recognized and reported?
4. Why do you think misstatement of revenues (e.g., recognizing revenues before they are earned) is one of the most common ways to manipulate financial statements?
5. Why is it important to have separate sales returns and allowances and sales discounts accounts? Wouldn't it be much easier to directly reduce the sales revenue account for these adjustments?
6. Why do companies usually have more controls for cash than for other assets?
7. What are three generally practiced controls for cash, and what is the purpose of each control?
8. Why do most companies tolerate having a small percentage of uncollectible accounts receivable?
9. Why does the accounting profession require the use of the allowance method of accounting for losses due to bad debts rather than the direct write-off method?
10. With the allowance method, why is the net balance, or net realizable value, of Accounts

Receivable the same after the write-off of a receivable as it was prior to the write-off of the uncollectible account?
11. Why is the "aging" of accounts receivable usually more accurate than basing the estimate on total receivables?
12. Why is it important to monitor operating ratios such as accounts receivable turnover?
13. Why must the customer service expense (warranty) sometimes be recorded in the period prior to when the actual customer services will be performed?

EXPANDED *material*

14. What are the major reasons that the balance of a bank statement is usually different from the cash book balance (Cash per the general ledger)?
15. Why don't the additions and deductions from the bank balance on a bank reconciliation require adjustment by the company?
16. Do all transactions by U.S. companies with foreign parties require special accounting procedures by the U.S. companies? Explain.

PRACTICE EXERCISES

PE 6-1   **Classifying Major Business Activities**
LO1   Classify each of the following business activities as an operating, investing, or financing activity.
   a. Acquiring inventory for resale.
   b. Buying and selling stocks and bonds of other companies.
   c. Selling shares of stock to investors for cash.
   d. Selling products or services.
   e. Buying property, plant, or equipment.
   f. Acquiring and paying for other operating items.
   g. Selling property, plant, or equipment.
   h. Borrowing cash from creditors.

PE 6-2
LO2

Revenue Recognition

In which one of the following situations should revenue be recognized?

a. The earnings process has begun and cash collectibility is reasonably assured.
b. The earnings process has begun and cash has been collected.
c. The earnings process is substantially complete and cash collectibility is not yet reasonably assured.
d. The earnings process will soon begin and cash has been collected.
e. The earnings process is substantially complete and cash collectibility is reasonably assured.

PE 6-3
LO2

Revenue Recognition

Make the journal entry necessary to record the sale of 120 books at $32 per book. Sixty-five of the books were sold for cash, and 55 were sold on credit.

PE 6-4
LO3

Cash Collection

Refer to the data in PE 6-3. Make the journal entry necessary when the company receives payment for the 55 books sold on credit.

PE 6-5
LO3

Sales Discounts

Refer to the data in PE 6-3. Assume that all of the books were sold to a single customer and that the terms of the credit sale were 2/10, n/30. Make the journal entry necessary to record the receipt of the cash payment assuming that (1) the customer paid the balance on the account five days after the purchase and (2) the customer paid the balance on the account 20 days after the purchase.

PE 6-6
LO3

Sales Returns and Allowances

Refer to the data in PE 6-3. Assume a customer found that 20 of the books were misprinted and returned the 20 books for a refund. Prepare the journal entry necessary in the records of the selling company to record the receipt of the returned books assuming that (1) the books were returned by a cash customer and (2) the books were returned by a credit customer.

PE 6-7
LO3

Computing Net Sales

Using the following data, compute net sales.

Sales discounts	$ 50,000
Accounts receivable, ending	125,000
Gross sales	2,500,000
Inventory, ending	200,000
Sales returns and allowances	75,000

PE 6-8
LO3

Control of Cash

Which one of the following is *not* an important control associated with cash?

a. All cash expenditures must be made with prenumbered checks.
b. The cash balance must never fall below the sum of inventory and accounts receivable.
c. All cash receipts must be deposited daily.
d. The handling of cash must be separated from the recording of cash.

PE 6-9
LO4

The Direct Write-Off Method

The company has an accounts receivable balance of $3,000,000 at the end of the year. The company decides that $90,000 of those accounts receivable are uncollectible because the customers associated with those accounts had filed for bankruptcy protection during the year. Using the direct write-off method of accounting for bad debt expense, make the journal entry necessary to record bad debt expense for the year.

PE 6-10   **The Allowance Method**

LO4   The company had credit sales of $2,500,000 during the year, its first year of business. The company has estimated that $50,000 of these sales on account will ultimately be uncollectible. In addition, a year-end review of accounts identified that of the $200,000 in accounts outstanding as of the end of the year, $43,000 were worthless because the business customers associated with those accounts had gone bankrupt. Using the allowance method of accounting for bad debt expense, make the journal entries necessary to record (1) bad debt expense for the year and (2) the write-off of uncollectible accounts at the end of the year.

PE 6-11   **Computing Net Accounts Receivable**

LO4   Refer to the data in PE 6-10. Taking into account the allowance for bad debts established at the end of the year, compute the net realizable value of accounts receivable (1) before the write-off of uncollectible accounts and (2) after the write-off of uncollectible accounts.

PE 6-12   **Collecting an Account Previously Written Off**

LO4   Refer to the data in PE 6-10. Assume that one customer, whose account had previously been written off, returned from exile in the Bahamas and paid his account of $7,000. Make the journal entry or entries necessary to record the receipt of this payment.

PE 6-13   **Estimating Uncollectible Accounts Receivable as a Percentage of Credit Sales**

LO4   The company had an Accounts Receivable balance of $85,000 and an Allowance for Bad Debts balance of $3,400 (credit) at the end of the year (before any adjusting entry). Credit sales for the year totaled $860,000. The accountant determined that 1% of this year's credit sales will ultimately be uncollectible. Make the journal entry necessary to record bad debt expense for the year.

PE 6-14   **Estimating Uncollectible Accounts Receivable as a Percentage**
LO4   **of Total Receivables**

The company had an Accounts Receivable balance of $85,000 and an Allowance for Bad Debts balance of $3,400 (credit) at the end of the year (before any adjusting entry). Credit sales for the year totaled $860,000. The accountant determined that 10% of the ending accounts receivable will ultimately be uncollectible. Make the journal entry necessary to record bad debt expense for the year.

PE 6-15   **Estimating Uncollectible Accounts Receivable Using Aging Accounts Receivable**

LO4   The company reports the following aging accounts receivable data:

Customer	Balance	Current	1–30	31–60	61–90	91–120	Over 120
					Days Past Due		
T. Gardner	$ 3,750	$ 2,250	$1,500				
J. Gammon	4,000	1,000		$2,500		$ 500	
M. Orser	2,000		2,000				
K. Saxton	1,000			750	$250		
K. Welch	4,000						$4,000
R. Beckstrom	10,900	8,000	2,900				
B. Roberts	3,900			3,900			
L. Wilcox	5,850	5,200			650		
J. Gagon	1,500					1,500	
A. Wycherly	1,750		1,750				
Totals	$38,650	$16,450	$8,150	$7,150	$900	$2,000	$4,000

(continued)

In addition, the company provides the following estimates for accounts that will ultimately be uncollectible:

Age	Percentage Estimated to Be Uncollectible
Current	1.75%
1–30 days past due	6
31–60 days past due	15
61–90 days past due	35
91–120 days past due	65
Over 120 days past due	90

Using this information, make the journal entry necessary to record bad debt expense. Assume that: (1) the balance in the allowance for bad debts account (before adjustment) is $2,000 (credit) and (2) the balance in the allowance for bad debts account (before adjustment) is $3,600 (debit).

PE 6-16
LO4

Evaluating Quality of Accounts Receivable

The company reports the following data for the past three years:

Year	Ending Accounts Receivable	Ending Allowance for Bad Debts
Year 3	$60,450	$10,360
Year 2	50,250	7,690
Year 1	43,200	4,400

Compute the allowance for bad debts as a percentage of accounts receivable and evaluate the quality of accounts receivable over the three-year period.

PE 6-17
LO5

Accounts Receivable Turnover

Using the following data, calculate the company's accounts receivable turnover.

Accounts receivable balance, December 31	$ 54,000
Inventory balance, December 31	59,000
Sales revenue	520,000
Cost of goods sold	310,000
Accounts receivable balance, January 1	46,000

PE 6-18
LO5

Average Collection Period

Refer to the data in PE 6-17. Calculate the company's average collection period.

PE 6-19
LO6

Warranty Expense

The company has determined, based on past experience, that 15% of all tires sold will need repairs within the warranty period. When customers request a tire repair under the warranty agreement, each visit costs an average of $20 in parts and labor. The company sold 600 tires during the year. Make the journal entry necessary to record warranty expense for the year.

PE 6-20
LO6

Repairs under Warranty

Refer to the data in PE 6-19. Assume that during the following year, 20 customers bring in 80 tires for warranty repairs. The labor and supplies associated with these repairs were $900 and $350, respectively. Make the journal entry necessary to record the performance of these warranty services.

PE 6-21	**Bank Reconciliation**
LO7	The company received a bank statement at the end of the month. The statement contained the following:

Ending balance	$33,000
Bank service charge for the month	250
Interest earned and added by the bank to the account balance	110

In comparing the bank statement to its own cash records, the company found the following:

Deposits made but not yet recorded by the bank	$11,200
Checks written and mailed but not yet recorded by the bank	21,300

Before making any adjustments suggested by the bank statement, the cash balance according to the books is $23,040. What is the correct cash balance as of the end of the month? Verify this amount by reconciling the bank statement with the cash balance on the books.

PE 6-22	**Journal Entries from a Bank Reconciliation**
LO7	Refer to PE 6-21. Make all journal entries necessary on the company's books to adjust the reported cash balance in response to the receipt of the bank statement.

PE 6-23	**Journal Entry to Record a Foreign Currency Transaction**
LO8	On November 6 of Year 1, the company provided services (on account) to a client located in Thailand. The contract price is 100,000 Thai baht. On November 6, the exchange rate was 50 baht for one U.S. dollar. On December 31, the exchange rate was 40 baht for one U.S. dollar. The company received payment on the account on March 23 of Year 2. On that date, the exchange rate was 100 baht for one U.S. dollar. Make the journal entry necessary on November 6 to record the performance of the service.

PE 6-24	**Computation of Foreign Exchange Gains and Losses**
LO8	Refer to PE 6-23. Compute the foreign exchange gain or loss that should be reported in (1) Year 1 and (2) Year 2.

EXERCISES

E 6-25	**Recognizing Revenue**
LO2	Supposedly, there is an over 200-year wait to buy **Green Bay Packers** season football tickets. The fiscal year-end (when they close their books) for the Green Bay Packers is March 30 of each year. If the Packers sell their season football tickets in February for the coming football season, when should the revenue from those ticket sales be recognized?

E 6-26	**Recognizing Revenue**
LO2	James Dee Company cleans the outside walls of buildings. The average job generates revenue of $800,000 and takes about two weeks to complete. Customers are required to pay for a job within 30 days after its completion. James Dee Company guarantees its work for five years—if the building walls get dirty within five years, James Dee will clean them again at no charge. James Dee is considering recognizing revenue using one of the following methods:

a. Recognize revenue when James Dee signs the contract to do the job.
b. Recognize revenue when James Dee begins the work.
c. Recognize revenue immediately after the completion of the job.

(continued)

d. Recognize revenue 30 days after the completion of the job when the cash is collected.

e. Wait until the five-year guarantee period is over before recognizing any revenue.

Which revenue recognition option would you recommend to James Dee? Explain your answer.

E 6-27
LO2

Recognizing Revenue–Long-Term Construction Projects

In the year 2002, Salt Lake City, Utah, hosted the Winter Olympics. To get ready for the Olympics, most of the major roads and highways in and around Salt Lake City were renovated. It took over three years to complete the highway projects, and **Wasatch Constructors**, the construction company performing the work, didn't want to wait until the work was completed to recognize revenue. How should the revenue on these highway construction projects have been recognized?

E 6-28
LO2

Revenue Recognition

Yummy, Inc., is a franchiser that offers for sale an exclusive franchise agreement for $30,000. Under the terms of the agreement, the purchaser of a franchise receives a variety of services associated with the construction of a Yummy Submarine and Yogurt Shop, access to various product supply services, and continuing management advice and assistance once the retail unit is up and running. The contract calls for the franchise purchaser to make cash payments of $10,000 per year for three years to Yummy, Inc.

How should Yummy, Inc., account for the sale of a franchise contract? Specifically, when should the revenue and receivable be recognized?

E 6-29
LO3

Control of Cash

Molly Maloney is an employee of Marshall Company, a small manufacturing concern. Her responsibilities include opening the daily mail, depositing the cash and checks received into the bank, and making the accounting entries to record the receipt of cash and the reduction of receivables. Explain how Maloney might be able to misuse some of Marshall's cash receipts. As a consultant, what control procedures would you recommend?

E 6-30
LO3

Recording Sales Transactions

On June 24, 2009, Sudweeks Company sold merchandise to Brooke Bowman for $70,000 with terms 2/10, n/30. On June 30, Bowman paid $39,200 on her account and was allowed a discount for the timely payment. On July 20, Bowman paid $21,000 on her account and returned $9,000 of merchandise, claiming that it did not meet contract terms.

Record the necessary journal entries for Sudweeks Company on June 24, June 30, and July 20.

E 6-31
LO3

Recording Sales Transactions

Lee Company sold merchandise on account to Peart Company for $16,000 on June 3, 2009, with terms 2/10, n/30. On June 7, 2009, Lee Company received $650 of returned merchandise from Peart Company and issued a credit memorandum for the appropriate amount. Lee Company received payment for the balance of the bill on June 21, 2009.

Record the necessary journal entries for Lee Company on June 3, June 7, and June 21.

E 6-32
LO4

Estimating Bad Debts

The trial balance of Sparkling Jewelry Company at the end of its 2009 fiscal year included the following account balances:

Account	
Accounts receivable	$66,400
Allowance for bad debts	1,300 (debit balance)

The company has *not yet* recorded any bad debt expense for 2009.

(continued)

Determine the amount of bad debt expense to be recognized by Sparkling Jewelry Company for 2009, assuming the following independent situations:

1. An aging accounts receivable analysis indicates that probable uncollectible accounts receivable at year-end amount to $3,900.
2. Company policy is to maintain a provision for uncollectible accounts receivable equal to 4% of outstanding accounts receivable.
3. Company policy is to estimate uncollectible accounts receivable as equal to 1% of the previous year's annual sales, which were $350,000.

E 6-33
LO4

Accounting for Bad Debts

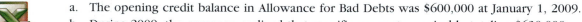

The following data were associated with the accounts receivable and uncollectible accounts of Julia Jay, Inc., during 2009:

a. The opening credit balance in Allowance for Bad Debts was $600,000 at January 1, 2009.
b. During 2009, the company realized that specific accounts receivable totaling $630,000 had gone bad and had been written off.
c. An account receivable of $35,000 was collected during 2009. This account had previously been written off as a bad debt in 2008.
d. The company decided that Allowance for Bad Debts would be $650,000 at the end of 2009.

1. Prepare journal entries to show how these events would be recognized in the accounting system using:
   a. The direct write-off method.
   b. The allowance method.
2. Discuss the advantages and disadvantages of each method with respect to the matching principle.

E 6-34
LO4

Accounting for Uncollectible Accounts Receivable

Dodge Company had the following information relating to its accounts receivable at December 31, 2008, and for the year ended December 31, 2009:

Accounts receivable balance at 12/31/08	$ 900,000
Allowance for bad debts at 12/31/08 (credit balance)	50,000
Gross sales during 2009 (all credit)	5,000,000
Collections from customers during 2009	4,500,000
Accounts written off as uncollectible during 2009	60,000
Estimated uncollectible receivables at 12/31/09	110,000

Dodge Company uses the percentage of receivables method to estimate bad debt expense.

1. At December 31, 2009, what is the balance of Dodge Company's Allowance for Bad Debts? What is the bad debt expense for 2009?
2. At December 31, 2009, what is the balance of Dodge Company's gross accounts receivable?

E 6-35
LO4

Aging of Accounts Receivable

Smoot Company's accounts receivable reveal the following balances:

Age of Accounts	Receivable Balance
Current	$720,000
1–30 days past due	395,000
31–60 days past due	105,000
61–90 days past due	52,000
91–120 days past due	13,000

(continued)

The credit balance in Allowance for Bad Debts is now $42,000. After a thorough analysis of its collection history, the company estimates that the following percentages of receivables will eventually prove uncollectible:

Current	0.5%
1–30 days past due	3.0
31–60 days past due	16.0
61–90 days past due	52.5
91–120 days past due	92.0

Prepare an aging schedule for the accounts receivable, and give the journal entry for recording the necessary change in the allowance for bad debts account.

E 6-36 **Aging of Accounts Receivable**

LO4 The following aging of accounts receivable is for Harry Company at the end of its first year of business:

Aging of Accounts Receivable **December 31, 2009**					
	Overall	**Less Than 30 Days**	**31 to 60 Days**	**61 to 90 Days**	**Over 90 Days**
Ken Nelson	$ 10,000	$ 8,000		$1,000	$1,000
Elaine Anderson	40,000	31,000	$ 4,000		5,000
Bryan Crist	12,000	3,000	4,000	2,000	3,000
Renee Warner	60,000	50,000	10,000		
Nelson Hsia	16,000	10,000	6,000		
Stella Valerio	25,000	20,000		5,000	
Totals	$163,000	$122,000	$24,000	$8,000	$9,000

Harry Company has collected the following bad debt information from a consultant familiar with Harry's industry:

Age of Account	**Percentage Ultimately Uncollectible**
Less than 30 days	2%
31–60 days	10
61–90 days	30
Over 90 days	75

1. Compute the appropriate Allowance for Bad Debts as of December 31, 2009.
2. Make the journal entry required to record this allowance. Remember that, since this is Harry's first year of operations, the allowance account at the beginning of the year was $0.
3. What is Harry's net accounts receivable balance as of December 31, 2009?

E 6-37 **Direct Write-Off versus Allowance Method**

LO4 The vice president for Tres Corporation provides you with the following list of accounts receivable written off in the current year. (These accounts were recognized as bad debt

(continued)

expense at the time they were written off; i.e., the company was using the direct write-off method.)

Date	Customer	Amount
March 30	Rasmussen Company	$12,000
July 31	Dodge Company	7,500
September 30	Larsen Company	10,000
December 31	Peterson Company	12,000

Tres Corporation's sales are all on a n/30 credit basis. Sales for the current year total $3,600,000, and analysis has indicated that uncollectible receivable losses historically approximate 1.5% of sales.

1. Do you agree or disagree with Tres Corporation's policy concerning recognition of bad debt expense? Why or why not?
2. If Tres were to use the percentage of sales method for recording bad debt expense, by how much would income before income taxes change for the current year?

E 6-38
LO4

Accounting for Uncollectible Receivables–Percentage of Sales Method

The trial balance of Beecher's Sporting Warehouse, Inc., shows a $110,000 outstanding balance in Accounts Receivable at the end of 2008. During 2009, 90% of the total credit sales of $4,400,000 was collected, and no receivables were written off as uncollectible. The company estimated that 1.5% of the credit sales would be uncollectible. During 2010, the account of Damon Shilling, who owed $7,300, was judged to be uncollectible and was written off. At the end of 2010, the amount previously written off was collected in full from Mr. Shilling.

Prepare the necessary journal entries for recording all the preceding transactions relating to uncollectibles on the books of Beecher's Sporting Warehouse, Inc.

E 6-39
LO4

Comparing the Percentage of Sales and the Percentage of Receivables Methods

Keefer Company uses the percentage of sales method for computing bad debt expense. As of January 1, 2009, the balance of Allowance for Bad Debts was $200,000. Write-offs of uncollectible accounts during 2009 totaled $240,000. Reported bad debt expense for 2009 was $320,000, computed using the percentage of sales method.

Keith & Harding, the auditors of Keefer's financial statements, compiled an aging accounts receivable analysis of Keefer's accounts at the end of 2009. This analysis has led Keith & Harding to estimate that, of the accounts receivable Keefer has as of the end of 2009, $700,000 will ultimately prove to be uncollectible.

Given their analysis, Keith & Harding, the auditors, think that Keefer should make an adjustment to its 2009 financial statements. What adjusting journal entry should Keith & Harding suggest?

E 6-40
LO5

Ratio Analysis

The following are summary financial data for Parker Enterprises, Inc., and Boulder, Inc., for three recent years:

	Year 3	Year 2	Year 1
Net sales (in millions):			
Parker Enterprises, Inc.	$ 3,700	$ 3,875	$ 3,882
Boulder, Inc.	17,825	16,549	15,242
Net accounts receivable (in millions):			
Parker Enterprises, Inc.	1,400	1,800	1,725
Boulder, Inc.	5,525	5,800	6,205

1. Using the above data, compute the accounts receivable turnover and average collection period for each company for years 2 and 3.
2. Which company appears to have the better credit management policy?

E 6-41
LO5

Assessing How Well Companies Manage Their Receivables

Assume that Hickory Company has the following data related to its accounts receivable:

	2008	2009
Net sales	$1,425,000	$1,650,000
Net receivables:		
Beginning of year	375,000	333,500
End of year	420,000	375,000

Use these data to compute accounts receivable turnover ratios and average collection periods for 2008 and 2009. Based on your analysis, is Hickory Company managing its receivables better or worse in 2009 than it did in 2008?

E 6-42
LO5

Measuring Accounts Receivable Quality

The following accounts receivable information is for Kayley Company:

	2009	2008	2007
Accounts receivable	$670,000	$580,000	$500,000
Allowance for bad debts	47,000	44,000	41,000

Did the creditworthiness of Kayley's customers increase or decrease between 2007 and 2009? Explain.

E 6-43
LO6

Accounting for Warranties

Rick Procter, president of Sharp Television Stores, has been concerned recently about declining sales due to increased competition in the area. Rick has noticed that many of the national stores selling television sets and appliances have been placing heavy emphasis on warranties in their marketing programs. In an effort to revitalize sales, Rick has decided to offer free service and repairs for one year as a warranty on his television sets. Based on experience, Rick believes that first-year service and repair costs on the television sets will be approximately 5% of sales. The first month of operations following the initiation of Rick's new marketing plan showed significant increases in sales of TV sets. Total sales of TV sets for the first three months under the warranty plan were $10,000, $8,000, and $12,000, respectively.

1. Assuming that Rick prepares adjusting entries and financial statements for his own use at the end of each month, prepare the appropriate entry to recognize customer service (warranty) expense for each of these first three months.
2. Prepare the appropriate entry to record services provided to repair sets under warranty in the second month, assuming that the following costs were incurred: labor (paid in cash), $550; supplies, $330.

E 6-44
LO6

Accounting for Warranties

Ainge Auto sells used cars and trucks. During 2009, it sold 53 cars and trucks for a total of $1,400,000. Ainge provides a 24-month, 30,000-mile warranty on the used cars and trucks sold. Ainge estimates that it will cost $25,000 in labor and $20,000 in parts to service (during the following year) the cars and trucks sold in 2009.

In January 2010, Joleen Glassett brought her truck in for warranty repairs. Ainge Auto fixed the truck under its warranty agreement. It cost Ainge $450 in labor and $310 in parts to fix Joleen Glassett's truck. Prepare the journal entries to record (1) Ainge Auto's estimated customer service liability as of December 31, 2009, and (2) the costs incurred in repairing the truck in January 2010.

E 6-45   **Preparing a Bank Reconciliation**

LO7   Prepare a bank reconciliation for Eugene Company at January 31, 2009, using the information shown.

1. Cash per the accounting records at January 31 amounted to $145,604; the bank statement on this same date showed a balance of $129,004.
2. The canceled checks returned by the bank included a check written by the LeRoy Company for $3,528 that had been deducted from Eugene's account in error.
3. Deposits in transit as of January 31, 2009, amounted to $21,856.
4. The following amounts were adjustments to Eugene Company's account on the bank statement:
    a. Service charges of $52.
    b. An NSF check of $2,800.
    c. Interest earned on the account, $80.
5. Checks written by Eugene Company that have not yet cleared the bank include four checks totaling $11,556.

E 6-46   **Preparing a Bank Reconciliation**

LO7   The records of Denna Corporation show the following bank statement information for December:

a. Bank balance, December 31, 2009, $87,450
b. Service charges for December, $50
c. Rent collected by bank, $1,000
d. Note receivable collected by bank (including $300 interest), $2,300
e. December check returned marked NSF (check was a payment of an account receivable), $200
f. Bank erroneously reduced Denna's account for a check written by Dunna Company, $1,000
g. Cash account balance, December 31, 2009, $81,200
h. Outstanding checks, $9,200
i. Deposits in transit, $5,000

1. Prepare a bank reconciliation for December.
2. Prepare the entry to correct the cash account as of December 31, 2009.

E 6-47   **Reconciling Book and Bank Balances**

LO7   Jensen Company has just received the September 30, 2009, bank statement summarized in the following schedule:

	Charges	Deposits	Balance
Balance, September 1			$ 5,100
Deposits recorded during September		$27,000	32,100
Checks cleared during September	$27,300		4,800
NSF check, J. J. Jones	50		4,750
Bank service charges	10		4,740
Balance, September 30			4,740

Cash on hand (recorded on Jensen's books but not deposited) on September 1 and September 30 amounted to $200. There were no deposits in transit or checks outstanding at September 1, 2009. The cash account for September reflected the following:

Cash

Sept. 1 Balance	5,300	Sept. Checks	28,000
Sept. Deposits	29,500		

(continued)

Answer the following questions. (*Hint:* It may be helpful to prepare a complete bank reconciliation.)

1. What is the ending balance per the cash account before adjustments?
2. What adjustments should be added to the depositor's books?
3. What is the total amount of the deductions from the depositor's books?
4. What is the total amount to be added to the bank's balance?
5. What is the total amount to be deducted from the bank's balance?

E 6-48
LO8

Foreign Currency Transaction

Apple Core, a U.S. company, sold 125,000 cases of tropical fruit to Minh Market, a Vietnamese firm, for 3.2 billion Vietnamese dong. The sale was made on November 17, 2009, when one U.S. dollar equaled 16,000 dong. Payment of 3.2 billion Vietnamese dong was due to Apple Core on January 16, 2010. At December 31, 2009, one U.S. dollar equaled 18,000 dong, and on January 16, 2010, one U.S. dollar equaled 18,400 dong.

1. What will be the value of the accounts receivable on December 31, 2009, in Vietnamese dong?
2. What will be the value of the accounts receivable on December 31, 2009, in U.S. dollars?
3. Will Apple Core recognize an exchange gain or loss at December 31, 2009? Explain.
4. Will Apple Core recognize an exchange gain or loss on January 16, 2010? Explain.
5. In connection with this sale, what amount will Apple Core report as Sales Revenue in its income statement for 2009?
6. In connection with this sale, what amount will Apple Core report as Cash Collected from Customers in its statement of cash flows for 2010?

E 6-49
LO8

Foreign Currency Transaction

American, Inc., sells one widget to Japanese Company at an agreed-upon price of 1,000,000 yen. On the day of the sale, one yen is equal to $0.01. American, Inc., maintains its accounting records in U.S. dollars. Therefore, the amount in yen must be converted to U.S. dollars.

1. Provide the journal entry that would be made by American, Inc., on the day of the sale, assuming Japanese Company pays for the widget on the day of the sale.
2. Most sales are on account, meaning that payment will not be received for 30 days or even longer. What issues will arise for American, Inc., if the sale is made with payment due in 30 days? (*Hint:* What might happen to the value of the yen in relation to the dollar during the 30-day period?)
3. Suppose that 30 days from the date of the sale the value of one yen is equal to $0.008. What journal entry would be made when the 1,000,000 yen are received by American, Inc.?

PROBLEMS

P 6-50
LO2

Recognizing Revenue

Brad Company sells ships. Each ship sells for over $25 million. Brad never starts building a ship until it receives a specific order from a customer. Brad usually takes about four years to build a ship. After construction is completed and during the first three years the customer uses the ship, Brad agrees to repair anything on the ship free of charge. The customers pay for the ships over a period of 10 years after the date of delivery.

Brad Company is considering the following alternatives for recognizing revenue from its sale of ships:

a. Recognize revenue when Brad receives the order to do the job.
b. Recognize revenue when Brad begins the work.
c. Recognize revenue proportionately during the four-year construction period.
d. Recognize revenue immediately after the customer takes possession of the ship.
e. Wait until the three-year guarantee period is over before recognizing any revenue.
f. Wait until the 10-year payment period is over before recognizing any revenue.

(continued)

Required:

1. Which of the methods, (a) through (f), should Brad use to recognize revenue? Support your answer.
2. **Interpretive Question:** A member of Congress has introduced a bill that would require the SEC to crack down on lenient revenue recognition practices by shipbuilding companies. This bill would require Brad Company to use method (f) above. The "logic" behind the congressperson's bill is that no revenue should ever be recognized until the complete amount of cash is in hand. You have been hired as a lobbyist by Brad Company to speak against this bill. What arguments would you use on Capitol Hill to sway representatives to vote against this bill?

P 6-51   **Recognizing Revenue**

LO2   The Ho Man Tin Tennis Club sells lifetime memberships for $20,000 each. A lifetime membership entitles a person to unlimited access to the club's tennis courts, weight room, exercise equipment, and swimming pool. Once a lifetime membership fee is paid, it is not refundable for any reason.

Judy Chan and her partners are the owners of Ho Man Tin Tennis Club. In order to overcome a cash shortage, they intend to seek investment funds from new partners. Judy and her partners are meeting with their accountant to provide information for preparation of financial statements. They are considering when they should recognize revenue from the sale of lifetime memberships.

Required:

Answer the following questions:

1. When should the lifetime membership fees be recognized as revenue? Remember, they are nonrefundable.
2. **Interpretive Question:** What incentives would Judy and her partners have for recognizing the entire amount of the lifetime membership fee as revenue at the time it is collected? Since the entire amount will ultimately be recognized anyway, what difference does the timing make?

P 6-52   **Sales Transactions**

LO3   Money Company and Profit Company entered into the following transactions:

a. Money Company sold merchandise to Profit Company for $60,000, terms 2/10, n/30.
b. Prior to payment, Profit Company returned $4,000 of the merchandise for credit.
c. Profit Company paid Money Company in full within the discount period.
d. Profit Company paid Money Company in full after the discount period. [Assume that transaction (c) did not occur.]

Required:

Prepare journal entries to record the transactions for Money Company (the seller).

P 6-53   **Cash Fraud**

LO3   Mac Faber was the controller of the Lewiston National Bank. In his position of controller, he was in charge of all accounting functions. He wrote cashier's checks for the bank and reconciled the bank statement. He alone could approve exceptions to credit limits for bank customers, and even the internal auditors reported to him. Unknown to the bank, Mac had recently divorced and was supporting two households. In addition, many of his personal investments had soured, including a major farm implement dealership that had lost $40,000 in the last year. Several months after Mac had left the bank for another job, it was discovered that a vendor had paid twice and that the second payment had been deposited in Mac's personal account. Because Mac was not there to cover his tracks (as he had been on previous occasions), an investigation ensued. It was determined that Mac had used his position in the bank to steal $117,000 over a period of two years. Mac was prosecuted and sentenced to 30 months in a federal penitentiary.

(continued)

Required:

1. What internal control weaknesses allowed Mac to perpetrate the fraud?
2. What motivated Mac to perpetrate the fraud?

P 6-54
LO4

Analysis of Allowance for Bad Debts

Boulder View Corporation accounts for uncollectible accounts receivable using the allowance method.

As of December 31, 2008, the credit balance in Allowance for Bad Debts was $130,000. During 2009, credit sales totaled $10,000,000, $90,000 of accounts receivable were written off as uncollectible, and recoveries of accounts previously written off amounted to $15,000. An aging of accounts receivable at December 31, 2009, showed the following:

Classification of Receivable	Accounts Receivable Balance as of December 31, 2009	Percentage Estimated Uncollectible
Current	$1,140,000	2%
1–30 days past due	600,000	10
31–60 days past due	400,000	23
Over 60 days past due	120,000	75
	$2,260,000	

Required:

1. Prepare the journal entry to record bad debt expense for 2009, assuming bad debts are estimated using the aging of receivables method.
2. Record journal entries to account for the actual write-off of $90,000 uncollectible accounts receivable and the collection of $15,000 in receivables that had previously been written off.

P 6-55
LO4

Accounting for Accounts Receivable

Assume that Dominum Company had the following balances in its receivable accounts on December 31, 2008:

Accounts receivable	$ 640,000
Allowance for bad debts	20,600 (credit balance)

Transactions during 2009 were as follows:

Gross credit sales	$2,100,000
Collections of accounts receivable	
($1,840,000 less cash discounts of $32,000)	1,808,000
Sales returns and allowances (from credit sales)	24,000
Accounts receivable written off as uncollectible	9,400
Balance in Allowance for Bad Debts on	
December 31, 2009 (based on percent of total accounts receivable)	21,800

Required:

1. Prepare entries for the 2009 transactions.
2. What amount will Dominum Company report for:
   a. Net sales in its 2009 income statement?
   b. Total accounts receivable on its balance sheet of December 31, 2009?

P 6-56
LO4

Analysis of Receivables

Juniper Company was formed in 1999. Sales have increased on the average of 5% per year during its first 10 years of existence, with total sales for 2008 amounting to $400,000. Since incorporation, Juniper Company has used the allowance method to account for uncollectible accounts receivable.

(continued)

On January 1, 2009, the company's Allowance for Bad Debts had a credit balance of $5,000. During 2009, accounts totaling $3,500 were written off as uncollectible.

Required:

1. What does the January 1, 2009, credit balance of $5,000 in Allowance for Bad Debts represent?
2. Since Juniper Company wrote off $3,500 in uncollectible accounts receivable during 2009, was the prior year's estimate of uncollectible accounts receivable overstated?
3. Prepare journal entries to record:
   a. The $3,500 write-off of receivables during 2009.
   b. Juniper Company's 2009 bad debt expense, assuming an aging of the December 31, 2009, accounts receivable indicates that potential uncollectible accounts at year-end total $9,000.

P 6-57

LO4

Computing and Recording Bad Debt Expense

During 2009, Wishbone Corporation had a total of $5,000,000 in sales, of which 80% were on credit. At year-end, the Accounts Receivable balance showed a total of $2,300,000, which had been aged as follows:

Age	Amount
Current	$1,900,000
1–30 days past due	200,000
31–60 days past due	100,000
61–90 days past due	70,000
Over 90 days past due	30,000
	$2,300,000

Prepare the journal entry required at year-end to record the bad debt expense under each of the following independent conditions. Assume, where applicable, that Allowance for Bad Debts had a credit balance of $5,500 immediately before these adjustments.

Required:

1. Use the direct write-off method. (Assume that $60,000 of accounts are determined to be uncollectible and are written off in a single year-end entry.)
2. Based on experience, uncollectible accounts existing at year-end are estimated to be 3% of total accounts receivable.
3. Based on experience, uncollectible accounts are estimated to be the sum of:

   1% of current accounts receivable
   6% of accounts 1–30 days past due
   10% of accounts 31–60 days past due
   20% of accounts 61–90 days past due
   30% of accounts over 90 days past due

P 6-58

LO4

Unifying Concepts: Aging of Accounts Receivable and Uncollectible Accounts

Capital Edge Company has found that, historically, 0.5% of its current accounts receivable, 3% of accounts 1 to 30 days past due, 4.5% of accounts 31 to 60 days past due, 8% of accounts 61 to 90 days past due, and 10% of accounts over 90 days past due are uncollectible. The following schedule shows an aging of the accounts receivable as of December 31, 2009:

			Days Past Due		
	Current	**1–30**	**31–60**	**61–90**	**Over 90**
Balance	$105,600	$31,400	$14,200	$3,600	$900

(continued)

The balances at December 31, 2009, in selected accounts are as follows. (Assume that the allowance method is used.)

Sales revenue	$560,100
Sales returns	10,300
Allowance for bad debts	1,100 (credit balance)

Required:
1. Given these data, make the necessary adjusting entry (or entries) for uncollectible accounts receivable on December 31, 2009, on Capital Edge's books.
2. On February 14, 2010, Shannon Johnson, a customer, informed Capital Edge Company that she was going bankrupt and would not be able to pay her account of $89. Make the appropriate entry (or entries).
3. On June 29, 2010, Shannon Johnson was able to pay the amount she owed in full. Make the appropriate entry (or entries).
4. Assume that Allowance for Bad Debts at December 31, 2009, had a debit balance of $1,100 instead of a credit balance of $1,100. Make the necessary adjusting journal entry that would be needed on December 31, 2009.

P 6-59

LO4

Estimating Uncollectible Accounts

Ulysis Corporation makes and sells clothing to fashion stores throughout the country. On December 31, 2009, before adjusting entries were made, it had the following account balances on its books:

Accounts receivable	$ 2,320,000
Sales revenue, 2009 (60% were credit sales)	16,000,000
Allowance for bad debts (credit balance)	4,000

Required:
1. Make the appropriate adjusting entry on December 31, 2009, to record the allowance for bad debts if uncollectible accounts receivable are estimated to be 3% of accounts receivable.
2. Make the appropriate adjusting entry on December 31, 2009, to record the allowance for bad debts if uncollectible accounts receivable are estimated on the basis of an aging of accounts receivable; the aging schedule reveals the following:

	Balance of Accounts Receivable	Percent Estimated to Become Uncollectible
Current	$1,200,000	0.5%
1–30 days past due	800,000	1
31–60 days past due	200,000	4
61–90 days past due	80,000	20
Over 90 days past due	40,000	30

3. Now assume that on March 3, 2010, it was determined that a $64,000 account receivable from Petite Corners is uncollectible. Record the bad debt, assuming:
   a. The direct write-off method is used.
   b. The allowance method is used.
4. Further assume that on June 4, 2010, Petite Corners paid this previously written-off debt of $64,000. Record the payment, assuming:
   a. The direct write-off method had been used on March 3 to record the bad debt.
   b. The allowance method had been used on March 3 to record the bad debt.
5. **Interpretive Question:** Which method of accounting for bad debts, direct write-off or allowance, is generally used? Why?

P 6-60

LO4

The Aging Method

The following aging of accounts receivable is for Coby Company at the end of 2009:

		Aging of Accounts Receivable December 31, 2009			
	Overall	Less Than 30 Days	31 to 60 Days	61 to 90 Days	Over 90 Days
Travis Campbell	$ 50,000	$ 40,000	$ 5,000	$ 2,000	$ 3,000
Linda Reed	35,000	31,000	4,000		
Jack Riding	110,000	100,000	10,000		
Joy Riddle	20,000	3,000	10,000	4,000	3,000
Afzal Shah	90,000	60,000	21,000	4,000	5,000
Edna Ramos	80,000	60,000	16,000		4,000
Totals	$385,000	$294,000	$66,000	$10,000	$15,000

Coby Company had a credit balance of $20,000 in its allowance for bad debts account at the beginning of 2009. Write-offs for the year totaled $16,500. Coby Company makes only one adjusting entry to record bad debt expense at the end of the year. Historically, Coby Company has experienced the following with respect to the collection of its accounts receivable:

Age of Account	Percentage Ultimately Uncollectible
Less than 30 days	1%
31–60 days	5
61–90 days	30
Over 90 days	90

Required:

1. Compute the appropriate balance of allowance for bad debts as of December 31, 2009.
2. Make the journal entry required to record this allowance for bad debts balance. Remember that the allowance account already has an existing balance.
3. What is Coby's net accounts receivable balance as of December 31, 2009?

P 6-61

LO5

Analysis of Accounts Receivable Quantity and Quality

The following accounts receivable information is for Rouge Company:

	2009	2008	2007
Accounts receivable	$ 98,000	$ 50,000	$ 70,000
Allowance for bad debts	5,000	2,800	4,000
Sales revenue	190,000	175,000	165,000

Required:

1. With the big increase in Allowance for Bad Debts in 2009, Rouge Company is concerned that the creditworthiness of its customers declined from 2008 to 2009. Is there any support for this view in the accounts receivable data? Explain.
2. **Interpretive Question:** Is there any cause for alarm in the accounts receivable data for 2009? Explain.

EXPANDED
material

P 6-62
LO7

Preparing a Bank Reconciliation

Milton Company has just received the following monthly bank statement for June 2009.

KA
KLOOSTER
& ALLEN

Date	Checks	Deposits	Balance
June 01			$25,000
June 02	$ 150		24,850
June 03		$ 6,000	30,850
June 04	750		30,100
June 05	1,500		28,600
June 07	8,050		20,550
June 09		8,000	28,550
June 10	3,660		24,890
June 11	2,690		22,200
June 12		9,000	31,200
June 13	550		30,650
June 17	7,500		23,150
June 20		5,500	28,650
June 21	650		28,000
June 22	700		27,300
June 23		4,140†	31,440
June 25	1,000		30,440
June 30	50*		30,390
Totals	$27,250	$32,640	

*Bank service charge.

†Note collected, including $140 interest.

Data from the cash account of Milton Company for June are as follows:

June 1 balance $20,440

Checks written:

June 1	$ 1,500
4	8,500
6	2,690
8	550
9	7,500
12	650
19	700
22	1,000
26	1,300
27	1,360
	$25,750

Deposits:

June 2	$ 6,000
5	8,000
10	9,000
18	5,500
30	6,000
	$34,500

At the end of May, Milton had three checks outstanding for a total of $4,560. All three checks were processed by the bank during June. There were no deposits outstanding at the end of May. It was discovered during the reconciliation process that a check for $8,050, written on June 4 for supplies, was improperly recorded on the books as $8,500.

Required:

1. Determine the amount of deposits in transit at the end of June.
2. Determine the amount of outstanding checks at the end of June.
3. Prepare a June bank reconciliation.
4. Prepare the journal entries to correct the cash account.
5. **Interpretive Question:** Why is it important that the cash account be reconciled on a timely basis?

P 6-63
LO7

Determining Where the Cash Went

Kim Lee, the bookkeeper for Briton Company, had never missed a day's work for the past 10 years until last week. Since that time, he has not been located. You now suspect that Kim may have embezzled money from the company. The following bank reconciliation, prepared by Kim last month, is available to help you determine if a theft occurred:

Briton Company
Bank Reconciliation for August 2009
Prepared by Kim Lee

Balance per bank statement	$192,056		Balance per books	$169,598
Additions to bank balance:			Additions to book balance:	
Deposits in transit	8,000		Note collected by bank	250
			Interest earned	600
Deductions from bank balance:			Deductions from book balance:	
Outstanding checks:			NSF check	(1,800)
#201	(19,200)		Bank service charges	(48)
#204	(5,000)			
#205	(4,058)			
#295	(195)			
#565	(1,920)			
#567	(615)			
#568	(468)			
Adjusted bank balance	**$168,600**		**Adjusted book balance**	**$168,600**

In examining the bank reconciliation, you decide to review canceled checks returned by the bank. You find that check stubs for check nos. 201, 204, 205, and 295 indicate that these checks were supposedly voided when written. All other bank reconciliation data have been verified as correct.

Required:

1. Compute the amount suspected stolen by Kim.
2. **Interpretive Question:** Describe how Kim accounted for the stolen money. What would have prevented the theft?

P 6-64
LO8

Accounting for a Foreign Currency Transaction

On December 19, 2009, Mr. Jones Company performed services for Lamour Company. The contracted price for the services was 35,000 euros, to be paid on March 23, 2010. On December 19, 2009, one euro equaled $0.97. On December 31, 2009, one euro equaled $0.99, and on March 23, 2010, one euro equaled $0.94. Mr. Jones is a U.S. company.

Required:

1. Make the journal entry on Mr. Jones' books to record the provision of services on December 19, 2009.
2. Make the necessary adjusting entry on Mr. Jones' books on December 31 to adjust the account receivable to its appropriate U.S. dollar value.
3. Make the journal entry on Mr. Jones' books to record the collection of the 35,000 euros on March 23.
4. **Interpretive Question:** Why would Mr. Jones, a U.S. company, agree to denominate the contract in euros instead of in U.S. dollars?

ANALYTICAL ASSIGNMENTS

AA 6-65
DISCUSSION

ZZZZ Best and Fictitious Receivables

ZZZZ Best was a Los Angeles-based company specializing in carpet cleaning and insurance restoration. Prior to allegations of fraud and its declaration of bankruptcy in 1988, ZZZZ Best was touted as one of the hottest stocks on Wall Street. In 1987, after only six years in

(continued)

business, the company had a market valuation exceeding $211 million, giving its "genius" president a paper fortune of $109 million. Lawsuits, however, alleged that the company was nothing more than a massive fraud scheme that fooled major banks, two CPA firms, an investment banker, and a prestigious law firm.

ZZZZ Best was started as a carpet-cleaning business by Barry Minkow, a 15-year-old high school student, in 1981. Although ZZZZ Best had impressive growth as a carpet-cleaning business, the growth was not nearly fast enough for the impatient Minkow. In 1985, ZZZZ Best announced that it was expanding into the insurance restoration business, restoring buildings that had been damaged by fire, floods, and other disasters. During 1985 and 1986, ZZZZ Best reported undertaking several large insurance restoration projects. The company reported high profits from these restoration jobs. A public stock offering in 1986 stated that 86% of ZZZZ Best Corporation's business was in the insurance restoration area.

Based on the company's high growth and reported income in 1987, a spokesperson for a large brokerage house was quoted in *Business Week* as saying that "Barry Minkow is a great manager and ZZZZ Best is a great company." He recommended that his clients buy ZZZZ Best stock. That same year, the Association of Collegiate Entrepreneurs and the Young Entrepreneurs' Organization placed Minkow on their list of the top 100 young entrepreneurs in America; and the mayor of Los Angeles honored Minkow with a commendation that said that he had "set a fine entrepreneurial example of obtaining the status of a millionaire at the age of 18."

Unfortunately, ZZZZ Best's insurance business, its impressive growth, and its high reported income were totally fictitious. In fact, the company never once made a legitimate profit. Barry Minkow himself later said that he was a "fraudster" who convincingly deceived almost everyone involved with the company. Through the use of widespread collusion among company officials, Minkow was even able to hide the fraud from ZZZZ Best's external auditor. For example, when ZZZZ Best reported an $8.2 million contract to restore a building in San Diego, the external auditor demanded to see the building; this was difficult since neither the building nor the job existed. However, officials of ZZZZ Best gained access to a construction site and led the auditor through a tour of an unfinished building in San Diego to show that the "restoration" work was ongoing. The situation became very complicated for ZZZZ Best when the auditor later asked to see the finished job. ZZZZ Best had to spend $1 million to lease the building and hire contractors to finish six of the eight floors in 10 days. The auditor was led on another tour and wrote a memo saying, "Job looks very good." The auditor was subsequently faulted for looking only at what ZZZZ Best officials chose to show, without making independent inquiries.

Minkow's house of cards finally came crashing down as it became apparent to banks, suppliers, investors, and the auditors that the increasing difficulty ZZZZ Best was having with paying its bills was entirely inconsistent with a company reporting so much revenue and profit. In January 1988, a federal grand jury in Los Angeles returned a 57-count indictment, charging 11 individuals—including ZZZZ Best founder and president, Barry Minkow—with engaging in a massive fraud scheme. Minkow was later convicted and sentenced to 25 years in a federal penitentiary in Colorado.

ZZZZ Best grossly inflated its operating results by reporting bogus revenue and receivables. What factors prevent a company from continuing to report fraudulent results indefinitely? What could the auditor have done to uncover the ZZZZ Best fraud?

Source: This description is based on articles in *The Wall Street Journal*, *Forbes*, and investigative proceedings of the U.S. House of Representatives, Subcommittee on Energy and Commerce hearings: *The Wall Street Journal*, July 7, 1987, p. 1; July 9, 1987, p. 1; August 23, 1988, p. 1; U.S. House of Representatives, Subcommittee on Oversight and Investigation of the Committee on Energy and Commerce, January 27, 1988; U.S. House of Representatives, Subcommittee on Oversight and Investigation of the Committee on Energy and Commerce, February 1, 1988; Daniel Akst, "How Barry Minkow Fooled the Auditors," *Forbes*, October 2, 1989, p. 126.

AA 6-66
DISCUSSION

Recognizing Revenue

HealthCare, Inc.,* operates a number of medical testing facilities around the United States. Drug manufacturers, such as **Merck** and **Bristol-Myers Squibb**, contract with HealthCare

---

*The name of the actual company has been changed.

(continued)

for testing of their newly developed drugs and other medical treatments. HealthCare advertises, gets patients, and then administers the drugs or other experimental treatments, under a doctor's care, to determine their effectiveness. The Food and Drug Administration requires such human testing before allowing drugs to be prescribed by doctors and sold by pharmacists. A typical contract might read as follows:

> HealthCare, Inc., will administer the new drug, "Lexitol," to 50 patients, once a week for 10 weeks, to determine its effectiveness in treating male baldness. Merck will pay HealthCare, Inc., $100 per patient visit, to be billed at the conclusion of the test period. The total amount of the contract is $50,000 (50 patients × 10 visits × $100 per visit).

Given these kinds of contracts, when should HealthCare recognize revenue—when contracts are signed, when patient visits take place, when drug manufacturers are billed, or when cash is collected?

AA 6-67
DISCUSSION

Credit Policy Review

The president, vice president, and sales manager of Moorer Corporation were discussing the company's present credit policy. The sales manager suggested that potential sales were being lost to competitors because of Moorer Corporation's tight restrictions on granting credit to consumers. He stated that if credit policies were loosened, the current year's estimated credit sales of $3,000,000 could be increased by at least 20% next year with an increase in uncollectible accounts receivable of only $10,000 over this year's amount of $37,500. He argued that because the company's cost of sales is only 25% of revenues, the company would certainly come out ahead.

The vice president, however, suggested that a better alternative to easier credit terms would be to accept consumer credit cards such as **Visa** or **Mastercard**. She argued that this alternative could increase sales by 40%. The credit card finance charges to Moorer Corporation would be 4% of the additional sales.

At this point, the president interrupted by saying that he wasn't at all sure that increasing credit sales of any kind was a good thing. In fact, he suggested that the $37,500 of uncollectible accounts receivable was altogether too high. He wondered whether the company should discontinue offering sales on account.

With the information given, determine whether Moorer Corporation would be better off under the sales manager's proposal or the vice president's proposal. Also, address the president's suggestion that credit sales of all types be abolished.

AA 6-68
JUDGMENT CALL

You Decide: Which method is better–the direct write-off method or the allowance method?

Your father-in-law has asked you to help him with some basic accounting duties dealing with a local irrigation company of which he is president. The company has issued shares of stock allowing shareholders the right to use a specified amount of water every week from a water canal that passes through town. Your main duties would consist of billing and collecting yearly dues from the shareholders and maintaining the books with a canned software system. There are less than 60 shareholders in the company. Should you write off receivables from customers when it is determined they will not pay, or should you estimate the percentage of receivables that will be uncollectible and establish an allowance? Your father-in-law does not want an allowance because he believes all customers will pay. What should you do?

AA 6-69
JUDGMENT CALL

You Decide: Can pre-billing customers increase revenues?

For the past year, you have been working as an accountant for a local Internet Service Provider. Business is growing steadily with the holiday season just around the corner. The

(continued)

company hopes to reach more customers next year through additional advertising. In order to do so, it will need a loan from the bank. You overheard your boss say that if revenues increase 5% by year-end, the company will be in good enough shape to receive the loan. Your boss asks you to send out invoices to a handful of customers charging them for a service that won't be provided until the next year and to recognize the billings as revenue. He says they will eventually receive the service but it is more important to recognize the sale now. What should you do?

AA 6-70
JUDGMENT CALL

You Decide: **Can a company overestimate bad debts in good years and then use lower estimates when times are bad?**

The company you work for has been highly profitable this year. Your boss tells you to overestimate the allowance for doubtful accounts. He says the income statement can handle the charge this year and the excess reserve can be used to increase earnings in future years. Is his proposal acceptable?

AA 6-71
REAL COMPANY ANALYSIS

Wal-Mart

The 2006 Form 10-K for **Wal-Mart** is included in Appendix A. Locate that Form 10-K and consider the following questions:

1. Provide the summary journal entry that Wal-Mart would have made to record its revenue for the fiscal year ended January 31, 2006 (assume all sales were on account).
2. Given Wal-Mart's beginning and ending balances in accounts receivable, along with your journal entry from part (1), estimate the amount of cash collected from customers during the year.
3. Locate Wal-Mart's note on revenue recognition. What is Wal-Mart's revenue recognition policy?

AA 6-72
REAL COMPANY ANALYSIS

Bank of America

Bank of America is one of the oldest banks in America, as well as one of the largest. Founded in the late 1800s, Bank of America has grown from a strictly California-based bank to one with operations in 29 states. Information from Bank of America's annual report follows. (Amounts are in millions.)

	2005	2004
Bad debt expense	$4,021	$2,868
Write-off of uncollectible accounts	5,834	4,147
Allowance for bad debts (year-end)	8,045	8,626

Using this information, answer the following questions:

1. Provide the journal entry made by Bank of America to record bad debt expense for 2005.
2. Provide the journal entry made by Bank of America to record the write-off of actual bad debts during 2005.
3. Estimate the amount of bad debts previously written off that Bank of America recovered in 2005.

AA 6-73
REAL COMPANY ANALYSIS

Microsoft and IBM

Information from comparative income statements and balance sheets for **Microsoft** and **IBM** is given below. (Amounts are in millions.)

	Microsoft		IBM	
	2005	2004	2005	2004
Sales	$39,788	$36,835	$91,134	$96,293
Accounts receivable	7,180	5,890	9,540	10,522

(continued)

Use this information to answer the following questions:

1. Without doing any computations, which company do you think has the lowest average collection period?
2. Compute Microsoft's average collection period for 2005.
3. Compute IBM's average collection period for 2005.

AA 6-74
INTERNATIONAL

Samsung

The economic downturn in South Korea in late 1997 focused world attention on what had heretofore been viewed as one of the world's economic powerhouses. Symptomatic of the economic collapse was the freefall in Korea's currency, the won, which declined in value from 845 won per U.S. dollar on December 31, 1996, to 1,695 won per dollar on December 31, 1997.

When Korea's economy soured, many sought to blame the economy's unusual structure, which concentrates a large fraction of the economic activity in the hands of just a few companies, called chaebol. Chaebol are large Korean conglomerates (groups of loosely connected firms with central ownership) that are usually centered around a family-owned parent company. The growth of the chaebol in the years since the Korean War has been aided by government nurturing—it is said that the chaebol have received government assistance in getting loans and obtaining trading licenses, for example.

In Korea there are now four super-chaebol—**Hyundai, Samsung, Daewoo,** and **Lucky Goldstar**. Collectively, these four conglomerates account for between 40 and 45% of South Korea's gross national product.

Samsung, one of the four super-chaebol, was founded in 1938 in Taegu, Korea. The company had humble beginnings; its original products included fruit, dried seafood, flour, and noodles, and its original exports were squid and apples. Now, Samsung has a worldwide presence in electronics, machinery, automobiles, chemicals, and financial services. To illustrate the size of Samsung's operations, it is estimated that one out of every five televisions or monitors in the world was made by Samsung.

The following information is from Samsung's 1997 annual report. All numbers are in trillions of Korean won.

	1997	1996
Net sales	91.519	74.641
Accounts receivable	10.064	6.233

1. Did Samsung's sales increase in 1997, relative to 1996, in terms of U.S. dollars? Explain. What exchange rate information would allow you to make a more accurate calculation?
2. Compute Samsung's average collection period for both 1996 and 1997. Instead of using the average accounts receivable balance, use the end-of-year balance.
3. Comment on the change in the average collection period from 1996 to 1997, especially in light of the economic conditions in Korea in 1997.
4. What do you think happened to Samsung's accounts payable balance in 1997, relative to 1996? Explain.

AA 6-75
ETHICS

Changing Our Estimates in Order to Meet Analysts' Expectations

John Verner is the controller for BioMedic, Inc., a biotechnology company. John is finishing his preparation of the preliminary financial statements for a meeting of the board of directors scheduled for later in the day. At the board's prior meeting, members discussed the need to report earnings of at least $1.32 per share. It was not mentioned specifically at the meeting, but everyone on the board knows that financial analysts have forecast that BioMedic will report earnings per share (EPS) of $1.32; failure to meet analysts' expectations could hurt BioMedic's chances of going forward with its planned initial public offering (IPO) later this year.

(continued)

Unfortunately for John and the company, the preliminary EPS figure is coming up short. John knows that the board will take a serious look at the estimates and assumptions made in preparing the income statement. In anticipation of the board's review, John has identified the following two issues:

1. In the past, bad debt expense has been computed using the percentage of sales method. The percentage used has varied between 3 and 3.5%. This year, John assumed a rate of 3%. If he were to modify his estimate of bad debt expense to 2.5% of sales, income would increase by $700,000.

2. BioMedic, Inc., offers a warranty on many of the products it sells. Like bad debt expense, warranty expense is computed as a percentage of sales. John is considering modifying his estimate of warranty expense from 1.4% of sales down to 1.1%. This modification would result in a $420,000 increase in net income.

These two changes, considered together, would result in BioMedic being able to report EPS of $1.33 per share, thereby allowing the company to publicly announce that it had exceeded analysts' expectations. Without these changes, BioMedic will report EPS of $1.21 per share.

What issues should John consider before he makes the changes to the income statement? Would John be doing something wrong by making these changes? Would John be breaking the law?

AA 6-76
WRITING

Revenue Recognition for Health Clubs

The health fitness business has become increasingly popular as the sedentary lifestyle of most Americans has caused a large percentage of the population to feel, and be, out of shape. Health clubs have popped up all over, and with these clubs come some interesting accounting issues. Members typically sign up for one year and pay an up-front fee, followed by a monthly payment. The up-front fee covers, among other things, a health assessment by a club expert as well as a customized training program. For the monthly fee, members get the use of the facilities. The big accounting question is: How should the up-front fee be accounted for? Can the entire amount of the up-front fee be recognized at the beginning of the contract, or should it be recognized over the course of the year? Prepare a one-page paper explaining your point of view.

AA 6-77
CUMULATIVE SPREADSHEET PROJECT

Creating a Forecasted Balance Sheet and Income Statement

This spreadsheet assignment is a continuation of the spreadsheet assignments given in earlier chapters. If you completed those spreadsheets, you have a head start on this one. If needed, review the spreadsheet assignment for Chapter 4 to refresh your memory on how to construct forecasted financial statements.

1. Handyman wishes to prepare a forecasted balance sheet and income statement for 2010. Use the original financial statement numbers for 2009 [given in part (1) of the Cumulative Spreadsheet Project assignment in Chapter 2] as the basis for the forecast, along with the following additional information:
   a. Sales in 2010 are expected to increase by 40% over 2009 sales of $700.
   b. In 2010, Handyman expects to acquire new property, plant, and equipment costing $80.
   c. The $160 in other operating expenses reported in 2009 includes $5 of depreciation expense.
   d. No new long-term debt will be acquired in 2010.
   e. No cash dividends will be paid in 2010.
   f. New short-term loans payable will be acquired in an amount sufficient to make Handyman's current ratio in 2010 exactly equal to 2.0.

Note: These statements were constructed as part of the spreadsheet assignment in Chapter 4; you can use that spreadsheet as a starting point if you have completed that assignment.

(continued)

For this exercise, the current assets are expected to behave as follows:

   i.   Cash and inventory will increase at the same rate as sales.

   ii.   The forecasted amount of accounts receivable in 2010 is determined using the forecasted value for the average collection period. For simplicity, do the computations using the end-of-period accounts receivable balance instead of the average balance. The average collection period for 2010 is expected to be 14.08 days.

Clearly state any additional assumptions that you make.

2. Repeat (1), with the following change in assumptions:

   a.   Average collection period is expected to be 9.06 days.

   b.   Average collection period is expected to be 20.00 days.

3. Comment on the differences in the forecasted values of accounts receivable in 2010 under each of the following assumptions about the average collection period: 14.08 days, 9.06 days, and 20.00 days. Under which assumption will Handyman's forecasted cash flow from operating activities be higher? Explain.

Inventory

(1) Identify what items and costs should be included in inventory and cost of goods sold. *Inventory is goods held for sale in the normal course of business. In a manufacturing firm, inventory is composed of raw materials, work in process, and finished goods. Inventory cost consists of all costs involved in buying the inventory and preparing it for sale. Proper calculation of inventory cost is absolutely critical for making financial reporting, production, pricing, and strategy decisions.*

(2) Account for inventory purchases and sales using both a perpetual and a periodic inventory system. *With a perpetual system, inventory records are updated whenever a purchase or a sale is made. With a periodic system, inventory records are not updated when a sale is made.*

(3) Calculate cost of goods sold using the results of an inventory count and understand the impact of errors in ending inventory on reported cost of goods sold. *Beginning inventory and purchases numbers are added to compute how much inventory was available for sale. An inventory count reveals how much was not sold; the difference is equal to the cost of goods sold. Overstating the amount of ending inventory causes profits to be overstated as well.*

(4) Apply the four inventory cost flow alternatives: specific identification, FIFO, LIFO, and average cost. *In order to calculate cost of goods sold and ending inventory, the accountant must make an assumption about which units are sold first. With FIFO, the oldest units are assumed to be sold first. With LIFO, the newest units are assumed to be sold first. With the average cost assumption, all units are assigned the same average cost, independent of their specific actual cost.*

(5) Use financial ratios to evaluate a company's inventory level. *The length of the operating cycle is the time from the purchase of inventory to the collection of cash from the sale of that inventory; this interval is equal to the number of days' sales in inventory plus the average collection period. The length of this interval should be compared to the average time taken to pay for inventory purchases.*

EXPANDED *material*

(6) Analyze the impact of inventory errors on reported cost of goods sold. *Overstating ending inventory this year causes profits to be overstated this year but understated next year. This reversal occurs because ending inventory for this year becomes beginning inventory for next year. The effects are reversed if ending inventory is understated this year.*

(7) Describe the complications that arise when LIFO or average cost is used with a perpetual inventory system. *When LIFO is used with a perpetual inventory system, the identification of the "newest unit" changes every time a purchase is made. Accordingly, identification of the units sold must be done sale by sale, using the specific timing of sales and purchases. Similarly, when the average cost assumption is made with a perpetual inventory system, the "average cost" changes every time a purchase is made.*

(8) Apply the lower-of-cost-or-market method of accounting for inventory. *Inventory should be reported in the balance sheet at the lower of its historical cost or its current market value. Current market value is computed by comparing replacement cost to the inventory's net realizable value (selling price less selling cost).*

(9) Explain the gross margin method of estimating inventories. *Knowledge of a company's historical gross profit percentage can be used to estimate a company's cost of goods sold. This estimate, combined with sales and purchases data, can be used to estimate the amount of inventory a company has.*

Sears, Roebuck & Company began as the result of an inventory mistake. In 1886, a shipment of gold watches was mistakenly sent to a jeweler in Redwood Falls, Minnesota. When the jeweler refused to accept delivery of the unwanted watches, they were purchased by an enterprising railroad agent who saw an opportunity to make some money. Richard Sears sold all of those watches, ordered more, and started the **R. W. Sears Watch Company**. The next year, Sears moved his operation to Chicago, where he found a partner in watchmaker Alvah Roebuck, and in 1893 they incorporated under the name "Sears, Roebuck & Co."

The company's initial growth was fueled by mail-order sales to farmers. Sears bought goods in volume from manufacturers. Then, taking advantage of cheap parcel post and rural free delivery (RFD) rates, Sears shipped the goods directly to the customers, thereby bypassing the profit markups of the chain of middlemen usually standing between manufacturers and farmers. Sales growth was partially driven by the persuasive advertising copy written by Richard Sears for the famous Sears catalog. In fact, his product descriptions have been politely called "fanciful." But the company compensated by backing its products with an unconditional money-back guarantee for dissatisfied customers.

Sears began as a retailer buying inventory in bulk and selling it to the masses. In the 1980s Sears diversified its operations and began selling auto insurance (through **Allstate**), financial services (through **Dean Witter**), and real estate (through **Coldwell Banker**). In the early 1990s, the diversified Sears empire began to show increasing weakness, culminating in a reported loss of almost $2.3 billion in 1992. The company's management responded by going back to the basics of retail marketing. The financial services operations and the real estate operations (along with the famous Sears Tower in Chicago) were sold. Sears focused on clothing sales in its mall-base stores and appliance and automotive product sales in its off-the-mall stores.

Sears is continuing to leverage one of its biggest assets—its in-house brand names such as Kenmore and Craftsman. In fact, sales of Sears appliances and tools make up two-thirds of the company's annual revenue. Currently, Sears is the leader in appliance sales and outsells the next 12 competitors combined. In an attempt to overhaul its clothing lines, Sears bought the well-known catalog and Internet retailer, **Land's End**, in June 2002 and in March 2005, Sears and **Kmart** merged forming a retailing powerhouse to compete with **Wal-Mart**.

Like Sears, every business has products or services that it sells. Some companies, usually referred to as diversified companies or conglomerates, sell many unrelated products and services, just as Sears did in the 1980s. Other companies focus on a core set of products or services, as Sears did in the 1990s.

In Chapter 6, the focus was on revenues and receivables arising from the sale of products and services. In this chapter, the focus is on accounting for the products and services that are sold.

Traditionally, companies have been divided into two groups: service companies and product companies. Companies such as hotels, cable TV networks, banks, carpet cleaners, and lawyers, accountants, and engineers all sell services. In contrast, supermarkets, steel mills, and book stores sell products. Because the practice of accounting evolved in a business environment dominated by manufacturing and merchandising firms, the accounting for service companies is significantly less developed than the accounting for companies that sell products. In this chapter we discuss traditional accounting for product companies, emphasizing cost of goods sold and inventory. In Chapter 8 we will discuss operating expenses that are common to both service and product firms. Further discussion of the developing area of accounting for service companies is included in Chapter 16 in the management accounting section of *Accounting: Concepts and Applications*.

Inventory accounting is considerably more complex for manufacturing firms than for merchandising firms. In a retail or wholesale business, the cost of goods sold is simply the costs incurred in purchasing the merchandise sold during the period; inventory is simply the cost of products purchased and not yet sold. Manufacturing firms, however, produce the goods they sell, so inventory and cost of goods sold must include all manufacturing costs of the products produced and sold. Because it is much

EXHIBIT 1 **How Much Inventory Do Companies Have?**

Inventory Levels for the 50 Largest Companies, 1979–2005

Source: Standard and Poor's COMPUSTAT.

SETTING THE STAGE

easier to understand the concept of inventory and cost of goods sold in the context of retail and wholesale firms, manufacturing firms will not be considered in detail in this chapter. The details of inventory accounting for manufacturing firms will be covered in Chapter 16 in the management accounting section of *Accounting: Concepts and Applications.*

Fifty years ago, inventory was arguably the most important asset on the balance sheet. However, changes in the economy have led to a decrease in the relative importance of inventory. For example, as illustrated in Exhibit 1, inventory for the 50 largest companies in the United States declined steadily from over 15% of total assets in 1979 to 6.8% of total assets in 2005. This trend is a result of two factors: more efficient management of inventory because of improved information technology and a decrease in the prominence of old-style, smokestack industries that carried large inventories. Companies in the growth industries of services, technology, and information often have little or no inventory.

STOP & THINK

The clear separation between product and service companies is disappearing. For example, does **Microsoft** sell a product or a service? What about **McDonald's**–product or service?

Inventory and Cost of Goods Sold

Identify what items and costs should be included in inventory and cost of goods sold.

1

Inventory is the name given to goods that are either manufactured or purchased for resale in the normal course of business (see page 286 for definition). A car dealer's inventory is comprised of automobiles; a grocery store's inventory consists of vegetables, meats, dairy products, canned goods, and bakery items; **Sears'** inventory is composed of shirts, Kenmore appliances, DieHard® batteries, and more. Like other items of value, such as cash or equipment, inventory is classified as an asset and reported on the balance sheet. When products are sold, they are no longer assets. The costs to purchase or manufacture the products must be removed from the asset classification (inventory) on the balance sheet and reported on the income statement as an expense—**cost of goods sold** (see page 286 for definition).

EXHIBIT 2	Time Line of Business Issues Involved with Inventory

Activity – Buying/Making and Selling Inventory*

	BUY	ADD	SELL	COMPUTE
	raw materials or goods for resale	value–labor and overhead	finished inventory	ending inventory and finished goods

Journal Entry	Inventory
	  A/P
		Inventory
		  A/P or Cash
			A/R
			  Sales
			COGS
			  Inventory
				COGS**
				  Inventory**

F/S Impact	Inventory (↑) A/P (↑)	Inventory (↑) Cash (↓) or A/P (↑)	A/R (↑) Sales (↑) Exp (↑) Inventory (↓)	Exp (↑) Inventory (↓)

 * Exhibit assumes the inventory account is updated with each purchase.
** A physical count of inventory may require an adjustment to the inventory and COGS accounts.

inventory

Goods held for resale.

cost of goods sold

The costs incurred to purchase or manufacture the merchandise sold during a period.

The time line in Exhibit 2 illustrates the business issues involved with inventory as well as the financial statement effects of those business issues. The accounting questions associated with the items in the time line are as follows:

- When is inventory considered to have been purchased—when it is ordered, shipped, received, or paid for?
- Similarly, when is the inventory considered to have been sold?
- Which of the costs associated with the "value added" process are considered to be part of the cost of inventory, and which are simply business expenses for that period?
- How should total inventory cost be divided between the inventory that was sold (cost of goods sold) and the inventory that remains (ending inventory)?

These questions are addressed in the following sections of the chapter.

What is Inventory?

In a merchandising firm, either wholesale or retail, inventory is composed of the items that have been purchased in order to be resold. In a supermarket, milk is inventory, a shopping cart is not. In a manufacturing company, there are three different types of inventory: raw materials, work in process, and finished goods.

raw materials

Materials purchased for use in manufacturing products.

Raw Materials   **Raw materials** are goods acquired in a relatively undeveloped state that will eventually compose a major part of the finished product. If you are making bicycles, one of the raw materials is tubular steel. For a computer assembler, raw materials inventory is composed of plastic, wires, and **Intel** Pentium® chips.

work in process

Partially completed units in production.

Work in Process   **Work in process** consists of partially finished products. When you take a tour of a manufacturing plant, you are seeing work-in-process inventory.

finished goods

Manufactured products ready for sale.

Finished Goods   **Finished goods** are the completed products waiting for sale. A completed car rolling off the automobile assembly line is part of finished goods inventory.

What Costs Are Included in Inventory Cost?

Inventory cost consists of all costs involved in buying the inventory and preparing it for sale. In the case of raw materials or goods acquired for resale by a merchandising firm, cost includes the purchase price, freight, and receiving and storage costs.

manufacturing overhead

The indirect manufacturing costs associated with producing inventory.

The cost of work-in-process inventory is the sum of the costs of the raw materials, the production labor, and some share of the **manufacturing overhead** required to keep the factory running. The cost of an item in finished goods inventory is the total of the materials, labor, and overhead costs used in the production process for that item. As you can imagine, accumulating these costs and calculating a cost per unit is quite a difficult task. The cost of a finished automobile includes the cost of the steel and rubber; the salaries and wages of assembly workers, inspectors, and testers; the factory insurance; the workers' pension benefits; and much more. This costing process is a key part of management accounting and is covered in Chapter 16 in the management accounting section of *Accounting: Concepts and Applications*.

The costs just described are all costs expended in order to get inventory produced and ready to sell. These costs are appropriately included in inventory costs. Those costs incurred in the sales effort itself are *not* inventory costs, but instead should be reported as operating expenses in the period in which they are incurred. For example, the costs of maintaining the finished goods warehouse or the retail showroom are period expenses. Salespersons' salaries are period expenses, as is the cost of advertising (a more detailed discussion of advertising is included in Chapter 8). In addition, general non-factory administrative costs are also period expenses. Examples are the costs of the corporate headquarters and the company president's salary.

FOB (free-on-board) destination

A business term meaning that the seller of merchandise bears the shipping costs and maintains ownership until the merchandise is delivered to the buyer.

Who Owns the Inventory?

As a general rule, goods should be included in the inventory of the business holding legal title. So, a merchandising firm is considered to have purchased inventory once it has legal title to the inventory. Similarly, the inventory is considered to be sold when legal title passes to the customer. In most cases, this "legal title" rule is easy to apply—if you go into a business and look around, it is probably safe to assume that the inventory you see belongs to that business. In the case of goods in transit and goods on consignment, however, this "legal title" rule can be rather difficult to apply.

FOB (free-on-board) shipping point

A business term meaning that the buyer of merchandise bears the shipping costs and acquires ownership at the point of shipment.

Goods in Transit When goods are being shipped from the seller to the buyer, who owns the inventory that is on a truck or railroad car—the seller or the buyer? If the seller pays for the shipping costs, the arrangement is known as **FOB (free-on-board) destination**, and the seller owns the merchandise from the time it is shipped until it is delivered to the buyer. If the buyer pays the shipping costs, the arrangement is known as **FOB (free-on-board) shipping point**, and the buyer owns the merchandise during transit. Thus, in determining which items should be counted and included in the inventory balance for a period, a company must note the amount of merchandise in transit and the terms under which it is being shipped. In all cases, merchandise should be included in the inventory of the party who owns it; for goods in transit, this is generally the party who is paying the shipping costs. The impact of shipping terms on the ownership of goods in transit is summarized in Exhibit 3.

consignment

An arrangement whereby merchandise owned by one party, the consignor, is sold by another party, the consignee, usually on a commission basis.

Goods on Consignment Sometimes the inventory a firm stocks in its warehouse has not actually been purchased from suppliers. With a **consignment** arrangement, suppliers (the consignors) provide inventory for resale while

EXHIBIT 3   **Ownership Transfer for Goods in Transit**

Seller

Buyer

FOB
Shipping Point

FOB
Destination

- Buyer owns goods in transit
- Ownership changes at shipping point

- Seller owns goods in transit
- Ownership changes at destination

retaining ownership of the inventory until it is sold. (This is referred to in the business world as a "sale-through" arrangement as opposed to a "sell-in" arrangement where sales to distributors are recorded as revenue.) The firm selling the merchandise (the consignee) merely stocks and sells the merchandise for the supplier/owner and receives a commission on any sales as payment for services rendered. Through a consignment arrangement, the manufacturer enables dealers to acquire a broad sample of inventory without incurring the purchase and finance charges required to actually buy the inventory. It is extremely important that goods being held on consignment not be included in the inventory of the firm holding the goods for sale even though they are physically on that firm's premises. It is equally important that the supplier/owner properly include all such goods in its records even though the inventory is not on its premises.

An example of a company that successfully uses consignment sales as part of its business strategy is **International Airline Support Group, Inc.** This company is a leading distributor of aircraft spare parts for large jet airplanes. The company uses consignments because, as stated in its annual report, this arrangement allows it "to obtain parts inventory on a favorable basis without committing its capital to purchasing inventory."

Ending Inventory and Cost of Goods Sold

cost of goods available for sale

The cost of all merchandise available for sale during the period; equal to the sum of beginning inventory and net purchases.

Inventory purchased or manufactured during a period is added to beginning inventory, and the total cost of this inventory is called the **cost of goods available for sale**. At the end of an accounting period, total cost of goods available for sale must be allocated between inventory still remaining (to be reported in the balance sheet as an asset) and inventory sold during the period (to be reported in the income statement as an expense, Cost of Goods Sold).

This cost allocation process is extremely important because the more cost that is said to remain in ending inventory, the less cost is reported as cost of goods sold in the income statement. This is why accurately determining who owns the inventory is such a big issue. Making a mistake with inventory ownership will result in misstating both the income statement and the balance sheet. For this reason, accountants must be careful of inventory errors because they directly affect reported net income. The impact of inventory errors is illustrated later in the chapter.

The cost allocation process also involves a significant amount of accounting judgment. Identical inventory items are usually purchased at varying prices throughout the year, so to calculate the amount of ending inventory and cost of goods sold, the accountant must determine which items (the low cost or high cost) remain and which were sold. Again, this decision can directly affect the amount of reported cost of goods sold and net income. The use of inventory cost flow assumptions is discussed later in the chapter.

> ### REMEMBER THIS...
>
> - Inventory is composed of goods held for sale in the normal course of business.
> - For a manufacturing firm, the three types of inventory are raw materials, work in process, and finished goods.
> - All costs incurred in producing and getting inventory ready to sell should be added to inventory cost.
> - Inventory should be recorded on the books of the company holding legal title.
> - At the end of an accounting period, the total cost of goods available for sale during the period must be allocated between ending inventory and cost of goods sold.

Account for inventory purchases and sales using both a perpetual and a periodic inventory system.

Accounting for Inventory Purchases and Sales

② To begin a more detailed study of inventory accounting, we must first establish a solid understanding of the journal entries used to record inventory transactions. The accounting procedures for recording purchases and sales using both a periodic and a perpetual inventory system are detailed in this section.

Overview of Perpetual and Periodic Systems

Some businesses track changes in inventory levels on a continuous basis, recording inventory increases and decreases with each individual purchase and sale to maintain a running total of the inventory balance. This is called a perpetual inventory system. Other businesses rely on quarterly or yearly inventory counts to reveal which inventory items have been sold. This is called a periodic inventory system.

Perpetual You own a discount appliance superstore. Your biggest-selling items are washers, dryers, refrigerators, microwaves, and dishwashers. You advertise your weekly sale items on local TV stations, and your sales volume is quite heavy. You have 50 salespeople who work independently of one another. You have found that customers get very upset if they come to buy an advertised item and you have run out. In this business environment, would it make sense to keep a running total of the quantity remaining of each inventory item and update it each time a sale is made? Yes, the benefit of having current information on each inventory item would make it worthwhile to spend a little extra time to update the inventory records when a sale is made.

perpetual inventory system

A system of accounting for inventory in which detailed records of the number of units and the cost of each purchase and sales transaction are prepared throughout the accounting period.

This appliance store would probably use a **perpetual inventory system**. With a perpetual system, inventory records are updated whenever a purchase or a sale is made. In this way, the inventory records at any given time reflect how many of each inventory item should be in the warehouse or out on the store shelves. A perpetual system is most often used when each individual inventory item has a relatively high value or when there are large costs to running out of or overstocking specific items.

Periodic You operate a newsstand in a busy metropolitan subway station. Almost all of your sales occur during the morning and the evening rush hours. You sell a diverse array of items—newspapers, magazines, pens, snacks, and other odds and ends. During rush hour, your business is a fast-paced pressure cooker; the longer you take with one customer, the more chance that the busy commuters waiting in line for service will tire of waiting and you will lose sales. In this business environment,

© DIGITAL VISION/GETTY IMAGES INC.

A newsstand will wait until the end of the day to count inventory by comparing what items it started with to what is left. This is an example of a periodic inventory system.

periodic inventory system

A system of accounting for inventory in which cost of goods sold is determined and inventory is adjusted at the end of the accounting period, not when merchandise is purchased or sold.

would it make sense to make each customer wait while you meticulously check off on an inventory sheet exactly which items were sold? No, the delay caused by this detailed bookkeeping would cause you to lose customers. It makes more sense to wait until the end of the day, count up what inventory you still have left, compare that to what you started with, and use those numbers to deduce how many of each inventory item you sold during the day.

This subway newsstand scenario is an example of a situation where a **periodic inventory system** is appropriate. With a periodic system, inventory records are not updated when a sale is made; only the dollar amount of the sale is recorded. Periodic systems are most often used when inventory is composed of a large number of diverse items, each with a relatively low value.

Impact of Information Technology Over the past 25 years, advances in information technology have lowered the cost of maintaining a perpetual inventory system. As a result, more businesses have adopted perpetual systems so that they can more closely track inventory levels. A visible manifestation of this trend is in supermarkets. Twenty years ago, the checkout clerk rang up the price of each item on a cash register. After the customers walked out of the store with their groceries, the store knew the total amount of the sale but did not know which individual items had been sold. This was a periodic inventory system. Now, with laser scanning equipment tied into the supermarket's computer system, most supermarkets operate under a perpetual system. The store manager knows exactly what you bought and exactly how many of each item should still be left on the store shelves.

Perpetual and Periodic Journal Entries

The following transactions for Grantsville Clothing Store will be used to illustrate the differences in bookkeeping procedures between a business using a perpetual inventory system and one using a periodic inventory system:

a. Purchased on account: 1,000 shirts at a cost of $10 each for a total of $10,000.
b. Purchased on account: 300 pairs of pants at a cost of $18 each for a total of $5,400.
c. Paid cash for separate shipping costs on the shirts purchased in (a), $970. The supplier of the pants purchased in (b) included the shipping costs in the $18 purchase price.
d. Returned 30 of the shirts (costing $300) to the supplier because they were stained.
e. Paid for the shirt purchase. A 2% discount was given on the $9,700 bill [(1,000 purchased − 30 returned) × $10] because of payment within the 10-day discount period (payment terms were 2/10, n/30).

(Continued)

f.   Paid $5,400 for the pants purchase. No discount was allowed because payment was made after the discount period.

g.   Sold on account: 600 shirts at a price of $25 each for a total of $15,000.

h.   Sold on account: 200 pairs of pants at a price of $40 each for a total of $8,000.

i.   Accepted return of 50 shirts by dissatisfied customers.

STOP & THINK

If you buy your groceries with a credit card or a bank debit card, what kind of information can the supermarket accumulate about you?

The journal entries for the perpetual inventory system should seem familiar to you—a perpetual system has been assumed in all earlier chapters of the text. A perpetual system was assumed because it is logical and is the system all companies would choose if there were no cost to updating the inventory records each time a sale or purchase is made. As mentioned, a periodic inventory system is sometimes a practical necessity.

Purchases   With a perpetual system, all purchases are added (debited) directly to Inventory. With a periodic system, the inventory balance is only updated using an inventory count at the end of the period; inventory purchases during the period are recorded in a temporary holding account called Purchases. As will be illustrated later, at the end of the period, the balance in Purchases is closed to Inventory in connection with the computation of cost of goods sold.

Entries (a) and (b) to record the shirt and pants purchases are given below.

	Perpetual			**Periodic**		
a.	Inventory	10,000		Purchases	10,000	
	Accounts Payable		10,000	Accounts Payable		10,000
b.	Inventory	5,400		Purchases	5,400	
	Accounts Payable		5,400	Accounts Payable		5,400

Transportation Costs   The cost of transporting the inventory is an additional inventory cost. Sometimes, as with the pants in the Grantsville Clothing example, the shipping cost is already included in the purchase price, so a separate entry to record the transportation costs is not needed. When a separate payment is made for transportation costs, it is recorded as follows:

	Perpetual			**Periodic**		
c.	Inventory	970		Freight In	970	
	Cash		970	Cash		970

With a perpetual inventory system, transportation costs are added directly to the inventory balance. With a periodic inventory system, another temporary holding account, Freight In, is created, and transportation costs are accumulated in this account during the period. Like the purchases account, Freight In is closed to Inventory at the end of the period in connection with the computation of cost of goods sold.

Purchase Returns   With a perpetual system, the return of unsatisfactory merchandise to the supplier results in a decrease in Inventory. In addition, since no payment will have to be made for the returned merchandise, Accounts Payable is reduced by the same amount. With a periodic system, the amount of the returned merchandise is recorded in yet another temporary holding account called Purchase Returns. Purchase Returns is a contra account to Purchases and is also closed to Inventory as part of the computation of cost of goods sold.

	Perpetual			Periodic		
d.	Accounts Payable	300		Accounts Payable	300	
	Inventory		300	Purchase Returns		300

If the returned merchandise had already been paid for, the supplier would most likely return the purchase price. In this case, the debit would be to Cash instead of to Accounts Payable.

Purchase Discounts   As discussed in Chapter 6, sellers sometimes offer inducements for credit customers to pay quickly. In this example, Grantsville Clothing takes advantage of purchase discounts to save money on the payment for the shirts. The amount of the purchase discount is $194 ($9,700 × 0.02), so the total payment for the shirts is $9,506 ($9,700 − $194). The amount recorded for inventory should reflect the actual amount paid to purchase the inventory. With a perpetual inventory system, this is shown by subtracting the purchase discount amount from the inventory account. With a periodic inventory system, another holding account is created to accumulate purchase discounts taken during the period.

	Perpetual			Periodic		
e.	Accounts Payable	9,700		Accounts Payable	9,700	
	Inventory		194	Purchase Discounts		194
	Cash		9,506	Cash		9,506
f.	Accounts Payable	5,400		Accounts Payable	5,400	
	Cash		5,400	Cash		5,400

Note that the payment for the pants is made after the discount period, so the full amount must be paid. Since this transaction had no impact on Inventory, the entry is the same for both the perpetual and the periodic system.

In terms of journal entries, you should recognize that the difference between a perpetual and a periodic inventory system is that all adjustments to inventory under a perpetual system are entered directly in the inventory account; with a periodic system, all inventory adjustments are accumulated in an array of temporary holding accounts: Purchases, Freight In, Purchase Returns, and Purchase Discounts.

Sales   The sales of shirts and pants would be recorded as follows:

	Perpetual			Periodic		
g.	Accounts Receivable	15,000		Accounts Receivable	15,000	
	Sales (600 × $25)		15,000	Sales		15,000
	Cost of Goods Sold	6,000				
	Inventory (600 × $10)		6,000			
h.	Accounts Receivable	8,000		Accounts Receivable	8,000	
	Sales (200 × $40)		8,000	Sales		8,000
	Cost of Goods Sold	3,600				
	Inventory (200 × $18)		3,600			

These entries reflect the primary difference between a perpetual and a periodic inventory system—with a periodic system, no attempt is made to recognize cost of goods sold on a transaction-by-transaction basis. In fact, with a periodic system, Grantsville Clothing would not even know how many shirts and how many pairs of pants had been sold. Instead, only total sales of $23,000 ($15,000 + $8,000) would be known.

For simplicity, we have recorded the cost of goods sold for the shirts as $10 each. The actual cost per shirt, after adjusting for freight in and purchase discounts, is $10.80, computed as follows:

Total purchase price (1,000 shirts)	$10,000
Plus: Freight in	970
Less: Purchase returns (30 shirts)	(300)
Less: Purchase discounts	(194)
Total cost of shirts (970 shirts)	$10,476
Total cost $10,476 ÷ 970 shirts = $10.80 per shirt	

In practice, it is unlikely that a firm using a perpetual inventory system would bother to adjust unit costs for the effects of freight cost and purchase discounts on an ongoing basis. The cost of doing these calculations could easily outweigh any resulting improvement in the quality of cost information.

Sales Returns   As discussed in Chapter 6, dissatisfied customers sometimes return their purchases. The journal entries to record the return of 50 shirts are as follows:

	Perpetual			**Periodic**		
i.	Sales Returns (50 × $25)	1,250		Sales Returns	1,250	
	Accounts Receivable		1,250	Accounts Receivable		1,250
	Inventory (50 × $10)	500				
	Cost of Goods Sold		500			

STOP & THINK

Should the returned inventory be recorded at its original cost of $10 per shirt?

Under the perpetual system, not only are the sales for the returned items canceled, but the cost of the returned inventory is also removed from Cost of Goods Sold and restored to the inventory account.

Closing Entries   After all of the journal entries are posted to the ledger, the T-accounts for Inventory and Cost of Goods Sold, under a perpetual system, would appear as follows:

	Inventory					**Cost of Goods Sold**			
(a)		10,000	(d)	300		(g)	6,000	(i)	500
(b)		5,400	(e)	194		(h)	3,600		
(c)		970	(g)	6,000					
(i)		500	(h)	3,600					
Bal.		6,776				Bal.	9,100		

These numbers, after being verified by a physical count of the inventory (as described in the next section), would be reported in the financial statements—the $6,776 of Inventory in the balance sheet and the $9,100 of Cost of Goods Sold in the income statement.

Review the journal entries (a) through (i) under the periodic inventory system and notice that none of the amounts have been entered in either Inventory or Cost of Goods Sold. As a result, both of these accounts will have zero balances at year-end. Actually, the inventory account would have the same balance it had at the beginning of the period, which, in this example, we will assume to be zero.

With a periodic inventory system, the correct balances are recorded in Inventory and Cost of Goods Sold through a series of closing entries. Two entries are made:

1. Transfer all the temporary holding accounts to the inventory account balance. At this point, the inventory account balance is equal to the cost of goods available for sale (beginning inventory plus the net cost of purchases for the period).

2. Reduce Inventory by the amount of Cost of Goods Sold. At this point, the inventory account balance is equal to the ending inventory amount, and the appropriate cost of goods sold amount is also recognized.

To illustrate, the information for Grantsville Clothing will be used. The entry to transfer all the temporary holding accounts to the inventory account is as follows:

Inventory	15,876	
Purchase Returns	300	
Purchase Discounts	194	
Freight In		970
Purchases		15,400
Closing of temporary inventory accounts for periodic system.		

net purchases

The net cost of inventory purchased during a period, after adding the cost of freight in and subtracting returns and discounts.

The inventory debit of $15,876 is the amount of **net purchases** for the period. Notice that, after this entry has been posted, the balances in all the temporary holding accounts will have been reduced to zero. As mentioned, after the addition of net purchases, the inventory account balance represents cost of goods available for sale (the sum of beginning inventory and net purchases). Remember that, in this example, beginning inventory is assumed to be zero.

The second closing entry involves the adjustment of Inventory to its appropriate ending balance and the creation of the cost of goods sold account. This cost of goods sold account would be closed when other nominal accounts (e.g., Sales Salaries, Interest Expense, etc.) are closed. If the year-end physical count indicates that the ending inventory balance should be $6,776, the appropriate entry is as follows:

Cost of Goods Sold	9,100	
Inventory ($15,876 − $6,776)		9,100
Adjustment of inventory account to appropriate ending balance.		

In this example, the values for both ending inventory ($6,776) and cost of goods sold ($9,100) are the same with either a perpetual or a periodic inventory system. So, what is the practical difference between the two systems? One difference is that a perpetual system can tell you the inventory balance and the cumulative cost of goods sold at any time during the period. With a periodic system, on the other hand, you must wait until the inventory is counted at the end of the period to compute the amount of inventory or cost of goods sold. Another difference is that, with a perpetual system, you can compare the inventory records to the amount of inventory actually on hand and thus determine whether any inventory has been lost or stolen. As described in the next section, this comparison is not possible with a periodic system.

REMEMBER THIS...

-   With a perpetual inventory system, the amount of inventory and cost of goods sold for the period are tracked on an ongoing basis.
-   With a periodic inventory system, inventory and cost of goods sold are computed using an end-of-period inventory count.
-   With a periodic system, inventory-related items are recorded in temporary holding accounts that are transferred to the inventory account at the end of the period.

Counting Inventory and Calculating Cost of Goods Sold

Calculate cost of goods sold using the results of an inventory count and understand the impact of errors in ending inventory on reported cost of goods sold.

(3) Regular physical counts of the existing inventory are essential to maintaining reliable inventory accounting records. With a perpetual system, the physical count can be compared to the recorded inventory balance to see whether any inventory has been lost or stolen. With a periodic system, a physical count is the only way to get the information necessary to compute cost of goods sold.

Taking a Physical Count of Inventory

No matter which inventory system a company is using, periodic physical counts are a necessary and important part of accounting for inventory. With a perpetual inventory system, the physical count either confirms that the amount entered in the accounting records is accurate or highlights shortages and clerical errors. If, for example, employees have been stealing inventory, the theft will show up as a difference between the balance in the inventory account and the amount physically counted.

A physical count of inventory involves two steps:

1. *Quantity count.* In most companies, physically counting all inventory is a time-consuming activity. Because sales transactions and merchandise deliveries can complicate matters, inventory is usually counted on holidays or after the close of business on the inventory day. Special care must be taken to ensure that all inventory owned, wherever its location, is counted and that inventory on hand but not owned (consignment inventory) is not counted.
2. *Inventory costing.* When the physical count has been completed, each type of merchandise is assigned a unit cost. The quantity of each type of merchandise is multiplied by its unit cost to determine the dollar value of the inventory. These amounts are then added to obtain the total ending inventory for the business. This is the amount reported as Inventory on the balance sheet. The ending balance in the inventory account may have to be adjusted for any shortages discovered.

To illustrate the impact of a physical inventory count on the accounting records for both a periodic and a perpetual system, we will refer back to the Grantsville Clothing Store example used earlier. Assume that a physical count, combined with inventory costing analysis, suggests that the correct amount for ending inventory is $5,950. This information can be combined with previous information from the accounting system as follows:

	Periodic System	Perpetual System
Beginning inventory	$ 0	$ 0
Plus: Net purchases	15,876	15,876
Cost of goods available for sale	$15,876	$15,876
Less: Ending inventory	5,950	6,776 (from inventory system)
Cost of goods sold	$ 9,926	$ 9,100 (from inventory system)
Goods lost or stolen	unknown	826 ($6,776 − $5,950)
Total cost of goods sold, lost, or stolen	$ 9,926	$ 9,926

Recall that, in this example, the beginning inventory is assumed to be zero. The amount of net purchases is a combination of the items affecting the amount paid for inventory purchases during the period: purchase price, freight in, purchase returns, and purchase discounts. The $15,876 amount for net purchases was computed earlier in connection with the closing entry for the periodic system.

This cost of goods sold computation highlights the key difference between a periodic and a perpetual inventory system. With a periodic system, the company does not know what ending inventory *should be* when the inventory count is performed. The best the company can do is count the inventory and assume that the difference between the cost of goods available for sale and the cost of goods still remaining (ending inventory) must represent the cost of goods that were sold. Actually, a business using a periodic system has no way of knowing whether these goods were sold, lost, stolen, or spoiled— all it knows for sure is that the goods are gone.

inventory shrinkage

The amount of inventory that is lost, stolen, or spoiled during a period; determined by comparing perpetual inventory records to the physical count of inventory.

With a perpetual system, the accounting records themselves yield the cost of goods sold during the period, as well as the amount of inventory that should be found when the physical count is made. In the Grantsville Clothing example, the predicted ending inventory is $6,776 (from the T-account shown earlier); the actual ending inventory, according to the physical count, is only $5,950. The difference of $826 ($6,776 - $5,950) represents inventory lost, stolen, or ruined during the period. This amount is called inventory shrinkage. The adjusting entry needed to record this **inventory shrinkage** is as follows:

Inventory Shrinkage	826	
Inventory ($6,776 - $5,950)		826
Adjustment of perpetual inventory balance to reflect inventory		
shrinkage.		

F Y I

CVS is a leader in the retail drugstore industry in the United States with net sales of $24.2 billion in fiscal 2002. Inventory shrinkage for CVS for 2002 was $288 million, or almost 1.2% of sales. The company has since ceased to report actual inventory shrinkage numbers and instead reported in 2005 that inventory shrinkage had improved.

For internal management purposes, the amount of inventory shrinkage would be tracked from one period to the next to detect whether the amount of "shrinkage" for any given period is unusually high. For external reporting purposes, the shrinkage amount would probably be combined with normal cost of goods sold, and the title "Cost of Goods Sold" would be given to the total. Notice that if this practice is followed, reported cost of goods sold would be the same under both a perpetual and a periodic inventory system. The difference is that, with a perpetual system, company management knows how much of the goods was actually sold and how much represents inventory shrinkage.

With a periodic inventory system, no journal entry for inventory shrinkage is made because the amount of shrinkage is unknown. Instead, the ending inventory amount derived from the physical count is used to make the second periodic inventory closing entry (refer back to the previous section). Using the $5,950 ending inventory amount, the appropriate periodic inventory closing entry is:

Cost of Goods Sold	9,926	
Inventory ($15,876 - $5,950)		9,926
Adjustment of inventory account to appropriate ending balance.		

The Income Effect of an Error in Ending Inventory

As shown in the previous section, the results of the physical inventory count directly affect the computation of cost of goods sold with a periodic system and inventory shrinkage with a perpetual system. Errors in the inventory count will cause the amount of cost of goods sold or inventory shrinkage to be misstated. To illustrate, assume that the correct inventory count for Grantsville Clothing is $5,950 but that the ending inventory value is mistakenly computed to be $6,450. The impact of this $500 ($6,450 − $5,950) inventory overstatement is as follows:

	Periodic System	Perpetual System
Beginning inventory	$ 0	$ 0
Plus: Net purchases	15,876	15,876
Cost of goods available for sale	$15,876	$15,876
Less: Ending inventory	6,450	6,776 (from inventory system)
Cost of goods sold	$ 9,426	$ 9,100 (from inventory system)
Goods lost or stolen	unknown	326 ($6,776 − $6,450)
Total cost of goods sold, lost, or stolen	$ 9,426	$ 9,426

The $500 inventory overstatement reduces the reported cost of goods sold, lost, or stolen by $500, from $9,926 (computed earlier) to $9,426. This is because if we mistakenly think that we have more inventory remaining, then we will also mistakenly think that we must have sold less. Conversely, if the physical count understates ending inventory, total cost of goods sold will be overstated.

Since an inventory overstatement decreases reported cost of goods sold, it will also increase reported gross margin and net income. For this reason, the managers of a firm that is having difficulty meeting profit targets are sometimes tempted to "mistakenly" overstate ending inventory. Because of this temptation, auditors must take care to review a company's inventory counting process and also to physically observe a sample of the actual inventory. Many new accounting graduates who are hired by public accounting firms spend a portion of their first year on the job checking the inventory counts done by clients. The benefits of this exposure are twofold: (1) these new auditors get an opportunity to see what a business actually does, and (2) the inventory count provides assurance that the inventory amount stated on the financial statements is accurate.

REMEMBER THIS...

- A physical inventory count is necessary to ensure that inventory records match the actual existing inventory.

- If a perpetual system is used, an inventory count can be used to compute the amount of inventory shrinkage during the period.

- An error in the reported ending inventory amount can have a significant effect on reported cost of goods sold, gross margin, and net income. For example, overstatement of ending inventory results in understatement of cost of goods sold and overstatement of net income.

Inventory Cost Flow Assumptions

Apply the four inventory cost flow alternatives: specific identification, FIFO, LIFO, and average cost.

(4) Consider the following transactions for the Ramona Rice Company for the year 2009.

Mar. 23	Purchased 10 kilos of rice, $4 per kilo.
Nov. 17	Purchased 10 kilos of rice, $9 per kilo.
Dec. 31	Sold 10 kilos of rice, $10 per kilo.

The surprisingly difficult question to answer with this simple example is "How much income did Ramona make in 2009?" As you can see, it depends on which rice was sold on December 31. There are three possibilities:

	Case #1 Sold Old Rice	Case #2 Sold New Rice	Case #3 Sold Mixed Rice
Sales ($10 × 10 kilos)	$100	$100	$100
Cost of goods sold (10 kilos)	40	90	65
Gross margin	$ 60	$ 10	$ 35

FIFO (first in, first out)

An inventory cost flow assumption whereby the first goods purchased are assumed to be the first goods sold so that the ending inventory consists of the most recently purchased goods.

LIFO (last in, first out)

An inventory cost flow assumption whereby the last goods purchased are assumed to be the first goods sold so that the ending inventory consists of the first goods purchased.

average cost

An inventory cost flow assumption whereby cost of goods sold and the cost of ending inventory are determined by using an average cost of all merchandise available for sale during the period.

specific identification

A method of valuing inventory and determining cost of goods sold whereby the actual costs of specific inventory items are assigned to them.

In Case #1, it is assumed that the 10 kilos of rice sold on December 31 were the old ones, purchased on March 23 for $4 per kilo. Accountants call this a **FIFO (first in, first out)** assumption. In Case #2, it is assumed that the company sold the new rice, purchased on November 17 for $9 per kilo. Accountants call this a **LIFO (last in, first out)** assumption. In Case #3, it is assumed that all the rice is mixed together, so the cost per kilo is the average cost of all the rice available for sale, or $6.50 per kilo [($40 + $90) ÷ 20 kilos]. Accountants call this an **average cost** assumption.

The point of the Ramona Rice example is this: in most cases, there is no feasible way to track exactly which units were sold. Accordingly, in order to compute cost of goods sold, the accountant must make an assumption. Note that this is not a case of tricky accountants trying to manipulate the reported numbers; instead, this is a case in which income simply cannot be computed unless the accountant uses his or her judgment and makes an assumption.

All three of the assumptions described in the example—FIFO, LIFO, and average cost—are acceptable under U.S. accounting rules. An interesting question is whether a company would randomly choose one of the three acceptable methods, or whether the choice would be made more strategically. For example, if Ramona Rice were preparing financial statements to be used to support a bank loan application, which assumption would you suggest that the company make? On the other hand, if Ramona were completing its income tax return, which assumption would be the best? This topic of strategic accounting choice will be discussed later in this chapter.

In the following sections, we will examine in more detail the different cost flow assumptions used by companies to determine inventories and cost of goods sold.

Specific Identification Inventory Cost Flow

An alternative to the assumptions just described is to specifically identify the cost of each particular unit that is sold. This approach, called **specific identification**, is often used by automobile dealers and other businesses that sell a limited number of units at a high price. To illustrate the specific identification inventory costing method, we will consider the September 2009 records of Nephi Company, which sells one type of bicycle.

Sept. 1   Beginning inventory consisted of 10 bicycles costing $200 each.
 3   Purchased 8 bicycles costing $250 each.
 18   Purchased 16 bicycles costing $300 each.
 20   Purchased 10 bicycles costing $320 each.
 25   Sold 28 bicycles, $400 each.

These inventory records show that during September the company had 44 bicycles (10 from beginning inventory and 34 that were purchased during the month) that it could have sold. However, only 28 bicycles were sold, leaving 16 on hand at the end of

September. Using the specific identification method of inventory costing requires that the individual costs of the actual units sold be charged against revenue as cost of goods sold. To compute cost of goods sold and ending inventory amounts with this alternative, a company must know which units were actually sold and what the unit cost of each was.

Suppose that of the 28 bicycles sold by Nephi on September 25, 8 came from the beginning inventory, 4 came from the September 3 purchase, and 16 came from the September 18 purchase. With this information, cost of goods sold and ending inventory are computed as follows:

	Bicycles	Costs
Beginning inventory	10	$ 2,000
Net purchases	34	10,000
Goods available for sale	44	$12,000
Ending inventory	16	4,600
Cost of goods sold	28	$ 7,400

The cost of ending inventory is the total of the individual costs of the bicycles still on hand at the end of the month, or:

2 bicycles from beginning inventory, $200 each	$ 400
4 bicycles purchased on September 3, $250 each	1,000
0 bicycles purchased on September 18, $300 each	0
10 bicycles purchased on September 20, $320 each	3,200
Total ending inventory (16 units)	$4,600

Similarly, the cost of goods sold is the total of the costs of the specific bicycles sold, or:

8 bicycles from beginning inventory, $200 each	$1,600
4 bicycles purchased on September 3, $250 each	1,000
16 bicycles purchased on September 18, $300 each	4,800
0 bicycles purchased on September 20, $320 each	0
Total cost of goods sold (28 units)	$7,400

For many companies, it is impractical, if not impossible, to keep track of specific units. In that case, an assumption must be made as to which units were sold during the period and which are still in inventory, as illustrated earlier in the Ramona Rice example.

It is very important to remember that the accounting rules do not require that the assumed flow of goods for costing purposes match the actual physical movement of goods purchased and sold. In some cases, the assumed cost flow may be similar to the physical flow, but firms are not required to match the assumed accounting cost flow to the physical flow. A grocery store, for example, usually tries to sell the oldest units first to minimize spoilage. Thus, the physical flow of goods would reflect a FIFO pattern, but the grocery store could use a FIFO, LIFO, or average cost assumption in determining the ending inventory and cost of goods sold numbers to be reported in the financial statements. On the other hand, a company that stockpiles coal must first sell the coal purchased last since it is on top of the pile. That company might use the LIFO cost assumption, which reflects physical flow, or it might use one of the other alternatives.

In the next few sections, we will illustrate the FIFO, LIFO, and average inventory costing methods. The bicycle inventory data for Nephi Company will again be used in illustrating the different inventory cost flows.

FIFO Cost Flow Assumption

With FIFO, it is assumed that the oldest units are sold and the newest units remain in inventory. Using the FIFO inventory cost flow assumption, the ending inventory and cost of goods sold for Nephi Company are:

	Bicycles	Costs
Beginning inventory	10	$ 2,000
Net purchases	34	10,000
Goods available for sale	44	$12,000
Ending inventory	16	5,000
Cost of goods sold	28	$ 7,000

The $7,000 cost of goods sold and $5,000 cost of ending inventory are determined as follows:

FIFO cost of goods sold (oldest 28 units):	
10 bicycles from beginning inventory, $200 each	$2,000
8 bicycles purchased on September 3, $250 each	2,000
10 bicycles purchased on September 18, $300 each	3,000
Total FIFO cost of goods sold	$7,000

FIFO ending inventory (newest 16 units):	
6 bicycles purchased on September 18, $300 each	$1,800
10 bicycles purchased on September 20, $320 each	3,200
Total FIFO ending inventory	$5,000

LIFO Cost Flow Assumption

LIFO is the opposite of FIFO. With LIFO, the cost of the most recent units purchased is transferred to cost of goods sold. When prices are rising, as they are in the Nephi Company example, LIFO provides higher cost of goods sold, and hence lower net income, than FIFO. This is because the newest (high-priced) goods are assumed to have been sold. Using the LIFO inventory cost flow assumption, the ending inventory and cost of goods sold for Nephi Company are:

	Bicycles	Costs
Beginning inventory	10	$ 2,000
Net purchases	34	10,000
Goods available for sale	44	$12,000
Ending inventory	16	3,500
Cost of goods sold	28	$ 8,500

The $8,500 cost of goods sold and $3,500 cost of ending inventory are determined as follows:

LIFO cost of goods sold (newest 28 units):	
10 bicycles purchased on September 20, $320 each	$3,200
16 bicycles purchased on September 18, $300 each	4,800
2 bicycles purchased on September 3, $250 each	500
Total LIFO cost of goods sold	$8,500

LIFO ending inventory (oldest 16 units):	
10 bicycles from beginning inventory, $200 each	$2,000
6 bicycles purchased on September 3, $250 each	1,500
Total LIFO ending inventory	$3,500

Average Cost Flow Assumption

With average costing, an average cost must be computed for all the inventory available for sale during the period. The average unit cost for Nephi Company during September is computed as follows:

	Bicycles	Costs
Beginning inventory	10	$ 2,000
Net purchases	34	10,000
Goods available for sale	44	$12,000

$12,000 ÷ 44 units = $272.73 per unit

With the average cost assumption, cost of goods sold is computed by multiplying the number of units sold by the average cost per unit. Similarly, the cost of ending inventory is computed by multiplying the number of units in ending inventory by the average cost per unit. These calculations are as follows:

Average Cost of Goods Sold: 28 Units × $272.73 per Unit = $7,636 (rounded)
Average Ending Inventory: 16 Units × $272.73 per Unit = $4,364 (rounded)

This information can be shown as follows:

	Bicycles	Costs
Beginning inventory	10	$ 2,000
Net purchases	34	10,000
Goods available for sale	44	$12,000
Ending inventory	16	4,364
Cost of goods sold	28	$ 7,636

A Comparison of All Inventory Costing Methods

The cost of goods sold and ending inventory amounts we have calculated using the three cost flow assumptions are summarized along with the resultant gross margins as follows:

	FIFO	LIFO	Average
Sales revenue (28 × $400)	$11,200	$11,200	$11,200
Cost of goods sold	7,000	8,500	7,636
Gross margin	$ 4,200	$ 2,700	$ 3,564
Ending inventory	$ 5,000	$ 3,500	$ 4,364

Note that the net result of each of the inventory cost flow assumptions is to allocate the total cost of goods available for sale of $12,000 between cost of goods sold and ending inventory.

Conceptual Comparison   From a conceptual standpoint, LIFO gives a better reflection of cost of goods sold in the income statement than does FIFO because the most recent goods ("last in"), with the most recent costs, are assumed to have been sold. Thus, LIFO cost of goods sold matches current revenues with current costs. Average cost is somewhere between LIFO and FIFO. On the balance sheet, however, FIFO gives a better measure of inventory value because, with the FIFO assumption, the "first in" units are sold and the remaining units are the newest ones with the most recent costs. In summary, LIFO gives a conceptually better measure of income, but FIFO gives a conceptually better measure of inventory value on the balance sheet.

Financial Statement Impact Comparison

As illustrated in the Nephi Company example, in times of rising inventory prices (the most common situation in the majority of industries today), cost of goods sold is highest with LIFO and lowest with FIFO. As a result, gross margin, net income, and ending inventory are lowest with LIFO and highest with FIFO. With the impact on the reported financial statement numbers being so uniformly bad, you may be wondering why any company would ever voluntarily choose to use LIFO (during times of inflation). It might further surprise you to learn that, since 1974, hundreds of U.S. companies have voluntarily switched from FIFO to LIFO and that over half of the large companies in the United States currently use LIFO in accounting for at least some of their inventories.

The attractiveness of LIFO can be explained with one word—TAXES. If a company uses LIFO in a time of rising prices, reported cost of goods sold is higher, reported taxable income is lower, and cash paid for income taxes is lower. In fact, LIFO was invented in the 1930s in the United States for the sole purpose of allowing companies to lower their income tax payments. In most instances where accounting alternatives exist, firms are allowed to use one accounting method for tax purposes and another for financial reporting. In 1939, however, when the Internal Revenue Service (IRS) approved the use of LIFO, it ruled that firms may use LIFO for tax purposes only if they also use LIFO for financial reporting purposes. Therefore, companies must choose between reporting higher profits and paying higher taxes with FIFO or reporting lower profits and paying lower taxes with LIFO.

STOP & THINK

Over the entire life of a company—from its beginning with zero inventory until its final closeout when the last inventory item is sold—is aggregate cost of goods sold more, less, or the same as aggregate purchases? How is this relationship affected by the inventory cost flow assumption used?

REMEMBER THIS...

- In most cases, an accountant must make an inventory cost flow assumption in order to compute cost of goods sold and ending inventory.
- With FIFO (first in, first out), it is assumed that the oldest inventory units are sold first.
- With LIFO (last in, first out), it is assumed that the newest units are sold first.
- With the average cost assumption, the total goods available for sale are used to compute an average cost per unit for the period; this average cost is then used in calculating cost of goods sold and ending inventory.
- LIFO produces a better matching of current revenues and current expenses in the income statement; FIFO yields a balance sheet inventory value that is closer to the current value of the inventory.
- The primary practical attraction of LIFO is that it lowers income tax payments during times of inflation.

Assessing How Well Companies Manage Their Inventories

⑤ Use financial ratios to evaluate a company's inventory level.

Money tied up in the form of inventories cannot be used for other purposes. Therefore, companies try hard to minimize the necessary investment in inventories while at the same time assuring that they have enough inventory on hand to meet customer demand. In recent years a method of inventory management called just-in-time (JIT) inventory has become popular. JIT, which will be described in Chapter 23 of *Accounting: Concepts and Applications*, is an inventory management method that attempts to have exactly enough inventory arrive just in time for sale. Its purpose is to minimize the amount of money needed to purchase and hold inventory.

Evaluating the Level of Inventory

inventory turnover

A measure of the efficiency with which inventory is managed; computed by dividing cost of goods sold by average inventory for a period.

Two widely used measurements of how effectively a company is managing its inventory are the inventory turnover ratio and number of days' sales in inventory. **Inventory turnover** provides a measure of how many times a company turns over, or replenishes, its inventory during a year. The calculation is similar to the accounts receivable turnover discussed in Chapter 6. It is calculated by dividing cost of goods sold by average inventory as follows:

$$\text{Inventory Turnover} = \frac{\text{Cost of Goods Sold}}{\text{Average Inventory}}$$

The average inventory amount is the average of the beginning and ending inventory balances. The inventory turnover ratios for **Sears**, **Safeway**, and **Caterpillar** for 2005 are as follows (dollar amounts are in billions):

	Sears	Safeway	Caterpillar
Cost of goods sold	$35.505	$27.303	$26.558
Beginning inventory	3.281	2.741	4.675
Ending inventory	9.068	2.766	5.224
Average inventory	6.175	2.754	4.950
Inventory turnover	5.75	9.91	5.37

number of days' sales in inventory

An alternative measure of how well inventory is being managed; computed by dividing 365 days by the inventory turnover ratio.

From this analysis, you can see that Safeway, the supermarket, turns its inventory over more frequently than Sears, the department store, and Caterpillar, the equipment dealer. This result is what we would have predicted given that the companies are in different businesses and have different types of inventory.

Inventory turnover can also be converted into the **number of days' sales in inventory**. This ratio is computed by dividing 365, or the number of days in a year, by the inventory turnover, as follows:

$$\frac{\text{Number of Days'}}{\text{Sales in Inventory}} = \frac{365}{\text{Inventory Turnover}}$$

Computing this ratio for Sears, Safeway, and Caterpillar yields the following:

	Number of Days' Sales in Inventory
Sears	63.5 days
Safeway	36.8 days
Caterpillar	68.0 days

CAUTION

Sometimes these two inventory ratios are computed using ending inventory rather than average inventory. This is appropriate if the inventory balance does not change much from the beginning to the end of the year.

Individuals analyzing how effective a company's inventory management is would compare these ratios with those of other firms in the same industry and with comparable ratios for the same firm in previous years.

Impact of the Inventory Cost Flow Assumption

As mentioned previously, in times of rising prices, the use of LIFO results in higher cost of goods sold and lower inventory values. All three of the companies in the ratio illustration above use LIFO. Each company includes supplemental disclosures in the financial statement notes that allow users to compute what reported inventory and cost of goods sold would have been if the company had used FIFO. To illustrate the impact that the choice of inventory cost flow assumption can have on the reported numbers, consider the following comparison for Caterpillar for 2005:

	Reported LIFO Numbers	Numbers if Using FIFO
Cost of goods sold	$26.558	$26.337
Average inventory	4.950	6.013
Inventory turnover	5.37	4.38
Number of days' sales in inventory	68.0 days	83.3 days

The difference in cost of goods sold for 2005 is not great because inflation was relatively low in that year. However, the difference in the reported average inventory balance reflects the cumulative effect of inflation for the many years since Caterpillar first started using LIFO. The impact on the ratio values is dramatic. Of course, the difference between LIFO and FIFO is not as great for most companies as shown here for Caterpillar, but the general point is that the choice of inventory cost flow assumption can affect the conclusions drawn about the financial statements—if the financial statement user is not careful.

Number of Days' Purchases in Accounts Payable

In Chapter 6, we introduced the average collection period ratio. In this chapter we have discussed the computation of the number of days' sales in inventory. Taken together, these two ratios indicate the length of a firm's operating cycle. The two ratios measure the amount of time it takes, on average, from the point when inventory is purchased to the point when cash is collected from the customer who purchased the inventory. For example, Sears' 131-day operating cycle for 2005 is depicted below.

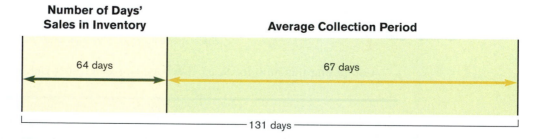

Is Sears' operating cycle too long, too short, or just right? That is difficult to tell without information from prior years and from competitors. But by including one additional ratio in the analysis, we can learn more about how Sears is managing its operating cash flow.

number of days' purchases in accounts payable

A measure of how well operating cash flow is being managed; computed by dividing total inventory purchases by average accounts payable and then dividing 365 days by the result.

The number of days' purchases in accounts payable reveals the average length of time that elapses between the purchase of inventory on account and the cash payment for that inventory. The **number of days' purchases in accounts payable** is computed by dividing total inventory purchases by average accounts payable and then dividing the result into 365 days:

$$\text{Number of Days' Purchases in Accounts Payable} = \frac{365 \text{ Days}}{\text{Purchases/Average Accounts Payable}}$$

The amount of inventory purchased during a year is computed by combining cost of goods sold with the change in the inventory balance for the year. If inventory increased during the year, then inventory purchases are equal to cost of goods sold plus the increase in the inventory balance. Similarly, if inventory decreased during the year, inventory purchases are equal to cost of goods sold minus the decrease in the inventory balance.

The number of days' purchases in accounts payable indicates how long a company takes to pay its suppliers. For example, Sears' number of days' purchases in accounts payable for 2005 is computed as follows (dollar figures are in millions):

Cost of goods sold for 2005	$35,505
Add increase in inventory during 2005	5,787
Inventory purchases during 2005	$41,292
Average accounts payable during 2005	$ 2,193

$$\text{Number of Days' Purchases in Accounts Payable} = \frac{365 \text{ Days}}{\$41,292/\$2,193}$$

$$= 19 \text{ days}$$

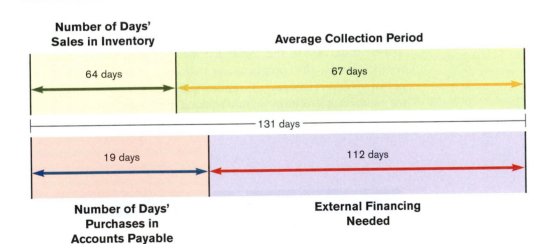

Number of Days' Sales in Inventory

64 days

Average Collection Period

67 days

131 days

19 days

112 days

Number of Days' Purchases in Accounts Payable

External Financing Needed

CAUTION

This computation of the number of days' purchases in accounts payable assumes that only inventory purchases on account are included in accounts payable. It is likely that the accounts payable balance also includes such items as supplies purchased on account. Nevertheless, the purchase of inventory is typically the most significant element of accounts payable.

Sears must pay its suppliers in 19 days but must wait for 131 days before receiving the cash from its customers. Sears must finance the remaining 112 days (131 days − 19 days) of its operating cycle with bank loans or additional stockholder investment or by charging interest to those using its credit card debt. Sears is famous for using the last option—charging customers for the use of credit. In 2005 alone, Sears reported revenue from its credit card activities of over $213 million.

These calculations illustrate that proper management of the sales/collection cycle, coupled with prudent financing of inventory purchases on account, can reduce a company's reliance on external financing.

REMEMBER THIS...

- Proper inventory management seeks a balance between keeping a lower inventory level to avoid tying up excess resources and maintaining a sufficient inventory balance to ensure smooth business operation.
- Companies assess how well their inventory is being managed by using two ratios: (1) inventory turnover and (2) number of days' sales in inventory.
- A company's choice of inventory cost flow assumption can significantly affect the values of these inventory ratios; intelligent ratio analysis requires considering possible accounting differences among companies.
- Comparison of the average collection period, number of days' sales in inventory, and number of days' purchases in accounts payable reveals how much of a company's operating cycle it must finance through external financing.

Thus far we have defined inventory and cost of goods sold; we have described the perpetual and periodic inventory systems, three inventory cost flow assumptions, and the use of financial ratios to evaluate a company's management of its inventory. These topics are all sufficient for a basic understanding of the nature of inventory and cost of goods sold, as well as the most common ways of accounting for inventory. The four topics that will be discussed in the expanded material are (1) the impact of more complicated inventory errors, (2) complications that arise in using LIFO and average cost with a perpetual inventory system, (3) reporting inventory at amounts below cost, and (4) a method for estimating inventory without taking a physical count.

Inventory Errors

Analyze the impact of inventory errors on reported cost of goods sold.

6 Incorrect amounts for inventory on the balance sheet and cost of goods sold on the income statement can result from errors in counting inventories, recording inventory transactions, or both. The effect of an error in the end-of-period inventory count was discussed earlier in the chapter. To examine the effects of other types of inventory errors, we will assume that Richfield Company had the following inventory records for 2009:

Inventory balance, January 1, 2009	$ 8,000
Purchases through December 30, 2009	20,000
Inventory balance, December 30, 2009	12,000

We will further assume that on December 31 the company purchased and received another $1,000 of inventory. The following comparison shows the kinds of inventory situations that might result:

The $1,000 of merchandise purchased on December 31 was	Incorrect*	Incorrect	Incorrect	Correct
	not recorded as a purchase and not counted as inventory	recorded as a purchase but not counted as inventory	not recorded as a purchase but counted as inventory	recorded as a purchase and counted as inventory
Beginning inventory	$ 8,000 (OK)**	$ 8,000 (OK)	$ 8,000 (OK)	$ 8,000 (OK)
Net purchases	20,000 (↓)	21,000 (OK)	20,000 (↓)	21,000 (OK)
Cost of goods available for sale	$28,000 (↓)	$29,000 (OK)	$28,000 (↓)	$29,000 (OK)
Ending inventory	12,000 (↓)	12,000 (↓)	13,000 (OK)	13,000 (OK)
Cost of goods sold	$16,000 (OK)	$17,000 (↑)	$15,000 (↓)	$16,000 (OK)

*This calculation produces the correct cost of goods sold but by an incorrect route—the errors in purchases and ending inventory offset each other.
**For the amount, ↓ indicates it is too low, ↑ means it is too high, and OK means it is correct.

In these calculations, the beginning inventory plus purchases equals the cost of goods that were "available for sale." In other words, everything that "could be sold" must have either been on hand at the beginning of the period (beginning inventory) or purchased during the period (net purchases). Then, ending inventory (what wasn't sold) was subtracted from the cost of goods available for sale. The result is the cost of goods that were sold. Everything on hand (available) had to be either sold or left in ending inventory. From this example, you can see how inventory and cost of goods sold can be misstated by the improper recording of inventory purchases or counting of inventory.

Similar errors can occur when inventory is sold. If a sale is recorded but the merchandise remains in the warehouse and is counted in the ending inventory, cost of goods sold will be understated, whereas gross margin and net income will be overstated. If a sale is not recorded but inventory is shipped and not counted in the ending inventory, gross margin and net income will be understated, and cost of goods sold will be overstated.

To illustrate these potential inventory errors, we will again consider the data of Richfield Company. Note that sales figures have been added and the ending inventory and the 2009 purchases now correctly include the $1,000 purchase of merchandise made on December 31, 2009.

Sales revenue through December 30, 2009 (200% of cost)	$32,000
Inventory balance, January 1, 2009	8,000
Net purchases during 2009	21,000
Inventory balance, December 31, 2009	13,000

In addition, assume that on December 31, inventory that cost $1,000 was sold for $2,000. The merchandise was delivered to the buyer on December 31. The following analysis shows the kinds of situations that might result:

The $2,000 sale on December 31 was	Incorrect	Incorrect	Incorrect	Correct
	not recorded and the merchandise was counted as inventory	recorded and the merchandise was counted as inventory	not recorded and the merchandise was excluded from inventory	recorded and the merchandise was excluded from inventory
Sales revenue	$32,000 (↓)*	$34,000 (OK)	$32,000 (↓)	$34,000 (OK)
Cost of goods sold:				
Beginning inventory	$ 8,000 (OK)	$ 8,000 (OK)	$ 8,000 (OK)	$ 8,000 (OK)
Net purchases	21,000 (OK)	21,000 (OK)	21,000 (OK)	21,000 (OK)
Cost of goods available for sale	$29,000 (OK)	$29,000 (OK)	$29,000 (OK)	$29,000 (OK)
Ending inventory	13,000 (↑)	13,000 (↑)	12,000 (OK)	12,000 (OK)
Cost of goods sold	$16,000 (↓)	$16,000 (↓)	$17,000 (OK)	$17,000 (OK)
Gross margin	$16,000 (↓)	$18,000 (↑)	$15,000 (↓)	$17,000 (OK)

*For the amount, ↓ indicates it is too low, ↑ means it is too high, and OK means it is correct.

To reduce the possibility of these types of inventory cutoff errors, most businesses close their warehouses at year-end while they count inventory. If they are retailers, they will probably count inventory after hours. During the inventory counting period, businesses do not accept or ship merchandise, nor do they enter purchase or sales transactions in their accounting records.

As explained, an error in inventory results in cost of goods sold being overstated or understated. This error has the opposite effect on gross margin and, hence, on net income. For example, if at the end of the accounting period $2,000 of inventory is not counted, cost of goods sold will be $2,000 higher than it should be, and gross margin and net income will be understated by $2,000. Such inventory errors affect gross margin and net income not only in the current year but in the following year as well. A recording delay resulting in an understatement of purchases in one year, for example, results in an overstatement in the next year.

To illustrate how inventory errors affect gross margin and net income, let us first assume the following correct data for Salina Corporation:

		2008		2009
Sales revenue		$50,000		$40,000
Cost of goods sold:				
Beginning inventory	$10,000		$ 5,000	
Net purchases	20,000		25,000	
Cost of goods available for sale	$30,000		$30,000	
Ending inventory	5,000		10,000	
Cost of goods sold		25,000		20,000
Gross margin		$25,000		$20,000
Operating expenses		10,000		10,000
Net income		$15,000		$10,000

Now suppose that ending inventory in 2008 was overstated; that is, instead of the correct amount of $5,000, the count erroneously showed $7,000 of inventory on hand. The following analysis shows the effect of the error on net income in both 2008 and 2009:

		2008		2009
Sales revenue		$50,000		$40,000
Cost of goods sold:				
Beginning inventory	$10,000		$ 7,000 (↑)	
Net purchases	20,000		25,000	
Cost of goods available for sale	$30,000		$32,000 (↑)	
Ending inventory	7,000 (↑)*		10,000	
Cost of goods sold		23,000 (↓)		22,000 (↑)
Gross margin		$27,000 (↑)		$18,000 (↓)
Operating expenses		10,000		10,000
Net income		$17,000 (↑)		$ 8,000 (↓)

*For the amount, ↑ means it is too high, ↓ means it is too low.

When the amount of ending inventory is overstated (as it was in 2008), both gross margin and net income are overstated by the same amount ($2,000 in 2008). If the ending inventory amount had been understated, net income and gross margin would also have been understated, again by the same amount.

Since the ending inventory in 2008 becomes the beginning inventory in 2009, the net income and gross margin for 2009 are also misstated. In 2009, however, beginning inventory is overstated, so gross margin and net income are understated, again by $2,000.

Thus, the errors in the two years offset or counterbalance each other, and if the count taken at the end of 2009 is correct, income in subsequent years will not be affected by this error.

> **REMEMBER THIS...**
>
> - A misstatement of an ending inventory balance affects net income, both in the current year and in the next year.
> - Errors in beginning and ending inventory have the opposite effect on cost of goods sold, gross margin, and net income.
> - Errors in inventory correct themselves after two years if the physical count at the end of the second year shows the correct amount of ending inventory for that period.

Complications of the Perpetual Method with LIFO and Average Cost

Describe the complications that arise when LIFO or average cost is used with a perpetual inventory system.

(7) In the Nephi Company bicycle example used earlier in the chapter, the simplifying assumption was made that all 28 bicycles were sold at the end of the month. In essence, this is the assumption made when a periodic inventory system is used—goods are assumed to be sold at the end of the period because the exact time when particular goods are sold is not recorded. Computation of average cost and LIFO under a perpetual system is complicated because the average cost of units available for sale changes every time a purchase is made, and the identification of the "last in" units also changes with every purchase.

These perpetual system complications are illustrated below using the same Nephi Company example used earlier, but now assuming that sales occurred at different times during the month.

Sept.	1	Beginning inventory consisted of 10 bicycles costing $200 each.
	3	Purchased 8 bicycles costing $250 each.
	5	Sold 12 bicycles, $400 each.
	18	Purchased 16 bicycles costing $300 each.
	20	Purchased 10 bicycles costing $320 each.
	25	Sold 16 bicycles, $400 each.

When a perpetual system is used and sales occur during the period, the identification of the "last in" units must be evaluated at the time of each individual sale, as follows:

September 5 sale of 12 bicycles, identification of "last in" units:		
8 bicycles purchased on September 3, $250 each	$2,000	
4 bicycles in beginning inventory, $200 each	800	$2,800
September 25 sale of 16 bicycles, identification of "last in" units:		
10 bicycles purchased on September 20, $320 each	$3,200	
6 bicycles purchased on September 18, $300 each	1,800	5,000
Total perpetual LIFO cost of goods sold		$7,800

This $7,800 amount for LIFO cost of goods sold under a perpetual inventory system compares to the $8,500 LIFO cost of goods sold computed earlier in the chapter assuming a periodic inventory system. Again, the difference arises because the "last in" units are identified at the end of the period with a periodic system; with a perpetual system, the "last in" units are identified at the time of each individual sale.

A similar difference arises with the average cost method because, with a perpetual system, a new average cost per unit must be determined at the time each individual sale is made. This process is illustrated as follows:

September 5 sale of 12 bicycles, determination of average cost:

10 bicycles in beginning inventory, $200 each	$2,000	
8 bicycles purchased on September 3, $250 each	2,000	
Total cost of goods available for sale on September 5		$4,000

Average cost on September 5: $4,000 ÷ 18 bicycles = $222.22 per bicycle
September 5 cost of goods sold:
    12 bicycles × $222.22 per bicycle = $2,667 (rounded)

September 25 sale of 16 bicycles, determination of average cost:

6 (18 − 12) bicycles; remaining cost ($4,000 − $2,667)	$1,333	
16 bicycles purchased on September 18, $300 each	4,800	
10 bicycles purchased on September 20, $320 each	3,200	
Total cost of goods available for sale on September 25		$9,333

Average cost on September 25: $9,333 ÷ 32 bicycles = $291.66 per bicycle
September 25 cost of goods sold:
    16 bicycles × $291.66 per bicycle = $4,667 (rounded)

Total cost of goods sold: $2,667 + $4,667 = $7,334

This $7,334 cost of goods sold under the perpetual average method compares with $7,636 cost of goods sold under the periodic average method. Again, the difference is that one overall average cost for all goods available for sale during the period is used with a periodic system; with a perpetual system, a new average cost is computed at the time of each sale.

By the way, no complications arise in using FIFO with a perpetual system. This is because, no matter when sales occur, the "first in" units are always the same ones. So, FIFO periodic and FIFO perpetual yield the same numbers for cost of goods sold and ending inventory.

Because of the complications associated with computing perpetual LIFO and perpetual average cost, many businesses that use average cost or LIFO for financial reporting purposes use a simple FIFO assumption in maintaining their day-to-day perpetual inventory records. The perpetual FIFO records are then converted to periodic average cost or LIFO for the financial reports.

REMEMBER THIS...

- Using the average cost and LIFO inventory cost flow assumptions with a perpetual inventory system leads to some complications.
- These complications arise because the identity of the "last in" units changes with each new inventory purchase, as does the average cost of units purchased up to that point.

Reporting Inventory at Amounts below Cost

Apply the lower-of-cost-or-market method of accounting for inventory.

(8) All the inventory costing alternatives we have discussed in this chapter have one thing in common: they report inventory at cost. Occasionally, however, it becomes necessary to report inventory at an amount that is less than cost. This happens when the future value of the inventory is in doubt—when it is damaged, used, or obsolete, or when it can be replaced new at a price that is less than its original cost.

Inventory Valued at Net Realizable Value

net realizable value

The selling price of an item less reasonable selling costs.

When inventory is damaged, used, or obsolete, it should be reported at no more than its **net realizable value**. This is the amount the inventory can be sold for, minus any selling costs. Suppose, for example, that an automobile dealer has a demonstrator car that originally cost $18,000 and now can be sold for only $16,000. The car should be reported at its net realizable value. If a commission of $500 must be paid to sell the car, the net realizable value is $15,500, or $2,500 less than cost. This loss is calculated as follows:

Cost		$18,000
Estimated selling price	$16,000	
Less selling commission	500	15,500
Loss		$ 2,500

To achieve a proper matching of revenues and expenses, a company must recognize this estimated loss as soon as it is determined that an economic loss has occurred (even before the car is sold). The journal entry required to recognize the loss and reduce the inventory amount of the car is:

Loss on Write-Down of Inventory (Expense)	2,500	
Inventory		2,500
To write down inventory to its net realizable value.		

By writing down inventory to its net realizable value, a company recognizes a loss when it happens and shows no profit or loss when the inventory is finally sold. Using net realizable values means that assets are not being reported at amounts that exceed their future economic benefits.

Inventory Valued at Lower of Cost or Market

lower-of-cost-or-market (LCM) rule

A basis for valuing inventory at the lower of original cost or current market value.

ceiling

The maximum market amount at which inventory can be carried on the books; equal to net realizable value.

Inventory must also be written down to an amount below cost if it can be replaced new at a price that is less than its original cost. In the electronics industry, for instance, the costs of computers and compact disc players have fallen dramatically in recent years. When goods remaining in ending inventory can be replaced with identical goods at a lower cost, the lower unit cost must be used in valuing the inventory (provided that the replacement cost is not higher than net realizable value or lower than net realizable value minus a normal profit). This is known as the **lower-of-cost-or-market (LCM) rule**. (In a sense, a more precise name would be the lower-of-actual-or-replacement-cost rule.)

The **ceiling**, or maximum market amount at which inventory can be carried on the books, is equivalent to net realizable value, which is the selling price less

floor

The minimum market amount at which inventory can be carried on the books; equal to net realizable value minus a normal profit.

estimated selling costs. The ceiling is imposed because it makes no sense to value an inventory item above the amount that can be realized upon sale. For example, assume that a company purchased an inventory item for $10 and expected to sell it for $14. If the selling costs of the item amounted to $3, the ceiling or net realizable value would be $11 ($14 − $3).

The **floor** is defined as the net realizable value minus a normal profit. Thus, if the inventory item costing $10 had a normal profit margin of 20%, or $2, the floor would be $9 (net realizable value of $11 less normal profit of $2). This is the lowest amount at which inventory should be carried in order to prevent showing losses in one period and large profits in subsequent periods.

In applying this LCM rule, you can follow certain basic guidelines:

1. Define market value as:
   a. replacement cost, if it falls between the ceiling and the floor.
   b. the floor, if the replacement cost is less than the floor.
   c. the ceiling, if the replacement cost is higher than the ceiling.
      (As a practical matter, when replacement cost, ceiling, and floor are compared, market is always the middle value.)
2. Compare the defined market value with the original cost and choose the lower amount.

The following chart gives four separate examples of the application of the LCM rule; the resulting LCM amount is highlighted in each case.

| | | | | Market | |
| | | | | Net Realizable Value (Ceiling) | Net Realizable Value Minus Normal Profit (Floor) |
Item	Number of Items in Inventory	Original Cost (LIFO FIFO, etc.)	Replacement Cost		
A	10	$17	$16	$15	$10
B	8	21	18	23	16
C	30	26	21	31	22
D	20	19	16	34	25

The LCM rule can be applied in one of three ways: (1) by computing cost and market figures for each item in inventory and using the lower of the two amounts in each case, (2) by computing cost and market figures for the total inventory and then applying the LCM rule to that total, or (3) by applying the LCM rule to categories of inventory. For a clothing store, categories of inventory might be all shirts, all pants, all suits, or all dresses.

To illustrate, we will use the above data to show how the LCM rule would be applied to each inventory item separately and to total inventory. (The third method is similar to the second, except that it may involve several totals, one for each category of inventory.)

Item	Number of Items in Inventory	Original Cost	Market Value	LCM for Individual Items
A	10	$17 × 10 units = $ 170	$15 × 10 units = $ 150	$ 150
B	8	$21 × 8 units = 168	$18 × 8 units = 144	144
C	30	$26 × 30 units = 780	$22 × 30 units = 660	660
D	20	$19 × 20 units = 380	$25 × 20 units = 500	380
		$1,498	$1,454	$1,334

$44

$164

Using the first method, applying the LCM rule to individual items, inventory is valued at $1,334, a write-down of $164 from the original cost. With the second method, using total inventory, the lower of total cost ($1,498) or total market value ($1,454) is used for a write-down of $44. The write-down is smaller when total inventory is used because the increase in market value of $120 in item D offsets decreases in items A, B, and C. In practice, each of the three methods is acceptable, but once a method has been selected, it should be followed consistently.

The journal entry to write down the inventory to the lower of cost or market applying the LCM rule to individual items is:

Loss on Write-Down of Inventory (Expense)	164	
Inventory		164
To write down inventory to lower of cost or market.		

The amount of this entry would have been $44 if the LCM rule had been applied to total inventory.

The LCM rule has gained wide acceptance because it reports inventory on the balance sheet at amounts that are consistent with future economic benefits. With this method, losses are recognized when they occur, not necessarily when a sale is made.

REMEMBER THIS...

- The recorded amount of inventory should be written down (1) when it is damaged, used, or obsolete and (2) when it can be replaced (purchased new) at an amount that is less than its original cost.
- In the first case, inventory is reported at its net realizable value, an amount that allows a company to break even when the inventory is sold.
- In the second case, inventory is written down to the lower of cost or market.
- When using the lower-of-cost-or-market rule, market is defined as falling between the ceiling and floor.
- Ceiling is defined as the net realizable value; floor is net realizable value minus a normal profit margin.
- In no case should inventory be reported at an amount that exceeds the ceiling or is less than the floor.
- These reporting alternatives are attempts to show assets at amounts that reflect realistic future economic benefits.

Method of Estimating Inventories

Explain the gross margin method of estimating inventories.

9 We have assumed that the number of inventory units on hand is known by a physical count that takes place at the end of each accounting period. For the periodic inventory method, this physical count is the only way to determine how much inventory is on hand at the end of a period. For the perpetual inventory method, the physical count verifies the quantity on hand or indicates the amount of inventory shrinkage or theft. There are times, however, when a company needs to know the dollar amount of ending inventory, but a physical count is either impossible or impractical. For example, many firms prepare quarterly, or even monthly, financial statements, but it is too expensive and time-consuming to count the inventory at the end of each period. In such cases, if the perpetual inventory method is being used, the balance in the inventory account is usually assumed to be

gross margin method

A procedure for estimating the amount of ending inventory; the historical relationship of cost of goods sold to sales revenue is used in computing ending inventory.

correct. With the periodic inventory method, however, some estimate of the inventory balance must be made. A common method of estimating the dollar amount of ending inventory is the gross margin method.

The Gross Margin Method

With the **gross margin method**, a firm uses available information about the dollar amounts of beginning inventory and purchases, and the historical gross margin percentage to estimate the dollar amounts of cost of goods sold and ending inventory. To illustrate, we will assume the following data for Payson Brick Company:

Net sales revenue, January 1 to March 31	$100,000
Inventory balance, January 1	15,000
Net purchases, January 1 to March 31	65,000
Gross margin percentage (historically determined percentage of net sales)	40%

With this information, the dollar amount of inventory on hand on March 31 is estimated as follows:

		Dollars	Percentage of Sales
Net sales revenue		$100,000	100%
Cost of goods sold:			
Beginning inventory	$15,000		
Net purchases	65,000		
Total cost of goods available for sale	$80,000		
Ending inventory ($80,000 − $60,000)	20,000 (3)*		
Cost of goods sold ($100,000 − $40,000)		60,000 (2)*	60%
Gross margin ($100,000 × 0.40)		$ 40,000 (1)*	40%

*The numbers indicate the order of calculation.

In this example, gross margin is first determined by calculating 40% of sales (step 1). Next, cost of goods sold is found by subtracting gross margin from sales (step 2). Finally, the dollar amount of ending inventory is obtained by subtracting cost of goods sold from total cost of goods available for sale (step 3). Obviously, the gross margin method of estimating cost of goods sold and ending inventory assumes that the historical gross margin percentage is appropriate for the current period. This assumption is a realistic one in many fields of business. In cases where the gross margin percentage has changed, this method should be used with caution.

The gross margin method of estimating ending inventories is also useful when a fire or other calamity destroys a company's inventory. In these cases, the dollar amount of inventory lost must be determined before insurance claims can be made. The dollar amounts of sales, purchases, and beginning inventory can be obtained from prior years' financial statements and from customers, suppliers, and other sources. Then the gross margin method can be used to estimate the dollar amount of inventory lost.

REMEMBER THIS...

- The gross margin method is a common technique for estimating the dollar amount of inventory.
- The historical gross margin percentage is used in conjunction with sales to estimate cost of goods sold.
- This estimated cost of goods sold amount is subtracted from cost of goods available for sale to yield an estimate of ending inventory.

REVIEW OF LEARNING OBJECTIVES

(1) Identify what items and costs should be included in inventory and cost of goods sold.

- Inventory:
  - is composed of goods held for sale in the normal course of business,
  - includes all costs incurred in producing and getting it ready to sell,
  - includes raw materials, work in process, and finished goods in a manufacturing company, and
  - should be recorded on the books of the company holding legal title.

(2) Account for inventory purchases and sales using both a perpetual and a periodic inventory system.

- With a perpetual inventory system, the amount of inventory and cost of goods sold for the period are tracked on an ongoing basis.
- With a periodic inventory system, inventory and cost of goods sold are computed using an end-of-period inventory count.

(3) Calculate cost of goods sold using the results of an inventory count and understand the impact of errors in ending inventory on reported cost of goods sold.

- If a perpetual system is used, an inventory count can be used to compute the amount of inventory shrinkage during the period.
- An error in the reported ending inventory amount can have a significant effect on reported cost of goods sold, gross margin, and net income. For example, overstatement of ending inventory results in understatement of cost of goods sold and overstatement of net income.

(4) Apply the four inventory cost flow alternatives: specific identification, FIFO, LIFO, and average cost.

Specific Identification	No assumptions made; costs of specific units included in ending inventory and in cost of goods sold.
FIFO	Assume that the oldest inventory units are sold and that the newest remain in ending inventory.
LIFO	Assume that the newest inventory units are sold and that the oldest remain in ending inventory.
Average Cost	Assign a common average cost per unit to all units, both in cost of goods sold and in ending inventory.

(5) Use financial ratios to evaluate a company's inventory level.

- Proper inventory management seeks a balance between keeping a lower inventory level to avoid tying up excess resources and maintaining a sufficient inventory balance to ensure smooth business operation.
- Companies assess how well their inventory is being managed by using two ratios: (1) inventory turnover and (2) number of days' sales in inventory.
- Comparison of the average collection period, number of days' sales in inventory, and number of days' purchases in accounts payable reveals how much of a company's operating cycle it must finance through external financing.

(6) Analyze the impact of inventory errors on reported cost of goods sold.

- A misstatement of an ending inventory balance affects net income, both in the current year and in the next year.
- Errors in beginning and ending inventory have the opposite effect on cost of goods sold, gross margin, and net income.
- Errors in inventory correct themselves after two years if the physical count at the end of the second year shows the correct amount of ending inventory for that period.

(7) Describe the complications that arise when LIFO or average cost is used with a perpetual inventory system.

- When LIFO is used with a perpetual inventory system, the identification of the "newest unit" changes every time a purchase is made. Accordingly, identification of the units sold must be done sale by sale, using the specific timing of sales and purchases.
- When the average cost assumption is made with a perpetual inventory system, the "average cost" changes every time a purchase is made.

(8) Apply the lower-of-cost-or-market method of accounting for inventory.

- When using the lower-of-cost-or-market rule, market is defined as falling between the ceiling and floor.
- Ceiling is defined as the net realizable value; floor is net realizable value minus a normal profit margin.
- In no case should inventory be reported at an amount that exceeds the ceiling or is less than the floor.

(9) Explain the gross margin method of estimating inventories.

- The historical gross margin percentage can be used in conjunction with sales to estimate cost of goods sold.
- This estimated cost of goods sold amount is subtracted from cost of goods available for sale to yield an estimate of ending inventory.

KEY TERMS & CONCEPTS

average cost, 298
consignment, 287
cost of goods available for sale, 288
cost of goods sold, 286
FIFO (first in, first out), 298
finished goods, 286
FOB (free-on-board) destination, 287
FOB (free-on-board) shipping point, 287

inventory, 286
inventory shrinkage, 296
inventory turnover, 303
LIFO (last in, first out), 298
manufacturing overhead, 287
net purchases, 294
number of days' purchases in accounts payable, 305

number of days' sales in inventory, 303
periodic inventory system, 290
perpetual inventory system, 289
raw materials, 286
specific identification, 298
work in process, 286

EXPANDED *material*

ceiling, 311
floor, 312
gross margin method, 314
lower-of-cost-or-market (LCM) rule, 311
net realizable value, 311

Inventory Cost Flow Alternatives

Lehi Wholesale Distributors buys printers from manufacturers and sells them to office supply stores. During January 2009, its periodic inventory records showed the following:

Jan. 1   Beginning inventory consisted of 26 printers at $200 each.
     10   Purchased 10 printers at $220 each.
     15   Purchased 20 printers at $250 each.
     28   Purchased 9 printers at $270 each.
     31   Sold 37 printers.

Required:

Calculate ending inventory and cost of goods sold, using:

1. FIFO inventory.
2. LIFO inventory.
3. Average cost.

Solution

When computing ending inventory and cost of goods sold, it is usually easiest to get an overview first. The following calculations are helpful:

Beginning inventory, 26 units at $200 each	$ 5,200
Purchases: 10 units at $220	$ 2,200
20 units at $250	5,000
9 units at $270	2,430
Total purchases (39 units)	$ 9,630
Cost of goods available for sale (65 units)	$14,830
Less ending inventory (28 units)	?
Cost of goods sold (37 units)	?

Given a beginning inventory, only ending inventory and cost of goods sold will vary with the different inventory costing alternatives. Because ending inventory and cost of goods sold are complementary numbers whose sum must equal total goods available for sale, you can calculate only one of the two missing numbers in each case and then compute the other by subtracting the first number from goods available for sale. Thus, in the calculations that follow, we will always calculate ending inventory first.

1. FIFO Inventory

Since we know that 28 units are left in ending inventory, we look for the last 28 units purchased because the first units purchased would all be sold. The last 28 units purchased were:

9 units at $270 each on January 28 =	$2,430
19 units at $250 each on January 15 =	4,750
Ending inventory	$7,180

Ending inventory is $7,180, and cost of goods sold is $7,650 ($14,830 – $7,180).

(continued)

2. LIFO Inventory

The first 28 units available would be considered the ending inventory (since the last ones purchased are the first ones sold). The first 28 units available were:

Beginning inventory: 26 units at $200 = $5,200
January 10 purchase: 2 units at $220 =   440
    Ending inventory $5,640

Thus,

Cost of goods available for sale $14,830
Ending inventory   5,640
Cost of goods sold . . . . $ 9,190

3. Average Cost

The total cost of goods available for sale is divided by total units available for sale to get a weighted average cost:

$$\frac{\text{Cost of Goods Available for Sale}}{\text{Units Available for Sale}} = \frac{\$14,830}{65} = \$228.15 \text{ per Unit}$$

Cost of goods available for sale $14,830
Less ending inventory (28 units at $228.15)   6,388
Cost of goods sold (37 units at $228.15) . . . . $ 8,442

Note: With the average cost alternative, the computed amounts may vary slightly due to rounding.

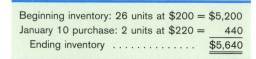
EXPANDED
material

Perpetual Inventory Cost Flow Alternatives

Using the above example, we assume Lehi Wholesale Distributors buys printers from manufacturers and sells them to office supply stores. During January 2009, its inventory records showed the following:

Jan. 1   Beginning inventory consisted of 26 printers at $200 each.
     10   Purchased 10 printers at $220 each.
     12   Sold 15 printers.
     15   Purchased 20 printers at $250 each.
     17   Sold 14 printers.
     19   Sold 8 printers.
     28   Purchased 9 printers at $270 each.

Required:

Calculate ending inventory and cost of goods sold, using:
  1. Perpetual FIFO inventory.
  2. Perpetual LIFO inventory.
  3. Perpetual average cost.

(continued)

Solution

When computing ending inventory and cost of goods sold, it is usually easiest to get an overview first. The following calculations are helpful:

Beginning inventory, 26 units at $200 each	$ 5,200
Purchases: 10 units at $220	$ 2,200
20 units at $250	5,000
9 units at $270	2,430
Total purchases (39 units)	$ 9,630
Cost of goods available for sale (65 units)	$14,830
Less ending inventory (28 units)	?
Cost of goods sold (37 units)	?

Given a beginning inventory, only ending inventory and cost of goods sold will vary with the different inventory costing alternatives. Because ending inventory and cost of goods sold are complementary numbers whose sum must equal total goods available for sale, you can calculate only one of the two missing numbers in each case, and then compute the other by subtracting the first number from goods available for sale. Thus, in the calculations that follow, we will always calculate ending inventory first.

1. Perpetual FIFO Inventory

With this alternative, records must be maintained throughout the period, as shown. The final calculation is:

Cost of goods available for sale	$14,830
Ending inventory [(19 × $250) + (9 × $270)]	7,180
Cost of goods sold	$ 7,650

PERPETUAL FIFO CALCULATIONS

	Purchased			Sold			Remaining		
Date	**Number of Units**	**Unit Cost**	**Total Cost**	**Number of Units**	**Unit Cost**	**Total Cost**	**Number of Units**	**Unit Cost**	**Total Cost**
Beginning inventory							26	$200	$5,200
January 10	10	$220	$2,200				36	26 at $200	$7,400
								10 at $220	
12				15	15 at $200	$3,000	21	11 at $200	$4,400
								10 at $220	
15	20	$250	5,000				41	11 at $200	$9,400
								10 at $220	
								20 at $250	
17				14	11 at $200	2,860	27	7 at $220	$6,540
					3 at $220			20 at $250	
19				8	7 at $220	1,790	19	19 at $250	$4,750
					1 at $250				
28	9	$270	2,430	—		—	28	19 at $250	$7,180
								9 at $270	
Totals	39		$9,630	37		$7,650			

(continued)

2. Perpetual LIFO Inventory

With this alternative, as shown below, the calculation is:

Cost of goods available for sale	$14,830
Ending inventory	6,230
Cost of goods sold	$ 8,600

PERPETUAL LIFO CALCULATIONS

	Purchased			Sold			Remaining		
Date	Number of Units	Unit Cost	Total Cost	Number of Units	Unit Cost	Total Cost	Number of Units	Unit Cost	Total Cost
Beginning inventory							26	$200	$5,200
January 10	10	$220	$2,200				36	26 at $200	$7,400
								10 at $220	
12				15	10 at $220	$3,200	21	21 at $200	$4,200
					5 at $200				
15	20	$250	5,000				41	21 at $200	$9,200
								20 at $250	
17				14	14 at $250	3,500	27	21 at $200	$5,700
								6 at $250	
19				8	6 at $250	1,900	19	19 at $200	$3,800
					2 at $200				
28	9	$270	2,430	—			28	19 at $200	$6,230
								9 at $270	
Totals	39		$9,630	37		$8,600			

3. Perpetual Average Cost

With this alternative, a new average cost of inventory items must be calculated each time a purchase is made, as shown in the following table:

Cost of goods available for sale	$14,830
Ending inventory	6,748
Cost of goods sold	$ 8,082

PERPETUAL AVERAGE COST CALCULATIONS

	Purchased	Sold	Remaining	Computations
Beginning inventory			26 units at $200.00 = $5,200	
January 10	10 units at $220 = $2,200		36 units at $205.56 = $7,400	$5,200 + $2,200 = $7,400; $7,400 ÷ 36 = $205.56
12		15 units at $205.56 = $3,083	21 units at $205.56 = $4,317	
15	20 units at $250 = $5,000		41 units at $227.24 = $9,317	$4,317 + $5,000 = $9,317; $9,317 ÷ 41 = $227.24
17		14 units at $227.24 = $3,181	27 units at $227.24 = $6,135	
19		8 units at $227.24 = $1,818	19 units at $227.24 = $4,318	
28	9 units at $270 = $2,430		28 units at $241.00 = $6,748	$4,318 + $2,430 = $6,748; $6,748 ÷ 28 = $241.00

DISCUSSION QUESTIONS

1. In wholesale and retail companies, inventory is composed of the items that have been purchased for resale. What types of inventory does a manufacturing firm have?
2. What comprises the cost of inventory?
3. Why is it more difficult to account for the inventory of a manufacturing firm than for that of a merchandising firm?
4. Who owns merchandise during shipment under the terms FOB shipping point?
5. When is the cost of inventory transferred from an asset to an expense?
6. Which inventory method (perpetual or periodic) provides better control over a firm's inventory?
7. Is the accounting for purchase discounts and purchase returns the same with the perpetual and the periodic inventory methods? If not, what are the differences?
8. Are the costs of transporting inventory into and out of a firm treated the same way? If not, what are the differences?
9. Why is it usually important to take advantage of purchase discounts?
10. Why are the closing entries for inventory under a periodic system more complicated than those for a perpetual system?
11. Why is it necessary to physically count inventory when the perpetual inventory method is being used?
12. What adjusting entries to Inventory are required when the perpetual inventory method is used?
13. What is the effect on net income when goods held on consignment are included in the ending inventory balance?

14. Explain the difference between cost flow and the movement of goods.
15. Which inventory cost flow alternative results in paying the least amount of taxes when prices are rising?
16. Would a firm ever be prohibited from using one inventory costing alternative for tax purposes and another for financial reporting purposes?
17. Why is it necessary to know which inventory cost flow alternative is being used before the financial performances of different firms can be compared?
18. What can the inventory turnover ratio tell us?

EXPANDED *material*

19. Is net income under- or overstated when purchased merchandise is counted and included in the inventory balance but not recorded as a purchase?
20. Is net income under- or overstated if inventory is sold and shipped but not recorded as a sale?
21. Why do the LIFO and average cost inventory cost flow assumptions result in different inventory numbers for the perpetual and periodic inventory methods?
22. When should inventory be valued at its net realizable value?
23. When should inventory be valued at the lower of cost or market?
24. When firms cannot count their inventory, how do they determine how much inventory is on hand for the financial statements?

PRACTICE EXERCISES

PE 7-1
LO1
Inventory Identification
Which one of the following is *not* an example of inventory?
a. Cranes at a construction site
b. Books on the shelves of a bookstore
c. Apples in a supermarket
d. Screws to be used in assembling tables at a carpentry shop
e. Computer software for sale at a computer store

PE 7-2
LO1
Costs Included in Inventory
Which one of the following costs is *not* included in inventory?
a. Salaries paid to assembly workers
b. Direct materials used in assembly
c. Salary paid to the company president
d. Rent paid for use of the company factory
e. Salary paid to the factory supervisor

PE 7-3 **Goods in Transit**

LO1 Collin Wholesale sold $2,500 inventory to Jennifer Company on December 27, year 1, with shipping terms of FOB destination. The inventory arrived on January 2, year 2. Which company owns the inventory at year-end (December 31, year 1)?

PE 7-4 **Computing Cost of Goods Sold**

LO1 Using the following data, compute cost of goods sold.

Inventory, December 31	$ 51,000
Inventory, January 1	63,000
Cash, December 31	19,000
Purchases during the year	287,000
Sales during the year	505,000

PE 7-5 **Perpetual and Periodic Inventory Systems**

LO2 For each of the following businesses, indicate whether the business would be more likely to use a perpetual or a periodic inventory system.

a. Automobile dealer   d. Large appliance retailer

b. Summer snow-cone stand   e. Newsstand

c. Supermarket   f. Discount clothing retailer

PE 7-6 **Inventory Purchases**

LO2 The company purchased (on account) 180 tables to be resold to customers. The cost of each table was $200. Make the journal entry to record this transaction under (1) a perpetual inventory system and (2) a periodic inventory system.

PE 7-7 **Transportation Costs**

LO2 The company incurred $830 in shipping costs related to the inventory purchases in PE 7-6. The company paid for the shipping costs in cash. Make the journal entry necessary to record this transaction under (1) a perpetual inventory system and (2) a periodic inventory system.

PE 7-8 **Purchase Returns**

LO2 The company returned 15 of the tables purchased in PE 7-6 because of defects in assembly. Make the journal entry necessary to record this return under (1) a perpetual inventory system and (2) a periodic inventory system.

PE 7-9 **Purchase Discounts**

LO2 The company paid for the tables purchased in PE 7-6 (less the tables returned in PE 7-8). Because the company paid within 10 days, it received a 2% discount on the purchase. Make the journal entry necessary to record this transaction under (1) a perpetual inventory system and (2) a periodic inventory system.

PE 7-10 **Sales**

LO2 The company sold 70 tables on account for $240 each. Make the journal entry or entries necessary to record this transaction under (1) a perpetual inventory system and (2) a periodic inventory system. Don't forget the impact of the 2% discount described in PE 7-9 and the transportation costs mentioned in PE 7-7.

PE 7-11 **Sales Returns**

LO2 A dissatisfied customer returned six of the tables that were sold in PE 7-10. Make the journal entry or entries necessary to record this transaction under (1) a perpetual inventory system and (2) a periodic inventory system.

PE 7-12 **Closing Inventory Entries for a Periodic System**

LO3 Refer to the data in PE 7-6 through PE 7-11. Assume the beginning balance in the inventory account was $0 for the periodic inventory system. A physical count of the inventory at the

(continued)

end of the period shows the ending balance of inventory is $19,970. Prepare the necessary entries for a periodic inventory system (1) to close the temporary accounts to the inventory account and (2) to adjust the inventory account to the appropriate ending balance.

PE 7-13   **Inventory Shrinkage**

LO3   The company's perpetual inventory records show that the ending inventory balance should be $182,000. However, a physical count of the inventory reveals the true ending balance of inventory to be $178,500. Prepare the journal entry necessary to record inventory shrinkage for the period.

PE 7-14   **Computing Cost of Goods Sold with a Periodic System**

LO3   The company uses a periodic inventory system. Beginning inventory was $6,000. Net purchases (including freight in, purchase returns, and purchase discounts) were $23,000. The physical count of inventory at the end of the year revealed ending inventory to be $7,500. Compute cost of goods sold.

PE 7-15   **Errors in Ending Inventory**

LO3   The company uses a periodic inventory system and overstated its ending inventory by $20,000. How will this inventory error affect reported net income for the company?

PE 7-16   **Specific Identification Inventory Cost Flow**

LO4   The company reports the following activity during October related to its inventory of cameras:

Oct. 1   Beginning inventory consisted of 8 cameras costing $100 each.
      3   Purchased 12 cameras costing $110 each.
     14   Purchased 7 cameras costing $115 each.
     20   Purchased 15 cameras costing $125 each.
     29   Sold 26 cameras for $150 each.

The 26 cameras sold on October 29 consisted of the following: 4 cameras from the beginning inventory, 5 cameras purchased on October 3, 3 cameras purchased on October 14, and 14 cameras purchased on October 20. Determine (1) the cost of goods sold for the month and (2) the ending inventory balance for October 31 using the specific identification cost flow assumption.

PE 7-17   **FIFO Cost Flow Assumption**

LO4   Refer to the data in PE 7-16. Determine (1) the cost of goods sold for the month and (2) the ending inventory balance for October 31 using the FIFO cost flow assumption.

PE 7-18   **LIFO Cost Flow Assumption**

LO4   Refer to the data in PE 7-16. Determine (1) the cost of goods sold for the month and (2) the ending inventory balance for October 31 using the LIFO cost flow assumption.

PE 7-19   **Average Cost Flow Assumption**

LO4   Refer to the data in PE 7-16. Determine (1) the cost of goods sold for the month and (2) the ending inventory balance for October 31 using the average cost flow assumption. Round unit costs to the nearest tenth of a cent.

PE 7-20   **Inventory Turnover**

LO5   Using the following data, compute inventory turnover.

Inventory, December 31, year 1	$ 82,000
Cost of goods sold	342,000
Sales	694,000
Inventory, January 1, year 1	74,000

PE 7-21   **Number of Days' Sales in Inventory**

LO5   Refer to the data in PE 7-20. Compute number of days' sales in inventory.

PE 7-22   **Number of Days' Purchases in Accounts Payable**

LO5   Using the following data, compute number of days' purchases in accounts payable.

Accounts payable, December 31, year 1	$ 52,000
Cost of goods sold	358,000
Accounts payable, January 1, year 1	46,000
Purchases	364,000

PE 7-23   **Inventory Errors–Multiple Years**

LO6   At the beginning of year 1, the company's inventory level was stated correctly. At the end of year 1, inventory was *understated* by $2,000. At the end of year 2, inventory was *overstated* by $450. Reported net income was $3,000 in year 1 and $3,000 in year 2. Compute the correct amount of net income in year 1.

PE 7-24   **Inventory Errors–Multiple Years**

LO6   Refer to PE 7-23. Compute the correct amount of net income in year 2.

PE 7-25   **LIFO and a Perpetual Inventory System**

LO7   The company reported the following inventory data for the year:

	Units	Cost per Unit
Beginning inventory	300	$17.50
Purchases:		
July 15	900	18.00
October 11	1,200	18.25
Units remaining at year-end: 300		

Sales occurred as follows:

	Units Sold
January 16	200
July 23	600
November 1	1,300
Total	2,100

Compute (1) cost of goods sold and (2) ending inventory making a LIFO cost flow assumption. The company uses a *perpetual* inventory system.

PE 7-26   **Average Cost and a Perpetual Inventory System**

LO7   Refer to PE 7-25. Compute (1) cost of goods sold and (2) ending inventory making an average cost assumption. The company uses a perpetual inventory system.

PE 7-27 **Lower of Cost or Market**

LO8 The following information pertains to the company's ending inventory:

	Original Cost	Net Realizable Value	Replacement Cost	Normal Profit
Item A	$ 720	$ 740	$ 710	$ 80
Item B	390	400	310	70
Item C	1,250	1,300	1,230	250

Apply lower-of-cost-or-market accounting to each inventory item individually. What total amount should be reported as inventory in the balance sheet?

PE 7-28 **Recording an Inventory Write-Down**

LO9 The company started business at the beginning of year 1. The company applies the lower-of-cost-or-market (LCM) rule to its inventory as a whole. Inventory cost and market value as of the end of year 1 were as follows:

	Cost	Market Value
Year 1	$1,200	$900

The market value number already includes consideration of the replacement cost, the ceiling, and the floor. Make the journal entry necessary to record the LCM adjustment at the end of year 1.

PE 7-29 **Estimating Inventory**

LO9 On August 17, the company's inventory was destroyed in a hurricane-related flood. For insurance purposes, the company must reliably estimate the amount of inventory on hand on August 17. The company uses a periodic inventory system. The following data have been assembled:

Inventory, January 1	$1,650,000
Purchases, January 1–August 17	4,130,000
Sales, January 1–August 17	6,500,000
Historical gross profit percentages:	
Last year	60%
Two years ago	65%

Estimate the company's inventory as of August 17 using (1) last year's gross profit percentage and (2) the gross profit percentage from two years ago.

EXERCISES

E 7-30 **Goods on Consignment**

LO1 Company A has consignment arrangements with Supplier B and with Customer C. In particular, Supplier B ships some of its goods to Company A on consignment, and Company A ships some of its goods to Customer C on consignment. At the end of 2009, Company A's accounting records showed:

Goods on consignment from Supplier B	$ 8,000
Goods on consignment with Customer C	10,000

(continued)

1. If a physical count of inventory reveals that $30,000 of goods are on hand, what amount of ending inventory should be reported?
2. If the amount of the beginning inventory for the year was $27,000 and purchases during the year were $59,000, then what is the cost of goods sold for the year? (Assume the ending inventory from question 1.)
3. If, instead of these facts, Company A had only $4,000 of goods on consignment with Customer C, but had $10,000 of consigned goods from Supplier B, and physical goods on hand totaled $36,000, what would the correct amount of the ending inventory be?
4. With respect to question 3, if beginning inventory totaled $24,000 and the cost of goods sold was $47,500, what were the purchases?

E 7-31   **Recording Sales Transactions–Perpetual Inventory Method**

LO2   On June 24, 2009, Reed Company sold merchandise to Emily Clark for $95,000 with terms 2/10, n/30. On June 30, Clark paid $44,100, receiving the cash discount on her payment, and returned $15,000 of merchandise, claiming that it did not meet contract terms.

Assuming that Reed uses the perpetual inventory method, record the necessary journal entries on June 24 and June 30. The cost of merchandise to Reed Company is 60% of its selling price.

E 7-32   **Perpetual Inventory Method**

LO2   Orser Furniture purchases and sells dining room furniture. Its management uses the perpetual method of inventory accounting. Journalize the following transactions that occurred during October 2009:

Oct.   2   Purchased on account $27,000 of inventory with payment terms 2/10, n/30, and paid $650 in cash to have it shipped from the vendor's warehouse to the Orser showroom.
         5   Sold inventory costing $4,900 for $8,250 on account.
        10   Paid $13,950 of accounts payable (from October 2 purchase) and received the cash discount.
        14   Returned two damaged tables purchased on October 2 (costing $550 each) to the vendor.
        19   Received payment of $4,560 from customers.
        20   Paid the balance of the account from October 2 purchase.
        22   Sold inventory costing $3,800 for $5,200 on account.
        24   A customer returned a dining room set that she decided didn't match her home. She paid $3,250 for it, and its cost to Orser was $1,800.

Assuming the balance in the inventory account is $12,000 on October 1, and no other transactions relating to inventory occurred during the month, what is the inventory balance at the end of October?

E 7-33   **Recording Sales Transactions–Periodic Inventory Method**

LO2   On June 24, 2009, Mowen Company sold merchandise to Jack Simpson for $80,000 with terms 2/10, n/30. On June 30, Simpson paid $39,200, receiving the cash discount on his payment, and returned $16,000 of merchandise, claiming that it did not meet contract terms.

Assuming that Mowen Company uses the periodic inventory method, record the necessary journal entries on June 24 and June 30.

E 7-34   **Cost of Goods Sold Calculations**

LO2   Complete the Cost of Goods Sold section for the income statements of the following five companies:

	Able Company	Baker Company	Carter Company	Delmont Company	Eureka Company
Beginning inventory	$16,000	$24,800	_____	_____	$19,200
Purchases	26,500	_____	$43,000	$89,500	_____
Purchase returns	_____	1,000	1,800	200	2,200
Cost of goods available for sale	42,100	_____	58,300	_____	81,500
Ending inventory	_____	22,200	15,200	28,800	_____
Cost of goods sold	33,400	67,200	_____	93,400	68,400

E 7-35   **Journalizing Inventory Transactions**

LO2   Shannon Parts uses the periodic method of inventory accounting.

1. Journalize the following transactions relating to the company's purchases in 2009:

   Jan. 24   Purchased $18,000 of inventory on credit, terms 2/10, n/30.

   30   Paid $17,640 to pay off the debt from the January 24 purchase.

   Mar. 14   Purchased $140,000 of inventory on credit, terms 2/10, n/30. Paid $1,150 in cash for transportation.

   Apr. 1   Returned defective machinery worth $25,000 from the March 14 purchase to manufacturer.

   13   Paid $115,000 to pay off the debt from the March 14 purchase.

2. Assuming these were the only purchases in 2009, compute the cost of goods sold. Beginning inventory was $23,400 and ending inventory was $26,250.

E 7-36   **Adjusting Inventory (Perpetual Method)**

LO3   Deer Company's perpetual inventory records show an inventory balance of $120,000. Deer Company's records also show cost of goods sold totaling $240,000. A physical count of inventory on December 31, 2009, showed $92,000 of ending inventory.

Adjust the inventory records assuming that the perpetual inventory method is used.

E 7-37   **Adjusting Inventory and Closing Entries (Periodic Method)**

LO3   As of December 31, 2009, Whitney Company had the following account balances:

Inventory (beginning)	$140,000
Purchases	230,000
Purchase returns	6,000

A physical count of inventory on December 31, 2009, showed $104,000 of ending inventory. Prepare the closing entries that are needed to adjust the inventory records and close the related purchases accounts, assuming that the periodic inventory method is used.

E 7-38   **Cost of Goods Sold Calculation**

LO3   The accounts of Berrett Company have the following balances for 2009:

Purchases	$520,000
Inventory, January 1, 2009	80,000
Purchase returns	15,280
Purchase discounts	1,760
Freight in	24,800
Freight out (selling expense)	4,800
Cash	8,000

The inventory count on December 31, 2009, is $96,000. Using the information given, compute the cost of goods sold for Berrett Company for 2009.

E 7-39   **Adjusting Inventory Records for Physical Counts**

LO3   Cleopatra, Inc., which uses the perpetual inventory method, recently had an agency count its inventory of frozen burritos. The agency left the following inventory sheet:

Type of Merchandise	Date Purchased	Quantity on Hand	Unit Cost	Inventory Amount
Chicken Burrito	2/12/09	50	$2.50	(a)
Beef Burrito	2/18/09	19	(b)	$60.80
Bean Burrito	2/08/09	(c)	$2.10	$65.10
Veggie Burrito	2/15/09	43	(d)	$81.70

Complete the inventory calculations for Cleopatra (items a–d) and provide the journal entry necessary to adjust ending inventory, if necessary. The balance in Inventory before the physical count was $321.10.

E 7-40   **Specific Identification Method**

LO4   E's Diamond Shop is computing its inventory and cost of goods sold for November 2009. At the beginning of the month, these items were in stock:

	Quantity	Cost	Total
Ring A	8	$600	$ 4,800
Ring A	10	650	6,500
Ring B	5	300	1,500
Ring B	6	350	2,100
Ring B	3	450	1,350
Ring C	7	200	1,400
Ring C	8	250	2,000
			$19,650

During the month, the shop purchased four type A rings at $600, two type B rings at $450, and five type C rings at $300 and made the following sales:

Ring Type	Quantity Sold	Price	Cost
A	2	$1,000	$600
A	3	1,050	600
A	1	1,200	650
B	2	850	450
B	2	800	350
C	4	450	200
C	3	500	250
C	1	550	250

Because of the high cost per item, E's uses specific identification inventory costing.
1. Calculate the cost of goods sold and ending inventory balances for November.
2. Calculate the gross margin for the month.

E 7-41   **Inventory Costing Methods**

LO4   For each of the descriptions listed below, identify the inventory costing method to which it applies. The costing methods are: average cost, LIFO, and FIFO.
1. The value of ending inventory does not include the cost of the most recently acquired goods.
2. In a period of rising prices, cost of goods sold is highest.
3. In a period of rising prices, ending inventory is highest.
4. Ending inventory is between the levels of the other two methods.
5. The balance of the inventory account may be unrealistic because inventory on hand is valued at old prices.

E 7-42
LO4

FIFO and LIFO Inventory Costing

Jefferson's Jewelry Store is computing its inventory and cost of goods sold for November 2009. At the beginning of the month, the following jewelry items were in stock (rings were purchased in the order listed):

	Quantity	Cost	Total
Ring A	8	$600	$ 4,800
Ring A	10	650	6,500
Ring B	5	300	1,500
Ring B	6	350	2,100
Ring B	3	450	1,350
Ring C	7	200	1,400
Ring C	8	250	2,000
			$19,650

During the month, the following rings were purchased: four type A rings at $600, two type B rings at $450, and five type C rings at $300. Also during the month, these sales were made:

Ring Type	Quantity Sold	Price
A	2	$1,000
A	3	1,050
A	1	1,200
B	2	850
B	2	800
C	4	450
C	3	500
C	1	550

Jefferson's uses the periodic inventory method. Calculate the cost of goods sold and ending inventory balances for November using FIFO and LIFO.

E 7-43
LO4

FIFO, LIFO, and Average Cost Calculations (Periodic Inventory Method)

The following transactions took place with respect to Model B computers in Jackson's Computer Store during November 2009:

Nov. 1	Beginning inventory	60 computers at $1,350
5	Purchase of Model B computers	14 computers at $1,400
11	Purchase of Model B computers	12 computers at $1,500
24	Purchase of Model B computers	18 computers at $1,750
30	Sale of Model B computers	40 computers at $2,700

Assuming the periodic inventory method, compute cost of goods sold and ending inventory using the following inventory costing alternatives: (a) FIFO, (b) LIFO, and (c) average cost.

E 7-44
LO5

Inventory Ratios

The following data are available for 2009, regarding the inventory of two companies:

	Atkins Computers	Burbank Electronics
Beginning inventory	$ 40,000	$ 80,000
Ending inventory	48,000	95,000
Cost of goods sold	690,000	910,000

Compute inventory turnover and number of days' sales in inventory for both companies. Which company is handling its inventory more efficiently?

E 7-45 **Analysis of the Operating Cycle**

LO5 The following information was taken from the records of Dallen Company for the year 2010:

Sales	$600,000
Beginning inventory	$114,000
Ending inventory	$87,000
Beginning accounts receivable	$68,000
Average collection period	44 days
Beginning accounts payable	$36,000
Ending accounts payable	$42,000
Gross profit percentage	37%

1. Compute the number of days' sales in inventory.
2. Compute the ending balance in Accounts Receivable.
3. Compute the number of days' purchases in accounts payable.
4. How many days elapse, on average, between the time Dallen must pay its suppliers for inventory purchases and the time Dallen collects cash from its customers for the sale of that same purchased inventory?
5. Repeat the computations in (1), (2), (3), and (4) using the end-of-year balance sheet balances rather than the average balances.

E 7-46 **Inventory Errors**

LO6 As the accountant for Synergy Solutions, you are in the process of preparing the income statement for the year ended December 31, 2009. In doing so, you have noticed that merchandise costing $3,500 was sold for $5,000 on December 31.

Before the effects of the $5,000 sale were taken into account, the relevant income statement figures were:

Sales revenue	$95,000
Beginning inventory	21,000
Purchases	38,000
Ending inventory	19,000

1. Prepare a partial income statement through gross margin under each of the following three assumptions:
   a. The sale is recorded in the 2009 accounting record; the inventory is included in the ending physical inventory count.
   b. The sale is recorded in 2009; the inventory is not included in ending inventory.
   c. The sale is not recorded in the 2009 accounting records; the merchandise is not included in the ending inventory count.
2. Under the given circumstances, which of the three assumptions is correct?
3. Which assumption overstates gross margin (and therefore net income)?

E 7-47 **FIFO, LIFO, and Average Cost Calculations (Perpetual Inventory Method)**

LO7 The July 2009 inventory records of Mario's Bookstore showed the following:

July	1	Beginning inventory	28,000 at $2.00 = $56,000
	5	Sold	4,000
	13	Purchased	6,000 at $2.25 = 13,500
	17	Sold	3,000
	25	Purchased	8,000 at $2.50 = 20,000
	27	Sold	5,000
			$89,500

(continued)

1. Using the perpetual inventory method, compute the ending inventory and cost of goods sold balances with (a) FIFO, (b) LIFO, and (c) average cost. Compute unit costs to the nearest cent.
2. Which of the three alternatives is best? Why?

E 7-48
LO8

Lower of Cost or Market

Prepare the necessary journal entries to account for the purchases and year-end adjustments of the inventory of Payson Manufacturing Company. All purchases are made on account. Payson uses the periodic inventory method.

1. Purchased 50 standard widgets for $8 each to sell at $14 per unit.
2. Purchased 15 deluxe widgets at $20 each to sell for $30 per unit.
3. At the end of the year, the standard widgets could be purchased for $9 and are selling for $15.
4. At the end of the year, the deluxe widgets could be purchased for $10 and are selling for $16 per unit. Selling costs are $4 per unit, and normal profit is $6 per unit. Inventory is 15 units.
5. At the end of the second year, standard widgets could be purchased for $6 and are selling for $8. Selling costs are $1 per widget, and normal profit is $2 per widget. Inventory is 50 units.
6. At the end of the second year, the deluxe widgets could be purchased for $9 and are selling for $20. Selling costs and normal profit remain as in (4). Inventory is 15 units.

E 7-49
LO8

Lower of Cost or Market

Duncan Company sells lumber. Inventory cost data per 1,000 board feet of lumber for Duncan Company are as follows:

Item	Plywood	Maple	Pine	Redwood
Quantity on hand	21	23	38	16
Original cost	$450	$1,900	$700	$1,600
Current replacement cost	400	1,700	550	1,650
Net realizable value	350	1,850	650	1,700
Net realizable value minus normal profit	250	1,600	600	1,500

1. By what amount, if any, should each item (considered separately) be written down?
2. Make the appropriate journal entry (or entries):
   a. Assuming that each inventory item is considered separately.
   b. Assuming that LCM is applied to total inventory.

E 7-50
LO9

Gross Margin Method of Estimating Inventory

Jason Company needs to estimate the inventory balance for its quarterly financial statements. The periodic inventory method is used. Records show that quarterly sales totaled $400,000, beginning inventory was $80,000, and net purchases totaled $280,000; the historical gross margin percentage has averaged approximately 40%.

1. What is the approximate amount of ending inventory?
2. If a physical count shows only $100,000 in inventory, what could be the explanation for the difference?

E 7-51
LO9

Estimating Inventory Amounts

Erin's Boutique was recently destroyed by fire. For insurance purposes, she must determine the value of the destroyed inventory. She knows the following information about her 2009 operations before the fire occurred:

Beginning inventory	$ 5,750
Net purchases	58,000
Sales	91,300
Profit margin	35%

Estimate the cost of Erin's destroyed inventory.

E 7-52   **Estimating Inventory**

LO9   Ted Smyth manages an electronics store. He suspects that some employees are stealing items from inventory. Determine the cost of the missing inventory. The following information is available from the accounting records:

Beginning inventory	$ 300,000
Sales	2,000,000
Net purchases	1,600,000
Actual ending inventory	450,000
Historical profit margin	30%

PROBLEMS

P 7-53   **What Should Be Included in Inventory?**

LO1   Howard is trying to compute the inventory balance for the December 31, 2008, financial statements of his automotive parts shop. He has computed a tentative balance of $61,800 but suspects that several adjustments still need to be made. In particular, he believes that the following could affect his inventory balance:

a. A shipment of goods that cost $2,000 was received on December 28, 2008. It was properly recorded as a purchase in 2008 but not counted with the ending inventory.

b. Another shipment of goods (FOB destination) was received on January 2, 2009, and cost $1,200. It was properly recorded as a purchase in 2009 but was counted with 2008's ending inventory.

c. A $3,400 shipment of goods to a customer on January 3 was recorded as a sale in 2009 but was not included in the December 31, 2008, ending inventory balance. The goods cost $2,300.

d. The company had goods costing $8,000 on consignment with a customer, and $6,000 of merchandise was on consignment from a vendor. Neither amount was included in the $61,800 figure.

e. The following amounts represent merchandise that was in transit on December 31, 2008, and recorded as purchases and sales in 2008 but not included in the December 31 inventory.

1. Ordered by Howard, $2,600, FOB destination.
2. Ordered by Howard, $900, FOB shipping point.
3. Sold by Howard, cost $3,400, FOB shipping point.
4. Sold by Howard, cost $5,100, FOB destination.

Required:

1. Determine the correct amount of ending inventory at December 31, 2008.
2. Assuming net purchases (before any adjustment, if any) totaled $79,200 and beginning inventory (January 1, 2008) totaled $38,700, determine the cost of goods sold in 2008.

P 7-54   **Perpetual and Periodic Journal Entries**

LO2   The following transactions for Goodmonth Tire Company occurred during the month of March 2009:

a. Purchased 500 automobile tires on account at a cost of $40 each for a total of $20,000.

b. Purchased 300 truck tires on account at a cost of $80 each for a total of $24,000.

c. Returned 12 automobile tires to the supplier because they were defective.

d. Paid for the automobile tires.

e. Paid for half the truck tires.

(continued)

f.   Paid the remaining balance owed on the truck tires.

g.   Sold on account 400 automobile tires at a price of $90 each for a total of $36,000.

h.   Sold on account 200 truck tires at a price of $150 each for a total of $30,000.

i.   Accepted return of 7 automobile tires from dissatisfied customers.

Required:

1.   Prepare journal entries to account for the above transactions assuming a periodic inventory system.

2.   Prepare journal entries to account for the above transactions assuming a perpetual inventory system.

3.   Assume that inventory levels at the beginning of March (before these transactions) were 100 automobile tires that cost $40 each and 70 truck tires that cost $80 each. Also, assume that a physical count of inventory at the end of March revealed that 184 automobile tires and 164 truck tires were on hand. Given these inventory amounts, prepare the closing entries to account for inventory and related accounts as of the end of March.

P 7-55

LO2

Income Statement Calculations

Stout Company has gross sales of 250% of cost of goods sold. It has also provided the following information for the calendar year 2009:

Inventory balance, January 1, 2009	$ 22,000
Total cost of goods available for sale	84,000
Sales returns	4,200
Purchase returns	2,000
Freight in	800
Sales (net of returns)	169,800
Operating expenses	7,500

Using the available information, compute the following. (Ignore income taxes.)

Required:

1.   Gross sales for 2009.

2.   Net purchases and gross purchases for 2009.

3.   Cost of goods sold for 2009.

4.   Inventory balance at December 31, 2009.

5.   Gross margin for 2009.

6.   Net income for 2009.

P 7-56

LO2

Income Statement Calculations

	Company A	Company B	Company C	Company D
Sales revenue	$2,000	(4) _____	$480	$1,310
Beginning inventory	200	76	0	600
Purchases	(1) _____	423	480	249
Purchase returns	(20)	(19)	(0)	(8) _____
Ending inventory	300	110	(6) _____	195
Cost of goods sold	1,200	370	(7) _____	(9) _____
Gross margin	(2) _____	(5) _____	155	(10) _____
Operating expenses	108	22	34	129
Net income	(3) _____	107	121	546

Required:

Complete the income statement calculations by filling in all missing numbers.

P 7-57

LO4

Inventory Cost Flow Alternatives

Stocks, Inc., sells weight-lifting equipment. The sales and inventory records of the company for January through March 2009 were as follows:

	Weight Sets	Unit Cost	Total Cost
Beginning inventory, Jan. 1	460	$30	$13,800
Purchase, Jan. 16	110	32	3,520
Sale, Jan. 25 ($45 per set)	216		
Purchase, Feb. 16	105	36	3,780
Sale, Feb. 27 ($40 per set)	307		
Purchase, March 10	150	28	4,200
Sale, March 30 ($50 per set)	190		

Required:

1. Determine the amounts for ending inventory, cost of goods sold, and gross margin under the following costing alternatives. Use the periodic inventory method, which means that all sales are assumed to occur at the end of the period no matter when they actually occurred. Round amounts to the nearest dollar.

   a. FIFO

   b. LIFO

   c. Average cost

2. **Interpretive Question:** Which alternative results in the highest gross margin? Why?

P 7-58

LO4

Periodic Inventory Cost Flow Method

Fresh Wholesale buys peaches from farmers and sells them to canneries. During May 2009, Fresh's inventory records showed the following:

			Cases	Price
May	1	Beginning inventory	5,100	$10.50
	4	Purchase	1,210	12.00
	9	Sale	1,020	19.65
	13	Purchase	1,050	12.50
	19	Sale	1,750	19.65
	26	Purchase	2,120	13.00
	30	Sale	2,340	19.65

Fresh Wholesale uses the periodic inventory method to account for its inventory, which means that all sales are assumed to occur at the end of the period no matter when they actually occurred.

Required:

Calculate the cost of goods sold and ending inventory using the following cost flow alternatives. (Calculate unit costs to the nearest cent.)

1. FIFO

2. LIFO

3. Average cost

P 7-59

LO5

Calculating and Interpreting Inventory Ratios

Captain Geech Boating Company sells fishing boats to fishermen. Its beginning and ending inventories for 2009 are $462 million and $653 million, respectively. It had cost of goods sold of $1,578 million for the year ended December 31, 2009. Merchant Marine Company also sells fishing boats. Its beginning and ending inventories for the year 2009 are $120 million and $90 million, respectively. It had cost of goods sold of $1,100 million for the year ended December 31, 2009.

(continued)

Required:

1. Calculate the inventory turnover and number of days' sales in inventory for the two companies.
2. **Interpretive Question:** Are the results of these ratios what you expected? Which company is managing its inventory more efficiently?

P 7-60

LO6

The Effect of Inventory Errors

The accountant for Steele Company reported the following accounting treatments for several purchase transactions (FOB shipping point) that took place near December 31, 2009, the company's year-end:

Date Inventory Was Shipped	Was the Purchase Recorded in the Books on or before December 31, 2009?	Amount	Was the Inventory Counted and Included in Inventory Balance on December 31, 2009?
2009:			
December 26	Yes	$1,100	Yes
December 29	Yes	800	No
December 31	No	1,800	Yes
2010:			
January 1	No	300	Yes
January 1	Yes	3,000	No
January 1	No	600	No

Required:

1. If Steele Company's records reported purchases and ending inventory balances of $80,800 and $29,800, respectively, for 2009, what would the proper amounts in these accounts have been?
2. What would be the correct amount of cost of goods sold for 2009, if the beginning inventory balance on January 1, 2009, was $20,200?
3. By how much would cost of goods sold be over- or understated if the corrections in question (1) were not made?

P 7-61

LO6

Correction of Inventory Errors

The annual reported income for Salazar Company for the years 2006–2009 is shown here. However, a review of the inventory records reveals inventory misstatements.

	2006	2007	2008	2009
Reported net income	$30,000	$40,000	$35,000	$45,000
Inventory overstatement, end of year		3,000		2,000
Inventory understatement, end of year	4,000		1,000	

Required:

Using the data provided, calculate the correct net income for each year.

P 7-62

LO6

The Effect of Inventory Errors

You have been hired as the accountant for Christman Company, which uses the periodic inventory method. In reviewing the firm's records, you have noted what you think are several accounting errors made during the current year, 2009. These potential mistakes are listed as follows:

a. A $51,000 purchase of merchandise was properly recorded in the purchases account, but the related accounts payable account was credited for only $4,000.   *(continued)*

b. A $4,400 shipment of merchandise received just before the end of the year was properly recorded in the purchases account but was not physically counted in the inventory and, hence, was excluded from the ending inventory balance.

c. A $5,600 purchase of merchandise was erroneously recorded as a $6,500 purchase.

d. A $1,200 purchase of merchandise was not recorded either as a purchase or as an account payable.

e. During the year, $3,100 of defective merchandise was sent back to a supplier. The original purchase had been recorded, but the merchandise return entry was not recorded.

f. During the physical inventory count, inventory that cost $800 was counted twice.

Required:

1. If the previous accountant had tentatively computed the 2009 gross margin to be $25,000, what would be the correct gross margin for the year?

2. If these mistakes are not corrected, by how much will the 2010 net income be in error?

P 7-63   **Unifying Concepts: Inventory Cost Flow Alternatives**

LO7   Stan's Wholesale buys canned tomatoes from canneries and sells them to retail markets. During August 2009, Stan's inventory records showed the following:

			Cases	Price
Aug.	1	Beginning inventory	4,100	$10.50
	4	Purchase	1,500	11.00
	9	Sale	950	19.95
	13	Purchase	1,000	11.00
	19	Sale	1,450	19.95
	26	Purchase	1,700	11.50
	30	Sale	1,900	19.95

Even though it requires more computational effort, Stan's uses the perpetual inventory method because management feels that the advantage of always having current knowledge of inventory levels justifies the extra cost.

Required:

Calculate the cost of goods sold and ending inventory using the following cost flow alternatives. (Calculate unit costs to the nearest cent.)

1. FIFO
2. LIFO
3. Average cost

P 7-64   **Perpetual Inventory Cost Flow Alternatives**

LO7   Pump-It, Inc., sells weight-lifting equipment. The sales and inventory records of the company for January through March 2009 were as follows:

	Weight Sets	Unit Cost	Total Cost
Beginning inventory, Jan. 1	460	$30	$13,800
Purchase, Jan. 16	110	32	3,520
Sale, Jan. 25 ($45 per set)	216		
Purchase, Feb. 16	105	36	3,780
Sale, Feb. 27 ($40 per set)	307		
Purchase, March 10	150	28	4,200
Sale, March 30 ($50 per set)	190		

(continued)

Required:

1. Determine the amounts for ending inventory, cost of goods sold, and gross margin under the following costing alternatives. Use the perpetual inventory method. Round amounts to the nearest dollar.
   a. FIFO
   b. LIFO
   c. Average cost (calculate unit costs to the nearest cent)
2. **Interpretive Question:** Which alternative results in the highest gross margin? Why?

P 7-65
LO9

Unifying Concepts: Inventory Estimation Method

McCarlie Clothing Store has the following information available:

	Cost	Selling Price	Other
Purchases during March 2009	$215,000	$400,000	
Inventory balance, March 1, 2009	60,000	95,000	
Sales during March		510,000	
Average gross margin rate for the last three years			52%

Required:

1. On the basis of this information, estimate the cost of inventory on hand at March 31, 2009, using the gross margin method. Round to the nearest whole percent.
2. How accurate do you think this method is?

ANALYTICAL ASSIGNMENTS

AA 7-66
DISCUSSION

Why Use a Perpetual System?

You are a consultant for the ABC Consulting Company. You have been hired by Eddie's Electronics, a company that owns 25 electronics stores selling radios, televisions, compact disc players, stereos, and other electronic equipment. Since the company began business 10 years ago, it has been using a periodic inventory system. However, Mark Eddie just returned from a seminar where some of his competitors told him he should be using the perpetual inventory method. Mr. Eddie is not sure he should believe his competitors. He wants you to advise him about his inventory choices and make a recommendation about the inventory method he should use.

AA 7-67
DISCUSSION

Should We Reduce Inventory?

It has now been two years since you advised Mr. Eddie to switch to the perpetual inventory method. He is very happy with the additional information he has about inventory levels and theft. He has hired you for advice once again. This time, Mr. Eddie has been to an inventory management seminar where he heard that most companies have too much money tied up in inventory. He wonders if his company could be much more profitable if it reduced its inventory levels. What would you tell him?

AA 7-68
JUDGMENT CALL

You Decide: Should inventory be recorded at cost or fair market value?

You recently ran into Bill Autograph, a friend from high school who has been really busy getting his sports collectible/memorabilia business off the ground. When he heard you were an accountant, he became very interested and wanted you to clarify something. One concept he seemed particularly confused about was the fact that when inventory is purchased, it is recorded on the books at cost but the books are not adjusted for subsequent increases in the value of the inventory. This concept is of particular importance to Bill because he often buys collectibles that will increase in value depending on how successful a particular player or team becomes. Can he record increases in the value of his sports memorabilia inventory?

AA 7-69
REAL COMPANY ANALYSIS

Wal-Mart

Using **Wal-Mart**'s 2006 Form 10-K in Appendix A, answer the following questions:
1. What type of items compose Wal-Mart's inventory?
2. Review Wal-Mart's balance sheet to determine the amount of inventory on hand on January 31, 2006.
3. What inventory method does Wal-Mart use?

AA 7-70
REAL COMPANY ANALYSIS

General Electric

Selected financial statement information relating to inventories for **General Electric (GE)** is given below.

December 31 (in millions)	2005	2004
Cost of goods sold	$46,169	$42,645
Inventory–FIFO valuation	11,171	10,439
Inventory–LIFO valuation	10,474	9,778

1. Compute GE's number of days' sales in inventory for 2005 using (a) the FIFO valuation for inventory and (b) the LIFO valuation for inventory. Are the differences significant enough to concern you?
2. Suppose that GE purchases its inventory with the terms "net 30 days." That is, GE's creditors expect payment in 30 days. Is GE going to have a cash flow problem?

AA 7-71
REAL COMPANY ANALYSIS

La-Z-Boy and McDonald's

The following information is taken from the 2005 financial statements of **La-Z-Boy, Inc.**, maker of recliners and other home furnishings, and the 2005 financial statements of **McDonald's**, maker of the Big Mac® and other fast foods.

	La-Z-Boy	McDonald's
Cost of goods sold	$1,583.14*	$14,136.00*
Beginning inventory	250.57	147.50
Ending inventory	260.56	147.00

*Amounts in millions.

1. Before you do any computations, forecast which of the two companies will have a lower number of days' sales in inventory.
2. Compute each company's number of days' sales in inventory. Was your forecast in (1) correct?
3. How can these two very successful companies have number of days' sales in inventory that are so different?

AA 7-72
INTERNATIONAL

Why No LIFO?

The LIFO method of accounting for inventory is primarily a U.S. invention. Many countries around the world will not allow LIFO to be used, and other countries discourage its use. For example, the International Accounting Standards Board calls LIFO an undesirable but "allowable" method. In the United Kingdom, LIFO is allowable under corporate law but is unacceptable under professional accounting standards.

Why do you think other countries have such an unfavorable opinion of LIFO? Think about these issues: In periods of rising prices, does the amount shown on the balance sheet relating to inventory reflect current cost? If a company's inventory on the balance sheet reflected costs from years past, what would happen to the income statement if those inventory costs were suddenly moved to Cost of Goods Sold? Would the result reflect a firm's actual performance?

AA 7-73
ETHICS

Shipping Bricks

In 1989 the U.S. Department of Justice Criminal Division discovered a massive inventory fraud that was being conducted by managers at **Miniscribe Corporation.** MiniScribe manufactured and sold computer disk drives. The fraud included placing bricks in disk drive boxes, shipping those boxes to customers, and recording a sale when the box was shipped. MiniScribe managers also knowingly shipped defective drives and recorded sales even though they knew those drives would be returned.

What would be the effect on the income statement and the balance sheet of shipping bricks and recording those shipments as sales? (*Hint:* Think about the journal entry that would have been made by MiniScribe accountants when a box of bricks was shipped to customers who were expecting disk drives.) Would company officials be able to fool financial statement users for a long time using this type of deception? What could financial statement users have looked for to detect this type of fraud?

AA 7-74
WRITING

Estimating Inventory

Jon Johnson, an accountant with a local CPA firm, has just completed an inventory count for Mom & Pop's Groceries. Mom and Pop provide audited financial statements to their bank annually, and part of that audit requires an inventory count. Don Squire, a partner with the CPA firm, has also conducted an analysis to estimate this period's ending inventory. Don used the gross margin method, a method whereby the prior period's gross margin percentage is used to infer this period's percentage, to estimate ending inventory. In addition, the store is equipped with cash registers that scan each product as it is sold and, as a result, provide a perpetual inventory record.

These three inventory analysis methods have resulted in three very different answers, which are summarized in the following table:

Method	Inventory Value
Inventory count	$ 98,500
Gross margin analysis	119,750
Point-of-sale scanners	111,500

In evaluating the results, Jon and Don are curious as to why the three methods result in such large differences. Since the inventory count reports actual inventory on hand, they begin to wonder if Mom and Pop have an inventory theft problem. Write a short memo explaining why the other two methods, gross margin analysis and point-of-sale scanners, can result in significantly different answers without there being a theft problem.

AA 7-75
CUMULATIVE SPREADSHEET PROJECT

Preparing New Forecasts

This spreadsheet assignment is a continuation of the spreadsheet assignments given in earlier chapters. If you completed those spreadsheets, you have a head start on this one. If needed, review the spreadsheet assignment for Chapter 4 to refresh your memory on how to construct forecasted financial statements.

1. Handyman wishes to prepare a forecasted balance sheet and income statement for 2010. Use the original financial statement numbers for 2009 [given in part (1) of the Cumulative Spreadsheet Project assignment in Chapter 2] as the basis for the forecast, along with the following additional information:
   a. Sales in 2010 are expected to increase by 40% over 2009 sales of $700.
   b. Cash will increase at the same rate as sales.
   c. The forecasted amount of accounts receivable in 2010 is determined using the forecasted value for the average collection period. For simplicity, do the computations using the end-of-period accounts receivable balance instead of the average balance. The average collection period for 2010 is expected to be 14.08 days.
   d. In 2010, Handyman expects to acquire new property, plant, and equipment costing $80.

(continued)

   e. The $160 in operating expenses reported in 2009 breaks down as follows: $5 depreciation expense, $155 other operating expenses.

   f. No new long-term debt will be acquired in 2010.

   g. No cash dividends will be paid in 2010.

   h. New short-term loans payable will be acquired in an amount sufficient to make Handyman's current ratio in 2010 exactly equal to 2.0.

Note: These statements were constructed as part of the spreadsheet assignment in Chapter 6; you can use that spreadsheet as a starting point if you have completed that assignment. *Clearly state any additional assumptions that you make.*

For this exercise, add the following additional assumptions:

   i. The forecasted amount of inventory in 2010 is determined using the forecasted value for the number of days' sales in inventory (computed using the end-of-period inventory balance). The number of days' sales in inventory for 2010 is expected to be 107.6 days.

   ii. The forecasted amount of accounts payable in 2010 is determined using the forecasted value for the number of days' purchases in accounts payable (computed using the end-of-period accounts payable balance). The number of days' purchases in accounts payable for 2010 is expected to be 48.34 days.

2. Repeat (1), with the following changes in assumptions:

   a. Number of days' sales in inventory is expected to be 66.2 days.

   b. Number of days' sales in inventory is expected to be 150.0 days.

3. Comment on the differences in the forecasted values of cash from operating activities in 2010 under each of the following assumptions about the number of days' sales in inventory: 107.6 days, 66.2 days, and 150.0 days.

4. Is there any impact on the forecasted level of accounts payable when the number of days' sales in inventory is changed? Why or why not?

5. What happens to the forecasted level of short-term loans payable when the number of days' sales in inventory is reduced to 66.2 days? Explain.

Completing the Operating Cycle

After studying this chapter, you should be able to:

LEARNING OBJECTIVES

1 **Account for the various components of employee compensation expense.** *In addition to wages and salaries, companies also compensate their employees through bonuses, stock options, pensions, and other benefits. Computing total compensation expense involves a significant element of estimation and assumption.*

2 **Compute income tax expense, including appropriate consideration of deferred tax items.** *Reported income tax expense reflects all of the tax implications of transactions and events occurring during the year. Because financial accounting rules and income tax rules are not the same, income tax expense this year sometimes reflects items that will not actually impact the legal computation of income taxes until future years.*

3 **Distinguish between contingent items that should be recognized in the financial statements and those that should be merely disclosed in the financial statement notes.** *A contingent item is an uncertain circumstance involving a potential gain or loss that will not be resolved until some future event occurs. Contingent losses are recognized when they* are probable and estimable; they are not recognized but are only disclosed when they are just possible.

4 **Understand when an expenditure should be recorded as an asset and when it should be recorded as an expense.** *Conceptually, a cost should be recorded as an asset whenever it has a probable future economic benefit. In practice, it is frequently quite difficult to tell when a cost should be recorded as an asset (capitalized) and when it should be recorded as an expense.*

5 **Prepare an income statement summarizing operating activities as well as other revenues and expenses, extraordinary items, and earnings per share.** *Because the items in the income statement are carefully arranged and sequenced, emphasis is placed on the portion of income that is generated by the ongoing core operations of the business.*

Before 1850, the primary use for petroleum was as a medicine. Known variously as Seneca oil, American oil, and rock oil, a mixture of water and petroleum was reportedly good for rheumatism, chronic cough, ague, toothache, corns, neuralgia, urinary disorders, indigestion, and liver ailments.

Gradually, additional properties of oil were discovered. It was found that oil could serve as a lubricant for the machinery that was becoming more common as the Industrial Revolution progressed. In addition, distilled oil was found to burn well in the household lamps that had traditionally burned vegetable oil or sperm whale oil. As the demand for petroleum increased, the search for oil began in earnest. In late August 1859, oil was struck in northwestern Pennsylvania at a depth of 69½ feet, creating an oil well that yielded 25 barrels per day. This discovery touched off an oil rush in western Pennsylvania, and the opportunities to get rich were soon fanned by the increased demand for lubricating oil associated with the North's war production during the Civil War.

In those early days, Cleveland, Ohio, was the center of oil refining, and one of the earliest players in the refining business was John D. Rockefeller. Rockefeller had started his business career in Cleveland as a bookkeeper(!) in 1855. By saving his earnings, he acquired some investment capital, and, with a partner, he put up $4,000 to begin a refinery in Cleveland in 1862. Rockefeller subsequently created an empire of oil companies located in various states. These companies were eventually consolidated into a holding company called the **Standard Oil Company of New Jersey**.

F Y I

John D. Rockefeller used some of his Standard Oil profits to found the University of Chicago in 1891.

In the early 1890s, the spirit of reform spread over the United States. Many people felt that Big Business was too powerful and must be reined in by the federal government. In 1911, the U.S. Supreme Court mandated the breakup of the Standard Oil Company into 34 smaller companies. Many of those companies are still very well known, as evidenced by the partial list contained in Exhibit 1.

The largest piece of the dismembered Standard Oil Trust was the Standard Oil Company of New Jersey, which changed its named to **Exxon** in 1972. Exxon now

F Y I

The oil boom did not hit Texas until 1901 when a well on Spindletop Hill, south of Beaumont, Texas, began to gush 100,000 barrels of oil a day.

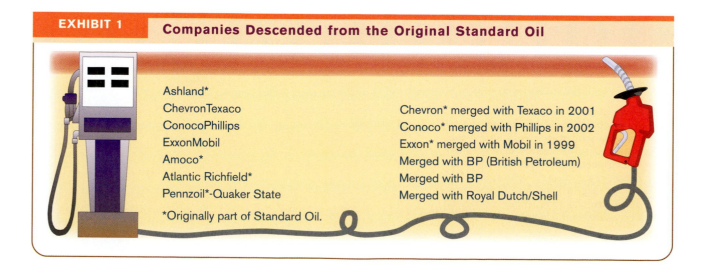

EXHIBIT 1   **Companies Descended from the Original Standard Oil**

Ashland*	
ChevronTexaco	Chevron* merged with Texaco in 2001
ConocoPhillips	Conoco* merged with Phillips in 2002
ExxonMobil	Exxon* merged with Mobil in 1999
Amoco*	Merged with BP (British Petroleum)
Atlantic Richfield*	Merged with BP
Pennzoil*-Quaker State	Merged with Royal Dutch/Shell

*Originally part of Standard Oil.

F Y I

The federal antitrust case against **Microsoft** was compared to the Standard Oil case of 1911, with Bill Gates playing the role of a modern-day Rockefeller.

operates in over 100 countries, exploring for oil, producing petrochemical products, and transporting oil and natural gas. In many places, the company is known as **Esso**, representing the initials "SO" for Standard Oil. On December 1, 1998, Exxon (the former Standard Oil Company of New Jersey) announced an agreement to merge with **Mobil** (the former **Standard Oil Company of New York**), thus reuniting these two pieces of the vast empire built by John D. Rockefeller. The formal joining of the two companies was completed on November 30, 1999, creating **ExxonMobil**.[1] To illustrate the size of ExxonMobil's operations, the company had worldwide proven oil reserves of 11.2 billion barrels and proven natural gas reserves of 66.9 trillion cubic feet as of December 31, 2005.

In Chapters 6 and 7, we discussed the accounting for sales and the cost of inventory sold. For firms that sell a product, the cost of the inventory sold typically represents the largest expense. For example, cost of goods sold was the largest expense category for **ExxonMobil** in 2005, totaling 57% of sales. For **Wal-Mart**, cost of goods sold was 77% of sales in 2005. Although cost of goods sold represents a significant expense for those companies such as ExxonMobil and Wal-Mart that manufacture and/or sell a product, it is certainly not the only expense. And for those companies that sell a service, other expenses such as employee compensation or advertising can be far more significant than cost of goods sold.

In this chapter, we discuss a number of these other significant operating issues. We will begin with a discussion of two significant operating expenses that are incurred by almost every firm: employee compensation and income taxes. We also discuss the accounting for the costs associated with contingencies, which are items that are not fully resolved at the time the financial statements are prepared. Two common examples of contingencies are lawsuits and environmental cleanup obligations. Also in this chapter we discuss how one determines whether a cost should be recorded as an asset (capitalized) or recorded as an expense. The expense versus capitalize issue has arisen many times over the years as accountants have wrestled with how to account for advertising costs, research costs, and others.

The financial statement items covered in this chapter are illustrated in Exhibit 2. Various operating items affecting the income statement are covered in the chapter. The two most significant are employee compensation and income taxes. The balance sheet items discussed are pension liabilities, deferred income tax liabilities, and contingent liabilities. The accounting aspects of these balance sheet items are intriguing in that both the pension and deferred tax items are sometimes reported as assets rather than liabilities. In addition, contingent liabilities are frequently not reported on the balance sheet at all. The details of all these topics, and more, are discussed in this chapter.

---

[1] Information for this description was obtained from Daniel J. Boorstin, *The Americans: The Democratic Experience* (New York: Random House, 1973) and Ida M. Tarbell, *The History of the Standard Oil Company* (New York: MacMillan Company, 1904).

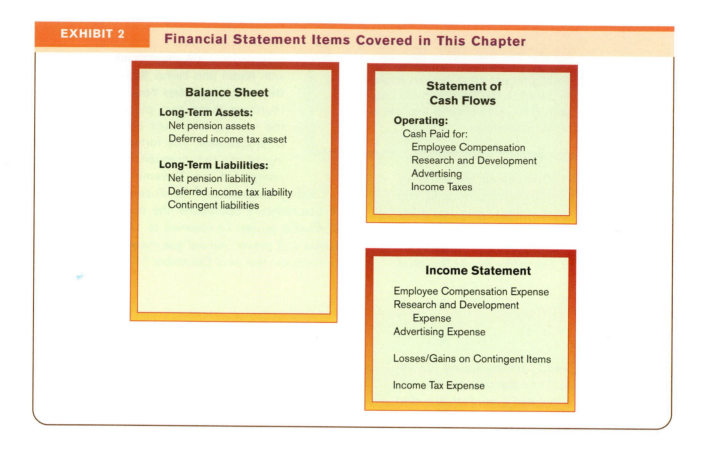

EXHIBIT 2 | **Financial Statement Items Covered in This Chapter**

Balance Sheet

Long-Term Assets:
Net pension assets
Deferred income tax asset

Long-Term Liabilities:
Net pension liability
Deferred income tax liability
Contingent liabilities

Statement of Cash Flows

Operating:
Cash Paid for:
Employee Compensation
Research and Development
Advertising
Income Taxes

Income Statement

Employee Compensation Expense
Research and Development
Expense
Advertising Expense

Losses/Gains on Contingent Items

Income Tax Expense

Employee Compensation

Account for the various components of employee compensation expense.

① Often, one of the largest operating expenses of a business is the salaries and wages of its employees. But the cost of employees is not simply the expense associated with the current period's wages. As the following time line illustrates, issues associated with employee compensation can extend long after the employee has retired.

Payroll relates to the salaries and wages earned by employees for work done in the current period. Wages are paid anywhere from weekly to monthly, depending on the company. Compensated absences exist when an employer agrees to pay workers for sick days or vacation days. These obligations must be estimated and accrued in the period that the employee earns those days off. Many employees are paid bonuses based on some measure of performance (such as income or sales

Employee Compensation Event Line

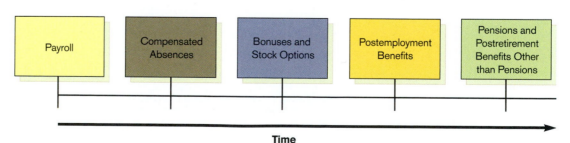

Payroll | Compensated Absences | Bonuses and Stock Options | Postemployment Benefits | Pensions and Postretirement Benefits Other than Pensions

Time

volume). Those bonuses are often paid quarterly or annually. One way to provide bonuses to employees is through the granting of stock options. In some cases, employees may earn what are termed "postemployment benefits," which kick in if an employee is laid off or terminated. Finally, firms offer benefits to their employees upon retirement. We will discuss each of these items in further detail in the sections that follow.

Payroll

In its simplest form, accounting for payroll involves debiting Salaries Expense and crediting Salaries Payable when employees work and then debiting Salaries Payable and crediting Cash when wages are paid. However, accounting for salaries and related payroll taxes is never quite that simple and can, in fact, be quite complex. This is primarily because every business is legally required to withhold certain taxes from employees' salaries and wages.

Social Security (FICA) taxes

Federal Insurance Contributions Act taxes imposed on the employee and the employer; used mainly to provide retirement benefits.

Very few people receive their full salary as take-home pay. For example, an employee who earns $30,000 a year probably takes home between $20,000 and $25,000. The remainder is withheld by the employer to pay the employee's federal and state income taxes, **Social Security (FICA) taxes,**[2] and any voluntary or contractual withholdings that the employee has authorized (such as union dues, medical insurance premiums, and charitable contributions). Thus, the accounting entry to record the expense for an employee's monthly salary (computed as 1/12 of $30,000) might be:

Salaries Expense	2,500	
FICA Taxes Payable, Employees		191
Federal Withholding Taxes Payable		400
State Withholding Taxes Payable		200
Salaries Payable		1,709
To record Mary Perrico's salary for July.		

All the credit amounts (which are arbitrary in this example) are liabilities that must be paid by the employer to the federal and state governments and to the employee. It should be noted that these withholdings do not represent an additional expense to the employer because the employee actually pays them. The employer merely serves as an agent for the governments for collecting and paying these withheld amounts.

In addition to remitting employees' income and FICA taxes, companies must also pay certain payroll-related taxes, such as the employer's portion of the FICA tax (an amount equal to the employee's portion) and state and federal unemployment taxes. The payroll-related taxes paid by employers are expenses to the company and are included in operating expenses on the income statement. An entry to record the company's share of payroll taxes relating to Mary Perrico's employment (again using arbitrary amounts) would be:

Payroll Tax Expense	279	
FICA Taxes Payable, Employer		191
Federal Unemployment Taxes Payable		18
State Unemployment Taxes Payable		70
To record employer payroll tax liabilities associated with Mary Perrico's salary for July.		

---

[2] Congress has split FICA taxes into two parts—Social Security and Medicare. For the purposes of this chapter, we will combine the two.

The different liabilities recorded in the preceding two entries for payroll would be eliminated as payments are made. The entries to account for the payments are:

FICA Taxes Payable	382	
Federal Withholding Taxes Payable	400	
Federal Unemployment Taxes Payable	18	
Cash		800
Paid July withholdings and payroll taxes to federal government.		
State Withholding Taxes Payable	200	
State Unemployment Taxes Payable	70	
Cash		270
Paid July withholdings and payroll taxes to state government.		
Salaries Payable	1,709	
Cash		1,709
Paid July salary to Mary Perrico.		

As these entries show, three checks are written for payroll-related expenses: one to the federal government, one to the state, and one to the employee.

One further point about salaries and wages needs to be made. The period of time covered by the payroll may not coincide with the last day of the year for financial reporting. Thus, if the reporting year ends on Wednesday, December 31, and the salaries and wages for that week will be paid Monday, January 5 of the following year, then the company must show the salaries and wages earned from Monday through Wednesday (December 29, 30, and 31) as a liability on the December 31 balance sheet. To accomplish this, the company would record an end-of-year adjusting entry to record the salaries and wages earned for those three days.

Compensated Absences

Suppose that you work for a business that provides each employee one day of sick leave for each full month of employment. When should that sick day (or compensated absence) be accounted for? When it is taken by the employee? When it is earned by the employee? And how much of an accrual should be associated with the compensated absences?

The matching principle requires that the expense associated with the compensated absence be accounted for in the period in which it is earned by the employee. Some of the conceptual issues associated with accounting for compensated absences are similar to those addressed in accounting for bad debts. In the case of bad debts, if we waited until we were sure a customer wasn't going to pay, then we could be certain about our bad debt expense. But we may not find out that we are not going to be paid until several periods later, and as a result, the bad debt expense would be reflected in the wrong accounting period. So instead of waiting until accounts are dishonored, we estimate the expense for each period. The same is true with compensated absences. Although we could wait until those sick days are taken and then know exactly what they will cost, it may be years before we know. Rather than wait, we estimate instead. For example, if you earn both $100 a day and one sick day per month, then it makes sense for your employer to recognize an expense (and accrue a liability) of $100 per month related to your sick pay. This would be done with the following journal entry:

Salaries Expense	100	
Sick Days Payable		100
To recognize accrued sick pay.		

When you take that sick day (and let's not forget that the government will take its share of your sick pay also), the journal entry would be:

Sick Days Payable	100	
Various Taxes Payable		20
Cash		80
To record payment of sick day net of FICA, federal, and state taxes.		

Now suppose that you don't take your sick day until next year. Assume also that you received a $10 raise per day. This makes our estimate of $100 incorrect, so we will fix that estimate in the period in which you take the sick day. The journal entry in this instance would be:

Sick Days Payable	100	
Salaries Expense	10	
Various Taxes Payable		22
Cash		88
To record payment of sick day net of FICA, federal, and state taxes.		

The same procedures would apply when accounting for accrued vacation pay or other types of compensated absences.

Bonuses

bonus

Additional compensation, beyond the regular compensation, that is paid to employees if certain objectives are achieved.

Many companies offer employee **bonus** plans that allow employees to receive additional compensation should certain objectives be achieved. These bonus plans sometimes apply to all employees although more often they are restricted to members of top management. In many instances, the terms of the bonus plan are defined using financial statement numbers. For example, in its 2005 proxy statement filed with the Securities and Exchange Commission (SEC), **ExxonMobil** disclosed that it paid $9.15 million in bonuses to its top six executives. ExxonMobil's chief executive officer (CEO), Lee R. Raymond, received the lion's share of that bonus amount at $4.9 million (this on top of his regular annual compensation of $4.0 million).

The purpose of an earnings-based bonus plan is to encourage managers to work harder and smarter to improve the performance of the company. However, such a plan also increases the incentive of managers to manipulate reported earnings. In fact, one of the factors looked at by auditors in evaluating the risk of financial statement fraud in a company is whether the company has an earnings-based management bonus plan.

Stock Options

employee stock options

Rights given to employees to purchase shares of stock of a company at a predetermined price.

Employee stock options have become an increasingly popular way to compensate top executives. Under a stock option plan, managers are given the option of purchasing shares of the company's stock in the future at a price that is specified today. For example, in 2002, Lee Raymond, CEO of ExxonMobil, was granted 1,050,000 options, each allowing him to buy one share of ExxonMobil stock in the future for $37.12, which was the market value of ExxonMobil shares on the date the options were granted. Raymond will make money from these options if he is able to improve the performance of ExxonMobil and increase its stock price. In August of 2006, a share of ExxonMobil stock was worth $68 making those options worth $32,424,000 [1,050,000 × ($68.00 − $37.12)]. Stock options are an attractive way to compensate top management because the options pay off only if the managers are able to increase the value of the company, which is exactly what the owners of the company (the stockholders) desire.

There has been significant debate in the United States about how to compute the compensation expense associated with employee stock options. The debate centered around the issue of what the value of an option is. The FASB has determined the proper way to value options is the fair value method. This method is described below.

Fair Value Method   The "fair value" of an option stems from the possibility that the employee may want to exercise the option in the future if the company's stock price goes up. For example, even if an option exercise price of $50 is equal to the stock price on the date the option is granted to an employee, there is a chance that the stock price may increase during the life of the option. This means that an option with no "intrinsic value" can still have substantial economic value because the employee holding the option may be able to buy the stock at less than its market value some time in the future. Exact computation of the fair value of options involves complex formulas derived using stochastic calculus, but commercially available software packages make option valuation no more difficult than using a spreadsheet.

Postemployment Benefits

postemployment benefits

Benefits paid to employees who have been laid off or terminated.

Postemployment benefits are perhaps the least common of the topics covered in this section on employee compensation. **Postemployment benefits** are those benefits that are incurred after an employee has ceased to work for an employer but before that employee retires. A common example is a company-provided severance package for employees who have been laid off. This severance package might include salary for a certain time period, retraining costs, education costs, and the like. Accounting standards require that the amount of the postemployment cost be estimated and accrued in the period in which the employee is actually terminated. For example, suppose a company decides to close a segment of its operations, thereby laying off a certain percentage of its labor force. The company must estimate the costs associated with the benefits offered to those laid-off employees and would record the following journal entry when the employees are actually terminated:

Salaries Expense	xxx	
Benefits Payable		xxx

To record postemployment benefits for laid-off employees.

pension

An agreement between an employer and employees that provides for benefits upon retirement.

When the benefits are paid, a journal entry would be made to reduce the payable and to record the cash outflow.

Pensions

A **pension** is cash compensation received by an employee after that employee has retired. Two primary types of pension plans exist. A **defined contribution plan** requires the company to place a certain amount of money into a pension fund each year on behalf of the employees. Then, after the employees retire, they receive the money contributed to the pension fund plus the earnings on those contributions. With a **defined benefit plan**, on the other hand, the company promises the employees a certain monthly cash amount after they retire, based on factors such as number of years worked by the employee, employee's highest salary, and so forth.

defined contribution plan

A pension plan under which the employer contributes a defined amount to the pension fund; after retirement, the employees receive the amount contributed plus whatever it has earned.

The accounting for a defined contribution plan is quite simple—a company merely reports pension expense equal to the amount of cash it is required to contribute to its employees' pension fund during the year. Normally, no balance sheet liability is reported in connection with a defined contribution plan because, once the company has made the required contribution to the pension fund, it has no remaining obligation to the employees.

defined benefit plan

A pension plan under which the employer defines the amount that retiring employees will receive and contributes enough to the pension fund to pay that amount.

The accounting issues associated with defined benefit plans are much more complex because the ultimate amount that a company will have to pay into its employees' pension fund depends on how long the employees work before retiring, what their highest salaries are, how long the employees live after they retire, and how well the investments in the pension fund perform. The accounting concept underlying this complexity, however, is still the same basic idea of matching: the income statement this year should contain all expenses related to generating revenue this year, whether those expenses are paid in cash this year (like cash wages) or are not expected to be paid for many years (like pension benefits).

STOP & THINK

Who bears the risks associated with a defined contribution plan—the employer or the employee? Which party bears the risks associated with a defined benefit plan?

Pension-Related Items in the Financial Statements   Each of the major balance sheet and income statement items related to pension accounting is briefly introduced below.

- *Pension fund.* When a company has a defined benefit pension plan, it is required by U.S. federal law to establish a separate pension fund to ensure that employees receive the defined benefits promised under the plan. The pension fund is basically a large investment fund of stocks and bonds. The company still owns these pension fund assets, but it cannot use them for any purpose except to pay pension benefits to employees.

- *Pension obligation.* The promise to make defined benefit pension payments to employees represents a liability to the company making the promise. The amount of this liability is quite difficult to estimate because it depends on future salary increases, employee turnover, employee life span, and so forth. The estimation of the liability is done by professionals called actuaries. These are the same individuals who provide the computations that life insurance companies use in setting premiums.

- *Net pension asset or liability.* One possible way to present the pension information on a balance sheet is to list the pension plan assets among the long-term assets and the pension liability as a long-term liability. However, the accounting standards stipulate that these two items be offset against one another and a single net amount be shown as either a net pension asset or a net pension liability.

- *Pension-related interest cost.* The estimated pension obligation represents an amount owed by a company to its employees. Accordingly, a pension-related interest cost is recognized each year; the amount of this interest cost is the increase in the pension obligation resulting from interest on the unpaid pension obligation.

- *Service cost.* The amount of a company's pension obligation increases each year as employees work and earn more pension benefits. This increase in the pension obligation is an expense associated with work done during the year and is called the pension service cost.

- *Return on pension fund assets.* The cost of a company's pension plan is partially offset by the return that the company earns on the assets in its pension fund.

- *Pension expense.* Just as pension liabilities and assets are offset against one another to arrive at a single net liability or asset to be reported on the balance sheet, the three components of pension expense (interest cost, service cost, and return on pension fund assets) are netted against one another to yield a single number that is reported on the income statement.

Illustration from ExxonMobil's Financial Statements   In the notes to its 2005 financial statements, ExxonMobil discloses the following about its pension benefit obligation and its pension fund. All numbers are in millions of dollars.

	U.S. Plans	Non-U.S. Plans	Total
Pension benefit obligation	$11,181	$19,310	$30,491
Pension fund assets	7,250	12,063	19,313
Net pension liability	$ 3,931	$ 7,247	$11,178

Note that ExxonMobil has separated its pension plans into those covering employees in the United States and those covering employees located outside the United States. This is a useful separation because the laws governing the maintenance of pension plans vary from country to country; U.S. laws are generally viewed as giving more protection to the rights of the employees covered by pension plans than foreign laws do. Also note that ExxonMobil's pension plans are "underfunded," meaning that the market value of the assets in the pension funds is less than the estimated pension liability. ExxonMobil also provides the following information about its pension expense in 2005. Again, all of the numbers are in millions.

	U.S. Plans	Non-U.S. Plans	Total
Service cost	$ 330	$ 382	$ 712
Interest cost	611	834	1,445
Less: Expected return on fund assets	(629)	(789)	(1,418)
Other miscellaneous items	397	434	831
Net pension expense	$ 709	$ 861	$1,570

Note the significant reduction in reported pension expense caused by the expected return on pension fund assets; without the return on the pension fund, ExxonMobil's pension expense would be more than twice as high.

CAUTION

The expected, not the actual, return on the pension fund assets is subtracted in computing pension expense. The accounting for the difference between expected and actual return involves deferring gains and losses, corridor amounts, and other complexities best left for an intermediate accounting course.

Postretirement Benefits Other Than Pensions

In addition to pension benefits, employers often offer employees other benefits after their retirement. For example, ExxonMobil promises its employees that it will continue to cover them with health-care and life insurance plans after retirement. These types of plans are typically less formal than pension plans and often are not backed by assets accumulated in a separate fund. For example, ExxonMobil has only a $456 million separate fund set up to cover its estimated $5.4 billion obligation to cover the post-retirement health-care needs of employees.

The accounting rules require companies to currently recognize the expense and long-term liability associated with the postretirement benefits that are earned in the current year, in keeping with the normal practice of matching expenses to the period in which they are initially incurred. The actual accounting is complex but similar to that required for pensions. The potential liabilities for these future payments can be quite significant for many firms. **General Motors** has the largest postretirement benefit plan in the United States, with a nonpension postretirement obligation totaling $84.941 billion as of December 31, 2005.

As illustrated in this section, compensation expense includes much more than just wages and salaries. Companies presumably have calculated that the value of the services provided by employees justifies the additional compensation cost beyond salaries and wages. The fact that employees earn benefits in one year that they do not receive until later, sometimes many years later, necessitates careful accounting to ensure that compensation expense is reported in the year in which it is earned.

REMEMBER THIS...

- Employee compensation is not limited to just the current period's payroll. The cost of employees also includes compensated absences, bonuses, stock options, postemployment benefits, pensions, and other postretirement benefits.
- Companies account for employee stock options using the fair value method.
- A pension obligation is reported on the balance sheet as the difference between the obligation and the amount in an associated pension fund.
- Pension expense is the sum of interest cost and service cost, less the expected return on the pension fund assets.

Taxes

Compute income tax expense, including appropriate consideration of deferred tax items.

(2) In addition to the payroll taxes described in the previous section, companies are responsible for paying several other taxes to federal, state, and/or local governments, including sales taxes, property taxes, and income taxes. The accounting for these taxes is described next.

Sales Taxes

Most states and some cities charge a sales tax on retail transactions. These taxes are paid by customers to the seller, who in turn forwards them to the state or city. Sales taxes collected from customers represent a current liability until remitted to the appropriate governmental agency. For example, assume that a sporting goods store in Denver prices a pair of skis at $200 and that the combination of state and city sales tax is 6.5%. When the store sells the skis, it collects $213 and records the transaction as follows:

Cash	213	
Sales Revenue		200
Sales Tax Payable		13
Sold a pair of skis for $200. Collected $213, including 6.5% sales tax.		

sales tax payable

Money collected from customers for sales taxes that must be remitted to local governments and other taxing authorities.

The sales revenue is properly recorded at $200, and the $13 is recorded as **Sales Tax Payable**, a liability. Then, on a regular basis, a sales tax return is completed and filed with the state or city tax commission, and sales taxes collected are paid to those agencies. Note that the collection of the sales tax from customers creates a liability to the state but does not result in the recognition of revenue when collected or an expense when paid to the state. The company acts as an agent of the state in collecting the sales tax and recognizes a liability only until the collected amount is remitted to the state.

Property Taxes

Property taxes are usually assessed by county or city governments on land, buildings, and other company assets. The period covered by the assessment of property taxes is often from July 1 of one year to June 30 of the next year. If a property taxpayer is on a calendar-year financial reporting basis (or on a fiscal-year basis ending on a day other than June 30), the property tax assessment year and the company's financial reporting year will not coincide. Therefore, when the company prepares its financial statements at calendar-year end, it must report a prepaid tax asset (if taxes are paid at the beginning of the tax year) or a property tax liability (if taxes are paid at the end of the tax year) for the taxes associated with the first portion of the assessment year. To illustrate, assume that Yokum Company pays its property taxes of $3,600 on June 30, 2008, for the period July 1, 2008, to June 30, 2009. If the company is on a calendar-year basis and records the prepayment as an asset, then the adjusting entry at December 31, 2008, would be:

Property Tax Expense	1,800	
Prepaid Property Taxes		1,800
To record property tax expense for six months.		

The prepaid property taxes account balance of $1,800 would be shown on Yokum's balance sheet at December 31, 2008, as a current asset. On June 30, 2009, property tax expense would be recognized for the period January 1, 2009, through June 30, 2009, with the following entry:

Property Tax Expense	1,800	
Prepaid Property Taxes		1,800
To record property tax expense for the property assessment period January 1–June 30, 2009.		

Income Taxes

Corporations pay income taxes just as individuals do. This corporate income tax is usually reported as the final expense on the income statement. For example, in 2005, three lines from **ExxonMobil**'s income statement relating to taxes were as follows, with all numbers in millions:

	2005	2004	2003
Income before income taxes	$59,432	$41,241	$31,966
Income taxes	23,302	15,911	11,006
Income from continuing operations	$36,130	$25,330	$20,960

The $23.302 billion in income tax expense reported by ExxonMobil in 2005 is not necessarily equal to the amount of cash paid for income taxes during the year. In fact, ExxonMobil paid $22.535 billion for income taxes in 2005. Reported income tax expense may differ from the actual amount of cash paid for taxes for two reasons. First, like many other expenses, income taxes are not necessarily paid in cash in the year in which they are incurred. The important point to remember is that reported income tax expense reflects the amount of income taxes attributable to income earned during the year, whether the tax was actually paid in cash during the year or not.

The second reason reported income tax expense may differ from the actual amount of cash paid for taxes is that income tax expense is based on reported financial accounting income, whereas the amount of cash paid for income taxes is dictated by the applicable government tax law. The $23.302 billion income tax expense reported by ExxonMobil in 2005 reflects the total estimated amount of income tax the company expects will eventually be paid based on the income reported in the current year's income statement. However, because the income computed using the tax rules is almost always different from the income computed using financial accounting standards, some of this tax may not have to be paid for several years. In addition, tax rules may require income tax to be paid on income before the financial accounting standards consider that income to be "earned." These differences in tax law income and financial accounting income give rise to deferred income tax items, which are discussed in this section.

Corporations in the United States compute two different income numbers—financial income for reporting to stockholders and taxable income for reporting to the Internal Revenue Service (IRS). The existence of these two "sets of books" seems unethical to some, illegal to others. However, the difference between the stockholders' need for information and the government's need for efficient revenue collection makes the computation of the two different income numbers essential. The different purposes of these reporting systems were summarized by the U.S. Supreme Court in the *Thor Power Tool case* (1979):

> The primary goal of financial accounting is to provide useful information to management, shareholders, creditors, and others properly interested; the major responsibility of the accountant is to protect these parties from being misled. The primary goal of the income tax system, in contrast, is the equitable collection of revenue.

In summary, U.S. corporations compute income in two different ways, and rightly so. Nevertheless, the existence of these two different numbers that can each be called "income before taxes" makes it surprisingly difficult to define what is meant by "income tax expense."

Deferred Tax Example

Assume that you invest $1,000 by buying shares in a mutual fund on January 1. Also assume that the income tax rate is 40%. According to the tax law, any economic gain you experience through an increase in the value of your mutual fund shares is not taxed until you actually sell your shares. The rationale behind this tax rule is that until you sell your shares, you don't have the cash to pay any tax. Now, assume further that the economy does well and that the value of your mutual fund shares increases to $1,600 by December 31. You decide to prepare partial financial statements to summarize your holdings and the performance of your shares during the year. These financial statements are as follows:

Balance Sheet		Income Statement	
Assets:		Revenues:	
Mutual Fund Shares	$1,600	Gain on Mutual Fund Investment	$600

A moment's consideration reveals that this balance sheet and income statement are misleading. Yes, it is true that your shares are now worth $1,600, but if and when you liquidate the shares, you will have to pay income tax of $240 [($1,600 − $1,000) × 0.40]. Thus, you are overstating your economic position by only reporting the $1,600 in mutual fund shares; you should also report that a liability of $240 exists in relation to these shares. Similarly, it is misleading to report the $600 gain on your income statement without also reporting that, at some future time, you will have to pay $240 in income tax on that gain. A more accurate set of financial statements would appear as follows:

Balance Sheet		Income Statement	
Assets:		Revenues:	
Mutual Fund Shares	$1,600	Gain on Mutual Fund Investment	$600
Liabilities:		Expenses:	
Deferred Income Tax Liability	$ 240	Income Tax Expense	$240

The appropriate journal entry to recognize income tax expense in this case is as follows:

Income Tax Expense	240	
Deferred Income Tax Liability		240

Note that the deferred income tax liability is not a legal liability because, as far as the IRS is concerned, you do not currently owe any tax on the increase in the value of your mutual fund. Nevertheless, the deferred tax liability is an economic liability that should be reported now because it reflects an obligation that will have to be paid in the future as a result of an event (the increase in the value of the mutual fund shares) that occurred this year.

Now, what if the mutual fund shares had decreased in value from $1,000 to $400? Consider whether the following set of financial statements would accurately reflect your economic position and performance:

Balance Sheet		**Income Statement**	
Assets:		Revenues:	
Mutual Fund Shares	$400	Loss on Mutual Fund Investment	$600

Again, these financial statements are somewhat misleading because they ignore the future tax implications of the change in the value of the mutual fund shares. In this case, when the shares are sold, you will realize a taxable loss of $600. If you have other investment income, that loss can be used to reduce your total taxable income by $600, which will save you $240 ($600 × 0.40) in income taxes. Thus, in a real sense, this loss on the mutual funds is not all bad because it will provide you with a $240 reduction in income taxes in the year in which you sell the shares. This reduction in taxes is an asset, a deferred income tax asset, because it represents a probable future economic benefit that has arisen from an event (the drop in the value of the mutual fund shares) that occurred this year. Similarly, the income statement effect of this future savings in taxes is to soften the blow of the reported $600 loss. The loss that occurred this year will result in an income tax benefit in the future, so the benefit is reported on this year's income statement, as follows:

Balance Sheet		**Income Statement**	
Assets:		Expenses:	
Mutual Fund Shares	$400	Loss on Mutual Fund Investment	$ 600
		Less: Income Tax Benefit	(240)
Deferred Income Tax Asset	$240		
		Net Loss	$ 360

The journal entry to recognize the income tax "expense" is as follows:

Deferred Income Tax Asset	240	
Income Tax Expense		240

Notice that Income Tax Expense is credited, or reduced, in this entry. If there are other income taxes for the year, this credit will result in a reduction in reported income tax expense. If there are no other income taxes, then the credit amount will be reported on the income statement as an addition to income under the title "income tax benefit."

The value of the deferred tax asset depends on your having other investment income in the future against which the loss on the mutual fund shares can be offset. Thus, accounting for deferred tax assets is complicated by the fact that one must make an assumption about the likelihood that a company will have enough taxable income in the future to be able to take advantage of the deferred tax benefit.

As this simple mutual fund example illustrates, the amount of income tax expense reported on a company's income statement is not necessarily the same as the amount of income tax the company must pay on taxable income generated during the year. There are literally hundreds of accounting areas in which income is taxed by the taxing authorities in a different year than the year in which the income is reported to the financial statement users in the income statement. The details of deferred income tax accounting are among the most complicated issues covered in intermediate accounting courses.

REMEMBER THIS...

- The amount of sales tax collected is reported as a liability until the funds are forwarded to the appropriate government agency.

- When property taxes are paid in advance, the amount is reported as a prepaid asset until the time period covered by the property tax has expired.

- Reported income tax expense is not merely the amount of income tax that a company legally owes for a given year.

- Because of differences between financial accounting rules and income tax rules, revenues and expenses can enter into the computation of income in different years for financial accounting purposes and for income tax purposes.

- Proper accounting for deferred income taxes ensures that reported income tax expense for a year represents all of the income tax consequences arising from transactions undertaken during the year.

Contingencies

Distinguish between contingent items that should be recognized in the financial statements and those that should be merely disclosed in the financial statement notes.

③

By its very nature, business is full of uncertainty. As discussed in relation to employee compensation and taxes, proper recording of an expense in the current period frequently requires making estimates about what will occur in future periods. Sometimes the very existence of an asset or liability depends on the occurrence, or nonoccurrence, of a future event. For example, whether a company will have to make a payment as a result of a lawsuit arising from events occurring this year depends on a judge or jury ruling that may not be known for several years. In accounting terms, a **contingency** is an uncertain circumstance involving a potential gain or loss that will not be resolved until some future event occurs. In this section, we discuss the conceptual issues associated with contingencies and the accounting for events for which the outcome is uncertain.

contingency

Circumstances involving potential losses or gains that will not be resolved until some future event occurs.

If you were a financial statement user, would you want to be informed of events known to management that might have an adverse effect on the company's future? Consider as an example a lawsuit filed against a company. Because litigation can take years, how should that company account for the possibility of a loss? Would you want the company to wait until the lawsuit is resolved before informing financial statement users of the litigation? Of course not. You would want to know about the lawsuit if the outcome could potentially materially affect the operations of the company. But would you want to know about every lawsuit filed against the company? Probably not.

Accounting standard-setters have addressed this issue and determined that the proper disclosure for a contingency depends upon the assessed outcome. The first thing to note is that accounting standard-setters determined that accounting for contingent gains is, in most cases, inappropriate. Contingent gains are typically not accounted for until the future event relating to the contingent gain resolves itself. Contingent liabilities are to be accounted for differently depending on an assessment of the likely outcome of the contingency. Exhibit 3 contains the relevant terms, definitions, and proper accounting for contingent liabilities.

If you think about it, this probability spectrum makes a great deal of sense. For example, if it is likely that your company will lose a lawsuit in which it is the defendant, then it would be appropriate to account for that outcome now by recognizing a loss and establishing a payable. If the likelihood of your company losing the case is slight, then it makes sense to do nothing. And if you are unsure of the outcome, then disclosure in the notes seems appropriate.

The problem in implementing these terms relates to assessing the likelihood of an outcome. Who is to say if your company will lose a lawsuit? The company must obtain objective assessments as to the possible outcome of future events. In the case of litigation, the company would ask its attorneys about the possible outcome. The firm auditing the company might use its own attorneys to assess the possible outcome. In any case, companies are required to make objective assessments as to the likely outcome of contingent events and then account for those events based on that assessment.

Wal-Mart's 2006 Form 10-K (see Appendix A) contains the company's disclosure relating to contingencies. At the time, the company was involved in several lawsuits regarding labor laws. Contrast Wal-Mart's disclosure with the 2005 disclosure provided by **Altria Group**, the parent of tobacco company **Philip Morris**, relating to its involvement in ongoing tobacco litigation. The company provides over eight pages of disclosure relating to its potential tobacco-related liability.

STOP & THINK

Why might a company hesitate to assess the likelihood of losing an ongoing lawsuit as being probable? If you were the attorney for the plaintiff, how could you use the resulting information from the financial statements?

environmental liabilities

Obligations incurred because of damage done to the environment.

Environmental Liabilities

Environmental liabilities have gained increasing attention of late because of their potential magnitude. **Environmental liabilities** are obligations incurred because of damage done by companies to the environment. Common environmental liabilities include cleanup costs associated with oil spills, toxic waste dumps,

EXHIBIT 3	Accounting for Contingent Liabilities	
Term	**Definition**	**Accounting**
Probable	The future event is likely to occur.	Estimate the amount of the contingency and make the appropriate journal entry; provide detailed disclosure in the notes.
Reasonably possible	The chance of the future event occurring is more than remote but less than likely.	Provide detailed disclosure of the possible liability in the notes.
Remote	The chance of the future event occurring is slight.	No disclosure required.

or air pollution. These liabilities are usually brought to the company's attention as a result of fines or penalties imposed by the federal government or when damage that is caused by the company is recognized. Although the accounting and disclosures associated with environmental liabilities fall under the guidelines for contingencies discussed in the previous section, environmental liabilities present a unique problem.

In the case of a lawsuit, one can typically make a reasonable estimate as to the upper bound of the potential settlement. For example, if your company is being sued for $4 million, it is unlikely that any potential settlement will be higher than that amount. In the case of environmental liabilities, it is often very difficult to estimate the cost of environmental cleanup. Thus, while the company may deem it probable that a liability exists, estimating that liability can be difficult. Recall that the contingency standard requires a liability to be recorded on the company's books if it is probable and estimable. If a potential liability is possible and estimable, the standards require note disclosure.

What about the situation where a potential liability is probable but cannot be estimated with much accuracy, as is often the case with environmental liabilities? Obviously, if a company cannot estimate a probable obligation, it makes sense to provide extensive note disclosure. Most companies will estimate at least a minimum amount and provide note disclosure as to the possibility of additional costs. As an illustration, **ExxonMobil** disclosed the information in Exhibit 4 in its 1991 and 2005 annual reports in connection

---

EXHIBIT 4	**ExxonMobil–1991 and 2005 Disclosures Concerning *Exxon Valdez* Oil Spill**

Disclosure in 1991

On March 24, 1989, the Exxon Valdez, a tanker owned by Exxon Shipping Company, a subsidiary of Exxon Corporation, ran aground on Bligh Reef in Prince William Sound off the port of Valdez, Alaska, and released approximately 260,000 barrels of crude oil. More than 315 lawsuits, including class actions, have been brought in various courts against Exxon Corporation and certain of its subsidiaries.

On October 8, 1991, the United States District Court for the District of Alaska approved a civil agreement and consent decree. . . . These agreements provided for guilty pleas to certain misdemeanors, the dismissal of all felony charges and the remaining misdemeanor charges by the United States, and the release of all civil claims against Exxon . . . by the United States and the state of Alaska. The agreements also released all claims related to or arising from the oil spill by Exxon. . . .

Payments under the plea agreement totaled $125 million–$25 million in fines and $100 million in payments to the United States and Alaska for restoration projects in Alaska. Payments under the civil agreement and consent decree will total $900 million over a ten-year period. The civil agreement also provides for the possible payment, between September 1, 2002, and September 1, 2006, of up to $100 million for substantial loss or decline in populations, habitats, or species in areas affected by the oil spill which could not have been reasonably anticipated on September 25, 1991.

The remaining cost to the corporation from the Valdez accident is difficult to predict and cannot be determined at this time. It is believed the final outcome, net of reserves already provided, will not have a materially adverse effect upon the corporation's operations or financial condition.

Disclosure in 2005

A number of lawsuits, including class actions, were brought in various courts against Exxon Mobil Corporation and certain of its subsidiaries relating to the accidental release of crude oil from the tanker Exxon Valdez in 1989. The vast majority of the compensatory claims have been resolved and paid. All of the punitive damage claims were consolidated in the civil trial that began in 1994. The first judgment from the United States District Court for the District of Alaska in the amount of $5 billion was vacated by the United States Court of Appeals for the Ninth Circuit as being excessive under the Constitution. The second judgment in the amount of $4 billion was vacated by the Ninth Circuit panel without argument and sent back for the District Court to reconsider in the light of the recent U.S. Supreme Court decision in *Campbell v. State Farm*. The most recent District Court judgment for punitive damages was for $4.5 billion plus interest and was entered in January 2004. ExxonMobil and the plaintiffs have appealed this decision to the Ninth Circuit. The Corporation has posted a $5.4 billion letter for credit. Oral arguments were held before the Ninth Circuit on January 27, 2006. Management believes that the likelihood of the judgment being upheld is remote. While it is reasonably possible that a liability may have been incurred from the Exxon Valdez grounding, it is not possible to predict the ultimate outcome or to reasonably estimate any such potential liability.

with lawsuits filed as a result of the *Exxon Valdez* oil spill. Note that in 1991, the company sounds quite optimistic that it has settled the bulk of the claims related to the oil spill and that any further claims "will not have a materially adverse effect" upon the company. This optimistic disclosure is particularly interesting in light of the $4.5 billion adverse judgment discussed in the 2005 disclosure.

REMEMBER THIS...

- Contingent liabilities depend on some future event to determine if a liability actually exists.
- Companies are required to assess the likelihood of certain future events occurring and then, based on that assessment, provide appropriate disclosure.
- If the company deems the future event to be likely, the journal entries are made and the liability is accrued.
- If the future event is deemed reasonably possible, note disclosure is required.
- For those events considered remote, no disclosure is required.
- Environmental liabilities represent a case where a liability exists but measurement is difficult. A minimum liability is typically established along with extensive note disclosure.

Capitalize versus Expense

Understand when an expenditure should be recorded as an asset and when it should be recorded as an expense.

4 To this point in the text, we have assumed that the decision of expensing a cost to the income statement or capitalizing an expenditure and placing it on the balance sheet as an asset is an easy one. In reality, that decision is often difficult and one that makes accounting judgment critical. For example, should a building that cost $1 million and is expected to benefit 20 future periods be capitalized and placed on the balance sheet? The answer is pretty clear—of course. What about office supplies that are used this period? Will they benefit future periods? No, and as a result, the costs of those supplies should be expensed. What about research and development costs? Should they be capitalized as an asset or expensed to the income statement? Now you see the problem. Sometimes it is difficult to determine whether an expenditure will benefit the future. Exhibit 5 provides an expense/asset continuum that demonstrates the difficulty of the decision to capitalize or expense a cost.

EXHIBIT 5   **Expense/Asset Continuum**

Office Supplies Used

Repairs

Research and Development

Land and Building

Expense ⟵   ⟶ Asset

The endpoints of the continuum are easy. The decision starts to get fuzzy, though, once you leave the endpoints. Do repairs and maintenance benefit future periods (and therefore need to be capitalized), or are they necessary expenditures just to keep a machine running (and should be expensed)? To illustrate the issues involved in deciding whether an expenditure should be capitalized or expensed, two specific areas will be discussed—research and development (R&D) and advertising.

Research and Development

Research is an activity undertaken to discover new knowledge that will be useful in developing new products, services, or processes. Development involves the application of research findings to develop a plan or design for new or improved products and processes. **ExxonMobil** reports that, from 2003 through 2005, it spent an average of $660 million per year on R&D activities.

Because of the uncertainty surrounding the future economic benefit of R&D activities, the FASB decided in 1974 that research and development expenditures should be expensed in the period incurred. Among the arguments for expensing R&D costs is the frequent inability to find a definite causal relationship between the expenditures and future revenues. Sometimes very large expenditures do not generate any future revenue, while relatively small expenditures lead to significant discoveries that generate large revenues. The FASB found it difficult to establish criteria that would distinguish between those R&D expenditures that would most likely benefit future periods and those that would not.

In summary, the FASB concluded that R&D expenditures are undertaken to benefit future periods, but that it is impractical to identify which R&D expenditures actually do provide future economic benefit. Accordingly, all R&D costs are to be recorded as expenses in the year they are incurred. This rule leads to a systematic overstatement of R&D expenses and a systematic understatement of R&D assets.

STOP & THINK

Would you expect that a rule requiring all firms to expense R&D outlays would cause R&D expenditures to decrease? Why or why not?

FYI

The International Accounting Standards Board (IASB) has established an R&D accounting rule that many think is superior to the FASB rule. The IASB rule requires research costs to be expensed and development costs to be capitalized. Research costs are defined as those R&D costs incurred before technological feasibility has been established.

Advertising

Every year in the two weeks of hype preceding the Super Bowl, we hear about the incredible number of media people covering the event and about how much money advertisers are paying for a 30-second spot during the broadcast. We also hear a little bit about the football teams. With advertising costs running in excess of $2 million for 30 seconds, one has to believe that the advertisers expect some future economic benefit from the advertising. So, should advertising costs be capitalized or expensed?

For accounting purposes, the general presumption is that advertising costs should be expensed because of the uncertainty of the future benefits. However, in selected cases in which the future benefits are more certain, advertising costs should be capitalized. This type of advertising involves targeted advertising to customers who have purchased products in the past. Such advertising is also characterized by the ability to estimate how many customers will respond favorably.

As these discussions of R&D and advertising illustrate, capitalize-or-expense decisions can be quite difficult from a conceptual standpoint. The general rule of thumb is that, when there is significant uncertainty about whether an expenditure should be capitalized or expensed, expense it. This approach is in line with the traditional conservatism of accounting, but be aware that it can result in a significant understatement of the economic assets of a company.

REMEMBER THIS...

- Conceptually, a cost should be recorded as an asset whenever it has a probable future economic benefit.

- In practice, it is frequently quite difficult to tell when a cost should be recorded as an asset (capitalized) and when it should be recorded as an expense.

- In some areas, such as research and development (R&D) and advertising, specific accounting rules have been developed to create more uniformity about which costs should be expensed and which should be capitalized.

Summarizing Operations on an Income Statement

Prepare an income statement summarizing operating activities as well as other revenues and expenses, extraordinary items, and earnings per share.

(5) Having now completed our discussion of operating revenues and expenses (in Chapters 6, 7, and thus far in 8), you are ready to examine an income statement, such as the one in Exhibit 6, and see how operating results are communicated to investors and creditors. The numbers in the income statement do not relate to any previous examples; they are shown here for illustrative purposes only.

This income statement shows that with net sales revenue of $2,475,000, P & L Company had net income of $385,000. The income statement classifies and accounts for the other $2,090,000 ($2,475,000 − $385,000). Sales revenue, cost of goods sold, and operating expenses (which are separated into selling expenses and general and administrative expenses on the income statement) have already been explained. It is important to note that operating income of $726,000 shows how much P & L Company earned from carrying on its major operations. These items constitute the major ongoing components of the income statement. Items shown at the bottom of the income statement are not part of the main operations of the business or are unusual and nonrecurring in nature.

Other Revenues and Expenses

other revenues and expenses

Items incurred or earned from activities that are outside of, or peripheral to, the normal operations of a firm.

Other revenues and expenses are those items incurred or earned from activities outside of, or peripheral to, the normal operations of a firm. For example, a manufacturing company that receives dividends from its investments in the stock of another firm would show those dividend revenues as "Other Revenues and Expenses." This way, investors can see how much of a firm's income is from its major operating activity and how much is from peripheral activities, such as investing in other companies. The most common items reported in this section are interest and investment revenues and expenses. The other revenues and expenses category also includes gains and losses from the sale of assets other than inventory, such as land and buildings.

Extraordinary Items

extraordinary items

Nonoperating gains and losses that are unusual in nature, infrequent in occurrence, and material in amount.

The **extraordinary items** section of an income statement is reserved for reporting special nonoperating gains and losses. This category is restrictive and

EXHIBIT 6	Sample Income Statement

P & L Company
Income Statement
For the Year Ended December 31, 2009

Revenues:			
Gross sales revenue		$2,500,000	
Less: Sales returns		(12,000)	
Less: Sales discounts		(13,000)	
Net sales revenue			$2,475,000
Cost of goods sold			1,086,000
Gross margin			$1,389,000
Operating expenses:			
Selling expenses:			
Sales salaries expense	$200,000		
Sales commissions expense	60,000		
Advertising expense	45,000		
Delivery expense	14,000		
Total selling expenses		$ 319,000	
General and administrative expenses:			
Administrative salaries expense	$278,000		
Rent expense, office equipment	36,000		
Property tax expense	22,000		
Miscellaneous expenses	8,000		
Total general and administrative expenses		344,000	
Total operating expenses			663,000
Operating income			$ 726,000
Other revenues and expenses:			
Dividend revenue		$ 5,000	
Gain on sale of land		4,000	
Interest expense		(85,000)	
Net other revenues and expenses			(76,000)
Income from operations before income taxes			$ 650,000
Income taxes on operations (30%)			195,000
Income before extraordinary item			$ 455,000
Extraordinary item:			
Flood loss		$ (100,000)	
Income tax effect (30%)		30,000	(70,000)
Net income			$ 385,000
Earnings per share (100,000 shares outstanding):			
Income before extraordinary item			$4.55
Extraordinary loss			(0.70)
Net income			$3.85

 FYI

Another item that is reported in a separate section of the income statement relates to discontinued operations. When a company decides to cease the operations of a segment or a division, it must provide careful disclosure as to the past profitability of the segment and the expected costs associated with closing the segment.

includes only those items that are (1) unusual in nature, (2) infrequent in occurrence, and (3) material in amount. They are separated from other revenues and expenses so that readers can identify them as onetime, or nonrecurring, events. Extraordinary items are rare but can include losses or gains from floods, fires, earthquakes, and so on. For example, in 1980 when Mount St. Helens erupted in Washington, mudslides and flooding adversely affected much of the **Weyerhaeuser Company**'s timberlands.

© INTERNETWORK MEDIA/PHOTODISC GREEN/GETTY IMAGES INC.

The 1980 eruption of Mount St. Helens caused **Weyerhaeuser Company** to report an extraordinary loss of $66.7 million. However, it's not likely Weyerhaeuser will have to worry about that extraordinary event happening again anytime soon!

Weyerhaeuser reported an extraordinary loss of $66.7 million in 1980 to cover standing timber, buildings, equipment, and other damaged items. Interestingly enough, the attack on the World Trade Center in September of 2001 was not accounted for as an extraordinary item. Accounting standard-setters determined that the economic effects of the World Trade Center attack were so pervasive as to make it impossible to separate the direct costs stemming from the attack from the economic costs (including lost revenue) created by the transformation of the economic landscape created by the attack.

If a firm has an extraordinary loss, its taxes are lower than they would be on the basis of ordinary operations. P & L Company, for example, actually paid only $165,000 ($195,000 based on operations less a $30,000 tax benefit from the extraordinary loss) in taxes. On the other hand, if a firm has an extraordinary gain, its taxes are increased. Therefore, to ensure that the full effect of the gain or loss is presented, extraordinary items are always shown together with their tax effects so that a net-of-tax amount can be seen. Thus, income tax expense may appear in two places on the income statement: below operating income before income taxes and in the extraordinary items section.

Earnings per Share

earnings per share (EPS)

The amount of net income (earnings) related to each share of stock; computed by dividing net income by the number of shares of stock outstanding during the period.

As noted in Chapter 2, a company is required to show **earnings per share (EPS)** on the income statement. If extraordinary items are included on the income statement, a firm will report EPS figures on income before extraordinary items, on extraordinary items, and on net income. Earnings per share is calculated by dividing a firm's net income by the number of shares of stock outstanding during the period. Exhibit 6 assumes that 100,000 shares of stock are outstanding. Earnings-per-share amounts are important because they allow potential investors to compare the profitability of all firms, whether large or small. Thus, the performance of a company earning $200 million and having 200,000 shares of stock outstanding can be compared with a company earning $60,000 and with 30,000 shares outstanding.

Income statements will often report two EPS figures—basic and diluted. The basic earnings per share figure is based on historical information. The diluted earnings per share number considers stock transactions that might occur in the future, the most common example being the exercise of stock options. Consider the following simplified example.

Burt Company reported net income for the year 2009 of $300,000. As of January 1, Burt had 100,000 shares of stock outstanding; those shares of stock were outstanding throughout the year. In addition, as of January 1, Burt had stock options outstanding that allowed certain executives to receive 50,000 shares of stock *for free* at a time of their choosing. As of December 31, the executives had not yet exercised the options.

basic earnings per share

An earnings per share figure that divides net income by the number of shares of stock outstanding.

diluted earnings per share

An earnings per share figure that considers the effect on net income and shares outstanding of events that will likely occur in the future, such as the exercising of favorable stock options.

Burt Company will compute two EPS numbers for 2009. The **basic earnings per share** is a straightforward computation based on Burt's reported net income and number of shares outstanding during the year. In this case, basic EPS is $3.00 per share ($300,000 net income/100,000 shares outstanding). Burt also computes **diluted earnings per share**. The diluted EPS number can be thought of as the earnings per share that would have been earned by each owner of one share *if* the holders of favorable contracts, such as the stock options in the case of Burt Company, had decided to exercise their rights at the beginning of the year. The diluted EPS number is really a future-oriented number; it gives the shareholders an indication of what their earnings per share next year might be if existing contracts, such as the options in this case, are exercised and new shares are issued. In this case, the diluted EPS is $2.00 per share [$300,000/(100,000 shares + 50,000 potential shares)]. Options are just one example of contracts that can "dilute" the earnings per share of existing shareholders; another example is bonds (basically corporate IOUs) that can be converted into shares of stock. Bonds are discussed in Chapter 10.

Differing Income Statement Formats

The income statement featured in Exhibit 6 demonstrates detailed disclosure of a company's operations. Most companies do not provide that level of detail. The information contained in income statements varies from company to company. For example, **Wal-Mart** (see Appendix A) summarizes the results of its operations in 19 lines. **IBM**, on the other hand, provides detailed revenue and cost figures on the face of its income statements for each of its five operating segments (hardware, global services, software, global financing, and enterprise investments). **Ford Motor Company** provides detail in its income statements as to the operations of its two very different lines of business—automotive and financial services. Keep in mind that the format of the income statement will vary across companies but the information contained in the income statement is the same—revenues and expenses.

REMEMBER THIS...

- The results of operating activities are summarized and reported on an income statement.
- On an income statement, cost of goods sold is subtracted from net sales to arrive at gross margin, or the amount a company marks up its inventory.
- Operating expenses are then subtracted from gross margin to arrive at operating income.
- Nonoperating items, such as other revenues and expenses, extraordinary items, and earnings per share, are reported on the income statement below operating income.

REVIEW OF
LEARNING OBJECTIVES

① Account for the various components of employee compensation expense.

Total employee compensation can involve some or all of the following:

- Payroll
- Compensated absences
- Bonuses
- Stock options
- Postemployment benefits
- Pensions
- Postretirement benefits other than pensions

② Compute income tax expense, including appropriate consideration of deferred tax items.

- Sales tax—Reported as a liability until the funds are forwarded to the appropriate government agency.
- Property tax—When paid in advance, the amount is reported as a prepaid asset until the time period covered by the property tax has expired.
- Income tax—Deferred income taxes reported to ensure that reported income tax expense for a year represents all of the income tax consequences arising from transactions undertaken during the year.

③ Distinguish between contingent items that should be recognized in the financial statements and those that should be merely disclosed in the financial statement notes.

- **Probable**—expense and liability recognized
- **Possible**—note disclosure required
- **Remote**—no disclosure required

④ Understand when an expenditure should be recorded as an asset and when it should be recorded as an expense.

- Conceptually, a cost should be recorded as an asset whenever it has a probable future economic benefit.
- In practice, it is frequently quite difficult to tell when a cost should be recorded as an asset (capitalized) and when it should be recorded as an expense.
- In some areas, such as research and development (R&D) and advertising, specific accounting rules have been developed to create more uniformity about which costs should be expensed and which should be capitalized.

⑤ Prepare an income statement summarizing operating activities as well as other revenues and expenses, extraordinary items, and earnings per share.

- On an income statement, cost of goods sold is subtracted from net sales to arrive at gross margin, or the amount a company marks up its inventory.
- Operating expenses are then subtracted from gross margin to arrive at operating income.
- Nonoperating items, such as other revenues and expenses, extraordinary items, and earnings per share, are reported on the income statement below operating income.

KEY TERMS & CONCEPTS

basic earnings per
   share, 363

bonus, 347

contingency, 355

defined benefit plan, 349

defined contribution
   plan, 348

diluted earnings per
   share, 363

earnings per share
   (EPS), 362

employee stock
   options, 347

environmental
   liabilities, 356

extraordinary
   items, 360

other revenues and
   expenses, 360

pension, 348

postemployment
   benefits, 348

sales tax payable, 351

Social Security (FICA)
   taxes, 345

REVIEW PROBLEM

The Income Statement

From the following information, prepare an income statement for Southern Corporation for the year ended December 31, 2009. Assume that there are 200,000 shares of stock outstanding.

Sales Returns	$ 50,000
Sales Discounts	70,000
Gross Sales Revenue	9,000,000
Flood Loss	80,000
Income Taxes on Operations	500,000
Administrative Salaries Expense	360,000
Sales Salaries Expense	800,000
Rent Expense (General and Administrative)	32,000
Utilities Expense (General and Administrative)	4,000
Supplies Expense (General and Administrative)	16,000
Delivery Expense (Selling)	6,300
Payroll Tax Expense (Selling)	6,000
Automobile Expense (General and Administrative)	3,800
Insurance Expense (General and Administrative)	34,000
Advertising Expense (Selling)	398,000
Interest Revenue	6,000
Interest Expense	92,000
Insurance Expense (Selling)	7,000
Entertainment Expense (Selling)	7,200
Miscellaneous Selling Expenses	15,000
Miscellaneous General and Administrative Expenses	10,800
Cost of Goods Sold	5,950,000
Tax rate applicable to flood loss	30%

Solution

The first step in preparing an income statement is classifying items, as follows:

Revenue Accounts	
Sales Returns	$ 50,000
Sales Discounts	70,000
Gross Sales Revenue	9,000,000

(continued)

Cost of Goods Sold Accounts	
Cost of Goods Sold	$5,950,000

Selling Expense Accounts	
Sales Salaries Expense	$800,000
Delivery Expense	6,300
Payroll Tax Expense	6,000
Advertising Expense	398,000
Insurance Expense	7,000
Entertainment Expense	7,200
Miscellaneous Selling Expenses	15,000

General and Administrative Expense Accounts	
Administrative Salaries Expense	$360,000
Rent Expense	32,000
Utilities Expense	4,000
Supplies Expense	16,000
Automobile Expense	3,800
Insurance Expense	34,000
Miscellaneous General and Administrative Expenses	10,800

Other Revenue and Expense Accounts	
Interest Revenue	$ 6,000
Interest Expense	92,000

Miscellaneous Accounts	
Income Taxes on Operations	$500,000

Extraordinary Item Accounts	
Flood Loss	$80,000
Tax rate	30%

Once the accounts are classified, the income statement is prepared by including the accounts in the following format:

	Net Sales Revenue (Gross Sales Revenue − Sales Returns − Sales Discounts)
−	Cost of Goods Sold
=	Gross Margin
−	Selling Expenses
−	General and Administrative Expenses
=	Operating Income
+/−	Other Revenues and Expenses (add Net Revenues, subtract Net Expenses)
=	Income before Income Taxes

(continued)

-     Income Taxes on Operations
=   Income before Extraordinary Items
+/−   Extraordinary Items (add Extraordinary Gains, subtract Extraordinary Losses, net of applicable taxes)
=   Net Income

After net income has been computed, earnings per share is calculated and added to the bottom of the statement. It is important that the proper heading be included.

Southern Corporation
Income Statement
For the Year Ended December 31, 2009

Revenues:			
Gross sales revenue		$9,000,000	
Less: Sales returns		(50,000)	
Less: Sales discounts		(70,000)	
Net sales revenue			$8,880,000
Cost of goods sold			5,950,000
Gross margin			$2,930,000
Operating expenses:			
Selling expenses:			
Sales salaries expense	$800,000		
Delivery expense	6,300		
Payroll tax expense	6,000		
Advertising expense	398,000		
Insurance expense	7,000		
Entertainment expense	7,200		
Miscellaneous expenses	15,000		
Total selling expenses		$1,239,500	
General and administrative expenses:			
Administrative salaries expense	$360,000		
Rent expense	32,000		
Utilities expense	4,000		
Supplies expense	16,000		
Automobile expense	3,800		
Insurance expense	34,000		
Miscellaneous expenses	10,800		
Total general and administrative expenses		460,600	
Total operating expenses			1,700,100
Operating income			$1,229,900
Other revenues and expenses:			
Interest revenue		$ 6,000	
Interest expense		(92,000)	
Net other revenues and expenses			(86,000)
Income from operations before income taxes			$1,143,900
Income taxes on operations			500,000
Income before extraordinary item			$ 643,900
Extraordinary item:			
Flood loss		$ (80,000)	
Income tax effect (30%)		24,000	(56,000)
Net income			$ 587,900
Earnings per share:			
Before extraordinary items		$ 3.22	($643,900 ÷ 200,000 shares)
Extraordinary loss		(0.28)	($ 56,000 ÷ 200,000 shares)
Net income		$ 2.94	($587,900 ÷ 200,000 shares)

DISCUSSION QUESTIONS

1. Why is the accounting for payroll-related liabilities more complicated than the accounting for other current liabilities?

2. If the period of time covered by a company's payroll does not coincide with the last day of the year for financial reporting, how is accounting for the payroll affected by this situation?

3. What is a compensated absence?

4. What danger is there in basing a manager's bonus on reported net income?

5. Why might a company offer stock options to an employee instead of simply paying the employee cash? Why might the employee accept stock options instead of asking to be paid in cash?

6. For a stock option to be valuable at some future point in time, what must happen to the company's stock price?

7. Severance benefits resulting from a company restructuring are reported as an expense in the period that the restructuring decision is made rather than when the benefits are actually paid. Why?

8. What is the difference between a defined contribution pension plan and a defined benefit pension plan?

9. How is a company's pension obligation reported in its balance sheet?

10. List and briefly discuss the three components of pension expense discussed in the chapter.

11. In what ways do postretirement health-care and life insurance benefit plans differ from postretirement pension plans?

12. Why is an end-of-year adjusting entry for property taxes often necessary?

13. In your opinion, what is the primary objective of determining pretax financial accounting income? How does this objective differ from the objectives of determining taxable income as defined by the IRS?

14. When and how does a company record the amount owed to the government for income taxes for a given year?

15. What causes deferred income taxes?

16. What is the difference between a "contingent liability" and a "liability"?

17. Escalating environmental liabilities are a major concern of companies today. How does a company know when to record such liabilities?

18. Currently **Microsoft** spends a tremendous amount of money on research and development costs to continuously develop new products. How are such R&D costs accounted for?

19. XYZ Corporation pays for advertising costs all the time. Sometimes the company records these payments as assets, and sometimes it records them as expenses. Why would XYZ use different accounting treatments?

20. What types of items would be included on an income statement as "other revenues and expenses"?

21. More than ever before, tremendous attention is being paid to a company's earnings-per-share number. Why do you think investors and creditors pay so much attention to earnings per share?

PRACTICE EXERCISES

PE 8-1 Salaries Expense Calculation
LO1 Using the following data, compute salaries expense.

State Withholding Taxes Payable	$ 6,100
FICA Taxes Payable, Employer	6,503
Salaries Payable	59,647
Federal Unemployment Taxes Payable	720
Federal Withholding Taxes Payable	12,750
State Unemployment Taxes Payable	2,380
FICA Taxes Payable, Employees	6,503

PE 8-2 Salaries Expense Journal Entry
LO1 Refer to the data in PE 8-1. Make the journal entry necessary to record salaries expense for the period.

PE 8-3 Payroll Tax Expense Calculation
LO1 Refer to the data in PE 8-1. Compute payroll tax expense.

PE 8-4 **Payroll Tax Expense Journal Entry**

LO1 Refer to the data in PE 8-1. Make the journal entry necessary to record payroll tax expense for the period.

PE 8-5 **Salaries and Payroll Tax Payments**

LO1 Refer to the data in PE 8-1. Make the journal entries necessary to record the payment of the payable accounts related to salaries expense and payroll tax expense to (1) the federal government, (2) the state government, and (3) the employees.

PE 8-6 **Accruing Compensated Absences**

LO1 Assume an employee earns $150 per day and accrues one sick day each month. Make the journal entry necessary at the end of the quarter to record the accrual of the sick days during the quarter.

PE 8-7 **Using Compensated Absences**

LO1 The employee mentioned in PE 8-6 used one sick day. For simplicity, combine the various taxes into one account called "Various Taxes Payable." The effective tax rate for all of the various taxes is 20%. Make the journal entry necessary to record the use of the sick day.

PE 8-8 **Accounting for Employee Stock Options**

LO1 An employee receives stock options as part of her compensation package. Those options allow the employee to purchase 1,000 shares of stock for $40 per share. If after one year the stock price has increased to $58 per share and the employee elects to exercise all of her stock options, how much will the employee net from the options?

PE 8-9 **Postemployment Benefits**

LO1 Because of a drop in demand for its products, the company found it necessary to lay off 350 employees. The employment contract grants termination benefits worth an estimated $10,000 to each employee. Make the journal entry necessary to record the termination of the employees.

PE 8-10 **Pension Terminology**

LO1 Identify which one of the following terms correctly matches the following definition: The amount a company's pension obligation increases as a result of employees working and earning more benefits.
  a. Pension fund
  b. Pension-related interest cost
  c. Service cost
  d. Pension expense
  e. Return on pension fund

PE 8-11 **Net Pension Asset/Liability**

LO1 Companies A, B, and C report the following information:

	A	B	C
Pension benefit obligation	$ 3,920	$ 9,230	$1,302
Service cost	235	500	150
Pension fund assets	2,004	11,023	1,350
Expected return on pension fund assets	200	1,000	120

For each of the companies, determine the amount of the net pension asset/liability. Be sure to specify whether the amount is an asset or a liability.

PE 8-12   **Pension Expense**

LO1   Using the following numbers, compute pension expense.

Expected return on fund assets	$ 445
Pension benefit obligation	3,200
Service cost	265
Interest cost	320
Pension fund assets	4,100

PE 8-13   **Sales Tax**

LO2   The company sold merchandise for $448; this price does *not* include sales tax. The state sales tax rate is 6.25%. Make the journal entry necessary to record this transaction.

PE 8-14   **Property Taxes**

LO2   The company paid $10,800 in advance for one year of property taxes on September 24. The property taxes are for the one-year period beginning October 1. Make the journal entries necessary to record (1) the payment of the property taxes and (2) the year-end adjusting entry on December 31.

PE 8-15   **Income Tax Expense**

LO2   Which one of the following statements correctly describes income tax expense?
a. The amount of cash paid for income taxes during the year.
b. The amount of income tax owed as of the end of the year.
c. The amount of cash that will be paid for income taxes next year.
d. The amount of income taxes attributable to the income earned during the year.
e. The amount of income taxes payable as reported in a company's income tax return.

PE 8-16   **Deferred Tax Liability**

LO2   The company invested $2,500 in a mutual fund on April 1. By December 31, the value of the mutual fund had increased to $3,100, and the company did *not* sell any portion of the mutual fund during the year. The company's income tax rate is 35%. Prepare the journal entry necessary to record the deferred income tax liability.

PE 8-17   **Deferred Tax Assets**

LO2   The company invested $5,600 in a mutual fund on August 1. By December 31, the value of the mutual fund had declined to $3,900, and the company did not sell any portion of the mutual fund during the year. The company's income tax rate is 25%. Prepare the journal entry necessary to record the deferred income tax asset.

PE 8-18   **Contingent Liabilities**

LO3   Which one of the following correctly describes the circumstances in which a contingent liability should be recognized as a liability in the financial statements?
a. The chance of the future event occurring is remote.
b. The chance of the future event occurring is possible.
c. The chance of the future event occurring is probable.
d. The chance of the future event occurring is slight.
e. The chance of the future event occurring is more likely than not.

PE 8-19   **Capitalize versus Expense**

LO4   Which one of the following statements is correct?
a. When there is significant uncertainty about whether an expenditure should be capitalized or expensed, capitalize it.
b. When there is significant uncertainty about whether an expenditure should be capitalized or expensed, expense it.

(continued)

c. Generally, advertising costs are capitalized because it is easy for firms to trace advertising dollars spent to revenue generated from such advertisements.

d. Expenditures made for equipment and buildings should be expensed in the period of the purchase.

e. Research and development expenditures are typically capitalized in the period in which they are incurred.

PE 8-20   **Income Statement Classification**

LO5   Using the following data, prepare a classified income statement. The income tax rate on all items is 25%. (*Hint:* Net income is $52,050.)

Advertising expense	$ 4,000
Sales returns	5,000
Cost of goods sold	80,000
Dividend revenue	2,000
Gain on sale of equipment	1,000
Interest expense	5,000
Rent expense	3,600
Sales discounts	10,000
Salaries expense	11,000
Gross sales	215,000
Tornado loss	30,000

PE 8-21   **Earnings per Share**

LO5   The company had 300,000 shares of stock outstanding throughout the year. In addition, as of January 1 the company had issued stock options that allowed employees to receive 50,000 shares of stock for free at a time of their choosing in the future. As of the end of the year, none of the options had been exercised. Net income for the year was $510,000. Compute (1) basic earnings per share and (2) diluted earnings per share.

EXERCISES

E 8-22   **Payroll Accounting**

LO1   Stockbridge Stores, Inc., has three employees, Frank Wall, Mary Jones, and Susan Wright. Summaries of their 2009 salaries and withholdings are as follows:

Employee	Gross Salaries	Federal Income Taxes Withheld	State Income Taxes Withheld	FICA Taxes Withheld
Frank Wall	$54,000	$6,500	$2,500	$4,131
Mary Jones	39,000	4,800	1,900	2,984
Susan Wright	34,000	4,250	1,500	2,601

1. Prepare the summary entry for salaries paid to the employees for the year 2009.

2. Assume that, in addition to FICA taxes, the employer has incurred $192 for federal unemployment taxes and $720 for state unemployment taxes. Prepare the summary journal entry to record the payroll tax liability for 2009, assuming no taxes have yet been paid.

3. **Interpretive Question:** What other types of items are frequently withheld from employees' paychecks in addition to income taxes and FICA taxes?

E 8-23
LO1

Bonus Computation and Journal Entry

Chris Anger is the president of Anger Company, and his brother, George Anger, is the vice president. Their compensation package includes bonuses of 5% for Chris Anger and 4% for George Anger of net income that exceeds $325,000. Net income for the year 2009 has just been computed to be $745,000.

1. Compute the amount of bonuses to be paid to Chris and George Anger.
2. Prepare the journal entries to record the accrual and payment of the bonuses. Summarize all withholding taxes related to the bonuses in an account called Various Taxes Payable. Taxes payable on the bonuses total $8,400 for Chris and $6,720 for George.

E 8-24
LO1

Stock Options: Fair Value Method

On January 1, 2009, the Magily Company established a stock option plan for its senior employees. A total of 60,000 options were granted that permit employees to purchase 60,000 shares of stock at $48 per share. Each option had a fair value of $11 on the date the options were granted. The market price for Magily stock on January 1, 2009, was $50. The employees are required to remain with Magily Company for the entire year of 2009 in order to be able to exercise these options.

Compute the total amount of compensation expense to be associated with these options under the fair value method.

E 8-25
LO1

Stock Options: Fair Value Method

Refer to the information in E 8-24. If those holding stock options can purchase a share of stock for $48 and the market value of a share of stock on 1/1/09 is $50, how can the option to purchase the share be worth $11. What factors would cause the option to be worth more than $2 ($50 − $48)? Remember, the options cannot be exercised until the end of the year.

E 8-26
LO1

Pensions on the Balance Sheet

Pension plan information for Brassfield Company is as follows:

December 31, 2009	
Pension obligation liability	$4,300,000
December 31, 2009	
Pension fund assets	4,640,000
During 2009	
Total pension expense	250,000

How will this information be reported on Brassfield's balance sheet as of December 31, 2009?

E 8-27
LO1

Computing Pension Expense

Chanelle Company reports the following pension information for 2009:

Pension-related interest cost for the year	$ 65,000
Pension fund assets, end of year	895,000
Pension obligation liability, end of year	930,000
Pension service cost for the year	90,000
Return on pension fund assets for the year	115,000

1. What pension amount would Chanelle report on its balance sheet as of the end of the year?
2. Compute the amount to be reported on the income statement as pension expense for the year.

E 8-28   **Pension Computations**

LO1   The following pension information is for three different companies. For each company, compute the missing amount or amounts.

	Company 1	Company 2	Company 3
Pension fund assets	$100,000	$75,000	$ (e)
Pension obligation liability	(a)	80,000	100,000
Net pension asset (liability)	20,000	(c)	(25,000)
Pension-related interest cost	$ 10,000	$ (d)	$ 20,000
Service cost	8,000	6,000	23,000
Return on pension plan assets	5,000	8,000	(f)
Pension expense	(b)	10,000	35,000

E 8-29   **Accounting for Property Taxes**

LO2   In June 2008, Hans Company received a bill from the county government for property taxes on its land and buildings for the period July 1, 2008, through June 30, 2009. The amount of the tax bill is $17,400, and payment is due August 1, 2008. Hans Company uses the calendar year for financial reporting purposes.

1. Prepare the journal entries to record payment of the property taxes on August 1, 2008.
2. Prepare the adjusting entry for property taxes on December 31, 2008.

E 8-30   **Deferred Income Taxes**

LO2   Yosef Company began operating on January 1, 2009. At the end of the first year of operations, Yosef reported $750,000 income before income taxes on its income statement but only $660,000 taxable income on its tax return. This difference arose because $90,000 in income earned during 2009 was not yet taxable according to the income tax regulations. The tax rate is 35%.

1. Compute the amount of income tax that Yosef legally owes for taxable income generated during 2009.
2. Compute the amount of income tax expense to be reported on Yosef's income statement for 2009.
3. State whether Yosef has a deferred income tax asset or a deferred income tax liability as of the end of 2009. What is the amount of the asset or liability?

E 8-31   **Deferred Income Taxes**

LO2   Oranjestad Company began operating on January 1, 2009. At the end of the first year of operations, Oranjestad reported $650,000 income before income taxes on its income statement but taxable income of $720,000 on its tax return. This difference arose because $70,000 in expenses incurred during 2009 were not yet deductible for income tax purposes according to the income tax regulations. The tax rate is 35%.

1. Compute the amount of income tax that Oranjestad legally owes for taxable income generated during 2009.
2. Compute the amount of income tax expense to be reported on Oranjestad's income statement for 2009.
3. State whether Oranjestad has a deferred income tax asset or a deferred income tax liability as of the end of 2009. What is the amount of the asset or liability?

E 8-32   **Contingent Liabilities**

LO3   Rayn Company is involved in the following legal matters:

a. A customer is suing Rayn for allegedly selling a faulty and dangerous product. Rayn's attorneys believe that there is a 40% chance of Rayn's losing the suit.
b. A federal agency has accused Rayn of violating numerous employee safety laws. The company faces significant fines if found guilty. Rayn's attorneys feel that the company

(continued)

has complied with all applicable laws, and they therefore place the probability of incurring the fines at less than 10%.

c. Rayn has been named in a gender discrimination lawsuit. In the past, Rayn has systematically promoted its male employees at a faster rate than it has promoted its female employees. Rayn's attorneys judge the probability that Rayn will lose this lawsuit at more than 90%.

For each item, determine the appropriate accounting treatment.

E 8-33   **Classifying Expenditures as Assets or Expenses**

LO4   Determining whether an expenditure should be expensed or capitalized is often difficult. Consider each of the following independent situations and indicate whether you would recommend that the cost be expensed or capitalized as an asset. Explain your answer.

1. Splash.com has spent $1.5 million for a 30-second advertisement to be aired during the Super Bowl. The ad introduces the company's new Web-based product, and the company expects the ad to increase sales for at least 18 months.

2. Chromosome.com has spent $8 million on research related to genetic diseases. The company expects this research to lead to substantial revenues, beginning in the next year.

3. Catalog.com is an online catalog sales company. Catalog.com has just spent $5 million designing a targeted advertising campaign that will encourage regular customers of the company's online catalog service to buy new products.

4. Food.com is an online seller of groceries. The company just spent $4 million building a new warehouse. The warehouse is expected to be useful for the next 15 years.

E 8-34   **Preparing an Income Statement**

LO5   Bateman Company is preparing financial statements for the calendar year 2009. The following totals for each account have been verified as correct:

Office Supplies on Hand	$ 730
Insurance Expense	420
Gross Sales Revenue	18,000
Cost of Goods Sold	8,700
Sales Returns	800
Interest Expense	150
Accounts Payable	490
Accounts Receivable	610
Extraordinary Loss	1,980
Selling Expenses	860
Office Supplies Used	240
Cash	750
Revenue from Investments	430
Number of shares of capital stock	200

Prepare an income statement. Assume a 35% income tax rate on both income from operations and extraordinary items. Include EPS numbers.

E 8-35   **Unifying Concepts: The Income Statement**

LO5   Use the following information to prepare an income statement for Fairchild Corporation for the year ended December 31, 2009. You should show separate classifications for revenues, cost of goods sold, gross margin, selling expenses, general and administrative expenses, operating income, other revenues and expenses, income before income taxes, income taxes, and net income. (*Hint:* Net income is $27,276.)

(continued)

Sales Returns	$ 4,280
Income Taxes	26,000
Interest Revenue	2,400
Office Supplies Expense (General and Administrative)	400
Utilities Expense (General and Administrative)	3,980
Office Salaries Expense (General and Administrative)	12,064
Miscellaneous Selling Expenses	460
Insurance Expense (Selling)	1,160
Advertising Expense	6,922
Sales Salaries Expense	40,088
Sales Discounts	3,644
Interest Expense	1,170
Miscellaneous General and Administrative Expenses	620
Insurance Expense (General and Administrative)	600
Payroll Tax Expense (General and Administrative)	3,600
Store Supplies Expense (Selling)	800
Delivery Expense (Selling)	2,198
Inventory, January 1, 2009	79,400
Sales Revenue	395,472
Cost of Goods Sold	262,610
Purchases	230,560
Purchases Discounts	3,050
Inventory, December 31, 2009	44,300
Average number of shares of stock outstanding	10,000

PROBLEMS

P 8-36

LO1

Payroll Accounting

Orange County Bank has three employees, Albert Myers, Juan Moreno, and Michi Endo. During January 2009, these three employees earned $6,000, $4,200, and $4,000, respectively. The following table summarizes the required withholding rates on each individual's income for the month of January:

Employee	Federal Income Tax Withholdings	State Income Tax Withholdings	FICA Tax
Albert Myers	33%	3%	7.65%
Juan Moreno	28	4	7.65
Michi Endo	28	5	7.65

You are also informed that the bank is subject to the following unemployment tax rates on the salaries earned by the employees during January 2009:

Federal unemployment tax	0.8%
State unemployment tax	3.0%

Required:
1. Prepare the journal entry to record salaries payable for the month of January.
2. Prepare the journal entry to record payment of the January salaries to employees.
3. Prepare the journal entry to record the bank's payroll taxes for the month of January.

P 8-37   **Determining Payroll Costs**

LO1   Parley Pharmaceuticals pays its salespeople a base salary of $2,000 per month plus a commission. Each salesperson starts with a commission of 1.5% of total gross sales for the month. The commission is increased thereafter according to seniority and productivity, up to a maximum of 5%. Parley has five salespeople with gross sales for the month of July and commission rates as follows:

	Commission Rate	Gross Sales
Jordan	3.0%	$140,000
Alisa	4.5	200,000
Kasey	1.5	110,000
Trevor	5.0	180,000
Chad	2.5	90,000

The FICA tax rate is 7.65%. In addition, state and federal income taxes of 20% are withheld from each employee.

Required:

1. Compute Parley's total payroll expense (base salary plus commissions) for the month.
2. Compute the total amount of cash paid to employees for compensation for the month.
3. **Interpretive Question:** Briefly outline the advantages and disadvantages of having no income taxes withheld, but instead relying on individual taxpayers to pay the entire amount of their income tax at the end of the year when they file their tax return.

P 8-38   **Stock Options**

LO1   On January 1, 2009, Tiger Man Company established a stock option plan for its senior employees. A total of 400,000 options were granted that permit employees to purchase 400,000 shares of stock at $20 per share. Each option had a fair value of $5 on the grant date. The market price for Tiger Man stock on January 1, 2009, was $20. The employees are required to remain with Tiger Man for three years (2009, 2010, and 2011) in order to be able to exercise these options. Tiger Man's net income for 2009, before including any consideration of compensation expense, is $675,000.

Required:

1. Compute the compensation expense associated with these options for 2009 under the fair value method. Note that the period of time that the employees must work to be able to exercise the options is three years.
2. **Interpretive Question:** You are a Tiger Man stockholder. What objections might you have to Tiger Man's employee stock option plan?

P 8-39   **Accounting for Pensions**

LO1   The following information is available from John Gammon Company relating to its defined benefit pension plan:

Balances as of January 1, 2009:	
Pension obligation liability	$4,300
Pension fund assets	3,800
Activity for 2009:	
Service cost	$ 550
Contributions to pension fund	240
Benefit payments to retirees	200
Return on plan assets	340
Pension-related interest cost	344

(continued)

Required:

1. Compute the amount of pension expense to be reported on the income statement for 2009.
2. Determine the net pension amount to be reported on the balance sheet at the end of the year. *Note:* The benefit payments to retirees are made out of the pension fund assets. These payments reduce both the amount in the pension fund and the amount of the remaining pension obligation.
3. **Interpretive Question:** You are an employee of John Gammon Company and have just received the above information as part of the company's annual report to the employees on the status of the pension plan. Does anything in this information cause you concern? Explain.

P 8-40

LO1

Accounting for Pensions

Marseille Company reported the following information relating to its pension plan for the years 2007 through 2010:

	Year-End Obligation	Year-End Plan Assets	Interest Cost	Service Cost	Return on Assets
2007	$792,300	$598,700	–	–	–
2008	846,807	616,044	$71,307	$74,200	$71,844
2009	917,455	643,669	76,213	79,435	73,925
2010	995,026	695,009	82,571	76,300	77,240

Required:

1. Compute the amount of pension expense to be reported on the income statement for each of the years 2008 through 2010.
2. Determine the net pension amount to be reported on the balance sheet at the end of each year 2007 through 2010. Clearly indicate whether the amount is an asset or a liability.
3. Each year, the amount of the pension obligation is increased by the interest cost and the service cost. The pension obligation is reduced by the amount of pension benefits paid. Compute the amount of pension benefits paid in each of the years 2008 through 2010.
4. Each year, the amount in the pension fund is increased by contributions to the fund and by the return earned on the fund assets. The pension fund amount is reduced by the amount of pension benefits paid. Compute the amount of contributions to the pension fund in each of the years 2008 through 2010.

P 8-41

LO2

Life Cycle of a Deferred Tax Item

Black Kitty Company recorded certain revenues of $10,000 and $20,000 on its books in 2007 and 2008, respectively. However, these revenues were not subject to income taxation until 2009. Company records reveal pretax financial accounting income and taxable income for the three-year period as follows:

	Financial Income	Taxable Income
2007	$44,000	$34,000
2008	38,000	18,000
2009	21,000	51,000

Assume Black Kitty's tax rate is 40% for all periods.

Required:

1. Determine the amount of income tax that will be paid each year from 2007 through 2009.
2. Determine the amount of income tax expense that will be reported on the income statement each year from 2007 through 2009.

(continued)

3. Compute the amount of deferred tax liability that would be reported on the balance sheet at the end of each year.

4. **Interpretive Question:** Why would the IRS allow Black Kitty to defer payment of taxes on some of the revenue earned in 2007 and 2008?

P 8-42

LO5

Unifying Concepts: The Income Statement

From the following information, prepare an income statement for Moriancumer, Inc., for the year ended December 31, 2009. (*Hint:* Net income is $98,500.) Assume that there are 15,000 shares of capital stock outstanding.

Gross Sales Revenue	$4,230,000
Income Taxes	99,000
Cost of Goods Sold	3,116,000
Sales Salaries Expense	350,000
Rent Expense (Selling)	16,000
Payroll Tax Expense (Selling)	4,900
Entertainment Expense (Selling)	1,500
Miscellaneous Selling Expenses	6,300
Miscellaneous General and Administrative Expenses	5,400
Automobile Expense (Selling)	3,500
Insurance Expense (General and Administrative)	700
Interest Expense	39,000
Interest Revenue	2,000
Sales Returns	8,000
Advertising and Promotion Expense	204,000
Insurance Expense (Selling)	17,000
Delivery Expense (Selling)	3,100
Office Supplies Expense (General and Administrative)	8,000
Utilities Expense (General and Administrative)	1,100
Administrative Salaries Expense	200,000
Fire Loss (net of tax)	50,000

P 8-43

LO5

Income Statement Analysis

The following table represents portions of the income statements of Brinkerhoff Company for the years 2007–2009:

	2009	2008	2007
Gross sales revenue	$56,000	$ (9)	$47,600
Sales discounts	0	300	200
Sales returns	0	100	400
Net sales revenue	56,000	(10)	(1)
Beginning inventory	(15)	8,700	(2)
Purchases	33,400	(11)	25,000
Purchases discounts	700	400	800
Freight-in	(16)	0	700
Cost of goods available for sale	40,500	37,800	(3)
Ending inventory	6,900	(12)	(4)
Cost of goods sold	(17)	(13)	(5)
Gross margin	(18)	20,400	(6)
Selling expenses	4,500	(14)	(7)
General and administrative expenses	(19)	3,100	2,800
Income before income taxes	14,300	14,000	11,900
Income taxes	4,250	4,200	(8)
Net income	(20)	9,800	8,400

Required:

Fill in the missing numbers. Assume that gross margin is 40% of net sales revenue.

ANALYTICAL ASSIGNMENTS

AA 8-44

DISCUSSION

Recording Liabilities and the Effect on Bonuses

John Flowers, president of Marquette Company, is paid a salary plus a bonus equal to 10% of pretax income. The company has just computed its pretax income to be $3.4 million. Based on this income, Flowers expects to receive a bonus of $340,000. However, the company has just been told by outside experts that it may have an environmental liability of $2.1 million and that, based on new actuarial estimates, the recorded amount of postretirement benefits is too low by $1.2 million. The experts recommend that both of these liabilities be recorded, which would reduce income to $100,000 and Flowers' bonus to $10,000. Flowers believes he does not need to record the adjustments for the following reasons: the environmental liability is not certain, the amount of the potential liability can't be accurately estimated, and "actuarial estimates" are always changing. Is Flowers violating GAAP if he refuses to allow the company to adjust pretax income, or is the decision to not record the adjustments acceptable because of the uncertainty of the liabilities and the amounts?

AA 8-45

DISCUSSION

Questioning the Accounting for Pensions, Research, and Income Taxes

Tatia Wilks, the president of Lewbacca Company, is concerned about the low earnings that Lewbacca is scheduled to report this year. She called the company's accounting staff into her office to question them about the accounting treatment of several items. She raised the following points:

a. Why do we have to report an expense this year associated with our pension plan? Our company is new, and none of our employees is within even 15 years of retirement. Accordingly, the pension plan won't cost us anything for at least 15 years.

b. Research to find new products and improve our old products is one of our key competitive advantages. However, you tell me that all of the money we spend on research is reported as an expense this year. This is silly because the results of our research comprise our biggest economic asset.

c. We have an excellent staff of tax planners who work hard to legally minimize the amount of income taxes we pay each year. However, I see in the notes to the financial statements that you are requiring our company to report a "deferred income tax expense" for taxes that we don't even owe yet! Why?

How would you respond to each of these points?

AA 8-46

JUDGMENT CALL

***You Decide:* Are stock options and bonus plans an appropriate incentive or a cause for corruption?**

Do employee bonus plans provide incentives to work harder and achieve personal and corporate goals, or are they a catalyst for corporate corruption? For example, assume you work for a Fortune 500 company. You are the chief financial officer of the company and are in charge of the company's accounting. The company is doing well; in fact, you have just been informed that members of top management will each receive 10,000 stock options to purchase company stock if earnings meet forecasts. Your associate tells you that the options will create pressure to meet the forecasts. Is he right?

AA 8-47

JUDGMENT CALL

***You Decide:* Should start-up costs be capitalized or expensed?**

Your spouse is setting up a home-based Web design business. Her purpose for setting up the business is to earn some extra income now and, in two to three years, sell the business. Your spouse is wondering whether she can capitalize the start-up costs or whether they must be expensed. She has heard from other business owners that in order to minimize taxes, it is a lot better to expense as much as you can. With this end goal in mind, what should your spouse do?

AA 8-48

REAL COMPANY
ANALYSIS

Wal-Mart

The 2006 Form 10-K for **Wal-Mart** is included in Appendix A. Locate that Form 10-K and consider the following questions:

1. Find Wal-Mart's financial statement note on "Income taxes."
   a. Using the current tax information and the information given on income before income taxes, compute Wal-Mart's 2005 effective tax rate for both U.S. and international income. The effective tax rate is computed by dividing current taxes by income before income taxes.
   b. As of January 31, 2006, Wal-Mart had $4,097 million in deferred income tax liabilities. What was the source of most of this deferred tax liability?
2. Find Wal-Mart's financial statement note concerning "share-based compensation plans."
   c. Briefly describe Wal-Mart's employee stock option plan.
   d. Wal-Mart's employee stock option plan allows employees to buy Wal-Mart stock at a fixed price in the future. If Wal-Mart's stock price continues to rise, these options could be very valuable. Wal-Mart is required to estimate the value of these options and expense the value of these options as employee compensation. How much stock compensation expense did Wal-Mart recognize in the year ended January 31, 2006?

AA 8-49

REAL COMPANY
ANALYSIS

General Motors

General Motors has the largest set of private pension plans in the world. The company has many different pension plans covering different groups of employees. The following information was extracted from the notes to GM's 2005 financial statements. All numbers are in millions of U.S. dollars. As you can see, for reporting purposes these plans are separated into U.S. plans and non-U.S. plans.

	U.S. Plans Pension Benefits		Non-U.S. Plans Pension Benefits	
	2005	**2004**	**2005**	**2004**
Fair value of plan assets at end of year	$95,250	$90,886	$ 9,925	$ 9,023
Projected benefit obligation at end of year	89,133	90,760	20,641	18,056
Funded status	$ 6,117	$ 126	$(10,716)	$(9,033)

1. The projected benefit obligation is the measure of the value of the pension benefits earned by GM's employees that has not yet been paid. What is GM's total projected benefit obligation?
2. To ensure that employees will be able to collect their pension benefits, GM is required by law to set aside funds in a pension plan. What is the total value of assets in all of these pension funds?
3. Why do you think GM is required to separate its disclosure of pension plans into U.S. and non-U.S. plans?

AA 8-50

REAL COMPANY
ANALYSIS

IBM

Note P to **IBM**'s 2005 financial statements describes how taxes affect IBM's operations. Among the information given is the following (all amounts are in millions of U.S. dollars):

For the year ended December 31:	2005	2004	2003
Income from continuing operations before income taxes:			
U.S. operations	$ 7,450	$ 4,400	$3,662
Non-U.S. operations	4,776	6,269	5,755
Total income from continuing operations before income taxes	$12,226	$10,669	$9,417

(continued)

The continuing operations provision for income taxes by geographic operations is as follows:

For the year ended December 31:	2005	2004	2003
U.S. operations	$2,988	$1,492	$ 937
Non-U.S. operations	1,244	1,680	1,892
Total continuing operations provision for income taxes	$4,232	$3,172	$2,829
Provision for social security, real estate, personal property, and other taxes	$3,501	$3,449	$3,372

1. a. Compute the effective tax rate (income taxes/earnings before income taxes) for both U.S. and non-U.S. operations for 2003, 2004, and 2005.
    b. For each year 2003–2005, compute the percentage of the total tax burden that was made up of income taxes.
2. A deferred tax asset is a tax deduction that has already occurred and has been reported as a financial accounting expense but cannot be used to reduce income taxes until a future year. As of December 31, 2005, IBM reports that it has a deferred tax asset of $3.039 billion related to retirement-related benefits. How would such a deferred tax asset arise?

AA 8-51

INTERNATIONAL

Hutchison Whampoa

In Hong Kong, Li Ka-shing is known as "Superman." Li's personal wealth is estimated to be in excess of $1 billion, and there is a saying in Hong Kong that for every dollar spent, five cents goes into Li's pocket. Li and his family fled from China in 1940 in order to escape the advancing Japanese army. Li dropped out of school at age 13 to support his family by selling plastic trinkets on the streets of Hong Kong. Later, he scraped together enough money to buy a company that produced plastic flowers. His big success came when he bought the real estate surrounding his factory and watched the land skyrocket in value. Today, Li continues his simple lifestyle even though the companies he controls comprise over 10% of the value of the Hong Kong stock market. When asked why his sons have much nicer houses and cars than he does, Li responded, "My sons have a rich father; I did not."

Li is chairman of **Hutchison Whampoa Limited**. Hutchison has five major business segments: property development, container port operations, retailing, telecommunications, and energy. In 2005, Hutchison Whampoa reported net income of HK$13.554 billion (equivalent to approximately US$1.738 billion).

1. Assume that one of Hutchison Whampoa's overseas subsidiaries earns income of $1,000. The income tax rate in Hong Kong is 15%. When this income of $1,000 is transferred to the parent company in Hong Kong, it will be taxed, but no income tax is owed until then. What journal entry should Hutchison Whampoa make to record the income tax consequences of this $1,000 in income?
2. In 2005, Hutchison Whampoa reported earnings per share of HK$3.36. How many shares were outstanding during the year? (*Note:* See the net income information given above.)
3. Hutchison Whampoa reports that it records as assets the costs it incurs to sign up new subscribers to its cellular phone service network. These signup costs are then systematically transferred to expense over the following three years. What is the theoretical justification for this accounting practice?

AA 8-52

ETHICS

Twisting the Contingency Rules to Save the Environment

You are a member of an environmental group that is working to clean up Valley River, which runs through your town. Right now, the group is focusing on forcing Allied Industrial, a manufacturer with a large plant located on the river, to conduct its operations in a more environmentally friendly way.

The leader of your group, Frank Bowers, is a political science major at the local university. Frank discovers that Allied Industrial is involved in ongoing litigation with respect to

(continued)

toxic waste cleanup at 13 factory sites in other states. Frank is shocked to learn that Allied itself estimates that the total cost to clean up the toxic waste at these 13 sites could be as much as $140 million yet has not reported any liability on its balance sheet. Frank found this information buried in the notes to Allied Industrial's financial statements.

Frank is convinced that he has found a public relations tool that can be used to force Allied Industrial to clean up Valley River. He has called a press conference and plans to accuse Allied of covering up its $140 million obligation to clean up the toxic waste at the 13 sites. His primary piece of evidence is the fact that the $140 million obligation is not mentioned anywhere in Allied's primary financial statements.

You have taken a class in accounting and are somewhat troubled by Frank's interpretation of Allied's financial statement disclosures. You look at Allied's annual report and see that it does give complete disclosure about the possible obligation although it does not report the $140 million as a liability. The report also states that, in the opinion of its legal counsel, it is possible but not probable that Allied will be found liable for the $140 million toxic waste cleanup cost.

The press conference is scheduled for 3 P.M. What should you do?

AA 8-53
WRITING

Computing the Total Compensation for a Professor

Eunice Burns is a new assistant professor of phrenology at the University of Winnemucca. Her academic year salary is $30,000. In addition, she receives a summer salary equal to two-ninths (approximately 22%) of her academic year salary. The university agrees to contribute an amount equal to 7% of Eunice's academic year salary to a pension fund. Eunice acquires legal title to these pension contributions only if she stays at the university for five years or more. Historically, approximately 60% of new assistant professors have remained with the university at least five years. The university withholds $840 per year from Eunice's salary as her contribution to medical coverage. It costs the university $3,000 per year per employee for medical coverage. Eunice has a term-life insurance policy through the university because of the favorable group rate she can get. The $300 annual cost is withheld from her salary. If she were to get the same insurance on her own, it would cost $450. The FICA tax rate is 7.65%. This amount is withheld from Eunice's pay, and in addition, the university must match this amount and pay it to the federal government. Federal income taxes totaling 15% of income are withheld from Eunice's pay. Both the FICA tax and the federal income tax withholding are applied only to Eunice's academic year salary; no amounts are withheld from her summer salary.

You have just been hired as an assistant to the chief financial officer of the university. You have been asked to compute the total cost to the university of having Eunice Burns on the faculty. Write a one-page memo to the chief financial officer of the university outlining your calculations. Be sure to explain any assumptions that you make.

AA 8-54
CUMULATIVE SPREADSHEET PROJECT

Computing Changes in Debt Ratio and Return on Equity

This spreadsheet assignment is a continuation of the spreadsheet assignments given in earlier chapters. If you completed those spreadsheets, you have a head start on this one.

This assignment is based on the spreadsheet prepared in part (1) of the spreadsheet assignment for Chapter 7. Review that assignment for a summary of the assumptions made in preparing a forecasted balance sheet and income statement for 2010 for Handyman Company. Using those financial statements, complete the following two independent sensitivity exercises.

1. Handyman is involved in a class-action lawsuit in which a number of customers allege that they injured their thumbs while using hammers purchased at Handyman. These customers are seeking $50 million in compensatory and punitive damages. (*Note:* All of the numbers in Handyman's financial statements are in millions.) In making the financial statement projections for Handyman for 2010, it has been assumed that losing this lawsuit is possible, but not probable. Compute how each of the following quantities would be affected if a loss in this lawsuit becomes probable during 2010:
   a. Debt ratio (total liabilities/total assets) as of the end of 2010.
   b. Return on equity (net income/ending stockholders' equity) for 2010.

(continued)

2. Ignore the lawsuit described in (1). It is expected that Handyman's total "other operating expenses" will be $217 million in 2010. Of this amount, $20 million is for expected development costs that would be capitalized if Handyman were allowed to use International Accounting Standards. Compute how the capitalization of these development costs in 2010 would affect the following quantities. (*Note:* This is a hypothetical exercise because, as a U.S. company, Handyman is not currently allowed to use International Accounting Standards in preparing its financial statements.)

    a. Debt ratio (total liabilities/total assets) as of the end of 2010.

    b. Return on equity (net income/ending stockholders' equity) for 2010.

Fray Enterprises is a small business that purchases electronic personal information managers (PIM) from manufacturers and sells them to consumers. These PIMs keep track of appointments, phone numbers, to-do lists, and the like. Fray conducts business via the Internet and, at this point, carries only one model of PIM, the ZL-420. Fray provides the following trial balance as of January 1, 2009.

Fray Enterprises
Trial Balance
January 1, 2009

	Debits	Credits
Cash	$ 9,200	
Accounts Receivable	26,800	
Allowance for Bad Debts		$ 804
Inventory	31,650	
Prepaid Rent	1,100	
Office Supplies	900	
Accounts Payable		19,100
Wages Payable		2,800
Taxes Payable		3,400
Common Stock (10,000 shares)		30,000
Retained Earnings		13,546
Total	$69,650	$69,650

Fray uses the periodic FIFO inventory method in accounting for its inventory. The inventory of ZL-420 consists of the following inventory layers:

Layer	Units	Price per Unit	Total Price
1 (oldest purchase)	50	$120	$ 6,000
2	80	130	10,400
3	70	135	9,450
4 (most recent purchase)	40	145	5,800
Total	240		$31,650

Fray provides the following additional relevant information:

- The company uses the percentage of receivables method in estimating bad debts; 2% of the ending receivables balance is deemed to be uncollectible.
- Fray conducts an actual physical count of its inventory and office supplies at the end of each month.
- Fray rents its warehouse, office facilities, and computer equipment. Rent on the computer equipment is paid at the beginning of each month. Rent on the warehouse and office space is paid on the 15th of each month.
- Payroll is paid on the 5th and the 20th (pay periods end on the 15th and the last day of the month).
- Taxes Payable represents payroll taxes that are due by the 5th of the following month.
- All sales and all inventory purchases are on account.

The following transactions occurred for Fray during January of 2009:

Jan.   1   Paid rent on the computer equipment, $1,400.
       5   Recorded sales for the week, 130 units at $210 per unit. (The company uses a periodic inventory system.)
       5   Paid wages payable and taxes payable from the prior period.
       5   Collected $19,000 from customers on account during the week.
       8   Purchased office supplies for cash, $300.
      10   Received 70 ZL-420s from the manufacturer at a cost of $145 per unit.
      11   Paid accounts payable, $16,900.
      12   Collected $22,000 from customers on account during the week.
      12   Recorded sales for the week, 120 units at $210 per unit.
      15   Paid monthly rent for the office and warehouse, $2,200.
      15   Received 130 ZL-420s from the manufacturer at a cost of $150 per unit.
      18   A customer returned a ZL-420 and requested a refund. A check was immediately mailed to the customer in the amount of $210.
      19   Collected $30,000 from customers on account during the week.
      19   Recorded sales for the week, 140 units at $210 per unit.
      20   Paid the semimonthly payroll for the pay period ending on January 15. Salaries and wages total $4,800 and payroll taxes were as follows: FICA taxes payable, employee, $367; FICA taxes payable, employer, $367; state withholding taxes payable, $310; federal withholding taxes payable, $780; federal unemployment taxes payable, $60; state unemployment taxes payable, $180.
      22   Received notice that a customer owing Fray $630 had filed bankruptcy and would be unable to pay.
      23   Paid the taxes payable from the payroll on January 20.
      24   Received 180 ZL-420s from the manufacturer at a cost of $150 per unit.
      25   Purchased office supplies for cash, $480.
      25   Paid accounts payable, $43,000.
      26   Collected $30,500 from customers on account during the week.
      26   Recorded sales for the week, 135 units at $220 per unit.
      29   Customers returned 7 ZL-420s and requested refunds. Checks were immediately mailed to each customer in the amount of $210 each.
      30   Received 140 ZL-420s from the manufacturer at a cost of $145 per unit.
      31   Collected $29,900 from customers on account.
      31   Recorded sales for the partial week, 70 units at $220 per unit.
      31   Accrued the semimonthly payroll for the pay period ending on January 31. Salaries and wages total $5,000 and payroll taxes were as follows: FICA taxes payable, employee, $382; FICA taxes payable, employer, $382; state withholding taxes payable, $230; federal withholding taxes payable, $810; federal unemployment taxes payable, $65; state unemployment taxes payable, $190.

Required:
1. Provide the required journal entries to record each of the above events.
2. Make the adjusting entries necessary (1) to record bad debt expense for the period and (2) to adjust inventory and office supplies. A count of inventory and office supplies revealed 165 ZL-420s on hand and supplies valued at $1,000.
3. Prepare a trial balance as of January 31, 2009.
4. Prepare an income statement and a balance sheet for Fray Enterprises.
5. Compute Fray's number of days' sales in inventory, number of days' sales in accounts receivable, and number of days' purchases in accounts payable ratios. What can you conclude about the company's liquidity position based on this analysis?

P A R T

3

Investing and Financing Activities

© AP PHOTO/SARA D. DAVIS

Investments in Property, Plant, and Equipment and in Intangible Assets

(1) Identify the two major categories of long-term operating assets: property, plant, and equipment and intangible assets. *A company needs an infrastructure of long-term operating assets in order to produce and distribute its products and services. In addition to property, plant, and equipment, long-term operating assets also include intangible items such as patents and licenses.*

(2) Understand the factors important in deciding whether to acquire a long-term operating asset. *A company should purchase a long-term operating asset if the future cash flows expected to be generated by the asset are "large" in comparison to the cost to purchase the asset.*

(3) Record the acquisition of property, plant, and equipment through a simple purchase as well as through a lease, by self-construction, and as part of the purchase of several assets at once. *The recorded cost of property, plant, or equipment includes all costs needed to purchase the asset and prepare it for its intended use. Assets can be acquired through purchase, leasing, exchange, self-construction, or through the purchase of an entire company.*

(4) Compute straight-line and units-of-production depreciation expense for plant and equipment. *Depreciation is the process of systematically allocating the cost of a long-term asset over the service life of that asset. If that service life is measured in years, then a reasonable way to allocate the cost is equally over the years; this is called straight-line depreciation.*

(5) Account for repairs and improvements of property, plant, and equipment. *Postacquisition costs that increase an asset's capacity or extend its life are called improvements and are capitalized meaning that they are added to the cost of the asset. Routine maintenance costs are called repairs and are expensed.*

(6) Identify whether a long-term operating asset has suffered a decline in value and record the decline. *When a long-term operating asset suffers a significant decline in value (as indicated by a decline in the cash flows expected to be generated by the asset), it is said to be impaired. When an asset is impaired, its recorded value is reduced and an impairment loss is recognized. Increases in asset values are not recognized in the financial statements.*

(7) Record the discarding and selling of property, plant, and equipment. *Upon the disposal of a long-term operating asset, a gain or loss is recognized if the disposal proceeds are more or less, respectively, than the remaining book value of the asset.*

(8) Account for the acquisition and amortization of intangible assets and understand the special difficulties associated with accounting for intangibles. *Because the traditional accounting model is designed for manufacturing and retail companies, many intangible assets go unrecorded. Intangible assets are recorded only when they are purchased, either individually or as part of a set of assets. Goodwill is the excess of the purchase price over the fair value of the net identifiable assets in a business acquisition.*

(9) Use the fixed asset turnover ratio as a measure of how efficiently a company is using its property, plant, and equipment. *The fixed asset turnover ratio is computed as sales divided by the amount of property, plant, and equipment (fixed assets). This ratio can be used as a general measure of how efficiently a company is using its property, plant, and equipment.*

EXPANDED *material*

(10) Compute declining-balance and sum-of-the-years'-digits depreciation expense for plant and equipment. *Many long-term operating assets wear out proportionately more in the early years of their lives. For these assets, more depreciation is recorded in the early years; this is called accelerated depreciation. Two mathematical techniques used to generate this accelerated pattern are declining-balance depreciation and sum-of-the-years'-digits depreciation.*

(11) Account for changes in depreciation estimates and methods. *Depreciation expense involves making estimates relating to pattern of use, estimated useful life, and salvage value. Changes in estimated salvage value or useful life and changes in depreciation method are reflected in the computation of depreciation expense for the current and future periods. The undepreciated book value is allocated over the remaining life based on the revised estimates or method.*

Thomas Edison received $300,000 in investment funds in 1878 in order to start his **Edison Electric Light Company**. Today, **General Electric** is the direct descendant of Edison's company and, with a market value of $354 billion (as of May 2006), is the second most valuable company in the world (behind **ExxonMobil**). General Electric has been a fixture in corporate America since the late 1800s and is the only one of the 12 companies in the original Dow Jones Industrial Average that is still included among the 30 companies making up the Dow today.[1]

The stated purpose of the creation of the Edison Electric Light Company was the development of an economically practical electric light bulb. After a year of experimentation, Thomas Edison discovered that carbonized bamboo would provide a long-lasting light filament that was also easy to produce. Edison quickly found that delivering electric light to people's homes required more than a light bulb, however. So, he developed an entire electricity generation and distribution system, inventing new pieces of equipment when he couldn't find what he needed. The first public electric light system was built in London, followed soon after by the Pearl Street Station system in New York City in 1882. In 1892, Edison's company merged with the **Thomson-Houston Electric Company** [developer of alternating-current

(AC) equipment that could transmit over longer distances than Edison's direct-current (DC) system], and the General Electric Company (GE) was born.

From the beginning, General Electric's strength has been research. In addition to improving the design of the light bulb (including the development in the early 1900s of gas-filled, tungsten-filament bulbs that are the model for bulbs still used today), GE was also instrumental in developing almost every familiar household appliance—the iron, washing machine, refrigerator, range, air conditioner, dishwasher, and more. In addition, GE research scientists helped create FM radio, aircraft jet engines, and nuclear-power reactors.

Today, General Electric operates in a diverse array of businesses, ranging from train locomotives to medical CT scanners to consumer financing to the NBC television network. To support its broad array of businesses, General Electric maintains a vast quantity of long-term assets that cost almost $112 billion to acquire. In 2005 alone, GE spent an additional $14.4 billion in acquiring long-term operating assets and received $6.0 billion for disposing of old assets. Its long-term assets include $3.3 billion in rail cars, $32.9 billion in aircraft, $15.6 billion in buildings, $25.8 billion in machinery, and $81.7 billion in "intangible" assets.

In Chapters 6 through 8, operating activities of a business and the assets and liabilities arising from those operations were discussed. In this and the next three chapters, investing and financing activities are covered. In this chapter, investments in long-term assets that are used in the business, such as buildings, property, land, and equipment, are discussed. In Chapter 10, long-term debt financing is covered. In Chapter 11, equity financing is discussed. Once you understand debt and equity securities, as discussed in Chapters 10 and 11, you will understand how these

long-term operating assets

Assets expected to be held and used over the course of several years to facilitate operating activities.

same securities can be purchased as investments. Therefore, in Chapter 12, investments in stocks and bonds (securities) of other companies are discussed. Exhibit 1 illustrates the time line of important business issues associated with long-term operating assets and shows the financial statement impact of the items that will be covered in this chapter.

The two primary categories of long-term assets discussed in this chapter are (1) property, plant, and equipment and (2) intangible assets. Because property, plant, and equipment and intangible assets are essential to a business in carrying out its operating activities, they are sometimes called long-term operating assets. Unlike inventories, these **long-term operating assets** are

[1] This description is based on General Electric Company History at **http://ge.com/en/company/companyinfo/at_a_glance/hist_leader.htm**; General Electric Company, *International Directory of Company Histories*, vol. 12 (Detroit: St. James Press, 1996), pp. 193–197; 1999 Annual Report of the General Electric Company.

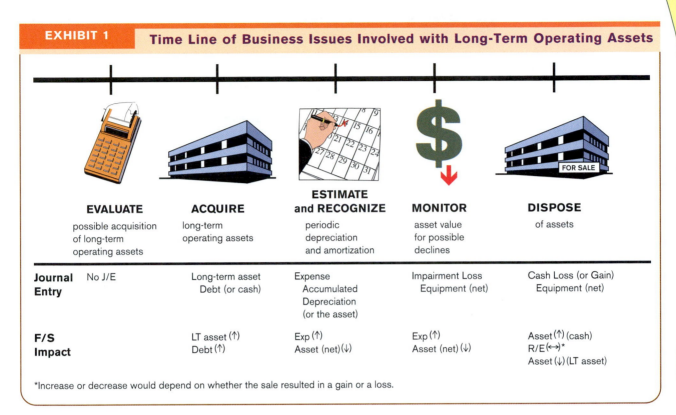

EXHIBIT 1   **Time Line of Business Issues Involved with Long-Term Operating Assets**

	EVALUATE	**ACQUIRE**	**ESTIMATE and RECOGNIZE**	**MONITOR**	**DISPOSE**
	possible acquisition of long-term operating assets	long-term operating assets	periodic depreciation and amortization	asset value for possible declines	of assets
Journal Entry	No J/E	Long-term asset Debt (or cash)	Expense Accumulated Depreciation (or the asset)	Impairment Loss Equipment (net)	Cash Loss (or Gain) Equipment (net)
F/S Impact		LT asset ($\uparrow$) Debt ($\uparrow$)	Exp ($\uparrow$) Asset (net)($\downarrow$)	Exp ($\uparrow$) Asset (net)($\downarrow$)	Asset ($\uparrow$) (cash) R/E($\leftrightarrow$)* Asset ($\downarrow$) (LT asset)

*Increase or decrease would depend on whether the sale resulted in a gain or a loss.

SETTING THE STAGE

not acquired for resale to customers but are held and used by a business to generate revenues. As illustrated by the numbers given for **General Electric** at the beginning of the chapter, long-term operating assets often comprise a significant portion of the total assets of a company.

Nature of Long-Term Operating Assets

① Identify the two major categories of long-term operating assets: property, plant, and equipment and intangible assets.

Businesses make money by selling products and services. A company needs an infrastructure of long-term operating assets in order to profitably produce and distribute these products and services. For example, **General Electric** needs factories in which to manufacture the locomotives and light bulbs that it sells. GE also needs patents on its unique technology to protect its competitive edge in the marketplace. A factory is an example of a long-term operating asset that is classified as property, plant, and equipment. A patent is an example of an intangible asset. **Property, plant, and equipment** refers to tangible, long-lived assets acquired for use in business operations. This category includes land, buildings, machinery, equipment, and furniture. **Intangible assets** are long-lived assets that are used in the operation of a business but do not have physical substance (see page 392 for definition). In most cases, they provide their owners with competitive advantages over other firms. Typical intangible assets are patents, licenses, franchises, and goodwill.

The following section outlines the process used in deciding whether to acquire a long-term operating asset. The subsequent sections discuss the accounting issues that arise when a long-term operating asset is acquired: accounting for the acquisition of the asset, recording periodic depreciation, accounting for new costs and changes in asset value, and properly removing the asset from the books upon disposition.

property, plant, and equipment

Tangible, long-lived assets acquired for use in business operations; include land, buildings, machinery, equipment, and furniture.

intangible assets

Long-lived assets without physical substance that are used in business, such as licenses, patents, franchises, and goodwill.

Understand the factors important in deciding whether to acquire a long-term operating asset.

Deciding Whether to Acquire a Long-Term Operating Asset

② As mentioned in the previous section, long-term operating assets are acquired to be used over the course of several years. The decision to acquire a long-term asset depends on whether the future cash flows generated by the asset are expected to be large enough to justify the asset cost. The process of evaluating a long-term project is called **capital budgeting**. This process is briefly introduced here and is covered in more detail in Chapter 22 in the management accounting section of *Accounting: Concepts and Applications*.

capital budgeting

Systematic planning for long-term investments in operating assets.

Assume that Yosef Manufacturing makes joysticks and other computer game accessories. Yosef is considering expanding its operations by buying an additional production facility. The cost of the new factory is $100 million. Yosef expects to be able to sell the joysticks and other items made in the factory for $80 million per year. At that level of production, the annual cost of operating the factory (wages, insurance, materials, maintenance, etc.) is expected to total $65 million. The factory is expected to remain in operation for 20 years. Should Yosef buy the new factory for $100 million?

To summarize the information in the preceding paragraph, Yosef must decide whether to pay $100 million for a factory that will generate a net profit of $15 million ($80 million − $65 million) per year for 20 years. At first glance, you might think that the decision is obvious because the factory costs only $100 million but will generate $300 million in profit ($15 million × 20 years) during its 20-year life. But this analysis ignores the important fact that dollars received in the future are not worth as much as dollars received right now. For example, if you can invest your money and earn 10%, receiving $1 today is the same as receiving $6.73 20 years from now because the $1 received today could be invested and would grow to $6.73 in 20 years. This important concept is called the **time value of money** and is essential to properly evaluating whether to acquire any long-term asset.

time value of money

The concept that a dollar received now is worth more than a dollar received in the future.

Using the time value of money calculations that will be explained in detail in Chapter 10, it can be shown that receiving the future cash flows from the factory of $15 million per year for 20 years is the same as receiving $128 million in one lump sum right now, if the prevailing interest rate is 10%. Thus, the decision to acquire the factory boils down to the following comparison: Should we pay $100 million to buy a factory now if the factory will generate future cash flows that are worth the equivalent of $128 million now? The decision is yes, because the $128 million value of the expected cash inflows is greater than the $100 million cost of the factory. On the other hand, if the factory were expected to generate only $10 million per year, then, using the computations that will be explained in Chapter 10, it can be calculated that the value of the cash flows would be only $85 million, and the factory should not be purchased for $100 million.

The important concept to remember here is that long-term operating assets have value because they are expected to help a company generate cash flows in the future. If events occur that change the expectation concerning those future cash flows, then the value of the asset changes. For example, if consumer demand for computer joysticks dries up, the value of a factory built to produce joysticks can plunge overnight even though the factory itself is still as productive as it ever was. Accounting for this type of decline in the value of a long-term operating asset is discussed later in the chapter.

REMEMBER THIS...

- Long-term operating assets have value because they help companies generate future cash flows.
- The decision to acquire a long-term operating asset involves comparing the cost of the asset to the value of the expected cash inflows, after adjusting for the time value of money.
- An asset's value can decline or disappear if events cause a decrease in the expected future cash flows generated by the asset.

Accounting for Acquisition of Property, Plant, and Equipment

Record the acquisition of property, plant, and equipment through a simple purchase as well as through a lease, by self-construction, and as part of the purchase of several assets at once.

③ Like all other assets, property, plant, and equipment are initially recorded at cost. The cost of an asset includes not only the purchase price but also any other costs incurred in acquiring the asset and getting it ready for its intended use. Examples of these other costs include shipping, installation, and sales taxes. The items that should be included in the acquisition cost of various types of property, plant, and equipment are outlined in Exhibit 2.

Property, plant, and equipment are usually acquired by purchase. In some cases, assets are acquired by leasing but are accounted for as assets in much the same way as purchased assets. Plant and equipment can also be constructed by a business for its own use. Also, a company can in one transaction purchase several different assets or even another entire company. The accounting for each of these types of acquisition is explained below and on the following pages.

EXHIBIT 2	Items Included in the Acquisition Cost of Property, Plant, and Equipment
Land	Purchase price, commissions, legal fees, escrow fees, surveying fees, clearing and grading costs.
Land improvements (e.g., landscaping, paving, fencing)	Cost of improvements, including expenditures for materials, labor, and overhead.
Buildings	Purchase price, commissions, reconditioning costs.
Equipment	Purchase price, taxes, freight, insurance, installation, and any expenditures incurred in preparing the asset for its intended use, e.g., reconditioning and testing costs.

Assets Acquired by Purchase

A company can purchase an asset by paying cash, incurring a liability, exchanging another asset, or by a combination of these methods. If a single asset is purchased for cash, the accounting is relatively simple. To illustrate, we assume that Wheeler Resorts, Inc., purchases a new delivery truck for $15,096 (purchase price, $15,000, less 2% discount for paying cash, plus sales tax of $396). The entry to record this purchase is:

Delivery Truck	15,096	
Cash		15,096
Purchased a delivery truck for $15,096		
($15,000 − $300 cash discount + $396 sales tax).		

In this instance, cash was paid for a single asset, the truck. An alternative would be to borrow part of the purchase price. If the company had borrowed $12,000 of the $15,096 from a bank, the entry would have been:

Delivery Truck	15,096	
Cash		3,096
Notes Payable		12,000
Purchased a delivery truck for $15,096; paid $3,096 cash		
and issued a note for $12,000 to Chemical Bank.		

lease

A contract that specifies the terms under which the owner of an asset (the lessor) agrees to transfer the right to use the asset to another party (the lessee).

The $12,000 represents the principal of the note; it does not include any interest charged by the lending institution. (The interest is recognized later as interest expense.)

When one long-term operating asset is acquired in exchange for another, the cost of the new asset is usually set equal to the market value of the asset given up in exchange.

Assets Acquired by Leasing

lessee

The party that is granted the right to use property under the terms of a lease.

Leases are often short-term rental agreements in which one party, the **lessee**, is granted the right to use property owned by another party, the **lessor**. For example, as a student, you may decide to lease (rent) an apartment to live in while you are attending college. The owner of the apartment (lessor) will probably require you to sign a lease specifying the terms of the arrangement. The lease states the period of time in which you will live in the apartment, the amount of rent you will pay, and when each rent payment is due. When the lease expires, you will either sign a new lease or move out of the apartment, which would then be rented to someone else.

lessor

The owner of property that is leased (rented) to another party.

Companies enter into similar types of lease arrangements. For example, Wheeler Resorts might decide to lease a building because it needs additional office space. Assume Wheeler signs a two-year lease requiring monthly rental payments of $1,000. When the lease expires, Wheeler will either move out of the building or negotiate a new lease with the owner. Accounting for this type of rental agreement, called an **operating lease**, is straightforward. When rent is paid each month, Wheeler records the following journal entry:

operating lease

A simple rental agreement.

Rent (or Lease) Expense	1,000	
Cash		1,000
To record monthly rent of office building.		

Some lease agreements, however, are not so simple. Suppose Wheeler has decided to expand its operations and wants to acquire a hotel in the Phoenix, Arizona, area.

A college student (lessee) often rents an apartment while attending college. The apartment owner (lessor) will require the student to sign a lease stating the terms of the arrangement.

© LELAND BOBBE/GETTY IMAGES INC.

Wheeler's alternatives are to buy land and build a new hotel, purchase an existing hotel, or lease a hotel. Assume Wheeler locates a desirable piece of land, and the owner of the land agrees to build a hotel and lease the property to Wheeler. The lease agreement is noncancelable and requires Wheeler to make annual lease payments of $100,000 for 20 years. At the end of 20 years, Wheeler will become the owner of the property. Clearly, this is not a simple rental agreement, even though the transaction is called a lease by the parties involved. In reality, this transaction is a purchase of the property with the payments being spread over 20 years. The result is the same as if Wheeler had borrowed money on a 20-year mortgage and purchased the property.

Generally accepted accounting principles require that the recording of a transaction reflect its true economic nature, not its form. Instead of recognizing the individual lease payments as an expense as was done with the operating lease, Wheeler records the property as an asset and also records a liability reflecting the obligation to the lessor. The amount to be recorded is the cash amount that Wheeler would have to pay right now in order to completely pay off the obligation to make the future lease payments. This amount is called the present value of the lease payments (in the Wheeler example, the present value of 20 annual payments of $100,000) and takes into account the time value of money. As mentioned earlier, the time value concept will be explained in more detail in Chapter 10.

Continuing the example, assume that, at the beginning of the lease term, the present value of the future lease payments is $851,360. Wheeler makes the following journal entry to record the lease:

Leased Property	851,360	
Lease Liability		851,360
To record hotel acquired under a 20-year noncancelable lease.		

capital lease

A leasing transaction that is recorded as a purchase by the lessee.

This type of lease is called a **capital lease** because the lessee records (capitalizes) the leased asset the same as if the asset had been acquired in an outright purchase. The asset is reported with Property, Plant, and Equipment on the lessee's balance sheet. The lessee (Wheeler Resorts) also shows the lease liability on the balance sheet as a long-term liability.

When annual lease payments are made, Wheeler will not record the payment as rent expense. Instead, the payment will be recorded as a reduction in the lease liability, with part of each payment being interest on the outstanding obligation. The difference between the total lease payments (20 years × $100,000, or $2 million) and the "cost" or present value of the property is the amount of interest that will be paid over the term of the lease. To illustrate, assume that the first payment is made one year after the lease term begins and includes interest of $85,136 and a $14,864 reduction in the liability. The payment is recorded as follows:

Lease Liability	14,864	
Interest Expense	85,136	
Cash		100,000

To record annual lease payment under capital lease.

Accounting for payments on capital leases is discussed in more detail in Chapter 10.

Classifying Leases   As illustrated, an operating lease is accounted for as a simple rental, whereas a capital lease is accounted for as a purchase of the leased asset. Because the accounting treatment of a lease can have a major impact on the financial statements, the accounting profession has established criteria for determining whether a lease should be classified as an operating or a capital lease. If a lease is noncancelable and meets any one of the following four criteria, it is recorded as a capital lease:

1. The lease transfers ownership of the leased asset to the lessee by the end of the lease term (as in the Wheeler Resorts example).
2. The lease contains an option allowing the lessee to purchase the asset at the end of the lease term at a bargain price, essentially guaranteeing that ownership will eventually transfer to the lessee.
3. The lease term is equal to 75% or more of the estimated economic life of the asset, meaning that the lessee will use the asset for most of its economic life.
4. The present value of the lease payments at the beginning of the lease is 90% or more of the fair market value of the leased asset. Meeting this criterion means that, in agreeing to make the lease payments, the lessee is agreeing to pay almost as much as the cash price to purchase the asset outright.

If just one of the above criteria is met, then the lease agreement is classified as a capital lease and is accounted for by the lessee as a debt-financed purchase. A lease that does not meet any of the capital lease criteria is considered an operating lease. Keep in mind that these two types of leases are not alternatives for the same transaction. If the terms of the lease agreement meet any one of the capital lease criteria, the lease must be accounted for as a capital lease.

The accounting for leases has been a thorn in the side of accounting standard-setters for at least 50 years. From the beginning, the crucial issue has been how to require companies to report leased assets and lease liabilities in the balance sheet when a lease constitutes an effective transfer of ownership. The four lease criteria outlined above were issued by the FASB in 1976, with the thought that the rigidity and strictness of the criteria would result in most leases being reported on lessee companies' balance sheets as capital leases. In practice, U.S. companies have taken these four criteria as a challenge and have carefully crafted their lease agreements so that none of the criteria is satisfied, allowing the leases to continue to be accounted for as operating leases.

One of the largest leasing companies in the United States is a subsidiary of **General Electric** called **GE Capital Services**. GE Capital Services leases industrial equipment, aircraft, factory buildings, rail cars, shipping containers, computers, medical equipment, and more. In 2005, the total original cost of assets leased by GE Capital Services to other companies was $72.4 billion.

FYI

One of the most interesting accounting manipulations involving the four lease criteria relates to the 90% threshold for the present value of the minimum lease payments. By hiring an insurance company to guarantee a portion of the lease payments, a lessee is able to exclude these payments from the present value computations, lowering the present value below the 90% threshold.

Assets Acquired by Self-Construction

Sometimes buildings or equipment are constructed by a company for its own use. This may be done to save on construction costs, to utilize idle facilities or idle workers, or to meet a special set of technical specifications. Self-constructed assets, like purchased assets, are recorded at cost, including all expenditures incurred to build the asset and make it ready for its intended use. These costs include the materials used to build the asset, the construction labor, and some reasonable share of the general company overhead (electricity, insurance, supervisors' salaries, etc.) during the time of construction.

Another cost that is included in the cost of a self-constructed asset is the interest cost associated with money borrowed to finance the construction project. Just as the cost to rent a crane to be used to construct a building would be included in the cost of the building, the cost to "rent" money to finance the construction project should also be included in the building cost. Interest that is recorded as part of the cost of a self-constructed asset is called **capitalized interest**. The amount of interest that should be capitalized is that amount that could have been saved if the money used on the construction project had instead been used to repay loans.

capitalized interest

Interest that is recorded as part of the cost of a self-constructed asset.

The following illustration demonstrates the computation of the cost of a self-constructed asset. Wheeler Resorts decided to construct a new hotel using its own workers. The construction project lasted from January 1 to December 31, 2009. Building materials costs for the project were $4,500,000. Total labor costs attributable to the project were $2,500,000. Total company overhead (costs other than materials and labor) for the year was $10,000,000; of this amount, it is determined that 15% can be reasonably assigned as part of the cost of the construction project. A construction loan was negotiated with Wheeler's bank; during the year, Wheeler was able to borrow from the bank to pay for materials, labor, etc. The total amount of interest paid on this construction loan during the year was $500,000. The total cost of the self-constructed hotel is computed as follows:

Materials	$4,500,000
Labor	2,500,000
Overhead allocation ($10,000,000 × 0.15)	1,500,000
Capitalized interest	500,000
Total hotel cost	$9,000,000

STOP & THINK

What is the difference between capitalized interest and regular interest?

The new hotel would be reported in Wheeler's balance sheet at a total cost of $9,000,000. As with other long-term operating assets, self-constructed assets are reported at the total cost necessary to get them ready for their intended use.

The amount of capitalized interest reported by several large U.S. companies, relative to their total interest expense, is displayed in Exhibit 3. As you can see, General Electric capitalized only an insignificant amount of its $15.187 billion in interest during 2005. On the other hand, **ExxonMobil** capitalized almost one-half of its interest during 2005.

Acquisition of Several Assets at Once

basket purchase

The purchase of two or more assets acquired together at a single price.

A **basket purchase** occurs when two or more assets are acquired together at a single price. A typical basket purchase is the purchase of a building along with the land on which the building sits. Because there are differences in the accounting for land and buildings, the purchase price must be allocated between the two assets on some reasonable basis. The relative fair market values of the

| EXHIBIT 3 | **Magnitude of Capitalized Interest for Several Large U.S. Companies** |

Company	Capitalized Interest	Interest Expense**	Capitalized, as a Percentage of Total Interest
General Electric*	$ 0	$15,187	0.0%
General Motors	45	15,768	0.3
ExxonMobil	434	496	46.7
McDonald's	5	356	1.4
Disney	77	597	11.4

Note: Numbers are for 2005 and are in millions of dollars.
*Once again, GE reports it capitalized only an "insignificant" amount.
**These amounts come from the income statement, and are net of capitalized interest, which explains the high percentage for ExxonMobil.

assets are usually used to determine the respective costs to be assigned to the land and the building.

To illustrate, we will assume that Wheeler Resorts purchases a 40,000-square-foot building on 2.6 acres of land for $3,600,000. How much of the total cost should be assigned to the land and how much to the building? If an appraisal indicates that the fair market values of the land and the building are $1,000,000 and $3,000,000, respectively, the resulting allocated costs would be $900,000 and $2,700,000, calculated as follows:

Asset	Fair Market Value	Percentage of Total Value	Apportionment of Lump-Sum Cost
Land	$1,000,000	25%	0.25 × $3,600,000 = $ 900,000
Building	3,000,000	75	0.75 × $3,600,000 = 2,700,000
Total	$4,000,000	100%	$3,600,000

In this case, the fair market value of the land is $1,000,000, or 25% of the total market value of the land and building. Therefore, 25% of the actual cost, or $900,000, is allocated to the land, and 75% of the actual cost, or $2,700,000, is allocated to the building. The journal entry to record this basket purchase is:

Land	900,000	
Building	2,700,000	
Cash		3,600,000
Purchased 2.6 acres of land and a 40,000-square-foot building.		

If part of the purchase price is financed by a bank, an additional credit to Notes Payable or Mortgage Payable would be included in the entry.

Sometimes one company will buy all the assets of another company. For example, in its 2006 annual report, **Wal-Mart** discloses that, in December 2005, it purchased **Sonae Distribuicao Brasil S.A.** (a retail operation in Southern Brazil) for $720 million in cash. The purchase of an entire company raises a number of accounting issues. The first, already discussed above, is how to allocate the purchase price to the various assets acquired. In general, all acquired assets are recorded on the books of the acquiring company at their fair values as of the acquisition date.

goodwill

An intangible asset that exists when a business is valued at more than the fair market value of its net assets, usually due to strategic location, reputation, good customer relations, or similar factors; equal to the excess of the purchase price over the fair market value of the net assets purchased.

The second major accounting issue associated with the purchase of an entire company is the recording of goodwill. **Goodwill** represents all the special competitive advantages enjoyed by a company, such as a trained staff, good credit rating, reputation for superior products and services, and an established network of suppliers and customers. These factors allow an established business to earn more profits than would a new business, even though the new business might have the same type of building, the same equipment, and the same type of production processes.

When one company purchases another established business, the excess of the purchase price over the value of the identifiable net assets is assumed to represent the purchase of goodwill. The accounting for goodwill is illustrated later in the chapter.

REMEMBER THIS...

- Property, plant, and equipment cost = All costs to purchase and get ready for use.
- Leases:
  - Operating lease—accounted for as a rental; nothing on the balance sheet.
  - Capital lease—accounted for as a purchase; asset and liability on the balance sheet.
- Self-construction cost = Materials, labor, reasonable overhead, and interest.
- When two or more assets are acquired for a single price in a basket purchase, the relative fair market values are used to determine the respective costs.

Calculating and Recording Depreciation Expense

Compute straight-line and units-of-production depreciation expense for plant and equipment.

(4) The second element in accounting for plant and equipment is the allocation of an asset's cost over its useful life. The matching principle requires that this cost be assigned to expense in the periods benefited from the use of the asset. The allocation procedure is called **depreciation**, and the allocated amount, recorded in a period-ending adjusting entry, is an expense that is deducted from revenues in order to determine income. It should be noted that the asset "plant" normally refers to buildings only; land is recorded as a separate asset and is not depreciated because it is usually assumed to have an unlimited useful life.

depreciation

The process of cost allocation that assigns the original cost of plant and equipment to the periods benefited.

Accounting for depreciation is often confusing because students tend to think that depreciation expense reflects the decline in an asset's value. The concept of depreciation is nothing more than a systematic write-off of the original cost of an asset. The undepreciated cost is referred to as **book value**, which represents that portion of the original cost not yet assigned to the income statement as an expense. A company never claims that an asset's recorded book value is equal to its market value. In fact, market values of assets could increase at the same time that depreciation expense is being recorded.

book value

For a long-term operating asset, the asset's original cost less any accumulated depreciation.

To calculate depreciation expense for an asset, you need to know (1) its original cost, (2) its estimated useful life, and (3) its estimated salvage, or residual, value. **Salvage value** is the amount expected to be received when the asset is sold at the end of its useful life (see page 400 for definition). When an asset is purchased, its actual life and salvage value are obviously unknown. They must be

salvage value

The amount expected to be received when an asset is sold at the end of its useful life.

straight-line depreciation method

The depreciation method in which the cost of an asset is allocated equally over the periods of an asset's estimated useful life.

units-of-production method

The depreciation method in which the cost of an asset is allocated to each period on the basis of the productive output or use of the asset during the period.

estimated as realistically as is feasible, usually on the basis of experience with similar assets. In some cases, an asset will have little or no salvage value. If the salvage value is not significant, it is usually ignored in computing depreciation.

Several methods can be used for depreciating the costs of assets for financial reporting. In the main part of this chapter, we describe two: straight-line and units-of-production. In the expanded material section of this chapter, we describe two more depreciation methods: sum-of-the-years'-digits and declining-balance.

The **straight-line depreciation method** assumes that an asset will benefit all periods equally and that the cost of the asset should be assigned on a uniform basis for all accounting periods. If an asset's benefits are thought to be related to its productive output (miles driven in an automobile, for example), the **units-of-production method** is usually appropriate.

To illustrate straight-line and units-of-production depreciation methods, we assume that Wheeler Resorts purchased a van on January 1 for transporting hotel guests to and from the airport. The following facts apply:

Acquisition cost	$24,000
Estimated salvage value	$2,000
Estimated life:	
In years	4 years
In miles driven	60,000 miles

Straight-Line Method of Depreciation

The straight-line depreciation method is the simplest depreciation method. It assumes that an asset's cost should be assigned equally to all periods benefited. The formula for calculating annual straight-line depreciation is:

$$\frac{\text{Cost} - \text{Salvage value}}{\text{Estimated useful life (years)}} = \text{Annual depreciation expense}$$

With this formula, the annual depreciation expense for the van is calculated as:

$$\frac{\$24,000 - \$2,000}{4 \text{ years}} = \$5,500 \text{ depreciation expense per year}$$

When the depreciation expense for an asset has been calculated, a schedule showing the annual depreciation expense, the total accumulated depreciation, and the asset's book value (undepreciated cost) for each year can be prepared. The depreciation schedule for the van (using straight-line depreciation) is shown in Exhibit 4.

EXHIBIT 4	Depreciation Schedule with Straight-Line Depreciation		
	Annual Depreciation Expense	**Accumulated Depreciation**	**Book Value**
Acquisition date	–	–	$24,000
End of year 1	$ 5,500	$ 5,500	18,500
End of year 2	5,500	11,000	13,000
End of year 3	5,500	16,500	7,500
End of year 4	5,500	22,000	2,000
	$22,000		

The entry to record straight-line depreciation each year is:

Depreciation Expense	5,500	
Accumulated Depreciation, Hotel Van		5,500
To record annual depreciation for the hotel van.		

FYI

A comparison of the amounts of cost and accumulated depreciation reveals how old the plant and equipment is relative to its total expected life.

Depreciation Expense is reported on the income statement. Accumulated Depreciation is a contra-asset account that is offset against the cost of the asset on the balance sheet. Book value is equal to the asset account balance, which retains the original cost of the asset as a debit balance, minus the credit balance in the accumulated depreciation account.

At the end of the first year, the acquisition cost, accumulated depreciation, and book value of the van are presented on the balance sheet as follows:

Property, Plant, and Equipment:	
Hotel van	$24,000
Less: Accumulated depreciation	5,500
Book value	$18,500

Similar information is provided in the annual reports of all companies with property, plant, and equipment. For example, **General Electric** reported the following in the notes to its 2005 financial statements:

	Original Cost (in millions)	
(December 31)	**2005**	**2004**
GE		
Land and improvements	$ 1,366	$ 1,562
Buildings, structures, and related equipment	10,044	9,617
Machinery and equipment	25,811	25,811
Leasehold costs and manufacturing plant under construction	2,157	2,157
	$ 39,378	$ 39,147
GE Capital Services		
Buildings and equipment	$ 5,547	$ 5,684
Equipment leased to others		
Aircraft	32,941	26,837
Vehicles	23,208	23,056
Railroad rolling stock	3,327	3,390
Mobile and modular space	2,889	2,965
Construction and manufacturing	1,609	1,772
All other	2,834	3,021
	$ 72,355	$ 66,725
	$111,733	$105,872
	Accumulated Depreciation and Amortization	
GE	$22,874	$22,391
GE Capital Services		
Buildings and equipment	2,431	2,389
Equipment leased to others	18,900	17,989
	$44,205	$42,769

Using this information, one can calculate that the property, plant, and equipment used by General Electric had been used for 58% ($22,874/$39,378) of its useful life as of the end of 2005. Similarly, the buildings and equipment used by **GE Capital Services** had been used for 44% ($2,431/$5,547) of its life, and the equipment leased by GE Capital Services to others had been used for 28% ($18,900/$66,808) of its useful life.

Units-of-Production Method of Depreciation

The units-of-production depreciation method allocates an asset's cost on the basis of use rather than time. This method is used primarily when a company expects that asset usage will vary significantly from year to year. If the asset's usage pattern is uniform from year to year, the units-of-production method will produce the same depreciation pattern as the straight-line method. Assets with varying usage patterns for which this method of depreciation may be appropriate include automobiles and other vehicles whose life is estimated in terms of number of miles driven. It is also used for certain machines whose life is estimated in terms of number of units produced or number of hours of operating life. The formula for calculating the units-of-production depreciation for the year is:

$$\frac{\text{Cost} - \text{Salvage value}}{\substack{\text{Total estimated life in} \\ \text{units, hours, or miles}}} \times \substack{\text{Number of units produced,} \\ \text{hours used, or miles driven} \\ \text{during the year}} = \text{Current year's depreciation expense}$$

To illustrate, we again consider Wheeler Resorts' van, which has an expected life of 60,000 miles. With the units-of-production method, if the van is driven 12,000 miles during the first year, the depreciation expense for that year is calculated as follows:

$$\frac{\$24,000 - \$2,000}{60,000 \text{ miles}} \times 12,000 \text{ miles} = \$4,400 \text{ depreciation expense}$$

The entry to record units-of-production depreciation at the end of the first year of the van's life is:

Depreciation Expense	4,400	
Accumulated Depreciation, Hotel Van		4,400
To record depreciation for the first year of the hotel van's life.		

The depreciation schedule for the four years is shown in Exhibit 5. This exhibit assumes that 18,000 miles were driven the second year, 21,000 the third year, and 9,000 the fourth year.

Note that part of the formulas for straight-line and units-of-production depreciation is the same. In both cases, cost − salvage value is divided by the asset's useful life. With straight-line, life is measured in years; with units-of-production, life is in miles or hours.

EXHIBIT 5	Depreciation Schedule with Units-of-Production Depreciation			
	Miles Driven	**Depreciation Expense**	**Accumulated Depreciation**	**Book Value**
Acquisition date	–	–	–	$24,000
End of year 1	12,000	$ 4,400	$ 4,400	19,600
End of year 2	18,000	6,600	11,000	13,000
End of year 3	21,000	7,700	18,700	5,300
End of year 4	9,000	3,300	22,000	2,000
		$22,000		

With units-of-production, the depreciation per mile or hour must then be multiplied by the usage for the year to determine depreciation expense.

What if the van lasts longer than four years or is driven for more than 60,000 miles? Once the $22,000 difference between cost and salvage value has been recorded as depreciation expense, there is no further expense to record. Thus, any additional years or miles are "free" in the sense that no depreciation expense will be recognized in connection with them. However, as other vans are purchased in the future, the initial estimates of their useful lives will be adjusted to reflect the experience with previous vans.

What if the van lasts less than four years or is driven fewer than 60,000 miles? This topic is covered later in the chapter in connection with the accounting for the disposal of property, plant, and equipment.

A Comparison of Depreciation Methods

The amount of depreciation expense will vary according to the depreciation method used by a company. Exhibit 6 compares the annual depreciation expense for Wheeler Resorts' van under the straight-line and units-of-production depreciation methods. As this schedule makes clear, the total amount of depreciation is the same regardless of which method is used.

Straight-line is by far the most commonly used depreciation method because it is the simplest to apply and makes intuitive sense. For example, in the notes to its 2006 financial statements (see Appendix A), **Wal-Mart** discloses that it depreciates its property, plant, and equipment using the straight-line method over useful lives ranging from 3 to 50 years.

Partial-Year Depreciation Calculations

Thus far, depreciation expense has been calculated on the basis of a full year. Businesses purchase assets at all times during the year, however, so partial-year depreciation calculations are often required. To compute depreciation expense for less than a full year, first calculate the depreciation expense for the year and then distribute it evenly over the number of months the asset is held during the year.

To illustrate, assume that Wheeler Resorts purchased its $24,000 van on July 1 instead of January 1. The depreciation calculations for the first one and one-half years, using straight-line depreciation, are shown in Exhibit 7. The units-of-production method has been omitted from the exhibit; midyear purchases do not complicate the calculations with this method because it involves number of miles driven, hours flown, and so on, rather than time periods.

In practice, many companies simplify their depreciation computations by taking a full year of depreciation in the year an asset is purchased and none in the year the asset is

EXHIBIT 6	Comparison of Depreciation Expense Using Different Depreciation Methods	
	Straight-Line Depreciation	**Units-of-Production Depreciation**
End of year 1	$ 5,500	$ 4,400
End of year 2	5,500	6,600
End of year 3	5,500	7,700
End of year 4	5,500	3,300
Totals	$22,000	$22,000

EXHIBIT 7	Partial-Year Depreciation		
Method	**Full-Year Depreciation**	**Depreciation 1st Year (6 months)**	**Depreciation 2nd Year (12 months)**
Straight-line	$5,500	$2,750 ($5,500 × ½)	$5,500

natural resources

Assets that are physically consumed or waste away, such as oil, minerals, gravel, and timber.

depletion

The process of cost allocation that assigns the original cost of a natural resource to the periods benefited.

sold. This is allowed because depreciation is based on estimates, and in the long run, the difference in the amounts is usually immaterial.

Units-of-Production Method with Natural Resources

Another common use for the units-of-production method is with natural resources. **Natural resources** include such assets as oil wells, timber tracts, coal mines, and gravel deposits. Like all other assets, newly purchased or developed natural resources are recorded at cost. This cost must be written off as the assets are extracted or otherwise depleted. This process of writing off the cost of natural resources is called **depletion** and involves the calculation of a depletion rate for each unit of the natural resource. Conceptually, depletion is exactly the same as depreciation; with plant and equipment, the accounting process is called depreciation, whereas with natural resources it is called depletion.

To illustrate, assume that Power-T Company purchases a coal mine for $1,200,000 cash. The entry to record the purchase is:

Coal Mine	1,200,000	
Cash		1,200,000
Purchased a coal mine for $1,200,000.		

If the mine contains an estimated 200,000 tons of coal deposits (based on a geologist's estimate), the depletion expense for each ton of coal extracted and sold will be $6 ($1,200,000/200,000 tons). Here, the unit of production is the extraction of one ton of coal. If 12,000 tons of coal are mined and sold in the current year, the depletion entry is:

Depletion Expense	72,000	
Accumulated Depletion, Coal Mine		72,000
To record depletion for the year: 12,000 tons at $6 per ton.		

After the first year's depletion expense has been recorded, the coal mine is shown on the balance sheet as follows:

Coal mine	$1,200,000
Less: Accumulated depletion	72,000
Book value	$1,128,000

But how do you determine the number of tons of coal in a mine? Because most natural resources cannot be counted, the amount of the resource owned is an estimate. The depletion calculation is therefore likely to be revised as new information becomes available. When an estimate is changed, a new depletion rate per unit is calculated and used to compute depletion during the remaining life of the natural resource or until another new estimate is made. Coverage of accounting for changes in estimates is included in the expanded material section of this chapter.

REMEMBER THIS...

- Depreciation is the process whereby the cost of an asset is allocated over its useful life.
- The straight-line and units-of-production methods allocate cost proportionately over an asset's life on the bases of time and use, respectively.
- Straight-line depreciation expense = (Cost − Salvage value) ÷ Estimated useful life
- Units-of-production depreciation expense =

  [(Cost − Salvage value) ÷ Estimated life in units] × Units produced
- Depreciation for natural resources is called depletion and is similar to units-of-production depreciation.

Account for repairs and improvements of property, plant, and equipment.

Repairing and Improving Property, Plant, and Equipment

⑤ Sometime during its useful life, an asset will probably need to be repaired or improved. The accounting issue associated with these postacquisition expenditures is whether they should be immediately recognized as an expense or be added to the cost of the asset (capitalized). Remember from the discussion in Chapter 8 that an expenditure should be capitalized if it is expected to have an identifiable benefit in future periods.

Two types of expenditures can be made on existing assets. The first is ordinary expenditures for repairs, maintenance, and minor improvements. For example, a truck requires oil changes and periodic maintenance. Because these types of expenditures typically benefit only the period in which they are made, they are expenses of the current period.

The second type is an expenditure that lengthens an asset's useful life, increases its capacity, or changes its use. These expenditures are capitalized; that is, they are added to the asset's cost instead of being expensed in the current period. For example, overhauling the engine of a delivery truck involves a major expenditure to extend the useful life of the truck. To qualify for capitalization, an expenditure should meet three criteria: (1) it must be significant in amount; (2) it should benefit the company over several periods, not just during the current one; and (3) it should increase the productive life or capacity of the asset.

To illustrate the differences in accounting for capital and ordinary expenditures, assume that Wheeler Resorts also purchases a delivery truck for $42,000. This truck has an estimated useful life of eight years and a salvage value of $2,000. The straight-line depreciation is $5,000 per year [($42,000 – $2,000)/8 years]. If the company spends $1,500 each year for normal maintenance, its annual recording of these expenditures is:

Repairs and Maintenance Expense	1,500	
Cash		1,500
Spent $1,500 for maintenance of delivery truck.		

This entry has no effect on either the recorded cost or the depreciation expense of the truck. Now suppose that at the end of the sixth year of the truck's useful life, Wheeler spends $8,000 to overhaul the engine. This expenditure will increase the truck's remaining life from two to four years, but will not change its estimated salvage value. The depreciation for the last four years will be $4,500 per year, calculated as shown below.

	Depreciation before Overhaul		Depreciation after Overhaul
Original cost	$42,000	Original cost	$42,000
Less salvage value	2,000	Accumulated depreciation	
Cost to be allocated (depreciable amount)	$40,000	(prior to overhaul)	30,000
Original life of asset	8 years	Remaining book value	$12,000
Original depreciation per year ($40,000/8)	$5,000	Capital expenditure (overhaul)	8,000
Usage before overhaul	× 6 years	New book value	$20,000
Accumulated depreciation prior to overhaul	$30,000	Less salvage value	2,000
		New depreciable amount	$18,000
		Remaining life	4 years
		New annual depreciation ($18,000/4)	$ 4,500

The journal entry to record the $8,000 capitalized expenditure is:

Delivery Truck	8,000	
Cash		8,000
Spent $8,000 to overhaul the engine of the $42,000 truck.		

Another example of a capital expenditure is the cost of land improvements. Certain improvements are considered permanent, such as moving earth to change the land contour. Such an expenditure would be capitalized as part of the land account. Other expenditures may have a limited life, such as those incurred in building a road, a sidewalk, or a fence. These expenditures would be capitalized in a separate land improvements account and be depreciated over their useful lives.

It is often difficult to determine whether a given expenditure should be capitalized or expensed. The two procedures produce a different net income, however, so it is extremely important that such expenditures be properly classified. When in doubt, accepted practice is to record an expenditure as an expense to ensure that the asset is not reported at an amount that exceeds its future benefit.

REMEMBER THIS...

- When an expenditure is capitalized, it is recorded as an addition to the cost of an asset.
- To be capitalized, an expenditure must:
  1. be significant in amount,
  2. provide benefits for more than one period, and
  3. increase the productive life or capacity of an asset.
- Ordinary expenditures, such as repairs, merely maintain an asset's productive capacity at the level originally projected and are expenses of the current period.

Recording Impairments of Asset Value

Identify whether a long-term operating asset has suffered a decline in value and record the decline.

(6) As mentioned earlier, the value of a long-term asset depends on the future cash flows expected to be generated by that asset. Occasionally, events occur after the purchase of an asset that significantly reduce its value. For example, a decline in the consumer demand for high-priced athletic shoes can cause the value of a shoe-manufacturing plant to plummet. Accountants call this **impairment**. When an asset is impaired, the event should be recognized in the financial statements, both as a reduction in the reported value of the asset in the balance sheet and as a loss in the income statement. Of course, the value of long-term assets can also increase after the purchase date. In the United States, these increases are not recorded, as explained more fully later in this section.

impairment

A decline in the value of a long-term operating asset.

Recording Decreases in the Value of Property, Plant, and Equipment

According to U.S. accounting rules, the value of an asset is impaired when the sum of estimated future cash flows from that asset is less than the book value of the asset. This computation ignores the time value of money. As illustrated in the example below, this is a strange impairment threshold—a more reasonable test would be to compare the book value to the fair value of the asset.

Once it has been determined that an asset is impaired, the amount of the impairment is measured as the difference between the book value of the asset and the fair value. To summarize, the existence of an impairment loss is determined using the sum of the estimated future cash flows from the asset, ignoring the time value of money. The amount of the impairment loss is measured using the fair value of the asset, which does incorporate the time value of money. The practical result of this two-step process is that an impairment loss is not recorded unless it is quite certain that the asset has suffered a permanent decline in value.

To illustrate, assume that Wheeler Resorts purchased a fitness center building five years ago for $600,000. The building has been depreciated using the straight-line method with a 20-year useful life and no residual value. Wheeler estimates that the building has a remaining useful life of 15 years, that net cash inflow from the building will be $25,000 per year, and that the fair value of the building is $230,000.

Annual depreciation for the building has been $30,000 ($600,000 ÷ 20 years). The current book value of the building is computed as follows:

Original cost	$600,000
Accumulated depreciation ($30,000 × 5 years)	150,000
Book value	$450,000

The book value of $450,000 is compared with the $375,000 ($25,000 × 15 years) sum of future cash flows (ignoring the time value of money) to determine whether the building is impaired. The sum of future cash flows is only $375,000, which is less than the $450,000 book value, so an impairment loss should be recognized. The loss is equal to the $220,000 ($450,000 – $230,000) difference between the book value of the building and its fair value. The impairment loss would be recorded as follows:

Accumulated Depreciation, Building	150,000	
Loss on Impairment of Building	220,000	
Building ($600,000 – $230,000)		370,000
Recognized $220,000 impairment loss on building.		

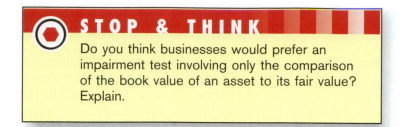

STOP & THINK

Do you think businesses would prefer an impairment test involving only the comparison of the book value of an asset to its fair value? Explain.

This journal entry basically records the asset as if it were being acquired brand new at its fair value of $230,000. The existing accumulated depreciation balance is wiped clean, and the new recorded value of the asset is its fair value of $230,000 ($600,000 − $370,000). After an impairment loss is recognized, no restoration of the loss is allowed even if the fair value of the asset later recovers.

The odd nature of the impairment test can be seen if the facts in the Wheeler example are changed slightly. Assume that net cash inflow from the building will be $35,000 per year and that the fair value of the building is $330,000. With these numbers, no impairment loss is recognized, even though the fair value of $330,000 is less than the book value of $450,000, because the sum of future cash flows of $525,000 ($35,000 × 15 years) exceeds the book value. Thus, in this case the asset would still be recorded at its book value of $450,000, even though its fair value is actually less. As mentioned above, the practical impact of the two-step impairment test is that no impairment losses are recorded unless the future cash flow calculations offer very strong evidence of a permanent decline in asset value. The impairment test is summarized in Exhibit 8.

AOL Time Warner set a world record when it recorded an impairment loss in 2002 of $99.737 billion. Over half of that amount related to a write-off of goodwill associated with the 2000 merger of **AOL** and **Time Warner**. This record write-off resulted in AOL Time Warner reporting a net loss for the year of $98.7 billion.

Recording Increases in the Value of Property, Plant, and Equipment

Under U.S. accounting standards, increases in the value of property, plant, and equipment are not recognized. Gains from increases in asset value are recorded only if and when the asset is sold. Thus, in the Wheeler example discussed above, if the fair value of the building rises to $800,000, the building would still be reported in the financial statements at its depreciated book value of $450,000. This is an example of the conservative bias that often exists in the accounting rules: losses are recognized when they occur, but the recognition of gains is deferred until the asset is sold.

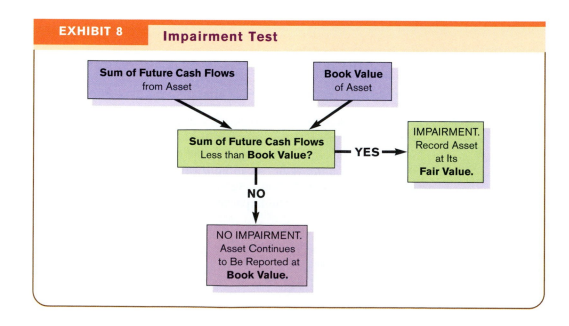

EXHIBIT 8   Impairment Test

Although increases in the value of property, plant, and equipment are not recognized in the United States, accounting rules in other countries do allow for their recognition. For example, companies in Great Britain often report their long-term operating assets at their fair values. Because this upward revaluation of property, plant, and equipment is allowable under international accounting standards, it will be interesting to watch over the next decade or so to see whether sentiment grows to allow this practice in the United States as well.

REMEMBER THIS...

- When an asset's value declines after it is purchased, it is said to be impaired.
- Recording an impairment loss is a two-step process.
  1. Compare the recorded book value of the asset to the sum of future cash flows expected to be generated by the asset.
  2. If the book value is higher, recognize a loss in an amount equal to the difference between the book value of the asset and its FAIR value.
- According to U.S. accounting rules, increases in the value of property, plant, and equipment are not recognized.

Disposal of Property, Plant, and Equipment

Record the discarding and selling of property, plant, and equipment.

(7) Plant and equipment eventually become worthless or are sold. When a company removes one of these assets from service, it has to eliminate the asset's cost and accumulated depreciation from the accounting records. There are basically three ways to dispose of an asset: (1) discard or scrap it, (2) sell it, or (3) exchange it for another asset.

Discarding Property, Plant, and Equipment

When an asset becomes worthless and must be scrapped, its cost and its accumulated depreciation balance should be removed from the accounting records. If the asset's total cost has been depreciated, there is no loss on the disposal. If, on the other hand, the cost is not completely depreciated, the undepreciated cost represents a loss on disposal.

To illustrate, we assume that Wheeler Resorts, Inc., purchases a computer for $15,000. The computer has a five-year life and no estimated salvage value and is depreciated on a straight-line basis. If the computer is scrapped after five full years, the entry to record the disposal is as follows:

Accumulated Depreciation, Computer	15,000	
Computer		15,000
Scrapped $15,000 computer.		

If Wheeler must pay $300 to have the computer dismantled and removed, the entry to record the disposal is:

Accumulated Depreciation, Computer	15,000	
Loss on Disposal of Computer	300	
Computer		15,000
Cash		300
Scrapped $15,000 computer and paid disposal costs of $300.		

If the computer had been scrapped after only four years of service (and after $12,000 of the original cost has been depreciated), there would have been a loss on disposal of $3,300 (including the disposal cost), and the entry would have been:

Accumulated Depreciation, Computer	12,000	
Loss on Disposal of Computer	3,300	
Computer		15,000
Cash		300
Scrapped $15,000 computer and paid disposal costs of $300.		

Don't think of the losses recognized above as "bad" or gains as "good." A loss on disposal simply means that, given the information we now have, it appears that we didn't record enough depreciation expense in previous years. As a result, the book value of the asset is higher than the amount we can get on disposal. Similarly, a gain means that too much depreciation expense was recognized in prior years, making the book value of the asset lower than its actual disposal value.

Selling Property, Plant, and Equipment

A second way of disposing of property, plant, and equipment is to sell it. If the sales price of the asset exceeds its book value (the original cost less accumulated depreciation), there is a gain on the sale. Conversely, if the sales price is less than the book value, there is a loss.

To illustrate, we refer again to Wheeler's $15,000 computer. If the computer is sold for $600 after five full years of service, assuming no disposal costs, the entry to record the sale is:

Cash	600	
Accumulated Depreciation, Computer	15,000	
Computer		15,000
Gain on Sale of Computer		600
Sold $15,000 computer at a gain of $600.		

Because the asset was fully depreciated, its book value was zero and the $600 cash received represents a gain. If the computer had been sold for $600 after only four years of service, there would have been a loss of $2,400 on the sale, and the entry to record the sale would have been:

Cash	600	
Accumulated Depreciation, Computer	12,000	
Loss on Sale of Computer	2,400	
Computer		15,000
Sold $15,000 computer at a loss of $2,400.		

The $2,400 loss is the difference between the sales price of $600 and the book value of $3,000 ($15,000 − $12,000). The amount of a gain or loss is thus a function of two factors: (1) the amount of cash received from the sale, and (2) the book value of the asset at the date of sale. The book value can vary from the market price of the asset for two reasons: (1) the accounting for the asset is not intended to show market value in the financial statements, and (2) it is difficult to estimate salvage value and useful life at the outset of an asset's life.

Exchanging Property, Plant, and Equipment

A third way of disposing of property, plant, and equipment is to exchange it for another asset. Such exchanges occur regularly with cars, trucks, machines, and other types of large equipment. When dissimilar assets are exchanged, such as a truck for a computer, the transaction is accounted for exactly as outlined previously: the acquired asset is recorded in the books at its fair market value, and a gain or loss may be recognized depending on the difference between this market value and the book value of the asset that was disposed of. Accounting for exchanges of similar assets can be more complicated and therefore is not discussed in this text. For a full treatment of the accounting for the exchange of similar assets, see an intermediate accounting text.

REMEMBER THIS...

- There are three ways of disposing of assets:
  1. discarding (scrapping),
  2. selling, and
  3. exchanging.
- If a scrapped asset has not been fully depreciated, a loss equal to the undepreciated cost or book value is recognized.
- When an asset is sold, there is a gain if the sales price exceeds the book value and a loss if the sales price is less than the book value.

Accounting for Intangible Assets

Account for the acquisition and amortization of intangible assets and understand the special difficulties associated with accounting for intangibles.

(8) Intangible assets are rights and privileges that are long-lived, are not held for resale, have no physical substance, and usually provide their owner with competitive advantages over other firms. Familiar examples are **patents**, franchises, licenses, and goodwill.

The importance of intangible assets can be illustrated by considering **General Electric**. As mentioned in Chapter 2, if the balance sheet were perfect, the amount of owners' equity would be equal to the market value of the company. On December 31, 2005, GE's reported equity was equal to $109.354 billion. The actual market value of GE on December 31, 2005, was $367 billion. The reason for the large difference between the recorded value and the actual value is that a traditional balance sheet excludes many important intangible economic assets. Examples of GE's important intangible economic assets are its track record of successful products and its entrenched market position in the many industries in which it operates. These intangible factors are by far the most valuable assets owned by GE, but they fall outside the traditional accounting process.

patent

An exclusive right granted for 20 years by the federal government to manufacture and sell an invention.

As with many accounting issues, accounting for intangibles involves a trade-off between relevance and reliability. Information concerning intangible assets is relevant, but to meet the standard for recognition in the financial statements, the recorded amount for the intangible must also be reliable. The most important distinction in intangible assets for accounting purposes is between those intangible assets that are internally generated and those that are externally purchased. This distinction is important because the transfer of externally-purchased intangible assets in an arm's-length market transaction provides reliable evidence that the intangibles have probable future economic benefit. Such reliable evidence does not exist for most internally-generated intangibles. Accordingly, as discussed in Chapter 8, most costs associated with generating and maintaining internally-generated intangibles are expensed as incurred.

Keep in mind, however, that an intangible asset that is internally generated (and therefore not recorded as an asset on a company's books) is still valued by the stock market. As an illustration, consider Exhibit 9, which lists the 10 most valuable brands in the

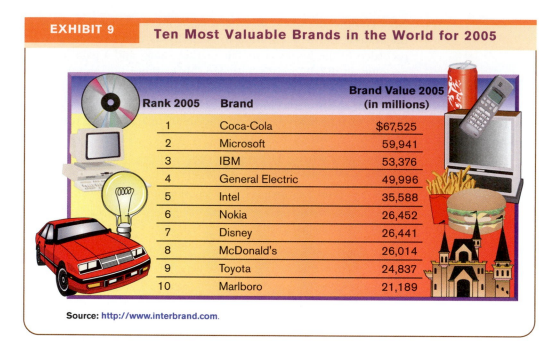

Rank 2005	Brand	Brand Value 2005 (in millions)
1	Coca-Cola	$67,525
2	Microsoft	59,941
3	IBM	53,376
4	General Electric	49,996
5	Intel	35,588
6	Nokia	26,452
7	Disney	26,441
8	McDonald's	26,014
9	Toyota	24,837
10	Marlboro	21,189

EXHIBIT 9   Ten Most Valuable Brands in the World for 2005

Source: http://www.interbrand.com.

world in 2005. Each of these brands represents a valuable economic asset that has been internally generated. For example, the $67.5 billion Coca-Cola brand name has been created over the years by **The Coca-Cola Company** through successful business operations and relentless marketing. But because the valuation of this asset is not deemed sufficiently reliable to meet the standard for financial statement recognition, it is not included in The Coca-Cola Company's balance sheet. However, as explained below, if another company were to buy The Coca-Cola Company, an important part of recording the transaction would be allocating the total purchase price to the various economic assets acquired, including previously unrecorded intangible assets.

In the future, financial reporting will move toward providing more information about internally-generated intangibles. Whether this will involve actual valuation and recognition of these intangibles in the financial statements, or simply more extensive note disclosure, remains to be seen.

A short description of some of the common types of intangible assets is given below.

Trademark   A trademark is a distinctive name, symbol, or slogan that distinguishes a product or service from similar products or services. Well-known examples include Coke, Windows, Yahoo!, and the Nike Swoosh. As shown in Exhibit 9 above, it was estimated in 2005 that the value of the Coca-Cola trademark was in excess of $67 billion. Because the Coca-Cola trademark is an internally-generated intangible asset, it is not reported in The Coca-Cola Company's balance sheet. However, the company has purchased other trademarks (such as Minute Maid), with a total cost of $2.3 billion; these are reported in The Coca-Cola Company's balance sheet.

Franchises   Franchise operations have become so common in everyday life that we often don't realize we are dealing with them. In fact, these days it is difficult to find a non-franchise business in a typical shopping mall. When a business obtains a **franchise**, the recorded cost of the franchise includes any sum paid specifically for the franchise right as well as legal fees and other costs incurred in obtaining it. Although the value of a franchise at the time of its acquisition may be substantially in excess of its cost, the amount recorded should be limited to actual outlays. For example, approximately 60% of **McDonald**'s locations are operated under franchise agreements. A McDonald's franchisee must contribute an initial cash amount of $200,000, which is used to buy some of the equipment and signs and also to pay the initial franchise fee. The value of a McDonald's franchise alone is much more

franchise

An entity that has been licensed to sell the product of a manufacturer or to offer a particular service in a given area.

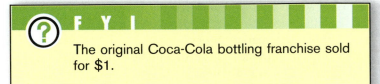

F Y I

The original Coca-Cola bottling franchise sold for $1.

than $200,000, but the franchisee would only record a franchise asset in his or her financial statements equal to the cost (not value) of the franchise. However, if a franchise right is included when one company purchases another company, presumably the entire value is included in the purchase price, and the fair value attributable to the franchise right is recorded as an intangible asset in the acquirer's books.

Goodwill   Goodwill is the business contacts, reputation, functioning systems, staff camaraderie, and industry experience that make a business much more than just a collection of assets. As mentioned above, if these factors are the result of a contractual right or are associated with intangibles that can be bought and sold separately, then the value of the factor should be reported as a separate intangible asset. In essence, goodwill is a residual number, the value of all of the synergies of a functioning business that cannot be specifically identified with any other intangible factor. Goodwill is recognized only when it is purchased as part of the acquisition of another company. In other words, a company's own goodwill, its homegrown goodwill, is not recognized. Goodwill will be discussed more in depth later in the chapter. Exhibit 10 provides a summary of a number of intangible assets and how they are valued.

Estimating the Fair Value of an Intangible   The most difficult part of recording an amount for an intangible asset is not in identifying the asset but instead is in estimating a fair value of the asset. The objective in estimating the fair value is to duplicate the

EXHIBIT 10	**Acquisition Costs of Goodwill and Other Intangible Assets**	
Patent	An exclusive right granted by a national government that enables an inventor to control the manufacture, sale, or use of an invention. In the United States, legal life is 20 years from patent application date.	**COST:** Purchase price, filing and registry fees, cost of subsequent litigation to protect right. Does not include internal research and development costs.
Trademark	An exclusive right granted by a national government that permits the use of distinctive symbols, labels, and designs, e.g., McDonald's golden arches, Nike's Swoosh, Apple's computer name and logo. Legal life is virtually unlimited.	**COST:** Same as Patent.
Copyright	An exclusive right granted by a national government that permits an author to sell, license, or control his/her work. In the United States, copyrights expire 50 years after the death of the author.	**COST:** Same as Patent.
Franchise agreement	An exclusive right or privilege received by a business or individual to perform certain functions or sell certain products or services.	**COST:** Expenditures made to purchase the franchise. Legal fees and other costs incurred in obtaining the franchise.
Acquired customer list	A list or database containing customer information such as name, address, past purchases, and so forth. Companies that originally develop such a list often sell or lease it to other companies, unless prohibited by customer confidentiality agreements.	**COST:** Purchase price when acquired from another company. Costs to internally develop a customer list are expensed as incurred.
Goodwill	Miscellaneous intangible resources, factors, and conditions that allow a company to earn above-normal income with its identifiable net assets. Goodwill is recorded only when a business entity is acquired by a purchase.	**COST:** Portion of purchase price that exceeds the sum of the current market value for all identifiable net assets, both tangible and intangible.

Source: Some of these illustrations are taken from SFAS No. 141, "Business Combinations," Appendix A.

price at which the intangible asset would change hands in an arm's-length market transaction. If there is a market for similar intangibles assets, then the best estimate of fair value is made with reference to these observable market prices.

To illustrate the accounting for the purchase of an intangible patent, assume that Wheeler Resorts, Inc., acquires, for $200,000, a patent granted seven years earlier to another firm. The entry to record the purchase of the patent is:

Patent	200,000	
Cash		200,000
Purchased patent for $200,000.		

The one exception to valuing purchased intangibles at market value involves goodwill, which arises when an entire business is purchased. Goodwill is best thought of as a residual amount, the amount of the purchase price of a business that is left over after all other tangible and intangible assets have been identified. As such, goodwill is that intangible something that makes the whole company worth more than its individual parts. In general, goodwill represents all the special advantages, not otherwise separately identifiable, enjoyed by an enterprise, such as a high credit standing, reputation for superior products and services, experience with development and distribution processes, favorable government relations, and so forth. These factors allow a business to earn above-normal income with the identifiable assets, tangible and intangible, employed in the business.

To illustrate the accounting for goodwill, assume that, in order to cater to the medicinal needs of its guests, Wheeler Resorts purchases Valley Drug Store for $400,000. At the time of purchase, the recorded assets and liabilities of Valley Drug have the following fair market values:

Inventory	$220,000
Long-term operating assets	110,000
Other assets (prepaid expenses, etc.)	10,000
Liabilities	(20,000)
Total net assets	$320,000

Note that Wheeler Resorts records these items at their fair market values on the date purchased, just as it does when purchasing individual assets.

Because Wheeler was willing to pay $400,000 for Valley Drug, there must have been other favorable, intangible factors worth approximately $80,000. These factors are called goodwill, and the entry to record the purchase of the drug store is:

Inventory	220,000	
Long-term Operating Assets	110,000	
Other Assets	10,000	
Goodwill	80,000	
Liabilities		20,000
Cash		400,000
Purchased Valley Drug Store for $400,000.		

Amortization of Intangible Assets

amortization

The process of cost allocation that assigns the original cost of an intangible asset to the periods benefited.

Like tangible assets, intangible assets are recorded at their historical costs. Unlike tangible assets, the costs associated with intangible assets are not always allocated as expenses over time. The periodic allocation to expense of an intangible asset's cost is called **amortization**. Conceptually, depreciation (with plant and equipment), depletion (with natural resources), and amortization (with intangible assets) are exactly the same thing. Straight-line amortization is generally used for intangible assets.

In accounting for an intangible asset after its acquisition, a determination first must be made as to whether the intangible asset has a finite life. If no economic, legal, or contractual factors cause the intangible to have a finite life, then its life is said to be indefinite, and the asset is not to be amortized until its life is determined to be finite. An indefinite life is one that extends beyond the foreseeable horizon. An example of an intangible asset that has an indefinite life is a broadcast license which includes an extension option that can be renewed indefinitely. If an intangible asset is determined to have a finite life, then the asset is to be amortized over its estimated life; the useful life estimate should be reviewed periodically.

To illustrate the amortization of an intangible asset, let us continue with the patent example with Wheeler Resorts, Inc., used earlier. Recall that the patent, with a legal life of 20 years, was purchased from another company after seven years. Because seven years of its 20-year legal life have already elapsed, the patent now has a legal life of only 13 years, although it may have a shorter useful life. If its useful life is assumed to be eight years, one-eighth of the $200,000 cost should be amortized each year for the next eight years. The entry each year to record the patent amortization expense is:

Amortization Expense, Patent	25,000	
Patent		25,000
To amortize one-eighth of the cost of the patent.		

Notice that in the above entry, the patent account was credited. Alternatively, a contra-asset account, such as Accumulated Amortization, could have been credited. In practice, however, crediting the intangible asset account directly is more common. This is different from the normal practice of crediting Accumulated Depreciation for buildings or equipment.

Many intangible assets that used to be amortized are no longer amortized. For example, goodwill used to be amortized over a 40-year period. Goodwill is now no longer amortized.

Impairment of Intangible Assets

While many intangible assets are not amortized, all intangible assets must be evaluated every year to determine if (1) their estimated useful life has changed and (2) the intangible asset has become impaired. Previously in this chapter the issue of asset impairment was discussed with regard to tangible assets. While the specifics of the various impairment tests associated with the different kinds of intangible assets are beyond the scope of this textbook, suffice it to say that when evaluating whether or not an intangible asset has become impaired, the objective is to ensure that the intangible assets recorded on the books of a company are not overstated. If an intangible asset is determined to be impaired, an impairment loss is recorded on the income statement and the intangible asset is reduced on the books of the company.

REMEMBER THIS...

- Intangible assets are long-term rights and privileges that have no physical substance but provide competitive advantages to owners. Common intangible assets are patents, franchises, licenses, and goodwill.
- Intangible assets are only recognized in the financial statements if they have been purchased through an arm's-length transaction.
- The cost of recorded intangible assets is expensed as follows:
  - Certain intangible assets are amortized over the economic life of the asset.
  - Many intangible assets are not amortized because their economic lives are not limited.
  - All intangible assets, including goodwill, must be analyzed to determine if impairment has occurred. If it has, then an impairment loss is recognized.

Use the fixed asset turnover ratio as a measure of how efficiently a company is using its property, plant, and equipment.

(9)

Measuring Property, Plant, and Equipment Efficiency

In this section we discuss the fixed asset turnover ratio, which uses financial statement data to give a rough indication of how efficiently a company is utilizing its property, plant, and equipment to generate sales. We also illustrate that the fixed asset turnover ratio must be interpreted carefully because, as with most other financial ratios, acceptable values for this ratio differ significantly from one industry to the next.

Evaluating the Level of Property, Plant, and Equipment

fixed asset turnover

The number of dollars in sales generated by each dollar of fixed assets; computed as sales divided by property, plant, and equipment.

Fixed asset turnover can be used to evaluate the appropriateness of the level of a company's property, plant, and equipment. Fixed asset turnover is computed as sales divided by average property, plant, and equipment (fixed assets) and is interpreted as the number of dollars in sales generated by each dollar of fixed assets. This ratio is also often called PP&E turnover. The computation of the fixed asset turnover for **General Electric** is given below. All financial statement numbers are in millions.

	2005	2004
Sales	$148,019	$133,417
Property, plant, and equipment		
Beginning of year	$ 63,103	$ 53,388
End of year	67,528	63,103
Average fixed assets	$ 65,316	$ 58,246
Fixed asset turnover	2.27 times	2.29 times

The fixed asset turnover calculations suggest that GE used its fixed assets to generate sales a little less efficiently in 2005 than in 2004. In 2005, each dollar of fixed assets generated $2.27 in sales, down from $2.29 in 2004.

Industry Differences in Fixed Asset Turnover

As with all ratios, the fixed asset turnover ratio must be used carefully to ensure that erroneous conclusions are not made. For example, fixed asset turnover ratio values for two companies in different industries cannot be meaningfully compared. This point can be illustrated using the fact that General Electric is composed of two primary parts—General Electric, the manufacturing company, and GE Capital Services, the financial services firm. The fixed asset turnover ratio computed earlier was for both these parts combined. Because GE Capital Services does not use property, plant, and equipment for manufacturing but instead leases the assets to other companies in order to earn financial revenue, one would expect its fixed asset turnover ratio to be quite unlike that for a manufacturing firm. In fact, as shown below, the fixed asset turnover ratio for the manufacturing segments of General Electric was 5.44 in 2005, over double the ratio value for the company as a whole.

	2005	**2004**
Fixed Asset Turnover Ratio		
General Electric–Manufacturing Segments Only		

	2005	**2004**
Sales	$90,430	$82,214
Property, plant, and equipment		
Beginning of year	$16,756	$14,566
End of year	16,504	16,756
Average fixed assets	$16,630	$15,661
Fixed asset turnover	5.44 times	5.25 times

REMEMBER THIS...

- The fixed asset turnover ratio can be used as a general measure of how efficiently a company is using its property, plant, and equipment.
- Fixed asset turnover is computed as sales divided by average property, plant, and equipment and is interpreted as the number of dollars in sales generated by each dollar of fixed assets.
- Standard values for this ratio differ significantly from industry to industry.

Two topics related to operational assets that are traditionally covered in introductory accounting classes were not covered in the main part of this chapter. These two topics relate to depreciation—accelerated depreciation methods and changes in depreciation estimates.

Accelerated Depreciation Methods

Compute declining-balance and sum-of-the-years'-digits depreciation expense for plant and equipment.

(10) Earlier in the chapter, straight-line and units-of-production depreciation methods were discussed. Both of these methods allocate the cost of an asset evenly over its life. With straight-line depreciation, each time period during the asset's useful life is assigned an equal amount of depreciation. With units-of-production depreciation, each mile driven, hour used, or other measurement of useful life is assigned an equal amount of depreciation. Sometimes, a depreciation method that does not assign costs equally over the life of the asset is preferred. For example, if most of an asset's benefits will be realized in the earlier periods of the asset's life, the method used should assign more depreciation to the earlier years and less to the later years. Examples of these "accelerated" depreciation methods are the declining-balance and the sum-of-the-years'-digits methods. These methods are merely ways of assigning more of an asset's depreciation to earlier periods and less to later periods.

To illustrate these depreciation methods, we will again use the Wheeler Resorts example from earlier in the chapter. Assume again that Wheeler Resorts purchased a van for transporting hotel guests to and from the airport. The following facts apply:

Acquisition cost	$24,000
Estimated salvage value	$2,000
Estimated life:	
In years	4 years
In miles driven	60,000 miles

Declining-Balance Method of Depreciation

declining-balance depreciation method

An accelerated depreciation method in which an asset's book value is multiplied by a constant depreciation rate (such as double the straight-line percentage, in the case of double-declining-balance).

The **declining-balance depreciation method** provides for higher depreciation charges in the earlier years of an asset's life than does the straight-line method. The declining-balance method involves multiplying a fixed rate, or percentage, by a decreasing book value. This rate is a multiple of the straight-line rate. Typically, it is twice the straight-line rate, but it also can be 175, 150, or 125% of the straight-line rate. Our depreciation of Wheeler's hotel van will illustrate the declining-balance method using a fixed rate equal to twice the straight-line rate. This method is often referred to as the double-declining-balance depreciation method.

Declining-balance depreciation differs from the other depreciation methods in two respects: (1) the initial computation ignores the asset's salvage value, and (2) a constant depreciation rate is multiplied by a decreasing book value. The salvage value is not ignored completely because the depreciation taken during the asset's life cannot reduce the asset's book value below the estimated salvage value.

The double-declining-balance (DDB) rate is twice the straight-line rate, computed as follows:

$$\frac{1}{\text{Estimated life (years)}} \times 2 = \text{DDB rate}$$

This rate is multiplied times the book value at the beginning of each year (cost − accumulated depreciation) to compute the annual depreciation expense for the year. If the 150% declining balance were being used instead, the 2 in the rate formula would be replaced by 1.5 and so on for any other percentages.

To illustrate, the depreciation calculation for the van using the 200% (or double) declining-balance method is:

Straight-line rate	4 years = 1/4 = 25%
Double the straight-line rate	25% × 2 = 50%
Annual depreciation	50% × undepreciated cost (book value)

Based on this information, the formula for double-declining-balance depreciation can be expressed as (straight-line rate × 2) × (cost − accumulated depreciation) = current year's depreciation expense. The double-declining-balance depreciation for the four years is shown in Exhibit 11. As you review this exhibit, note that the book value of the van at the end of year 4 is $2,000, its salvage value.

 CAUTION

With declining-balance depreciation, the asset is not depreciated below its salvage value, though this figure is ignored in the initial computations.

EXHIBIT 11	Depreciation Schedule with Double-Declining-Balance Depreciation

	Computation	Annual Depreciation Expense	Accumulated Depreciation	Book Value
Acquisition date	–	–	–	$24,000
End of year 1	$24,000 × 0.50	$12,000	$12,000	12,000
End of year 2	12,000 × 0.50	6,000	18,000	6,000
End of year 3	6,000 × 0.50	3,000	21,000	3,000
End of year 4	*	1,000	22,000	2,000
		$22,000		

*In year 4, depreciation expense cannot exceed $1,000 because the book value cannot be reduced below salvage value.

If Wheeler had applied the declining-balance method to depreciate the hotel van on the basis of 150% of the straight-line rate, the fixed rate would have been 37.5%, computed as follows: 25% × 1.50 = 37.5%. Using the 37.5% fixed rate, the annual depreciation of the hotel van would have been as follows:

First year:	$24,000 × 37.5% = $9,000
Second year:	$24,000 − $9,000 = $15,000 × 37.5% = $5,625
Third year:	$15,000 − $5,625 = $9,375 × 37.5% = $3,516
Fourth year:	$9,375 − $3,516 = $5,859 − $2,000 salvage value = $3,859

Since a total book value of $5,859 remains at the end of year 3, the remaining book value less the estimated salvage value is expensed in year 4.

Depreciation for Income Tax Purposes   Net income reported on the financial statements prepared for stockholders, creditors, and other external users often differs from taxable income reported on income tax returns. The most common cause of differences between financial reporting and tax returns is the computation of depreciation. Depreciation for income tax purposes must be computed in accordance with federal income tax law, which specifies rules to be applied in computing tax depreciation for various categories of assets. Income tax rules are designed to achieve economic objectives, such as stimulating investment in productive assets.

The income tax depreciation system in the United States is called the Modified Accelerated Cost Recovery System (MACRS). MACRS is based on declining-balance depreciation and is designed to allow taxpayers to quickly deduct the cost of assets acquired. Allowing this accelerated depreciation deduction for income tax purposes gives companies tax benefits for investing in new productive assets. Presumably, this will spur investment, create jobs, and make voters more likely to reelect their representatives.

Sum-of-the-Years'-Digits Method of Depreciation

sum-of-the-years'-digits (SYD) depreciation method

The accelerated depreciation method in which a constant balance (cost minus salvage value) is multiplied by a declining depreciation rate.

Like the declining-balance method, the **sum-of-the-years'-digits (SYD) depreciation method** provides for a proportionately higher depreciation expense in the early years of an asset's life. It is therefore appropriate for assets that provide greater benefits in their earlier years (such as trucks, machinery, and equipment) as opposed to assets that benefit all years equally (as buildings do). The formula for calculating SYD is:

$$\frac{\text{Number of years of life remaining at beginning of year}}{\text{Sum-of-the-years'-digits}} \times (\text{Cost} - \text{Salvage value}) = \text{Depreciation expense}$$

The numerator is the number of years of estimated life remaining at the beginning of the current year. The van, with a four-year life, would have four years remaining at the beginning of the first year, three at the beginning of the second, and so on. The denominator is the sum of the years of the asset's life. The sum of the years' digits for the van is 10 (4 + 3 + 2 + 1). In other words, the numerator decreases by one year each year, whereas the denominator remains the same for each year's calculation of depreciation. Also note that the asset's cost is reduced by the salvage value in computing the annual depreciation expense as is done for the straight-line method but not for the declining-balance method.

The depreciation on the van for the first two years is:

First year:	4/10 × ($24,000 − $2,000) = $8,800
Second year:	3/10 × ($24,000 − $2,000) = $6,600

The depreciation schedule for four years is shown in Exhibit 12.

EXHIBIT 12	Depreciation Schedule with Sum-of-the-Years'-Digits Depreciation		
	Annual Depreciation Expense	**Accumulated Depreciation**	**Book Value**
Acquisition date	–	–	$24,000
End of year 1	$ 8,800	$ 8,800	15,200
End of year 2	6,600	15,400	8,600
End of year 3	4,400	19,800	4,200
End of year 4	2,200	22,000	2,000
Total	$22,000		

The entry to record the sum-of-the-years'-digits depreciation for the first year is:

Depreciation Expense   8,800
    Accumulated Depreciation, Hotel Van   8,800
      To record the first year's depreciation for the hotel van.

Subsequent years' depreciation entries would show depreciation expense of $6,600, $4,400, and $2,200.

When an asset has a long life, the computation of the denominator (the sum-of-the-years'-digits) can become quite involved. There is, however, a simple formula for determining the denominator. It is:

$$\frac{n(n + 1)}{2}$$ where n is the life (in years) of the asset

Given that the van has a useful life of four years, the formula works as follows:

$$\frac{4(5)}{2} = 10$$

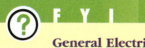

General Electric is one of the few large companies that continues to use the sum-of-the-years'-digits method of depreciation.

As you can see, the answer is the same as if you had added the years' digits (4 + 3 + 2 + 1). If an asset has a 10-year life, the sum of the years' digits is:

$$\frac{10 (11)}{2} = 55$$

The depreciation fraction in year 1 would be 10/55, in year 2, 9/55, and so on.

A Comparison of Depreciation Methods

Now that you have been introduced to the four most common depreciation methods, we can compare them both graphically and by using the Wheeler Resorts van example. Exhibit 13 compares the straight-line, sum-of-the-years'-digits, and declining-balance depreciation methods with regard to the relative amount of depreciation expense incurred in each year for an asset that has a five-year life. The units-of-production method is not illustrated because there would not be a standard pattern of cost allocation. Exhibit 14 shows the results for the Wheeler Resorts' van for all four depreciation methods.

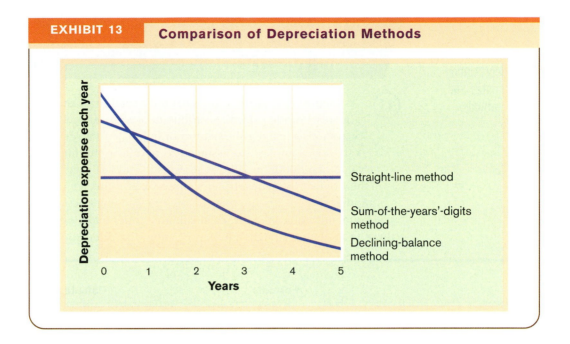

EXHIBIT 13   Comparison of Depreciation Methods

EXHIBIT 14   Comparison of Depreciation Expense Using Different Depreciation Methods

	Straight-Line Depreciation	Units-of-Production Depreciation	DDB Depreciation	SYD Depreciation
Year 1	$ 5,500	$ 4,400	$12,000	$ 8,800
Year 2	5,500	6,600	6,000	6,600
Year 3	5,500	7,700	3,000	4,400
Year 4	5,500	3,300	1,000	2,200
Totals	$22,000	$22,000	$22,000	$22,000

REMEMBER THIS...

- Two depreciation methods that allow for more depreciation expense in the early years of an asset's life are the declining-balance and the sum-of-the-years'-digits methods.
- The declining-balance method involves multiplying the asset's declining book value by a fixed rate that is a multiple of the straight-line rate.
- Sum-of-the-years'-digits depreciation is computed by multiplying (cost − salvage value) by a declining ratio based on the number of years in the asset's estimated life.

Account for changes in depreciation estimates and methods.

(11)

Changes in Depreciation Estimates and Methods

As mentioned earlier in the chapter, useful lives and salvage values are only estimates. In addition, the various depreciation methods are simply alternative ways for estimating the pattern of usage of an asset over time. Wheeler Resorts' van, for example, was assumed to have a useful life of four years and a salvage value of $2,000. In reality, the van's life and salvage value may be different from the original estimates. If, after three years, Wheeler realizes that the van will last another three years and that the salvage value will be $3,000 instead of $2,000, the accountant would need to calculate a new depreciation expense for the remaining three years. Using straight-line depreciation, the calculations would be as follows:

	Formula	Calculation	Total Depreciation
Annual depreciation for the first three years	$\dfrac{\text{Cost} - \text{Salvage value}}{\text{Estimated useful life}} = \dfrac{\text{Depreciation}}{\text{expense}}$	$\dfrac{\$24,000 - \$2,000}{4 \text{ years}} = \$5,500$	$16,500
Book value after three years	$\dfrac{\text{Cost} - \text{Accumulated}}{\text{depreciation to date}} = \text{Book value}$	$24,000 − $16,500 = $7,500	
Annual depreciation for last three years (based on new total life of six years and new salvage value of $3,000	$\dfrac{\text{Book value} - \text{Salvage value}}{\text{Remaining useful life}} = \dfrac{\text{Depreciation}}{\text{expense}}$	$\dfrac{\$7,500 - \$3,000}{3 \text{ years}} = \$1,500$	4,500
Total depreciation			$21,000

F Y I

To illustrate the uncertainty about depreciation life estimates, consider that **Boeing** 727 airplanes are lasting a lot longer than initially expected. The first Boeing 727 was delivered in 1963; the last was built in 1984. As of January 2001, almost 1,300 of the 1,831 727s delivered were still in service.

The example shows that a change in the estimate of useful life or salvage value does not require a modification of the depreciation expense already taken. New information affects depreciation only in future years. Exhibit 15 shows the revised depreciation expense. Similar calculations, although more complex, would apply if either the sum-of-the-years'-digits or the declining-balance depreciation method had been

EXHIBIT 15	**Depreciation Schedule When There Is a Change in Estimate**

	Annual Depreciation Expense	Accumulated Depreciation	Book Value
Acquisition date	–	–	$24,000
Year 1	$ 5,500	$ 5,500	18,500
Year 2	5,500	11,000	13,000
Year 3	5,500	16,500	7,500
Change			
Year 4	1,500	18,000	6,000
Year 5	1,500	19,500	4,500
Year 6	1,500	21,000	3,000
Total	$21,000		

used. Had the company changed from the straight-line method to another method, the procedures used would be the same. The book value on the date the change is made would be used and the assumptions associated with the new depreciation method would be applied to this book value.

REMEMBER THIS...

- Because depreciation is only an estimate, changes in estimates of useful life, salvage value, or pattern of use may be required as new information becomes available.
- When there is a change in estimate, past periods' depreciation amounts remain the same.
- The change is reflected in future years' depreciation, as follows:
  - Change in life—The remaining book value (less old salvage value) is allocated over the new life.
  - Change in salvage value—The remaining book value, less the new salvage value, is allocated over the old life.
  - Change in method—The remaining book value, less the old salvage value, is allocated over the remaining life using the new method.

REVIEW OF LEARNING OBJECTIVES

(1) **Identify the two major categories of long-term operating assets: property, plant, and equipment and intangible assets.**

Categories of Long-Term Operating Assets	Examples
Property, Plant, and Equipment	Land, buildings, machines
Intangible Assets	Patents, licenses, goodwill

(2) **Understand the factors important in deciding whether to acquire a long-term operating asset.**

- Long-term operating assets have value because they help companies generate future cash flows. An asset's value can decline or disappear if events cause a decrease in the expected future cash flows generated by the asset.
- The decision to acquire a long-term operating asset (called capital budgeting) involves comparing the cost of the asset to the value of the expected cash inflows, after adjusting for the time value of money.

(3) **Record the acquisition of property, plant, and equipment through a simple purchase as well as through a lease, by self-construction, and as part of the purchase of several assets at once.**

Ways to Acquire Property, Plant, and Equipment	Things to Remember
Simple Purchase	Include all costs to purchase the asset and get it ready for its intended use.
Leasing	• Operating lease—accounted for as a rental; nothing on the balance sheet. • Capital lease—accounted for as a purchase; asset and liability on the balance sheet.
Self Construction	Include the cost of materials, labor, reasonable overhead, and interest.
Basket Purchase	Allocate the basket purchase price based on relative fair values.

(4) Compute straight-line and units-of-production depreciation expense for plant and equipment.

Straight-Line Depreciation	(Cost − Salvage value) ÷ Estimated useful life
Units-of-Production Depreciation	[(Cost − Salvage value) ÷ Estimated life in units] × Units produced
Depletion	Same as units-of-production depreciation

(5) Account for repairs and improvements of property, plant, and equipment.

Record an expenditure as an asset (that is, capitalize it) when–	The expenditure is: • significant in amount, • provides benefits for more than one period, and • increases the productive life or capacity of an asset.
Record an expenditure as an expense when–	The expenditure merely maintains an asset's productive capacity at the level originally projected.

(6) Identify whether a long-term operating asset has suffered a decline in value and record the decline.

- Recording an impairment loss is a two-step process.
  (1) Compare the recorded book value of the asset to the sum of future cash flows expected to be generated by the asset.
  (2) If the book value is higher, recognize a loss in an amount equal to the difference between the book value of the asset and its FAIR value.
- According to U.S. accounting rules, increases in the value of property, plant, and equipment are not recognized.

(7) Record the discarding and selling of property, plant, and equipment.

- If a scrapped asset has not been fully depreciated, a loss equal to the undepreciated cost or book value is recognized.
- When an asset is sold, there is a gain if the sales price exceeds the book value and a loss if the sales price is less than the book value.

(8) Account for the acquisition and amortization of intangible assets and understand the special difficulties associated with accounting for intangibles.

- Intangible assets are only recognized in the financial statements if they have been purchased through an arm's-length transaction.
- The cost of recorded intangible assets is expensed as follows:
  - Certain intangible assets are amortized over the economic life of the asset.
  - Many intangible assets are not amortized because their economic lives are not limited.
  - All intangible assets, including goodwill, must be analyzed to determine if impairment has occurred. If it has, then an impairment loss is recognized.

(9) Use the fixed asset turnover ratio as a measure of how efficiently a company is using its property, plant, and equipment.

- Fixed asset turnover is computed as sales divided by average property, plant, and equipment and is interpreted as the number of dollars in sales generated by each dollar of fixed assets.
- Standard values for this ratio differ significantly from industry to industry.

(10) Compute declining-balance and sum-of-the years'-digits depreciation expense for plant and equipment.

- The declining-balance method involves multiplying the asset's declining book value by a fixed rate that is a multiple of the straight-line rate.
- Sum-of-the-years'-digits depreciation is computed by multiplying (cost – salvage value) by a declining ratio based on the number of years in the asset's estimated life.

(11) Account for changes in depreciation estimates and methods.

- A change in depreciation estimate is reflected in future years' depreciation, as follows:
  - Change in life—The remaining book value (less old salvage value) is allocated over the new life.
  - Change in salvage value—The remaining book value, less the new salvage value, is allocated over the old life.
  - Change in method—The remaining book value, less the old salvage value, is allocated over the remaining life using the new method.

KEY TERMS & CONCEPTS

amortization, 414
basket purchase, 397
book value, 399
capital budgeting, 392
capital lease, 395
capitalized interest, 397
depletion, 404
depreciation, 399
fixed asset turnover, 416

franchise, 412
goodwill, 399
impairment, 407
intangible assets, 392
lease, 394
lessee, 394
lessor, 394
long-term operating assets, 390

natural resources, 404
operating lease, 394
patent, 411
property, plant, and equipment, 391
salvage value, 400
straight-line depreciation method, 400
time value of money, 392

units-of-production method, 400

declining-balance depreciation method, 418
sum-of-the-years'-digits (SYD) depreciation method, 419

REVIEW PROBLEMS

Property, Plant, and Equipment

Swift Motor Lines is a trucking company that hauls crude oil in the Rocky Mountain states. It currently has 20 trucks. The following information relates to a single truck:

a. Date truck was purchased, July 1, 2006.
b. Cost of truck:

Truck	$125,000
Paint job	3,000
Sales tax	7,000

c. Estimated useful life of truck, 120,000 miles.
d. Estimated salvage value of truck, $27,000.
e. 2008 expenditures on truck:
  (1) $6,000 on new tires and regular maintenance.
  (2) On January 1, spent $44,000 to completely rework the truck's engine; increased the total life to 200,000 miles but left expected salvage value unchanged.

(continued)

f. Miles driven:

2006	11,000
2007	24,000
2008 (after reworking of engine)	20,000
2009	14,000

Required:

Record journal entries to account for the following. (Use the units-of-production depreciation method.)

1. The purchase of the truck.
2. The expenditures on the truck during 2008.
3. Depreciation expense for:
    a. 2006
    b. 2007
    c. 2008
    d. 2009

Solution

1. Truck Purchase

The cost of the truck includes both the amount paid for it and all costs incurred to get it in working condition. In this case, the cost includes both the paint job and the sales tax. Thus, the entry to record the purchase is:

Truck	135,000	
Cash		135,000
Purchased truck for cash.		

2. Expenditures

The expenditure of $6,000 is an ordinary expenditure and is expensed in the current year. The engine overhaul is capitalized. The entries are:

Repairs and Maintenance Expense	6,000	
Cash		6,000
Recorded purchase of new tires and regular maintenance on truck.		

Truck	44,000	
Cash		44,000
Recorded major overhaul to truck's engine.		

3. Depreciation Expense

The formula for units-of-production depreciation on the truck is:

$$\frac{\text{Cost} - \text{Salvage value}}{\text{Total miles expected to be driven}} \times \frac{\text{Number of miles}}{\text{driven in any year}} = \text{Depreciation expense}$$

Journal entries and calculations are as follows:

a. 2006:

Depreciation Expense	9,900	
Accumulated Depreciation, Truck		9,900
Recorded depreciation expense for 2006.		

$$\frac{\$135,000 - \$27,000}{120,000 \text{ miles}} \times 11,000 \text{ miles} = \$9,900 \text{ or } \$0.90 \text{ per mile} \times 11,000 \text{ miles}$$

(continued)

b.   2007:

Depreciation Expense	21,600	
Accumulated Depreciation, Truck		21,600
Recorded depreciation expense for 2007.		

$$\$0.90 \times 24{,}000 \text{ miles} = \$21{,}600$$

c.   2008:

Depreciation Expense	14,600	
Accumulated Depreciation, Truck		14,600
Recorded depreciation expense for 2008.		

$$\frac{\$135{,}000 - \$9{,}900 - \$21{,}600 + \$44{,}000 - \$27{,}000}{\substack{165{,}000 \text{ miles} \\ (200{,}000 - 11{,}000 - 24{,}000)}} \times 20{,}000 \text{ miles} = \$14{,}600 \text{ or } \$0.73^* \text{ per mile} \times 20{,}000 \text{ miles}$$

*Rounded to the nearest cent.

d.   2009:

Depreciation Expense	10,220	
Accumulated Depreciation, Truck		10,220
Recorded depreciation expense for 2009.		

$$\$0.73 \times 14{,}000 \text{ miles} = \$10{,}220$$

Property, Plant, and Equipment

Swift Motor Lines is a trucking company that hauls crude oil in the Rocky Mountain states. It currently has 20 trucks. The following information relates to a single truck:

a. Date truck was purchased, July 1, 2006.
b. Cost of truck:

Truck	$125,000
Paint job	3,000
Sales tax	7,000

c. Estimated useful life of truck, eight years.
d. Estimated salvage value of truck, $27,000.
e. 2008 expenditures on truck:
   (1) $6,000 on new tires and regular maintenance.
   (2) On January 1, spent $44,000 to completely rework the truck's engine. As a result of the engine work, the remaining life of the truck is increased to nine years, but the expected salvage value remains the same.

Required:

Record journal entries to account for the following. (Use the sum-of-the-years'-digits depreciation method.)

1. The purchase of the truck.
2. Depreciation expense for:
   a. 2006
   b. 2007
   c. 2008
3. The expenditures on the truck during 2008.

(continued)

Solution

1. Truck Purchase

The cost of the truck includes both the amount paid for it and all costs incurred to get it in working condition. In this case, the cost includes both the paint job and the sales tax. Thus, the entry to record the purchase is:

Truck	135,000	
Cash		135,000
Purchased truck for cash.		

2. Depreciation Expense

The formula for sum-of-the-years'-digits depreciation on the truck is:

$$\frac{\text{Number of years of life remaining at beginning of year}}{\text{Sum-of-the-years'-digits}} \times (\text{Cost} - \text{Salvage value}) = \text{Depreciation expense}$$

Depreciation for the three years is calculated as follows:

$$2006: \frac{8}{36} \times (\$135,000 - \$27,000) = \$24,000; \$24,000 \times 1/2 \text{ year} = \$12,000$$

$$2007: \frac{7.5}{36} \times (\$135,000 - \$27,000) = \$22,500$$

$$2008: \frac{9}{45} \times [(\$135,000 + \$44,000) - (\$12,000 + \$22,500) - \$27,000] = \$23,500$$

The depreciation entries are:

a.   2006:

Depreciation Expense	12,000	
Accumulated Depreciation, Truck		12,000
Recorded depreciation expense for 2006.		

b.   2007:

Depreciation Expense	22,500	
Accumulated Depreciation, Truck		22,500
Recorded depreciation expense for 2007.		

c.   2008:

Depreciation Expense	23,500	
Accumulated Depreciation, Truck		23,500
Recorded depreciation expense for 2008.		

3. Expenditures

The first expenditure of $6,000 is an ordinary expenditure and is expensed in the current year. The $44,000 expenditure is capitalized because it lengthens the truck's life. The entries are:

Repairs and Maintenance Expense	6,000	
Cash		6,000
Recorded purchase of new tires and regular maintenance on truck.		

Truck	44,000	
Cash		44,000
Recorded major overhaul of truck engine.		

DISCUSSION QUESTIONS

1. What are the major characteristics of property, plant, and equipment?
2. When buying a long-term asset such as a building or piece of equipment, the time value of money must be considered. With respect to time value, it is often said that the last payment (say, 20 years in the future) doesn't cost as much as the next payment today. Explain.
3. Why are expenditures other than the net purchase price included in the cost of an asset?
4. Why would a company include leased assets in the property, plant, and equipment section of its balance sheet when the assets are owned by another entity?
5. A company that borrows money to construct its own building generally should include the interest paid on the loan during the construction period in the cost of the building. Why?
6. Why are fair market values used to determine the cost of operating assets acquired in a basket purchase?
7. Companies usually depreciate assets such as buildings even though those assets may be increasing in value. Why?
8. How does the company accountant decide whether an expenditure should be capitalized or expensed?
9. If a firm is uncertain whether an expenditure will benefit one or more than one accounting period, or whether it will increase the capacity or useful life of an operational asset, most firms will expense rather than capitalize the expenditure. Why?
10. Sometimes long-term assets experience sudden dramatic decreases in value. For example, a waste dump might suddenly be constructed next to an office building. When such impairment of value occurs, should the decrease in value be recognized immediately, or should the same amount of depreciation expense be recognized as in past years?
11. Accountants in other countries sometimes write up the recorded amounts of long-term assets when their values increase. Why are U.S. accountants reluctant to increase the recorded value of property, plant, and equipment when their value increases?
12. Why is it common to have a gain or loss on the disposal of a long-term operating asset? Is it true that if the useful life and salvage value of an asset could be known with certainty and were realized, there would never be such a gain or loss?
13. When recording the disposal of a long-term operating asset, why is it necessary to debit the accumulated depreciation of the old asset?
14. Why are intangible assets considered assets although they have no physical substance?
15. Goodwill can be recorded only when a business is purchased. Does this result in similar businesses having incomparable financial statements?
16. How is fixed asset turnover calculated, and what does the resulting ratio value mean?

EXPANDED *material*

17. Which of the depreciation methods discussed in this chapter will usually result in the highest net income in the early years of an asset's life?
18. How does the declining-balance method of depreciation differ from other methods of depreciation?
19. Modified accelerated cost recovery system (MACRS) depreciation is allowed by the IRS but usually is not used in financial reporting. Why do you think this is the case?
20. When changing the estimate of the useful life of an asset, should depreciation expense for all the previous years be recalculated? If not, how do you account for a change in this estimate?
21. Why is it often necessary to recalculate the depletion rate for natural resources?

PRACTICE EXERCISES

PE 9-1 **Long-Term Operating Assets**
LO1 Which one of the following is not an example of a long-term operating asset?
a. Buildings
b. Land
c. Goodwill
d. Equipment
e. Office Supplies

PE 9-2 **Decision of Long-Term Asset Acquisition**
LO2 Pekka Inc. has the option to purchase a new drilling machine for $50,000 today. The company expects a net cash flow of $13,000 per year from using the machine, and the machine

(continued)

will last five years. According to the time value of money, the value today of $13,000 per year for five years is $46,862. Should the company purchase the new drilling machine?

PE 9-3
LO3

Asset Purchased with Cash

The company used cash to purchase a stamping machine. The retail price on the machine is $35,000, but the company received a 2% discount. It also paid $2,150 in sales tax for the purchase. Make the necessary journal entry(ies) to record this transaction.

PE 9-4
LO3

Asset Purchased Partially with Cash

Refer to the data in PE 9-3. Assume the company borrowed $15,000 of the purchase price from a bank. Make the necessary journal entry(ies) to record this transaction.

PE 9-5
LO3

Operating Lease

On January 1, XYZ Company entered into a lease for equipment rental. The company agreed to pay $4,500 per year for ten years. The present value of all ten lease payments is $27,651. Assuming the company classified the lease as an operating lease, make the necessary journal entry(ies) to record the payment of the first year's rent expense for the equipment. The first lease payment is made at the end of the year.

PE 9-6
LO3

Capital Lease Acquisition

On January 1, XYZ Company entered into a lease for equipment rental. The company agreed to pay $4,500 per year for ten years. The present value of all ten lease payments is $27,651. Assuming the company classified the lease as a capital lease, make the necessary journal entry(ies) to record the acquisition of the equipment. The first lease payment is made at the end of the year.

PE 9-7
LO3

Capital Lease Payments

Refer to the data in PE 9-6. The interest included in the first lease payment is $2,765. Make the necessary journal entry(ies) to record the first $4,500 lease payment at the end of the first year.

PE 9-8
LO3

Classifying Leases

Which one of the following characteristics of a lease would not cause the lease to be classified as a capital lease?

a. Lease ownership transfers to the lessee at the end of the lease.
b. The present value of the lease payments at the beginning of the lease is 90% or more of the fair market value of the leased asset.
c. The lease term is equal to 50% of the estimated economic life of the asset.
d. The lease contains a bargain purchase option.

PE 9-9
LO3

Assets Acquired by Self-Construction

Using the following data, compute the total cost of a self-constructed office building.

Percentage of overhead attributable to construction of office building	30%
Direct materials	$1,450,000
Capitalized interest	140,000
Direct labor	860,000
Total overhead incurred during year	2,450,000

PE 9-10
LO3

Acquisition of Several Assets at Once

The company purchased a building and the accompanying land for $890,000 cash. Independent appraisers estimated the fair market value of the building and the land to be $720,000 and 240,000, respectively. Make the necessary journal entry(ies) to record this transaction.

PE 9-11
LO4

Straight-Line Method of Depreciation

Using the following data and the straight-line method of depreciation, compute depreciation expense, and make the necessary journal entry to record depreciation expense for the first year.

(continued)

Cost of machine	$1,000,000
Estimated useful life (years)	8 years
Salvage value	$40,000
Estimated useful life (units)	1,600,000
Units produced during the first year	180,000

PE 9-12
LO4

Units-of-Production Method of Depreciation

Refer to the data in PE 9-11. Using the units-of-production method of depreciation, compute depreciation expense, and make the necessary journal entry to record depreciation expense for the first year.

PE 9-13
LO4

Partial-Year Depreciation Calculations

On September 30, the company purchased a $25,000 delivery truck. The company estimates the truck will last five years and have a salvage value of $5,000 at the end of five years. Using the straight-line method of depreciation, compute the amount of depreciation in the first two years of the truck's service.

PE 9-14
LO4

Units-of-Production Method with Natural Resources

The company purchased an oil field for $4,200,000 cash. The oil field contains an estimated 600,000 barrels of oil. During the first year of operation, the company extracts and sells 70,000 barrels of oil. Compute the amount of depletion expense, and make the necessary journal entry(ies) to record depletion expense for the year.

PE 9-15
LO5

Repairing and Improving Property, Plant, and Equipment

The company has a molding machine with a historical cost of $150,000 and accumulated depreciation of $110,000. On January 1, the company performed a major motor overhaul costing $24,000. The company expects the machine will last seven more years and have a salvage value of $8,000. Compute depreciation expense for the current year using the straight-line method.

PE 9-16
LO6

Determining Asset Impairment

The company purchased a building 14 years ago for $720,000. The building has accumulated depreciation of $504,000 and a fair market value of $150,000. The company expects the building will generate a net cash inflow of $30,000 per year for the next six years. Determine whether, from an accounting point of view, the building is impaired.

PE 9-17
LO6

Recording Decreases in the Value of Property, Plant, and Equipment

Using the information in PE 9-16, determine the amount of impairment and record the impairment loss.

Original cost	$720,000
Accumulated depreciation	504,000
Book value	$216,000
Sum of future cash flows ($30,000 × 6 years)	$180,000

PE 9-18
LO7

Discarding Property, Plant, and Equipment

The company scrapped a truck with a historical cost of $60,000 and accumulated depreciation of $48,000. In addition, the company had to pay $500 to discard the truck. Make the necessary journal entry(ies) to record this transaction.

PE 9-19
LO7

Selling Property, Plant, and Equipment

The company sold a truck with a historical cost of $30,000 and accumulated depreciation of $24,000 for $7,000 cash. Make the necessary journal entry(ies) to record this transaction.

PE 9-20   **Patents**

LO8   On January 1, the company purchased a 13-year-old patent from another company for $210,000. The patent has a seven-year legal life remaining. Make the necessary journal entry(ies) to record amortization for the year the patent was acquired.

PE 9-21   **Goodwill**

LO8   Parent Company purchased Daughter Company for $200,000. At the time of purchase, the fair market value of Daughter Company's assets and liabilities was as follows:

Inventory	$ 25,000
Property, plant, and equipment	140,000
Other assets	64,000
Liabilities	59,000

Make the necessary journal entry(ies) (on Parent's books) to record the purchase of Daughter Company.

PE 9-22   **Fixed Asset Turnover**

LO9   Using the following data, compute the fixed asset turnover.

Current assets, end of year	$ 35,000
Fixed assets, end of year	180,000
Fixed assets, beginning of year	195,000
Sales during the year	595,000

PE 9-23   **Declining-Balance Method of Depreciation**

LO10   Using the following data and the declining-balance method of depreciation, compute depreciation expense for the first two years.

Cost of machine	$1,500,000
Estimated useful life (years)	10 years
Salvage value	$100,000

PE 9-24   **Sum-of-the-Years'-Digits Method of Depreciation**

LO10   Using the data in PE 9-23 and the sum-of-the-years'-digits method of depreciation, compute depreciation expense for the first two years.

PE 9-25   **Changes in Depreciation Estimates**

LO11   Using the information in PE 9-11, the company computed depreciation expense of $120,000 per year. After two years, the company determined that the machine would last 10 more years (for a total of 12 years). Compute depreciation expense for the third year.

EXERCISES

E 9-26   **Acquisition Decision**

LO3   Johnson Company is considering acquiring a new airplane. It has looked at two financing options. The first is to lease the airplane for 10 years with lease payments of $70,000 each year. The second is to purchase the airplane, making a down payment of $250,000 and

(continued)

annual payments of $40,000 for 10 years. If the present value of the two financing options is the same, what other factors must be considered in deciding whether to purchase or to lease?

E 9-27
LO3

Accounting for the Acquisition of a Long-Term Asset

Action Jackson Company acquired a new machine in order to expand its productive capacity. The costs associated with the machine purchase were as follows:

Purchase price	$25,000
Installation costs	750
Cost of initial testing	900
Sales tax	1,563

1. Make the journal entry to record the acquisition of the machine. Assume that all costs were paid in cash.
2. Make the journal entry to record the acquisition of the machine. Assume that Action Jackson Company signed a note payable for the $25,000 purchase price and paid the remaining costs in cash.

E 9-28
LO3, LO4

Computing Asset Cost and Depreciation Expense

Freddy's Restoration Company decided to purchase a new floor-polishing machine for its shop in New York City. After a long search, it found the appropriate polisher in Chicago. The machine costs $45,000 and has an estimated 15-year life and no salvage value. Freddy's Restoration Company made the following additional expenditures with respect to this purchase:

Sales tax	$2,000
Delivery costs (FOB shipping point)	1,000
Assembly cost	1,400
Painting of machine to match the décor	600

1. What is the cost of the machine to Freddy's Restoration Company?
2. What is the amount of the first full year's depreciation if Freddy's uses the straight-line method?

E 9-29
LO3, LO4

Acquisition and Depreciation of Assets

Vandre Oil Company, which prepares financial statements on a calendar-year basis, purchased new drilling equipment on July 1, 2009, using check numbers 1035 and 1036. The check totals are shown here, along with a breakdown of the charges.

1035 (Payee–Oil Equipment, Inc.):	
Cost of drilling equipment	$150,000
Cost of cement platform	50,000
Installation charges	26,000
Total	$226,000
1036 (Payee–Red Ball Freight):	
Freight costs for drilling equipment	$ 4,000

Assume that the estimated life of the drilling equipment is 10 years and its salvage value is $7,000.

1. Record the disbursements on July 1, 2009, assuming that no entry had been recorded for the drilling equipment.
2. Disregarding the information given about the two checks, assume that the drilling equipment was recorded at a total cost of $195,000. Calculate the depreciation expense for 2009 using the straight-line method.

E 9-30   **Accounting for Leased Assets**

LO3   On January 1, 2009, Hanks Company leased a copy machine with an integrated laser printer from Officeneeds, Inc. The five-year lease is noncancelable and requires monthly payments of $200 at the end of each month, with the first payment due on January 31, 2009. At the end of five years, Hanks will own the equipment. The present value of the lease payments at the beginning of the lease is determined to be $9,413.

1. Prepare journal entries to record:
    a. The lease agreement on January 1, 2009.
    b. The first lease payment on January 31, 2009, assuming that $78 of the $200 payment is interest.

2. Now assume that the lease expires after one year at which time a new lease can be negotiated or Hanks can return the equipment to Officeneeds. Prepare any journal entries relating to the lease that would be required on January 1 and January 31, 2009.

E 9-31   **Interest Capitalization**

LO3   Litton Company is constructing a new office building. Costs of the building are as follows:

Wages paid to construction workers	$185,000
Building materials purchased	456,000
Interest expense on construction loan	13,800
Interest expense on mortgage loan during the first year subsequent to the building's completion	22,000

Given the above costs, at what amount should the building be recorded in the accounting records?

E 9-32   **Accounting for the Acquisition of Assets–Basket Purchase**

LO3   Sealise Corporation purchased land, a building, and equipment for a total cost of $450,000. After the purchase, the property was appraised. Fair market values were determined to be $120,000 for the land, $280,000 for the building, and $80,000 for the equipment. Given these appraisals, record the purchase of the property by Sealise Corporation.

E 9-33   **Depreciation Calculations**

LO4   Garns Photography Company purchased a new car on July 1, 2008, for $26,000. The estimated life of the car was five years or 110,000 miles, and its salvage value was estimated to be $1,000. The car was driven 9,000 miles in 2008 and 24,000 miles in 2009.

1. Compute the amount of depreciation expense for 2008 and 2009 using the following methods:
    a. Straight-line.
    b. Units-of-production.

2. Which depreciation method more closely reflects the used-up service potential of the car? Explain.

E 9-34   **Depreciation Calculations**

LO4   Denver Hardware Company has a giant paint mixer that cost $31,500 plus $400 to install. The estimated salvage value of the paint mixer at the end of its useful life in 15 years is estimated to be $1,900. Denver estimates that the machine can mix 850,000 cans of paint during its lifetime. Compute the second full year's depreciation expense, using the following methods:

1. Straight-line.
2. Units-of-production, assuming that the machine mixes 51,000 cans of paint during the second year.

E 9-35   **Acquisition and Improvement of Assets**

LO3, LO5   Prepare entries in the books of Sanmara, Inc., to reflect the following. (Assume cash transactions.)

(continued)

1. Purchased a lathing machine to be used by the firm in its production process.

Invoice price	$45,000
Cash discount taken	900
Installation costs	1,200
Sales tax on machine	1,800

2. Performed normal periodic maintenance on the lathing machine at a cost of $200.
3. Added to the lathing machine a governor costing $400, which is expected to increase the machine's useful life.

E 9-36
LO6

Asset Impairment

Consider the following three independent scenarios:

	1	2	3
Original cost of asset	$1,400	$1,400	$1,400
Accumulated depreciation	400	400	400
Sum of future cash flows	1,500	1,500	900
Fair value of the asset	1,100	800	800

1. For each of the three scenarios, answer the following questions:
   a. Is the asset impaired?
   b. At what amount (net of accumulated depreciation) should the asset be reported?
2. Make the journal entry required in Scenario 3.

E 9-37
LO6

Asset Impairment

In 2004, Yorkshire Company purchased land and a building at a cost of $700,000, of which $150,000 was allocated to the land and $550,000 was allocated to the building. As of December 31, 2008, the accounting records related to these assets were as follows:

Land	$150,000
Building	550,000
Accumulated Depreciation, Building	150,000

On January 1, 2009, it is determined that there is toxic waste under the building and the future cash flows associated with the land and building are less than the recorded total book value for those two assets. The fair value of the land and building together is now only $120,000, of which $50,000 is land and $70,000 is the building. How should this impairment in value be recognized? Make the entry on January 1, 2009, to record the impairment of the land and building.

E 9-38
LO7

Accounting for the Disposal of Assets

Canlas Concrete Company has a truck that it wants to sell. The truck had an original cost of $80,000, was purchased four years ago, and was expected to have a useful life of eight years with no salvage value.

Using straight-line depreciation, and assuming that depreciation expense for four full years has been recorded, prepare journal entries to record the disposal of the truck under each of the following independent conditions:

1. Canlas Concrete Company sells the truck for $45,000 cash.
2. Canlas Concrete Company sells the truck for $38,000 cash.
3. The old truck is wrecked and Canlas Concrete Company hauls it to the junkyard.

E 9-39
LO7

Disposal of an Asset

Aeronautics Company purchased a machine for $115,000. The machine has an estimated useful life of eight years and a salvage value of $7,000. Journalize the disposal of the machine under each of the following conditions. (Assume straight-line depreciation.)

1. Sold the machine for $97,000 cash after two years.
2. Sold the machine for $36,000 cash after five years.

E 9-40
LO8

Accounting for Intangible Assets

Gaylord Research, Inc., has the following intangible assets:

Asset	Cost	Date Purchased	Expected Useful or Legal Life
Goodwill	$ 16,000	January 1, 2000	Unlimited
Patent	136,000	January 1, 2002	20 years

1. Record the amortization expense for both of these intangible assets for 2009 assuming neither of the assets is impaired.
2. Prepare the intangible assets section of the balance sheet for Gaylord Research, Inc., as of December 31, 2009.

E 9-41
LO8

Intangible Assets

On January 1, 2008, Landon Company purchased a patent for $250,000 to allow it to improve its product line. On July 1, 2008, Landon Company purchased another existing business in a nearby city for a total cost of $750,000. The market value of the land, building, equipment, and other tangible assets was $550,000. The excess $200,000 was recorded as goodwill.

Assuming Landon Company amortizes patents over a 20-year period, record the following:

1. The purchase of the patent on January 1, 2008.
2. The amortization of the patent at December 31, 2008.
3. Under what conditions would goodwill be amortized on the books of Landon?

E 9-42
LO8

Computing Goodwill

Stringtown Company purchased Stansbury Island Manufacturing for $1,800,000 cash. The book value and fair value of the assets of Stansbury Island as of the date of the acquisition are listed below:

	Book Value	Market Value
Cash	$ 30,000	$ 30,000
Accounts receivable	300,000	300,000
Inventory	350,000	600,000
Property, plant, and equipment	500,000	900,000
Totals	$1,180,000	$1,830,000

In addition, Stansbury Island had liabilities totaling $400,000 at the time of the acquisition.

1. At what amounts will the individual assets of Stansbury Island be recorded on the books of Stringtown, the acquiring company?
2. How will Stringtown account for the liabilities of Stansbury Island?
3. How much goodwill will be recorded as part of this acquisition?

E 9-43   **Fixed Asset Turnover**

LO9   The Store Next Door reported the following asset values in 2008 and 2009:

	2009	2008
Cash	$ 45,000	$ 27,000
Accounts receivable	500,000	430,000
Inventory	550,000	480,000
Land	300,000	280,000
Buildings	800,000	660,000
Equipment	150,000	110,000

In addition, The Store Next Door had sales of $3,200,000 in 2009. Cost of goods sold for the year was $1,900,000.

   Compute The Store Next Door's fixed asset turnover ratio for 2009.

E 9-44   **Acquisition and Depreciation of Assets**

LO3, LO4, LO10   Brough Oil Company, which prepares financial statements on a calendar-year basis, purchased new drilling equipment on July 1, 2009. A breakdown of the cost follows:

Cost of drilling equipment	$125,000
Cost of cement platform	35,000
Installation charges	22,000
Freight costs for drilling equipment	3,000
Total	$185,000

Assuming that the estimated life of the drilling equipment is 20 years and its salvage value is $10,000:

1. Record the purchase on July 1, 2009.
2. Assume that the drilling equipment was recorded at a total cost of $140,000. Calculate the depreciation expense for 2009 using the following methods:
   a. Sum-of-the-years'-digits.
   b. Double-declining-balance.
   c. 150% declining-balance.
3. Prepare the journal entry to record the depreciation for 2009 in accordance with part (2)a.

E 9-45   **Acquisition and Depreciation**

LO3, LO4, LO10   At the beginning of 2009, Beef's Steak House constructed a new walk-in freezer that had a useful life of 10 years. At the end of 10 years, the motor could be salvaged for $3,500. In addition to construction costs that totaled $15,000, the following costs were incurred:

Sales taxes on components	$1,100
Delivery costs	700
Installation of motor	300
Painting of both interior and exterior of freezer	200

1. What is the cost of the walk-in freezer to Beef's Steak House?
2. Compute the amount of depreciation to be taken in the first year assuming Beef's Steak House uses the
   a. Double-declining-balance method.
   b. Sum-of-the-years'-digits method.

E 9-46   **Depreciation Computations**
LO10

Hsin-Yo Company purchases an $850,000 piece of equipment on January 2, 2007, for use in its manufacturing process. The equipment's estimated useful life is 10 years with no salvage value. Hsin-Yo uses 150% declining-balance depreciation for all its equipment.

1. Compute the depreciation expense for 2007, 2008, and 2009.
2. Compute the book value of the equipment on December 31, 2009.

E 9-47   **Depreciation Calculations**
LO10

Letha Enterprises purchased a new van on January 1, 2008, for $35,000. The estimated life of the van was four years or 76,000 miles, and its salvage value was estimated to be $3,000. Compute the amount of depreciation expense for 2008, 2009, and 2010 using the following methods:

1. Double-declining-balance.
2. 175% declining-balance.
3. Sum-of-the-years'-digits.

E 9-48   **Depreciation Calculations**
LO10

On January 1, 2008, MAC Corporation purchased a machine for $60,000. The machine cost $800 to deliver and $2,000 to install. At the end of 10 years, MAC expects to sell the machine for $2,000. Compute depreciation expense for 2008 and 2009 using the following methods:

1. Double-declining-balance.
2. 150% declining-balance.
3. Sum-of-the-years'-digits.

E 9-49   **Accounting for Natural Resources**
LO3, LO4, LO11

On January 1, 2008, Georgetown Holdings Corporation purchased a coal mine for cash, having taken into consideration the favorable tax consequences and the inevitable energy crunch in the future. Georgetown paid $960,000 for the mine. Shortly before the purchase, an engineer estimated that there were 120,000 tons of coal in the mine.

1. Record the purchase of the mine on January 1, 2008.
2. Record the depletion expense for 2008, assuming that 30,000 tons of coal were mined during the year.
3. Assume that on January 1, 2009, the company received a new estimate that the mine now contained 150,000 tons of coal. Record the entry (if any) to show the change in estimate.
4. Record the depletion expense for 2009, assuming that another 30,000 tons of coal were mined.

E 9-50   **Change in Estimated Useful Life**
LO4, LO11

On January 1, 2007, Landon Excavation Company purchased a new bulldozer for $120,000. The equipment had an estimated useful life of 10 years and an estimated residual value of $10,000. On January 1, 2009, Landon determined that the bulldozer would have a total useful life of only 8 years instead of 10 years with no change in residual value. Landon uses straight-line depreciation.

Compute depreciation expense on this bulldozer for 2007, 2008, and 2009.

PROBLEMS

P 9-51   **Acquisition, Depreciation, and Disposal of Assets**
LO3, LO4, LO7

On January 2, 2009, Dale Company purchased a building and land for $580,000. The most recent appraisal values for the building and the land are $420,000 and $180,000, respectively. The building has an estimated useful life of 25 years and a salvage value of $30,000.

(continued)

Required:

1. Assuming cash transactions and straight-line depreciation, prepare journal entries to record:
   a. Purchase of the building and land on January 2, 2009.
   b. Depreciation expense on December 31, 2009.
2. Assume that after three years the property (land and building) was sold for $470,000. Prepare the journal entry to record the sale.

P 9-52   **Purchasing Property, Plant, and Equipment**

LO3   Jordon Company is considering replacing its automated stamping machine. The machine is specialized and very expensive. Jordon is considering three acquisition alternatives. The first is to lease a machine for 10 years at $1 million per year, after which time Jordon can buy the machine for $1 million. The second alternative is to pay cash for the machine at a cost of $7 million. The third alternative is to make a down payment of $3 million, followed by 10 annual payments of $550,000. The company is trying to decide which alternative to select.

Required:

1. Assuming the present value of the lease payments is $7.2 million and the present value of the 10 loan payments of $550,000 is $4.1 million, determine which alternative Jordon should choose.
2. **Interpretive Question:** Your decision in part (1) was based only on financial factors. What other qualitative issues might influence your decision?

P 9-53   **Acquisition of an Asset**

LO3   Ray's Printing Company purchased a new printing press. The invoice price was $184,250. The company paid for the press within 10 days, so it was allowed a 2% discount. The freight cost for delivering the press was $3,000. A premium of $1,200 was paid for a special insurance policy to cover the transportation of the press. The company spent $3,400 to install the press and an additional $655 in start-up costs to get the press ready for regular production.

Required:

1. At what amount should the press be recorded as an asset?
2. What additional information must be known before the depreciation expense for the first year of operation of the new press can be computed?
3. **Interpretive Question:** What criterion is used to determine whether the start-up costs of $655 are included in the cost of the asset? Explain.

P 9-54   **Accounting for Leased Assets**

LO3   On January 2, 2009, Yardley Company contracted to lease a computer on a noncancelable basis for six years at an annual rental of $55,000, payable at the end of each year. The computer has an estimated economic life of seven years. There is no bargain purchase option, and the computer will be returned to the lessor at the end of the six-year term of the lease. At the beginning of the lease, the computer has a fair market value of $245,000, and the present value of the lease payments equals $239,539.

Required:

1. Is this a capital lease or an operating lease? Explain.
2. Assuming that the lease is an operating lease, prepare the journal entries for Yardley Company for 2009.
3. Assuming that the lease is a capital lease, prepare the journal entries for Yardley Company for 2009. Assume the lease payment at the end of 2009 includes interest of $23,954.

P 9-55   **Accounting for Leased Assets**

LO3   The board of directors of Swogen Company authorized the president to lease a corporate jet to facilitate her travels to domestic and international subsidiaries of the company. After

(continued)

extensive investigation of the alternatives, the company agreed to lease a jet for $300,548 each year for five years, payable at the end of each year. Title to the jet will pass to Swogen Company at the end of five years with no further payments required. The lease agreement starts on January 2, 2009. The jet has an economic life of eight years. The lease contract is noncancelable and contains an interest rate of 8%, resulting in a present value of the lease payments of $1,200,000 as of January 2, 2009.

Required:

1. Does this lease contract meet the requirements to be accounted for as a capital lease? Why or why not?
2. Assuming that the lease contract is to be accounted for as a capital lease, prepare the journal entries for Swogen Company for 2009. Interest included in the first payment is $96,000.

P 9-56
LO3

Interest Capitalization

Jennifer Cosmetics wants to construct a new building. It has two building options, as follows:

a. Hire a contractor to do all the work. Jennifer has a bid of $850,000 from a reputable contractor to complete the project.

b. Construct the building itself by taking out a construction loan of $800,000. Using this alternative, Jennifer believes materials and labor will cost $800,000, and interest on the construction loan will be calculated as follows:

$200,000 @ 12% for 9 months
$300,000 @ 12% for 6 months
$200,000 @ 12% for 3 months
$100,000 @ 12% for 1 month

Required:

1. What will be the recorded cost of the building under each alternative?
2. Assuming the building is depreciated over a 20-year period using straight-line depreciation with no salvage value, how much is the annual depreciation expense under each alternative?

P 9-57
LO4

Depreciation Calculations

On January 1, Clauser Company purchased a $79,000 machine. The estimated life of the machine was four years, and the estimated salvage value was $4,000. The machine had an estimated useful life in productive output of 90,000 units. Actual output for the first two years was: year 1, 25,000 units; year 2, 18,000 units.

Required:

1. Compute the amount of depreciation expense for the first year, using each of the following methods:
   a. Straight-line.
   b. Units-of-production.
2. What was the book value of the machine at the end of the first year, assuming that straight-line depreciation was used?
3. If the machine is sold at the end of the third year for $20,000, how much should the company report as a gain or loss (assuming straight-line depreciation)?

P 9-58
LO3, LO4

Purchase of Multiple Assets for a Single Sum

On April 1, 2009, Cajun Company paid $210,000 in cash to purchase land, a building, and equipment. The appraised fair market values of the assets were as follows: land, $70,000; building, $120,000; and equipment, $60,000. The company incurred legal fees of $8,000 to determine that it would have a clear title to the land. Before the facilities could be used, Cajun had to spend $4,000 to grade and landscape the land, $3,500 to put the equipment in working order, and $14,000 to renovate the building. The equipment was then estimated

(continued)

to have a useful life of seven years with no salvage value, and the building would have a useful life of 20 years with a net salvage value of $10,000. Both the equipment and the building are to be depreciated on a straight-line basis. The company is on a calendar-year reporting basis.

Required:
1. Allocate the single purchase price to the individual assets acquired.
2. Prepare the journal entry to acquire the land, building, and equipment.
3. Prepare the journal entry to record the title search, landscape, put the equipment in working order, and renovate the building.
4. Prepare the journal entries on December 31, 2009, to record the depreciation on the building and the equipment.

P 9-59

LO3, LO4

Basket Purchase and Partial-Year Depreciation

On April 1, 2009, Rosenberg Company purchased for $200,000 a tract of land on which was located a fully equipped factory. The following information was compiled regarding this purchase:

	Market Value	Seller's Book Value
Land	$ 75,000	$ 30,000
Building	100,000	75,000
Equipment	50,000	60,000
Totals	$225,000	$165,000

Required:
1. Prepare the journal entry to record the purchase of these assets.
2. Assume that the building is depreciated on a straight-line basis over a remaining life of 20 years and the equipment is depreciated on a straight-line basis over five years. Neither the building nor the equipment is expected to have any salvage value. Compute the depreciation expense for 2009 assuming the assets were placed in service immediately upon acquisition.

P 9-60

LO3, LO4, LO7

Acquisition, Depreciation, and Sale of an Asset

On January 2, 2007, Union Oil Company purchased a new airplane. The following costs are related to the purchase:

Airplane, base price	$112,000
Cash discount	3,000
Sales tax	4,000
Delivery charges	1,000

Required:
1. Prepare the journal entry to record the payment of these items on January 2, 2007.
2. Ignore your answer to part (1) and assume that the airplane cost $90,000 and has an expected useful life of five years or 1,500 hours. The estimated salvage value is $3,000. Using units-of-production depreciation and assuming that 300 hours are flown in 2008, calculate the amount of depreciation expense to be recorded for the second year.
3. Ignore the information in parts (1) and (2) and assume that the airplane costs $90,000, that its expected useful life is five years, and that its estimated salvage value is $5,000. The company now uses the straight-line depreciation method. On January 1, 2010, the following balances are in the related accounts:

(continued)

Airplane	$90,000
Accumulated Depreciation, Airplane	51,000

Prepare the necessary journal entries to record the sale of this airplane on July 1, 2010, for $40,000.

P 9-61

LO3, LO4, LO7

Acquisition, Depreciation, and Sale of an Asset

On July 1, 2009, Philip Ward bought a used pickup truck at a cost of $5,300 for use in his business. On the same day, Ward had the truck painted blue and white (his company's colors) at a cost of $800. Mr. Ward estimates the life of the truck to be three years or 40,000 miles. He further estimates that the truck will have a $450 scrap value at the end of its life, but that it will also cost him $50 to transfer the truck to the junkyard.

Required:

1. Record the following journal entries:
   a. July 1, 2009: Paid all bills pertaining to the truck. (No previous entries have been recorded concerning these bills.)
   b. December 31, 2009: The depreciation expense for the year, using the straight-line method.
   c. December 31, 2010: The depreciation expense for 2010, again using the straight-line method.
   d. January 2, 2011: Sold the truck for $2,600 cash.
2. What would the depreciation expense for 2009 have been if the truck had been driven 8,000 miles and the units-of-production method of depreciation had been used?
3. **Interpretive Question:** In part (1)d, there is a loss of $650. Why did this loss occur?

P 9-62

LO4

Accounting for Natural Resources

On May 31, 2007, Barren Oil Company purchased an oil well, with estimated reserves of 200,000 barrels of oil, for $2.0 million cash.

Required:

Prepare journal entries for the following:
1. Record the purchase of the oil well.
2. During 2007, 16,000 barrels of oil were extracted from the well. Record the depletion expense for 2007.
3. During 2008, 21,000 barrels of oil were extracted from the well. Record the depletion expense for 2008.

P 9-63

LO6

Asset Impairment

Delta Company owns plant and equipment on the island of Lagos. The cost and book value of the building are $2,800,000 and $2,400,000, respectively. Until this year, the market value of the factory was $7 million. However, a new dictator just came to power and declared martial law. As a result of the changed political status, the future cash inflows from the use of the factory are expected to be greatly reduced. Delta now believes that the output from the factory will generate cash inflows of $100,000 per year for the next 20 years. In addition, the market value of the factory building is now just $1,300,000. Delta is not sure how to account for the sudden impairment in value.

Required:

1. Explain how to decide whether an impairment loss is to be recognized.
2. Prepare the necessary journal entry, if any, to account for an impairment in the value of the factory.

P 9-64

LO8

Accounting for Intangible Assets (Goodwill)

On January 1, 2009, InterGalactic Company purchased the following assets and liabilities from Immensity Company for $325,000:

(continued)

	Book Value	Fair Market Value
Inventory	$ 60,000	$ 70,000
Building	100,000	130,000
Land	70,000	90,000
Accounts receivable	30,000	30,000
Accounts payable	(15,000)	(15,000)

Required:
Prepare a journal entry to record the purchase of Immensity by InterGalactic.

P 9-65

LO8

Accounting for Goodwill

On January 1, 2009, Fishing Creek Company purchased Skull Valley Technologies for $8,800,000 cash. The book value and fair value of Skull Valley's assets as of the date of the acquisition are listed below.

	Book Value	Market Value
Cash	$ 100,000	$ 100,000
Accounts receivable	500,000	500,000
Inventory	950,000	1,200,000
Property, plant, and equipment	1,500,000	1,900,000
Trademark	0	2,000,000
Totals	$3,050,000	$5,700,000

In addition, Skull Valley had liabilities totaling $4,000,000 at the time of the acquisition.

Required:
1. At what amount will Skull Valley's trademark be recorded on the books of Fishing Creek, the acquiring company?
2. How much goodwill will be recorded as part of this acquisition?
3. **Interpretive Question:** What was Skull Valley's recorded stockholders' equity immediately before the acquisition? Under what circumstances does stockholders' equity yield a poor measure of the fair value of a company?

P 9-66

LO9

Fixed Asset Turnover Ratio

Waystation Company reported the following asset values in 2008 and 2009:

	2009	2008
Cash	$ 40,000	$ 30,000
Accounts receivable	500,000	400,000
Inventory	700,000	500,000
Land	300,000	200,000
Buildings	800,000	600,000
Equipment	400,000	300,000

In addition, Waystation had sales of $4,000,000 in 2009. Cost of goods sold for the year was $2,500,000.

As of the end of 2008, the fair value of Waystation's total assets was $2,500,000. Of the excess of fair value over book value, $50,000 resulted because the fair value of Waystation's inventory was greater than its recorded book value. As of the end of 2009, the fair value of Waystation's total assets was $3,500,000. As of December 31, 2009, the fair

(continued)

value of Waystation's inventory was $100,000 greater than the inventory's recorded book value.

Required:

1. Compute Waystation's fixed asset turnover ratio for 2009.
2. Using the fair value of fixed assets instead of the book value of fixed assets, recompute Waystation's fixed asset turnover ratio for 2009. State any assumptions that you make.
3. **Interpretive Question:** Waystation's primary competitor is Handy Corner. Handy Corner's fixed asset turnover ratio for 2009, based on publicly available information, is 2.8 times. Is Waystation more or less efficient at using its fixed assets than is Handy Corner? Explain your answer.

P 9-67

LO10

Depreciation Calculations

Neilson's Hardware Company has a giant paint mixer that cost $51,300 plus $700 to install. The estimated salvage value of the paint mixer at the end of its useful life in eight years is estimated to be $4,000. Neilson's estimates that the machine can mix 720,000 cans of paint during its lifetime.

Required:

Compute the second full year's depreciation expense, using the following methods:

1. Double-declining-balance.
2. Sum-of-the-years'-digits.

P 9-68

LO3, LO10

Depreciation Calculations

On January 1, Top Flight Company purchased a $68,000 machine. The estimated life of the machine was five years, and the estimated salvage value was $5,000. The machine had an estimated useful life in productive output of 75,000 units. Actual output for the first two years was: year 1, 20,000 units; year 2, 15,000 units.

Required:

1. Compute the amount of depreciation expense for the first year, using each of the following methods:
   a. Straight-line.
   b. Units-of-production.
   c. Sum-of-the-years'-digits.
   d. Double-declining-balance.
2. What was the book value of the machine at the end of the first year, assuming that straight-line depreciation was used?
3. If the machine is sold at the end of the fourth year for $15,000, how much should the company report as a gain or loss (assuming straight-line depreciation)?

P 9-69

LO3, LO10

Financial Statement Effects of Depreciation Methods

On July 1, 2008, the consulting firm of Little, Smart, and Quick bought a new computer for $120,000 to help it service its clients more efficiently. The new computer was estimated to have a useful life of five years with an estimated salvage value of $20,000 at the end of five years. It was further estimated that the computer would be in operation about 1,500 hours in each of the five years with some variation of use from year to year. Janet Little, who manages the firm's internal operations, has asked you to help her decide which depreciation method should be selected for the new computer. The methods being considered are straight-line, double-declining-balance, and sum-of-the-years'-digits.

(continued)

Required:

1. Prepare a schedule showing depreciation for 2008, 2009, and 2010 for each of the three methods being considered.
2. For each of the three methods, compute the asset book value that would be reported on the balance sheet at December 31, 2010.
3. **Interpretive Question:** Which method would maximize income for the three years (2008–2010), and which would minimize income for the same period?

P 9-70

LO3, LO10

Depreciation Calculations

Gretchen, Inc., a firm that makes oversized boots, purchased a machine for its factory. The following data relate to the machine:

Price	$46,000
Delivery charges	$350
Installation charges	$650
Date purchased	May 1, 2008
Estimated useful life:	
In years	10 years
In hours of production	25,000 hours of operating time
Salvage value	$2,000

During 2008, the machine was used 1,800 hours. During 2009, the machine was used 2,900 hours.

Required:

Determine the depreciation expense and the year-end book values for the machine for the years 2008 and 2009, assuming that:

1. The straight-line method is used.
2. The double-declining-balance method is used.
3. The units-of-production method is used.
4. The sum-of-the-years'-digits method is used.
5. **Interpretive Question:** If you were Gretchen, which method would you use in order to report the highest profits in 2008 and 2009 combined?

P 9-71

LO5, LO11

Changes in Depreciation Estimates and Capitalization of Expenditures

Ironic Metal Products, Inc., acquired a machine on January 2, 2007, for $76,600. The useful life of the machine was estimated to be eight years with a salvage value of $4,600. Depreciation is recorded on December 31 of each year using the sum-of-the-years'-digits method.

At the beginning of 2009, the company estimated the remaining useful life of the machine to be four years and changed the estimated salvage value from $4,600 to $2,600. On January 2, 2010, major repairs on the machine cost the company $34,000. The repairs added two years to the machine's useful life and increased the salvage value to $3,000.

Required:

1. Prepare journal entries to record:
   a. The purchase of the machine.
   b. Annual depreciation expense for the years 2007 and 2008.
   c. Depreciation in 2009 under the revised estimates of useful life and salvage value.
   d. The expenditure for major repairs in 2010.
   e. Depreciation expense for 2010.
2. Compute the book value of the machine at the end of 2010.

P 9-72

LO3, LO4, LO11

Unifying Concepts: Accounting for Natural Resources

Forest Products, Inc., buys and develops natural resources for profit. Since 2006, it has had the following activities:

1/1/06   Purchased for $800,000 a tract of timber estimated to contain 1,600,000 board feet of lumber.

1/1/07   Purchased for $600,000 a silver mine estimated to contain 30,000 tons of silver ore.

7/1/07   Purchased for $60,000 a uranium mine estimated to contain 5,000 tons of uranium ore.

1/1/08   Purchased for $500,000 an oil well estimated to contain 100,000 barrels of oil.

Required:

1. Provide the necessary journal entries to account for the following:
   a. The purchase of these assets.
   b. The depletion expense for 2008 on all four assets, assuming that the following were extracted:
      (1) 200,000 board feet of lumber.
      (2) 5,000 tons of silver.
      (3) 1,000 tons of uranium.
      (4) 10,000 barrels of oil.

2. Assume that on January 1, 2009, after 20,000 tons of silver had been mined, engineers' estimates revealed that only 4,000 tons of silver remained. Record the depletion expense for 2009, assuming that 2,000 tons were mined.

3. Compute the book values of all four assets as of December 31, 2009, assuming that the total extracted to date is:
   a. Timber tract, 800,000 board feet.
   b. Silver mine, 22,000 tons [only 2,000 tons are left per part (2)].
   c. Uranium mine, 3,000 tons.
   d. Oil well, 80,000 barrels.

P 9-73

LO3, LO4, LO5

Unifying Concepts: Property, Plant, and Equipment

Logan Corporation owns and operates three sawmills that make lumber for building homes. The operations consist of cutting logs in the forest, hauling them to the various sawmills, sawing the lumber, and shipping it to building supply warehouses throughout the western part of the United States. To haul the logs, Logan has several trucks. Relevant data pertaining to one truck are:

a. Date of purchase, July 1, 2007.

b. Cost:

Truck	$40,000
Trailer	25,000
Paint job (to match company colors)	3,000
Sales tax	4,000

c. Estimated useful life of the truck, 120,000 miles.

d. Estimated salvage value, zero.

e. 2008 expenditures on truck:
   (1) Spent $4,500 on tires, oil changes, greasing, and other miscellaneous items.
   (2) Spent $18,000 to overhaul the engine and replace the transmission on January 1, 2008. This expenditure increased the life of the truck by 85,000 miles.

Required:

Record journal entries to account for:

1. The purchase of the truck.

2. The 2007 depreciation expense using units-of-production depreciation and assuming the truck was driven 35,000 miles.

(continued)

3. The expenditures relating to the truck during 2008.
4. The 2008 depreciation expense using the units-of-production method and assuming the truck was driven 50,000 miles.

ANALYTICAL ASSIGNMENTS

AA 9-74
DISCUSSION

Intangible Assets

Renford Company owns two restaurants. One, located in Tacoma, was purchased from a previous owner and the other, located in Seattle, was built by Renford Company. The restaurant was built nine years ago. The Tacoma restaurant was purchased last year and has goodwill of $550,000 on the books. As it turns out, the Seattle restaurant does twice as much business as the Tacoma restaurant and is much more profitable. The Seattle restaurant is in a prime location, and business keeps increasing each year. The Tacoma restaurant does about the same amount of business each year, and it doesn't look as if it will ever do any better. Does it make sense to you to have goodwill on the books of the less profitable restaurant? Should Renford record goodwill on the books of the Seattle restaurant, or should it write off the goodwill on the Tacoma restaurant's books?

AA 9-75
DISCUSSION

EXPANDED
material

Straight-Line versus Accelerated Depreciation

Dennis Company currently depreciates its assets using the straight-line method for both tax and financial accounting. Total depreciation expense for this year will be $250,000 using straight-line depreciation. A consultant has just advised the company that it should use accelerated depreciation methods for both tax and financial accounting because "paying lower taxes is better than recognizing higher income." Using accelerated depreciation methods, total depreciation expense this year would be $400,000. The company has an effective tax rate of 40%. Do you agree with the consultant? Why or why not?

AA 9-76
JUDGMENT CALL

You Decide: Should companies leasing equipment be required to record the equipment and leases as assets and liabilities on the balance sheet or as expenses on the income statement?

Current rules require that leases meeting any one of the following requirements should be classified as an asset and liability on the balance sheet:

- A transfer of ownership.
- A bargain purchase option.
- A lease term equal to 75% or more of the economic life of the asset.
- The present value of the payments are 90% or more of the fair market value of the asset at the beginning of the lease term.

However, what if a company leasing the asset decides to structure the lease so that the lease term is 73% of the economic life of the asset or the present value of the lease payments equals 88% of the fair market value of the asset? Should a company be able to use creative techniques in order to structure a lease so that it does not appear on the balance sheet?

AA 9-77
REAL COMPANY ANALYSIS

Wal-Mart

Using **Wal-Mart**'s 2006 Form 10-K contained in Appendix A, answer the following questions:

1. As a percentage of total assets, is Wal-Mart's investment in property, plant, and equipment increasing or decreasing over time? Which of Wal-Mart's assets is increasing the

(continued)

fastest as a percentage of total assets? What does that indicate Wal-Mart is doing? *Hint:* Include property under capital lease as PP&E in calculating percentages.

2. Reference the notes to the financial statements. Which depreciation method does Wal-Mart use? Estimate the average useful life of Wal-Mart's depreciable assets (i.e., not including land) by dividing the ending balance in the depreciable asset accounts by the depreciation expense for the year. Does the resulting estimated useful life seem reasonable? *Hint:* Include property under capital lease as PP&E in your calculations.

3. Wal-Mart notes in its statement of cash flows that $14.563 billion of property, plant, and equipment was purchased in 2005. Using that information along with the detailed information from the balance sheet, compute (a) the original cost of the equipment disposed of during 2005 and (b) the accumulated depreciation associated with that equipment. (*Hint:* For property, plant, and equipment, beginning balance + purchases − disposals = ending balance; a similar calculation is used for accumulated depreciation.)

AA 9-78

REAL COMPANY ANALYSIS

FedEx

FedEx delivers packages around the world. To accomplish this task, FedEx has made huge investments in long-term assets.

1. Identify what you consider to be the major long-term assets of FedEx. Review the information shown below from FedEx's balance sheet (numbers are in millions) to see how well you did.

May 31	2005	2004
Property and Equipment, at Cost		
Aircraft and related equipment	$ 7,610	$ 7,001
Package handling and ground support equipment	3,366	3,395
Computer and electronic equipment	3,893	3,537
Vehicles	1,994	1,919
Facilities and other	5,154	4,459
	$22,017	$20,311
Less accumulated depreciation and amortization	12,374	11,274
Net property and equipment	$ 9,643	$ 9,037

2. FedEx uses the straight-line depreciation method in depreciating most of its assets. For each major category—aircraft and related equipment, package handling and ground support equipment, computer and electronic equipment, vehicles (mainly trucks and buildings), and facilities and other—provide an estimate (or a range) as to what you would deem a reasonable useful life for each category.

3. Using the information above, compute the accumulated depreciation associated with the property and equipment sold during 2005 given that depreciation for the year was $1.438 billion.

AA 9-79

REAL COMPANY ANALYSIS

U.S. Steel

1. **U.S. Steel** provides the following information in the notes to its financial statements relating to its use of the straight-line method of depreciation. Can you interpret the information contained in the note?

Property, plant and equipment—U.S. Steel records depreciation on a modified straight-line or straight-line method utilizing a composite or group asset approach based upon estimated lives of assets. The modified straight-line method is utilized for domestic steel producing assets and is based upon raw steel production levels. The modification factors applied to straight-line calculations range from a minimum of 85% at a production level below 81% of capability, to a maximum of 105% for a 100% production level. No modification is made at the 95% production level, considered the normal long-range level.

(continued)

2. U.S. Steel also provides information relating to the balances in its individual property, plant and equipment accounts, as shown below. In very general terms, how old is the company's property, plant, and equipment? Provide support for your answer.

	December 31	
(in millions)	**2005**	**2004**
Land and depletable property	$ 165	$ 175
Buildings	727	673
Machinery and equipment	10,235	9,827
Leased machinery and equipment	189	189
Total	$11,316	$10,864
Less accumulated depreciation, depletion and amortization	7,301	7,237
Net	$ 4,015	$ 3,627

AA 9-80

INTERNATIONAL

Swire Pacific

Swire Pacific, Ltd., based in Hong Kong, is one of the largest companies in the world. The primary operations of the company are in the regions of Hong Kong, China, and Taiwan where it has operated for over 125 years. Swire operates **Cathay Pacific Airways** and has extensive real estate holdings in Hong Kong.

Swire includes in its fixed assets those long-term assets held as investment properties. In 2002, the company noted that it revalued those assets each year for increases and decreases in fair value. During 2002, Swire reduced the value of those assets on their books by $5.161 billion in Hong Kong dollars.

1. Can you compose the journal entry made by Swire Pacific accountants to write the assets down in value? What would be the debit portion of the journal entry? (*Hint:* Although you may not know the exact answer, think about it and make an educated guess. Would the debit be to another asset account? Would it be to a liability account?)

2. Suppose that in the next year, the assets were again revalued and it was determined that a difference existed between market value and book value of only $3 billion Hong Kong dollars. How would this year's journal entry differ from the previous year's?

AA 9-81

ETHICS

Strategic Accounting Method Choices

You saw in Chapter 6 that a company's management selects the percentage to be used when computing bad debt expense. You noted in Chapter 7 that management is allowed to choose the method for valuing inventory. In this chapter you found that management gets to choose the method used for depreciating assets, the estimated salvage value, and the estimated useful life.

Suppose that you are involved in negotiations with the local labor union regarding wages for your company's employees. Labor leaders are asking that their members be given an average annual raise of 12%. The company president has asked you to prepare a set of financial statements that portrays the company's performance as being mediocre at best. The president also makes it clear that she does not want you to prepare fraudulent financial statements. All estimates must be within the bounds of reason.

So you come up with the following:

- Change the percentage used for estimating bad debts from 1.5% to 2%.
- Elect to use the LIFO method for valuing inventory because the prices associated with inventory have been rising.
- Change the average estimated salvage value of long-term assets from 15% to 10% of historical cost.
- Change the depreciation method from straight-line to an accelerated method.
- Change the average estimated useful life of long-term assets from 10 years to 7 years.

(continued)

As you know, each of these changes will result in net income being lower. Each of these changes is also still within the bounds of reason required by the company president.

1. Would it be appropriate to make the changes described above in order to obtain favorable terms from the labor union negotiators?
2. If the above changes are made, what sort of disclosure do you think should be required?

AA 9-82
WRITING

Gains Are Good, Losses Are Bad–Right?

When a long-term asset is sold for more than its book value, we record a gain. When a long-term asset is sold for less than its book value, we record a loss.

Your assignment is to write a two-page memo addressing the following questions:

1. What factors affect a long-term asset's book value?
2. What factors affect a long-term asset's fair value?
3. Should financial statement users expect an asset's book value to equal its fair value?
4. In the case of an asset sold for a loss, if we knew when we purchased the asset what we know at the point of sale, how would depreciation expense have differed if our objective was to ensure that book value equaled fair value when the asset was sold?
5. Is recognizing a loss on the sale of a long-term asset a bad thing? Is a gain good?

AA 9-83
CUMULATIVE SPREADSHEET PROJECT

Preparing New Forecasts

This spreadsheet project is a continuation of the spreadsheet projects in earlier chapters. If you completed those spreadsheets, you have a head start on this one.

1. Handyman wishes to prepare a forecasted balance sheet and income statement for 2010. Use the original financial statement numbers for 2009 [given in part (1) of the Cumulative Spreadsheet Project assignment in Chapter 2] as the basis for the forecast, along with the following additional information:

   a. Sales in 2010 are expected to increase by 40% over 2009 sales of $700.
   b. Cash will increase at the same rate as sales.
   c. The forecasted amount of accounts receivable in 2010 is determined using the forecasted value for the average collection period. For simplicity, do the computations using the end-of-period accounts receivable balance instead of the average balance. The average collection period for 2010 is expected to be 14.08 days.
   d. The forecasted amount of inventory in 2010 is determined using the forecasted value for the number of days' sales in inventory (computed using the end-of-period inventory balance). The number of days' sales in inventory for 2010 is expected to be 107.6 days.
   e. The forecasted amount of accounts payable in 2010 is determined using the forecasted value for the number of days' purchases in accounts payable (computed using the end-of-period accounts payable balance). The number of days' purchases in accounts payable for 2010 is expected to be 48.34 days.
   f. The $160 in operating expenses reported in 2009 breaks down as follows: $5 depreciation expense, $155 other operating expenses.
   g. No new long-term debt will be acquired in 2010.
   h. No cash dividends will be paid in 2010.
   i. New short-term loans payable will be acquired in an amount sufficient to make Handyman's current ratio in 2010 exactly equal to 2.0.

   Note: These statements were constructed as part of the spreadsheet assignment in Chapter 7; you can use that spreadsheet as a starting point if you have completed that assignment.

   Clearly state any additional assumptions that you make.

   For this exercise, add the following additional assumptions:

   j. The forecasted amount of property, plant, and equipment (PP&E) in 2010 is determined using the forecasted value for the fixed asset turnover ratio. For simplicity,

(continued)

compute the fixed asset turnover ratio using the end-of-period gross PP&E balance. The fixed asset turnover ratio for 2010 is expected to be 3.518 times.

k. In computing depreciation expense for 2010, use straight-line depreciation and assume a 30-year useful life with no residual value. Gross PP&E acquired during the year is only depreciated for half the year. In other words, depreciation expense for 2010 is the sum of two parts: (1) a full year of depreciation on the beginning balance in PP&E, assuming a 30-year life and no residual value, and (2) a half-year of depreciation on any new PP&E acquired during the year, based on the change in the gross PP&E balance.

Clearly state any additional assumptions that you make.

2. Repeat (1), with the following changes in assumptions:
   a. Fixed asset turnover ratio is expected to be 6.000 times.
   b. Fixed asset turnover ratio is expected to be 2.000 times.

3. Comment on the differences in the forecasted values of the following items in 2010 under each of the following assumptions about the fixed asset turnover ratio: 3.518 times, 6.000 times, and 2.000 times:
   a. Property, plant, and equipment.
   b. Depreciation expense.
   c. Income tax expense.
   d. Paid-in capital.

4. Return the fixed asset turnover ratio to 3.518 times. Now, repeat (1), with the following changes in assumptions:
   a. Estimated useful life is expected to be 15 years.
   b. Estimated useful life is expected to be 60 years.

5. Comment on the differences in the forecasted values of the following items in 2010 under each of the following assumptions about the estimated useful life of property, plant, and equipment: 30 years, 15 years, and 60 years.
   a. Depreciation expense.
   b. Income tax expense.

CHAPTER

10

Long-Term Debt Financing

After studying this chapter, you should be able to:

LEARNING OBJECTIVES

1. **Use present value concepts to measure long-term liabilities.** *The proper measure of the economic obligation associated with a long-term liability is the present value of the future cash flows instead of the simple sum of the future cash flows.*

2. **Account for long-term liabilities, including notes payable and mortgages payable.** *Long-term notes payable are frequently repaid through regular interest payments with the entire balance of the note (the principal) being repaid at the end of the term of the note. With a mortgage, the liability is typically repaid through a series of equal payments, with some interest and some principal repayment included in each payment amount.*

3. **Account for capital lease obligations and understand the significance of operating leases being excluded from the balance sheet.** *For accounting purposes, leases are considered to be either rentals (called operating leases) or asset purchases with borrowed money (called capital leases). A company using a leased asset tries to have the lease classified as an operating lease in order to keep the lease obligation off the balance sheet.*

4. **Account for bonds, including the original issuance, the payment of interest, and the retirement of bonds.** *Bonds are a way to borrow funds from many difference sources rather than borrowing the entire amount from one source, such as a bank. Depending on the market interest rate at the time it is issued, a bond can be issued for more or less than its face value.*

5. **Use debt-related financial ratios to determine the degree of a company's financial leverage and its ability to repay loans.** *Debt-related financial ratios give an indication of the degree of a company's leverage and how much cushion operating profits give in terms of being able to make periodic interest payments.*

EXPANDED material

6. **Amortize bond discounts and bond premiums using either the straight-line method or the effective-interest method.** *A bond discount arises when the coupon rate on the bonds is less than the market interest rate; a premium arises when the coupon rate is more than the market rate. Premium and discount balances are gradually reduced to zero over the life of the bond. A premium reduces bond interest expense; a discount increases bond interest expense.*

© MARK ASHMAN/HANDOUT/REUTERS/CORBIS

In 1923, two brothers, Walt and Roy Disney, founded the **Disney Brothers Studio** as a partnership to produce animated features for film. Five years later, the Disney Brothers Studio released its first animated film with sound effects and dialogue, *Steamboat Willie*, featuring a soon-to-become-famous mouse, Mickey. Pluto was introduced to American audiences in 1930, and Goofy was created just two years later. Donald Duck appeared on the scene in 1934, and in 1937 *Snow White and the Seven Dwarfs* was released, accompanied by the first comprehensive merchandising campaign.

But Walt Disney's vision encompassed more than animated films. In 1952, Disney began designing and creating Disneyland, which opened on July 17, 1955. Beginning in the late 1950s, the television shows *Disneyland* (which ran for 29 seasons under various names) and The *Mickey Mouse Club* were also successful Disney ventures. Though Walt Disney passed away in 1966, his influence is still felt around the world. We have Walt Disney World in Florida and Disneylands in Anaheim, California; Paris; Tokyo; and Hong Kong.

Disney's company has expanded far beyond what even he could have foreseen. **The Walt Disney Company** is now involved in television and radio stations; international film distribution; home video production; live theatrical entertainment; online computer programs; interactive computer games; telephone company partnerships; cruise lines; Disney Stores; newspaper, magazine, and book publishing; Internet marketing; and the convention business. In the past decade, The Walt Disney Company has grown over 300%. How has the company financed this growth? In part through very successful operations, but these have not been enough. The company has also borrowed to finance its expansion. As of October 1, 2005, The Walt Disney Company had long-term debt totaling over $10 billion. This long-term financing includes loans with U.S. banks as well as loans denominated (or made) in Hong Kong dollars and euros. The effective interest rates on Disney's loans range from 2.13 to 9.07%.[1]

F Y I

Not everything that Disney touches turns to gold. Disney opened an indoor theme park–DisneyQuest–in Chicago in June 1999 and closed the park in September 2001 citing a lack of long-range financial return potential.

In this chapter, we will introduce various types of long-term liabilities. We will explain a concept used in measuring the present value of an obligation due in the future. This concept–the time value of money–is useful for computing the value of bonds and notes, as in the Disney example, as well as for computing mortgage payments and pension obligations. In the main part of this chapter, we discuss the measurement of long-term liabilities and introduce numerous types of long-term liabilities–notes, mortgages, leases, and bonds. The basic accounting procedures associated with several of these liabilities are also discussed. In the expanded material, the complexities associated with the amortization of a bond issued at a premium or discount are discussed. Exhibit 1 highlights the financial statement accounts discussed in this chapter.

---

[1] The information for this scenario was obtained from Disney's Web site at **http://www.disney.com**.

EXHIBIT 1	Financial Statement Items Discussed in This Chapter

Balance Sheet

Long-term liabilities
Long-term debt

Statement of Cash Flows

Operating activities
Payments for interest

Financing activities
Proceeds from borrowing
Repayments of borrowing

Income Statement

Other revenues and expenses
Interest expense

Measuring Long-Term Liabilities

Use present value concepts to measure long-term liabilities.

① Conceptually, the value of a liability is the cash that would be required to pay the liability in full today. Because money has a time value—usually referred to as interest, most people are willing to accept less money today than they would if a liability were paid in the future. Therefore, with the exception of short-term Accounts Payable, liabilities to be paid in the future usually involve interest.

Accounting for **long-term liabilities** is complex because usually payments of interest, or in some cases principal and interest, are made periodically over the period in which the liability is outstanding. Further, in some cases the amount of the liability in a noncash transaction may not be readily apparent. The time value of money concept is used in measuring and recording these liabilities.

Present Value and Future Value Concepts

long-term liabilities

Debts or other obligations that will not be paid within one year.

The concepts of present value and future value are used to measure the effect of time on the value of money. To illustrate, if you are to receive $100 one year from today, is it worth $100 today? Obviously not, because if you had the $100 today you could either spend it now or invest it and earn interest. If the $100 won't be received for one year, those options are not available. The **present value of $1** is the value today of $1 to be received or paid in the future, given a specified interest rate. To determine the value today of money to be received or paid in the future, we must "discount" the future amount (reduce the future amount to its present value) by an appropriate interest rate. For example, if money can earn 10% per year, $100 to be received one year from now is approximately equal to $90.91 received today.

present value of $1

The value today of $1 to be received or paid at some future date, given a specified interest rate.

Putting it another way, if $90.91 is invested today in an account that earns 10% interest for one year, the interest earned will be $9.09 ($90.91 × 10% × 1 year = $9.09). The sum of the $90.91 principal and the $9.09 interest will equal $100 at the end of one year. Thus, the present value of $100 to be received (or paid) in one year at 10% interest is $90.91. This present value relationship can be diagrammed as follows:

Present Value (Computed) $90.91 — (One-Year Period @ 10%) — Future Amount (Known) $100

$90.91 is the present value of the $100 future amount.

The relationships in this diagram can be described in two ways. We have just seen that the $90.91 is the present value of $100 to be received one year from now when interest is 10%. In this example, the $100 to be received one year from now is known, and the present value of $90.91 must be computed. We are computing a present value amount from a known future value amount.

Another way to look at the relationship is on a future value basis. Future values apply when the amount today ($90.91) is known, and the future amount must be calculated. Future values are exactly the opposite of present values. Thinking in terms of future values, $100 is the future amount we can expect to receive in one year, given a present known amount of $90.91 when the interest rate is 10%. We can diagram this relationship as follows:

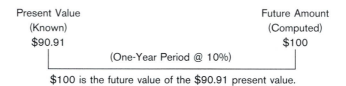

Present Value (Known) $90.91 — (One-Year Period @ 10%) — Future Amount (Computed) $100

$100 is the future value of the $90.91 present value.

Present and future values can be calculated using formulas. If more than one period is involved, however, the formula is exponential, and the calculations become rather complicated. Therefore, it is more convenient to use either a present value table or a calculator that gives the present value of $1 for various numbers of periods and interest rates (see Table I, page 484) or a future value table that gives the future value of $1 for various numbers of periods and interest rates (see Table III, page 486). We will illustrate the use of both a present value table and a future value table as well as the keystrokes needed when using a standard business calculator.

Computing the Present Value of a Single Amount
To use a present value table, you simply locate the appropriate number of periods in the leftmost column and the interest rate in the row at the top of the table. The intersection of the row and column is the factor representing the present value of $1 for the number of periods and the relevant interest rate. To find the present value of an amount other than $1, multiply the factor in the table by that amount.

To illustrate the use of a present value table (Table I) to find the present value of a known future amount, assume that $10,000 is to be paid four years from today when the interest rate is 10%. What is the present value of the $10,000 payment?

Amount of payment	$ 10,000
Present value factor of $1 to be paid in 4 periods at 10% interest (from Table I)	× 0.6830
Present value of payment	$ 6,830

This present value amount, $6,830, is the amount that could be paid today to satisfy the obligation that is due four years from now if money earns 10% annually. As indicated, this procedure is sometimes referred to as "discounting." Thus, we say that $10,000 discounted for four years at 10% is $6,830. Stated another way, if $6,830 is invested today in an account that pays 10% interest, in four years the balance in that account will be $10,000.

Another way to compute this same amount is to use a business calculator. The keystrokes described below are for a Hewlett-Packard 10BII business calculator; similar keystrokes are used with other business calculators. To compute the present value of $10,000 to be received four years from today, with a prevailing interest rate of 10%, make the following keystrokes:

Hewlett-Packard Keystrokes:
a. Always **CLEAR ALL** before doing anything else. With a Hewlett-Packard 10BII, one does this by pressing the yellow key, then pressing "C." This has the effect of clearing out any information left over from a prior computation.
b. Always set **P/YR** (payments per year) to the correct number—"1" in this case. With a Hewlett-Packard 10BII, one does this by pressing "1," then pressing the yellow key, then pressing "PMT." This has the effect of telling the calculator that each year is being viewed as a separate period. As described later in this chapter, interest can be compounded over different periods, such as monthly, quarterly, daily, or even continuously. Setting **P/YR** equal to 1 means that the interest rate is compounded annually. Sometimes, the default for this amount is "12" because the calculator is set to compute monthly payments. Until you are comfortable using your calculator, your best strategy is to set this amount to "1" to avoid having the calculator doing too many mysterious things automatically.

1. 10,000   Press **FV**.
2. 4   Press **N**.
3. 10   Press **I/YR**.
4. Press **PV** for the answer of $6,830.13.

Computing the Future Value of a Single Amount

To find the future value of an amount that is known today, use a future value table. When using a future value table, simply locate the appropriate number of periods in the leftmost column and the interest rate in the row at the top of the table. The intersection of the row and column is the factor representing the future value of $1 for the number of periods and the relevant interest rate. To find the future value of an amount other than $1, multiply the factor in the table by that amount.

To illustrate the use of a future value table (Table III), we will use the same information as before, except that we will now assume that the present value of $6,830 is known, not the future amount of $10,000. Assume that we have a savings account with a current balance of $6,830 that earns interest of 10%. What will be the balance in that account in four years?

Present value in savings account	$ 6,830*
Future value factor of $1 in 4 periods at 10% interest (from Table III)	× 1.4641*
Future value	$ 10,000*

*Rounded; other calculations in chapter will also be rounded.

Hewlett-Packard Keystrokes:
a. **CLEAR ALL**.
b. Set **P/YR** to 1.

1. 6,830   Press **PV**.
2. 4   Press **N**.
3. 10   Press **I/YR**.
4. Press **FV** for the answer of $9,999.80. (You would round to $10,000.)

When computing future values, we often use the term *compounding* to mean the frequency with which interest is added to the principal. Thus, we say that interest of 10% has been compounded once a year (annually) to arrive at a future value at the end of four years of $10,000. If the interest is added more or less frequently than once a year, the future amount will be different.

compounding period

The period of time for which interest is computed.

The preceding example assumed annual **compounding periods** for interest. If the 10% interest had been compounded semiannually (twice a year) for four years, the calculation would have used a 5% (one-half of the 10%) rate for eight periods (4 years × 2 periods per year) instead of 10% for four periods. To illustrate, what is the present value of $10,000 to be paid in four years if interest of 10% is compounded semiannually?

Amount of payment	$ 10,000
Present value factor of $1 to be paid in 8 periods	
at 5% interest (from Table I)	× 0.6768
Present value of payment	$ 6,768

Thus, the present value of $10,000 to be paid in four years is $6,768 if interest is compounded semiannually. Likewise, if semiannual compounding is used to determine the future value of $6,768 in four years at 10% compounded semiannually, the result is as follows:

Present value in savings account	$ 6,768
Future value factor of $1 in 8 periods	
at 5% interest (from Table III)	× 1.4775
Future value	$ 10,000

Note that the present value ($6,768) is lower with semiannual compounding than with annual compounding ($6,830). The more frequently interest is compounded, the greater the total amount of interest deducted (in computing present values) or added (in computing future values).

For practice using semiannual compounding with a business calculator, try the following set of keystrokes:

Hewlett-Packard Keystrokes:
a. **CLEAR ALL**.
b. Set **P/YR** to 1. There is a simple way to tell the calculator to automatically compute the impact of semiannual compounding. Look in your calculator instruction book if you are interested in knowing how to do this. Alternatively, you can do some of the calculations yourself (divide the interest rate by two and double the number of periods) and use the keystrokes below.

1. 6,768   Press **PV**.
2. 8   Press **N**.
3. 5   Press **I/YR**.
4. Press **FV** for the answer of $9,999.42.

STOP & THINK

Without referencing the present value tables, answer these questions: As interest rates increase, would you expect the present value factors to increase or decrease? Why?

Because interest may also be compounded quarterly, monthly, or for some other period, you should learn the relationship of interest to the compounding period. Semiannual interest means that you double the interest periods and halve the annual interest rate; with quarterly interest, you quadruple the periods and take one-fourth of the annual interest rate. The formula for interest rate is:

$$\frac{\text{Yearly interest rate}}{\text{Compounding periods per year}} = \frac{\text{Interest rate per}}{\text{compounding period}}$$

The number of interest periods is simply the number of periods per year times the number of years. That formula is:

$$\frac{\text{Compounding}}{\text{periods per year}} \times \frac{\text{Number of}}{\text{years}} = \frac{\text{Number of}}{\text{interest periods}}$$

Computing the Present Value of an Annuity

annuity

A series of equal amounts to be received or paid at the end of equal time intervals.

present value of an annuity

The value today of a series of equally spaced, equal-amount payments to be made or received in the future given a specified interest rate.

In discussing present values and future values, we have assumed only a single present value or future value with one of the amounts known and the other to be computed. With liabilities, we generally know the future amount that must be paid and would like to compute the present value of that future payment. Because this chapter focuses on liabilities, we will concentrate on present value calculations.

Many long-term liabilities involve a series of payments rather than one lump-sum payment. For example, a company might purchase equipment under an installment agreement requiring payments of $5,000 each year for five years. Determining the value today (present value) of a series of equally spaced, equal-amount payments (called an **annuity**) is more complicated than determining the present value of a single future payment. If you were to try to calculate the **present value of an annuity** by hand, you would have to discount the first payment for one period, the second payment for two periods, and so on, and then add all the present values together. Because such calculations are time-consuming, a table is generally used (see Table II, page 485). The factors in the table are the sums of the individual present values of all future payments. Based on the present value of an annuity of $1, the table provides factors for various interest rates and number of payments.

CAUTION

Use care when referencing the present value and future value tables. You can do all your computations correctly, but if you pull the factor from the wrong table, your answer will be wrong.

To illustrate the use of a present value of an annuity table (Table II), we will assume that $10,000 is to be paid at the end of each of the next 10 years. This series of payments is illustrated below.

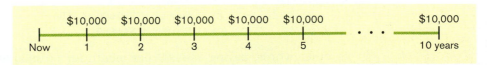

If the interest rate is 12% compounded annually, Table II shows a present value factor of 5.6502. This factor means that the present value of $1 paid each year for 10 years discounted at 12% is approximately $5.65. Applying this factor to payments of $10,000 results in the following:

Amount of the annual payment	$ 10,000
Present value factor of an annuity of $1	
discounted for 10 payments at 12%	× 5.6502
Present value	$ 56,502

This amount, $56,502, is the amount (present value) that could be paid today to satisfy the obligation to pay $10,000 per year for 10 years if the interest rate is 12%.

The present value of an annuity can also be computed with a business calculator as follows:

Hewlett-Packard Keystrokes:
a. **CLEAR ALL**.
b. Set **P/YR** to 1.

1. 10,000   Press **PMT**.
2. 10   Press **N**.
3. 12   Press **I/YR**.
4. Press **PV** for the answer of $56,502.23.

Computing Periodic Payments

With some modifications, the same calculations used to compute the present value of an annuity can be used to compute the proper amount of a periodic loan payment. For example, consider the task of computing the appropriate monthly payment on an automobile loan of $20,000 if the interest rate is 12% compounded monthly (i.e., 1% per month) and the loan period is 60 months. This problem can be viewed as follows:

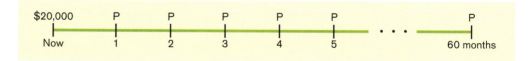

In this case, we know the present value of the annuity—it is $20,000, or the amount we would have to pay today to pay off the entire loan. What we want to know is what series of 60 payments (P in the diagram) has a present value exactly equal to the $20,000 that we owe. The calculation of the payment amount can be set up as follows:

Amount of the annual payment	Payment
Present value factor of an annuity of $1	
discounted for 60 payments at 1%	× 44.9550
Present value	$ 20,000

In equation format, this can be written as follows:

$$\$20{,}000 = \text{Payment} \times 44.9550$$
$$\text{Payment} = \$20{,}000/44.9550$$
$$\text{Payment} = \$444.89$$

In other words, paying $444.89 per month for 60 months is the same as paying $20,000 right now, if the interest rate on borrowed money is 12% compounded monthly (1% per month). (Note that the total paid would be $26,693.40 ($444.89 × 60) and that the total interest would be $6693.40.)

This payment amount can also be computed with a business calculator as follows:

Hewlett-Packard Keystrokes:
a. **CLEAR ALL**.
b. Set **P/YR** to 1.

1. 20,000   Press **PV**.
2. 60   Press **N**.
3. 1   Press **I/YR**.
4. Press **PMT** for the answer of $444.88895.

REMEMBER THIS...

- Long-term liabilities are debts or other obligations that will not be paid or satisfied within one year. Present value concepts, which equate the value of money received or paid in different periods, are used to measure long-term liabilities.

- An annuity is a series of equal payments to be made or received in the future. A lump sum is one payment to be made or received in the future.

- Future value computations are performed to calculate how much a lump-sum payment or an annuity will have grown, because of interest, at some point in the future.

- Present value computations are performed to calculate how much money right now is economically equivalent to a lump sum or annuity to occur in the future.

- Present and future value amounts can be computed using tables, a business calculator, or a spreadsheet.

- In calculating present and future values, you must consider the compounding period and the interest rate. For other than annual payments, the number of periods used is the number of periods per year times the number of years; the interest rate used is the annual rate divided by the number of periods per year.

- The same type of computations used to compute the present value of an annuity can also be used to compute the proper amount of a periodic payment, such as the monthly payment on a car loan.

Accounting for Long-Term Liabilities

Account for long-term liabilities, including notes payable and mortgages payable.

② Now that we have explained how present value concepts are applied in measuring long-term liabilities, we are ready to discuss the accounting for those liabilities. The time line in Exhibit 2 illustrates the business events associated with long-term liabilities.

A company's first decision is to determine the type of long-term financing to use. In this chapter, we will discuss four different types of financing: notes payable, mortgages payable, leasing, and bonds. There are advantages and disadvantages to each type of financing. For example, bonds (which are sold in $1,000 increments) allow a company to borrow a little bit of money from a lot of different people, whereas notes involve borrowing a lot of money from one lender (or perhaps a consortium of lenders). The benefit of a mortgage is typically a lower interest rate because the property being purchased is used as collateral on the loan, thereby providing the lender with less risk. Leases have the advantage of typically requiring a lower

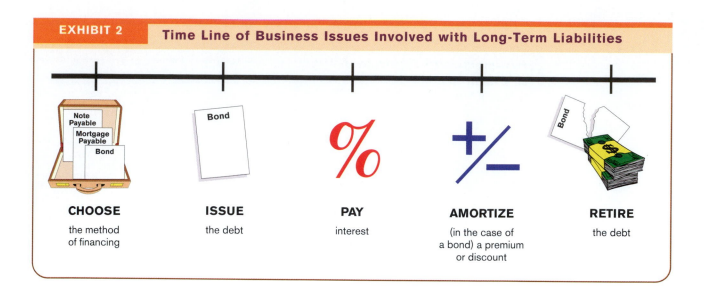

EXHIBIT 2   Time Line of Business Issues Involved with Long-Term Liabilities

CHOOSE
the method
of financing

ISSUE
the debt

PAY
interest

AMORTIZE
(in the case of
a bond) a premium
or discount

RETIRE
the debt

down payment as there are no risks associated with product obsolescence. (At the end of many leases, the asset being leased is returned to the original owner.) Once the pros and cons of the various types of financing are analyzed, and the company selects an option, the accounting differs, depending upon the type of financing chosen. In this section, we will discuss the recording of long-term debt, including notes payable and mortgages payable.

Interest-Bearing Notes

To illustrate the accounting for a long-term interest-bearing note payable, assume that on January 1, 2009, Giraffe Company borrowed $10,000 from City Bank for three years at 10% interest. Assume also that interest is payable annually on December 31. The entries to account for the note are:

2009				
Jan.	1	Cash	10,000	
		Note Payable		10,000
		Borrowed $10,000 from City Bank for three years.		
Dec.	31	Interest Expense	1,000	
		Cash		1,000
		Made first annual interest payment on City Bank note ($10,000 × 0.10).		
2010				
Dec.	31	Interest Expense	1,000	
		Cash		1,000
		Made second annual interest payment on City Bank note ($10,000 × 0.10).		
2011				
Dec.	31	Interest Expense	1,000	
		Note Payable	10,000	
		Cash		11,000
		Made final interest payment ($10,000 × 0.10) and repaid principal on City Bank note.		

A long-term note such as this three-year note should be recorded in the books at the present value of the future cash payments to be made in connection with the note. If the market interest rate is 10%, then the present value of the cash payments on the note is computed as follows:

Present value of interest payments:		
Amount of each interest payment	$ 1,000	
Table II factor for 3 payments at 10%	× 2.4869	
Present value of annuity		$ 2,487
Present value of principal payment:		
Amount of principal payment	$10,000	
Table I factor for 3 periods at 10%	× 0.7513	
Present value of single payment		7,513
Present value of interest and principal		$10,000

The total present value is the sum of the present values of the interest payments (an annuity) and the single principal payment due in three years. In this case, the present value of the cash payments on the note is exactly equal to the note's face amount of $10,000. This is because the annual interest payments of 10% are equal to the market rate of interest, or the rate of interest that lenders would insist on earning for lending money in exchange for the note.

In the notes to its 2005 financial statements, **The Walt Disney Company** reported the existence of a variety of notes payable, including notes for which the amounts to be repaid were stated in euros, Hong Kong dollars, and U.S. dollars. These notes included various types of debt instruments including "fixed or floating rate notes, U.S. dollar or foreign currency denominated notes, redeemable notes, index linked and dual currency notes."

Mortgages Payable

mortgage payable

A written promise to pay a stated amount of money at one or more specified future dates; a mortgage is secured by the pledging of certain assets, usually real estate, as collateral.

A **mortgage payable** is similar to a note payable in that it is a written promise to pay a stated sum of money at one or more specified future dates. It differs from a note in the way it is applied. Whereas money borrowed with a note can often be used for any business purpose, mortgage money is usually related to a specific asset, typically real estate. Assets purchased with a mortgage are usually pledged as security or collateral on the loan. Individuals commonly obtain home mortgages, and companies frequently use plant mortgages. In either case, a mortgage generally requires periodic (usually monthly) payments of principal plus interest.

To illustrate the accounting for a mortgage, we will assume that McGiven Automobile Company borrows $100,000 on January 1 to purchase a new showroom and signs a mortgage agreement pledging the showroom as collateral on the loan. If the mortgage is at 8% for 30 years, and the monthly payment is $733.76, payable on January 31 with subsequent payments due at the end of each month thereafter, the entries to record the acquisition of the mortgage and the first monthly payment are:

Jan. 1	Cash	100,000	
	Mortgage Payable		100,000
	Borrowed $100,000 to purchase the automobile showroom.		
Jan. 31	Mortgage Payable	67.09	
	Interest Expense	666.67	
	Cash		733.76
	Made first month's mortgage payment.		

As this entry shows, only $67.09 of the $733.76 payment is applied to reduce the mortgage; the remainder is interest ($100,000 × 0.08 × $\frac{1}{12}$). In each successive month, the amount applied to reduce the mortgage will increase slightly until, toward the end of

EXHIBIT 3	Mortgage Amortization Schedule – Year 1 ($100,000, 30-Year Mortgage at 8%)

Payment	Monthly Payment	Interest Portion	Principal Portion	Outstanding Mortgage Balance
				$100,000.00
1	$733.76	$666.67	$67.09	99,932.91
2	733.76	666.22	67.54	99,865.37
3	733.76	665.77	67.99	99,797.38
4	733.76	665.32	68.44	99,728.93
5	733.76	664.86	68.90	99,660.03
6	733.76	664.40	69.36	99,590.67
7	733.76	663.94	69.82	99,520.85
8	733.76	663.47	70.29	99,450.56
9	733.76	663.00	70.76	99,379.80
10	733.76	662.53	71.23	99,308.58
11	733.76	662.06	71.70	99,236.87
12	733.76	661.58	72.18	99,164.69

mortgage amortization schedule

A schedule that shows the breakdown between interest and principal for each payment over the life of a mortgage.

the 30-year mortgage, almost all of the payment will be reductions in the mortgage balance. A **mortgage amortization schedule** identifies how much of each mortgage payment is interest and how much is principal reduction, as shown in Exhibit 3 (for the first year of the mortgage). A similar table could be prepared for each year of the mortgage.

The following table shows how much the monthly payment and total amount paid and what the qualifying annual income (the monthly payment is recommended not to exceed 28% of a person's monthly gross income) would have to be on a $100,000, 25-year mortgage. You can see that as the interest rate increases, so does the monthly payment and total amount paid over the life of the loan.

$100,000, 25-Year Mortgage			
Interest Rate	Monthly Payment	Total Amount Paid	Qualifying Annual Income
7%	$ 707	$212,100	$30,300
8%	772	231,600	33,086
9%	839	251,700	35,957
10%	909	272,700	38,957
11%	980	294,000	42,000
12%	1,053	315,900	45,129
13%	1,128	338,400	48,343
14%	1,204	361,200	51,600

At the end of each year, a mortgage is reported on the balance sheet in two places: (1) the principal to be paid during the next year is shown as a current liability, and (2) the balance of the mortgage payable is shown as a long-term liability. Further, any accrued interest on the mortgage is reported as a current liability, and the interest expense for the year is included with other expenses on the income statement.

REMEMBER THIS...

- Long-term interest-bearing notes are obligations that will be repaid over several years.
- Interest on the note is computed by multiplying the outstanding balance of the note by the rate of interest.
- Mortgages payable are long-term liabilities that arise when companies borrow money to buy land, construct buildings, or purchase additional operating assets. Mortgages are tied to specific assets.
- Mortgages are amortized over a period of time and involve periodic, usually monthly, payments that include both principal and interest.

Accounting for Lease Obligations

(3) Account for capital lease obligations and understand the significance of operating leases being excluded from the balance sheet.

As discussed in Chapter 9, a company may choose to lease rather than purchase an asset. If a lease is a simple, short-term rental agreement, called an operating lease, lease payments are recorded as Rent Expense by the lessee and as Rent Revenue by the lessor. However, if the terms of a lease agreement meet specific criteria (see Chapter 9, page 396), the transaction is classified as a capital lease and is accounted for as if the asset had been purchased with long-term debt. The lessee records the leased property as an asset and recognizes a liability to the lessor.

In Chapter 9, we focused on the recording of assets acquired under capital leases, using assumed amounts for the present value. Here we will explain how the present value of a capital lease is determined. To illustrate the measurement and recording of a capital lease, we will assume that Malone Corporation leases a mainframe computer from Macro Data, Inc., on December 31, 2008. The lease requires annual payments of $10,000 for 10 years, with the first payment due on December 31, 2009.[2] The rate of interest applicable to the lease is 14% compounded annually.

Assuming the lease meets the criteria for a capital lease, Malone Corporation will record the computer and the related liability at the present value of the future lease payments. From Table II, on page 485, the factor for the present value of an annuity for 10 payments at 14% is 5.2161. This factor is multiplied by the annual lease payment to determine the present value. The entry to record the lease on Malone's books is:

? FYI

Many companies structure their lease agreements so as not to meet the lease capitalization criteria. In these cases, the companies must still disclose their expected future lease payments in the notes to the financial statements.

2008			
Dec. 31	Leased Computer	52,161	
	Lease Liability		52,161
	Leased a computer from Macro Data, Inc., for		
	$10,000 a year for 10 years discounted at 14%		
	($10,000 × 5.2161 = $52,161).		

---

[2] Readers should be aware that the illustration of a capital lease presented here assumes that lease payments are made at the end of each year, with the present values based on an ordinary annuity. Usually, lease payments are made at the beginning of each lease period, which requires present value calculations using the concept of an annuity in advance or "annuity due." These calculations are explained in intermediate accounting texts.

A construction company may choose to lease large equipment rather than purchase such an asset.

© GETTY IMAGES INC.

If Malone Corporation uses a calendar year for financial reporting, the December 31, 2009, balance sheet will report the leased asset in the property, plant, and equipment section and the lease liability in the liabilities section.

A schedule of the computer lease payments is presented in Exhibit 4. Each year the lease liability account balance is multiplied by 14% to determine the amount of interest included in each of the annual $10,000 lease payments.

Note that this is the same procedure used with a mortgage when determining the amount of each payment that is applied to reduce the principal and the amount that is considered interest expense. As you can see, in the table the interest expense is first calculated by multiplying the interest rate times the lease account balance; the principle amount of the payment is calculated by deducting the interest expense from the payment and the lease account balance for the subsequent year is determined by subtracting the principal amount of the payment from the previous years' lease account balance.

The remainder of the payment is a reduction in the liability. For example, the first lease payment is recorded as follows:

2009			
Dec. 31	Interest Expense	7,303	
	Lease Liability	2,697	
	Cash		10,000
	Paid annual lease payment for computer		
	($52,161 × 0.14 = $7,303; $10,000 − $7,303 = $2,697).		

Similar entries would be made in each of the remaining nine years of the lease, except that the principal payment (reduction in Lease Liability) would increase while the interest expense would decrease. Interest expense decreases over the lease term because a constant rate (14%) is applied to a decreasing principal balance.

EXHIBIT 4	**Schedule of Computer Lease Payments**			
Year	**Annual Payment**	**Interest Expense (0.14 × Lease Liability)**	**Principal**	**Lease Liability**
				$52,161
1	$10,000	(0.14 × $52,161) = $7,303	$2,697	49,464
2	10,000	(0.14 × 49,464) = 6,925	3,075	46,389
3	10,000	(0.14 × 46,389) = 6,494	3,506	42,883
4	10,000	(0.14 × 42,883) = 6,004	3,996	38,887
5	10,000	(0.14 × 38,887) = 5,444	4,556	34,331
6	10,000	(0.14 × 34,331) = 4,806	5,194	29,137
7	10,000	(0.14 × 29,137) = 4,079	5,921	23,216
8	10,000	(0.14 × 23,216) = 3,250	6,750	16,466
9	10,000	(0.14 × 16,466) = 2,305	7,695	8,771
10	10,000	(0.14 × 8,771) = 1,229*	8,771	0

*Rounded.

Although the asset and liability accounts have the same balance at the beginning of the lease term, they seldom remain the same during the lease period. The asset and the liability are accounted for separately, with the asset being depreciated using one of the methods discussed in Chapter 9.

Operating Leases

When a lease is accounted for as a capital lease, the lease obligation (and an associated leased asset) will appear on the balance sheet of the company using the leased asset. If, on the other hand, a company is able to classify a lease as an operating lease according to the criteria outlined in Chapter 9, *nothing will appear on the balance sheet.* Neither the leased asset nor the lease liability will be recognized. For this reason, an operating lease is often referred to as a form of "off-balance-sheet financing"—the economic obligation associated with the financing arrangement entered into to secure the use of an asset is not reported on the balance sheet.

Because operating leases are not reported on the balance sheet, accounting rules require companies to disclose operating lease details in the financial statement notes so that financial statement users will be aware of these off-balance-sheet obligations. The information from the operating lease note from **Disney's** 2005 financial statements is reproduced below.

Contractual commitments for broadcast programming rights, future minimum lease payments under non-cancelable operating leases and creative talent and other commitments totaled $23.3 billion at October 1, 2005, payable as follows:

	Broadcast Programming	Operating Leases	Other	Total
2006	$ 4,174	$ 279	$ 887	$ 5,340
2007	2,836	253	484	3,573
2008	2,445	204	324	2,973
2009	1,944	171	196	2,311
2010	2,093	149	92	2,334
Thereafter	6,065	580	96	6,741
	$19,557	$1,636	$2,079	$23,272

Recall that the obligation to make this $23.3 billion in operating lease payments is not reported as a liability on Disney's balance sheet.

REMEMBER THIS...

- A lease is a contract whereby the lessee makes periodic payments to the lessor for the use of an asset.
- A simple short-term rental agreement, or operating lease, involves only the recording of rent expense by the lessee and rent revenue by the lessor.
- A capital lease is accounted for as a debt-financed purchase of the leased asset. Both the asset and the liability are initially recorded by the lessee at the present value of the future lease payments discounted at the applicable interest rate. The asset is subsequently depreciated. The liability is recorded as being repaid, with interest.
- Operating leases are a form of off-balance-sheet financing because the obligation to make future operating lease payments is not recognized as a liability on the balance sheet.
- Companies are required to disclose the amount of their future operating lease payments in the notes to the financial statements.

The Nature of Bonds

Account for bonds, including the original issuance, the payment of interest, and the retirement of bonds.

④ A **bond** is a contract between the borrowing company (issuer) and the lender (investor) in which the borrower promises to pay a specified amount of interest at the end of each period the bond is outstanding and to repay the principal at the maturity date of the bond contract. Bonds generally have maturity dates exceeding 10 years and, as a result, are another example of a long-term liability.

Types of Bonds

Bonds can be categorized on the basis of various characteristics. The following classification system considers three characteristics:

bond

A contract between a borrower and a lender in which the borrower promises to pay a specified rate of interest for each period the bond is outstanding and repay the principal at the maturity date.

1. The extent to which bondholders are protected.
   a. **Debentures** (or **unsecured bonds**). Bonds that have no underlying assets pledged as security, or collateral, to guarantee their repayment.
   b. **Secured bonds.** Bonds that have a pledge of company assets, such as land or buildings, as a protection for lenders. If the company fails to meet its bond obligations, the pledged assets can be sold and used to pay the bondholders. Bonds that are secured with the issuer's assets are often referred to as "mortgage bonds."
2. How the bond interest is paid.
   a. **Registered bonds.** Bonds for which the issuing company keeps a record of the names and addresses of all bondholders and pays interest only to those whose names are on file.
   b. **Coupon bonds.** Unregistered bonds for which the issuer has no record of current bondholders but instead pays interest to anyone who can show evidence of ownership. Usually, these bonds have a printed coupon for each interest payment. When a payment is due, the bondholder clips the coupon from the certificate and sends it to the issuer as evidence of bond ownership. The issuer then sends an interest payment to the bondholder.
3. How the bonds mature.
   a. **Term bonds.** Bonds that mature in one single sum on a specified future date.
   b. **Serial bonds.** Bonds that mature in a series of installments.
   c. **Callable bonds.** Term or serial bonds that the issuer can redeem at any time at a specified price.
   d. **Convertible bonds.** Term or serial bonds that can be converted to other securities, such as stocks, after a specified period, at the option of the bondholder. (The accounting for this type of bond is discussed in advanced accounting texts.)

debentures (unsecured bonds)

Bonds for which no collateral has been pledged.

secured bonds

Bonds for which assets have been pledged in order to guarantee repayment.

registered bonds

Bonds for which the names and addresses of the bondholders are kept on file by the issuing company.

coupon bonds

Unregistered bonds for which owners receive periodic interest payments by clipping a coupon from the bond and sending it to the issuer as evidence of ownership.

Two other types of bonds that are often encountered are zero-coupon bonds and junk bonds. **Zero-coupon bonds** are issued with no promise of interest payments. The company issuing the bonds promises only to repay a fixed amount at the maturity date. While the idea of having to make no interest payments might be initially appealing to the issuer, remember that the present value of the bond is affected by both the single payment at the end of the bond's life and the annuity payment. If this annuity (interest) payment will not be part of the bond, potential buyers will pay much less for the bond. For this reason, zero-coupon bonds are often referred to as *deep-discount bonds*.

Junk bonds are high-risk bonds issued by companies in weak financial condition or with large amounts of debt already outstanding. These bonds typically

term bonds

Bonds that mature in one single sum at a specified future date.

serial bonds

Bonds that mature in a series of installments at specified future dates.

callable bonds

Bonds for which the issuer reserves the right to pay the obligation before its maturity date.

convertible bonds

Bonds that can be traded for, or converted to, other securities after a specified period of time.

zero-coupon bonds

Bonds issued with no promise of interest payments; only a single payment will be made.

junk bonds

Bonds issued by companies in weak financial condition with large amounts of debt already outstanding; these bonds yield high rates of return because of high risk.

yield returns of at least 12%, but some may return in excess of 20%. Of course, with these high returns comes greater risk.

Characteristics of Bonds

When an organization issues bonds, it usually sells them to underwriters (brokers and investment bankers), who in turn sell them to various institutions and to the public. At the time of the original sale, the company issuing the bonds chooses a trustee to represent the bondholders. In most cases, the trustee is a large bank or trust company to which the company issuing the bonds delivers a contract called a bond indenture, deed of trust, or trust indenture. The **bond indenture** specifies that in return for an investment of cash by investors, the company promises to pay a specific amount of interest (based on a specified, or stated, rate of interest) each period the bonds are outstanding and to repay the **principal** (also called **face value** or **maturity value**) of the bonds at a specified future date (the **bond maturity date**) (see page 470 for definitions). It is the duty of the trustee to protect investors and to make sure that the bond issuer fulfills its responsibilities.

The total value of a single "bond issue" often exceeds several million dollars. A bond issue is generally divided into a number of individual bonds, which may be of varying denominations. The principal, or face value, of each bond is usually $1,000 or a multiple thereof. Note that the price of bonds is quoted as a percentage of $1,000 face value. Thus, a bond quoted at 98 is selling for $980 (98% × $1,000), and a bond quoted at 103 is selling for $1,030 (103% × $1,000). By issuing bonds in small denominations, a company increases the chances that a broad range of investors will be able to compete for the purchase of the bonds. This increased demand usually results in the bonds selling for a higher price.

In most cases, the market price of bonds is influenced by (1) the riskiness of the bonds and (2) the interest rate at which the bonds are issued. The first factor, riskiness of the bonds, is determined by general economic conditions and the financial status of the company selling the bonds, as measured by organizations (**Moody's** or **Standard and Poor's**, for instance) that regularly assign a rating, or a grade, to all corporate bonds.

Companies strive to earn as high a bond rating as possible because the higher the rating, the lower the interest rate they will have to pay to attract buyers. For example, using the widely cited Moody's bond rating, an Aaa bond is a bond of the highest quality with the least risk of nonpayment. As of May 2006, bonds with this rating were paying interest of approximately 5.9%. A high-risk bond, on the other hand, will have a low rating, which means the company will have to offer a higher rate of interest to attract buyers. For example, as of March 2006, the bonds of financially troubled **General Motors** were rated B by Moody's, a rating indicating that the bonds were "highly speculative."

Determining a Bond's Issuance Price

When a company issues bonds, it is generally promising to make two types of payments: (1) a payment of interest of a fixed amount at equal intervals (usually semiannually but sometimes quarterly or annually) over the life of the bond and (2) a single payment—the principal, or face value, of the bond—at the maturity date. For example,

F Y I

Another type of bond that has arisen in recent years is the "Yankee bond." A Yankee bond is a bond issued by a non-U.S. company with all bond-related payments made in U.S. dollars. Non-U.S. companies sometimes choose to pay principal and interest on bonds in U.S. dollars because U.S. dollar amounts are associated with less risk of currency exchange fluctuations than are payments in less stable currencies such as the Indonesian rupiah. Lower risk means that the company can pay a lower interest rate to lenders.

bond indenture

A contract between a bond issuer and a bond purchaser that specifies the terms of a bond.

assume that Denver Company issues 10%, five-year bonds with a total face value of $800,000. Interest is to be paid semiannually. This information tells us that Denver Company agrees to pay $40,000 ($800,000 × 0.10 × ½ year) in interest every six months and also agrees to pay to the investors the principal amount of $800,000 at the end of five years. The following diagram reflects this agreement between Denver Company and the bond investors:

principal (face value or maturity value)

The amount that will be paid on a bond at the maturity date.

bond maturity date

The date at which a bond principal or face amount becomes payable.

In this example, we assumed that the bonds were issued at their face value of $800,000. However, bonds are frequently issued at a price that is more or less than their face value. The actual price at which bonds are issued is affected by the interest rate investors are seeking at the time the bonds are sold in relation to the interest rate specified by the borrower in the bond indenture. How, then, is the issuance price of bonds determined?

Essentially, present value concepts are used to measure the effect of time on the value of money. The price should equal the present value of the interest payments (an annuity) plus the present value of the bond's face value at maturity. These present values are computed using the **market rate of interest** (also called the **effective rate** or **yield rate**), which is the rate investors expect to earn on their investment. It is contrasted with the **stated rate of interest**, which is the rate printed on the bond (10% in the Denver Company example).

 FYI

Bonds are bought and sold on trading markets just like stocks. The New York Bond Exchange is the largest exchange of this type.

If the effective rate is equal to the stated rate, the bonds will sell at face value (that is, at $800,000). If the effective rate is higher than the stated rate, the bonds will sell at a **bond discount** (at less than the face value) because the investors desire a higher rate than the company is promising to pay. Likewise, if the effective rate is lower than the stated rate, the bonds will sell at a **bond premium** (at more than face value) because the company is promising to pay a higher rate than the market is paying at that time.

 STOP & THINK

If the market rate of interest is higher than the rate of interest stated on the bonds, will the bonds sell at a price higher or lower than the face value? Think about the question this way: Is the higher rate more attractive to investors, and if it is, what would investors do as a result?

Consider the following scenario: If Company A is issuing bonds with a stated rate of 12% and the market rate for similar

market rate (effective rate or yield rate) of interest

The actual interest rate earned or paid on a bond investment.

bonds is 10%, what will happen to the price of Company A's bonds? Investors, eager to receive a 12% return, will bid the price of the bonds up until the price at which the bonds sell yields a 10% return. The amount paid for the bonds over and above the maturity value is the bond premium. If Company A were issuing bonds with a stated rate of 8%, no one would buy the bonds until the price was lowered sufficiently to allow investors to earn a return of 10%. The

stated rate of interest

The rate of interest printed on the bond.

bond discount

The difference between the face value and the sales price when bonds are sold below their face value.

bond premium

The difference between the face value and the sales price when bonds are sold above their face value.

difference between the selling price and the maturity value would be the amount of the bond discount.

We will use the Denver Company bonds example (from page 470) to explain how the price is computed in each situation.

Bonds Issued at Face Value Denver Company has agreed to issue $800,000 bonds and pay 10% interest, compounded semiannually. Assume that the effective interest rate demanded by investors for bonds of this level of risk is also 10%. Using the effective interest rate, which happens to be the same as the stated rate, the calculation to determine the price at which the bonds will be issued is shown below. (Note that because the interest is compounded semiannually, the interest rate is halved and the five-year bond life is treated as 10 six-month periods.)

The calculation shows why the bonds sell at face value. At the effective rate, the sum of the present value of the interest payments and the payment at maturity is $800,000, which is the issuance price at the stated rate. This equality of present values will occur only when the effective rate and the stated rate are the same.

1. Semiannual interest payments	$ 40,000	
Present value of an annuity of		
10 payments of $1 at 5% (Table II)	× 7.7217	
Present value of interest payments		$308,868
2. Maturity value of bonds	$800,000	
Present value of $1 received 10 periods		
in the future discounted at 5% (Table I)	× 0.6139	
Present value of principal amount		491,132*
3. Issuance price of bonds (total present value)		$800,000

*Difference is due to the rounding of the present value factor.

The value of the bonds can also be computed using a business calculator as follows:

Hewlett-Packard Keystrokes:
a. **CLEAR ALL**.
b. Set **P/YR** to 1.

1. 800,000   Press **FV**.
2. 40,000   Press **PMT**.
3. 10   Press **N**.
4. 5   Press **I/YR**.
5. Press **PV** for the answer of $800,000.

Bonds Issued at a Discount Denver Company will sell its bonds at less than the face value of $800,000 (at a discount) if the stated rate of interest is less than the effective rate that investors are seeking. To illustrate the issuance of bonds at a discount, assume that the effective rate is 12% compounded semiannually; the stated rate remains 10% compounded semiannually. In this case, the bonds will be issued at a price of $741,124, as shown here:

1. Semiannual interest payments	$ 40,000	
Present value of an annuity of		
10 payments of $1 at 6% (Table II)	× 7.3601	
Present value of interest payments		$294,404
2. Maturity value of bonds	$800,000	
Present value of $1 received		
10 periods in the future discounted at 6% (Table I)	× 0.5584	
Present value of principal amount		446,720
3. Issuance price of bonds (total present value)		$741,124

CAUTION

The most common mistake made in computing bond values is to use the stated rate of interest in calculating the present value of the cash flows. The stated rate of interest is used *only* to compute the amount of the semiannual interest payments. The present value computations are done using the current market rate (i.e., effective or yield rate) of interest.

Denver Company will receive less than the $800,000 face value because the stated rate of interest is lower than the effective rate. In this case, there is a discount of $58,876 ($800,000 − $741,124).

The following keystrokes are used to compute the value of the bonds using a business calculator:

Hewlett-Packard Keystrokes:
a. **CLEAR ALL**.
b. Set **P/YR** to 1.

1. 800,000   Press **FV**.
2. 40,000   Press **PMT**.
3. 10   Press **N**.
4. 6   Press **I/YR**.
5. Press **PV** for the answer of $741,119.30. This answer differs slightly from the value computed using the tables because of rounding.

Bonds Issued at a Premium   The Denver Company bonds will be issued for more than $800,000 (at a premium) when the stated interest rate is higher than the effective rate. Let us now assume that the effective rate is 8% compounded semiannually and that the stated rate is still 10% compounded semiannually. In this case, the bonds will be issued at $864,916, as shown here:

1. Interest payments	$ 40,000	
Present value of an annuity of		
10 payments of $1 at 4% (Table II)	× 8.1109	
Present value of interest payments		$324,436
2. Maturity value of bonds	$800,000	
Present value of $1 received		
10 periods in the future discounted at 4% (Table I)	× 0.6756	
Present value of principal amount		540,480
3. Issuance price of bonds (total present value)		$864,916

Denver Company will receive more than the $800,000 face value when the bonds are issued because the company has agreed to pay the investors a higher rate of interest than the market rate.

The same calculation can be done using a business calculator as follows:

Hewlett-Packard Keystrokes:
a. **CLEAR ALL.**
b. Set **P/YR** to 1.

1. 800,000   Press **FV.**
2. 40,000   Press **PMT.**
3. 10   Press **N.**
4. 4   Press **I/YR.**
5. Press **PV** for the answer of $864,887.17. This answer differs slightly from the value computed using the tables because of rounding.

In all three situations, the 10% stated rate determined the amount of each interest payment. The price of the bonds was determined by discounting the $40,000 of interest payments and the $800,000 face amount at maturity by the effective rate of interest, which may vary from day to day, depending on market conditions. In essence, the issuance price depends on four factors: (1) face value of the bonds, (2) periodic interest payments (face value × stated interest rate), (3) time period, and (4) effective interest rate. Although the bond price is the exact amount that allows investors to earn the interest rate they are seeking, it also reflects the real cost of money to the borrowing company.

Now that you know how to calculate bond values, you may feel ready to move to New York City and become a Wall Street bond trader. Not so fast. There are four steps to computing bond values, as outlined below.

1. Determine the market interest rate.
2. Compute the present value of the maturity amount (using the market interest rate as the discount rate).
3. Compute the present value of the annuity of annual interest payments (using the market interest rate as the discount rate).
4. Add the quantities computed in (2) and (3).

Three of these steps—2, 3, and 4—are very straightforward. These are the steps that you have learned in this chapter. The initial step of determining the market interest rate is where the art and analysis of bond trading are brought to bear. For example, how can you tell whether a company's riskiness requires that the market interest rate on its bonds should be 7.2% or 7.3%? This is an extremely difficult determination to make, and yet it is exactly the type of decision that bond traders must make many times each day.

Accounting for Bonds Payable Issued at Face Value

When a company issues bonds, it must account for the issuance (sale) of the bonds, for the interest payments, and for the amortization of any bond premium or discount. Then, at or before maturity, the company must account for the bond's retirement.

The accounting for these four elements depends on the issuance price of the bonds and on the date of issuance in relation to the date on which interest is paid. In the following sections, we explain the accounting for bonds when the issue price is equal to face value. The accounting for bonds issued at a premium or at a discount is discussed in the expanded material section of the chapter. For most of this discussion, we will use the following data:

Issuing company	Central Trucking Company
Accounting year	Calendar year ending December 31
Face value of bonds issued	$100,000
Stated interest rate	12%
Effective interest rate when issued	12%
Initial date of issuance	January 1, 2009
Date of maturity	January 1, 2019
Interest payment dates	January 1 and July 1

Central Trucking Company issued $100,000 bonds with a stated interest rate of 12% on January 1, 2009. The bonds were issued at face value because 12% is the effective, or market, rate of interest for similar bonds. The journal entry to record their issuance on January 1, 2009, is as follows:

Cash	100,000	
Bonds Payable		100,000
Issued $100,000, 12%, 10-year bonds at face value.		

The entry to record the first semiannual payment of interest on July 1, 2009, is:

Bond Interest Expense	6,000	
Cash		6,000
Paid semiannual interest on the $100,000, 12%,		
10-year bonds ($100,000 × 0.12 × ½ year).		

Because Central Trucking operates on a calendar-year basis, it will need to make the following adjusting entry on December 31, 2009, to account for the interest expense between July 1 and December 31, 2009:

Bond Interest Expense	6,000	
Bond Interest Payable		6,000
To recognize expense for the six months July 1 to		
December 31, 2009 ($100,000 × 0.12 × ½ year).		

At the end of the accounting period (December 31, 2009), the financial statements will report the following:

Income Statement

Bond interest expense ($6,000 × 2)	$ 12,000

Balance Sheet

Current liabilities:	
Bond interest payable	$ 6,000
Long-term liabilities:	
Bonds payable (12%, due January 1, 2019)	$100,000

On January 1, 2010, when the semiannual interest is paid, the bond interest payable account is eliminated. The January 1 entry is:

Bond Interest Payable	6,000	
Cash		6,000
Paid semiannual bond interest.		

The entries to record the interest expense payments during the remaining nine years will be the same as those made during 2009 and on January 1, 2010. The only other entry required in accounting for these bonds is the recording of their retirement on January 1, 2019. That entry, assuming that all interest has been accounted for, will be:

Bonds Payable	100,000	
Cash		100,000
Retired the $100,000, 10-year, 12% bonds.		

As the preceding entries illustrate, accounting for the issuance of bonds, the payment of the interest, and the retirement of the bonds is relatively simple when the bonds are issued at face value.

Bond Retirements before Maturity

Bond issues are, by definition, an inflexible form of long-term debt. The issuing company has a set schedule of interest payments and a specified maturity date, usually at least 5 or 10 years from the issuance date. In many cases, however, a company may want to pay off (redeem) and retire its bonds before maturity. This situation might occur when interest rates fall—a company uses the money obtained by issuing new bonds at a lower interest rate to retire the older, higher-interest bonds. As a result, the company retains the money it needs for expansion or other long-range projects but pays less interest for using that money.

As noted earlier, callable bonds are issued with an early redemption provision. Although the company usually has to pay a premium (penalty) for the privilege of redeeming (calling) the bonds, the amount of the penalty will probably be less than the amount gained by paying a lower interest rate. With bonds that are not callable, the company simply purchases the bonds in the open market, as available, at the going price.

To illustrate the retirement of bonds before maturity, assume that the Central Trucking Company bonds are now selling in the bond market at 109 and are callable at 110. The company decides to take advantage of the lower interest rate (8%) by issuing new bonds and using the proceeds to pay off the outstanding bonds. Given that the bonds were issued at their face value, the penalty (the call premium) is $10,000. The entry to record the retirement of the bonds at 110 is:

Bonds Payable	100,000	
Loss on Bond Retirement	10,000	
Cash ($100,000 × 1.10)		110,000
To retire $100,000 of bonds at a call price of 110.		

In this case, the bonds were retired at a loss of $10,000. The loss is probably tolerable because the company expects to pay significantly less interest over the life of the new bond issue than it would have had to continue to pay on the old bonds. Gains and losses on the early retirement of bonds are reported on the income statement.

REMEMBER THIS...

- Bonds are certificates of debt issued by companies or government agencies, guaranteeing a stated interest rate and repayment of the principal at a specified maturity date.
- Bonds can be classified by their level of security (debentures versus secured bonds), by the way interest is paid (registered versus coupon bonds), and by the way they mature (term bonds, serial bonds, callable bonds, and convertible bonds).
- The bond's face value, or principal, and future interest payments (face value $\times$ stated interest rate) are discounted by the interest rate desired by investors (the effective yield or market rate) to arrive at the issuance price of the bonds.
- Bonds will sell at their face value if the stated interest rate is equal to the effective rate. If the effective rate is higher than the stated rate, the bonds will sell at a discount. If the effective rate is lower than the stated rate, the bonds will sell at a premium.
- Accounting for bonds involves three steps: (1) accounting for their issuance, (2) accounting for the periodic interest payments, and (3) accounting for their retirement.
- When bonds are retired at maturity, there is no gain or loss because the amount paid is equal to the face value of the bonds. When bonds are retired before maturity, a gain or loss often results because the price paid to retire the bonds can be different from the carrying value of the bonds.

Using Debt-Related Financial Ratios

Use debt-related financial ratios to determine the degree of a company's financial leverage and its ability to repay loans.

⑤ As illustrated earlier in the chapter in Exhibit 2, an important business issue associated with long-term debt is the determination of how a company wishes to obtain the money it needs to buy necessary assets. A company's leverage is the degree to which the company has borrowed the funds needed for asset acquisitions. This section describes the financial ratios that are commonly used to evaluate the level of a company's financial leverage.

Debt Ratio and Debt-to-Equity Ratio

The **debt ratio** measures the amount of assets supplied by lenders. It is calculated as follows:

debt ratio

A measure of leverage, computed by dividing total liabilities by total assets.

$$\text{Debt ratio} = \frac{\text{Total liabilities}}{\text{Total assets}}$$

The computed value of the debt ratio indicates the percentage of a company's funding that has come through borrowing.

The debt ratio for **Disney** for 2005 is calculated as follows (the numbers are in millions):

debt-to-equity ratio

The number of dollars of borrowed funds for every dollar invested by owners; computed as total liabilities divided by total stockholders' equity.

$$\text{Debt ratio} = \frac{\$26,948}{\$53,158} = 50.7\%$$

Thus, 51% of Disney's assets are provided by lenders and 49% by stockholders and company earnings that have been retained.

The **debt-to-equity ratio** also measures the balance of funds being provided by creditors and stockholders. This ratio is calculated by dividing total liabilities by total stockholders' equity. The higher the debt-to-equity ratio, the more debt the company has. The debt-to-equity ratio for Disney is calculated as follows:

$$\text{Debt-to-equity ratio} = \frac{\text{Total liabilities}}{\text{Total stockholders' equity}}$$

$$\text{Debt-to-equity ratio} = \frac{\$26,948}{\$26,210} = 1.03$$

In this case, the debt-to-equity ratio indicates that Disney's debt is about 3% higher than its equity. Note that the debt ratio and the debt-to-equity ratio both indicate the same thing—that Disney has acquired just a little bit more of its total financing from borrowing than from stockholders and retained earnings. It doesn't matter which of these two ratios you use to measure a company's leverage; the important thing is that you are consistent and that any ratios you use for comparison have been computed using the same formula.

Times Interest Earned Ratio

times interest earned

A measure of a borrower's ability to make required interest payments; computed as income before interest and taxes divided by annual interest expense.

Lenders like to have an indication of the borrowing company's ability to meet the required interest payments. **Times interest earned** is the ratio of the income that is available for interest payments to the annual interest expense. Times interest earned is computed as follows:

$$\text{Times interest earned} = \frac{\text{Income before interest and taxes (operating profit)}}{\text{Annual interest expense}}$$

To illustrate the computation of this ratio, we will return to Disney. For year-end 2005, Disney's interest expense was $597 million, and its operating profit was $4,584 million. This results in times interest earned of 7.7 times, computed as follows:

$$\text{Times interest earned} = \frac{\$4,584}{\$597} = 7.7 \text{ times}$$

Disney's times interest earned value of 7.7 times means that its operations in 2005 generated enough profit to be able to pay Disney's interest expense for the year 7.7 times. This suggests that Disney's creditors have a substantial cushion before they need to be concerned about Disney's ability to meet its required periodic interest payments.

REMEMBER THIS...

- Both the debt ratio and the debt-to-equity ratio measure the level of a company's leverage.
    - Debt ratio = Total liabilities divided by total assets
    - Debt-to-equity ratio = Total liabilities divided by total stockholders' equity
- The times interest earned ratio (operating income divided by interest expense) measures how much cushion a company has in terms of being able to make its periodic interest payments.

EXPANDED *material*

The present value techniques discussed in this chapter are useful in determining the value of obligations due at some future time. The computations and accounting are similar for interest-bearing notes, mortgages, capital leases, and bonds. However, there are certain complexities associated with these liabilities that deserve additional attention. In this section of the chapter, we discuss the procedures associated with the amortization of a bond discount or premium.

Amortize bond discounts and bond premiums using either the straight-line method or the effective-interest method.

⑥

Bonds Issued at a Discount or at a Premium

As we have explained, bonds may be issued at a discount or a premium because their stated interest rate may be (and often is) lower or higher than the effective rate. The two rates often differ because economic conditions in the marketplace change between the date the stated interest is set and the date the bonds are actually sold. Various factors determine this second date—for example, the time it takes to print the bonds and the investment banker's decision regarding the best time to offer the bonds. Because the cost to the company for the use of the bond money is really the effective interest rate rather than the stated rate, the discount or premium must be written off (amortized) over the period the bonds are outstanding, and the amortization is treated as an adjustment to bond interest expense.

There are two methods of amortizing bond discounts and bond premiums: straight-line amortization and effective-interest amortization. With **straight-line amortization**, a company writes off the same amount of discount or premium each period the bonds are held. For example, with a $4,000 discount on a 10-year bond, $400 is amortized each year. **Effective-interest amortization** takes the time value of money into consideration. The amount of discount or premium amortized is the difference between the interest actually incurred (based on the effective rate) and the interest actually paid (based on the stated rate). The straight-line amortization method will be used to explain the accounting for the amortization of discounts and premiums; then the effective-interest method will be explained and illustrated.

straight-line amortization

A method of systematically writing off a bond discount or premium in equal amounts each period until maturity.

effective-interest amortization

A method of systematically writing off a bond premium or discount that takes into consideration the time value of money and results in an equal interest rate being used for amortization for each period.

Accounting for Bonds Issued at a Discount

When bonds are issued at a discount, a contra-liability account is used to keep a separate record of the discounted amount. To illustrate, we will assume that the $100,000, 10-year, 12% bonds issued by Central Trucking on January 1, 2009, sold for $98,000. The entry to record the issuance of the bonds is:

Cash	98,000	
Discount on Bonds	2,000	
Bonds Payable		100,000
Issued $100,000, 12%, 10-year bonds at 98.		

The discount on bonds account represents the difference between the face value of the bonds and the issuance price. This discount is accounted for as additional bond interest expense over the life of the bonds. In other words, if the company receives only $98,000 when the bonds are issued and is required to pay $100,000 at maturity, the $2,000 difference is additional interest. The following analysis shows that total interest on the bonds is $122,000, comprised of the periodic interest payments ($120,000) plus the $2,000 discount.

Amount to be paid to bondholders:	
Interest paid each year for 10 years ($100,000 × 0.12 × 10)	$120,000
Face value to be paid at maturity	100,000
Total amount to be paid to bondholders	$220,000
Proceeds received from sale of bonds ($100,000 × 0.98)	98,000
Total interest expense	$122,000
Average annual interest expense ($122,000/10 years)	$ 12,200

Although the $2,000 of additional interest arising from the discount will not be paid until the bonds mature, interest accrues, or accumulates, over time. Thus, each year that the bonds are outstanding, Central Trucking will record bond interest expense for the amount paid at the stated rate ($100,000 × 0.12 = $12,000) and will also recognize a portion of the discount as bond interest expense. In recording the additional bond interest expense, the contra account Discount on Bonds is amortized or written off over the life of the bonds. Using straight-line amortization, an even amount is amortized each period. In the Central Trucking Company example, the semiannual amortization would be $100 ($2,000 discount/10 years × ½). Bond amortization is recorded when interest payments are made, and the entry on July 1, 2009, is:

Bond Interest Expense	6,100	
Discount on Bonds		100
Cash		6,000
Paid semiannual interest on the $100,000, 12%, 10-year bonds ($100,000 × 0.12 × ½ year) and amortized the bond discount ($2,000/10 years × ½ year).		

As illustrated, amortization of a discount increases bond interest expense. In this case, the bond interest expense is $6,100, or the sum of the semiannual interest payment and the semiannual amortization of the bond discount. Over the 10-year life of the bonds, the bond interest expense will be increased by $2,000 (20 periods × $100), the amount of the discount. Thus, these bonds pay an effective interest rate of approximately 12.45%[3] per year ($12,200 interest/$98,000 received on the bonds).

The adjusting entry to record the bond interest expense on December 31, 2009, is:

Bond Interest Expense	6,100	
Discount on Bonds		100
Bond Interest Payable		6,000
To recognize bond interest expense for the six months July 1 to December 31, 2009.		

The financial statements prepared at December 31, 2009, would report the following:

Income Statement

Bond interest expense ($6,100 × 2)	$12,200

Balance Sheet

Current liabilities:		
Bond interest payable		$ 6,000
Long-term liabilities:		
Bonds payable (12%, due January 1, 2019)	$100,000	
Less unamortized discount ($2,000 − $200)	1,800	$98,200

The entries to account for the bond interest expense and bond discount amortization during the remaining nine years will be the same as those illustrated. And because the bond discount will be completely amortized at the end of the 10 years, the entry to record

---

[3] Because straight-line amortization was used, this effective rate of 12.45% is only an approximation that will change slightly each period. An accurate effective rate can be calculated only if the effective-interest method of amortization is used.

the retirement of the bonds will be the same as that for bonds issued at face value. That entry is:

Bonds Payable	100,000	
Cash		100,000
Retired the $100,000, 12%, 10-year bonds.		

Accounting for Bonds Issued at a Premium

Like discounts, premiums must be amortized over the life of the bonds. To illustrate the accounting for bonds sold at a premium, we will assume that Central Trucking was able to sell its $100,000, 12%, 10-year bonds at 103 (that is, at 103% of face value). The entry to record the issuance of these bonds on January 1, 2009, is:

Buying

Cash	103,000	
Premium on Bonds		3,000
Bonds Payable		100,000
Sold $100,000, 12%, 10-year bonds at 103.		

Premium on Bonds is added to Bonds Payable on the balance sheet and, like Discount on Bonds, is amortized using either the straight-line method or the effective-interest method. Thus, if Central Trucking uses the straight-line method, the annual amortization of the premium will be $300 ($3,000/10 years), or $150 every six months. The entry to record the first semiannual interest payment and the premium amortization of July 1, 2009, is:

Interest (paying)

Bond Interest Expense	5,850	
Premium on Bonds	150	
Cash		6,000
Paid semiannual interest on the $100,000, 12%, 10-year bonds		
($100,000 × 0.12 × ½ year) and amortized the bond premium		
($3,000/10 years × ½).		

The amortization of a premium on bonds reduces the actual bond interest expense. The following analysis shows why bond interest expense is reduced when bonds are sold at a premium:

Amount to be paid to bondholders:	
[($12,000 interest × 10 years) + $100,000 face value]	$220,000
Proceeds received from sale of bonds	103,000
Total interest to be paid	$117,000
Average annual interest expense ($117,000/10 years)	$ 11,700

CAUTION

If bonds issued at a premium or discount are retired before maturity, remember that the bond payable and any associated premium or discount would have to be eliminated from the books.

In this case, the annual payments of $12,000 include interest of $11,700 and $300, which represents a partial repayment (one-tenth) of the bond premium. Thus, the effective interest rate is approximately 11.36% ($11,700/$103,000), which is less than the stated rate of 12%.

The adjusting entry to record the accrual of the interest expense on December 31, 2009, is:

Bond Interest Expense	5,850	
Premium on Bonds	150	
Bond Interest Payable		6,000
To recognize bond interest expense for the six months *July 1 to December 31, 2009.*		

The financial statements prepared at December 31, 2009, would report the following:

Income Statement

Bond interest expense ($5,850 × 2)	$ 11,700

Balance Sheet

Current liabilities:		
Bond interest payable		$ 6,000
Long-term liabilities:		
Bonds payable (12%, due January 1, 2019)	$100,000	
Plus unamortized premium ($3,000 – $300)	2,700	$102,700

Effective-Interest Amortization

Companies can often justify use of the straight-line method of amortizing bond premiums and discounts on the grounds that its results are not significantly different from those of the theoretically more accurate effective-interest method. Nevertheless, because the effective-interest method considers the time value of money, it is required by generally accepted accounting principles if it leads to results that differ significantly from those obtained by the straight-line method.

The effective-interest method amortizes a varying amount each period, which is the difference between the interest actually incurred and the cash actually paid. The amount actually incurred is the changing **bond carrying value** (the face value of the bond minus the unamortized discount or plus the unamortized premium) multiplied by a constant rate, the effective-interest rate.

To illustrate the effective-interest method, let's continue with the Central Trucking Company example we have used previously. We will assume that the Central Trucking Company $100,000, 12%, 10-year bonds were issued on January 1, 2009, for $112,463. The bonds pay interest semiannually on January 1 and July 1, so their effective interest rate is approximately 10%[4] a year, or 5% every six months. Because the actual bond interest expense for each interest period is equal to the effective rate of 5% multiplied by the bond carrying value, the amortization (rounded to the nearest $1) for the 10 years is calculated as shown in the following table.

bond carrying value

The face value of bonds minus the unamortized discount or plus the unamortized premium.

Note that the table on the next page looks a lot like the mortgage amortization schedule on page 464 and the schedule of computer lease payments on page 466. The reason is that these other schedules also use the effective-interest amortization method.

---

[4] The 10% rate is the rate that will discount the face value of the bonds and the semiannual interest payments to a present value that equals the issuance price of the bonds, computed as follows:

Present value of $100,000 at 5% for 20 periods	$100,000 × 0.3769 = $ 37,690
Present value of $6,000 at 5% for 20 payments	$ 6,000 × 12.4622 = 74,773
Total present value = issuance price of the bonds	$112,463

Period	1 Cash Paid for Interest	2 Semiannual Interest Expense (0.05 × Bond Carrying Value)	3 Premium Amortization (1) − (2)	4 Carrying Value
Issuance date				$112,463
Year 1, first six months	$6,000	$5,623	$377	112,086
Year 1, second six months	6,000	5,604	396	111,690
Year 2, first six months	6,000	5,585	415	111,275
Year 2, second six months	6,000	5,564	436	110,839
Year 3, first six months	6,000	5,542	458	110,381
Year 3, second six months	6,000	5,519	481	109,900
Year 4, first six months	6,000	5,495	505	109,395
Year 4, second six months	6,000	5,470	530	108,865
Year 5, first six months	6,000	5,443	557	108,308
Year 5, second six months	6,000	5,415	585	107,723
Year 6, first six months	6,000	5,386	614	107,109
Year 6, second six months	6,000	5,355	645	106,464
Year 7, first six months	6,000	5,323	677	105,787
Year 7, second six months	6,000	5,289	711	105,076
Year 8, first six months	6,000	5,254	746	104,330
Year 8, second six months	6,000	5,217	783	103,547
Year 9, first six months	6,000	5,177	823	102,724
Year 9, second six months	6,000	5,136	864	101,860
Year 10, first six months	6,000	5,093	907	100,953
Year 10, second six months	6,000	5,047	953	100,000

In this computation, the $6,000 in column (1) is the actual cash paid each six months. Column (2) shows the interest expense for each six months, which is the amount that will be reported on the income statement. Column (3), which is the difference between columns (1) and (2), represents the amortization of the premium. Column (4) shows the carrying, or book, value of the bonds (that is, the total of the bonds payable and the unamortized bond premium), which is the amount that will be reported on the balance sheet each period. Using the effective-interest method, the bond carrying value is always equal to the present value of the bond obligation. As the carrying value decreases, while the effective rate of interest remains constant, the interest expense also decreases from one period to the next, as illustrated in column (2) of the amortization schedule.

To help you translate this table into the entries for the interest payments and premium amortization at the end of each six-month period, we have provided the semiannual journal entries for year 3.

Year 3, End of First Six Months

Bond Interest Expense	5,542	
Bond Premium	458	
Cash		6,000

To record effective-interest expense on Central Trucking Company bonds for the first six months of year 3.

Year 3, End of Second Six Months

Bond Interest Expense	5,519	
Bond Premium	481	
Bond Interest Payable		6,000

To record effective-interest expense on Central Trucking Company bonds for the second six months of year 3.

Because the straight-line method would show a constant amortization ($12,463/20 = $623.15 per six-month period) on a decreasing bond balance, the straight-line interest rate cannot be constant. When the straight-line results differ significantly from the effective-interest results, generally accepted accounting principles require use of the effective-interest method.

The effective-interest method of amortizing a bond discount is essentially the same as amortizing a bond premium. The main difference is that the bond carrying value is increasing instead of decreasing.

REMEMBER THIS...

- When bonds are issued at a premium or a discount, the premium or discount must be amortized over the life of the bond.

- When a bond premium or discount exists, bond interest expense recognized on the income statement is not equal to the amount of cash paid for interest.

- Two methods of amortization are available—the straight-line method and the effective-interest method.

- The straight-line method amortizes an equal amount of premium or discount every period.

- When the effective-interest method is used, the amount of discount or premium amortized each period is equal to the market rate of interest multiplied by the bond's carrying value.

TABLE I   The Present Value of $1 Due in *n* Periods*

Period	1%	2%	3%	4%	5%	6%	7%	8%	9%	10%	12%	14%	15%	16%	18%	20%
1	.9901	.9804	.9709	.9615	.9524	.9434	.9346	.9259	.9174	.9091	.8929	.8772	.8696	.8621	.8475	.8333
2	.9803	.9612	.9426	.9246	.9070	.8900	.8734	.8573	.8417	.8264	.7972	.7695	.7561	.7432	.7182	.6944
3	.9706	.9423	.9151	.8890	.8638	.8396	.8163	.7938	.7722	.7513	.7118	.6750	.6575	.6407	.6086	.5787
4	.9610	.9238	.8885	.8548	.8227	.7921	.7629	.7350	.7084	.6830	.6355	.5921	.5718	.5523	.5158	.4823
5	.9515	.9057	.8626	.8219	.7835	.7473	.7130	.6806	.6499	.6209	.5674	.5194	.4972	.4761	.4371	.4019
6	.9420	.8880	.8375	.7903	.7462	.7050	.6663	.6302	.5963	.5645	.5066	.4556	.4323	.4104	.3704	.3349
7	.9327	.8706	.8131	.7599	.7107	.6651	.6227	.5835	.5470	.5132	.4523	.3996	.3759	.3538	.3139	.2791
8	.9235	.8535	.7894	.7307	.6768	.6274	.5820	.5403	.5019	.4665	.4039	.3506	.3269	.3050	.2660	.2326
9	.9143	.8368	.7664	.7026	.6446	.5919	.5439	.5002	.4604	.4241	.3606	.3075	.2843	.2630	.2255	.1938
10	.9053	.8203	.7441	.6756	.6139	.5584	.5083	.4632	.4224	.3855	.3220	.2697	.2472	.2267	.1911	.1615
11	.8963	.8043	.7224	.6496	.5847	.5268	.4751	.4289	.3875	.3503	.2875	.2366	.2149	.1954	.1619	.1346
12	.8874	.7885	.7014	.6246	.5568	.4970	.4440	.3971	.3555	.3186	.2567	.2076	.1869	.1685	.1372	.1122
13	.8787	.7730	.6810	.6006	.5303	.4688	.4150	.3677	.3262	.2897	.2292	.1821	.1625	.1452	.1163	.0935
14	.8700	.7579	.6611	.5775	.5051	.4423	.3878	.3405	.2992	.2633	.2046	.1597	.1413	.1252	.0985	.0779
15	.8613	.7430	.6419	.5553	.4810	.4173	.3624	.3152	.2745	.2394	.1827	.1401	.1229	.1079	.0835	.0649
16	.8528	.7284	.6232	.5339	.4581	.3936	.3387	.2919	.2519	.2176	.1631	.1229	.1069	.0930	.0708	.0541
17	.8444	.7142	.6050	.5134	.4363	.3714	.3166	.2703	.2311	.1978	.1456	.1078	.0929	.0802	.0600	.0451
18	.8360	.7002	.5874	.4936	.4155	.3503	.2959	.2502	.2120	.1799	.1300	.0946	.0808	.0691	.0508	.0376
19	.8277	.6864	.5703	.4746	.3957	.3305	.2765	.2317	.1945	.1635	.1161	.0829	.0703	.0596	.0431	.0313
20	.8195	.6730	.5537	.4564	.3769	.3118	.2584	.2145	.1784	.1486	.1037	.0728	.0611	.0514	.0365	.0261
25	.7798	.6095	.4776	.3751	.2953	.2330	.1842	.1460	.1160	.0923	.0588	.0378	.0304	.0245	.0160	.0105
30	.7419	.5521	.4120	.3083	.2314	.1741	.1314	.0994	.0754	.0573	.0334	.0196	.0151	.0116	.0070	.0042
40	.6717	.4529	.3066	.2083	.1420	.0972	.0668	.0460	.0318	.0221	.0107	.0053	.0037	.0026	.0013	.0007
50	.6080	.3715	.2281	.1407	.0872	.0543	.0339	.0213	.0134	.0085	.0035	.0014	.0009	.0006	.0003	.0001
60	.5504	.3048	.1697	.0951	.0535	.0303	.0173	.0099	.0057	.0033	.0011	.0004	.0002	.0001	†	†

*The formula used to derive the values in this table was PV = F $\frac{1}{(1 + i)^n}$ where PV = present value, F = future amount to be discounted, *i* = interest rate, and *n* = number of periods.

†The value of 0 to four decimal places.

TABLE II The Present Value of an Annuity of $1 per Number of Payments*

Number of Payments	1%	2%	3%	4%	5%	6%	7%	8%	9%	10%	12%	14%	15%	16%	18%	20%
1	0.9901	0.9804	0.9709	0.9615	0.9524	0.9434	0.9346	0.9259	0.9174	0.9091	0.8929	0.8772	0.8596	0.8621	0.8475	0.8333
2	1.9704	1.9416	1.9135	1.8861	1.8594	1.8334	1.8080	1.7833	1.7591	1.7355	1.6901	1.6467	1.6257	1.6052	1.5656	1.5278
3	2.9410	2.8839	2.8286	2.7751	2.7232	2.6730	2.6243	2.5771	2.5313	2.4869	2.4018	2.3216	2.2832	2.2459	2.1743	2.1065
4	3.9820	3.8077	3.7171	3.6299	3.5460	3.4651	3.3872	3.3121	3.2397	3.1699	3.0373	2.9137	2.8550	2.7982	2.6901	2.5887
5	4.8884	4.7135	4.5797	4.4518	4.3295	4.2124	4.1002	3.9927	3.8897	3.7908	3.6048	3.4331	3.3522	3.2743	3.1272	2.9906
6	5.7985	5.6014	5.4172	5.2421	5.0757	4.9173	4.7665	4.6229	4.4859	4.3553	4.1114	3.8887	3.7845	3.6847	3.4976	3.3255
7	6.7282	6.4720	6.2303	6.0021	5.7864	5.5824	5.3893	5.2064	5.0330	4.8684	4.5638	4.2883	4.1604	4.0386	3.8115	3.6046
8	7.6517	7.3255	7.0197	6.7327	6.4632	6.2098	5.9713	5.7466	5.5348	5.3349	4.9676	4.6389	4.4873	4.3436	4.0776	3.8372
9	8.5660	8.1622	7.7861	7.4353	7.1078	6.8017	6.5152	6.2469	5.9952	5.7590	5.3282	4.9464	4.7716	4.6065	4.3030	4.0310
10	9.4713	8.9826	8.5302	8.1109	7.7217	7.3601	7.0236	6.7101	6.4177	6.1446	5.6502	5.2161	5.0188	4.8332	4.4941	4.1925
11	10.3676	9.7868	9.2526	8.7605	8.3064	7.8869	7.4987	7.1390	6.8052	6.4951	5.9377	5.4527	5.2337	5.0286	4.6560	4.3271
12	11.2551	10.5733	9.9540	9.3851	8.8633	8.3838	7.9427	7.5361	7.1607	6.8137	6.1944	5.6603	5.4206	5.1971	4.7932	4.4392
13	12.1337	11.3484	10.6350	9.9856	9.3936	8.8527	8.3577	7.9038	7.4869	7.1034	6.4235	5.8424	5.5831	5.3423	4.9095	4.5327
14	13.0037	12.1062	11.2961	10.5631	9.8986	9.2950	8.7455	8.2442	7.7862	7.3667	6.6282	6.0021	5.7245	5.4675	5.0081	4.6106
15	13.8651	12.8493	11.9379	11.1184	10.3797	9.7122	9.1079	8.5595	8.0607	7.6061	6.8109	6.1422	5.8474	5.5755	5.0916	4.6755
16	14.7179	13.5777	12.5611	11.6523	10.8378	10.1059	9.4466	8.8514	8.3126	7.8237	6.9740	6.2651	5.9542	5.6685	5.1624	4.7296
17	15.5623	14.2919	13.1661	12.1657	11.2741	10.4773	9.7632	9.1216	8.5436	8.0216	7.1196	6.3729	6.0472	5.7487	5.2223	4.7746
18	16.3983	14.9920	13.7535	12.6593	11.6896	10.8276	10.0591	9.3719	8.7556	8.2014	7.2497	6.4674	6.1280	5.8178	5.2732	4.8122
19	17.2260	15.6785	14.3238	13.1339	12.0853	11.1581	10.3356	9.6036	8.9501	8.3649	7.3658	6.5504	6.1982	5.8775	5.3162	4.8435
20	18.0456	16.3514	14.8775	13.5903	12.4622	11.4699	10.5940	9.8181	9.1285	8.5136	7.4694	6.6231	6.2593	5.9288	5.3527	4.8696
25	22.0232	19.5235	17.4131	15.6221	14.0939	12.7834	11.6536	10.6748	9.8226	9.0770	7.8431	6.8729	6.4641	6.0971	5.4669	4.9476
30	25.8077	22.3965	19.6004	17.2920	15.3725	13.7648	12.4090	11.2578	10.2737	9.4269	8.0552	7.0027	6.5660	6.1772	5.5168	4.9789
40	32.8347	27.3555	23.1148	19.7928	17.1591	15.0463	13.3317	11.9246	10.7574	9.7791	8.2438	7.1050	6.6418	6.2335	5.5482	4.9966
50	39.1961	31.4236	25.7298	21.4822	18.2559	15.7619	13.8007	12.2335	10.9617	9.9148	8.3045	7.1327	6.6605	6.2463	5.5641	4.9995
60	44.9550	34.7609	27.6756	22.6235	18.9293	16.1614	14.0392	12.3766	11.0480	9.9672	8.3240	7.1401	6.6651	6.2482	5.5553	4.9999

*The formula used to derive the values in this table was $PV = F\left(\dfrac{1 - \dfrac{1}{(1 + i)^n}}{i}\right)$ where PV = present value, F = periodic payment to be discounted, i = interest rate, and n = number of payments.

TABLE III Amount of $1 Due in *n* Periods

Period	1%	2%	3%	4%	5%	6%	7%	8%	9%	10%	12%	14%	15%	16%	18%	20%
1	1.0100	1.0200	1.0300	1.0400	1.0500	1.0600	1.0700	1.0800	1.0900	1.1000	1.1200	1.1400	1.1500	1.1600	1.1800	1.2000
2	1.0201	1.0404	1.0609	1.0816	1.1025	1.1236	1.1449	1.1664	1.1881	1.2100	1.2544	1.2996	1.3225	1.3456	1.3924	1.4400
3	1.0303	1.0612	1.0927	1.1249	1.1576	1.1910	1.2250	1.2597	1.2950	1.3310	1.4049	1.4815	1.5209	1.5609	1.6430	1.7280
4	1.0406	1.0824	1.1255	1.1699	1.2155	1.2625	1.3108	1.3605	1.4116	1.4641	1.5735	1.6890	1.7490	1.8106	1.9388	2.0736
5	1.0510	1.1041	1.1593	1.2167	1.2763	1.3382	1.4026	1.4693	1.5386	1.6105	1.7623	1.9254	2.0114	2.1003	2.2878	2.4883
6	1.0615	1.1262	1.1941	1.2653	1.3401	1.4185	1.5007	1.5869	1.6771	1.7716	1.9738	2.1950	2.3131	2.4364	2.6996	2.9860
7	1.0721	1.1487	1.2299	1.3159	1.4071	1.5036	1.6058	1.7138	1.8280	1.9487	2.2107	2.5023	2.6600	2.8262	3.1855	3.5832
8	1.0829	1.1717	1.2668	1.3686	1.4775	1.5938	1.7182	1.8509	1.9926	2.1436	2.4760	2.8526	3.0590	3.2784	3.7589	4.2998
9	1.0937	1.1951	1.3048	1.4233	1.5513	1.6895	1.8385	1.9990	2.1719	2.3579	2.7731	3.2519	3.5179	3.8030	4.4355	5.1598
10	1.1046	1.2190	1.3439	1.4802	1.6289	1.7908	1.9672	2.1589	2.3674	2.5937	3.1058	3.7072	4.0456	4.4114	5.2338	6.1917
11	1.1157	1.2434	1.3842	1.5395	1.7103	1.8983	2.1049	2.3316	2.5804	2.8531	3.4785	4.2262	4.6524	5.1173	6.1759	7.4031
12	1.1268	1.2682	1.4258	1.6010	1.7959	2.0122	2.2522	2.5182	2.8127	3.1384	3.8960	4.8179	5.3502	5.9360	7.2876	8.9161
13	1.1381	1.2936	1.4685	1.6651	1.8856	2.1329	2.4098	2.7196	3.0658	3.4523	4.3635	5.4924	6.1528	6.8858	8.5994	10.699
14	1.1495	1.3195	1.5126	1.7317	1.9799	2.2609	2.5785	2.9372	3.3417	3.7975	4.8871	6.2613	7.0757	7.9875	10.147	12.839
15	1.1610	1.3459	1.5580	1.8009	2.0789	2.3966	2.7590	3.1722	3.6425	4.1772	5.4736	7.1379	8.1371	9.2655	11.973	15.407
16	1.1726	1.3728	1.6047	1.8730	2.1829	2.5404	2.9522	3.4259	3.9703	4.5950	6.1304	8.1372	9.3576	10.748	14.129	18.488
17	1.1843	1.4002	1.6528	1.9479	2.2920	2.6928	3.1588	3.7000	4.3276	5.0545	6.8660	9.2765	10.761	12.467	16.672	22.186
18	1.1961	1.4282	1.7024	2.0258	2.4066	2.8543	3.3799	3.9960	4.7171	5.5599	7.6900	10.575	12.375	14.462	19.673	26.623
19	1.2081	1.4568	1.7535	2.1068	2.5270	3.0256	3.6165	4.3157	5.1417	6.1159	8.6128	12.055	14.231	16.776	23.214	31.948
20	1.2202	1.4859	1.8061	2.1911	2.6533	3.2071	3.8697	4.6610	5.6044	6.7275	9.6463	13.743	16.366	19.460	27.393	38.337
30	1.3478	1.8114	2.4273	3.2434	4.3219	5.7435	7.6123	10.062	13.267	17.449	29.959	50.950	66.211	85.849	143.37	237.37
40	1.4889	2.2080	3.2620	4.8010	7.0400	10.285	14.974	21.724	31.409	45.259	93.050	188.88	267.86	378.72	750.37	1469.7
50	1.6446	2.6916	4.3839	7.1067	11.467	18.420	29.457	46.901	74.357	117.39	289.00	700.23	1083.6	1670.7	3927.3	9100.4
60	1.8167	3.2810	5.8916	10.519	18.679	32.987	57.946	101.25	176.03	304.48	897.59	2595.9	4383.9	7370.1	20555.	56347.

TABLE IV	Amount of an Annuity of $1 per Number of Payments															

Number of Payments	1%	2%	3%	4%	5%	6%	7%	8%	9%	10%	12%	14%	15%	16%	18%	20%
1	1.0000	1.0000	1.0000	1.0000	1.0000	1.0000	1.0000	1.0000	1.0000	1.0000	1.0000	1.0000	1.0000	1.0000	1.0000	1.0000
2	2.0100	2.0200	2.0300	2.0400	2.0500	2.0600	2.0700	2.0800	2.0900	2.1000	2.1200	2.1400	2.1500	2.1600	2.1800	2.2000
3	3.0301	3.0604	3.0909	3.1216	3.1525	3.1836	3.2149	3.2464	3.2781	3.3100	3.3744	3.4396	3.4725	3.5056	3.5724	3.6400
4	4.0604	4.1216	4.1836	4.2465	4.3101	4.3746	4.4399	4.5061	4.5731	4.6410	4.7793	4.9211	4.9934	5.0665	5.2154	5.3680
5	5.1010	5.2040	5.3091	5.4163	5.5256	5.6371	5.7507	5.8666	5.9847	6.1051	6.3528	6.6101	6.7424	6.8771	7.1542	7.4416
6	6.1520	6.3081	6.4684	6.6330	6.8019	6.9753	7.1533	7.3359	7.5233	7.7156	8.1152	8.5355	8.7537	8.9775	9.4420	9.9299
7	7.2135	7.4343	7.6625	7.8983	8.1420	8.3938	8.6540	8.9228	9.2004	9.4872	10.0890	10.7305	11.0668	11.4139	12.1415	12.9159
8	8.2857	8.5830	8.8923	9.2142	9.5491	9.8975	10.2598	10.6366	11.0285	11.4359	12.2997	13.2328	13.7268	14.2401	15.3270	16.4991
9	9.3685	9.7546	10.1591	10.5828	11.0266	11.4913	11.9780	12.4876	13.0210	13.5795	14.7757	16.0853	16.7858	17.5185	19.0859	20.7989
10	10.4622	10.9497	11.4639	12.0061	12.5779	13.1808	13.8164	14.4866	15.1929	15.9374	17.5487	19.3373	20.3037	21.3215	23.5213	25.9587
11	11.5668	12.1687	12.8078	13.4864	14.2068	14.9716	15.7836	16.6455	17.5603	18.5312	20.6546	23.0445	24.3493	25.7329	28.7551	32.1504
12	12.6825	13.4121	14.1920	15.0258	15.9171	16.8699	17.8885	18.9771	20.1407	21.2843	24.1331	27.2707	29.0017	30.8502	34.9311	39.5805
13	13.8093	14.6803	15.6178	16.6268	17.7130	18.8821	20.1406	21.4953	22.9534	24.5227	28.0291	32.0887	34.3519	36.7862	42.2187	48.4966
14	14.9474	15.9739	17.0863	18.2919	19.5986	21.0151	22.5505	24.2149	26.0192	27.9750	32.3926	37.5811	40.5047	43.6720	50.8180	59.1959
15	16.0969	17.2934	18.5989	20.0236	21.5786	23.2760	25.1290	27.1521	29.3609	31.7725	37.2797	43.8424	47.5804	51.6595	60.9653	72.0351
16	17.2579	18.6393	20.1569	21.8248	23.6575	25.6725	27.8881	30.3243	33.0034	35.9497	42.7535	50.9804	55.7178	60.9250	72.9390	87.4421
17	18.4304	20.0121	21.7616	23.6975	25.8404	28.2129	30.8402	33.7502	36.9737	40.5447	48.8837	59.1176	65.0751	71.6730	87.0680	105.9306
18	19.6147	21.4123	23.4144	25.6454	28.1324	30.9057	33.9990	37.4502	41.3013	45.5992	55.7497	68.3941	75.8364	84.1407	103.7403	128.1167
19	20.8190	22.8406	25.1169	27.6712	30.5390	33.7600	37.3790	41.4463	46.0185	51.1591	63.4397	78.9692	88.2118	98.6032	123.4135	154.7400
20	22.0190	24.2974	26.8704	29.7781	33.0660	36.7856	40.9955	45.7620	51.1601	57.2750	72.0524	91.0249	102.4436	115.3797	146.6280	186.6880
30	34.7849	40.5681	47.5754	56.0849	66.4388	79.0582	94.4608	113.2832	136.3075	164.4940	241.3327	356.7868	434.7451	530.3117	790.9480	1181.8816
40	48.8864	60.4020	75.4013	95.0255	120.7998	154.7620	199.6351	259.0565	337.8824	442.5926	767.0914	1342.0251	1779.0903	2360.7572	4163.2130	7343.8578
50	64.4632	84.5794	112.7969	152.6671	209.3480	290.3359	406.5289	573.7702	815.0836	1163.9085	2400.0182	4994.5213	7217.7163	10435.6488	21813.0937	45497.1908
60	81.6697	114.0515	163.0534	237.9907	353.5837	533.1282	813.5204	1253.2133	1944.7921	3034.8164	7471.6411	18535.1333	29919.9916	46057.5085	114189.6665	281732.5718

REVIEW OF LEARNING OBJECTIVES

(1) Use present value concepts to measure long-term liabilities.

- Long-term liabilities are recorded at their present value.
- Terms associated with the time value of money include the following:
  - Present value—amount of money right now to which a future lump sum or annuity is economically equivalent.
  - Future value—amount to which a lump sum or annuity will accumulate in the future.
  - Annuity—a series of equal payments to be made or received in the future.
  - Lump sum—one payment to be made or received in the future.
  - Compounding—adding interest to the principal amount so that subsequent interest is computed on the original principal plus accumulated interest.

(2) Account for long-term liabilities, including notes payable and mortgages payable.

- Interest-bearing notes are recorded on the books of the issuer at face value.
  - Interest expense is incurred based on the rate of interest, the carrying value of the note, and the passage of time.
  - Interest Expense is debited for the amount of interest incurred and Cash or Interest Payable is credited.
- Mortgage liabilities are paid by a series of regular payments that include interest expense and a reduction of the principal of the mortgage note.
  - The balance sheet liability at any given time is the present value of the remaining mortgage payments.

(3) Account for capital lease obligations and understand the significance of operating leases being excluded from the balance sheet.

- A lease is a contract whereby the lessee makes periodic payments to the lessor for the use of an asset.

Operating Lease	Capital Lease
Accounted for as a rental agreement	Accounted for as a debt-financed purchase of an asset.
Leased asset: Not on the balance sheet	Leased asset: Initially recorded at the present value of the future lease payments, subsequently depreciated.
Lease liability: Not on the balance sheet	Lease liability: Initially recorded at the present value of the future lease payments, subsequently recorded as being repaid, with interest.

(4) Account for bonds, including the original issuance, the payment of interest, and the retirement of bonds.

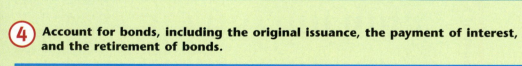

Accounting for bond issuance	• If bonds are sold at face value, Cash is debited and Bonds Payable is credited.
	• If bonds are sold at a discount, the discount is debited and subtracted from Bonds Payable on the balance sheet.
	• If bonds are sold at a premium, the premium is credited and added to Bonds Payable on the balance sheet.

(continued)

Accounting for bond interest payments	• When interest is paid, Bond Interest Expense is debited and Cash is credited.
	• An adjustment is made to bond interest expense if the bond is sold at a premium or discount.
Accounting for bond retirement	• At the date a bond matures, the borrowing company pays the face value to the investors, and the bonds are canceled.
	• If the bonds are retired before maturity, a gain or loss will be recognized when the carrying value of the bonds differs from the amount paid to retire the bonds.

⑤ Use debt-related financial ratios to determine the degree of a company's financial leverage and its ability to repay loans.

• Both the debt ratio and the debt-to-equity ratio measure the level of a company's leverage.
  • Debt ratio = Total liabilities divided by total assets
  • Debt-to-equity ratio = Total liabilities divided by total stockholders' equity
• The times interest earned ratio (operating income divided by interest expense) measures how much cushion a company has in terms of being able to make its periodic interest payments.

⑥ Amortize bond discounts and bond premiums using either the straight-line method or the effective-interest method.

• When bonds are issued at a premium or a discount, the premium or discount must be amortized over the life of the bond.
• When a bond premium or discount exists, bond interest expense recognized on the income statement is not equal to the amount of cash paid for interest.
• The straight-line method amortizes an equal amount of premium or discount every period.
• When the effective-interest method is used, the amount of discount or premium amortized each period is equal to the market rate of interest multiplied by the bond's carrying value.

KEY TERMS & CONCEPTS

annuity, 459
bond, 468
bond discount, 471
bond indenture, 470
bond maturity date, 470
bond premium, 471
callable bonds, 469
compounding
  period, 458
convertible bonds, 469
coupon bonds, 468

debentures (unsecured
  bonds), 468
debt ratio, 476
debt-to-equity ratio, 476
junk bonds, 469
long-term liabilities, 455
market rate (effective
  rate or yield rate) of
  interest, 470
mortgage amortization
  schedule, 464

mortgage payable, 463
present value of $1, 455
present value of an
  annuity, 459
principal (face value or
  maturity value), 470
registered bonds, 468
secured bonds, 468
serial bonds, 469
stated rate of
  interest, 471

term bonds, 469
times interest earned, 477
zero-coupon bonds, 469

bond carrying value, 481
effective-interest
  amortization, 478
straight-line
  amortization, 478

REVIEW PROBLEMS

Accounting for Long-Term Liabilities

Energy Corporation had the following transactions relating to its long-term liabilities for the year:

a. Issued a $30,000, three-year, 8% note payable to White Corporation for a truck purchased on January 2. Interest is payable annually on December 31 of each year.

b. Issued $300,000 of 12%, 10-year bonds on July 1. The market rate on the date of issuance was 12%. Interest payments are made on June 30 and December 31 of each year.

c. Purchased a warehouse on December 1 by borrowing $250,000. The terms of the mortgage call for monthly payments of $2,194 for 30 years to be made at the end of each month. The interest rate on the mortgage is 10%.

Required:

Make all journal entries required during the year to account for the above liabilities. Energy Corporation reports on a calendar-year basis.

Solution

Jan. 2 Truck	30,000	
Note Payable		30,000
Purchased a truck by issuing a note.		

July 1 Cash	300,000	
Bonds Payable		300,000
Issued 12%, 10-year bonds with a face value of $300,000.		

Dec. 1 Warehouse	250,000	
Mortgage Payable		250,000
Purchased a warehouse by issuing a 10%, 30-year		
mortgage.		

31 Interest Expense	2,400	
Cash		2,400
Paid yearly interest on the 3-year, 8% note		
($30,000 × 8% = $2,400).		

31 Bond Interest Expense	18,000	
Cash		18,000
Paid semiannual interest payment on 12%, 10-year		
bonds ($300,000 × 0.12 × ⁶/₁₂ = $18,000).		

Interest Expense	2,083	
Mortgage Payable	111	
Cash		2,194
Paid first monthly payment on 30-year mortgage		
(interest: $250,000 × 0.10 × ¹/₁₂ = $2,083;		
reduction in principal: $2,194 − $2,083 = $111).		

EXPANDED
material

Bonds Payable

Scientific Engineering Company received authorization on July 1, 2009, to issue $300,000 of 12% bonds. The maturity date of the bonds is July 1, 2029. Interest is payable on January 1 and July 1 of each year. The bonds were sold for $289,200 on July 1, 2009 (the same day as authorized). Scientific Engineering uses straight-line amortization.

Required:

1. Compute the approximate effective interest rate for the bonds.

(continued)

2. Record the journal entries on:
   a. July 1, 2009.
   b. December 31, 2009.
   c. January 1, 2010.
   d. July 1, 2010.
   e. December 31, 2010.
3. Record the journal entries on July 1, 2029, for the final interest payment and the retirement of the bonds.

Solution

1. Effective Interest Rate

Because the bonds sold at a discount, the actual or effective rate of interest is higher than the stated interest rate of 12%. The effective interest rate can be approximated as follows:

Bond discount amortized per year = $10,800/20 periods = $540
Annual interest expense = ($300,000 × 12%) + $540 = $36,540
Effective interest rate = $36,540/$289,200 = 12.63%

2. Journal Entries

a. 2009

July	1	Cash	289,200	
		Discount on Bonds	10,800	
		Bonds Payable		300,000

   To record the sale of $300,000 of 12% bonds due on July 1, 2029.

b. 2009

Dec. 31	Bond Interest Expense	18,270	
	Discount on Bonds		270
	Bond Interest Payable		18,000

   To record semiannual bond interest expense on $300,000, 12%, 20-year bonds ($300,000 × 0.12 × ½ year) and amortize bond discount ($10,800 ÷ 20 years × ½ year).

c. 2010

Jan. 1	Bond Interest Payable	18,000	
	Cash		18,000

   Paid semiannual interest on $300,000 bonds.

d. 2010

July 1	Bond Interest Expense	18,270	
	Discount on Bonds		270
	Cash		18,000

   Paid semiannual interest on $300,000 bonds and amortized bond discount.

e. 2010

Dec. 31	Bond Interest Expense	18,270	
	Discount on Bonds		270
	Bond Interest Payable		18,000

   To record semiannual bond interest expense on $300,000 bonds and amortize bond discount.

3. Retirement of the Bonds

2029

July 1	Bond Interest Expense	18,270	
	Discount on Bonds		270
	Bond Interest Payable		18,000

   To record the bond interest expense and discount amortization up to the date of maturity.

(continued)

Bonds Payable 300,000	
Bond Interest Payable 18,000	
Cash	318,000

*To record the payment of interest for six months
and retire the bonds at maturity.*

The first entry on July 1, 2029, updates the amortization of the bond discount to the retirement date and reflects the cash owed for interest for the period January 1–July 1, 2029. The second entry reflects payment for retiring the bonds plus payment of the interest owed. Alternatively, Cash could have been credited for $18,000 in the first entry. If Cash had been credited, the second entry would have included only a debit to Bonds Payable and a credit to Cash for $300,000.

DISCUSSION QUESTIONS

1. The higher the interest rate, the lower the present value of a future amount. Why?
2. What is an annuity?
3. When does the stated amount of a liability equal its present value?
4. What is the difference between a note payable and a mortgage payable?
5. When a mortgage payment is made, a portion of it is applied to interest, and the balance is applied to reduce the principal. How is the amount applied to reduce the principal computed?
6. If a lease is recorded as a capital lease, what is the relationship of the lease payments and the lease liability?
7. Why do companies prefer to classify leases as operating leases rather than as capital leases?
8. To whom do companies usually sell bonds?
9. What are two important characteristics that determine the issuance price of a bond?
10. Identify four different ways in which bonds can mature or be eliminated as liabilities.
11. If a bond's stated interest rate is below the market interest rate, will the bond sell at a premium or at a discount? Why?
12. If you think the market interest rate is going to drop in the near future, should you invest in bonds?

13. When do you think bonds will sell at or near face value?
14. Explain why bonds retired before maturity may result in a gain or loss to the issuing company.
15. What does the debt ratio measure?
16. From the standpoint of a lender, which is more attractive: a high times interest earned ratio or a low times interest earned ratio? Explain.

EXPANDED *material*

17. What type of account is Discount on Bonds?
18. Why does the amortization of a bond discount increase the book value of bonds?
19. Why is the effective-interest amortization method more theoretically appropriate than the straight-line amortization method?
20. What is the carrying value of a bond?
21. How does the carrying value of a bond affect the accounting for bonds payable under the effective-interest method?
22. If the effective rate of interest for a bond is greater than its stated rate of interest, explain why the annual bond interest expense will be different from the periodic cash interest payments to the bondholders.

PRACTICE EXERCISES

PE 10-1 **Present Value of a Single Amount**
LO1 The company will receive $20,000 in five years when the interest rate is 8%. Compute the present value of this payment.

PE 10-2 **Future Value of a Single Amount**
LO1 The company invests $61,000 today in a savings account that earns 10% compounded annually. What will be the balance in the savings account ten years from today (e.g., future value)?

PE 10-3   **Interest Rate per Compounding Period**
LO1   The interest rate is 16% compounded quarterly for six years. Compute the interest rate per compounding period.

PE 10-4   **Number of Interest Periods**
LO1   The interest rate is 12% compounded monthly for seven years. Compute the number of interest periods.

PE 10-5   **Future Value of Single Amount Compounded Monthly**
LO1   Compute the future value of $10,000 invested today at 24% interest compounded monthly for five years.

PE 10-6   **Computing the Present Value of an Annuity**
LO1   The company will receive $1,600 every six months for eight years. The company's interest rate is 10% compounded semiannually. Compute the present value of this annuity payment.

PE 10-7   **Computing Periodic Payment Amount**
LO1   The company borrowed $50,000 to be repaid in equal monthly installments at 12% interest over five years. Compute the periodic payment amount.

PE 10-8   **Interest-Bearing Notes**
LO2   The company borrowed $20,000 at 8% interest by issuing a note payable. The terms of the note require yearly interest payments for seven years and repayment of the principal at the end of seven years. Make the necessary journal entries to record the following transactions:
1. Issuance of the note payable.
2. Payment of the first interest expense.

PE 10-9   **Mortgages Payable Issuance and First Payment**
LO2   On January 1, the company borrowed $500,000 to purchase a new building and signed a mortgage agreement pledging the building as collateral on the loan. The mortgage is at 12% for 30 years, and the monthly payment is $5,143 payable on January 31 with subsequent payments due at the end of each month thereafter. Make the necessary journal entries to record the following transactions:
1. Acquisition of the mortgage.
2. January 31 (first month) payment on mortgage.

PE 10-10   **Mortgages Payable Second Payment**
LO2   Refer to the data in PE 10-9. Make the necessary journal entry(ies) to record the second month's mortgage payment on February 28. Round to the nearest penny.

PE 10-11   **Capital Lease Acquisition**
LO3   The company leased a delivery truck on January 1, 2009. The lease requires annual payments of $7,500 for seven years at a 12% rate of interest payable at the end of each year. The company classifies this lease as a capital lease. Make the necessary journal entry(ies) to record the lease of this asset.

PE 10-12   **Capital Lease Payment**
LO3   Refer to the data in PE 10-11. Make the necessary journal entry(ies) to record the first lease payment on December 31, 2009. Round amounts to the nearest penny.

PE 10-13   **Types of Bonds**
LO4   Which one of the following statements is false?
a. Debentures are bonds that have no underlying assets pledged as collateral to guarantee their payment.

(continued)

b. Serial bonds mature in one single sum on a specified future date.

c. Callable bonds can be redeemed by the issuer at any time at a specified price.

d. Companies keep a record of the names and addresses of all registered bondholders and pay interest only to those whose names are on file.

PE 10-14
LO4

Bonds Issued at Face Value

The company issued 15-year, $100,000 bonds with a stated rate of interest of 12%, compounded quarterly. The effective interest rate demanded by investors for bonds of this level of risk is also 12%. Calculate the issuance price of the bond (e.g., the total present value).

PE 10-15
LO4

Bonds Issued at a Discount

The company issued five-year, $25,000 bonds with a stated rate of interest of 8%, compounded semiannually. The effective interest rate demanded by investors for bonds of this level of risk is 12%. Calculate the issuance price of the bond (e.g., the total present value).

PE 10-16
LO4

Bonds Issued at a Premium

The company issued seven-year, $100,000 bonds with a stated rate of interest of 8%, compounded semiannually. The effective interest rate demanded by investors for bonds of this level of risk is 6%. Calculate the issuance price of the bond (e.g., the total present value).

PE 10-17
LO4

Accounting for Bonds Payable Issued at Face Value

The company issued 20-year, $450,000 bonds with a stated rate of interest of 11%, compounded semiannually. The effective interest rate demanded by investors for bonds of this level of risk is also 11%. Since these bonds are issued at face value (i.e., the stated rate of interest is equal to the interest rate demanded by investors for bonds of this level of risk), the issuance price is also $450,000. Make the necessary journal entries for:

1. The issuance of the bonds.
2. The first interest payment.

PE 10-18
LO4

Accounting for Retirement of Bonds Payable Issued at Face Value

Refer to the data in PE 10-17. Assuming all interest has been accounted for, make the necessary journal entry(ies) to record the retirement of the bonds at the end of 20 years.

PE 10-19
LO4

Bond Retirements before Maturity

The company had $300,000 in callable bonds in the open market. The company's bonds were selling in the open market at 106 and were callable at 107. The company decided to retire the bonds early. Make the necessary journal entry(ies) to record the retirement of these bonds.

PE 10-20
LO5

Debt Ratio

Using the following information, compute the debt ratio.

Total liabilities	$247,500
Annual interest expense	5,204
Total assets	542,850
Income before interest and taxes	62,030

PE 10-21
LO5

Debt-to-Equity Ratio

Refer to the data in PE 10-20. Compute the debt-to-equity ratio.

PE 10-22
LO5

Times Interest Earned Ratio

Refer to the data in PE 10-20. Compute the times interest earned ratio.

EXERCISES

E 10-23
LO1

Computing the Present Value of a Single Sum

Find the present value (rounded to the nearest dollar) of:

1. $20,000 due in 4 years at 6% compounded annually.
2. $40,000 due in 6½ years at 4% compounded semiannually.
3. $15,000 due in 5 years at 16% compounded quarterly.
4. $11,000 due in 25 years at 10% compounded semiannually.

E 10-24
LO1

Computing the Future Value of a Single Sum

Compute the future value (rounded to the nearest dollar) of the following investments:

1. $15,842 invested to earn interest at 6% compounded annually for 4 years.
2. $30,920 invested to earn interest at 4% compounded semiannually for 6½ years.
3. $6,846 invested to earn interest at 16% compounded quarterly for 5 years.
4. $959 invested to earn interest at 10% compounded semiannually for 25 years.

E 10-25
LO1

Computing the Present Value of an Annuity

What is the present value (rounded to the nearest dollar) of an annuity of $12,000 per year for seven years if the interest rate is:

1. 9% compounded annually.
2. 12% compounded annually.

E 10-26
LO1

Computing the Amount of Periodic Payments

Howard Company has just borrowed $250,000. The loan is to be repaid in regular annual payments made at the end of each year. What is the amount of each annual payment under the following sets of terms:

1. Interest rate of 8% compounded annually; repayment in four annual payments.
2. Interest rate of 7% compounded annually; repayment in eight annual payments.

E 10-27
LO2

Accounting for Long-Term Note Payable

Maloney Company borrowed $60,000 on a two-year, 8% note dated October 1, 2008. Interest is payable annually on October 1, 2009, and October 1, 2010, the maturity date of the note. The company prepares its financial statements on a calendar-year basis. Prepare all journal entries relating to the note for 2008, 2009, and 2010.

E 10-28
LO2

Accounting for Long-Term Note Payable

Silmaril, Inc., borrowed $25,000 from First National Bank by issuing a three-year, 10% note dated July 1, 2008. Interest is payable semiannually on December 31 and June 30. The principal amount is to be repaid in full on June 30, 2011. Silmaril, Inc., reports on a calendar-year basis. Prepare all journal entries relating to the note during 2008, 2009, 2010, and 2011.

E 10-29
LO2

Accounting for a Mortgage

Kohler Kleaners borrowed $50,000 on June 1, 2009, to finance the purchase of a building. The mortgage requires payments of $525 to be made at the end of every month for 12 years with the first payment being due on June 30, 2009. The interest rate on the mortgage is 8%.

1. Prepare a mortgage amortization schedule for 2009.
2. How much interest will be paid in 2009?
3. By how much will the principal amount of the mortgage be reduced by the end of 2009?

E 10-30
LO2

Accounting for a Mortgage

On January 1, 2009, Paik, Inc., borrowed $75,000 to finance the purchase of machinery. The terms of the mortgage require payments to be made at the end of every month with the first payment being due on January 31, 2009. The length of the mortgage is five years, and the mortgage carries an interest rate of 24%.

(continued)

1. Compute the amount of the monthly payment.
2. Prepare a mortgage amortization schedule for 2009.
3. Prepare the journal entry to be made on January 31, 2009, when the first payment is made.
4. For the remainder of the year, how will the journal entries relating to the mortgage differ from the one made on January 31?

E 10-31
LO3

Lease Accounting

Logan Electronics signed a lease to use a machine for five years. The annual lease payment is $14,200 payable at the end of each year.

1. Record the lease, assuming that the lease should be accounted for as a capital lease and the applicable interest rate is 12%. (Round to the nearest dollar.)
2. For the initial year, record the annual lease payment.

E 10-32
LO3

Lease Accounting

Digital, Inc., leased computer equipment from Young Leasing Company on January 2, 2009. The terms of the lease required annual payments of $4,141 for five years beginning on December 31, 2009. The interest rate on the lease is 14%.

1. Assuming the lease qualifies as an operating lease, what journal entry would be made on January 2 to record the leased asset?
2. If the lease qualifies as an operating lease, what journal entry would be made when the first payment is made on December 31, 2009?
3. Provide the journal entry made on January 2, 2009, assuming the lease qualifies as a capital lease.
4. Provide the journal entry made on December 31, 2009, to record the first lease payment, assuming a capital lease.

E 10-33
LO4

Issuance Price of Bonds

Neukoelln Company issued seven-year bonds on January 1. The face value of the bonds is $72,000. The stated interest rate on the bonds is 12%. The market rate of interest at the time of issuance was 10%. The bonds pay interest semiannually. Calculate the issuance price of the bonds.

E 10-34
LO4

Issuance Price of Bonds

Hopeful Company issued seven-year bonds on January 1. The face value of the bonds is $80,000. The stated interest rate on the bonds is 7%. The market rate of interest at the time of issuance was 10%. The bonds pay interest semiannually. Calculate the issuance price of the bonds.

E 10-35
LO4

Accounting for Bonds Issued at Face Value

Romulus, Inc., issued $500,000 of 10%, five-year bonds at face value on July 1, 2009. Interest on the bonds is payable semiannually on December 31 and June 30.

1. Provide the journal entry to record the issuance of the bonds on July 1, 2009.
2. Provide the journal entry made on December 31, 2009, to account for these bonds.
3. On September 30, 2010, Romulus elected to retire the bonds early. The market price of the bonds on this date was $486,000. Provide the journal entries to record the early retirement.
4. Why do you think Romulus elected to retire the bonds early?

E 10-36
LO4

Accounting for Bonds Issued at Face Value

Schwedt Company issued $280,000 of 9%, 10-year bonds at face value on September 1, 2009. The bonds pay interest on March 1 and September 1. Schwedt uses the calendar year for financial reporting purposes.

1. Provide the journal entry to record the bond issuance on September 1, 2009.
2. Provide the journal entry to record interest expense on December 31, 2009.

(continued)

3. Provide the journal entries made during 2010 relating to the bond.

4. On February 20, 2011, Schwedt elected to retire the bond issue early. The market price on the day of retirement was $300,000. Provide the journal entries to record the bond retirement.

5. Why do you think Schwedt elected to retire the bonds early?

E 10-37
LO5

Computation of Debt-Related Financial Ratios

The following information comes from the financial statements of Gwynn Company:

Long-term debt	$50,000
Total liabilities	78,000
Total stockholders' equity	40,000
Operating income	16,000
Interest expense	6,000

Compute the following ratio values:

1. Debt ratio.
2. Debt-to-equity ratio.
3. Times interest earned.

E 10-38
LO3, LO5

Impact of Capitalizing the Value of Operating Leases

The following information comes from the financial statements of Karlla Peterson Company:

Total liabilities	$100,000
Total stockholders' equity	80,000

In addition, Karlla Peterson has a large number of operating leases. The payments on these operating leases total $20,000 per year for the next 15 years. The present value of the economic obligation associated with these operating leases is $150,000. Of course, because these are operating leases, this economic obligation is off the balance sheet.

Compute the following ratio values:

1. Debt ratio. *Hint:* Remember the accounting equation.
2. Debt-to-equity ratio.
3. Debt-to-equity ratio assuming that Karlla Peterson's operating leases are accounted for as capital leases.
4. Debt ratio assuming that Karlla Peterson's operating leases are accounted for as capital leases.

EXPANDED *material*

E 10-39
LO4, LO6

Accounting for Bonds Issued at a Discount

Kontiki Alarm Company issued $250,000 of 10%, five-year bonds at 98 on June 30, 2009. Interest is payable on June 30 and December 31. The company uses the straight-line method to amortize bond premiums and discounts. The company's fiscal year is from February 1 through January 31.

Prepare all necessary journal entries to account for the bonds from the date of issuance through June 30, 2010. Also record the retirement of the bonds on June 30, 2014, assuming that all interest has been paid and that the discount has been fully amortized.

E 10-40
LO4, LO6

Accounting for Bonds Issued at a Premium

Sealon Corporation issued $100,000 of 10%, 10-year bonds at 102 on April 1, 2009. Interest is payable semiannually on April 1 and October 1. Sealon Corporation uses the calendar year for financial reporting.

(continued)

1. Record the necessary entries to account for these bonds on the following three dates. (Use the straight-line method to amortize the bond premium.)
   a. April 1, 2009.
   b. October 1, 2009.
   c. December 31, 2009.
2. Show how the bonds would be reported on the balance sheet of Sealon Corporation on December 31, 2009.

E 10-41
LO6

Effective-Interest Calculation

Determine the *approximate* effective rate of interest for $300,000, 8%, five-year bonds issued at 95. (Assume straight-line amortization.)

E 10-42
LO6

Bond Amortization Schedule

The following is a partially completed amortization schedule prepared for the Liggett Company to account for its three-year bond issue with a face value of $50,000. The schedule covers the first three semiannual interest payment dates. Amounts are rounded to the nearest dollar. Compute the missing numbers.

Year	Interest Paid	Bond Expense	Premium Amortized	Bonds Payable Carrying Value
0				$52,537
½	(1)	$2,627	(2)	52,164
1	$3,000	(3)	$392	(4)
1½	(5)	(6)	(7)	(8)

E 10-43
LO4, LO6

Accounting for Bonds

Brown & Co., a calendar-year firm, is authorized to issue $500,000 of 11%, 15-year bonds dated May 1, 2009, with interest payable semiannually on May 1 and November 1.

Amortization of bond premiums or discounts is recorded using the straight-line amortization method. Prepare journal entries to record the following events, assuming that the bonds are sold at 97 on May 1, 2009.

1. The bond issuance on May 1, 2009.
2. Payment of interest on November 1, 2009.
3. Adjusting entry on December 31, 2009.
4. Payment of interest on May 1, 2010.

PROBLEMS

P 10-44
LO1

Present and Future Value Computations

Required:

1. Determine the present value in each of the following situations:
   a. A $9,000 loan to be repaid in full at the end of five years. Interest on the loan is payable quarterly. The interest rate is 8% compounded quarterly.
   b. A six-year note for $12,000 bearing interest at an annual rate of 12%, compounded semiannually. Interest is payable semiannually.
   c. A one-year mortgage to be paid in monthly installments of $6,000. The interest rate is 12% compounded monthly.
2. Determine the future value in each of the following situations:
   a. An investment of $20,000 today to earn interest at 8% compounded semiannually to provide for a down payment on a house four years from now.
   b. An investment of $40,000 today to earn interest at 12% compounded quarterly that is designated for a charitable contribution 15 years from now when the donor retires.

P 10-45
LO1

Present and Future Value Computations

Required:

1. Compute the present value for each of the following situations, assuming an interest rate of 10% compounded annually. (Round amounts to the nearest dollar.)
   a. A single payment of $30,000 due on a mortgage five years from now.
   b. A series of payments of $5,000 each, due at the end of each year for five years.
   c. A five-year, 10% loan of $25,000, with interest payable annually, and the principal due in five years.

2. Compute the future value amounts (rounded to the nearest dollar) in each of the following situations:
   a. A $20,000 lump-sum investment today that will earn interest at 10% compounded annually over five years.
   b. A $5,000 lump-sum investment today that will earn interest at 8%, compounded quarterly to provide money for a child's college education 15 years from now.

P 10-46
LO1

Computing the Amount of Periodic Payments

Nathan Smith has just purchased a new car for $28,000. He paid $8,000 down and signed a note for the remaining $20,000. The interest rate on the note is 12% compounded monthly, or 1% per month.

Required:

1. Compute the amount of Mr. Smith's monthly payment if he plans to pay off the $20,000 note in 30 monthly payments. Remember: The interest rate is 1% per month.
2. Repeat part (1) assuming that Mr. Smith wishes to repay the note in 60 monthly payments.
3. Assume that Mr. Smith decides to repay the note in 60 monthly payments. What is the balance remaining on the note immediately after he makes the 30th payment? *Hint:* Compute the present value of the remaining 30 payments.

P 10-47
LO2

Accounting for Notes Payable

Sweet's Candy Company needed cash for its current business operations. On January 1, 2008, the company borrowed $8,000 on a two-year, interest-bearing note from Peterson Bank at an annual interest rate of 10%. Interest is payable annually on January 1, and the note matures January 1, 2010. Sweet's Candy Company also borrowed $4,500 from Laurence National Bank on January 1, 2008, signing a three-year, 11% note due on January 1, 2011, with interest payable annually on January 1.

Required:

Prepare all journal entries relating to the two notes for 2008, 2009, 2010, and 2011. Assume that Sweet's Candy Company uses the calendar year for financial reporting. (Round all amounts to the nearest dollar.)

P 10-48
LO2

Accounting for Notes Payable

During 2008, Schmaal Corporation had the following transactions relating to long-term liabilities:

May 1   Purchased a machine costing $600,000 from Kretschmar Corporation. Issued a three-year, interest-bearing note with interest payable on May 1 of each year. The note matures on May 1, 2011, and carries an interest rate of 7%.

July 1   Borrowed $25,000 from South-Central National Bank. The terms of the note require semiannual payments of interest on December 31 and June 30. The note matures in two years and carries an interest rate of 6%.

Required:

1. Prepare the journal entries made on May 1 and July 1 to record the issuance of these two notes.
2. Prepare all journal entries made on December 31, 2008.
3. Prepare all journal entries made during 2009.

P 10-49
LO2

Accounting for a Mortgage

On November 1, 2009, Nydegger Company arranges with an insurance company to borrow $400,000 on a 30-year mortgage to purchase land and a building to be used in its operations. The land and the building are pledged as collateral for the loan, which has an annual interest rate of 12%, compounded monthly. The monthly payments of $4,114 are made at the end of each month, beginning on November 30, 2009.

Required:

1. Prepare the journal entry to record the purchase of the land and building, assuming that $75,000 of the purchase price is assignable to the land.
2. Prepare the journal entries on November 30 and December 31 for the monthly payments on the mortgage.
3. **Interpretive Question:** Explain generally how the remaining liability at December 31, 2009, will be reported on the company's balance sheet dated December 31, 2009.

P 10-50
LO3

Lease Accounting

On January 1, 2008, Linda Lou Foods, Inc., leased a tractor. The lease agreement qualifies as a capital lease and calls for payments of $7,000 per year (payable each year on January 1, starting in 2009) for eight years. The annual interest rate on the lease is 8%. Linda Lou Foods uses a calendar-year reporting period.

Required:

1. Prepare the journal entries for the following dates:
   a. January 1, 2008, to record the leasing of the tractor.
   b. December 31, 2008, to recognize the interest expense for the year 2008.
   c. January 1, 2009, to record the first lease payment.
2. Prepare the appropriate journal entries at December 31, 2009, and January 1, 2010.
3. **Interpretive Question:** Explain briefly how the leased asset is accounted for annually.

P 10-51
LO3

Lease Accounting

Empire, Inc., leased a starship on January 2, 2009. Terms of the lease require annual payments of $135,746 per year for 14 years. The interest rate on the lease is 10%, and the first payment is due on December 31, 2009.

Required:

1. Compute the present value of the lease payments.
2. Assuming the lease qualifies as a capital lease, prepare the journal entry to record the lease.
3. Prepare the journal entry to record the first lease payment on December 31, 2009, and to depreciate the leased asset. Empire, Inc., uses the straight-line method for depreciating all long-term assets.
4. **Interpretive Question:** How would the leased asset, and its associated liability, be disclosed on the balance sheet prepared on December 31, 2009?

P 10-52
LO4

Issuance Price of Bonds

Patterson Company issued 30-year bonds on June 30. The face value of the bonds was $750,000. The stated interest rate on the bonds was 6%. The market rate of interest at the time of issuance was 4%. Patterson also issued another set of bonds on August 31. These bonds were 20-year bonds and had a face value of $556,000. The stated rate of interest on these bonds was 5%. The market rate of interest at the time these bonds were issued was 8%. Both sets of bonds pay interest semiannually.

Required:

Calculate the issuance price of these bonds.

P 10-53
LO4

Accounting for Bonds

On July 1, 2009, Paramount, Inc. issued $500,000, 8%, 30-year bonds with interest paid semiannually on January 1 and July 1. The bonds were sold when the market rate of interest

(continued)

was 8%. On October 1, 2012, the bonds were retired when their fair market value was $495,000.

Required:

1. Demonstrate, using the present value tables, that the bonds were sold for $500,000.
2. Provide the journal entry made on July 1 to record the issuance of the bonds.
3. Provide the journal entry made on December 31, 2009, relating to interest.
4. Provide the journal entries to record the retirement of the bonds.

P 10-54

LO4

Accounting for Bonds

Lihue Enterprises issued $1.5 million, 9%, 20-year bonds on November 1, 2008. Interest payment dates are May 1 and November 1. The bonds were sold at face value.

Required:

1. Provide the journal entry to record the initial issuance of the bonds.
2. Provide the required journal entry on December 31, 2008.
3. Provide all journal entries relating to the bonds made during 2009.

P 10-55

LO5

Reporting Liabilities on the Balance Sheet

The following list of accounts is taken from the adjusted trial balance of Goforth Company.

Accounts Payable	$45,000
Notes Payable (due in 6 months)	24,000
Income Taxes Payable	18,000
Unearned Sales Revenue	27,500
Notes Payable (due in 2 years)	40,000
Prepaid Insurance	6,200
Accounts Receivable	53,000
Current Portion of Mortgage Payable	12,300
Mortgage Payable (due beyond 1 year)	93,000
Retained Earnings	91,400
Property Taxes Payable	8,700
Salaries & Wages Payable	15,200
Sales Tax Payable	3,100

Required:

Prepare the liabilities section of the company's balance sheet.

P 10-56

LO5

Reporting Liabilities on the Balance Sheet

The following amounts are shown on Plymouth Company's adjusted trial balance for the year 2009:

Accounts Payable	$ 36,000
Property Taxes Payable	6,300
Short-Term Notes Payable	44,000
Mortgage Payable (due within 1 year)	28,000
Mortgage Payable (due after 1 year)	300,000
Accrued Interest on Mortgage Payable	3,000
Lease Liability (current portion)	58,000
Lease Liability (long term)	414,000
Rent Payable	70,000
Income Taxes Payable	50,000
Federal & State Unemployment Taxes Payable	16,000

Required:

Prepare the liabilities section of Plymouth Company's balance sheet at December 31, 2009.

P 10-57   **Computation of Debt-Related Financial Ratios**

LO5   The following information comes from the financial statements of Walker Company:

Long-term debt	$430,000
Total liabilities	490,000
Total stockholders' equity	360,000
Current assets	140,000
Earnings before income taxes	28,000
Interest expense	50,000

Required:

Compute the following ratio values. State any assumptions that you make.

1. Debt ratio.
2. Debt-to-equity ratio.
3. Times interest earned.
4. **Interpretive Question:** You are a bank manager considering making a new $35,000 loan to Walker that would replace part of the existing long-term debt. You expect Walker to repay your loan in two years. Which of the ratios computed in parts (1) through (3) would be most useful to you in evaluating whether to make the loan to Walker?

P 10-58   **Impact of Capitalizing the Value of Operating Leases**

LO5   The following information comes from the financial statements of Travis Campbell Company:

Total liabilities	$100,000
Total stockholders' equity	80,000
Property, plant, and equipment	110,000
Sales	500,000
Earnings before income taxes	11,000
Interest expense	23,000

In addition, Travis Campbell has a large number of operating leases. The payments on these operating leases total $30,000 per year for the next 10 years. The present value of the economic obligation associated with these operating leases is $180,000. Of course, because these are operating leases, this economic obligation is off the balance sheet.

Required:

Compute the following ratio values:

1. Debt ratio. *Hint:* Remember the accounting equation.
2. Debt ratio assuming that Travis Campbell's operating leases are accounted for as capital leases.
3. Asset turnover (sales/total assets).
4. Asset turnover assuming that Travis Campbell's operating leases are accounted for as capital leases.
5. **Interpretive Question:** You are Travis Campbell's banker. You are concerned that the times interest earned ratio is not accurately reflecting the risk that Travis Campbell will not meet its fixed annual payments because most of those fixed payments are operating lease payments, not interest payments. Design an alternative ratio that will reflect the fact that, like interest payments, operating lease payments are fixed obligations that must be covered through operating profits each year. Compute the value for the ratio that you have designed.

P 10-59
LO4, LO6

Accounting for Bonds

Nemo Company authorized and sold $90,000 of 10%, 15-year bonds on April 1, 2009. The bonds pay interest each April 1, and Nemo's year-end is December 31.

Required:

1. Prepare journal entries to record the issuance of Nemo Company's bonds under each of the following three assumptions:
   a. Sold at 97.
   b. Sold at face value.
   c. Sold at 105.
2. Prepare adjusting entries for the bonds on December 31, 2009, under all three assumptions. (Use the straight-line amortization method.)
3. Show how the bond liabilities would appear on the December 31, 2009, balance sheet under each of the three assumptions.
4. **Interpretive Question:** What condition would cause the bonds to sell at 97? At 105?

P 10-60
LO4, LO6

Accounting for Bonds Issued at a Premium

On March 1, 2009, Roger Corporation issued $90,000 of 12%, five-year bonds at 110. The bonds were dated March 1, 2009, and interest is payable on March 1 and September 1. Roger records amortization using the straight-line method. Roger's financial reporting year ends on December 31.

Required:

Provide all necessary journal entries on each of the following dates:

1. March 1, 2009.
2. September 1, 2009.
3. December 31, 2009.
4. March 1, 2014.

P 10-61
LO4, LO6

Bonds Retired at Maturity

Stottard Company issued $450,000 of 10%, 10-year bonds on June 1, 2008, at 103. The bonds were dated June 1, and interest is payable on June 1 and December 1 of each year.

Required:

1. Record the issuance of the bonds on June 1, 2008.
2. Record the interest payment on December 1, 2008. Stottard uses the straight-line method of amortization.
3. Record the interest accrual on December 31, 2008, including amortization.
4. Record the journal entries required on June 1, 2018, when the bonds mature.

P 10-62
LO4, LO6

Straight-Line versus Effective-Interest Amortization

Cyprus Corporation issued $150,000 of bonds on January 1, 2009, to raise funds to buy some special machinery. The maturity date of the bonds is January 1, 2014, with interest payable each January 1 and July 1. The stated rate of interest is 10%. When the bonds were sold, the effective rate of interest was 12%. The company's financial reporting year ends December 31.

Required:

1. Determine the price at which the bonds would be sold.
2. Prepare the amortization schedule using the effective-interest method.
3. Prepare a comparative schedule of interest expense for each year (2009–2014) for the effective-interest and straight-line methods of amortization.
4. Record the journal entry for the last payment using the amortization schedule in part (2).
5. Record the journal entry for the retirement of the bonds.

(continued)

6. **Interpretive Question:** Is the difference between the interest expense each year between the straight-line and effective-interest methods sufficient to require the use of the effective-interest method? How do you think this question would be answered in practice?

P 10-63

LO4, LO6

Effective-Interest Amortization

Royce Corporation issued $200,000 of three-year, 12% bonds on January 1, 2008. The bonds pay interest on January 1 and July 1 each year. The bonds were sold to yield a 10% return, compounded semiannually.

Required:

1. At what price were the bonds issued?
2. Prepare a schedule to amortize the premium or discount on the bonds using the effective-interest amortization method.
3. Use the information in the amortization schedule prepared for part (2) to record the interest payment on July 1, 2010, including the appropriate amortization of the premium or discount.
4. **Interpretive Question:** Explain why these bonds sold for more or less than face value.

P 10-64

LO4, LO6

Accounting for Bonds

Bell Company sold $200,000 of 10-year bonds on January 1, 2008, to Brown Corporation. The bond indenture included the following information:

Face value	$200,000
Date of bonds	January 1, 2008
Maturity date	January 1, 2018
Stated rate of interest	14%*
Effective (market) rate of interest	12%*

*Compounded semiannually

Required:

1. Prepare the journal entry to record the issuance of the bonds.
2. What is the interest expense on the Bell Company books for the years ending December 31, 2008, and December 31, 2009, using straight-line amortization?
3. Show how the bonds would be presented on Bell's balance sheet at December 31, 2009.

P 10-65

LO4, LO6

Straight-Line versus Effective-Interest Amortization

Foster Corporation issued three-year bonds with a $180,000 face value on March 1, 2008, in order to pay for a new computer system. The bonds mature on March 1, 2011, with interest payable on March 1 and September 1. The contract rate of interest is 10%. (Interest is compounded semiannually.) When the bonds were sold, the effective rate of interest was 12%. The company's fiscal year ends on February 28.

Required:

1. At what price were the bonds issued based on the information presented?
2. Prepare an amortization schedule using the effective-interest method.
3. Prepare a schedule of interest expense for each year (2008–2011), comparing the annual interest expense for straight-line and effective-interest amortization.
4. Using the amortization schedule prepared in part (2), prepare the journal entry to record the interest payment on September 1, 2008.
5. Prepare the adjusting journal entry to record accrued interest on February 28, 2009.
6. Prepare the journal entry to retire the bonds on March 1, 2011, assuming all interest has been paid prior to retirement.

P 10-66

LO4, LO6

Bonds Retired before Maturity

Amity Construction Company issued $100,000 of 10% bonds on January 1, 2009. The maturity date of the bonds is January 1, 2019. Interest is payable January 1 and July 1. The bonds

(continued)

were sold at 111.4 on July 1, 2009. The company uses the straight-line method of amortizing bond premiums and discounts.

Required:
1. Make the required journal entries for each of the following dates:
   a. July 1, 2009.
   b. December 31, 2009.
   c. January 1, 2010.
   d. July 1, 2010.
2. Because of a substantial decline in the market rate of interest, Amity Construction Company purchased all the bonds on the open market at face value (100) on July 1, 2012. The following entry had just been made on that day:

Bond Interest Expense	4,400	
Premium on Bonds	600	
Cash		5,000
Made semiannual interest payment on the bonds		
and amortized bond premium for six months.		

Prepare the journal entry to record the retirement of the bonds on July 1, 2012.

P 10-67
LO4, LO6

Unifying Concepts: Accounting for Bonds Payable

Gonzalez Corporation was authorized to issue $100,000 of 7%, four-year bonds, dated May 1, 2009. All the bonds were sold on that date when the effective interest rate was 8%. Interest is payable on May 1 and November 1 each year. The company follows a policy of amortizing premium or discount using the effective-interest method. The company closes its books on December 31 of each year.

Required:
1. Calculate the issuance price of the bonds.
2. Prepare an amortization schedule that covers the life of the bond.
3. Prepare journal entries at the following dates based on the information shown in the amortization schedule prepared for part (2).
   a. December 31, 2009.
   b. May 1, 2010.
   c. November 1, 2010.
   d. December 31, 2010.
4. Based on the journal entries prepared for part (3), how much interest expense related to this bond issue did the company report on its income statement for the year 2010?
5. What was the carrying value of this bond issue on the balance sheet of the company at December 31, 2010?
6. **Interpretive Question:** Explain why another company in the same industry, which issued bonds with the same amount of face value, the same date of issuance, and the same stated rate of interest, might have had an issuance price of more or less than the price you computed for the issuance of the Gonzalez Corporation bonds.

P 10-68
LO4, LO6

Analysis of Bonds

Bonds with a face value of $200,000 and a stated interest rate of 12% were issued on March 1, 2009. The bonds pay interest each February 28 and August 31 and mature on March 1, 2019. The issuing company uses the calendar year for financial reporting.

Required:
Using these data, complete the following tables for each of the conditions listed. (Show computations and assume straight-line amortization.)
1. The bonds sold at face value.
2. The bonds sold at 97.
3. The bonds sold at 103.

(continued)

	Case 1	Case 2	Case 3
Cash received at issuance date	_____	_____	_____
Total cash paid to bondholders through maturity	_____	_____	_____
Income statement for 2009:			
Bond interest expense	_____	_____	_____
Balance sheet at December 31, 2009:			
Long-term liabilities:			
Bonds payable, 12%	_____	_____	_____
Unamortized discount	_____	_____	_____
Unamortized premium	_____	_____	_____
Bond carrying value	_____	_____	_____
Approximate effective interest rate*	_____	_____	_____

*Round to the nearest tenth of a percent.

ANALYTICAL ASSIGNMENTS

AA 10-69

DISCUSSION

Present Value Concepts

Hamburg Company recently began business and purchased a large facility to make beach clothing. Hamburg Company managed to make a small profit in its initial year of operations, although it used all its cash to purchase inventory and equipment. After preparing its tax return for the year, Hamburg's managers realized that they could pay less taxes than they thought. Because IRS accelerated depreciation methods allow for higher depreciation expense than the straight-line method the company is using for financial-reporting purposes, Hamburg can claim more depreciation expense than it thought it could and can reduce taxable income by $30,000. However, Hamburg's managers know that the two depreciation methods will eventually even out because the difference is only temporary and will create a deferred income tax liability, which must be recorded on the books. The managers are very conservative, though, and would rather pay the additional taxes now than record a liability that must be paid in the future, even if they must borrow the money from a bank to pay the extra taxes. They have come to you for advice. What would you tell them?

AA 10-70

DISCUSSION

Debt and Equity Financing

Berlin Company is in a world of hurt. For the past 15 years, the company has been the exclusive toy supplier to Infants-R-Us toy stores. Unfortunately for Berlin Company, Infants-R-Us just declared bankruptcy and went out of business. Berlin is the supplier for a few local toy stores, but Infants-R-Us was by far its largest customer. Berlin's managers believe that they can save the company if they can raise enough money to develop a new product line of a popular toy, "Nano Babies." Developing the new product line will require a considerable investment, however. Berlin is trying to decide the best way to finance the investment. It has found a bank that will loan it the money at 18%, a very high rate but the only one it can get because of its precarious financial position. Berlin can also issue bonds to raise the money, but because of investors' concerns about the future viability of the company, the only kind of bonds investors will buy are high-interest junk bonds at an interest rate of 17%. Even then, there is concern that the bonds will be discounted when they are marketed. Which financing alternative would you recommend to the company? If you were an investor, would you buy Berlin Company's bonds?

AA 10-71

JUDGMENT CALL

You Decide: Should the following bonds be classified as debt or equity on the balance sheet?

A company has recently issued bonds that are convertible into stock at the bondholder's request. The interest rate on the bonds is ridiculously low because it is expected that most holders will exercise the conversion options! How should the bonds be reported?

AA 10-72
JUDGMENT CALL

***You Decide:* If a young company has a negative "times interest earned" ratio, should the company be refused or given a loan by lenders?**

Design Arts Inc. is a young computer game design company that has been in business for two years. The company has been working on a computer game that is scheduled for release in six months. However, it has exhausted all its financial resources and needs one last loan of $100,000 to help it meet its deadline. The company has not had any revenues up to this point but knows that once the game hits the market, it will be extremely profitable. Would you make a loan to this company?

AA 10-73
REAL COMPANY
ANALYSIS

Wal-Mart

The 2006 Form 10-K for **Wal-Mart** is included in Appendix A. Locate that Form 10-K and consider the following questions:

1. Examine Wal-Mart's balance sheet as of January 31, 2006. What percent of the increase in Wal-Mart's total assets from 2005 to 2006 was financed with an increase in the company's long-term debt?
2. Compute Wal-Mart's debt ratio for 2006 and 2005. Is the ratio increasing or decreasing? Identify the primary reason for the change.

AA 10-74
REAL COMPANY
ANALYSIS

IBM

International Business Machines (IBM) included the following information in Note K to its 2005 financial statements:

Long-Term Debt At December 31, 2005 (dollars in millions)			
At December 31:	**Maturities**	**2005**	**2004**
U.S. dollars:			
Debentures:			
5.875%	2032	$ 600	$ 600
6.22%	2027	469	469
6.5%	2028	313	313
7.0%	2025	600	600
7.0%	2045	150	150
7.125%	2096	850	850
7.5%	2013	532	532
8.375%	2019	750	750
3.43% convertible notes	2007	238	278
Notes: 5.4% average	2006–2013	2,713	2,724
Medium-term note program: 4.4% average	2006–2018	5,620	3,627
Other: 4.1% average	2006–2011	1,833	1,555
		$14,668	$12,448
Other currencies (average interest rate at December 31, 2005, in parentheses):			
Euros (3.1%)	2006–2010	$ 1,280	$ 1,095
Japanese yen (1.4%)	2006–2015	1,450	3,435
Canadian dollars (7.7%)	2008–2011	5	9
Swiss francs (1.5%)	2008	378	220
Other (6.1%)	2006–2011	406	513
		$18,187	$17,720

1. IBM lists eight different issues of debentures. What is a debenture?
2. What is unusual about the 7.125% debentures?
3. IBM has borrowed the equivalent of $3.519 billion in the form of foreign currency loans. Why would IBM get loans denominated in foreign currencies rather than get all of its loans in U.S. dollars?

(continued)

4. The average interest rates on the foreign currency loans range from a low of 1.4% for loans of Japanese yen to 7.7% for loans of Canadian dollars. What factors would cause IBM to pay a higher interest rate when it borrows Canadian dollars than when it borrows Japanese yen?

AA 10-75
REAL COMPANY ANALYSIS

Citigroup

The **City Bank of New York** was chartered on June 16, 1812, just two days before the start of the War of 1812 between the United States and Great Britain. To get around twentieth-century bank holding laws, a holding company was organized to own the bank. This holding company took the name of **Citicorp** in 1974. In 1998, **Citicorp** and **Travelers Group** merged to become **Citigroup Inc**.

A simplified balance sheet for Citigroup as of December 31, 2005, and a schedule outlining the interest rate on Citigroup's outstanding long-term debt are given below.

Citigroup
Balance Sheet
December 31, 2005

	(millions of dollars)
Cash	$ 28,373
Investment securities	180,597
Loans receivable	573,721
Other assets	711,346
Total	$1,494,037
Deposit liabilities	$ 592,595
Other liabilities	571,406
Long-term debt	217,499
Stockholders' equity	112,537
Total	$1,494,037

Interest Rates Prevailing on Parent and Subsidiary Loans
for Loans Outstanding on December 31, 2005

Type of Loan	Average Interest Rate
Parent Company	
Senior notes	4.42%
Subordinated notes	5.45%
Parent Company and Subsidiaries	
Senior notes	4.75%
Subordinated notes	5.71%

1. Citigroup's simplified balance sheet is representative of most banks' balance sheets. Using the information about relative sizes of assets and liabilities given in that balance sheet, write a brief description of the primary operating activity of a bank.
2. Compute Citigroup's debt ratio (total liabilities divided by total assets). Comment on whether the value seems high or low to you.
3. In its long-term debt of $217.5 billion, Citigroup has both fixed-rate loans and floating-rate (or variable-rate) loans. What is the advantage of borrowing with a fixed-rate loan? What is the advantage of borrowing with a variable-rate loan?
4. Citigroup states that some of the subsidiary long-term debt is guaranteed by Citigroup. When Citigroup guarantees the long-term debt of one of its subsidiaries, does that raise or lower the interest rate that the subsidiary must pay on the debt? Explain. Is the interest rate on a loan higher when it is secured by assets or when it is unsecured? Explain.

AA 10-76

INTERNATIONAL

British Petroleum

In May 1901, William Knox D'Arcy convinced the Shah of Persia (present-day Iran) to allow him to hunt for oil. The oil discovered in Persia in 1908 was the first commercially significant amount of oil found in the Middle East. The company making the discovery called itself the **Anglo-Persian Oil Company**, later named **British Petroleum**, or BP. Today, BP is one of the largest oil and gas exploration and refining companies in the world.

The information below comes from Note 39 (Finance debt) of British Petroleum's 2005 financial statements.

(millions of dollars)	Loans	Finance Leases
Payments due within:		
1 year	$ 5,418	$ 78
2 to 5 years	8,421	320
Thereafter	4,542	838
	$18,381	$1,236
Less finance charge	0	455
Net obligation	$18,381	$ 781

1. In Great Britain, a finance lease is what we in the United States would call a capital lease. According to Note 39, British Petroleum expects to make total lease payments of $1.236 billion under finance leases. However, a liability of only $781 million is reported. Why is there a difference between the two amounts?

2. The $1.236 billion payment amount for the finance leases reflects the total of all lease payments that will be made under the agreements. Does the $18.381 billion amount reported for loans reflect the amount of all payments that will be made under the loan agreements? Explain.

3. The future loan and finance lease payments are separated into amounts to be repaid within one year, within two to five years, and after five years. How would a financial statement user find this payment timing information to be useful?

AA 10-77

ETHICS

Hiding an Obligation By Calling It a Lease

You and your partner own Miss Karma's Preschool, which provides preschool and day care services for about 100 children per day. Business is booming, and you are right in the middle of expanding your operation. Three months ago you took your financial statements to the local bank and applied for a five-year, $145,000 loan. The bank approved the loan, but it included as part of the loan agreement a condition that you would incur no other long-term liabilities during the five-year loan period. You cheerfully agreed to this condition because you didn't anticipate any further financing needs.

Two weeks ago a state government inspector came to your facility and said that your square footage was not enough for the number of children enrolled in your programs. The inspector gave you one month to find another facility, or else you would have to shut down. Luckily, you were able to find another building to use. However, the owner of the building insists on having you sign a 20-year lease. Alternatively, you can buy the building for $220,000. To buy the building, you would have to get a mortgage, which would, of course, violate the agreement on your five-year bank loan.

Your partner suggests that the lease is the way to solve all of your problems. Your partner has studied some accounting and reports that you can sign the lease but carefully construct the lease contract so that the lease will be accounted for as an operating lease. In this way, the lease obligation will not be reported as an accounting liability, the loan agreement will not be violated, and you can move to the new facility without any problem.

Is your partner right? Is it possible to avoid reporting the 20-year lease contract as an accounting liability? By signing the lease, are you violating the bank loan agreement? What do you think is the best course of action?

AA 10-78
WRITING

My Contract's Bigger Than Your Contract!

You are an agent for professional athletes. One of your clients is a superstar in the NBA. Last month you negotiated a new deal for your client that pays him $22 million per year for each of the next six years. Your client was very pleased with this $132 million contract, especially because it was a bigger contract than any of the other players on his team received.

This morning, while you were relaxing in your Jacuzzi, you got an angry cellular call from your client. It seems that one of his teammates just signed a $150 million deal, paying him $15 million per year for each of the next 10 years. Your client is outraged because you guaranteed that no one on his team would be receiving a bigger contract this season. Your client has threatened to terminate his agreement with you and also to spread the word among all his friends that you are not trustworthy.

Write a one-page memo to your client explaining that the actual value of his $132 million contract is greater than the $150 million contract signed by his teammate. Your client has a marketing degree from an ACC school, so he has had some exposure to the concept of the time value of money.

AA 10-79
CUMULATIVE
SPREADSHEET
PROJECT

Preparing New Forecasts

This spreadsheet assignment is a continuation of the spreadsheet assignments given in earlier chapters. If you completed those spreadsheets, you have a head start on this one.

1. Handyman wishes to prepare a forecasted balance sheet and income statement for 2010. Use the original financial statement numbers for 2009 [given in part (1) of the Cumulative Spreadsheet Project assignment in Chapter 2] as the basis for the forecast, along with the following additional information:

    a. Sales in 2010 are expected to increase by 40% over 2009 sales of $700.
    b. Cash will increase at the same rate as sales.
    c. The forecasted amount of accounts receivable in 2010 is determined using the forecasted value for the average collection period. For simplicity, do the computations using the end-of-period accounts receivable balance instead of the average balance. The average collection period for 2010 is expected to be 14.08 days.
    d. The forecasted amount of inventory in 2010 is determined using the forecasted value for the number of days' sales in inventory (computed using the end-of-period inventory balance). The number of days' sales in inventory for 2010 is expected to be 107.6 days.
    e. The forecasted amount of accounts payable in 2010 is determined using the forecasted value for the number of days' purchases in accounts payable (computed using the end-of-period accounts payable balance). The number of days' purchases in accounts payable for 2010 is expected to be 48.34 days.
    f. The $160 in operating expenses reported in 2009 breaks down as follows: $5 depreciation expense, $155 other operating expenses.
    g. See item (l) for the assumption concerning the amount of new long-term debt that will be acquired in 2010.
    h. No cash dividends will be paid in 2010.
    i. New short-term loans payable will be acquired in an amount sufficient to make Handyman's current ratio in 2010 exactly equal to 2.0.
    j. The forecasted amount of property, plant, and equipment (PP&E) in 2010 is determined using the forecasted value for the fixed asset turnover ratio. For simplicity, compute the fixed asset turnover ratio using the end-of-period gross PP&E balance. The fixed asset turnover ratio for 2010 is expected to be 3.518 times.
    k. In computing depreciation expense for 2010, use straight-line depreciation and assume a 30-year useful life with no residual value. Gross PP&E acquired during the year is depreciated for only half the year. In other words, depreciation expense for 2010 is the sum of two parts: (1) a full year of depreciation on the beginning balance in PP&E, assuming a 30-year life and no residual value and (2) a half-year of depreciation on any new PP&E acquired during the year, based on the change in the gross PP&E balance.

(continued)

Note: These statements were constructed as part of the spreadsheet assignment in Chapter 9; you can use that spreadsheet as a starting point if you have completed that assignment. *Clearly state any additional assumptions that you make.*

For this exercise, add the following additional assumptions:

l. New long-term debt will be acquired (or repaid) in an amount sufficient to make Handyman's debt ratio (total liabilities divided by total assets) in 2010 exactly equal to 0.80.

m. Assume an interest rate on short-term loans payable of 6.0% and on long-term debt of 8.0%. Only a half-year's interest is charged on loans taken out during the year. For example, if short-term loans payable at the end of 2010 are $15 and given that short-term loans payable at the end of 2009 were $10, total short-term interest expense for 2010 would be $0.75 [($10 × 0.06) + ($5 × 0.06 × 1/2)].

Clearly state any additional assumptions that you make.

2. Repeat (1), with the following changes in assumptions:
   a. The debt ratio in 2010 is exactly equal to 0.70.
   b. The debt ratio in 2010 is exactly equal to 0.90.

3. Prepare a table displaying the forecasted values of long-term debt and paid-in capital in 2010 under each of the following assumptions about the debt ratio: 0.70, 0.80, and 0.90. The sum of these two items can be viewed as the total amount of long-term financing (both debt and equity) received from outsiders. Comment on why the total of these two items is not the same under each debt ratio assumption.

Equity Financing

LEARNING OBJECTIVES

After studying this chapter, you should be able to:

(1) Distinguish between debt and equity financing, and describe the advantages and disadvantages of organizing a business as a proprietorship or a partnership. *Equity financing entitles the investor to share in the profits of the company; debt financing only entitles the lender to a fixed repayment amount. A business can be organized as a sole proprietorship, a partnership, or a corporation. Both proprietorships and partnerships can be easily formed; they both have the disadvantage of exposing the owner or owners to unlimited liability.*

(2) Describe the basic characteristics of a corporation and the nature of common and preferred stock. *Two advantages of the corporate form are the ease in transferability of ownership and the limited liability of the shareholders. The common stockholders of a corporation collectively choose the board of directors who then choose managers to conduct the day-to-day operation of the corporation. Preferred stockholders give up some of the advantages of ownership in exchange for some of the protection enjoyed by lenders.*

(3) Account for the issuance and repurchase of common and preferred stock. *When a company issues shares of stock, a portion of the proceeds is typically reported as the par value of the stock, with the remainder being called paid-in capital in excess of par. Treasury stock is shares of a company's own stock that have been repurchased. The amount spent to repurchase treasury stock is shown as a reduction in stockholders' equity.*

(4) Understand the factors that affect retained earnings, describe the factors determining whether a company can and should pay cash dividends, and account for cash dividends. *Cash dividends represent a distribution of accumulated profits to shareholders. Cash dividends reduce retained earnings. Preferred stock dividends must be paid before any dividends can be paid to common stockholders.*

(5) Describe the purpose of reporting comprehensive income in the equity section of the balance sheet, and prepare a statement of stockholders' equity. *Accumulated other comprehensive income is the portion of the balance sheet equity section where the equity impact of certain unrealized gains and losses is summarized.*

In 1882, two young newspaper reporters, Charles Dow and Edward Jones, teamed up to provide the Wall Street financial community with handwritten news bulletins. In 1889, when the staff of **Dow Jones & Company** had grown to 50, they decided to convert the bulletin service into a daily newspaper. The first issue of *The Wall Street Journal* appeared on July 8, 1889. Clarence Barron, who operated a financial news service in Boston, was the paper's first out-of-town reporter. Barron purchased Dow Jones & Company in 1902 for $130,000, and his heirs still hold majority control of the company today.

The Wall Street Journal is the flagship of the company, but the name "Dow Jones" is best known because of the Dow Jones Industrial Average that is cited in the news every day. "The Dow" is widely used to reflect the general health of the U.S. economy. So, what is it? Simply put, the Dow Jones Industrial Average measures the average movement of the stock prices of selected U.S. companies. The very first value of the average was 40.94 on May 26,

1896. Charles Dow computed this value by adding the share prices of 12 important companies chosen by him (**General Electric** was one of them) and then dividing by 12. Thus, the average price per share for these 12 companies was $40.94. Since 1928, the average has included 30 companies selected by the editors of *The Wall Street Journal*. The average is no longer computed by simply averaging share prices, but the underlying concept remains the same. Changes in the companies included in the average are rare. Nevertheless, since 1990, 14 companies have been replaced to reflect the decreasing importance of manufacturing in the U.S. economy. For example, **Bethlehem Steel**, which had been in "The Dow" since 1928, was replaced in March 1997 by **Wal-Mart**. In 1999, the first two NASDAQ companies were added to "The Dow"– **Microsoft** and **Intel**. The 30 companies included in the average as of June 1, 2006, are listed in Exhibit 1. The 30 companies in the average are listed every day in *The Wall Street Journal*, often on page C3.[1]

EXHIBIT 1	The 30 Firms Included in the Dow Jones Industrial Average (as of June 1, 2006)

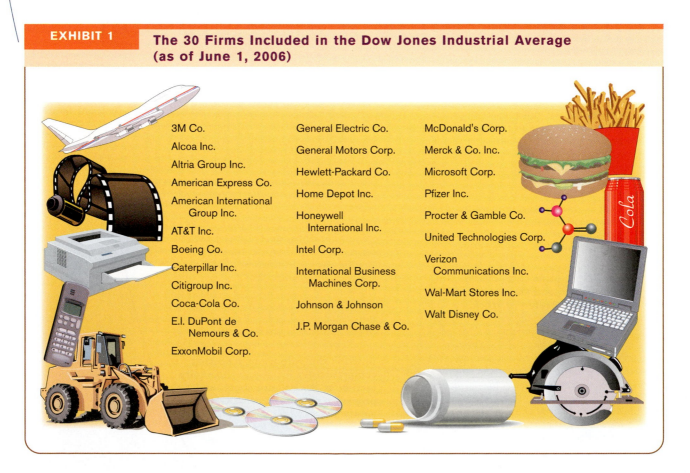

3M Co.
Alcoa Inc.
Altria Group Inc.
American Express Co.
American International Group Inc.
AT&T Inc.
Boeing Co.
Caterpillar Inc.
Citigroup Inc.
Coca-Cola Co.
E.I. DuPont de Nemours & Co.
ExxonMobil Corp.

General Electric Co.
General Motors Corp.
Hewlett-Packard Co.
Home Depot Inc.
Honeywell International Inc.
Intel Corp.
International Business Machines Corp.
Johnson & Johnson
J.P. Morgan Chase & Co.

McDonald's Corp.
Merck & Co. Inc.
Microsoft Corp.
Pfizer Inc.
Procter & Gamble Co.
United Technologies Corp.
Verizon Communications Inc.
Wal-Mart Stores Inc.
Walt Disney Co.

---

[1] This description is based on information obtained from Dow Jones & Company History at **http://dowjones.com**; Dow Jones & Company, *International Directory of Company Histories*, vol. 19 (Detroit: St. James Press, 1998), pp. 128–131.

Dow Jones & Company is an appropriate symbol of capitalism–a corporation that has done business in and around the spiritual heart of capitalistic finance, the New York Stock Exchange, for over one hundred years. With the disintegration of the former Soviet Union and the rapid conversion of China into a "socialist market" economy, it seems that the economic battle of capitalism and communism has been won by capitalism. As the history of many of the companies profiled in earlier chapters (Microsoft, Sears, Yahoo!, General Electric) illustrates, the true story of capitalism is not the story of rich "capitalists" exploiting the masses, but rather the story of unknown individuals using a free market to find outside investor financing that will turn their ideas into reality. Accounting for investor financing is the topic of this chapter.

This is the second chapter on financing activities. In the previous chapter, financing through borrowing (debt) was discussed. Another way organizations raise money to finance operations is from investments by owners. In corporations, those investments take the form of stock purchases. In proprietorships and partnerships, they take the form of capital investments in the business. Exhibit 2 shows the financial statement items that will be covered in this chapter.

Certain basic characteristics are common to all investor financing, no matter what the form of business. The first is that owner investments affect the equity accounts of the business. Second, together with the liabilities, these owners' equity accounts show the sources of the cash that was used to buy the assets. There are three primary ways to bring money into a business: borrowing (debt financing), selling owners' interests (equity financing), and earning profits (also reflected in the equity accounts through the retained earnings account). In this chapter, we illustrate the accounting for equity financing in the context of corporations.

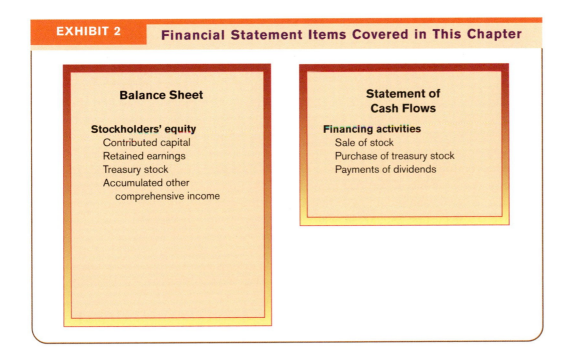

EXHIBIT 2   **Financial Statement Items Covered in This Chapter**

Balance Sheet

Stockholders' equity
   Contributed capital
   Retained earnings
   Treasury stock
   Accumulated other
     comprehensive income

**Statement of
Cash Flows**

Financing activities
   Sale of stock
   Purchase of treasury stock
   Payments of dividends

Raising Equity Financing

1 Most business owners do not have enough excess personal cash to establish and expand their companies. Therefore, they eventually need to look for money from outsiders, either in the form of loans or as funds contributed by investors. The business issues associated with investor financing are summarized in the time line in Exhibit 3.

The factors affecting the choice between borrowing and seeking additional investment funds are described in this section of the chapter. This section also outlines the advantages and disadvantages of organizing a business as a proprietorship or a partnership. The decision to incorporate and the process that a corporation follows in soliciting investor funds are described in the next section. The bulk of the chapter is devoted to the accounting procedures used to give a proper reporting of stockholders' equity to the investors. Of course, proper financial reporting to current and potential investors is one of the primary reasons for the existence of financial accounting.

Difference between a Loan and an Investment

Imagine that you own a small business and need $40,000 for expansion. What is the difference between borrowing the $40,000 and finding a partner who will invest the $40,000? If you borrow the money, you must guarantee to repay the $40,000 with interest. If you fail to make these payments, the lender can haul you into court and use the power of the law to force repayment. On the other hand, if your company does very well and you generate more than enough cash to repay the $40,000 plus interest, the lender does not get to share in your success. You owe the lender $40,000 plus interest and not a penny more. So, a loan is characterized by a fixed, legal obligation to repay a specified amount, whether the borrowing company performs poorly or performs well.

If you receive $40,000 in investment funds from a new partner, the partner now shares in your company's failures and successes. If business is bad and the investor is never able to recover his or her $40,000 investment—well, that's the way it goes. The law will not help the investor recover the investment because the very nature of an investment is that the investor accepts the risk of losing everything. However, in exchange for accepting this risk, the investor also gets to share in the success if the company does well. For example, if you had loaned $40,000 to Sam Walton for **Wal-Mart**'s expansion back in 1970, you would have been repaid the $40,000 plus a little interest. If you had invested that same $40,000 in Wal-Mart, however, your investment would have grown in value to $240.5 million by June 2006. Thus, an investment is characterized by a higher

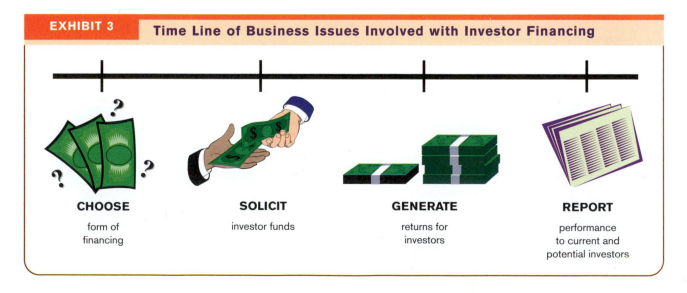

EXHIBIT 3   **Time Line of Business Issues Involved with Investor Financing**

CHOOSE
form of financing

SOLICIT
investor funds

GENERATE
returns for investors

REPORT
performance to current and potential investors

F Y I

The law does not help investors recover lost investment funds unless the investors can show that they were tricked (by false financial reports, for example) into making the investment.

risk of losing your money, balanced by the chance of sharing in the wealth if the company does well.

Proprietorships and Partnerships

As explained in Chapter 2, a business can be organized as a proprietorship, a partnership, or a corporation. These three types of organization are merely different types of legal contracts that define the rights and responsibilities of the owner or owners of the business. The advantages and disadvantages of proprietorships and partnerships are discussed below. Corporations are discussed in the next section.

proprietorship

A business owned by one person.

A **proprietorship** is a business owned by one person. A **partnership** is a business owned by two or more persons or entities. In most respects, proprietorships and partnerships are similar to each other but very different from corporations. Both a proprietorship and a partnership are characterized by ease of formation, limited life, and unlimited liability.

partnership

An association of two or more individuals or organizations to carry on economic activity.

Ease of Formation   Proprietorships and partnerships can be formed with few legal formalities. When a person decides to establish a proprietorship, he or she merely acquires the necessary cash, inventory, equipment, and other assets; obtains a business license; and begins providing goods or services to customers. The same is true for a partnership, except that because two or more persons are involved, they must decide together which assets will be acquired and how business will be conducted.

Limited Life   Because proprietorships and partnerships are not legal entities that are separate and distinct from their owners, they are easily terminated. In the case of a proprietorship, the owner can decide to dissolve the business at any time. For a partnership, anything that terminates or changes the contract between the partners legally dissolves the partnership. Among the events that dissolve a partnership are:

1. the death or withdrawal of a partner,
2. the bankruptcy of a partner,
3. the admission of a new partner,
4. the retirement of a partner, or
5. the completion of the project for which the partnership was formed.

The occurrence of any of these events does not necessarily mean that a partnership must cease business; rather, the existing partnership is legally terminated, and another partnership must be formed.

Unlimited Liability   Proprietorships and partnerships have unlimited liability, which means that the proprietor or partners are personally responsible for all debts of the business. If a partnership is in poor financial condition, creditors first attempt to satisfy their claims from the assets of the partnership. After those assets are exhausted, creditors may seek payment from the personal assets of the partners. In addition, because partners are responsible for one another's actions (within the scope of the partnership), creditors may seek payment for liabilities created by a departed or bankrupt partner from the personal assets of the remaining partners. This unlimited liability feature is probably the single most significant disadvantage of a proprietorship or partnership. It can deter a wealthy person from joining a partnership for fear of losing personal assets. (For more information relating to proprietorship and partnership accounting, access this book's Web site at **http://www.thomsonedu.com/accounting/albrecht.**)

> **REMEMBER THIS...**
>
> - A loan is a fixed, legal obligation to repay a specified amount, whether the borrowing company performs poorly or performs well.
> - With an investment, the investor risks losing the investment funds if the company performs poorly but shares in the wealth if the company does well.
> - A proprietorship is a business owned by one person.
> - A partnership is a business owned by two or more persons.
> - Both a proprietorship and a partnership are easy to start and easy to terminate.
> - A major disadvantage of proprietorships and partnerships is the unlimited liability of the owner or partners.

Describe the basic characteristics of a corporation and the nature of common and preferred stock.

Corporations and Corporate Stock

② Corporations are the dominant form of business enterprise in the United States. Established as separate legal entities, **corporations** are legally distinct from the persons responsible for their creation. In many respects, they are accorded the same rights as individuals; they can conduct business, be sued, enter into contracts, and own property. Firms are incorporated by the state in which they are organized and are subject to that state's laws and requirements.

Characteristics of a Corporation

Corporations have several characteristics that distinguish them from proprietorships and partnerships. These characteristics are discussed below.

corporation

A legal entity chartered by a state; ownership is represented by transferable shares of stock.

limited liability

The legal protection given stockholders whereby they are responsible for the debts and obligations of a corporation only to the extent of their capital contributions.

Limited Liability   **Limited liability** means that in the event of corporate bankruptcy, the maximum financial loss any stockholder can sustain is his or her investment in the corporation (unless fraud can be proved). Because a corporation is a separate legal entity and is responsible for its own acts and obligations, creditors usually cannot look beyond the corporation's assets for satisfaction of their claims. This limited liability feature is probably the main reason for the phenomenal growth of the corporate form of business because it protects investors from sustaining losses beyond their investments. In most cases of bankruptcy, however, stockholders will lose most of their investment because the claims of creditors must be satisfied before stockholders receive anything.

Easy Transferability of Ownership   Shares of stock in a corporation can be bought, sold, passed from one generation to another, or otherwise transferred without affecting the legal or economic status of the corporation. In other words, most corporations have perpetual existence—the life of the corporation continues by the transfer of shares of stock to new owners.

Ability to Raise Large Amounts of Capital   Raising large amounts of capital can be easier for a corporation than for a proprietorship or a partnership because a corporation can sell shares of its stock. The sale of shares of stock permits many investors, both large and small, to participate in ownership of the business. Some corporations actually have thousands of individual stockholders. In its 2005 annual report, **Dow Jones & Company** reports that it has approximately 14,000 stockholders of record. Because of this widespread ownership, large corporations are said to be publicly owned.

© RYAN MCVAY/PHOTODISC RED/
GETTY IMAGES INC.

Corporations are the dominant form of business in the United States. A corporation is a legal entity, and its ownership is represented by transferable shares of stock.

Double Taxation Because corporations are separate legal entities, they are taxed independently of their owners. This often results in a disadvantage, however, because the portion of corporate profits that is paid out in dividends is taxed twice. First, the profits are taxed to the corporation; second, the owners, or stockholders, are taxed on their dividend income.

Close Government Regulation

Because large corporations may have thousands of stockholders, each with only a small ownership interest, the government has assumed the task of monitoring certain corporate activities. For example, the government requires that all major corporations be audited and that they issue periodic financial statements. As a result, in certain respects, major corporations often enjoy less freedom than do partnerships and proprietorships.

Starting a Corporation

Suppose that you want to start a corporation. First, you should study your state's corporate laws (usually with the aid of an attorney). Then you must apply to the appropriate state official for a charter. Your application will include the intended name of your corporation, its purpose (that is, the type of activity it will engage in), the type and amount of stock you plan to have authorized for your corporation, and, in some cases, the names and addresses of the potential stockholders. Finally, if the state approves your application, you will be issued a "charter" (also called "articles of incorporation"), giving legal status to your corporation.

Of course, one of the purposes of forming a corporation is to then sell stock in the corporation in order to obtain business financing. If the business you intend to establish will operate across state lines and if you intend to seek investment funds from the general public, then you must register your intended stock issue with the Securities and Exchange Commission in Washington, D.C. You are required to provide a **prospectus** to each potential investor; the prospectus outlines your business plan, sources of financing, significant risks, and the like. Finally, you can sell your shares to the public in what is called an "initial public offering" (IPO). You will receive the proceeds from the IPO, minus the commission charged by the investment banker sponsoring the issue.

When an investor buys stock in a corporation, he or she receives a stock certificate as evidence of ownership. For convenience, these stock certificates are frequently held by the stockbroker through whom the investor purchased the shares. The investors in a corporation are called **stockholders**, and they govern

F Y I

There are some hybrid organizations that have characteristics of both partnerships and corporations. For example, several of the large international accounting firms are organized as limited liability partnerships (LLPs). An LLP offers the advantages of a partnership structure but also provides each partner with limited liability for the costs of lawsuits caused by the actions of his or her partners.

F Y I

An LLC (limited liability company) offers the limited liability legal protection of a corporation as well as the favorable partnership treatment for income tax purposes.

prospectus

A report provided to potential investors that represents a company's financial statements and explains its business plan, sources of financing, and significant risks.

stockholders

Individuals or organizations that own a portion (shares of stock) of a corporation.

board of directors

Individuals elected by the stockholders to govern a corporation.

the corporation through an elected **board of directors**. In most corporations, the board of directors then chooses a management team to direct the daily affairs of the corporation. In smaller companies, the board of directors is usually made up of members of that management team.

Several types of stock can be authorized by the charter and issued by the corporation. The most familiar types are common stock and preferred stock, and the major difference between them concerns the degree to which their holders are allowed to participate in the rights of ownership of the corporation.

Common Stock

common stock

The most frequently issued class of stock; usually, it provides a voting right but is secondary to preferred stock in dividend and liquidation rights.

Certain basic rights are inherent in the ownership of **common stock**. These rights are as follows:

1. The right to vote in corporate matters such as the election of the board of directors or the undertaking of major actions such as the purchase of another company.
2. The preemptive right, which permits existing stockholders to purchase additional shares whenever stock is issued by the corporation. This allows common stockholders to maintain the same percentage of ownership in the company if they choose to do so.
3. The right to receive cash dividends if they are paid. As explained later, corporations do not have to pay cash dividends, and the amount received by common stockholders is sometimes limited.
4. The right to ownership of all corporate assets once obligations to everyone else have been satisfied. This means that once all loans have been repaid and the claims of the preferred stockholders have been met (as discussed below), all the excess assets belong to the common stockholders.

 F Y I

Occasionally, a corporation will have more than one class of common stock. For example, Dow Jones & Company has common stock and Class B common stock. Each Class B share gets 10 votes in corporate matters, and most of the Class B shares are owned by the descendants of Clarence Barron.

In essence, the common stockholders of a corporation are the true owners of the business. They delegate their decision-making authority to the board of directors, who in turn delegate authority for day-to-day operations to managers hired for that purpose. Thus, a distinguishing characteristic of business ownership as a common stockholder of a corporation is a clear separation between owning the business and operating the business.

Preferred Stock

preferred stock

A class of stock that usually provides dividend and liquidation preferences over common stock.

The term "preferred stock" is somewhat misleading because it gives the impression that **preferred stock** is better than common stock. Preferred stock isn't better; it's different. A good way to think of preferred stock is that preferred stockholders usually give up some of the ownership rights of the common stockholders in exchange for some of the protection enjoyed by lenders.

In most cases, preferred stockholders are not allowed to vote for the corporate board of directors. In addition, preferred stockholders are usually allowed to receive only a fixed cash dividend, meaning that if the company does well, preferred stockholders do not get to share in the success. In exchange for these limitations, in the event that the corporation is liquidated, preferred stockholders are entitled to receive their cash dividends and have their claims fully paid before any cash is paid to common stockholders.

convertible preferred stock

Preferred stock that can be converted to common stock at a specified conversion rate.

Preferred stock may also include other types of privileges, the most common of which is convertibility. **Convertible preferred stock** is preferred stock that can be converted to common stock at a specified conversion rate. For example, in the notes to **Microsoft**'s 1999 financial statements, Microsoft detailed the terms of 12.5 million shares of Microsoft convertible preferred stock that was sold in December 1996. Holders of those shares of preferred stock were able to exchange them for Microsoft common stock beginning in December 1999. On December 15, 1999, each preferred share was converted into 1.1273 common shares. Convertible preferred stock can be very appealing to investors. They can enjoy the dividend privileges of the preferred stock while having the option to convert to common stock if the market value of the common stock increases significantly. By issuing shares of stock with varying rights and privileges, companies can appeal to a wider range of investors.

REMEMBER THIS...

- The five major features of a corporation are:
  1. limited liability for stockholders,
  2. easy transferability of ownership,
  3. the ability to raise large amounts of capital,
  4. separate taxation, and
  5. for large corporations, closer regulation by government.
- Common stock confers four basic rights upon its owners:
  1. the right to vote in corporate matters,
  2. the right to maintain proportionate ownership,
  3. the right to receive cash dividends, and
  4. the ownership of all excess corporate assets upon liquidation of the corporation.
- Preferred stock typically carries preferential claims to dividend and liquidation privileges but has no voting rights.

Accounting for Stock

③ In this section we focus on the accounting for the issuance of stock as well as the accounting for stock repurchases.

Account for the issuance and repurchase of common and preferred stock.

Issuance of Stock

Each share of common stock usually has a **par value** printed on the face of the stock certificate. For example, the common stock of **Dow Jones & Company** has a $1 par value. This par value has little to do with the market value of the shares. In May 2006, each Dow Jones common share with a $1 par value was selling for about $34 per share. When par-value stock sells for a price above par, it is said to sell at a premium. In most states it is illegal to issue stock for a price below par value. If stock were issued at a discount (below par), stockholders could later be held liable to make up the difference between their investment and the par value of the shares they purchased. The par value multiplied by the total number of shares outstanding is usually equal to a company's "legal capital," and it represents the amount of the invested funds that cannot be returned to the investors as long as the corporation is in existence. This legal capital requirement was originally intended to protect a company's creditors; without it, excessive dividends could be paid, leaving nothing for creditors. The par value really was of more importance a hundred years ago and is something of a historical oddity today. These days, most states allow the sale of no-par stock.

par value

A nominal value assigned to and printed on the face of each share of a corporation's stock.

When par-value stock is issued by a corporation, usually Cash is debited, and the appropriate stockholders' equity accounts are credited. For par-value common stock, the equity accounts credited are Common Stock, for an amount equal to the par value, and Paid-In Capital in Excess of Par, Common Stock, for the premium on the common stock.

To illustrate, we will assume that the Boston Lakers Basketball Team (a corporation) issued 1,000 shares of $1 par-value common stock for $50 per share. The entry to record the stock issuance is:

Cash (1,000 shares × $50)	50,000	
Common Stock (1,000 shares × $1 par value)		1,000
Paid-In Capital in Excess of Par,		
Common Stock (1,000 shares × $49)		49,000
Issued 1,000 shares of $1 par-value common stock at $50 per share.		

A similar entry would be made if the stock being issued were preferred stock. The total par value of the common and preferred stock, along with the associated amounts of paid-in capital in excess of par, constitutes a corporation's **contributed capital**.

contributed capital

The portion of owners' equity contributed by investors (the owners) in exchange for shares of stock.

This illustration points out two important elements in accounting for the issuance of stock: (1) the equity accounts identify the type of stock being issued (common or preferred), and (2) the proceeds from the sale of the stock are divided into the portion attributable to its par value and the portion paid in excess of par value. These distinctions are important because the owners' equity section of the balance sheet should correctly identify the specific sources of capital so that the respective rights of the various stockholders can be known.

If the stock being issued has no par value, only one credit is included in the entry. To illustrate, assume that the Lakers' stock does not have a par value and that the corporation issued 1,000 shares for $50 per share. The entry to record this stock issuance would be:

Cash	50,000	
Common Stock		50,000
Issued 1,000 shares of no-par stock at $50 per share.		

Although stock is usually issued for cash, other considerations may be involved. To illustrate the kinds of entries made when stock is issued for noncash considerations, we will assume that a prospective stockholder exchanged a piece of land for 5,000 shares of the Boston Lakers' $1 par-value common stock. Assuming the market value of the stock at the date of the exchange was $40 per share, the entry is:

Land (5,000 shares × $40)	200,000	
Common Stock (5,000 shares × $1)		5,000
Paid-In Capital in Excess of Par,		
Common Stock (5,000 shares × $39)		195,000
Issued 5,000 shares of $1 par-value common stock for land		
(5,000 shares × $40 per share = $200,000).		

When noncash considerations are received in payment for stock, the assets or services received should be recorded at the current market value of the stock issued. If the market value of the stock cannot be determined, the market value of the assets or services received should be used as the basis for recording the transaction.

Accounting for Stock Repurchases

Sometimes, when a company has excess cash or needs some of its shares of stock back from investors, it may purchase some of its own outstanding stock. This repurchased stock is called **treasury stock** by accountants. There are many reasons for a firm to buy its own stock. Five of the most common are that management:

> **treasury stock**
>
> Issued stock that has subsequently been reacquired by the corporation.

1. wants the stock for a profit-sharing, bonus, or stock-option plan for employees,
2. feels that the stock is selling for an unusually low price and is a good buy,
3. wants to stimulate trading in the company's stock,
4. wants to remove some shares from the market in order to avoid a hostile takeover, or
5. wants to increase reported earnings per share by reducing the number of shares of stock outstanding.

Many successful U.S. companies have ongoing stock repurchase plans. For example, **Wal-Mart** disclosed in its 2006 Form 10-K (Appendix A) that it spent $3.580 billion in 2006 to repurchase 74 million of its own shares. **Coca-Cola** spent $5.255 billion in the years 2003–2005 repurchasing its own shares. The most aggressive stock buyback program is **General Electric**'s—a number of years ago GE announced its intention to buy back its own shares. In December 2004, GE's board of directors authorized a three-year $15 billion share repurchase program. Subsequently in 2005, the board increased the authorized repurchase amount to $25 billion. As of the end of 2005, GE had spent a cumulative total of $17.3 billion on net stock repurchases, $5.3 billion of which occurred in 2005.

When a firm purchases stock of another company, the investment is included as an asset on the balance sheet. However, a corporation cannot own part of itself, so treasury stock is not considered an asset. Instead, it is a contra-equity account and is included on the balance sheet as a deduction from stockholders' equity. Think of it this way: when a corporation issues shares, its equity is increased; when the corporation buys those shares back, its equity is reduced. The reporting of treasury stock is illustrated in the stockholders' equity section of the balance sheet for General Electric in Exhibit 4.

Notice that the $17.326 billion spent by General Electric to buy back its own shares as of December 31, 2005, is shown as a subtraction from total share owners' equity. By the way, the "other capital" included in GE's equity section is primarily composed of paid-in capital in excess of par. Also, the "accumulated nonowner changes other than earnings" item is quite interesting and controversial, as will be explained in a later section.

Treasury stock is usually accounted for on a cost basis; that is, the stock is debited at its cost (market value) on the date of repurchase. To illustrate, we assume that 100 shares

EXHIBIT 4	Share Owners' Equity for General Electric

General Electric Company
December 31, 2005 and 2004
Share Owners' Equity
(in millions of U.S. dollars)

	2005	2004
Common stock	$ 669	$ 669
Accumulated nonowner changes other than earnings	2,667	7,238
Other capital	25,227	24,265
Retained earnings	98,117	91,411
Less common stock held in treasury	(17,326)	(12,762)
Total share owners' equity	$109,354	$110,821

of the $1 par-value common stock were reacquired by the Boston Lakers for $60 per share. The entry to record the repurchase is:

Treasury Stock, Common	6,000	
Cash (100 shares × $60)		6,000
Purchased 100 shares of treasury stock at $60 per share.		

 FYI

An alternative way to account for stock repurchases is called the par-value method. This method, though not used as frequently as the cost method illustrated in this section, is the method of choice for a number of large U.S. companies including **Microsoft**, **Intel**, and **Wal-Mart**. The par-value method of accounting for stock repurchases is covered in intermediate accounting courses.

The effect of this entry is to reduce both total assets (Cash) and total stockholders' equity by $6,000.

When treasury stock is reissued, the treasury stock account must be credited for the original amount paid to reacquire the stock. If the treasury stock's reissuance price is greater than its cost, an additional credit must be made to an account called Paid-In Capital, Treasury Stock. Together, these credits show the net increase in total stockholders' equity. At the same time, the cash account is increased by the total amount received upon reissuance of the treasury stock.

To illustrate, we assume that 40 of the 100 shares of the treasury stock that were originally purchased for $60 per share are reissued at $80 per share. The entry to record that reissuance is:

Cash (40 shares × $80)	3,200	
Treasury Stock, Common (40 shares × $60 cost)		2,400
Paid-In Capital, Treasury Stock [40 × ($80 − $60)]		800
Reissued 40 shares of treasury stock at $80 per share.		

The company now has a balance of $3,600 in the treasury stock account (60 shares at $60 per share).

 CAUTION

Do not credit a gain when treasury stock is reissued at a price greater than its cost. Gains are associated with a company's operations, not with a company buying and selling its own shares.

Sometimes the reissuance price of treasury stock is less than its cost. As before, the entry involves a debit to Cash for the amount received and a credit to Treasury Stock for the cost of the stock. However, because an amount less than the repurchase cost has been received, an additional debit is required. The debit is to Paid-In Capital, Treasury Stock if there is a balance in that account from previous transactions, or to Retained Earnings if there is no balance in the paid-in capital, treasury stock account.

To illustrate, we will consider two more treasury stock transactions. First, we assume that another 30 shares of treasury stock are reissued for $40 per share, $20 less than their cost. Because Paid-In Capital, Treasury Stock has a balance of $800, the entry to record this transaction is:

Cash (30 shares × $40)	1,200	
Paid-In Capital, Treasury Stock	600	
Treasury Stock, Common (30 shares × $60 cost)		1,800
Reissued 30 shares of treasury stock at $40 per share; original cost was $60 per share.		

Note that after this transaction is recorded, the balance in Paid-In Capital, Treasury Stock is $200 ($800 − $600).

Next, we assume that the company reissues 20 additional shares at $45 per share. The entry to record this transaction is:

Cash (20 shares × $45)	900	
Paid-In Capital, Treasury Stock	200	
Retained Earnings	100	
Treasury Stock (20 shares × $60 cost)		1,200
Reissued 20 shares of treasury stock at $45 per share; original cost		
was $60 per share.		

In this transaction, the selling price was $300 less than the cost of the treasury stock. Because the paid-in capital, treasury stock account had a balance of only $200, Retained Earnings was debited for the remaining $100.

Balance Sheet Presentation

We have discussed the ways in which stock transactions affect owners' equity accounts. We will now show how these accounts are summarized and presented on the balance sheet. The following data, with the addition of the preferred stock information in (1), summarize the stock transactions of the Boston Lakers shown earlier:

1. $40 par-value preferred stock: issued 1,000 shares at $45 per share.
2. $1 par-value common stock: issued 1,000 shares at $50 per share.
3. $1 par-value common stock: issued 5,000 shares for land with a fair market value of $200,000.
4. Treasury stock, common: purchased 100 shares at $60; reissued 40 shares at $80; reissued 30 shares at $40; reissued 20 shares at $45.

With these data, and assuming a Retained Earnings balance of $100,000, the stockholders' equity section would be as shown in Exhibit 5.

EXHIBIT 5   **Stockholders' Equity for Boston Lakers**

Boston Lakers Basketball Team
Stockholders' Equity

Preferred stock ($40 par value, 1,000 shares issued and outstanding)	$ 40,000
Common stock ($1 par value, 6,000 shares issued, 5,990 shares outstanding)*	6,000
Paid-in capital in excess of par, preferred stock	5,000
Paid-in capital in excess of par, common stock	244,000
Total contributed capital	$295,000
Retained earnings (to be discussed)	100,000
Total contributed capital and retained earnings	$395,000
Less treasury stock (10 shares of $1 par common at cost of $60 per share)	(600)
Total stockholders' equity	$394,400

*Treasury shares are described as being issued but not outstanding. Thus, 6,000 common shares have been issued, but only 5,990 are outstanding because 10 are held by the Boston Lakers as treasury shares.

REMEMBER THIS...

- When a company issues stock, it debits Cash or a noncash account (Property, for example) and credits various stockholders' equity accounts.
- Shares typically are assigned a par value, which is usually small in relation to the market value of the shares. Amounts received upon issuance of shares are divided into par value and paid-in capital in excess of par.
- A company's own stock that is repurchased is known as treasury stock and is included in the financial statements as a contra-stockholders' equity account.

Retained Earnings

(4) Understand the factors that affect retained earnings, describe the factors determining whether a company can and should pay cash dividends, and account for cash dividends.

Common stockholders can invest money in a corporation in two ways. First, as described in the previous section, common stockholders can buy shares of stock. Second, when the corporation makes money, the common stockholders can allow the corporation to keep those earnings to be reinvested in the business. **Retained earnings** is the name given to the aggregate amount of corporate earnings that have been reinvested in the business. The retained earnings balance is increased each year by net income and decreased by losses, dividends, and some treasury stock transactions (as illustrated earlier).

Remember, retained earnings is not the same as cash. In fact, a company can have a large Retained Earnings balance and be without cash, or it can have a lot of cash and a very small Retained Earnings balance. For example, on December 31, 2005, **Dow Jones & Company** had a Cash balance of $11 million but a Retained Earnings balance of $817 million. Although both Cash and Retained Earnings are usually increased when a company has earnings, they typically are increased by different amounts. This occurs for two reasons: (1) the company's net income, which increases Retained Earnings, is accrual-based, not cash-based; and (2) cash from earnings may be invested in productive assets such as inventories, used to pay off loans, or spent in any number of ways, many of which do not affect net income or retained earnings. In summary, cash is an asset; retained earnings is one source of financing (along with borrowing and direct stockholder investment) that a corporation can use to get funds to acquire assets.

retained earnings

The portion of a corporation's owners' equity that has been earned from profitable operations and not distributed to stockholders.

Cash Dividends

If you had your own business and wanted to withdraw money for personal use, you would simply withdraw it from the company's checking account or cash register. In a corporation, a formal action by the board of directors is required before money can be distributed to the owners. In addition, such payments must be made on a pro rata basis. That is, each owner must receive a proportionate amount on the basis of ownership percentage. These pro rata distributions to owners are called **dividends**. When paid in the form of cash, they are called **cash dividends**. The amount of dividends an individual stockholder receives depends on the number of shares owned and on the per-share amount of the dividend.

dividends

Distributions to the owners (stockholders) of a corporation.

cash dividend

A cash distribution of earnings to stockholders.

Should a Company Pay Cash Dividends?   Note that a company does not have to pay cash dividends. Theoretically, a company that does not pay dividends should be able to reinvest its earnings in assets that will enable it to grow more rapidly than its dividend-paying competitors. This added growth will presumably be reflected in increases in the per-share price of the stock. In practice, most public companies pay regular cash dividends, but some well-known companies do not. For example, **Berkshire Hathaway** has never paid cash dividends to its common stockholders.

So, should a corporation pay cash dividends or not? Well, the surprising answer is that no one knows the answer to that question. Ask your finance professor what he or she thinks. Although no one knows the theoretically best dividend policy, three general observations can be made:

- Stable companies pay out a large portion of their income as cash dividends.
- Growing companies pay out a small portion of their income, if any, as cash dividends. They keep the funds inside the company for expansion.
- Companies are very cautious about raising dividends to a new level because once investors come to expect a certain level of dividends, they see it as very bad news if the company reduces the dividends back to the old level.

STOP & THINK

If you were a **Microsoft** shareholder, would you want to receive a high level of cash dividends, or would you prefer that Microsoft use your share of the profits for business expansion?

Although cash dividends are the most common type of dividend, corporations can distribute other types of dividends as well. A stock dividend is a distribution of additional shares of stock to stockholders. A property dividend is a distribution of corporate assets (for example, the stock of another firm) to stockholders. Property dividends are quite rare. In this section, only the accounting for cash dividends will be discussed.

declaration date

The date on which a corporation's board of directors formally decides to pay a dividend to stockholders.

Accounting for Cash Dividends Three important dates are associated with dividends: (1) declaration date, (2) date of record, and (3) payment date. The first is when the board of directors formally declares its intent to pay a dividend. On this **declaration date**, the company becomes legally obligated to pay the dividend. Assuming that the board of directors votes on December 15, 2009, to declare an $8,000 dividend, this liability may be recorded as follows:

Dividends	8,000	
Dividends Payable		8,000
Declared dividend on December 15, 2009.		

At the end of the year, the dividends account is closed to Retained Earnings by the following entry:

Retained Earnings	8,000	
Dividends		8,000
To close Dividends to Retained Earnings.		

From this entry, you can see that a declaration of dividends reduces Retained Earnings and, eventually, the amount of cash on hand. Thus, though not considered to be an expense, dividends do reduce the amount a company could otherwise invest in productive assets.

Alternatively, a declaration of dividends can be recorded by debiting Retained Earnings directly. However, using the dividends account instead of Retained Earnings allows a company to keep separate records of dividends paid to preferred and common stockholders. Whichever method is used, the end result is the same: a decrease in Retained Earnings.

date of record

The date selected by a corporation's board of directors on which the stockholders of record are identified as those who will receive dividends.

The second important dividend date is the **date of record**. Falling somewhere between the declaration date and the payment date, this is the date selected by the board of directors on which the stockholders of record are identified as those who will receive dividends. Because many corporate stocks are in flux—being bought and sold daily—it is important that the stockholders who will receive the dividends be identified. No journal entry is required on the date of record; the date of record is simply noted in the minutes of the directors' meeting and in a letter to stockholders.

dividend payment date

The date on which a corporation pays dividends to its stockholders.

As you might expect, the third important date is the **dividend payment date**. This is the date on which, by order of the board of directors, dividends will be paid. The entry to record a dividend payment would typically be:

Dividends Payable	8,000	
Cash		8,000
Paid dividends declared on December 15, 2009.		

The following press release, made by **Ford Motor Company** on March 8, 2006 (declaration date), identifies both the date of record and the dividend payment date:

> The Board of Directors of Ford Motor Company (NYSE: F) today declared a second quarter dividend of 10 cents a share on the company's Class B and common stock. This is the same level of dividend paid in the first quarter of 2006. The second quarter dividend is payable on June 1, 2006 to shareholders of record on May 2, 2006.

As mentioned earlier, once a dividend-paying pattern has been established, the expectation of dividends is built into the per-share price of the stock. A reduction in the dividend usually produces a sharp drop in the price. Similarly, an increased dividend usually triggers an increase in the stock price. Dividend increases are usually considered to set a precedent, indicating that future dividends will be at this per-share amount or more. With this in mind, boards of directors are careful about increasing or decreasing dividends.

Dividend Preferences

When cash dividends are declared by a corporation that has both common and preferred stock outstanding, how the dividends are allocated to the two classes of investors depends on the rights of the preferred stockholders. These rights are identified when the stock is approved by the state. Two "dividend preferences," as they are called, are (1) current-dividend preference and (2) cumulative-dividend preference.

Current-Dividend Preference.

Preferred stock has a dividend percentage associated with it and is typically described as follows: "5% preferred, $40 par-value stock, 1,000 shares outstanding." The first figure—"5%" in this example—is a percentage of the par value and can be any amount, depending on the particular stock. So, $2 per share (0.05 × $40 par) is the amount that will be paid in dividends to preferred stockholders each year that dividends are declared. The fact that preferred stock dividends are fixed at a specific percentage of their par value makes them somewhat similar to the interest paid to bondholders. The **current-dividend preference** requires that when dividends are paid, this percentage of the preferred stock's par value be paid to preferred stockholders before common stockholders receive any dividends.

current-dividend preference

The right of preferred stockholders to receive current dividends before common stockholders receive dividends.

To illustrate the payment of different types of dividends, the following data from the Boston Lakers Basketball Team will be used throughout this section. (The various combinations of dividend preferences illustrated over the next few pages are summarized in Cases 1 to 4 in Exhibit 6.) As a reminder, the outstanding stock includes:

- Preferred stock: 5%, $40 par value, 1,000 shares issued and outstanding.
- Common stock: $1 par value, 6,000 shares issued, 5,990 shares outstanding.

To begin, note that, as with all preferred stock, the Lakers' 5% preferred stock has a current-dividend preference: Before any dividends can be paid to common stockholders, preferred stockholders must be paid a total of $2,000 ($40 × 0.05 × 1,000 shares). Thus, if only $1,500 of dividends are declared (Case 1), preferred stockholders will receive the

EXHIBIT 6	Dividend Preferences: Summary of Cases 1 to 4				
Case	Preferred Dividend Feature	Years in Arrears	Total Dividend	Preferred Dividend	Common Dividend
1	5%, Noncumulative	Not applicable	$ 1,500	$1,500	$ 0
2	5%, Noncumulative	Not applicable	3,000	2,000	1,000
3	5%, Cumulative	2	5,000	5,000	0
4	5%, Cumulative	2	11,000	6,000	5,000

entire dividend payment. If $3,000 are declared (Case 2), preferred stockholders will receive $2,000 and common stockholders, $1,000.

Cumulative-Dividend Preference. The **cumulative-dividend preference** can be quite costly for common stockholders because it requires that preferred stockholders be paid current dividends plus all unpaid dividends from past years before common stockholders receive anything. If dividends have been paid in all previous years, then only the current 5% must be paid to preferred stockholders. But if dividends on preferred stock were not paid in full in prior years, the cumulative deficiency must be paid before common stockholders receive anything.

With respect to the cumulative feature, it is important to repeat that companies are not required to pay dividends. Any past unpaid dividends are called **dividends in arrears**. Because they do not have to be paid unless dividends are declared in the future, dividends in arrears do not represent actual liabilities and thus are not recorded in the accounts. Instead, they are reported in the notes to the financial statements.

To illustrate the distribution of dividends for cumulative preferred stock, we will assume that the Boston Lakers Basketball Team has not paid any dividends for the last two years but has declared a dividend in the current year. The Lakers must pay $6,000 in dividends to preferred stockholders before they can give anything to the common stockholders. The calculation is as follows:

Dividends in arrears, 2 years	$4,000
Current-dividend preference	
($40 × 0.05 × 1,000 shares)	2,000
Total	$6,000

Therefore, if the Lakers pay only $5,000 in dividends (Case 3), preferred stockholders will receive all the dividends, common stockholders will receive nothing, and there will still be dividends in arrears of $1,000 the next year. If $11,000 in dividends are paid (Case 4), preferred stockholders will receive $6,000, and common stockholders will receive $5,000.

The entries to record the declaration and payment of dividends in Case 4 are:

Date of Declaration

Dividends, Preferred Stock	6,000	
Dividends, Common Stock	5,000	
Dividends Payable		11,000
Declared dividends on preferred and common stock.		

Date of Payment

Dividends Payable	11,000	
Cash		11,000
Paid dividends on preferred and common stock.		

Constraints on Payment of Cash Dividends

Earlier in this section, the question was asked whether a company should pay cash dividends. A related question is: Can the company legally pay cash dividends? To illustrate, consider the following exaggerated scenario. Tricky Company obtains a corporate charter, borrows $1 million from Naïve Bank, pays out a $1 million cash dividend to the stockholders, and all the stockholders disappear to the Bahamas. Is this a legal possibility? No, it isn't, because the corporate right to declare cash dividends is regulated by state law in order to protect creditors. The right to declare cash dividends is often linked to a company's Retained Earnings balance.

In many states, a company is **not** allowed to pay cash dividends in an amount that would cause the retained earnings balance to be negative. Thus, if the retained earnings balance of the Boston Lakers were $8,500, the $11,000 dividend in Case 4 discussed previously could not be paid, even if the Lakers had the available cash to make the payment. The incorporation laws in many states are less restrictive and allow the payment of cash dividends in excess of the retained earnings balance if, for example, current earnings are strong or the market value of the assets is high.

Frequently, lenders do not rely on state incorporation laws to protect them from excess cash dividend payments by corporations to which they lend money. Instead, the loan contract itself includes restrictions on the payment of cash dividends during the period that the loan is outstanding. In this way, lenders are able to prevent cash that should be used to repay loans from being paid to stockholders as dividends.

Dividend Payout Ratio

dividend payout ratio

A measure of the percentage of earnings paid out in dividends; computed by dividing cash dividends by net income.

A ratio of interest to stockholders is the **dividend payout ratio**. This ratio indicates the percentage of net income paid out during the year in the form of cash dividends and is computed as follows:

$$\text{Dividend payout ratio} = \frac{\text{Cash dividends}}{\text{Net income}}$$

Dividend payout ratio values for Dow Jones, Microsoft, and General Electric for 2005 are computed below. The numbers are in millions.

	Dow Jones	**Microsoft**	**General Electric**
Cash dividends	$81.59	$36,968.00	$9,647.00
Net income	$60.40	$12,254.00	$16,353.00
Dividend payout ratio	135.08%	301.68%	58.99%

Both Dow Jones and Microsoft paid out more in dividends than they earned in income for the year. This is not typical. Microsoft's high ratio was as a result of a one-time large cash dividend. General Electric's payout ratio of 59% is at the high end of what corporation's typically pay out. Most large U.S. corporations pay out approximately 40 to 60% of their annual income as dividends.

REMEMBER THIS...

- The retained earnings account reflects the total undistributed earnings of a business since incorporation. It is increased by net income and decreased by dividends, net losses, and some treasury stock transactions.
- The important dates associated with a cash dividend are:
  - the date of declaration,
  - the date of record, and
  - the payment date.
- Preferred stockholders can be granted a current and a cumulative preference for dividends over the rights of common stockholders.
- In some states, the payment of cash dividends is limited to an amount not to exceed the existing Retained Earnings balance.
- The dividend payout ratio (cash dividends divided by net income) reveals the percentage of net income that is paid out as cash dividends.

Other Equity Items

In addition to the two major categories of contributed capital and retained earnings, the equity section of a balance sheet often includes a number of miscellaneous items. These items are gains or losses that bypass the income statement when they are recognized. A further discussion of these items is given below.

Equity Items That Bypass the Income Statement

Since 1980, the equity sections of U.S. balance sheets have begun to fill up with a strange collection of items, each the subject of an accounting controversy. Two of these items are summarized below.

- *Foreign currency translation adjustment.* The foreign currency translation adjustment arises from the change in the equity of foreign subsidiaries (as measured in terms of U.S. dollars) that occurs as a result of changes in foreign currency exchange rates. For example, if the Japanese yen weakens relative to the U.S. dollar, the equity of Japanese subsidiaries of U.S. firms will decrease, in dollar terms. Before 1981, these changes were recognized as losses or gains on the income statement. Multinational firms disliked this treatment because it added volatility to reported earnings. The FASB changed the accounting rule, and now these changes are reported as direct adjustments to equity on the balance sheet, insulating the income statement from this aspect of foreign currency fluctuations.
- *Unrealized gains and losses on available-for-sale securities.* As will be explained in Chapter 12, available-for-sale securities are securities that a company purchased without intending to resell them immediately but also not necessarily planning to hold them forever. When the FASB was considering requiring securities to be reported at their market values on the balance sheet, companies complained about the income volatility that would be caused by recognizing these changes as gains or losses on the income statement. The FASB made the standard more acceptable to businesses by allowing unrealized gains and losses on available-for-sale securities to bypass the income statement and go straight to the equity section of the balance sheet.

The hodgepodge of direct equity adjustments described above is conceptually unsatisfying. These adjustments have arisen on a case-by-case basis as part of the FASB's effort to establish accounting standards that are accepted by the business community. As mentioned, many businesspeople are opposed to including these categories on the income statement because, they say, the income statement would become cluttered with gains and losses from market value changes, distracting from the purpose of the income statement, which is to focus on reporting profits from the activities of the business. The compromise that allows market values in the balance sheet while keeping the income statement uncluttered is the creation of a separate category of equity called **accumulated other comprehensive income**. Accumulated other comprehensive income is composed of certain market-related gains and losses that are not included in the computation of net income. It is important to remember that accumulated other comprehensive income is not income at all, but an equity category that summarizes the changes in equity that result during the period from market-related increases and decreases in the reported values of assets and liabilities. The reporting of accumulated other comprehensive income is illustrated in the 2005 equity section of **Dow Jones & Company**, shown in Exhibit 7.

accumulated other comprehensive income

Certain market-related gains and losses that are not included in the computation of net income; for example, foreign currency translation adjustments and unrealized gains or losses on investments.

EXHIBIT 7	Equity Section for Dow Jones & Company

Dow Jones & Company's Equity Section
(amounts in million of dollars)

	2005	2004
Common stock, par value $1.00 per share	$ 81,738	$ 81,572
Class B common stock, convertible, par value $1.00 per share	20,443	20,609
	$ 102,181	$ 102,181
Additional paid-in capital	137,290	124,082
Retained earnings	817,168	839,446
Accumulated other comprehensive income:		
Unrealized gain on investments	2,636	4,949
Unrealized (loss) gain on hedging	(198)	227
Foreign currency translation adjustment	3,430	6,826
Minimum pension liability, net of deferred taxes	(28,861)	(13,942)
	$1,033,646	$1,063,769
Less, treasury stock	871,381	913,226
Total stockholders' equity	$ 162,265	$ 150,543

statement of comprehensive income

A statement outlining the changes in accumulated comprehensive income that arose during the period.

A **statement of comprehensive income** provides a place, outside the regular income statement, for reporting all the unrealized gains and losses that are reported as equity adjustments. The appeal of comprehensive income is that this approach preserves the traditional income statement (calming the fears of the business community) but allows unrealized gains and losses to be reported. In essence, comprehensive income makes it possible to recognize unrealized gains and losses so that current market values can be reported on the balance sheet without having those unrealized gains and losses affect the income statement.

The statement of comprehensive income is very new; U.S. companies have been required to present it starting December 31, 1998. Dow Jones & Company's comprehensive income presentation for 2005 is shown in Exhibit 8. Note that net income is one component in the computation of comprehensive income. For Dow Jones, 2005 was a particularly bad year, with all five of the reported elements of comprehensive income being negative.

 STOP & THINK

Which will have a greater impact on a company's stock price: net income of $100 million or a $100 million unrealized gain from a change in exchange rates or securities prices? Explain your answer.

EXHIBIT 8	Statement of Comprehensive Income for Dow Jones & Company

(in thousands)	2005	2004	2003
Net income	$60,395	$ 99,548	$170,599
Unrealized gain (loss) on investments	(254)	(734)	4,118
Unrealized gain (loss) on hedging	(198)	227	453
Foreign currency translation adjustments	(1,179)	3,009	3,551
Minimum pension liability	(14,919)	(13,719)	9,756
Other	(4,503)	(453)	(2,059)
Comprehensive income (loss)	$39,342	$ 87,878	$186,418

Statement of Stockholders' Equity

statement of stockholders' equity

A financial statement that reports all changes in stockholders' equity.

Companies that have numerous changes in their stockholders' equity accounts during the year usually include a **statement of stockholders' equity** (also called a statement of changes in stockholders' equity) with their financial statements. This statement reconciles the beginning and ending balances for all stockholders' equity accounts reported on the balance sheet.

An illustrative statement of stockholders' equity from the 2005 annual report of Dow Jones & Company is presented in Exhibit 9. Note the following items in the statement:

- As mentioned earlier in the chapter, Dow Jones has two classes of common stock. Class B common shares with a par value of $166,000 were converted into ordinary common shares during the year.
- Dow Jones paid a dividend during the year of $82.673 million.
- The company reissued $41.8 million of its treasury shares during the year.

The last column in the statement reflects the total beginning and ending stockholders' equity account balances and all increases and decreases. Both the individual account

Exhibit 9	**Statement of Stockholders' Equity for Dow Jones & Company**

Consolidated Statement of Stockholders' Equity
Dow Jones & Company, Inc.
For the Year Ended December 31, 2005
(amounts in thousands of U.S. dollars)

	Common Stock	Class B Common Stock	Additional Paid-In Capital	Retained Earnings	Accumulated Other Comprehensive Income (Loss)	Treasury Stock Shares	Treasury Stock Amount	Total
Balance, December 31, 2004	$81,572	$20,609	$124,082	$839,446	$ (1,940)	(20,136,426)	$(913,226)	$150,543
Net income–2005				60,395				$ 60,395
Adjustment for realized gain on investments in income					(1,101)			(1,101)
Reclassification Adjustment					(958)			(958)
Unrealized loss on investment					(254)			(254)
Unrealized loss on hedging					(198)			(198)
Adjustment for realized gain on hedging included in net income					(227)			(227)
Translation adjustment, net of deferred taxes of $635					(1,179)			(1,179)
Adjustment for realized translation adjustment in net income					(2,217)			(2,217)
Minimum pension liability, net of deferred taxes of $8,377					(14,919)			(14,919)
Comprehensive income								$ 39,342
Dividends, $1.00 per share				(82,673)				$ (82,673)
Conversion of class B common stock into common stock	166	(166)						
Issuance of stock options related to acquisition of MarketWatch			24,902					24,902
Sales under stock compensation plans			(11,694)			1,061,785	41,845	30,151
Balance, December 31, 2005	$81,738	$20,443	$137,290	$817,168	$(22,993)	(19,074,641)	$(871,381)	$162,265

balances and total Stockholders' Equity at December 31, 2005, are reported on the balance sheet of Dow Jones & Company.

REMEMBER THIS...

- Accumulated other comprehensive income is not income at all, but an equity category that summarizes the effect on equity of certain market-related gains and losses.
- Two examples of items giving rise to accumulated other comprehensive income are:
  1. market fluctuations in the value of some investment securities and
  2. changes in the value of assets and liabilities held by foreign subsidiaries that are caused by exchange rate changes.
- A statement of stockholders' equity summarizes the changes affecting all the different categories of equity during the year.

REVIEW OF LEARNING OBJECTIVES

(1) Distinguish between debt and equity financing, and describe the advantages and disadvantages of organizing a business as a proprietorship or a partnership.

- A lender receives a fixed repayment amount.
- An investor receives a variable amount, depending on whether the company does well.

Proprietorship	Partnership
Owned by one person	Owned by two or more persons
Easy to start, easy to terminate	Easy to start, easy to terminate
Unlimited liability	Unlimited liability

(2) Describe the basic characteristics of a corporation and the nature of common and preferred stock.

Features of a corporation	(1) limited liability for stockholders,
	(2) easy transferability of ownership,
	(3) the ability to raise large amounts of capital,
	(4) separate taxation, and
	(5) for large corporations, closer regulation by government.
Basic rights of common stockholders	(1) the right to vote in corporate matters,
	(2) the right to maintain proportionate ownership,
	(3) the right to receive cash dividends, and
	(4) the ownership of all excess corporate assets upon liquidation of the corporation.

- Preferred stock typically carries preferential claims to dividend and liquidation privileges but has no voting rights.

③ Account for the issuance and repurchase of common and preferred stock.

- When a company issues stock, it debits Cash or a noncash account (Property, for example) and credits various stockholders' equity accounts.
- Shares typically are assigned a par value, which is usually small in relation to the market value of the shares. Amounts received upon issuance of shares are divided into par value and paid-in capital in excess of par.
- A company's own stock that is repurchased is known as treasury stock and is included in the financial statements as a contra-stockholders' equity account.

④ Understand the factors that affect retained earnings, describe the factors determining whether a company can and should pay cash dividends, and account for cash dividends.

- The retained earnings are:
  - increased by net income,
  - decreased by dividends, net losses, and some treasury stock transactions.
- The important dates associated with a cash dividend are:
  - the date of declaration,
  - the date of record, and
  - the payment date.
- Preferred stockholders can be granted a current and a cumulative preference for dividends over the rights of common stockholders.
- The dividend payout ratio (cash dividends divided by net income) reveals the percentage of net income that is paid out as cash dividends.

⑤ Describe the purpose of reporting comprehensive income in the equity section of the balance sheet, and prepare a statement of stockholders' equity.

- Accumulated other comprehensive income is an equity account.
- Two examples of items giving rise to accumulated other comprehensive income are:
  - market fluctuations in the value of some investment securities, and
  - changes in the value of assets and liabilities held by foreign subsidiaries that are caused by exchange rate changes.
- A statement of stockholders' equity summarizes the changes affecting all the different categories of equity during the year.

KEY TERMS & CONCEPTS

accumulated other comprehensive income, 531
board of directors, 520
cash dividend, 526
common stock, 520
contributed capital, 522
convertible preferred stock, 520

corporation, 518
cumulative-dividend preference, 529
current-dividend preference, 528
date of record, 527
declaration date, 527
dividend payment date, 527

dividend payout ratio, 530
dividends, 526
dividends in arrears, 529
limited liability, 518
par value, 521
partnership, 517
preferred stock, 520
proprietorship, 517
prospectus, 519

retained earnings, 526
statement of comprehensive income, 532
statement of stockholders' equity, 533
stockholders, 519
treasury stock, 523

REVIEW PROBLEM

Stockholders' Equity

Clarke Corporation was organized during 1979. At the end of 2009, the equity section of the balance sheet was:

Contributed capital:	
Preferred stock (8%, $30 par, 6,000 shares authorized,	
5,000 shares issued and outstanding)	$150,000
Common stock ($5 par, 50,000 shares authorized,	
20,000 shares issued, 17,000 shares outstanding)	100,000
Paid-in capital in excess of par, common stock	80,000
Total contributed capital	$330,000
Retained earnings	140,000
Total contributed capital plus retained earnings	$470,000
Less treasury stock (3,000 shares of common stock	
at cost, $10 per share)	(30,000)
Total stockholders' equity	$440,000

During 2009, the following stockholders' equity transactions occurred in chronological sequence:

a. Issued 800 shares of common stock at $11 per share.

b. Reissued 1,200 shares of treasury stock at $12 per share.

c. Issued 300 shares of preferred stock at $33 per share.

d. Reissued 400 shares of treasury stock at $9 per share.

e. Declared and paid a dividend large enough to meet the current-dividend preference on the preferred stock and to pay the common stockholders $1.50 per share.

f. Net income for 2009 was $70,000, which included $400,000 of revenues and $330,000 of expenses.

g. Closed the dividends accounts for 2009.

Required:

1. Journalize the transactions.
2. Set up T-accounts with beginning balances and post the journal entries to the T-accounts, adding any necessary new accounts. (Assume a beginning balance of $20,000 for the cash account.)
3. Prepare the stockholders' equity section of the balance sheet as of December 31, 2009.

Solution

1. Journalize the Transactions

a.	Cash	8,800	
	Common Stock		4,000
	Paid-In Capital in Excess of Par, Common Stock		4,800
	Issued 800 shares of common stock at $11 per share.		

Cash received is $11 × 800 shares; common stock is par value times the number of shares ($5 × 800); paid-in capital is the excess.

b.	Cash	14,400	
	Treasury Stock		12,000
	Paid-In Capital, Treasury Stock		2,400
	Reissued 1,200 shares of treasury stock at $12 per share.		

Cash is $12 × 1,200 shares; treasury stock is the cost times the number of shares sold ($10 × 1,200 shares); paid-in capital is the excess.

c.	Cash	9,900	
	Preferred Stock		9,000
	Paid-In Capital in Excess of Par, Preferred Stock		900
	Issued 300 shares of preferred stock at $33 per share.		

(continued)

Cash is $33 × 300 shares; preferred stock is par value times the number of shares issued ($30 × 300); paid-in capital is the excess.

d.	Cash	3,600	
	Paid-In Capital, Treasury Stock	400	
	Treasury Stock		4,000

Reissued 400 shares of treasury stock at $9 per share.

Cash is $9 × 400 shares; treasury stock is the cost times the number of shares sold ($10 × 400); paid-in capital is decreased for the difference. If no Paid-In Capital, Treasury Stock balance had existed, Retained Earnings would have been debited.

e.	Dividends, Preferred Stock	12,720	
	Dividends, Common Stock	29,100	
	Cash		41,820

Declared and paid cash dividend.

Calculations:

Preferred Stock	Number of Shares	Par-Value Amount
Original balance	5,000	$150,000
Entry (c)	300	9,000
Total	5,300	$159,000
		× 0.08
		$ 12,720

Common Stock	Number of Shares
Original balance (excludes treasury stock)	17,000
Entry (a)	800
Entry (b)	1,200
Entry (d)	400
Total	19,400 shares
	× $1.50
	$29,100
Total preferred stock dividend	$12,720
Total common stock dividend	29,100
Total dividend	$41,820

f.	Revenues (individual revenue accounts)	400,000	
	Expenses (individual expense accounts)		330,000
	Retained Earnings		70,000

To close net income to Retained Earnings.

g.	Retained Earnings	41,820	
	Dividends, Preferred Stock		12,720
	Dividends, Common Stock		29,100

To close the dividends accounts for 2009.

2. Set up T-Accounts and Post to the Accounts

Cash

Beg.			
Bal.	20,000	(e)	41,820
(a)	8,800		
(b)	14,400		
(c)	9,900		
(d)	3,600		
Bal.	14,880		

Preferred Stock

		Beg.	
		Bal.	150,000
		(c)	9,000
		Bal.	159,000

Paid-In Capital in Excess of Par, Preferred Stock

		(c)	900
		Bal.	900

(continued)

Common Stock

	Beg.		
	Bal.	100,000	
	(a)	4,000	
	Bal.	104,000	

Paid-In Capital in Excess of Par, Common Stock

	Beg.		
	Bal.	80,000	
	(a)	4,800	
	Bal.	84,800	

Treasury Stock

	Beg.			
	Bal.	30,000	(b)	12,000
			(d)	4,000
	Bal.	14,000		

Paid-In Capital, Treasury Stock

(d)	400	(b)	2,400
		Bal.	2,000

Retained Earnings

			Beg.	
(g)	41,820		Bal.	140,000
			(f)	70,000
			Bal.	168,180

Dividends, Preferred Stock

(e)	12,720	(g)	12,720
Bal.	0		

Dividends, Common Stock

(e)	29,100	(g)	29,100
Bal.	0		

Revenues

			Beg.	
(f)	400,000		Bal.	400,000
			Bal.	0

Expenses

	Beg.			
	Bal.	330,000	(f)	330,000
	Bal.	0		

3. Prepare Stockholders' Equity Section of the Balance Sheet

Clarke Corporation
Partial Balance Sheet
December 31, 2009

Stockholders' Equity
Contributed capital:

Preferred stock (8%, $30 par, 6,000 shares authorized, 5,300 shares issued and outstanding)	$159,000
Common stock ($5 par, 50,000 shares authorized, 20,800 shares issued, 19,400 outstanding)	104,000
Paid-in capital in excess of par, preferred stock	900
Paid-in capital in excess of par, common stock	84,800
Paid-in capital, treasury stock	2,000
Total contributed capital	$350,700
Retained earnings	168,180
Total contributed capital plus retained earnings	$518,880
Less treasury stock (1,400 shares of common stock at cost, $10 per share)	(14,000)
Total stockholders' equity	$504,880

Transaction	Common Stock Issued	Common Stock Authorized	Treasury Stock
Number of shares originally issued	20,000	50,000	3,000
Entry (a)	800		
Entry (b)			(1,200)
Entry (d)			(400)
Total	20,800	50,000	1,400

DISCUSSION QUESTIONS

1. What are the primary differences between debt financing and equity financing?
2. What are the major differences between a partnership and a corporation?
3. How is a proprietorship or partnership established?
4. Does the death of a partner legally terminate a partnership? If so, does it mean that the partnership must cease operating?
5. Are partners legally liable for the actions of other partners? Explain.
6. In which type of business entity do all owners have limited liability?
7. In what way are corporate profits subject to double taxation?
8. How do common and preferred stock differ?
9. What is the purpose of having a par value for stock?
10. Why would a company repurchase its own shares of stock that it had previously issued?
11. Is treasury stock an asset? If not, why not?
12. How is treasury stock usually accounted for?
13. In what way does the stockholders' equity section of a balance sheet identify the sources of the assets?
14. What factors affect the Retained Earnings balance of a corporation?
15. Is it possible for a firm to have a large Retained Earnings balance and no cash? Explain.
16. When is a company legally barred from paying cash dividends?
17. Why should a potential common stockholder carefully examine the dividend preferences of a company's preferred stock?
18. The dividend payout ratio for Deedle Company is 40%. What does this mean?
19. What is accumulated other comprehensive income? Why was this concept adopted by accounting standard-setters?
20. Give two examples of other equity items (items that bypass the income statement and go directly to the equity section of the balance sheet).

PRACTICE EXERCISES

PE 11-1
LO1
Characteristics of Proprietorships and Partnerships
Which one of the following is *not* a usual characteristic of either a proprietorship or a partnership?
a. Limited size.
b. Limited life.
c. Ease of formation.
d. Unlimited liability.

PE 11-2
LO2
Characteristics of Corporations
Which one of the following is *not* a usual characteristic of a corporation?
a. Limited liability.
b. Limited life.
c. Close government regulation.
d. Easy transferability of ownership.
e. Ability to raise large amounts of capital.

PE 11-3
LO2
Characteristics of Common Stock and Preferred Stock
Which one of the following statements is true regarding common stock and preferred stock?
a. Preferred stockholders always have the right to vote in corporate matters.
b. Common stockholders are the residual owners of the business after all other obligations have been paid.
c. Preferred stock is better than common stock.
d. Common stockholders receive dividends before preferred stockholders.
e. Preferred stock can never be converted into common stock.

PE 11-4
LO3
Issuance of No-Par Common Stock
The company issued 5,000 shares of no-par common stock at $25 per share for cash. Make the necessary journal entry(ies) to record this transaction.

PE 11-5
LO3
Issuance of Common Stock for Cash

The company issued 3,000 shares of $1 par-value common stock for $40 per share for cash. Make the necessary journal entry(ies) to record this transaction.

PE 11-6
LO3
Issuance of Common Stock for Other Assets

The company issued 7,200 shares of $1 par-value common stock in exchange for a building. The market value of the stock at the date of the exchange was $30 per share. Make the necessary journal entry(ies) to record this transaction.

PE 11-7
LO3
Accounting for Stock Repurchases

The company repurchased 1,500 shares of $1 par-value common stock for $32 per share from the open market. Make the necessary journal entry(ies) to record this transaction.

PE 11-8
LO3
Accounting for Sale of Treasury Stock at Price Higher than Cost

Refer to the data in PE 11-7. The company resells 400 shares of treasury stock for $40 per share. Make the necessary journal entry(ies) to record this transaction.

PE 11-9
LO3
Accounting for Sale of Treasury Stock at Price Lower than Cost

Refer to the data in PE 11-7 and PE 11-8. The company resells 300 shares of treasury stock for $28 per share. Make the necessary journal entry(ies) to record this transaction.

PE 11-10
LO3
Accounting for Sale of Treasury Stock at Price Lower than Cost

Refer to the data in PE 11-7 through PE 11-9. The paid-in capital, treasury stock account currently has a $2,500 credit balance. The company resells 800 shares of treasury stock for $26 per share. Make the necessary journal entry(ies) to record this transaction.

PE 11-11
LO4
Dividend Declaration Accounting

The company has the following two types of stock:
1. 2,000 shares of 10% cumulative preferred stock with a $20 par value.
2. 5,000 shares of common stock with a $1 par value.

The company declared a $21,000 cash dividend. Make the necessary journal entry(ies) to record this event.

PE 11-12
LO4
Dividend Payment Accounting

Refer to the data in PE 11-11. Make the necessary journal entry(ies) to record the payment of the cash dividend.

PE 11-13
LO4
Dividend Closing Entry(ies)

Refer to the data in PE 11-11. Make the necessary journal entry(ies) to close the dividend accounts to retained earnings at the end of the year.

PE 11-14
LO4
Dividend Payout Ratio

Using the following data, compute the dividend payout ratio.

Cash dividends	$ 19,000
Sales	512,000
Net income	76,000

PE 11-15
LO5
Balance Sheet Preparation

Using the following data, prepare a statement of stockholders' equity for the company.

(continued)

Paid-in capital in excess of par, common stock	$492,000
Retained earnings	200,000
Common stock ($1 par value, 8,400 shares issued, 8,000 outstanding)	8,000
Treasury stock (400 shares of $1 common at cost of $45)	18,000
Preferred stock ($20 par value, 2,500 shares issued and outstanding)	50,000

PE 11-16
LO5

Statement of Comprehensive Income

Using the following items, compute the company's comprehensive income.

1. The company's investment in a foreign subsidiary increased by $4,000 because the Euro strengthened relative to the U.S. dollar during the year.
2. Net income for the year was $52,000.
3. Unrealized loss on investments for the year was $11,000.

EXERCISES

E 11-17
LO3

Issuance of Stock

Brockbank Corporation was organized on July 15, 2009. Record the journal entries for Brockbank to account for the following:

a. The state authorized 30,000 shares of 7% preferred stock ($20 par) and 100,000 shares of no-par common stock.
b. The company gave 6,000 shares of common stock to its attorney in return for her help in incorporating the business. Fees for this work are normally about $18,000. (*Note:* The debit is to Legal Expense.)
c. Brockbank Corporation gave 15,000 shares of common stock to an individual who contributed a building worth $50,000.
d. Brockbank Corporation issued 5,000 shares of preferred stock at $25 per share.
e. Peter Brockbank paid $70,000 cash for 30,000 shares of common stock.
f. Another individual donated a $15,000 machine and received 4,000 shares of common stock.
g. The attorney sold all her shares to her brother-in-law for $18,000.

E 11-18
LO3

No-Par Stock Transactions

Harmsen Maintenance Corporation was organized in early 2009 with 60,000 shares of no-par common stock authorized. During 2009, the following transactions occurred:

a. Issued 31,000 shares of stock at $24 per share.
b. Issued another 3,900 shares of stock at $28 per share.
c. Issued 3,000 shares for a building appraised at $90,000.
d. Declared dividends of $1.50 per share.
e. Earned net income of $187,000 for the year, including $405,000 of revenues and $218,000 of expenses, and closed these accounts.
f. Closed the dividends accounts.

Given this information:

1. Journalize the transactions.
2. Present the stockholders' equity section of the balance sheet as it would appear on December 31, 2009.

E 11-19
LO3

Treasury Stock Transactions

Provide the necessary journal entries to record the following:

a. Washington Corporation was granted a charter authorizing the issuance of 200,000 shares of $10 par-value common stock.

(continued)

b. The company issued 50,000 shares of common stock at $15 per share.

c. The company reacquired 3,000 shares of its own stock at $19 per share, to be held in treasury.

d. Another 1,500 shares of stock were reacquired at $21 per share.

e. Of the shares reacquired in (c), 1,200 were reissued for $24 per share.

f. Of the shares reacquired in (d), all 1,500 were reissued for $16 per share.

g. Given the preceding transactions, what is the balance in the treasury stock account?

E 11-20
LO3, LO4

Stock Issuance and Cash Dividends

Lindstrom Corporation was organized in January 2009. The state authorized 200,000 shares of no-par common stock and 75,000 shares of 8%, $24 par, preferred stock. Record the following transactions that occurred in 2009:

a. Issued 20,000 shares of common stock at $35 per share.

b. Issued 3,500 shares of preferred stock for a building appraised at $100,000.

c. Declared a cash dividend sufficient to meet the current-dividend preference on preferred stock and pay common shareholders $3.50 per share.

E 11-21
LO3, LO4

Stock Issuance, Treasury Stock, and Dividends

On January 1, 2009, Vaness Corporation was granted a charter authorizing the following capital stock: common stock, $5 par, 200,000 shares; preferred stock, $10 par, 7%, 50,000 shares. Record the following 2009 transactions:

a. Issued 95,000 shares of common stock at $22 per share.

b. Issued 18,000 shares of preferred stock at $13 per share.

c. Bought back 10,000 shares of common stock at $30 per share.

d. Reissued 1,000 shares of treasury stock at $27 per share.

e. Declared cash dividends of $27,400 to be allocated between common and preferred stockholders. (The preferred stock, which has a current-dividend preference, is noncumulative.)

f. Paid dividends of $27,400.

E 11-22
LO3, LO4

Stock Issuance, Treasury Stock, and Dividends

On January 1, 2009, Snow Company was authorized to issue 100,000 shares of common stock, par value $10 per share and 10,000 shares of 8% preferred stock, par value $20 per share. Record the following transactions for 2009:

a. Issued 70,000 shares of common stock at $25 per share.

b. Issued 8,000 shares of preferred stock at $30 per share.

c. Reacquired 5,000 shares of common stock at $20 per share.

d. Reissued 2,000 shares of treasury stock for $46,000.

e. Declared a cash dividend sufficient to meet the current-dividend preference on preferred stock and pay common shareholders $1 per share.

E 11-23
LO3, LO4

Stock Transactions and Dividends

Fowler Corporation was organized in January 2009. The state authorized 150,000 shares of no-par common stock and 50,000 shares of 12%, $8 par, preferred stock. Record the following transactions that occurred in 2009:

a. Issued 28,000 shares of common stock at $32 per share.

b. Issued 15,000 shares of preferred stock for a piece of land appraised at $200,000.

c. Declared a cash dividend sufficient to meet the current-dividend preference on preferred stock and paid common shareholders $2 per share.

d. How would your answer to (c) change if the dividend declared were not sufficient to meet the current-dividend preference on preferred stock?

E 11-24
LO4

Dividend Calculations

On January 1, 2009, Oldroyd Corporation had 130,000 shares of common stock issued and outstanding. During 2009, the following transactions occurred (in chronological order):

(continued)

a. Oldroyd issued 10,000 new shares of common stock.
b. The company reacquired 2,000 shares of stock for use in its employee stock option plan.
c. At the end of the option period, 1,200 shares of treasury stock had been purchased by corporate officials.

Given this information, compute the following:
1. After the foregoing three transactions have occurred, what amount of dividends must Oldroyd Corporation declare in order to pay 50 cents per share? To pay $1 per share?
2. What is the dividend per share if $236,640 is paid?
3. If all 2,000 treasury shares had been purchased by corporate officials through the stock option plan, what would the dividends per share have been, again assuming $236,640 in dividends were paid? (Round to the nearest cent.)

E 11-25

LO4

Dividend Calculations

Churchill Corporation has the following stock outstanding:

Preferred stock (6%, $20 par value, 40,000 shares)	$800,000
Common stock ($2 par value, 400,000 shares)	800,000

For the two independent cases that follow, compute the amount of dividends that would be paid to preferred and common shareholders. Assume that total dividends paid are $200,000. No dividends have been paid for the past three years.

Case A, Preferred is noncumulative.
Case B, Preferred is cumulative.

E 11-26

LO3, LO4

Stock Issuance, Treasury Stock, and Dividends

During 2009, Doxey Corporation had the following transactions and related events:

Jan. 15   Issued 6,500 shares of common stock at par ($16 per share), bringing the total number of shares outstanding to 121,300.

Feb. 6   Declared a 50-cent-per-share dividend on common stock for stockholders of record on March 6.

Mar. 6   Date of record.

     8   Pedro Garcia, a prominent banker, purchased 20,000 shares of Doxey Corporation common stock from the company for $346,000.

Apr. 6   Paid dividends declared on February 6.

June 19   Reacquired 800 shares of common stock as treasury stock at a total cost of $9,350.

Sept. 6   Declared dividends of 55 cents per share to be paid to common stockholders of record on October 15, 2009.

Oct. 6   The Dow Jones Industrial Average plummeted 300 points, and Doxey's stock price fell $3 per share.

     15   Date of record.

Nov. 16   Paid dividends declared on September 6.

Dec. 15   Declared and paid a 6% cash dividend on 18,000 outstanding shares of preferred stock (par value $32).

Given this information:
1. Prepare the journal entries for these transactions.
2. What is the total amount of dividends paid to common and preferred stockholders during 2009?

E 11-27
LO4

Dividend Payout Ratio

The following numbers are for three different companies:

	A	B	C
Total assets	$3,100	$3,500	$2,900
Cash dividends	30	200	340
Total liabilities	2,600	1,600	2,000
Net income	310	420	460

For each company, compute the dividend payout ratio.

E 11-28
LO5

Analysis of Stockholders' Equity

The stockholders' equity section of Kay Corporation at the end of the current year showed:

Preferred stock (6%, $40 par, 10,000 shares authorized, 6,000 shares issued and outstanding)	$?
Common stock ($6 par, 80,000 shares authorized, 53,000 issued, 52,650 shares outstanding)	318,000
Paid-in capital in excess of par, preferred stock	?
Paid-in capital in excess of par, common stock	129,000
Retained earnings	86,000
Less treasury stock (350 shares at cost)	(2,000)
Total stockholders' equity	$?

1. What is the dollar amount to be reported for preferred stock?
2. What is the average price for which common stock was issued? (Round to the nearest cent.)
3. If preferred stock was issued at an average price of $43 per share, what amount should appear in the paid-in capital in excess of par, preferred stock account?
4. What is the average cost per share of treasury stock? (Round to the nearest cent.)
5. Assuming that the preferred stock was issued for an average price of $43 per share, what is total stockholders' equity?
6. If net income for the year were $67,000 and if only dividends on preferred stock were paid, by how much would retained earnings increase?

E 11-29
LO5

Preparing the Stockholders' Equity Section

The following account balances, before any closing entries, appear on the books of Spring Company as of December 31, 2009:

Retained Earnings (balance at Jan. 1, 2009)	$240,000
Dividends, Preferred Stock	15,000
Dividends, Common Stock	35,000
Common Stock ($5 par, 100,000 shares authorized, 70,000 issued and outstanding)	350,000
Paid-In Capital in Excess of Par, Common Stock	350,000
Preferred Stock (6%, $50 par, 50,000 shares authorized, 5,000 issued and outstanding)	250,000
Paid-In Capital in Excess of Par, Preferred Stock	25,000

Based on these account balances, and assuming net income for 2009 of $80,000, prepare the stockholders' equity section of the December 31, 2009, balance sheet for Spring Company.

E 11-30
LO5

Comprehensive Income

The following information relates to Larkin Company:
a. Larkin Company's net income for the year was $23,000.

(continued)

b. Larkin Company has an investment portfolio for long-term investment purposes. That portfolio decreased in value by $2,600 during the year.

c. Larkin Company has several foreign subsidiaries. The currencies in the countries where those subsidiaries are located increased in value (relative to the U.S. dollar) during the year. Accordingly, the computed value of the equity of those subsidiaries, in U.S. dollars, decreased by $1,700.

Compute Larkin's comprehensive income for the year.

E 11-31
LO5

Other Equity Items

Red Rider Company has the following stockholders' equity section on its balance sheet as of December 31, 2009 and 2008.

Red Rider Company (in millions)		
	2009	**2008**
Stockholders' Equity		
Preferred stock	$ 2.0	$ 2.0
Common stock	32.0	32.0
Paid-in capital–various	12.4	11.2
Retained earnings	24.5	24.6
Subtotal	$ 70.9	$69.8
Accumulated foreign currency translation adjustments	5.2	4.5
Net unrealized gains on investments in certain debt and equity securities	25.6	20.0
Total stockholders' equity	$101.7	$94.3

Based on this stockholders' equity section, answer the following questions:

1. At the end of 2009, what was the total amount of equity financing provided by Red Rider's investors?
2. At the end of 2009, how much of Red Rider's earnings had not been distributed to investors?
3. What is the total amount of "other equity items" contained in the 2009 stockholders' equity section?
4. What contributed most to the increased equity from 2008 to 2009?

PROBLEMS

P 11-32
LO3, LO4

Stock Transactions and Analysis

The following selected items and amounts were taken from the balance sheet of Quale Company as of December 31, 2009:

Cash	$ 93,000
Property, plant, and equipment	850,000
Accumulated depreciation	150,000
Liabilities	50,000
Preferred stock (7%, $100 par, noncumulative, 10,000 shares authorized, 5,000 shares issued and outstanding)	500,000
Common stock ($10 par, 100,000 shares authorized, 80,000 shares issued and outstanding)	800,000
Paid-in capital in excess of par, preferred stock	1,000
Paid-in capital in excess of par, common stock	125,000
Paid-in capital, treasury stock	1,000
Retained earnings	310,000

(continued)

Required:

For each of parts (1) to (5), (a) prepare the necessary journal entry (or entries) to record each transaction, and (b) calculate the amount that would appear on the December 31, 2009, balance sheet as a consequence of this transaction only for the account given. (*Note:* In your answer to each part of this problem, consider this to be the only transaction that took place during 2009.)

1. Quale Company issued 200 shares of common stock in exchange for cash of $4,000.
   a. Entry
   b. Paid-In Capital in Excess of Par, Common Stock
2. The company issued 200 shares of preferred stock at a price of $102 per share.
   a. Entry
   b. Paid-In Capital in Excess of Par, Preferred Stock
3. The company issued 500 shares of common stock in exchange for a building. The common stock is not actively traded, but the building was recently appraised at $11,000.
   a. Entry
   b. Property, Plant, and Equipment
4. The company reacquired 1,000 shares of common stock from a stockholder for $23,000 and subsequently reissued the shares to a different investor for $21,500. (*Note:* Make two entries.)
   a. Entries
   b. Paid-In Capital, Treasury Stock
5. The board of directors declared dividends of $75,000. This amount includes the current-year dividend preference on preferred stock, with the remainder to be paid to common shareholders.
   a. Entry
   b. Retained Earnings

P 11-33

LO3, LO4, LO5

Stock Transactions and the Stockholders' Equity Section

The following is Saratoga Springs Company's stockholders' equity section of the balance sheet on December 31, 2008:

Preferred stock (7%, $50 par, noncumulative, 22,000 shares authorized, 9,000 shares issued and outstanding)	$450,000
Common stock ($8 par, 110,000 shares authorized, 94,000 shares issued and outstanding)	752,000
Paid-in capital in excess of par, preferred stock	125,000
Paid-in capital in excess of par, common stock	326,000
Retained earnings	540,000

Required:

1. Journalize the following 2009 transactions:
   a. Issued 3,000 preferred shares at $62 per share.
   b. Reacquired 2,500 common shares for the treasury at $17 per share.
   c. Declared and paid a $1.50-per-share dividend on common stock in addition to paying the required preferred dividends. (*Note:* Debit Retained Earnings directly.)
   d. Reissued 900 treasury shares at $20 per share.
   e. Reissued the remaining treasury shares at $16 per share.
   f. Earnings for the year were $83,000, including $350,000 of revenues and $267,000 of expenses.
2. Prepare the stockholders' equity section of the balance sheet for the company at December 31, 2009.

P 11-34

LO3

Recording Stockholders' Equity Transactions

Zina Corporation was organized during 2008. At the end of 2008, the stockholders' equity section of the balance sheet appeared as follows:

(continued)

Contributed capital:	
Preferred stock (5%, $30 par, 15,000 shares authorized,	
8,000 shares issued and outstanding)	$240,000
Common stock ($22 par, 36,000 shares authorized, 18,000 issued,	
15,000 outstanding)	396,000
Paid-in capital in excess of par, preferred stock	56,000
Total contributed capital	$692,000
Retained earnings	244,000
Total contributed capital plus retained earnings	$936,000
Less treasury stock (3,000 shares at cost of $28 per share)	(84,000)
Total stockholders' equity	$852,000

During 2009, the following transactions occurred in the order given:

a. Issued 1,200 shares of common stock at $25 per share.

b. Reissued 1,600 shares of treasury stock at $30 per share.

c. Reissued 750 shares of treasury stock at $21 per share.

Required:

Record the transactions.

P 11-35

LO3, LO4, LO5

Stock Transactions and Stockholders' Equity Section

The balance sheet for Lakeland Corporation as of December 31, 2008, is as follows:

Assets		$750,000
Liabilities		$410,000
Stockholders' equity:		
Preferred stock, convertible (5%, $20 par)	$ 50,000	
Common stock ($10 par)	150,000	
Paid-in capital in excess of par, common stock	30,000	
Retained earnings	116,000	
	$346,000	
Less treasury stock, common (500 shares at cost)	(6,000)	340,000
Total liabilities and stockholders' equity		$750,000

During 2009, the following transactions were completed in the order given:

a. The company reacquired 750 shares of outstanding common stock at $7 per share.

b. The company reacquired 150 shares of common stock in settlement of an account receivable of $1,500.

c. Semiannual cash dividends of 75 cents per share on common stock and 50 cents per share on preferred stock were declared and paid.

d. Each share of preferred stock is convertible into three shares of common stock. Five hundred shares of preferred stock were converted into common stock. (*Hint:* Shares are converted at par values, and any excess reduces Retained Earnings.)

e. The 900 shares of common treasury stock acquired during 2009 were sold at $13. The remaining treasury shares were exchanged for a machine with a fair market value of $6,300.

f. The company issued 3,000 shares of common stock in exchange for land appraised at $39,000.

g. Semiannual cash dividends of 75 cents per share on common stock and 50 cents per share on preferred stock were declared and paid.

h. Closed net income of $35,000 to Retained Earnings, which included $135,000 of revenues and $100,000 of expenses.

i. Closed dividends accounts to Retained Earnings.

(continued)

Required:

1. Give the necessary journal entries to record the transactions listed.
2. Prepare the stockholders' equity section of the balance sheet as of December 31, 2009.

P 11-36

LO3, LO4, LO5

Stockholders' Equity, Dividends, and Treasury Stock

The stockholders' equity section of Nielsen Corporation's December 31, 2008, balance sheet is as follows:

Stockholders' equity:	
Preferred stock (10%, $50 par, 10,000 shares authorized,	
1,000 shares issued and outstanding)	$ 50,000
Common stock ($15 par, 100,000 shares authorized,	
5,000 shares issued and outstanding)	75,000
Paid-in capital in excess of par, preferred stock	2,000
Paid-in capital in excess of par, common stock	25,000
Total contributed capital	$152,000
Retained earnings	102,000
Total stockholders' equity	$254,000

During 2009, Nielsen Corporation had the following transactions affecting stockholders' equity:

Jan.	20	Paid a cash dividend of $2 per share on common stock. The dividend was declared on December 15, 2008.
Aug.	15	Reacquired 1,000 shares of common stock at $20 per share.
Sept.	30	Reissued 500 shares of treasury stock at $21 per share.
Oct.	15	Declared and paid cash dividends of $3 per share on the common stock.
Nov.	1	Reissued 200 shares of treasury stock at $18 per share.
Dec.	15	Declared and paid the 10% preferred cash dividend.
	31	Closed net income of $40,000 to Retained Earnings. (Revenues were $260,000; expenses were $220,000.) Also closed the dividends accounts to Retained Earnings.

Required:

1. Journalize the transactions.
2. Prepare the stockholders' equity section of Nielsen Corporation's December 31, 2009, balance sheet.
3. **Interpretive Question:** What is the effect on earnings per share when a company purchases treasury stock?

P 11-37

LO4

Dividend Calculations

Snowy Peaks Corporation was organized in January 2006 and issued shares of preferred and common stock as shown. As of December 31, 2009, there have been no changes in outstanding stock.

Preferred stock (10%, $15 par, 10,000 shares issued and outstanding)	$150,000
Common stock ($20 par, 15,000 shares issued and outstanding)	300,000

Required:

For each of the following independent situations, compute the amount of dividends that would be paid for each class of stock in 2008 and 2009. Assume that total dividends of $8,000 and $92,000 are paid in 2008 and 2009, respectively.

1. Preferred stock is noncumulative.
2. Preferred stock is cumulative, and no dividends are in arrears in 2008.
3. Preferred stock is cumulative, and no dividends have been paid during 2006 and 2007.

P 11-38   **Dividend Calculations**

LO4

Lowe Corporation had authorization for 80,000 shares of 8% preferred stock, par value $20 per share, and 24,000 shares of common stock, par value $120 per share, all of which are issued and outstanding. During the years beginning in 2008, Lowe Corporation maintained a policy of paying out 50% of net income in cash dividends. One-half the net income for the three years beginning in 2008 was $50,000, $280,000, and $340,000. There are no dividends in arrears for years prior to 2008.

Required:

Compute the amount of dividends paid to each class of stock for each year under the following separate cases:

1. Preferred stock is noncumulative.
2. Preferred stock is cumulative.
3. **Interpretive Question:** Why is it important that a common stockholder know about the dividend privileges of the preferred stock?

P 11-39   **Dividend Transactions and Calculations**

LO3, LO4

As of December 31, 2008, Nibley Corporation has 300,000 shares of $12 par-value common stock authorized, with 120,000 of these shares issued and outstanding.

Required:

1. Prepare journal entries to record the following 2009 transactions:

Jan.   1   Received authorization for 150,000 shares of 5%, cumulative preferred stock with a par value of $15.

      2   Issued 14,000 shares of the preferred stock at $20 per share.

June   1   Reacquired 30% of the common stock outstanding for $25 per share.

      2   Declared a cash dividend of $20,000. The date of record is June 15.

   30   Paid the previously declared cash dividend of $20,000.

2. Determine the proper allocation to preferred and common stockholders of a $150,000 cash dividend declared on December 31, 2009. (This dividend is in addition to the June 2 dividend.)
3. **Interpretive Question:** Why didn't the preferred stockholders receive their current-dividend preference of $10,500 in part (2)?

P 11-40   **Dividend Payout Ratio**

LO4

The following numbers are for three different companies:

	A	B	C
Cash	$ 300	$ 500	$ 700
Retained earnings	900	1,000	4,100
Cash dividends	0	100	600
Paid-in capital	3,200	2,000	2,500
Total liabilities	800	900	700
Sales	8,000	6,000	7,000
Net income	400	700	900

Required:

1. For each company, compute the dividend payout ratio.
2. **Interpretive Question:** Which of the three companies is most likely to be a high-growth Internet company? Which is most likely to be an old, stable company? Explain.

P 11-41   **Preparing the Stockholders' Equity Section and Recording Dividends**

LO4, LO5

In 2007, Lee Ann Adams and some college friends organized The Candy Jar, a gourmet candy company. In 2007, The Candy Jar issued 150,000 of the 300,000 authorized shares of

(continued)

common stock, par value $15, for $3,000,000 and all the 50,000 authorized shares of 10%, $20 par, cumulative preferred stock for $1,100,000. Combined earnings for 2007, 2008, 2009, and 2010 amounted to $1,250,000. Dividends paid in the four years were as follows: 2007—$100,000; 2008—$300,000; 2009—$0; 2010—$150,000.

Required:

1. Prepare the stockholders' equity section of the balance sheet as of December 31, 2010, for The Candy Jar.
2. Prepare the journal entry that would be necessary to record the dividends paid in 2010.

P 11-42

LO3, LO4, LO5

Stockholders' Equity Calculations

A computer virus destroyed important financial information pertaining to Paseo Company's stockholders' equity section. Your expertise is needed to compute the missing account balances. The only information you can recover from the computer's backup system is as follows:

a. During 2009, 7,000 shares of common stock with a par value of $1 were issued when the market price per share was $12.
b. Cash dividends of $25,000 were paid to preferred shareholders.
c. Paseo Company acquired 3,000 shares of common stock at $14 to hold as treasury stock.
d. Paseo Company reissued 2,500 shares of treasury stock for $16.

	December 31, 2008	December 31, 2009
Preferred stock	$ 3,000	$ 3,000
Common stock	8,000	?
Paid-in capital in excess of par, preferred stock	1,500	1,500
Paid-in capital in excess of par, common stock	12,000	?
Paid-in capital, treasury stock	0	?
Retained earnings	18,200	7,400
Treasury stock	0	(7,000)
Total stockholders' equity	42,700	?

Required:

1. Calculate the account balances for the following accounts:
   a. Common Stock
   b. Paid-In Capital in Excess of Par, Common Stock
   c. Paid-In Capital, Treasury Stock
   d. Stockholders' Equity
2. How much net income did Paseo Company report for 2009?

P 11-43

LO3, LO5

Stock Calculations and the Stockholders' Equity Section

The following account balances appear on the books of World Corporation as of December 31, 2009:

Preferred stock (7%, $40 par, 70,000 shares authorized, 50,000 shares issued and outstanding)	$2,000,000
Common stock ($3 par, 500,000 shares authorized, 300,000 shares issued and outstanding)	900,000
Paid-in capital in excess of par, preferred stock	310,000
Paid-in capital in excess of par, common stock	490,000
Net income for 2009	130,000
Dividends paid during 2009	70,000
Retained earnings, January 1, 2009	1,360,000

(continued)

Required:

1. If the preferred stock is selling at $45 per share, what is the maximum amount of cash that World Corporation can obtain by issuing additional preferred stock given the present number of authorized shares?

2. If common stock is selling for $12 per share, what is the maximum amount of cash that can be obtained by issuing additional common stock given the present number of authorized shares?

3. Given the account balances at December 31, 2009, and ignoring parts (1) and (2), prepare, in good form, the stockholders' equity section of the balance sheet.

P 11-44

LO3, LO5

Unifying Concepts: Stock Transactions and the Stockholders' Equity Section

Richard Corporation was founded on January 1, 2009, and entered into the following stock transactions during 2009:

a. Received authorization for 100,000 shares of $20 par-value common stock, 50,000 shares of 6% preferred stock with a par value of $5, and 50,000 shares of no-par common stock.

b. Issued 25,000 shares of the $20 par-value common stock at $24 per share.

c. Issued 10,000 shares of the preferred stock at $8 per share.

d. Issued 5,000 shares of the no-par common stock at $22 per share.

e. Reacquired 1,000 shares of the $20 par-value common stock at $25 per share.

f. Reacquired 500 shares of the no-par common stock at $20 per share.

g. Reissued 250 of the 1,000 reacquired shares of $20 par-value common stock at $23 per share.

h. Reissued all the 500 reacquired shares of no-par common stock at $23 per share.

i. Closed the $14,000 net income to Retained Earnings. Revenues and expenses for the year were $90,000 and $76,000, respectively.

Required:

1. Prepare journal entries to record the 2009 transactions in Richard Corporation's books.

2. Prepare the stockholders' equity section of Richard Corporation's balance sheet at December 31, 2009. Assume that the transactions represent all the events involving equity accounts during 2009.

P 11-45

LO3, LO5

Unifying Concepts: Stock Transactions, the Stockholders' Equity Section, and the Statement of Stockholders' Equity

The condensed balance sheet of JCB Corporation at December 31, 2008, is shown below.

JCB Corporation Balance Sheet December 31, 2008	
Assets	
Cash	$ 550,000
All other assets	828,000
	$1,378,000
Liabilities and Stockholders' Equity	
Current liabilities	$ 145,000
Long-term liabilities	220,000
	$ 365,000
Contributed capital:	
Common stock ($10 par, 150,000 shares authorized,	
70,000 shares outstanding)	$ 700,000
Paid-in capital in excess of par, common stock	140,000
Retained earnings	173,000
	$1,013,000
	$1,378,000

(continued)

During 2009, the following transactions affected stockholders' equity:

Feb. 15   Purchased 6,000 shares of JCB outstanding common stock at $18 per share.
May 21   Sold 3,500 of the shares purchased on February 15 at $21 per share.
Sept. 15   Issued 12,000 shares of previously unissued common stock at $22 per share.
Dec. 21   Sold the remaining 2,500 shares of treasury stock at $23 per share.
      31   Closed net income of $91,600 to Retained Earnings. Revenues were $291,600; expenses were $200,000.

Required:

1. Prepare the journal entries to record the 2009 transactions.
2. Prepare the stockholders' equity section of the balance sheet at December 31, 2009.
3. Prepare a statement of stockholders' equity for the year ended December 31, 2009.

P 11-46

LO3, LO4, LO5

Unifying Concepts: Stockholders' Equity

Icon Corporation was organized during 2007. At the end of 2008, the equity section of its balance sheet appeared as follows:

Contributed capital:	
Preferred stock (6%, $20 par, 10,000 shares authorized,	
5,000 shares issued and outstanding)	$100,000
Common stock ($10 par, 50,000 shares authorized,	
11,000 shares issued, 10,000 outstanding)	110,000
Paid-in capital in excess of par, preferred stock	20,000
Total contributed capital	$230,000
Retained earnings	100,000
Total contributed capital plus retained earnings	$330,000
Less treasury stock (1,000 shares of common at cost)	(12,000)
Total stockholders' equity	$318,000

During 2009, the following stockholders' equity transactions occurred (in chronological sequence):

a. Issued 500 shares of common stock at $13 per share.
b. Reissued 500 shares of treasury stock at $13 per share.
c. Issued 1,000 shares of preferred stock at $25 per share.
d. Reissued 500 shares of treasury stock at $10 per share.
e. Declared a dividend large enough to meet the current-dividend preference of the preferred stock and to pay the common stockholders $2 per share. Dividends are recorded directly in the retained earnings account.
f. Closed net income of $65,000 to Retained Earnings. Revenues were $400,000; expenses were $335,000.

Required:

1. Journalize the transactions.
2. Prepare the stockholders' equity section of the balance sheet at December 31, 2009.

P 11-47

LO5

Comprehensive Income

The following information relates to Loveland Company:

Sales	$60,000
Cost of goods sold	36,000
Other operating expenses	8,000
Interest expense	500
Income tax expense	5,400

(continued)

In addition, the following events occurred during the year:

a. Loveland Company has an investment portfolio for long-term investment purposes. That portfolio decreased in value by $9,000 during the year.

b. Loveland Company owns a substantial amount of land. During the year, the land increased in value by $34,000.

c. Loveland Company has several foreign subsidiaries. The currencies in the countries where those subsidiaries are located declined in value (relative to the U.S. dollar) during the year. Accordingly, the computed value of the equity of those subsidiaries, in U.S. dollars, decreased by $3,700.

Required:

1. Compute Loveland's comprehensive income for the year.

2. **Interpretive Question:** Is comprehensive income a good measure of the change in a company's value during the year?

P 11-48

LO5

Stockholders' Equity Section with Selected "Other Information"

The stockholders' equity section of Glory Company's balance sheet was as follows as of December 31, 2009, and December 31, 2008:

Glory Company
Stockholders' Equity Sections of Balance Sheet
December 31, 2009 and 2008
(in millions)

	2009	2008
Preferred stock	$ 21.4	$ 21.4
Common stock	48.4	43.2
Paid-in capital, various types	22.6	15.3
Retained earnings	51.8	41.2
Subtotal	$144.2	$121.1
Accumulated foreign currency translation adjustments	21.4	57.3
Net unrealized gains (losses) on investments in certain debt and equity securities	(46.4)	(8.8)
Total stockholders' equity	$119.2	$169.6

Required:

Based on the stockholders' equity section for Glory Company, answer the following questions:

1. Do you believe Glory Company made a profit during the year 2009? Assuming that only net income and dividends changed the retained earnings balance from 2008 to 2009, by how much did net income exceed dividends?

2. What was the total amount of money raised during 2009 from the selling of stock? (Assume that only the selling of stock affected the contributed capital accounts.)

3. Did the market value of Glory Company's securities that affect the equity section increase or decrease in 2009? By how much?

4. **Interpretive Question:** The board of directors believes it should fire the current management of the company because total stockholders' equity decreased substantially. Do you agree? Why or why not?

ANALYTICAL ASSIGNMENTS

AA 11-49

DISCUSSION

Does Stockholders' Equity Tell the Real Story?

Last year, Shades International (a hypothetical company) invented the famous Shades Sunglasses that are widely popular around the world and especially in Japan and the Far East. Citizens of these countries love the new-age sunglasses and are buying them as fast as they can. Shades International owns the patent but contracts out to other companies to

(continued)

manufacture the glasses. Shades International also leases its research and development facility, the only building it occupies. Royalties from the glasses exceeded $10 million last year and are expected to increase dramatically this year. Selected data (in millions of dollars) from Shades International's financial statements are as follows:

Patent	$ 0.3
Other assets	0.9
Total liabilities	4.5
Total stockholders' equity	(3.3)

In the next two months, Shades International will be offering stock for sale to the public. Your friend is encouraging you to buy some of the stock. You are leery about the negative stockholders' equity balance. Is Shades International worth even considering as a possible investment?

AA 11-50

DISCUSSION

To Pay or Not To Pay Dividends

Assume Lenny Company manufactures specialized computer peripheral parts such as speakers and modems. It is a new company that has been in operation for just two years. During those two years, Lenny Company's stock price has increased over 400%. Lenny Company does not pay dividends nor does the company plan to do so in the future. However, the company's stock seems to be heavily traded. Why do you think there is so much interest in buying Lenny Company's stock if stockholders do not receive dividends?

AA 11-51

JUDGMENT CALL

You Decide: Should partners of a business be held personally liable for the debts of the business, or should their business activities and debts be kept separate from their personal activities?

John and Jeff formed a partnership and started selling cookies based on a secret recipe they created. After one year of strong sales, Jeff left the company with $30,000 cash and was never heard of again. Now, the creditors are requesting payment from John to satisfy a loan Jeff signed. If John can't make the payments from what is left in the business, who will the bank look to for payment?

AA 11-52

JUDGMENT CALL

You Decide: Should the U.S. government change the current corporate tax system from double to single taxation, or is the present system (taxing corporate profits and then dividends to shareholders) adequate?

You were recently at a family gathering when the topic of conversation turned political. Your father, a retired CEO of a regional grocery chain, commented on his dissatisfaction with the current corporate tax system. He said, "It was very frustrating to see profits of my company taxed once at the corporate level and then again when the shareholders receive dividends. Something should be done about that!" Do you agree with your father?

AA 11-53

JUDGMENT CALL

You Decide: Should companies be required to pay cash dividends on their stock to shareholders, or should it be left up to the companies' discretion whether they pay dividends or reinvest those funds back in the company?

Your father asked you why his investment in a publicly-traded stock is not paying him any dividends. He said, "As far as I know, they never have. I invested in the company to get something back and so far, I haven't received anything. Shouldn't the company be looking after its shareholders?" Should all companies be required to pay dividends?

AA 11-54

REAL COMPANY ANALYSIS

Wal-Mart

The 2006 Form 10-K for **Wal-Mart** is included in Appendix A. Wal-Mart's stockholders' equity statements provide details of equity transactions of the company during the 2006 fiscal year. Locate the statements and consider the following questions:

1. What was the major reason that stockholders' equity increased for the year?
2. How much did common stockholders receive in dividends during the year?
3. Did Wal-Mart issue more shares than it repurchased during the year or vice versa? How can you tell?

AA 11-55

REAL COMPANY ANALYSIS

Union Pacific Corporation

Union Pacific's statement of shareholders' equity for the year 2005 is reproduced below.

Millions of Dollars Thousands of Shares	Common Shares	Treasury Shares	Common Shares	Paid-In-Surplus	Retained Earnings	Treasury Stock	Accumulated Other Comprehensive Income/(Loss)			Total
							Minimum Pension Liability Adj.	Foreign Currency Trans. Adj.	Derivative Adj.	
Balance at Jan. 1, 2003	275,579	(21,920)	$ 689	$ 3,946	$ 7,597	$ (1,347)	$ (232)	$ (9)	$ 7	$ 10,651
Comprehensive income/(loss):										
Net income			–	–	1,585	–	–	–	–	1,585
Other comp. income/(loss) from continuing operations [a]			–	–	–	–	39	(9)	(4)	26
Other comp. income/(loss) from discontinued operations [b]			–	–	–	–	84	–	–	84
Total comprehensive income/(loss)			–	–	1,585	–	123	(9)	(4)	1,695
Conversion, exercises of stock options, forfeitures, and other	114	4,388	–	(10)	–	270	–	–	–	260
Dividends declared ($0.99 per share)	–	–	–	–	(252)	–	–	–	–	(252)
Balance at Dec. 31, 2003	275,693	(17,532)	$ 689	$ 3,936	$ 8,930	$ (1,077)	$ (109)	$ (18)	$ 3	$12,354
Comprehensive income/(loss):										
Net income			–	–	604	–	–	–	–	604
Other comp. income/(loss) [a]			–	–	–	–	(103)	–	(10)	(113)
Total comprehensive income/(loss)			–	–	604	–	(103)	–	(10)	491
Conversion, exercises of stock options, forfeitures, and other	2	2,357	–	(19)	–	141	–	–	–	122
Dividends declared ($1.20 per share)	–	–	–	–	(312)	–	–	–	–	(312)
Balance at Dec. 31, 2004	275,695	(15,175)	$ 689	$ 3,917	$ 9,222	$ (936)	$ (212)	$ (18)	$ (7)	$12,655
Comprehensive income/(loss):										
Net income			–	–	1,026	–	–	–	–	1,026
Other comp. income/(loss) [a]			–	–	–	–	1	5	1	7
Total comprehensive income/(loss)			–	–	1,026	–	1	5	1	1,033
Conversion, exercises of stock options, forfeitures, and other	104	6,011	–	(2)	–	337	–	–	–	335
Dividends declared ($1.20 per share)	–	–	–	–	(316)	–	–	–	–	(316)
Balance at Dec. 31, 2005	275,799	(9,164)	$ 689	$ 3,915	$ 9,932	$ (599)	$ (211)	$ (13)	$ (6)	$13,707

(continued)

1. Based on the dividends paid during 2005, how many shares of stock were outstanding when the dividends were paid?
2. Why isn't the number of shares receiving dividends exactly the same as the number of shares outstanding on December 31 as indicated in the statement?
3. Compute Union Pacific's dividend payout ratio for each year. Has that number increased or decreased over time?

AA 11-56

INTERNATIONAL

The EMI Group

The shareholders' equity section of the balance sheet of **The EMI Group**, a company based in the United Kingdom, is reproduced below. Review this information and answer the questions below.

The EMI Group Balance Sheets at 31 March 2005	Group	
	2005 £m	2004 £m
Capital and reserves		
Called-up share capital	110.6	110.4
Share premium account	447.3	445.8
Capital redemption reserve	495.8	495.8
Other reserves	252.2	255.7
Profit and loss reserve (including goodwill previously written off)	(2,101.3)	(2,091.7)
Equity shareholders' funds	(795.4)	(784.0)
Minority interests (equity)	48.3	67.6
	(747.1)	(716.4)

1. What do you think the term "called-up share capital" means?
2. What do you think the term "share premium account" means?
3. What does the term "profit and loss reserve" mean?

AA 11-57

ETHICS

Buying Your Own Shares Back

You are the chief financial officer for Esoteric, Inc., a company whose stock is publicly traded. The stock market has recently experienced an overall downturn, and the price of your company's stock has decreased by about 15%. This significantly affects the compensation of the executives of your company as their bonuses are based on the company's stock price. The bonus plan rewards company executives who take actions to increase the value of the company to shareholders. The reasoning is that if management increases the value of the company to shareholders, management should be rewarded.

As you consider ways to increase the value of the company, when the market itself is slumping, the following idea pops into your head: We will buy back our own stock. That will cause the remaining outstanding stock to increase in value, which is good for those individuals holding that stock. And it will also result in you and the other corporate executives receiving sizable bonuses.

Do you think this plan of action to increase stock price was what the designers of the compensation plan had in mind when they linked executive bonuses to company stock price? Does buying back the company's own stock add value to the company as a whole? Should the compensation plan prohibit activities like buying stock back? Consider these issues and be prepared to discuss them.

AA 11-58
WRITING

Other Comprehensive Income

In this chapter you learned that certain transactions that changed a company's net assets were not reflected on the income statement but instead were reflected on the statement of stockholders' equity under the heading of accumulated other comprehensive income. Prepare a two-page memo summarizing the following points:

1. Why aren't all items included under accumulated other comprehensive income simply disclosed on the income statement? What is it about these transactions that keep their effects off the income statement?

2. In your opinion, do you think there should be a separate accumulated other comprehensive income statement or is disclosing the amount in the statement of stockholders' equity sufficient to get investor's attention?

AA 11-59
CUMULATIVE
SPREADSHEET
PROJECT

Preparing New Forecasts

This spreadsheet assignment is a continuation of the spreadsheet assignments given in earlier chapters. If you completed those spreadsheets, you have a head start on this one.

1. Handyman wishes to prepare a forecasted balance sheet and income statement for 2010. Use the original financial statement numbers for 2009 [given in part (1) of the Cumulative Spreadsheet Project assignment in Chapter 2] as the basis for the forecast, along with the following additional information:

   a. Sales in 2010 are expected to increase by 40% over 2009 sales of $700.

   b. Cash will increase at the same rate as sales.

   c. The forecasted amount of accounts receivable in 2010 is determined using the forecasted value for the average collection period. For simplicity, do the computations using the end-of-period accounts receivable balance instead of the average balance. The average collection period for 2010 is expected to be 14.08 days.

   d. The forecasted amount of inventory in 2010 is determined using the forecasted value for the number of days' sales in inventory (computed using the end-of-period inventory balance). The number of days' sales in inventory for 2010 is expected to be 107.6 days.

   e. The forecasted amount of accounts payable in 2010 is determined using the forecasted value for the number of days' purchases in accounts payable (computed using the end-of-period accounts payable balance). The number of days' purchases in accounts payable for 2010 is expected to be 48.34 days.

   f. The $160 in operating expenses reported in 2009 breaks down as follows: $5 depreciation expense, $155 other operating expenses.

   g. New long-term debt will be acquired (or repaid) in an amount sufficient to make Handyman's debt ratio (total liabilities divided by total assets) in 2010 exactly equal to 0.80.

   h. No cash dividends will be paid in 2010.

   i. New short-term loans payable will be acquired in an amount sufficient to make Handyman's current ratio in 2010 exactly equal to 2.0.

   j. The forecasted amount of property, plant, and equipment (PP&E) in 2010 is determined using the forecasted value for the fixed asset turnover ratio. For simplicity, compute the fixed asset turnover ratio using the end-of-period gross PP&E balance. The fixed asset turnover ratio for 2010 is expected to be 3.518 times.

   k. In computing depreciation expense for 2010, use straight-line depreciation and assume a 30-year useful life with no residual value. Gross PP&E acquired during the year is depreciated for only half the year. In other words, depreciation expense for 2010 is the sum of two parts: (1) a full year of depreciation on the beginning balance in PP&E, assuming a 30-year life and no residual value and (2) a half-year of depreciation on any new PP&E acquired during the year, based on the change in the gross PP&E balance.

   l. Assume an interest rate on short-term loans payable of 6.0% and on long-term debt of 8.0%. Only a half-year's interest is charged on loans taken out during the year.

(continued)

For example, if short-term loans payable at the end of 2010 are $15 and given that short-term loans payable at the end of 2009 were $10, total short-term interest expense for 2010 would be $0.75 [($10 × 0.06) + ($5 × 0.06 × ½)].

Note: These statements were constructed as part of the spreadsheet assignment in Chapter 10; you can use that spreadsheet as a starting point if you have completed that assignment.

For this exercise, add the following additional assumptions:
- In addition to preparing forecasted financial statements for 2010, Handyman also wishes to prepare forecasted financial statements for 2011. All assumptions applicable to 2010 are also assumed to be applicable to 2011. Sales in 2011 are expected to be 40% higher than sales in 2010.

Clearly state any additional assumptions that you make.

2. For each forecasted year, 2010 and 2011, state whether Handyman is expected to issue new shares of stock or to repurchase shares of stock.
3. Repeat (2), with the following changes in assumptions:
   a. The debt ratio in 2010 and 2011 is exactly equal to 0.70.
   b. The debt ratio in 2010 and 2011 is exactly equal to 0.95.
4. Comment on how it is possible for a company to have negative paid-in capital.

12

Investments in Debt and Equity Securities

After studying this chapter, you should be able to:

LEARNING OBJECTIVES

(1) Understand why companies invest in other companies. *Companies sometimes make investments in securities in order to provide a safety cushion of available funds or to store a temporary excess of cash. Companies also invest in other companies in order to earn a return, to secure influence, or to gain control.*

(2) Understand the different classifications for securities. *For accounting purposes, stocks and bonds purchased as investment securities are classified as trading, available-for-sale, or held-to-maturity investments, or as equity investments. These classifications, and the associated accounting treatment, reflect the underlying reasons for the investment.*

(3) Account for the purchase, recognition of revenue, and sale of trading and available-for-sale securities. *The cost of an investment includes the purchase price plus any brokerage fees. Interest and dividends received on trading and available-for-sale securities are reported as revenue. When a security is sold, the gain or loss on the sale is called a realized gain or loss.*

(4) Account for changes in the value of securities. *Both trading and available-for-sale securities are reported in the balance sheet at market value. Unrealized gains and losses are reported in the income statement for trading securities and as an equity adjustment for available-for-sale securities.*

EXPANDED
material

(5) Account for held-to-maturity securities. *Held-to-maturity securities are reported in the balance sheet at amortized cost, which reflects the gradual adjustment of the book value of the investment from its original cost to its ultimate maturity value.*

(6) Account for securities using the equity method. *When a company owns between 20% and 50% of another company, the equity method is used to account for the investment. Income from the investment is computed as the investing company's share of the net income of the investee. Dividends received are viewed as a partial return of the original amount invested.*

(7) Understand the basics of consolidated financial statements. *Consolidated financial statements are prepared when a parent owns more than 50% of one or more subsidiaries. All of the assets, liabilities, revenues, and expenses of the parent and the majority-owned subsidiaries are added in preparing the consolidated financial statements.*

Warren Buffett, who has been called "the world's greatest investor," has lived most of his life not far from the house in which he grew up in Omaha, Nebraska.[1] He attended the Wharton School at the University of Pennsylvania (but dropped out because he thought he wasn't learning anything); received a bachelor's degree from the University of Nebraska; applied for admission to do graduate work at Harvard but was rejected; and instead earned a master's degree in economics at Columbia.

Buffett began his professional career as a stock trader and eventually created an investment fund called the Buffett Partnership, which earned a 32% average annual return over its life from 1956 to 1969. Buffett also began purchasing shares in a small textile manufacturer

called **Berkshire Hathaway**. His first 2,000 shares of Berkshire Hathaway stock cost $7.50 per share (plus $0.10 per share in commissions). Buffett transformed Berkshire Hathaway from a textile manufacturer into a holding company that invests in the stock of other companies. A selection of the companies controlled by Berkshire Hathaway, along with some of Berkshire Hathaway's major investments, is shown in Exhibit 1.

How has Berkshire Hathaway's stock performed under Warren Buffett's leadership? Well, on September 1, 2006, the company's stock closed at $96,000 per share! How has Warren Buffett done personally? He receives a salary of only $100,000 per year (making him the lowest paid CEO among the nation's top

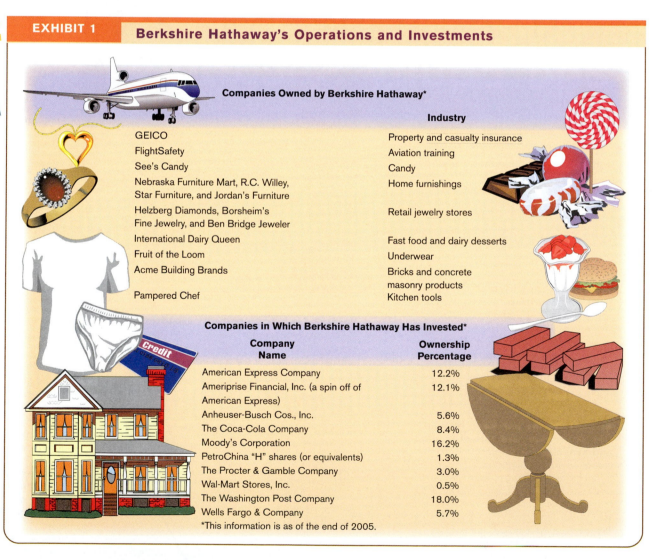

EXHIBIT 1   **Berkshire Hathaway's Operations and Investments**

Companies Owned by Berkshire Hathaway*

Company	Industry
GEICO	Property and casualty insurance
FlightSafety	Aviation training
See's Candy	Candy
Nebraska Furniture Mart, R.C. Willey, Star Furniture, and Jordan's Furniture	Home furnishings
Helzberg Diamonds, Borsheim's Fine Jewelry, and Ben Bridge Jeweler	Retail jewelry stores
International Dairy Queen	Fast food and dairy desserts
Fruit of the Loom	Underwear
Acme Building Brands	Bricks and concrete masonry products
Pampered Chef	Kitchen tools

Companies in Which Berkshire Hathaway Has Invested*

Company Name	Ownership Percentage
American Express Company	12.2%
Ameriprise Financial, Inc. (a spin off of American Express)	12.1%
Anheuser-Busch Cos., Inc.	5.6%
The Coca-Cola Company	8.4%
Moody's Corporation	16.2%
PetroChina "H" shares (or equivalents)	1.3%
The Procter & Gamble Company	3.0%
Wal-Mart Stores, Inc.	0.5%
The Washington Post Company	18.0%
Wells Fargo & Company	5.7%

*This information is as of the end of 2005.

---

[1] Janet Lowe, *Warren Buffett Speaks: Wit and Wisdom from the World's Greatest Investor* (New York: John Wiley & Sons, 1997).

200 companies). But don't feel sorry for Mr. Buffett. He was smart enough to purchase a large number of Berkshire Hathaway shares when the price was low. With a personal worth of approximately $42 billion, he ranks second on the list of the world's richest people.[2]

In this chapter we focus on why companies invest in other companies and how to account for those investments. When a company purchases the debt or equity securities of another company, several accounting issues are raised: how to account for the initial purchase, how to account for the receipt of dividends or interest, how to account for any subsequent changes in value of the security, and how to account for the security if it is sold or matures. The remainder of this chapter focuses on each of these issues. First, we examine how securities are classified and the different accounting implications of these classifications. We then introduce proper accounting for the purchase, receipt of revenue, sale, and valuation of securities. In the expanded material section of the chapter, we review the computations and accounting for a bond premium or discount from the point of view of the purchaser (we focused on the seller's perspective in Chapter 10). We also introduce the equity method of accounting and discuss when its application is appropriate. Exhibit 2 highlights the financial statement accounts that will be discussed in this chapter.

SETTING THE STAGE

Why Companies Invest in Other Companies

Understand why companies invest in other companies.

1 Companies invest in the debt and equity securities of other companies for a variety of reasons. A major reason is to earn a return on their excess cash. Most businesses are cyclical or seasonal; that is, their cash inflows and outflows vary significantly throughout the year. At certain times (particularly when inventories are being purchased), a company's cash supply is low. At other times (usually during or shortly after heavy selling seasons), there is excess cash on hand. A typical cash flow pattern for a retail firm is illustrated in Exhibit 3. The time line shows that the company has insufficient cash for inventory buildup for the Christmas rush, followed by large amounts of accounts receivable (from credit sales), and then an excess of cash immediately after Christmas.

When a company needs cash to meet current obligations, funds can be obtained through such means as borrowing from financial institutions or selling (factoring) accounts receivable or other assets. During those periods of time when excess cash exists, firms usually prefer to invest that money and earn a return. One possibility is to place the money in a bank and earn a fixed return. Most firms, however, are not satisfied with the low interest rates offered by financial institutions and have turned to other investment alternatives. Investing in the stocks (equity) and bonds (debt) of other companies allows a firm to earn a higher rate of return by accepting a higher degree of risk. **Berkshire Hathaway** is perhaps the most famous example of a company whose sole purpose is to invest in the debt and equity securities of other companies.

---

[2] If you have never had the pleasure of reading one of Warren Buffett's "Chairman's Letter to the Shareholders," you should take the opportunity now. No one writes a funnier, more insightful letter than Mr. Buffett. The company's Internet address is **http://www.berkshirehathaway.com.**

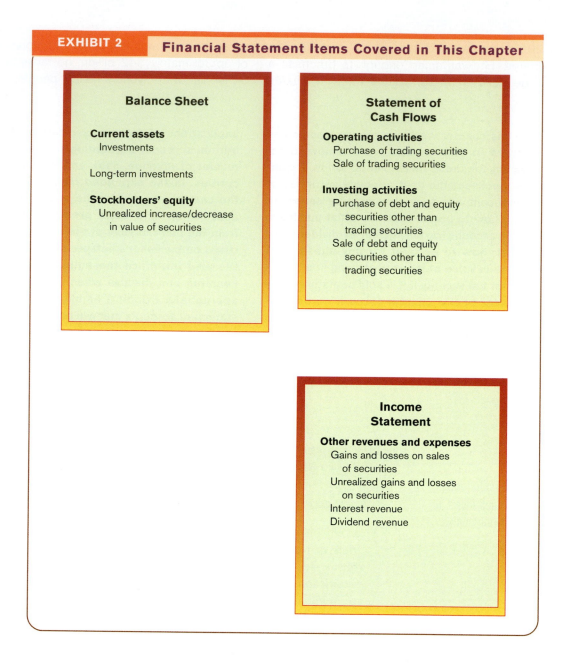

EXHIBIT 2 — Financial Statement Items Covered in This Chapter

Balance Sheet

Current assets
Investments

Long-term investments

Stockholders' equity
Unrealized increase/decrease
in value of securities

Statement of Cash Flows

Operating activities
Purchase of trading securities
Sale of trading securities

Investing activities
Purchase of debt and equity
securities other than
trading securities
Sale of debt and equity
securities other than
trading securities

Income Statement

Other revenues and expenses
Gains and losses on sales
of securities
Unrealized gains and losses
on securities
Interest revenue
Dividend revenue

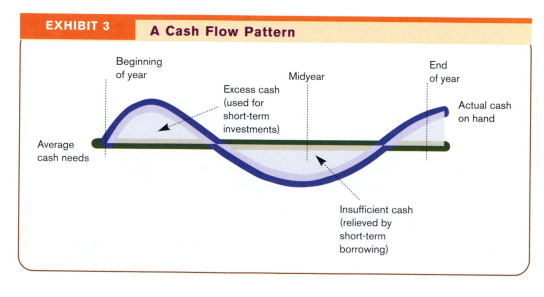

EXHIBIT 3   A Cash Flow Pattern

Beginning of year — Midyear — End of year

Excess cash (used for short-term investments)

Average cash needs

Actual cash on hand

Insufficient cash (relieved by short-term borrowing)

© JACK ANDERSEN/GETTY IMAGES INC.

The Coca-Cola Company owns significant stakes in companies that bottle its products. Such investments allow Coca-Cola to ensure that its bottling facilities remain available and that its soft-drink products consistently meet the company's quality standards.

Firms also invest in other companies for reasons other than to earn a return. The desire to purchase strategic resources, to influence the board of directors, or to diversify its product offerings are additional reasons for a company to invest in other companies. For example, **The Coca-Cola Company** owns 36% of **Coca-Cola Enterprises**, 40% of **Coca-Cola Femsa**, and 32% of **Coca-Cola Amatil Ltd**. These three companies bottle many of Coke's products, and The Coca-Cola Company maintains a significant ownership percentage to ensure that the bottling facilities remain available. As indicated in Exhibit 1, Berkshire Hathaway owns a number of companies outright and has significant investments in other companies. These investments allow Berkshire Hathaway to significantly influence or even control the operating decisions of those companies.

Rather than investing in the research and development required to develop a product or an area of expertise, many companies find it cheaper to purchase all or part of another company that has already expended the effort and the time to develop the desired product or know-how. As an example, to complement its existing software, **Novell** (a computer company specializing in networking) purchased WordPerfect and Quattro Pro, word-processing and spreadsheet software packages, respectively. This purchase then allowed Novell to assemble a menu of software packages to compete with **Microsoft's** Word, Excel, PowerPoint, and Access software packages. Novell's attempt to compete with Microsoft failed, however, and the company eventually sold WordPerfect to **Corel**.

STOP & THINK

Can you think of additional reasons why companies would purchase interests in other companies?

REMEMBER THIS...

- Companies invest in other companies for a variety of reasons. In most cases, the objective is to earn a return on the investment, either through the receipt of interest or dividends, or through an increase in the value of the investment.

- A firm may also invest in other companies so that it will be able to influence their operating decisions.

- In some cases, companies find it cheaper to buy another company to gain access to its assets than to expend the resources necessary to develop the assets on their own.

Classifying a Security

② Two general types of securities are purchased by companies—debt securities and equity securities. **Debt securities** are financial instruments that carry with them the promise of interest payments and the repayment of the principal amount. Bonds are the most common type of debt security. Debt securities are issued by companies when the need for cash arises. These securities are often traded on public exchanges such as the New York Bond Exchange. Investors often prefer debt securities to equity securities because of the certainty of the income stream (interest) and the relative safety (low risk) of debt as an investment. Investors in corporate debt securities have priority over investors in equity securities, both for the yearly interest payments and for the return of principal if the issuing corporation gets into financial difficulty. Bonds issued by corporations are the most common type of debt securities (recall from Chapter 10 that bonds are typically issued in multiples of $1,000). Once the bonds are issued, ownership of the entire bond issuance, or just a portion, can change hands frequently.

Unlike bonds, **equity securities** (or **stock**), which are also traded on public exchanges, represent actual ownership interest in a corporation. The owner of equity securities is allowed to vote on such corporate matters as executive compensation policies, who will serve on the board of directors of the corporation, and who will be the outside auditor. In addition to voting, the owner of stock often receives a return on that investment in the form of a dividend. A second type of return often accumulates to the stockholder as well—appreciation in stock price. Many investors invest in a company not for the dividend but for the potential increase in stock price. With the potential for increased stock price also comes a risk—the stock price could fall. Holders of debt securities, barring extreme financial difficulties by the issuer, will always receive the face amount of the bond upon maturity. Equity holders do not have that same promise. Stock can greatly increase in value or become worthless.

As mentioned earlier, investors can purchase both debt and equity securities with different goals in mind. Some may purchase to receive interest or dividend payments or to realize quick gains on price changes, while others may invest for more long-term reasons. Accounting standard-setters have developed different methods of accounting for investments depending on the intentions of the holder of the security. Exhibit 4 outlines the major classifications of debt and equity securities.

debt securities

Financial instruments issued by a company that carry with them a promise of interest payments and the repayment of principal.

equity securities (stock)

Shares of ownership in a corporation that can change significantly in value and that provide for a return to investors in the form of dividends.

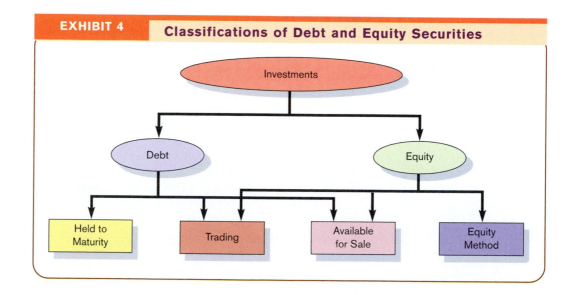

EXHIBIT 4   **Classifications of Debt and Equity Securities**

Held-to-Maturity Securities

held-to-maturity security

A debt security purchased by an investor with the intent of holding the security until it matures.

If an investor purchases a debt security with the intent of holding the security until it matures, it is classified as a **held-to-maturity security** and is accounted for using techniques similar to those discussed in Chapter 10 for the bond issuer. The investor and the issuer record the same amounts but in a different way. With bond liabilities, the face value of the bonds is recorded in Bonds Payable, and a separate contra account is maintained for any discount or premium. Amortization of the discount or premium is then recorded in these contra accounts. With bond investments, the actual amount paid for the bonds (the cost of the asset), not the face value, is originally debited to the investment account. The amortization of any bond premium or discount is then recorded directly in the investment account. Thus, if you recall the accounting for Bonds Payable as presented in Chapter 10, you already know most of the accounting for a bond investment that is expected to be held to maturity. The procedures relating to amortizing premiums and discounts for the investors are discussed in the expanded material section of this chapter. Note that equity securities cannot be classified as held-to-maturity securities; equity securities typically do not mature.[3]

F Y I

Equity securities cannot be classified as held-to-maturity securities.

Equity Method Securities

equity method

A method used to account for an investment in the stock of another company when significant influence can be imposed (presumed to exist when 20 to 50% of the outstanding voting stock is owned).

consolidated financial statements

Statements that report the combined operating results, financial position, and cash flows of two or more legally separate but affiliated companies as if they were one economic entity.

In the case of equity securities, accounting standard-setters have determined that if securities are held with the objective of significantly influencing the operations of the investee, then the securities should be accounted for using the **equity method**. The equity method records changes in the value of the investment as the net assets of the investee change. The assumption underlying the equity method is that if the investor can influence the operating decisions of the investee, then any change in the net assets of the investee should be reflected on the books of the investor. In determining what constitutes significant influence, the Accounting Principles Board suggests that, unless evidence exists to the contrary, ownership of at least 20% of the outstanding common stock of a company, but less than 50%, indicates the existence of significant influence. Because accounting for a security using the equity method can get complicated, details of the equity method are presented in the expanded material section of this chapter. If ownership exceeds 50%, then a controlling interest is assumed, and the accounting becomes far more complex. The FASB is examining the issue of control and has suggested that companies look beyond ownership percentage and examine other factors that may indicate control.[4] Two factors the FASB has highlighted are (1) ownership of a large minority voting interest (approximately 40%) with no other group owning a significant interest and (2) a company's domination of the process for electing the investee's board of directors. In cases where it is determined that control exists, the parent company (the acquiring company) and the subsidiary company (the acquired company) are required to combine their financial statements into one set of statements as if they were one economic entity. Such combined statements are called **consolidated financial statements**. The preparation of consolidated financial statements is briefly covered in the expanded material of this chapter.

---

[3] There are exceptions to this rule, as in the case of "mandatorily redeemable preferred stock," but the accounting for these types of securities is beyond the scope of this text.

[4] Exposure Draft: Consolidated Financial Statements, Including Accounting and Reporting of Noncontrolling Interests in Subsidiaries—a replacement of ARB No. 51 (Norwalk: Financial Accounting Standards Board, 2005).

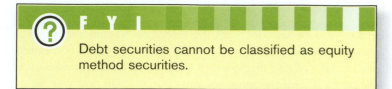

Debt securities cannot be classified as equity method securities.

trading securities

Debt and equity securities purchased with the intent of selling them should the need for cash arise or to realize short-term gains.

available-for-sale securities

Debt and equity securities not classified as trading, held-to-maturity, or equity method securities.

Trading and Available-for-Sale Securities

In those instances where securities are not being held to maturity (in the case of debt) or to control or significantly influence an investee (in the case of equity), the Financial Accounting Standards Board has developed two other classes of securities—trading and available-for-sale. **Trading securities** are those debt and equity securities held with the intent of selling the securities should the need for cash arise or to realize gains arising from short-term changes in price. These types of securities are purchased simply to earn a return on excess cash. **Available-for-sale securities** are publicly-traded securities that are classified as neither held-to-maturity nor trading (in the case of debt securities). In the case of equity securities, they represent securities that are not classified as trading securities or accounted for using the equity method.

Why the Different Classifications?

Why are there different classifications for debt and equity securities? Why not simply classify all securities as "investments"? The reason for the distinction lies in the different treatments of accounting for changes in market value. In the case of securities classified as held-to-maturity, changes in the securities' value between the date of purchase and the maturity date do not affect the amount to be received at maturity. That amount is fixed on the day the bonds are issued. Thus, temporary changes in the value of securities classified as held-to-maturity are not recognized on the investor's books. Similar reasoning applies to securities accounted for under the equity method. These securities are purchased, not with the intent of selling them in the future, but instead to be able to exercise influence over a corporation. Again, temporary changes in the value of these securities are not recognized on the investor's books.

Trading securities are purchased with the intent of earning a return—through interest or dividends and through short-term resale of the securities. Firms are required to recognize these two types of returns on the income statement. For example, assume that XYZ Company purchases 100 shares of ABC, Inc. stock for $5 per share. During the year, ABC pays a $1 dividend per share, and the value of the stock increases to $7 per share. XYZ will recognize, as income, $100 in dividend income as well as $200 in unrealized market gains. While the $100 in dividends was actually received, the $200 gain was not.

Many companies avoid the issue of what to include on the income statement by classifying all their investment securities as being available-for-sale. Berkshire Hathaway and **Microsoft** are examples of companies that use this classification scheme.

The securities would have to have been sold in order to actually receive the $200 increase in value. Recognizing this gain, even though it was not realized through an arm's-length transaction, represents a major departure from the historical cost principle that has guided accounting for centuries. In 1994, the FASB determined that because the fair market value of many debt and equity securities can be objectively determined (via market quotes) and they can easily be sold (one phone call to a broker), it would be appropriate to include any unrealized gains or losses on changes in value of trading securities on the income statement.

Changes in the value of securities classified as available-for-sale are recorded on the balance sheet. However, no gain or loss is realized on the income statement. Instead, an adjustment is made directly to a stockholders' equity account—Unrealized Increase/Decrease in Value of Available-for-Sale Securities-Equity. The obvious question is "Why aren't changes in the value of these securities reflected on the income statement?"

The answer lies in the intent behind holding the securities. Trading securities will probably be sold sooner rather than later. We cannot make that same assumption with available-for-sale securities. We are less certain they will be sold. Because of this uncertainty as to when the change in value will actually be realized, the FASB elected to go around the income statement in reporting changes in value relating to available-for-sale securities. Whatever the classification used, companies disclose their classification in the notes to the financial statements. For example, **Berkshire Hathaway** provides the following note disclosure relating to its investments:

> Berkshire's management determines the appropriate classifications of investments in fixed maturity securities and equity securities at the acquisition date and re-evaluates the classifications at each balance sheet date. Berkshire's investments in fixed maturity and equity securities are primarily classified as available-for-sale, except for certain securities held by finance businesses which are classified as held-to-maturity. Held-to-maturity investments are carried at amortized cost, reflecting Berkshire's intent and ability to hold the securities to maturity. Available-for-sale securities are stated at fair value with net unrealized gains or losses reported as a component of accumulated other comprehensive income.

As you can see, Berkshire Hathaway classifies virtually every security as available-for-sale and is very specific as to what this classification means for the financial statements: current values go on the balance sheet, with unrealized gains and losses disclosed in stockholders' equity, while realized gains and losses are reported on the income statement.

Exhibit 5 summarizes the classification and disclosure issues relating to investments in debt and equity securities.

EXHIBIT 5	**Classification and Disclosure of Securities**		
Classification of Securities	**Types of Securities**	**Disclosed at**	**Reporting of Temporary Changes in Fair Value**
Trading	Debt and equity	Fair value	Income statement
Available-for-sale	Debt and equity	Fair value	Stockholders' equity
Held-to-maturity	Debt	Amortized cost	Not recognized
Equity method	Equity	Cost adjusted for changes in net assets of investee	Not recognized

REMEMBER THIS...

- Securities are classified depending upon the intent of management. If management's intent is to hold the investment until maturity (debt) or to influence the decisions of an investee (equity), then the held-to-maturity (debt) and equity method (equity) classifications are appropriate.

- If the securities are being held for other reasons, then management may classify them as either trading or available-for-sale. The importance of the classification becomes apparent when accounting for changes in value.

Account for the purchase, recognition of revenue, and sale of trading and available-for-sale securities.

③

Accounting for Trading and Available-for-Sale Securities

Four issues are associated with accounting for securities: (1) accounting for the purchase, (2) accounting for the revenue earned, (3) accounting for the sale, and (4) accounting for the changes in value. The first three issues are fairly straightforward and are presented in this section. Accounting for changes in the value of securities is discussed in the following section. The time line in Exhibit 6 illustrates the important business issues associated with buying and selling investment securities.

Accounting for the Purchase of Securities

Investments in securities, like all other assets, are recorded at cost when purchased. This is the case whether the security being purchased is debt or equity or whether it is being held with the intent to sell it quickly or hold it for the long term. Cost includes the market price of the security plus any extra expenditures required in making the purchase (such as a stockbroker's fee).

To illustrate the accounting for securities, we will use the following information throughout the chapter. On July 1, 2009, Far Side, Inc., purchased the following securities:

Security	Type	Classification	Cost (including Broker's Fees)
1	Debt	Trading	$ 5,000
2	Equity	Trading	27,500
3	Debt	Available-for-sale	17,000
4	Equity	Available-for-sale	9,200

The initial entry to record the investments is as follows:

Investment in Trading Securities	32,500	
Investment in Available-for-Sale Securities	26,200	
Cash		58,700

EXHIBIT 6	Time Line of Business Issues Associated with Buying and Selling Investment Securities

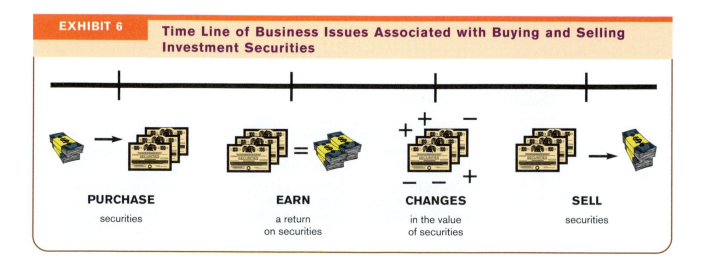

| **PURCHASE** | **EARN** | **CHANGES** | **SELL** |
| securities | a return on securities | in the value of securities | securities |

Though investments in securities are all recorded at cost, each of the four classifications of securities is accounted for differently subsequent to purchase. As a result, separate accounts are used to record the initial purchase. Management purchased Securities 1 and 2 with the intent of earning a return on the investment and selling the securities should the need for cash arise. Therefore, those securities are classified as "trading." Securities 3 and 4 were also purchased to earn a return on excess cash, but management has classified them as "available-for-sale." While the journal entry illustrated above combines all securities of the same classification into one account, subsidiary records will be kept for each individual security purchased.

Accounting for the Return Earned on an Investment

When a firm invests in the debt or equity of another firm with the intent of earning a return on its investment, how that return is accounted for varies depending on the classification of the investment. Recall from Chapter 10 that when debt securities are sold, a premium or discount can arise as a result of differences between the stated rate of interest and the market rate of interest. The resulting premium or discount must then be amortized over the life of the investment, thereby affecting the amount of interest expense recorded by the issuer. Theoretically, the purchaser of that debt security must also account for the difference between the purchase price and the eventual maturity value. In the discussion that follows, however, we are assuming that the time for which the investor anticipates holding debt securities classified as "trading" or as "available-for-sale" is not long enough for any amortization of premium or discount to materially affect interest expense. Amortization of premiums and discounts on debt securities is illustrated for "held-to-maturity" securities in the expanded material section of this chapter.

With this caveat in mind, the accounting for dividends and interest received on trading and available-for-sale securities becomes relatively straightforward. Cash received relating to interest and dividends is credited to Interest Revenue and Dividend Revenue, respectively. Interest earned but not yet received or dividends that have been declared but not paid are also recorded as revenue with a corresponding receivable. Continuing our example, interest and dividends received during 2009 relating to Far Side's securities investments were as follows:

Security	Interest	Dividends
1	$225	
2		$825
3	850	
4		644

The appropriate journal entry to record the receipt of interest and dividends is:

Cash	2,544	
Interest Revenue		1,075
Dividend Revenue		1,469

Accounting for the Sale of Securities

Suppose that Far Side sells all of its investment in Security 2 for $28,450 on October 31, 2009. As Security 2 was purchased for $27,500, the security has increased in value and that increase must be recorded. The journal entry to record the sale is:

Cash	28,450	
Investment in Trading Securities		27,500
Realized Gain on Sale of Trading Securities		950

If Security 2 had been sold for less than $27,500, a loss would have been recorded. If a broker's fee had been charged on the transaction, the fee would reduce the amount of cash received and decrease the gain recognized. If the broker's fee exceeded $950, a loss would be recorded on the books of the seller.

At the end of the accounting period, any gain or loss on the sale of securities must be included on the income statement. In the above example, the "Realized Gain on Sale of Trading Securities" would be included with Other Revenues and Expenses on the income statement. Note the term *realized*. **Realized gains and losses** indicate that an arm's-length transaction has occurred and that the securities have actually been sold. This distinction is important because in the next section we focus on accounting for unrealized gains and losses—those gains and losses that occur while a security is still being held and no arm's-length transaction has taken place.

realized gains and losses

Gains and losses resulting from the sale of securities in an arm's-length transaction.

On its statement of cash flows, **Berkshire Hathaway** reported proceeds of $4,872 million from the sale of debt securities and equity securities. On its income statement, the company reported net realized gains of $427 million from the sale of securities. With this information, we can compute the historical cost of the securities sold during the period. Proceeds of $4,872 million less a gain of $427 million indicate that the cost of the securities was $4,445 million. A summary journal entry indicating the effects of these transactions for Berkshire Hathaway is as follows:

Cash	4,872	
Available-for-Sale Securities		4,445
Realized Gain on Sale of Securities		427

REMEMBER THIS...

- Investments in debt and equity securities are recorded at cost, which includes the fair value of the securities plus any other expenditures required to purchase the securities.
- When purchased, the securities are classified into one of four categories: held-to-maturity, equity method, trading, or available-for-sale securities.
- Revenues from securities take the form of interest, dividends, or gains or losses from selling the securities and are included under Other Revenues and Expenses on the income statement.

Accounting for Changes in the Value of Securities

Account for changes in the value of securities.

4 Investments in debt and equity securities are initially recorded at cost. If the value of a security changes after it is purchased, should that change in value be recorded on the investor's books? As stated previously in the chapter, the answer is "it depends." It depends on management's intent regarding that security. In the case of trading and available-for-sale securities, changes in market value are recorded on the books of the investor. For held-to-maturity securities and equity method securities, changes in value are not recorded unless they are considered permanent. To illustrate the accounting for changes in value of securities, we will continue the Far Side example. On December 31, 2009, the following market values were available:[5]

Security	Classification	Historical Cost	Market Value (December 31, 2009)
1	Trading	$ 5,000	$ 5,200
3	Available-for-sale	17,000	16,700
4	Available-for-sale	9,200	9,250

Changes in the Value of Trading Securities

At the end of 2009, Far Side computes the market value of its trading securities portfolio and compares it to the historical cost of the portfolio. In this instance, market value is $200 greater than historical cost. The journal entry to record this increase in value is:

Market Adjustment–Trading Securities	200	
Unrealized Gain on Trading Securities–Income		200

unrealized gains and losses

Gains and losses resulting from changes in the value of securities that are still being held.

market adjustment— trading securities

An account used to track the difference between the historical cost and the market value of a company's portfolio of trading securities.

This journal entry recognizes the $200 increase in the value of the trading securities and records the unrealized gain on the income statement. **Unrealized gains and losses** indicate that the securities have changed in value and are still being held. This journal entry also introduces a new account—**Market Adjustment—Trading Securities**. This account is combined with the trading securities account and reported on the balance sheet. Thus, the balance sheet will reflect the trading securities at their fair market value. Why not adjust the trading securities account directly instead of creating this market adjustment account? The reason is that the use of a valuation account, Market Adjustment—Trading Securities, allows a record of historical cost to be maintained. With this approach, a company can easily determine realized and unrealized gains. Perhaps the most important reason for keeping a record of historical cost is that, for tax purposes, only realized gains and losses are relevant. Other decisions made within a firm also rely on this historical cost information.

Changes in the Value of Available-for-Sale Securities

A market adjustment account is also employed when adjusting available-for-sale securities to their fair market value. However, the change in value is not recorded on the income statement but is instead recorded in the account "Unrealized

---

[5] Remember that Security 2 was sold on October 31, 2009.

STOP & THINK

In Chapter 7, we were not to write inventory up if its value increased, though we were to write it down if its value declined. In Chapter 9, we were not to write property, plant, and equipment up if its value increased, though we were to write it down if its value declined. Why can we write up the value of securities if their price increases above the original cost?

Increase/Decrease in Value of Available-for-Sale Securities—Equity." The "equity" used in the account title refers to the fact that this account is disclosed in the stockholders' equity section of the balance sheet, and its balance is carried forward from year to year. To illustrate, the available-for-sale portfolio of Far Side has a fair market value of $25,950 at year-end and a historical cost of $26,200. The appropriate adjustment is:

Unrealized Increase/Decrease in Value of Available-for-Sale Securities–Equity	250	
Market Adjustment–Available-for-Sale Securities		250

This journal entry adjusts the portfolio of available-for-sale securities to its fair market value at year-end and records the difference in the equity account.

Subsequent Changes in Value

Assume that no securities were bought or sold by Far Side, Inc., during 2010. At the end of 2010, its portfolio of securities had the following fair market values:

Security	Classification	Historical Cost	Market Value (December 31, 2010)
1	Trading	$ 5,000	$ 4,850
3	Available-for-sale	17,000	16,900
4	Available-for-sale	9,200	9,150

The value of the trading securities has declined to $4,850. Since the market adjustment account relating to trading securities should reflect the difference between historical cost and market, an entry is made to adjust the balance in Market Adjustment—Trading Securities from its previous $200 debit balance to the required $150 credit balance ($5,000 − $4,850). Where did this $200 debit balance come from? It came from the adjusting entry made on December 31, 2009. Remember that the market adjustment account is a real (balance sheet) account and is not closed at the end of an accounting period. Its balance carries forward from year to year. The required adjusting entry is:

Unrealized Loss on Trading Securities–Income	350	
Market Adjustment–Trading Securities		350

When this entry is posted, the Market Adjustment—Trading Securities T-account will appear as follows:

**Market Adjustment–
Trading Securities**

12/31/09	200		
		Adjustment	350
		12/31/10	150

CAUTION

The amount of the adjustment for the current period depends on the balance in the market adjustment account. Don't forget to factor that balance into your calculations.

The $150 credit balance will be netted against the $5,000 balance in the trading securities account and disclosed on the balance sheet as "Investment in Trading Securities (net)" for $4,850. The $350 unrealized loss will be included in the current period's net income and reported on the income statement. This adjustment procedure ensures that changes in the value of the trading securities portfolio are reflected in the period in which those changes in value occurred.

A similar procedure is employed in valuing the available-for-sale securities portfolio, except that the stockholders' equity account is used instead of the income statement account. For Far Side, the market value of the available-for-sale securities portfolio is $26,050. In comparing this to the historical cost of $26,200, a $150 credit balance in the market adjustment account is required. Take a moment and read the information again. An adjustment *to* get to a $150 credit balance is required—not an adjustment *of* $150. Given the previous credit balance in Market Adjustment—Available-for-Sale Securities of $250, the following adjusting entry is required:

Market Adjustment–Available-for-Sale Securities	100	
Unrealized Increase/Decrease in Value of Available-for-Sale Securities–Equity		100

Once this entry is posted, Market Adjustment—Available-for-Sale Securities will have the required $150 credit balance as follows:

**Market Adjustment–
Available-for-Sale Securities**

		12/31/09	250
Adjustment	100		
		12/31/10	150

When individual securities from a portfolio are sold, a realized gain or loss is recognized for the difference between the original cost of the securities and the selling price, without regard to previous adjustments made to a market adjustment account. At the end of the period, the cost of the remaining securities is compared to the fair market value of the remaining securities, and the market adjustment account is updated to account for the difference.

As mentioned earlier, **Berkshire Hathaway** classifies all of its securities as available-for-sale. To determine how well Warren Buffett has managed the portfolio during the year, the financial statement reader must review both the income statement and the statement of stockholders' equity. Comparing the performance of the company's portfolio of securities for the years 2003 through 2005 results in the following (in millions):

	2003	2004	2005
Realized investment gains (from the income statement)	$ 2,914	$1,746	$5,728
Unrealized appreciation of investments (from the statement of shareholders' equity)	10,842	2,599	2,081
Total portfolio performance	$13,756	$4,345	$7,809

REMEMBER THIS...

- When the value of a trading or available-for-sale security changes, that change is reflected on the balance sheet using a market adjustment account.
- For trading securities, the unrealized gain or loss is reflected on the income statement for the period.
- For available-for-sale securities, the unrealized increase or decrease is recorded in a stockholders' equity account.

EXPANDED

In this section of the chapter, we turn our attention to some of the complexities associated with purchasing debt and equity securities. First, we examine held-to-maturity securities and how any associated premium or discount associated with these securities is amortized. We also address the issue of purchasing a debt security between interest payment dates. The accounting issues associated with an equity security accounted for under the equity method are also presented, and the chapter concludes with a brief discussion of consolidated financial statements.

Account for
held-to-maturity
securities.

Accounting for Held-to-Maturity Securities

5 Held-to-maturity securities are debt securities issued by companies to raise needed funding for expansion, acquisitions, or other business reasons. Bonds (discussed in Chapter 10 from the point of view of the issuer) are by far the most common type of debt instrument that can be readily bought and sold. Because bonds represent the most common type of publicly-traded debt instrument, the following discussion will focus on bonds purchased as investments to be held to maturity.

Accounting for the Initial Purchase

Bonds can be purchased at amounts either above face value (at a premium), below face value (at a discount), or at face value. Regardless of the purchase price, like all other assets, bonds are initially recorded at cost. The cost is the total amount paid to acquire the bonds; this includes the actual price paid for the bonds and any other purchasing expenditures, such as commissions or broker's fees.

To illustrate, assume that Far Side, Inc., purchased a fifth security and classified it as held-to-maturity. Security 5 consists of twenty $1,000 bonds of Chicago Company. The bonds were issued on July 1, 2009, and will mature five years from the date of issuance. The bonds will pay interest at a stated annual rate of 12%, with payments to be made semi-annually on June 30 and December 31. In determining the value of the bonds, the present value of these future cash flows must be determined at the market rate on the date of the purchase. Assuming the market rate on bonds of similar risk is 16%, the purchase price of the bonds is obtained by adding the present value of $20,000 (received 10 periods in the future and discounted at 8%) to the present value of the annuity of the 10 interest payments of $1,200 each (discounted at 8%). The reason 8% is used is that interest is received semiannually; recall that in calculating present value, you must halve the interest rate (16%/2) for semiannual compounding periods. Likewise, you must double the number of years to determine the number of periods (5 years × 2 periods per year = 10 periods). The calculations are:

1.	Semiannual interest payment	$ 1,200	
	Present value of an annuity of 10 payments of $1 at 8% (Table II, page 485)	× 6.7101	
	Present value of interest payments		$ 8,052
2.	Principal (face value) of bonds	$20,000	
	Present value of $1 received 10 periods in the future discounted at 8% (Table I, page 484)	× 0.4632	
	Present value of principal		9,264
3.	Total present value of investment		$17,316

In this example, 16% is the effective rate of interest because that is the amount of interest actually earned; 12% is the stated, or nominal, rate of interest on Chicago Company's bonds. Note that the 12% stated rate determines the size of the annuity payments ($20,000 × 0.12 × ¹/₂ year) but not the purchase price of the bonds; the purchase price varies according to market conditions. The 16% effective rate depends on three amounts: the purchase price, the interest payments, and the face value of the bonds. The $17,316 bond price is the amount that earns Far Side exactly 16%. The journal entry to record the acquisition is:

Investment in Held-to-Maturity Securities	17,316	
Cash		17,316

Note that the investment account is debited for the cost of the bonds with no separate amount shown for the discount of $2,684 ($20,000 – $17,316). Although the discount could be recorded in a separate contra-asset account, in practice it is more common for investors to record the asset cost in the investment account as shown.

Accounting for Bonds Purchased between Interest Dates

The preceding entry assumes that the investing company purchased the bonds on the issuance date, which was also the beginning date for the first interest period. In many cases, however, the date bonds are actually issued does not coincide with an interest date. Further, investors often acquire bonds in the "secondary market"; that is, they purchase bonds from other investors rather than from the issuing company. The secondary market for bonds includes the New York Bond Exchange. Since bonds are traded actively in this market each weekday, investors often acquire bonds between interest dates.

An investor who buys bonds between interest dates, either from the issuing company or in the secondary market, has to pay for the interest that has accrued since the last interest payment date. As explained in Chapter 10, this is necessary because whoever owns the bonds at the time interest is paid receives interest for one full interest period, usually six months, regardless of how long the bonds have been held.

To illustrate, we will assume that Far Side purchased the Chicago Company bonds in the secondary market for $17,316 on November 1, 2009. Semiannual interest of $1,200 ($20,000 × 0.12 ×¹/₂) is paid on the bonds on June 30 and December 31 of each year. On December 31, 2009, Far Side will receive $1,200 even though the bonds were purchased only two months earlier. Since the previous owner is entitled to 4 months' interest on November 1, Far Side will have to pay that individual or company the interest for the period July 1 to October 31. This is illustrated in Exhibit 7.

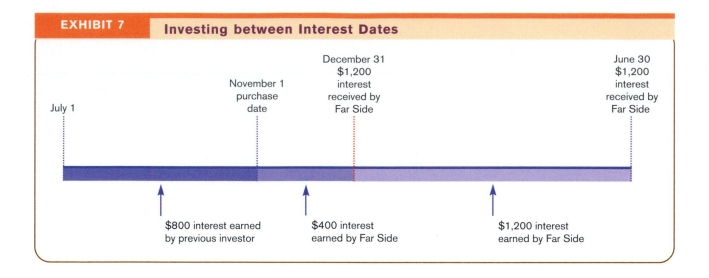

EXHIBIT 7   **Investing between Interest Dates**

The entry to record the investment in bonds on November 1 (between interest dates) is:

Investment in Held-to-Maturity Securities	17,316	
Bond Interest Receivable	800	
Cash		18,116
Purchased $20,000 of Chicago Company bonds for $17,316		
and paid four months' accrued interest.		

When Far Side receives $1,200 in interest on December 31, it will make the following entry:

Cash	1,200	
Interest Receivable		800
Interest Revenue		400
Received interest on Chicago Company bonds.		

Accounting for the Amortization of Bond Discounts and Premiums

Only in those rare instances when the stated interest rate of a bond is exactly equivalent to the prevailing market (or yield) rate for similar investments is a bond purchased at face value. At all other times, bonds are purchased either at a discount (below face value) or at a premium (above face value). Because the face amount of a bond is received at maturity, discounts and premiums must be written off (amortized) over the period that a bond is held.

straight-line amortization

A method of systematically writing off a bond discount or premium in equal amounts each period until maturity.

As you learned in Chapter 10, there are two common methods of amortizing bond discounts and premiums: the straight-line method and the effective-interest method. Because straight-line amortization is simpler, it will be used first to illustrate the amortization process; then the effective-interest method will be described.

Straight-Line Amortization   To illustrate the **straight-line amortization** of a bond discount, we will assume again that Far Side purchased the Chicago Company $20,000, 12%, five-year bonds for $17,316 on the issuance date, July 1, 2009. The entry to record this investment was given on page 575. Far Side will record amortization of $268.40 ($2,684/5 years $\times \frac{1}{2}$) on each interest date. Thus, every six months, beginning on December 31, 2009, Far Side will make the following entry:

Cash	1,200.00	
Investment in Held-to-Maturity Securities	268.40	
Bond Interest Revenue		1,468.40
Received semiannual bond interest and amortized		
bond discount.		

At the end of five years, the investment in the held-to-maturity securities account will have a balance of $20,000.

The discount amortization is revenue earned on the bonds; when the bonds mature, Far Side will receive $20,000 (the face value) in return for an original investment of $17,316. It is this additional revenue of $2,684 that increases the return the investor actually earns from the 12% stated interest rate to the effective interest rate of 16%. The following analysis shows how this works:

Maturity value to be received	$20,000
Interest to be received ($1,200 $\times$ 10 payments)	12,000
Total amount to be received	$32,000
Investment	17,316
Total interest revenue to be earned	$14,684

Interest earned per year:

Stated amount of interest ($20,000 $\times$ 0.12)	$2,400.00	12%
Additional interest from discount ($2,684/5 years)	536.80	4%*
Total	$2,936.80	16%

*This is an approximation; with the straight-line method, the actual interest earned each year changes.

When accounting for the amortization of a bond discount, a company must be careful to amortize the discount only over the period the bonds are actually held. For example, if Far Side had purchased the Chicago Company bonds four months after the issuance date, the discount would have been amortized over a period of 56 months (4 full years plus 8 months of the first year). The amortization for the first year would then have been approximately $383.43 ($2,684 $\times$ ^{8}/56), and the amortization for each of the succeeding four years would be approximately $575.14 ($2,684 $\times$ ^{12}/56).

Accounting for the amortization of a premium on investments is essentially the opposite of accounting for a discount. Amortization of a premium decreases revenue earned, and the effect of the amortization entry is to reduce Investment in Held-to-Maturity Securities to the face value of the bonds by the maturity date.

To illustrate the amortization of a bond premium by the investor, assume that Far Side acquired the $20,000, 12%, five-year Chicago Company bonds for $21,540 on July 1, 2009, the date of issuance. The entry to record the purchase is:

Investment in Held-to-Maturity Securities	21,540	
Cash		21,540
Purchased $20,000 of Chicago Company bonds for $21,540.		

At each interest payment date, beginning December 31, 2009, Far Side will make the following entry:

Cash	1,200	
Investment in Held-to-Maturity Securities		154
Bond Interest Revenue		1,046
Received semiannual bond interest and amortized bond premium		
($1,540/5 years × ½).		

The effect of the amortization entries is to reduce the return earned on the bonds from the stated annual interest rate of 12% to the rate actually earned on the investment (approximately 10%).

Effective-Interest Amortization   To illustrate the computations involved in using the **effective-interest amortization** method, we will again consider Far Side's purchase of the 12%, five-year, $20,000 bonds of Chicago Company for $17,316 on the issuance date. The amount of discount amortized in each of the five years using the effective-interest method is computed as shown in Exhibit 8.

effective-interest amortization

A method of systematically writing off a bond premium or discount that takes into consideration the time value of money and results in an equal rate of amortization for each period.

In the computation, column (2) represents the cash received at the end of each interest period; column (3) shows the amount of effective interest earned, which is the amount that will be reported on the income statement each period; column (4) is the difference between columns (3) and (2) and so represents the amortization; and column (5) shows the investment balance that will be reported on the balance sheet at the end of each period. Note that the interest rate used to compute the actual interest earned is the effective rate of 8% (16%/2) and not the stated rate of 12%. Also note that the total discount is the same as it was when the straight-line method was used, $2,684.

When bonds are purchased at a discount, the amount of amortization increases each successive period. This is so because the investment balance of the bonds increases, and a constant interest rate times an increasing balance results in an increasing amount of interest income. If bonds are purchased at a premium, the effective-interest amortization method will involve a constant interest rate being multiplied by a declining investment balance each period. The result will be a decline in actual interest earned each period.

EXHIBIT 8	Amortization Table for Chicago Company Bonds

(1) Time Period	(2) Cash Received	(3) Interest Actually Earned (0.16 × 1/2 × Investment Balance)	(4) Amount of Amortization (3) – (2)	(5) Investment Balance
Acquisition date				$17,316
Year 1, first six months	$1,200	(0.08 × $17,316) = $1,385	$ 185	17,501
Year 1, second six months	1,200	(0.08 × $17,501) = 1,400	200	17,701
Year 2, first six months	1,200	(0.08 × $17,701) = 1,416	216	17,917
Year 2, second six months	1,200	(0.08 × $17,917) = 1,433	233	18,150
Year 3, first six months	1,200	(0.08 × $18,150) = 1,452	252	18,402
Year 3, second six months	1,200	(0.08 × $18,402) = 1,472	272	18,674
Year 4, first six months	1,200	(0.08 × $18,674) = 1,494	294	18,968
Year 4, second six months	1,200	(0.08 × $18,968) = 1,517	317	19,285
Year 5, first six months	1,200	(0.08 × $19,285) = 1,543	343	19,628
Year 5, second six months	1,200	(0.08 × $19,628) = 1,572*	372	20,000
			$2,684	

*Difference due to rounding.

FYI

Note the similarities between this table and the amortization tables prepared in Chapter 10. The computations are identical—the only difference is that in Chapter 10, we were paying cash, whereas in Chapter 12, we are receiving cash.

Since the effective-interest amortization method takes into account the time value of money, and thus shows the true revenue earned each period (whereas the straight-line method represents only approximations), companies normally should use the effective-interest amortization method. As an exception to this rule, companies are allowed to use the straight-line method when the two methods produce amortization amounts that are not significantly different. Because that is often the case, both methods continue to be used.

Accounting for the Sale or Maturity of Bond Investments

If bonds are held until their maturity date, the accounting for the bond proceeds at maturity includes a debit to Cash and a credit to the investment account for the principal amount. For example, if Far Side, Inc., holds the $20,000, 12% bonds from Chicago Company to maturity, the entry to record the receipt of the bond principal on the maturity date will be:

Cash	20,000	
Investment in Held-to-Maturity Securities		20,000
Received the principal of Chicago Company bonds at maturity.		

This entry assumes, of course, that all previous receipts of interest and bond amortizations have been properly recorded.

Because held-to-maturity securities are usually traded on major exchanges, thus providing a continuous and ready market, they can be sold to other investors prior to their maturity. When these securities are sold prior to their maturity, the difference between the sales price and the investment balance is recognized as a gain or loss on the sale of the investment.

To illustrate, we will assume that Sawyer Company purchased ten $1,000, 8%, five-year bonds of REX Company. We will also assume that the bonds were originally purchased on January 1, 2009, at 101% of their face value; on January 1, 2010, Sawyer showed a balance of $10,040 for these bonds. If the bonds are sold on that day for $10,300, the entry to record the sale and recognize the gain is (assuming no sales commission):

Cash	10,300	
Gain on Sale of Bonds		260
Investment in Held-to-Maturity Securities		10,040
Sold the REX bonds for $10,300.		

If held-to-maturity securities are sold prior to their maturity date, it is important that the amortization of the bond premium or discount be recorded up to the date of sale. If the amortization of the discount or premium is not updated, the gain or loss recognized on the sale will be incorrect.

REMEMBER THIS...

- Accounting for investments in held-to-maturity securities involves four steps:
  1. accounting for the purchase of the securities,
  2. accounting for interest received on the securities,
  3. accounting for amortization of the premium or discount, and
  4. accounting for the sale or maturity of the securities.
- Amortization of premiums and discounts is usually accounted for by the simple straight-line amortization method or the theoretically more correct effective-interest method. The amortization adjusts the interest earned on the bonds from the stated to the effective rate.
- Investments in held-to-maturity securities are generally reported at cost (adjusted for premium or discount amortization), regardless of whether the current market value is less than or greater than their historical cost.
- When held-to-maturity securities are sold before maturity, the premium or discount must be amortized to the date of sale; a gain or loss would be reflected in the income statement for the difference between the selling price and the carrying value on the date of sale.
- Debt securities held until maturity result in no gain or loss on retirement because the carrying value after amortization of a premium or discount should be equal to the face value of the securities.

Account for securities using the equity method.

Accounting for Equity Investments Using the Equity Method

(6) When enough of the outstanding common stock of a company is purchased by another company, the acquiring company may have the ability to significantly influence the operating decisions of the investee. If the ability to influence is present, then accounting standards require the use of the equity method in accounting for the investment. As stated previously, significant influence is presumed if a company owns between 20 and 50% of a company. Keep in mind that the percentage ownership criterion serves only as a guideline. The ability to influence is the key criterion. For example, assume that a company owns 35% of a firm that is headquartered in a foreign country whose government is undergoing a period of volatility. Some of the radical leaders in that country are calling for more internal investment and less outside interference from U.S. corporations. These leaders, if able to gain positions of power, have threatened to expropriate (take over all operations owned by U.S. companies). Even though the U.S. company meets the percentage ownership criterion, it may not be able to significantly influence the operations of the foreign subsidiary. Consider another example of a firm whose ownership is widespread, with no single shareholder owning more than 2% of the corporation. If one stockholder were able to acquire 15% of the outstanding common stock, that investor might be able to influence the decisions of the investee simply because of the size of the ownership percentage relative to that of all other stockholders. The important point is that the ability to influence is the key criterion for using the equity method of accounting.

Under the equity method, dividend payments represent a return of investment; they do not represent revenue, as they do when accounting for trading or available-for-sale securities. Revenue is recognized when the investee company has earnings. When earnings

FYI

Although temporary changes in the value of equity method securities are not accounted for, permanent changes are recognized.

CAUTION

A common mistake in accounting for equity method securities is to debit or credit the investment account for the entire amount of the investee's income or dividends. Remember, the investor accounts only for its share of the investee's income and dividends.

FYI

Coca-Cola, a company in which **Berkshire Hathaway** owns over 8%, has a number of subsidiaries that it accounts for using the equity method. In 2005, Coca-Cola reported equity income from those subsidiaries of $680 million accounted for using the equity method.

are announced, the carrying (book) value of the investment is increased because the investor owns a fixed percentage of a company that is worth more now than it was when the investment was originally made.

In accounting for investments with the equity method, the original investment is first recorded on the books at cost and is subsequently modified to reflect the investor's share of the investee's reported income, losses, and dividends. In this way, book value is increased to recognize the investor's share of earnings and decreased by the dividends received or to recognize the investor's share of losses. Temporary changes in value of investments accounted for using the equity method are not recorded.

There are two reasons why the procedures employed under the equity method are preferred over those used when accounting for trading or available-for-sale securities. First, the equity method assumes that significant influence can be exerted. Thus, the accounting procedures prevent the investing company from manipulating earnings by dictating the dividend policy of the investee. For a trading or available-for-sale security, where dividend payments are reported as revenue, an influential investor could increase its income by putting pressure on the investee to pay larger and more frequent dividends. With the equity method, dividends do not affect earnings. Second, the equity method provides more timely recognition of the investee's earnings and losses than do the procedures employed for trading or available-for-sale securities.

Illustrating the Equity Method

To illustrate the accounting for the equity method, we will use the following information: Kimball, Inc. purchases 20% (2,000 shares) of Holland Enterprises outstanding common stock (10,000 shares), paying $100 per share. Later in the year, Kimball receives a dividend of $2.50 per share; at year-end, Kimball receives Holland's income statement showing that the company earned $50,000 for the year. To ensure that you understand how the equity method differs from the accounting demonstrated earlier in the chapter, we will proceed with two scenarios: (1) Kimball is not able to exercise significant influence on Holland and, as a result, classifies the security as available-for-sale, and (2) Kimball is able to exercise significant influence and uses the equity method.

The accounting for this purchase of stock and subsequent events is shown in Exhibit 9. Column 1 shows the journal entries assuming that the Holland stock is considered an available-for-sale security. Column 2 illustrates the equity method. It is assumed that the Holland stock is selling for $102 per share at year-end.

Although accounting for the holding of equity method securities is different from the accounting for available-for-sale or trading securities, accounting for the sale of a stock investment is the same regardless of the classification. If the selling price exceeds the balance in the investment account, the difference is recognized as a gain. If the selling price is less than the recorded investment balance, the difference is recognized as a loss. To illustrate, assume that Kimball sells its 2,000 shares of Holland Enterprises stock (previously accounted for under the equity method) for $225,000 shortly after the year-end recognition of its $10,000 share of Holland's earnings. The entry to record the sale is:

EXHIBIT 9	**Accounting for Equity Securities**	
	(1) **Available-for-Sale Security**	**(2)** **Equity Method Security**

Accounting for the
 initial purchase of
 the stock
	Investment in Available-for-Sale
	 Securities 200,000
	     Cash 200,000
		Investment in Equity Method
		 Securities 200,000
		     Cash 200,000

Payment of a $2.50
 per share dividend by
 Holland Company
	Cash 5,000
	     Dividend Revenue 5,000
		Cash 5,000
		     Investment in Equity
		       Method Securities 5,000

Announcement by Holland of net income for the year of $50,000	No entry	Investment in Equity Method Securities .... 10,000 Revenue from Investments..... 10,000

Holland stock is
 selling at $102 per
 share at year-end
	Market Adjustment–
	 Available-for-Sale Securities 4,000
	     Unrealized Increase
	     in Available-for-Sale
	     Securities–Equity 4,000
		No entry

Cash	225,000	
Investment in Equity Method Securities		205,000
Realized Gain on Sale of Investment		20,000

The $205,000 is obtained by adding Kimball's share of Holland's reported net income to the original investment cost and subtracting the dividends received from Holland ($200,000 + $10,000 − $5,000).

REMEMBER THIS...

- When the percentage of outstanding voting common stock owned is sufficient to exercise influence (as is usually true with ownership of 20 to 50%), the equity method is used.

- This method involves increasing the book value of the investment for earnings and decreasing it for dividends and losses.

Consolidated Financial Statements

Understand the basics of consolidated financial statements.

(7) The equity method is used when an investor is able to exercise significant influence over an investee's operations. If the investor is able to control decisions made by the investee, then consolidated financial statements are appropriate. The objective with consolidated financial statements is to reflect in one set of financial statements the results of all companies owned or controlled by the parent corporation.

To show how consolidation works, a simple example of a parent company owning part or all of three other companies will be used. The income statement and balance sheet data for the four companies are given at the top of the next page.

	Parent	Percentage of the Parent's Ownership		
		100% Sub1	80% Sub2	30% Sub3
Assets				
Cash	$ 48	$ 20	$ 20	$ 20
Accounts receivable	200	80	80	80
Plant and equipment	500	100	100	100
Investment in Sub 1 ($120 × 1.00)	120			
Investment in Sub 2 ($120 × 0.80)	96			
Investment in Sub 3 ($120 × 0.30)	36			
Total assets	$ 1,000	$ 200	$ 200	$ 200
Liabilities	$ 600	$ 80	$ 80	$ 80
Equity	400	120	120	120
Total liabilities and stockholders' equity	$ 1,000	$ 200	$ 200	$ 200
Revenues				
Sales	$ 4,790	$ 2,000	$ 2,000	$ 2,000
Income from Sub 1 ($100 × 1.00)	100			
Income from Sub 2 ($100 × 0.80)	80			
Income from Sub 3 ($100 × 0.30)	30			
Expenses	(3,000)	(1,900)	(1,900)	(1,900)
Net income	$ 2,000	$ 100	$ 100	$ 100

Note that in the parent company's books, ownership of all three subsidiaries has been accounted for using the equity method. So, in each case the parent reports an investment asset equal to its share of the net assets, or equity, of the subsidiary, and investment income equal to its share of the net income of the subsidiary.

The objective of consolidation is to create financial statements for the parent and its controlled subsidiaries to report their performance as if they were one company. Operationally, this means that the individual assets, liabilities, revenues, and expenses of the parent and all subsidiaries of which it owns more than 50% are added together and included in the consolidated financial statements. Companies of which the parent owns less than 50% but more than 20% are accounted for using the equity method, as described in the preceding section. The consolidated balance sheet and income statement for the parent company and its subsidiaries are shown in Exhibit 10.

You should note four things concerning these consolidated results:

1. The consolidated balance sheet and income statement include *all* assets, liabilities, revenues, and expenses of the parent and the subsidiaries it controls. Thus, even though the parent owns only 80% of Sub 2, all of that subsidiary's assets, liabilities, revenues, and expenses are included in the consolidated total. An example of the intuition here is that the parent, with its 80% ownership, completely *controls* the assets of Sub 2 even though it doesn't own them completely.

2. *None* of the individual assets, liabilities, revenues, and expenses of Sub 3 are included in the consolidated financial statements because that subsidiary is not controlled by the parent. Instead, the parent's ownership of 30% of Sub 3 is accounted for using the equity method.

3. The fact that all of the assets, liabilities, revenues, and expenses of Sub 2 have been included in the consolidated total and yet the parent owns only 80% of that subsidiary is reflected in the minority interest items. In the consolidated balance sheet, **minority interest** is the amount of equity investment made by outside shareholders to consolidated subsidiaries that are not 100% owned by the parent. In the consolidated income statement, minority interest income (shown as a subtraction) reflects the amount of

minority interest

The amount of equity investment made by outside shareholders to consolidated subsidiaries that are not 100% owned by the parent.

EXHIBIT 10	Consolidated Financial Statements

Parent Company and Subsidiaries
Consolidated Balance Sheet

Assets

Cash ($48 + $20 + $20)	$ 88
Accounts receivable ($200 + $80 + $80)	360
Plant and equipment ($500 + $100 + $100)	700
Investment in Sub 3 ($120 × 0.30)	36
Total assets	$ 1,184
Liabilities ($600 + $80 + $80)	$ 760
Minority interest ($120 × 0.20)	24
Equity	400
Total liabilities and equities	$ 1,184

Parent Company and Subsidiaries
Consolidated Income Statement

Revenues

Sales ($4,790 + $2,000 + $2,000)	$ 8,790
Income from Sub 3 ($100 × 0.30)	30
Expenses ($3,000 + $1,900 + $1,900)	(6,800)
Minority interest income ($100 × 0.20)	(20)
Net income	$ 2,000

income belonging to outside shareholders of consolidated subsidiaries that are not 100% owned.

4. Total consolidated equity of $400 in this example is the same as total equity reported by the parent. Consolidated equity can be thought of as the amount invested by the group of shareholders who control the entire consolidated economic entity; this group of shareholders is the shareholders of the parent company. Of course, some of this equity investment, along with some funds borrowed by the parent, has been used to purchase 100% of Sub 1, 80% of Sub 2, and 30% of Sub 3. But to add portions of the equity of each of those subsidiaries in computing consolidated equity would essentially result in double counting the original investment made by the parent shareholders.

REMEMBER THIS...

- Consolidated financial statements are prepared when a parent owns more than 50% of one or more subsidiaries.
- All of the assets, liabilities, revenues, and expenses of the parent and the majority-owned subsidiaries are added in preparing the consolidated financial statements.

REVIEW OF LEARNING OBJECTIVES

(1) Understand why companies invest in other companies. Companies usually invest in other companies for one of the following reasons:

- To earn a return on excess cash.
- To gain influence, or even control, over the other company.

(2) Understand the different classifications for securities.

Classification of Securities	Types of Securities	Disclosed at	Reporting of Temporary Changes in Fair Value
Trading	Debt and equity	Fair value	Income statement
Available-for-sale	Debt and equity	Fair value	Stockholders' equity
Held-to-maturity	Debt	Amortized cost	Not recognized
Equity method	Equity	Cost adjusted for changes in net assets of investee	Not recognized

(3) Account for the purchase, recognition of revenue, and sale of trading and available-for-sale securities.

- Investments in debt and equity securities are recorded at cost, which includes the fair value of the securities plus any other expenditures required to purchase the securities.
- Revenues from securities take the form of:
  - interest,
  - dividends, or
  - gains or losses from selling the securities.

(4) Account for changes in the value of securities.

- Changes in value of trading or available-for-sale securities are reflected on the balance sheet using a market adjustment account.
- For trading securities, the unrealized gain or loss is reflected on the income statement for the period.
- For available-for-sale securities, the unrealized increase or decrease is recorded in a stockholders' equity account.

(5) Account for held-to-maturity securities.

- Amortization of premiums and discounts on held-to-maturity securities is accounted for by:
  - the straight-line amortization method or
  - the effective-interest method.
- The amortization adjusts the interest earned on the bonds from the stated to the effective rate.
- Investments in held-to-maturity securities are generally reported at cost (adjusted for premium or discount amortization), regardless of whether the current market value is less than or greater than their historical cost.

6 **Account for securities using the equity method.**

- When the percentage of outstanding voting common stock owned is sufficient to exercise influence (as is usually true with ownership of 20 to 50%), the equity method is used.
- This method involves:
  - increasing the book value of the investment for a percentage share of earnings and
  - decreasing it for a percentage share of dividends and losses.

7 **Understand the basics of consolidated financial statements.**

- Consolidated financial statements are prepared when a parent owns more than 50% of one or more subsidiaries.
- All of the assets, liabilities, revenues, and expenses of the parent and the majority-owned subsidiaries are added in preparing the consolidated financial statements.

KEY TERMS & CONCEPTS

available-for-sale
  securities, 566
consolidated financial
  statements, 565
debt securities, 564
equity method, 565

equity securities
  (stock), 564
held-to-maturity
  security, 565
Market Adjustment—
  Trading Securities, 571

realized gains and
  losses, 570
trading
  securities, 566
unrealized gains and
  losses, 571

effective-interest
  amortization, 578
minority interest, 583
straight-line
  amortization, 576

REVIEW PROBLEM

Investments in Debt and Equity Securities

On January 1, 2009, Schultz, Inc., purchased the following securities:

Security	Type	Classification	Cost
1	Debt	Trading	$2,500
2	Debt	Trading	1,500
3	Equity	Trading	1,750
4	Debt	Available-for-sale	4,300
5	Equity	Available-for-sale	2,750

On March 31, one-half of Security 2 was sold for $900. During the year, interest and dividends were received as follows:

Security	Interest	Dividends
1	$200	
2	85	
3		none
4	435	
5		$200

(continued)

The following fair market values are available on December 31, 2009. Schultz had no balance in its market adjustment accounts on January 1, 2009.

Security	Market Value
1	$2,400
2	950
3	1,600
4	4,250
5	2,900

Required:

Record all necessary journal entries to account for these investments during 2009.

Solution

To account for these investments, four events must be accounted for:

1. The initial purchase on January 1.
2. The sale of one-half of Security 2 on March 31.
3. The receipt of interest and dividends during the year.
4. The changes in value as of December 31.

The initial purchase

Jan. 1	Investment in Trading Securities	5,750	
	Investment in Available-for-Sale Securities	7,050	
	Cash		12,800

To record the purchase of trading and available-for-sale securities.

The sale of one-half of Security 2 on March 31

Mar. 31	Cash	900	
	Realized Gain on Sale of Securities		150
	Investment in Trading Securities		750

Sold one-half of Security 2 ($750 book value) for $900.
Recorded the $150 realized gain ($900 − $750).

The receipt of interest and dividends during the year

	Cash	920	
	Interest Revenue		720
	Dividend Revenue		200

Received $720 in interest during the year and $200 in dividends.

Note: Even if cash were not received by year-end, the interest and dividends earned would need to be recorded, with the offsetting debit to a receivable account(s).

The changes in value as of December 31, 2009

Dec. 31	Unrealized Loss on Trading Securities	50	
	Market Adjustment–Trading Securities		50

To account for the difference between book value ($5,000) and fair market value ($4,950) of trading securities.

Note: Remember that one-half of Security 2 was sold during the year.

Dec. 31	Market Adjustment–Available-for-Sale Securities	100	
	Unrealized Increase/Decrease in Value of		
	Available-for-Sale Securities–Equity		100

To account for the difference between book value ($7,050) and fair market value ($7,150) of available-for-sale securities.

DISCUSSION QUESTIONS

1. Why do firms invest in assets that are not directly related to their primary business operations?
2. Describe the risk and return trade-off of investments.
3. What are the four different classifications of debt and equity securities?
4. When will a security be classified as "trading"?
5. What types of securities can be classified as "held-to-maturity"?
6. To be classified as an equity method security, the investor must typically own at least a certain percentage of the outstanding common stock of the investee. What is that minimum percentage? That percentage of ownership represents the investor's ability to do what?
7. Identify the different types of returns an investor can realize when investing in debt and equity securities.
8. When a security is sold, what information must be known to account for that transaction?
9. What is the difference between a realized gain or loss and an unrealized gain or loss?
10. What does the account "Market Adjustment" represent?
11. How are changes in the value of trading securities accounted for on the books of the investor?
12. How are changes in the value of available-for-sale securities accounted for on the books of the investor?
13. What is the process for adjusting the value of a trading or available-for-sale security after a valuation account has been established?
14. Why aren't premiums and discounts on available-for-sale securities amortized?
15. Why aren't changes in the value of held-to-maturity and equity method securities accounted for on the books of the investor?

16. How does the accounting for changes in the value of trading and available-for-sale securities differ?

17. What future cash inflows is a company buying when it purchases a held-to-maturity security?
18. When would a company be willing to pay more than the face amount (a premium) for a held-to-maturity security?
19. Why does the amortization of a discount increase the amount of interest revenue earned on a held-to-maturity security?
20. Why must an investor purchasing held-to-maturity securities between interest payment dates pay the previous owner for accrued interest on those securities?
21. Why is the effective-interest amortization method theoretically superior to the straight-line method?
22. What is the key criterion for using the equity method of accounting for equity securities?
23. What guidelines have been provided to determine if the ability to significantly influence the decisions of an investee exists?
24. How does the equity method of accounting for securities differ from the procedures employed for a trading security?
25. Under what circumstances should consolidated financial statements be prepared?
26. What financial statement accounts are shown only in consolidated financial statements and never in the financial statements of individual companies?

PRACTICE EXERCISES

PE 12-1
LO1
Why Companies Invest in Other Companies
Which one of the following is *not* a primary reason companies invest in other companies?

a   To earn return on excess cash.
b. To eliminate risk in other investments.
c. To gain influence over another company.
d. To gain control over another company.

PE 12-2
LO2
Classifying a Security
Which one of the following types of investments is *always* an example of a debt security?

a. Available-for-sale securities.
c. Held-to-maturity securities.
b. Trading securities.
d. Equity method securities.

PE 12-3   **Equity Method Securities**

LO2   What is the general rule for what percentage an entity must own in another company to account for the investment using the equity method?

a.   The entity should own 20 to 50% of the other company's outstanding voting stock.

b.   The entity should own 5 to 10% of the other company's outstanding voting stock.

c.   The entity should own 50 to 90% of the other company's outstanding voting stock.

d.   The entity should own 10 to 20% of the other company's outstanding voting stock.

PE 12-4   **Disclosure of Securities**

LO2   Which two of the following classifications of securities are valued at fair value on a company's balance sheet?

a.   Available-for-sale securities.

b.   Equity method securities.

c.   Trading securities.

d.   Held-to-maturity securities.

PE 12-5   **Accounting for the Purchase of Trading and Available-for-Sale Securities**

LO3   The company purchased the following securities with cash:

Security	Type	Classification	Cost (including Broker's Fees)
1	Equity	Trading	$28,000
2	Equity	Available-for-sale	61,000
3	Debt	Available-for-sale	18,600
4	Debt	Trading	37,400

Make the necessary journal entry(ies) to record the purchase of these securities.

PE 12-6   **Accounting for the Return Earned on an Investment**

LO3   Refer to the data in PE 12-5. The company received the following interest and dividends from its securities investments during the year:

Security	Interest	Dividends
1		$340
2		560
3	$154	
4	305	

Make the necessary journal entry(ies) to record the receipt of interest and dividends during the year.

PE 12-7   **Accounting for the Sale of Securities**

LO3   Refer to the data in PE 12-5. Near the end of the year, the company sold Security 1 for $25,200. Make the necessary journal entry(ies) to record the sale.

PE 12-8   **Changes in Value of Trading Securities**

LO4   At the end of the year, the company had the following securities:

Security	Classification	Historical Cost	Market Value (December 31)
1	Available-for-sale	$52,000	$52,400
2	Available-for-sale	12,300	11,500
3	Trading	23,500	24,250

Make the necessary journal entry(ies) to record the change in value of the company's trading security (Security 3).

PE 12-9
LO4

Changes in Value of Available-for-Sale Securities

Refer to the data in PE 12-8. Make the necessary journal entry(ies) to record the change in value of the company's available-for-sale securities.

PE 12-10
LO4

Subsequent Changes in Value of Trading Securities

At the end of year 2, the company owned the following security (which was originally purchased for $41,600 and had a market value at the end of year 1 of $42,700).

Classification	Historical Cost	Market Value (December 31, Year 2)
Trading	$41,600	$40,800

Make the necessary journal entry(ies) to record the change in value of the security in the second year.

EXPANDED *material*

PE 12-11
LO5

Computing the Value of Held-to-Maturity Securities

On January 1, 2009, the company purchased thirty $1,000 held-to-maturity bonds of another company. The bonds mature in four years from the date of issuance and pay interest at a stated annual rate of 8%, with payments to be made quarterly on March 31, June 30, September 30, and December 31. The market rate on bonds of similar risk is 12%. Compute the present value of this investment.

PE 12-12
LO5

Accounting for the Initial Purchase of Held-to-Maturity Securities

Using the information from PE 12-11, make the necessary journal entry to record the purchase of this held-to-maturity security.

PE 12-13
LO5

Straight-Line Amortization of Bond Discounts

The company purchased $40,000, 10%, three-year bonds for $35,939. Interest on the bonds is payable semiannually. Using straight-line amortization of the bond discounts, make the necessary journal entry(ies) to be made at each interest payment date to record the semiannual interest payment.

PE 12-14
LO5

Straight-Line Amortization of Bond Premiums

The company purchased $65,000, 10%, three-year bonds for $68,407.39. Interest on the bonds is payable semiannually. Using straight-line amortization of the bond premiums, make the necessary journal entry(ies) to be made at each interest payment date to record the semiannual interest payment.

PE 12-15
LO5

Effective-Interest Amortization of Bond Premiums

Refer to the data in PE 12-14. Using the effective-interest method of bond premium amortization, make the necessary journal entries to record the first two interest payments received on the bonds.

PE 12-16
LO5

Accounting for the Sale of Bond Investments

Refer to the data in PE 12-14 and 12-15. The company decided to sell the bonds for $67,000 immediately after receiving the second interest payment. Make the necessary journal entry(ies) to record the sale of these bonds.

PE 12-17 **Accounting for Investments Using the Equity Method**

LO6 Manwill Company owns 40% (30,000 shares) of Hall Company's voting stock. Since Manwill has a significant interest in Hall Company, it uses the equity method of accounting for the investment. Hall Company reported the following information for the year:

1. Hall reported net income of $80,000.
2. Hall paid dividends of $20,000.
3. Hall's stock value increased from $40 to $45.

Make the necessary journal entry(ies) to record the change in value of Manwill Company's investment in Hall Company.

PE 12-18 **Consolidated Financial Statements**

LO7 Parent Company owns 90% of the outstanding stock of Sub Company. At the end of the year, Sub Company reports revenues of $1,000 and expenses of $850. What will Parent Company report on its own financial statements as "Income from Sub"? On the consolidated financial statements, how much of Sub Company's revenues and expenses will be reported?

EXERCISES

E 12-19 **Investment in Trading Securities–Journal Entries**

LO3, LO4 Prepare the journal entries to account for the following investment transactions of Samuelson Company:

2008

July 1   Purchased 350 shares of Bateman Company stock at $22 per share plus a brokerage fee of $600. The Bateman stock is classified as trading.

Oct. 31   Received a cash dividend of $2.00 per share on the Bateman Company stock.

Dec. 31   At year-end, Bateman Company stock had a market price of $19 per share.

2009

Feb. 20   Sold 175 shares of the Bateman Company stock for $26 per share.

Oct. 31   Received a cash dividend of $2.20 per share on the Bateman Company stock.

Dec. 31   At year-end, Bateman Company stock had a market price of $29 per share.

E 12-20 **Investment in Trading Securities–Journal Entries**

LO3, LO4 In June 2009, Hatch Company had no investment securities but had excess cash that would not be needed for nine months. Management decided to use this money to purchase trading securities as a short-term investment. The following transactions relate to the investments:

July 16   Purchased 4,000 shares of Eli Corporation stock. The price paid, including brokerage fees, was $41,880.

Sept. 23   Received a cash dividend of $0.90 per share on the Eli stock.

   28   Sold 2,000 shares of Eli Corporation stock at $11 per share. Paid a selling commission of $160.

Dec. 31   The market value of Eli's stock was $11.25 per share.

Given these data, prepare the journal entries to account for Hatch's investment in Eli Corporation stock.

E 12-21 **Investment in Available-for-Sale Securities–Journal Entries**

LO3, LO4 Bird Beak Corporation made the following available-for-sale securities transactions:

Jan. 14   Purchased 4,000 shares of Pinegar Corporation common stock at $20.80 per share.

Mar. 31   Received a cash dividend of $0.25 per share on the Pinegar Corporation stock.

Aug. 28   Sold 1,600 shares of Pinegar Corporation stock at $22.60 per share.

Dec. 31   The market value of the Pinegar Corporation stock was $24 per share.

Prepare journal entries to record the transactions.

E 12-22

LO3, LO4

Investment in Securities

In January 2007, Solitron, Inc., determined that it had excess cash on hand and decided to invest in Horner Company stock. The company intends to hold the stock for a period of three to five years, thereby making the investment an available-for-sale security. The following transactions took place in 2007, 2008, and 2009:

2007

Jan. 17   Purchased 2,750 shares of Horner Company stock for $89,500.
May 10   Received a cash dividend of $1.30 per share on Horner Company stock.
Dec. 31   The market value of the Horner Company stock was $30 per share.

2008

May 22   Purchased 750 shares of Horner Company stock at $40 per share.
July 18   Received a cash dividend of $0.90 per share on the Horner Company stock.
Dec. 31   The market value of the Horner Company stock was $42 per share.

2009

June 7   Received a cash dividend of $1 per share on the Horner Company stock.
Oct. 5   Sold the Horner Company stock at $27 per share for cash.
Dec. 31   The market value of the Horner Company stock was $25 per share.

Prepare the journal entries required to record each of these events.

E 12-23

LO4

Investment in Equity Securities

During 2007, Riverbend Company purchased trading securities as a short-term investment. The costs of the securities and their market values on December 31, 2009, are listed below.

Security	Cost	Market Value (December 31, 2009)
A	$250,000	$130,000
B	160,000	169,000
C	315,000	350,000

Riverbend had no trading securities in the years before 2009. Before any adjustments related to these trading securities, Riverbend had net income of $630,000 in 2009.

1. What is net income (ignoring income taxes) after making any necessary trading security adjustments?
2. What would net income be if the market value of Security A were $240,000?

E 12-24

LO3, LO4

Investment in Debt and Equity Securities

In February 2009, Packard Corporation purchased the following securities. Prior to these purchases, Packard had no portfolio of investment securities.

Security	Type	Classification	Cost
1	Debt	Trading	$11,500
2	Equity	Trading	9,000
3	Equity	Available-for-sale	7,250
4	Debt	Available-for-sale	12,300

During 2009, Packard received $2,400 in interest and $1,800 in dividends. On December 31, 2009, Packard's portfolio of securities had the following market values:

Security	Fair Market Value
1	$12,000
2	8,750
3	7,500
4	12,500

Prepare the journal entries required to record each of these transactions.

E 12-25

LO3, LO4

Investment in Debt and Equity Securities

Andrews, Inc., purchased the following securities during 2009:

Security	Type	Classification	Cost
1	Debt	Trading	$ 2,400
2	Equity	Trading	3,500
3	Debt	Available-for-sale	4,200
4	Equity	Available-for-sale	1,800
5	Debt	Held-to-maturity	11,000

During 2009, Andrews received interest of $1,400 and dividends of $600 on its investments. On September 29, 2009, Andrews sold one-half of Security 1 for $1,600. On December 31, 2009, the portfolio of securities had the following fair market values:

Security	Fair Market Value
1	$ 1,700
2	3,600
3	4,000
4	1,900
5	12,000

Andrews had no balance in its market adjustment accounts at the beginning of the year. Prepare the journal entries required to record the purchase of the securities, the receipt of interest and dividends, the sale of securities, and the adjustments required at year-end.

E 12-26

LO4

Investment in Securities–Changes in Value

Sharp, Inc., had the following portfolio of investment securities on January 1, 2009:

Security	Type	Classification	Historical Cost	Fair Market Value (1/1/09)
1	Debt	Trading	$1,000	$ 800
2	Equity	Trading	1,250	1,100
3	Debt	Trading	1,700	1,650
4	Debt	Available-for-sale	2,200	2,150
5	Debt	Held-to-maturity	1,800	1,750

Appropriate adjustments have been made in prior years. No securities were bought or sold during 2009. On December 31, 2009, Sharp's portfolio of securities had the following fair market values:

Security	Fair Market Value (12/31/09)
1	$ 650
2	1,200
3	1,700
4	2,250
5	1,850

Prepare the necessary adjusting entry(ies) on December 31, 2009.

E 12-27

LO4

Investment in Securities–Changes in Value

Indonesia, Inc., held the following portfolio of securities on December 31, 2008 (the end of its first year of operations):

	Cost	Market Value (12/31/08)
Trading securities	$16,300	$14,800
Available-for-sale securities	24,100	25,000
Held-to-maturity securities	19,000	20,300

No additional securities were bought or sold during 2009. On December 31, 2009, Indonesia's securities had a fair market value of:

Trading securities	$15,900
Available-for-sale securities	25,200
Held-to-maturity securities	18,900

Prepare the entries required at the end of 2008 and 2009 to properly adjust Indonesia's portfolio of securities.

E 12-28

LO3, LO5

Accounting for the Purchase of Securities

The Running Store is a chain of sporting goods stores. The Running Store is interested in using some of its excess cash to invest in securities. It decides to buy the following securities:

Security	Type	Price
Steven Company	Available-for-sale	$ 2,750
Nick, Inc.	Trading	11,040
Ryan Company	Available-for-sale	6,830
Jacob Company	Held-to-maturity	15,000

Prepare the journal entry to record the purchase of these securities.

E 12-29

LO3, LO5

Accounting for the Sale of Securities

Shay Company owns the following securities, which it is interested in selling:

Security	Type	Cost	Market Adjustments	Market Price
London Company	Available-for-sale	$5,000	$ 600 increase	$6,400
Brown Company	Trading	6,100	800 decrease	6,300
Shaw Company	Available-for-sale	8,400	1,000 increase	8,700
Robbins Company	Held-to-maturity	7,200	None	9,800

Prepare the journal entry to record the sale of these securities.

EXPANDED *material*

E 12-30

LO5

Held-to-Maturity Security Price Determination

1. How much should an investor pay for $100,000 of debenture bonds that pay interest every six months at an annual rate of 8%, assuming that the bonds mature in 10 years and that the effective interest rate at the date of purchase is also 8%?

2. How much should an investor pay for $100,000 of debenture bonds that pay $5,000 of interest every six months, have a maturity date in 10 years, and are sold to yield 8% interest, compounded semiannually?

E 12-31

LO5

Held-to-Maturity Security Price Determination

McMinville Corporation has decided to purchase bonds of La Verkin Corporation as a long-term investment. The 10-year bonds have a stated rate of interest of 12%, with interest payments being made semiannually. How much should McMinville be willing to pay for $150,000 of the bonds if:

1. A rate of return of 14% is deemed necessary to justify the investment?
2. A rate of return of 10% is considered to be an adequate return?

E 12-32

LO5

Investments in Held-to-Maturity Securities

Control Group purchased thirty $1,000, 10%, 20-year bonds of Natchez Corporation on January 1, 2009, as a long-term investment. The bonds mature on January 1, 2029, and interest is payable every January 1 and July 1. Control Group's reporting year ends December 31, and the company uses the straight-line method of amortizing premiums and discounts.

Make all necessary journal entries relating to the bonds for 2009, assuming:

1. The purchase price is 104% of face value.
2. The purchase price is 94% of face value.

E 12-33

LO5

Straight-Line Amortization of Premium

On their issuance date, Salina Company purchased thirty-five $1,000, 10%, six-year bonds of AF Corporation as a long-term investment for $38,285. Interest payments are made semiannually. Prepare a schedule showing the amortization of the bond premium over the six-year life of the bonds. Use the straight-line method of amortization.

E 12-34

LO5

Effective-Interest Amortization of Premium

Assume the same facts as in E 12-33. Prepare a schedule showing the amortization of the bond premium over the six-year life of the bonds. Use the effective-interest method of amortization. (*Hint:* The effective rate of interest earned on the bonds is 8% compounded semiannually.)

E 12-35

LO6

Investments in Stock–Equity Method

On January 3, 2009, Jorgenson, Inc., purchased 30,000 shares of the outstanding common stock of Horace Corporation. At the time of this transaction, Horace has 100,000 shares of common stock outstanding. The cost of the purchase (including brokerage fees) was $19 per share. During the year, Horace reported income of $32,000 and paid dividends of $4,000. On December 31, 2009, Horace's stock was valued at $23 per share.

Provide the entries necessary to record the above transactions.

E 12-36

LO6

Equity Method

Foster Enterprises purchased 20% of the outstanding common stock of Novelties, Inc., on January 2, 2009, paying $150,000. During 2009, Novelties, Inc., reported net income of $20,000 and paid dividends to shareholders of $15,000. On December 31, 2009, Foster's investment in Novelties stock had a fair market value of $158,000. Assuming this is the only security owned by Foster, prepare all journal entries required by Foster in 2009 assuming:

1. The security is classified as a trading security.
2. The security is classified as an available-for-sale security.
3. The equity method is applied to the investment.

E 12-37

LO6

Investments in Stock–Equity Method

During 2009, Genco Corporation purchased 10,000 shares of Wiener Company stock for $85 per share. Wiener had a total of 40,000 shares of stock outstanding.

1. Prepare journal entries for the following transactions:

Jan. 1 Purchased 10,000 shares of common stock at $85.

Dec. 31 Wiener Company declared and paid a $4.60-per-share dividend.

31 Wiener Company reported net income for 2009 of $360,000.

(continued)

2. On December 31, 2009, the market price of Wiener's stock was $79 per share. Show how this investment would be reported on Genco's balance sheet at December 31, 2009, assuming that this is the only stock investment owned by Genco.

E 12-38

LO7

Consolidated Financial Statements–Balance Sheet

Ecotec Inc. purchased 70% of the outstanding common stock of Beatrix Co. on January 1, 2007, paying $875,000. On that day, the balance sheets of the two companies immediately after the purchase are as follows:

(in thousands)	Ecotec	Beatrix
Cash	$ 410	$ 260
Other current assets	1,875	1,240
Property, plant, & equipment	1,100	850
Investment in Beatrix	875	0
Total assets	$4,260	$2,350
Current liabilities	$1,225	$ 800
Long-term liabilities	775	300
Common stock	800	500
Retained earnings	1,460	750
Total liabilities & equities	$4,260	$2,350

1. Compute the amount that will be disclosed on the consolidated balance sheet as "Minority Interest."
2. Prepare a consolidated balance sheet as of January 1, 2007.

E 12-39

LO7

Consolidated Financial Statements–Income Statement

On January 1, 2007, Limbo Inc. purchased 80% of the outstanding common stock of Euphoria Co. at a price of $960,000. At the end of 2007, each company prepared separate income statements, which are presented below.

(in thousands)	Limbo	Euphoria
Sales	$3,650	$1,245
Income from Euphoria	112	0
Interest revenue	108	15
	$3,870	$1,260
Cost of goods sold	1,900	640
Other operating expenses	1,020	450
Interest expense	210	30
Net income	$ 740	$ 140

1. Compute the amount that will be reported on the consolidated income statement as "Minority Interest Income."
2. Prepare a consolidated income statement.
3. Compare Limbo's reported net income with consolidated net income. Explain the relationship.

PROBLEMS

P 12-40

LO3

Investment in Securities–Recording and Analysis

The following data pertain to the securities of Linford Company during 2009, the company's first year of operations:

a. Purchased 400 shares of Corporation A stock at $40 per share plus a commission of $200. This security is classified as trading.

(continued)

b. Purchased $6,000 of Corporation B bonds. These bonds are classified as trading.

c. Received a cash dividend of $0.50 per share on the Corporation A stock.

d. Sold 100 shares of Corporation A stock for $46 per share.

e. Received interest of $240 on the Corporation B bonds.

f. Purchased 50 shares of Corporation C stock for $3,500. Classified the stock as available-for-sale.

g. Received interest of $240 on the Corporation B bonds.

h. Sold 150 shares of Corporation A stock for $28 per share.

i. Received a cash dividend of $1.40 per share on the Corporation C stock.

j. Interest receivable at year-end on the Corporation B bonds amounts to $60.

Required:

Prepare journal entries to record the preceding transactions. Post the entries to T-accounts, and determine the amount of each of the following for the year:

1. Dividend revenue.

2. Bond interest revenue.

3. Net gain or loss from selling securities.

P 12-41

LO3, LO4

Buying and Selling Trading Securities

Iron Company incurred the following transactions relating to the common stock of Bronze Company:

July 14, 2007	Purchased 12,000 shares at $41 per share.
Sept. 4, 2008	Sold 2,100 shares at $46 per share.
Aug. 24, 2009	Sold 1,500 shares at $40 per share.

The end-of-year market prices for the shares were as follows:

Dec. 31, 2007	$38 per share
Dec. 31, 2008	$49 per share
Dec. 31, 2009	$36 per share

Iron Company classifies the Bronze stock as trading securities.

Required:

1. Determine the amount of (a) realized gain or loss and (b) unrealized gain or loss to be reported on the income statement each year relating to the Bronze stock.

2. How would your answer to part (1) change if the securities were classified as available-for-sale? Explain.

P 12-42

LO3, LO4

Trading and Available-for-Sale Securities

Lorien Technologies, Inc., purchased the following securities during 2008:

Security	Classification	Cost	Market Value (12/31/08)
A	Trading	$ 5,000	$ 4,000
B	Trading	7,000	10,000
C	Available-for-sale	10,000	8,000
D	Available-for-sale	6,000	3,500

The following transactions occurred during 2009:

a. On January 1, 2009, Lorien purchased Security E for $12,000. Security E is classified as available-for-sale.

b. On March 23, 2009, Security B was sold for $4,700.

c. On July 23, 2009, Security C was sold for $19,500.

(continued)

The remaining securities had the following market values as of December 31, 2009:

Security	Market Value
A	$ 4,500
D	5,000
E	13,000

Required:

1. Determine the amount of (a) realized gain or loss and (b) unrealized gain or loss to be reported relating to Lorien's trading securities for 2009.
2. Determine the amount of (a) realized gain or loss and (b) unrealized gain or loss to be reported relating to Lorien's available-for-sale securities for 2009. Which amounts will appear on the income statement?

P 12-43

LO3

Investments in Trading Securities

In December 2009, the treasurer of Toth Company concluded that the company had excess cash on hand and decided to invest in Soren Corporation stock. The company intends to hold the stock for a period of 6 to 12 months and classifies the security as trading. The following transactions took place:

Jan.	1	Purchased 7,600 shares of Soren Corporation stock for $152,000.
Apr.	24	Received a cash dividend of $1.20 per share on the Soren Corporation stock.
May	5	Sold 2,000 shares of the Soren Corporation stock at $23 per share for cash.
July	21	Received a cash dividend of $1.30 per share on the Soren Corporation stock.
Aug.	9	Sold the balance of the Soren Corporation stock at $15 per share for cash.

Required:

Prepare the appropriate journal entries to record each of these transactions.

P 12-44

LO3, LO4

Investments in Debt and Equity Securities

Wilbur Company often invests in the debt and equity securities of other companies as short-term investments. During 2009, the following events occurred:

July   1   Wilbur purchased the securities listed here:

Security	Type	Classification	Cost
1	Debt	Trading	$41,200
2	Equity	Trading	23,940
3	Equity	Trading	51,250
4	Equity	Available-for-sale	21,300

Sept.	30	Wilbur received a cash dividend of $2,460 on Security 2.
Dec.	1	Wilbur sold Security 4 for $18,300.
	31	Wilbur received interest of $4,300 on Security 1.
	31	The market prices were quoted as follows: Security 1, $40,900; Security 2, $25,550; Security 3, $44,000.

Required:

1. Prepare journal entries to record the events.
2. Illustrate how these investments would be reported on the balance sheet at December 31.
3. What items and amounts would be reported on the income statement for the year?

P 12-45

LO3, LO4

Unifying Concepts: Short-Term Investments in Stocks and Bonds

JAG Manufacturing Company produces and sells one main product. There is significant seasonality in demand, and the unit price is quite high. As a result, during the heavy selling season, the company generates cash that is idle for a few months. The company

(continued)

uses this cash to acquire investments. The following transactions relate to JAG's investments during 2009:

Mar. 15   Purchased 1,200 shares of Gates Corporation stock at $21 per share, plus broker-age fees of $815. This stock is classified as trading.

Apr. 1   Purchased $39,000 of 10% bonds of Micro Company. This investment is classi-fied as available-for-sale.

June 3   Received a cash dividend of $0.75 per share on the Gates Corporation stock.

Oct. 1   Received a semiannual interest payment of $1,950 on the Micro Company bonds.

     10   Sold 400 shares of the Gates Corporation stock at $26 per share less a $295 bro-kerage fee.

Dec. 31   Recorded $975 of interest earned on the Micro Company bonds for the period October 1, 2009, through December 31, 2009.

     31   The market price of the Gates Corporation stock was $19 per share; the market price of the Micro Company bonds was $38,560.

Required:
Prepare journal entries to record these transactions.

P 12-46
LO3, LO4

Recording Investment Transactions

The following data pertain to the investments of Sumner Company during 2009, the company's first year of operations:

a. Purchased 200 shares of Corporation A stock at $40 per share, plus brokerage fees of $100. Classified as trading.
b. Purchased $10,000 of Corporation B bonds at face value. Classified as trading.
c. Received a cash dividend of $0.50 per share on the Corporation A stock.
d. Received interest of $600 on the Corporation B bonds.
e. Purchased 50 shares of Corporation C stock for $3,500. Classified as available-for-sale.
f. Received interest of $600 on the Corporation B bonds.
g. Sold 80 shares of Corporation A stock for $32 per share due to a significant decline in the market.
h. Received a cash dividend of $1.40 per share on the Corporation C stock.
i. Interest receivable at year-end on the Corporation B bonds amounts to $200.
j. Market value of securities at year-end: Corporation A stock, $42 per share; Corporation B bonds, $10,200; Corporation C stock, $3,450.

Required:
Enter these transactions in T-accounts, and determine each of the following for the year:
 1. Dividend revenue.
 2. Bond interest revenue.
 3. Net gain or loss from selling securities.
 4. Unrealized gain or loss from holding securities.

P 12-47
LO3, LO4

Investments in Available-for-Sale Securities

Lindorf Company often purchases common stocks of other companies as long-term invest-ments. At the end of 2008, Lindorf held the common stocks listed. (Assume that Lindorf Company exercises no significant influence over these companies; that is, they are classified as available-for-sale securities.)

Corporation	Number of Shares	Cost per Share
A	2,500	$ 40
B	2,000	26
C	2,300	153
D	750	75

(continued)

Additional information for 2008:

Sept. 30   Lindorf received a cash dividend of $1.15 per share on Corporation A stock.
Dec. 31   The market prices were quoted as follows:
           Corporation A stock, $35; Corporation B stock, $28;
           Corporation C stock, $154; Corporation D stock, $70.

Required:

1. Illustrate how these investments would be reported on the balance sheet at December 31, 2008, and prepare the adjusting entry at that date.
2. What items and amounts would be reported on the income statement for 2008?
3. Prepare the journal entry for the sale of Corporation D stock for $71 per share in 2009.
4. **Interpretive Question:** Why are losses from the write-down of available-for-sale securities not included in the current year's income, whereas similar losses for trading securities are included?

P 12-48

LO3

Unifying Concepts: Investments in Debt and Equity Securities

On January 1, Heiress Company had surplus cash and decided to make some long-term investments. The following transactions occurred during the year:

Jan.   1   Purchased thirty $1,000, 11% bonds of McComb Corporation at face value. Semiannual interest payment dates are January 1 and July 1 each year. The bonds are classified as available-for-sale.
Feb. 15   Purchased 3,000 shares of Gordon Corporation stock at $28 per share, plus brokerage fees of $1,100. The stock is classified as available-for-sale.
July   1   Received a semiannual interest payment on the McComb Corporation bonds.
Sept. 30   Received an annual cash dividend of $1.00 per share on Gordon Corporation stock.
Oct. 15   Sold 1,000 shares of the Gordon Corporation stock at $33 per share.
Dec. 31   Adjusted the accounts to accrue interest on the McComb Corporation bonds.

Required:

1. Prepare journal entries for these transactions.
2. The market quote for McComb Corporation's bonds at closing on December 31 was 103. The Gordon Corporation stock closed at $32 per share. Prepare a partial balance sheet showing all the necessary data for these securities. Assume that Heiress exercises no significant influence over its investees.

P 12-49

LO3, LO4

Investments in Equity Securities

On March 15, 2009, Boston Company acquired 5,000 shares of Richfield Corporation common stock at $45 per share as a long-term investment. Richfield has 50,000 shares of outstanding voting common stock. Boston does not own any other stocks. The following additional events occurred during the fiscal year ended December 31, 2009:

Dec.   1   Boston received a cash dividend of $2.50 per share from Richfield Corporation.
      31   Richfield Corporation announced earnings for the year of $150,000.
      31   Richfield common stock had a closing market price of $42 per share.

Required:

1. What accounting method should be used to account for this investment? Why?
2. Prepare journal entries for the above transactions.
3. Prepare a partial income statement and balance sheet to show how the investments accounts would be shown on the financial statements.

P 12-50

LO4

Investment Portfolio

General Corporation has the following investments in equity securities at December 31, 2008 (there are no existing balances in the market adjustment account):

Company	Classification	Shares	Percentage of Shares Owned	Cost	Market Price at 12/31/05
Clarke Corporation	Trading	1,000	2%	$75	$78
Marlin Company	Available-for-sale	4,000	15	34	32
Air Products, Inc.	Available-for-sale	3,000	10	46	43

Required:

1. Prepare any adjusting entries required at December 31, 2008.
2. Illustrate how these investments would be presented on General Corporation's balance sheet at December 31, 2008. The available-for-sale securities are expected to be held for two to five years.
3. Prepare the journal entry on April 10, 2009, when General Corporation sold the Clarke Corporation investment for $72 per share.
4. Assume that General Corporation still owns its investment in Marlin Company and Air Products at December 31, 2009; the market prices on that date are $37 for Marlin and $44 for Air Products. Prepare all adjusting journal entries needed at December 31, 2009.

P 12-51

LO5

Investments in Held-to-Maturity Securities

Eysser Corporation purchased $50,000 of Hillside Construction Company's 10% bonds at $103\frac{1}{3}$ plus accrued interest on February 1, 2008. The bonds mature on April 1, 2015, and interest is payable on April 1 and October 1. Eysser Corporation uses the straight-line method of amortizing bond premiums and discounts.

Required:

1. Record all journal entries to account for this investment during the years 2008 and 2009, assuming that Eysser closes its books annually on December 31.
2. **Interpretive Question:** At the time these bonds were purchased (February 1, 2008), was the market rate of interest above or below 10%? Explain.

P 12-52

LO5

Investments in Held-to-Maturity Securities

On January 1, 2009, Eurowest Company purchased a $25,000, 12% bond at 104 as a long-term investment. The bond pays interest annually on each December 31 and matures on December 31, 2011.

Assuming straight-line amortization, answer the following questions:

Required:

1. What will be the net amount of cash received (total inflows minus total outflows) from this investment over its life?
2. How much cash will be collected each year?
3. How much premium will be amortized each year?
4. By how much will Investment in Held-to-Maturity Securities decrease each year?
5. How much revenue will be reported on the income statement each year relating to this security?

P 12-53

LO5

Determining the Purchase Price of Held-to-Maturity Securities and Effective-Interest Amortization

Corbett Corporation decided to purchase twenty $1,000, 10%, six-year bonds of Texas Manufacturing Company as a long-term investment on February 1, 2008. The bonds mature

(continued)

on February 1, 2014, and interest payments are made semiannually on February 1 and
August 1.

Required:

1. How much should Corbett Corporation be willing to pay for the bonds if the current interest rate on similar bonds is 8%?
2. Prepare a schedule showing the amortization of the bond premium or discount over
   the remaining life of the bonds, assuming that Corbett Corporation uses the effective-
   interest method of amortization.
3. How much bond interest revenue would be recorded each year if the straight-line
   method of amortization were used? Show how these amounts differ from the annual
   interest recognized using the effective-interest method. (Assume a fiscal year ending
   July 31.)
4. **Interpretive Question:** Which of the two amortization methods is preferable? Why?

P 12-54

LO5

Investments in Held-to-Maturity Securities

Walsh Equipment Company made the following purchases of debt securities during 2009.
All are classified as held-to-maturity, and all pay interest semiannually.

Purchase Date	Corp.	Face Amount	Cost	Interest Rate, %	Maturity Date	Last Interest Payment Date
10/15/09	A	$10,000	97	8	1/1/14	7/1/09
11/30/09	B	15,000	103	10	4/1/12	10/1/09
12/15/09	C	20,000	99	14	6/1/13	12/1/09
12/31/09	D	16,000	105	12	5/1/10	11/1/09

Required:

1. Prepare journal entries for the purchases.
2. Show all adjusting entries relating to the bonds on December 31, 2009, assuming that
   Walsh Equipment Company closes its book on that date and uses the straight-line amortization method.

P 12-55

LO3, LO4, LO6

Long-Term Investments in Equity Securities

Century Corporation acquired 8,400 common shares of Fidelity Company on January 10,
2009, for $12 per share and acquired 15,000 common shares of Essem Corporation on
January 25, 2009, for $22 per share. Fidelity has 60,000 shares of common stock outstand-
ing, and Essem has 50,000 shares outstanding. At December 31, 2009, the following information was obtained about the operations of Fidelity and Essem:

	Fidelity	Essem
Net income	$36,000.00	$100,000.00
Dividends paid per share	0.40	1.00
Market value per share at December 31, 2009	10.00	20.00

Assume that Century Corporation exerted significant influence over the policies of Essem
Corporation, but influenced the policies of Fidelity Corporation only to a very limited extent. Century classified its investment in Fidelity as an available-for-sale security.

Required:

1. How should Century account for its investments in Essem Corporation?
2. Prepare the journal entries for each investment for the year 2009 using the method or
   methods you selected in part (1).

P 12-56
LO6

Investments in Stocks–Equity Method

On March 20, 2009, Reeder Company acquired 80,000 shares of Needed Industries common stock at $32 per share as a long-term investment. Needed has 200,000 shares of outstanding voting common stock. The following additional information is presented for the calendar year ended December 31, 2009:

Nov. 15   Reeder received a cash dividend of $1.50 per share from Needed Industries.
Dec. 31   Needed announced earnings for the year of $250,000.
       31   Needed Industries common stock had a closing market price of $28 per share.

Required:
   1. **Interpretive Question:** What accounting method should be used by Reeder Company to account for this investment? Why?
   2. Prepare journal entries for the transactions and events described.

P 12-57
LO3, LO4, LO6

Long-Term Investments in Stock–Available-for-Sale and Equity Method

The following activities relate to Merrill Company during the years 2008 and 2009:

2008
Feb. 15   Merrill purchased 10,000 shares of Hendershot Equipment stock for $40 per share.
Dec. 1   Merrill received an $0.80-per-share cash dividend from Hendershot Equipment.
       31   Hendershot Equipment common stock had a closing market price of $37 per share. Hendershot's 2008 net income was $120,000.

2009
July   1   Merrill sold all 10,000 shares of Hendershot Equipment stock for $42 per share.

Additional information: Hendershot Equipment had 50,000 shares of common stock outstanding on January 1, 2008.

Required:
   1. Prepare journal entries to record the transactions assuming:
      a.   The securities are classified as available-for-sale.
      b.   The equity method is used.
   2. Show the amounts that would be reported on the financial statements of Merrill Company at December 31, 2008, under each assumption.
   3. **Interpretive Question:** What is the minimum number of shares of stock that Hendershot could have outstanding in order for Merrill to use the equity method?

P 12-58
LO3, LO4, LO6

Long-Term Investments in Equity Securities

During January 2009, Danbury, Inc., acquired 40,000 shares of Corporation A common stock for $24 per share. In addition, it purchased 5,000 shares of Corporation B preferred (nonvoting) stock for $112 per share. Corporation A has 160,000 shares of common stock outstanding, and Corporation B has 12,000 shares of nonvoting stock outstanding. Danbury anticipates holding both securities for at least five years.

The following data were obtained from operations during 2009:

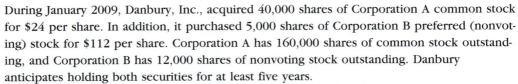

	2009
Net income:	
Corporation A	$190,000
Corporation B	80,000
Dividends paid (per share):	
Corporation A	$0.60
Corporation B	2.50
Market value per share at December 31:	
Corporation A	$ 25
Corporation B	109

(continued)

Required:

1. **Interpretive Question:** What method should Danbury, Inc., use in accounting for the investment in Corporation A stock? Why? What accounting method should be used in accounting for Corporation B nonvoting stock? Why?
2. Prepare the journal entries necessary to record the transactions for 2009.

P 12-59

LO5, LO6

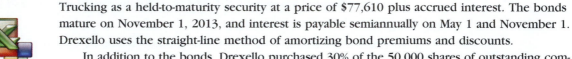

Unifying Concepts: Long-Term Investments in Stocks and Bonds

On January 2, 2009, Drexello, Inc., purchased $75,000 of 10%, five-year bonds of Greasy Trucking as a held-to-maturity security at a price of $77,610 plus accrued interest. The bonds mature on November 1, 2013, and interest is payable semiannually on May 1 and November 1. Drexello uses the straight-line method of amortizing bond premiums and discounts.

In addition to the bonds, Drexello purchased 30% of the 50,000 shares of outstanding common stock of Mellon Company at $42 per share, plus brokerage fees of $450, on January 10, 2009. On December 31, 2009, Mellon announced that its net income for the year was $150,000 and paid an annual dividend of $2 per share as advised by the board of directors of Drexello. The closing market price of Mellon common stock on December 31 was $38 per share.

Required:

1. Record all the 2009 transactions relating to these two investments in general journal form.
2. Show how the long-term investments and the related revenues would be reported on the financial statements of Drexello at December 31, 2009.

P 12-60

LO7

Consolidated Financial Statements

Parent Company owns parts of three different subsidiaries. The balance sheets and income statements for these four companies are listed below. Note that, in the financial statements of Parent Company, its ownership interest in the three subsidiaries has been accounted for using the equity method.

		Percentage of the Parent's Ownership		
		90%	**60%**	**40%**
	Parent	**Sub 1**	**Sub 2**	**Sub 3**
Assets				
Cash	$ 120	$ 40	$ 30	$ 60
Accounts receivable	500	120	90	50
Plant and equipment	1,050	400	160	300
Investment in Sub 1	288			
Investment in Sub 2	78			
Investment in Sub 3	84			
Total assets	$ 2,120	$ 560	$ 280	$ 410
Liabilities	$ 900	$ 240	$ 150	$ 200
Equity	1,220	320	130	210
Total liabilities and stockholders' equity	$ 2,120	$ 560	$ 280	$ 410
Sales	$ 6,420	$ 3,000	$ 3,000	$ 8,000
Income from Sub 1	360			
Income from Sub 2	480			
Income from Sub 3	160			
Expenses	(4,200)	(2,600)	(2,200)	(7,600)
Net income	$ 3,220	$ 400	$ 800	$ 400

Required:

1. Prepare a consolidated balance sheet for Parent Company and its subsidiaries.
2. Prepare a consolidated income statement for Parent Company and its subsidiaries.
3. **Interpretive Question:** Return on sales is net income divided by total sales. Without doing any computations, state what would happen to consolidated return on sales if Sub 3 were consolidated rather than accounted for using the equity method. Explain.

ANALYTICAL ASSIGNMENTS

AA 12-61
DISCUSSION

Which Investment Should We Make?

Pentron Data Corporation has a significant amount of excess cash on hand and has decided to make a long-term investment in either debt or equity securities. After a careful analysis, the investment committee has recommended to the company treasurer that Pentron purchase either one of the following two investments. The first investment involves purchasing sixty $1,000, 8% bonds issued by Andrea Company. The bonds mature in four years, pay interest semiannually, and are currently selling at 92. The second investment alternative involves purchasing 3,000 shares of Franklin Corporation common stock at $30 per share (including brokerage fees). The investment committee believes that the Franklin stock will pay an annual dividend of $3.50 per share and is likely to be salable at the end of four years for $36 per share.

Discuss the following questions:

1. If Pentron wants to earn 12% per year, should it make either investment?
2. Which of the two investments would you advise the treasurer to invest in assuming the inherent risk is approximately equal? Your decision should be based on which investment provides the more attractive return, ignoring income tax effects.

AA 12-62
DISCUSSION

Classification of Securities

Memphis Company has just purchased five securities; it intends to hold the stock until the price increases to a sufficiently high level, at which time it plans to sell the stock. In fact, it is unlikely that the company will hold the securities for more than a few months. Nevertheless, Memphis's management has decided to classify the securities as available-for-sale rather than as trading securities. Why is Memphis choosing this type of classification, and would you allow it if you were the auditor?

AA 12-63
JUDGMENT CALL

You Decide: Should the trading securities that companies own be left on the books at historical cost, or should they be adjusted annually to their current market price (as is now required by GAAP)?

When physical assets are purchased, they are recorded on the balance sheet at cost and left there until the asset is sold. For example, when land is purchased, the cost of the land is recorded on the books. If the land increases in value, no adjustment is made. The company realizes the gain in value when it sells the land at a gain. Why don't we do this for marketable securities? Why should the assets for land and securities be different?

AA 12-64
REAL COMPANY
ANALYSIS

Microsoft

(Since **Wal-Mart** doesn't report investments activity, we will refer to **Microsoft**'s 2005 annual report for the case.) Locate Microsoft's 2005 annual report at **http://www.microsoft .com** to answer the following questions:

1. Find Microsoft's note on accounting policies. Using the information in that note (under the heading "Financial Instruments"), determine what fraction of Microsoft's investment securities are classified as "available-for-sale."
2. In its note on "Cash and short-term investments," Microsoft lists the general types of investments that make up its $60.592 billion portfolio. Certificates of deposit are listed both as "cash and cash equivalents" and as "short-term investments." What is the difference between these two categories? *Hint:* Go back to the note you looked at to answer (1).
3. Look at Microsoft's stockholders' equity statement. Where in the equity section does Microsoft report the unrealized gains and losses from available-for-sale securities?

AA 12-65

REAL COMPANY
ANALYSIS

Berkshire Hathaway

The following note comes from the 2005 annual report of **Berkshire Hathaway:**

(6) Investments in equity securities

Data with respect to investments in equity securities are shown below.
Amounts are in millions.

December 31, 2005	Cost	Unrealized Gains	Fair Value
Common stock of:			
American Express Company	$ 1,287	$ 6,515	$ 7,802
The Coca-Cola Company	1,299	6,763	8,062
The Procter & Gamble Company*	5,963	(175)	5,788
Wells Fargo & Company	2,754	3,221	5,975
Other equity securities	10,036	9,058	19,094
	$21,339	$25,382	$46,721

December 31, 2004	Cost	Unrealized Gains	Fair Value
Common stock of:			
American Express Company	$ 1,470	$ 7,076	$ 8,546
The Coca-Cola Company	1,299	7,029	8,328
The Gillette Company*	600	3,699	4,299
Wells Fargo & Company	463	3,045	3,508
Other equity securities	5,505	7,531	13,036
	$ 9,337	$28,380	$37,717

*The Gillette Company was acquired by The Procter & Gamble Company during 2005.

Berkshire Hathaway also discloses that it classifies each of these investments as an available-for-sale security.

1. All securities included in the tables in Berkshire Hathaway's Note 6 are classified as available-for-sale. Make all journal entries that were required in 2005 to account for Berkshire Hathaway's investments in:
   a. **The Coca-Cola Company**.
   b. Other equity securities.
2. Did the performance of Berkshire Hathaway's portfolio of equity securities have any bright spots in 2005?
3. How has Berkshire Hathaway's portfolio of equity securities performed over time?

AA 12-66

INTERNATIONAL

Sony

Sony Corporation was organized in 1946 under the name **Tokyo Tsushin Kogyo**. The name "Sony" is a combination of the Latin word sonus (sound) and the English word sonny; it was given to a small transistor radio sold by the company in the United States, starting in 1954. The radio was so popular that the entire company changed its name to Sony in 1958.

In its 2006 annual report, Sony included the note to its financial statements shown on the following page.

(continued)

8. Marketable securities and securities investments and other

	Yen in millions							
	March 31, 2005				**March 31, 2006**			
	Cost	**Gross unrealized gains**	**Gross unrealized losses**	**Fair value**	**Cost**	**Gross unrealized gains**	**Gross unrealized losses**	**Fair value**
Available-for-sale:								
Debt securities	¥2,090,605	¥ 58,161	¥(2,464)	¥2,146,302	¥2,522,864	¥ 17,021	¥(22,810)	¥2,517,075
Equity securities	107,126	49,350	(814)	155,662	227,079	171,921	(1,589)	397,411
Held-to-maturity								
securities	27,431	530	(13)	27,948	33,193	132	(221)	33,104
Total	¥2,225,162	¥108,041	¥(3,291)	¥2,329,912	¥2,783,136	¥189,074	¥(24,620)	¥2,947,590

	Dollars in millions			
	March 31, 2006			
	Cost	**Gross unrealized gains**	**Gross unrealized losses**	**Fair value**
Available-for-sale:				
Debt securities	$21,563	$ 145	$(195)	$21,513
Equity securities	1,941	1,470	(14)	3,397
Held-to-maturity				
securities	283	1	(1)	283
Total	$23,787	$1,616	$(210)	$25,193

1. In the notes to its English-language financial statements, Sony states that those statements "conform with accounting principles generally accepted in the United States." However, Sony's official accounting records are maintained using Japanese accounting principles. Why would Sony go to the trouble of preparing a separate set of English-language financial statements using U.S. accounting principles?

2. Assuming that approximately the same available-for-sale securities were on hand in both 2005 and 2006, how well did Sony's investments perform in 2006?

3. What journal entries did Sony make during the year to record the revaluation of available-for-sale securities? Use only the total amounts (that is, don't use the separate amounts for debt and equity securities), and ignore the fact that securities were bought and sold during the year.

AA 12-67

ETHICS

Is It OK to Strategically Classify Securities?

You have recently been hired as a staff assistant in the office of the chairman of the board of directors of Clefton, Inc. Because you have some background in accounting, the chairman has asked you to review the preliminary financial statements that have been prepared by the company's accounting staff. After the financial statements are approved by the chairman of the board, they will be audited by external auditors. This is the first year that Clefton has had its financial statements audited by external auditors.

In examining the financial statement note on investment securities, you notice that all of the securities that had unrealized gains for the year have been classified as trading, whereas all of the securities that had unrealized losses have been classified as available-for-sale. You realize that this has the impact of placing all the gains on the income statement and hiding all the losses in the equity section of the balance sheet. You call the chief accountant who confirms that the securities are not classified until the end of the year and that the classification depends on whether a particular security has experienced a gain or

(continued)

a loss during the year. The chief accountant states that this policy was adopted, with the approval of the chairman of the board, in order to maximize the reported net income of the company. The chief accountant tells you that investment security classification is based on how management intends to use those securities; therefore, management is free to classify the securities in any way it wishes.

You are uncomfortable with this investment security classification strategy. You are also dismayed that the chief accountant and the chairman of the board seem to have agreed on this scheme to maximize reported income. You are also worried about what the external auditors will do when they find out about this classification scheme. You have been asked to report to the chairman of the board this afternoon to give your summary of the status of the preliminary financial statements. What should you do?

AA 12-68
WRITING

Why Doesn't the Gain Go on the Income Statement?

You are the controller for Chong Lai Company. You just received a very strongly worded e-mail message from the president of the company. The president has learned that a $627,000 gain on a stock investment made by the company last year will not be reported in the income statement because you have classified the security as available-for-sale. With the gain, the company would report a record profit for the year. Without the gain, profits are actually down slightly from the year before. The president wants an explanation—now.

It has been your policy for the past several years to routinely classify all investments as available-for-sale. Your company is not in the business of actively buying and selling stocks and bonds. Instead, all investments are made to strengthen relationships with either suppliers or major customers. As such, your practice is to buy securities and hold them for several years.

Write a one-page memo to the president explaining the rationale behind your policy of security classification.

AA 12-69
CUMULATIVE SPREADSHEET PROJECT

Adding an Investment Portfolio

This spreadsheet assignment is a continuation of the spreadsheet assignments given in earlier chapters. If you completed those spreadsheets, you have a head start on this one.

This assignment is based on the spreadsheet prepared in part (1) of the spreadsheet assignment for Chapter 9. Review that assignment for a summary of the assumptions made in preparing a forecasted balance sheet, income statement, and statement of cash flows for 2010 for Handyman Company. Using those financial statements, complete the following exercise.

Handyman has decided that, in 2010, it will create an available-for-sale investment portfolio. Handyman plans to invest $20 million in a variety of stocks and bonds. (Recall that the numbers in the Handyman spreadsheet are in millions.) As of the end of 2009, Handyman has no investment portfolio. Adapt your spreadsheet to include this expected $20 million investment portfolio as a current asset in 2010. Ignore the possibility of any interest, dividends, gains, or losses on this portfolio. Answer the following questions:

1. With the assumptions built into your spreadsheet, where will Handyman get the $20 million in funding necessary to acquire these investment securities?
2. Where in the statement of cash flows did you put the cash outflow associated with the acquisition of these investment securities? Explain your placement.

COMPREHENSIVE PROBLEM   9-12

Warner Company started business on January 1, 2009. The following transactions and events occurred in 2009 and 2010. For simplicity, information for sales, inventory purchases, collections on account, and payments on account is given in summary form at the end of each year.

2009

Jan.	1	Issued 150,000 shares of $1-par common stock to investors at $15 per share.
	1	Purchased a building for $720,000. The building has a 25-year expected useful life and a $70,000 expected salvage value. Warner uses the straight-line method of depreciation.
	1	Leased equipment under a ten-year lease. The five lease payments of $20,000 each are to be made on December 31 of each year. The cash price of the equipment is $134,202. This lease is accounted for as a capital lease with an implicit interest rate of 8%. The equipment has a ten-year useful life and zero expected salvage value; Warner uses straight-line depreciation with all of its equipment.
Feb.	1	Borrowed $1.8 million from Foley Bank. The loan bears a 9% annual interest rate. Interest is to be paid each year on February 1. The principal on the loan will be repaid in four years.
Mar.	1	Purchased 50,000 shares of Ryan Company for $30 per share. Warner classifies this as an investment in trading securities. These securities are reported as a current asset.
July	15	Purchased 55,000 shares of Anson Company for $23 per share. Warner classifies this as an investment in available-for-sale securities. These securities are reported as a long-term asset.
Nov.	17	Declared a cash dividend of $0.30 per share, payable on January 15, 2010.
Dec.	31	Made the lease payment.
	31	The Ryan Company shares had a market value of $26 per share. The Anson Company shares had a market value of $28 per share.

Summary:

a. Sales for the year (all on credit) totaled $900,000. The cost of inventory sold was $480,000.
b. Cash collections on credit sales for the year were $420,000.
c. Inventory costing $540,000 was purchased on account. (Warner Company uses the perpetual inventory method.)
d. Payments on account totaled $500,000.

2010

Jan.	1	Issued $400,000 in bonds at par value. The bonds have a stated interest rate of 10%, payable semiannually on July 1 and January 1.
	1	The estimated useful life and salvage value for the building were changed. It is now estimated that the building has a remaining life (as of January 1, 2010) of 20 years. Also, it is now estimated that the building will have no salvage value. These changes in estimate are to take effect for the year 2010 and subsequent years.
	15	Paid the cash dividend declared in November 2009.

Feb.	1	Warner Company repurchased 15,000 shares of its own common stock to be held as treasury stock. The price paid was $32 per share.
	1	Paid the interest on the loan from Foley Bank.
Apr.	10	Sold all 50,000 shares of the Ryan Company stock. The shares were sold for $25 per share.
July	1	Paid the interest on the bonds.
Oct.	1	Retired the bonds that were issued on January 1. Warner had to pay $380,000 to retire the bonds. This amount included interest that had accrued since July 1.
Nov.	20	Declared a cash dividend of $0.30 per share. The dividend applies only to outstanding shares, not to treasury shares.
Dec.	31	Made the lease payment.
	31	After recording depreciation expense for the year, the building was evaluated for possible impairment. The building is expected to generate cash flows of $18,000 per year for its 19-year remaining life. The building has a current market value of $320,000.
	31	The Anson Company shares had a market value of $19 per share.

Summary:

a. Sales for the year (all on credit) totaled $1.8 million. The cost of inventory sold was $950,000.

b. Cash collections on credit sales for the year were $1.54 million.

c. Inventory costing $1,000,000 was purchased on account.

d. Payments on account totaled $970,000.

Required:

1. Prepare all journal entries to record the information for 2009. Also prepare any necessary adjusting entries.

2. Prepare a trial balance as of December 31, 2009. There is no need to show your ledger T-accounts; however, preparing and posting to T-accounts may aid in the preparation of the trial balance.

3. Prepare an income statement for the year ended December 31, 2009, and a balance sheet as of December 31, 2009.

4. Prepare all journal entries to record the information for 2010. Also prepare any necessary adjusting entries.

5. Prepare a trial balance as of December 31, 2010. (As you compute the amounts to include in the trial balance, don't forget the beginning balances left over from 2009.)

6. Prepare an income statement for the year ended December 31, 2010, and a balance sheet as of December 31, 2010.

PART

4

Other Dimensions of Financial Reporting

The Statement of Cash Flows

After studying this chapter, you should be able to:

① Understand the purpose of a statement of cash flows. *The statement of cash flows provides information that is not readily apparent by looking at just the balance sheet and the income statement. Operating cash flow is particularly useful in selected cases when net income does not give an accurate refection of a company's performance.*

② Recognize the different types of information reported in the statement of cash flows. *Cash flows are partitioned into three categories—operating, investing, and financing. In normal circumstances, a company has positive cash from operations and negative cash from investing activities. Whether cash from financing activities is positive or negative typically depends on how fast a company is growing.*

③ Prepare a simple statement of cash flows. *Preparing a statement of cash flows is a simple process if one has access to the record of a company's detailed cash transactions. One simply scans the list of cash transactions and sorts them into operating, investing, and financing items.*

④ Analyze financial statements to prepare a statement of cash flows. *When detailed cash flow information is not available, a statement of cash flows can be prepared using knowledge of how the three primary financial statements articulate. Operating cash flow can be reported using either the direct or the indirect method.*

⑤ Use information from the statement of cash flows to make decisions. *Knowledge of how the three primary financial statements tie together allows one to forecast how interactions among management decisions might affect a company's future financial position.*

Home Depot is the leading retailer in the "do-it-yourself" home handyman market. In January 2006, Home Depot had 1,984 stores in the United States, Canada, and Mexico. With each store averaging 105,000 square feet (and an additional 23,000 square feet in the outside garden center), a lot of shelf space is filled with paint, lumber, hardware, and plumbing fixtures. If plumbing fixtures don't seem very exciting to you, consider this: Home Depot is the 14th largest company in the United States (in terms of revenues), with 2006 revenues of $81.5 billion and market value of $91.1 billion.[1] And if lumber and hardware seem obsolete in this high-tech world, consider that, for the past 10 years, Home Depot's earnings per share (EPS) has grown an average of 23.1% per year. In fiscal 2006, Home Depot's net income reached $5.8 billion.[2]

But Home Depot's prospects weren't always so rosy. Back in 1985, when sales were only $700 million, Home Depot experienced cash flow problems, in large part due to rapid increases in the level of inventory. Part of this inventory increase was the natural result of Home Depot's expansion. But Home Depot stores were also starting to fill up with excess inventory because of lax inventory management. In 1983, the average Home Depot store contained enough inventory to support average sales for 75 days.

By 1985, the number of days' sales in inventory had increased to 83 days. Combined with Home Depot's rapid growth, this inventory inefficiency caused total inventory to increase by $69 million in 1985. This increase in inventory was instrumental in Home Depot's negative cash flow from operations of $43 million. Concerns about this declining profitability and negative cash flow caused Home Depot's stock value to take a dive in 1985, and the beginning of 1986 found Home Depot wondering where it would find the investors and creditors to finance its aggressive expansion plans. Exhibit 1 summarizes the differences between Home Depot's reported net income and the company's cash flow from operations for the fiscal years 1984 through 1986 and the company's recent performance.

Home Depot's current success is the result of an incredible operating cash flow turnaround that began in fiscal 1987. Operating income almost tripled in 1987 compared to fiscal 1986, and net income increased from $8.2 million to $23.9 million. A computerized inventory management program was instituted, and the number of days' sales in inventory dropped to 80 days. Improved profitability and more efficient management of inventory combined to transform the negative $43 million operating cash flow in fiscal 1986 into positive cash from operations of $66 million in fiscal 1987.

EXHIBIT 1	**Home Depot's Net Income and Cash Flows from Operations**		
		Fiscal Year Ended	
(in thousands)	February 2, 1986	February 3, 1985	January 29, 1984
Net earnings	$ 8,219	$14,122	$ 10,261
Net cash provided by operations	(43,120)	(3,056)	(10,574)
		Fiscal Year Ended	
(in thousands)	January 29, 2006	January 30, 2005	February 1, 2004
Net earnings	$5,838,000	$5,001,000	$4,304,000
Net cash provided by operations	6,484,000	6,904,000	6,545,000

---

[1] See the Fortune 500 listing at **http://www.fortune.com**.
[2] January 30, 2006, 10-K filing of The Home Depot, Inc.

I n this chapter, we will study the statement of cash flows. You will learn that this statement provides one of the earliest warning signs of cash concerns of the type experienced by Home Depot. The statement of cash flows alerts financial statement readers to increases and decreases in cash as well as to the reasons and trends for the changes.

In today's business environment, it is not enough simply to monitor earnings and earnings per share measurements. An entity's financial position and especially its inflows and outflows of cash are also critical to its financial success.

The three primary financial statements were introduced and illustrated in Chapter 2. In subsequent chapters, we examined in detail the components of the balance sheet and income statement. For our discussion of the statement of cash flows, we will first describe the purpose and general format of a statement of cash flows. We will then show how easy it is to prepare a statement of cash flows if detailed cash flow information is available. A statement of cash flows can also be prepared based on an analysis of balance sheet and income statement accounts. We will also distinguish between the direct and indirect methods of reporting operating cash flows and discuss the usefulness of the statement of cash flows. Finally, we will explain how the statement of cash flows can be used to make investment and lending decisions.

What's the Purpose of a Statement of Cash Flows?

Understand the purpose of a statement of cash flows.

① The **statement of cash flows**, as its name implies, summarizes a company's cash flows for a period of time. The statement of cash flows explains how a company's cash was generated during the period and how that cash was used.

You might think that the statement of cash flows is a replacement for the income statement, but the two statements have very different objectives. The income statement, as you know, measures the results of operations for a period of time. Net income is the accountant's best estimate at reflecting a company's economic performance for a period. The income statement provides details as to how the retained earnings account changes during a period and ties together, in part, the owners' equity sections of comparative balance sheets.

statement of cash flows

The financial statement that shows an entity's cash inflows (receipts) and outflows (payments) during a period of time.

The statement of cash flows, on the other hand, provides details as to how the cash account changed during a period. The statement of cash flows reports the period's transactions and events in terms of their impact on cash. In Chapter 4, we compared the cash-basis and accrual-basis methods of measuring income and explained why accrual-basis income is considered a better measure of periodic income. The statement of cash flows provides important information from a cash-basis perspective that complements the income statement and balance sheet, thus providing a more complete picture of a company's operations and financial position. It is important to note that the statement of cash flows does not include any transactions or accounts that are not already reflected in the balance sheet or the income statement. Rather, the statement of cash flows simply provides information relating to the cash flow effects of those transactions.

Users of financial statements, particularly investors and creditors, need information about a company's cash flows in order to evaluate the company's ability to generate positive net cash flows in the future to meet its obligations and to pay dividends. In some cases, careful analysis of cash flows can provide early warning of impending financial problems, as was the case with **Home Depot**.

Before moving on, it is important to reiterate that the statement of cash flows does not replace the income statement. The income statement summarizes the results of a company's operations, whereas the statement of cash flows summarizes a company's inflows and outflows of cash. Information contained in the income statement can be used to facilitate the preparation of a statement of cash flows; information in the statement of cash flows sheds some light on the company's ability to generate income in the future. The statement of cash flows and the income statement provide complementary information about different aspects of a business.

> **REMEMBER THIS...**
>
> • The statement of cash flows, one of the three primary financial statements, provides information about the cash receipts and payments of an entity during a period.
>
> • The statement of cash flows provides important information that complements the income statement and balance sheet.

Recognize the different types of information reported in the statement of cash flows.

What Information Is Reported in the Statement of Cash Flows?

(2) Accounting standards include specific requirements for the reporting of cash flows. The general format for a statement of cash flows, with details and dollar amounts omitted, is presented in Exhibit 2. As illustrated, the inflows and outflows of cash must be divided into three main categories: operating activities, investing activities, and financing activities. Further, the statement of cash flows is presented in a manner that reconciles the beginning and ending balances of cash and cash equivalents. **Cash equivalents** are short-term, highly liquid investments that can easily be converted into cash. Generally, only investments with maturities of three months or less qualify as cash equivalents. Examples are U.S. Treasury bills, money market funds, and commercial paper (short-term debt issued by corporations). In this chapter, as is common in practice, the term *cash* will be used to include cash and cash equivalents.

cash equivalents

Short-term, highly liquid investments that can easily be converted into cash.

Major Classifications of Cash Flows

Exhibit 3 shows the three main categories of cash inflows and outflows—operating, investing, and financing. Exhibit 4 summarizes the specific activities included in each category. Beginning with operating activities, each of the cash flow categories will be explained. We will also discuss the reporting of significant noncash transactions and events.

operating activities

Transactions and events that enter into the determination of net income.

Operating Activities   **Operating activities** include those transactions and events that enter into the calculation of net income. Cash receipts from

EXHIBIT 2	General Format for a Statement of Cash Flows

Cash provided by (used in):
Cash from operating activities	$XXX
+ Cash from investing activities	XXX
+ Cash from financing activities	XXX
= Net increase (decrease) in cash and cash equivalents	$XXX
+ Cash and cash equivalents at beginning of year	XXX
= Cash and cash equivalents at end of year	$XXX

EXHIBIT 3 **The Flow of Cash**

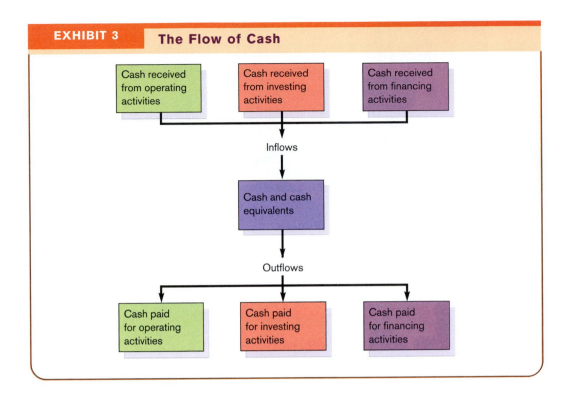

EXHIBIT 4 **Major Classifications of Cash Flows**

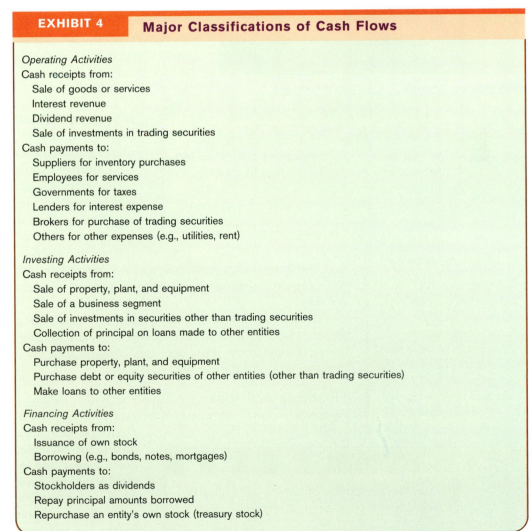

Operating Activities
Cash receipts from:
  Sale of goods or services
  Interest revenue
  Dividend revenue
  Sale of investments in trading securities
Cash payments to:
  Suppliers for inventory purchases
  Employees for services
  Governments for taxes
  Lenders for interest expense
  Brokers for purchase of trading securities
  Others for other expenses (e.g., utilities, rent)

Investing Activities
Cash receipts from:
  Sale of property, plant, and equipment
  Sale of a business segment
  Sale of investments in securities other than trading securities
  Collection of principal on loans made to other entities
Cash payments to:
  Purchase property, plant, and equipment
  Purchase debt or equity securities of other entities (other than trading securities)
  Make loans to other entities

Financing Activities
Cash receipts from:
  Issuance of own stock
  Borrowing (e.g., bonds, notes, mortgages)
Cash payments to:
  Stockholders as dividends
  Repay principal amounts borrowed
  Repurchase an entity's own stock (treasury stock)

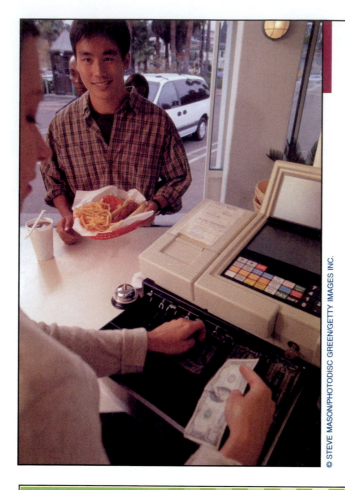

Operating activities, including the sale of goods, help determine net income and are reported on the statement of cash flows.

the sale of goods or services are the major cash inflows for most businesses. Other inflows include cash receipts for interest revenue, dividend revenue, and similar items. Major outflows of cash are for the purchase of inventory and for the payment of wages, taxes, interest, utilities, rent, and similar expenses. As we will explain later, the amount of cash provided by (or used in) operating activities is a key figure and should be highlighted on the statement of cash flows.

Note that our focus in analyzing operating activities is to determine cash flows from operations. An analysis is required to convert income from an accrual-basis to a cash-basis number.

To do this, we begin with the net income figure, remove all items relating to investing activities (such as depreciation and gains/losses on the sale of equipment) and financing activities (such as gains/losses on retirement of debt), and then adjust for changes in those current assets and current liabilities that involve cash and relate to operations (which are most of the current assets and current liabilities).

FYI

Although cash inflows from interest and dividends logically might be classified as financing activities, the FASB has decided to classify them as operating activities, which conforms to their presentation on the income statement.

investing activities

Transactions and events that involve the purchase and sale of securities (excluding cash equivalents), property, plant, equipment, and other assets not generally held for resale, and the making and collecting of loans.

Investing Activities   Transactions and events that involve the purchase and sale of securities (other than trading securities), property, buildings, equipment, and other assets not generally held for resale, and the making and collecting of loans are classified as **investing activities**. These activities occur regularly and result in cash inflows and outflows. They are not classified under operating activities because they relate only indirectly to the entity's central, ongoing operations, which usually involve the sale of goods or services.

The analysis of investing activities involves identifying those accounts on the balance sheet relating to investments (typically long-term asset accounts) and then explaining how those accounts changed and how those changes affected the cash flows for the period.

Financing Activities   **Financing activities** include transactions and events whereby resources are obtained from or paid to owners (equity financing) and creditors (debt financing). Dividend payments, for example, fit this definition. As noted earlier, the receipt of dividends and interest and the payment of interest are classified under operating activities simply because they are reported as a part of income on the income statement. The receipt or

FYI

The purchase and sale of trading securities is classified as an operating activity.

financing activities

Transactions and events whereby resources are obtained from, or repaid to, owners (equity financing) and creditors (debt financing).

payment of the principal amount borrowed or repaid (but not the interest) is considered a financing activity.

Analyzing the cash flow effects of financing activities involves identifying those accounts relating to financing (typically long-term debt and common stock) and explaining how changes in those accounts affected the company's cash flows. Exhibit 5 summarizes the activities reflected on the statement of cash flows and indicates how the balance sheet and income statement accounts relate to the various activities.

 F Y I

On the statement of cash flows, the activities are typically listed in this order: operating, investing, and financing. However, there is no requirement that they be listed in this way. **Microsoft**, for example, uses this order: operating, financing, and investing.

Noncash Investing and Financing Activities

Some investing and financing activities do not affect cash. For example, equipment may be purchased with a note payable, or land may be acquired by issuing stock. These noncash transactions are not reported in the statement of cash flows. However, if a company has significant noncash financing and investing activities, they should be disclosed in a separate schedule or in a narrative explanation. The disclosures may be presented below the statement of cash flows or in the notes to the financial statements.

Cash Flow Patterns

Most U.S. companies (about 60%) report positive cash flows from operations. That shouldn't come as a big surprise because companies need to generate cash from operating activities to survive in the long term. In addition, about 80% of U.S. companies report negative cash flows from investing activities. Again, this is expected as companies must expand, enhance, or replace long-term assets. Predicting whether the sign for cash from financing activities will be positive or negative is more difficult. That sign depends on

EXHIBIT 5	How Balance Sheet and Income Statement Accounts Relate to the Statement of Cash Flows		
Cash Flow Activity	Related Balance Sheet and Income Statement Accounts	Examples	Chapters in Which Accounts Were Covered
Operating	All income statement accounts **except** those income statement items relating to:	Sales, Cost of Goods Sold, Salaries Expense, etc.	Chs. 6–8
	• Investing	Depreciation, Gains/Losses on Sale of Equipment	Ch. 9
	• Financing	Gains/Losses on Retirement of Debt	Ch. 10
	Current assets	Accounts Receivable	Ch. 6
		Inventory	Ch. 7
	Current liabilities	Accounts Payable	Ch. 7
Investing	Long-term assets	Property, Plant, and Equipment	Ch. 9
	Long-term investments	Available-for-Sale and Held-to-Maturity Securities	Ch. 12
Financing	Long-term debt	Bonds and Mortgages	Ch. 10
	Stockholders' equity (except for	Common Stock	Ch. 11
	net income in Retained Earnings)	Dividends	Ch. 11

FYI

Many companies report positive cash flows from operations even though they have net losses. This is primarily because depreciation and amortization are added to net income when calculating cash flow from operations. In fact, many companies focus on a number called EBITDA which is earnings before income taxes, depreciation, and amortization.

whether the company is young, growing, and in need of cash, or mature, stable, and flush with cash. As a company proceeds through the normal life cycle of a business, cash from financing typically will vary between positive and negative. As an example, in fiscal 2005 Home Depot reported positive cash flows from operations ($6.5 billion), negative cash flows from investing ($4.6 billion), and negative cash flows from financing ($1.6 billion).

REMEMBER THIS...

- The statement of cash flows is presented in a manner that highlights three major categories of cash flows:
  - operating activities,
  - investing activities, and
  - financing activities.
- Any significant noncash investing and financing activities should be disclosed separately, either below the statement of cash flows or in the notes to the financial statements.

Prepare a simple statement of cash flows.

③

Preparing a Statement of Cash Flows—A Simple Example

Now that we have reviewed the three types of cash flow activities disclosed on the statement of cash flows, let's start with a simple example to see how easy (conceptually) a statement of cash flows is to prepare. For this example, we will begin with the following trial balance information for Silmaril, Inc.

Silmaril, Inc.
Trial Balance
January 1, 2009

	Debit	Credit
Cash	$ 300	
Accounts Receivable	2,500	
Inventory	1,900	
Property, Plant, and Equipment	4,000	
Accumulated Depreciation		$1,200
Accounts Payable		1,700
Taxes Payable		40
Long-Term Debt		2,200
Common Stock		1,000
Retained Earnings		2,560
Totals	$8,700	$8,700

The following transactions were conducted by Silmaril, Inc., during 2009:

1. Sales on account, $13,500.
2. Collections on account, $14,000.
3. Purchased inventory on account, $7,900.
4. Cost of goods sold, $8,000.
5. Paid accounts payable, $8,100.
6. Purchased property, plant, and equipment for cash, $1,700.
7. Sold property, plant, and equipment for cash, $500 (original cost, $1,200; accumulated depreciation, $800).
8. Paid long-term debt, $200.
9. Issued stock at par value, $450.
10. Recorded depreciation expense, $500.
11. Paid interest on debt, $180.
12. Recorded interest owed (accrued) but not paid, $20.
13. Paid miscellaneous expenses (e.g., wages, supplies, etc.) for the period, $3,200.
14. Recorded tax expense for the period, $450.
15. Paid taxes during the period, $440.

With this information, we can reconstruct the journal entries made by Silmaril, Inc., during the year:

1.	Accounts Receivable	13,500	
	Sales		13,500
2.	Cash	14,000	
	Accounts Receivable		14,000
3.	Inventory	7,900	
	Accounts Payable		7,900
4.	Cost of Goods Sold	8,000	
	Inventory		8,000
5.	Accounts Payable	8,100	
	Cash		8,100
6.	Property, Plant, and Equipment	1,700	
	Cash		1,700
7.	Cash	500	
	Accumulated Depreciation	800	
	Property, Plant, and Equipment		1,200
	Gain on Sale of Equipment		100
8.	Long-Term Debt	200	
	Cash		200
9.	Cash	450	
	Common Stock		450
10.	Depreciation Expense	500	
	Accumulated Depreciation		500
11.	Interest Expense	180	
	Cash		180
12.	Interest Expense	20	
	Interest Payable		20
13.	Miscellaneous Expenses	3,200	
	Cash		3,200
14.	Tax Expense	450	
	Taxes Payable		450
15.	Taxes Payable	440	
	Cash		440

When these journal entries are posted, the following trial balance results:

Silmaril, Inc.

Trial Balance

December 31, 2009

	Debit	Credit
Cash	$ 1,430	
Accounts Receivable	2,000	
Inventory	1,800	
Property, Plant, and Equipment	4,500	
Accumulated Depreciation		$ 900
Accounts Payable		1,500
Interest Payable		20
Taxes Payable		50
Long-Term Debt		2,000
Common Stock		1,450
Retained Earnings		2,560
Sales		13,500
Gain on Sale of Equipment		100
Cost of Goods Sold	8,000	
Depreciation Expense	500	
Interest Expense	200	
Tax Expense	450	
Miscellaneous Expenses	3,200	
Totals	$22,080	$22,080

To this point, this is all a review—journalizing transactions, posting journal entries, and preparing a trial balance. From this trial balance, we can easily prepare an income statement and a balance sheet; but our objective here is to prepare a statement of cash flows. With information from the Cash T-account, we can prepare a statement of cash flows. The Cash T-account would contain the following information (journal entry reference numbers are in parentheses):

Cash

Beg. Bal.	300		
(2)	14,000	(5)	8,100
(7)	500	(6)	1,700
(9)	450	(8)	200
		(11)	180
		(13)	3,200
		(15)	440
End. Bal.	1,430		

Our task at this point is simply to categorize each cash inflow and outflow as an operating, investing, or financing activity. The inflows and outflows break down as follows:

Operating Activities:

Collections on account (2)		$14,000
Payments for inventory (5)	$ 8,100	
Payments for miscellaneous expenses (13)	3,200	
Payment for interest (11)	180	
Payment for taxes (15)	440	(11,920)
Cash flows from operating activities		$ 2,080

Investing Activities:

Sold equipment (7)	$ 500	
Purchased equipment (6)	(1,700)	
Cash flows from investing activities		(1,200)

Financing Activities:

Issued stock (9)		$ 450	
Paid debt (8)		(200)	
Cash flows from financing activities			250
Net increase in cash			$ 1,130
Beginning cash balance			300
Ending cash balance			$ 1,430

As you can see, if we have access to the detailed transaction data from the Cash T-account, preparing a statement of cash flows involves determining the proper cash flow category (operating, investing, or financing) for each inflow or outflow and then properly formatting the statement. More advanced accounting software programs allow financial statement preparers to categorize each cash inflow and outflow as an operating, investing, or financing activity and to prepare a statement of cash flows with the press of a key. Once considered one of the most difficult parts of accounting, preparing a statement of cash flows has been greatly simplified as a result of computer technology.

If information is properly coded when input into a computerized accounting system, the preparation of a statement of cash flows is easy. As mentioned, the more advanced accounting software facilitates this process. But what happens if an accounting system does not classify cash transactions according to their activities? In the next section, we discuss how a statement of cash flows is prepared if one does not have ready access to detailed cash inflow and outflow information.

REMEMBER THIS...

- If transactions are properly classified when input into the accounting system, the preparation of a statement of cash flows is straightforward.

- Cash inflows and outflows are segregated according to type of activity (operating, investing, or financing), and a statement of cash flows is prepared based on that information.

Analyze financial statements to prepare a statement of cash flows.

Analyzing the Other Primary Financial Statements to Prepare a Statement of Cash Flows

④ If detailed cash flow information is not accessible, the preparation of a statement of cash flows is more difficult. The income statement and comparative balance sheets must be analyzed to determine how cash was generated and how cash was used by a business. How can we determine a company's cash inflows and outflows by looking at balance sheets and an income statement? The secret lies in remembering the basics of double-entry accounting: each journal entry has two parts—a debit and a credit. In the case of the cash account, every time Cash is debited, some other account is credited; every time Cash is credited, some other account is debited. If we don't have access to the details of the cash account, we can infer those details based on our knowledge of accounting and by analyzing changes in accounts other than Cash.

For example, consider the accounts receivable account. A debit to that account means what? Ninety-nine percent of the time, a debit to Accounts Receivable is associated with a sale on account. A credit to Accounts Receivable means what? Most likely, cash was collected. If we have the beginning and ending balances for the accounts receivable account (from comparative balance sheets) and sales for the period (from the income statement), we can infer the cash collected for the period. Consider the information taken from Silmaril's beginning trial balance and the year-end trial balance relating to Accounts Receivable (remember, we are assuming that the detailed journal entries are not available to us, only the resulting financial statements):

Accounts Receivable

Beg. Bal.	2,500		
Sales	13,500	Collections	?
End. Bal.	2,000		

To reconcile the accounts receivable account, we can only assume that cash collections of $14,000 occurred. With any other amount the account will not reconcile.[3] In other words, we can infer that the following journal entry must have been made:

Cash 14,000

    Accounts Receivable 14,000

As you can see from this analysis, we don't necessarily need the detailed cash account information to prepare a statement of cash flows. We can use our knowledge of double-entry accounting to infer those details.

A similar analysis is conducted for every balance sheet account (except Cash). The analyses draw on our knowledge of the relationship between the income statement and balance sheet accounts and of what accounts are associated with operating, investing, and financing activities. Consider another example—Common Stock. First of all, we know that changes in the common stock account are considered financing activities. Second, what do we know about credits to the common stock account? They typically are associated with the issuance (sale) of stock. What about debits to the common stock account? They are associated with the retirement of common stock. Assume we are given comparative balance sheet information (transactions in a company's own stock are not reflected on the income statement) relating to the common stock account of Silmaril, Inc., as follows:

	Beginning Balance	Ending Balance
Common stock	$1,000	$1,450

What would you infer about Silmaril's cash flow activities relating to its common stock account? Without any additional information, it would be safe to assume that the company sold stock for $450. If something out of the ordinary happened in the common stock account (like the retirement of stock), that information would generally be available in the notes to the financial statements and would be used to modify the analysis.

As an illustration of this type of complexity, consider Silmaril's property, plant, and equipment (PP&E) account. First of all,

---

[3] Some of you may be thinking that Accounts Receivable can be credited when accounts are written off. This is true, and write-offs would affect our analysis. However, our purpose here is to understand the concepts. A more complicated analysis including write-offs will be covered in an intermediate accounting class.

the PP&E account is associated with what type of cash flow activity? Investing. Increases in property, plant, and equipment correspond to purchases of PP&E, and decreases relate to the sale of PP&E. Because the sale of PP&E is typically an out-of-the-ordinary type of transaction, we could look at the notes to the financial statements for information relating to any sales. In the case of Silmaril, Inc., we find that equipment costing $1,200, with accumulated depreciation of $800, was sold for $500. Based on this information, and using information from the comparative balance sheets, we can infer the purchases made during the period as follows:

Property, Plant, and Equipment

Beg. Bal.	4,000		
Purchases	?	Sold	1,200
End. Bal.	4,500		

How much PP&E was purchased during the period? The only amount that will reconcile the PP&E account is $1,700. The journal entry would have been a debit to PP&E and a credit to Cash. Again, we find that we don't need the details of the cash account to be able to infer the cash inflows and outflows for the company. Our knowledge of double-entry accounting allows us to do a little detective work and infer what went on in the cash account.

A Six-Step Process for Preparing a Statement of Cash Flows

Is there a systematic method for analyzing the income statement and comparative balance sheets to prepare a statement of cash flows? Yes, the following six-step process can be used in preparing a statement of cash flows:

1. Compute the change in the cash and cash-equivalent accounts for the period of the statement. Seldom is one handed a check figure in real life, but such is the case when preparing a statement of cash flows. The statement of cash flows is not complete until you have explained the change from the beginning balance in the cash account to the balance at year-end.

2. Convert the income statement from an accrual-basis to a cash-basis summary of operations. This is done in three steps: (1) eliminate from the income statement those expenses that do not involve cash (such **noncash items** would include depreciation expense that does not involve an outflow of cash in the current period even though income was reduced); (2) eliminate from the income statement the effects of nonoperating activity items (such items include gains and losses on the sale of long-term assets and gains and losses associated with the retirement of debt); and (3) identify those current asset and current liability accounts associated with the income statement accounts, and adjust those income statement accounts for the changes in the associated current assets and current liabilities. For example, Sales will be adjusted for the change between the beginning and ending balance in Accounts Receivable to derive the cash collections for the period. The final result will be cash flows from operating activities.

3. Analyze the long-term assets to identify the cash flow effects of investing activities. Changes in property, plant, and equipment and in long-term investments may indicate that cash has either been spent or been received.

4. Analyze the long-term debt and stockholders' equity accounts to determine the cash flow effects of any financing transactions. These transactions could be borrowing or repaying debt, issuing or buying back stock, or paying dividends.

noncash items

Items included in the determination of net income on an accrual basis that do not affect cash; for example, depreciation and amortization.

STOP & THINK

Why must gains (losses) on the sale of equipment be subtracted (added) when computing cash flows from operations?

CAUTION

Make sure that the total net cash flows from the statement (the sum of net cash flows from operating, investing, and financing activities) are equal to the net increase (decrease) in cash as computed in step 1.

5. Prepare a formal statement of cash flows by classifying all cash inflows and outflows according to operating, investing, and financing activities. The net cash flows provided by (used in) each of the three main activities of an entity should be highlighted. The net cash flows amount for the period is then added (subtracted) from the beginning Cash balance to report the ending Cash balance.

6. Report any significant investing or financing transactions that did not involve cash in a narrative explanation or in a separate schedule to the statement of cash flows. This would include such transactions as the purchase of land by issuing stock or the retirement of bonds by issuing stock.

An Illustration of the Six-Step Process

We will illustrate this six-step process for preparing the statement of cash flows using the information from the Silmaril, Inc., example presented earlier. Remember that in this case we are assuming that we do not have access to the detailed cash flow information. Thus, we are going to have to make inferences about cash flows by examining all other balance sheet and income statement accounts other than the cash account.

Step 1. Compute the Change in the Cash and Cash-Equivalent Accounts for the Period of the Statement

Recall that Silmaril began the year with a Cash balance of $300 and ended with a Cash balance of $1,430. Thus, our objective in preparing the statement of cash flows is to explain why the cash account changed by $1,130 during the year.

Step 2. Convert the Income Statement from an Accrual Basis to a Cash Basis

From the trial balance prepared at the end of the year, we can prepare the following income statement for Silmaril, Inc.:

Sales	$13,500
Cost of goods sold	8,000
Gross margin	$ 5,500
Miscellaneous expenses	3,200
Depreciation expense	500
Income from operations	$ 1,800
Interest expense	(200)
Gain on sale of equipment	100
Income before taxes	$ 1,700
Tax expense	450
Net income	$ 1,250

Our objective at this point is to convert the income statement to cash flows from operations. Recall that this involves three steps: (1) eliminating expenses not involving cash, (2) eliminating the effects of nonoperating activities, and (3) adjusting the remaining figures from an accrual basis to a cash basis. We will use a work sheet to track the adjustments that will be made. The first two adjustments involve removing depreciation expense (because it does not involve an outflow of cash) and eliminating the gain on the sale of the equipment (because the sale of equipment is an investing activity, the effect of which will be disclosed in the investing activities section of the statement). The following work sheet reflects these adjustments:

	Income Statement	Adjustments	Cash Flows from Operations
Sales	$13,500		
Cost of goods sold	(8,000)		
Miscellaneous expenses	(3,200)		
Depreciation expense	(500)	**+ 500 (not a cash flow item)**	0
Interest expense	(200)		
Gain on sale of equipment	100	**− 100 (not an operating activity)**	0
Tax expense	(450)		
	$ 1,250		

Note that because depreciation expense was initially subtracted to arrive at net income, our adjustment involves adding $500 back because no cash actually flowed out of the company relating to depreciation. The cash flow effect of the sale of the equipment should be reflected in the investing activities section of the statement of cash flows. Therefore, the effect of the gain must be removed from the operating activities section.

CAUTION

When equipment is initially purchased, the cash outflow is reported as an investing activity. When the equipment is used, this use is recorded as depreciation and does not involve any cash flow even though it is reported as an expense on the income statement.

Because the gain was initially added, we must subtract $100 as an adjustment to remove the effects of this investing activity from the operating activities section.

The adjustments now involve converting the remaining revenue and expense items from an accrual basis to a cash basis. Recall from our analysis earlier in this section that the amount of cash collected from customers differed from sales for the period. In fact, collections exceeded sales by $500 (explaining how the accounts receivable account declined by $500). An adjustment must be made to increase the accrual-basis sales figure to its cash-basis counterpart. We add $500 as illustrated below.

	Income Statement	Adjustments	Cash Flows from Operations
Sales	$13,500	**+ 500 (decrease in accounts receivable)**	$14,000
Cost of goods sold	(8,000)		
Miscellaneous expenses	(3,200)		
Depreciation expense	(500)	**+ 500 (not a cash flow item)**	0
Interest expense	(200)		
Gain on sale of equipment	100	**− 100 (not an operating activity)**	0
Tax expense	(450)		
	$ 1,250		

Next, we turn our attention to Cost of Goods Sold. The statement of cash flows should reflect the amount of cash paid for inventory during the period. We can compute that amount by adjusting Cost of Goods Sold to reflect the inventory used this period but purchased last period, as well as inventory that was purchased last period and paid for this period.

Because Inventory declined for the period from a beginning balance of $1,900 to an ending balance of $1,800, we must adjust Cost of Goods Sold to reflect that it includes inventory that was purchased last period and used this period (explaining how the inventory balance declined). To reduce Cost of Goods Sold, our adjustment involves adding $100. The resulting number represents the amount of inventory purchased during the year. A similar adjustment is made for the change in the balance in Accounts Payable and reflects

CAUTION

Remember that Cost of Goods Sold is subtracted from Sales. Adding $100 serves to reduce the negative number, and subtracting $200 makes the cost of goods sold figure a larger negative number.

the amount of inventory paid for during the year. What event would cause Accounts Payable to decline? Obviously, Accounts Payable would most likely decline because more was paid for this period than was purchased this period. If more was paid for this period, we are required to subtract an additional $200 to reflect the additional cash outflow. The net effect of these two adjustments is to convert the accrual-basis Cost of Goods Sold figure to the amount of inventory paid for during the year. The following T-account analysis shows the net effect of these two adjustments:

Cash	Inventory		Accounts Payable	Cost of Goods Sold
8,100^C	Beg. Bal. 1,900	8,000^A	Beg. Bal. 1,700	8,000^A
	7,900^B	8,100^C	7,900^B	
	End. Bal. 1,800		End. Bal. 1,500	

^{A} Cost of inventory sold during the period (from the income statement).
^{B} Inventory purchased during the period [solved for based on the beginning and ending inventory balances and the cost of goods sold (A)].
^{C} Inventory paid for during the period [solved for based on the beginning and ending Accounts Payable balances and the inventory purchased during the period (B)].

Updating our work sheet results in the following:

	Income Statement	Adjustments	Cash Flows from Operations
Sales	$13,500	+500 (decrease in accounts receivable)	$14,000
Cost of goods sold	(8,000)	**+100 (decrease in inventory)**	(8,100)
		−200 (decrease in accounts payable)	
Miscellaneous expenses	(3,200)		
Depreciation expense	(500)	+500 (not a cash flow item)	0
Interest expense	(200)		
Gain on sale of equipment	100	−100 (not an operating activity)	0
Tax expense	(450)		
	$ 1,250		

Because neither a miscellaneous expenses payable account nor a prepaid expenses account exists, we can safely assume that all the miscellaneous expenses were paid for in cash. Therefore, there would be no adjustment.

Both Interest Expense and Tax Expense require adjustments similar to that done for Accounts Payable and/or Inventory. Let's first adjust Interest Expense from an accrual basis to a cash basis. Note that Interest Payable increased from $0 at the beginning of the period to $20 at the end of the period. How would that happen? Obviously, if a payable account increases, the company owes for products and services it has purchased or used. In this case what was used is money. Interest expense for the period was $200, of which Silmaril has yet to pay $20. Thus, the cash flow related to interest must be $180— requiring an adjustment of $20.

Tax Expense is adjusted in a similar fashion. Because the amount of taxes owed increased from the beginning to the end of the period, Silmaril must have paid a lesser amount relating to taxes than is reflected on the income statement. Reviewing the T-account for Taxes Payable helps us see how that can be:

Taxes Payable

		Beg. Bal.	40
Taxes paid		Amount related	
during the period	?	to tax expense	450
		End. Bal.	50

As you can determine, the only amount that will balance the above T-account is $440—the amount paid for taxes during the period. Because the income statement reflects expense of $450 related to taxes, yet the cash outflow was only $440, we must make an adjustment of $10. The work sheet, with these final adjustments, appears as follows:

	Income Statement	Adjustments	Cash Flows from Operations
Sales	$13,500	+500 (decrease in accounts receivable)	$14,000
Cost of goods sold	(8,000)	+100 (decrease in inventory)	(8,100)
		−200 (decrease in accounts payable)	
Miscellaneous expenses	(3,200)	+0	(3,200)
Depreciation expense	(500)	+500 (not a cash flow item)	0
Interest expense	(200)	**+20 (increase in interest payable)**	(180)
Gain on sale of equipment	100	−100 (not an operating activity)	0
Tax expense	(450)	**+10 (increase in taxes payable)**	(440)
	$ 1,250	+830 net adjustment	$ 2,080

Note that the cash flows from operations figure obtained through an analysis of the income statement accounts and current asset and current liability accounts is the same figure obtained previously when we assumed access to the detailed cash account information. We should always get the same answer when the question is the same—"What were cash flows from operations?"

The Direct and Indirect Methods.   Our final task relating to cash flows from operations relates to preparing the operating activities section of the statement of cash flows. At this point, we have two alternatives—the indirect method or the direct method.

indirect method

A method of reporting net cash flows from operations that involves converting accrual-basis net income to a cash basis.

The **indirect method** begins with net income as reported on the income statement and then details the adjustments made to arrive at cash flows from operations. For Silmaril, Inc., it involves beginning with the net income figure and then listing the adjustments from the work sheet. In other words, the following highlighted portions of the work sheet are used.

	Income Statement	Adjustments	Cash Flows from Operations
Sales	$13,500	+500 (decrease in accounts receivable)	$14,000
Cost of goods sold	(8,000)	+100 (decrease in inventory)	(8,100)
		−200 (decrease in accounts payable)	
Miscellaneous expenses	(3,200)	+0	(3,200)
Depreciation expense	(500)	+500 (not a cash flow item)	0
Interest expense	(200)	+20 (increase in interest payable)	(180)
Gain on sale of equipment	100	−100 (not an operating activity)	0
Tax expense	(450)	+10 (increase in taxes payable)	(440)
	$ 1,250	+830 net adjustment	$ 2,080

The operating activities section is formatted as follows:

Operating Activities:		
Net income		$1,250
Add: Depreciation expense	$ 500	
Decrease in accounts receivable	500	
Decrease in inventory	100	
Increase in interest payable	20	
Increase in taxes payable	10	
Less: Gain on sale of equipment	(100)	
Decrease in accounts payable	(200)	830
Cash flows from operations		$2,080

direct method

A method of reporting net cash flows from operations that shows the major classes of cash receipts and payments for a period of time.

Using the **direct method**, the operating activities section of a statement of cash flows is, in effect, a cash-basis income statement. Unlike the indirect method, the direct method does not start with net income. Instead, this method directly reports the major classes of operating cash receipts and payments of an entity during a period. This information is obtained from the last column of the work sheet as follows:

	Income Statement	Adjustments	Cash Flows from Operations
Sales	$13,500	+500 (decrease in accounts receivable)	$14,000
Cost of goods sold	(8,000)	+100 (decrease in inventory)	(8,100)
		−200 (decrease in accounts payable)	
Miscellaneous expenses	(3,200)	+0	(3,200)
Depreciation expense	(500)	−500 (not a cash flow item)	0
Interest expense	(200)	+20 (increase in interest payable)	(180)
Gain on sale of equipment	100	−100 (not an operating activity)	0
Tax expense	(450)	+10 (increase in taxes payable)	(440)
	$ 1,250	+830 net adjustment	$ 2,080

The resulting operating activities section, given below, looks a lot like the operating activities section we prepared when we had access to the detailed cash flow information.

Operating Activities:		
Collections from customers		$ 14,000
Payments for inventory	$8,100	
Payments for miscellaneous expenses	3,200	
Payments for interest	180	
Payments for taxes	440	(11,920)
Cash flows from operating activities		$ 2,080

STOP & THINK

Now that you have seen both methods for preparing the operating activities section of the statement of cash flows, which method do you prefer? Which method do you think is used most often by companies?

Note that the same amount of cash flows from operating activities is derived using either the indirect method or the direct method.

Why Two Methods? You may be wondering, "Why are there two methods for preparing a statement of cash flows when both methods always result in the same answer?" Good question. Each method has advantages and disadvantages. Most companies prefer and use the indirect method because it is relatively easy to apply and reconciles the difference between net income and the net cash flows provided by operations. Many users of financial statements favor the direct method because it reports the sources of cash inflows and outflows directly without the potentially confusing adjustments to net income. The accounting standard-setters considered the arguments for both methods, and although they preferred the clarity of the direct method, they permitted either method to be used. Because they can choose either method and already have to compute net income, approximately 95% of large U.S. corporations use the indirect method when preparing a statement of cash flows.

Some Rules of Thumb. Although all this analysis may seem complex, the guidelines below will help you as you analyze accounts and prepare a statement of cash flows.

Accounts	Direction of Change during the Period	Adjustment to Be Made
Current assets	Increase	Subtracted
Current assets	Decrease	Added
Current liabilities	Increase	Added
Current liabilities	Decrease	Subtracted

When current assets increase (decrease) during the period, the difference between the beginning and ending balances is subtracted (added) from the appropriate income statement account to arrive at cash flows for the period. As an example, if accounts receivable increase during the period, that means sales exceed collections and Sales on the income statement must be reduced to reflect the cash collected for the period. The reverse would be true when accounts receivable decrease.

CAUTION

These guidelines will help you to understand how certain adjustments are made, but they will not help you understand why the adjustments are being made. To understand why, you must use your knowledge of accounting.

In the case of current liabilities, an increase (decrease) requires that an adjustment be made to add (subtract) the difference between the beginning and ending balances. For example, when interest payable increases from the beginning to the end of the period, interest expense exceeds the cash paid during the period. Interest Expense must be reduced (by adding back) to reflect the cash paid during the period. Again, the reverse would be true if interest payable were to decrease during the period. Exhibit 6 summarizes the procedures for converting selected accounts from an accrual to a cash basis.

Step 3. Analyze the Long-Term Assets to Identify the Cash Flows Effect of Investing Activities

The only long-term asset account for Silmaril, Inc., is the property, plant, and equipment (PP&E) account with its associated accumulated depreciation. The balance in the PP&E account increased by $500 during the period. What does an increase in the PP&E account indicate? Obviously, something was purchased. If we had no additional information, we would assume that PP&E was purchased by paying $500. But we do have additional information. We know that PP&E was purchased during the period by paying $1,700. With that information, we can prepare the following PP&E T-account:

Property, Plant, and Equipment

Beg. Bal.	4,000		
Purchased	1,700	Sold	?
End. Bal.	4,500		

EXHIBIT 6	Guidelines for Converting from Accrual to Cash Basis

Accrual Basis	±	Adjustments Required	=	Cash Basis
Net sales	+	Beginning accounts receivable*	=	Cash receipts
	−	Ending accounts receivable*		from customers
Other revenues (e.g., rent and interest):				
Rent revenue	+	Ending unearned rent	=	Cash received
	−	Beginning unearned rent		for rent
Interest revenue	+	Beginning interest receivable	=	Cash received
	−	Ending interest receivable		for interest
Cost of goods sold	+	Ending inventory		
	−	Beginning inventory		Cash paid
	+	Beginning accounts payable	=	for inventory
	−	Ending accounts payable		
Operating expenses** (e.g., insurance and wages): Insurance				
expense	+	Ending prepaid insurance	=	Cash paid
	−	Beginning prepaid insurance		for insurance
Wages expense	+	Beginning wages payable	=	Cash paid
	−	Ending wages payable		for wages
Income tax	+	Beginning income taxes payable	=	Cash paid for
expense	−	Ending income taxes payable		income taxes
				Net cash flows provided by (used in) operating activities

*Net of allowance for uncollectible accounts.
**Excluding depreciation and other noncash items.

To make the T-account balance, equipment must have been sold. What was the original cost of the equipment that was sold? It must have been $1,200 (that is the only number that will make the T-account balance). What was the accumulated depreciation associated with the sold equipment? Let's take a look at the accumulated depreciation T-account. Entries on the debit side of that account track the accumulated depreciation associated with equipment that has been sold. Entries to the credit side are associated with depreciation expense for the period. Because we know depreciation expense for the period (from the income statement), and we know the beginning and ending balances in the account (from the balance sheet), we can infer the accumulated depreciation associated with the equipment that was sold.

Accumulated Depreciation

		Beg. Bal.	1,200
		Depreciation	
Sold	?	Expense	500
		End. Bal.	900

The accumulated depreciation associated with the equipment that was sold must have been $800. In addition, we know from the income statement that the sale resulted in a gain of $100. With this information, we can infer that the following journal entry was made relating to the sale of PP&E:

Cash	500	
Accumulated Depreciation	800	
Property, Plant, and Equipment		1,200
Gain on Sale of Equipment		100

As you can see, we can determine the amount of cash received from the sale of PP&E by monitoring the change in other related accounts on the income statement and balance sheet.

As Silmaril's only investing activity related to the PP&E account, we have analyzed all the changes in that account and are now ready to prepare the investing activities section of the statement of cash flows. Had Silmaril bought or sold available-for-sale or held-to-maturity securities during the year, we would need to analyze these accounts to determine any cash flow effects. The investing activities section of the statement of cash flows for Silmaril, Inc., would be as follows:

Investing Activities:

Proceeds from the sale of property, plant, and equipment	$ 500	
Purchased property, plant, and equipment	(1,700)	
Cash flows from investing activities		(1,200)

Step 4. Analyze the Long-Term Debt and Stockholders' Equity Accounts to Determine the Cash Flow Effects of any Financing Transactions

Consider long-term debt accounts. What would make them increase? What would make them decrease? Obviously, these debt accounts would increase when a company borrows more money (an inflow of cash) and decrease when the company pays back the debt (an outflow of cash). In the case of Silmaril, we observe that the company's long-term debt account declined from $2,200 to $2,000. Unless something unusual happened (such as additional debt was issued and then some debt was repaid), we assume that the reason for the decrease was that cash was used to reduce the liability.

In the case of stockholders' equity accounts, we examine both the common stock and retained earnings accounts for increases and decreases resulting from cash flows. The common stock account will increase as a result of the sale of stock and decrease if any stock is repurchased and retired. Because the common stock account increased by $450 during the period, we assume that the increase resulted from the sale of stock. Again, if an unusual transaction had occurred, information relating to the transaction would be available in the notes. Retained Earnings increases from the recognition of net income (an operating activity) and decreases as a result of net losses (also an operating activity) or through the payment of dividends (a financing activity). In the case of Silmaril, Inc., because no dividends are disclosed on the trial balance, the entire change in Retained Earnings results from net income; the cash flow effect has already been included in operating activities.

Silmaril, Inc., would prepare the following information relating to its financing activities:

Financing Activities:		
Proceeds from the sale of stock	$ 450	
Repayment of long-term debt	(200)	
Cash flows from financing activities		250

Step 5. Prepare a Formal Statement of Cash Flows

Based on our analysis of all income statement and balance sheet accounts, we have identified all inflows and outflows of cash for Silmaril, Inc., and categorized those cash flows based on the type of activity. The resulting statement of cash flows (prepared using the direct method)[4] would be as follows:

Operating Activities:			
Collections from customers			$ 14,000
Payments for inventory	$ 8,100		
Payments for miscellaneous expenses	3,200		
Payments for interest	180		
Payments for taxes	440	(11,920)	
Cash flows from operating activities			$ 2,080
Investing Activities:			
Proceeds from the sale of property, plant, and equipment	$ 500		
Purchased property, plant, and equipment	(1,700)		
Cash flows from investing activities		(1,200)	
Financing Activities:			
Proceeds from the sale of stock	$ 450		
Repayment of long-term debt	(200)		
Cash flows from financing activities		250	
Net increase in cash		$ 1,130	
Beginning cash balance		300	
Ending cash balance		$ 1,430	

Additional disclosure is required in the notes to the financial statements depending on the method used. Other disclosures required by FASB Statement No. 95 include the amounts paid for interest and income taxes. When the indirect method is used to report cash flows from operating activities, cash paid for interest and income taxes is disclosed as supplemental. When the direct method is used to report cash flows from operating activities, these amounts are included in the statement of cash flows.

An additional disclosure required when the direct method is used is a schedule reconciling net income with net cash flows provided by (used in) operating activities. This schedule is, in effect, the same as the operating activities section of a statement of cash flows prepared using the indirect method.

noncash transactions

Investing and financing activities that do not affect cash; if significant, they are disclosed below the statement of cash flows or in the notes to the financial statements.

Step 6. Report Any Significant Investing or Financing Transactions That Did Not Involve Cash

If Silmaril had any significant **noncash transactions**, such as purchasing PP&E by issuing debt or trading Silmaril stock for that of another company, these transactions would be disclosed in the notes to the financial statements or in a separate schedule below the statement of cash flows. In this example, no such transactions occurred.

---

[4] A statement of cash flows prepared using the indirect method is shown in the Review Problem on pages 639–641. The statement of cash flows for **Wal-Mart**, shown in Appendix A, was also prepared using the indirect method.

REMEMBER THIS...

- Operating activities include those transactions that enter into the determination of net income.
- The direct or the indirect method may be used to show the net cash flows provided by (used in) operating activities.
- The indirect method starts with net income, as reported on the income statement, and adds or subtracts adjustments to convert accrual net income to net cash flows from operations.
- When using the indirect method, adjustments to net income are made for increases and decreases in operating account balances, noncash items such as depreciation, and gains and losses from the sale of assets.
- The direct method shows the major classes of operating cash receipts and payments. The direct method requires analysis of cash transactions or an analysis of accrual revenues and expenses in order to convert them to cash receipts and payments.
- Investing activities involve the purchase or sale of long-term assets such as property, plant, and equipment or investment securities.
- Financing activities include transactions in which cash is obtained from or paid to owners and creditors.

Using Information from the Statement of Cash Flows to Make Decisions

Use information from the statement of cash flows to make decisions.

5 To this point in the text, we have reviewed numerous financial statement analysis techniques involving the income statement and the balance sheet. We have used numerous ratios that were computed using numbers from the income statement and the balance sheet. We can also use information from the statement of cash flows for analysis purposes.

Analysis using cash flow information is often restricted to examining the relationships among the categories in the statement of cash flows. Although the statement of cash flows, like the other financial statements, reports information about the past, careful analysis of this information can help investors, creditors, and others assess the amounts, timing, and uncertainty of future cash flows. Specifically, the statement helps users answer questions such as how a company is able to pay dividends when it had a net loss, or why a company is short of cash despite increased earnings. A statement of cash flows may show, for example, that external borrowing or the issuance of capital stock provided the cash from which dividends were paid even though a net loss was reported for that year. Similarly, a company may be short on cash, even with increased earnings, because of increased inventory purchases, plant expansion, or debt retirement.

Trends are often more important than absolute numbers for any one period. Accordingly, cash flow statements usually are presented on a comparative basis. This enables users to analyze a company's cash flows over time.

Because companies are required to highlight cash flows from operating, investing, and financing activities, a company's operating cash flows and investing and financing policies can be compared with those of other companies. We can learn much about a company by examining patterns that appear among the three cash flow categories in the statement of cash flows. Exhibit 7 shows eight possible cash flow patterns and provides some insight into what each cash flow pattern indicates about the company.

Positive cash flows from operations are necessary if a company is to succeed over the long term (patterns 1 through 4). The most common cash flow pattern is 2. Companies

EXHIBIT 7	Analysis of Cash Flows Statement: Patterns			
	CF from Operating	**CF from Investing**	**CF from Financing**	**General Explanation**
#1	+	+	+	Company is using cash generated from operations, from sale of assets, and from financing to build up pile of cash—very liquid company—possibly looking for acquisition.
#2	+	−	−	Company is using cash flows generated from operations to buy fixed assets and to pay down debt or pay owners.
#3	+	+	−	Company is using cash from operations and from sale of fixed assets to pay down debt or pay owners.
#4	+	−	+	Company is using cash from operations and from borrowing (or from owner investment) to expand.
#5	−	+	+	Company's operating cash flow problems are covered by sale of fixed assets, by borrowing, or by stockholder contributions. The negative cash flow from operations could cause long-term problems if it persists.
#6	−	−	+	Company is growing rapidly, but has shortfalls in cash flows from operations and from purchase of fixed assets financed by long-term debt or new investment.
#7	−	+	−	Company is financing operating cash flow shortages and payments to creditors and/or stockholders via sale of fixed assets.
#8	−	−	−	Company is using cash reserves to finance operation shortfall and pay long-term creditors and/or investors.

Source: Michael T. Dugan, Benton E. Gup, and William D. Samson, "Teaching the Statement of Cash Flows," *Journal of Accounting Education*, Vol. 9, 1991, p. 36.

use cash flows from operations to purchase fixed assets or to pay down debt. Growing companies follow cash flow pattern 6. Cash is being borrowed to cover a shortage of cash from operations as well as to purchase fixed assets. Most (about 80%) of the publicly-traded companies in the United States follow patterns 2, 4, and 6.

REMEMBER THIS...

- An analysis of the relationships among the categories on the statement of cash flows can provide insight into a company's performance.
- Positive cash flows from operations are necessary if a company is to succeed over the long term.

REVIEW OF LEARNING OBJECTIVES

(1) Understand the purpose of a statement of cash flows.

- The statement of cash flows is one of the three primary financial statements presented by companies in their annual reports.
- The primary purpose of the statement of cash flows is to provide information about the cash receipts and payments of an entity during a period.
- The statement of cash flows also explains the changes in the balance sheet accounts and the cash effects of the accrual-basis amounts reported in the income statement.

(2) Recognize the different types of information reported in the statement of cash flows.

Operating activities	• Receipts from the sale of goods or services and from interest, and the payments for inventory, wages, utilities, taxes, and interest.
Investing activities	• Purchase and sale of land, buildings, or equipment. • Purchase and sale of certain investment securities.
Financing activities	• Selling stock, paying cash dividends, and borrowing money and repaying loans.
Significant noncash transactions	• One example is the purchase of land by the issuance of stock.

(3) Prepare a simple statement of cash flows.

- If transactions are properly classified when input into the accounting system, the preparation of a statement of cash flows is straightforward.
- Cash inflows and outflows are segregated according to type of activity (operating, investing, or financing), and a statement of cash flows is prepared based on that information.

(4) Analyze financial statements to prepare a statement of cash flows. A six-step process can be employed to assist in the analysis of balance sheet and income statement data to prepare a statement of cash flows.

(1) Compute the change in the cash balance for the period.
(2) Convert the income statement from an accrual basis to a cash basis. The result is cash flows from operating activities.
(3) Analyze long-term assets to determine the cash flow effects of investing activities.
(4) Analyze long-term liabilities and stockholders' equity accounts to determine the cash flow effects of financing activities.
(5) Prepare a formal statement of cash flows.
(6) Disclose significant noncash transactions in the notes to the financial statements or in a separate schedule at the bottom of the statement of cash flows.

(5) Use information from the statement of cash flows to make decisions.

- A statement of cash flows helps investors and creditors observe trends related to a company's use of operating income and its use of external sources of capital.
- Used with the income statement and the balance sheet, the statement of cash flows is a valuable source of information.

KEY TERMS & CONCEPTS

cash equivalents, 616	indirect method, 629	noncash	statement of cash
direct method, 630	investing activities, 618	transactions, 634	flows, 615
financing activities, 619	noncash items, 625	operating activities, 616	

REVIEW PROBLEMS

Classifying Cash Flows

Anna Dimetros is the bookkeeper for Russia Imports, Inc. (RII), a New York City–based company. Anna has collected the following cash flow information about RII for the most current year of operations. The cash balance at the beginning of the year was $105,000.

Cash receipts:	
Cash received from issuance of stock	$ 50,000
Cash received from customers	252,300
Cash received from interest at bank	4,600
Cash received from borrowing at bank	25,000
Total cash receipts	$331,900
Cash payments:	
Cash paid for wages of employees	$134,600
Cash paid to stockholders as dividends	5,500
Cash paid to bank for interest	7,200
Cash paid to bank to repay earlier loan	10,000
Cash paid for taxes	23,500
Cash paid for operating expenses	128,100
Cash paid for equipment	15,000
Total cash payments	$323,900

Required:

1. From the information provided, classify the cash flows for Russia Imports, Inc., according to operating, investing, and financing activities.
2. Determine the ending cash balance.

Solution

Russia Imports, Inc.			
Cash Flows			
20XX			
1. *Cash flows from operating activities:*			
Cash receipts from:			
Customers		$252,300	
Bank (interest)		4,600	$256,900
Cash payments to:			
Employees (wages)		$134,600	
Bank (interest)		7,200	
Government (taxes)		23,500	
Various entities (operating expenses)		128,100	293,400
Net cash flows used in operating activities			$ (36,500)

(continued)

Cash flows from investing activities:		
Cash payments to:		
Purchase equipment	$(15,000)	
Net cash flows used in investing activities		$ (15,000)
Cash flows from financing activities:		
Cash receipts from:		
Issuance of stock	$ 50,000	
Borrowing at bank	25,000	$ 75,000
Cash payments to:		
Stockholders (dividends)	$ (5,500)	
Repay earlier loan	(10,000)	(15,500)
Net cash flows provided by financing activities ...		$ 59,500
Total net cash flows for period		$ 8,000
2. Beginning cash balance		$ 105,000
Total net cash flows for period		8,000
Ending cash balance		$ 113,000*

*Alternatively, beginning balance ($105,000) + receipts ($331,900) − payments ($323,900) = ending balance ($113,000).

Preparing a Statement of Cash Flows

Snow Corporation produces clock radios. Comparative income statements and balance sheets for the years ended December 31, 2009 and 2008, are presented.

Snow Corporation

Comparative Income Statements

For the Years Ended December 31, 2009 and 2008

	2009	2008
Net sales revenue	$600,000	$575,000
Cost of goods sold	500,000	460,000
Gross margin	$100,000	$115,000
Operating expenses	66,000	60,000
Operating income	$ 34,000	$ 55,000
Interest expense	4,000	3,000
Income before taxes	$ 30,000	$ 52,000
Income taxes	12,000	21,000
Net income	$ 18,000	$ 31,000

Snow Corporation

Comparative Balance Sheets

December 31, 2009 and 2008

	2009	2008
Assets		
Current assets:		
Cash and cash equivalents	$ 11,000	$ 13,000
Accounts receivable (net)	92,000	77,000
Inventory	103,000	92,000
Prepaid expenses	6,000	5,000
Total current assets	$ 212,000	$ 187,000

(continued)

	2009	2008
Property, plant, and equipment:		
Land	$ 69,000	$ 66,000
Machinery and equipment	172,000	156,000
Accumulated depreciation, machinery and equipment	(113,000)	(102,000)
Total property, plant, and equipment	$ 128,000	$ 120,000
Total assets	$ 340,000	$ 307,000
Liabilities and Stockholders' Equity		
Current liabilities:		
Accounts payable	$ 66,000	$ 78,000
Dividends payable	2,000	0
Income taxes payable	3,000	5,000
Total current liabilities	$ 71,000	$ 83,000
Long-term debt	75,000	42,000
Total liabilities	$ 146,000	$ 125,000
Stockholders' equity:		
Common stock, no par	$ 26,000	$ 26,000
Retained earnings	168,000	156,000
Total stockholders' equity	$ 194,000	$ 182,000
Total liabilities and stockholders' equity	$ 340,000	$ 307,000

The following additional information is available.

a. Dividends declared during 2009 were $6,000.

b. The market price per share of stock on December 31, 2009, was $14.50.

c. Equipment worth $16,000 was acquired by the issuance of a long-term note ($10,000) and by paying cash ($6,000).

d. Land was acquired for $3,000 cash.

e. Depreciation of $11,000 was included in operating expenses for 2009.

f. There were no accruals or prepaid amounts for interest.

Required:

Analyze the data provided to prepare a statement of cash flows. Use (1) the indirect method and (2) the direct method to report cash flows from operating activities.

Solution

1. Indirect Method

Snow Corporation
Statement of Cash Flows (Indirect Method)
For the Year Ended December 31, 2009

Cash flows from operating activities:		
Net income	$ 18,000	
Add (deduct) adjustments to cash basis:		
Depreciation expense	11,000	
Increase in accounts receivable	(15,000)	
Increase in inventory	(11,000)	
Increase in prepaid expenses	(1,000)	
Decrease in accounts payable	(12,000)	
Decrease in income taxes payable	(2,000)	
Net cash flows used in operating activities		$(12,000)

(continued)

Cash flows from investing activities:

Cash payments for:

Land	$ (3,000)	
Machinery and equipment	(6,000)	
Net cash flows used in investing activities		(9,000)

Cash flows from financing activities:

Cash receipts from long-term borrowing	$ 23,000	
Cash payments for dividends	(4,000)*	
Net cash flows provided by financing activities		19,000
Net decrease in cash		$ (2,000)
Cash and cash equivalents at beginning of year		13,000
Cash and cash equivalents at end of year		$ 11,000

*Cash dividends declared ($6,000) less increase in dividends payable ($2,000)

Supplemental disclosure:

Cash payments for:

Interest	$ 4,000	
Income taxes		14,000

Noncash transaction:

Equipment was purchased by issuing a long-term note for $10,000.

The statement of cash flows for Snow Corporation shows that although reported net income was positive for 2009, the net cash flows generated from operating activities were negative. Only by borrowing cash was Snow Corporation able to pay dividends and purchase land and equipment. Even then the cash account decreased by $2,000 during the period.

2. Direct Method

Snow Corporation
Statement of Cash Flows (Direct Method)
For the Year Ended December 31, 2009

Cash flows from operating activities:

Cash receipts from customers		$ 585,000

Cash payments for:

Inventory	$523,000	
Operating expenses	56,000	
Interest expense	4,000	
Income tax expense	14,000	(597,000)
Net cash flows used in operating activities		$ (12,000)

Cash flows from investing activities:

Cash payments for:

Land	$ (3,000)	
Machinery and equipment	(6,000)	
Net cash flows used in investing activities		(9,000)

Cash flows from financing activities:

Cash receipts from long-term borrowing	$ 23,000	
Cash payments for dividends	(4,000)	
Net cash flows provided by financing activities		19,000
Net decrease in cash		$ (2,000)
Cash and cash equivalents at beginning of year		13,000
Cash and cash equivalents at end of year		$ 11,000

*Supplemental Disclosure**

Equipment was purchased by issuing a long-term note for $10,000.

*A schedule reconciling net income with net cash flow used by operating activities would also be presented, either with the statement of cash flows or in the notes to the financial statements. The information provided in the schedule is the same as the operating activities section of the statement of cash flows prepared using the indirect method (see part 1).

DISCUSSION QUESTIONS

1. What is the main purpose of a statement of cash flows?
2. What are cash equivalents, and how are they treated on a statement of cash flows?
3. Distinguish among cash flows from operating, investing, and financing activities, providing examples for each type of activity.
4. How are significant noncash investing and financing transactions to be reported?
5. Describe the process of converting from accrual revenues to cash receipts.
6. Describe the six-step process that can be used to prepare a statement of cash flows by analyzing the income statement and comparative balance sheets.

7. Distinguish between the indirect and direct methods of reporting net cash flows provided by (used in) operating activities.
8. How are depreciation and similar noncash items treated on a statement of cash flows?
9. What supplemental disclosures are likely to be required in connection with a statement of cash flows?
10. How might investors and creditors use a statement of cash flows?

PRACTICE EXERCISES

PE 13-1
LO2

Categories of Cash Inflows and Outflows

Which one of the following is *not* one of the three main sections in the statement of cash flows for a company?
a. Earning activities.
b. Financing activities.
c. Operating activities.
d. Investing activities.

PE 13-2
LO2

Identifying Operating Activities

Which one of the following is an example of an operating activity?
a. Cash payments to repay principal amounts borrowed.
b. Cash payments to suppliers for inventory purchases.
c. Cash receipts from sale of a business segment.
d. Cash receipts from issuance of own stock.

PE 13-3
LO2

Identifying Investing Activities

Which one of the following is an example of an investing activity?
a. Cash payments to lenders for interest expense.
b. Cash receipts from borrowing notes.
c. Cash receipts from sale of goods or services.
d. Cash payments to purchase property, plant, and equipment.

PE 13-4
LO2

Identifying Financing Activities

Which one of the following is an example of a financing activity?
a. Cash payments to purchase debt or equity securities of other entities (other than trading securities).
b. Cash payments to stockholders as dividend.
c. Cash receipts from dividend revenue.
d. Cash receipts from collection of principal on loans made to other entities.

PE 13-5
LO3

Computing Net Change in Cash for the Period

The company had a beginning cash balance of $215. In addition, the company reported the following amounts of cash provided by (used in) each category of the statement of cash flows:

(continued)

Operating activities	$ 3,460
Investing activities	(3,730)
Financing activities	298

Using the above information, compute the company's ending cash balance.

PE 13-6
LO3

Computation of Cash from Operating Activities

Using the following information, compute the amount of cash provided by operating activities.

Payments for miscellaneous expenses	$1,031
Payment to stockholders as dividends	350
Payment for taxes	135
Payment for interest	43
Collections on account	4,286
Payments for inventory	2,874

PE 13-7
LO3

Solving for Cash from Investing Activities

Using the following information, compute the amount of cash provided by (used in) investing activities:

Cash from operating activities	$136,190
Cash from financing activities	86,340
Beginning cash balance	12,540
Ending cash balance	13,405

PE 13-8
LO4

Using Accounts Receivable to Compute Cash Collections

Assume all of the company's sales are on account. The accounts receivable balance at the beginning of the year was $512, and the ending balance was $481. During the year, the company had sales of $4,526. Compute the amount of cash collections on sales.

PE 13-9
LO4

Identifying Noncash Flow Items and Nonoperating Activity Items

Using the following income statement accounts, identify the items that are noncash items and/or should not be included in the operating activities section of the statement of cash flows. (These items will be added to or subtracted from net income to compute cash flow from operating activities.)

Sales revenues	$23,236
Gain on sale of land	540
Cost of goods sold	(15,304)
General and administrative expenses	(2,634)
Depreciation expense	(1,785)
Interest expense	(429)
Tax expense	(1,450)

PE 13-10
LO4

Using Inventory and Accounts Payable to Compute Cash Paid for Inventory

Using the following information and assuming that all inventory is purchased on account, compute cash paid for inventory:

Cost of goods sold	$36,843
Inventory, beginning balance	3,110
Inventory, ending balance	2,982
Accounts payable, beginning balance	2,576
Accounts payable, ending balance	2,718

PE 13-11

LO4

Using Taxes Payable to Compute Cash Paid for Taxes

Using the following information, compute cash paid for taxes.

Income tax expense	$3,464
Taxes payable, beginning balance	237
Taxes payable, ending balance	276

PE 13-12

LO4

Indirect Method

Using the following information, prepare the operating activities section of the statement of cash flows using the indirect method.

	Income Statement		Adjustments	Cash Flows from Operations
Sales	$ 32,840	−340	(increase in accounts receivable)	$ 32,500
Cost of goods sold	(21,352)	−103	(increase in inventory)	(21,310)
		+145	(increase in accounts payable)	
Miscellaneous expenses	(4,670)	+130	(decrease in prepaid expenses)	(4,540)
Depreciation expense	(4,503)	+4,503	(not a cash flow item)	0
Interest expense	(362)	−24	(decrease in interest payable)	(386)
Loss on sale of land	(1,030)	+1,030	(not an operating activity)	0
Income tax expense	(369)	+14	(increase in taxes payable)	(355)
Net income	$ 554	+5,355	(net adjustment)	$ 5,909

PE 13-13

LO4

Direct Method

Refer to the data in PE 13-12. Prepare the operating activities section of the statement of cash flows using the direct method.

PE 13-14

LO4

Computing Cash Paid for Property, Plant, and Equipment

The company reported the following information related to its long-term assets:

Property, plant, and equipment, beginning balance	$195,410
Property, plant, and equipment, ending balance	210,850
Accumulated depreciation, beginning balance	74,330
Accumulated depreciation, ending balance	73,680
Depreciation expense	8,240

In addition, the company disclosed that it sold equipment with a historical cost of $18,700 for $14,270.

Using this information, compute cash paid for property, plant, and equipment.

PE 13-15

LO4

Computing Gain on Sale of Property, Plant, and Equipment

Refer to the data in PE 13-14. Compute the realized gain on the sale of equipment.

PE 13-16

LO4

Computing Cash from Financing Activities

Using the following information, compute the amount of cash from financing activities:
1. The company purchased $12,000 of its own common stock to be held in the treasury.
2. The company paid cash dividends of $2,350 to its stockholders.
3. The company repaid $25,000 of long-term debt.

PE 13-17

LO5

Using Information from the Statement of Cash Flows to Make Decisions

Using the following information about a company, decide whether you would want to loan money to the company.

(continued)

	2007	2008	2009
Net income	$ 2,045	$ 1,295	$ 2,540
Cash provided by (used in) operating activities	121	(2,023)	(6,843)
Cash provided by (used in) investing activities	(6,300)	(1,450)	(2,460)
Cash provided by (used in) financing activities	4,010	5,300	9,200

EXERCISES

E 13-18
LO2

Classification of Cash Flows

Indicate whether each of the following items would be associated with a cash inflow (I), cash outflow (O), or noncash item (N) and under which category each would be reported on a statement of cash flows: Operating Activities (OA); Investing Activities (IA); Financing Activities (FA); or not on the statement (NOS). An example is provided.

Item	Classified as	Reported under
Example: Sales Revenue	I	OA

1. Fees collected for services
2. Interest paid
3. Proceeds from sale of equipment
4. Cash (principal) received from bank on long-term note
5. Purchase of treasury stock for cash
6. Collection of loan made to company officer
7. Cash dividends paid
8. Taxes paid
9. Depreciation expense
10. Wages paid to employees
11. Cash paid for inventory purchases
12. Proceeds from sale of common stock
13. Interest received on loan to company officer
14. Purchase of land by issuing stock
15. Utility bill paid

E 13-19
LO2

Classification of Cash Flows

The following items summarize certain transactions that occurred during the past year for Alta Inc. Show in which section of the statement of cash flows the information would be reported by placing an X in the appropriate column. (Assume the direct method is used to report operating cash flows.)

Transaction	Reported in Statement of Cash Flows			Not Reported in Statement of Cash Flows
	Operating	Investing	Financing	
a. Collections from customers				
b. Depreciation expense				
c. Wages and salaries paid				
d. Cash dividends paid				
e. Taxes paid				
f. Utilities paid				
g. Building purchased in exchange for stock				
h. Stock of Western Co. purchased				
i. Inventory purchased for cash				
j. Interest on Alta's note to local bank paid				
k. Interest received from a note with a customer				
l. Delivery truck sold at no gain or loss				

E 13-20   **Transaction Analysis**

LO2   Following are the transactions of McKinley Company:
a. Sold equipment for $3,600. The original cost was $11,100; the book value is $3,050.
b. Purchased equipment costing $77,000 by paying cash of $27,000 and signing a $50,000 long-term note at 10% interest.
c. Received $8,200 of the principal and $490 in interest on a long-term note receivable.
d. Received $6,300 in cash dividends on stock held as a trading security.
e. Purchased treasury stock for $2,400. (Assume that the cost method is used.)

Complete the following:
1. Prepare journal entries for each of the transactions. (Omit explanations.)
2. For each transaction, indicate the amount of cash inflow or outflow. Then, note how each transaction would be classified on a statement of cash flows.

E 13-21   **Transaction Analysis**

LO3   The Vikon Company had the following selected transactions during the past year:
a. Sold (issued) 1,000 shares of common stock, $10 par, for $25 per share.
b. Collected $100,000 of accounts receivable.
c. Paid dividends to current stockholders in the amount of $50,000 (assume dividends declared earlier establishing a dividends payable account).
d. Received $1,500 interest on a note receivable from a company officer.
e. Paid the annual insurance premium of $1,200.
f. Recorded depreciation expense of $5,000.

Complete the following:
1. Prepare appropriate journal entries for each of the above transactions. (Omit explanations.)
2. For each transaction, indicate the amount of cash inflow or outflow and also how each cash flow would be classified on a statement of cash flows.

E 13-22   **Preparing a Simple Cash Flow Statement**

LO3   Assume you have access to the ledger (specifically, the detail of the cash account) for Stern Company, represented by the following T-account:

Cash

Beg. Bal.	29,870	(2)	60,000
(1)	145,500	(3)	64,000
(4)	4,750	(5)	4,000
(6)	45,000	(7)	10,500
(8)	17,000	(9)	25,000
End. Bal.	78,620		

The transactions that are represented by posting entries (1) through (9) in the cash account are as follows:
1. Collections on account
2. Payments for wages and salaries
3. Payments for inventory
4. Proceeds from sale of equipment
5. Payments of dividends
6. Proceeds from new bank loan
7. Payments for other cash operating expenses
8. Proceeds from sale of nontrading securities
9. Payments for taxes

From these data, prepare a statement of cash flows for Stern Company for the year ended December 31, 2008.

E 13-23

LO4

Determining Cash Receipts and Payments

Assuming the following data, compute:

1. Cash collected from customers.
2. Cash paid for wages and salaries.
3. Cash paid for inventory purchases.
4. Cash paid for taxes.

	Income Statement Amount for Year	Balance Sheet	
		Beg. of Year	End of Year
Sales revenue	$450,000		
Accounts receivable (net)		$28,000	$33,000
Wages and salaries expense	95,000		
Wages and salaries payable		11,000	8,000
Cost of goods sold	220,000		
Accounts payable		23,500	21,000
Inventory		22,000	25,000
Income tax expense	40,000		
Income taxes payable		19,000	20,500

E 13-24

LO4

Adjustments to Cash Flows from Operations (Indirect Method)

Assume that you are using the indirect method of preparing a statement of cash flows. For each of the changes listed, indicate whether it would be added to or subtracted from net income in computing net cash flows provided by (used in) operating activities. If the change does not affect net cash flows provided by (used in) operating activities, so indicate.

1. Increase in Accounts Receivable (net)
2. Decrease in Accounts Payable
3. Increase in securities classified as cash equivalents
4. Gain on sale of equipment
5. Decrease in Inventory
6. Increase in Prepaid Insurance
7. Depreciation
8. Increase in Wages Payable
9. Decrease in Dividends Payable
10. Decrease in Interest Receivable

E 13-25

LO4

Cash Flows from Operations (Direct Method)

Neil Brown is the proprietor of a small company. The results of operations for last year are shown, along with selected balance sheet data. From the information provided, determine the amount of net cash flows provided from operations, using the direct method.

Sales revenue	$510,000	
Cost of goods sold	320,000	
Gross margin		$190,000
Operating expenses:		
Wages expense	$ 75,000	
Utilities expense	2,500	
Rent expense	35,400	
Insurance expense	6,900	119,800
Net income		$ 70,200

(continued)

	Beginning of Year	End of Year
Accounts receivable (net)	$42,000	$39,000
Inventory	38,000	39,000
Prepaid insurance	2,200	1,800
Accounts payable	16,000	19,000
Wages payable	10,000	8,800

E 13-26
LO4

Cash Flows from Operations (Indirect Method)

Given the data in E 13-25, show how the amount of net cash flows from operating activities would be calculated using the indirect method.

E 13-27
LO4

Cash Flows Provided by Operations (Direct Method)

The following information was taken from the comparative financial statements of Imperial Corporation for the years ended December 31, 2008 and 2009:

Net income for 2009	$ 90,000
Sales revenue	500,000
Cost of goods sold	300,000
Depreciation expense for 2009	60,000
Amortization of goodwill for 2009	10,000
Interest expense on short-term debt for 2009	3,500
Dividends declared and paid in 2009	65,000

	Dec. 31, 2009	Dec. 31, 2008
Accounts receivable (net)	$30,000	$43,000
Inventory	50,000	42,000
Accounts payable	56,000	59,400

Use the direct method to compute cash flows provided by operating activities in 2009.
(*Hint:* You need to calculate cash paid for operating expenses.)

E 13-28
LO4

Cash Flows Provided by Operations (Indirect Method)

Given the data in E 13-27, show how the amount of cash provided by operations for 2009 is computed using the indirect method.

E 13-29
LO4

Cash Flows Provided by Operations (Direct Method)

The following information was taken from the comparative financial statements of Dougal Industries, Inc., for the years ended December 31, 2008 and 2009:

Net income for 2009	$ 60,000
Sales revenue	900,000
Cost of goods sold	720,000
Depreciation expense for 2009	50,000
Interest expense on short-term debt for 2009	7,400
Dividends declared and paid in 2009	20,000
Utilities expense	4,100

(continued)

	Dec. 31, 2009	Dec. 31, 2008
Accounts receivable (net)	$51,000	$46,000
Inventory	83,100	72,400
Accounts payable	65,200	68,700

Use the direct method to compute cash flows provided by operating activities in 2009. (*Hint:* You need to calculate cash paid for operating expenses.)

E 13-30
LO4

Cash Flows Provided by Operations (Indirect Method)

Given the data in E 13-29, show how the amount of cash flows provided by operations for 2009 is computed using the indirect method.

E 13-31
LO4

Net Cash Flows (Indirect Method)

Given the following selected data for Milton Corporation, using the indirect method to report cash flows from operating activities, determine the net increase (decrease) in cash for the year ended December 31, 2009.

Net income	$ 95,000
Depreciation	25,000
Other operating expenses	140,000
Cost of goods sold	240,000
Sales revenue	500,000
Increase in accounts receivable (net)	10,000
Decrease in accounts payable	5,000
Decrease in inventory	3,000
Increase in prepaid assets	7,000
Increase in wages payable	15,000
Equipment purchased for cash	40,000
Increase in bonds payable	100,000
Dividends declared and paid	40,000
Decrease in dividends payable	2,000

E 13-32
LO4

Net Cash Flows (Direct Method)

Based on the following information, determine the net increase (decrease) in cash for Luther Corp. for the year ended December 31, 2009. Use the direct method to report cash flows from operating activities.

Cash received from interest revenue	$ 16,000
Cash paid for dividends	80,000
Cash collected from customers	712,000
Cash paid for wages	476,000
Depreciation expense for the period	65,000
Cash received from issuance of common stock	350,000
Cash paid for retirement of bonds at par	150,000
Cash received on sale of equipment at book value	13,000
Cash paid for land	210,000

E 13-33
LO4

Statement of Cash Flows (Indirect Method)

North Western Company provides the following financial information. Prepare a statement of cash flows for 2009, using the indirect method to report cash flows from operating activities.

(continued)

North Western Company
Comparative Balance Sheets
December 31, 2009 and 2008

	2009	2008
Assets		
Cash and cash equivalents	$ 4,500	$ 9,000
Accounts receivable (net)	33,000	36,000
Inventory	75,000	60,000
Plant and equipment (net)	262,500	225,000
Total assets	$375,000	$330,000
Liabilities and Stockholders' Equity		
Accounts payable	$ 60,000	$ 54,000
Capital stock	225,000	217,500
Retained earnings	90,000	58,500
Total liabilities and stockholders' equity	$375,000	$330,000

North Western Company
Income Statement
For the Year Ended December 31, 2009

Sales	$412,500
Cost of goods sold	225,000
Gross margin	$187,500
Operating expenses	135,000
Net income	$ 52,500

Note: Dividends of $21,000 were declared and paid during 2009. Depreciation expense for the year was $22,500.

E 13-34   **Statement of Cash Flows (Direct Method)**
LO4   By analyzing the information in E 13-33, prepare a statement of cash flows. Use the direct method to report cash flows from operating activities.

E 13-35   **Cash Flow Patterns**
LO5   Below are recent financial statement data for the following companies:
- **Amazon.com**
- **Coca-Cola**
- **ExxonMobil**
- **Microsoft**

Use the financial statement data to match each company with its numbers. All numbers are in millions.

	Net Income	Cash Flow from Operating Activities	Cash Flow from Investing Activities	Cash Flow from Financing Activities
1	$ (720)	$ (91)	$ (922)	$ 1,104
2	7,910	15,013	(10,985)	(4,779)
3	7,785	10,030	(11,191)	2,245
4	2,431	3,883	(3,421)	(471)

(continued)

Consider the following information as you match the companies:

1. Start-ups have high positive financing cash flows relative to investing cash flows.
2. Companies with lots of property, plant, and equipment have cash from operations that is greater than net income because of lots of depreciation expense.
3. Old cash cows are spending money on investing but still have plenty left over for a net cash outflow from financing activities.

E 13-36

LO5

Analyzing Cash Flows

Study the comparative cash flow statements for **Wal-Mart** in Appendix A. What observations do you have about Wal-Mart's cash flow position? From a liquidity standpoint, is the trend over the last few years positive or negative? Explain.

PROBLEMS

P 13-37

LO4

Transaction Analysis

Klein Corporation reports the following summary data for the current year:

a. Sales revenue totaled $125,750.
b. Interest revenue for the period was $1,100.
c. Interest expense for the period was $400.
d. Cost of goods sold for the period was $78,000.
e. Operating expenses, all paid in cash (except for depreciation of $7,500), were $24,000.
f. Income tax expense for the period was $4,000.
g. Accounts receivable (net) increased by $5,000 during the period.
h. Accounts payable increased by $2,500 during the period.
i. Inventory at the beginning and end of the period was $17,500 and $12,500, respectively.
j. Cash increased during the period by $2,500.

Assume all other current asset and current liability accounts remained constant during the period.

Required:

1. Compute the amount of cash collected from customers.
2. Compute the amount of cash paid for inventory.
3. Compute the amount of cash paid for operating expenses.
4. Compute the amount of cash flows provided by (used in) operations.
5. **Interpretive Question:** What must have been the combined amount of cash flows provided by (used in) investing and financing activities?

P 13-38

LO3, LO4

Analysis of the Cash Account

The following information, in T-account format, is provided for Mars Company for the year 2009:

Cash Account

Beg. Bal.	16,300	(b)	45,500
(a)	168,000	(c)	29,000
(d)	5,000	(f)	40,800
(e)	22,000	(g)	2,100
		(h)	3,300
End. Bal.	90,600		

(continued)

Additional information:

a. Sales revenue for the period was $164,000. Accounts receivable (net) decreased $4,000 during the period.

b. Net purchases of $48,000 were made during 2009, all on account. Accounts payable increased $2,500 during the period.

c. The equipment account increased by $21,000 during the year.

d. One piece of equipment that cost $8,000, with a net book value of $4,000, was sold for a $1,000 gain.

e. The company borrowed $22,000 from its bank during the year.

f. Various operating expenses were all paid in cash, except for depreciation of $2,400. Total operating expenses were $43,200.

g. Interest expense for the year was $1,800. The interest payable account decreased by $300 during the year.

h. Income tax expense for the year was $4,200. The income taxes payable account increased by $900 during the year.

Required:

1. From the information given, reconstruct the journal entries that must have been made during the year (omit explanations).

2. Prepare a statement of cash flows for Mars Company for the year ended December 31, 2009.

P 13-39

LO4

Analyzing Cash Flows

The following information was provided by the treasurer of Surety, Inc., for the year 2009:

a. Cash sales for the year were $50,000; sales on account totaled $60,000.

b. Cost of goods sold was 50% of total sales.

c. All inventory is purchased on account.

d. Depreciation on equipment was $31,000 for the year.

e. Amortization of goodwill was $2,000.

f. Collections of accounts receivable were $38,000.

g. Payments on accounts payable for inventory equaled $39,000.

h. Rent expense paid in cash was $11,000.

i. The company issued 20,000 shares of $10-par stock for $240,000.

j. Land valued at $106,000 was acquired by issuance of a bond with a par value of $100,000.

k. Equipment was purchased for cash at a cost of $84,000.

l. Dividends of $46,000 were declared but not yet paid.

m. The company paid $15,000 of dividends that had been declared the previous year.

n. A machine used on the assembly line was sold for $12,000. The machine had a book value of $7,000.

o. Another machine with a book value of $500 was scrapped and was reported as an ordinary loss. No cash was received on this transaction.

p. The cash account increased $191,000 during the year to a total of $274,000.

Required:

1. Compute the beginning balance in the cash account.

2. How much cash was provided by (or used in) operating activities?

3. How much cash was provided by (or used in) investing activities?

4. How much cash was provided by (or used in) financing activities?

5. Would all the above items, (a) through (p), be reported on a cash flow statement? Explain.

P 13-40
LO4

Cash Flows from Operations (Indirect Method)

Gardner Enterprises reported a net loss of $40,000 for the year just ended. Relevant data for the company follow.

	Beginning of Year	End of Year
Cash and cash equivalents	$ 50,000	$ 20,000
Accounts receivable (net)	80,000	65,000
Inventory	123,000	130,000
Prepaid expenses	7,500	4,500
Accounts payable	55,000	60,000
Accrued liabilities	10,000	4,000
Dividends payable	25,000	35,000
Depreciation for the year, $43,000		
Dividends declared, $35,000		

Required:

1. Using the indirect method, determine the net cash flows provided by (used in) operating activities for Gardner Enterprises.
2. **Interpretive Question:** Explain how Gardner Enterprises can pay cash dividends during a year when it reports a net loss.

P 13-41
LO4

Cash Flows from Operations (Direct Method)

Saturday Shoppers, Inc., shows the following information in its accounting records at year-end:

Sales revenue	$740,000
Interest revenue	24,000
Cost of goods sold	380,000
Wages expense	190,000
Depreciation expense	42,000
Other (cash) operating expenses	68,000
Dividends declared	30,000

Selected balance sheet data are as follows:

	Beginning of Year	End of Year
Accounts receivable (net)	$ 63,000	$ 74,000
Interest receivable	9,000	6,000
Inventory	210,000	219,000
Accounts payable	41,000	44,000
Wages payable	32,000	34,000
Dividends payable	25,000	30,000

Required:

1. Using the direct method, compute the net cash flows provided by (used in) operating activities for Saturday Shoppers, Inc.
2. **Interpretive Question:** Explain the main differences between the net amount of cash flows from operations and net income (loss).

P 13-42   **Cash Flows from Operations (Indirect and Direct Methods)**

LO4   The following combined income and retained earnings statement, along with selected balance sheet data, are provided for McDuffie Company:

McDuffie Company		
Combined Income and Retained Earnings Statement		
For the Year Ended December 31, 2009		
Net sales revenue		$105,000
Other revenues		3,000*
Total revenues		$108,000
Expenses:		
Cost of goods sold	$55,000	
Selling and administrative expenses	15,200	
Depreciation expense	5,400	
Interest expense	1,200	
Total expenses		76,800
Income before taxes		$ 31,200
Income taxes		9,360
Net income		$ 21,840
Retained earnings, January 1, 2009		33,500
		$ 55,340
Dividends declared and paid		4,000
Retained earnings, December 31, 2009		$ 51,340

*Gain on sale of equipment (cost, $8,400; book value, $6,000; sales price $9,000).

	Beginning of Year	End of Year
Accounts receivable (net)	$12,300	$11,000
Inventory	16,800	18,000
Prepaid expenses	950	1,100
Accounts payable	7,200	7,000
Interest payable	750	1,000
Income taxes payable	2,200	2,500

Required:

1. Using the indirect method, compute the net cash flows from operations for McDuffie Company for 2009.
2. Using the direct method, compute the net cash flows from operations for McDuffie Company for 2009.
3. What is the impact of dividends paid on net cash flows from operations? Explain.

P 13-43   **Computation of Net Income from Cash Flows from Operations (Direct Method)**

LO4   The following partially completed work sheet is provided for ATM Corporation, which uses the direct method in computing net cash flows from operations:

(continued)

ATM Corporation

Partial Work Sheet–Cash Flows from Operations

(Direct Method)

For the Year Ended December 31, 2009

	Accrual Basis	Adjustments		Cash Basis
		Debits	**Credits**	
Net sales revenue				$150,000
Expenses:				
Cost of goods sold				$ 75,000
Depreciation				0
Loss on sale of equipment				0
Other (cash) expenses				26,000
Total expenses				$101,000
Net income (net cash flows from operations)				$ 49,000

Key:

1. Decrease in Accounts Receivable (net), $4,500.
2. Loss on sale of equipment, $1,500.
3. Increase in Inventory, $10,000.
4. Increase in Accounts Payable, $3,000.
5. Depreciation for the year, $8,000.
6. Decrease in Prepaid Expenses, $1,000.
7. Increase in Accrued Liabilities, $2,500.

Required:

Complete the work sheet with the key items above and compute the net income (loss) to be reported by ATM Corporation on its income statement for 2009.

P 13-44
LO4

Income Statement from Cash Flow Data

Parker Corporation computed the amount of cash flows from operations using both the direct and indirect methods, as follows:

Direct method:	
Collections from customers	$ 525,000
Payments to suppliers	(170,000)
Payments for operating expenses	(198,000)
Cash flows provided by operating activities	$ 157,000
Indirect method:	
Net income	$ 95,000
Depreciation	62,100
Gain on sale of equipment	(4,000)
Decrease in inventory	2,400
Decrease in accounts receivable (net)	3,600
Decrease in accounts payable	(6,800)
Increase in miscellaneous accrued payable	4,700
Cash flows provided by operating activities	$ 157,000

Required:

Using the data provided, prepare an income statement for Parker Corporation for the year 2009.

P 13-45   **Statement of Cash Flows (Indirect Method)**

LO4   JEM Company's comparative balance sheets for 2008 and 2009 are provided.

JEM Company Comparative Balance Sheets December 31, 2009 and 2008	2009	2008
Assets		
Cash and cash equivalents	$ 30,500	$ 10,000
Accounts receivable (net)	64,500	51,000
Inventory	100,000	115,000
Equipment	55,000	30,000
Accumulated depreciation–equipment	(21,500)	(14,000)
Total assets	$228,500	$192,000
Liabilities and Stockholders' Equity		
Accounts payable	$ 52,500	$ 46,000
Long-term notes payable	70,000	50,000
Capital stock	60,000	60,000
Retained earnings	46,000	36,000
Total liabilities and stockholders' equity	$228,500	$192,000

The following additional information is available:

a. Net income for the year 2009 (as reported on the income statement) was $50,000.

b. Dividends of $40,000 were declared and paid.

c. Equipment that cost $8,000 and had a book value of $1,000 was sold during the year for $2,500.

Required:

Based on the information provided, prepare a statement of cash flows for JEM Company for the year ended December 31, 2009. Use the indirect method to report cash flows from operating activities.

P 13-46   **Statement of Cash Flows (Direct Method)**

LO4   Financial statement data for Bankhead, Inc., are provided. (All numbers are shown rounded to the nearest thousand, with 000's omitted.)

Bankhead, Inc. Income and Retained Earnings Statements For the Year Ended December 31, 2009	
Sales revenue	$1,450
Cost of goods sold	1,030
Gross margin	$ 420
Operating expenses:	
Sales and administrative expenses	$ 110
Depreciation expense	17
Other expenses	81
Total operating expenses	$ 208
Income before taxes	$ 212
Income taxes	53
Net income	$ 159
Dividends paid	25
Increase in retained earnings	$ 134

(continued)

Bankhead, Inc.

Comparative Balance Sheets

December 31, 2009 and 2008

	2009	2008
Assets		
Cash and cash equivalents	$ 783	$ 612
Accounts receivable (net)	456	448
Inventory	245	980
Land	1,450	1,300
Store fixtures	255	255
Accumulated depreciation, store fixtures	(72)	(55)
Total assets	$3,117	$3,540
Liabilities and Stockholders' Equity		
Liabilities:		
Accounts payable	$ 170	$ 366
Short-term notes payable	574	735
Long-term debt	824	1,024
Total liabilities	$1,568	$2,125
Stockholders' equity:		
Common stock	$ 145	$ 145
Paid-in capital in excess of par	550	550
Retained earnings	854	720
Total stockholders' equity	$1,549	$1,415
Total liabilities and stockholders' equity	$3,117	$3,540

Required:

1. Compute the net cash flows from operations using the direct method.
2. **Interpretive Question:** Comment on the difference between net income and net cash flows from operations.
3. Prepare a statement of cash flows for Bankhead, Inc., for the year ended December 31, 2009.

P 13-47

LO4

Statement of Cash Flows (Indirect Method)

1. Using the data from P 13-46, prepare a statement of cash flows. Use the indirect method to report cash flows from operating activities.
2. **Interpretive Question:** What are the main differences between a statement of cash flows prepared using the indirect method and one prepared using the direct method?

P 13-48

LO4, LO5

Unifying Concepts: Analysis of Operating, Investing, and Financing Activities

Jonathan Beecher is the manager and one of three brothers who own the Mile High Sporting Goods Company in Denver, Colorado. Jonathan is pleased that sales were up last year and that his new, small company has been able to expand and open a second store in Denver. After reviewing the balance sheet, however, Jonathan is concerned that Cash shows a negative balance. He can't understand how his company can show net income, based on increased sales, yet have a negative Cash position. He is concerned about what his banker is going to say when they meet next month to discuss a loan for the company to expand to a third store. Jonathan provides the following financial information and asks for your help.

(continued)

Mile High Sporting Goods Company
Income Statement
For the Year Ended December 31, 2009

Sales		$210,000
Less cost of goods sold		96,000
Gross margin		$114,000
Operating expenses:		
Salary and wages	$41,000	
Depreciation	6,800	
Other operating expenses	14,200	62,000
Operating income		$ 52,000
Income taxes		12,300
Net income		$ 39,700

Mile High Sporting Goods Company
Comparative Balance Sheets
As of December 31, 2009 and 2008

	2009	2008
Assets		
Current assets:		
Cash	$ (2,900)	$ 4,300
Accounts receivable (net)	3,800	3,100
Inventory	60,000	51,000
Total current assets	$ 60,900	$ 58,400
Other assets:		
Property, plant, and equipment	$ 94,800	$ 46,300
Less accumulated depreciation	(19,200)	(12,400)
Total other assets	$ 75,600	$ 33,900
Total assets	$136,500	$ 92,300
Liabilities and Stockholders' Equity		
Current liabilities:		
Accounts payable	$ 8,200	$ 10,400
Wages payable	1,300	3,200
Taxes payable	1,000	2,400
Total current liabilities	$ 10,500	$ 16,000
Other liabilities:		
Notes payable	35,000	25,000
Total liabilities	$ 45,500	$ 41,000
Stockholders' equity:		
Capital stock	$ 40,000	$ 40,000
Retained earnings	51,000	11,300
Total stockholders' equity	$ 91,000	$ 51,300
Total liabilities and stockholders' equity	$136,500	$ 92,300

Required:
1. Using the direct method, compute the net cash flows from operations. Also determine net cash flows for investing and financing activities.
2. **Interpretive Question:** Is Mile High Sporting Goods Company in a good liquidity position? As Mr. Beecher's banker, would you loan him more money to fund the company's expansion?

ANALYTICAL ASSIGNMENTS

AA 13-49

DISCUSSION

Should We Make the Loan?

Save More, Inc., a discount department store, has applied to its bankers for a loan. Although the company has been profitable, it is short of cash. The loan application includes the following information about current assets, current liabilities, net income, depreciation expense, and dividends for the past five years. (All numbers are rounded to the nearest thousand, with the 000's omitted.)

	Dec. 31, 2004	Dec. 31, 2005	Dec. 31, 2006	Dec. 31, 2007	Dec. 31, 2008
Cash and cash equivalents	$ 5	$ 73	$ 10	$158	$ (189)
Accounts receivable (net)	403	555	516	576	654
Inventory	253	142	383	385	1,022
Accounts payable	19	17	281	253	52
Net income	454	492	467	440	481
Depreciation expense	50	50	55	60	60
Dividends paid	177	197	208	211	211

As a bank loan officer, you have been asked to review these figures in order to determine whether the bank should loan money to Save More, Inc.

1. Compute the net cash flows from operations for the last four years.
2. What caused the sudden decrease in cash flows from operations?
3. What factors would you focus on, and what additional information would you need before deciding whether to make the loan?

AA 13-50

DISCUSSION

Analyzing the Cash Position of Good Time, Inc.

The following data show the account balances of Good Time, Inc., at the beginning and end of the company's fiscal year:

	Aug. 31, 2009	Sept. 1, 2008
Debits		
Cash and cash equivalents	$ 88,200	$ 29,000
Accounts receivable (net)	15,000	13,300
Inventory	10,500	12,700
Prepaid insurance	2,800	2,000
Long-term investments (cost equals market)	3,000	8,400
Equipment	40,000	33,000
Treasury stock (at cost)	5,000	10,000
Cost of goods sold	184,000	
Operating expenses	93,500	
Income taxes	18,800	
Loss on sale of equipment	500	
Total debits	$461,300	$108,400

(continued)

	Aug. 31, 2009	Sept. 1, 2008
Credits		
Accumulated depreciation–equipment	$ 9,500	$ 9,000
Accounts payable	3,500	5,600
Interest payable	500	1,000
Income taxes payable	6,000	4,000
Notes payable–long-term	8,000	12,000
Common stock	55,000	50,000
Paid-in capital in excess of par	16,000	15,000
Retained earnings	9,800*	11,800
Sales	352,000	
Gain on sale of long-term investments	1,000	
Total credits	$461,300	$108,400

*Preclosing balance

The following information concerning this year was also available:

a. All purchases and sales were on account.

b. Equipment with an original cost of $5,000 was sold for $1,500; a loss of $500 was recognized on the sale.

c. Among other items, the operating expenses included depreciation expense of $3,500; interest expense of $1,400; and insurance expense of $1,200.

d. Equipment was purchased by issuing common stock and paying the balance ($6,000) in cash.

e. Treasury stock was sold for $2,000 less than it cost; the decrease in stockholders' equity was recorded by reducing Retained Earnings.

f. No dividends were paid this year.

You are to examine Good Time's cash position by:

1. Preparing schedules showing the amount of cash collected from accounts receivable, cash paid for accounts payable, cash paid for interest, and cash paid for insurance.

2. Preparing a statement of cash flows for Good Time for the fiscal year 2009 using the direct method.

3. Identifying the major reasons why Good Time's cash and cash equivalents increased so dramatically during the year.

4. Comment on whether the dividend policy seems appropriate under the current circumstances.

AA 13-51

DISCUSSION

Analyzing Cash Flow Patterns

Paula Dalton is a security analyst for DJM, Inc. She claims that she can tell a great deal about companies by analyzing their cash flow patterns. Specifically, she looks at the negative or positive cash flow trends in the three categories on cash flow statements. Paula thinks this information is even more valuable than net income trend data from income statements. She illustrates her theory with the following patterns of cash flows for Abbott Company over the past three years.

	2009	2008	2007
Net income	–	+	+
Cash flows from:			
Operating activities	–	–	+
Investing activities	+	+	+
Financing activities	+	+	+

How do you think Paula would analyze these results? Do you agree that analyzing cash flow patterns provides superior analytical information?

AA 13-52
JUDGMENT CALL

You Decide: **Which method is better at reporting information on the statement of cash flows—the indirect or direct method?**

Your finance professor said that the indirect method is a better way to prepare the statement of cash flows because it starts with a known number—net income. However, in your accounting course, your professor teaches that the direct method gives you more information on *how* the cash is used and, therefore, contains more useful information. Which professor do you agree with?

AA 13-53
JUDGMENT CALL

You Decide: **Ignoring all other factors, will a company that is generating negative cash flows from operating activities be a good or bad investment?**

When evaluating a company, you notice the following on its cash flow statement: negative cash flow from operating activities, negative cash from investing activities, and positive cash flow from financing activities. A fellow student commented, "I wouldn't invest in a company that cannot generate cash from its core business activities!" However, in 1985, **Home Depot** had a very large negative cash flow from operating activities and later turned into a very large, successful company. How would you answer your friend?

AA 13-54
REAL COMPANY ANALYSIS

Wal-Mart

The 2006 Form 10-K for **Wal-Mart** appears in Appendix A. Locate that Form 10-K and consider the following questions:

1. Does Wal-Mart present the three cash flow statement categories—operating, investing, and financing—in the same order as that illustrated in the chapter?
2. In 2006 Wal-Mart subtracted $456 million in arriving at cash flow from operations relating to an increase in receivables. Why would an increase in receivables be subtracted?
3. In 2006, Wal-Mart spent $14.183 billion on various investing activities. Were the cash flows from operations sufficient to pay for these investments?
4. Did Wal-Mart pay any cash dividends to common stockholders during 2006? Did Wal-Mart make any payments to common stockholders during the year?

AA 13-55
REAL COMPANY ANALYSIS

The Coca-Cola Company

The 2005 statement of cash flows for **The Coca-Cola Company** is given on page 662. Use the statement to answer the following questions:

1. Compute Coca-Cola's "Net cash provided by operations after reinvestment." This amount is computed by subtracting "Net cash used in investing activities" from "Net cash provided by operating activities." Interpret the results of the calculation for Coca-Cola for the period 2003–2005.
2. In its operating activities section, Coca-Cola subtracts gains on sales of assets in computing net cash provided by operating activities. Why are these gains subtracted?
3. Think of the dealings that The Coca-Cola Company has with its shareholders. The shareholders give money to the company by purchasing new shares of stock. In turn, the company returns cash to shareholders by paying cash dividends and by repurchasing shares of stock. For the three-year period 2003–2005, did The Coca-Cola Company receive more cash from its shareholders than it paid back to them, or did it pay more cash to its shareholders than it received? Show your calculations.
4. Look carefully at the statement of cash flows. Did the U.S. dollar get stronger or weaker during the three-year period 2003–2005?

(continued)

The Coca-Cola Company and Subsidiaries
Consolidated Statements of Cash Flows
For the Years Ended December 31, 2003, 2004, 2005
(in millions)

	2005	2004	2003
Operating activities:			
Net income	$ 4,872	$ 4,847	$ 4,347
Depreciation and amortization	932	893	850
Stock-based compensation expense	324	345	422
Deferred income taxes	(88)	162	(188)
Equity income or loss, net of dividends	(446)	(476)	(294)
Foreign currency adjustments	47	(59)	(79)
Gain on issuances of stock by equity investees	(23)	(24)	(8)
Gains on sales of assets, including bottling interests	(9)	(20)	(5)
Other operating changes	85	480	330
Other items	299	437	249
Net change in operating assets and liabilities	430	(617)	(168)
Net cash provided by operating activities	$ 6,423	$ 5,968	$ 5,456
Investing activities:			
Acquisitions and investments, principally trademarks and bottling companies	$ (637)	$ (267)	$ (359)
Purchases of investments and other assets	(53)	(46)	(177)
Proceeds from disposals of investments and other assets	33	161	147
Purchases of property, plant and equipment	(899)	(755)	(812)
Proceeds from disposals of property, plant and equipment	88	341	87
Other investing activities	(28)	63	178
Net cash used in investing activities	$(1,496)	$ (503)	$ (936)
Financing activities:			
Issuances of debt	$ 178	$ 3,030	$ 1,026
Payments of debt	(2,460)	(1,316)	(1,119)
Issuances of stock	230	193	98
Purchases of stock for treasury	(2,055)	(1,739)	(1,440)
Dividends	(2,678)	(2,429)	(2,166)
Net cash used in financing activities	$(6,785)	$(2,261)	$(3,601)
Effect of exchange rate changes on cash and cash equivalents	$ (148)	$ 141	$ 183
Cash and cash equivalents:			
Net increase during the year	$(2,006)	$ 3,345	$ 1,102
Balance at beginning of year	6,707	3,362	2,260
Balance at end of year	$ 4,701	$ 6,707	$ 3,362

AA 13-56

INTERNATIONAL

GlaxoSmithKline

GlaxoSmithKline, a British company, is one of the largest pharmaceutical firms in the world. The name "Glaxo" comes from the company's first major product line, baby food products that were sold with the slogan, "Builds Bonnie Babies." Growth of the company in recent years has been driven by sales of Zantac, an anti-ulcer drug.

GlaxoSmithKline's 2005 statement of cash flows is shown on the next page. Look at the statement and answer the following questions.

1. International accounting standards treat interest paid and interest received differently than those items are treated in the United States. Interest paid and interest received are classified as operating activities in the United States. Where are they classified on GlaxoSmithKline's statement and cash flow and what do you think is the reasoning behind the classification?

(continued)

2. Note that GlaxoSmithKline includes a reconciliation of operating profit to operating cash flow separate from the operating activities section of the statement of cash flows. Why do you think it would do that?

GlaxoSmithKline plc

Consolidated Statement of Cash Flows

31st December 2005

(in millions of £)

Reconciliation of operating profit to operating cash flows	2005 £m	2004 £m	2003 £m
Operating profit	6,874	5,756	6,050
Depreciation	710	691	704
Impairment and assets written off	193	94	255
Amortization of goodwill and intangible fixed assets	194	168	127
(Profit)/Loss on sale of property, plant and equipment	(19)	2	–
(Profit)/Loss on sales of intangible assets	(203)	1	(7)
Profit on sale of equity investments	(15)	(33)	(89)
Fair value loss on inventory sold	–	13	–
Decrease/(increase) in inventories	47	(33)	(76)
Increase in trade and other receivables	(397)	(235)	(369)
Increase/(decrease) in trade and other payables	491	163	(74)
(Decrease)/increase in pension and other provisions	(453)	(351)	71
Share-based incentive plans	236	333	375
Other	7	(42)	38
Net cash inflow from operating activities	7,665	6,527	7,005
Cash flow statement			
Cash flows from operating activities			
Cash generated from operations	7,665	6,527	7,005
Taxation paid	(1,707)	(1,583)	(1,917)
Net cash inflow from operating activities	5,958	4,944	5,088
Cash flow from investing activities			
Purchase of property, plant and equipment	(903)	(788)	(746)
Proceeds from sale of property, plant and equipment	54	53	46
Proceeds from sale of intangible assets	221	–	–
Purchase of intangible assets	(278)	(255)	(316)
Purchase of equity instruments	(23)	(103)	(63)
Proceeds from sale of equity instruments	35	58	125
Share transactions with minority shareholders	(36)	–	–
Purchase of businesses, net of cash acquired	(1,026)	(297)	(12)
Disposal of businesses and interest in associates	(2)	230	3
Investments in associates and joint ventures	(2)	(2)	(3)
Interest received	290	173	104
Dividends from associates and joint ventures	10	11	1
Net cash outflow from investing activities	(1,660)	(920)	(861)

(continued)

Reconciliation of operating profit to operating cash flows	2005 £m	2004 £m	2003 £m
Cash flow from financing activities			
Decrease/(increase) in liquid investments	550	(53)	(373)
Proceeds from own shares for employee share options	68	23	26
Issue of share capital	252	42	41
Share capital purchased for cancellation	–	(201)	(980)
Purchase of Treasury shares	(999)	(799)	–
Redemption of preference shares issued by subsidiary	–	(489)	–
Increase in long-term loans	982	1,365	1,046
Repayment of long-term loans	(70)	(15)	(23)
Net repayment of short-term loans	(857)	(407)	(442)
Net repayment of obligations under finance leases	(36)	(22)	–
Interest paid	(381)	(350)	(236)
Dividends paid to shareholders	(2,390)	(2,475)	(2,333)
Dividends paid to minority interests	(86)	(73)	(84)
Dividends paid on preference shares	–	(2)	(15)
Other financing cash flows	53	49	82
Net cash outflow from financing activities	(2,914)	(3,407)	(3,291)
Exchange adjustments	233	(93)	(110)
Increase in cash and bank overdrafts	1,617	524	826

AA 13-57

ETHICS

Manipulating the Federal Budget Deficit

Assume that you are the paymaster in charge of all U.S. Department of Defense (DOD) payroll matters. The total amount that you disburse in payroll checks in any given week is in excess of $1 billion.

Assume also that tax receipts have been lower than expected and that a federal budget deficit, and not a surplus, is now projected. Currently, Congress is struggling to reduce the projected budget deficit. It is an election year, and the members of Congress are worried that they will be stuck with a "tax and spend" label if the government runs a deficit this year. Of course, the DOD budget has been scrutinized very carefully to reduce reported expenditures as much as possible.

Yesterday, a congressional leader came to your office with a disturbing proposal. Because the federal budget numbers are reported on a cash basis, rather than on an accrual basis, expenses are reported when they are paid instead of when they are incurred. This year, the final DOD payday of the year happens to fall on the last day of the federal government's fiscal year (September 30). The congressional leader suggested that you delay issuing the payroll checks by one day. This would push the actual payment of the cash into the next fiscal year. Thus, even though the payment would be for services performed in the current fiscal year, the expense wouldn't be reported until next year. With this simple trick, the reported deficit for this year (an election year) can be reduced by $1 billion.

What should you do?

AA 13-58

WRITING

Convincing the Old-Timers of the Need for Cash Flow Data

You are the chief accountant for Harry Monst Company. The president of the company is a former accountant who worked her way up through the management ranks over the course of 30 years. She is a great manager, but her knowledge of accounting is outdated.

Harry Monst Company has a revolving line of credit with Texas Commercial Bank. A new loan officer has just been put in charge of the Harry Monst account. The new loan officer is surprised to see that Harry Monst has not been submitting a statement of cash flows along with the rest of the financial statements that comprise the annual loan review packet. The new loan officer called you and asked for a statement of cash flows.

You were surprised when you took the completed statement of cash flows to the president for her signature. She refused to sign, stating that she had never looked at or prepared a statement of cash flows in her career and she wouldn't start now.

(continued)

Write a one-page memo to the president with the objective of convincing her of the usefulness of the statement of cash flows.

AA 13-59
CUMULATIVE
SPREADSHEET
PROJECT

Preparing New Forecasts

This spreadsheet assignment is a continuation of the spreadsheet assignments given in earlier chapters. If you completed those spreadsheets, you have a head start on this one.

1. Handyman wishes to prepare a forecasted balance sheet, income statement, and statement of cash flows for 2010. Use the original financial statement numbers for 2009 [given in part (1) of the Cumulative Spreadsheet Project assignment in Chapter 2] as the basis for the forecast along with the following additional information:
   a. Sales in 2010 are expected to increase by 40% over 2009 sales of $700.
   b. In 2010, Handyman expects to acquire new property, plant, and equipment costing $80.
   c. The $160 in operating expenses reported in 2009 breaks down as follows: $5 depreciation expense, $155 other operating expenses.
   d. No new long-term debt will be acquired in 2010.
   e. No cash dividends will be paid in 2010.
   f. New short-term loans payable will be acquired in an amount sufficient to make Handyman's current ratio in 2010 exactly equal to 2.0.

Construction of the forecasted statement of cash flows for 2010 involves analyzing the forecasted income statement for 2010, along with the balance sheets for 2009 (actual) and 2010 (forecasted).

For this exercise, the current assets are expected to behave as follows:
   a. Cash will increase at the same rate as sales.
   b. The forecasted amount of accounts receivable in 2010 is determined using the forecasted value for the average collection period (computed using the end-of-period Accounts Receivable balance). The average collection period for 2010 is expected to be 14.08 days. This is from the *Chapter 6 spreadsheet*.
   c. The forecasted amount of inventory in 2010 is determined using the forecasted value for the number of days' sales in inventory (computed using the end-of-period Inventory balance). The number of days' sales in inventory for 2010 is expected to be 107.6 days. This is from the *Chapter 7 spreadsheet*.
   d. The forecasted amount of accounts payable in 2010 is determined using the forecasted value of the number of days' purchases in accounts payable (computed using the end-of-period Accounts Payable balance). The number of days' purchases in accounts payable for 2010 is expected to be 48.34 days. This is from the *Chapter 7 spreadsheet*.

Clearly state any additional assumptions that you make.

2. Repeat (1), with the following changes in assumptions:
   a. The average collection period is expected to be 9.06 days with days' sales in inventory remaining at 107.6 days and days' purchases in payables remaining at 48.34 days.
   b. The average collection period is expected to be 20 days with days' sales in inventory remaining at 107.6 days and days' purchases in payables remaining at 48.34 days.
   c. Days' sales in inventory are expected to be 66.2 days with the average collection period remaining at 14.08 days and days' purchases in payables remaining at 48.34 days.
   d. Days' sales in inventory are expected to be 150 days with the average collection period remaining at 14.08 days and days' purchases in payables remaining at 48.34 days.

Comment on the forecasted values of cash from operating activities in 2010 under each of the scenarios given in (2).

© AP PHOTO/RICHARD VOGEL

Introduction to Financial Statement Analysis

After studying this chapter, you should be able to:

LEARNING OBJECTIVES

(1) Explain the purpose of financial statement analysis. *Analysis of financial statement numbers can be used to diagnose existing problems and to forecast how a company will perform in the future.*

(2) Understand the relationships between financial statement numbers and use ratios in analyzing and describing a company's performance. *Financial ratios are relationships between two financial statement numbers and are often used in analyzing and describing a company's performance.*

(3) Use common-size financial statements to perform comparison of financial statements across years and between companies. *Common-size financial statements allow comparison of financial statements across years and between companies and are prepared by dividing all financial statement numbers by sales for the year.*

(4) Understand the DuPont framework and how return on equity can be decomposed into its profitability, efficiency, and leverage components. *The DuPont framework decomposes return on equity into its profitability, efficiency, and leverage components.*

(5) Conduct a focused examination of a company's efficiency by using asset-specific ratios. *Accounts receivable turnover, inventory turnover, and fixed asset turnover can be used to measure how efficiently a company is using those assets.*

(6) Determine the degree of a company's financial leverage and its ability to repay loans using debt-related financial ratios. *Debt-related financial ratios give an indication of the degree of a company's leverage and how much cushion operating profits give in terms of being able to make periodic interest payments.*

(7) Use cash flow information to evaluate cash flow ratios. *Cash flow ratios are frequently overlooked because traditional analysis models are based on the balance sheet and the income statement.*

(8) Understand the limitations of financial statement analysis. *Analysis of financial statements can be misleading if statements are not comparable or if statements exclude significant information. In addition, analysis of historical data can distract one's attention from relevant current information.*

Microsoft was founded in 1975 by Bill Gates and Paul Allen. How successful has the company been? In terms of stock price, Microsoft's per-share stock price (adjusted for stock splits) has gone from $0.07 in 1986 to almost $27 in April of 2006 (see Exhibit 1). But as the graph illustrates, Microsoft's stock price is down from its historic high of $60 per share in 1999. An analysis of Microsoft's financial statements reveals some of the reasons for the declining stock price. That is the topic of this chapter—an introduction to financial statement analysis. With some basic analysis tools (called ratios), we will be able to conduct some fundamental analysis of a company's financial statements. Our analysis will provide us with insights as to a company's performance and will help us identify areas of concern. Keep in mind that this is merely an introduction to financial statement analysis. There are entire textbooks devoted to the analysis of financial statements. Our objective here is to expose you to some of the basic tools to help you start to understand what financial statements can tell us about the operations of a business. To illustrate the analysis techniques introduced in this chapter, we will reference the 2005 financial statements of Microsoft.

EXHIBIT 1 **History of Microsoft's Stock Price per Share**

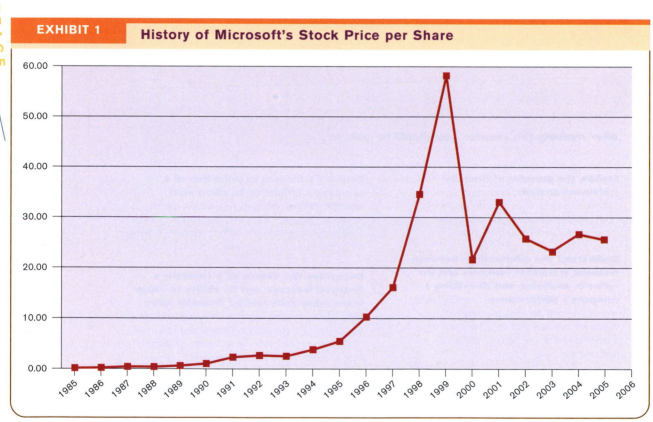

The Need for Financial Statement Analysis

Explain the purpose of financial statement analysis.

(1) Consider the following questions related to financial statement information for **Microsoft** in 2005:

- Microsoft's net income in 2005 was $12.254 billion. That seems like a lot, but does it represent a large amount for a company the size of Microsoft?
- Total assets for Microsoft at the end of 2005 were $70.815 billion. Given the volume of business that Microsoft does, is this amount of assets too much, too little, or just right?
- By the end of 2005, Microsoft's liabilities totaled $22.700 billion. Is this level of debt too much for Microsoft?

financial statement analysis

The examination of both the relationships among financial statement numbers and the trends in those numbers over time.

financial ratios

Relationships between financial statement amounts.

The important point to recognize is that just having the financial statement numbers is not enough to answer the questions that financial statement users want answered. Without further analysis, the raw numbers themselves don't tell much of a story.

Financial statement analysis involves the examination of both the relationships among financial statement numbers and the trends in those numbers over time. One purpose of financial statement analysis is to use the past performance of a company to predict how it will do in the future. Another purpose is to evaluate the performance of a company with an eye toward identifying problem areas. In sum, financial statement analysis is both diagnosis—identifying where a firm has problems—and prognosis—predicting how a firm will perform in the future.

Relationships between financial statement amounts are called **financial ratios**. Net income divided by sales, for example, is a financial ratio called return on sales, which tells you how many pennies of profit a company makes on each dollar of sales. The return on sales for Microsoft is 30.8%, meaning that Microsoft makes almost 31 cents' worth of profit for every dollar of product or service sold. There are hundreds of different financial ratios, each shedding light on a different aspect of the health of a company.

Exhibit 2 illustrates how financial statement analysis fits into the decision cycle of a company's management. Notice that the preparation of the financial statements is just the starting point of the process. After the statements are prepared, they are analyzed using techniques akin to those to be introduced in this chapter. Analysis of the summary information in the financial statements usually doesn't provide detailed answers to management's questions, but it does identify areas in which further data should be gathered. Decisions are then made and implemented, and the accounting system captures the results of these decisions so that a new set of financial statements can be prepared. The process then repeats itself.

 FYI

Financial information is almost always compared to what was reported in the previous year. For example, when Microsoft publicly announced on January 26, 2006, that its quarterly revenues were $11.84 billion, the press release also stated that this amount represented a 9% increase over the same period in the prior year.

 FYI

Financial statement analysis often points to areas in which additional data must be gathered, including details of significant transactions, market share information, competitors' plans, and customer demand forecasts.

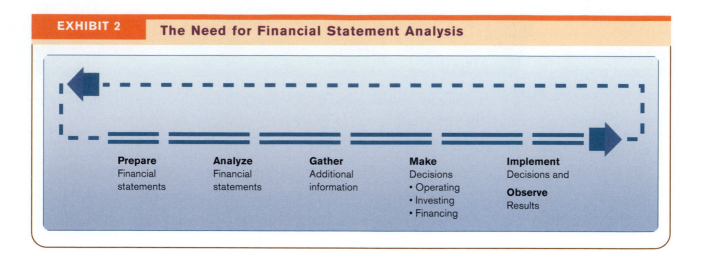

EXHIBIT 2 **The Need for Financial Statement Analysis**

Prepare Financial statements

Analyze Financial statements

Gather Additional information

Make Decisions
• Operating
• Investing
• Financing

Implement Decisions and

Observe Results

For external users of financial statements, such as investors and creditors, financial statement analysis plays the same role in the decision-making process. Whereas management uses the analysis to help in making operating, investing, and financing decisions, investors and creditors analyze financial statements to decide whether to invest in, or loan money to, a company.

In analyzing a company's financial statements, merely computing a list of financial ratios is not enough. Most pieces of information are meaningful only when they can be compared with some benchmark. For example, knowing that Microsoft's return on sales in 2005 was 30.8% tells you a little, but you can evaluate the ratio value much better if you know that Microsoft's return on sales was 22.2% and 23.4% in 2004 and 2003, respectively. In short, the usefulness of financial ratios is greatly enhanced when they are compared with past values and with values for other firms in the same industry.

REMEMBER THIS...

- Financial statement analysis is used:
  - to predict a company's future profitability and cash flows from its past performance and
  - to evaluate the performance of a company with an eye toward identifying problem areas.
- The informativeness of financial ratios is greatly enhanced when they are compared:
  - with past values and
  - with values for other firms in the same industry.

Widely Used Financial Ratios

Understand the relationships between financial statement numbers and use ratios in analyzing and describing a company's performance.

Before diving into a comprehensive treatment of financial ratio analysis, we'll first get our feet wet with the most widely used ratios. Familiarity with financial ratios will allow you to hold your own in most casual business conversations and will enable you to understand most ratios used in the popular business press. Data from Microsoft's 2005 financial statements will be used to illustrate the ratio calculations. The data are displayed in Exhibit 3.

Debt Ratio

debt ratio

A measure of leverage, computed by dividing total liabilities by total assets.

Comparing the amount of liabilities with the amount of assets indicates the extent to which a company has borrowed money to leverage the owners' investments and increase the size of the company. One frequently used measure of leverage is the **debt ratio**, computed as total liabilities divided by total assets. An intuitive interpretation of the debt ratio is that it represents the proportion of borrowed funds used to acquire the company's assets. For Microsoft, the debt ratio is computed as follows:

$$\text{Debt Ratio:} \quad \frac{\text{Total Liabilities}}{\text{Total Assets}} = \frac{\$22,700}{\$70,815} = 32.1\%$$

In other words, Microsoft borrowed 32.1% of the money it needed to buy its assets.

Is 32.1% a good or bad debt ratio, or is it impossible to tell? If you are a banker thinking of lending money to Microsoft, you want Microsoft to have a low debt ratio because a smaller amount of other liabilities increases your chances of being repaid. If you are a Microsoft stockholder, you want a higher debt ratio because you want the company to add borrowed funds to your investment dollars to expand the business.

 CAUTION

The debt ratio is often confused with the debt-to-equity ratio and the asset-to-equity ratio. Each of these ratios is a measure of a company's leverage. However, each is computed slightly differently. Make sure when discussing a leverage ratio, it is understood which one is being used.

Thus, there is some happy middle ground where the debt ratio is not too high for creditors but not too low for investors. The general rule of thumb across all industries is that debt ratios should be around 50%, but this benchmark varies widely from one industry to the next. By comparison, **Apple Computer**'s 2005 debt ratio was 35.4%.

Current Ratio

liquidity

A company's ability to pay its debts in the short run.

An important concern about any company is its **liquidity**, or ability to pay its debts in the short run. If a firm can't meet its obligations in the short run, it may

---

EXHIBIT 3   **Selected Financial Data for Microsoft for 2005**

Current assets	$ 48,737*
Total assets	70,815
Current liabilities	16,877
Total liabilities	22,700
Stockholders' equity	48,115
Sales	39,788
Net income	12,254
Market value of shares (as of June 30, 2006)	263,573

*All numbers are in millions of dollars.

current ratio

A measure of the liquidity of a business; equal to current assets divided by current liabilities.

not survive to enjoy the long run. The most commonly used measure of liquidity is the **current ratio**, which is a comparison of current assets (cash, receivables, and inventory) with current liabilities. Current ratio is computed by dividing total current assets by total current liabilities. For Microsoft, the current ratio is computed as follows:

$$\text{Current Ratio:} \quad \frac{\text{Current Assets}}{\text{Current Liabilities}} = \frac{\$48,737}{\$16,877} = 2.888$$

Historically, the rule of thumb has been that a current ratio below 2 suggests the possibility of liquidity problems. However, advances in information technology have enabled companies to be much more effective in minimizing the need to hold cash, inventories, and other current assets. As a result, current ratios for successful companies these days are frequently less than 1. Current ratios for selected U.S. companies are shown in Exhibit 4.

Return on Sales

return on sales

A measure of the amount of profit earned per dollar of sales, computed by dividing net income by sales.

As mentioned earlier, Microsoft makes 30.8 cents of profit on each dollar of sales. This ratio is called **return on sales** and, using Microsoft's numbers, is computed as follows:

$$\text{Return on Sales:} \quad \frac{\text{Net Income}}{\text{Sales}} = \frac{\$12,254}{\$39,788} = 30.8\%$$

As with all ratios, the return-on-sales value for Microsoft must be evaluated in light of the appropriate industry. For example, the 2004 return on sales for Microsoft was 22.2%. At the other end of the spectrum, return on sales in the supermarket industry is frequently between 1% and 2%. These values, because they come from outside Microsoft's industry, do not really provide a useful benchmark against which Microsoft's return on sales can be compared. A better comparison for Microsoft is the 2005 return-on-sales value for Apple Computer, which was 9.6%. So, it appears that return on sales for Microsoft was substantially above the industry average in 2005; why this happened will be examined later in the chapter.

Asset Turnover

asset turnover

A measure of company efficiency, computed by dividing sales by total assets.

Microsoft's balance sheet reveals total assets of $70.815 billion. Are those assets being used efficiently? A financial ratio that gives an overall measure of company efficiency is called **asset turnover** and is computed as follows:

$$\text{Asset Turnover:} \quad \frac{\text{Sales}}{\text{Total Assets}} = \frac{\$39,788}{\$70,815} = 0.56$$

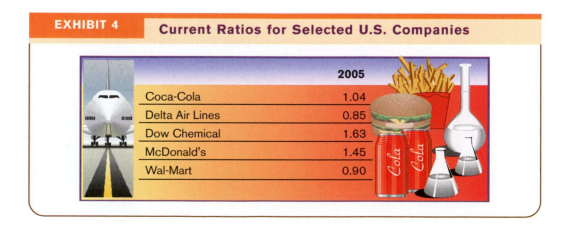

EXHIBIT 4	**Current Ratios for Selected U.S. Companies**

	2005
Coca-Cola	1.04
Delta Air Lines	0.85
Dow Chemical	1.63
McDonald's	1.45
Wal-Mart	0.90

CAUTION

The computed asset turnover ratio can be misleading, as discussed in the concluding section of this chapter, because not all economic assets are recorded as assets on the balance sheet. Thus, the denominator of the ratio can be understated, sometimes very significantly.

Microsoft's asset turnover ratio of 0.56 means that for each dollar of assets Microsoft is able to generate $0.56 in sales. The higher the asset turnover ratio, the more efficient the company is at using its assets to generate sales. In evaluating Microsoft's asset turnover, note that asset turnover for Apple Computer in 2005 was 1.21, indicating that Microsoft was less efficient than its competitor at using its assets to generate sales.

Return on Equity

return on equity

A measure of the amount of profit earned per dollar of investment, computed by dividing net income by equity.

What investors really want to know is not how many pennies of profit are earned on a dollar of sales or what the current ratio is—they want to know how much profit they earn for each dollar they invest. This amount, called **return on equity**, is the overall measure of the performance of a company. Return on equity for Microsoft is computed as follows:

$$\text{Return on Equity:} \quad \frac{\text{Net Income}}{\text{Stockholders' Equity}} = \frac{\$12,254}{\$48,115} = 25.5\%$$

Microsoft's return on equity of 25.5% means that 25.5 cents of profit were earned for each dollar of stockholder investment in 2005. By comparison, Apple Computer's return on equity in 2005 was 17.9%. Good companies typically have return on equity values between 15% and 25%. Return on equity is the fundamental measure of overall company performance and forms the basis of the DuPont framework discussed later on.

Price-Earnings Ratio

price-earnings ratio

A measure of growth potential, earnings stability, and management capabilities; computed by dividing market value of a company by net income.

If a company earned $100 this year, how much should I pay to buy that company? If I expect the company to make more in the future, I'd be willing to pay a higher price than if I expected the company to make less. Also, I'd probably be willing to pay a bit more for a stable company than for one that experiences wild swings in earnings. The relationship between the market value of a company and that company's current earnings is measured by the **price-earnings ratio**, or PE ratio, and is computed by dividing the market value of the shares outstanding by the company's net income.[1] Microsoft's PE ratio at the end of 2005 was:

$$\text{PE Ratio:} \quad \frac{\text{Market Value of Shares}}{\text{Net Income}} = \frac{\$263,573}{\$12,254} = 21.5$$

In the United States, PE ratios typically range between 5 and 30. High PE ratios are associated with firms for which strong growth is predicted in the future. **Google**, for example, has a high PE ratio, but it is not found on the list of companies with high net income. The reason Google is valued so highly is that it is expected to continue to grow so rapidly in the future that its current income is small compared with what investors are expecting in the future. This expected future growth is reflected in Google's PE ratio of about 80 (in 2006). Sample PE ratios for several companies as of April 14, 2006, are included in Exhibit 5.

A summary of the financial ratios discussed in this section is presented in Exhibit 6.

---

[1] The PE ratio can be equivalently computed using per share amounts: PE ratio = Market price per share/Earnings per share.

EXHIBIT 5	Sample PE Ratios for Several U.S. Companies		

Company Name	Stock Ticker Symbol	PE Ratio
Yahoo!	Yhoo	24.4
Wal-Mart	wmt	17.1
Berkshire Hathaway	brka	15.7
Home Depot	hd	15.1
Sears	shld	24.9

EXHIBIT 6	Summary of Selected Financial Ratios	

1. Debt ratio	$\dfrac{\text{Total liabilities}}{\text{Total assets}}$	Percentage of funds needed to purchase assets that were obtained through borrowing.
2. Current ratio	$\dfrac{\text{Current assets}}{\text{Current liabilities}}$	Measure of liquidity; number of times current assets could cover current liabilities.
3. Return on sales	$\dfrac{\text{Net income}}{\text{Sales}}$	Number of pennies earned during the year on each dollar of sales.
4. Asset turnover	$\dfrac{\text{Sales}}{\text{Total assets}}$	Number of dollars of sales during the year generated by each dollar of assets.
5. Return on equity (ROE)	$\dfrac{\text{Net income}}{\text{Stockholders' equity}}$	Number of pennies earned during the year on each dollar invested.
6. Price-earnings ratio (PE)	$\dfrac{\text{Market value of shares}}{\text{Net income}}$	Amount investors are willing to pay for each dollar of earnings; indication of growth potential.

Note that the PE ratio is different from the other ratios in that it is not the ratio of two financial statement numbers. Instead, the PE ratio is a comparison of a financial statement number to a market value number. The large majority of financial ratios, however, are (1) a comparison of two amounts found in the same financial statement (such as return on sales, which compares two income statement amounts) or (2) a comparison of two amounts from different financial statements (such as asset turnover, which compares an income statement and a balance sheet amount). These two types of ratios are illustrated in Exhibit 7.

In looking at Exhibit 7, you might justifiably conclude that the cash flow statement is completely ignored when computing financial ratios. Unfortunately, that is often true. Relative to the other two primary financial statements, the statement of cash flows is relatively new (the balance sheet and the income statement have been a part of accounting since its invention—the statement of cash flows has only been required since 1988). As a result, ratios involving balance sheet and income statement accounts have been in existence for decades. Given the newness of the statement of cash flows, standardized ratios are still developing. The **Enron** accounting scandal highlighted the usefulness of ratios involving cash flow information (see Analytical Assignment 14-73 in the end-of-chapter material). To make sure you don't fall victim to the oversight of ignoring cash flow ratios, we include a special section on cash flow ratios later in this chapter.

EXHIBIT 7 **Financial Ratios and the Relationships among the Financial Statements**

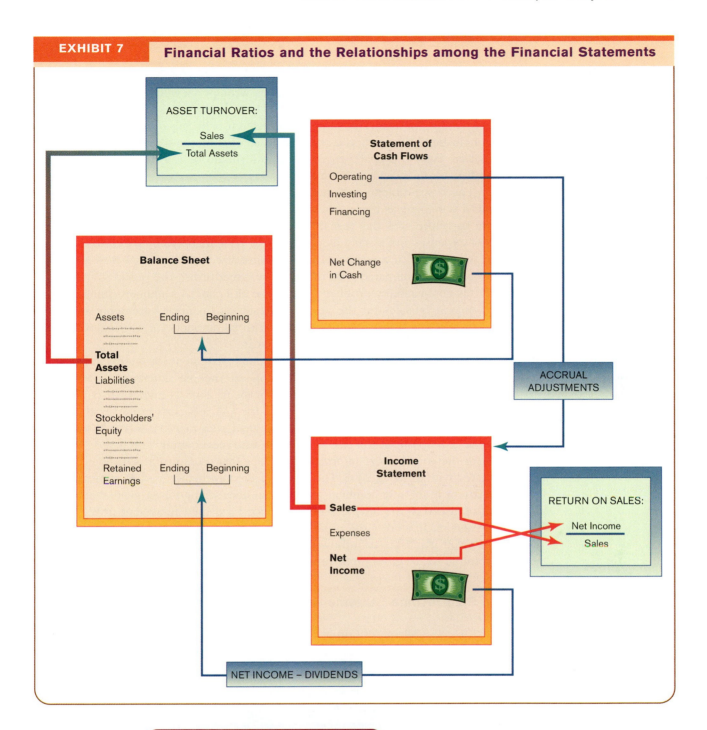

REMEMBER THIS...

Financial ratios result from the relationship between two financial statement numbers.

- **Debt ratio:** Percentage of company funding that is borrowed.
- **Current ratio:** Indication of a company's ability to pay its short-term debts.
- **Return on sales:** Pennies in profit on each dollar of sales.
- **Asset turnover:** Measure of efficiency; number of sales dollars generated by each dollar of assets.
- **Return on equity:** Pennies in profit for each dollar invested by stockholders.
- **Price-earnings ratio:** Number of dollars an investor must pay to "buy" the future rights to each dollar of current earnings.

Common-Size Financial Statements

Use common-size financial statements to perform comparison of financial statements across years and between companies.

③ Financial statement analysis is sometimes wrongly viewed as just the computation of a bunch of financial ratios—divide every financial statement number by every other number. This shotgun approach usually fails to lead to any concrete conclusions. This section explains the use of common-size financial statements that are easy to prepare, easy to use, and should be the first step in any comprehensive financial statement analysis.

The first problem encountered when using comparative data to analyze financial statements is that the scale, or size, of the numbers is usually different. If a firm has more sales this year than last year, it is now a larger company and the levels of expenses and assets this year can't be meaningfully compared to the levels last year. In addition, if a company is of medium size in its industry, how can its financial statements be compared with those of the larger firms? The quickest and easiest solution to this comparability problem is to divide all financial statement numbers for a given year by sales for the year. The resulting financial statements are called

common-size financial statements

Financial statements achieved by dividing all financial statement numbers by total sales for the year.

common-size financial statements, with all amounts for a given year being shown as a percentage of sales for that year.

Exhibit 8 contains a common-size income statement for Microsoft for 2005. To illustrate the usefulness of a common-size income statement, consider the question of whether Microsoft's gross profit in 2005 is higher. In comparison with the gross profit of $30,119 in 2004, the $33,588 gross profit for 2005 looks pretty good. But sales in 2005 are higher than sales in 2004, so the absolute levels of gross profit in the two years cannot be meaningfully compared. But looking at the common-size information, we see that gross profit is 81.8% of sales in 2004 compared with 84.4% in 2005. The common-size information reveals something that was not apparent in the raw numbers—in 2004 an item selling for $1 yielded an average gross profit of just 81.8¢; in 2005 an item selling for $1 yielded an average gross profit of 84.4¢. Microsoft made more gross profit from each dollar of sales in 2005 than in 2004. The news is even better because the 2005 gross profit represents a continuation of the increase from the 81.2% gross profit percentage in 2003.

EXHIBIT 8	**Common-Size Income Statement for Microsoft**

Microsoft Corporation
Income Statement
For Years Ended June 30
(in millions)

Year Ended June 30	2003	%	2004	%	2005	%
Revenue	32,187	100.0%	36,835	100.0%	39,788	100.0%
Cost of revenue	6,059	18.8%	6,716	18.2%	6,200	15.6%
Gross profit on sales	26,128	81.2%	30,119	81.8%	33,588	84.4%
Operating expenses:						
Research and development	6,595	20.5%	7,779	21.1%	6,184	15.5%
Sales and marketing	7,562	23.5%	8,309	22.6%	8,677	21.8%
General and administrative	2,426	7.5%	4,997	13.6%	4,166	10.5%
Total operating expenses	16,583	51.5%	21,085	57.2%*	19,027	47.8%
Operating income	9,545	29.7%	9,034	24.5%*	14,561	36.6%
Investment income and other	1,509	4.7%	3,162	8.6%	2,067	5.2%
Income before income taxes	11,054	34.3%*	12,196	33.1%	16,628	41.8%
Provision for income taxes	3,523	10.9%	4,028	10.9%	4,374	11.0%
Net income	7,531	23.4%	8,168	22.2%	12,254	30.8%

*Note: Because of rounding, the percentages don't always add up exactly. This is a minor arithmetic problem that shouldn't get in the way of the analysis.

CAUTION

Notice in Exhibit 8 that the results for 2005, the most recent year reported, are shown in the far right column. This is the way Microsoft reports in its annual report. However, most companies choose to report the most recent information in the far left column.

Each item on the income statement can be analyzed in the same way. In 2005, income before income taxes was 41.8% of sales compared with 33.1% in 2004. Operating expenses as a percentage of sales decreased sharply from 2004 to 2005 (57.2% vs. 47.8%) indicating the increase in operating income in 2005 related mainly to a decrease in the operating expense percentage. With a common-size income statement, each of the income statement items can be examined in this way, yielding much more information than just looking at the raw income statement numbers.

At this point, you should be saying to yourself: "Yes, but what is the exact explanation for Microsoft's increase in gross profit percentage in 2005? And why did regular operating expenses decrease?" These questions illustrate the usefulness and the limitations of financial statement analysis. Our quick analysis of Microsoft's income statement has pointed out the major areas in which Microsoft has experienced significant income statement change in the past two years. But the

FYI

The SEC requires publicly-traded companies to provide three years of income statements and two years of balance sheets when providing financial reports to the public.

only way to find out why these financial statement numbers changed is to gather information from outside the financial statements—ask management, read press releases, talk to financial analysts who follow the firm, read industry newsletters, and dig into the notes to the financial statements. In short, financial statement analysis usually doesn't tell you the final answers, but it

does suggest which questions you should be asking and where you should look to find the answers.

A common-size balance sheet also expresses each amount as a percentage of sales for the year. As an illustration, a comparative balance sheet for Microsoft with each item expressed in both dollar amounts and percentages is shown in Exhibit 9.

The most informative section of the common-size balance sheet is the asset section, which can be used to determine how efficiently a company is using its assets. For example, looking at total assets for Microsoft in 2004 and 2005, you see the company's total assets were $70,815 in 2005. Did Microsoft manage its assets more efficiently in 2005 than in 2004 when total assets were $94,368? Comparing the raw numbers can't give a clear answer because Microsoft's level of sales is different in the two years. The common-size balance sheet indicates that each dollar of sales in 2004 required assets in place of $2.562, whereas each dollar of sales in 2005 required assets of just $1.780. So in which of the two years was Microsoft more efficient at using its assets to generate sales? Microsoft was more efficient in 2005, when each dollar of sales required a lower level of assets.

FYI

A common-size balance sheet can also be prepared using total assets to standardize each amount instead of using total sales, in which case the asset percentages are a good indication of the company's asset mix.

Specific ratios related to asset efficiency have been introduced in earlier chapters. Those ratios will be reviewed in a later section of this chapter.

Common-size financial statements are not a sophisticated analytical tool, and they don't constitute a complete analysis. However, they are the easiest, most intuitive, and fastest tool available, and they should be included in the initial stages of any comprehensive analysis of financial statements.

EXHIBIT 9	Common-Size Balance Sheet for Microsoft

30-Jun	2004		2005	
Assets				
Current assets:				
Cash and equivalents	14,304	38.8%	4,851	12.2%
Short-term investments	46,288	125.7%	32,900	82.7%
Total cash and short-term investments	60,592	164.5%	37,751	94.9%
Accounts receivable, net	5,890	16.0%	7,180	18.0%
Inventories	421	1.1%	491	1.2%
Deferred income taxes	2,097	5.7%	1,701	4.3%
Other	1,566	4.3%	1,614	4.1%
Total current assets	70,566	191.6%	48,737	122.5%
Property and equipment, net	2,326	6.3%	2,346	5.9%
Equity and other investments	12,210	33.1%	11,004	27.7%
Goodwill	3,115	8.5%	3,309	8.3%
Intangible assets, net	569	1.5%	499	1.3%
Deferred income taxes	3,808	10.3%	3,621	9.1%
Other long-term assets	1,774	4.8%	1,299	3.3%
Total assets	94,368	256.2%*	70,815	178.0%*
Liabilities and stockholders' equity				
Current liabilities:				
Accounts payable	1,717	4.7%	2,086	5.2%
Accrued compensation	1,339	3.6%	1,662	4.2%
Income taxes	3,478	9.4%	2,020	5.1%
Short-term unearned revenue	6,514	17.7%	7,502	18.9%
Other	1,921	5.2%	3,607	9.1%
Total current liabilities	14,969	40.6%	16,877	42.4%*
Long-term unearned revenue	1,663	4.5%	1,665	4.2%
Other long-term liabilities	2,911	7.9%	4,158	10.5%
Total liabilities	19,543	53.1%*	22,700	57.1%
Stockholders' equity:				
Common stock and paid-in capital	56,396	153.1%	60,413	151.8%
Retained earnings, including accumulated other comprehensive income of $1,119 and $1,426	18,429	50.0%	(12,298)	(30.9%)
Total stockholders' equity	74,825	203.1%	48,115	120.9%
Total liabilities and stockholders' equity	94,368	256.2%*	70,815	178.0%

*Note: Because of rounding, the percentages don't always add up exactly. This is a minor arithmetic problem that shouldn't get in the way of the analysis.

REMEMBER THIS...

- Common-size financial statements are generated by dividing all financial statement amounts for a given year by sales for that year.

- A common-size income statement reveals the number of pennies of each expense for each dollar of sales.

- The asset section of a common-size balance sheet tells how many pennies of each asset are needed to generate each dollar of sales.

DuPont Framework

As discussed earlier, return on equity (net income ÷ equity) is the single measure that summarizes the financial health of a company. Return on equity can be interpreted as the number of cents of net income an investor earns in one year by investing one dollar in the company. As a very rough rule of thumb, return on equity (ROE) consistently above 15% is a sign of a company in good health; ROE consistently below 15% is a sign of trouble. Return on equity for Microsoft for the years 2005 and 2004 is computed as follows.

	2005	2004
Net income	$12,254	$8,168
Stockholders' equity	$48,115	$74,825
Return on equity	25.5%	10.9%

What can we say about Microsoft's overall performance in 2005? It was good relative to the rough ROE benchmark of 15%, and it increased significantly when compared to the ROE of 2004. But how do we pin down the exact reason or reasons for any change in a company's ROE? The answer is the focus of this section.

The **DuPont framework** (named after a system of ratio analysis developed 70 years ago at DuPont by F. Donaldson Brown) provides a systematic approach to identifying general factors causing ROE to deviate from normal. The DuPont system also provides a framework for computation of financial ratios to yield a more in-depth analysis of a company's areas of strength and weakness. The insight behind the DuPont framework is that ROE can be decomposed into three components as shown in Exhibit 10.

For each of the three ROE components—profitability, efficiency, and leverage—there is one ratio that summarizes a company's performance in that area. These ratios are as follows:

DuPont framework

A systematic approach for breaking down return on equity into three ratios: return on sales, asset turnover, and assets-to-equity ratio.

assets-to-equity ratio

A measure of the number of dollars of assets a company is able to acquire using each dollar of equity; calculated by dividing assets by equity.

- **Return on sales** is computed as net income divided by sales and is interpreted as the number of pennies in profit generated from each dollar of sales.
- **Asset turnover** is computed as sales divided by assets and is interpreted as the number of dollars in sales generated by each dollar of assets.
- **Assets-to-equity ratio** is computed as assets divided by equity and is interpreted as the number of dollars of assets acquired for each dollar invested by stockholders.

The DuPont analysis of Microsoft's ROE for 2005 and 2004 is as follows:

			Profitability	×	Efficiency	×	Leverage
	Return on Equity	=	$\dfrac{\text{Net Income}}{\text{Sales}}$	×	$\dfrac{\text{Sales}}{\text{Assets}}$	×	$\dfrac{\text{Assets}}{\text{Equity}}$
2005	25.5%	=	$\dfrac{\$12{,}254}{\$39{,}788}$	×	$\dfrac{\$39{,}788}{\$70{,}815}$	×	$\dfrac{\$70{,}815}{\$48{,}115}$
		=	30.8%	×	0.56	×	1.47
2004	10.9%	=	$\dfrac{\$8{,}168}{\$36{,}835}$	×	$\dfrac{\$36{,}835}{\$94{,}368}$	×	$\dfrac{\$94{,}368}{\$74{,}825}$
		=	22.2%	×	0.39	×	1.26

EXHIBIT 10	Analysis of ROE Using the DuPont Framework

Return on Equity = Profitability $\times$ Efficiency $\times$ Leverage

= Return on Sales $\times$ Asset Turnover $\times$ Assets-to-Equity Ratio

$$= \frac{\text{Net Income}}{\text{Sales}} \times \frac{\text{Sales}}{\text{Assets}} \times \frac{\text{Assets}}{\text{Equity}}$$

Profitability = The company's ability to generate net income per dollar of sales
Efficiency = The ability of the company to generate sales through the use of assets
Leverage = The degree to which a company uses borrowed funds instead of invested funds

The results of the DuPont analysis suggest that Microsoft's ROE was lower in 2004 for the following reasons:

1. In 2004, each sale was less profitable than in 2005: each dollar of sales produced 30.8¢ of profit in 2005, compared to 22.2¢ in 2004.
2. In 2004, assets were used less efficiently to generate sales: each dollar of assets generated $0.39 in sales in 2004 compared to $0.56 in sales in 2005.

In 2005, Microsoft was also slightly more effective at leveraging stockholders' investment. Through the use of liabilties, Microsoft was able to turn each dollar of invested funds in 2005 into $1.47 of assets, more than the $1.26 in assets in 2004.

The DuPont analysis allows a financial statement user to begin to answer the question of "Why?" Why did a company's return on equity increase (or decrease) during a period? What has been the trend over time in each of the three areas of profitability, efficiency, and leverage? Answers to these questions will allow the user to begin to focus attention on those areas of the business that have experienced changes as reflected in the ratios.

This preliminary DuPont analysis is only the beginning of a proper ratio analysis. If a DuPont analysis suggests problems in any of the three ROE components, additional ratios in each area can shed more light on the exact nature of the problem.

One of the insights behind the DuPont framework is that overall company performance is a function of both the profitability of each sale, measured by return on sales, and the ability to use assets to generate sales, measured by asset turnover. For example, comparing Microsoft and Apple indicates that Microsoft is better than Apple Computer in terms of profitability (2005 return on sales of 30.8% for Microsoft compared to just 9.6% for Apple) but is worse in terms of efficiency (2005 asset turnover of 0.56 for Microsoft and 1.21 for Apple).

Profitability Ratios

When the DuPont calculations indicate that a company has a profitability problem, then a common-size income statement can be used to identify which expenses are causing the problem. Referring back to the common-size income statement in Exhibit 8, cost of goods sold as a percentage of sales was higher in 2004 than in 2005 (18.2% vs. 15.6%). In addition, operating expenses were also higher in 2004 (57.2% compared to just 47.8% in 2005). To summarize, the return on sales indicates overall whether a firm has a problem with the profitability of each dollar of sales; the common-size income statement can be used to pinpoint exactly which expenses are causing the problem.

Efficiency Ratios

The asset turnover ratio suggests that Microsoft was less efficient at using its assets to generate sales in 2004 than it was in 2005. But which assets were causing this decreased efficiency? One way to get a quick indication is to review the common-size balance sheet in Exhibit 9, whose numbers indicate that in 2004 Microsoft had a much higher amount of cash and short-term investments as a percentage of sales (164.5%) than in 2005 (94.9%), suggesting that Microsoft was not using a very large part of the company's assets in an income-producing fashion in 2004.

In addition to the common-size balance sheet, specific financial ratios have been developed to indicate whether a firm is holding too much or too little of a particular asset. Some of these additional ratios were introduced earlier in the text. These efficiency ratios are reviewed later in this chapter.

Leverage Ratios

leverage

Borrowing that allows a company to purchase more assets than its stockholders are able to pay for through their own investment.

Leverage ratios are an indication of the extent to which a company is using other people's money to purchase assets. **Leverage** is borrowing that allows a company to purchase more assets than its stockholders are able to pay for through their own investment. The assets-to-equity ratios for Microsoft for 2004 and 2005 indicate that leverage was higher in 2005 (1.26 in 2004; 1.47 in 2005). Higher leverage increases return on equity through the following chain of events:

- More borrowing means that more assets can be purchased without any additional equity investment by stockholders.
- More assets mean that more sales can be generated.
- More sales mean that net income should increase.

STOP & THINK

Company Z has an assets-to-equity ratio of 2.5. Can you compute what its debt ratio would be?

Investors generally prefer high leverage in order to increase the size of their company without increasing their investment, but lenders prefer low leverage to increase the safety of their debt. The field of corporate finance deals with how to optimally balance these opposing tendencies and choose the perfect capital structure for a firm. As mentioned earlier, a general rule of thumb is that large U.S. companies borrow about half of the funds they use to purchase assets. There are specific ratios that allow financial statement users to analyze the leverage of a firm. Those ratios were introduced in the chapter on debt (Chapter 10). Those ratios are reviewed later in this chapter.

Exhibit 11 show the DuPont framework ratios for a number of familiar companies for 2005.

Note that although **Wal-Mart** has the lowest return on sales, it does have one of the highest returns on equity. The reason becomes readily apparent by looking at the components of return on equity. Wal-Mart has the highest asset turnover of the companies

| EXHIBIT 11 | DuPont Framework Ratios for Selected U.S. Companies |

	ROE	Return on Sales	Asset Turnover	Assets-to-Equity Ratio
Disney	9.7%	7.9%	0.6	2.0
Wal-Mart	21.1%	3.6%	2.3	2.6
Home Depot	21.7%	7.2%	1.8	1.7
Federal Express	13.0%	4.3%	1.5	2.1
Southwest Airlines	8.2%	7.2%	0.5	2.1

© DIGITAL VISION/GETTY IMAGES INC.

Information for financial analysis comes from many sources. Electronic media offer a wealth of information that can be timelier than print sources of financial information.

included in the list as well as having the highest assets-to-equity ratio. Wal-Mart's efficiency and leverage combine to make for a high return on equity.

Remember, the preparation of financial statements by the accountant is not the end of the process but just the beginning. The statements are then analyzed by investors, creditors, and management to detect signs of existing deficiencies in performance and to predict how the firm will perform in the future. As repeated throughout this section, proper interpretation of a ratio depends on comparing the ratio value to the value for the same firm in the previous year and to values for other firms in the same industry. Finally, ratio analysis doesn't reveal the answers to a company's problems, but it does highlight areas in which further information should be gathered to find those answers.

> **REMEMBER THIS...**
>
> The DuPont framework decomposes return on equity (ROE) into three areas:
>
> - **Profitability.** Return on sales is computed as net income divided by sales and is interpreted as the number of pennies in profit generated from each dollar of sales.
> - **Efficiency.** Asset turnover is computed as sales divided by assets and is interpreted as the number of dollars in sales generated by each dollar of assets.
> - **Leverage.** Assets-to-equity ratio is computed as assets divided by equity and is interpreted as the number of dollars of assets a company is able to acquire using each dollar invested by stockholders.

More Efficiency Ratios

Conduct a focused examination of a company's efficiency by using asset-specific ratios.

⑤ In earlier chapters, we learned how accounts receivable turnover, inventory turnover, and fixed asset turnover can be used to measure how efficiently a company is using those assets. Those discussions are summarized in this section. In the preceding sections of this chapter, we have used the financial numbers for Microsoft to illustrate the computation of ratios. Because Microsoft has a relatively low level of inventory and property, plant, and equipment, different company illustrations are used in this section. The two companies that will be used to illustrate the computation of the asset efficiency ratios are **ExxonMobil** and **Chevron**, both in the oil production, refining, and retailing business. Selected financial statement numbers for these two companies for 2005 are as follows:

(in millions of dollars)	ExxonMobil	Chevron
Sales	$370,680	$198,200
Cost of goods sold	185,219	127,968
Accounts receivable (average)	26,422	14,807
Inventory (average)	7,994	2,962
Property, plant, and equipment (average)	107,825	54,074

Accounts Receivable Efficiency

The accounts receivable turnover ratio is a computation of how many times during the year a company is "turning over" or collecting its receivables. It is a measure of how many times old receivables are collected and replaced by new receivables. Accounts receivable turnover is calculated as follows:

$$\text{Accounts Receivable Turnover} = \frac{\text{Sales Revenue}}{\text{Average Accounts Receivable}}$$

The accounts receivable turnover ratios for ExxonMobil and Chevron for 2005 are computed as follows:

$$\text{ExxonMobil} = \frac{\$370,680}{\$26,422} = 14.03 \text{ times}$$

$$\text{Chevron} = \frac{\$198,200}{\$14,807} = 13.39 \text{ times}$$

It appears that ExxonMobil turns its receivables over slightly more frequently than does Chevron.

Accounts receivable turnover can be converted into the number of days it takes to collect receivables by computing average collection period. Average collection period is computed by dividing 365 (or the number of days in a year) by the accounts receivable turnover as follows:

$$\text{Average Collection Period} = \frac{365}{\text{Accounts Receivable Turnover}}$$

The average collection periods for ExxonMobil and Chevron for 2005 are computed as follows:

$$\text{ExxonMobil} = \frac{365}{14.03 \text{ times}} = 26.0 \text{ days}$$

$$\text{Chevron} = \frac{365}{13.39 \text{ times}} = 27.3 \text{ days}$$

The computation of average collection period allows us to more easily see that there really isn't much difference between the receivables collection practices of ExxonMobil and Chevron—ExxonMobil collects its receivables just 1.3 days sooner, on average.

Inventory Efficiency

Inventory turnover provides a measure of how many times a company turns over, or replenishes, its inventory during a year. The calculation is similar to the calculation for accounts receivable turnover.

$$\text{Inventory Turnover} = \frac{\text{Cost of Goods Sold}}{\text{Average Inventory}}$$

The inventory turnover ratios for ExxonMobil and Chevron for 2005 are computed as follows:

$$\text{ExxonMobil} = \frac{\$185,219}{\$7,994} = 23.17 \text{ times}$$

$$\text{Chevron} = \frac{\$127,968}{\$2,962} = 43.20 \text{ times}$$

From these computations we can see that Chevron is managing its level of inventory much more aggressively than is ExxonMobil. Inventory turnover can also be converted into the number of days' sales in inventory. This ratio is computed by dividing 365 by the inventory turnover, as follows:

$$\text{Number of Days' Sales in Inventory} = \frac{365}{\text{Inventory Turnover}}$$

The number of days' sales in inventory for ExxonMobil and Chevron for 2005 are computed as follows:

$$\text{ExxonMobil} = \frac{365}{23.17 \text{ times}} = 15.8 \text{ days}$$

$$\text{Chevron} = \frac{365}{43.20 \text{ times}} = 8.4 \text{ days}$$

ExxonMobil has a level of inventory that is almost twice as large, in terms of the number of days' sales that the inventory level represents, as Chevron's inventory. A deeper understanding of the underlying reasons for this substantial difference would require an in-depth analysis of the specific inventory management practices of the two companies.

Property, Plant, and Equipment Efficiency

Fixed asset turnover can be used to evaluate the appropriateness of the level of a company's property, plant, and equipment. Fixed asset turnover is computed as sales divided by average property, plant, and equipment (fixed assets) and is interpreted as the number of dollars in sales generated by each dollar of fixed assets. This ratio is also often called PP&E turnover. The computations of the fixed asset turnover for ExxonMobil and Chevron are shown below.

$$\text{ExxonMobil} = \frac{\$370,680}{\$107,825} = 3.44 \text{ times}$$

$$\text{Chevron} = \frac{\$198,200}{\$54,074} = 3.67 \text{ times}$$

These fixed asset turnover calculations suggest that Chevron is slightly more efficient at using its property, plant, and equipment to generate sales than is ExxonMobil. However, unlike what we found in our analysis of the two companies' inventory management practices, the difference in fixed asset turnover is relatively small.

REMEMBER THIS...

Ratios to assess the level of accounts receivable:
- Accounts receivable turnover (Sales Revenue ÷ Average Accounts Receivable)
- Average collection period (365 ÷ Accounts Receivable Turnover)

Ratios to assess the level of inventory:
- Inventory turnover (Cost of Goods Sold ÷ Average Inventory)
- Number of days' sales in inventory (365 ÷ Inventory Turnover)

Ratio to assess the level of property, plant, and equipment:
- Fixed asset turnover (Sales Revenue ÷ Average Property, Plant, and Equipment)

More Leverage Ratios

Determine the degree of a company's financial leverage and its ability to repay loans using debt-related financial ratios.

6 As we saw in our consideration of the DuPont framework earlier in this chapter, the amount of a company's financial leverage has a direct impact on that company's return on equity—the higher the leverage, the higher the return on equity. One leverage-related ratio, the debt ratio, was discussed earlier in this chapter in the section on widely-used ratios. This section reviews the debt-to-equity ratio and the times interest earned ratio which were first introduced in Chapter 10. As with the preceding section on efficiency ratios, 2005 financial statement information for ExxonMobil and Chevron will be used to illustrate the computation of these ratios. That information is given below.

(in millions of dollars)	ExxonMobil	Chevron
Total assets	$208,335	$125,833
Total liabilities	97,149	63,157
Total stockholders' equity	111,186	62,676
Operating profit	59,928	25,679
Interest expense	496	482

Debt-to-Equity Ratio

The debt-to-equity ratio reflects the mix of sources of financing for a company. This ratio is calculated by dividing total liabilities by total stockholders' equity. The ratio has a value of 1.0 if the amount of borrowing is exactly equal to the amount of stockholder investment. The higher the debt-to-equity ratio, the more debt the company has. The debt-to-equity ratios for ExxonMobil and Chevron for 2005 are computed as follows:

$$\text{ExxonMobil} = \frac{\$97,149}{\$111,186} = 0.87$$

$$\text{Chevron} = \frac{\$63,157}{\$62,676} = 1.01$$

Chevron's liabilities are a little higher than its stockholders' equity yielding a debt-to-equity ratio of 1.01. Another way to view this is that Chevron has borrowed a little bit more than half of its total financing needs which is a somewhat higher proportion than what ExxonMobil has borrowed.

Students are frequently confused about the differences among the debt ratio, the debt-to-equity ratio, and the assets-to-equity ratio. All three of these ratios represent the same thing—the relationship between the amount of a company's borrowing and the amount of a company's stockholder investment. However, because each of the ratios is computed a little differently, the resulting numbers are not comparable. This is exactly analogous to the interpretation of temperatures from different scales. A temperature of 0° on the Celsius scale corresponds to 32° on the Fahrenheit scale. If someone tells you that the temperature is 40°, in order to interpret that information you first need to know what temperature scale is being used—40° on the Celsius scale is a lot different from 40° on the Fahrenheit scale. Similarly, a debt-related ratio of 1.00 (or 100%) means the following very different things for each of the three debt-related ratios mentioned above.

- Debt-to-equity ratio—A ratio value of 1.00 means that total liabilities and total stockholders' equity are equal.
- Debt ratio—A ratio value of 1.00, or 100%, means that ALL of the company's financing has come from debt and that there is no stockholder investment at all.
- Assets-to-equity ratio—A ratio value of 1.00 means that total assets and total stockholders' equity are equal to each other, implying that there are no liabilities.

Whenever you see a computed value for a debt-related ratio, make sure that you first know what formula was used in computing the ratio before you start to interpret the meaning of the ratio value.

Times Interest Earned Ratio

Lenders like to have an indication of the borrowing company's ability to meet the required interest payments. Times interest earned is the ratio of the income that is available for interest payments to the annual interest expense. Times interest earned is computed as follows:

$$\text{Times Interest Earned} = \frac{\text{Income Before Interest and Taxes (Operating Profit)}}{\text{Annual Interest Expense}}$$

The times interest earned ratios for ExxonMobil and Chevron for 2005 are computed as follows:

$$\text{ExxonMobil} = \frac{\$59,928}{\$496} = 120.8 \text{ times}$$

$$\text{Chevron} = \frac{\$25,679}{\$482} = 53.3 \text{ times}$$

Both of these ratio values are very high indicating that the lenders who have loaned money to ExxonMobil or to Chevron have no reason to doubt that the two companies will be able to continue to make their interest payments in the future.

REMEMBER THIS...

- The debt ratio, the debt-to-equity ratio, and the assets-to-equity ratio all measure the level of a company's leverage.
  - Debt ratio = Total liabilities divided by total assets
  - Debt-to-equity ratio = Total liabilities divided by total stockholders' equity
  - Assets-to-equity ratio = Total assets divided by total stockholders' equity
- The times interest earned ratio (operating income divided by interest expense) measures how much cushion a company has in terms of being able to make its periodic interest payments.

Cash Flow Ratios

Use cash flow information to evaluate cash flow ratios.

7 The requirement that companies provide a cash flow statement is very recent (since 1988), especially when you remember that double-entry accounting itself is over 500 years old. Because the cash flow statement is relatively new, it often fails to get the emphasis it deserves as one of the three primary financial statements. Most of the age-old tools of financial statement analysis, such as the DuPont framework, do not incorporate cash flow data. Accordingly, information from the cash flow statement is not yet ingrained in the analytical tradition, but it will be. In fact, one way to impress others that you are a modern, well-trained, future-looking professional is to become proficient in analyzing cash flow data.

Usefulness of Cash Flow Ratios

Analysis of cash flow information is especially important in those situations in which net income does not give an accurate picture of the economic performance of a company. Three such situations are discussed briefly below.

Large Noncash Expenses When a company reports large noncash expenses, such as write-offs and depreciation, earnings may give a gloomier picture of current operations than is warranted. In fact, a company may report record losses in the same years it is reporting positive cash flow from operations. In such cases, cash flow from operations is a better indicator of whether the company can continue to honor its commitments to creditors, customers, employees, and investors in the near term. Don't misunderstand this to mean that a reported loss is nothing to worry about so long as cash flow is positive: the positive cash flow indicates that business can continue for the time being, but the reported loss may hint at looming problems in the future. As an example, consider the case of **AOL Time Warner** (now called just **Time Warner**). In 2002, the company reported the largest net loss in the history of American business—$98.7 billion. However, much of that loss related to the impairment of certain assets—a noncash expenditure for the year. For 2002, AOL Time Warner reported a positive cash flow from operations of $7 billion.

> **FYI**
>
> Although net income may sometimes paint a misleading picture of a company's performance, in most cases net income is the single best measure of a firm's economic performance.

Rapid Growth Cash flow analysis is also a valuable tool for evaluating rapidly growing companies that use large amounts of cash to expand inventory. In addition, cash collections on growing accounts receivable often lag behind the need to pay creditors. In these cases, reported earnings may be positive but operations are actually consuming rather than generating cash. For example, **Pixar**, the company that has produced such films as *Toy Story* and *Monsters, Inc.*, experienced revenue growth in 2002 of 77%. The company reported record net income in 2002 of $90 million. However, cash flow from operations was a negative $4.5 million. The message: For high-growth companies, positive earnings are no guarantee that sufficient cash flows are there to service current needs.

Window Dressing Time Cash flow analysis offers important insights into companies that are striving to present a stellar financial record. Accrual accounting involves making assumptions in order to adjust raw cash flow data into a better measure of economic performance—net income. For companies entering phases in which it's critical that reported earnings look good, accounting assumptions and adjustments can be stretched—sometimes to the breaking point. Such phases include the period just before a company applies for a large loan, just before an initial public offering of stock (when founding entrepreneurs cash in all those years of struggle and sweat), and just before a company is being bought out by another company. In these cases, cash flow from operations, which is not impacted by accrual assumptions, provides an excellent reality check for reported earnings.

To illustrate the computation of selected cash flow ratios, the data in Exhibit 12 from Microsoft's 2005 and 2004 financial statements are used.

Cash Flow to Net Income

Perhaps the most important cash flow relationship is that between cash from operations and reported net income. The **cash flow-to-net income ratio** reflects the extent to which accrual accounting assumptions and adjustments have been

cash flow-to-net income ratio

A ratio that reflects the extent to which accrual accounting assumptions and adjustments have been included in computing net income.

EXHIBIT 12	Selected Cash Flow Data for Microsoft for 2005 and 2004*		
		2005	**2004**
Net income		$12,254	$ 8,168
Cash from operations		16,605	14,626
Cash paid for capital expenditures		1,019	1,113

*All amounts are in millions of dollars.

included in computing net income. For Microsoft, computation of the cash flow-to-net income ratio (in millions of dollars) is as follows:

	2005	**2004**
Cash from operations	$16,605	$14,626
Net income	$12,254	$8,168
Cash flow-to-net income ratio	1.36	1.79

STOP & THINK

Can you think of some accrual accounting adjustments that might cause a difference between net income and cash from operations?

In general, the cash flow-to-net income ratio will have a value greater than one because of significant noncash expenses (such as depreciation) that reduce reported net income but have no impact on cash flow. For a given company, the cash flow-to-net income ratio should remain fairly stable from year to year. A significant change in the ratio indicates that accounting assumptions were instrumental in reducing reported net income.

cash flow adequacy ratio

Cash from operations divided by expenditures for fixed asset additions and acquisitions of new businesses.

Cash Flow Adequacy

A "cash cow" is a business that is generating enough cash from operations to completely pay for all new plant and equipment purchases with cash left over to repay loans or distribute to investors. The **cash flow adequacy ratio**, computed as cash from operations divided by expenditures for fixed asset additions and acquisitions of new businesses, indicates whether a business is a cash cow. Computation of the cash flow adequacy ratio for Microsoft is as follows:

	2005	**2004**
Cash from operations	$16,605	$14,626
Cash paid for capital expenditures	$1,019	$1,113
Cash flow adequacy ratio	16.30	13.14

The calculations indicate that in 2005 and in 2004 Microsoft's cash from operations was sufficient to pay for its capital expansion with something left over. This means that Microsoft could pay for its expansion without incurring any new debt or seeking funds from investors. It would be fair to say that Microsoft could be considered a cash cow. 2005 cash flow ratios for a group of companies are presented in Exhibit 13.

Southwest Airlines reports cash flow from operations as being more than four times its reported net income. In addition, all of the companies in the list each generated

EXHIBIT 13	2005 Cash Flow Ratios for Selected U.S. Companies	
	Cash Flow/ Net Income	Cash Flow Adequacy Ratio
Disney	1.7	2.4
Wal-Mart	1.6	1.2
Home Depot	1.1	1.0
Federal Express	2.0	1.4
Southwest Airlines	4.1	1.8

 F Y I

Cash paid for dividends is sometimes added to the denominator of the cash flow adequacy ratio. With this formulation, the ratio indicates whether operating cash flow is sufficient to pay for both capital additions and regular dividends to stockholders.

enough cash flow from operations in 2005 to more than pay for all their capital expenditures for the year.

Remember that cash flow ratios fall outside many financial statement analysis models because the cash flow statement hasn't been around long enough to work its way into traditional models. Rebel against tradition and don't forget cash flow!

REMEMBER THIS...

- Because the statement of cash flows is a relatively recent requirement, time-tested ratios using information from that statement are still developing.
- Cash flow ratios are useful in that they can identify instances where accrual basis accounting measures are not providing a complete picture.
- The ratio of cash flow to net income highlights when there are significant differences between cash from operations and net income.
- The cash flow adequacy ratio demonstrates a company's ability to finance its capital expansion through cash from operations.

Potential Pitfalls

Understand the limitations of financial statement analysis.

8 Financial statement analysis, as emphasized previously, usually does not give answers but instead points in directions where further investigation is needed. This section discusses several reasons why we must be careful not to place too much weight on an analysis of financial statement numbers themselves.

Financial Statements Don't Contain All Information

Accountants, including the authors, should be forgiven for mistakenly thinking that all knowledge in the universe can be summarized in numerical form in financial statements. Accountants love numbers, they love things that balance, and they love condensing and summarizing the complexity of business—in short, accountants love financial statements. Businesspeople don't have this emotional relationship with financial statements and therefore should be able to take a more detached view. Businesspeople should remember that financial statements represent just one part of the information spectrum. Microsoft's financial statements, for example, tell nothing about the morale of Microsoft's employees, about new products being developed in Microsoft's research laboratories, or about the strategic plans of Microsoft's competitors. In addition, as discussed in Chapter 2, many valuable economic assets, such as the value of a company's own homegrown reputation, brand recognition, and customer loyalty, are not recognized in financial statements. The danger in financial statement analysis is that, in computing dozens of ratios and comparing common-size financial statements across years and among competitors, we can forget there is lots of decision-relevant information to be found *outside* financial statements. Don't let the attractiveness of the apparent precision of financial statement numbers distract you from searching for all relevant information, no matter how imprecise and nonquantitative.

Lack of Comparability

Ratio analysis is most meaningful when ratios can be benchmarked to comparable values for the same company in prior years and to ratio values for other companies in the same industry. A problem arises when reported financial statement numbers that seem to be comparable are actually measurements of different things. For example, some companies list depreciation expense separately and include advertising expense as part of selling, general, and administrative expense whereas others do not list depreciation expense separately but do report a separate line for advertising expense. This classification difference makes it more difficult to compare the income statements of the two companies.

conglomerates

A company comprised of a number of divisions with those divisions often operating in different industries.

Another benchmarking difficulty arises because many large U.S. companies are **conglomerates**, meaning that they are composed of divisions operating in different industries, sometimes quite unrelated to one another. Throughout this chapter **Apple Computer**, for example, was used as a benchmark competitor for **Microsoft**, but in addition to operating in the software industry, Apple is also heavily involved in the computer hardware business. Thus, a true benchmark firm for Microsoft would be to use (if available) only the results for the software segment of Apple Computer.

Finally, comparison difficulties arise because all companies don't use the same accounting practices. Companies can choose different methods of computing depreciation expense, cost of goods sold, and bad debt expense. Some companies report leased assets as part of property, plant, and equipment in the balance sheet, and some companies don't report leased assets anywhere at all on the balance sheet.

Search for the Smoking Gun

Financial case studies are very useful and fun because they allow students to discover key business insights for themselves in the context of real situations. When analyzing a case, one feels a bit like Sherlock Holmes scouring financial statements to see whether a company's problems are caused by poor inventory management, short-sighted tax planning, or growing difficulties collecting receivables. This detective mentality can be counterproductive, however, because not every company you analyze is going to be a candidate for a Harvard Business School case that illustrates one particular management principle. For example, not every company suffering from poor profitability has one stupendous flaw that will leap out at you as you do your ratio analysis. If you focus too much on trying to "solve" the case and find the smoking gun, you may overlook indications of a collection of less spectacular problems.

Anchoring, Adjustment, and Timeliness

Financial statements are based on historical data. A large part of the value of this historical data lies in its ability to indicate how a company will perform in the future. The danger in performing ratio analysis on several years of past data is that we might then tend to focus on the company's past performance and ignore current year information. All of the analysis performed in this chapter using historical data for Microsoft for 2005 and before may tell us less about Microsoft's operating position than the news that Microsoft and the U.S. Department of Justice had reached an agreement on a three-year-old antitrust dispute. The careful analyst must balance what he or she learns from an analysis of historical financial statement data with more current data available from different sources.

REMEMBER THIS . .

- There is more to a company and its future than just the information contained in the financial statements.
- Care must be taken to ensure that when comparing financial statement information across time or across companies at the same point in time, that similar accounting practices have been used.
- Care must be taken to ensure that current information is included when analyzing past data.

REVIEW OF LEARNING OBJECTIVES

1 Explain the purpose of financial statement analysis.

- Financial statement analysis is used:
  - to predict a company's future profitability and cash flows from its past performance and
  - to evaluate the performance of a company with an eye toward identifying problem areas.
- The informativeness of financial ratios is greatly enhanced when they are compared:
  - with past values and
  - with values for other firms in the same industry.

2 Understand the relationships between financial statement numbers and use ratios in analyzing and describing a company's performance. Six of the most commonly used financial ratios are as follows:

- **Debt ratio:** Percentage of company funding that is borrowed.
- **Current ratio:** Indication of a company's ability to pay its short-term debts.
- **Return on sales:** Pennies in profit on each dollar of sales.
- **Asset turnover:** Measure of efficiency; number of sales dollars generated by each dollar of assets.
- **Return on equity:** Pennies in profit for each dollar invested by stockholders.
- **Price-earnings ratio:** Number of dollars an investor must pay to "buy" the future rights to each dollar of current earnings.

3 Use common-size financial statements to perform comparison of financial statements across years and between companies.

- Common-size financial statements are the easiest, most intuitive, and fastest tool available for starting an analysis of a company's financial statements.

- A common-size income statement reveals the number of pennies of each expense for each dollar of sales.
- The asset section of a common-size balance sheet tells how many pennies of each asset are needed to generate each dollar of sales.

(4) Understand the DuPont framework and how return on equity can be decomposed into its profitability, efficiency, and leverage components. The DuPont framework decomposes return on equity (ROE) into three areas:

- **Profitability:** Return on sales is computed as net income divided by sales and is interpreted as the number of pennies in profit generated from each dollar of sales.
- **Efficiency:** Asset turnover is computed as sales divided by assets and is interpreted as the number of dollars in sales generated by each dollar of assets.
- **Leverage:** Assets-to-equity ratio is computed as assets divided by equity and is interpreted as the number of dollars of assets a company is able to acquire using each dollar invested by stockholders.

(5) Conduct a focused examination of a company's efficiency by using asset-specific ratios.

	Ratios	Formulas
Accounts Receivable	• Accounts Receivable Turnover • Average Collection Period	• Sales ÷ Average Accounts Receivable • 365 ÷ Accounts Receivable Turnover
Inventory	• Inventory Turnover • Number of Days' Sales in Inventory	• Cost of Goods Sold ÷ Average Inventory • 365 ÷ Inventory Turnover
Property, Plant, and Equipment	• Fixed Asset Turnover	• Sales ÷ Average Property, Plant, and Equipment

(6) Determine the degree of a company's financial leverage and its ability to repay loans using debt-related financial ratios.

- The debt ratio, the debt-to-equity ratio, and the assets-to-equity ratio all measure the level of a company's leverage.
  - Debt ratio = Total liabilities divided by total assets
  - Debt-to-equity ratio = Total liabilities divided by total stockholders' equity
  - Assets-to-equity ratio = Total assets divided by total stockholders' equity
- The times interest earned ratio (operating income divided by interest expense) measures how much cushion a company has in terms of being able to make its periodic interest payments.

(7) Use cash flow information to evaluate cash flow ratios.

- Cash flow ratios are particularly useful:
  - when net income is impacted by large noncash expenses,
  - when rapid growth causes cash from operations to be much less than reported net income, and
  - when company management has a strong incentive to bias reported net income in order to get a loan or issue shares at a favorable price.
- The ratio of cash flow to net income highlights when there are significant differences between cash from operations and net income.
- The cash flow adequacy ratio demonstrates a company's ability to finance its capital expansion through cash from operations.

⑧ **Understand the limitations of financial statement analysis.** Financial statement analysis usually does not provide answers but only points out areas in which more information should be gathered.

We must be careful not to base a decision solely on an analysis of financial statement numbers because:

- financial statements don't contain all the relevant information;

- financial statements sometimes can't be properly compared among companies because of differences in classification, industry mix, and accounting methods;

- most sets of financial statements will not reveal a smoking gun that, if fixed, will solve all of a company's problems; and

- focusing on historical financial statement data may cause us to overlook important current information.

KEY TERMS & CONCEPTS

asset turnover, 672

assets-to-equity ratio, 679

cash flow adequacy ratio, 688

cash flow-to-net income ratio, 687

common-size financial statements, 676

conglomerates, 690

current ratio, 672

debt ratio, 671

DuPont framework, 679

financial ratios, 669

financial statement analysis, 669

leverage, 681

liquidity, 671

price-earnings ratio, 673

return on equity, 673

return on sales, 672

REVIEW PROBLEM

Financial Statement Analysis

The comparative income statements and balance sheets for Montana Corporation for the years ending December 31, 2009 and 2008, are given here.

Montana Corporation Income Statements For the Years Ended December 31, 2009 and 2008		
	2009	**2008**
Net sales	$600,000	$575,000
Cost of goods sold	500,000	460,000
Gross margin	$100,000	$115,000
Expenses:		
Selling and administrative expenses	$ 66,000	$ 60,000
Interest expense	4,000	3,000
Total expenses	$ 70,000	$ 63,000
Income before taxes	$ 30,000	$ 52,000
Income taxes	12,000	21,000
Net income	$ 18,000	$ 31,000
Earnings per share	$1.80	$3.10

(continued)

Montana Corporation
Balance Sheets
December 31, 2009 and 2008

	2009	2008
Assets		
Current assets:		
Cash	$ 11,000	$ 13,000
Accounts receivable (net)	92,000	77,000
Inventory	103,000	92,000
Prepaid expenses	6,000	5,000
Total current assets	$212,000	$187,000
Property, plant, and equipment:		
Land and building	$ 61,000	$ 59,000
Machinery and equipment	172,000	156,000
Total property, plant, and equipment	$233,000	$215,000
Less accumulated depreciation	113,000	102,000
Net property, plant, and equipment	$120,000	$113,000
Other assets	$ 8,000	$ 7,000
Total assets	$340,000	$307,000
Liabilities and Stockholders' Equity		
Current liabilities:		
Accounts payable	$ 66,000	$ 55,000
Notes payable	–	23,000
Dividends payable	2,000	–
Income taxes payable	3,000	5,000
Total current liabilities	$ 71,000	$ 83,000
Long-term debt	75,000	42,000
Total liabilities	$146,000	$125,000
Stockholders' equity:		
Common stock ($1 par)	$ 10,000	$ 10,000
Paid-in capital in excess of par	16,000	16,000
Retained earnings	168,000	156,000
Total stockholders' equity	$194,000	$182,000
Total liabilities and stockholders' equity	$340,000	$307,000
Additional information:		
Dividends declared in 2009		$6,000
Market price per share, December 31, 2009		$14.50
Cash Flow Information:		
Cash from operations for 2009		$11,000
Cash paid for capital expenditures for 2009		$19,000

Required:

Prepare a comprehensive financial statement analysis of Montana Corporation for 2009. Note that though financial statement analysts usually compare data from two or more years, we are more concerned here with the methods of analysis than the results, so we will use only one year, 2009.

(continued)

Solution

1. Key Relationships

The computation of the four key ratios for 2009 provides the analyst with an overall view of the company's performance and gives an indication of how well management performed with respect to operations, asset turnover, and debt-equity management.

Computation of Key Ratios (2009)

Operating Performance		Asset Turnover		Debt-Equity Management		Return on Stockholders' Equity
$\dfrac{\text{Net Income}}{\text{Net Sales}}$	$\times$	$\dfrac{\text{Net Sales}}{\text{Average Total Assets}}$	$\times$	$\dfrac{\text{Average Total Assets}}{\text{Average Stockholders' Equity}}$	$=$	$\dfrac{\text{Net Income}}{\text{Average Stockholders' Equity}}$
$\dfrac{\$18,000}{\$600,000}$	$\times$	$\dfrac{\$600,000}{\$323,500}$	$\times$	$\dfrac{\$323,500}{\$188,000}$	$=$	$\dfrac{\$18,000}{\$188,000}$
3.00%	$\times$	1.85 times	$\times$	1.72 times	$=$	9.57%*

*The factors do not multiply to the product because of rounding.

2. Analysis of Operating Performance

Operating performance is measured by means of vertical and horizontal analyses of the income statement.

Vertical analysis of the income statement: When the income statement is analyzed vertically, net sales is set at 100%, and each expense and net income are shown as percentages of net sales.

Montana Corporation
Vertical Analysis of Income Statement
For the Year Ended December 31, 2009

Net sales	$600,000	100.0%
Cost of goods sold	500,000	83.3
Gross margin	$100,000	16.7%
Expenses:		
Selling and administrative expenses	$ 66,000	11.0%
Interest expense	4,000	0.7
Total expenses	$ 70,000	11.7%
Income before taxes	$ 30,000	5.0%
Income taxes	12,000	2.0
Net income	$ 18,000	3.0%

(continued)

3. Analysis of Asset Turnover and Utilization

Asset turnover and utilization are analyzed by performing vertical analysis of the balance sheet.

Montana Corporation
Vertical Analysis of the Balance Sheet (as a % of sales)
December 31, 2009

Assets

Current assets:

Cash	$ 11,000	1.8%
Accounts receivable (net)	92,000	15.3
Inventory	103,000	17.2
Prepaid expenses	6,000	1.0
Total current assets	$212,000	35.3%

Property, plant, and equipment:

Land and building	$ 61,000	10.2%
Machinery and equipment	172,000	28.7
Total property, plant, and equipment	$233,000	38.8%*
Less accumulated depreciation	113,000	18.8
Net property, plant, and equipment	$120,000	20.0%
Other assets	$ 8,000	1.3%
Total assets	$340,000	56.7%*

Liabilities and Stockholders' Equity

Current liabilities:

Accounts payable	$ 66,000	11.0%
Dividends payable	2,000	0.3
Income taxes payable	3,000	0.5
Total current liabilities	$ 71,000	11.8%
Long-term debt	75,000	12.5
Total liabilities	$146,000	24.3%
Stockholders' equity	194,000	32.3
Total liabilities and stockholders' equity	$340,000	56.7%*

*Note: Because of rounding, the percentages don't always add up exactly.

4. Common Ratios

a. Debt Ratio:

$$\frac{\text{Total Liabilities}}{\text{Total Assets}} = \frac{\$146,000}{\$340,000} = 42.9\%$$

b. Current Ratio:

$$\frac{\text{Current Assets}}{\text{Current Liabilities}} = \frac{\$212,000}{\$71,000} = 2.99$$

c. Return on Sales:

$$\frac{\text{Net Income}}{\text{Net Sales}} = \frac{\$18,000}{\$600,000} = 0.03$$

d. Asset Turnover Ratio:

$$\frac{\text{Net Sales}}{\text{Average Total Assets}} = \frac{\$600,000}{\dfrac{\$340,000 + \$307,000}{2}} = \frac{\$600,000}{\$323,500} = 1.85$$

(continued)

e. Return on Stockholders' Equity:

$$\frac{\text{Net Income}}{\text{Average Stockholders' Equity}} = \frac{\$18,000}{\dfrac{\$194,000 + \$182,000}{2}} = \frac{\$18,000}{\$188,000} = 9.6\%$$

f. Price-Earnings Ratio:

$$\frac{\text{Market Price per Share}}{\text{Earnings per Share}} = \frac{\$14.50}{\$1.80} = 8.1$$

DISCUSSION QUESTIONS

1. Financial statement analysis can be used to identify a company's weak areas so that management can work toward improvement. Can financial statement analysis be used for any other purpose? Explain.
2. "An analysis of a company's financial ratios reveals the underlying reasons for the company's problems." Do you agree or disagree? Explain.
3. What benchmarks can be used to add meaning to a computed financial ratio value?
4. What characteristic of a company does current ratio measure?
5. Company A has a return on sales of 6%. Is this a high value for return on sales?
6. How does the price-earnings ratio differ from most other financial ratios?
7. What is a common-size financial statement? What are its advantages?
8. What other types of information should be gathered if an analysis of common-size financial statements suggests that a company has problems?
9. What is the most informative section of the common-size balance sheet? Explain.
10. What is the purpose of the DuPont framework?
11. Identify the three ROE components represented in the DuPont framework and tell what ratio

summarizes a company's performance in each area.
12. What further analysis can be done if the DuPont calculations suggest that a company has a profitability problem?
13. What can the inventory turnover ratio tell us?
14. How is fixed asset turnover calculated, and what does the resulting ratio value mean?
15. What does the debt-to-equity ratio measure?
16. From the standpoint of a lender, which is more attractive: a high times interest earned ratio or a low times interest earned ratio? Explain.
17. Why are cash flow ratios often excluded from financial analysis models?
18. Why is it especially important to look at cash flow data when examining a firm that is preparing to make an application for a large loan?
19. What does it mean when the value of a company's cash flow adequacy ratio is less than one?
20. What factors can reduce comparability among financial statements?
21. What is the danger in focusing a financial analysis solely on the data found in the historical financial statements?

PRACTICE EXERCISES

PE 14-1   **What Is a Financial Ratio?**
LO1   Choose the letter of the correct answer. A financial ratio is a
     a. key source of external financing for most publicly-traded companies.
     b. relationship between financial statement amounts.
     c. stockbroker who performs financial statement analysis.
     d. trend in a number over time.
     e. complete set of the three primary financial statements.

PE 14-2   **Usefulness of Financial Ratios**

LO1   Choose the letter of the correct answer. The usefulness of financial ratios is greatly enhanced when the values are

a. computed by the SEC.

b. compared to values for companies in different industries.

c. compared to past values of the same ratio for the same company.

d. compared to the retained earnings balance.

e. included in the body of the statement of cash flows.

PE 14-3   **Financial Ratios Defined**

LO2   Write the formula for computing each of the following financial ratios.

a. Debt ratio

b. Current ratio

c. Return on sales

d. Asset turnover

e. Return on equity

f. Price-earnings ratio

PE 14-4   **Debt Ratio**

LO2   Using the following data, compute the debt ratio.

Accounts Payable	$ 2,400
Accounts Receivable	6,750
Building	65,000
Cash	2,100
Capital Stock	26,150
Inventory	4,100
Land	14,000
Long-Term Notes Payable	32,000
Market Value of Equity	103,000
Net Income	9,000
Retained Earnings (ending)	24,000
Sales	86,000
Short-Term Notes Payable	5,700
Stockholders' Equity	50,150
Unearned Revenue	1,700

PE 14-5   **Current Ratio**

LO2   Refer to the data in PE 14-4. Compute the current ratio.

PE 14-6   **Return on Sales**

LO2   Refer to the data in PE 14-4. Compute return on sales.

PE 14-7   **Asset Turnover**

LO2   Refer to the data in PE 14-4. Compute asset turnover.

PE 14-8   **Return on Equity**

LO2   Refer to the data in PE 14-4. Compute return on equity.

PE 14-9   **Price-Earnings Ratio**

LO2   Refer to the data in PE 14-4. Compute the price-earnings ratio.

PE 14-10
LO3

Common-Size Income Statement

Using the following data, prepare a common-size income statement.

Sales		$75,000
Cost of goods sold		40,000
Gross profit		$35,000
Operating expenses:		
Sales and marketing	$3,000	
General and administrative	8,000	
Total operating expenses		11,000
Operating income		$24,000
Interest expense		4,000
Income before income taxes		$20,000
Income tax expense		3,500
Net income		$16,500

PE 14-11
LO3

Comparative Common-Size Income Statements

Using the following data, (1) prepare comparative common-size income statements for Years 1 and 2 and (2) briefly outline why return on sales is lower in Year 2 (1.8%) compared to Year 1 (7.0%).

	Year 2	Year 1
Sales	$100,000	$80,000
Cost of goods sold	70,000	50,000
Gross profit	$ 30,000	$30,000
Operating expenses	25,000	20,000
Operating income	$ 5,000	$10,000
Interest expense	2,000	2,000
Income before income taxes	$ 3,000	$ 8,000
Income tax expense	1,200	2,400
Net income	$ 1,800	$ 5,600

PE 14-12
LO3

Common-Size Balance Sheet

Using the following data, prepare a common-size balance sheet. Sales for the year were $75,000.

Assets		
Current assets:		
Cash	$4,800	
Accounts receivable	9,300	
Inventory	6,000	
Total current assets		$20,100
Property, plant, and equipment (net)		33,000
Goodwill		5,700
Total assets		$58,800
Liabilities and stockholders' equity		
Current liabilities:		
Accounts payable	$7,200	
Unearned revenue	3,800	
Total current liabilities		$11,000
Long-term debt		18,000
Total liabilities		$29,000
Capital stock		15,000
Retained earnings		14,800
Total liabilities and stockholders' equity		$58,800

PE 14-13   **Common-Size Balance Sheet Standardized Using Total Assets**
LO3

Refer to the data in PE 14-12. Prepare a common-size balance sheet using total assets to standardize each amount instead of using total sales.

PE 14-14   **Comparative Common-Size Balance Sheets**
LO3

Using the following data, (1) prepare comparative common-size balance sheets for Years 1 and 2 (standardized by sales) and (2) briefly outline any significant changes from Year 1 to Year 2. Sales for Year 1 were $80,000, and sales for Year 2 were $100,000.

	Year 2	Year 1
Assets		
Cash	$ 4,000	$ 3,200
Accounts receivable	8,000	6,400
Inventory	17,000	15,000
Property, plant, and equipment (net)	25,000	25,000
Total assets	$54,000	$49,600
Liabilities and stockholders' equity		
Accounts payable	$ 9,000	$ 7,200
Long-term debt	20,000	20,000
Total liabilities	$29,000	$27,200
Capital stock	15,000	15,000
Retained earnings	10,000	7,400
Total liabilities and stockholders' equity	$54,000	$49,600

PE 14-15   **DuPont Framework Defined**
LO4

(1) List the three ratios that combine to form the DuPont framework. Also list the formulas used to compute each ratio. (2) Give a brief intuitive explanation of the interpretation of the values of each of the three ratios.

PE 14-16   **Computation of Return on Equity Using the DuPont Framework**
LO4

Using the following DuPont framework ratios, compute return on equity for Year 1, Year 2, and Year 3.

	Year 3	Year 2	Year 1
Return on sales	25.9%	23.4%	22.5%
Asset turnover	0.71	0.67	0.60
Assets-to-equity ratio	1.52	1.45	1.20

PE 14-17   **Analysis of Return on Equity Using the DuPont Framework**
LO4

Refer to the data in PE 14-16. Briefly explain why the company's return on equity increased from Year 1 to Year 3.

PE 14-18   **DuPont Framework Computations**
LO4

Using the following data, compute return on equity, return on sales, asset turnover, and the assets-to-equity ratio.

Total assets	$120,000
Interest expense	$5,000
Total stockholders' equity	$70,000
Sales	$190,000
Net income	$17,000
Total liabilities	$50,000
Market value of equity	$112,000
Current ratio	2.48

PE 14-19
LO4

DuPont Framework Computations

Using the following data, compute return on equity, return on sales, asset turnover, and the assets-to-equity ratio.

Sales	$450,000
Cash flow from operating activities	$12,000
Net income	$20,000
Total assets	$300,000
Total liabilities	$120,000
Price-earnings ratio	17.4

PE 14-20
LO4

DuPont Framework Intuition Test

Return on equity can be computed by dividing net income by stockholders' equity. It can also be computed by multiplying return on sales, asset turnover, and the assets-to-equity ratio. Using the definitions of the various ratios, show why both of these approaches yield the same answer.

PE 14-21
LO5

Accounts Receivable Turnover

Using the following data, calculate the company's accounts receivable turnover.

Accounts receivable balance, December 31	$ 54,000
Inventory balance, December 31	59,000
Sales revenue	520,000
Cost of goods sold	310,000
Accounts receivable balance, January 1	46,000

PE 14-22
LO5

Average Collection Period

Refer to the data in PE 14-21. Calculate the company's average collection period.

PE 14-23
LO5

Inventory Turnover

Using the following data, compute inventory turnover.

Inventory, December 31, year 1	$ 82,000
Cost of goods sold	342,000
Sales	694,000
Inventory, January 1, year 1	74,000

PE 14-24
LO5

Number of Days' Sales in Inventory

Refer to the data in PE 14-23. Compute number of days' sales in inventory.

PE 14-25
LO5

Fixed Asset Turnover

Using the following data, compute the fixed asset turnover.

Current assets, end of year	$ 35,000
Fixed assets, end of year	180,000
Fixed assets, beginning of year	195,000
Sales during the year	595,000

PE 14-26
LO6

Debt Ratio

Using the following information, compute the debt ratio.

Total liabilities	$247,500
Annual interest expense	5,204
Total assets	542,850
Income before interest and taxes	62,030

PE 14-27   **Debt-to-Equity Ratio**

LO6   Refer to the data in PE 14-26. Compute the debt-to-equity ratio.

PE 14-28   **Times Interest Earned Ratio**

LO6   Refer to the data in PE 14-26. Compute the times interest earned ratio.

PE 14-29   **When Operating Cash Flow Information Is Particularly Valuable**

LO7   Which one of the following is *not* a situation in which cash flow data can provide a better picture of a company's economic performance than does net income?

a. A company preparing for an initial public offering.

b. A company experiencing rapid growth.

c. A company reporting large noncash expenses.

d. A company with high asset turnover.

e. A company preparing to apply for a large loan.

PE 14-30   **Cash Flow-to-Net Income Ratio**

LO7   Using the following data, compute the cash flow-to-net income ratio.

Total revenues	$225,000
Cash expenses	98,000
Noncash expenses	111,000
Cash paid for capital expenditures	48,000
Cash from operations	25,000

PE 14-31   **Cash Flow Adequacy Ratio**

LO7   Refer to the data in PE 14-30. Compute the cash flow adequacy ratio.

PE 14-32   **Potential Pitfalls of Financial Statement Analysis**

LO8   Which one of the following statements is true with respect to financial statement analysis?

a. All aspects of a business can be summarized neatly into the three primary financial statements.

b. Comparing the financial statements of different companies is relatively easy because all companies are required to use the same financial statement formats and classifications.

c. Every company examined using financial statement analysis will be found to have at least one prominent flaw.

d. Analysts should use only historical ratio analysis, rather than information about current events, in deciding how to rate a company's future prospects.

e. Financial statement analysis usually does not give answers but instead points in directions where further investigation is needed.

EXERCISES

E 14-33   **Computation of Ratios**

LO2   The balance sheet for Tony Corporation is as follows:

Tony Corporation	
Balance Sheet	
December 31, 2009	
Assets	
Current assets:	
Cash	$ 11,000
Accounts receivable	18,000
Total current assets	$ 29,000
Long-term investments	25,000
Property, plant, and equipment	55,000
Total assets	$109,000

(continued)

Liabilities and stockholders' equity
Current liabilities:

Accounts payable	$ 15,000
Salaries payable	5,000
Total current liabilities	$ 20,000
Long-term liabilities	17,500
Total liabilities	$ 37,500

Stockholders' equity:

Paid-in capital	$ 50,000
Retained earnings	21,500
Total stockholders' equity	$ 71,500
Total liabilities and stockholders' equity	$109,000

In addition, the following information for 2009 has been assembled:

Sales	$265,000
Net income	33,000
Market value at December 31, 2009	150,000

Compute the following ratios:

1. Debt ratio
2. Current ratio
3. Return on sales
4. Asset turnover
5. Return on equity
6. Price-earnings ratio

E 14-34
LO2

Ratios and Computing Missing Values

The balance sheet for Rodman Company is as follows:

Rodman Company
Balance Sheet
December 31, 2009

Assets
Current assets:

Cash	$	(a)
Accounts receivable		55,000
Total current assts	$	(b)
Long-term investments		35,000
Property, plant, and equipment		120,000
Total assets	$	(c)

Liabilities and stockholders' equity
Current liabilities:

Account payable	$ 64,000	
Income taxes payable		(d)
Total current liabilities	$ 80,000	
Long-term liabilities		(e)
Total liabilities	$	(f)

Stockholders' equity:

Paid-in capital	$	(g)
Retained earnings		78,500
Total stockholders' equity	$	(h)
Total liabilities and stockholders' equity	$	(i)

(continued)

In addition, the following information for 2009 has been assembled:

Debt ratio	50%
Current ratio	1.2

Compute the missing values (a) through (i).

E 14-35

LO2

Computations Using Ratios

The following information for Chong Lai Company for 2009 has been assembled:

Market value at December 31, 2009	$600,000
Total liabilities	$100,000
Debt ratio	40%
Return on sales	10%
Asset turnover	2.0

Compute the following:
1. Total assets
2. Sales
3. Net income
4. Price-earnings ratio

E 14-36

LO3

Common-Size Income Statement

Comparative income statements for King Engineering Company for 2009 and 2008 are given below.

	2009	2008
Sales	$ 885,000	$ 545,000
Cost of goods sold	(570,000)	(305,000)
Gross profit on sales	$ 315,000	$ 240,000
Selling and general expenses	(106,000)	(84,000)
Operating income	$ 209,000	$ 156,000
Interest expense	(35,000)	(20,000)
Income before income tax	$ 174,000	$ 136,000
Income tax expense	(52,000)	(41,000)
Net income	$ 122,000	$ 95,000

1. Prepare common-size income statements for King Engineering Company for 2009 and 2008.
2. Return on sales for King Engineering is lower in 2009 than in 2008. What expense or expenses are causing this lower profitability?

E 14-37

LO3

Common-Size Balance Sheet

The following data are taken from the comparative balance sheet prepared for Warren Road Company:

	2009	2008
Cash	$ 34,000	$ 25,000
Accounts receivable	43,000	40,000
Inventories	68,000	30,000
Property, plant, and equipment	91,000	55,000
Total assets	$236,000	$150,000

(continued)

Sales for 2009 were $1,000,000. Sales for 2008 were $800,000.

1. Prepare the asset section of a common-size balance sheet for Warren Road Company for 2009 and 2008.
2. Overall, Warren Road is less efficient at using its assets to generate sales in 2009 than in 2008. What asset or assets are responsible for this decreased efficiency?

E 14-38
LO3

Common-Size Balance Sheet

The following data are taken from the comparative balance sheet prepared for Elison Company:

	2009	2008
Cash	$ 68,000	$ 50,000
Accounts receivable	86,000	80,000
Inventories	136,000	60,000
Property, plant, and equipment	182,000	110,000
Total assets	$472,000	$300,000

Sales for 2009 were $2,000,000. Sales for 2008 were $1,600,000.

1. Prepare the asset section of a common-size balance sheet for Elison Company for 2009 and 2008.
2. Overall, Elison is less efficient at using its assets to generate sales in 2009 than in 2008. What asset or assets are responsible for this decreased efficiency?

E 14-39
LO3

Common-Size Income Statement

Comparative income statements for Callister Company for 2009 and 2008 are given below.

	2009	2008
Sales	$1,600,000	$900,000
Cost of goods sold	1,020,000	480,000
Gross profit	$ 580,000	$420,000
Selling and administrative expenses	200,000	160,000
Operating income	$ 380,000	$260,000
Interest expense	80,000	60,000
Income before taxes	$ 300,000	$200,000
Income tax expense	90,000	60,000
Net income	$ 210,000	$140,000

1. Prepare common-size income statements for Callister Company for 2009 and 2008.
2. The profit margin for Callister is lower in 2009 than in 2008. What expense or expenses are causing this lower profitability?

E 14-40
LO3

Income Statement Analysis

You have obtained the following data for Lindsey Garns Company:

Sales	$230,000
Gross profit (as a percentage of sales)	30%
Return on sales	10%
Operating expenses (as a percentage of sales)	15%

Based on the above data, determine the following:

1. Cost of goods sold
2. Net income
3. Operating expenses
4. Income taxes (assume there are no other expenses or revenues)

E 14-41   **Income Statement and Balance Sheet Analysis**

LO2   Answer each of the following independent questions:

1. Nicholas Toy Company had a net income for the year ended December 31, 2009, of $72,000. Its total assets at December 31, 2009, were $1,860,000. Its total stockholders' equity at December 31, 2009, was $910,000. Calculate Nicholas Toy's return on equity.

2. On January 1, 2009, Andrew's Bookstore had current assets of $293,000 and current liabilities of $185,000. By the end of the year, its current assets had increased to $324,000 and its current liabilities to $296,000. Did the current ratio change during the year? If so, by how much?

3. The total liabilities and stockholders' equity of Ryan James Corporation is $750,000. Its current assets equal 40% of total assets and the current ratio is 1.5. Further, the ratio of stockholders' equity to total liabilities is 3 to 1. Determine (a) the amount of current liabilities and (b) the debt ratio.

E 14-42   **DuPont Framework**

LO4   The following information is for Calle Concordia Company:

	2009	2008	2007
Current assets	$ 30,000	$ 25,000	$ 35,000
Total assets	100,000	80,000	90,000
Current liabilities	20,000	15,000	15,000
Total liabilities	45,000	40,000	50,000
Stockholders' equity	55,000	40,000	40,000
Sales	400,000	300,000	300,000
Net income	20,000	10,000	5,000

For the years 2007, 2008, and 2009, compute:

1. Return on equity
2. Return on sales
3. Asset turnover
4. Assets-to-equity ratio

E 14-43   **DuPont Framework**

LO4   The numbers below are for Iffy Company and Model Company for the year 2009:

	Iffy	Model
Cash	$ 120	$ 900
Accounts receivable	600	4,500
Inventory	480	6,000
Property, plant, and equipment	3,440	15,000
Total liabilities	3,190	18,150
Stockholders' equity	1,450	8,250
Sales	10,000	75,000
Cost of goods sold	9,200	66,750
Wage expense	700	5,250
Net income	100	3,000

1. Compute return on equity, return on sales, asset turnover, and the assets-to-equity ratio for both Iffy and Model.
2. Briefly explain why Iffy's return on equity is lower than Model's.

E 14-44

LO4

DuPont Framework

The numbers for Faulty Company and Benchmark Company for the year 2009 are as follows:

	Faulty	Benchmark
Cash	$ 140	$ 500
Accounts receivable	900	2,740
Inventory	2,200	6,100
Property, plant, and equipment	1,800	6,300
Total liabilities	3,780	11,730
Stockholders' equity	1,260	3,910
Sales	12,000	45,000
Cost of goods sold	7,650	32,100
Wage expense	1,300	4,200
Other expenses	2,940	7,760
Net income	110	940

1. Compute return on equity, return on sales, asset turnover, and the assets-to-equity ratio for both Faulty and Benchmark.
2. Briefly explain why Faulty's return on equity is lower than Benchmark's.

E 14-45

LO4

DuPont Framework

The following information is for Ina Company:

	2009	2008	2007
Total assets	$200,000	$160,000	$180,000
Total liabilities	90,000	80,000	100,000
Stockholders' equity	110,000	80,000	80,000
Sales	800,000	600,000	600,000
Net income	40,000	20,000	10,000

For the years 2007, 2008, and 2009, compute:
1. Return on equity
2. Profit margin
3. Asset turnover
4. Assets-to-equity ratio

E 14-46

LO4

DuPont Framework for Analyzing Financial Statements

The income statement and balance sheet for Rollins Company are provided below. Using the DuPont framework, compute the profit margin, asset turnover, assets-to-equity ratio, and resulting return on equity for the year 2009.

Rollins Company		
Income Statement		
For the Year Ended December 31, 2009		
Revenue from services		$151,920
Operating expenses:		
Insurance expense	$ 5,480	
Rent expense	500	
Office supplies expense	2,960	
Salaries expense	55,000	63,940
Net income		$ 87,980

(continued)

Rollins Company
Balance Sheet
December 31, 2009

Assets		Liabilities and Owners' Equity	
Cash	$ 22,000	Accounts payable	$ 54,800
Accounts receivable	40,000	Capital stock	50,000
Notes receivable	12,800	Retained earnings	150,000
Machinery	180,000	Total liabilities	
Total assets	$254,800	and owners' equity	$254,800

E 14-47

LO4

DuPont Framework for Analyzing Financial Statements

Using the income statement and balance sheet for Kau and Sons Company, compute the three components of return on equity—profitability, efficiency, and leverage—based on the DuPont framework, for the year 2009.

Kau and Sons Co.
Income Statement
For the Year Ended December 31, 2009

Revenues		$320,000
Expenses:		
Supplies expense	$124,000	
Salaries expense	33,200	
Utilities expense	7,100	
Rent expense	29,000	
Other expenses	7,700	201,000
Net income		$119,000

Kau and Sons Co.
Balance Sheet
December 31, 2009

Assets		Liabilities and Owners' Equity	
Cash	$ 52,100	Accounts payable	$ 29,800
Accounts receivable	34,900	Notes payable	56,200
Supplies	46,700	Capital stock	80,000
Land	70,000	Retained earnings	304,800
Buildings	267,100	Total liabilities	
Total assets	$470,800	and owners' equity	$470,800

E 14-48

LO4

DuPont Framework

DuPont framework data for four industries are presented below.

	Assets-to-Equity Ratio	Asset Turnover	Return on Sales
Retail jewelry stores	1.578	1.529	0.050
Retail grocery stores	1.832	5.556	0.014
Electric service companies	2.592	0.498	0.069
Legal services firms	1.708	3.534	0.083

(continued)

For the four industries, compute:

1. Return on assets
2. Return on equity

E 14-49   **Financial Statement Analysis**

LO2   You have obtained the following data for the Jacob Company for the year ended December 31, 2009. (Some income statement items are missing.)

Cost of goods sold	$485,000
General and administrative expenses	80,000
Interest expense	8,500
Net income	12,000
Sales	790,000
Tax expense	8,000

Answer each of the following questions:

1. What is the total gross profit?
2. What is the amount of operating income?
3. What is the amount of other operating expenses (in addition to general and administrative expenses)?
4. What is the gross profit percentage (that is, gross profit as a percentage of sales)?
5. If the return on assets is 4%, what are the total assets?
6. If the return on stockholders' equity is 8%, what is the stockholders' equity?
7. What is the return on sales?
8. What is the income tax rate? (Tax Expense/Income before Taxes)

E 14-50   **Accounts Receivable Efficiency**

LO5   The following are summary financial data for Parker Enterprises, Inc., and Boulder, Inc., for three recent years:

	Year 3	Year 2	Year 1
Net sales (in millions):			
Parker Enterprises, Inc.	$ 3,700	$ 3,875	$ 3,882
Boulder, Inc.	17,825	16,549	15,242
Net accounts receivable (in millions):			
Parker Enterprises, Inc.	1,400	1,800	1,725
Boulder, Inc.	5,525	5,800	6,205

1. Using the above data, compute the accounts receivable turnover and average collection period for each company for years 2 and 3.
2. Which company appears to be managing its accounts receivable more efficiently?

E 14-51   **Inventory Ratios**

LO5   The following data are available for 2009, regarding the inventory of two companies:

	Atkins Computers	Burbank Electronics
Beginning inventory	$ 40,000	$ 80,000
Ending inventory	48,000	95,000
Cost of goods sold	690,000	910,000

Compute inventory turnover and number of days' sales in inventory for both companies. Which company is managing its inventory more efficiently?

E 14-52   **Fixed Asset Turnover**

LO5   The Store Next Door reported the following asset values in 2008 and 2009:

	2009	2008
Cash	$ 45,000	$ 27,000
Accounts receivable	500,000	430,000
Inventory	550,000	480,000
Land	300,000	280,000
Buildings	800,000	660,000
Equipment	150,000	110,000

In addition, The Store Next Door had sales of $3,200,000 in 2009. Cost of goods sold for the year was $1,900,000.

Compute The Store Next Door's fixed asset turnover ratio for 2009.

E 14-53   **Computation of Debt-Related Financial Ratios**

LO5, LO6   The following information comes from the financial statements of Gwynn Company:

Long-term debt	$50,000
Total liabilities	78,000
Total stockholders' equity	40,000
Operating income	16,000
Interest expense	6,000

Compute the following ratio values:

1. Debt ratio
2. Debt-to-equity ratio
3. Times interest earned

E 14-54   **Cash Flow Ratios**

LO7   Below are data extracted from the financial statements for Pagoda Company.

Pagoda Company		
Selected Financial Statement Data		
For the Years Ended December 31, 2009 and 2008		
	2009	2008
Net income	$51,000	$ 63,500
Cash from operating activities	38,200	205,000
Cash paid for purchase of fixed assets	47,000	215,000
Cash paid for interest	21,000	26,000
Cash paid for income taxes	23,000	50,100

Compute the following for both 2008 and 2009:

1. Cash flow-to-net income ratio
2. Cash flow adequacy ratio

PROBLEMS

P 14-55
LO2

Computing and Using Common Ratios

The following information is for the year 2009 for Millard Company and Grantsville Company, which are in the same industry:

	Millard	Grantsville
Current assets	$20,000	$75,000
Long-term assets	$40,000	$140,000
Current liabilities	$8,000	$60,000
Long-term liabilities	$15,000	$110,000
Sales	$200,000	$850,000
Net income	$4,000	$10,000
Market price per share	$15	$50
Number of shares outstanding	6,000 shares	3,000 shares

Required:

Compute the following:

1. Current ratio
2. Debt ratio
3. Return on sales
4. Asset turnover
5. Return on equity
6. Price-earnings ratio

P 14-56
LO2

Financial Ratios

The following information for SuperStar Company is provided:

Current assets	$215,000
Long-term assets	$780,000
Current liabilities	$120,000
Long-term liabilities	$330,000
Owners' equity	$545,000
Sales for year	$1,875,000
Net income for year	$178,000
Average market price per share	$90.00
Average number of shares outstanding	50,000

Required:

1. Compute the current ratio, debt ratio, return on sales, return on equity, asset turnover, and price-earnings ratio.
2. **Interpretive Question:** What do these ratios show for SuperStar Company?

P 14-57
LO2

Working Backwards Using Common Ratios

The following information for Steven Benjamin Company for 2009 has been assembled:

Price-earnings ratio	39.0
Stockholders' equity	$150,000
Debt ratio	80%
Net income	$41,000
Asset turnover	0.75
Current liabilities	$135,000
Long-term assets	$280,000

Required:

Compute the following:

1. Return on equity
2. Total assets
3. Sales
4. Return on sales
5. Current ratio
6. Total market value of shares

P 14-58   **Common-Size Income Statement**

LO3   Operations for Janelle Company for 2008 and 2009 are summarized below.

	2009	2008
Net sales	$600,000	$560,000
Cost of goods sold	430,000	300,000
Gross profit on sales	$170,000	$260,000
Selling and general expenses	130,000	150,000
Operating income	$ 40,000	$110,000
Interest expense	50,000	45,000
Income (loss) before income tax	$ (10,000)	$ 65,000
Income tax (refund)	3,000	20,000
Net income (loss)	$ (7,000)	$ 45,000

Required:

1. Prepare common-size income statements for 2009 and 2008.
2. What caused Janelle's profitability to decline so dramatically in 2009?

P 14-59   **Common-Size Financial Statements**

LO3   Below are financial statement data for Wong Shek Company for the years 2008 and 2009.

Wong Shek Company		
Financial Statements		
For 2008 and 2009		
Cash	$ 14	$ 10
Receivables	35	27
Inventory	230	153
Property, plant, and equipment	221	190
Total assets	$ 500	$ 380
Accounts payable	$ 106	$ 74
Long-term debt	217	217
Total liabilities	$ 323	$ 291
Paid-in capital	$ 113	$ 50
Retained earnings	64	39
Total liabilities and equity	$ 500	$ 380
Sales	$1,000	$ 700
Cost of goods sold	(700)	(500)
Gross profit	$ 300	$ 200
Operating expenses	(240)	(160)
Operating profit	$ 60	$ 40
Interest expense	(22)	(22)
Income before taxes	$ 38	$ 18
Income tax expense	(13)	(6)
Net income	$ 25	$ 12

Required:

1. Prepare common-size financial statements for Wong Shek for 2008 and 2009.
2. Did Wong Shek do better or worse in 2009 compared with 2008? Explain your answer.

P 14-60   **Common-Size Financial Statements**

LO3   The comparative income statements and balance sheets for Clarksville Corporation for the years 2007, 2008, and 2009 are given below.

(continued)

Clarksville Corporation
Comparative Income Statements
For the Years Ended December 31

	2009	2008	2007
Net sales	$5,700,000	$6,600,000	$3,800,000
Cost of goods sold	4,000,000	4,800,000	2,520,000
Gross profit on sales	$1,700,000	$1,800,000	$1,280,000
Selling expense	$1,120,000	$1,200,000	$ 960,000
General expense	400,000	440,000	400,000
Total operating expenses	$1,520,000	$1,640,000	$1,360,000
Operating income (loss)	$ 180,000	$ 160,000	$ (80,000)
Other revenue (expense)	80,000	130,000	160,000
Income before taxes	$ 260,000	$ 290,000	$ 80,000
Income tax	80,000	85,000	20,000
Net income	$ 180,000	$ 205,000	$ 60,000

Clarksville Corporation
Comparative Balance Sheets
December 31

	2009	2008	2007
Assets:			
Current assets	$ 855,000	$ 955,500	$ 673,500
Land, building, and equipment	1,275,000	1,075,000	925,000
Intangible assets	100,000	100,000	100,000
Other assets	48,000	60,500	61,500
Total assets	$2,278,000	$2,191,000	$1,760,000
Liabilities:			
Current liabilities	$ 410,000	$ 501,000	$ 130,000
Long-term liabilities	400,000	600,000	400,000
Total liabilities	$ 810,000	$1,101,000	$ 530,000
Stockholders' equity:			
Paid-in capital	$1,100,000	$ 800,000	$1,000,000
Retained earnings	368,000	290,000	230,000
Total stockholders' equity	$1,468,000	$1,090,000	$1,230,000
Total liabilities and stockholders' equity	$2,278,000	$2,191,000	$1,760,000

Required:

1. Prepare common-size income statements and balance sheets for Clarksville Corporation for the years 2007, 2008, and 2009.
2. Summarize any trends you see in Clarksville's numbers from 2007 to 2009.

P 14-61

LO4

DuPont Analysis

Financial information (in thousands of dollars) relating to three different companies follows.

	Company A	Company B	Company C
Net sales	$ 60,000	$28,000	$21,000
Net income	9,600	1,850	360
Total assets	155,400	21,500	3,200
Total equity	61,000	11,300	1,690

(continued)

Required:

1. Compute the following ratios:
   a. Return on sales
   b. Asset turnover
   c. Assets-to-equity ratio
   d. Return on equity
2. **Interpretive Question:** Assume the three companies are (a) a large department store, (b) a large supermarket, and (c) a large electric utility. Based on the above information, identify each company. Explain your answer.

P 14-62   **DuPont Analysis**

LO4   Refer to the financial statement information in P 14-60 for Clarksville Corporation.

Required:

For the years 2007, 2008, and 2009, compute the following ratios:
1. Return on sales
2. Asset turnover
3. Assets-to-equity ratio
4. Return on equity

P 14-63   **Ratio Analysis**

LO2   The following financial data are taken from the records of Big Brother Company.

Big Brother Company Comparative Balance Sheet December 31		
	2009	**2008**
Assets:		
Cash	$ 38,000	$ 23,000
Accounts receivable	11,000	15,000
Inventory	220,000	195,000
Property, plant, and equipment	70,000	70,000
Total assets	$339,000	$303,000
Liabilities and stockholders' equity:		
Current liabilities	$ 52,000	$ 36,000
Noncurrent liabilities	175,000	170,000
Stockholders' equity	112,000	97,000
Total liabilities and stockholders' equity	$339,000	$303,000

Big Brother Company Comparative Income Statement For the Years Ended December 31		
	2009	**2008**
Sales	$463,000	$345,000
Cost of goods sold	240,000	182,000
Gross margin on sales	$223,000	$163,000
Operating expenses	133,000	121,000
Interest expense	15,000	10,000
Income tax expense	30,000	12,000
Net income	$ 45,000	$ 20,000

(continued)

Required:

1. Compute the following ratios for 2008 and 2009:
   a. Current ratio
   b. Debt ratio
   c. Asset turnover
   d. Return on sales
   e. Return on equity
2. Have the firm's performance and financial position improved from 2008 to 2009? Explain.

P 14-64

LO2

Ratio Analysis

The following data are taken from the records of John Spencer Corporation.

John Spencer Corporation
Comparative Balance Sheet
December 31

	2009	2008
Assets:		
Cash	$ 4,000	$ 6,000
Accounts receivable	16,000	14,000
Inventory	40,000	20,000
Property, plant, and equipment	100,000	100,000
Other assets	16,000	20,000
Total assets	$176,000	$160,000
Liabilities and stockholders' equity:		
Current liabilities	$ 44,000	$ 50,000
Long-term liabilities	24,000	10,000
Paid-in capital	60,000	60,000
Retained earnings	48,000	40,000
Total liabilities and stockholders' equity	$176,000	$160,000

John Spencer Corporation
Comparative Income Statement
For the Years Ended December 31

	2009	2008
Sales	$530,000	$448,000
Cost of goods sold	372,000	338,000
Gross margin on sales	$158,000	$110,000
Operating expense	102,000	68,000
Operating income	$ 56,000	$ 42,000
Interest expense	4,000	2,000
Income before taxes	$ 52,000	$ 40,000
Income taxes	13,000	12,000
Net income	$ 39,000	$ 28,000

Required:

1. Compute the following ratios for 2008 and 2009:
   a. Current ratio
   b. Debt ratio
   c. Asset turnover

(continued)

d. Return on sales
e. Return on equity

2. Have the firm's performance and financial position improved from 2008 to 2009? Explain.

P 14-65
LO5

Analysis of Accounts Receivable Management

The following accounts receivable information is for Rouge Company:

	2009	2008	2007
Accounts receivable	$ 98,000	$ 50,000	$ 70,000
Sales revenue	190,000	175,000	165,000

Required:

Is there any cause for alarm in the accounts receivable data for 2009? Explain.

P 14-66
LO5

Calculating and Interpreting Inventory Ratios

Captain Geech Boating Company sells fishing boats to fishermen. Its beginning and ending inventories for 2009 are $462 million and $653 million, respectively. It had cost of goods sold of $1,578 million for the year ended December 31, 2009. Merchant Marine Company also sells fishing boats. Its beginning and ending inventories for the year 2009 are $120 million and $90 million, respectively. It had cost of goods sold of $1,100 million for the year ended December 31, 2009.

Required:

1. Calculate the inventory turnover and number of days' sales in inventory for the two companies.
2. **Interpretive Question:** Are the results of these ratios what you expected? Which company is managing its inventory more efficiently?

P 14-67
LO5

Fixed Asset Turnover Ratio

Waystation Company reported the following asset values in 2008 and 2009:

	2009	2008
Cash	$ 40,000	$ 30,000
Accounts receivable	500,000	400,000
Inventory	700,000	500,000
Land	300,000	200,000
Buildings	800,000	600,000
Equipment	400,000	300,000

In addition, Waystation had sales of $4,000,000 in 2009. Cost of goods sold for the year was $2,500,000.

As of the end of 2008, the fair value of Waystation's total assets was $2,500,000. Of the excess of fair value over book value, $50,000 resulted because the fair value of Waystation's inventory was greater than its recorded book value. As of the end of 2009, the fair value of Waystation's total assets was $3,500,000. As of December 31, 2009, the fair value of Waystation's inventory was $100,000 greater than the inventory's recorded book value.

Required:

1. Compute Waystation's fixed asset turnover ratio for 2009.
2. Using the fair value of fixed assets instead of the book value of fixed assets, recompute Waystation's fixed asset turnover ratio for 2009. State any assumptions that you make.

(continued)

3. **Interpretive Question:** Waystation's primary competitor is Handy Corner. Handy Corner's fixed asset turnover ratio for 2009, based on publicly available information, is 2.8 times. Is Waystation more or less efficient at using its fixed assets than is Handy Corner? Explain your answer.

P 14-68
LO6

Computation of Debt-Related Financial Ratios

The following information comes from the financial statements of Walker Company:

Long-term debt	$430,000
Total liabilities	490,000
Total stockholders' equity	360,000
Current assets	140,000
Earnings before income taxes	28,000
Interest expense	50,000

Required:

Compute the following ratio values. State any assumptions that you make.

1. Debt ratio.
2. Debt-to-equity ratio.
3. Times interest earned.
4. **Interpretive Question:** You are a bank manager considering making a new $35,000 loan to Walker that would replace part of the existing long-term debt. You expect Walker to repay your loan in two years. Which of the ratios computed in parts (1) through (3) would be most useful to you in evaluating whether to make the loan to Walker?

P 14-69
LO7

Cash Flow Analysis

Below are data extracted from the financial statements for Mushu Company.

Mushu Company **Selected Financial Statement Data** **For the Years Ended December 31, 2009 and 2008** **(in millions of dollars)**		
	2009	**2008**
Total assets	$112,000	$103,000
Stockholders' equity	24,000	22,000
Sales	96,000	78,000
Net income	8,100	5,400
Cash from operations	10,300	14,800
Cash paid for capital expenditures	7,500	6,400
Cash paid for acquisitions	3,400	1,100
Cash paid for interest	2,100	1,200
Cash paid for income taxes	3,400	3,200

Required:

1. Compute the following for 2008 and 2009:
   a. Return on sales
   b. Return on equity
   c. Cash flow-to-net income ratio
   d. Cash flow adequacy ratio
2. In which year did Mushu Company perform better: 2008 or 2009? Explain your answer.

ANALYTICAL ASSIGNMENTS

AA 14-70
DISCUSSION

Analyzing Earnings

Roger Donahoe owns two businesses: a drug store and a retail department store.

	Drug Store	Department Store
Net sales	$1,050,000	$670,000
Cost of goods sold	1,000,000	600,000
Average total assets	50,000	200,000
Other expenses	39,500	36,500

Which business is more profitable? Which business is more efficient? Overall, which business would you consider to be a more attractive investment?

AA 14-71
DISCUSSION

Can a Ratio Be Too Good?

Tony Christopher is analyzing the financial statements of Shaycole Company and has computed the following ratios:

	Shaycole	Industry Comparison
Current ratio	4.7	1.9
Asset turnover	1.8 times	1.4 times
Debt ratio	0.317	0.564

Andy Martinez, Tony's colleague, tells Tony that Shaycole looks great. Andy points out that, although Shaycole's ratios deviate significantly from the industry norms, all the deviations suggest that Shaycole is doing better than other firms in its industry. Is Andy right?

AA 14-72
DISCUSSION

Evaluating Alternative Investments

Judy Snow is considering investing $10,000 and wishes to know which of two companies offers the better alternative.

The Hoffman Company earned net income of $63,000 last year on average total assets of $280,000 and average stockholders' equity of $210,000. The company's shares are selling for $100 per share; 6,300 shares of common stock are outstanding.

The McMahon Company earned $24,375 last year on average total assets of $125,000 and average stockholders' equity of $100,000. The company's common shares are selling for $78 per share; 2,500 shares are outstanding.

Which stock should Judy buy?

AA 14-73
JUDGMENT CALL

You Decide: Could we see Enron coming?

Sherron Watkins, the whistle-blower at **Enron**, made the following statement at a conference that one of the authors attended: "If anyone would have been watching the cash flows of Enron, they could have figured out that there were problems." While traditional ratios don't reveal the problems, the following ratio provides some interesting results when looked at on a quarterly basis:

$$\frac{\text{Net Income from Operations} - \text{Cash Flows from Operations}}{\text{Net Income from Operations}}$$

(continued)

During the period 1998 and 2001, this ratio revealed the following:

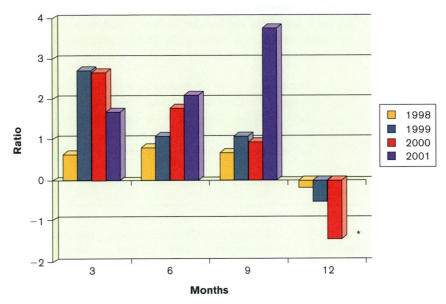

*Note: The Enron fraud was discovered in the 4th quarter of 2001. As a result, comparable 12-month numbers are not available.

Does this ratio look normal or as expected for a nonfraud committing company? What would you expect this ratio to look like? Why do the yearly results look so different than the quarterly results?

AA 14-74
JUDGMENT CALL

You Decide: Ratios and debt covenants

XYZ Company has some leases on buildings that are structured so they do not have to be reported on the balance sheet as assets and liabilities (synthetic leases). However, as a term of the agreement, the lessor—a financial institution—requires that the company maintain an amount of cash in its institution so that the buildings could be purchased if the company misses some restrictive covenant agreements (i.e., certain ratio requirements, such as a current ratio of 2:1, etc.). The total amount of cash required to be held by the bank is $60 million. So far, XYZ has been including the $60 million in its cash account when calculating its current ratio. Your auditor has suggested that since the $60 million is restricted for a certain purpose, it should be reported as a long-term investment rather than as cash. Reclassifying the $60 million from cash to long-term investments would throw all kinds of ratios in default and you definitely don't want to do it. What is the appropriate accounting?

AA 14-75
REAL COMPANY ANALYSIS

Wal-Mart

Using **Wal-Mart**'s 2006 Form 10-K contained in Appendix A, answer the following questions:

1. Compute the following ratios for Wal-Mart for 2005 and compare those results to the 2006 results—debt ratio, current ratio, return on sales, asset turnover, and return on equity. For which of these ratios did Wal-Mart improve from 2005 to 2006?
2   Wal-Mart's fiscal 2006 inventory represents what percentage of sales? What percentage of total assets does this line item represent? Why do you think Wal-Mart has so much money tied up in inventory?

AA 14-76

DuPont

In this chapter, you were introduced to the DuPont framework. Let us take a moment and apply that framework to the **DuPont Company**. DuPont is a company made up of many business segments and has the challenge of how to manage the diverse set of businesses operating under the control of the DuPont management team. In its 2005 annual report, DuPont described its business segments as follows:

> The company has six reporting segments. Five of the segments constitute the company's growth platforms: Agriculture & Nutrition; Coatings & Color Technologies; Electronic & Communication Technologies; Performance Materials; and Safety & Protection. The Pharmaceuticals segment is limited to income from the company's interest in two drugs, Cozaar and Hyzaar.

Summary segment results for 2005 are as follows:

2005	Agriculture & Nutrition	Coatings & Color Technologies	Electronic & Communication Technologies	Per-formance Materials	Pharma-ceuticals	Safety & Protection	Others
Total segment sales	$6,394	$6,234	$3,506	$6,750	$ –	$5,230	$ 52
Pretax operating income (loss)	862	564	532	523	751	980	(78)
Segment net assets	6,084	3,633	2,189	3,563	169	2,686	148

1. Using segment pretax operating income as a substitute for total company net income, tell which segment has the highest return on sales? The lowest?
2. Which segment has the highest asset turnover? The lowest?

AA 14-77

The Walt Disney Company

Information from the 2005 financial statements of **The Walt Disney Company** is listed below. This information reports Disney's performance, by geographic area.

	United States and Canada	Europe	Asia Pacific	Latin America and Other
Sales	$24,806	$5,207	$1,451	$480
Operating income	3,512	688	377	77
Identifiable assets	45,809	5,120	2,110	119

1. Disney divides its worldwide operations into four geographic areas: the United States and Canada, Europe, Asia Pacific, and Latin America and Other. Which of these four has the best 2005 profitability as measured by return on sales?
2. Which of Disney's four geographic areas has the best overall asset efficiency in 2005 as measured by asset turnover?
3. Discuss why return on equity cannot be computed for each geographic area.

AA 14-78

Which Is the Stronger Partner in the Merger?

In May 1998, **Daimler-Benz** and **Chrysler** announced their intention to merge. Daimler-Benz was the largest industrial company in Europe, and Chrysler was Number 3 of the Big Three automakers in the United States. The merger resulted in **DaimlerChrysler** becoming (at the time) the second largest automobile company in the world with 2000 sales exceeding $150 billion (**General Motors** reported sales in 2000 of $160 billion).

An interesting question is, "At the time of the merger, which of the two companies was the stronger?" Below are summary data for the two companies, both overall and for their respective automotive divisions.

(continued)

	Daimler-Benz		Chrysler	
	Overall	**Automotive**	**Overall**	**Automotive**
Sales	DM 124,050	DM 91,632	$61,147	$58,662
Net income	8,042	3,501	2,805	4,238
Total assets	137,099	46,955	60,418	44,483

The amounts are in millions of Deutsche marks for Daimler-Benz and millions of U.S. dollars for Chrysler.

For the automotive segment information, net income is the operating income for the segment and total assets are the assets that are identifiable with the segment.

1. Compute the following for both companies for overall results and automotive division results:
   a. Return on sales
   b. Asset turnover
2. In comparing the ratios calculated in (1), why don't you have to make adjustments for currency differences?
3. Which company had more worldwide automotive sales in 1997? *Note:* Don't forget the currency difference.

AA 14-79

ETHICS

Does the Bonus Plan Reward the Right Thing?

Roaring Springs Booksellers is an Internet book company. Customers choose their purchases from an online catalog and make their orders online. Roaring Springs then assembles the books from its warehouse inventory, packs the order, and ships it to the customer within three working days. The rapid turnaround time on orders requires Roaring Springs to have a large warehouse staff; wage expense averages almost 20% of sales.

Each member of Roaring Springs's top management team receives an annual bonus equal to 1% of his or her salary for every 0.1% that Roaring Springs's return on sales exceeds 5.0%. For example, if return on sales is 5.3%, each top manager would receive a bonus of 3% of salary. Historically, return on sales for Roaring Springs has ranged between 4.5% and 5.5%.

The management of Roaring Springs has come up with a plan to dramatically increase return on sales, perhaps to as high as 6.5% to 7.0%. The plan is to acquire a sophisticated, computerized packing machine that can receive customer order information, mechanically assemble the books for each order, box the order, print an address label, and route the box to the correct loading dock for pickup by the delivery service. Acquisition of this machine will allow Roaring Springs to lay off 100 warehouse employees, resulting in a significant savings in wage expense. Top management intends to acquire the machine by using new investment capital from stockholders and thus avoid an increase in interest expense. Because the depreciation expense on the new machine will be much less than the savings in reduced wage expense, return on sales will increase.

All the top managers of Roaring Springs are excited about the new plan because it could increase their bonuses to as much as 20% of salary. As assistant to the chief financial officer of Roaring Springs, you have been asked to prepare a briefing for the board of directors explaining exactly how this new packing machine will increase return on sales. As part of your preparation, you decide to examine the impact of the machine acquisition on the other two components of the DuPont framework—efficiency and leverage. You find that even with the projected increase in return on sales, the decrease in asset turnover and in the assets-to-equity ratio will cause total return on equity to decline from its current level of 18% to around 14%.

Your presentation is scheduled for the next board of directors meeting in two weeks. What should you do?

AA 14-80
WRITING

Who Should Get a Holiday Loan?

You are head of the loan department at Wilshire National Bank and have been approached by two firms in the retail toy business. Each firm is requesting a nine-month term loan to purchase inventory for the holiday season. You must make your recommendations to the loan committee and have gathered the following data in order to make your analysis. Fun Toy Company was organized in early 2008. The first year of operations was fairly successful, as the firm earned net income of $45,000. Total sales for the year were $600,000, and total assets at year-end December 31, 2008, were $350,000. A condensed balance sheet at September 30, 2009, follows. The firm is requesting a $100,000 loan.

Assets:		Liabilities and stockholders' equity:	
Cash	$ 60,000	Accounts payable	$ 70,000
Accounts receivable	65,000	Note payable, due 10/5/09	100,000
Inventory	125,000	Stockholders' equity	240,000
Prepaid expenses	5,000		
Furniture and fixtures	155,000	Total liabilities and	
Total assets	$410,000	stockholders' equity	$410,000

The Toy Store, the other firm, has been in business for many years. The firm's net income was $100,000 on total sales of $2,000,000 in the most recent fiscal year. A balance sheet as of September 30, 2009, is given below. The firm is seeking a $200,000 loan.

Assets:		Liabilities and stockholders' equity:	
Cash	$ 60,000	Accounts payable	$ 350,000
Accounts receivable	100,000	Current bank loan payable	150,000
Inventory	400,000	Long-term debt	400,000
Supplies	10,000	Stockholders' equity	500,000
Prepaid expenses	5,000		
Property, plant, and			
equipment	825,000	Total liabilities and	
Total assets	$1,400,000	stockholders' equity	$1,400,000

Write a one-page memo to the loan committee containing your recommendation about making loans to Fun Toy Company and to The Toy Store. You should use selected financial ratios in making your recommendation. Remember, your memo is only one page, so you can't just present a list of every possible ratio computation. Build your recommendation around a few key numbers.

AA 14-81
**CUMULATIVE
SPREADSHEET
PROJECT**

Projecting Financial Performance

The financial statement numbers and ratio assumptions used in constructing this series of cumulative spreadsheet projects in the text, starting in Chapter 2, are based on the actual experience of **Home Depot**. The original financial statement numbers in the spreadsheet project are adapted from Home Depot's actual 1985 financial statements. The projected financial statements that you will prepare in (1) below are a projection of how Home Depot would have performed in the years after 1985 if Home Depot had not made significant changes to its operations.

1. Handyman wishes to prepare forecasted balance sheets, income statements, and statements of cash flows for five years—2010, 2011, 2012, 2013, and 2014. Use the original financial statement numbers for 2009 (given in part (1) of the Cumulative Spreadsheet Project assignment in Chapter 2) as the basis for the forecast, along with the following additional information:
   a. Sales in 2010 are expected to increase by 40% over 2009 sales of $700. Sales are expected to increase 40% in each year thereafter.
   b. Cash will increase at the same rate as sales.

(continued)

   c. The forecasted amount of accounts receivable is determined using the forecasted value for the average collection period. The average collection period is expected to be 14.08 days. To make the calculations simpler, this value of 14.08 days is based on forecasted end-of-year accounts receivable rather than on average accounts receivable.

   d. The forecasted amount of inventory is determined using the forecasted value for the number of days' sales in inventory. The number of days' sales in inventory is expected to be 107.6 days. To make the calculations simpler, this value of 107.6 days is based on forecasted end-of-year inventory rather than on average inventory.

   e. The forecasted amount of accounts payable is determined using the forecasted value for the number of days' purchases in accounts payable. The number of days' purchases in accounts payable is expected to be 48.34 days. To make the calculations simpler, this value of 48.34 days is based on forecasted end-of-year accounts payable rather than on average accounts payable.

   f. The $160 in operating expenses reported in 2009 breaks down as follows: $5 depreciation expense, $155 other operating expenses.

   g. New long-term debt will be acquired (or repaid) in an amount sufficient to make Handyman's debt ratio (total liabilities divided by total assets) in each year exactly equal to 0.80.

   h. No cash dividends will be paid in any year.

   i. New short-term loans payable will be acquired in an amount sufficient to make Handyman's current ratio exactly equal to 2.0 in each year.

   j. The forecasted amount of property, plant, and equipment (PPE) is determined using the forecasted value for the fixed asset turnover ratio. For simplicity, compute the fixed asset turnover ratio using the end-of-period Gross PPE balance. The fixed asset turnover ratio is expected to be 3.518 times.

   k. In computing depreciation expense, use straight-line depreciation and assume a 30-year useful life with no residual value. Gross PPE acquired during the year is only depreciated for half the year. In other words, depreciation expense is the sum of two parts: (1) a full year of depreciation on the beginning balance in PPE, assuming a 30-year life and no residual value and (2) a half year of depreciation on any new PPE acquired during the year, based on the change in the Gross PPE balance.

   l. Assume an interest rate on short-term loans payable of 6.0% and on long-term debt of 8.0%. Only a half year's interest is charged on loans taken out during the year. For example, if short-term loans payable at the end of 2010 is $15 and given that short-term loans payable at the end of 2009 were $10, total short-term interest expense for 2010 would be $0.75 [($10 × .06) + ($5 × .06 × 1/2)].

2. Repeat (1), with the following changes in assumptions:

• Average Collection Period	9.06 days
• Number of Days' Sales in Inventory	66.23 days
• Fixed Asset Turnover	3.989 times
• Gross Profit Percentage	27.55%
• Other Operating Expenses/Sales	19.86%
• Number of Days' Purchases in Accounts Payable	50.37 days

Note: After making these changes in ratio values, your spreadsheet may have negative amounts for Short-Term Loans Payable. This is impossible. Adjust your spreadsheet so that Short-Term Loans Payable is never less than zero. This will require a relaxation of the requirement that the current ratio be at least 2.0.

3. Discuss why Handyman has a projected current ratio of less than 2.0 in some years when using the ratios in (2).

4. Which company would you rather loan money to—a company with the projected financial statements prepared in (1) or a company with the projected financial statements prepared in (2)? Explain your answer.

Management's Discussion and Analysis of Results of Operations and Financial Condition
WAL-MART

Overview

Wal-Mart Stores, Inc. ("Wal-Mart" or the "Company") is a global retailer committed to improving the standard of living for our customers throughout the world. We earn the trust of our customers every day by providing a broad assortment of quality merchandise and services at every day low prices ("EDLP") while fostering a culture that rewards and embraces mutual respect, integrity and diversity. EDLP is our pricing philosophy under which we price items at a low price every day so that our customers trust that our prices will not change erratically under frequent promotional activity. Our focus for SAM'S CLUB is to provide exceptional value on brand-name merchandise at "members only" prices for both business and personal use. Internationally, we operate with similar philosophies. Our fiscal year ends on January 31.

We intend for this discussion to provide the reader with information that will assist in understanding our financial statements, the changes in certain key items in those financial statements from year to year, and the primary factors that accounted for those changes, as well as how certain accounting principles affect our financial statements. The discussion also provides information about the financial results of the various segments of our business to provide a better understanding of how those segments and their results affect the financial condition and results of operations of the Company as a whole. This discussion should be read in conjunction with our financial statements and accompanying notes as of January 31, 2006, and the year then ended.

Throughout this Management's Discussion and Analysis of Results of Operations and Financial Condition, we discuss segment operating income and comparative store sales. Segment operating income refers to income from continuing operations before net interest expense, income taxes and minority interest. Segment operating income does not include unallocated corporate overhead. Comparative store sales is a measure which indicates the performance of our existing stores by measuring the growth in sales for such stores for a particular period over the corresponding period in the prior year. For fiscal 2006 and prior years, we considered comparative store sales to be sales at stores that were open as of February 1st of the prior fiscal year and had not been expanded or relocated since that date. Stores that were expanded or relocated during that period are not included in the calculation. Comparative store sales is also referred to as "same-store" sales by others within the retail industry. The method of calculating comparative store sales varies across the retail industry. As a result, our calculation of comparative store sales is not necessarily comparable to similarly titled measures reported by other companies. Beginning in fiscal 2007, we changed our method of calculating comparative store sales. These changes are described in our Current Report on Form 8-K that we furnished to the SEC on February 2, 2006.

On May 23, 2003, we consummated the sale of McLane Company, Inc. ("McLane"), one of our wholly-owned subsidiaries, for $1.5 billion. As a result of this sale, we classified McLane as a discontinued operation in the financial statements for fiscal 2004. McLane's external sales prior to the divestiture were $4.3 billion in fiscal 2004. McLane continues to be a supplier to the Company.

Operations

Our operations are comprised of three business segments: Wal-Mart Stores, SAM'S CLUB and International.

Our Wal-Mart Stores segment is the largest segment of our business, accounting for approximately 67.2% of our fiscal 2006 net sales. This segment consists of three traditional retail formats, all of which are located in the United States, and Wal-Mart's online retail format, Walmart.com. Our traditional Wal-Mart Stores retail formats include:

- Supercenters, which average approximately 187,000 square feet in size and offer a wide assortment of general merchandise and a full-line supermarket;
- Discount stores, which average approximately 102,000 square feet in size and offer a wide assortment of general merchandise and a limited assortment of food products; and
- Neighborhood Markets, which average approximately 42,000 square feet in size and offer a full-line supermarket and a limited assortment of general merchandise.

Our SAM'S CLUB segment consists of membership warehouse clubs in the United States and the segment's online retail format, samsclub.com. SAM'S CLUB accounted for approximately 12.7% of our fiscal 2006 sales. Our SAM'S CLUBs in the United States average approximately 129,000 square feet in size.

As of January 31, 2006, our International operations were located in nine countries and Puerto Rico. Internationally, we generated approximately 20.1% of our fiscal 2006 sales. Outside the United States, we operate several different formats of retail stores and restaurants, including supercenters, discount stores and SAM'S CLUBs. Additionally, at January 31, 2006, we owned an unconsolidated 33.3% minority interest in Central American Retail Holding Company ("CARHCO"), a retailer operating in five Central American countries. In February 2006, we acquired a controlling interest in CARHCO.

The Retail Industry

We operate in the highly competitive retail industry in both the United States and abroad. We face strong sales competition from other discount, department, drug, variety and specialty stores and supermarkets, many of which are national chains. Additionally, we compete with a number of companies for prime retail site locations, as well as in attracting and retaining quality employees ("associates"). We, along with other retail companies, are influenced by a number of factors including, but not limited to: cost of goods, consumer debt levels, economic conditions, interest rates, customer preferences, employment, labor costs, inflation, currency exchange fluctuations, fuel prices, weather patterns and insurance costs. Our SAM'S CLUB segment faces strong sales competition from other wholesale club operators, as well as other retailers. Further information on risks to our Company can be located in Item 1A, Risk Factors, in our Annual Report on Form 10-K for the year ended January 31, 2006.

Management's Discussion and Analysis of Results of Operations and Financial Condition
WAL-MART

Key Items in Fiscal 2006
Significant financial items during fiscal 2006 include:

- Net sales increased 9.5% from fiscal 2005 to $312.4 billion in fiscal 2006, and net income increased 9.4% to $11.2 billion. Foreign currency exchange rates favorably impacted sales and operating income by $1.5 billion and $64 million, respectively, in fiscal 2006.
- Net cash provided by operating activities was $17.6 billion for fiscal 2006. During fiscal 2006, we repurchased $3.6 billion of our common stock under our share repurchase program and paid dividends of $2.5 billion. Additionally during fiscal 2006, we issued $7.7 billion in long-term debt, repaid $2.7 billion of long-term debt and funded a net decrease in commercial paper of $704 million.
- Total assets increased 15.0%, to $138.2 billion at January 31, 2006, when compared to January 31, 2005. During fiscal 2006, we made $14.6 billion of capital expenditures which was an increase of 13.0% over capital expenditures of $12.9 billion in fiscal 2005.
- When compared to fiscal 2005, our Wal-Mart Stores segment experienced an 8.2% increase in operating income and a 9.4% increase in net sales in fiscal 2006.
- SAM'S CLUB's continued focus on our business members helped drive an 8.2% increase in operating income on a 7.2% increase in net sales when comparing fiscal 2006 with fiscal 2005.
- Our International segment generated a net sales and operating income increase of 11.4% compared to fiscal 2005.

Company Performance Measures
Management uses a number of metrics to assess the Company's performance. The following are the more frequently used metrics:

- Comparative store sales is a measure which indicates the performance of our existing stores by measuring the growth in sales for such stores for a particular period over the corresponding period in the prior year. Our Wal-Mart Stores segment's comparative store sales were 3.0% for fiscal 2006 versus 2.9% for fiscal 2005. Our SAM'S CLUB segment's comparative club sales were 5.0% in fiscal 2006 versus 5.8% in fiscal 2005.
- Operating income growth greater than net sales growth has long been a measure of success for us. For fiscal 2006, our operating income increased by 8.4% when compared to fiscal 2005, while net sales increased by 9.5% over the same period. Our SAM'S CLUB segment met this target; however, the Wal-Mart Stores segment fell short of the target, while the International segment grew operating income at the same rate as net sales.
- Inventory growth at a rate less than that of net sales is a key measure of our efficiency. However, our increased purchases of imported merchandise and recent acquisition activity impact this measure. Total inventories at January 31, 2006, were up 8.2% over levels at January 31, 2005, and net sales were up 9.5% when comparing fiscal 2006 with fiscal 2005. Approximately 150 basis points of the fiscal 2006 increase in inventory was from increased levels of imported merchandise, which carries a longer lead time, and an additional 170 basis points was from the consolidation of The Seiyu, Ltd. and the purchase of Sonae Distribuição Brasil S.A.
- With an asset base as large as ours, we are focused on continuing to make certain our assets are productive. It is important for us to sustain our return on assets. Return on assets is defined as income from continuing operations before minority interest divided by average total assets. Return on assets for fiscal 2006, 2005 and 2004 was 8.9%, 9.3% and 9.2%, respectively. Return on assets in fiscal 2006 was impacted by acquisition activity in the fourth quarter.

Results of Operations
The Company and each of its operating segments had net sales (in millions), as follows:

Fiscal Year Ended January 31,	2006			2005			2004	
	Net sales	Percent of total	Percent increase	Net sales	Percent of total	Percent increase	Net sales	Percent of total
Wal-Mart Stores	$209,910	67.2%	9.4%	$191,826	67.3%	10.1%	$174,220	68.0%
SAM'S CLUB	39,798	12.7%	7.2%	37,119	13.0%	7.5%	34,537	13.5%
International	62,719	20.1%	11.4%	56,277	19.7%	18.3%	47,572	18.5%
Total net sales	$312,427	100.0%	9.5%	$285,222	100.0%	11.3%	$256,329	100.0%

Our total net sales increased by 9.5% and 11.3% in fiscal 2006 and 2005 when compared to the previous fiscal year. Those increases resulted from our expansion programs and comparative store sales increases in the United States. Comparative store sales increased 3.4% in fiscal 2006 and 3.3% in fiscal 2005. As we continue to add new stores in the United States, we do so with an understanding that additional stores may take sales away from existing units. We estimate that comparative store sales in fiscal 2006, 2005 and 2004 were negatively impacted by the opening of new stores by approximately 1% per year. We expect that this effect of opening new stores on comparable store sales will continue during fiscal 2007 at a similar rate.

During fiscal 2006 and 2005, foreign currency exchange rates had a $1.5 billion and $3.2 billion favorable impact, respectively, on the International segment's net sales, causing an increase in the International segment's net sales as a percentage of total net sales relative to the Wal-Mart Stores and SAM'S CLUB segments. Additionally, the decrease in the SAM'S CLUB segment's net sales as a percent of total Company sales in fiscal 2006 and 2005 when compared to the previous fiscal years resulted from the more rapid development of new stores in the International and Wal-Mart Stores segments than the SAM'S CLUB segment. We expect this trend to continue for the foreseeable future.

Our total gross profit as a percentage of net sales (our "gross margin") was 23.1%, 22.9% and 22.5% in fiscal 2006, 2005 and 2004, respectively. Our Wal-Mart Stores and International segment sales yield higher gross margins than our SAM'S CLUB segment. Accordingly, the greater increases in net sales for the Wal-Mart Stores and International segments in fiscal 2006 and 2005 had a favorable impact on the Company's total gross margin.

Operating, selling, general and administrative expenses ("operating expenses") as a percentage of net sales were 18.2%, 17.9% and 17.5% for fiscal 2006, 2005 and 2004, respectively. The increase in operating expenses as a percentage of total net sales was primarily due to a faster rate of growth in operating expenses in our Wal-Mart Stores and International segments, which have higher operating expenses as a percentage of segment net sales than our SAM'S CLUB segment. Operating expenses in fiscal 2006 were higher as a percentage of net sales because of increases in utilities, maintenance and repairs and advertising. Increases in these expenses in fiscal 2006 were partially offset by reduced payroll costs as a percentage of net sales. Operating expenses in fiscal 2005 were impacted by the Wal-Mart Stores and SAM'S CLUB segments' implementation of a new job classification and pay structure for hourly field associates in the United States. The job classification and pay structure, which was implemented in the second quarter of fiscal 2005, was designed to help maintain internal equity and external competitiveness.

Operating expenses in fiscal 2004 were impacted by the adoption of Emerging Issues Task Force Issue No. 02-16, "Accounting by a Reseller for Cash Consideration Received from a Vendor" ("EITF 02-16"). The adoption of EITF 02-16 resulted in an after-tax reduction in fiscal 2004 net income of approximately $140 million.

Interest, net, as a percentage of net sales increased from fiscal 2004 through fiscal 2006. The increase was due to higher borrowing levels and higher interest rates during the period from fiscal 2004 through fiscal 2006. The $186-million increase in interest, net, in fiscal 2006 consisted of a $221-million increase due to higher borrowing levels and $99 million due to higher interest rates, partially offset by a benefit from refund of IRS interest paid, reversal of interest on income tax accruals for prior years, and reduced levels of interest on fiscal 2006 income tax accruals. The $154-million increase in interest, net, in fiscal 2005 consisted of a $139-million increase due to higher borrowing levels, a $26-million decrease due to changing interest rates and a $41-million increase in interest on income tax accruals.

Our effective income tax rates for fiscal 2006, 2005 and 2004 were 33.4%, 34.7% and 36.1%, respectively. The fiscal 2006 rate was less than the fiscal 2005 rate due primarily to adjustments in deferred income taxes and resolutions of certain federal and state tax contingencies. The fiscal 2005 rate was less than the fiscal 2004 rate due to the October 2004 passage of the Working Families Tax-Relief Act of 2004, which retroactively extended the work opportunity tax credit for fiscal 2005. In addition, the fiscal 2004 effective tax rate was impacted by an increase in the deferred tax asset valuation allowance as a result of tax legislation in Germany. This legislation required us to reevaluate the recoverability of deferred tax assets in Germany, resulting in a $150 million increase in the fiscal 2004 provision for income taxes.

In fiscal 2006, we earned net income of $11.2 billion, a 9.4% increase over fiscal 2005. In fiscal 2005, we earned income from continuing operations of $10.3 billion, a 15.9% increase over fiscal 2004. Net income in fiscal 2005 increased 13.4% from fiscal 2004 largely as a result of the increase in income from continuing operations described above, net of the $193 million provided from the discontinued operations and sale of McLane in fiscal 2004.

Wal-Mart Stores Segment

Fiscal Year	Segment Net Sales Increase from Prior Fiscal Year	Segment Operating Income (in millions)	Segment Operating Income Increase from Prior Fiscal Year	Operating Income as a Percentage of Segment Sales
2006	**9.4%**	**$15,324**	**8.2%**	**7.3%**
2005	10.1%	14,163	9.7%	7.4%
2004	10.9%	12,916	9.1%	7.4%

The segment net sales increases in fiscal 2006 and fiscal 2005 from the prior fiscal years resulted from comparative store sales increases of 3.0% in fiscal 2006 and 2.9% in fiscal 2005, in addition to our expansion program. Market development strategies in fiscal 2006 continued to put pressures on comparative stores sales increases as new stores were opened within the trade area of established stores. We have developed several initiatives to help mitigate this pressure and to grow comparable store sales through becoming more relevant to the customer by creating a better store shopping experience, continual improvement in product assortment and an aggressive store upgrade program to be instituted over the next 18 months.

Management's Discussion and Analysis of Results of Operations and Financial Condition

WAL-MART

Our expansion programs consist of opening new units, converting discount stores to supercenters, relocations that result in more square footage, as well as expansions of existing stores. Segment expansion during fiscal 2006 included the opening of 24 discount stores, 15 Neighborhood Markets and 267 supercenters (including the conversion and/or relocation of 166 existing discount stores into supercenters). Two discount stores closed in fiscal 2006. During fiscal 2006, our total expansion program added approximately 39 million of store square footage, an 8.6% increase. Segment expansion during fiscal 2005 included the opening of 36 discount stores, 21 Neighborhood Markets and 242 supercenters (including the conversion and/or relocation of 159 existing discount stores into supercenters). Two discount stores closed in fiscal 2005. During fiscal 2005, our total expansion program added approximately 36 million of store square footage, an 8.6% increase.

Fiscal 2006 segment operating income was down 0.1% as a percentage of segment net sales. This decrease was driven by a 4 basis point decline in gross margin and an 8 basis point increase in operating expenses, partially offset by a slight increase in other income as a percentage of segment net sales. This gross margin decrease from

fiscal 2005 can be attributed to the continued increase in sales of our lower-margin food items as a percentage of total segment net sales, rising transportation costs, and the unfavorable impact of an adjustment to our product warranty liabilities in fiscal 2006. The segment's operating expenses as a percentage of segment net sales in fiscal 2006 were higher than fiscal 2005 primarily due to expense pressures from utilities and advertising costs.

While our fiscal 2005 segment operating income as a percentage of segment net sales was unchanged from fiscal 2004, segment gross margin and operating expenses as a percentage of segment net sales were each up 0.4% for the year. Our gross margin improvement in fiscal 2005 can be primarily attributed to our global sourcing effort and reductions in markdowns and shrinkage as a percentage of segment net sales for fiscal 2005 when compared to fiscal 2004. The segment's operating expenses in fiscal 2005 as a percentage of segment net sales were higher than fiscal 2004 primarily due to expense pressures from associate wages and accident costs. Wages primarily increased due to our new job classification and pay structure, which was implemented in the second quarter of fiscal 2005.

SAM'S CLUB Segment

Fiscal Year	Segment Net Sales Increase from Prior Fiscal Year	Segment Operating Income (in millions)	Segment Operating Income Increase from Prior Fiscal Year	Operating Income as a Percentage of Segment Sales
2006	**7.2%**	**$1,385**	**8.2%**	**3.5%**
2005	7.5%	1,280	13.7%	3.4%
2004	8.9%	1,126	10.1%	3.3%

Growth in net sales for the SAM'S CLUB segment in fiscal 2006 and fiscal 2005 resulted from comparative club sales increases of 5.0% in fiscal 2006 and 5.8% in fiscal 2005, along with our expansion program. Comparative club sales in fiscal 2006 increased at a slower rate than in fiscal 2005 primarily due to lower growth rates in certain fresh and hardline categories. The impact of fuel sales contributed 130 basis points and 121 basis points to fiscal 2006 and 2005 comparative club sales, respectively. We believe that a greater focus on providing a quality in-club experience for our members will improve overall sales, including sales in these categories. Segment expansion consisted of the opening of 17 new clubs in fiscal 2006 and 13 clubs in fiscal 2005. One club closed in fiscal 2006. Our total expansion program added approximately 3 million of additional club square footage, or 3.8%, in fiscal 2006 and approximately 3 million, or 3.7%, of additional club square footage in fiscal 2005.

Segment operating income as a percentage of segment net sales increased slightly in fiscal 2006 when compared to fiscal 2005. The increase was due to an improvement in operating expenses and other income as a percentage of segment net sales, partially offset by a slight decrease in gross margin as a percentage of segment net sales. Operating expenses as a percentage of segment net sales improved primarily due to lower wage and accident costs in fiscal 2006 when

compared to fiscal 2005, partially offset by the impact of increased utility costs. The increase in other income as a percentage of segment net sales was primarily the result of income recognized from higher membership sales in fiscal 2006. Gross margin as a percentage of net sales decreased due to strong sales in certain lower margin categories, including fuel and tobacco, during fiscal 2006.

Segment operating income as a percentage of segment net sales increased slightly in fiscal 2005 when compared to fiscal 2004 due to an improvement in gross margin, partially offset by an increase in operating expenses as a percentage of segment net sales and the impact of the adoption of EITF 02-16 in fiscal 2004. The improvement in gross margin was primarily a result of strong sales in higher margin categories. Operating expenses as a percentage of segment net sales increased due to higher wage costs resulting from our new job classification and pay structure, which was implemented in the second quarter of fiscal 2005. The adoption of EITF 02-16 resulted in a decrease to the segment's operating income in fiscal 2004 of $44 million.

International Segment

Fiscal Year	Segment Net Sales Increase from Prior Fiscal Year	Segment Operating Income (in millions)	Segment Operating Income Increase from Prior Fiscal Year	Operating Income as a Percentage of Segment Sales
2006	**11.4%**	**$3,330**	**11.4%**	**5.3%**
2005	18.3%	2,988	26.1%	5.3%
2004	16.6%	2,370	18.6%	5.0%

At January 31, 2006, our International segment was comprised of wholly-owned operations in Argentina, Brazil, Canada, Germany, South Korea, Puerto Rico and the United Kingdom, the operation of joint ventures in China and the operations of majority-owned subsidiaries in Japan and Mexico.

The fiscal 2006 increase in the International segment's net sales primarily resulted from improved operating execution, our international expansion program and the impact of changes in foreign currency exchange rates. In fiscal 2006, the International segment opened 698 units, net of relocations and closings, which added 52 million, or 39.2%, of additional unit square footage. This includes the acquisition of Sonae Distribuição Brasil S.A. ("Sonae") in Southern Brazil, which added 139 stores and 11 million square feet in December 2005, and the consolidation of The Seiyu, Ltd. in Japan, which added 398 stores and 29 million square feet in December 2005. Additionally, the impact of changes in foreign currency exchange rates favorably affected the translation of International segment sales into U.S. dollars by an aggregate of $1.5 billion in fiscal 2006.

The fiscal 2005 increase in the International segment's net sales primarily resulted from improved operating execution, our international expansion program and the impact of foreign currency exchange rate changes. In fiscal 2005, the International segment opened 232 units, net of relocations and closings, which added 18 million, or 15.6%, of additional unit square footage. This includes the acquisition of Bompreço S.A. Supermercados do Nordeste in Brazil, which added 118 stores and approximately 8 million square feet in February 2004. Additionally, the impact of changes in foreign currency exchange rates favorably affected the translation of International segment sales into U.S. dollars by an aggregate of $3.2 billion in fiscal 2005.

Fiscal 2006 sales at our United Kingdom subsidiary, ASDA, were 42.7% of the International segment net sales. Sales for ASDA included in our consolidated income statement during fiscal 2006, 2005, and 2004 were $26.8 billion, $26.0 billion, and $21.7 billion, respectively.

While fiscal 2006 International segment operating income as a percentage of segment net sales was unchanged from fiscal 2005, segment gross margin was up 0.5%. This improvement in segment gross margin was offset by an increase in operating expenses and a decrease in other income, both as a percentage of segment net sales. The International segment's improvement in gross margin is primarily due to a favorable shift in the mix of products sold toward general merchandise categories which carry a higher margin. The 0.3% increase in operating expenses was driven primarily by increased advertising, utility and insurance expenditures. Other income declined 0.2% in fiscal 2006 primarily due to a reduction

in current year rental income in Canada and a payroll tax recovery in Mexico in fiscal 2005. Fiscal 2006 operating income includes a favorable impact of $64 million from changes in foreign currency exchange rates.

The fiscal 2005 increase in segment operating income as a percentage of segment net sales compared with fiscal 2004 resulted primarily from a 0.3% improvement in gross margin. The improvement in gross margin was due to a favorable shift in the mix of products sold toward general merchandise categories. Fiscal 2005 operating income includes a favorable impact of $150 million from changes in foreign currency exchange rates.

Future financial results for our foreign operations could be affected by factors such as changes in foreign currency exchange rates, weak economic conditions, changes in tax law and government regulations in the foreign markets in which we operate.

Liquidity and Capital Resources

Overview
Cash flows provided by operating activities supply us with a significant source of liquidity. Our cash flows from operating activities were $17.6 billion in fiscal 2006 compared with $15.0 billion in fiscal 2005. The increase in cash flows provided by operating activities was primarily attributable to improved income from operations and improved inventory management resulting in accounts payable growing at a faster rate than inventory.

Our cash flows from operating activities of continuing operations were $15.0 billion in fiscal 2005, compared with $15.9 billion in fiscal 2004. This decrease was primarily attributable to differences in the timing of payroll, income and other taxes, supplier payments and the timing of the collection of receivables in fiscal 2005 compared with fiscal 2004.

In fiscal 2006, we paid dividends of $2.5 billion, made $14.6 billion in capital expenditures, paid $3.6 billion to repurchase shares of our common stock, received $7.7 billion from the issuance of long-term debt, repaid $2.7 billion of long-term debt and repaid $704 million of commercial paper (net of issuances).

Working Capital
Current liabilities exceeded current assets at January 31, 2006, by $5.0 billion, an increase of $622 million from January 31, 2005. Our ratio of current assets to current liabilities was 0.9 to 1 at January 31, 2006 and 2005. At January 31, 2006, we had total assets of $138.2 billion compared with total assets of $120.2 billion at January 31, 2005.

Management's Discussion and Analysis of Results of Operations and Financial Condition
WAL-MART

Company Share Repurchase Program

From time to time, we repurchase shares of our common stock under a $10.0 billion share repurchase program authorized by our Board of Directors in September 2004. During the first half of fiscal 2006, we repurchased $3.6 billion of shares under this repurchase program. No shares of our common stock were repurchased under this program in the third or fourth quarters of fiscal 2006. During fiscal 2005, we repurchased $4.5 billion of shares under the current and past authorizations. At January 31, 2006, approximately $6.1 billion of additional shares may be repurchased under the current authorization.

There is no expiration date for or other restriction limiting the period over which we can make our share repurchases under the program, which will expire only when and if we have repurchased $10.0 billion of our shares under the program. Under the program, repurchased shares are constructively retired and returned to unissued status. We consider several factors in determining when to make share repurchases, including among other things, our current cash needs, the ratio of our debt to our total capitalization, our cost of borrowings, and the market price of the stock.

Common Stock Dividends

We paid dividends totaling approximately $2.5 billion or $0.60 per share in fiscal 2006. The dividends paid in fiscal 2006 represent a 15.4% increase over fiscal 2005. The fiscal 2005 dividend of $0.52 per share represented a 44.4% increase over fiscal 2004. We have increased our dividend every year since the first dividend was declared in March 1974.

On March 2, 2006, the Company's Board of Directors approved an increase in annual dividends to $0.67 per share. The annual dividend will be paid in four quarterly installments on April 3, 2006, June 5, 2006, September 5, 2006, and January 2, 2007 to holders of record on March 17, May 19, August 18 and December 15, 2006, respectively.

Contractual Obligations and Other Commercial Commitments

The following table sets forth certain information concerning our obligations and commitments to make contractual future payments, such as debt and lease agreements, and contingent commitments:

(In millions)		Payments due during fiscal years ending January 31,			
	Total	2007	2008-2009	2010-2011	Thereafter
Recorded Contractual Obligations					
Long-term debt	$31,024	$ 4,595	$ 6,178	$ 7,516	$ 12,735
Commercial paper	3,754	3,754	–	–	–
Capital lease obligations	6,380	592	1,138	1,040	3,610
Unrecorded Contractual Obligations:					
Non-cancelable operating leases	9,683	797	1,461	1,220	6,205
Interest on long-term debt	14,823	1,419	2,374	1,848	9,182
Undrawn lines of credit	5,296	5,296	–	–	–
Trade letters of credit	2,593	2,593	–	–	–
Standby letters of credit	2,800	2,800	–	–	–
Purchase obligations	19,872	10,519	9,023	218	112
Total commercial commitments	$96,225	$32,365	$20,174	$11,842	$31,844

Purchase obligations include all legally binding contracts such as firm commitments for inventory purchases, utility purchases, as well as commitments to make capital expenditures, software acquisition/license commitments and legally binding service contracts. Purchase orders for the purchase of inventory and other services are not included in the table above. Purchase orders represent authorizations to purchase rather than binding agreements. For the purposes of this table, contractual obligations for purchase of goods or services are defined as agreements that are enforceable and legally binding and that specify all significant terms, including: fixed or minimum quantities to be purchased; fixed, minimum or variable price provisions; and the approximate timing of the transaction. Our purchase orders are based on our current inventory needs and are fulfilled by our suppliers within short time periods. We also enter into contracts for outsourced services; however, the obligations under these contracts are not significant and the contracts generally contain clauses allowing for cancellation without significant penalty.

The expected timing for payment of the obligations discussed above is estimated based on current information. Timing of payments and actual amounts paid may be different depending on the timing of receipt of goods or services or changes to agreed-upon amounts for some obligations.

Off Balance Sheet Arrangements

In addition to the unrecorded contractual obligations discussed and presented above, the Company has made certain guarantees as discussed below for which the timing of payment, if any, is unknown.

In connection with certain debt financing, we could be liable for early termination payments if certain unlikely events were to occur. At January 31, 2006, the aggregate termination payment was $89 million. These two arrangements expire in fiscal 2011 and fiscal 2019.

In connection with the development of our grocery distribution network in the United States, we have agreements with third parties which would require us to purchase or assume the leases on certain unique equipment in the event the agreements are terminated. These agreements, which can be terminated by either party at will, cover up to a five-year period and obligate the Company to pay up to approximately $233 million upon termination of some or all of these agreements.

There are no recourse provisions which would enable us to recover from third parties any amounts paid under the above guarantees. No liability for these guarantees has been recorded in our financial statements.

The Company has entered into lease commitments for land and buildings for 60 future locations. These lease commitments with real estate developers provide for minimum rentals ranging from five to 35 years, which, if consummated based on current cost estimates, will approximate $95 million annually over the lease terms.

Capital Resources

During fiscal 2006, we issued $7.7 billion of long-term debt. The net proceeds from the issuance of such long-term debt were used to repay outstanding commercial paper indebtedness and for other general corporate purposes.

At January 31, 2006 and 2005, the ratio of our debt to our total capitalization was 42% and 39%, respectively. The fiscal 2006 consolidation of Seiyu and purchase of Sonae increased our debt to total capitalization at January 31, 2006, by 2.5 percentage points. Our objective is to maintain a debt to total capitalization ratio averaging approximately 40%.

Management believes that cash flows from operations and proceeds from the sale of commercial paper will be sufficient to finance any seasonal buildups in merchandise inventories and meet other cash requirements. If our operating cash flows are not sufficient to pay dividends and to fund our capital expenditures, we anticipate funding any shortfall in these expenditures with a combination of commercial paper and long-term debt. We plan to refinance existing long-term debt as it matures and may desire to obtain additional long-term financing for other corporate purposes. We anticipate no difficulty in obtaining long-term financing in view of our credit rating and favorable experiences in the debt market in the recent past. The following table details the ratings of the credit rating agencies that rated our outstanding indebtedness at January 31, 2006.

Rating agency	Commercial paper	Long-term debt
Standard and Poor's	A-1+	AA
Moody's Investors Service	P-1	Aa2
Fitch Ratings	F1+	AA
Dominion Bond Rating Service	R-1(middle)	AA

In February 2006, we entered into a £150 million revolving credit facility in the United Kingdom. Interest on borrowings under the credit facility accrues at LIBOR plus 25 basis points.

Future Expansion

Capital expenditures for fiscal 2007 are expected to be approximately $17.5 billion, including additions of capital leases. These fiscal 2007 expenditures will include the construction of 20 to 30 new discount stores, 270 to 280 new supercenters (with relocations or expansions accounting for approximately 160 of those supercenters), 15 to 20 new Neighborhood Markets, 30 to 40 new SAM'S CLUBs (with relocations or expansions accounting for 20 of those SAM'S CLUBs) and 220 to 230 new units in our International segment (with relocations or expansions accounting for approximately 35 of those units). We plan to finance this expansion, and any acquisitions of other operations that we may make during fiscal 2007, primarily out of cash flows from operations.

Market Risk

In addition to the risks inherent in our operations, we are exposed to certain market risks, including changes in interest rates and changes in foreign currency exchange rates.

The analysis presented for each of our market risk sensitive instruments is based on a 10% change in interest or foreign currency exchange rates. These changes are hypothetical scenarios used to calibrate potential risk and do not represent our view of future market changes. As the hypothetical figures indicate, changes in fair value based on the assumed change in rates generally cannot be extrapolated because the relationship of the change in assumption to the change in fair value may not be linear. The effect of a variation in a particular assumption is calculated without changing any other assumption. In reality, changes in one factor may result in changes in another, which may magnify or counteract the sensitivities.

At January 31, 2006 and 2005, we had $31.0 billion and $23.8 billion, respectively, of long-term debt outstanding. Our weighted average effective interest rate on long-term debt, after considering the effect of interest rate swaps, was 4.79% and 4.08% at January 31, 2006 and 2005, respectively. A hypothetical 10% increase in interest rates in effect at January 31, 2006 and 2005, would have increased annual interest expense on borrowings outstanding at those dates by $48 million and $25 million, respectively.

At January 31, 2006 and 2005, we had $3.8 billion of outstanding commercial paper obligations. The rate, including fees, on these obligations at January 31, 2006 and 2005, was 3.9% and 2.9%, respectively. A hypothetical 10% increase in commercial paper rates in effect at January 31, 2006 and 2005, would have increased annual interest expense on the outstanding balances on those dates by $14 million and $11 million, respectively.

Management's Discussion and Analysis of Results of Operations and Financial Condition
WAL-MART

We enter into interest rate swaps to minimize the risks and costs associated with financing activities, as well as to maintain an appropriate mix of fixed- and floating-rate debt. Our preference is to maintain approximately 50% of our debt portfolio, including interest rate swaps, in floating-rate debt. The swap agreements are contracts to exchange fixed- or variable-rates for variable- or fixed-interest rate payments periodically over the life of the instruments. The aggregate fair value of these swaps was a gain of approximately $133 million and $472 million at January 31, 2006 and 2005, respectively. A hypothetical increase (or decrease) of 10% in interest rates from the level in effect at January 31, 2006, would result in a (loss) or gain in value of the swaps of ($103 million) or $104 million, respectively. A hypothetical increase (or decrease) of 10% in interest rates from the level in effect at January 31, 2005, would result in a (loss) or gain in value of the swaps of ($123 million) or $126 million, respectively.

We hold currency swaps to hedge the foreign currency exchange component of our net investments in the United Kingdom and Japan. In addition, we hold a cross-currency swap which hedges the foreign currency risk of debt denominated in currencies other than the local currency. The aggregate fair value of these swaps at January 31, 2006 and 2005, was a loss of $244 million and $169 million, respectively. A hypothetical 10% increase (or decrease) in the foreign currency exchange rates underlying these swaps from the market rate would result in a (loss) or gain in the value of the swaps of ($96 million) and $78 million at January 31, 2006, and ($90 million) and $71 million at January 31, 2005. A hypothetical 10% change in interest rates underlying these swaps from the market rates in effect at January 31, 2006 and 2005, would have an insignificant impact on the value of the swaps.

In addition to currency swaps, we have designated debt of approximately £2.0 billion as of January 31, 2006 and 2005, as a hedge of our net investment in the United Kingdom. At January 31, 2006, a hypothetical 10% increase (or decrease) in value of the U.S. dollar relative to the British pound would result in a gain (or loss) in the value of the debt of $359 million. At January 31, 2005, a hypothetical 10% increase (or decrease) in value of the U.S. dollar relative to the British pound would result in a gain (or loss) in the value of the debt of $380 million. In addition, we have designated debt of approximately ¥87.1 billion as of January 31, 2006 as a hedge of our net investment in Japan. At January 31, 2006, a hypothetical 10% increase (or decrease) in value of the U.S. dollar relative to the Japanese yen would result in a gain (or loss) in the value of the debt of $75 million.

Summary of Critical Accounting Policies
Management strives to report the financial results of the Company in a clear and understandable manner, although in some cases accounting and disclosure rules are complex and require us to use technical terminology. In preparing our consolidated financial statements, we follow accounting principles generally accepted in the United States. These principles require us to make certain estimates and apply judgments that affect our financial position and results of operations as reflected in our financial statements. These judgments and estimates are based on past events and expectations of future outcomes. Actual results may differ from our estimates.

Management continually reviews its accounting policies, how they are applied and how they are reported and disclosed in our financial statements. Following is a summary of our more significant accounting policies and how they are applied in preparation of the financial statements.

Inventories
We value our inventories at the lower of cost or market as determined primarily by the retail method of accounting, using the last-in, first-out ("LIFO") method for substantially all merchandise inventories in the United States, except SAM'S CLUB merchandise and merchandise in our distribution warehouses, which is based on the cost LIFO method. Inventories for international operations are primarily valued by the retail method of accounting and are stated using the first-in, first-out ("FIFO") method.

Under the retail method, inventory is stated at cost, which is determined by applying a cost-to-retail ratio to each merchandise grouping's retail value. The cost-to-retail ratio is based on the fiscal year purchase activity. The retail method requires management to make certain judgments and estimates that may significantly impact the ending inventory valuation at cost as well as the amount of gross margin recognized. Judgments made include the recording of markdowns used to sell through inventory and shrinkage. Markdowns designated for clearance activity are recorded at the time of the decision rather than at the point of sale, when management determines the salability of inventory has diminished. Factors considered in the determination of markdowns include current and anticipated demand, customer preferences and age of merchandise, as well as seasonal and fashion trends. Changes in weather patterns and customer preferences related to fashion trends could cause material changes in the amount and timing of markdowns from year to year.

When necessary, the Company records a LIFO provision each quarter for the estimated annual effect of inflation, and these estimates are adjusted to actual results determined at year-end. Our LIFO provision is calculated based on inventory levels, markup rates and internally generated retail price indices except for grocery items, for which we use a consumer price index. At January 31, 2006 and 2005, our inventories valued at LIFO approximated those inventories as if they were valued at FIFO.

The Company provides for estimated inventory losses ("shrinkage") between physical inventory counts on the basis of a percentage of sales. The provision is adjusted annually to reflect the historical trend of the actual physical inventory count results. Historically, shrinkage has not been volatile.

Impairment of Assets
We evaluate long-lived assets other than goodwill for indicators of impairment whenever events or changes in circumstances indicate their carrying values may not be recoverable. Management's judgments regarding the existence of impairment indicators are based on market conditions and our operational performance, such as operating income and cash flows. The variability of these factors depends on a number of conditions, including uncertainty about future events, and thus our accounting estimates may change from period

to period. These factors could cause management to conclude that impairment indicators exist and require that impairment tests be performed, which could result in management determining that the value of long-lived assets is impaired, resulting in a writedown of the long-lived assets.

Goodwill is not amortized, but is evaluated for impairment annually or whenever events or changes in circumstances indicate that the value of certain goodwill may be impaired. This evaluation requires management to make judgments relating to future cash flows, growth rates, and economic and market conditions. These evaluations are based on discounted cash flows that incorporate the impact of existing Company businesses. Historically, the Company has generated sufficient returns to recover the cost of goodwill and other intangible assets. Because of the nature of the factors used in these tests, if different conditions occur in future periods, future operating results could be materially impacted.

Income Taxes

The determination of our provision for income taxes requires significant judgment, the use of estimates, and the interpretation and application of complex tax laws. Significant judgment is required in assessing the timing and amounts of deductible and taxable items. We establish reserves when, despite our belief that our tax return positions are fully supportable, we believe that certain positions may be successfully challenged. When facts and circumstances change, we adjust these reserves through our provision for income taxes.

Self-Insurance

We use a combination of insurance, self-insured retention and self-insurance for a number of risks, including, without limitation, workers' compensation, general liability, vehicle liability and the Company's portion of employee-related health care benefits. Liabilities associated with the risks that we retain are estimated in part by considering historical claims experience, including frequency, severity, demographic factors, and other actuarial assumptions. In calculating our liability, we analyze our historical trends, including loss development, and apply appropriate loss development factors to the incurred costs associated with the claims made against our self-insured program. The estimated accruals for these liabilities could be significantly affected if future occurrences or loss development differ from these assumptions. For example, for workers' compensation and liability, a 1% increase or decrease to the assumptions for claims costs and loss development factors would increase or decrease our self-insurance accrual by $23 million and $62 million, respectively.

For a summary of our significant accounting policies, please see Note 1 to our consolidated financial statements that appear after this discussion.

Forward-Looking Statements

This Annual Report contains statements that Wal-Mart believes are "forward-looking statements" within the meaning of the Private Securities Litigation Reform Act of 1995. Those statements are intended to enjoy the protection of the safe harbor for forward-looking statements provided by that Act. These forward-looking statements include statements under the caption "Results of Operations" regarding the effect of the opening of new stores on existing stores' sales and the trend in the percentages that the net sales of certain of our business segments represent of our total net sales, under the caption "SAM'S CLUB Segment" regarding the improvement in net sales in the SAM'S CLUB Segment and under the caption "Liquidity and Capital Resources" in Management's Discussion and Analysis of Financial Condition and Results of Operations with respect to our capital expenditures, our ability to fund certain cash flow shortfalls by the sale of commercial paper and long-term debt securities, our ability to sell our long-term securities and our anticipated reasons for repurchasing shares of our common stock. These statements are identified by the use of the words "anticipate," "believe," "contemplate," "expect," "plan," and other, similar words or phrases. Similarly, descriptions of our objectives, strategies, plans, goals or targets are also forward-looking statements. These statements discuss, among other things, expected growth, future revenues, future cash flows, future capital expenditures, future performance and the anticipation and expectations of Wal-Mart and its management as to future occurrences and trends. These forward-looking statements are subject to certain factors, in the United States and internationally, that could affect our financial performance, business strategy, plans, goals and objectives. Those factors include the cost of goods, labor costs, the cost of fuel and electricity, the cost of healthcare benefits, insurance costs, catastrophic events, competitive pressures, inflation, accident-related costs, consumer buying patterns and debt levels, weather patterns, transport of goods from foreign suppliers, currency exchange fluctuations, trade restrictions, changes in tariff and freight rates, changes in tax and other laws and regulations that affect our business, the outcome of legal proceedings to which we are a party, unemployment levels, interest rate fluctuations, changes in employment legislation and other capital market, economic and geo-political conditions. Moreover, we typically earn a disproportionate part of our annual operating income in the fourth quarter as a result of the seasonal buying patterns. Those buying patterns are difficult to forecast with certainty. The foregoing list of factors that may affect our performance is not exclusive. Other factors and unanticipated events could adversely affect our business operations and financial performance. We discuss certain of these matters more fully, as well as certain risk factors that may affect our business operations, financial condition and results of operations, in other of our filings with the SEC, including our Annual Report on Form 10-K. We filed our Annual Report on Form 10-K for the year ended January 31, 2006, with the SEC on or about March 29, 2006. Actual results may materially differ from anticipated results described or implied in these forward-looking statements as a result of changes in facts, assumptions not being realized or other circumstances. You are urged to consider all of these risks, uncertainties and other factors carefully in evaluating the forward-looking statements. The forward-looking statements included in this Annual Report are made only as of the date of this report, and we undertake no obligation to update these forward-looking statements to reflect subsequent events or circumstances, except as may be required by applicable law.

Consolidated Statements of Income
WAL-MART

(Amounts in millions except per share data)

Fiscal Year Ended January 31,	2006	2005	2004
Revenues:			
Net sales	$312,427	$285,222	$256,329
Other income, net	3,227	2,910	2,352
	315,654	288,132	258,681
Costs and expenses:			
Cost of sales	240,391	219,793	198,747
Operating, selling, general and administrative expenses	56,733	51,248	44,909
Operating income	18,530	17,091	15,025
Interest:			
Debt	1,171	934	729
Capital leases	249	253	267
Interest income	(248)	(201)	(164)
Interest, net	1,172	986	832
Income from continuing operations before income taxes and minority interest	17,358	16,105	14,193
Provision for income taxes:			
Current	5,932	5,326	4,941
Deferred	(129)	263	177
	5,803	5,589	5,118
Income from continuing operations before minority interest	11,555	10,516	9,075
Minority interest	(324)	(249)	(214)
Income from continuing operations	11,231	10,267	8,861
Income from discontinued operation, net of tax	–	–	193
Net income	$ 11,231	$ 10,267	$ 9,054
Basic net income per common share:			
Income from continuing operations	$ 2.68	$ 2.41	$ 2.03
Income from discontinued operation	–	–	0.05
Basic net income per common share	$ 2.68	$ 2.41	$ 2.08
Diluted net income per common share:			
Income from continuing operations	$ 2.68	$ 2.41	$ 2.03
Income from discontinued operation	–	–	0.04
Diluted net income per common share	$ 2.68	$ 2.41	$ 2.07
Weighted-average number of common shares:			
Basic	4,183	4,259	4,363
Diluted	4,188	4,266	4,373
Dividends per common share	$ 0.60	$ 0.52	$ 0.36

See accompanying notes.

Consolidated Balance Sheets
WAL-MART

(Amounts in millions except per share data)

January 31,	2006	2005
Assets		
Current assets:		
Cash and cash equivalents	$ 6,414	$ 5,488
Receivables	2,662	1,715
Inventories	32,191	29,762
Prepaid expenses and other	2,557	1,889
Total current assets	43,824	38,854
Property and equipment, at cost:		
Land	16,643	14,472
Buildings and improvements	56,163	46,574
Fixtures and equipment	22,750	21,461
Transportation equipment	1,746	1,530
Property and equipment, at cost	97,302	84,037
Less accumulated depreciation	21,427	18,637
Property and equipment, net	75,875	65,400
Property under capital lease:		
Property under capital lease	5,578	4,556
Less accumulated amortization	2,163	1,838
Property under capital lease, net	3,415	2,718
Goodwill	12,188	10,803
Other assets and deferred charges	2,885	2,379
Total assets	**$138,187**	**$120,154**
Liabilities and shareholders' equity		
Current liabilities:		
Commercial paper	$ 3,754	$ 3,812
Accounts payable	25,373	21,987
Accrued liabilities	13,465	12,120
Accrued income taxes	1,340	1,281
Long-term debt due within one year	4,595	3,759
Obligations under capital leases due within one year	299	223
Total current liabilities	48,826	43,182
Long-term debt	26,429	20,087
Long-term obligations under capital leases	3,742	3,171
Deferred income taxes and other	4,552	2,978
Minority interest	1,467	1,340
Commitments and contingencies		
Shareholders' equity:		
Preferred stock ($0.10 par value; 100 shares authorized, none issued)	–	–
Common stock ($0.10 par value; 11,000 shares authorized, 4,165 and 4,234 issued and outstanding at January 31, 2006 and January 31, 2005, respectively)	417	423
Capital in excess of par value	2,596	2,425
Accumulated other comprehensive income	1,053	2,694
Retained earnings	49,105	43,854
Total shareholders' equity	53,171	49,396
Total liabilities and shareholders' equity	**$138,187**	**$120,154**

See accompanying notes.

Consolidated Statements of Shareholders' Equity
WAL-MART

(Amounts in millions except per share data)	Number of Shares	Common Stock	Capital in Excess of Par Value	Accumulated Other Comprehensive Income	Retained Earnings	Total
Balance – January 31, 2003	4,395	$ 440	$ 1,954	$ (509)	$ 37,576	$ 39,461
Comprehensive income:						
Net income from continuing operations					8,861	8,861
Net income from discontinued operation					193	193
Other comprehensive income:						
Foreign currency translation				1,685		1,685
Net unrealized depreciation of derivatives				(341)		(341)
Minimum pension liability				16		16
Total comprehensive income						10,414
Cash dividends ($0.36 per share)					(1,569)	(1,569)
Purchase of Company stock	(92)	(9)	(182)		(4,855)	(5,046)
Stock options exercised and other	8		363			363
Balance – January 31, 2004	4,311	431	2,135	851	40,206	43,623
Comprehensive income:						
Net income from continuing operations					10,267	10,267
Other comprehensive income:						
Foreign currency translation				2,130		2,130
Net unrealized depreciation of derivatives				(194)		(194)
Minimum pension liability				(93)		(93)
Total comprehensive income						12,110
Cash dividends ($0.52 per share)					(2,214)	(2,214)
Purchase of Company stock	(81)	(8)	(136)		(4,405)	(4,549)
Stock options exercised and other	4		426			426
Balance – January 31, 2005	4,234	423	2,425	2,694	43,854	49,396
Comprehensive income:						
Net income from continuing operations					11,231	11,231
Other comprehensive income:						
Foreign currency translation				(1,920)		(1,920)
Net unrealized depreciation of derivatives				228		228
Minimum pension liability				51		51
Total comprehensive income						9,590
Cash dividends ($0.60 per share)					(2,511)	(2,511)
Purchase of Company stock	(74)	(7)	(104)		(3,469)	(3,580)
Stock options exercised and other	5	1	275			276
Balance – January 31, 2006	4,165	$417	$2,596	$1,053	$49,105	$53,171

See accompanying notes.

Consolidated Statements of Cash Flows
WAL-MART

(Amounts in millions)

Fiscal Year Ended January 31,	2006	2005	2004
Cash flows from operating activities			
Income from continuing operations	$ 11,231	$ 10,267	$ 8,861
Adjustments to reconcile net income to net cash			
provided by operating activities:			
Depreciation and amortization	4,717	4,264	3,852
Deferred income taxes	(129)	263	177
Other operating activities	620	378	173
Changes in certain assets and liabilities, net of effects of acquisitions:			
Decrease (increase) in accounts receivable	(456)	(304)	373
Increase in inventories	(1,733)	(2,494)	(1,973)
Increase in accounts payable	2,390	1,694	2,587
Increase in accrued liabilities	993	976	1,896
Net cash provided by operating activities of continuing operations	17,633	15,044	15,946
Net cash provided by operating activities of discontinued operation	–	–	50
Net cash provided by operating activities	17,633	15,044	15,996
Cash flows from investing activities			
Payments for property and equipment	(14,563)	(12,893)	(10,308)
Investment in international operations, net of cash acquired	(601)	(315)	(38)
Proceeds from the disposal of fixed assets	1,049	953	481
Proceeds from the sale of McLane	–	–	1,500
Other investing activities	(68)	(96)	78
Net cash used in investing activities of continuing operations	(14,183)	(12,351)	(8,287)
Net cash used in investing activities of discontinued operation	–	–	(25)
Net cash used in investing activities	(14,183)	(12,351)	(8,312)
Cash flows from financing activities			
Increase (decrease) in commercial paper	(704)	544	688
Proceeds from issuance of long-term debt	7,691	5,832	4,099
Purchase of Company stock	(3,580)	(4,549)	(5,046)
Dividends paid	(2,511)	(2,214)	(1,569)
Payment of long-term debt	(2,724)	(2,131)	(3,541)
Payment of capital lease obligations	(245)	(204)	(305)
Other financing activities	(349)	113	111
Net cash used in financing activities	(2,422)	(2,609)	(5,563)
Effect of exchange rate changes on cash	(102)	205	320
Net increase in cash and cash equivalents	926	289	2,441
Cash and cash equivalents at beginning of year	5,488	5,199	2,758
Cash and cash equivalents at end of year	$ 6,414	$ 5,488	$ 5,199
Supplemental disclosure of cash flow information			
Income tax paid	$ 5,962	$ 5,593	$ 4,538
Interest paid	1,390	1,163	1,024
Capital lease obligations incurred	286	377	252

See accompanying notes.

Notes to Consolidated Financial Statements
WAL-MART

1 SUMMARY OF SIGNIFICANT ACCOUNTING POLICIES

Consolidation

The consolidated financial statements include the accounts of Wal-Mart Stores, Inc. and its subsidiaries ("Wal-Mart" or the "Company"). Significant intercompany transactions have been eliminated in consolidation. Investments in which the Company has a 20 percent to 50 percent voting interest and where the Company exercises significant influence over the investee are accounted for using the equity method.

The Company's operations in Argentina, Brazil, China, Germany, Japan, Mexico, South Korea and the United Kingdom are consolidated using a December 31 fiscal year-end, generally due to statutory reporting requirements. There were no significant intervening events which materially affected the financial statements. The Company's operations in Canada and Puerto Rico are consolidated using a January 31 fiscal year-end.

The Company consolidates the accounts of certain variable interest entities where it has been determined that Wal-Mart is the primary beneficiary of those entities' operations. The assets, liabilities and results of operations of these entities are not material to the Company.

Cash and Cash Equivalents

The Company considers investments with a maturity of three months or less when purchased to be cash equivalents. The majority of payments due from banks for third-party credit card, debit card and electronic benefit transactions ("EBT") process within 24-48 hours, except for transactions occurring on a Friday, which are generally processed the following Monday. All credit card, debit card and EBT transactions that process in less than seven days are classified as cash and cash equivalents. Amounts due from banks for these transactions classified as cash totaled $575 million and $549 million at January 31, 2006 and 2005, respectively.

Receivables

Accounts receivable consist primarily of receivables from insurance companies resulting from our pharmacy sales, receivables from suppliers for marketing or incentive programs, receivables from real estate transactions and receivables from property insurance claims. Additionally, amounts due from banks for customer credit card, debit card and EBT transactions that take in excess of seven days to process are classified as accounts receivable.

Inventories

The Company values inventories at the lower of cost or market as determined primarily by the retail method of accounting, using the last-in, first-out ("LIFO") method for substantially all merchandise inventories in the United States, except SAM'S CLUB merchandise and merchandise in our distribution warehouses, which is based on the cost LIFO method. Inventories of foreign operations are primarily valued by the retail method of accounting, using the first-in, first-out ("FIFO") method. At January 31, 2006 and 2005, our inventories valued at LIFO approximate those inventories as if they were valued at FIFO.

Financial Instruments

The Company uses derivative financial instruments for purposes other than trading to manage its exposure to interest and foreign exchange rates, as well as to maintain an appropriate mix of fixed and floating-rate debt. Contract terms of a hedge instrument closely mirror those of the hedged item, providing a high degree of risk reduction and correlation. Contracts that are effective at meeting the risk reduction and correlation criteria are recorded using hedge accounting. If a derivative instrument is a hedge, depending on the nature of the hedge, changes in the fair value of the instrument will either be offset against the change in fair value of the hedged assets, liabilities or firm commitments through earnings or recognized in other comprehensive income until the hedged item is recognized in earnings. The ineffective portion of an instrument's change in fair value will be immediately recognized in earnings. Instruments that do not meet the criteria for hedge accounting, or contracts for which the Company has not elected hedge accounting, are marked to fair value with unrealized gains or losses reported in earnings during the period of change.

Capitalized Interest

Interest costs capitalized on construction projects were $157 million, $120 million, and $144 million in fiscal 2006, 2005 and 2004, respectively.

Long-Lived Assets

Long-lived assets are stated at cost. Management reviews long-lived assets for indicators of impairment whenever events or changes in circumstances indicate that the carrying value may not be recoverable. The evaluation is performed at the lowest level of identifiable cash flows, which is typically at the individual store level. Cash flows expected to be generated by the related assets are estimated over the asset's useful life based on updated projections. If the evaluation indicates that the carrying amount of the asset may not be recoverable, any potential impairment is measured based on a projected discounted cash flow method using a discount rate that is considered to be commensurate with the risk inherent in the Company's current business model.

Goodwill and Other Acquired Intangible Assets

Goodwill is not amortized; rather it is evaluated for impairment annually or whenever events or changes in circumstances indicate that the value of certain goodwill may be impaired. Other acquired intangible assets are amortized on a straight-line basis over the periods that expected economic benefits will be provided. These evaluations are based on discounted cash flows and incorporate the impact of existing Company businesses. The analyses require significant management judgment to evaluate the capacity of an acquired business to perform within projections. Historically, the Company has generated sufficient returns to recover the cost of the goodwill and other intangible assets.

Goodwill is recorded on the balance sheet in the operating segments as follows (in millions):

January 31,	2006	2005
International	$11,883	$10,498
SAM'S CLUB	305	305
Total goodwill	$12,188	$10,803

The fiscal 2006 consolidation of The Seiyu, Ltd. and acquisition of Sonae Distribuição Brasil S.A. and the fiscal 2005 acquisition of Bompreço S.A. Supermercados do Nordeste resulted in increases to goodwill. In addition, changes in the International segment's goodwill result from foreign currency exchange rate fluctuations.

Leases

The Company estimates the expected term of a lease by assuming the exercise of renewal options where an economic penalty exists that would preclude the abandonment of the lease at the end of the initial non-cancelable term and the exercise of such renewal is at the sole discretion of the Company. This expected term is used in the determination of whether a store lease is a capital or operating lease and in the calculation of straight-line rent expense. Additionally, the useful life of leasehold improvements is limited by the expected lease term. If significant expenditures are made for leasehold improvements late in the expected term of a lease, judgment is applied to determine if the leasehold improvements have a useful life that extends beyond the original expected lease term or if the leasehold improvements have a useful life that is bound by the end of the original expected lease term.

Rent abatements and escalations are considered in the calculation of minimum lease payments in the Company's capital lease tests and in determining straight-line rent expense for operating leases.

Foreign Currency Translation

The assets and liabilities of all foreign subsidiaries are translated using exchange rates at the balance sheet date. The income statements of foreign subsidiaries are translated using average exchange rates. Related translation adjustments are recorded as a component of accumulated other comprehensive income.

Revenue Recognition

The Company recognizes sales revenue net of estimated sales returns at the time it sells merchandise to the customer, except for layaway transactions. The Company recognizes revenue from layaway transactions when the customer satisfies all payment obligations and takes possession of the merchandise. Customer purchases of Wal-Mart and SAM'S CLUB shopping cards are not recognized as revenue until the card is redeemed and the customer purchases merchandise by using the shopping card.

SAM'S CLUB Membership Fee Revenue Recognition

The Company recognizes SAM'S CLUB membership fee revenues both in the United States and internationally over the term of the membership, which is 12 months. The following table details unearned revenues, membership fees received from members and the amount of revenues recognized in earnings for each of the fiscal years 2006, 2005 and 2004 (in millions):

Fiscal Year Ended January 31,	2006	2005	2004
Deferred membership fee revenue, beginning of year	$ 458	$ 449	$ 437
Membership fees received	940	890	840
Membership fee revenue recognized	(908)	(881)	(828)
Deferred membership fee revenue, end of year	$ 490	$ 458	$ 449

SAM'S CLUB membership revenue is included in other income, net in the revenues section of the Consolidated Statements of Income.

The Company's deferred membership fee revenue is included in accrued liabilities in the Consolidated Balance Sheets. The Company's analysis of historical membership fee refunds indicates that such refunds have been nominal. Accordingly, no reserve existed for membership fee refunds at January 31, 2006 and 2005.

Cost of Sales

Cost of sales includes actual product cost, change in inventory, the cost of transportation to the Company's warehouses from suppliers, the cost of transportation from the Company's warehouses to the stores and clubs and the cost of warehousing for our SAM'S CLUB segment.

Payments from Suppliers

Wal-Mart receives money from suppliers for various programs, primarily volume incentives, warehouse allowances and reimbursements for specific programs such as markdowns, margin protection and advertising. Substantially all allowances are accounted for as a reduction of purchases and recognized in our Consolidated Statements of Income when the related inventory is sold.

Operating, Selling, General and Administrative Expenses

Operating, selling, general and administrative expenses include all operating costs of the Company that are not related to the transportation of products from the supplier to the warehouse or from the warehouse to the store. Additionally, the cost of warehousing and occupancy for our Wal-Mart Stores segment distribution facilities are included in operating, selling, general and administrative expenses. Because we do not include the cost of our Wal-Mart Stores segment distribution facilities in cost of sales, our gross profit and gross margin may not be comparable to those of other retailers that may include all costs related to their distribution facilities in costs of sales and in the calculation of gross profit and gross margin.

Notes to Consolidated Financial Statements
WAL-MART

Advertising Costs

Advertising costs are expensed as incurred and were $1.6 billion, $1.4 billion and $966 million in fiscal 2006, 2005 and 2004, respectively. Advertising costs consist primarily of print and television advertisements.

Pre-Opening Costs

The costs of start-up activities, including organization costs and new store openings, are expensed as incurred.

Share-Based Compensation

The Company recognizes expense for its share-based compensation based on the fair value of the awards that are granted. The fair value of stock options is estimated at the date of grant using the Black-Scholes-Merton option valuation model which was developed for use in estimating the fair value of exchange traded options that have no vesting restrictions and are fully transferable. Option valuation methods require the input of highly subjective assumptions, including the expected stock price volatility. Measured compensation cost is recognized ratably over the vesting period of the related share-based compensation award.

Share-based compensation awards that may be settled in cash are accounted for as liabilities and marked to market each period.

Insurance/Self-Insurance

The Company uses a combination of insurance, self-insured retention and self-insurance for a number of risks, including, without limitation, workers' compensation, general liability, vehicle liability and the Company-funded portion of employee-related health care benefits. Liabilities associated with these risks are estimated in part by considering historical claims experience, demographic factors, frequency and severity factors and other actuarial assumptions.

Depreciation and Amortization

Depreciation and amortization for financial statement purposes are provided on the straight-line method over the estimated useful lives of the various assets. Depreciation expense, including amortization of property under capital leases for fiscal years 2006, 2005 and 2004 was $4.7 billion, $4.3 billion and $3.9 billion, respectively. For income tax purposes, accelerated methods of depreciation are used with recognition of deferred income taxes for the resulting temporary differences. Leasehold improvements are depreciated over the shorter of the estimated useful life of the asset or the remaining lease term. Estimated useful lives for financial statement purposes are as follows:

Buildings and improvements	5 – 50 years
Fixtures and equipment	3 – 12 years
Transportation equipment	3 – 15 years

Income Taxes

Income taxes are accounted for under the asset and liability method. Deferred tax assets and liabilities are recognized for the estimated future tax consequences attributable to differences between the financial statement carrying amounts of existing assets and liabilities and their respective tax bases. Deferred tax assets and liabilities are measured using enacted tax rates in effect for the year in which those temporary differences are expected to be recovered or settled. The effect on deferred tax assets and liabilities of a change in tax rate is recognized in income in the period that includes the enactment date. Valuation allowances are established when necessary to reduce deferred tax assets to the amounts more likely than not to be realized.

In determining the quarterly provision for income taxes, the Company uses an annual effective tax rate based on expected annual income and statutory tax rates. The effective tax rate also reflects the Company's assessment of the ultimate outcome of tax audits. Significant discrete items are separately recognized in the income tax provision in the quarter in which they occur.

The determination of the Company's provision for income taxes requires significant judgment, the use of estimates, and the interpretation and application of complex tax laws. Significant judgment is required in assessing the timing and amounts of deductible and taxable items. Reserves are established when, despite management's belief that the Company's tax return positions are fully supportable, management believes that certain positions may be successfully challenged. When facts and circumstances change, these reserves are adjusted through the provision for income taxes.

Net Income Per Common Share

Basic net income per common share is based on the weighted-average outstanding common shares. Diluted net income per common share is based on the weighted-average outstanding shares adjusted for the dilutive effect of stock options and restricted stock grants. The dilutive effect of stock options and restricted stock was 5 million, 7 million and 10 million shares in fiscal 2006, 2005 and 2004, respectively. The Company had approximately 57 million, 59 million and 50 million option shares outstanding at January 31, 2006, 2005 and 2004, respectively, which were not included in the diluted net income per share calculation because their effect would be antidilutive as the underlying option price exceeded the average market price of the stock for the period.

Estimates and Assumptions

The preparation of consolidated financial statements in conformity with generally accepted accounting principles requires Management to make estimates and assumptions. These estimates and assumptions affect the reported amounts of assets and liabilities. They also affect the disclosure of contingent assets and liabilities at the date of the consolidated financial statements and the reported amounts of revenues and expenses during the reporting period. Actual results may differ from those estimates.

Reclassifications

Certain reclassifications have been made to prior periods to conform to current presentations.

2 COMMERCIAL PAPER AND LONG-TERM DEBT

Information on short-term borrowings and interest rates is as follows (dollars in millions):

Fiscal Year	**2006**	2005	2004
Maximum amount outstanding at any month-end	**$9,054**	$7,782	$4,957
Average daily short-term borrowings	**5,719**	4,823	1,498
Weighted-average interest rate	**3.4%**	1.6%	1.1%

At January 31, 2006 and 2005, short-term borrowings consisted of $3.8 billion of commercial paper. At January 31, 2006, the Company had committed lines of credit of $5.0 billion with 57 firms and banks, which were used to support commercial paper, and committed and informal lines of credit with various banks totaling an additional $693 million.

Long-term debt at January 31, consists of (in millions):

Interest Rate	Due by Fiscal Year	**2006**	2005
2.130 – 6.875%	Notes due 2010	**$ 4,527**	$ 4,500
5.250%	Notes due 2036	**4,279**	1,883
1.100 – 13.250%, LIBOR less 0.140%	Notes due 2007	**3,415**	3,164
2.875 – 8.380%, LIBOR less 0.1025%	Notes due 2008	**3,311**	1,500
0.1838 – 0.880%	Notes due 2011[1]	**3,308**	500
0.750 – 7.250%	Notes due 2014	**2,885**	2,883
3.000 – 3.375%	Notes due 2009	**2,800**	1,000
1.200 – 4.125%	Notes due 2012	**2,015**	2,000
5.750 – 7.550%	Notes due 2031	**1,890**	1,941
3.150 – 6.630%	Notes due 2016	**767**	–
2.950 – 5.006%	Notes due 2019[1]	**516**	500
5.300 – 6.750%	Notes due 2024	**266**	250
2.100 – 2.875%	Notes due 2015	**53**	–
2.000 – 2.500%	Notes due 2017	**41**	–
3.750 – 5.000%	Notes due 2018	**31**	–
5.170%	Notes due 2021	**25**	–
1.000 – 2.300%	Notes due 2013	**23**	–
4.150 – 5.875%, LIBOR less 0.0425%	Notes due 2006	**–**	2,597
	Other [2]	**872**	1,128
Total		**$31,024**	$23,846

(1) Includes put option on $500 million.
(2) Includes adjustments to debt hedged by derivatives.

The Company has two separate issuances of $500 million debt with embedded put options. For the first issuance, beginning June 2001, and each year thereafter, the holders of $500 million of the debt may require the Company to repurchase the debt at face value, in addition to accrued and unpaid interest. The holders of the other $500 million issuance may require the Company to repurchase the debt at par plus accrued interest at any time. Both of these issuances have been classified as a current liability in the Consolidated Balance Sheets.

Under the Company's most significant borrowing arrangements, the Company is not required to observe financial covenants. However, under certain lines of credit totaling $5.0 billion, which were undrawn as of January 31, 2006, the Company has agreed to observe certain covenants, the most restrictive of which relates to minimum net worth levels and amounts of additional secured debt and long-term leases. In addition, one of our subsidiaries has restrictive financial covenants on $2.0 billion of long-term debt that requires it to maintain certain equity, sales, and profit levels. The Company was in compliance with these covenants at January 31, 2006.

Long-term debt is unsecured except for $1.1 billion, which is collateralized by property with an aggregate carrying value of approximately $1.4 billion. Annual maturities of long-term debt during the next five years and thereafter are (in millions):

Fiscal Year Ended January 31,	Annual Maturity
2007	$ 4,595
2008	3,320
2009	2,858
2010	4,639
2011	2,877
Thereafter	12,735
Total	$31,024

The Company has entered into sale/leaseback transactions involving buildings while retaining title to the underlying land. These transactions were accounted for as financings and are included in long-term debt and the annual maturities schedule above. The resulting obligations are amortized over the lease terms. Future minimum lease payments during the next five years and thereafter are (in millions):

Fiscal Year Ended January 31,	Minimum Payments
2007	$ 9
2008	10
2009	10
2010	10
2011	10
Thereafter	211
Total	$260

Notes to Consolidated Financial Statements
WAL-MART

The Company had trade letters of credit outstanding totaling $2.6 billion at January 31, 2006 and 2005. At January 31, 2006 and 2005, the Company had standby letters of credit outstanding totaling $2.3 billion and $2.0 billion, respectively. These letters of credit were issued primarily for the purchase of inventory and insurance.

3 FINANCIAL INSTRUMENTS

The Company uses derivative financial instruments for hedging and non-trading purposes to manage its exposure to interest and foreign exchange rates. Use of derivative financial instruments in hedging programs subjects the Company to certain risks, such as market and credit risks. Market risk represents the possibility that the value of the derivative instrument will change. In a hedging relationship, the change in the value of the derivative is offset to a great extent by the change in the value of the underlying hedged item. Credit risk related to derivatives represents the possibility that the counterparty will not fulfill the terms of the contract. The notional, or contractual, amount of the Company's derivative financial instruments is used to measure interest to be paid or received and does not represent the Company's exposure due to credit risk. Credit risk is monitored through established approval procedures, including setting concentration limits by counterparty, reviewing credit ratings and requiring collateral (generally cash) when appropriate. The majority of the Company's transactions are with counterparties rated "AA-" or better by nationally recognized credit rating agencies.

Fair Value Instruments

The Company enters into interest rate swaps to minimize the risks and costs associated with its financing activities. Under the swap agreements, the Company pays variable-rate interest and receives fixed-rate interest payments periodically over the life of the instruments. The notional amounts are used to measure interest to be paid or received and do not represent the exposure due to credit loss. All of the Company's interest rate swaps that receive fixed interest rate payments and pay variable interest rate payments are designated as fair value hedges. As the specific terms and notional amounts of the derivative instruments exactly match those of the instruments being hedged, the derivative instruments were assumed to be perfect hedges and all changes in fair value of the hedges were recorded on the balance sheet with no net impact on the income statement.

Net Investment Instruments

At January 31, 2006, the Company is party to cross-currency interest rate swaps that hedge its net investments in the United Kingdom and Japan. The agreements are contracts to exchange fixed-rate payments in one currency for fixed-rate payments in another currency. The Company also has outstanding approximately £2.0 billion of debt that is designated as a hedge of the Company's net investment in the United Kingdom and ¥87.1 billion of debt that is designated as a hedge of the Company's net investment in Japan. All changes in the fair value of these instruments are recorded in other comprehensive income, offsetting the foreign currency translation adjustment that is also recorded in other comprehensive income.

Cash Flow Instruments

The Company is party to a cross-currency interest rate swap to hedge the foreign currency risk of certain foreign-denominated debt. The swap is designated as a cash flow hedge of foreign currency exchange risk. The agreement is a contract to exchange fixed-rate payments in one currency for fixed-rate payments in another currency. Changes in the foreign currency spot exchange rate result in reclassification of amounts from other accumulated comprehensive income to earnings to offset transaction gains or losses on foreign-denominated debt. The instrument matures in fiscal 2007.

The Company expects that the amount of gain or loss existing in other accumulated comprehensive income to be reclassified into earnings within the next 12 months will not be significant.

Fair Value of Financial Instruments

Instrument Fiscal Year Ended January 31, (in millions)	Notional Amount		Fair Value	
	2006	2005	**2006**	2005
Derivative financial instruments designated for hedging:				
Receive fixed-rate, pay floating rate interest rate swaps designated as fair value hedges	**$ 6,945**	$ 8,042	**$ 133**	$ 477
Receive fixed-rate, pay fixed-rate cross-currency interest rate swaps designated as net investment hedges (Cross-currency notional amount: GBP 795 at 1/31/2006 and 1/31/2005)	**1,250**	1,250	**(107)**	(14)
Receive fixed-rate, pay fixed-rate cross-currency interest rate swap designated as a cash flow hedge (Cross-currency notional amount: CAD 503 at 1/31/2006 and 1/31/2005)	**325**	325	**(120)**	(87)
Receive fixed-rate, pay fixed-rate cross-currency interest rate swap designated as a net investment hedge (Cross-currency notional amount: ¥52,056 at 1/31/2006 and 1/31/2005)	**432**	432	**(17)**	(68)
Receive floating rate, pay fixed-rate interest rate swap designated as a cash flow hedge	**–**	1,500	**–**	(5)
Total	**$ 8,952**	$11,549	**$ (111)**	$ 303
Non-derivative financial instruments:				
Long-term debt	**$31,024**	$23,846	**$31,580**	$25,016

Hedging instruments with an unrealized gain are recorded on the Consolidated Balance Sheets in other current assets or other assets and deferred charges, based on maturity date. Those instruments with an unrealized loss are recorded in accrued liabilities or deferred income taxes and other, based on maturity date.

Cash and cash equivalents: The carrying amount approximates fair value due to the short maturity of these instruments.

Long-term debt: Fair value is based on the Company's current incremental borrowing rate for similar types of borrowing arrangements.

Fair value instruments and net investment instruments: The fair values are estimated amounts the Company would receive or pay to terminate the agreements as of the reporting dates.

4 ACCUMULATED OTHER COMPREHENSIVE INCOME

Comprehensive income is net income plus certain other items that are recorded directly to shareholders' equity. Amounts included in accumulated other comprehensive income for the Company's derivative instruments and minimum pension liability are recorded net of the related income tax effects. The following table gives further detail regarding changes in the composition of accumulated other comprehensive income during fiscal 2006, 2005 and 2004 (in millions):

	Foreign Currency Translation	Derivative Instruments	Minimum Pension Liability	Total
Balance at January 31, 2003	$ (1,125)	$ 822	$ (206)	$ (509)
Foreign currency translation adjustment	1,685			1,685
Change in fair value of hedge instruments		(444)		(444)
Reclassification to earnings		103		103
Subsidiary minimum pension liability			16	16
Balance at January 31, 2004	560	481	(190)	851
Foreign currency translation adjustment	2,130			2,130
Change in fair value of hedge instruments		(235)		(235)
Reclassification to earnings		41		41
Subsidiary minimum pension liability			(93)	(93)
Balance at January 31, 2005	**$ 2,690**	**$ 287**	**$ (283)**	**$ 2,694**
Foreign currency translation adjustment	**(1,920)**			**(1,920)**
Change in fair value of hedge instruments		**157**		**157**
Reclassification to earnings		**71**		**71**
Subsidiary minimum pension liability			**51**	**51**
Balance at January 31, 2006	$ 770	$515	$(232)	$ 1,053

5 INCOME TAXES

The income tax provision consists of the following (in millions):

Fiscal Year Ended January 31,	**2006**	2005	2004
Current:			
Federal	**$4,646**	$4,116	$4,039
State and local	**449**	640	333
International	**837**	570	569
Total current tax provision	**5,932**	5,326	4,941
Deferred:			
Federal	**(62)**	311	31
State and local	**56**	(71)	2
International	**(123)**	23	144
Total deferred tax provision	**(129)**	263	177
Total provision for income taxes	**$5,803**	$5,589	$5,118

Income from continuing operations before income taxes and minority interest by jurisdiction is as follows (in millions):

Fiscal Year Ended January 31,	**2006**	2005	2004
United States	**$14,447**	$13,599	$12,075
Outside the United States	**$ 2,911**	2,506	2,118
Total income from continuing operations before income taxes and minority interest	**$17,358**	$16,105	$14,193

Notes to Consolidated Financial Statements
WAL-MART

Items that give rise to significant portions of the deferred tax accounts are as follows (in millions):

January 31,	2006	2005
Deferred tax liabilities		
Property and equipment	$2,355	$2,210
International, principally asset		
basis differences	1,141	1,054
Inventory	336	187
Other	265	230
Total deferred tax liabilities	$4,097	$3,681
Deferred tax assets		
International loss carryforwards and		
asset basis differences	$2,082	$1,460
Amounts accrued for financial		
reporting purposes not yet		
deductible for tax purposes	1,668	1,361
Stock-based compensation expense	248	258
Other	353	263
Total deferred tax assets	4,351	3,342
Valuation allowance	(1,054)	(526)
Total deferred tax assets, net of		
valuation allowance	$3,297	$2,816
Net deferred tax liabilities	$ 800	$ 865

The change in the Company's net deferred tax liability is impacted by foreign currency translation.

A reconciliation of the significant differences between the effective income tax rate and the federal statutory rate on pretax income is as follows:

Fiscal Year Ended January 31,	2006	2005	2004
Statutory tax rate	35.00%	35.00%	35.00%
State income taxes, net of			
federal income tax benefit	1.86%	2.30%	1.53%
Income taxes outside the			
United States	(1.75%)	(1.81%)	(0.20%)
Other	(1.68%)	(0.79%)	(0.27%)
Effective income tax rate	33.43%	34.70%	36.06%

Federal and state income taxes have not been provided on accumulated but undistributed earnings of foreign subsidiaries aggregating approximately $6.8 billion at January 31, 2006 and $5.3 billion at January 31, 2005, as such earnings have been permanently reinvested in the business. The determination of the amount of the unrecognized deferred tax liability related to the undistributed earnings is not practicable.

The Company had foreign net operating loss carryforwards of $4.7 billion at January 31, 2006. Of this amount, $1.3 billion related to the December 2005 consolidation of The Seiyu, Ltd. The recording of the related deferred tax asset of $525 million resulted in a corresponding increase in the valuation allowance. Any tax benefit ultimately realized from the Japan net operating loss carryforward will adjust goodwill. Net operating loss carryforwards of $1.4 billion expire in various years through 2011.

6 ACQUISITIONS AND DISPOSAL

Acquisitions

During December 2005, the Company purchased an additional interest in The Seiyu, Ltd. ("Seiyu"), for approximately $570 million, bringing the Company's total investment in Seiyu, including adjustments arising from the equity method of accounting, to $1.2 billion. Seiyu is a retailer in Japan, which operates 398 stores selling apparel, general merchandise, food and certain services. Following this additional purchase, the Company owns approximately 53.3% of Seiyu. Beginning on the date of the controlling interest purchase, the Company began consolidating Seiyu as a majority-owned subsidiary using a December 31 fiscal year-end. Seiyu's results of operations were not material to the Company. As a result of the consolidation of Seiyu, total assets and liabilities of $6.8 billion and $5.6 billion, respectively, were recorded in our financial statements. Goodwill recorded in the consolidation amounted to approximately $1.6 billion. The amount of assets and liabilities recorded in the consolidation of Seiyu are preliminary estimates made by management and will be finalized upon completion of the valuation of tangible and intangible assets and liabilities.

The minority interest in Seiyu is represented, in part, by shares of Seiyu's preferred stock which are convertible into shares of Seiyu common stock. If the minority holder of Seiyu's preferred stock proposes to sell or convert its shares of preferred stock, the Company has the right to purchase those shares at a predetermined price.

Through a warrant exercisable through December 2007, the Company can contribute approximately ¥154.6 billion, or $1.3 billion at a January 31, 2006, exchange rate of 117.75 yen per dollar, for approximately 538 million additional common shares of Seiyu stock. If the warrant is exercised, we would own approximately 71% of the stock of Seiyu by the end of December 2007. These calculations assume no conversion of Seiyu's preferred stock into common shares and no other issuances of Seiyu common shares.

In December 2005, the Company completed the purchase of Sonae Distribuição Brasil S.A. ("Sonae"), a retail operation in Southern Brazil consisting of 139 hypermarkets, supermarkets and warehouse units. The purchase price was approximately $720 million. Assets recorded in the acquisition of Sonae were $1.3 billion and liabilities assumed were $566 million. As a result of the Sonae acquisition, we recorded goodwill of $305 million and other identifiable intangible assets of $89 million. Sonae's results of operations, which were not material to the Company, are included in our consolidated financial statements following the date of acquisition using a December 31 fiscal year-end. The amount of assets and liabilities recorded in the purchase of Sonae are preliminary estimates made by management and will be finalized upon completion of the valuation of tangible and intangible assets and liabilities.

In September 2005, the Company acquired a 33.3% interest in Central American Retail Holding Company ("CARHCO"), a retailer with more than 360 supermarkets and other stores in Costa Rica, El Salvador, Guatemala, Honduras and Nicaragua. The purchase price was approximately $318 million, including transaction costs. In fiscal 2006, the Company accounted for its investment in CARHCO under the equity method. Concurrent with the purchase of the investment in CARHCO, the Company entered into an agreement to purchase an additional 17.7% of CARHCO in the first quarter of fiscal 2007 and an option agreement that will allow the Company to purchase up to an additional 24% beginning in September 2010. To the extent that the Company does not exercise its option to purchase the additional 24% of CARHCO, the minority shareholders will have certain put rights that could require the Company to purchase the additional 24% after September 2012. In February 2006, the Company purchased the additional 17.7% of CARHCO for a purchase price of approximately $212 million.

In February 2004, the Company completed its purchase of Bompreço S.A. Supermercados do Nordeste ("Bompreço"), a supermarket chain in northern Brazil with 118 hypermarkets, supermarkets and mini-markets. The purchase price was approximately $315 million, net of cash acquired. The results of operations for Bompreço, which were not material to the Company, have been included in the Company's consolidated financial statements since the date of acquisition.

Disposal

On May 23, 2003, the Company completed the sale of McLane Company, Inc. ("McLane"). The Company received $1.5 billion in cash for the sale. The accompanying consolidated financial statements and notes reflect the gain on the sale and the operations of McLane as a discontinued operation.

Following is summarized financial information for McLane (in millions):

Fiscal Year Ended January 31,	2004
Net sales	$4,328
Income from discontinued operation	$ 67
Income tax expense	25
Net operating income from discontinued operation	42
Gain on sale of McLane, net of $147 income tax expense	151
Income from discontinued operation, net of tax	$ 193

The effective tax rate on the gain from the sale of McLane was 49% as a result of the non-deductibility of $99 million of goodwill recorded in the original McLane acquisition.

7 SHARE-BASED COMPENSATION PLANS

As of January 31, 2006, the Company has awarded share-based compensation to executives and other associates of the Company through various share-based compensation plans. The compensation cost recognized for all plans was $244 million, $204 million, and $183 million for fiscal 2006, 2005, and 2004, respectively. The total income tax benefit recognized for all share-based compensation plans was $82 million, $71 million, and $66 million for fiscal 2006, 2005, and 2004, respectively.

On February 1, 2003, the Company adopted the expense recognition provisions of Statement of Financial Accounting Standards No. 123 ("SFAS 123"), restating results for prior periods. In December 2004, the Financial Accounting Standards Board issued a revision of SFAS 123 ("SFAS 123(R)"). The Company adopted the provisions of SFAS 123(R) upon its release. The adoption of SFAS 123(R) did not have a material impact on our results of operations, financial position or cash flows. All share-based compensation is accounted for in accordance with the fair-value based method of SFAS 123(R).

The Company's Stock Incentive Plan of 2005 (the "Plan"), which is shareholder-approved, permits the grant of stock options, restricted (non-vested) stock and performance share compensation awards to its associates for up to 210 million shares of common stock. The Company believes that such awards better align the interests of its associates with those of its shareholders.

Under the Plan and prior plans, stock option awards have been granted with an exercise price equal to the market price of the Company's stock at the date of grant. Generally, outstanding options granted before fiscal 2001 vest over seven years. Options granted after fiscal 2001 generally vest over five years. Shares issued upon the exercise of options are newly issued. Options granted generally have a contractual term of 10 years. The fair value of each stock option award is estimated on the date of grant using the Black-Scholes-Merton option valuation model that uses various assumptions for inputs, which are noted in the following table. Generally, the Company uses historical volatilities and risk free interest rates that correlate with the expected term of the option. To determine the expected life of the option, the Company bases its estimates on historical grants with similar vesting periods. The following tables represents a weighted-average of the assumptions used by the company to estimate the fair values of the Company's stock options at the grant dates:

Fiscal Year Ended January 31,	**2006**	2005	2004
Dividend yield	**1.9%**	1.1%	0.9%
Volatility	**24.9%**	26.2%	32.3%
Risk-free interest rate	**4.2%**	3.5%	2.8%
Expected life in years	**6.1**	5.3	4.5

Notes to Consolidated Financial Statements
WAL-MART

A summary of the stock option award activity for fiscal 2006 is presented below:

Options	Shares	Weighted-Average Exercise Price	Weighted-Average Remaining Life in Years	Aggregate Intrinsic Value
Outstanding at January 31, 2005	68,115,000	$ 46.79		
Granted	4,281,000	50.74		
Exercised	(4,208,000)	23.26		
Forfeited or expired	(8,645,000)	51.92		
Outstanding at January 31, 2006	59,543,000	$48.02	6.5	$163,326,000
Exercisable at January 31, 2006	32,904,000	$45.20	5.3	$162,240,000

The weighted-average grant-date fair value of options granted during the fiscal years ended January 31, 2006, 2005 and 2004, was $12.29, $11.92 and $14.89, respectively. The total intrinsic value of options exercised during the years ended January 31, 2006, 2005 and 2004, was $108.3 million, $221.6 million and $231.0 million, respectively.

Under the Plan, the Company grants various types of awards of restricted (non-vested) stock to certain associates. These grants include awards for shares that vest based on the passage of time, performance criteria, or both. Vesting periods vary. The restricted stock awards may be settled in stock, or deferred as stock or cash, based upon the associate's election. Consequently, these awards are classified as liabilities in the accompanying balance sheets unless the associate has elected for the award to be settled or deferred in stock. The fair value of the restricted stock liabilities is remeasured each reporting period. The total liability for restricted stock awards at January 31, 2006, was $61.1 million.

A summary of the Company's restricted (non-vested) stock award activity for fiscal 2006 is presented below:

Non-Vested Stock Awards	Shares	Weighted-Average Grant-Date Fair Value
Restricted Stock Awards at January 31, 2005	3,423,000	$ 46.63
Granted	2,955,000	$ 44.81
Vested	(383,000)	$ 44.78
Forfeited	(551,000)	$ 45.02
Restricted Stock Awards at January 31, 2006	5,444,000	$46.08

As of January 31, 2006, there was $157.9 million of total unrecognized compensation cost related to restricted stock granted under the Plan, which is expected to be recognized over a weighted-average period of 5.9 years. The total fair value of shares vested during the fiscal years ended January 31, 2006, 2005, and 2004, was $19.9 million, $33.9 million and $8.0 million, respectively.

During fiscal 2005, the Company began issuing performance share awards under the Plan, the vesting of which is tied to the achievement of performance criteria. These awards accrue to the associate based on the extent to which revenue growth and return on investment goals are attained or exceeded over a one- to three-year period. Based on the extent to which the targets are achieved, vested shares may range from 0% to 150% of the original award amount. Because the performance shares may be settled in stock or cash, the performance shares are accounted for as liabilities in the accompanying balance sheets. Outstanding performance shares, the related liability and unrecognized compensation cost as of January 31, 2006 and 2005, were not significant.

The Company's United Kingdom subsidiary, ASDA, also offers two other stock option plans to its associates. The first plan, The ASDA Colleague Share Ownership Plan 1999 ("CSOP"), grants options to certain associates. Options granted under the CSOP Plan generally expire six years from the date of grant, with half vesting on the third anniversary of the grant and the other half on the sixth anniversary of the date of grant. Shares in the money at the vesting date are exercised while shares out of the money at the vesting date expire. The second plan, The ASDA Sharesave Plan 2000 ("Sharesave"), grants options to certain associates at 80% of market value on the date of grant. Sharesave options become exercisable after either a three-year or five-year period and generally lapse six months after becoming exercisable. Outstanding options under these plans as well as the related aggregate intrinsic value as of January 31, 2006, were not significant.

8 LITIGATION
The Company is involved in a number of legal proceedings. In accordance with Statement of Financial Accounting Standards No. 5, "Accounting for Contingencies," the Company has made accruals with respect to these matters, where appropriate, which are reflected in the Company's consolidated financial statements. The Company may enter into discussions regarding settlement of these matters, and may enter into settlement agreements, if it believes settlement is in the best interests of the Company's shareholders. The matters, or groups of related matters, discussed below, if decided adversely to or settled by the Company, individually or in the aggregate, may result in liability material to the Company's financial condition or results of operations.

The Company is a defendant in numerous cases containing class-action allegations in which the plaintiffs have brought claims under the Fair Labor Standards Act ("FLSA"), corresponding state statutes, or other laws. The plaintiffs in these lawsuits are current and former hourly associates who allege, among other things, that the Company forced them to work "off the clock," or failed to provide work breaks, or otherwise claim they were not paid for work performed. The complaints generally seek unspecified monetary damages, injunctive relief, or both. Class certification has yet to be addressed in a majority of the cases. Class certification has been denied or overturned in cases pending in Arizona, Arkansas, Florida, Georgia, Indiana, Louisiana, Maryland, Michigan, Nevada, New Jersey, North Carolina, Ohio, Texas, West Virginia and Wisconsin. Some or all of the requested classes have been certified in cases pending in California, Colorado, Massachusetts, Minnesota, Missouri, New Mexico, Oregon, Pennsylvania and Washington. Conditional certifications for notice purposes under the FLSA have been allowed in cases in Georgia, Michigan and Texas. The Company cannot estimate the possible loss or range of loss which may arise from these lawsuits.

The Company is a defendant in *Savaglio v. Wal-Mart Stores, Inc.*, a class-action lawsuit in which the plaintiffs allege that they were not provided meal and rest breaks in accordance with California law, and seek monetary damages and injunctive relief. A jury trial on the plaintiffs' claims for monetary damages concluded on December 22, 2005. The jury returned a verdict of $57,216,673 in statutory penalties and $115 million in punitive damages. The Company believes that it has substantial defenses to the claims at issue, and intends to challenge the verdict in post-trial motions and, if necessary, on appeal. Meanwhile, the plaintiffs' claims for injunctive relief have been tentatively set for trial in June 2006.

A putative class action is pending in California challenging the methodology of payments made under various Associate incentive bonus plans, and a second putative class action in California asserts that the Company has omitted to include bonus payments in calculating associates' regular rate of pay for purposes of determining overtime. As to the first case (*Cruz v. Wal-Mart Stores, Inc.*), the Company cannot estimate the possible loss or range of loss which may arise. The parties have entered into an agreement to settle the second case (*Fries v. Wal-Mart Stores, Inc.*), which must be approved by the court in order to become effective. If approved by the court, the settlement will include all class members who do not opt out of the settlement class. The amount to be paid by Wal-Mart under the settlement will not have a material impact on the Company's financial condition or results of operations.

The Company is currently a defendant in five putative class actions brought on behalf of assistant store managers who challenge their exempt status under state and federal laws, which are pending in California, Michigan, New Mexico and Tennessee. Conditional certification for notice purposes under the FLSA has been granted in one of these cases (*Comer v. Wal-Mart Stores, Inc.*). Otherwise, no determination has been made as to class certification in any of these cases. The Company cannot estimate the possible loss or range of loss which may arise from these lawsuits.

The Company is a defendant in *Dukes v. Wal-Mart Stores, Inc.*, a class-action lawsuit commenced in June 2001 and pending in the United States District Court for the Northern District of California. The case was brought on behalf of all past and present female employees in all of the Company's retail stores and warehouse clubs in the United States. The complaint alleges that the Company has engaged in a pattern and practice of discriminating against women in promotions, pay, training and job assignments. The complaint seeks, among other things, injunctive relief, front pay, back pay, punitive damages, and attorneys' fees. Following a hearing on class certification on September 24, 2003, on June 21, 2004, the District Court issued an order granting in part and denying in part the plaintiffs' motion for class certification. The class, which was certified by the District Court for purposes of liability, injunctive and declaratory relief, punitive damages, and lost pay, subject to certain exceptions, includes all women employed at any Wal-Mart domestic retail store at any time since December 26, 1998, who have been or may be subjected to the pay and management track promotions policies and practices challenged by the plaintiffs. The class as certified currently includes approximately 1.6 million present and former female associates.

The Company believes that the District Court's ruling is incorrect. The United States Court of Appeals for the Ninth Circuit has granted the Company's petition for discretionary review of the ruling. The Court of Appeals heard oral argument from counsel in the case on August 8, 2005. There is no indication at this time as to when a decision will be rendered. If the Company is not successful in its appeal of class certification, or an appellate court issues a ruling that allows for the certification of a class or classes with a different size or scope, and if there is a subsequent adverse verdict on the merits from which there is no successful appeal, or in the event of a negotiated settlement of the litigation, the resulting liability could be material to the Company. The plaintiffs also seek punitive damages which, if awarded, could result in the payment of additional amounts material to the Company. However, because of the uncertainty of the outcome of the appeal from the District Court's certification decision, because of the uncertainty of the balance of the proceedings contemplated by the District Court, and because the Company's liability, if any, arising from the litigation, including the size of any damages award if plaintiffs are successful in the litigation or any negotiated settlement, could vary widely, the Company cannot reasonably estimate the possible loss or range of loss which may arise from the litigation.

The Company is a defendant in *Mauldin v. Wal-Mart Stores, Inc.*, a class-action lawsuit that was filed on October 16, 2001, in the United States District Court for the Northern District of Georgia, Atlanta Division. The class was certified on August 23, 2002. On September 30, 2003, the court denied the Company's motion to reconsider that ruling. The class is composed of female Wal-Mart associates who were participants in the Associates Health and Welfare Plan at any time from March 8, 2001, to the present and who were using prescription contraceptives. The class seeks amendment of the Plan to include coverage for prescription contraceptives, back pay for all members in the form of reimbursement of the cost of prescription contraceptives, pre-judgment interest, and attorneys'

Notes to Consolidated Financial Statements
WAL-MART

fees. The complaint alleges that the Company's Health Plan violates Title VII's prohibition against gender discrimination in that the Health Plan's Reproductive Systems provision does not provide coverage for prescription contraceptives. The Company cannot estimate the possible loss or range of loss which may arise from this litigation.

The Company is a defendant in a lawsuit that was filed on August 24, 2001, in the United States District Court for the Eastern District of Kentucky. *EEOC (Janice Smith) v. Wal-Mart Stores, Inc.* is an action brought by the EEOC on behalf of Janice Smith and all other females who made application or transfer requests at the London, Kentucky, distribution center from 1995 to the present, and who were not hired or transferred into the warehouse positions for which they applied. The class seeks back pay for those females not selected for hire or transfer during the relevant time period. The class also seeks injunctive and prospective affirmative relief. The complaint alleges that the Company based hiring decisions on gender in violation of Title VII of the 1964 Civil Rights Act as amended. The EEOC can maintain this action as a class without certification. The Company cannot estimate the possible loss or range of loss which may arise from this litigation.

On November 8, 2005, the Company received a grand jury subpoena from the United States Attorney's Office for the Central District of California, seeking documents and information relating to the Company's receipt, transportation, handling, identification, recycling, treatment, storage and disposal of certain merchandise that constitutes hazardous materials or hazardous waste. The Company has been informed by the U.S. Attorney's Office for the Central District of California that it is a target of a criminal investigation into potential violations of the Resource Conservation and Recovery Act ("RCRA"), the Clean Water Act, and the Hazardous Materials Transportation Statute. This U.S. Attorney's Office contends, among other things, that the use of Company trucks to transport certain returned merchandise from the Company's stores to its return centers is prohibited by RCRA because those materials may be considered hazardous waste. The government alleges that, to comply with RCRA, the Company must ship from the store certain materials as "hazardous waste" directly to a certified disposal facility using a certified hazardous waste carrier. The Company contends that the practice of transporting returned merchandise to its return centers for subsequent disposition, including disposal by certified facilities, is compliant with applicable laws and regulations.

Additionally, the U.S. Attorney's Office in the Northern District of California has initiated its own investigation regarding the Company's handling of hazardous materials and hazardous waste and the Company has received administrative document requests from the California Department of Toxic Substances Control requesting documents and information with respect to two of the Company's distribution facilities. Further, the Company also received a subpoena from the Los Angeles County District Attorney's Office for documents and administrative interrogatories requesting information, among other things, regarding the Company's handling of materials and hazardous waste. California state and local government authorities and the State of Nevada have also initiated investigations into these matters. The Company is cooperating fully with the respective authorities.

The Company cannot estimate the possible loss or range of loss which may arise from this matter.

9 COMMITMENTS

The Company and certain of its subsidiaries have long-term leases for stores and equipment. Rentals (including, for certain leases, amounts applicable to taxes, insurance, maintenance, other operating expenses and contingent rentals) under operating leases and other short-term rental arrangements were $1.3 billion, $1.2 billion and $1.1 billion in 2006, 2005 and 2004, respectively. Aggregate minimum annual rentals at January 31, 2006, under non-cancelable leases are as follows (in millions):

Fiscal Year	Operating Leases	Capital Leases
2007	$ 797	$ 592
2008	751	588
2009	710	550
2010	634	526
2011	586	514
Thereafter	6,205	3,610
Total minimum rentals	$9,683	6,380
Less estimated executory costs		39
Net minimum lease payments		6,341
Less imputed interest at rates ranging from 3.0% to 29.0%		2,300
Present value of minimum lease payments		$4,041

The Company has entered into sale/leaseback transactions involving buildings and the underlying land that were accounted for as capital and operating leases. Included in the annual maturities schedule above are $429 million of capital leases and $140 million of operating leases.

Certain of the Company's leases provide for the payment of contingent rentals based on a percentage of sales. Such contingent rentals amounted to $27 million, $32 million and $38 million in 2006, 2005 and 2004, respectively. Substantially all of the Company's store leases have renewal options, some of which may trigger an escalation in rentals.

In connection with certain debt financing, we could be liable for early termination payments if certain unlikely events were to occur. At January 31, 2006, the aggregate termination payment was $89 million. These two arrangements expire in fiscal 2011 and fiscal 2019.

In connection with the development of our grocery distribution network in the United States, we have agreements with third parties which would require us to purchase or assume the leases on certain unique equipment in the event the agreements are terminated. These agreements, which can be terminated by either party at will, cover up to a five-year period and obligate the Company to pay up to approximately $233 million upon termination of some or all of these agreements.

There are no recourse provisions which would enable us to recover from third parties any amounts paid under the above guarantees. No liability for these guarantees has been recorded in our financial statements.

The Company has entered into lease commitments for land and buildings for 60 future locations. These lease commitments with real estate developers provide for minimum rentals ranging from 5 to 35 years, which if consummated based on current cost estimates, will approximate $95 million annually over the lease terms.

10 RETIREMENT-RELATED BENEFITS

In the United States, the Company maintains a Profit Sharing and 401(k) Retirement Savings Plan under which most full-time and many part-time associates become participants following one year of employment. The Profit Sharing component of the plan is entirely funded by the Company, with an additional contribution made by the Company to the associates' 401(k) component of the plan. In addition to the Company contributions to the 401(k) Retirement Savings component of the plan, associates may elect to contribute a percentage of their earnings. During fiscal 2006, participants could contribute up to 25% of their pretax earnings, but not more than statutory limits.

Associates may choose from among 13 different investment options for the 401(k) Retirement Savings component of the plan. For associates who did not make an election, their 401(k) balance in the plan is placed in a balanced fund. Associates are immediately vested in their 401(k) funds and may change their investment options at any time. Additionally, fully vested associates have the same 13 investment options for the Profit Sharing component of the plan. Associates are fully vested in the Profit Sharing component of the plan after seven years of service.

Annual contributions made by the Company to the United States and Puerto Rico Profit Sharing and 401(k) Retirement Savings Plans are made at the sole discretion of the Company, and were $827 million, $756 million and $662 million for fiscal 2006, 2005 and 2004, respectively.

Employees in foreign countries who are not U.S. citizens are covered by various post-employment benefit arrangements. These plans are administered based upon the legislative and tax requirements in the country in which they are established. Annual contributions to foreign retirement savings and profit sharing plans are made at the discretion of the Company, and were $244 million, $199 million and $123 million in fiscal 2006, 2005 and 2004, respectively.

The Company's subsidiaries in the United Kingdom and Japan have defined benefit pension plans. The plan in the United Kingdom was underfunded by $332 million and $419 million at January 31, 2006 and 2005, respectively. The plan in Japan was underfunded by $228 million at January 31, 2006.

11 SEGMENTS

At January 31, 2006, the Company and its subsidiaries were principally engaged in the operation of retail stores located in all 50 states, Argentina, Brazil, Canada, Germany, South Korea, Puerto Rico and the United Kingdom, through joint ventures in China, and through majority-owned subsidiaries in Japan and Mexico. The Company identifies segments based on management responsibility within the United States and in total for international units.

The Wal-Mart Stores segment includes the Company's supercenters, discount stores and Neighborhood Markets in the United States, as well as Walmart.com. The SAM'S CLUB segment includes the warehouse membership clubs in the United States as well as samsclub.com. At January 31, 2006, the International segment consisted of the Company's operations in Argentina, Brazil, China, Germany, Mexico, South Korea, Japan and the United Kingdom, which are consolidated using a December 31 fiscal year-end, generally due to statutory reporting requirements. There were no significant intervening events which materially affected the financial statements. The Company's operations in Canada and Puerto Rico are consolidated using a January 31 fiscal year-end. The amounts under the caption "Other" in the following table include unallocated corporate overhead. The Company's portion of the results of our unconsolidated minority interest in Seiyu prior to December 20, 2005, and our unconsolidated minority interest in CARHCO are also included under the caption "Other."

Notes to Consolidated Financial Statements
WAL-MART

The Company measures the profit of its segments as "segment operating income," which is defined as income from continuing operations before net interest expense, income taxes and minority interest. Information on segments and the reconciliation to income from continuing operations before income taxes and minority interest are as follows (in millions):

Fiscal Year Ended January 31, 2006	Wal-Mart Stores	SAM'S CLUB	International	Other	Consolidated
Revenues from external customers	$209,910	$39,798	$62,719	$ –	$312,427
Intercompany real estate charge (income)	3,454	547	–	(4,001)	–
Depreciation and amortization	1,922	296	1,043	1,456	4,717
Operating income (loss)	15,324	1,385	3,330	(1,509)	18,530
Interest expense, net					(1,172)
Income from continuing operations before income taxes and minority interest					$ 17,358
Total assets of continuing operations	$ 32,809	$ 5,686	$51,581	$48,111	$138,187

Fiscal Year Ended January 31, 2005	Wal-Mart Stores	SAM'S CLUB	International	Other	Consolidated
Revenues from external customers	$ 191,826	$ 37,119	$ 56,277	$ –	$ 285,222
Intercompany real estate charge (income)	2,754	513	–	(3,267)	–
Depreciation and amortization	1,561	274	919	1,510	4,264
Operating income (loss)	14,163	1,280	2,988	(1,340)	17,091
Interest expense, net					(986)
Income from continuing operations before income taxes and minority interest					$ 16,105
Total assets of continuing operations	$ 29,489	$ 5,685	$ 40,981	$ 43,999	$ 120,154

Fiscal Year Ended January 31, 2004	Wal-Mart Stores	SAM'S CLUB	International	Other	Consolidated
Revenues from external customers	$ 174,220	$ 34,537	$ 47,572	$ –	$ 256,329
Intercompany real estate charge (income)	2,468	484	–	(2,952)	–
Depreciation and amortization	1,482	249	810	1,311	3,852
Operating income (loss)	12,916	1,126	2,370	(1,387)	15,025
Interest expense, net					(832)
Income from continuing operations before income taxes and minority interest					$ 14,193
Total assets of continuing operations	$ 27,028	$ 4,751	$ 35,230	$ 38,396	$ 105,405

Certain information for fiscal years 2005 and 2004 has been reclassified to conform to current-year presentation.

In the United States, long-lived assets, net, excluding goodwill and other assets and deferred charges were $55.5 billion and $48.4 billion as of January 31, 2006 and 2005, respectively. In the United States, additions to long-lived assets were $11.8 billion, $9.8 billion and $8.1 billion in fiscal 2006, 2005 and 2004, respectively. Outside of the United States, long-lived assets, net, excluding goodwill and other assets and deferred charges were $23.8 billion and $19.7 billion in fiscal 2006 and 2005, respectively. Outside of the United States, additions to long-lived assets were $2.8 billion, $3.1 billion and $2.2 billion in fiscal 2006, 2005 and 2004, respectively. The International segment includes all real estate outside the United States. The operations of the Company's ASDA subsidiary are significant in comparison to the total operations of the International segment. ASDA sales during fiscal 2006, 2005 and 2004 were $26.8 billion, $26.0 billion and $21.7 billion, respectively. At January 31, 2006 and 2005, ASDA long-lived assets, consisting primarily of property and equipment, net, and goodwill, net, totaled $17.7 billion and $18.9 billion, respectively. The decline in ASDA's long-lived assets from January 31, 2005 to January 31, 2006 was largely due to foreign currency translation.

12 QUARTERLY FINANCIAL DATA (UNAUDITED)

(Amounts in millions except per share information)	April 30,	July 31,	October 31,	January 31,
		Quarters ended		
Fiscal 2006				
Net sales	**$70,908**	**$76,811**	**$75,436**	**$89,273**
Cost of sales	**54,571**	**58,787**	**57,988**	**69,045**
Gross profit	**$16,337**	**$18,024**	**$17,448**	**$20,228**
Net income	**$ 2,461**	**$ 2,805**	**$ 2,374**	**$ 3,589**
Basic and diluted net income per common share	**$ 0.58**	**$ 0.67**	**$ 0.57**	**$ 0.86**
Fiscal 2005				
Net sales	$64,763	$69,722	$68,520	$82,216
Cost of sales	49,969	53,533	52,567	63,723
Gross profit	$14,794	$16,189	$15,953	$18,493
Net income	$ 2,166	$ 2,651	$ 2,286	$ 3,164
Basic and diluted net income per common share	$ 0.50	$ 0.62	$ 0.54	$ 0.75

The sum of quarterly financial data will not agree to annual amounts due to rounding.

13 SUBSEQUENT EVENTS

On March 2, 2006, the Company's Board of Directors approved an increase in the Company's annual dividend to $0.67 per share. The annual dividend will be paid in four quarterly installments on April 3, 2006, June 5, 2006, September 5, 2006, and January 2, 2007 to holders of record on March 17, May 19, August 18 and December 15, 2006, respectively.

In February 2006, we entered into a £150 million revolving credit facility in the United Kingdom. Interest on borrowings under the credit facility accrues at LIBOR plus 25 basis points.

Report of Independent Registered Public Accounting Firm
WAL-MART

The Board of Directors and Shareholders,
Wal-Mart Stores, Inc.

We have audited the accompanying consolidated balance sheets of Wal-Mart Stores, Inc. as of January 31, 2006 and 2005, and the related consolidated statements of income, shareholders' equity and cash flows for each of the three years in the period ended January 31, 2006. These financial statements are the responsibility of the Company's management. Our responsibility is to express an opinion on these financial statements based on our audits.

We conducted our audits in accordance with the standards of the Public Company Accounting Oversight Board (United States). Those standards require that we plan and perform the audit to obtain reasonable assurance about whether the financial statements are free of material misstatement. An audit includes examining, on a test basis, evidence supporting the amounts and disclosures in the financial statements. An audit also includes assessing the accounting principles used and significant estimates made by management, as well as evaluating the overall financial statement presentation. We believe that our audits provide a reasonable basis for our opinion.

In our opinion, the financial statements referred to above present fairly, in all material respects, the consolidated financial position of Wal-Mart Stores, Inc. at January 31, 2006 and 2005, and the consolidated results of its operations and its cash flows for each of the three years in the period ended January 31, 2006, in conformity with U.S. generally accepted accounting principles.

We also have audited, in accordance with the standards of the Public Company Accounting Oversight Board (United States), the effectiveness of Wal-Mart Stores, Inc.'s internal control over financial reporting as of January 31, 2006, based on criteria established in *Internal Control – Integrated Framework* issued by the Committee of Sponsoring Organizations of the Treadway Commission and our report dated March 27, 2006 expressed an unqualified opinion thereon.

Ernst & Young LLP

Rogers, Arkansas
March 27, 2006

Report of Independent Registered Public Accounting Firm on Internal Control Over Financial Reporting
WAL-MART

The Board of Directors and Shareholders,
Wal-Mart Stores, Inc.

We have audited management's assessment, included in the accompanying Management's Report to Our Shareholders under the caption "Report on Internal Control Over Financial Reporting," that Wal-Mart Stores, Inc. maintained effective internal control over financial reporting as of January 31, 2006, based on criteria established in *Internal Control – Integrated Framework* issued by the Committee of Sponsoring Organizations of the Treadway Commission (the COSO criteria). Wal-Mart Stores, Inc.'s management is responsible for maintaining effective internal control over financial reporting and for its assessment of the effectiveness of internal control over financial reporting. Our responsibility is to express an opinion on management's assessment and an opinion on the effectiveness of the company's internal control over financial reporting based on our audit.

We conducted our audit in accordance with the standards of the Public Company Accounting Oversight Board (United States). Those standards require that we plan and perform the audit to obtain reasonable assurance about whether effective internal control over financial reporting was maintained in all material respects. Our audit included obtaining an understanding of internal control over financial reporting, evaluating management's assessment, testing and evaluating the design and operating effectiveness of internal control, and performing such other procedures as we considered necessary in the circumstances. We believe that our audit provides a reasonable basis for our opinion.

A company's internal control over financial reporting is a process designed to provide reasonable assurance regarding the reliability of financial reporting and the preparation of financial statements for external purposes in accordance with generally accepted accounting principles. A company's internal control over financial reporting includes those policies and procedures that (1) pertain to the maintenance of records that, in reasonable detail, accurately and fairly reflect the transactions and dispositions of the assets of the company; (2) provide reasonable assurance that transactions are recorded as necessary to permit preparation of financial statements in accordance with generally accepted accounting principles, and that receipts and expenditures of the company are being made only in accordance with authorizations of management and directors of the company; and (3) provide reasonable assurance regarding prevention or timely detection of unauthorized acquisition, use, or disposition of the company's assets that could have a material effect on the financial statements.

Because of its inherent limitations, internal control over financial reporting may not prevent or detect misstatements. Also, projections of any evaluation of effectiveness to future periods are subject to the risk that controls may become inadequate because of changes in conditions, or that the degree of compliance with the policies or procedures may deteriorate.

As indicated in the accompanying Management's Report to Our Shareholders, management's assessment of and conclusion on the effectiveness of internal control over financial reporting did not include the internal controls of The Seiyu, Ltd., and Sonae Distribuição Brasil S.A., both of which were acquired in fiscal 2006 and are included in the fiscal 2006 consolidated financial statements of Wal-Mart Stores, Inc. These entities represented, in the aggregate, 5.8% and 0.1% of total assets and total net sales, respectively, of the Company as of, and for the year ended, January 31, 2006. These acquisitions are more fully discussed in Note 6 to the consolidated financial statements for fiscal 2006. Our audit of internal control over financial reporting of Wal-Mart Stores, Inc. also did not include an evaluation of the internal control over financial reporting for these fiscal 2006 acquisitions.

In our opinion, management's assessment that Wal-Mart Stores, Inc. maintained effective internal control over financial reporting as of January 31, 2006, is fairly stated, in all material respects, based on the COSO criteria. Also, in our opinion, Wal-Mart Stores, Inc., maintained, in all material respects, effective internal control over financial reporting as of January 31, 2006, based on the COSO criteria.

We also have audited, in accordance with the standards of the Public Company Accounting Oversight Board (United States), the consolidated balance sheets of Wal-Mart Stores, Inc. as of January 31, 2006 and 2005, and the related consolidated statements of income, shareholders' equity and cash flows for each of the three years in the period ended January 31, 2006 and our report dated March 27, 2006 expressed an unqualified opinion thereon.

Ernst & Young LLP

Rogers, Arkansas
March 27, 2006

Management's Report to Our Shareholders
WAL-MART

Management of Wal-Mart Stores, Inc. ("Wal-Mart" or the "Company") is responsible for the preparation, integrity and objectivity of Wal-Mart's consolidated financial statements and other financial information contained in this Annual Report to Shareholders. Those consolidated financial statements were prepared in conformity with accounting principles generally accepted in the United States. In preparing those consolidated financial statements, management was required to make certain estimates and judgments, which are based upon currently available information and management's view of current conditions and circumstances.

The Audit Committee of the Board of Directors, which consists solely of independent directors, oversees our process of reporting financial information and the audit of our consolidated financial statements. The Audit Committee stays informed of the financial condition of Wal-Mart and regularly reviews management's financial policies and procedures, the independence of our independent auditors, our internal control and the objectivity of our financial reporting. Both the independent auditors and the internal auditors have free access to the Audit Committee and meet with the Audit Committee periodically, both with and without management present.

We have retained Ernst & Young LLP, an independent registered public accounting firm, to audit our consolidated financial statements found in this annual report. We have made available to Ernst & Young LLP all of our financial records and related data in connection with their audit of our consolidated financial statements.

We have filed with the Securities and Exchange Commission ("SEC") the required certifications related to our consolidated financial statements as of and for the year ended January 31, 2006. These certifications are attached as exhibits to our Annual Report on Form 10-K for the year ended January 31, 2006. Additionally, we have also provided to the New York Stock Exchange the required annual certification of our Chief Executive Officer regarding our compliance with the New York Stock Exchange's corporate governance listing standards.

Report on Internal Control Over Financial Reporting.
Management has responsibility for establishing and maintaining adequate internal control over financial reporting. Internal control over financial reporting is a process designed to provide reasonable assurance regarding the reliability of financial reporting and the preparation of financial statements for external reporting purposes in accordance with accounting principles generally accepted in the United States. Because of its inherent limitations, internal control over financial reporting may not prevent or detect misstatements. Management has assessed the effectiveness of the Company's internal control over financial reporting as of January 31, 2006. In making its assessment, management has utilized the criteria set forth by the Committee of Sponsoring Organizations ("COSO") of the Treadway Commission in *Internal Control – Integrated Framework*. Management concluded that based on its assessment, Wal-Mart's internal control over financial reporting was effective as of January 31, 2006. Management's assessment of the effectiveness of the Company's internal control over financial reporting as of January 31, 2006, has been audited by Ernst & Young LLP, an independent registered public accounting firm, as stated in their report which appears in this Annual Report to Shareholders.

Management's assessment of the effectiveness of the Company's internal control over financial reporting excluded The Seiyu, Ltd. and Sonae Distribuição Brasil S.A., both of which were acquired in fiscal 2006. These entities represented, in the aggregate, 5.8% and

0.1% of consolidated total assets and consolidated net sales, respectively, of the Company as of and for the year ended January 31, 2006. These acquisitions are more fully discussed in Note 6 to our consolidated financial statements for fiscal 2006. Under guidelines established by the SEC, companies are allowed to exclude acquisitions from their first assessment of internal control over financial reporting following the date of the acquisition.

Evaluation of Disclosure Controls and Procedures.
We maintain disclosure controls and procedures designed to provide reasonable assurance that information required to be timely disclosed is accumulated and communicated to management in a timely fashion. Management has assessed the effectiveness of these disclosure controls and procedures as of January 31, 2006, and determined they were effective as of that date to provide reasonable assurance that information required to be disclosed by us in the reports we file or submit under the Securities Exchange Act of 1934, as amended, was accumulated and communicated to management, as appropriate, to allow timely decisions regarding required disclosure and were effective to provide reasonable assurance that such information is recorded, processed, summarized and reported within the time periods specified by the SEC's rules and forms.

Report on Ethical Standards.
Our Company was founded on the belief that open communications and the highest standards of ethics are necessary to be successful. Our long-standing "Open Door" communication policy helps management be aware of and address issues in a timely and effective manner. Through the open door policy all associates are encouraged to inform management at the appropriate level when they are concerned about any matter pertaining to Wal-Mart.

Wal-Mart has adopted a Statement of Ethics to guide our associates in the continued observance of high ethical standards such as honesty, integrity and compliance with the law in the conduct of Wal-Mart's business. Familiarity and compliance with the Statement of Ethics is required of all associates who are part of management. The Company also maintains a separate Code of Ethics for our senior financial officers. Wal-Mart also has in place a Related-Party Transaction Policy. This policy applies to Wal-Mart's senior officers and directors and requires material related-party transactions to be reviewed by the Audit Committee. The senior officers and directors are required to report material related-party transactions to Wal-Mart. We maintain an ethics office which oversees and administers an ethics hotline. The ethics hotline provides a channel for associates to make confidential and anonymous complaints regarding potential violations of our statements of ethics, including violations related to financial or accounting matters.

H. Lee Scott
President and Chief Executive Officer

Thomas M. Schoewe
Executive Vice President and Chief Financial Officer

Fiscal 2006 End-of-Year Store Count
WAL-MART

State	Discount Stores	Supercenters	SAM'S CLUBs	Neighborhood Markets
Alabama	13	76	11	2
Alaska	7	0	3	0
Arizona	15	42	13	9
Arkansas	20	60	5	6
California	146	13	35	0
Colorado	13	44	15	0
Connecticut	28	4	3	0
Delaware	4	4	1	0
Florida	48	128	39	9
Georgia	15	101	21	0
Hawaii	8	0	2	0
Idaho	3	14	1	0
Illinois	79	51	28	0
Indiana	27	61	16	4
Iowa	18	37	7	0
Kansas	18	35	6	3
Kentucky	22	59	7	2
Louisiana	23	60	13	1
Maine	10	12	3	0
Maryland	33	8	12	0
Massachusetts	41	3	4	0
Michigan	37	40	25	0
Minnesota	31	21	13	0
Mississippi	12	53	6	1
Missouri	40	77	15	0
Montana	4	7	1	0
Nebraska	3	23	3	0
Nevada	8	15	5	6
New Hampshire	19	7	4	0
New Jersey	40	1	9	0
New Mexico	3	26	6	1
New York	48	35	18	0
North Carolina	34	78	19	0
North Dakota	7	1	2	0
Ohio	52	72	27	0
Oklahoma	29	53	8	15
Oregon	17	12	0	0
Pennsylvania	46	70	23	0
Rhode Island	7	1	1	0
South Carolina	14	49	9	0
South Dakota	1	10	2	0
Tennessee	16	81	16	6
Texas	62	253	70	30
Utah	2	26	7	5
Vermont	4	0	0	0
Virginia	20	61	13	0
Washington	21	19	3	0
W. Virginia	6	26	4	0
Wisconsin	34	43	11	0
Wyoming	1	8	2	0
U.S. Totals	**1,209**	**1,980**	**567**	**100**

International/Worldwide

Country	Discount Stores	Supercenters	SAM'S CLUBs	Neighborhood Markets
Argentina	0	11	0	0
Brazil	255*	23	15	2*
Canada	272	0	6	0
China	0	51	3	2
Germany	0	88	0	0
Japan	2‡	96‡	0	300‡
South Korea	0	16	0	0
Mexico	599†	105	70	0
Puerto Rico	9	5	9	31**
United Kingdom	294§	21	0	0
International Totals	**1,431**	**416**	**103**	**335**
Grand Totals	**2,640**	**2,396**	**670**	**435**

* Brazil includes 2 Todo Dias, 116 Bompreço and 139 Sonae.

‡ Japan includes 2 GM only, 96 general merchandise, apparel and food stores and 300 supermarkets. Japan excludes 45 Wakana units, which are take-out restaurants generally less than 1,000 square feet in size.

† Mexico includes 187 Bodegas, 16 Mi Bodegas, 1 Mi Bodega Express, 1 Mercamas, 53 Suburbias, 55 Superamas, 286 Vips and does not include Vips franchises.

** Puerto Rico includes 31 Amigos.

§ United Kingdom includes 236 ASDA stores, 10 George stores, 5 ASDA Living and 43 ASDA small stores.

APPENDIX B: Glossary

A

account An accounting record in which the results of transactions are accumulated; shows increases, decreases, and a balance.

accounting A system for providing quantitative, financial information about economic entities that is useful for making sound economic decisions. Accounting is often called the "language of business" because it provides the means of recording and communicating business activities and the results of those activities.

accounting cycle The procedure for analyzing, recording, summarizing, and reporting the transactions of a business.

accounting equation An algebraic equation that expresses the relationship between assets (resources), liabilities (obligations), and owner's equity (net assets, or the residual interest in a business after all liabilities have been met): Assets = Liabilities + Owners' Equity.

accounting model The basic accounting assumptions, concepts, principles, and procedures that determine the manner of recording, measuring, and reporting a company's transactions.

accounting system The procedures and processes used by a business to analyze transactions, handle routine bookkeeping tasks, and structure information so it can be used to evaluate the performance and health of the business.

accounts receivable A current asset representing money due for services performed or merchandise sold on credit.

accounts receivable turnover A measure used to indicate how fast a company collects its receivables; computed by dividing sales by average accounts receivable.

accrual-basis accounting A system of accounting in which revenues and expenses are recorded as they are earned and incurred, not necessarily when cash is received or paid.

accumulated other comprehensive income Certain market-related gains and losses that are not included in the computation of net income; for example, foreign currency translation adjustments and unrealized gains or losses on investments.

adjusting entries Entries required at the end of each accounting period to recognize, on an accrual basis, revenues and expenses for the period and to report proper amounts for asset, liability, and owners' equity accounts.

aging accounts receivable The process of categorizing each account receivable by the number of days it has been outstanding.

allowance for bad debts A contra account, deducted from Accounts Receivable, that shows the estimated losses from uncollectible accounts.

allowance method The recording of estimated losses due to uncollectible accounts as expenses during the period in which the sales occurred.

American Institute of Certified Public Accountants (AICPA) The national organization of CPAs in the United States.

amortization The process of cost allocation that assigns the original cost of an intangible asset to the periods benefited.

annual report A document that summarizes the results of operations and financial status of a company for the past year and outlines plans for the future.

annuity A series of equal amounts to be received or paid at the end of equal time intervals.

arm's-length transactions Business dealings between independent and rational parties who are looking out for their own interests.

articulation The interrelationships among the financial statements.

asset turnover A measure of company efficiency, computed by dividing sales by total assets.

assets Economic resources that are owned or controlled by a company.

assets-to-equity ratio A measure of the number of dollars of assets a company is able to acquire using each dollar of equity; calculated by dividing assets by equity.

audit committee Members of a company's board of directors who are responsible for dealing with the external and internal auditors.

audit report A report issued by an independent CPA that expresses an opinion about whether the financial statements fairly present a company's financial position, operating results, and cash flows in accordance with generally accepted accounting principles.

available-for-sale securities Debt and equity securities not classified as trading, held-to-maturity, or equity method securities.

average collection period A measure of the average number of days it takes to collect a credit sale; computed by dividing 365 days by the accounts receivable turnover.

average cost An inventory cost flow assumption whereby cost of goods sold and the cost of ending inventory are determined by using an average cost of all merchandise available for sale during the period.

B

bad debt An uncollectible account receivable.

bad debt expense An account that represents the portion of the current period's credit sales that are estimated to be uncollectible.

balance sheet (statement of financial position) The financial statement that reports a company's assets, liabilities, and owners' equity at a particular date.

bank reconciliation The process of systematically comparing the cash balance as reported by the bank with the cash balance on the company's books and explaining any differences.

basic earnings per share An earnings per share figure that divides net income by the number of shares of stock outstanding.

basket purchase The purchase of two or more assets acquired together at a single price.

board of directors Individuals elected by the stockholders to govern a corporation.

bond A contract between a borrower and a lender in which the borrower promises to pay a specified rate of interest for each period the bond is outstanding and repay the principal at the maturity date.

bond carrying value The face value of bonds minus the unamortized discount or plus the unamortized premium.

bond discount The difference between the face value and the sales price when bonds are sold below their face value.

bond indenture A contract between a bond issuer and a bond purchaser that specifies the terms of a bond.

bond maturity date The date at which a bond principal or face amount becomes payable.

bond premium The difference between the face value and the sales price when bonds are sold above their face value.

bonus Additional compensation, beyond the regular compensation, that is paid to employees if certain objectives are achieved.

book value The value of a company as measured by the amount of owners' equity; that is, assets less liabilities.

bookkeeping The preservation of a systematic, quantitative record of an activity.

business An organization operated with the objective of making a profit from the sale of goods or services.

business documents Records of transactions used as the basis for recording accounting entries; include invoices, check stubs, receipts, and similar business papers.

C

calendar year An entity's reporting year, covering 12 months and ending on December 31.

callable bonds Bonds for which the issuer reserves the right to pay the obligation before its maturity date.

capital budgeting Systematic planning for long-term investments in operating assets.

capital lease A leasing transaction that is recorded as a purchase by the lessee.

capital stock The portion of a stockholders' equity that represents investment by owners in exchange for shares of stock. Also referred to as paid-in capital.

capitalized interest Interest that is recorded as part of the cost of a self-constructed asset.

cash Coins, currency, money orders, checks, and funds on deposit with financial institutions; the most liquid of assets.

cash dividend A cash distribution of earnings to stockholders.

cash equivalents Short-term, highly liquid investments that can easily be converted into cash.

cash flow adequacy ratio Cash from operations divided by expenditures for fixed asset additions and acquisitions of new businesses.

cash flow-to-net income ratio A ratio that reflects the extent to which accrual accounting assumptions and adjustments have been included in computing net income.

cash-basis accounting A system of accounting in which transactions are recorded and revenues and expenses are recognized only when cash is received or paid.

ceiling The maximum market amount at which inventory can be carried on the books; equal to net realizable value.

certified public accountant (CPA) A special designation given to an accountant who has passed a national uniform examination and has met other certifying requirements.

chart of accounts A systematic listing of all accounts used by a company.

classified balance sheet A balance sheet in which assets and liabilities are subdivided into current and long-term categories.

closing entries Entries that reduce all nominal, or temporary, accounts to a zero balance at the end of each accounting period, transferring their preclosing balances to a permanent balance sheet account.

common stock The most frequently issued class of stock; usually, it provides a voting right but is secondary to preferred stock in dividend and liquidation rights.

common-size financial statements Financial statements achieved by dividing all financial statement numbers by total sales for the year.

comparative financial statements Financial statements in which data for two or more years are shown together.

compound journal entry A journal entry that involves more than one debit or more than one credit or both.

compounding period The period of time for which interest is computed.

comprehensive income A measure of the overall change in a company's wealth during a period; consists of net income plus changes in wealth resulting from changes in investment values and exchange rates.

conglomerates A company comprised of a number of divisions with those divisions often operating in different industries.

consignment An arrangement whereby merchandise owned by one party, the consignor, is sold by another party, the consignee, usually on a commission basis.

consolidated financial statements Statements that report the combined operating results, financial position, and cash flows of two or more legally separate but affiliated companies as if they were one economic entity.

contingency Circumstances involving potential losses or gains that will not be resolved until some future event occurs.

contra account An account that is offset or deducted from another account.

contributed capital The portion of owners' equity contributed by investors (the owners) in exchange for shares of stock.

control activities (procedures) Policies and procedures used by management to meet their objectives.

control environment The actions, policies, and procedures that reflect the overall attitudes of top management about control and its importance to the entity.

convertible bonds Bonds that can be traded for, or converted to, other securities after a specified period of time.

convertible preferred stock Preferred stock that can be converted to common stock at a specified conversion rate.

corporation A legal entity chartered by a state; ownership is represented by transferable shares of stock.

cost of goods available for sale The cost of all merchandise available for sale during the period; equal to the sum of beginning inventory and net purchases.

cost of goods sold The costs incurred to purchase or manufacture the merchandise sold during a period.

cost principle The idea that transactions are recorded at their historical costs or exchange prices at the transaction date.

coupon bonds Unregistered bonds for which owners receive periodic interest payments by clipping a coupon from the bond and sending it to the issuer as evidence of ownership.

credit An entry on the right side of a T-account.

cumulative-dividend preference The right of preferred stockholders to receive current dividends plus all dividends in arrears before common stockholders receive any dividends.

current assets Cash and other assets that can be easily converted to cash within a year.

current liabilities Liabilities expected to be satisfied within a year or the current operating cycle, whichever is longer.

current ratio A measure of the liquidity of a business; equal to current assets divided by current liabilities.

current-dividend preference The right of preferred stockholders to receive current dividends before common stockholders receive dividends.

D

date of record The date selected by a corporation's board of directors on which the stockholders of record are identified as those who will receive dividends.

debentures (unsecured bonds) Bonds for which no collateral has been pledged.

debit An entry on the left side of a T-account.

debt ratio A measure of leverage, computed by dividing total liabilities by total assets.

debt securities Financial instruments issued by a company that carry with them a promise of interest payments and the repayment of principal.

debt-to-equity ratio The number of dollars of borrowed funds for every dollar invested by owners; computed as total liabilities divided by total stockholders' equity.

declaration date The date on which a corporation's board of directors formally decides to pay a dividend to stockholders.

declining-balance depreciation method An accelerated depreciation method in which an asset's book value is multiplied by a constant depreciation rate (such as double the straight-line percentage, in the case of double-declining-balance).

defined benefit plan A pension plan under which the employer defines the amount that retiring employees will receive and contributes enough to the pension fund to pay that amount.

defined contribution plan A pension plan under which the employer contributes a defined amount to the pension fund; after retirement, the employees receive the amount contributed plus whatever it has earned.

depletion The process of cost allocation that assigns the original cost of a natural resource to the periods benefited.

depreciation The process of cost allocation that assigns the original cost of plant and equipment to the periods benefited.

detective controls Internal control activities that are designed to detect the occurrence of errors and fraud.

diluted earnings per share An earnings per share figure that considers the effect on net income and shares outstanding of events that will likely occur in the future, such as the exercising of favorable stock options.

direct method A method of reporting net cash flows from operations that shows the major classes of cash receipts and payments for a period of time.

direct write-off method The recording of actual losses from uncollectible accounts as expenses during the period in which accounts receivable are determined to be uncollectible.

dividend payment date The date on which a corporation pays dividends to its stockholders.

dividend payout ratio A measure of the percentage of earnings paid out in dividends; computed by dividing cash dividends by net income.

dividends Distributions to the owners (stockholders) of a corporation.

dividends in arrears Missed dividends for past years that preferred stockholders have a right to receive under the cumulative-dividend preference if and when dividends are declared.

double-entry accounting A system of recording transactions in a way that maintains the equality of the accounting equation.

DuPont framework A systematic approach for breaking down return on equity into three ratios: return on sales, asset turnover, and assets-to-equity ratio.

E

earnings (loss) per share (EPS) The amount of net income (earnings) related to each share of stock; computed by dividing net income by the number of shares of stock outstanding during the period.

effective-interest amortization A method of systematically writing off a bond premium or discount that takes into consideration the time value of money and results in an equal interest rate being used for amortization for each period.

employee stock options Rights given to employees to purchase shares of stock of a company at a predetermined price.

entity An organizational unit (a person, partnership, or corporation) for which accounting records are kept and about which accounting reports are prepared.

environmental liabilities Obligations incurred because of damage done to the environment.

equity method A method used to account for an investment in the stock of another company when significant influence can be imposed (presumed to exist when 20 to 50% of the outstanding voting stock is owned).

equity securities (stock) Shares of ownership in a corporation that can change significantly in value and that provide for a return to investors in the form of dividends.

expenses Costs incurred in the normal course of business to generate revenues.

external auditors Independent CPAs who are retained by organizations to perform audits of financial statements.

extraordinary items Nonoperating gains and losses that are unusual in nature, infrequent in occurrence, and material in amount.

F

FIFO (first in, first out) An inventory cost flow assumption whereby the first goods purchased are assumed to be the first goods sold so that the ending inventory consists of the most recently purchased goods.

financial accounting The area of accounting concerned with reporting financial information to interested external parties.

Financial Accounting Standards Board (FASB) The private organization responsible for establishing the standards for financial accounting and reporting in the United States.

financial ratios Relationships between financial statement amounts.

financial statement analysis The examination of both the relationships among financial statement numbers and the trends in those numbers over time.

financial statements Reports such as the balance sheet, income statement, and statement of cash flows, which summarize the financial status and results of operations of a business entity.

financing activities Activities whereby cash is obtained from or repaid to owners and creditors.

finished goods Manufactured products ready for sale.

fiscal year An entity's reporting year, covering a 12-month accounting period.

fixed asset turnover The number of dollars in sales generated by each dollar of fixed assets; computed as sales divided by property, plant, and equipment.

floor The minimum market amount at which inventory can be carried on the books; equal to net realizable value minus a normal profit.

FOB (free-on-board) destination A business term meaning that the seller of merchandise bears the shipping costs and maintains ownership until the merchandise is delivered to the buyer.

FOB (free-on-board) shipping point A business term meaning that the buyer of merchandise bears the shipping costs and acquires ownership at the point of shipment.

Foreign Corrupt Practices Act (FCPA) Legislation requiring any company that has publicly-traded stock to have an adequate system of internal accounting controls.

foreign currency transaction A sale in which the price is denominated in a currency other than the currency of the seller's home country.

franchise An entity that has been licensed to sell the product of a manufacturer or to offer a particular service in a given area.

G

GAAP oval A diagram that represents the flexibility a manager has, within GAAP, to report one earnings number from among many possibilities based on different methods and assumptions.

gains (losses) Money made or lost on activities outside the normal operation of a company.

generally accepted accounting principles (GAAP) Authoritative guidelines that define accounting practice at a particular time.

generally accepted auditing standards (GAAS) Auditing standards developed by the PCAOB for public companies and AICPA for private companies.

going concern assumption The idea that an accounting entity will have a continuing existence for the foreseeable future.

goodwill An intangible asset that exists when a business is valued at more than the fair market value of its net assets, usually due to strategic location, reputation, good customer relations, or similar factors; equal to the excess of the purchase price over the fair market value of the net assets purchased.

gross margin method A procedure for estimating the amount of ending inventory; the historical relationship of cost of goods sold to sales revenue is used in computing ending inventory.

gross profit (gross margin) The excess of net sales revenue over the cost of goods sold.

gross sales Total recorded sales before deducting any sales discounts or sales returns and allowances.

H

held-to-maturity security A debt security purchased by an investor with the intent of holding the security until it matures.

historical cost The dollar amount originally exchanged in an arms'-length transaction; an amount assumed to reflect the fair market value of an item at the transaction date.

I

impairment A decline in the value of a long-term operating asset.

income smoothing The practice of carefully timing the recognition of revenues and expenses to even out the amount of reported earnings from one year to the next.

income statement (statement of earnings) The financial statement that repots the amount of net income earned by a company during a period.

independent checks Procedures for continual internal verification of other controls.

indirect method A method of reporting net cash flows from operations that involves converting accrual-basis net income to a cash basis.

intangible assets Long-lived assets without physical substance that are used in business, such as licenses, patents, franchises, and goodwill.

internal auditors An independent group of experts (in controls, accounting, and operations) who monitor operating results and financial records, evaluate internal controls, assist with increasing the efficiency and effectiveness of operations, and detect fraud.

internal control structure Safeguards in the form of policies and procedures established to provide management with reasonable assurance that the objectives of an entity will be achieved.

internal earnings targets Financial goals established within a company.

Internal Revenue Service (IRS) A government agency that prescribes the rules and regulations that govern the collection of tax revenues in the United States.

International Accounting Standards Board (IASB) The committee formed in 1973 to develop worldwide accounting standards.

inventory Goods held for resale.

inventory shrinkage The amount of inventory that is lost, stolen, or spoiled during a period; determined by comparing perpetual inventory records to the physical count of inventory.

inventory turnover A measure of the efficiency with which inventory is managed; computed by dividing cost of goods sold by average inventory for a period.

investing activities Activities associated with buying and selling long-term assets.

J

journal An accounting record in which transactions are first entered; provides a chronological record of all business activities.

journal entry A recording of a transaction where debits equal credits; usually includes a date and an explanation of the transaction.

journalizing Recording transactions in a journal.

junk bonds Bonds issued by companies in weak financial condition with large amounts of debt already outstanding; these bonds yield high rates of return because of high risk.

L

lease A contract that specifies the terms under which the owner of an asset (the lessor) agrees to transfer the right to use the asset to another party (the lessee).

ledger A book of accounts in which data from transactions recorded in journals are posted and thereby summarized.

lessee The party that is granted the right to use property under the terms of a lease.

lessor The owner of property that is leased (rented) to another party.

leverage Borrowing that allows a company to purchase more assets than its stockholders are able to pay for through their own investment.

liabilities Obligations to pay cash, transfer other assets, or provide services to someone else.

LIFO (last in, first out) An inventory cost flow assumption whereby the last goods purchased are assumed to be the first goods sold so that the ending inventory consists of the first goods purchased.

limited liability The legal protection given stockholders whereby they are responsible for the debts and obligations of a corporation only to the extent of their capital contributions.

liquidity The ability of a company to pay its debts in the short run.

long-term assets Assets that a company needs in order to operate its business over an extended period of time.

long-term liabilities Liabilities that are not expected to be satisfied within a year.

long-term operating assets Assets expected to be held and used over the course of several years to facilitate operating activities.

lower-of-cost-or-market (LCM) rule A basis for valuing inventory at the lower of original cost or current market value.

M

management accounting The area of accounting concerned with providing internal financial reports to assist management in making decisions.

manufacturing overhead The indirect manufacturing costs associated with producing inventory.

Market Adjustment-Trading Securities An account used to track the difference between the historical cost and the market value of a company's portfolio of trading securities.

market rate (effective rate or yield rate) of interest The actual interest rate earned or paid on a bond investment.

market value The value of a company as measured by the number of shares of stock outstanding multiplied by the current market price of the stock; the current value of a business.

matching principle The concept that all costs and expenses incurred in generating revenues must be recognized in the same reporting period as the related revenues.

minority interest The amount of equity investment made by outside shareholders to consolidated subsidiaries that are not 100% owned by the parent.

monetary measurement The idea that money, as the common medium of exchange, is the accounting unit of measurement, and that only economic activities measurable in monetary terms are included in the accounting model.

mortgage amortization schedule A schedule that shows the breakdown between interest and principal for each payment over the life of a mortgage.

mortgage payable A written promise to pay a stated amount of money at one or more specified future dates; a mortgage is secured by the pledging of certain assets, usually real estate, as collateral.

N

natural resources Assets that are physically consumed or waste away, such as oil, minerals, gravel, and timber.

net assets The owners' equity of a business; equal to total assets minus total liabilities.

net income (net loss) An overall measure of the performance of a company; equal to revenues minus expenses for the period.

net purchases The net cost of inventory purchased during a period, after adding the cost of freight in and subtracting returns and discounts.

net realizable value The selling price of an item less reasonable selling costs.

net realizable value of accounts receivable The net amount that would be received if all receivables considered collectible were collected; equal to total accounts receivable less the allowance for bad debts.

net sales Gross sales less sales discounts and sales returns and allowances.

nominal accounts Accounts that are closed to a zero balance at the end of each accounting period; temporary accounts generally appearing on the income statement.

noncash items Items included in the determination of net income on an accrual basis that do not affect cash; for example, depreciation and amortization.

noncash transactions Investing and financing activities that do not affect cash; if significant, they are disclosed below the statement of cash flows or in the notes to the financial statements.

nonprofit organization An entity without a profit objective, oriented toward providing services efficiently and effectively.

notes to the financial statements Explanatory information considered an integral part of the financial statements.

NSF (not sufficient funds) check A check that is not honored by a bank because of insufficient cash in the check writer's account.

number of days' purchases in accounts payable A measure of how well operating cash flow is being managed; computed by dividing total inventory purchases by average accounts payable and then dividing 365 days by the result.

number of days' sales in inventory An alternative measure of how well inventory is being managed; computed by dividing 365 days by the inventory turnover ratio.

O

operating activities Activities that are part of the day-to-day business of a company.

operating lease A simple rental agreement.

organizational structure Lines of authority and responsibility.

other revenues and expenses Items incurred or earned from activities that are outside of, or peripheral to, the normal operations of a firm.

owners' equity The ownership interest in the net assets of an entity; equals total assets minus total liabilities.

P

par value A nominal value assigned to and printed on the face of each share of a corporation's stock.

partnership An association of two or more individuals or organizations to carry on economic activity.

patent An exclusive right granted for 20 years by the federal government to manufacture and sell an invention.

pension An agreement between an employer and employees that provides for benefits upon retirement.

periodic inventory system A system of accounting for inventory in which cost of goods sold is determined and inventory is adjusted at the end of the accounting period, not when merchandise is purchased or sold.

perpetual inventory system A system of accounting for inventory in which detailed records of the number of units and the cost of each purchase and sales transaction are prepared throughout the accounting period.

physical safeguards Physical precautions used to protect assets and records, such as locks on doors, fireproof vaults, password verification, and security guards.

post-closing trial balance A listing of all real account balances after the closing process has been completed; provides a means of testing whether total debits equal total credits for all real accounts prior to beginning a new accounting cycle.

postemployment benefits Benefits paid to employees who have been laid off or terminated.

posting The process of transforming amounts from the journal to the ledger.

preferred stock A class of stock that usually provides dividend and liquidation preferences over common stock.

prepaid expenses Payments made in advance for items normally charged to expense.

present value of $1 The value today of $1 to be received or paid at some future date, given a specified interest rate.

present value of an annuity The value today of a series of equally spaced, equal-amount payments to be made or received in the future given a specified interest rate.

preventative controls Internal control activities that are designed to prevent the occurrence of errors and fraud.

price-earnings ratio A measure of growth potential, earnings stability, and management capabilities; computed by dividing market value of a company by net income.

primary financial statements The balance sheet, income statement, and statement of cash flows, used by external groups to assess a company's economic standing.

principal (face value or maturity value) The amount that will be paid on a bond at the maturity date.

property, plant, and equipment Tangible, long-lived assets acquired for use in business operations; include land, buildings, machinery, equipment, and furniture.

proprietorship A business owned by one person.

prospectus A report provided to potential investors that represents a company's financial statements and explains its business plan, sources of financing, and significant risks.

Public Company Accounting Oversight Board (PCAOB) Board of five full-time members established by the Sarbanes-Oxley Act to oversee the accounting and auditing profession.

R

raw materials Materials purchased for use in manufacturing products.

real accounts Accounts that are not closed to a zero balance at the end of each accounting period; permanent accounts appearing on the balance sheet.

realized gains and losses Gains and losses resulting from the sale of securities in an arm's-length transaction.

receivables Claims for money, goods, or services.

registered bonds Bonds for which the names and addresses of the bondholders are kept on file by the issuing company.

retained earnings The amount of accumulated earnings of the business that have not been distributed to owners.

return on equity A measure of the amount of profit earned per dollar of investment, computed by dividing net income by equity.

return on sales A measure of the amount of profit earned per dollar of sales, computed by dividing net income by sales.

revenue Increase in a company's resources from the sale of goods or services.

revenue recognition The process of recording revenue in the accounting records; occurs after (1) the work has been substantially completed and (2) cash collection is reasonably assured.

revenue recognition principle The idea that revenues should be recorded when (1) the earnings process has been substantially completed and (2) cash has either been collected or collectibility is reasonably assured.

S

sales discount A reduction in the selling price that is allowed if payment is received within a specified period.

sales returns and allowances A contra-revenue account in which the return of, or allowance for reduction in the price of, merchandise previously sold is recorded.

sales tax payable Money collected from customers for sales taxes that must be remitted to local governments and other taxing authorities.

salvage value The amount expected to be received when an asset is sold at the end of its useful life.

Sarbanes-Oxley Act A law passed by Congress in 2002 that gives the SEC significant oversight responsibility and control over companies issuing financial statements and their external auditors.

secured bonds Bonds for which assets have been pledged in order to guarantee repayment.

Securities and Exchange Commission (SEC) The government body responsible for regulating the financial reporting practices of most publicly-owned corporations in connection with the buying and selling of stocks and bonds.

segregation of duties A strategy to provide an internal check on performance through separation of authorization of transactions from custody of related assets, separation of operational responsibilities from record-keeping responsibilities, and separation of custody of assets from accounting personnel.

separate entity concept The idea that the activities of an entity are to be separated from those of the individual owners.

serial bonds Bonds that mature in a series of installments at specified future dates.

Social Security (FICA) taxes Federal Insurance Contributions Act taxes imposed on the employee and the employer; used mainly to provide retirement benefits.

specific identification A method of valuing inventory and determining cost of goods sold whereby the actual costs of specific inventory items are assigned to them.

stated rate of interest The rate of interest printed on the bond.

statement of cash flows The financial statement that reports the amount of cash collected and paid out by a company during a period of time.

statement of comprehensive income A statement outlining the changes in accumulated comprehensive income that arose during the period.

statement of retained earnings A report that shows the changes in retained earnings during a period of time.

statement of stockholders' equity A financial statement that reports all changes in stockholders' equity.

stockholders (shareholders) The owners of a corporation.

stockholders' equity The owners' equity section of a corporate balance sheet.

straight-line amortization A method of systematically writing off a bond discount or premium in equal amounts each period until maturity.

straight-line depreciation method The depreciation method in which the cost of an asset is allocated equally over the periods of an asset's estimated useful life.

sum-of-the years' digits (SYD) depreciation method The accelerated depreciation method in which a constant balance (cost minus salvage value) is multiplied by a declining depreciation rate.

T

T-account A simplified depiction of an account in the form of a letter T.

term bonds Bonds that mature in one single sum at a specified future date.

time value of money The concept that a dollar received now is worth more than a dollar received in the future.

time-period concept The idea that the life of a business is divided into distinct and relatively short time periods so that accounting information can be timely.

times interest earned A measure of a borrower's ability to make required interest payments; computed as income before interest and taxes divided by annual interest expense.

trading securities Debt and equity securities purchased with the intent of selling them should the need for cash arise or to realize short-term gains.

transactions Exchange of goods or services between entities (whether individuals, businesses, or other organizations), as well as other events having an economic impact on a business.

treasury stock Issued stock that has subsequently been reacquired by the corporation.

trial balance A listing of all account balances; provides a means of testing whether total debits equal total credits for all accounts.

U

unearned revenues Cash amounts received before they have been earned.

units-of-production method The depreciation method in which the cost of an asset is allocated to each period on the basis of the productive output or use of the asset during the period.

unrealized gains and losses Gains and losses resulting from changes in the value of securities that are still being held.

unrecorded liabilities Expenses incurred during a period that have not been recorded by the end of that period.

unrecorded receivables Revenues earned during a period that have not been recorded by the end of that period.

V

venture capital firm A company that provides needed cash to companies in return for an ownership interest.

W

work in process Partially completed units in production.

work sheet A tool used by accountants to facilitate the preparation of financial statements.

Z

zero-coupon bonds Bonds issued with no promise of interest payments; only a single payment will be made.

APPENDIX C: Check Figures*

Chapter 1

Not Applicable

Chapter 2

Exercises

2-20	(8) BS/A
2-22	(Z) Expenses in 2009 = $330
2-24	Total assets = $560,000
2-26	(4) EPS = $2.45
2-28	(1) Net income = $510,000
2-30	6/30/09 Retained earnings = $83,900
2-32	(1) Net cash provided by operating activities = $78,000
2-34	N/A
2-36	N/A

Problems

2-38	(2) Total long-term assets = $576,000
2-40	(2) Retained earnings $33,000
2-42	EPS = $34.14
2-44	Net income = $34,515
2-46	(2) 5/31/09 Retained earnings $216,910
2-48	(2) Net income for 2009 = $25,000
2-50	Cash at beginning of year $676,000

Chapter 3

Exercises

3-24	N/A
3-26	(2) OE—R
3-28	(3) Net income for 2009 = $17,500
3-30	(4) Debit to Accounts Payable = $15,000
3-32	(1) Debit to Compensation Expense = $105,000
3-34	N/A
3-36	7/23 Paid rent of $2,000
3-38	Retained Earnings = $40,300

Problems

3-40	(1)(c) Debit to Utilities Expense = $720
3-42	9/9 Debit to Insurance Expense = $1,500
3-44	3/4/09 Credit to Accounts Receivable = $2,500

3-46	5/15/09 Debit to Notes Payable = $2,500
3-48	(2) Total Debits = $134,000

Chapter 4

Exercises

4-24	(1) (b) Accrual-basis Net income = $39,533
4-26	(3) Unrecorded liability
4-28	(2) Adjusting entry—Debit to Subscription Expense = $131
4-30	(2) (b) Debit to Salaries Expense = $90,000
4-32	(2) Debit to Interest Expense = $5,625
4-34	(4) No adjusting entry
4-36	(1) Supplies on Hand = $2,000
4-38	(12) N
4-40	Credit to Retained Earnings = $107,100
4-42	Debit to Sales Revenue = $906,000
4-44	(2) Retained Earnings = $41,200

Problems

4-46	(d) Credit to Rent Revenue = $33,900
4-48	(1) Wages Expense for 2009 = $30,000
4-50	N/A
4-52	(1) Credit to Retained Earnings = $76,580
4-54	(1) Total assets = $820,000
4-56	(2) Ending Cash balance = $33,000

Chapter 5

Exercises

5-2	Total assets = $7,801,300

Chapter 6

Exercises

6-26	N/A
6-28	N/A
6-30	6/30 Debit to Sales Discounts = $800
6-32	(1) Bad debt expense = $5,200
6-34	(2) Ending Accounts Receivable = $1,340,000

---

* Note: Check figures are provided for even-numbered exercises and problems, where applicable.

6-36   (3) 12/31/09 Net accounts receivable = $149,010

6-38   2009 Debit to Bad Debt Expense = $66,000

6-40   (1) Boulder, Inc. Average Collection Period for Year 3 = 118 days

6-42   N/A

6-44   January 2010 Debit to Estimated Liability for Service = $760

6-46   (2) Debit to Miscellaneous Expenses = $50

6-48   (1) 3.2 billion Vietnamese dong

Problems

6-50   N/A

6-52   (b) Debit to Sales Returns and Allowances = $4,000

6-54   (1) Debit to Bad Debt Expense = $209,800

6-56   (3) (a) Debit to Allowance for Bad Debts = $3,500

6-58   (2) Credit to Accounts Receivable = $89

6-60   (3) 12/31/09 Net accounts receivable = $362,260

6-62   (1) Deposits in transit = $6,000

6-64   (2) Credit to Exchange Gain = $700

Chapter 7

Exercises

7-30   (4) Net purchases = $53,500

7-32   Ending inventory = $31,371

7-34   (5) Beginning inventory = $17,100

7-36   Debit to Inventory Shrinkage = $28,000

7-38   Cost of goods sold = $511,760

7-40   (1) Cost of goods sold = $7,050

7-42   Net purchases = $4,800

7-44   Burbank number of days' sales in inventory = 35.1 days

7-46   (1) (a) Gross margin = $60,000

7-48   (2) Debit to Purchases = $300

7-50   (1) Ending inventory = $120,000

7-52   Ending inventory = $500,000

Problems

7-54   (1) (d) Debit to Accounts Payable = $19,520

7-56   (10) Gross margin = $675

7-58   (2) Ending inventory LIFO = $45,885

7-60   (1) Net Purchases = $79,600

7-62   (1) 2009 Correct gross margin = $31,400

7-64   (1) (a) Gross margin FIFO = $9,336

Chapter 8

Exercises

8-22   (2) Credit to FICA Taxes Payable, Employer = $9,716

8-24   Total compensation expense = $660,000

8-26   Net pension asset = $340,000

8-28   (b) Pension expense = $13,000

8-30   (2) Income tax expense = $262,500

8-32   N/A

8-34   Gross margin = $8,500

Problems

8-36   (2) Debit to Salaries Payable = $8,289.70

8-38   (1) Compensation expense for 2009 = $666,667

8-40   (3) 2008 Pension obligation = $846,807

8-42   Operating income = $284,500

Chapter 9

Exercises

9-26   N/A

9-28   (1) Total cost = $50,000

9-30   (1) (b) Debit to Interest Expense = $78

9-32   Debit to Land = $112,500

9-34   (1) Depreciation expense = $2,000 per year

9-36   (2) Debit to Loss on Impairment = $200

9-38   (2) Debit to Loss on Sale of Truck = $2,000

9-40   (1) Debit to Amortization Expense, Patent = $6,800

9-42   (3) Market value of the net assets = $1,430,000

9-44   (1) Debit to Drilling Equipment = $185,000

9-46   (2) 2009 Book value = $522,006

9-48   (1) 2009 Depreciation expense = $10,048

9-50   2009 Depreciation expense = $14,667

Problems

9-52   N/A

9-54   (3) 12/31/09 Debit to Interest Expense = $23,954

9-56   (2) Alternative b = $42,150 per year

9-58   (2) Debit to Equipment = $50,400
9-60   (1) Credit to Cash = $114,000
9-62   (3) Debit to Depletion Expense = $210,000
9-64   Debit to Goodwill = $20,000
9-66   (1) Fixed asset turnover = 3.08
9-68   (3) Depreciation = $50,400
9-70   (2) 2009 Depreciation Expense = $7,520
9-72   (3) (c) Uranium Book Value = $24,000

Chapter 10
Exercises

10-24   (4) $10,997
10-26   (1) Payment = $75,481
10-28   12/31/09 Credit to Cash = $1,250
10-30   (2) Total Interest Paid = $17,072
10-32   (2) Debit to Rent (or Lease) Expense = $4,141
10-34   Total issuance price = $68,124
10-36   (3) 3/1/10 Debit to Bond Interest Expense = $4,200
10-38   (1) Debt ratio = 55.6%
10-40   (1) (b) Debit to Premium on Bonds = $100
10-42   (4) Bonds Payable Carrying Value = $51,772

Problems

10-44   (2) (a) $27,372
10-46   (2) Payment = $444.89
10-48   (2) 12/31/08 Debit to Interest Expense = $750
10-50   (1) (c) Debit to Lease Liability = $3,782
10-52   June 30 Issuance price of bonds = $1,010,720
10-54   (2) Debit to Bond Interest Expense = $22,500
10-56   Total liabilities = $1,025,300
10-58   (2) Debt ratio = 77.8%
10-60   (1) Debit to Cash = $99,000
10-62   (1) Issuance price of bonds = $138,961
10-64   (1) Credit to Premium on bonds = $22,939
10-66   (1) (d) Debit to Bond Interest Expense = $4,400
10-68   Case 2 Approximate effective interest rate = 12.7%

Chapter 11
Exercises

11-18   (2) Retained earnings = $130,150
11-20   (c) Credit to Dividends Payable = $76,720
11-22   (e) Credit to Dividends Payable = $79,800
11-24   (3) $1.69 per share
11-26   (2) Total dividends paid = $172,485
11-28   (2) $8.43 per share
11-30   Comprehensive income = $22,100

Problems

11-32   (3) (b) $861,000
11-34   (b) Credit to Treasury Stock = $44,800
11-36   (2) Total stockholders' equity = $269,600
11-38   (2) 2009 Preferred Stock Dividends = $206,000
11-40   Case B Dividend payout ratio = 0.143
11-42   (1) (b) $89,000
11-44   (2) Total stockholders' equity = $786,250
11-46   (1) (e) Debit to Retained Earnings = $30,200
11-48   N/A

Chapter 12
Exercises

12-20   12/31 Credit to Unrealized Gain on Trading Securities—Income = $1,560
12-22   12/31/09 Debit to Unrealized Increase/Decrease in Value of Available-for-Sale Securities—Equity = $27,500
12-24   Debit to Investment in Trading Securities = $20,500
12-26   Debit to Market Adjustment—Available-for-Sale Securities = $100
12-28   Credit to Cash = $35,620
12-30   (2) Total present value = $113,592
12-32   (1) 12/31 Debit to Bond Interest Receivable = $1,500
12-34   Total amount of Amortization = $3,285
12-36   (2) Credit to Dividend Revenue = $3,000
12-38   (1) Minority interest = $375

Problems

12-40   (c) Credit to Dividend Revenue = $200
12-42   (1) $2,500 unrealized loss

12-44   (1) 12/31 Credit to Bond Interest
Revenue = $4,300
12-46   (3) Loss on sale of securities = $680
12-48   (1) 7/1 Debit to Cash = $1,650
12-50   (3) Debit to Realized Loss on Sale of
Trading Securities = $3,000
12-52   (2) $3,000
12-54   (2) 12/31/09 Debit to Bond Interest
Receivable = $418.90
12-56   (2) 3/20 Debit to Investment in Equity
Method Securities = $2,560,000
12-58   (2) Corporation B Credit to Dividend
Revenue = $12,500
12-60   N/A

Chapter 13
Exercises

13-18   N/A
13-20   (1) (d) Credit to Dividend Revenue =
$6,300
13-22   Net increase in cash = $48,750
13-24   N/A
13-26   Net cash flows provided by operating
activities = $74,400
13-28   Net cash flows provided by operating
activities = $161,600
13-30   Net cash flows provided by operating
activities = $90,800
13-32   Net cash flows used in investing
activities = ($197,000)
13-34   Cash receipts from Customers =
$415,500
13-36   N/A

Problems

13-38   (2) Net increase in cash = $74,300
13-40   (1) Net cash flows provided by operating

activities = $13,000
13-42   (1) Net cash flows from operations =
$24,540
13-44   Net income = $122,100
13-46   (1) Cash from operating activities = $707
13-48   (1) Cash paid for taxes = $13,700

Chapter 14
Exercises

14-34   (f) Total liabilities = $125,500
14-36   (1) 2009 Income tax expense as
percentage of sales = 5.9%
14-38   (1) 2009 Total assets as percentage of
sales = 23.6%
14-40   (1) Cost of goods sold = $161,000
14-42   (2) 2009 Return on sales = 5.0%
14-44   (1) Faulty's ROE = 8.7%
14-46   Profit Margin = 57.9%
14-48   (1) Retail jewelry stores' Return on
Assets = 7.6%
14-54   (1) 2009 Cash flow-to-net income
ratio = 0.75

Problems

14-56   (1) Current ratio = 1.79
14-58   (1) 2009 Operating income as percentage
of sales = 7%
14-60   (1) 2009 Total operating expenses as a
percentage of sales = 26.7%
14-62   (2) 2009 Asset turnover = 2.50
14-64   (1) (b) 2009 Debt ratio = 38.6%
14-66   N/A
14-68   N/A